Mathematics to Level 8

An Intermediate GC

L Bostock BSc

A Shepherd BSc

S Chandler BSc

E Smith MSc

Bishop Auckland College
Woodhouse Lane,
Bishop Auckland,
County Durham,
DL14 6JZ.
Tel: 01388 603052

BISHOP AUCKLAND COLLEGE
LEARNING RESOURCE LIBRARY
ACCESSION NO. 203467
CLASS NO. 510

Stanley Thornes (Publishers) Ltd

© L. Bostock, S. Chandler, A. Shepherd, E. Smith, 1993

All rights reserved. No part of this publication may be reproduced or transmitted in any form or by any means, electronic or mechanical, including photocopy, recording, or any information storage and retrieval system, without permission in writing from the publisher or under licence from the Copyright Licensing Agency Limited. Further details of such licences (for reprographic reproduction) may be obtained from the Copyright Licensing Agency Limited, of 90 Tottenham Court Road, London W1P 9HE.

The right of L. Bostock, S. Chandler, A. Shepherd and E. Smith to be identified as authors of this work has been asserted by them in accordance with the Copyright, Designs and Patents Act 1988.

First published in 1993 by:
Stanley Thornes (Publishers) Ltd
Ellenborough House
Wellington Street
CHELTENHAM GL50 1YD

Reprinted 1994 (twice)
Reprinted 1995

Typeset by Tech-Set, Gateshead, Tyne & Wear
Printed and bound in Great Britain by
BPC Paulton Books Ltd, Paulton

A catalogue record for this book is available from the British Library.

ISBN 0 7487 1664 5

SYMBOLS AND ABBREVIATIONS USED

$=$	is equal to
$\approx$	is approximately equal to
$\neq$	is not equal to
$>$	is greater than
$<$	is less than
$\geqslant$	is greater than or equal to
$\leqslant$	is less than or equal to
$\therefore$	therefore
$\Rightarrow$	gives, giving, implies or implying that
$\equiv$	is equivalent to or is congruent with
$\parallel$	is parallel to
$\perp$	is perpendicular to
LHS	left-hand side
RHS	right-hand side
(3 s.f.)	corrected to 3 significant figures
(2 d.p.)	corrected to 2 decimal places
+ve	positive
−ve	negative
$\triangle$	triangle
$\propto$	is proportional to

CONTENTS

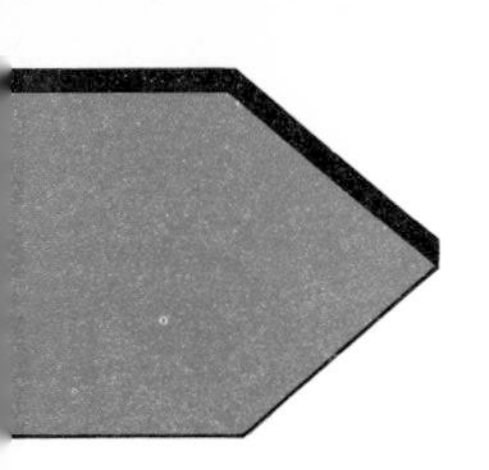

HOW TO USE THIS BOOK

ADVICE TO THE STUDENT

What the Book Contains

This book covers the National Curriculum in Mathematics up to and including Level 8. It is a reference book, a manual and a practice book, providing detailed explanations, numerous worked examples and a plentiful supply of exercises. It aims to prepare you for the intermediate tier of GCSE, Key Stage 4. It should be noted that the National Curriculum intermediate tier GCSE papers cover work up to the equivalent of Grade B and that this includes topics not included in the syllabuses that it replaces. Some of you may prefer to omit some Level 8 topics; a matrix which matches topics in this book to National Curriculum levels is available on request from Stanley Thornes (Publishers) Ltd.

This book can be used either as a complete one or two year course, as a consolidation and top-up book for those of you in your final year of preparation for GCSE, or as a revision course for those retaking GCSE and hoping for a better grade.

Self-Assessment

All of you will have done some mathematics so it is unlikely that anyone will need to cover all the work in this book. However, knowledge and confidence about particular topics will vary from one person to another and, to help assess which topics need to be covered in full, we have provided a self-assessment exercise at the end of each chapter. These exercises are designed to reflect the work contained in the chapter, starting with the basic work and progressing to the harder applications of the topic. Some of you may choose to do the self-assessment exercise before looking at the relevant chapter. If you find that you can do hardly any of the exercise, this indicates that the whole chapter needs to be worked thoroughly. When about half to three quarters of the questions present no problems, it is advisable to read through the chapter, stopping to concentrate only on those areas that do present problems. Those who manage at least 80 per cent of the questions without real difficulty can reasonably assume competence on the topics covered by that chapter though some questions within the chapter similar to those that gave difficulty should be worked.

The self-assessment exercises can also be used after working through a chapter to see if the work has been understood, or they can be used later for revision purposes.

Using Exercises

Each chapter contains exercises to test your understanding of the topic being studied and which enable you to practise and consolidate the skills needed to become proficient in mathematics. Many contain large numbers of questions. Individuals vary in the number of questions that they need to work through in order to gain confidence and skill in a particular topic. It is not necessary for you to work every question in every exercise. Once it is obvious to you that you know what you are doing with a particular type of question it is sensible to go on to the next type. There are many worked examples within the exercises. These show how work can be set out. The comments in small type give the thought processes and background information needed. These do not need to be written down.

Investigations and Coursework

Ideas for investigations and practical work are included near the end of several chapters. These vary in difficulty, extent and purpose. Some are suitable for group work and others for individual study. Some are open-ended while others lead to one result only. It is not intended that all of them should be tried. You may find certain of these investigations more interesting than others. Time spent on a few of these investigations will give enjoyment and insight that it is not easy to achieve in other ways. It will also give practice in coursework, which forms a part of most GCSE mathematics schemes. Some of the ideas may be suitable for use as part of the GCSE coursework but this must be checked with the appropriate authorities as syllabuses vary in their requirements. Because of the nature of these investigations it is not possible to provide answers. If you are working alone, some competent advice on work done should be sought.

Materials Needed

Apart from ordinary writing paper, you will need a supply of 5 mm squared paper and 2 mm squared graph paper. A small quantity of tracing paper is useful. You will also need a ruler, a protractor, a pair of compasses and a calculator. The calculator should be a scientific one with statistical functions and preferably capable of working in fractions; most of the cheapest scientific calculators have all the functions you will need (and many that you will not). Detailed instructions on the use of calculators are not included in this book as there is no universal standard for the layout of keys or of operation; you will need to consult your manual, and we suggest that you keep the manual with the calculator for reference.

To get the most out of this course you will need access to a computer with graph-drawing software, and database and spreadsheet software with a statistical package. This is not essential but highly desirable. You will find reference in this book to graphical calculators; these are expensive and not essential but if you have access to one it is worth learning how to use it.

Answers and Accuracy

Many problems ask for an answer to a given degree of accuracy, for example a length may be required to be given to the nearest centimetre. When the degree of accuracy is not specified, answers should be given in a form appropriate to the situation – it would be ridiculous to give the distance between London and Paris, say, to the nearest centimetre.

A problem with accuracy can sometimes arise when a value, calculated and given as an answer to the required degree of accuracy, is then used again to calculate a further value. This may be the cause of a difference between the last figure of your answer and that given in the answer in this book. Wherever possible, uncorrected values should be used for further calculation.

One last word about answers – before checking your answer with that given in this book, get into the habit of checking yourself that it is reasonable. For example, if you need to find three-quarters of £288 and come up with £484 as an answer, you should not get as far as even thinking of looking up the answer in the back. However complicated a problem is, you should have some idea of the size of answer expected.

1 WHOLE NUMBERS

NATURAL NUMBERS

The numbers $1, 2, 3, \ldots$ are called the *natural numbers.*
They can be added, subtracted, multiplied and divided.

Number Bonds

The ability to do mental calculations is important. There are many everyday situations where you need to calculate quickly and accurately and, when working on paper with simple numbers, using your brain is quicker than resorting to a calculator.

Mental accuracy and speed depend on knowing the following number bonds:

multiplication tables up to 12×12
pairs of numbers that add up to 10
the sum of any two numbers less than or equal to 10.

By 'know' we mean instant recall; there is only one way to acquire this skill and that is by repeated practice.

The addition facts are needed for subtraction because addition and subtraction are related operations. For example, $8 - 6$ means 'the number that when added to 6 makes 8', i.e. to evaluate $8 - 6$ you need to know that $6 + 2 = 8$.

Similarly you need to know the multiplication facts for evaluating divisions,
e.g. $54 \div 6$ is the number of 6s that make 54, so you need to know that $9 \times 6 = 54$.

Adding a String of Numbers

Remember that the order in which numbers are added does not matter, so when adding several numbers together it is sensible to look for pairs of numbers that add up to 10,

e.g.
$$\begin{aligned} 2 + 5 + 7 + 8 + 3 &= 10 + 10 + 5 \\ &= 25 \end{aligned}$$

Note that the result of adding two numbers is called their *sum.*
The *difference* between two numbers is the result of taking the smaller number from the larger number.

Multiplying a String of Numbers

The order in which numbers are multiplied does not matter so, when multiplying several numbers together, we do not have to work from left to right but can first choose to find the product of any two numbers from the string,

e.g. $2 \times 3 \times 4 \times 5 = 10 \times 12$

$= 120$

Note that the result of multiplying two numbers is called their *product.*
The result of dividing one number by another is called the *quotient.*

Multiplication and Division by Powers of 10

To multiply a number by 10, 100, ... we move the figures 1, 2, ... places to the left,

e.g. $27 \times 100 = 2700$ and $34 \times 1000 = 34\,000$

To divide a number by 10, 100, ... we move the figures 1, 2, ... places to the right,

e.g. $4300 \div 10 = 430.0$ and $290 \div 100 = 2.90$

$= 430$ $= 2.9$

(Decimals are fully explained in chapter 2.)

To multiply a number by 500, say, we can first multiply by 5 and then multiply by 100,

e.g. $27 \times 500 = 27 \times 5 \times 100$

$= 135 \times 100$

$= 13\,500$

MIXED OPERATIONS

When a calculation involves addition and subtraction only, the order in which the operations are done does not matter. *But it is important to remember that a + sign or a − sign tells you what to do with just the number following that sign;* it has no relevance to any further numbers, e.g. in the calculation $2-3+5$, we subtract *only 3;* we do *not* subtract 3 *and* 5.

So $2-3+5$ can be worked by first adding 2 and 5,

i.e. $2-3+5 = 7-3 = 4$

Similarly, in a calculation involving only multiplication and division, the order in which the operations are done does not matter, but it does matter that you remember that a × or ÷ sign tells you what to do only to the number or bracket immediately after that sign,

e.g. $2 \div 3 \times 6 = 2 \times 6 \div 3$

$= 12 \div 3 = 4$

When part of a calculation is in brackets, that part must be worked first because the sign before the bracket applies to the whole bracket,

e.g. $8-(3+2) = 8-5 = 3$

When a calculation involves a mixture of addition, subtraction, multiplication and division then, if there are no brackets,

multiplication and division
must be done before addition and subtraction

e.g.
$$\begin{aligned} 2+5\div 3\times 6 &= 2+(5\div 3\times 6) \\ &= 2+(30\div 3) \\ &= 2+10 \\ &= 12 \end{aligned}$$

When a number will not divide into another number exactly, the part left over is called a *remainder*, e.g. $10\div 3 = 3$, remainder 1 (i.e. $10 = 3\times 3+1$).

To find the remainder when larger numbers are involved, it is sensible to set the calculation out in an organised way. For example, to find the remainder when 127 is divided by 9, we can set the calculation out as follows:

$$\begin{array}{r} 14\ \text{r}\ 1 \\ 9\overline{)1\,2^{3}7} \end{array}$$

i.e. $127\div 9 = 14$, remainder 1
($\text{Check: } 14\times 9+1 = 126+1 = 127$)

Exercise 1a

This exercise should be used to practise speed and accuracy. Do not use a calculator.

1. Copy this table and fill in the blank squares. You should be able to do it accurately in less than four minutes.

×	1	2	3	4	5	6	7	8	9	10
1										
2										
3										
4										
5										
6										
7										
8										
9										
10										

2. Make another copy of the table but this time write the numbers 1 to 9 in any order across the top and down the side. Now fill in the blank squares. You should be able to do this accurately in less than four minutes.

3. Make another copy of the table in question 1, but this time put a '+' sign in the corner. Use it to test your speed and accuracy of addition.

4. Make another copy of the table in question 2, but with a '+' sign in the corner. Test your speed and accuracy again.

5. Do each of the following calculations in your head and write down the answer.

(a) 6×9
(b) 40×30
(c) $84 + 15$
(d) 30×70
(e) 200×40
(f) 11×12
(g) $210 \div 30$
(h) 9×7
(i) $250 \div 5$
(j) 9×12
(k) $56 \div 7$
(l) $18 + 7$
(m) $640 \div 8$
(n) $46 + 16$
(p) $3600 \div 90$
(q) $34 + 21$
(r) 120×12
(s) $9 + 42$
(t) $42 \div 6$
(u) $18 + 27$

6. Write down the answer to each of the following calculations.

(a) $54 + 31$
(b) $264 - 18$
(c) $69 + 27$
(d) $750 - 28$
(e) 5×130
(f) 7×15
(g) $2 \times 4 \times 3$
(h) 52×5
(i) $4 \times 3 \times 5$
(j) $12 + 5 + 4$
(k) $182 - 54$
(l) $132 \div 11$
(m) $96 - 27$
(n) $13 + 9 + 7$
(p) $2 \times 2 \times 3$
(q) 14×9
(r) $287 + 155$
(s) 3×46
(t) $162 \div 6$
(u) $147 \div 7$

7. Write down the remainder in each of the following divisions.

(a) $58 \div 5$
(b) $36 \div 7$
(c) $73 \div 4$
(d) $64 \div 3$
(e) $93 \div 6$
(f) $78 \div 8$
(g) $85 \div 4$
(h) $106 \div 3$
(i) $130 \div 9$
(j) $125 \div 4$
(k) $103 \div 11$
(l) $250 \div 6$
(m) $176 \div 9$
(n) $143 \div 12$
(p) $233 \div 9$
(q) $416 \div 7$

8. Write down the answer to each of the following calculations.

(a) $2 + 2 \times 3$
(b) $2 \times 3 + 2 \times 4$
(c) $3 \times 4 - 2 \times 3$
(d) $10 - 12 + 5$
(e) $2 - 7 + 9$
(f) $4 \div 3 \times 6$
(g) $6 \times 3 - 8 \div 2$
(h) $12 \times 4 - 7$
(i) $8 \times 4 - 3$
(j) $16 - 21 \div 7$
(k) $15 + 14 \div 2$
(l) $3 \div 6 \times 10$

9. Write down the answer to each of the following calculations.

(a) $5 \times (2 + 7)$
(b) 130×7
(c) $(25 - 14) \times 2$
(d) $12 + 15 + 8$
(e) $24 \div (5 - 2)$
(f) $12 + 16 \div 4$
(g) 200×30
(h) $(34 + 16) \times 50$

10. (a) Find two numbers whose sum is 6 and whose product is 8.

(b) Find two numbers whose sum is 15 and whose product is 44.

(c) Find two numbers whose sum is 12 and whose product is 35.

11. (a) How many 7s can you take away from 45 and what number is left?

(b) How many 9s can you take away from 100 and what number is left?

(c) How many 4s can you add to 60 before the total is greater than 100?

12. Starting from 25 count up in 7s until the total is greater than 100. Write down this number.

13. How much change do you get when you buy as many 19p stamps as possible with £2?

14. Eggs are packed into boxes that each hold six eggs. How many boxes are needed to pack 730 eggs?

15. How many pieces of wire, each 9 cm long, can be cut from a 250 cm length of wire?

16. Take any three digit number, where at least two of the digits are different, e.g. 771 is acceptable, but 777 is not. Now write the digits in reverse order and find the difference between the two numbers. Repeat this process with the difference. Continue to repeat with each successive difference until you see a pattern. Try the same process with some other three digit numbers. Comment on your results.

LONG MULTIPLICATION

To multiply 537 by 56 without using a calculator, we break it up into stages: multiply 537 by 6, then multiply 537 by 50 and add the results.
This is the conventional way to set out a long multiplication calculation:

$$\begin{array}{rl} 537 & \\ \times 56 & \\ \hline 3222 & (\times 6) \\ 26850 & (\times 50) \\ \hline 30072 & (+) \end{array}$$

LONG DIVISION

To divide 4788 by 37 without using a calculator, we work from the left:
4(thousand) ÷ 37 = 0, remainder 4(thousand)
then add the remainder to the next figure and divide by 37,
47(hundred) ÷ 37 = 1(hundred), remainder 10(hundred),
then add the remainder to the next figure and divide again, and so on.
This process is much easier to keep track of if it is set out in the conventional way:

$$\begin{array}{r l} 1\ 2\ 9 & \\ 37\overline{)4\ 7\ 8\ 8} & \\ 3\ 7 & \\ \hline 1\ 0\ 8 & \text{1st remainder is 10 hundreds} \\ 7\ 4 & \\ \hline 3\ 4\ 8 & \text{2nd remainder is 34 tens} \\ 3\ 3\ 3 & \\ \hline 1\ 5 & \end{array}$$

i.e. 4788 ÷ 37 = 129, remainder 15

Exercise 1b

Use pen and paper only to evaluate

1. 492 × 27
2. 393 × 46
3. 655 × 82
4. 190 × 36
5. 278 × 84
6. 4878 × 23
7. 944 × 153
8. 45 × 5337
9. 537 ÷ 17
10. 699 ÷ 22
11. 365 ÷ 31
12. 850 ÷ 47
13. 905 ÷ 28
14. 7400 ÷ 19
15. 3899 ÷ 122
16. 5050 ÷ 321

FACTORS

A factor of a number divides into the number exactly leaving no remainder, e.g. the factors of 12 are 1, 2, 3, 4, 6 and 12.
The following tests for divisibility are useful:

an even number will divide by 2
a number whose digits add up to a multiple of 3 will divide by 3
a number ending in 5 or zero will divide by 5
a number whose digits add up to a multiple of 9 will divide by 9.

Prime Numbers

A prime number has just two different factors: 1 and itself, e.g. 5 is a prime number, as the only factors of 5 are 1 and 5.

Note that 1 is *not* a prime number (it has only one factor, 1).

Index Notation

The expression 2^4 is an example of index notation.

It means 'four 2s multiplied together',

i.e. $2^4 = 2 \times 2 \times 2 \times 2$

The superscript 4 is called the *index* or *power*, and 2^4 is read as 'two to the power four'.

In general, 2^n is read as 'two to the power n', or simply as 'two to the n'.
However when the power is 2 or 3, special names are used; 2^2 is called '2 squared' and 2^3 is called '2 cubed'.

EXPRESSING A NUMBER AS THE PRODUCT OF ITS PRIME FACTORS

To write a number as a product of its prime factors, start by trying to divide by 2 and continue until 2 will no longer divide in exactly. Next try 3 in the same way, then 5 and so on, until a prime number is left as the last factor,

e.g. $24 = 2 \times 12 = 2 \times 2 \times 6 = 2 \times 2 \times 2 \times 3 = 2^3 \times 3$

and
$$\begin{aligned} 2100 = 2 \times 1050 &= 2 \times 2 \times 525 \\ &= 2 \times 2 \times 3 \times 175 \\ &= 2 \times 2 \times 3 \times 5 \times 35 \\ &= 2 \times 2 \times 3 \times 5 \times 5 \times 7 \\ &= 2^2 \times 3 \times 5^2 \times 7 \end{aligned}$$

Highest Common Factor (HCF)

The highest common factor of two or more numbers is the *largest* number that divides exactly into both of them.

If the numbers are less than 100, the HCF can be found by inspection, e.g. the HCF of 56 and 48 is 8.

If the HCF is not obvious, it can be found by first expressing each number as a product of its prime factors and then picking out the largest product of primes that is a factor of both of them,

e.g. $108 = 2^2 \times 3^3$ and $204 = 2^2 \times 3 \times 17$

Now we can see that $2^2 \times 3$, i.e. 12, is the highest number that is a factor of both 108 and 204.

MULTIPLES

A multiple of a number contains the first number as a factor,
e.g. some multiples of 3 are 3, 6, 24, 300.

Lowest Common Multiple (LCM)

The lowest common multiple of two or more numbers is the *smallest* number that is a multiple of both of them, i.e. each of them is a factor of their LCM.

For example, the smallest number for which 6 and 8 are each factors is 24, so 24 is the LCM of 6 and 8.

If the LCM of a set of numbers is not obvious then it can be found by expressing each number as a product of its prime factors and then picking out the smallest product that includes all the factors of both numbers,

e.g. $108 = 2^2 \times 3^3$ and $204 = 2^2 \times 3 \times 17$

so $2^2 \times 3^3 \times 17$ is the lowest number of which each of 108 and 204 are factors,

i.e. 1836 is the LCM of 108 and 204.

Exercise 1c

1. List all the factors of each number.

(a) 6 (e) 16 (i) 18

(b) 8 (f) 20 (j) 36

(c) 21 (g) 11 (k) 27

(d) 30 (h) 25 (l) 45

2. Using a ten by ten square, list all the numbers from 1 to 100. Ring all the prime numbers in the square.

3. Starting with the number itself, write down the four lowest multiples of each number.

(a) 2 (c) 5 (e) 12

(b) 4 (d) 3 (f) 8

4. Find the highest common factor of each set of numbers.

(a) 2, 3
(b) 4, 6
(c) 8, 12
(d) 36, 45
(e) 24, 51
(f) 26, 65
(g) 12, 15
(h) 12, 18
(i) 6, 12
(j) 48, 110
(k) 39, 13, 26
(l) 12, 36, 42

5. Find the lowest common multiple of each set of numbers.

(a) 2, 3
(b) 4, 6
(c) 3, 5
(d) 4, 18
(e) 6, 15
(f) 4, 10
(g) 12, 15
(h) 18, 24
(i) 15, 18
(j) 24, 36
(k) 9, 12, 18
(l) 12, 16, 24

6. Find the value of

(a) 3^3
(b) $2^2 \times 2^3$
(c) 5^3
(d) $3^2 - 2^3$
(e) 4^3
(f) 2^4
(g) $5^2 - 4^2$
(h) 9^2
(i) $3^3 - 4^2$
(j) 3^4
(k) $(2^3)^2$
(l) $7^2 \times 2^2$
(m) $11^2 + 2^5$
(n) $12^3 \div 3^2$
(p) $(3^3)^2$
(q) $2^3 - 2^2$

7. Express each number as a product of its prime factors and write the answers in index notation.

(a) 136
(b) 720
(c) 216
(d) 450
(e) 84
(f) 528
(g) 726
(h) 314
(i) 784
(j) 405

8. From the set of numbers $\{1, 3, 4, 5, 6, 8, 10, 11, 15, 17, 21, 27\}$ write down those numbers that are

(a) prime numbers,
(b) multiples of 3,
(c) factors of 60.

9. Write down the value of

(a) 3 squared
(b) 2 cubed
(c) 5 squared
(d) 4 cubed

10. Find the smallest length of tape that can be cut into an exact number of either 3 m lengths or 8 m lengths or 12 m lengths.

11. Two model trains travel round a double track. One train completes the circuit in 12 seconds and the other completes the circuit in 15 seconds. If they start side by side how long will it be before they are side by side again ?

12. A rectangular floor measures 450 cm by 350 cm. What is the side of the largest square tile that can be used to cover the floor without any cutting ?

13. What is the smallest sum of money that can be made up of an exact number of $20 notes or of $50 notes ?

14. Rectangular tiles measure 15 cm by 9 cm. What is the length of the side of the smallest square area that can be covered with these tiles ?

15. A rectangular shaped patio measures 550 cm by 330 cm. What is the largest sized square stone that can be used to pave the area without any cutting ?

16. Steve, Sally and Darren all go to Mrs James for music lessons. Steve goes every fourth day, Sally every eighth day and Darrel every sixth day. They all go for a lesson on Monday, 1st February. On what date and day of the week will they next all have a lesson on the same day ?

NEGATIVE NUMBERS

There are many quantities whose values can fall below a natural zero. Temperature is an obvious example.

Measuring in degrees Celsius (°C), 0 °C is the temperature at which water freezes. To describe temperatures below the freezing point of water we use the numbers $-1, -2, -3, \dots$ These are called negative numbers. Therefore a temperature of -2 °C means 'two degrees below freezing point'.

Most people would call -2 °C 'minus 2 °C' but it is better referred to as 'negative 2 °C' as 'minus' also means 'subtract'.

POSITIVE NUMBERS

To describe temperatures above freezing point we use positive numbers, i.e. $+1, +2, +3 \dots$

A temperature of 2 °C above freezing point can be written as $+2$ °C and called 'positive 2 °C', although most people would call it simply 2 °C and write it without the + sign. In fact *any number without a symbol in front of it is assumed to be a positive number.*

DIRECTED NUMBERS

Positive and negative numbers are collectively known as *directed numbers.* As well as temperature, they can be used to describe any measurement that goes above or below an obvious zero level, e.g. distance above or below sea-level, time after or before an event.

Directed numbers can also be used to describe quantities that involve one of two possible directions. For example, if a car is travelling along a road at 20 m.p.h. and another car is travelling at 20 m.p.h. in the opposite direction, then we could describe them as moving at $+20$ m.p.h. and at -20 m.p.h. respectively (or as 20 m.p.h. and -20 m.p.h.).

The Number Line

Positive and negative numbers can be represented on a number line.

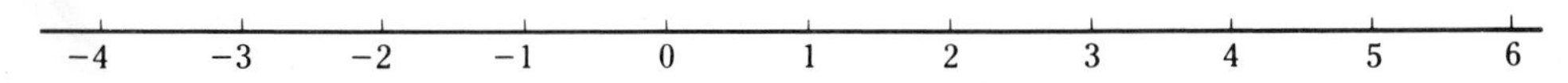

On this number line, 5 is to the *right* of 3

and we say that 5 is *greater than* 3

or $5 > 3$ where '>' means 'is greater than'.

Any number to the right of another number is greater than that second number, i.e. $-1 > -4$ and $6 > -2$

Conversely, any number to the *left* of another number is *less than* the second number. Therefore, using '<' to mean 'is less than', we have

$-3 < 1$ and $2 < 6$

Addition and Subtraction of Directed Numbers

If, at midnight, the temperature was 5 °C and if the temperature fell by 7 degrees in the next two hours, then we can represent this mathematically as

$$5\,°C - 7\,°C$$

The resulting temperature can be found by starting at 5 °C and then counting 7 degrees down the temperature scale, giving $5\,°C - 7\,°C = -2\,°C$

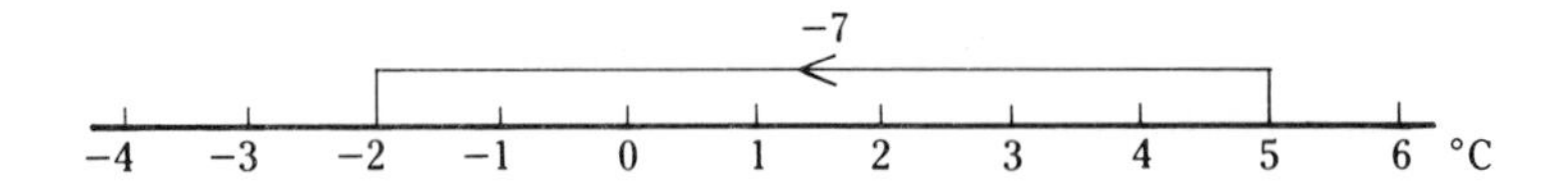

A similar argument applies to any application of directed numbers, so we can abstract the general rule: to take away a positive number, we move to the left along the number line.

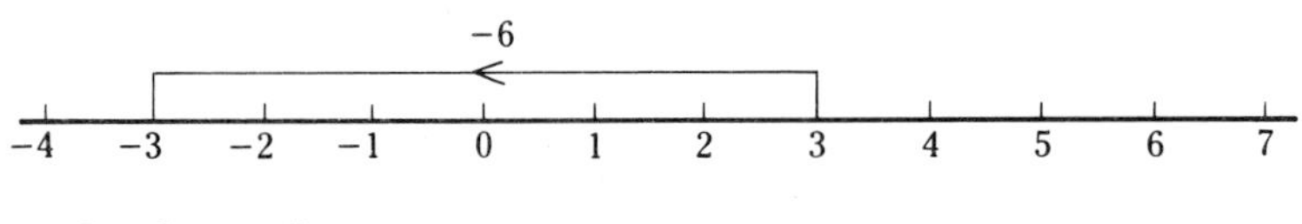

e.g. $3 - 6 = -3$

Extending the argument, to add a positive number move to the right along the number line.

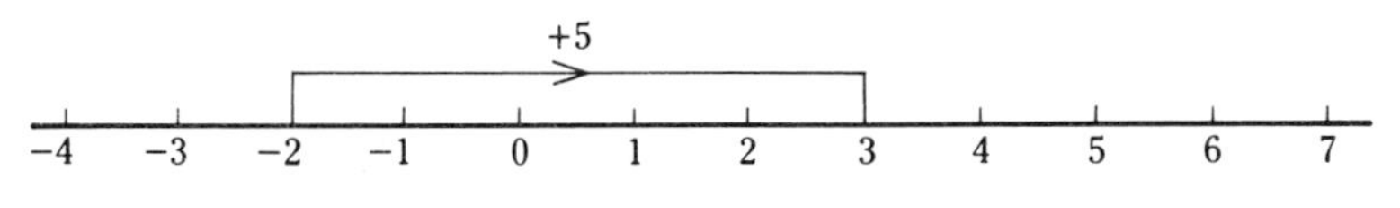

e.g. $-2 + 5 = 3$

The rules for addition and subtraction of negative numbers can also be deduced from temperature problems.

To freeze water we have to reduce its temperature and we can think of this either as adding coldness (negative heat) or as taking away warmth (positive heat), so

adding a negative number
is the same as taking away a positive number,

e.g. $+(-4) = -(+4) = -4$

If you want to melt an ice cube then you have to take away its frozen state, which means you have to add warmth.

If the temperature of the ice cube starts at −6 °C, then to melt it we have to increase its temperature by 6 °C, i.e. $-(-6\,°C) = +6\,°C$

Therefore,

taking away a negative number
is the same as adding a positive number,

e.g. $-(-5) = +5$

Exercise 1d

1. Insert > or < between each pair of numbers.

(a) 3 4		(g) 2 −5	
(b) 5 2		(h) 6 0	
(c) −1 5		(i) −15 −25	
(d) −3 −6		(j) 0 10	
(e) −2 −4		(k) −7 −5	
(f) 0 −1		(l) 12 −10	

2. Evaluate
   (a) $2-9$
   (b) $-3+2$
   (c) $4-3$
   (d) $-2-7$
   (e) $7-10+6$
   (f) $-3-2+6$
   (g) $5-12+4$
   (h) $8-9-12$
   (i) $-6+2+4$
   (j) $-8+5-2$
   (k) $7-4-6$
   (l) $5+7-9$
   (m) $6+7-8-3+6$
   (n) $-8-6-4+7-3$
   (p) $5-7+9-11$
   (q) $16-20+4-3-6$

Evaluate
(a) $3+(-4)$
(b) $-2-(4-2)-(7-12)$

(a) $3+(-4) = 3-4 = -1$

(b) $-2-(4-2)-(7-12)$

$= -2-(2)-(-5)$

$= -2-2+5$

$= 1$

3. Evaluate
   (a) $-2+(-4)$
   (b) $8+(-4)$
   (c) $3-(-4)$
   (d) $-5-(-4)$
   (e) $-7+(-2)$
   (f) $-2-(-7)$
   (g) $6+(-4)$
   (h) $9-(-6)$
   (i) $3+(-3)-3$
   (j) $7+(-1)-(-4)$
   (k) $(-2)+(-2)+(-2)$
   (l) $4-(-3)+(-6)$

MULTIPLICATION AND DIVISION OF DIRECTED NUMBERS

The rules for multiplication and division of directed numbers are extensions of those for addition and subtraction.

Consider $2\times(-3)$; this means '2 lots of −3' which is −6,

i.e. $2\times(-3) = -6$

The order in which two numbers are multiplied does not matter, so

$$2\times(-3) = (-3)\times 2 = -6$$

Hence when a positive number and a negative number are multiplied, the result is negative.

Now consider $-2\times(-3)$.

This can be interpreted as meaning 'subtract 2 lots of -3'
i.e. $-2\times(-3) = -(-6)$ and we know that $-(-6) = 6$

Therefore $$-2\times(-3) = 6$$

so multiplying two negative numbers gives a positive result.

Now consider $-6\div(-2)$

This means 'the number of (-2)s needed to make -6', which is 3

i.e. $$-6\div(-2) = 3$$

so dividing a negative number by a negative number gives a positive result.

Lastly consider $-6\div 2$, which means 'the number of 2s needed to make -6'

Now to get *negative* 6 we need to multiply 2 by a negative number, so

$$-6\div 2 = -3$$

A similar argument shows that $6\div(-2) = -3$, so dividing one number by another with the opposite sign gives a negative result.

We know that multiplying or dividing two positive numbers gives a positive result, so the rules can be summarised as follows.

When two numbers are multiplied or divided, then
if the signs are the same (both + or both −), the result is positive,
if the signs are different (one + and one −), the result is negative.

Exercise 1e

Evaluate (a) $4+3(-7)$ (b) $-5-6\div(-2)$

(a) $4+3(-7) = 4-21 = -17$ Remember, × and ÷ before + and −

(b) $-5-6\div(-2) = -5+3 = -2$

1. Evaluate
   (a) $2-4(-2)$
   (b) $4+3(-4)$
   (c) $-4\div -2$
   (d) $(3-5)\div(-2)$
   (e) $5-2\div(-1)$
   (f) $8-3(-5)$
   (g) $8\div(4-6)$
   (h) $12+3(-6)$
   (i) $(-2)^3$
   (j) $2\times(-2)\times(-3)$
   (k) $(-4)^2$
   (l) $(-3)^2\times(-2)^5$

2. Evaluate
   (a) $(-2)\times 3+4\times(-5)$
   (b) $(5-8)\div(2-5)$
   (c) $(2-10)\div(-4\times 2)$
   (d) $(-2)^2\times 3-10\div(-2)$
   (e) $(-1)^5\times(-2)^2\times 2$
   (f) $(7-18)\times(4+(-2))$

3. There are two numbers, each of which satisfies the condition that when it is multiplied by itself the answer is 25. What are these two numbers?

4. What number has to be multiplied by -6 to get 42?

5. What is the relationship between consecutive numbers in this set?

$$-3,\ 9,\ -27,\ 81,\ -243$$

6. Consider this list of numbers:

$$-4,\ 8,\ -16,\ 32,\ -64$$

   (a) What is the relationship between consecutive numbers?

   (b) Keeping the relationship between consecutive numbers the same, extend *each* end of the list by two numbers.

7. Insert $=$ and any of the symbols $+$, $-$, $\times$, $\div$ and brackets, to connect each set of numbers, keeping the numbers in the order given, e.g. for (a) $4 = 1-(-3)$. (There may be more than one way to connect the numbers.)

   (a) 4 1 −3
   (b) 5 −2 7
   (c) 2 3 5
   (d) 2 −2 4
   (e) 1 −2 −3
   (f) 5 −4 9

8. Find as many ways as you can of connecting the numbers in the following set. They do not have to be kept in the same order.

$$8 \quad -2 \quad 5 \quad 2$$

(One way is $8+2 = -5\times(-2)$)

TYPES OF NUMBER

Sets of numbers that have properties in common are classified by name.

The *integers* are all the positive and negative whole numbers, and zero,

i.e. $\ldots,\ -2,\ -1,\ 0,\ 1,\ 2,\ldots$

(Note that zero is neither positive nor negative.)

The *natural numbers* are the positive whole numbers, $1,\ 2,\ 3,\ 4,\ldots$
These are also called counting numbers, or positive integers.

Even numbers are integers that are exactly divisible by 2,

i.e. $\ldots,\ -4,\ -2,\ 2,\ 4,\ 6,\ldots$

All even numbers end with 0, 2, 4, 6 or 8.

Odd numbers are integers that are not exactly divisible by 2

i.e. $\ldots,\ -3,\ -1,\ 1,\ 3,\ 5,\ldots$

All odd numbers end with 1, 3, 5, 7 or 9.

A *prime number* is a positive integer that has only two distinct factors, itself and 1
Note that 1 is not a prime number.

A *square number* is a positive integer for which the number of dots representing the number can be arranged in a square pattern. For example, 25 is a square number because 25 dots can be arranged as a 5 by 5 square. Square numbers are also called perfect squares. A square number can be expressed as the product of two equal factors,

e.g. $25 = 5\times 5 = 5 \text{ squared} = 5^2$

A *triangular number* is a positive integer that is equal to the number of dots in any one triangle in this continuing pattern:

So the first four triangular numbers are 1, 3, 6 and 10

Note that not all numbers fit into one of these categories and we will meet other types of number later in this book.

SEQUENCES

This list of numbers is a sequence: 2, 4, 8, 16 . . .
The numbers are in order, i.e. 2 is the first number in the sequence, 4 is the second number, and so on.
Each number in this sequence is double the previous number, so the sequence can be continued, i.e. 2, 4, 8, 16, 32, 64, . . . and so on as far as we like.

A sequence is a set of numbers or shapes that has the two general properties illustrated above, i.e. the numbers are in a given order and there is a rule or procedure for continuing the sequence.
Sometimes the rule is given, in which case we can write down as many terms in the sequence as we wish. Sometimes the first few terms of the sequence are given and we have to discover the rule from these.

Each member of a sequence is called a *term* of the sequence.

Exercise 1f

1. Write down the next two terms in each of the following sequences.
   (a) 1, 2, 3, 4, . . .
   (b) -5, -3, -1, 1, 3, . . .
   (c) 1, 3, 6, 10, . . .
   (d) 2, 3, 5, 7, 11, . . .

2. In each sequence in question 1, all the terms are numbers of a particular type. For each sequence write down the name of the type of number.

3. Each of the following sequences is described in words. Write down the first four terms of each sequence.
   (a) the integers in descending order starting with 1
   (b) the prime numbers in ascending order starting with 13

4. For each of the following sequences, the first term and the rule for obtaining the next and subsequent terms is given. Write down the first five terms of the sequence.
   (a) 1; add 2 to the previous term.
   (b) 1; multiply the previous term by -2.
   (c) 96; divide the previous term by -2.
   (d) 1; each term is the sum of all the factors of the number representing its position (e.g. the 10th term is the sum of all the factors of 10, i.e. $1+2+5+10 = 18$).
   (e) 1; the square numbers in order of size.
   (f) 3; subsequent multiples of three.
   (g) 1; the second term is 2 and each subsequent term is the product of the two previous terms.
   (h) 2; the second term is 3 and each subsequent term is the sum of all the previous terms.

Investigations

Some of the suggestions that follow can take a great deal of time. If a computer is available and you have some programming skills, some of these investigations can be taken further. A calculator at least is essential.

1. Using no more than four numbers, each of which must be either 2 or 3, and the ordinary rules of addition, subtraction and multiplication, it is possible to make other numbers.

For example, $1 = 3 - 2$ and $10 = (3 \times 3) + 3 - 2$

(a) Show that there are other ways of making 10

(b) Find as many ways as possible of making the numbers 6, 7 and 8

(c) Investigate which numbers greater than 10 can be made.

(d) If there is no restriction on the number of 2s and 3s allowed, show that all numbers can be made.

2. *Perfect numbers*
A perfect number is equal to the sum of its factors including 1 but excluding itself. What is the smallest perfect number ? Try to find some more.

3. *Prime primes*
A prime prime number is a prime such that if the right-hand digits are successively removed, the remaining numbers are also prime. For example, 3797 (which is prime) gives 379, 37 and 3, each of which is prime. Try to find some more prime primes.

4. *Palindromes*
A number that reads the same forwards and backwards, e.g. 14641, is called a palindrome. There is a conjecture (i.e. it has not been proved) that if we take any number, reverse the digits and add the two numbers together, then do the same with the result and so on, we will end up with a palindrome.

Try to find some (non-palindromic) two digit numbers for which the palindrome appears after the first sum.

(a) Write down a palindrome that has
(i) 3 digits (ii) 4 digits (iii) 6 digits (iv) 7 digits

(b) If two palindromes are added together, is the result always a palindrome ?

(c) Is the difference between two palindromes a palindrome ? Justify your answer with examples.

(d) Is it possible to multiply a palindrome by another palindrome and get an answer that is also a palindrome ?

(e) What is the only year this century that is a palindrome ?

(f) How many dates can you find between 1990 and the end of the century that are palindromes ? (E.g. 29-11-92, i.e. 29th November 1992.)

Self-Assessment 1

1. Write down the value of (a) $24 + 36 \div 12$ (b) $4 + 3 \times 6$

2. Find (a) the highest common factor (b) the lowest common multiple, of 12 and 18.

3. Evaluate (a) $5^2 - 2^3$ (b) $4^3 - (-2)^3$

4. Find the value of $7 - 2(5 - 8)$

5. Write down the next two terms in the sequence $2, -6, 18, -54, \ldots$

6. Using any or all of the figures 2, 3, 5, 6 and 7, write down
   (a) a multiple of 9
   (b) a prime number greater than 20
   (c) an odd number greater than 100
   (d) a number that gives -4 when subtracted from 58
   (e) a square number.

7. Without using a calculator, evaluate 305×126

8. Find the remainder when 385 is divided by 87.

9. Without using a calculator, write down the value of
   (a) 120×30 (b) $2400 \div 60$ (c) $2 \times 3 \times 2$

10. Find two numbers whose sum is 24 and whose product is 140.

11. Evaluate $12 + 7 + 5 + 8 + 6 + 13$

12. The first two terms of a sequence are 3, 6. Subsequent terms are obtained by subtracting the previous term from the one before it. Write down the next five terms of the sequence.

13. A box measures 12 cm by 15 cm by 9 cm. The box is to be filled with cubes so that no space is left. What is the length of the side of the largest cube that will do this ?

2 FRACTIONS AND DECIMALS

FRACTIONS

The word fraction means part, so part of a quantity is called a fraction of it.

The bottom number in a fraction is called the *denominator*. The denominator gives the fraction its name and describes the number of equal-sized parts into which the whole has been divided.
The top number in a fraction is called the *numerator* and states how many of the equal parts are being considered.

For example, $\frac{3}{5}$ of a bar of chocolate means that the bar has been divided into 5 equal-sized parts and that 3 of these parts are being considered.

Equivalent Fractions

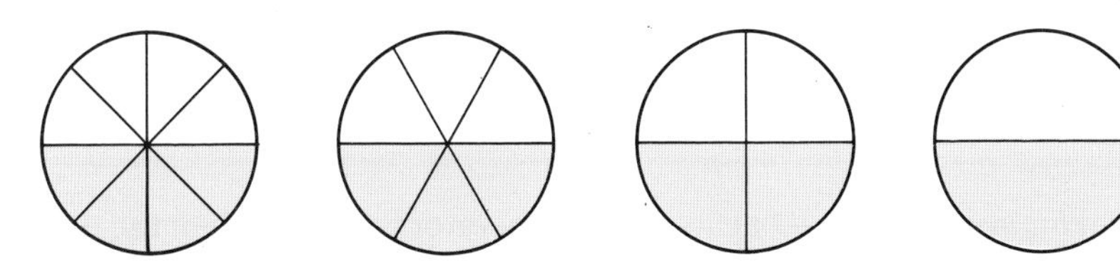

From the diagrams it is clear that $\frac{4}{8}$, $\frac{3}{6}$, $\frac{2}{4}$ and $\frac{1}{2}$ of the circle are all the same part of the circle.

The fractions $\frac{4}{8}$, $\frac{3}{6}$, $\frac{2}{4}$ and $\frac{1}{2}$ are called *equivalent fractions.*

Equivalent fractions are found by multiplying (or dividing) the numerator and the denominator by the same number,

e.g. $\quad \frac{1}{5} = \frac{1 \times 3}{5 \times 3} = \frac{3}{15} \quad$ and $\quad \frac{4}{9} = \frac{4 \times 5}{9 \times 5} = \frac{20}{45}$

When the numerator and denominator are divided by the same number, we get an equivalent fraction with smaller numerator and denominator. This is called simplifying the fraction or *cancelling.*

When the fraction has been simplified to give the smallest possible numerator and denominator, it is said to be expressed in its lowest possible terms,

e.g. $\quad \frac{15}{75} = \frac{15 \div 5}{75 \div 5} = \frac{3}{15} = \frac{3 \div 3}{15 \div 3} = \frac{1}{5}$

(This is normally set out as $\frac{\overset{1}{\cancel{\overset{3}{\cancel{15}}}}}{\underset{5}{\cancel{\underset{15}{\cancel{75}}}}} = \frac{1}{5}$)

Comparing the Sizes of Fractions

The sizes of $\frac{2}{9}$ and $\frac{1}{6}$ can be compared easily if both are expressed as equivalent fractions with the same denominator. The denominator of the equivalent fractions must therefore be a multiple of both 6 and 9. To keep the numbers involved as small as possible it is sensible to choose the lowest common multiple (LCM) of 6 and 9, which is 18.

Now $$\frac{2}{9} = \frac{4}{18} \quad \text{and} \quad \frac{1}{6} = \frac{3}{18}$$

from which we can see that $\frac{1}{6}$ is smaller than $\frac{2}{9}$.

Mixed Numbers and Improper Fractions

Fractions that are less than a whole unit are called *proper fractions.*

In the diagram below there are one and a half circles. This is written as $1\frac{1}{2}$ circles. $1\frac{1}{2}$ is called a *mixed number* because it contains a whole number and a fraction.

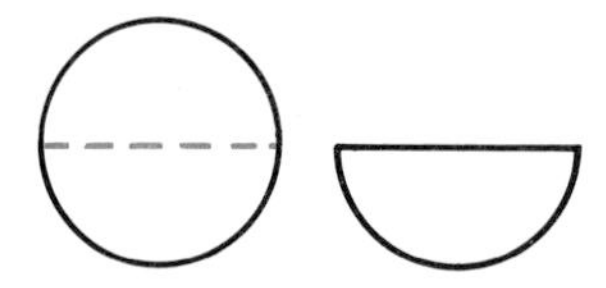

From the diagram, it is clear that $1\frac{1}{2}$ circles is the same as three half-circles, i.e. $\frac{3}{2}$ circles, so $\frac{3}{2} = 1\frac{1}{2}$.

We call $\frac{3}{2}$ an *improper fraction* because the numerator is greater than the denominator.

To change an improper fraction to a mixed number, divide the numerator by the denominator to give the number of units; the remainder is the number of fractional parts,

e.g. $$\frac{17}{5} = 3 \text{ and } \frac{2}{5} = 3\frac{2}{5}.$$

To change a mixed number to an improper fraction, multiply the units by the denominator and add the result to the numerator,

e.g. $$2\frac{1}{3} = \frac{6+1}{3} = \frac{7}{3}$$

EXPRESSING ONE QUANTITY AS A FRACTION OF ANOTHER QUANTITY

Many quantities can be divided into equal parts. For instance, there are seven days in a week, so one day is $\frac{1}{7}$ of a week and three days is $\frac{3}{7}$ of a week.

Similarly, 15 minutes can be expressed as a fraction of $1\frac{1}{2}$ hours.
There are 90 minutes in $1\frac{1}{2}$ hours so 15 minutes is $\frac{15}{90}$, i.e. $\frac{1}{6}$, of $1\frac{1}{2}$ hours.

To express one quantity as a fraction of another, first express both quantities in the same unit and then put the first quantity over the second quantity.

The Meaning of Division

$17 \div 5$ means the number of fives in 17

There are 3 fives in 17 with 2 left over. Now that remainder, 2, is $\frac{2}{5}$ of five, so we can say that there are $3\frac{2}{5}$ fives in 17,

i.e. $$17 \div 5 = 3\frac{2}{5}$$

But $$3\frac{2}{5} = \frac{17}{5}$$

therefore $$\frac{17}{5} = 17 \div 5$$

i.e. $17 \div 5 = 3$ remainder 2 or $17 \div 5 = \frac{17}{5} = 3\frac{2}{5}$

Exercise 2a

Do not use a calculator for this exercise.

1. Express each of the following fractions as eighths.

   (a) $\frac{1}{2}$ (b) $\frac{1}{4}$ (c) $\frac{3}{4}$

2. Express each of the following fractions as twelfths.

   (a) $\frac{1}{2}$ (b) $\frac{2}{3}$ (c) $\frac{3}{4}$ (d) $\frac{5}{6}$

3. Copy the following, filling in the missing numbers.

   $\frac{2}{5} = \frac{\quad}{10} = \frac{6}{\quad} = \frac{\quad}{25} = \frac{40}{\quad}$

4. Express each of the following fractions in its lowest terms.

   (a) $\frac{2}{6}$ (c) $\frac{5}{60}$ (e) $\frac{27}{36}$ (g) $\frac{99}{132}$

   (b) $\frac{3}{9}$ (d) $\frac{16}{56}$ (f) $\frac{48}{84}$ (h) $\frac{25}{115}$

5. Write each of the following improper fractions as a mixed number.

   (a) $\frac{5}{2}$ (c) $\frac{9}{4}$ (e) $\frac{53}{10}$ (g) $\frac{43}{8}$

   (b) $\frac{5}{3}$ (d) $\frac{37}{5}$ (f) $\frac{27}{4}$ (h) $\frac{69}{11}$

6. Write each of the following mixed numbers as an improper fraction.

   (a) $1\frac{1}{4}$ (c) $1\frac{2}{5}$ (e) $2\frac{2}{3}$ (g) $3\frac{2}{5}$

   (b) $2\frac{1}{3}$ (d) $3\frac{1}{4}$ (f) $1\frac{7}{8}$ (h) $6\frac{3}{4}$

7. Evaluate each of the following divisions, giving the answer as a mixed number.

   (a) $25 \div 4$ (e) $33 \div 8$

   (b) $13 \div 3$ (f) $27 \div 6$

   (c) $36 \div 5$ (g) $42 \div 10$

   (d) $50 \div 12$ (h) $17 \div 9$

8. Express both $\frac{5}{7}$ and $\frac{2}{3}$ as equivalent fractions with a denominator of 21.
Which is larger, $\frac{5}{7}$ or $\frac{2}{3}$?

9. Find equivalent fractions for $\frac{2}{3}$ and $\frac{4}{5}$ that have the same denominator. Hence write down the smaller of $\frac{2}{3}$ and $\frac{4}{5}$.

10. What fraction of one hour is (a) 1 minute (b) 10 minutes (c) 50 minutes ?

11. In the month of June it rained on 6 days. On what fraction of the total number of days in June did rain fall ?

12. What fraction of the stones in this patio are cracked ?

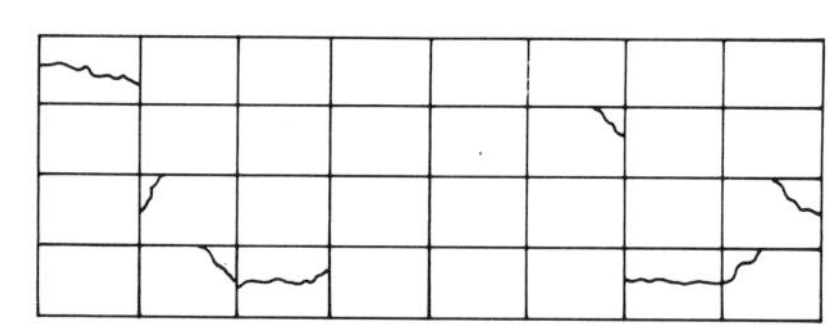

13. A tennis club has 144 members, 63 of whom are junior members, the rest being adult members. What fraction of the members are adult ?

14. Arrange each set of fractions in ascending order of size.

(a) $\frac{2}{3}, \frac{1}{2}, \frac{3}{5}, \frac{11}{30}$ (b) $\frac{2}{5}, \frac{3}{8}, \frac{17}{20}, \frac{7}{10}$

15. Arrange each set of fractions in descending order of size.

(a) $\frac{1}{3}, \frac{5}{6}, \frac{1}{2}, \frac{7}{12}$ (b) $\frac{7}{10}, \frac{3}{5}, \frac{17}{25}, \frac{3}{4}$

16. Arrange each set of numbers in ascending order of size.

(a) $\frac{14}{5}, 3, 2\frac{7}{8}, \frac{17}{6}$ (b) $\frac{12}{7}, \frac{7}{3}, \frac{27}{14}, 2\frac{1}{6}$

ADDITION AND SUBTRACTION OF FRACTIONS

Fractions of the same kind (e.g. fifths) can be added or subtracted by adding or subtracting their numerators,

e.g. $$\frac{2}{5}+\frac{1}{5}=\frac{3}{5} \quad \text{and} \quad \frac{5}{8}-\frac{3}{8}=\frac{2}{8}=\frac{1}{4}$$

Fractions with different denominators must first be expressed as equivalent fractions with a common denominator before they can be added or subtracted.

For example, to evaluate $\frac{3}{4}-\frac{2}{3}$ we note that 12 is a multiple of 3 and of 4 so we express both $\frac{3}{4}$ and $\frac{2}{3}$ as twelfths,

i.e. $$\frac{3}{4}-\frac{2}{3}=\frac{3\times3}{4\times3}-\frac{2\times4}{3\times4}=\frac{9}{12}-\frac{8}{12}=\frac{1}{12}$$

When mixed numbers are added or subtracted, it is sensible to add or subtract the units and then deal with the fractions,

e.g. $$2\frac{1}{2}+1\frac{3}{5}=3+\frac{1}{2}+\frac{3}{5}=3+\frac{5}{10}+\frac{6}{10}=3+\frac{11}{10}=3+1\frac{1}{10}=4\frac{1}{10}$$

and $$2\frac{1}{2}-1\frac{3}{5}=1+\frac{5}{10}-\frac{6}{10}=1-\frac{1}{10}=\frac{9}{10}$$

FRACTIONS OF QUANTITIES

To find $\frac{1}{4}$ of the number of tiles on this floor, we need to find $\frac{1}{4}$ of 12, i.e. $12 \div 4$, which is 3.

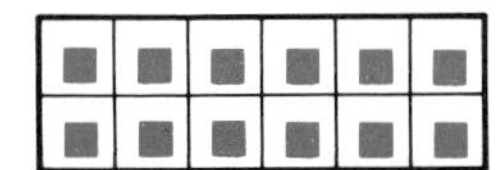

To find $\frac{3}{4}$ of the number of tiles on the floor we need $\frac{3}{4}$ of 12, i.e. $3 \times (12 \div 4)$, which is 9.

Hence to find a fraction of a quantity, multiply by the numerator and divide by the denominator.

MULTIPLYING FRACTIONS

Now $\frac{3}{4}$ of 12 can be written as $\frac{3}{4} \times 12 = \frac{3}{4} \times \frac{12}{1}$

But $\frac{3}{4}$ of $12 = 3 \times 12 \div 4 = \frac{3 \times 12}{4}$

i.e. $$\frac{3}{4} \times \frac{12}{1} = \frac{3 \times 12}{4 \times 1}$$

Fractions are multiplied by multiplying the numerators and multiplying the denominators.

When mixed numbers are multiplied, they must first be changed into improper fractions, e.g.

$$2\frac{1}{2} \times \frac{3}{4} = \frac{5}{2} \times \frac{3}{4} = \frac{5 \times 3}{2 \times 4} = \frac{15}{8} = 1\frac{7}{8}$$

and $$1\frac{1}{2} \times 2\frac{2}{3} = \frac{3}{2} \times \frac{8}{3} = \frac{{}^{1}\cancel{3} \times \cancel{8}^{4}}{{}_{1}\cancel{2} \times \cancel{3}_{1}} = \frac{4}{1} = 4$$

Notice that, in the second example, we simplified the fraction before doing the multiplication. This is sensible, because it is easier to see the numbers that divide exactly into the numerator and denominator when they are expressed as a product of factors, rather than waiting until they are multiplied out.

RECIPROCALS

If the product of two numbers is 1 then each number is called the *reciprocal* of the other.

Now $\frac{2}{3}\times\frac{3}{2} = 1$ so $\frac{2}{3}$ is the reciprocal of $\frac{3}{2}$ and vice versa.

Also $\frac{3}{4}\times\frac{4}{3} = 1$ so $\frac{3}{4}$ is the reciprocal of $\frac{4}{3}$ and vice versa.

Hence the reciprocal of a fraction is found by inverting the fraction. To find the reciprocal of a mixed number, first change it to an improper fraction and then invert it,

e.g. the reciprocal of $1\frac{1}{2}$ is the reciprocal of $\frac{3}{2}$, which is $\frac{2}{3}$

Any number can be written as a fraction, e.g. $3 = \frac{3}{1}$ and $2.5 = \frac{2.5}{1}$

Therefore the reciprocal of 3 is $\frac{1}{3}$, which is $1 \div 3$

and the reciprocal of 2.5 is $\frac{1}{2.5}$, which is $1 \div 2.5$

The reciprocal of a number is given when 1 is divided by that number.

DIVIDING BY A FRACTION

Consider $\frac{1}{2} \div \frac{1}{4}$

This means the number of $\frac{1}{4}$s in $\frac{1}{2}$.

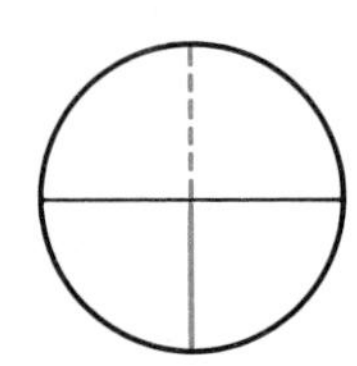

From the diagram we see that there are two $\frac{1}{4}$s in $\frac{1}{2}$, i.e. $\frac{1}{2} \div \frac{1}{4} = 2$

Now $1 \div \frac{1}{4}$ is the reciprocal of $\frac{1}{4}$, i.e. $\frac{4}{1}$, so $1 \div \frac{1}{4} = 1 \times \frac{4}{1}$

Hence $$\frac{1}{2} \div \frac{1}{4} = \frac{1}{2} \times \frac{4}{1} = 2$$

To divide by a fraction, multiply by its reciprocal. (Remember to convert any mixed numbers to improper fractions.)

Exercise 2b

Do not use a calculator for this exercise.

1. Find as a fraction in its lowest terms

(a) $\frac{2}{5}+\frac{1}{4}$
(b) $\frac{1}{4}+\frac{7}{10}$
(c) $\frac{7}{10}-\frac{1}{2}$
(d) $\frac{2}{3}-\frac{1}{2}$
(e) $\frac{1}{3}+\frac{1}{5}$
(f) $\frac{2}{3}+\frac{1}{4}$
(g) $\frac{5}{6}-\frac{2}{3}$
(h) $\frac{3}{8}-\frac{1}{7}$

2. Find as a fraction in its lowest terms

(a) $1\frac{2}{3}-\frac{5}{6}$
(b) $2\frac{1}{2}+\frac{1}{3}$
(c) $1\frac{1}{2}-\frac{2}{3}$
(d) $2\frac{1}{2}+\frac{3}{4}$
(e) $3\frac{1}{4}+1\frac{1}{5}$
(f) $3\frac{1}{3}-1\frac{1}{2}$
(g) $2\frac{1}{4}+\frac{4}{5}$
(h) $2\frac{1}{4}-1\frac{2}{3}$

3. Find as a fraction in its lowest terms

(a) $\frac{3}{4}+\frac{1}{2}-\frac{2}{5}$
(b) $\frac{3}{5}+\frac{2}{25}-\frac{3}{20}$
(c) $\frac{1}{3}-\frac{5}{18}+\frac{4}{9}$
(d) $\frac{2}{3}-\frac{1}{5}+\frac{1}{2}$
(e) $\frac{4}{5}-\frac{7}{10}+\frac{1}{2}$
(f) $4\frac{1}{5}-5\frac{1}{2}+1\frac{3}{10}$
(g) $\frac{1}{2}+\frac{7}{8}-1\frac{1}{4}$
(h) $6\frac{1}{3}-1\frac{2}{5}+1\frac{8}{15}$

4. Find

(a) $\frac{1}{4}$ of $\$24$
(b) $\frac{1}{3}$ of 1 hour
(c) $\frac{1}{5}$ of $\$35$
(d) $\frac{1}{9}$ of 27 cm
(e) $\frac{2}{3}$ of $\$48$
(f) $\frac{2}{5}$ of 85 kg
(g) $\frac{2}{7}$ of a week
(h) $\frac{2}{3}$ of 1 minute
(i) $\frac{3}{4}$ of 36 cm
(j) $\frac{5}{8}$ of 36 ft
(k) $\frac{3}{5}$ of 1 year
(l) $\frac{3}{4}$ of $\$96$

5. Find

(a) $\frac{2}{5}\times\frac{1}{3}$
(b) $\frac{5}{6}\times\frac{1}{4}$
(c) $\frac{7}{8}\times\frac{4}{21}$
(d) $\frac{3}{4}\times\frac{16}{21}$
(e) $\frac{3}{4}\times\frac{6}{7}$
(f) $\frac{2}{5}\times\frac{3}{5}$
(g) $\frac{2}{7}\times\frac{3}{7}$
(h) $\frac{8}{9}\times\frac{3}{40}$
(i) $\frac{3}{7}\times\frac{5}{9}\times\frac{14}{15}$
(j) $\frac{3}{10}\times\frac{5}{9}\times\frac{6}{7}$
(k) $2\frac{1}{2}\times\frac{7}{10}$
(l) $4\frac{2}{3}\times2\frac{2}{5}$

6. Write down the reciprocal of

(a) $\frac{3}{5}$
(b) $\frac{2}{5}$
(c) $\frac{7}{9}$
(d) $\frac{3}{4}$
(e) $\frac{2}{9}$
(f) $\frac{5}{12}$
(g) 4
(h) 6
(i) $2\frac{1}{2}$
(j) $3\frac{1}{4}$
(k) $2\frac{3}{4}$
(l) $1\frac{1}{2}$

7. Find

(a) $\frac{21}{32}\div\frac{7}{8}$
(b) $\frac{3}{56}\div\frac{9}{14}$
(c) $\frac{8}{75}\div\frac{4}{15}$
(d) $\frac{8}{21}\div\frac{4}{7}$
(e) $\frac{3}{7}\div\frac{9}{14}$
(f) $\frac{9}{26}\div\frac{60}{52}$
(g) $4\div\frac{2}{3}$
(h) $2\div\frac{2}{5}$
(i) $18\div\frac{14}{25}$
(j) $3\frac{1}{8}\div3\frac{3}{4}$
(k) $\frac{1}{5}\div1\frac{7}{20}$
(l) $6\frac{4}{9}\div1\frac{1}{3}$

Find $\left(2\frac{1}{4} \div \frac{3}{14}\right) \times 2\frac{1}{7}$

$\left(2\frac{1}{4} \div \frac{3}{14}\right) \times 2\frac{1}{7} = \left(\frac{9}{4} \div \frac{3}{14}\right) \times \frac{15}{7}$ changing mixed numbers to improper fractions

$= \frac{9}{4} \times \frac{14}{3} \times \frac{15}{7}$ inverting $\frac{3}{14}$ and multiplying

$= \frac{\cancel{9}^{3} \times \cancel{14}^{2\,1} \times 15}{\cancel{4}_{2} \times \cancel{3}_{1} \times \cancel{7}_{1}} = \frac{45}{2} = 22\frac{1}{2}$

8. Find

(a) $\frac{5}{8} \times 1\frac{1}{2} \div \frac{15}{16}$

(b) $\frac{2}{5} \times \frac{9}{10} \div \frac{27}{40}$

(c) $\left(\frac{3}{5} \div \frac{18}{55}\right) \times \frac{9}{11}$

(d) $\frac{1}{2} \times \frac{3}{5} \div \frac{5}{9}$

9. Find

(a) $\left(\frac{3}{7} \div \frac{8}{21}\right) \times \frac{2}{5}$

(b) $\frac{14}{25} \times \frac{5}{9} \div \frac{7}{18}$

(c) $2\frac{1}{2} \times 2\frac{2}{5} \div \frac{3}{5}$

(d) $\left(3\frac{1}{3} \div 2\frac{1}{6}\right) \times \frac{1}{4}$

Find (a) $\dfrac{\frac{3}{4} + \frac{2}{3}}{\frac{5}{6}}$ (b) $\frac{4}{9} + 1\frac{1}{2} \div \frac{3}{5} - 2\frac{1}{3}$

Remember: brackets first, then multiply and divide, lastly add and subtract.

(a) $\dfrac{\frac{3}{4} + \frac{2}{3}}{\frac{5}{6}} = \left(\frac{3}{4} + \frac{2}{3}\right) \div \frac{5}{6}$ the fraction line acts as a bracket

$= \left(\frac{9}{12} + \frac{8}{12}\right) \div \frac{5}{6}$ bracket first

$= \frac{17}{\cancel{12}_{2}} \times \frac{\cancel{6}^{1}}{5}$ division

$= \frac{17}{10} = 1\frac{7}{10}$

(b) $\frac{4}{9} + 1\frac{1}{2} \div \frac{3}{5} - 2\frac{1}{3} = \frac{4}{9} + \frac{3}{2} \div \frac{3}{5} - \frac{7}{3}$ improper fractions

$= \frac{4}{9} + \frac{3}{2} \times \frac{5}{3} - \frac{7}{3}$ division

$= \frac{4}{9} + \frac{5}{2} - \frac{7}{3}$ multiplication

$= \frac{8}{18} + \frac{45}{18} - \frac{42}{18}$ addition and subtraction

$= \frac{11}{18}$

10. Find

(a) $\frac{1}{2}+\frac{2}{3}\times\frac{5}{6}$

(b) $\frac{1}{3}-\frac{1}{2}\times\frac{1}{4}$

(c) $\frac{3}{4}\div\frac{1}{2}+\frac{1}{8}$

(d) $\frac{2}{3}\times\frac{1}{2}+\frac{1}{4}$

(e) $\frac{1}{7}+\frac{5}{8}\div\frac{1}{4}$

(f) $\frac{3}{5}\times\left(\frac{2}{3}+\frac{1}{2}\right)$

(g) $\dfrac{\frac{1}{2}-\frac{1}{5}}{\frac{4}{7}}$

(h) $\dfrac{\frac{3}{10}+\frac{2}{5}}{\frac{7}{15}}$

(i) $\dfrac{\frac{7}{8}}{\frac{3}{4}+\frac{2}{3}}$

The remaining part of this exercise contains a variety of questions involving fractions. Do not use a calculator.

11. How many $2\frac{1}{4}$s are there in $13\frac{1}{2}$?

12. A box holds 1 kg of flour. What fraction of its weight remains after 250 g of flour is used ?

13. The profit made at a jumble sale was \$270; $\frac{1}{3}$ of this profit was spent on new equipment and then $\frac{1}{4}$ of the remaining profit was spent on paint. What sum of money was left ?

14. What is $\frac{4}{7}$ of $4\frac{2}{3}$ divided by $1\frac{1}{9}$?

15. Which of the following statements are true ?

(a) $3\frac{2}{3}\div 1 = 3\frac{2}{3}\times 1$

(b) the reciprocal of $1\frac{1}{2}$ is $\frac{2}{3}$

(c) $\frac{3}{2}+\frac{1}{2}\div 2 = 1$

(d) $\frac{73}{7} = 1\frac{3}{7}$

16. How many $1\frac{1}{2}$ cm lengths of wire can be cut from a wire that is 35 cm long ? What length is left over ?

17. If it takes $2\frac{1}{2}$ minutes to read 120 lines of text, how long does it take to read one line ?

18. It takes three-quarters of an hour to travel 6 miles in heavy traffic. How long does it take to travel 1 mile ?

19. Carpet tiles are $\frac{3}{8}''$ thick.

(a) What is the depth of the box needed for 12 tiles ?

(b) How many tiles will fit into a box that is 12 inches deep ?

20. The diagram shows a round peg that is placed in the middle of a circular hole.

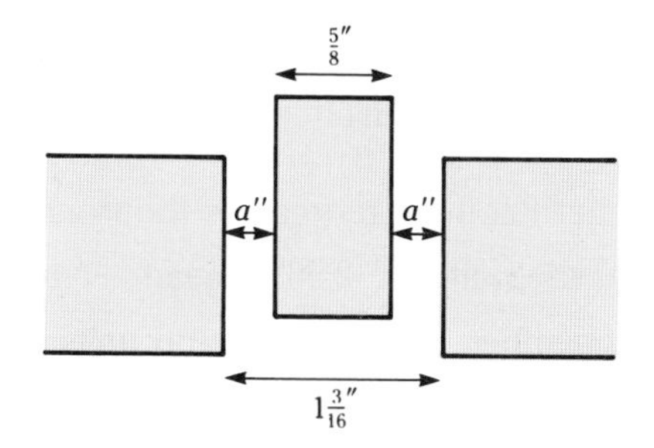

The diameter of the peg is $\frac{5}{8}''$ and the diameter of the hole is $1\frac{3}{16}''$. Find the distance marked a'' on the diagram.

21. One 5 litre container is half-filled with water and the other half is filled with oil.

A second 5 litre container is two-thirds filled with water and one-third with oil.

The contents of both containers are then carefully emptied into a 10 litre container.

What fraction of this container is

(a) filled with water

(b) filled with oil.

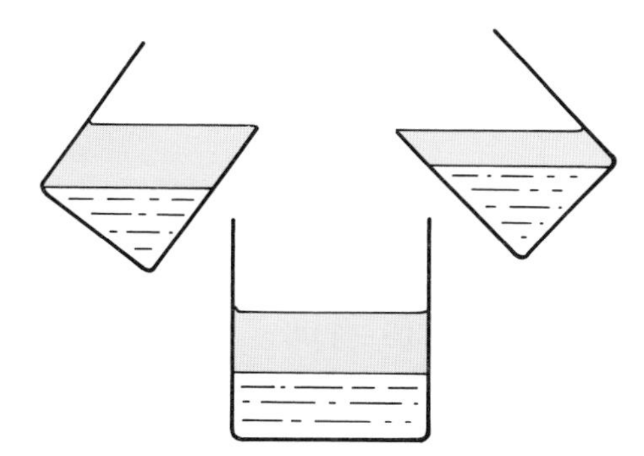

DECIMALS

The position of a figure in a number is called its *place value* and it tells us the value of that figure.

Consider the whole number 2058.
Counting from the right, the 8 in the first column represents 8 units, the 5 in the second column is 5 tens. There is 0 in the third column so there are no hundreds and the 2 in the fourth column represents 2 thousands.

Parts of a unit written in the form $\frac{2}{5}$ are properly called *vulgar fractions*.

Parts of a unit can also be written as *decimal fractions* (called decimals for short) by placing a point after the units column and continuing the columns to the right, for example 2.503

The first column after the decimal point represents tenths and this is called the first decimal place,
the second column after the point represents hundredths and is called the second decimal place,
the third column represents thousandths and so on.

Thus the number 2.503 means 2 units, 5 tenths, no hundredths and 3 thousandths.

The number 0.05 means no units, no tenths and 5 hundredths.

Changing Decimals to Fractions

As the positions of the figures after the decimal point tell us their value, it is easy to change from decimals to fractions.

For example, 0.15 means $\frac{1}{10}$ and $\frac{5}{100}$.

Now $\frac{1}{10}$ is $\frac{10}{100}$, therefore $0.15 = \frac{15}{100}$, which cancels to $\frac{3}{20}$.

Similarly, $1.025 = 1\frac{25}{1000} = 1\frac{1}{40}$

Addition and Subtraction of Decimals

Decimals can be added or subtracted in the same way as for whole numbers, provided that tenths are added to tenths and so on. To make sure that this is done it is sensible to write the numbers in a column with the decimal points under one another,

e.g. $1.6 + 3 + 0.05$ is written

$$\begin{array}{r} 1.60 \\ 3.00 \\ +0.05 \\ \hline 4.65 \end{array}$$

Notice that zeros have been added so that each number has the same number of decimal places.

Similarly $3.5 - 1.06$ is written

$$\begin{array}{r} 3.50 \\ -1.06 \\ \hline 2.44 \end{array}$$

Multiplying and Dividing by 10, 100, ...

If a number is multiplied by 10, then tens become hundreds, units become tens, tenths become units, hundredths become tenths and so on, i.e. all figures move one place to the left,

e.g. $12.72 \times 10 = 127.2$

If a number is divided by 10, then tens become units, units become tenths and so on, i.e. all figures move one place to the right,

e.g. $12.72 \div 10 = 1.272$

Extending this argument to multiplication by 100, 1000 and so on, we see that

when a number is multiplied by 10, 100, 1000, ...
the figures move 1, 2, 3, ... places to the left,

when a number is divided by 10, 100, 1000, ...
the figures move 1, 2, 3, ... places to the right.

MULTIPLICATION AND DIVISION OF DECIMALS

Decimals can be multiplied or divided by whole numbers in the usual way,

e.g. $1.3 \times 2 = 2.6$

and $1.3 \times 200 = 1.3 \times 2 \times 100 = 2.6 \times 100 = 260$

Similarly, $2.7 \div 2 = 1.35$ add zeros if necessary, i.e. $2\overline{)2.70}$ with quotient 1.35

and $2.7 \div 200 = 2.7 \div 2 \div 100 = 1.35 \div 100 = 0.0135$

Division by a decimal can be changed to division by a whole number, e.g.

$$2.8 \div 0.2 = \frac{2.8}{0.2} = \frac{2.8 \times 10}{0.2 \times 10} = \frac{28}{2} = 14$$

The method used in this example can be extended to give a general rule for division by a decimal.

To change division by a decimal
to division by a whole number, multiply
***both* the top *and* the bottom**
by 10 or 100 or ... as necessary
to change the bottom into a whole number.

The rule for multiplying by a decimal also comes from fractions,

e.g. $\underset{(1\text{ d.p.})}{1.6} \times \underset{(2\text{ d.p.})}{0.02} = \frac{16}{10} \times \frac{2}{100} = \frac{32}{1000} = \underset{(3\text{ d.p.})}{0.032}$

Notice that the sum of the numbers of decimal places in the numbers being multiplied together is equal to the number of decimal places in the result. This observation leads to the general rule that

to multiply by a decimal, first ignore the point and multiply the numbers as whole numbers. Then insert the point so that the number of decimal places in the result is equal to the sum of the numbers of decimal places in the numbers being multiplied.

CHANGING FRACTIONS TO DECIMALS

The fraction $\frac{3}{8}$ can be interpreted as meaning $3 \div 8$

By placing zeros after the decimal point, this division can be evaluated as a decimal,

i.e. $8\overline{)3.000}$ giving 0.375, hence $\frac{3}{8} = 0.375$

Any fraction can be treated in the same way, i.e.

to change a fraction to a decimal, divide the numerator by the denominator.

Exercise 2c

Do not use a calculator for this exercise.

1. Write down the value of the figure 7 in each of the following numbers.

(a) 3.07 (b) 2.74 (c) 73 (d) 57.5 (e) 30.07 (f) 0.007

2. Change each of the following decimals to a fraction in its lowest terms.

(a) 0.2 (b) 0.5 (c) 0.25 (d) 0.08 (e) 0.001 (f) 0.7 (g) 1.4 (h) 0.125 (i) 1.05 (j) 0.0025 (k) 2.06 (l) 5.005

3. Write down the value of

(a) $1.6 + 0.3$ (b) $2.8 - 1$ (c) $1.5 + 3$ (d) $1.8 - 0.5$ (e) $2.3 + 0.5$ (f) $1.6 - 0.2$ (g) $3.7 + 8$ (h) $4.4 - 1.2$

4. Find the value of

(a) $0.24 + 1.7$ (b) $0.5 - 0.04$ (c) $2.04 - 0.4$ (d) $0.09 + 1.57$ (e) $2.7 + 0.07$ (f) $0.26 - 0.08$ (g) $1.77 + 3.9$ (h) $2.44 - 1.74$ (i) $6.04 + 1.96$ (j) $3.74 - 1.27$ (k) $0.531 + 1.8$ (l) $2.5 - 1.063$

5. Write down the value of

(a) 2.5×100
(b) 0.066×10
(c) $24.4 \div 10$
(d) $12 \div 10$
(e) $0.35 \div 100$
(f) 0.044×100
(g) $32 \div 1000$
(h) 2.66×1000

6. Write down the value of

(a) 0.3×300
(b) $1.6 \div 20$
(c) 1.2×30
(d) 0.7×200
(e) $1.5 \div 50$
(f) $14.4 \div 120$
(g) 400×0.6
(h) $0.84 \div 40$

Find the value of (a) 1.4×0.04
(b) $1.4 \div 0.04$

(a) 1.4×0.04
$= 0.056$
(1 + 2) decimal places)

$$\begin{array}{r} 14 \\ \times 4 \\ \hline 56 \end{array}$$

(b) $1.4 \div 0.04 = \dfrac{1.4}{0.04}$

$= \dfrac{140}{4}$

$= 35$

7. Write down the value of

(a) $0.3 \div 0.1$
(b) $2 \div 0.2$
(c) $1.4 \div 0.07$
(d) $0.36 \div 1.2$
(e) $0.1 \div 0.01$
(f) $1.2 \div 6$
(g) $2.4 \div 0.06$
(h) $25 \div 0.05$

8. Write down the value of

(a) 1.2×0.1
(b) $(0.1)^2$
(c) 45×0.01
(d) $(0.01)^2$
(e) 2.5×0.05
(f) $(0.5)^2$
(g) 1.05×0.2
(h) $(0.2)^3$

9. Evaluate

(a) 2.56×1.2
(b) 1.33×0.2
(c) 4.5×0.03
(d) 0.7×6.3
(e) 1.05×0.12
(f) 0.06×10.5
(g) 6.4×0.05
(h) 2.5×0.08

10. Evaluate

(a) $8.4 \div 2.1$
(b) $3.6 \div 0.12$
(c) $4.5 \div 1.5$
(d) $0.056 \div 0.8$
(e) $1.32 \div 0.11$
(f) $5.4 \div 0.18$
(g) $0.0144 \div 1.2$
(h) $44.4 \div 0.02$

11. Evaluate

(a) $1.35 - 0.8$
(b) 1.35×0.8
(c) $121 \div 1.1$
(d) $15 + 8.7$
(e) $(0.2)^5$
(f) $2.66 + 1.04$
(g) $144 \div 0.16$
(h) $20 - 0.2$
(i) $3.6 + 1.09$
(j) 3.7×400

12. Evaluate

(a) $0.016 \div 80$
(b) $52 - 6.99$
(c) $1.56 \div 0.13$
(d) $0.17 + 1.9$
(e) $6 - 4.75$
(f) 8.1×400
(g) $6.9 - 4.09$
(h) $1.08 \div 200$
(i) $(0.4)^3$
(j) $0.73 + 4.37$

13. Express each of the following fractions as a decimal.

(a) $\frac{1}{5}$
(b) $\frac{1}{8}$
(c) $\frac{3}{4}$
(d) $\frac{3}{5}$
(e) $\frac{3}{20}$
(f) $\frac{1}{4}$
(g) $\frac{7}{8}$
(h) $\frac{6}{25}$

14. In the number 25.73, calculate twice the value of the figure 7 added to the value of the figure 5.

15. A piece of wire, 12.55 m long is cut into 50 pieces of equal length. How long is each piece?

16. In the number 12.08, take four times the value of the figure 8 away from twice the value of the figure 2.

17. In the number 0.95, find the product of the value of the figure 5 and the value of the figure 9.

ROUNDING NUMBERS

A statement of the number attending a football match has more impact if it is given to the nearest thousand (rather than the exact figure). It is not possible to measure the length of a dining table exactly and for most purposes a length given to the nearest centimetre is satsifactory. In each case, the number is rounded.

Consider the number 138; to the nearest ten, this is 140.
We write this 138 = 140 to the nearest ten.
However, the number 132 is 130 to the nearest ten.
This is written 132 = 130 to the nearest ten.

Notice that 138 is rounded up to 140 whereas 132 is rounded down to 130.

Now consider 135, which is exactly half-way between 130 and 140. In a case like this the rule is to *round up* to give it to the nearest ten, i.e. 135 = 140 to the nearest ten.

Correcting to a Specified Number of Decimal Places

Giving a number to the nearest tenth, hundredth and so on, is done in the same way.
For example, 1.38 is 1.4 to the nearest tenth.
As tenths are represented by the first decimal place, we write

1.38 = 1.4 correct to 1 decimal place (1 d.p.)

Numbers given to the nearest hundredth, thousandth and so on, are said to be correct to 2 decimal places, correct to 3 decimal places and so on.

The rule for giving a number
correct to a specified number of decimal places is:
look at the figure in the next decimal place.
If this figure is less than 5, round down.
If this figure is 5 or more, round up.

SIGNIFICANT FIGURES

A person's height could be given as 1.73 metres or as 173 cm or as 1730 mm or (although unlikely) as 0.001 73 km.

Each of these measurements has the same degree of accuracy, i.e. each is given to the nearest centimetre. In each number, the figure 1 has a different place value although the figure 1 is the first figure in each number. It is called the *first significant figure*. Similarly, 7 is the second significant figure and 3 is the third significant figure.

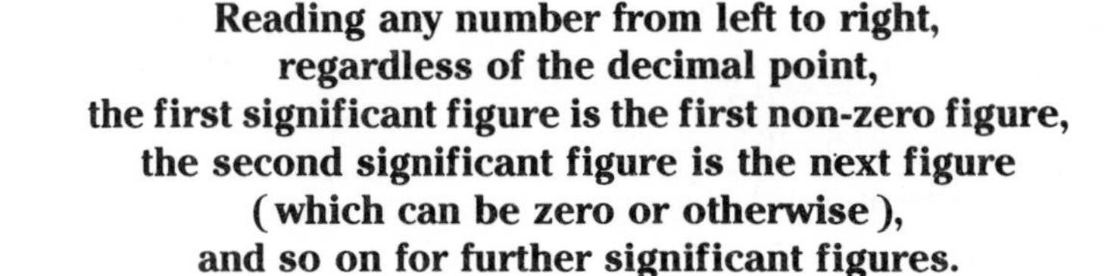

Reading any number from left to right,
regardless of the decimal point,
the first significant figure is the first non-zero figure,
the second significant figure is the next figure
(which can be zero or otherwise),
and so on for further significant figures.

For quantities such as length it is sensible to give numbers correct to a specified number of significant figures rather than a given number of decimal places. The rule for giving a number correct to a specified number of significant figures is the same as for correcting to a number of decimal places, i.e. look at the next significant figure; if it is 5 or more then round up, if it is less than 5 then round down.

For example
1.05|9 = 1.06 correct to 3 significant figures (3 s.f.)
0.33|3 = 0.33 correct to 2 significant figures
169|8 = 1700 correct to 3 significant figures
1.99|9 = 2.00 correct to 3 significant figures

Notice that the corrected number must be the same order of size as the original number. Notice also that zeros are placed after the point when necessary to give the required number of significant figures.

ESTIMATING THE RESULT OF A CALCULATION

Using a calculator makes calculations such as 1.578×16.805 almost trivial. However it is very easy to make mistakes when keying in numbers, so it is essential that you know roughly what answer to expect so that you can check the calculator result for reasonableness.

An estimate for a calculation can be obtained by correcting each number involved to 1 significant figure,

e.g. $1.578 \times 16.805 \approx 2 \times 20 = 40$

A better estimate can be obtained by correcting to the nearest unit,

e.g. $1.578 \times 16.805 \approx 2 \times 17 = 34$

However the first estimate is good enough to act as a check and has the advantage that the numbers involved can easily be multiplied mentally. Note however, that in both cases the numbers have been rounded up, so the estimated answer is greater than the actual product.

Using a Calculator

Most calculators display answers correct to 7 significant figures.
Most problems, however, do not require this degree of accuracy; either the context of the problem will dictate the degree of accuracy needed or it will be specified.

Using a calculator to find 1.578×16.805 correct to 3 decimal places we find that the display gives the result to 7 s.f., but it is not necessary to write all these figures down. As the answer is required correct to three decimal places, we need to copy the result as far as the fourth decimal place only,

i.e. $1.578 \times 16.805 = 26.5182\ldots$

$= 26.518$ (3 d.p.)

For an answer correct to 3 s.f. we would copy the number in the display as far as the fourth significant figure,

i.e. $1.578 \times 16.805 = 26.51\ldots$

$= 26.5$ (3 s.f.)

Recurring Decimals

If we try to express $\frac{1}{3}$ as a decimal, we get 0.33333 ... and so on for ever, i.e. the figure 3 recurs. 0.3333 ... is called a *recurring decimal*. Any decimal with a recurring figure or pattern of figures is called a recurring decimal.

For example, $\frac{1}{13} = 0.076923076923076\ldots$ where 076923 recurs.

Exercise 2d

1. Write down each number to the nearest number given in the bracket.
   (a) 2177 (ten)
   (b) 2578 (hundred)
   (c) 26.87 (unit)
   (d) 3532 (thousand)
   (e) 20.73 (unit)
   (f) 0.479 (unit)
   (g) 298.2 (ten)
   (h) 439 (hundred)
   (i) 139.78 (unit)
   (j) 905 (ten)
   (k) 12.58 (unit)
   (l) 375 (hundred)

2. Write down each number correct to the number of decimal places given in the bracket.
   (a) 0.6942 (2)
   (b) 13.479 (1)
   (c) 0.9999 (2)
   (d) 2.2525 (3)
   (e) 0.058055 (3)
   (f) 28.75 (1)
   (g) 40.378 (2)
   (h) 77.99841 (3)
   (i) 0.0507702 (5)
   (j) 1.002 793 (4)

3. Write down each number in question 1 correct to 2 significant figures.

4. Write down each number in question 2 correct to 3 significant figures.

5. For each of the following fractions, (i) show that it gives a recurring decimal and give the set of figures that recur, (ii) express it as a decimal correct to 3 s.f.
   (a) $\frac{2}{3}$
   (b) $\frac{1}{7}$
   (c) $\frac{1}{6}$
   (d) $\frac{2}{9}$
   (e) $\frac{1}{11}$
   (f) $\frac{1}{30}$
   (g) $\frac{4}{15}$
   (h) $\frac{5}{13}$
   (i) $\frac{7}{9}$

6. Write down an estimate for the value of each of the following calculations.
   (a) 12.5×1.4
   (b) $54.04 \div 9.89$
   (c) $23.893 - 4.678$
   (d) $0.0794 + 0.289$
   (e) $(0.046)^2$
   (f) $(0.198)^3$
   (g) 1.6×3.142
   (h) $37.88 \div 17.6$

7. Write down an estimate for the value of each of the following calculations.
   (a) $\dfrac{2.8 \times 3.79}{1.84}$
   (b) $\dfrac{3.75}{0.94 + 1.8}$
   (c) $\dfrac{12.06 - 8.62}{125.7}$
   (d) $\dfrac{2.05 \times 0.3}{0.59}$
   (e) $\dfrac{2.88 + 3.72}{0.578 \times 37}$
   (f) $\dfrac{7.08 - 0.7556}{(8.67)^2}$
   (g) $\dfrac{0.0335 \times 2.09}{1.0956 \times 3.94}$
   (h) $\dfrac{(0.678)^2}{1.85 - 0.99}$

8. Use a calculator to evaluate each part of questions 6 and 7, giving the answer correct to 3 significant figures.

9. Express each fraction as a decimal correct to 3 decimal places and hence arrange these numbers in ascending order:

$$1.57,\ \tfrac{5}{3},\ 1.49,\ 1\tfrac{2}{7},\ \tfrac{15}{11}$$

10. Arrange these numbers in descending order:

$$0.05,\ \tfrac{3}{16},\ 0.105,\ \tfrac{2}{13},\ \tfrac{6}{25}$$

In each of the following questions, give your answer to the degree of accuracy appropriate to the problem.

11. A path is made by laying 57 paving slabs, each 0.87 m long, end to end. How long is the path ?

12. A pile of 16 identical boxes is 2.43 m high. How high is each box ?

13. A clock which is running slow takes 1.06 seconds per tick instead of 1 second. How many ticks are there in 10 minutes ?

14. What should 4.9 be multiplied by to give 8.428 ?

15. One wall of a room is 7.28 m long. The floor is covered by square carpet tiles of side 0.52 m. How many tiles fit along the wall ?

16. A builders' merchant marks goods net of VAT. The price to be paid is calculated by multiplying the marked price by 1.175. What will be charged for a tin of paint marked at £6.97 ?

17. Pills, each weighing 0.57 grams, are packed in foil strips each containing 28 pills. Four foil strips are put into a box and 450 of these boxes are put into a carton. What is the weight of pills in a carton ?

18. The label on a box of carpet tiles states that each tile measures 45 cm by 45 cm. The tiles are to be placed on a floor to form a square with 12 tiles along a side. How long will the side of the square be ?

19. Bricks are packed on pallets, each holding 378 bricks. A lorry is loaded with 15 pallets. If each brick weighs 1.2 kg, what weight of bricks is the lorry carrying ?

ROOTS AND POWERS

Square Roots

When a number is expressed as the product of two equal factors, each factor is called a square root of the number.

For example, $4 = 2 \times 2$, so 2 is a square root of 4
Notice also that $4 = (-2) \times (-2)$, so -2 is also a square root of 4

Any positive number has two square roots, a positive one and a negative one.

A negative number cannot have a square root because a negative number cannot be expressed as the product of two *equal* factors (a negative number results from multiplying a negative number and a positive number).

The symbol $\sqrt{\ }$ is used for 'square root', so $\sqrt{12}$ means the positive square root of 12, and $-\sqrt{12}$ means the negative square root of 12.

The value of $\sqrt{12}$ can be found from a calculator by pressing [1] [2] [√] ;

$\sqrt{12} = 3.464$ (3 d.p.).

(Check the result by squaring the answer, i.e. $(3.464)^2 = 11.999\ldots = 12.00$ (4 s.f.).)

Cube Roots

When a number is expressed as a product of three equal factors, each factor is called a cube root of the number.

Some numbers have exact cube roots. The cube root of 8 is 2 since $8 = 2 \times 2 \times 2$

The symbol $\sqrt[3]{\ }$ is used to mean 'the cube root of', e.g. $\sqrt[3]{8} = 2$

Notice that as $2 \times 2 \times 2$ can be written as 2^3,

we have $\quad 8 = 2^3$ so $\sqrt[3]{8} = 2$

Similarly, $\quad 25 = 5^2$ so $\sqrt{25} = 5$

Extending the argument, the fourth root of a number is the value of the factor such that the product of four of them gives the number,

e.g. $\quad \sqrt[4]{81} = 3$ since $81 = 3^4$

The *n*th root of a number is the factor such that the product of *n* of them gives the number.

MULTIPLYING AND DIVIDING NUMBERS WRITTEN IN INDEX FORM

Now $2^3 \times 2^2 = 2 \times 2 \times 2 \times 2 \times 2 = 2^5$

therefore $2^3 \times 2^2 = 2^{3+2} = 2^5$

We can multiply together powers of the *same number* by adding the powers. (Powers of different numbers cannot be multiplied in this way because the numbers multiplied together are not all the same.)

Also $2^3 \div 2^2 = \dfrac{2 \times 2 \times 2}{2 \times 2} = 2$

Therefore $2^3 \div 2^2 = 2^{3-2} = 2^1 = 2$

We can divide different powers of the same number by subtracting the powers.

Negative Indices

Consider $3^2 \div 3^5$

Subtracting the indices gives $3^2 \div 3^5 = 3^{2-5} = 3^{-3}$

But $\quad 3^2 \div 3^5 = \dfrac{3 \times 3}{3 \times 3 \times 3 \times 3 \times 3} = \dfrac{1}{3^3}$

Therefore 3^{-3} means $\dfrac{1}{3^3}$, i.e. 3^{-3} is the reciprocal of 3^3.

a^{-b} means the reciprocal of a^b

For example, $5^{-2} = \dfrac{1}{5^2} = \dfrac{1}{25}$ and $3^{-1} = \dfrac{1}{3}$

The Zero Index

If we consider $3^2 \div 3^2$

subtracting the indices gives $3^2 \div 3^2 = 3^0$

But $3^2 \div 3^2 = 1, \text{ so } 3^0 = 1$

In general, $a^b \div a^b = 1$

subtracting the indices gives $a^b \div a^b = a^0, \text{ so } a^0 = 1$, i.e.

 **any number to the power zero is equal to 1** 

Fractional Indices

Consider $4^{\frac{1}{2}} \times 4^{\frac{1}{2}}$

Adding the indices gives $4^{\frac{1}{2}} \times 4^{\frac{1}{2}} = 4^1 = 4$

This means that 4 is the square of $4^{\frac{1}{2}}$ so $4^{\frac{1}{2}}$ must mean the square root of 4, i.e. $4^{\frac{1}{2}} = \sqrt{4}$

Similarly, $8^{\frac{1}{3}} \times 8^{\frac{1}{3}} \times 8^{\frac{1}{3}} = 8^1$, so $8^{\frac{1}{3}} = \sqrt[3]{8}$

In general, $a^{1/n}$ means the nth root of a.

Using a Calculator to find Powers and Roots

Note that calculators vary both in the way that keys are marked and in their operation, so consult your instruction book if you do not get the correct results.

To find $(1.7)^4$ by using a calculator with a $\boxed{y^x}$ button, follow this sequence of key strokes.

$\boxed{1}\ \boxed{\cdot}\ \boxed{7}\ \boxed{y^x}\ \boxed{4}\ \boxed{=}$ The display will show 8.3521

To find $\sqrt[4]{1.7}$ first write $\sqrt[4]{1.7}$ as $1.7^{\frac{1}{4}}$

Then if you have a key $\boxed{y^{1/x}}$ use this sequence $\boxed{1}\ \boxed{\cdot}\ \boxed{7}\ \boxed{y^{1/x}}\ \boxed{4}\ \boxed{=}$

If you do not have the key $\boxed{y^{1/x}}$ you can use the key $\boxed{y^x}$ as follows

$\boxed{1}\ \boxed{\cdot}\ \boxed{7}\ \boxed{y^x}\ \boxed{0}\ \boxed{\cdot}\ \boxed{2}\ \boxed{5}\ \boxed{=}$ The display will show 1.1418 . . .

More complicated calculations involving roots and powers can be performed in one step on a calculator.

For example, to find the value of $\frac{2}{7}\sqrt{\frac{2.9}{5.87}}$, $2.9 \div 5.87$ can be worked out first, then its square root found, and the result multiplied by 2 and divided by 7. The intermediate calculations can be found using the $\boxed{=}$ key, but the result does not need to be written down. This key sequence can be used:

$\boxed{2}\ \boxed{\cdot}\ \boxed{9}\ \boxed{\div}\ \boxed{5}\ \boxed{\cdot}\ \boxed{8}\ \boxed{7}\ \boxed{=}\ \boxed{\sqrt{\ }}\ \boxed{\times}\ \boxed{2}\ \boxed{\div}\ \boxed{7}\ \boxed{=}$

If brackets (sometimes called parentheses in the manual) are used, the [=] key need not be used until the end, and the numbers can be keyed in, in the given order i.e.

[2] [÷] [7] [×] [(] [2] [·] [9] [÷] [5] [·] [8] [7] [)] [√] [=]

In either case, the display should show 0.200822 . . .

STANDARD FORM

Very large numbers and very small numbers are more conveniently written in *standard form.*

A number in standard form is written as a number between 1 and 10 multiplied by the appropriate power of 10.

For example 70 000 000 000 becomes 7×10^{10} when written in standard form,

and 0.000 000 004 5 becomes 4.5×10^{-9} in standard form.

To express a number in standard form, first place a decimal point between the first and second significant figures to give a number between 1 and 10. Then count to find the power of 10 by which this number should be multiplied (or divided) to restore it to its original size.

For example, to write 5800 in standard form, first place the point between 5 and 8 which gives 5.8; counting then shows that to change 5.8 to 5800, we need to multiply by 10^3

so $$5800 = 5.8 \times 10^3$$

To write 0.005 03 in standard form, the point goes between the 5 and 0 to give 5.03. To change 5.03 to 0.005 03 we need to divide by 10^3. But dividing by 10^3 is equivalent to multiplying by $\frac{1}{10^3}$, i.e. by 10^{-3}

so $$0.005\,03 = 5.03 \times 10^{-3}$$

Scientific calculators display very large and very small numbers in scientific notation or engineering notation, but only the power of ten is shown and not the ten itself.

Note that scientific or engineering notation is similar to standard form but the number is not always between 1 and 10.

Try $2\,500\,000^2$ on your calculator: the display will look something like [6.25 12] and this means 6.25×10^{12}

0.0025^2 will give [6.25 −06] on the display and this means 6.25×10^{-6}.

Exercise 2e

Do not use a calculator for questions 1, 4, 5 and 6.

1. Find the value of

(a) 4^2 (e) 2^{-1} (i) 5^{-2}

(b) 4^{-2} (f) 9^3 (j) 8^{-2}

(c) 4^0 (g) 5^0 (k) 3^{-3}

(d) 2^{-5} (h) 3^{-1} (l) 10^0

2. Find, correct to 3 s.f., the value of

(a) $\sqrt{12}+\sqrt{3}$ (b) $4\sqrt{5}-\sqrt{20}$

3. Find, correct to 3 s.f., the value of

(a) $\dfrac{2}{\sqrt{2}}+\sqrt{8}$ (b) $\dfrac{1}{2\sqrt{5}}+\sqrt{5}$

4. Write each of these numbers in ordinary form

(a) 1.2×10^3 (e) 9.0704×10^5

(b) 3.14×10^{-2} (f) 7.605×10^{-4}

(c) 3.17×10^5 (g) 1.15×10^{-10}

(d) 9.55×10^{-3} (h) 2.8×10^{12}

Find the value of

(a) $\left(\dfrac{1}{3}\right)^{-1}$ (b) $\left(\dfrac{2}{3}\right)^{-2}$ (c) 6^{-2}

(a) $\left(\dfrac{1}{3}\right)^{-1}=\dfrac{3}{1}$ (b) $\left(\dfrac{2}{3}\right)^{-2}=\left(\dfrac{3}{2}\right)^{2}=\dfrac{9}{4}$ (c) $6^{-2}=\left(\dfrac{6}{1}\right)^{-2}=\left(\dfrac{1}{6}\right)^{2}=\dfrac{1}{36}$

5. Find the value of

(a) $\left(\dfrac{1}{4}\right)^{-1}$ (c) $\left(\dfrac{1}{2}\right)^{0}$ (e) $\left(\dfrac{2}{3}\right)^{-1}$

(b) $\left(\dfrac{5}{2}\right)^{-2}$ (d) $\left(\dfrac{3}{4}\right)^{-3}$ (f) $\left(\dfrac{5}{6}\right)^{0}$

6. Find the value of

(a) $25^{1/2}$ (e) $81^{1/4}$ (i) $64^{1/3}$

(b) $27^{1/3}$ (f) $125^{1/3}$ (j) $121^{1/2}$

(c) $16^{1/4}$ (g) $49^{1/2}$ (k) $625^{1/4}$

(d) $32^{1/5}$ (h) $625^{1/2}$ (l) $144^{1/2}$

Use your calculator to find the value of 1.007^6

$1.007^6 = 1.042\ldots$

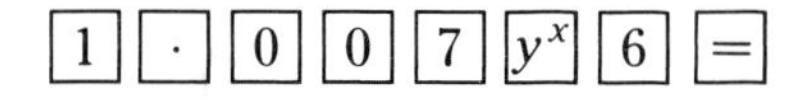

$= 1.04$ correct to 3 s.f.

7. Use your calculator to find the value of each of the following numbers giving your answer correct to 3 significant figures.

(a) 1.7^6 (e) 0.67^5 (i) $1500^{1/2}$

(b) $\sqrt[3]{5}$ (f) $\sqrt[4]{10}$ (j) $1.8^{3/2}$

(c) 2.1^{-4} (g) 1.05^8 (k) 56^{-3}

(d) $\sqrt[3]{12}$ (h) $\sqrt[5]{4.61}$ (l) 1.09^{-4}

8. Find the value of each of the following expressions correct to three significant figures and write down the sequence of keys that you used.

(a) $\dfrac{1}{2}\sqrt{\dfrac{126}{51}}$

(b) $\frac{2}{3}\sqrt{87+29.43}$

9. Work out each of the following calculations, giving your answer correct to three significant figures.

(a) $\dfrac{\sqrt[3]{3}}{\sqrt{2.8+7.29}}$ (b) $\sqrt{\dfrac{1.2-0.67^2}{0.26\times 1.05}}$

10. Write each of the following numbers in standard form.

(a) 26 500 (e) 0.002 21
(b) 0.008 23 (f) 1 070 030
(c) 204 000 (g) 6.2
(d) 0.050 99 (h) 4788

If $a = 4.6\times 10^4$ and $b = 2.3\times 10^5$ find, in standard form, the value of
(a) $a\times b$ (b) $a+b$

(a) $a\times b = (4.6\times 10^4)\times(2.3\times 10^5) = 4.6\times 10^4\times 2.3\times 10^5$

$= 4.6\times 2.3\times 10^9 = 10.58\times 10^9 = 1.058\times 10^{10}$

(b) $a+b = (4.6\times 10^4)+(2.3\times 10^5)$

$= 46\,000 + 230\,000 = 276\,000 = 2.76\times 10^5$

11. Find, in standard form, the value of

(a) $(1.2\times 10^4)\times(5.3\times 10^6)$
(b) $(7.2\times 10^{-4})\times(1.5\times 10^3)$
(c) $(3.6\times 10^6)\div(1.2\times 10^4)$
(d) $(3.3\times 10^{-3})\div(6.6\times 10^{-6})$
(e) $(1.8\times 10^3)+(1.2\times 10^2)$
(f) $(8.4\times 10^{-1})-(9.3\times 10^{-2})$

12. If $a = 2.4\times 10^5$, $b = 3.6\times 10^7$ and $c = 2.5\times 10^{-3}$ find

(a) $a\times b$ (c) $a+b$ (e) $b\div c$
(b) $a\div b$ (d) $a\times c$ (f) $a-b$

13. Find the value of each of the following

(a) $(\frac{1}{8})^{-2}$ (c) 6^3
(b) $(\frac{2}{3})^0$ (d) $(2^2)^3$

14. At a time when Jupiter, Pluto and the Sun are in line, the distances of Jupiter and Pluto from the Sun are respectively 7.88×10^8 km and 5.95×10^9 km.
What is the distance between Pluto and Jupiter when

(a) the planets on opposite sides of the Sun
(b) the planets on the same side of the Sun ?

Investigations

1. To express the fraction $\frac{16}{64}$ in its simplest terms, Ken cancelled the sixes and gave $\frac{1}{4}$ as his answer.

(a) Was his answer correct ?
(b) What was wrong with his method ?
(c) What happens to the fraction $\frac{49}{98}$ if you apply Ken's method ?
(d) Try Ken's method on the fractions $\frac{26}{65}$ and $\frac{16\,666}{66\,664}$.
(e) Find the denominator of the fraction $\frac{19}{?}$ so that Ken's method of simplifying gives the correct answer.
(f) Would you recommend Ken's method for simplifying the following fractions ? Give reasons for your answers.

$\frac{16}{62}, \frac{37}{74}, \frac{68}{86}$

2. When Winston used his calculator to find $1 \div 7$, the display showed 0.1428571

(a) Without using a calculator, multiply 0.142 8571 by 7

(b) Use your answer to decide if the number on the display of Winston's calculator is exactly equal to $1 \div 7$, or if it is a rounded value. If you decide that it is a rounded value, state whether it has been rounded up or down. Give reasons for your answers.

(c) Use your calculator to find (i) $\frac{13}{128}$ (ii) $\frac{5}{13}$. In each case write down the number shown in the display and decide whether this number is exact or rounded up or down.

(d) Use your calculator to express $\frac{1}{7}$ as a decimal. Write down the result and clear the display. Now use your calculator to find $\frac{1}{13}$ as a decimal. Write down the result and clear the display. Add your two results together. Now use your calculator to find $\frac{1}{7} + \frac{1}{13}$ in one step. Compare this answer with the previous answer. Investigate.

3. The first three terms of a sequence are

$$1 + \frac{1}{2}, \quad 1 + \cfrac{1}{2 + \cfrac{1}{2}}, \quad 1 + \cfrac{1}{2 + \cfrac{1}{2 + \cfrac{1}{2}}}$$

(a) Write down the next two terms in the sequence.

(b) The value of the second term is $1 + \frac{1}{2.5} = 1 + 0.4 = 1.4$

Find the value, correct to 4 decimal places where necessary, of each of the first 5 terms.

(c) The sequence can be continued indefinitely (this kind of pattern is called a *continued fraction*). Find the value of a few more terms and compare them with the value of $\sqrt{2}$. What seems to be happening ?

(d) Investigate the value of the continued fraction

$$1 + \cfrac{2}{1 + \cfrac{2}{1 + \cfrac{2}{1 + \cfrac{2}{1 + \dots}}}}$$

Self-Assessment 2

Do not use a calculator.

1. Find the reciprocal of

   (a) $\frac{3}{4}$ (b) $1\frac{1}{2}$

2. Evaluate

   (a) $1\frac{1}{3} \div \frac{2}{9}$ (b) $1\frac{1}{3} - \frac{2}{9}$ (c) $2\frac{1}{2} \times 1\frac{2}{5}$

3. What fraction of $3\frac{1}{2}$ hours is 45 minutes ?

4. A company has 350 employees. Three-fifths of the employees are female and two-sevenths of these work part-time. What fraction of the employees are female part-time workers and how many of them are there ?

5. Arrange these numbers in ascending order of size; $\frac{2}{3}$, 0.65, $\frac{5}{9}$, 0.7

6. Find the value of $2\frac{1}{2} + \frac{3}{4} \times \frac{4}{7}$

7. Find, correct to three significant figures, the value of $\sqrt{18} + \sqrt{\frac{72}{95}}$.
Show the sequence of buttons that you pressed on your calculator.

8. In the number 2.057, find ten times the value of the digit 5 multiplied by one quarter of the value of the digit 2.

9. Find the value of

(a) $1.2 + 0.42$ (d) $3 - 0.67$

(b) 0.5×0.7 (e) $(0.3)^2$

(c) $0.1 \div 0.01$ (f) $0.02 \div 0.4$

10. Find the value of

(a) 2^6 (c) 2^{-4} (e) $27^{2/3}$

(b) 2^0 (d) $\left(\frac{2}{5}\right)^{-1}$

11. Write each of these numbers in standard form

(a) 4 500 000 (b) 0.0024

12. Write each of these numbers correct to 3 significant figures

(a) 12.678 (b) 0.004 712 (c) 9.978

3 BASIC GEOMETRY

POINTS

A point has position but no size. A point has no dimensions.

Only one straight line can be drawn through two chosen points. The straight line joining two points is called a *line segment.* A line has one dimension.

ANGLES

An angle measures the amount of turning.
One complete turn or revolution is divided into 360°.

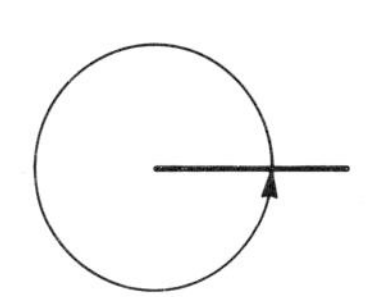

A quarter of a revolution is called a *right angle.*
A right angle is equal to 90°.

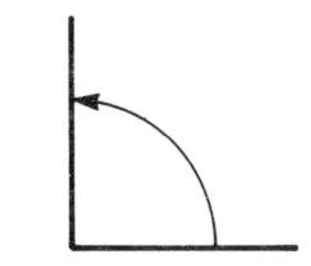

The sign for a right angle is 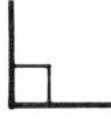

Half a revolution is two right angles.

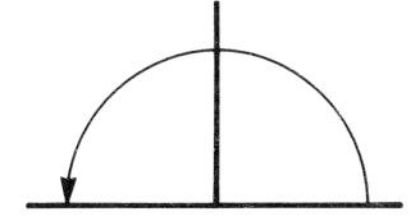

Acute, Obtuse and Reflex Angles

Any angle that is smaller than a right angle is called an *acute* angle.

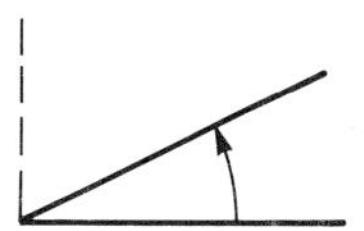

(When a line turns about a point we shall consider the *anticlockwise* direction as *positive* and the *clockwise* direction as *negative.*)

Any angle that is greater than one right angle and less than two right angles is called an *obtuse* angle.

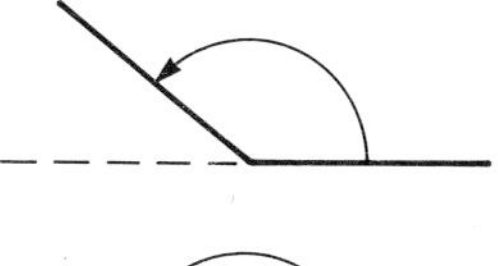

Any angle that is greater than two right angles is called a *reflex* angle.

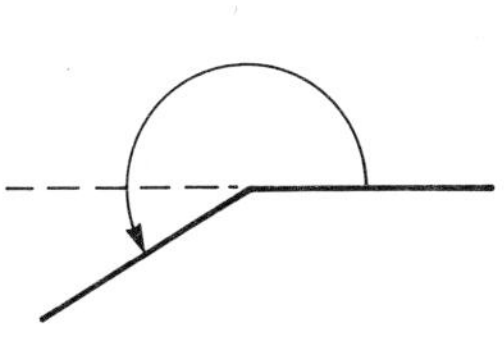

Parallel and Perpendicular Lines

Lines that are in the same direction are called *parallel lines.* They never meet and are always the same distance apart.

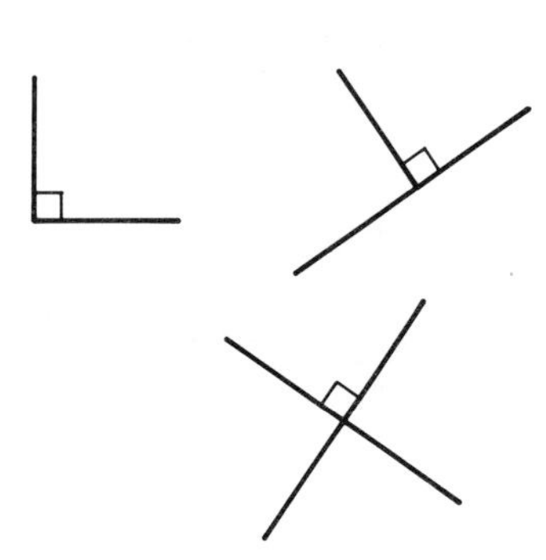

Lines that meet at right angles are said to be *perpendicular.*

ANGLE FACTS

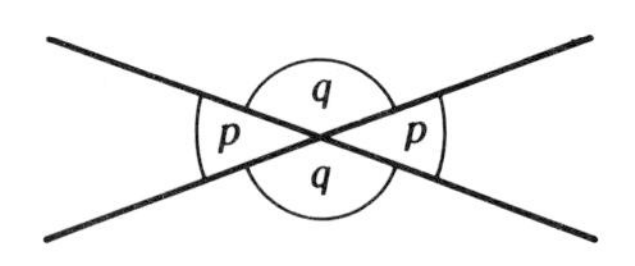

Vertically opposite angles are equal.

Complementary angles add up to 90°.

$$\hat{a} + \hat{b} = 90°$$

$\hat{a}$ is the complement of $\hat{b}$

and $\hat{b}$ is the complement of $\hat{a}$

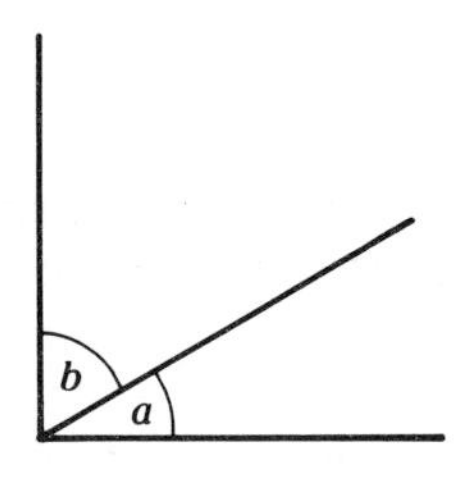

(If we use a to name an angle we will write the size of the angle as $\hat{a}$ or $\angle a$.
Hence $\hat{a} + \hat{b} = 90°$ or $\angle a + \angle b = 90°$)

Angles on a straight line add up to 180°.

$$\hat{a} + \hat{b} + \hat{c} = 180°$$

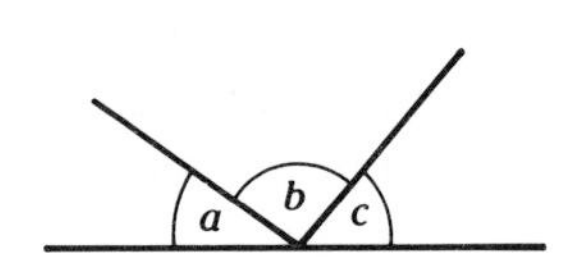

Two angles that add up to 180° are *supplementary* angles.

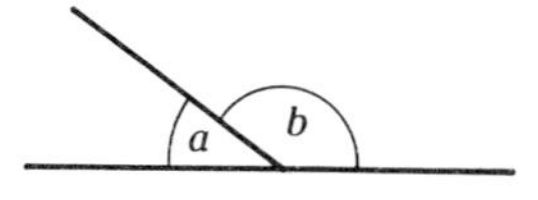

$$\widehat{a} + \widehat{b} = 180°$$

$\widehat{a}$ is the supplement of $\widehat{b}$

and $\widehat{b}$ is the supplement of $\widehat{a}$

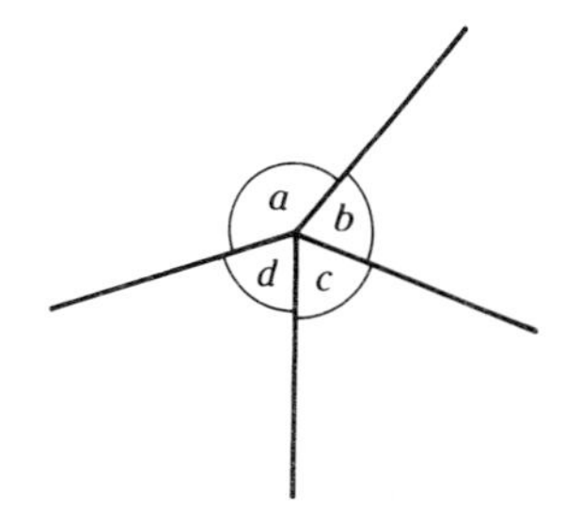

Angles at a point add up to 360°.

$$\widehat{a} + \widehat{b} + \widehat{c} + \widehat{d} = 360°$$

Exercise 3a

1. How many degrees are there
   (a) in half a revolution
   (b) in three-quarters of a turn
   (c) in two complete revolutions
   (d) in two-thirds of a turn ?

2. What angle, in degrees, corresponds to
   (a) $\frac{1}{3}$ of a right angle
   (b) 2 right angles
   (c) 0.4 of a right angle
   (d) 1.7 of a right angle ?

3. How many degrees does the hand of a clock turn through when
   (a) it starts at 2 and stops at 3
   (b) it starts at 2 and stops at 11 ?

   In each case state whether the angle is acute, obtuse or reflex.

4. For each angle in this question
   (a) state whether it is acute, obtuse or reflex
   (b) estimate its size
   (c) check your estimate by using a protractor. (Remember to choose the scale that starts at 0° on the arm of the angle on which you place the base line of the protractor. Using this scale, read off the value at the other arm.)

   (i)

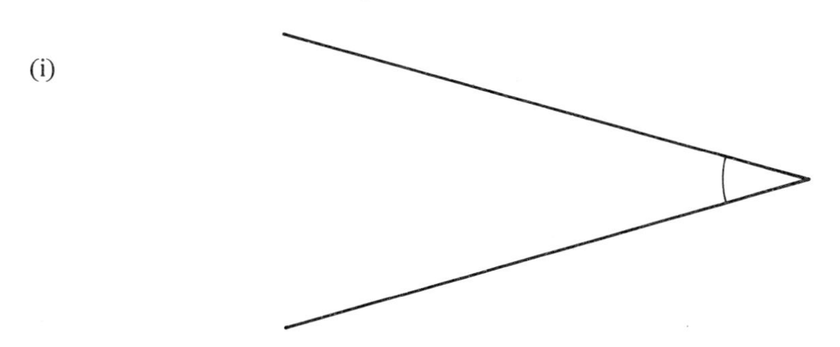

(ii)

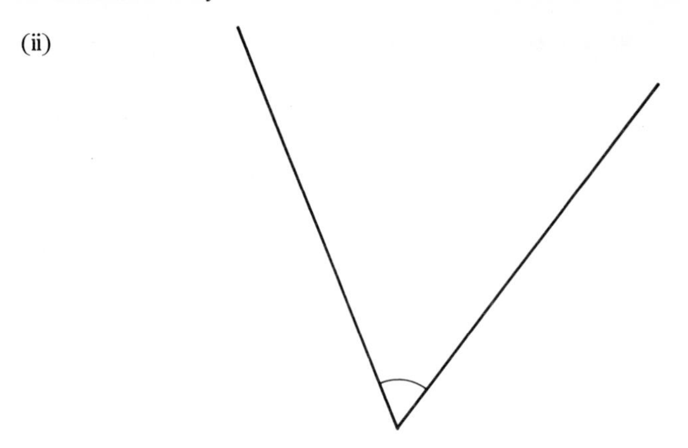

(iii)

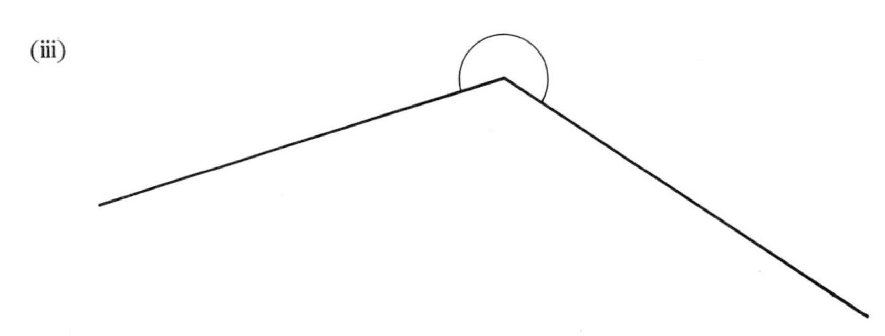

(iv)

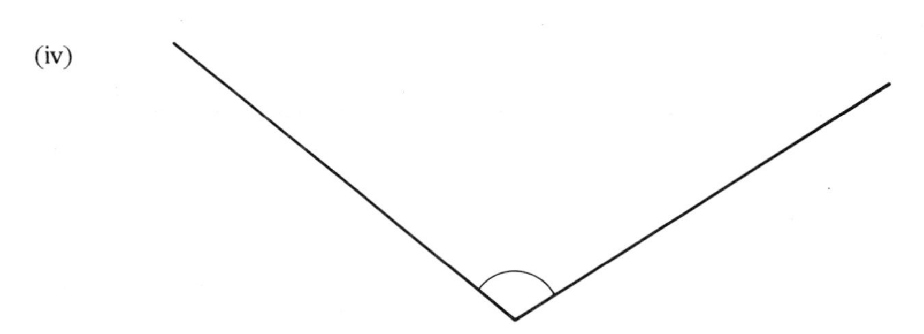

(v)

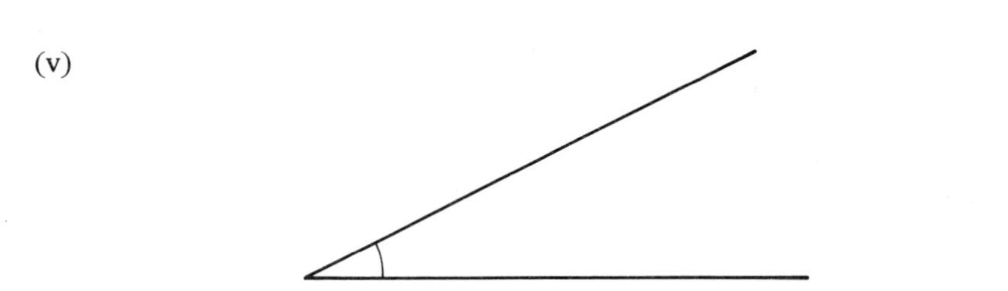

In questions 5 to 10 calculate the size of each angle marked with a letter.

5.

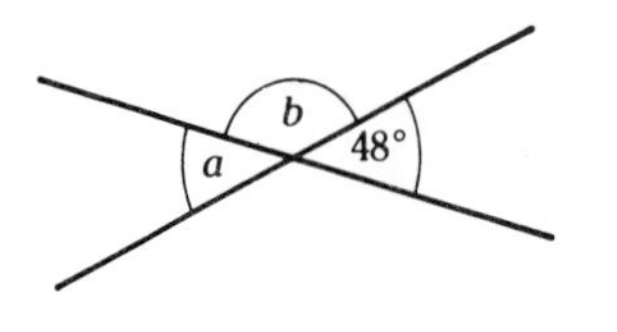

6.

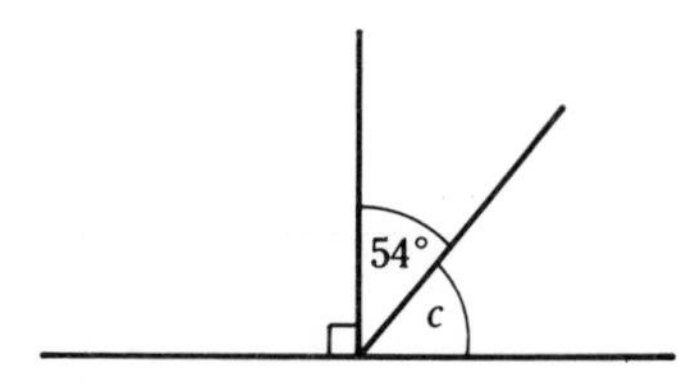

7.

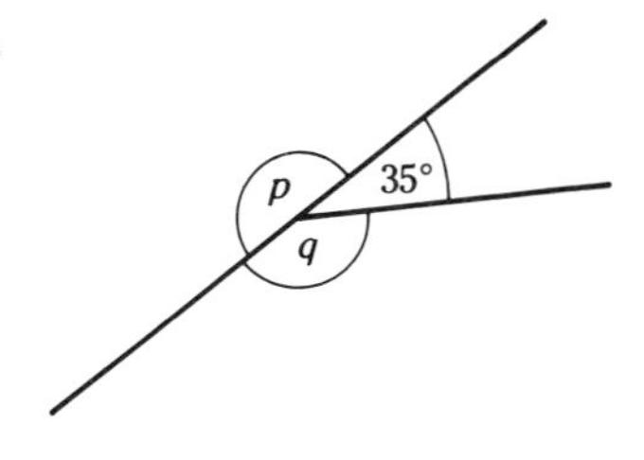

8.

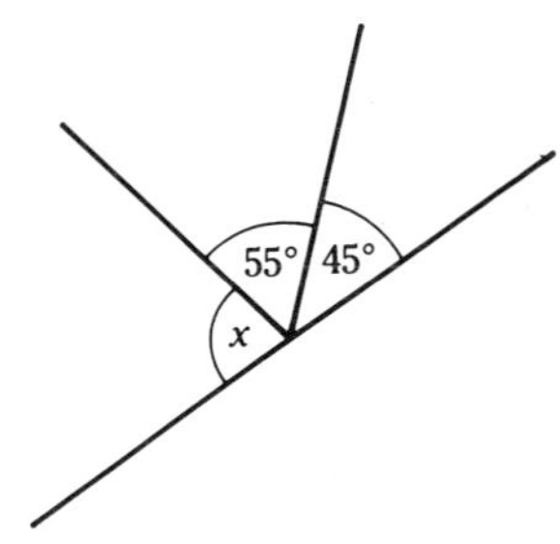

9.

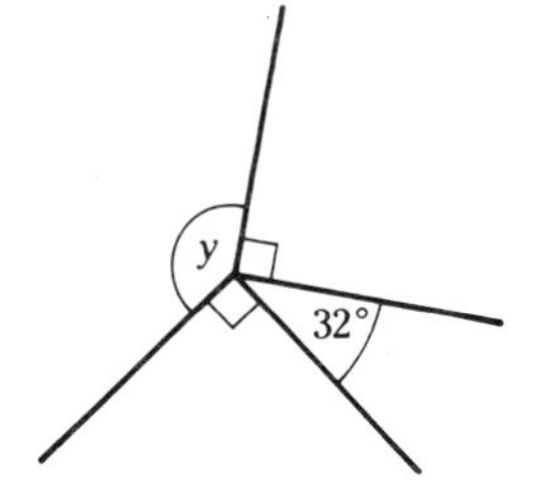

10.

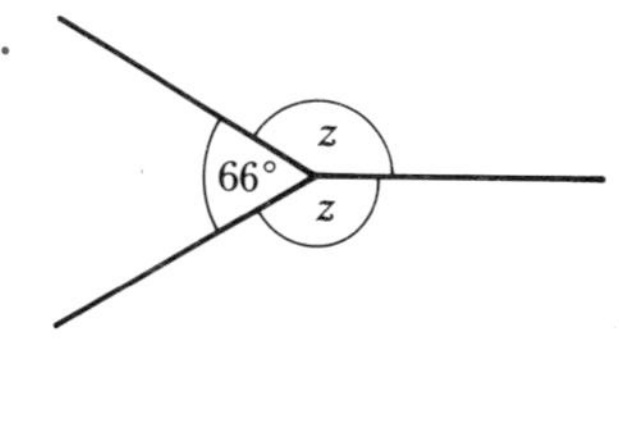

ANGLES AND PARALLEL LINES

When a transversal cuts a pair of parallel lines, various angles are formed.

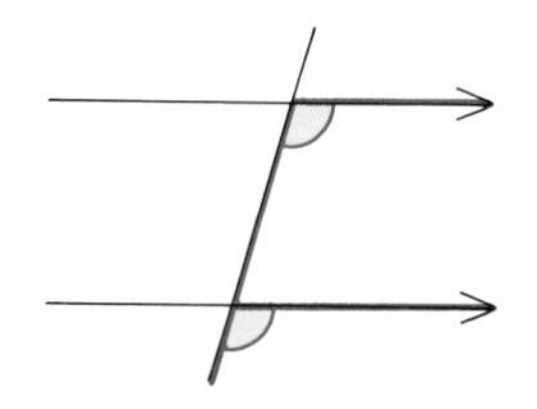

Corresponding angles are equal.
(Look for the letter **F**.)

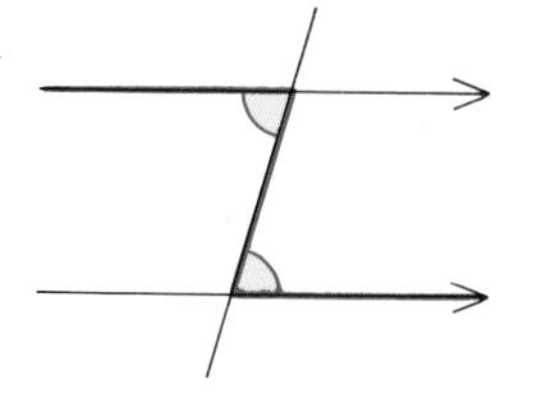

Alternate angles are equal.
(Look for the letter **Z**.)

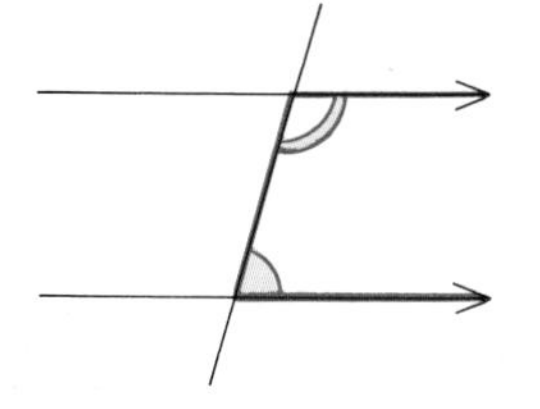

Interior angles add up to 180°.
(Look for the **U** shape.)

ANGLES OF A TRIANGLE

Draw a large triangle of any shape, using a straight edge to draw the sides. Measure each angle in your triangle, turning your page to a convenient position when necessary. Add the sizes of the three angles.

Draw another triangle of a different shape. Again measure each angle and add them.

Now try this: on a piece of paper draw a triangle of any shape and cut it out. Next tear off each corner and place the three different corners together.

They should look like this:

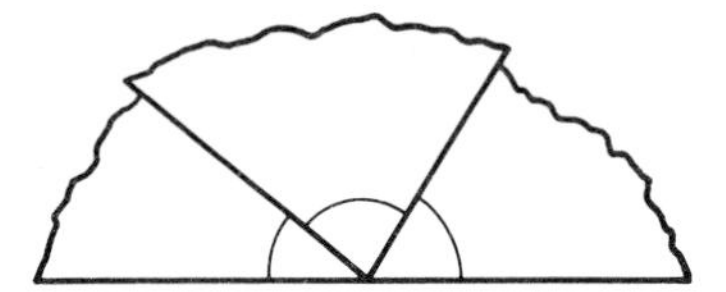

These experiments suggest that

 **the three angles of a triangle add up to 180°.** 

The three corners of a triangle are called its *vertices* (one corner is a *vertex*).

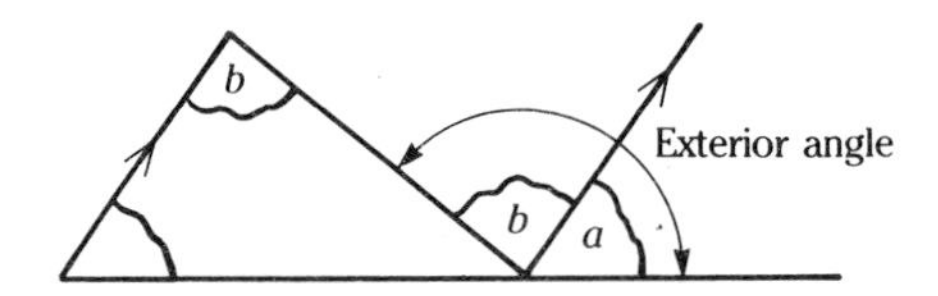

We can also see that it looks as though an exterior angle of a triangle is equal to the sum of the two interior opposite angles.

Exercise 3b

For each diagram in questions 1 and 2, write down the angle that corresponds to the angle marked x.

1. (a)

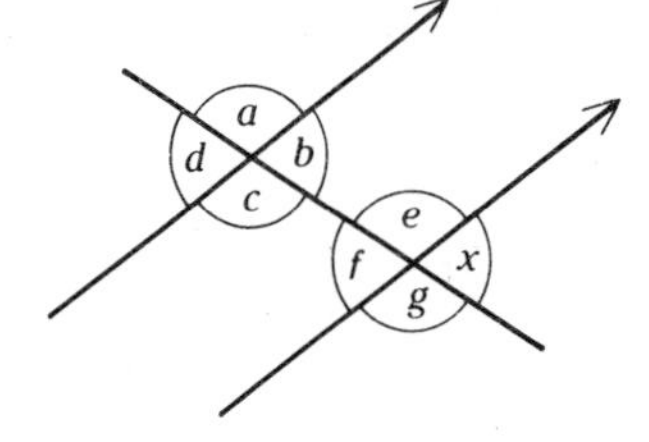

(b)

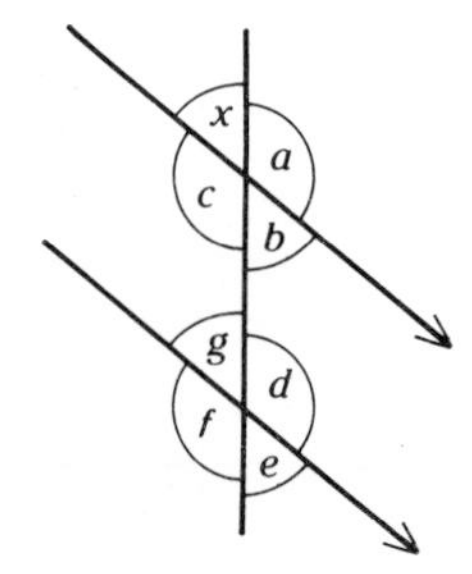

2. (a)

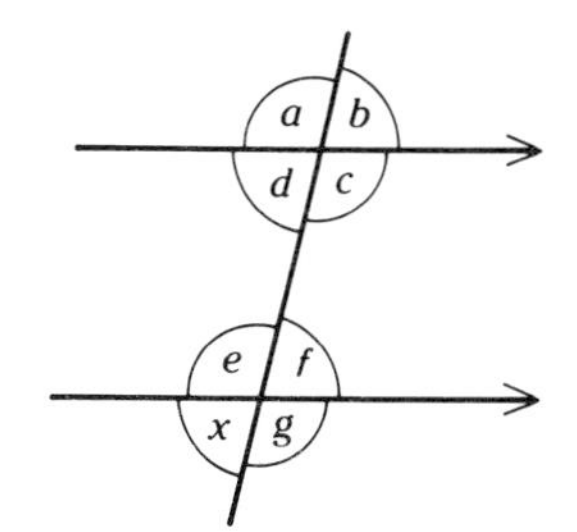

(b)

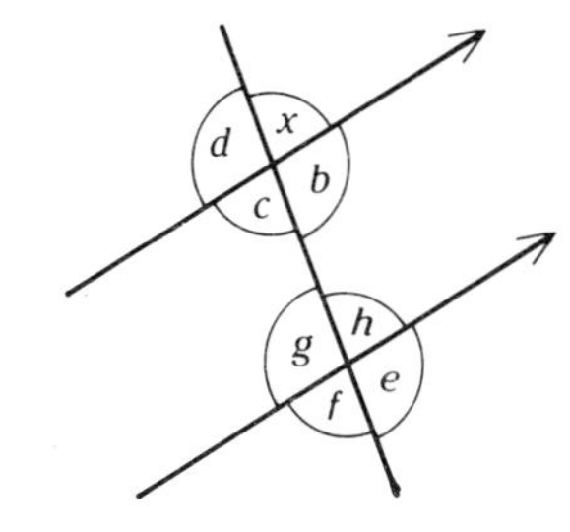

3. For this question refer to the diagrams in questions 1 and 2.
   (a) In the diagram 1(a) write down the angle that is alternate to *f*.
   (b) In diagram 1(b) write down the angle that is alternate to *d*.
   (c) In diagram 2(a) write down the angle that is alternate to *e*.
   (d) In diagram 2(b) write down the angle that is alternate to *g*.

4. Write down any pairs of interior angles you can find in the four diagrams given in questions 1 and 2.

In questions 5 to 11 find the size of each marked angle.

5.

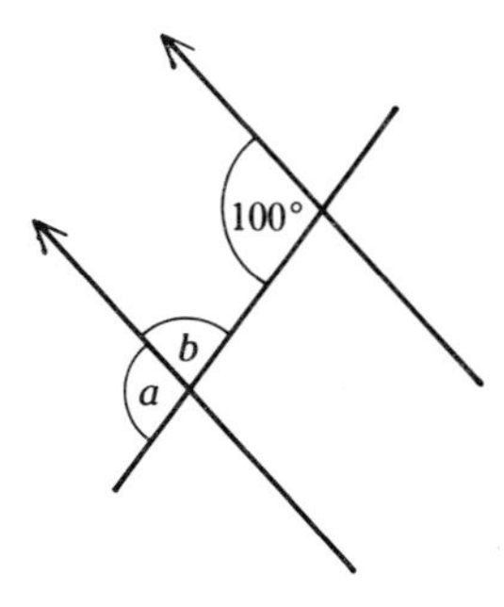

6.

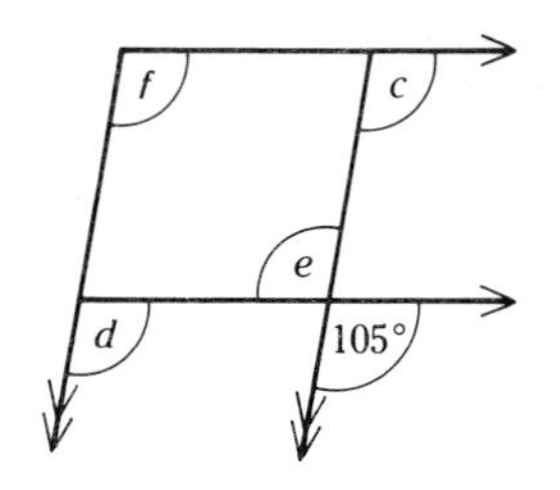

7.

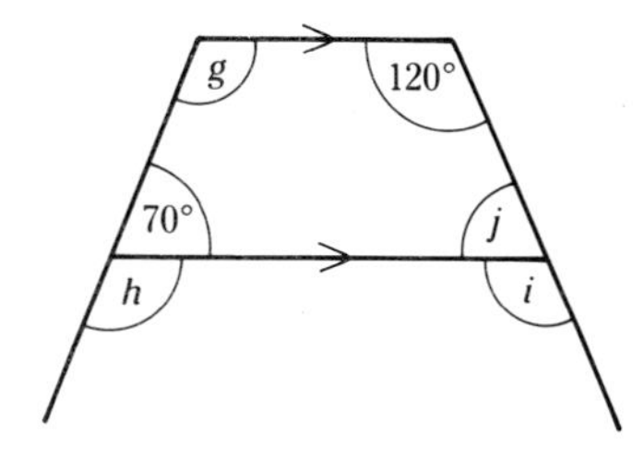

8.

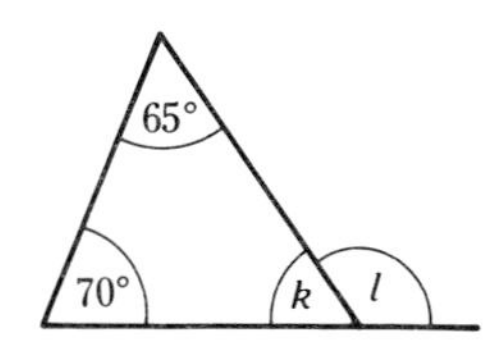

9.

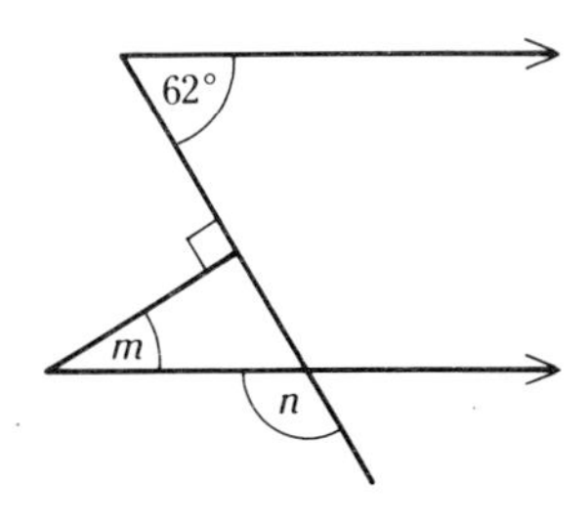

10.

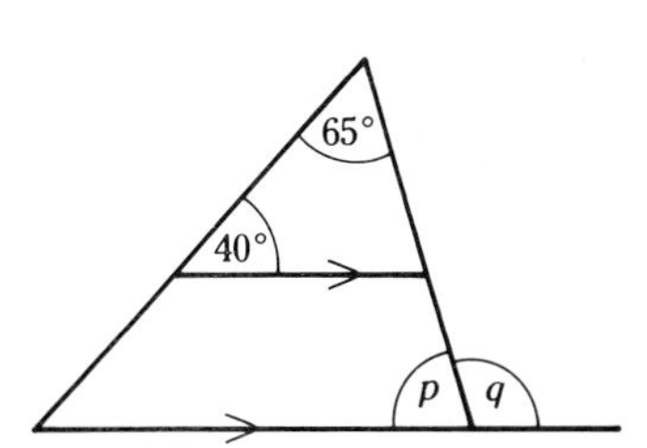

11.

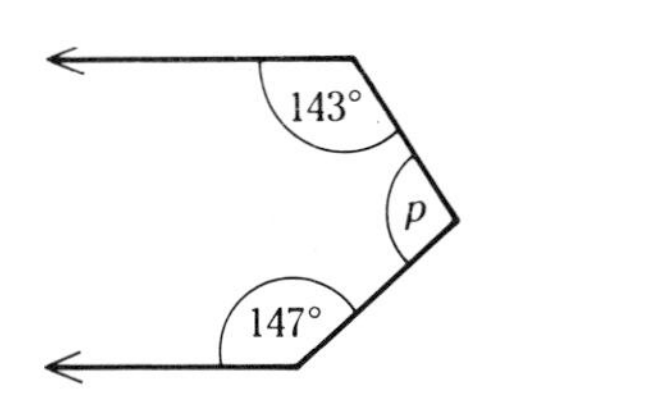

USING CAPITAL LETTERS TO LABEL VERTICES

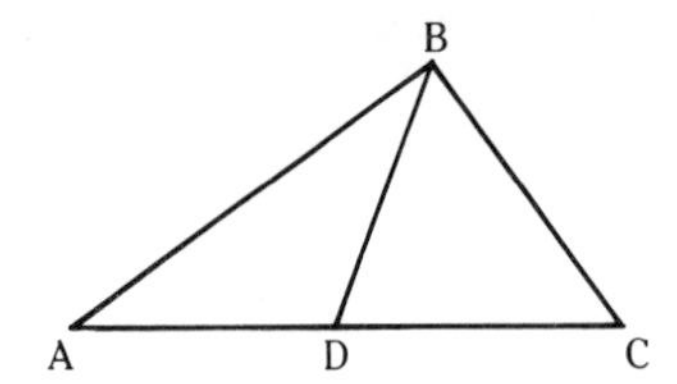

So that we can refer to one particular side, or to one particular angle, we often use capital letters to label the vertices of a figure. In the above diagram we use the letters A, B and C so that we can talk about 'the triangle ABC', which can be abbreviated to '$\triangle$ABC'. The side joining A and B is called 'the side AB' or just AB, with similar meanings for BC and AC.

The angle at the vertex A is called 'angle A' or $\hat{A}$ for short.

Sometimes there is ambiguity if we use a single letter. In the above diagram there are three different angles inside triangles at B. We can get over this problem by using the three letters round the arms of an angle to describe it. The three angles inside triangles at B are $A\hat{B}C$, $A\hat{B}D$ and $D\hat{B}C$.

TYPES OF TRIANGLE

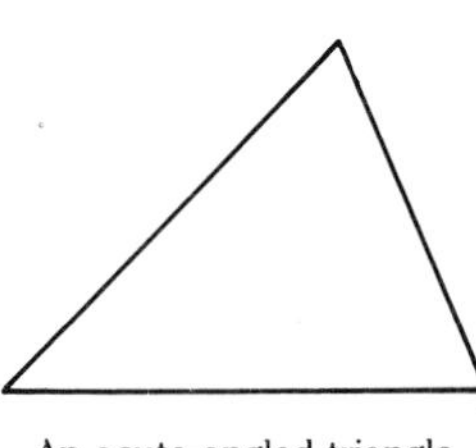

An acute-angled triangle

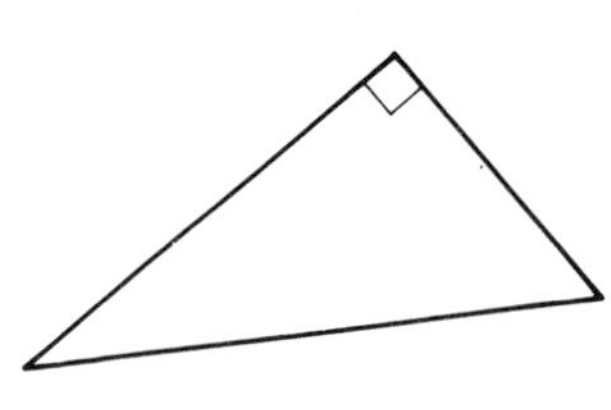

A right-angled triangle

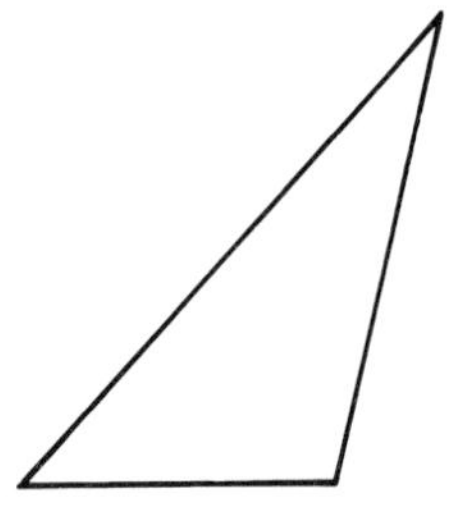

An obtuse-angled triangle

All three of these triangles are examples of *scalene* triangles – in each one the three sides have different lengths.

Some Special Triangles

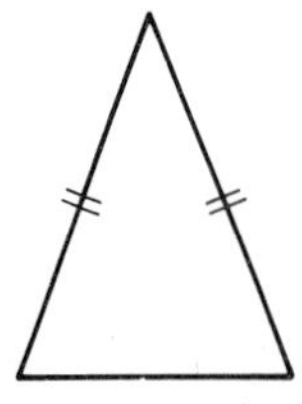

An *isosceles* triangle has two equal sides and the base angles are equal.

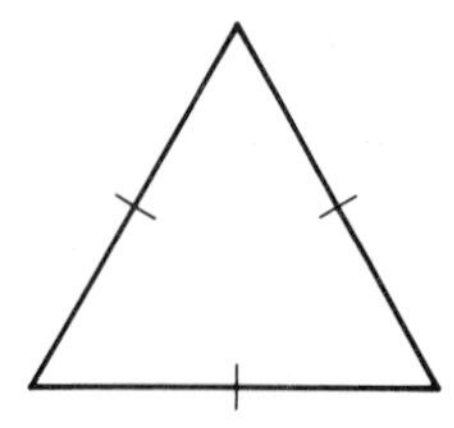

An *equilateral* triangle has three equal sides and each angle is 60°.

GENERAL QUADRILATERAL

A quadrilateral is a plane figure bounded by four straight lines.

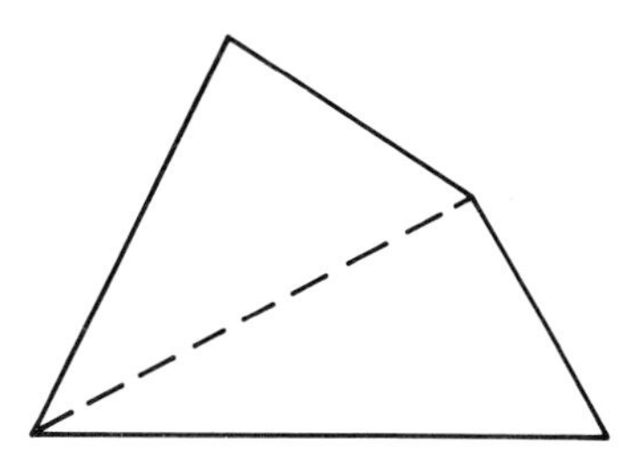

A *diagonal* is a line joining two opposite vertices. Either diagonal divides a quadrilateral into two triangles. The sum of the angles of a triangle is 180° so the sum of the angles of a quadrilateral is twice as big.

The sum of the interior angles of a quadrilateral is 360°.

At each vertex the sum of the interior and exterior angles is 180°. There are four vertices so the sum of all the exterior and interior angles is

$4 \times 180°$ i.e. 720°.

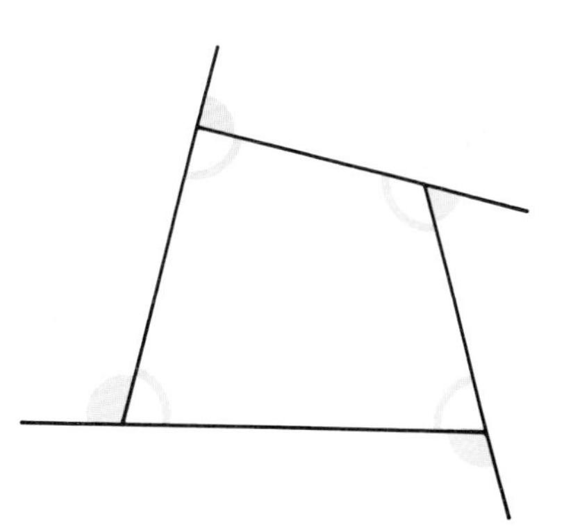

The sum of the interior angles is 360° so

the sum of the exterior angles of a quadrilateral is 360°.

Exercise 3c

Find the size of each marked angle.

1.

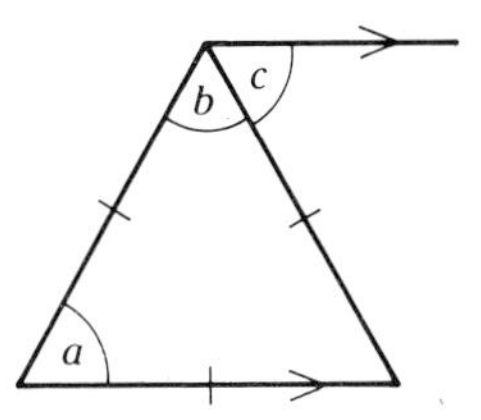

2.

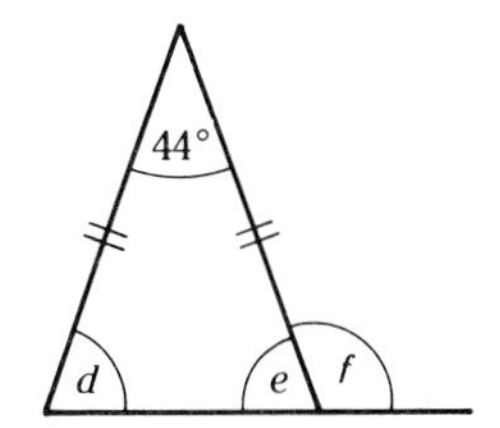

3.

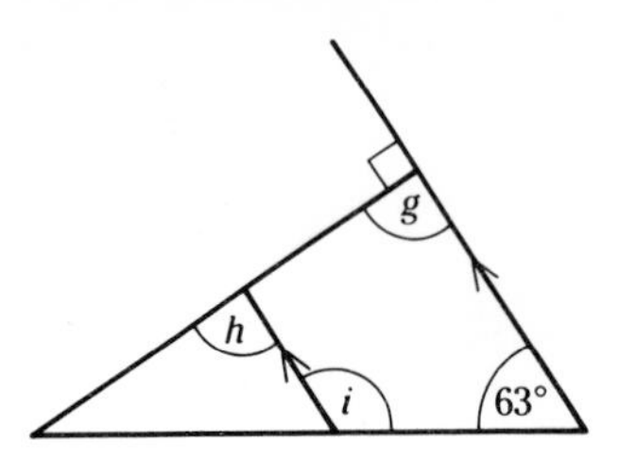

4.

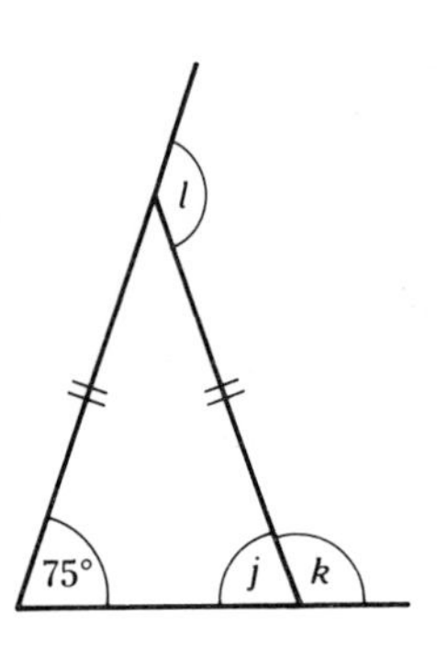

5.

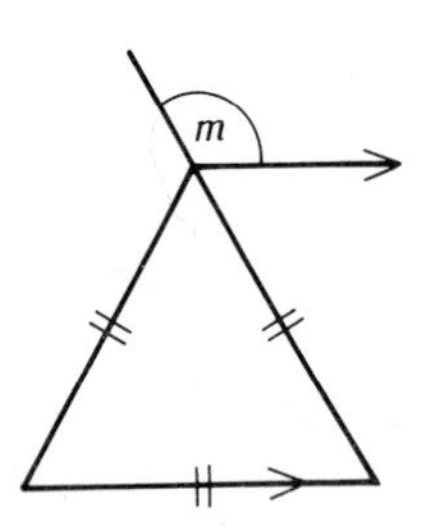

6.

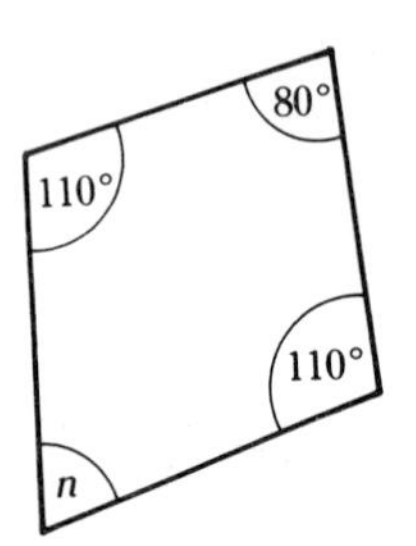

7.

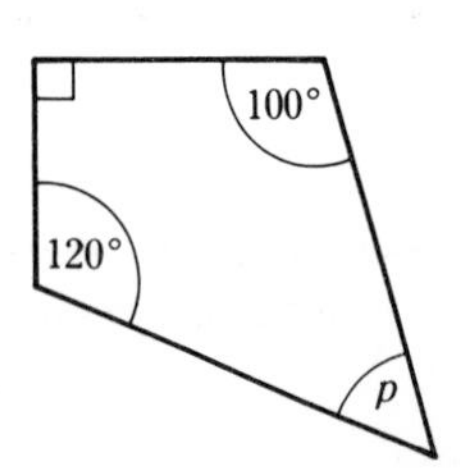

8.

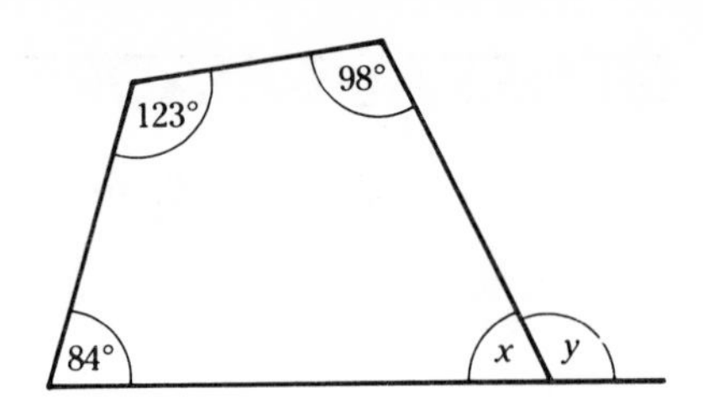

9.

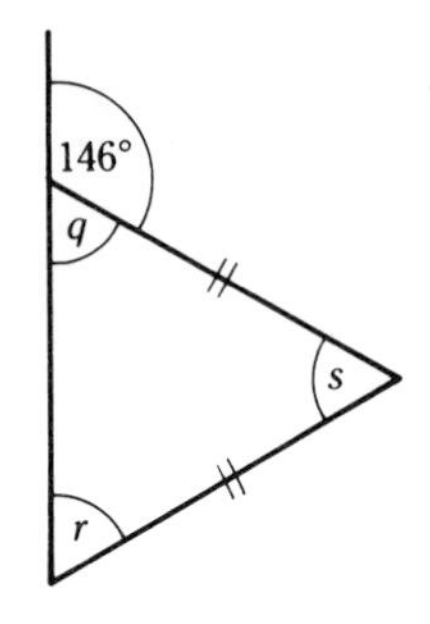

10.

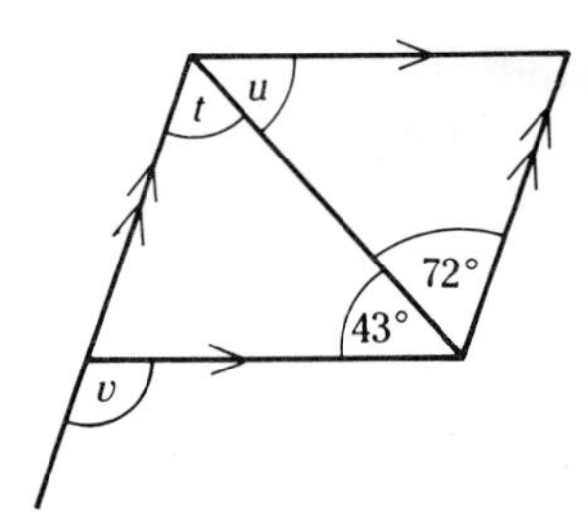

11.

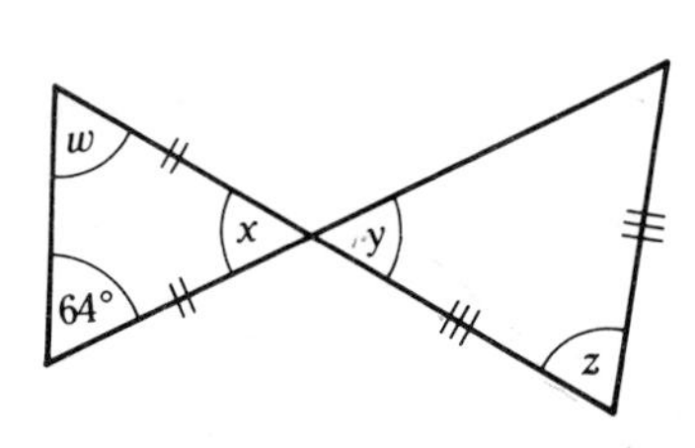

12.

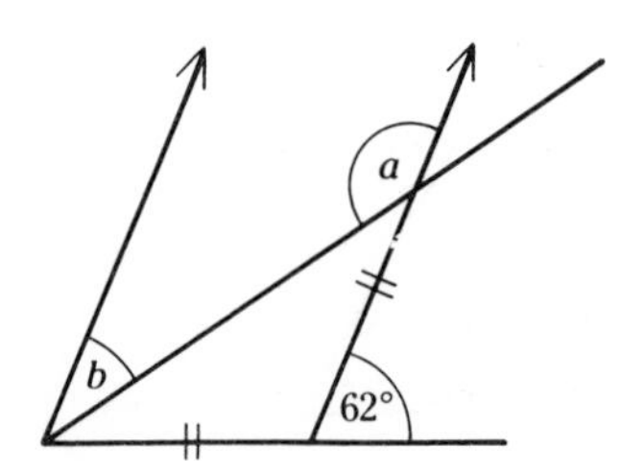

13.

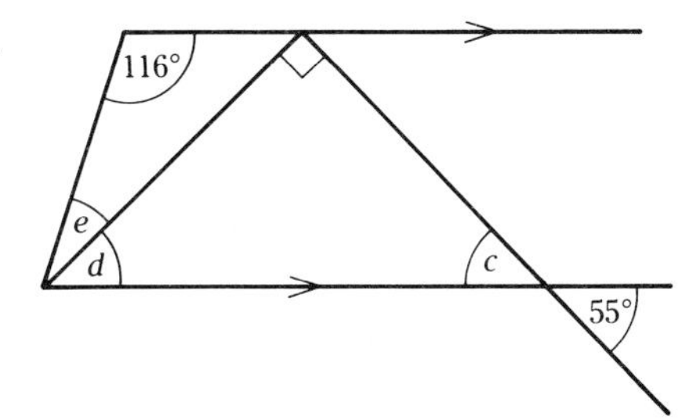

14.

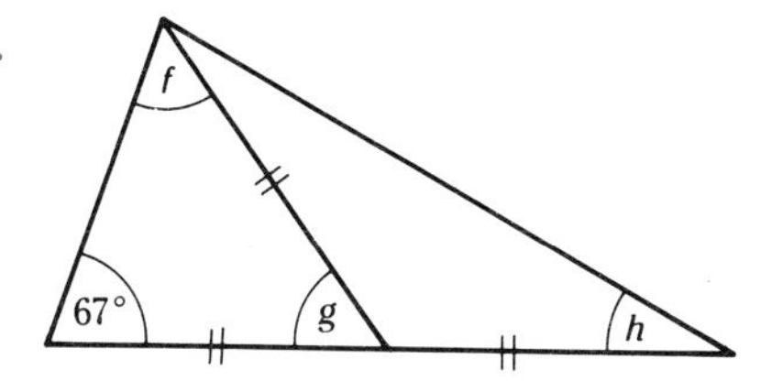

15.

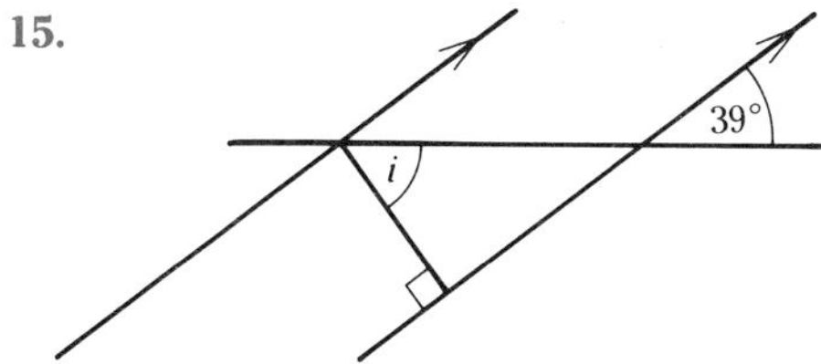

16.

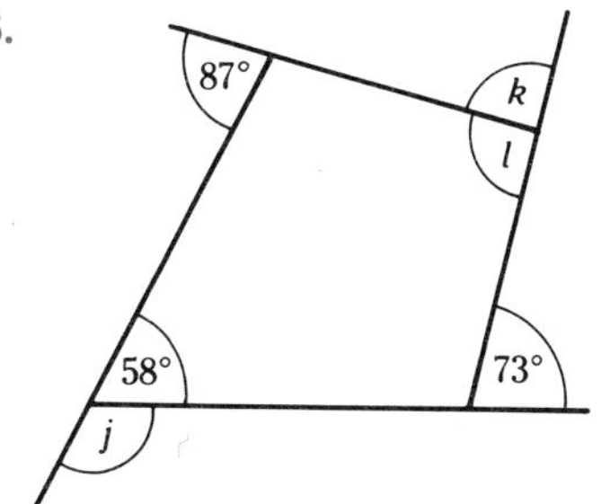

17.

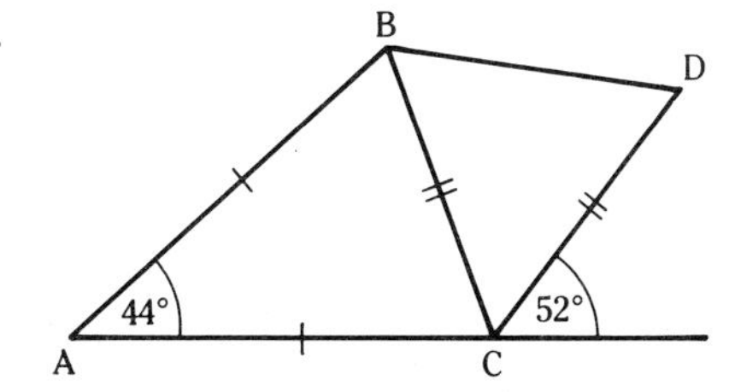

(a) Calculate (i) $A\hat{B}C$ (ii) each of the angles in $\triangle BCD$.

(b) What special type of triangle is $\triangle BCD$?

18.

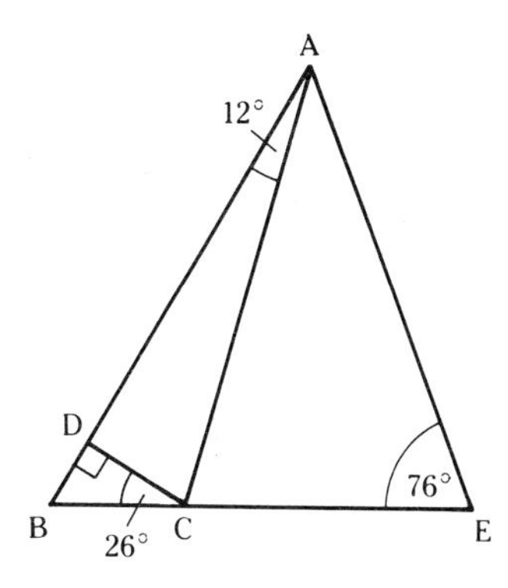

(a) Find the size of (i) $A\hat{B}C$ (ii) $A\hat{C}E$ (iii) $C\hat{A}E$.

(b) Name an isosceles triangle.

(c) What type of triangle is $\triangle ADC$?

(d) Is AE parallel to DC ?

19.

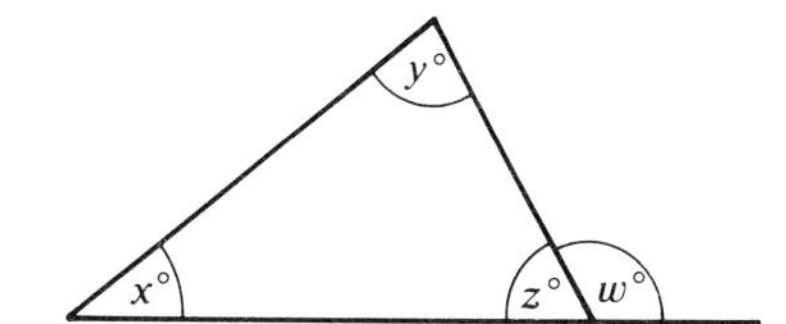

Using the diagram given above, find the sizes of the marked angles when

(a) $x = 48,\ y = 67$

(b) $x = 52,\ w = 108$

(c) $y = 70,\ z = 54$

(d) $y = 58,\ w = 124$

20.

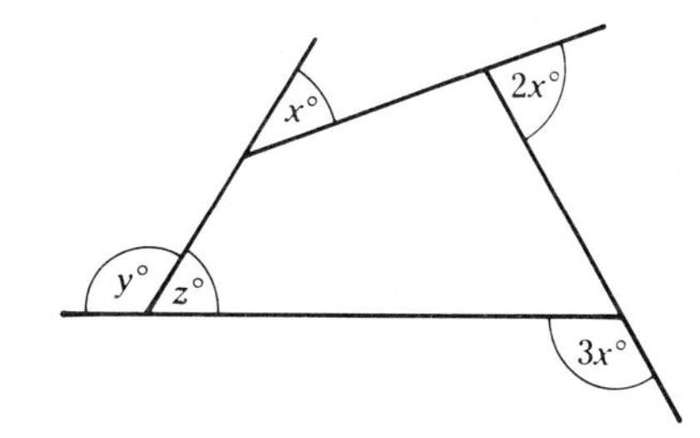

Using the diagram given above, find the sizes of the marked angles when

(a) $x = 42$

(b) $y = 138$

(c) $z = 66$

(d) $y = 4x$

21. In $\triangle ABC$, AB is extended to D to form an exterior angle CBD. If
$\widehat{BDC} = 40°, \widehat{BCD} = 38°$ and $\widehat{BAC} = 80°$, draw a diagram to show this information and find the other two angles of $\triangle ABC$.

22. ABCD is a quadrilateral. $\widehat{A} = 104°$ and $\widehat{B} = 84°$. The diagonal AC cuts $\widehat{DAB}$ in half and $AC = AD$.
Find $\widehat{BCD}$.

23. In $\triangle ABC$, $AB = AC$ and $\widehat{ACB} = 66°$. A line is drawn through C perpendicular to AB, to cut AB at D.
Find the angles of $\triangle BDC$.

24.

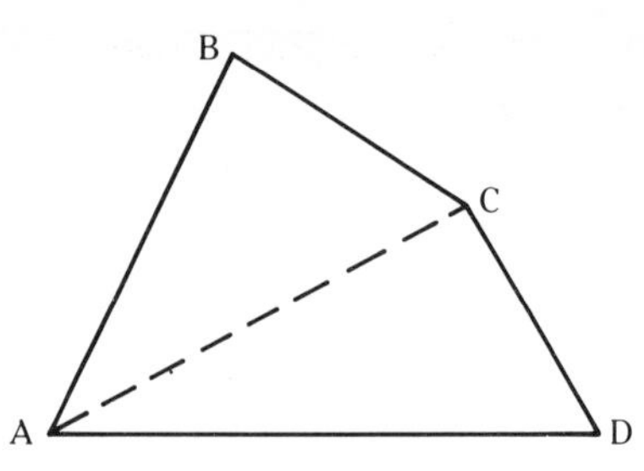

In quadrilateral ABCD, $\widehat{ABC} = \widehat{ACD} = 90°$, $\widehat{BCA} = 60°$ and $BC = CD$.

(a) Find $\widehat{BAC}$.

(b) Find the angles of $\triangle BCD$.

(c) BD and AC cut at E. Find the angles of $\triangle BEA$.

(d) If it is possible, find all the angles of $\triangle AED$.
If it is not possible, find out what you can about them.

ACCURATE DRAWING OF TRIANGLES

Given One Side and Two Angles

Construct $\triangle ABC$ in which $AB = 7$ cm, $\widehat{A} = 35°$, and $\widehat{B} = 40°$.

First make a rough sketch of $\triangle ABC$ and mark all the given data on your sketch.

Now draw the line AB, making it 7 cm long. Label both ends.

Then use your protractor to make an angle of 35° at A.

Next make an angle of 40° at B. If necessary extend the arms of the angles until they cross. The point where they cross is C.

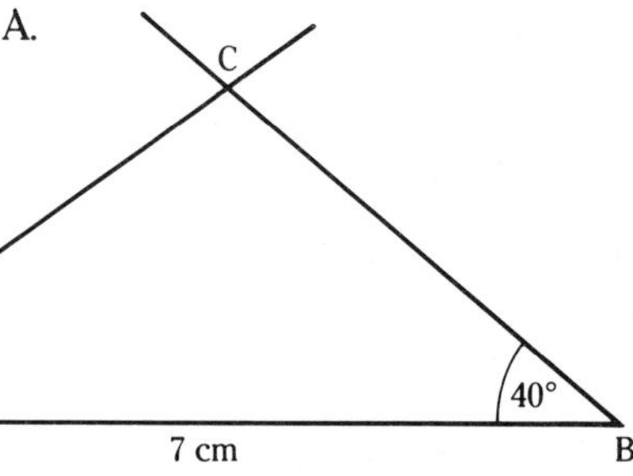

Since $\widehat{A} + \widehat{B} + \widehat{C} = 180°$ we can calculate that $\widehat{ACB} = 105°$.
As a check on the construction we can measure $\widehat{C}$.

Sometimes it may be necessary to calculate another angle.
For example if AB = 9 cm, $\hat{A} = 53°$ and $\hat{C} = 64°$, the sketch of △ABC is:

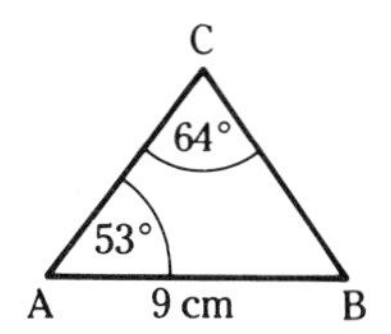

We can draw AB and $\hat{A}$ from the given information but we must calculate $\hat{B}$ before we can continue. ($\hat{C}$ cannot be drawn as we do not know where the point C is.)

Given Two Sides and the Angle between those Two Sides

Construct △PQR in which PQ = 4.5 cm, PR = 5.5 cm and $\hat{P} = 54°$.

First draw a rough sketch and put in all the measurements.

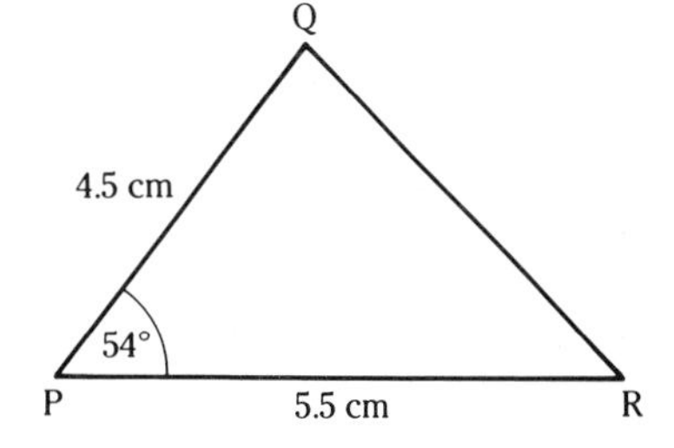

Draw one of the sides whose length you know. We will draw PR.

Now using a protractor make an angle of 54° at P.
Make the arm of the angle quite long.

Use a ruler to set your compasses to the length of PQ.

Then with the point of your compasses at P,
draw an arc to cut the arm of the angle.
This is the point Q.

Finally join R and Q.

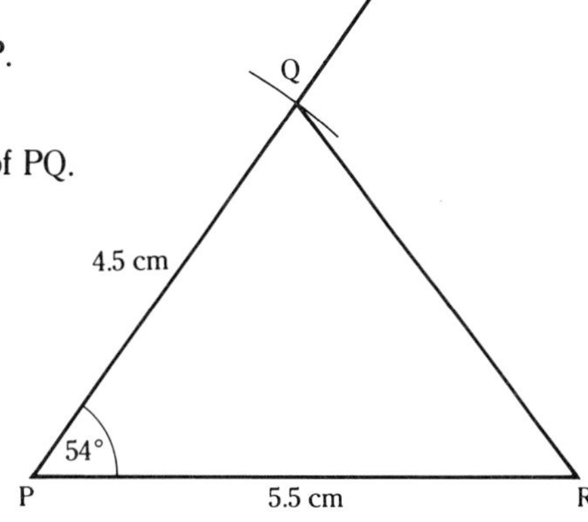

Given the Lengths of Three Sides

Construct $\triangle XYZ$ in which $XY = 5.5$ cm, $XZ = 3.5$ cm, $YZ = 6.5$ cm.

First draw a rough sketch and mark the measurements on it.

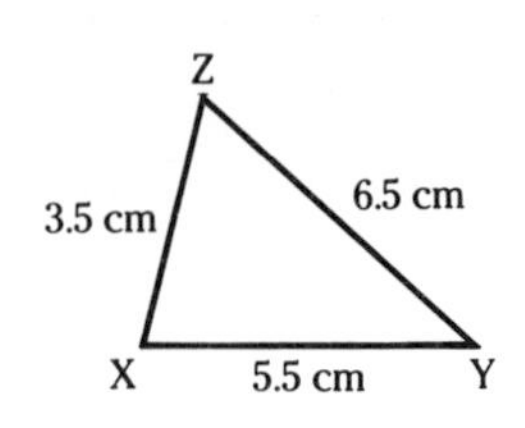

Next draw one side. We will draw XY.

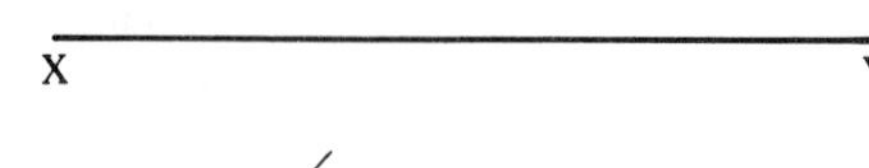

Set your compasses to the length of XZ using a ruler. With the point of the compasses at X draw a wide arc.

Next set your compasses to the length of YZ from a ruler and, with the point at Y, draw another arc to cut the first arc at Z.

Join ZX and ZY.

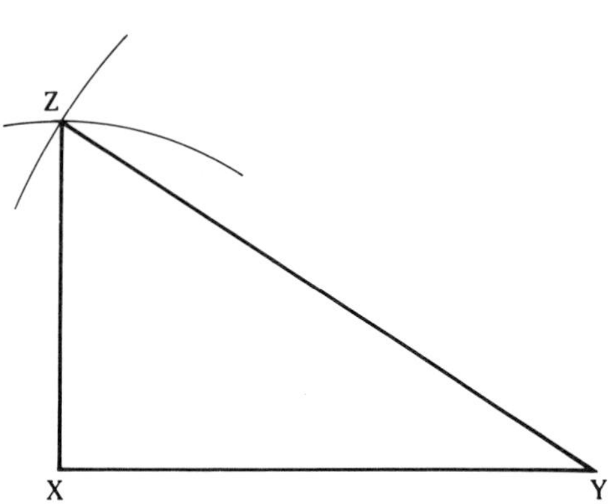

Exercise 3d

Construct the following triangles. Remember to draw a rough diagram first. It may be necessary to calculate the third angle.

1. $\triangle ABC$ in which $AB = 6$ cm, $\hat{A} = 50°$, $\hat{B} = 65°$. Measure BC.

2. $\triangle PQR$ in which $\hat{P} = 100°$, $PQ = 8.5$ cm, $\hat{Q} = 43°$. Measure PR.

3. $\triangle LMN$ in which $\hat{N} = 73°$, $LN = 4.1$ cm, $MN = 6.3$ cm. Measure $\hat{L}$.

4. $\triangle XYZ$ in which $\hat{Y} = 65°$, $XY = 3.8$ cm, $YZ = 4.2$ cm. Measure XZ.

5. $\triangle ABC$ in which $AB = 7.3$ cm, $BC = 6.1$ cm, $AC = 4.7$ cm. Measure $\hat{A}$, $\hat{B}$ and $\hat{C}$.

6. $\triangle DEF$ in which $DE = 10.4$ cm, $EF = 7.4$ cm, $DF = 8.2$ cm. Measure $\hat{D}$, $\hat{E}$ and $\hat{F}$.

7. (a) Try to construct two triangles that fit the following measurements: $\triangle PQR$ in which $\hat{P} = 60°$, $PQ = 6$ cm, $QR = 5.5$ cm.
   (b) Repeat part (a) if $QR = 6.6$ cm
   (c) Repeat part (a) if $QR = 4.5$ cm
   What conclusion can you draw from this question ?

8. Construct a quadrilateral ABCD in which $AB = 5$ cm, $\hat{A} = 70°$, $AD = 3$ cm, $BC = 5$ cm and $DC = 5$ cm. Measure AC. Measure all four angles and find their sum.

9. Construct a quadrilateral PQRS in which $PQ = 7$ cm, $PS = 6$ cm, $QR = 5.3$ cm, $\hat{P} = 65°$ and $\hat{Q} = 72°$. Measure PR.

10. Construct a quadrilateral WXYZ in which $WX = 6.8$ cm, $XY = 4.5$ cm, $\hat{W} = 90°$, $\hat{X} = 75°$ and $\hat{Y} = 125°$. Measure WZ and YZ.

Investigations

1. This investigates the sum of the interior angles of figures (flat shapes) with different numbers of sides.

(a) These figures all have interior angles that are less than 180 ° (they are convex).

Number of sides	3	4	5
Number of triangles	1	2	3
Sum of interior angles	180 °	360 °	540 °

(i) Copy and complete the table and extend it to 7-sided and 8-sided figures.

(ii) What is the sum of the interior angles of a figure with 10 sides ?

(iii) What is the relationship between the number of sides and the sum of the interior angles ?

(b) These figures have one interior angle that is greater than 180 °. (They are concave.)

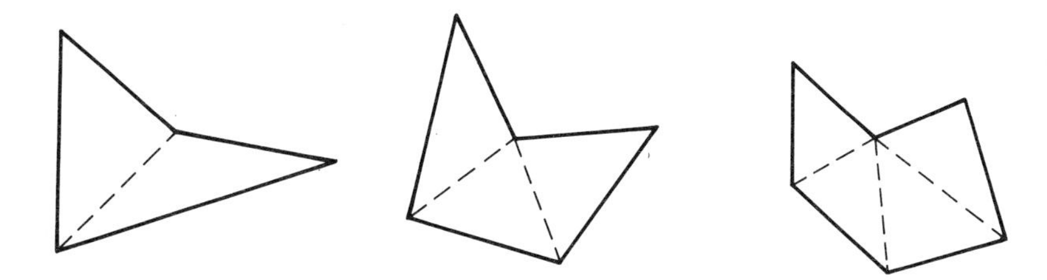

(i) Is it possible to draw such a figure with three sides ?

(ii) Investigate the relationship between the sum of the interior angles and the number of sides of these concave figures.

(c) Investigate what the angle sum is if more than one reflex angle is allowed.

2. A triangle has three sides and three angles. If you have worked through Exercise 3d, you will have found that we do not need to know the size of all six of these in order to construct a triangle whose shape and size is fixed. Suppose that you want a triangle cut from a sheet of steel. Investigate what measurements you can give to make sure that the triangle cut is exactly the shape and size you need.

Self-Assessment 3

1. How many degrees does the hand of a clock turn through when it starts at 4 and stops at 9 ?

2. Calculate the size of each angle marked with a letter.

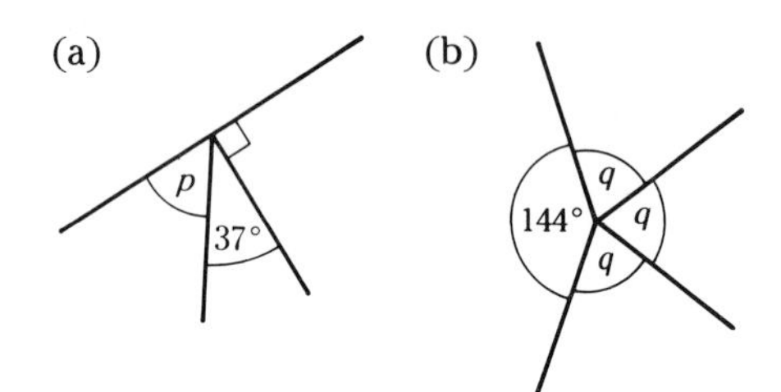

3.

(a) Which angle is alternate to e ?

(b) Name a pair of corresponding angles, one of which is d.

(c) Name a pair of interior angles, one of which is c.

(d) Name a pair of vertically opposite angles, one of which is f.

4. Find the size of each marked angle.

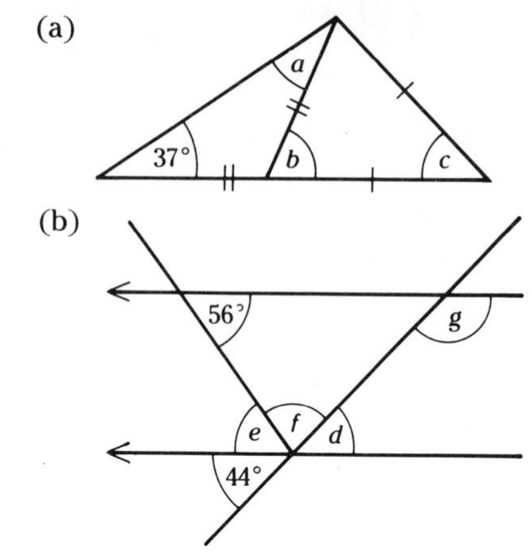

5. Construct △ABC in which AB = 8.4 cm, $\hat{A} = 38°$ and $\hat{B} = 72°$. Measure BC.

6. Construct △PQR in which PR = 8.2 cm, PQ = 5.7 cm and $\hat{P} = 65°$. Measure QR.

7. Construct △DEF in which DE = 10.4 cm. DF = 8.7 cm and EF = 6.9 cm. Measure $\hat{D}$ and $\hat{E}$.

8. Find x and y.

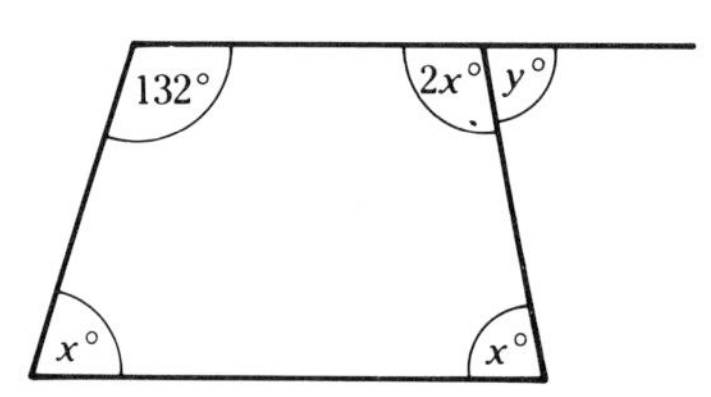

4 SYMMETRY AND TRANSFORMATIONS

LOCATING A POINT IN A PLANE

The most common way of giving the position of a point in a plane is based on using two fixed perpendicular lines called *the axes of coordinates* or the x and y axes. They meet at a point O, called *the origin.* The scales used on the two axes include both positive and negative numbers.

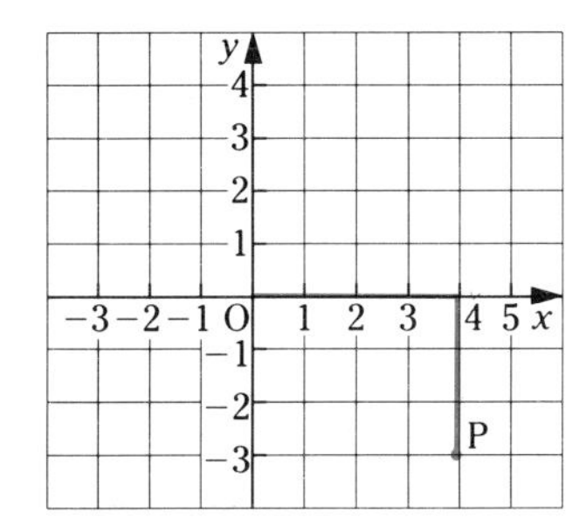

In all the work in this chapter the same scale is used on both axes. Ideally we would always use equal scales but sometimes this is not convenient as, for example, when drawing the graph of $y = x^2$.

Cartesian Coordinates

The position of a point is defined by its Cartesian coordinates. These are its horizontal distance from the y-axis (i.e. in the direction of Ox), followed by its vertical distance from the x-axis (i.e. in the direction of Oy). Distances measured upwards or right are positive, while distances measured downwards or left are negative. The point P in the diagram above is $(4, -3)$. The x-coordinate is 4 and the y-coordinate is -3.

Exercise 4a

1. Write down the Cartesian coordinates of each point.

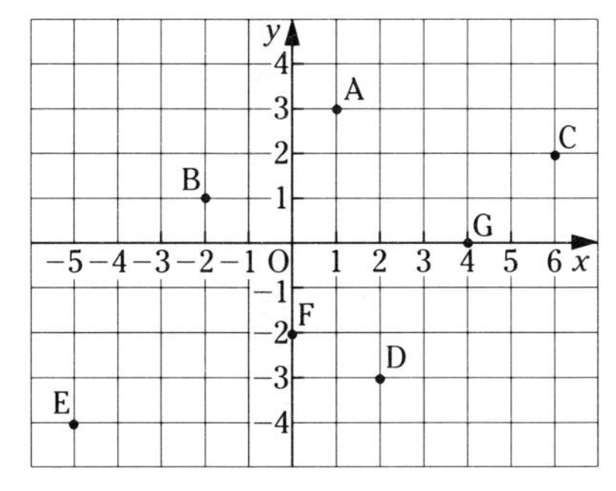

2. Using 5 mm squared paper plot each set of points, join them in order and give the name of the figure so formed.

   (a) $(0, 5)$, $(-6, 0)$, $(0, -5)$, $(6, 0)$

   (b) $(1, 0)$, $(0, 3)$, $(-6, 1)$, $(-5, -2)$

   (c) $(5, 1)$, $(1, 6)$, $(-3, 1)$

   (d) $(1, -3)$, $(6, -3)$, $(4, 2)$, $(-1, 2)$

   (e) $(2, 3)$, $(-1, 2)$, $(2, 1)$, $(3, 2)$

SYMMETRY

Line Symmetry

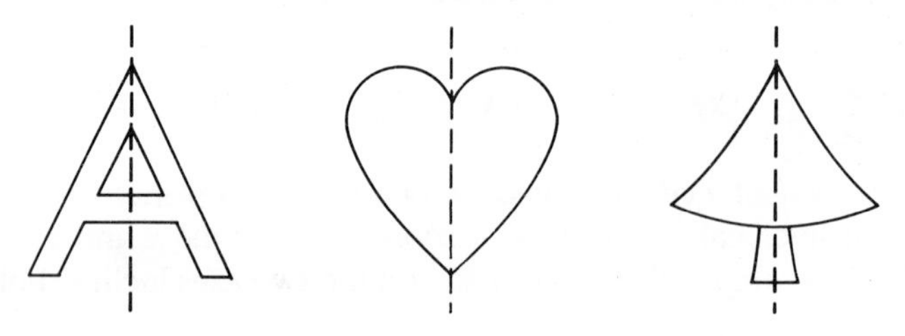

Each of these shapes is symmetrical about the broken line.
If the shape were folded along this *line of symmetry,* one half would fit exactly over the other.

Some shapes have more than one line of symmetry. The examples shown below are symmetrical about each broken line.

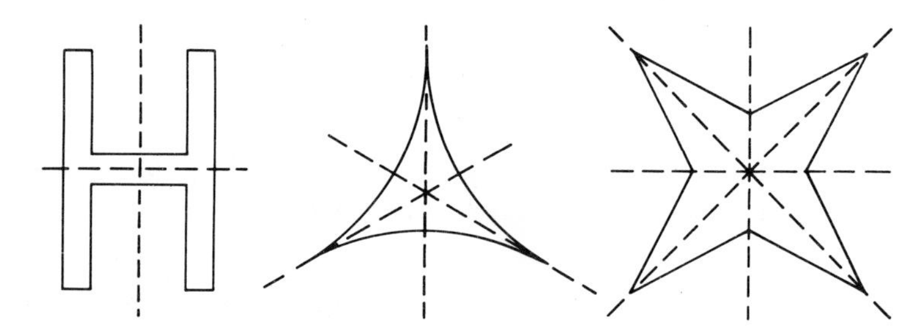

Rotational Symmetry

Some shapes can be rotated about a fixed point to a *new* position and still look the same as before. Such shapes have rotational symmetry, e.g.

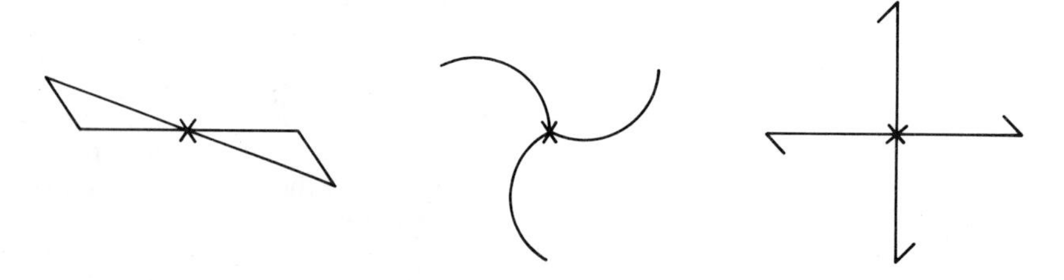

This shape needs to be turned through one-third of a revolution before it first looks the same, then two more such turns are needed, i.e. three in total, before it returns to its original position.

The shape has *rotational symmetry of order 3.*

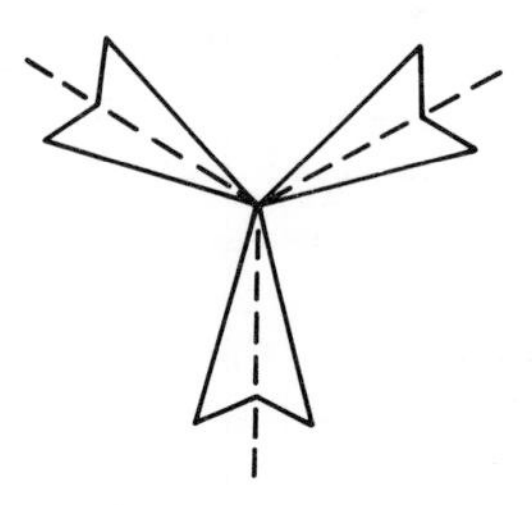

Exercise 4b

1. Some of these shapes have no line of symmetry, some have one line of symmetry and others have more than one. Copy those that are symmetrical and draw all the lines of symmetry.

(a) 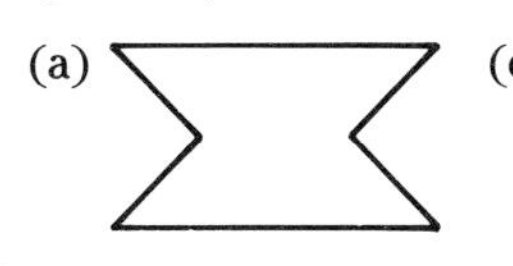

(d) 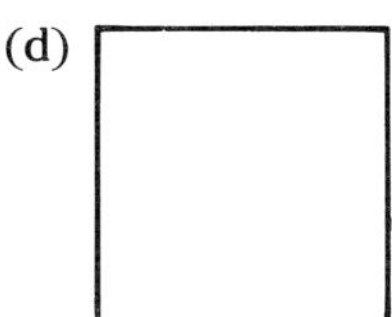

(b) 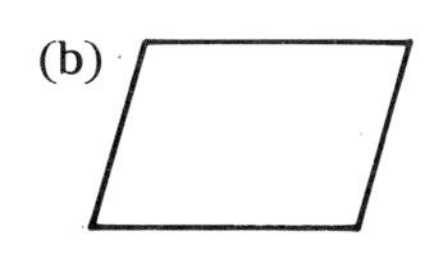

(e) 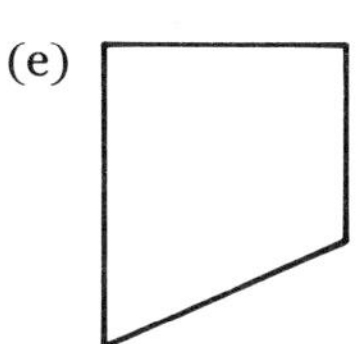

(c) 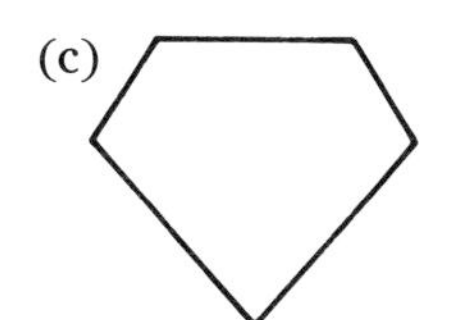

(f) 

2. On squared paper copy and complete each drawing using the broken lines as lines of symmetry.

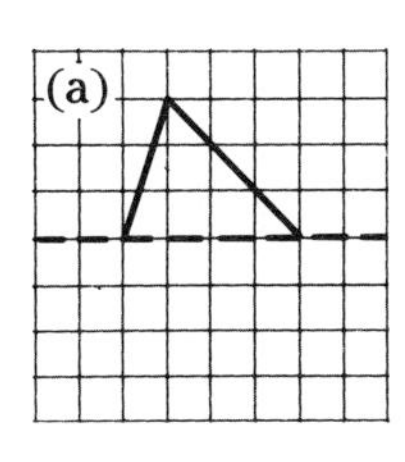

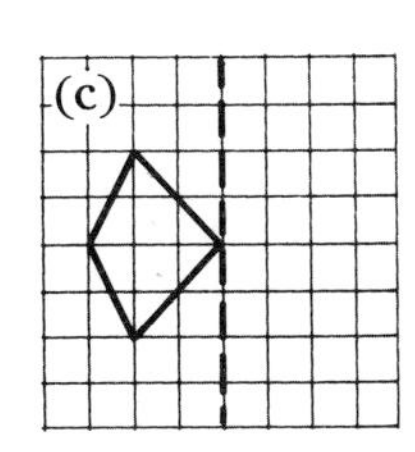

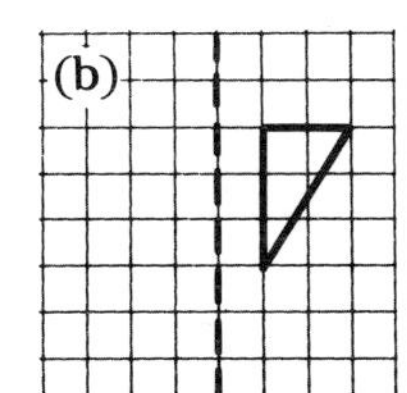

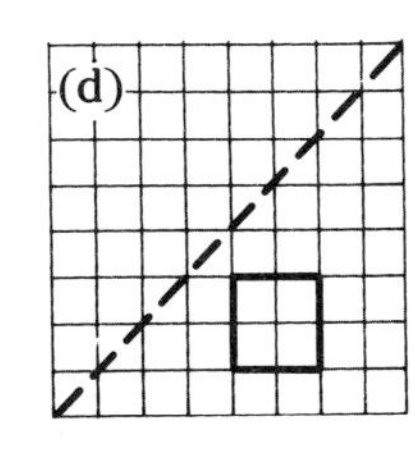

3. State which of the shapes in question 1 have rotational symmetry and give the order of that symmetry.

4. State which of the following shapes have (i) line symmetry only (ii) rotational symmetry only (iii) both

(a) 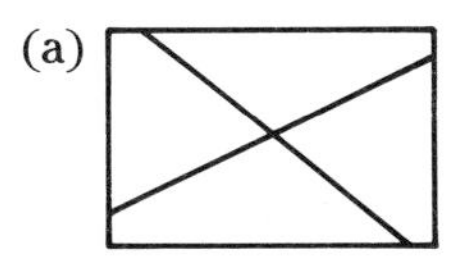

(d) 

(b) 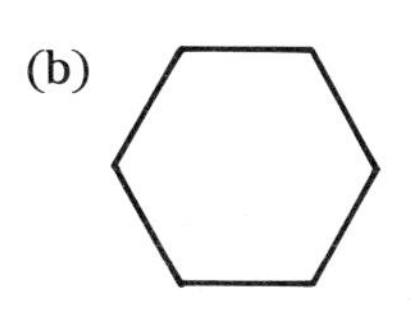

(e) 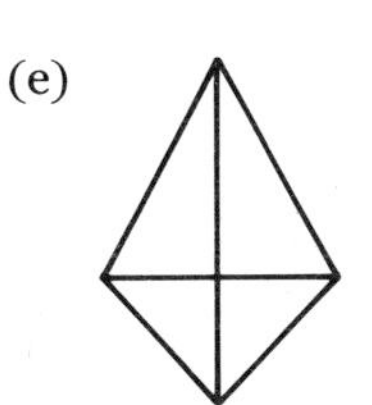

(c) 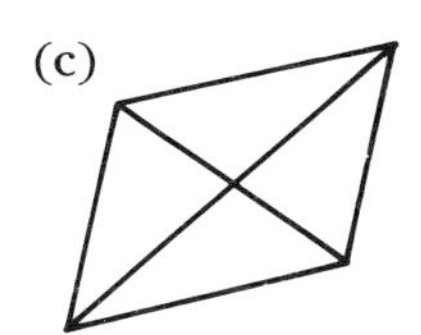

(f) 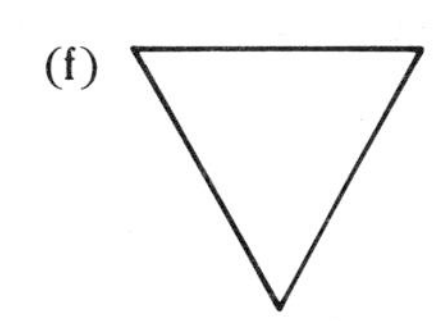

5. On squared paper draw x and y axes and mark each scale from -3 to 8. Plot the given points and join them as instructed. In each case state whether the shape has (i) line symmetry only (ii) rotational symmetry only (iii) both.

   (a) A(4, 6), B(6, 6), C(5, 1). Draw AB, BC and CA.

   (b) A(2, 2), B(2, 5), C(8, 5) and D(8, 2). Draw AB, BC, CD, DA, AC and BD.

   (c) A(1, -2), B(4, -1), C(0, 3), D(-3, 2). Draw AB, BC, CD, DA, AC and BD.

6. Draw axes as described in question 5. Plot the points A(6, 6), B(-1, 6), C(-3, -1) and D(-3, -3).

   (a) Draw AB, BC and CD and add points E and F so that ABCDEF forms a figure with one line of symmetry.

   (b) Draw the given diagram again and add E and F so that ABCDEF has rotational symmetry only.

TRANSFORMATIONS

A *transformation* is an operation that can change the position and/or the shape and/or size of an object.

We say that a transformation *maps* an object to its image.

Different transformations produce different effects and each of these transformations has a particular name.

Reflection

When an object is reflected in a mirror, the object and its *image* are symmetrical about the mirror line, which is the axis of symmetry.

The object is always 'turned over' to give the image.

Part of the object may be in contact with the mirror line, in which case the image is also in contact.

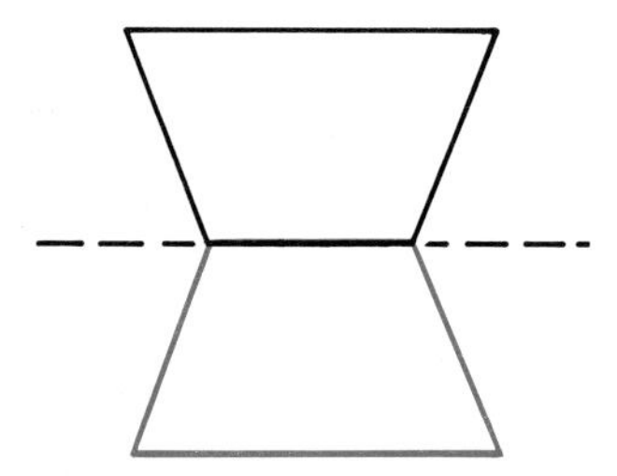

On the other hand, when the object is some distance away from the mirror line, the image and the object are equidistant from the mirror line.

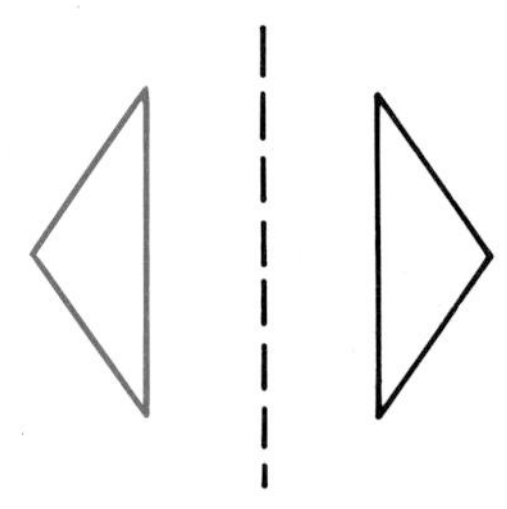

If the mirror line passes through the object it also crosses the image.

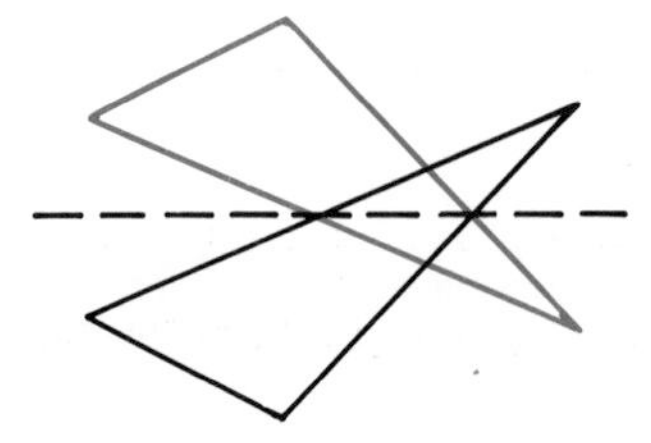

Exercise 4c

1. Use squared paper to copy each diagram (which shows an object and a mirror line). In each case draw the image of the object when it is reflected in the mirror line. Label the vertices of the image as A′, B′, C′, ... to correspond with the vertices A, B, C, ... of the object.

(a)

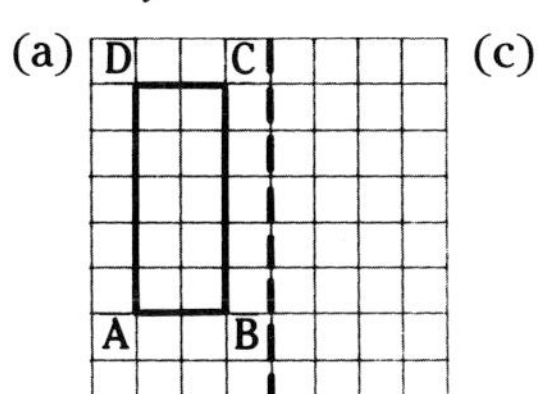

(c)

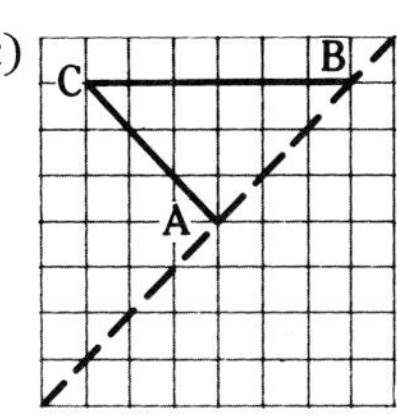

(b)

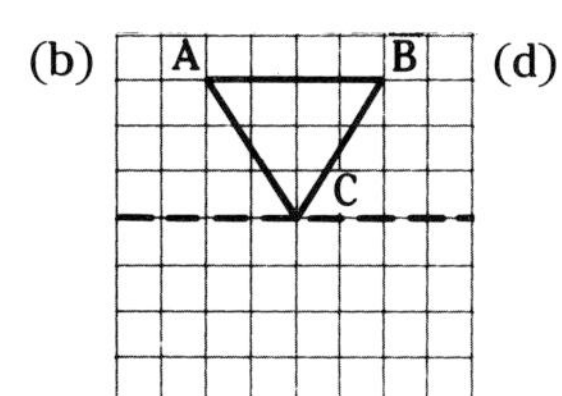

(d)

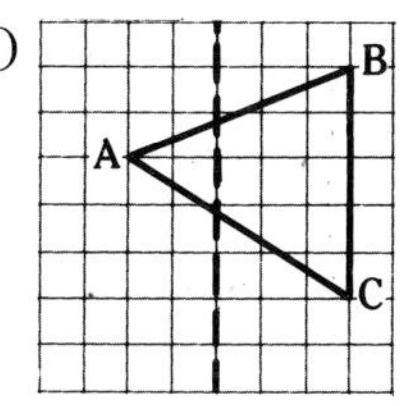

2. On squared paper, and using 1 cm for 1 unit, draw axes for x and y, each from -5 to 5. Draw $\triangle ABC$ where A is the point $(1, 2)$, B is $(2, 4)$ and C is $(3, 2)$. Draw
   (a) $\triangle A_1B_1C_1$, the image produced when $\triangle ABC$ is reflected in the x-axis
   (b) $\triangle A_2B_2C_2$, the image of $\triangle ABC$ in the y-axis.

3. On squared paper draw x and y axes graduated from -5 to 5 with $1\text{ cm} \equiv 1$ unit on each axis. P, Q and R are the points $(4, 0)$, $(1, -1)$ and $(5, -1)$ respectively. Draw $\triangle PQR$ and
   (a) its image $P_1Q_1R_1$ when reflected in the x-axis
   (b) its image $P_2Q_2R_2$ when reflected in the y-axis

4. Using axes graduated from -6 to 8 plot the points $A(-3, -4)$, $B(-2, -1)$ and $C(-6, -2)$ and join them to form $\triangle ABC$. Draw the following images of triangle ABC.
   (a) $A_1B_1C_1$ by reflection in the x-axis
   (b) $A_2B_2C_2$ by reflection in the horizontal line through $(0, -2)$
   (c) $A_3B_3C_3$ by reflection in the vertical line through $(-1, 0)$.

5. Using axes graduated from -8 to 8 plot the points $A(6, 2)$, $B(6, -1)$, $C(1, -1)$ and $D(1, 2)$ and join them to form rectangle ABCD. Draw the following images of ABCD.
   (a) $A_1B_1C_1D_1$ by reflection in the x-axis
   (b) $A_2B_2C_2D_2$ by reflection in the y-axis
   (c) $A_3B_3C_3D_3$ by reflecting $A_1B_1C_1D_1$ in the y-axis.
   (d) Describe how to obtain $A_3B_3C_3D_3$ by reflecting $A_2B_2C_2D_2$.

Find the mirror line if $\triangle A'B'C'$ is the image of $\triangle ABC$.

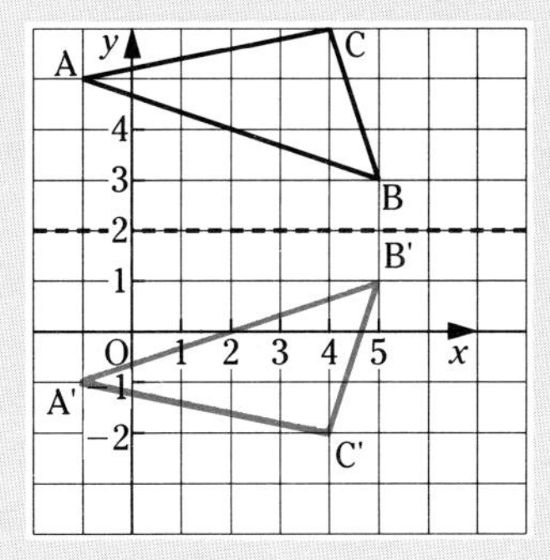

The mirror line is half-way between A and A′ and also half-way between B and B′ (or C and C′).

The horizontal line through the point $(0, 2)$ is the mirror line.

6. Copy each diagram and draw the mirror line.

(a)

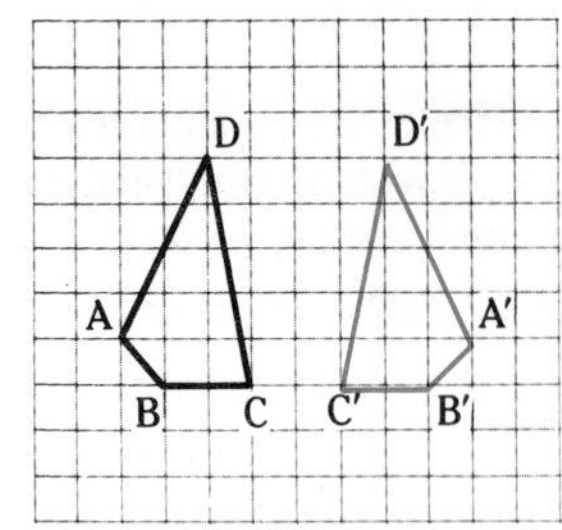

(b)

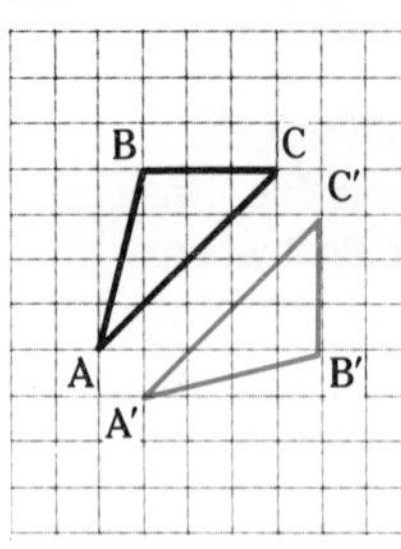

(c)

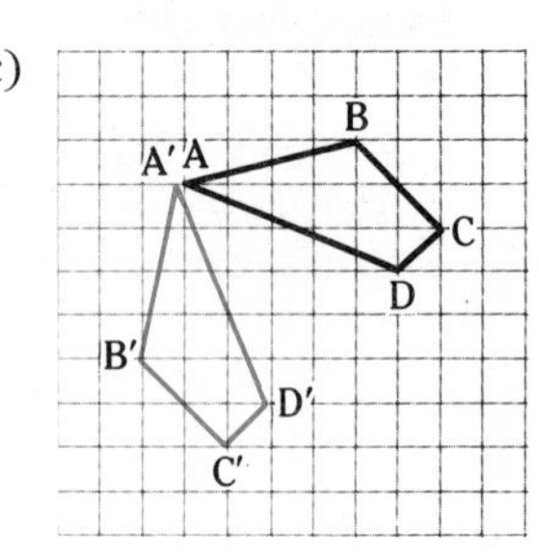

7. Draw $\triangle PQR$ where P is (2, 1), Q is (4, 4) and R is (−2, 4). Draw also $\triangle P'Q'R'$ where P′ is (2, 1), Q is (4, −2) and R′ is (−2, −2). Given that $\triangle P'Q'R'$ is the image of $\triangle PQR$, draw the mirror line.

Translation

Consider the transformations of $\triangle ABC$ shown in this diagram.

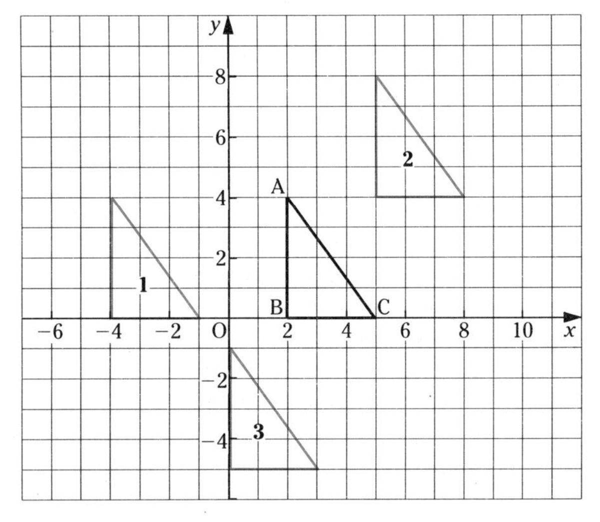

In each of these movements the side AB remains parallel to the y-axis and the orientation of the triangle (i.e. the way it faces) is unchanged. Transformations of this type are called *translations*.

Although no mirror is involved the words object and image are still used. A translation can be defined by giving the amount of movement parallel to each of the axes.
In the diagram above, for example, the translations that map triangle ABC to the image triangles are:

for image 1,
a translation of 6 units to the left parallel to the x-axis;

for image 2,
a translation of 3 units to the right parallel to the x-axis
and 4 units upward parallel to the y-axis;

for image 3,
a translation of 2 units to the left parallel to the x-axis
and 5 units downward parallel to the y-axis.

Exercise 4d

1. The diagram below shows six images of the black triangle. Which of the images are given by translation and which by reflection?

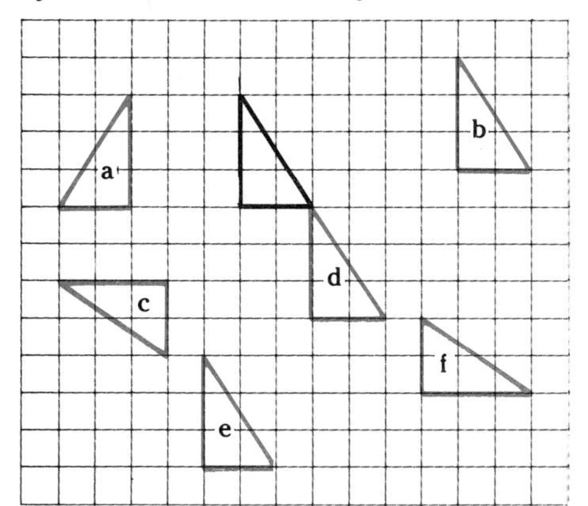

2. On squared paper draw x and y axes, each from -3 to 8 and mark the points A(3, 5), B(2, 1) and C(-1, 4). Mark and label $A_1B_1C_1$, $A_2B_2C_2$, etc., the images of triangle ABC under translations of
   (a) 2 units to the left parallel to Ox and 3 units down parallel to Oy
   (b) 4 units to the right parallel to Ox and 1 unit up parallel to Oy
   (c) 5 units to the right parallel to Ox and 3 units down parallel to Oy.

3. Describe the translation that maps the rectangle ABCD to
   (a) the rectangle $A_1B_1C_1D_1$
   (b) the rectangle $A_2B_2C_2D_2$
   (c) the rectangle $A_3B_3C_3D_3$

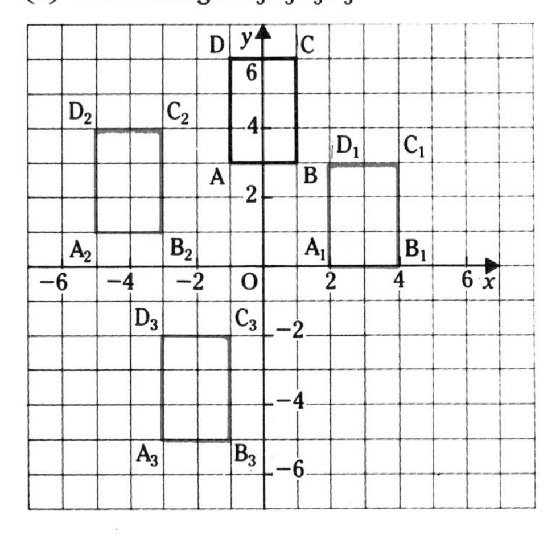

4. Copy the diagram.
   (a) The square ABCD is translated a distance equal to AB and in the direction of AB. Draw the image and label it 1.
   (b) Square ABCD is translated in the direction of AC a distance equal to AC. Draw this image and label it 2.
   (c) Describe the translation that maps 1 to 2.

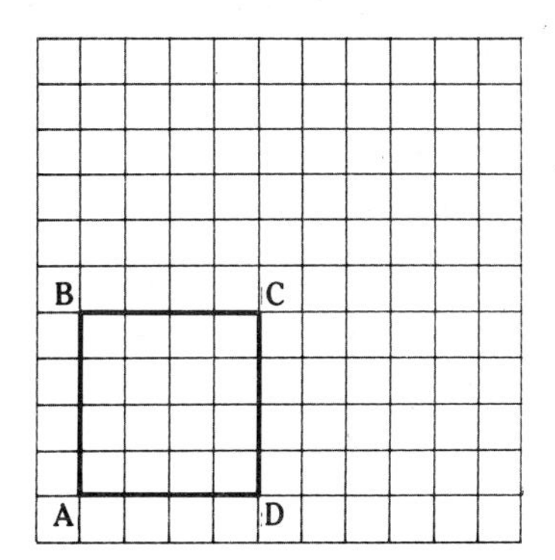

5. Copy the diagram.
   (a) Reflect the triangle labelled A in the x-axis and label the image B.
   (b) Translate B 5 units to the left and 1 unit down. Label the image C.
   (c) Reflect C in the x-axis and label the image D.
   (d) What transformation will map A to D?

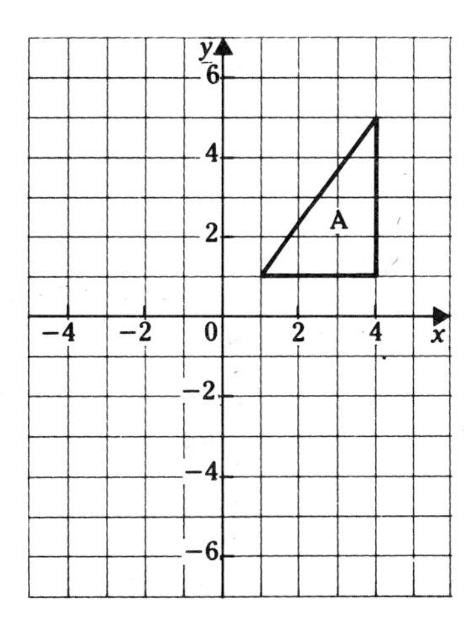

ROTATION

(a)

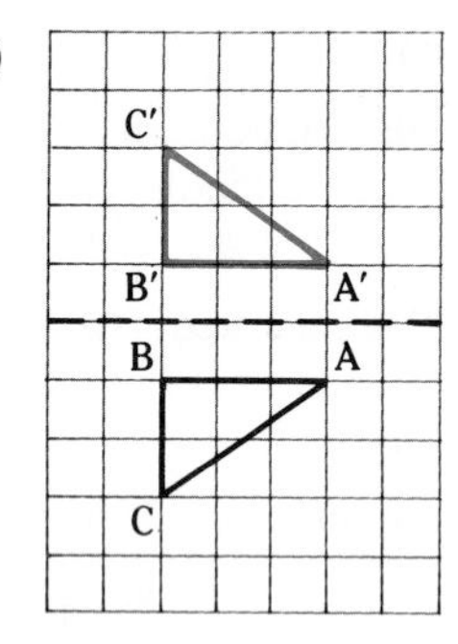

(b)

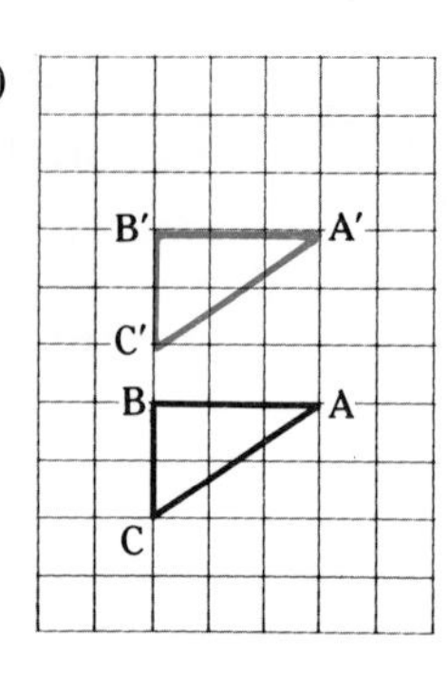

(c)

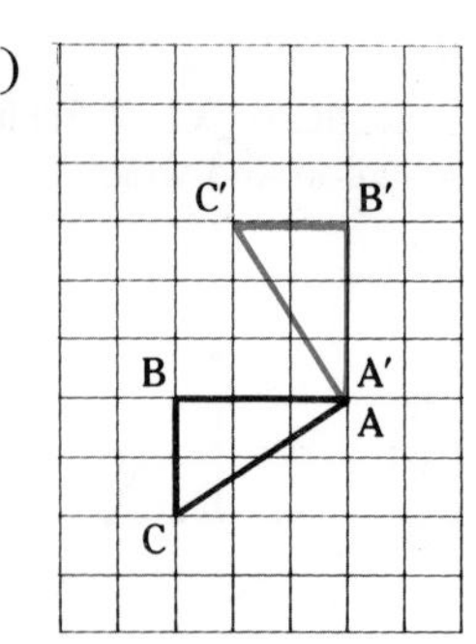

So far a shape has been transformed by reflection, as in (a), and translation, as in (b), but to carry out the transformation in (c) a rotation is needed.

In (c), △ABC is rotated through 90° clockwise ↻ about A. Or we could say that the rotation is 270° anticlockwise ↺. The point about which rotation takes place is the *centre of rotation;* in this case A is the centre of rotation.

Exercise 4e

State the angle of rotation when △PQR is mapped to △P'Q'R'.

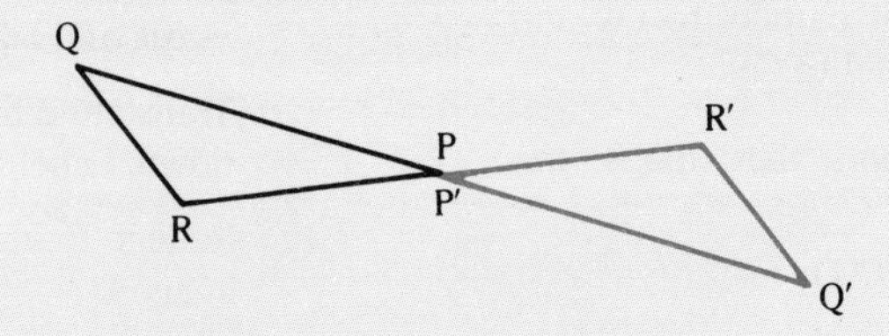

To see the angle of rotation, consider the angle between *one* line and its image.
The angle between PQ and its image P'Q' is 180° and for this angle it is not necessary to say whether it is clockwise or anticlockwise.

The angle of rotation is 180°.

Note that, to find the angle between one line and its image, it may be necessary to extend both lines until they cut.

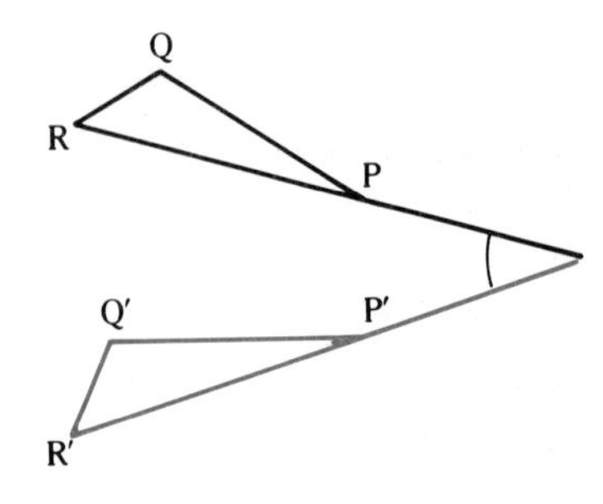

1. State the angle of rotation when $\triangle ABC$ is mapped to $\triangle A'B'C'$. The centre of rotation is marked with a cross.

(a)
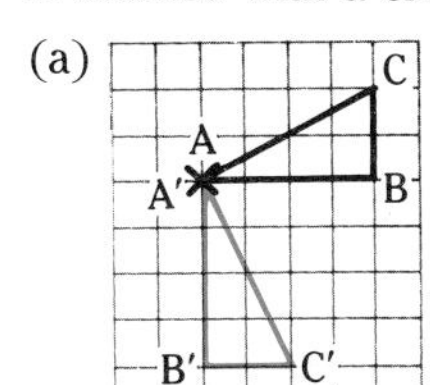

(c)
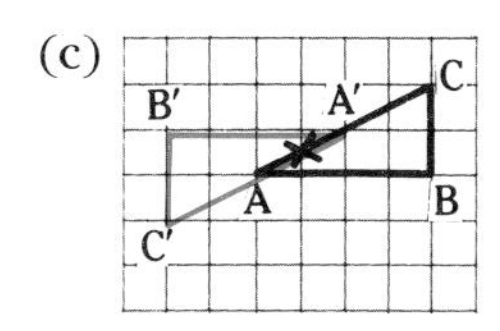

(b)
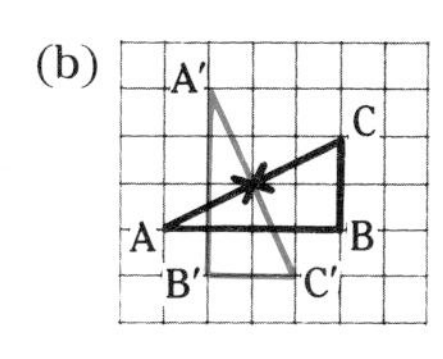

(d)
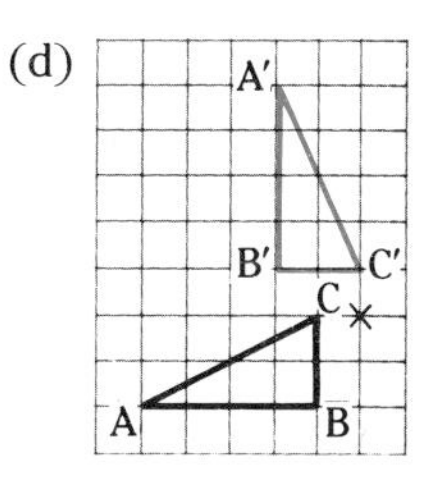

2. Write down the coordinates of A′ and B′, the images of A and B respectively, when AB undergoes the specified rotation.

(a) A(1, 0), B(5, 0);
90° clockwise about (3, 0)

(b) A(2, 3), B(−1, 0);
180° about (0, 1)

(c) A(3, 2), B(3, 4);
90° anticlockwise about (2, 1)

(d) A(−1, −1), B(−3, 3);
270° clockwise about O

3. Copy each diagram and draw the image of $\triangle PQR$ under the given rotation. Label the vertices of the image triangle so that P′ is the image of P, etc.

(a)
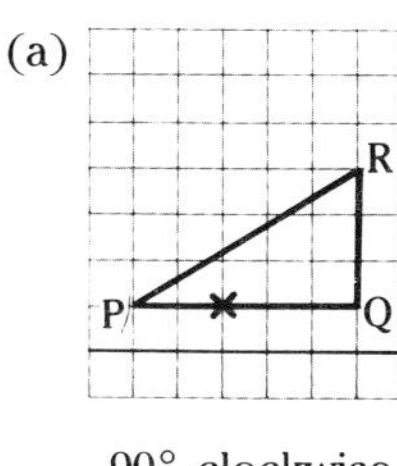

90° clockwise

(c)
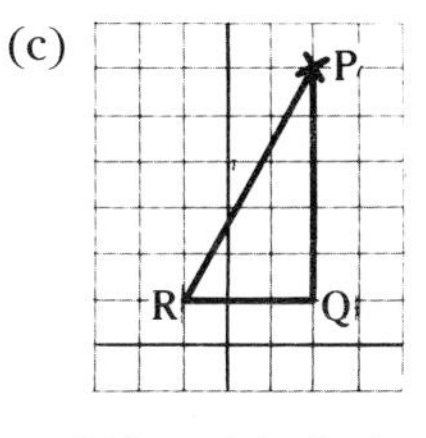

90° anticlockwise

(b)
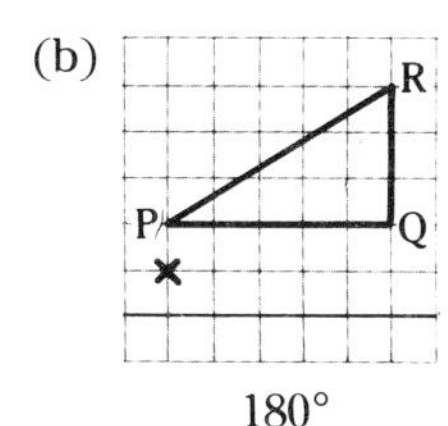

180°

(d)
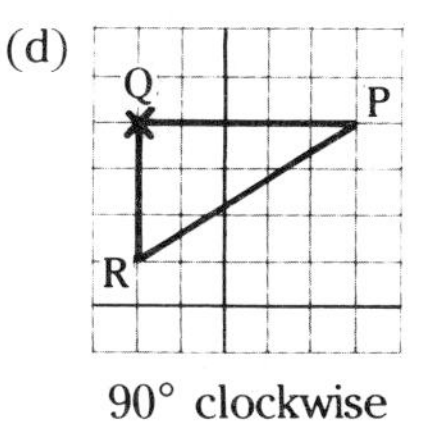

90° clockwise

Finding the Centre of Rotation

Quite often we can look at an object and its image by rotation and locate the centre of rotation by observation. This is not always possible, however, and then we use the following fact:
the distance of the centre of rotation, X, from any point on the object, A, say, is equal to the distance of X from A′.

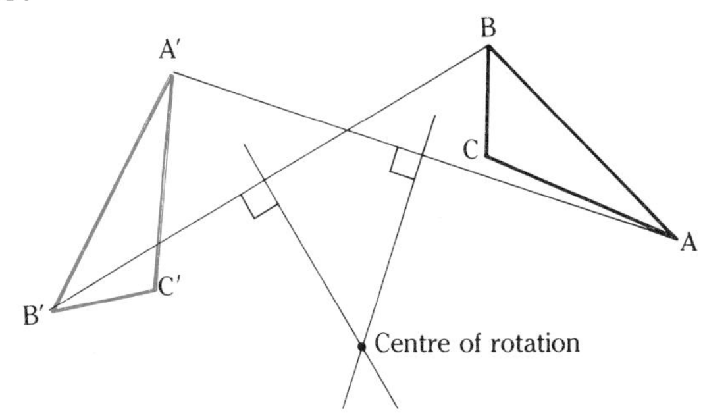

To locate the centre of rotation in this diagram, first we mark the point midway between A and its image A′. Then through this point a line at right angles to AA′ is drawn. Any point on this *perpendicular bisector* is equidistant from A and A′. (This fact can be checked by measurement.)

This process is repeated with either B and B′ or C and C′. The perpendicular bisectors meet at the centre of rotation.

Exercise 4f

In each diagram the purple shape is the image by rotation of the black shape. Trace the diagram and find the centre of rotation.

1.

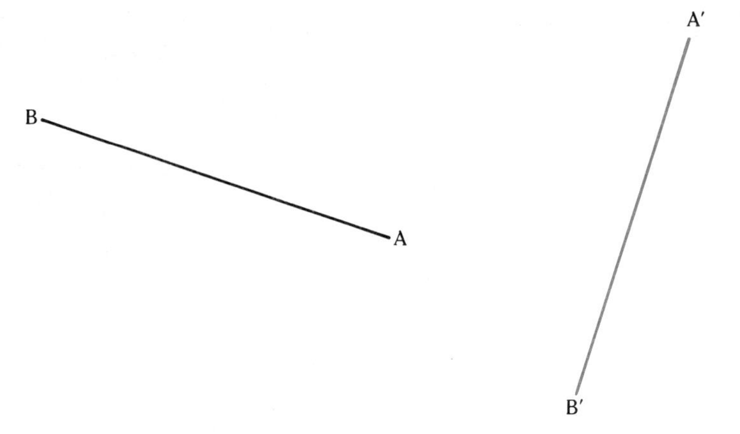

2.

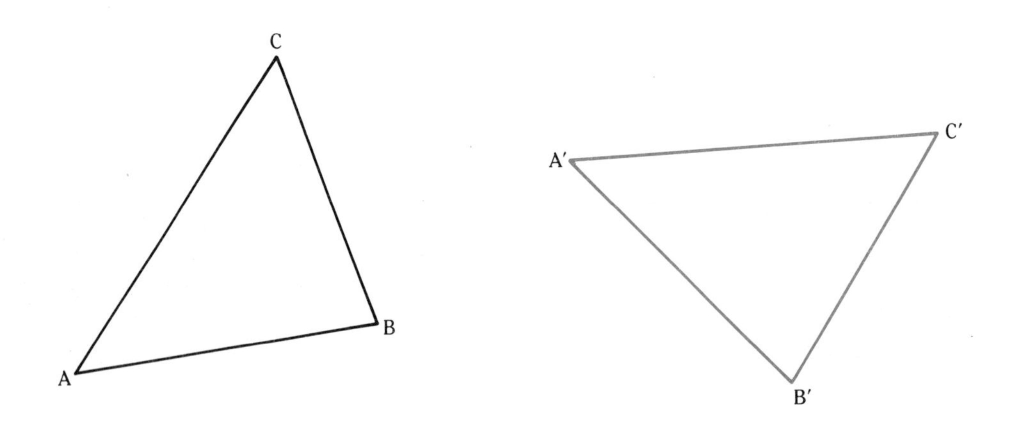

Reflections, translations and rotations all appear in the remaining questions in this exercise.

In questions 3 to 8 name the transformation that maps the black shape to the purple one (A′ is the image of A, etc.). Describe each transformation as fully as possible.

3.

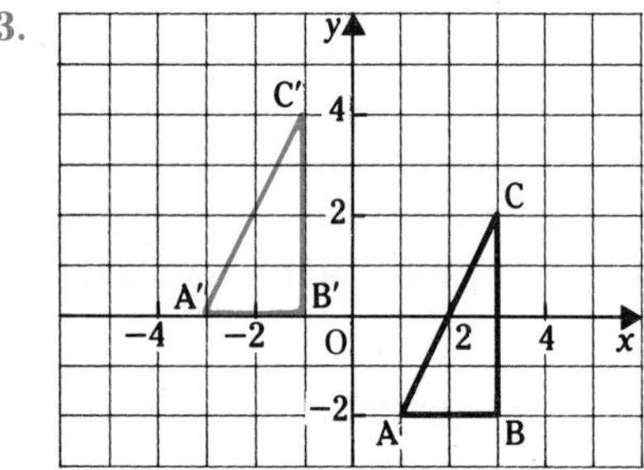

4.

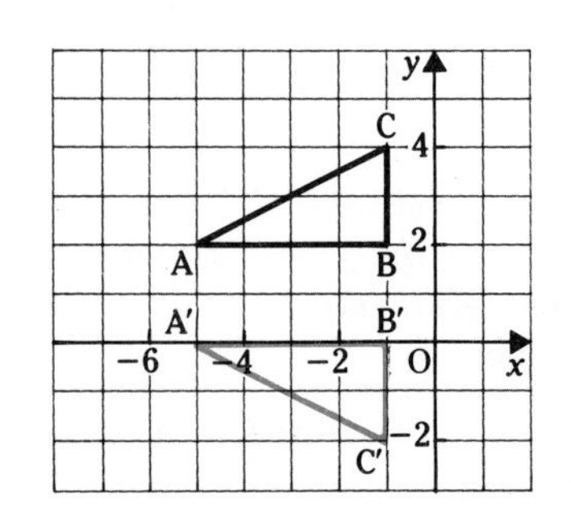

5.

6.

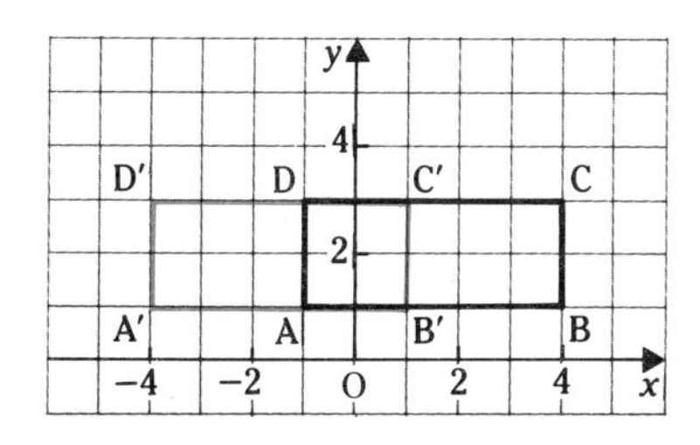

7.

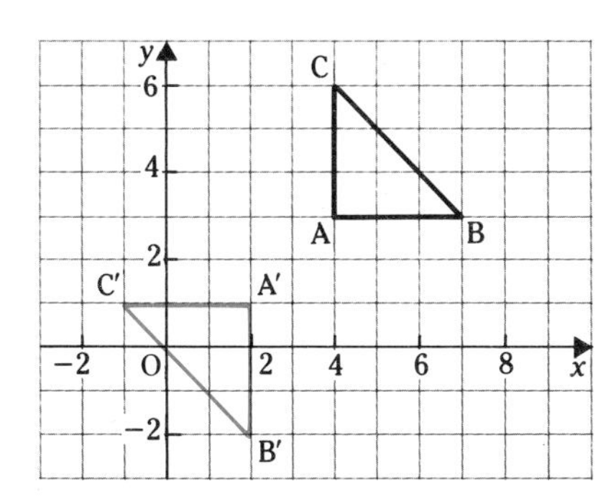

8.

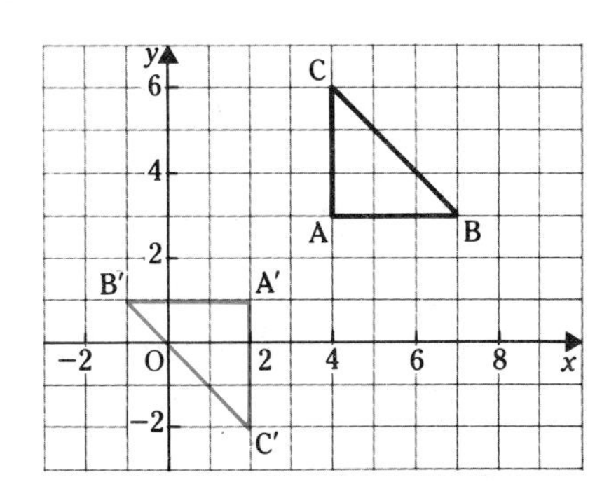

If when a shape is transformed we do not know which point is the image of a particular object point, there may be more than one possible transformation.

In questions 9 to 12 name as many different transformations as you can find that map the black shape to the purple one. The number of transformations that you should spot is given in brackets.
(Do not count a rotation of 90° clockwise and a rotation of 270° anticlockwise as different transformations.)

9. (3)

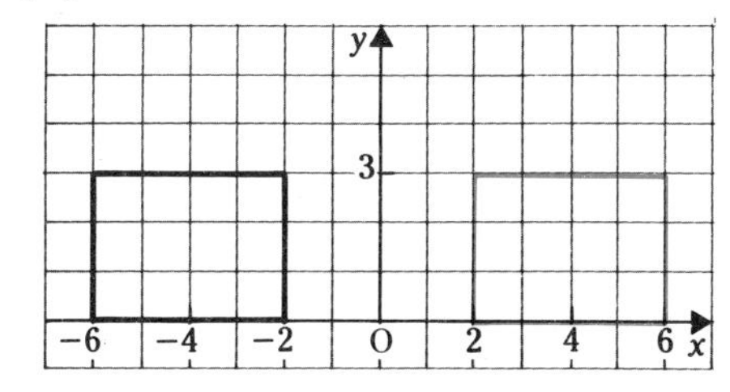

10. (2)

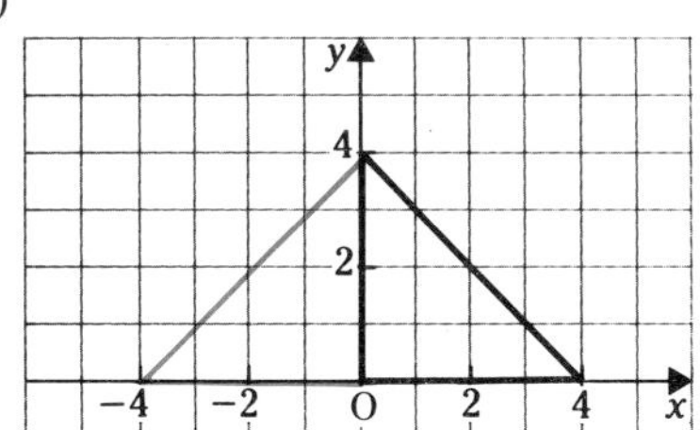

11. (5)

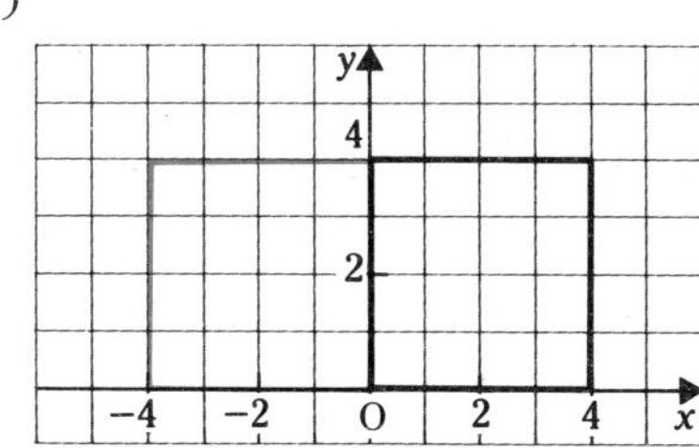

12. (4)

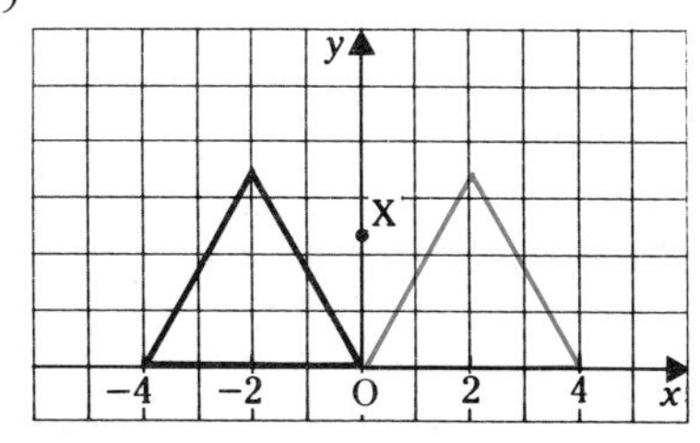

13. Taking the shaded shape in this diagram as the object, state what types of transformation could be used to map the object to the other shapes in the pattern.

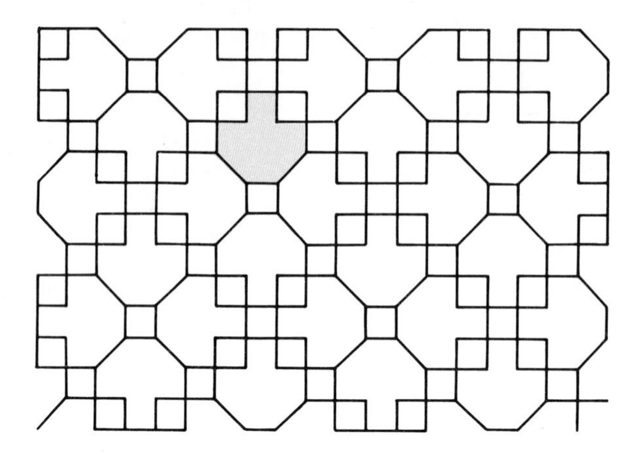

PATTERNS

Question 13 in the last exercise gives an indication of how transformations and symmetry can be used to form patterns.

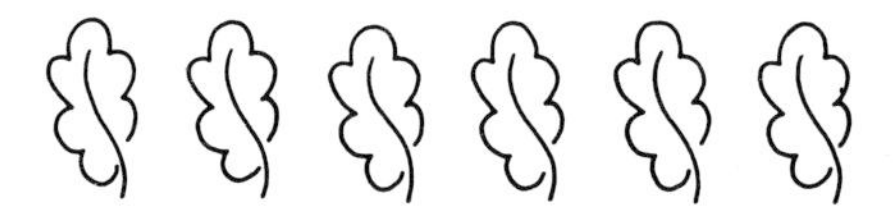

This is a simple border pattern.

One element, i.e. one shape, has been translated successively along the border.

The pattern can be made more interesting if the basic element is either reflected in a horizontal line, or rotated, and then translated as before.

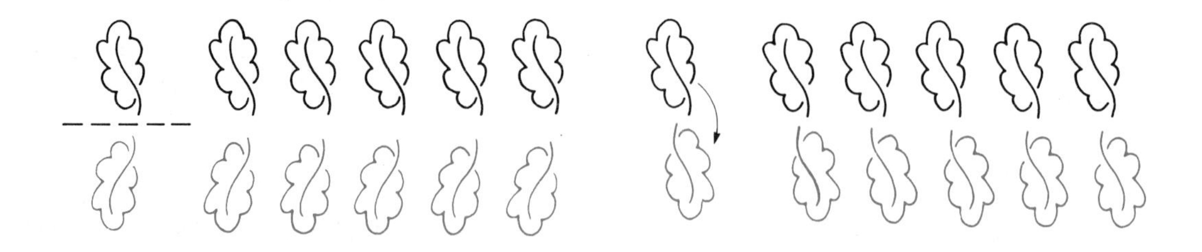

Clearly there is vast scope for creating patterns starting with just one simple element.

Nor need there be a restriction to border patterns; all-over patterns can also be formed from transformations of an element as the example at the top of the page shows.

Exercise 4g

1. Describe the transformations used to produce each of the following border patterns from the given element.

(a)

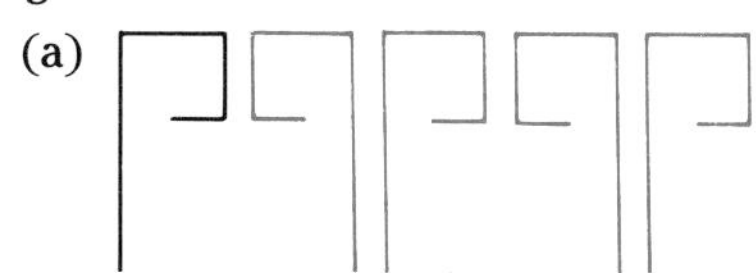

(b)

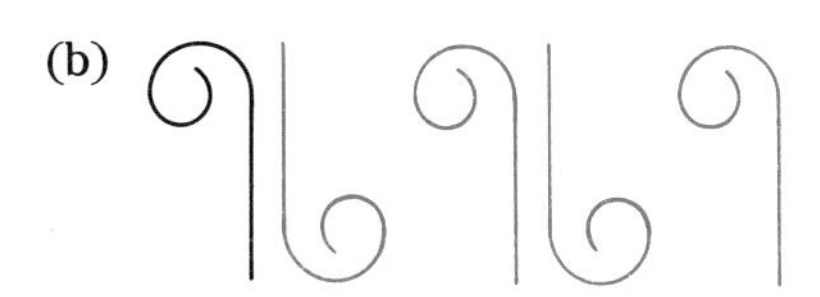

(c)

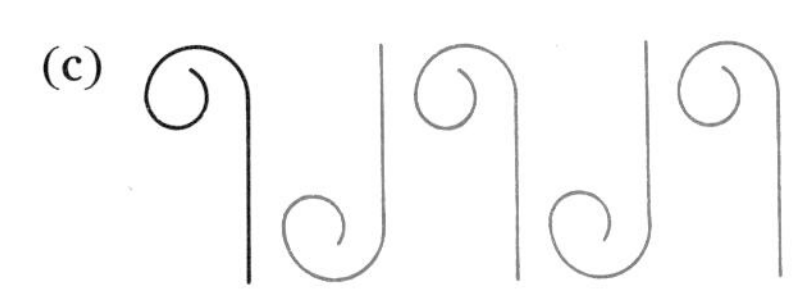

(d)

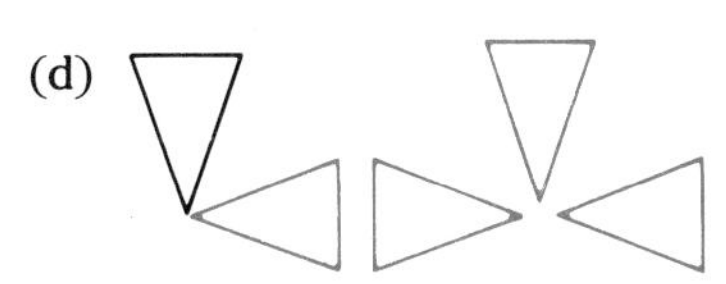

2. State the transformations used to produce each of the following all-over patterns.

(a)

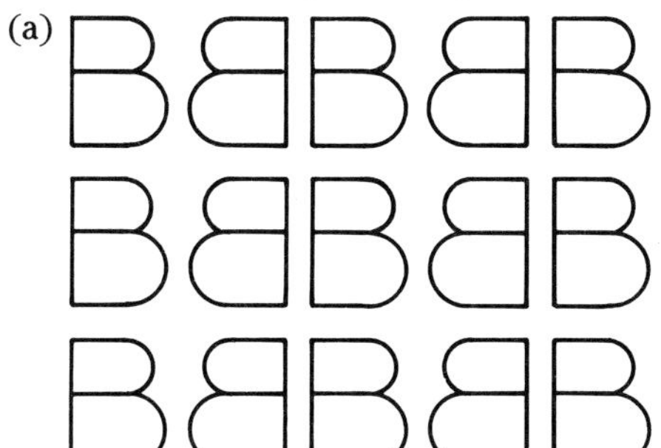

(b)

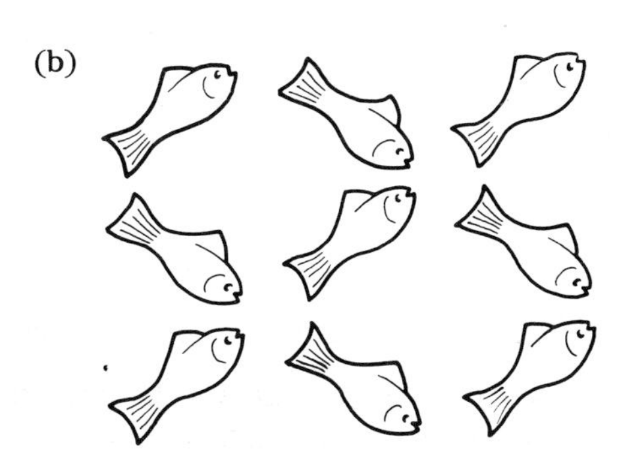

3.

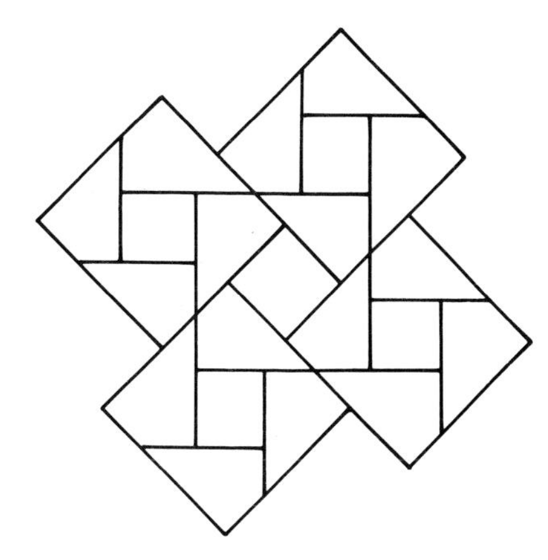

In each of these patterns,

(a) identify a basic shape which repeats. If there is more than one possible basic shape, consider each in turn

(b) investigate the types of transformation used on the basic shape to form the continuing pattern, copying and extending the pattern if necessary.

4. Make your own pattern using a basic shape such as a square or an equilateral triangle.

CONGRUENT FIGURES

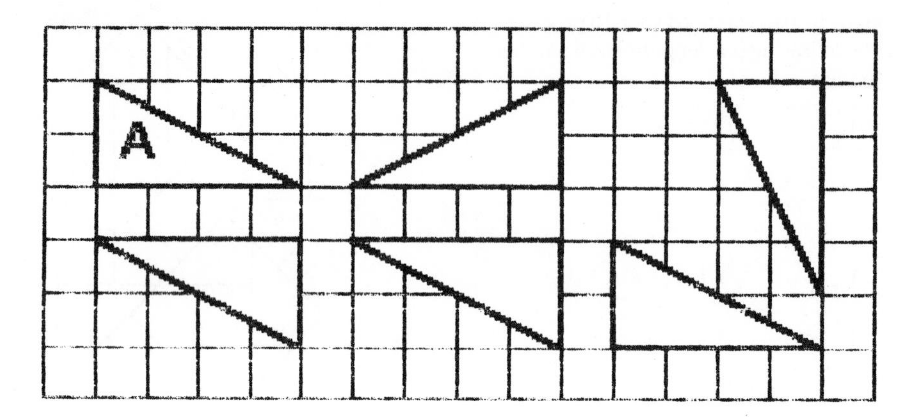

This diagram was drawn on a computer. Triangle A was drawn first and then transformed in various ways to give the other triangles.

All the triangles have exactly the same shape and size and are called *congruent* triangles.

Two figures with exactly the same shape *and* size are called congruent figures.

(Two figures with the same shape but *different in size* are called *similar* figures.)

Transformations and Congruent Figures

Some transformations leave the size and shape of a figure unchanged, i.e. the object and image are congruent. Reflection produces congruent shapes:

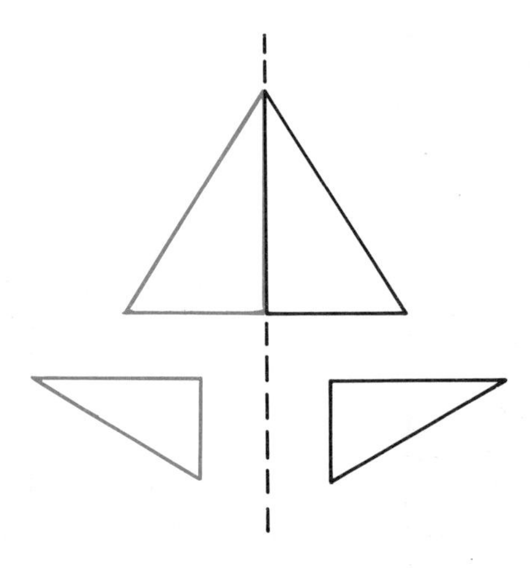

Rotation produces congruent shapes:

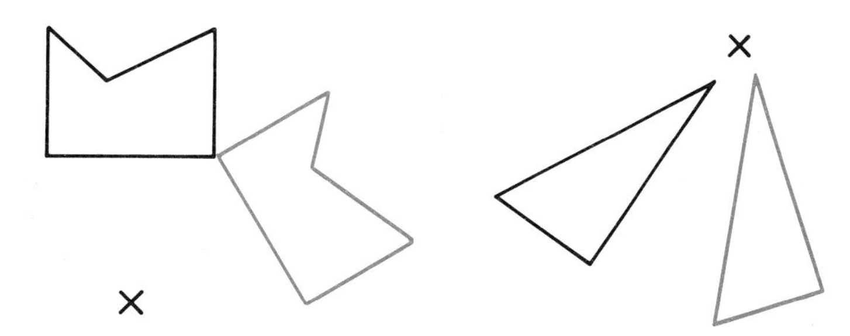

Translation produces congruent shapes:

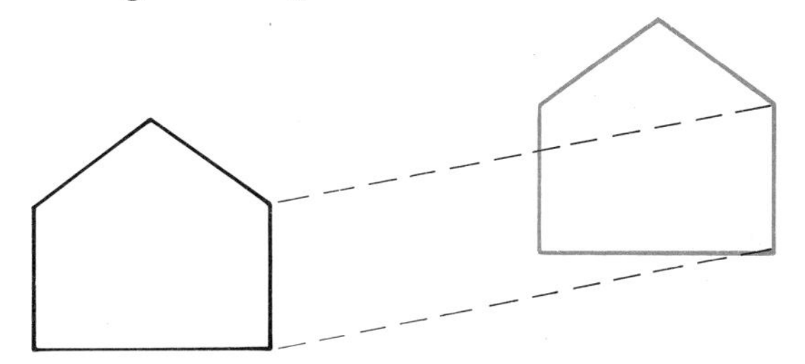

Exercise 4h

In questions 1 to 6 state whether or not the two figures are congruent. If they are congruent, state which transformation has been applied.

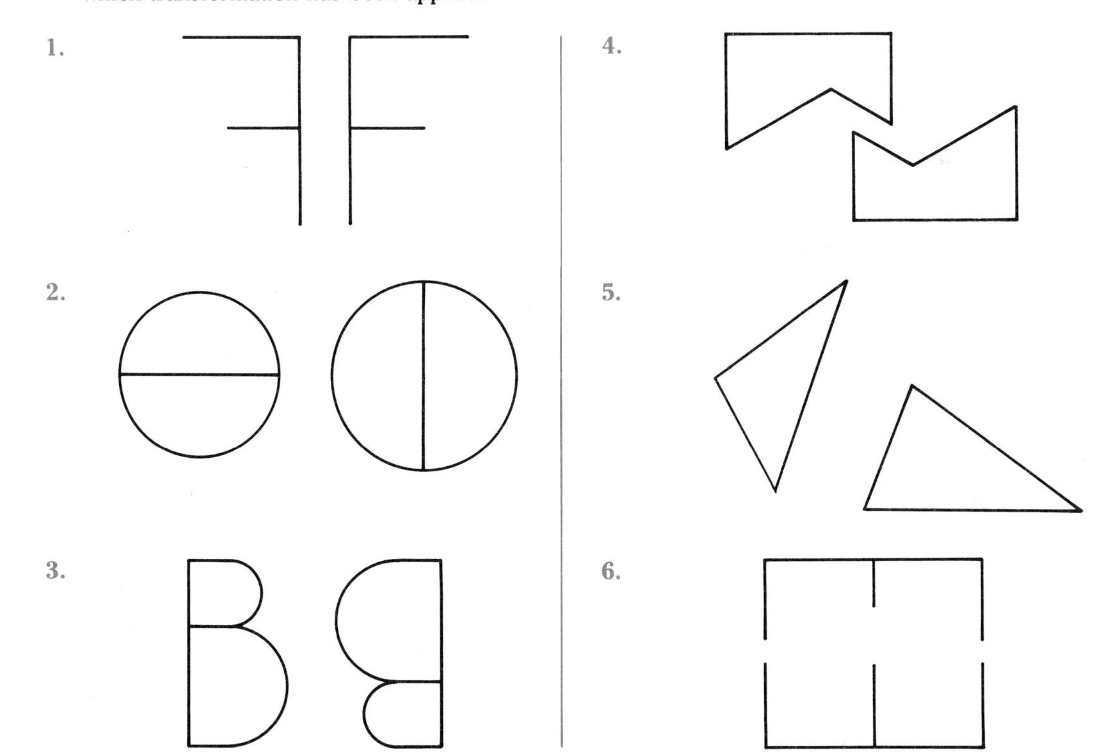

In each of the following questions

(a) describe a transformation, if there is one, that maps the black shape to the purple one

(b) state whether or not the object and the image are congruent.

7.

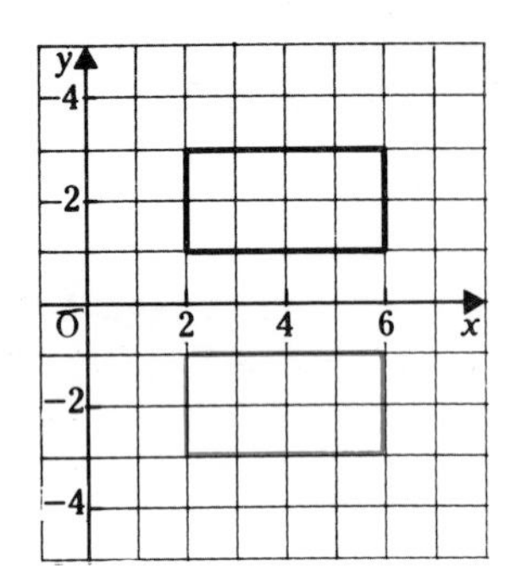

8.

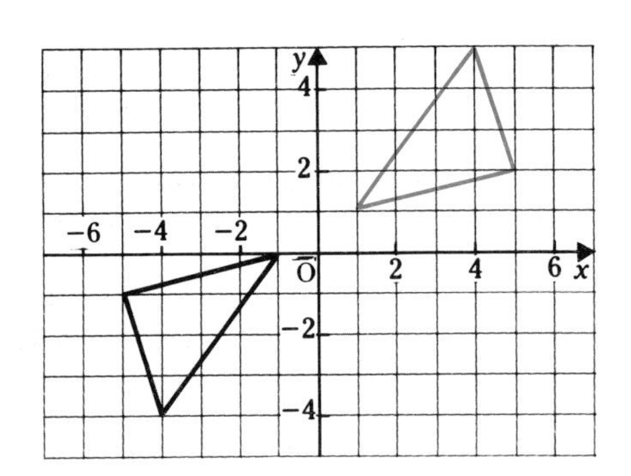

9.

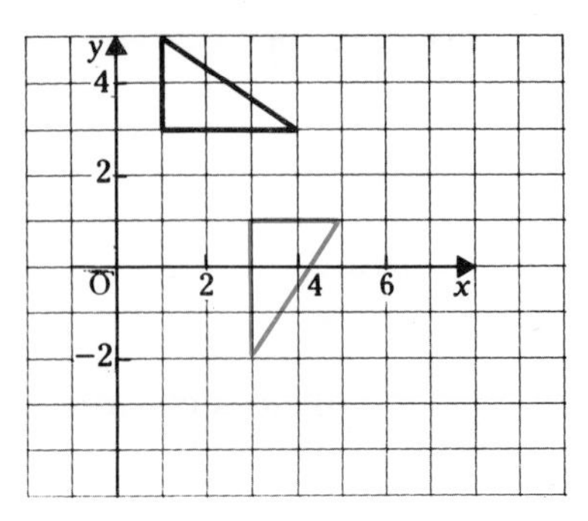

10.

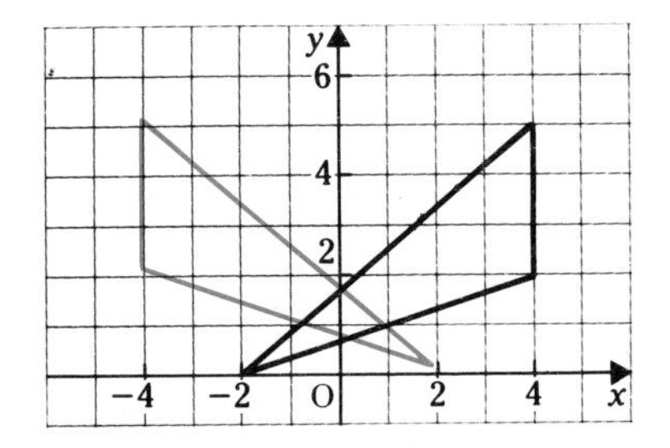

Investigations

1. Using 1 cm as 1 unit on each axis, draw x and y axes from -6 to 6. Mark the points A(4, 1), B(4, 2), C(2, 1) and draw $\triangle$ABC. Draw the line L through the points $(-6, -6)$ and (6, 6).

(a) When $\triangle$ABC is reflected in the line L the image is $\triangle A_1B_1C_1$. Draw this image and rotate it through 180° about O to produce $\triangle A_2B_2C_2$.
Describe the transformation that would map $\triangle$ABC to $\triangle A_2B_2C_2$.

(b) Rotate $\triangle$ABC through 180° about O and then reflect the image in the line L. Is the final image the triangle $\triangle A_2B_2C_2$?

Do the same comparison with other pairs of reflections and rotations, in each case finding the single transformation that is equivalent to the pair.

Investigate whether the order in which the transformations are applied affects the result and whether the single transformations themselves are always reflections or rotations.

Try different vertices for $\triangle$ABC to see whether these have any effect on your conclusions.

2. (a) Start with two parallel mirror lines, L_1 and L_2, and a triangle ABC as shown. Investigate what happens when $\triangle ABC$ is reflected in L_1, the image $\triangle A_1B_1C_1$ is then reflected in L_2 and this image, $\triangle A_2B_2C_2$, is reflected in L_1 and so on.

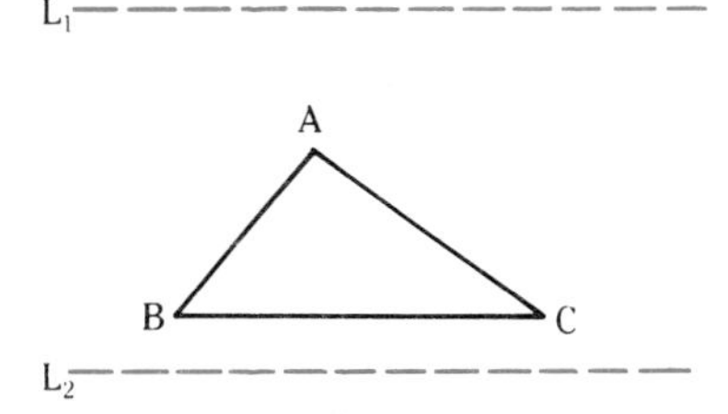

(b) Try a similar sequence of reflections in two non-parallel mirror lines. Start with mirror lines that intersect at P and are inclined at 45°. Investigate the positions of the images of one vertex at a time, relative to P.
Is there a similar relationship when the mirror lines are inclined at a different angle ?

Self-Assessment 4

1. State whether each of the following diagrams has:

    line symmetry, rotational symmetry, both or neither.

    For those shapes that have line symmetry, state the number of lines and for those with rotational symmetry state the order of the symmetry.

(a)
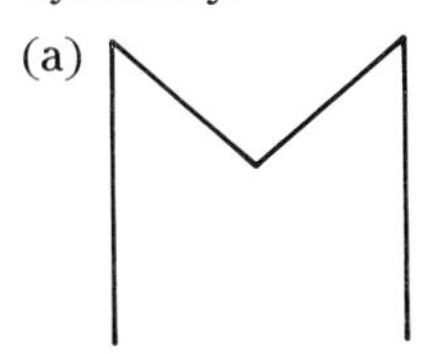

(b)
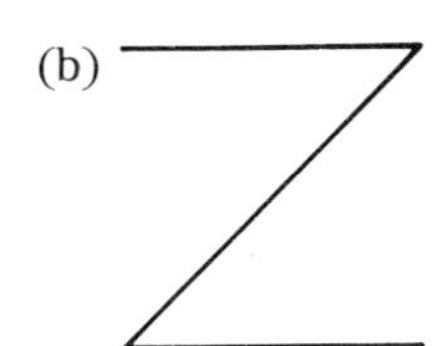

(c)
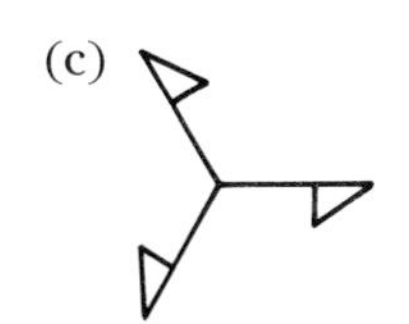

(d)
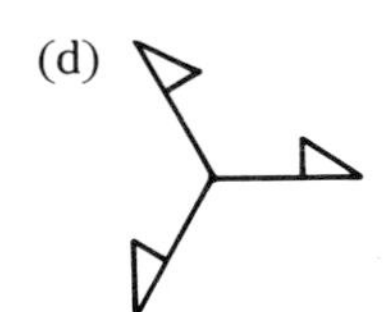

(e)
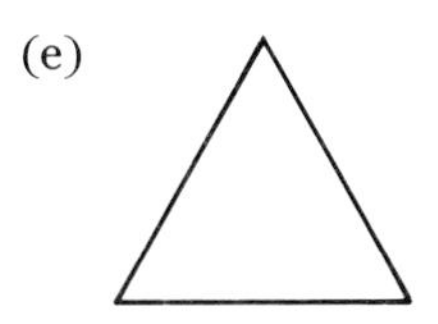

(f)
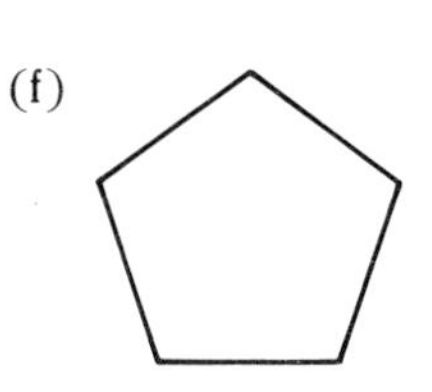

(g)
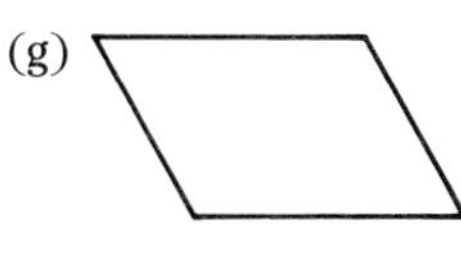

(h)
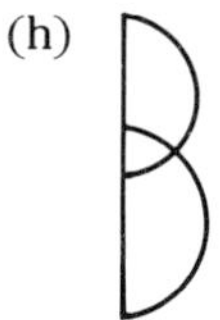

2. On squared paper, using the side of a square as 1 unit, draw x and y axes scaled from -4 to 7.
Mark the following points, A(-3, 1), B(1, 4), C(6, 4) and D(2, 1), and draw the quadrilateral ABCD.

    (a) Does ABCD have line symmetry ? If it has, name the mirror line or lines.

    (b) Does ABCD have rotational symmetry ? If it has, give the coordinates of the centre of rotation.

    (c) Repeat the question with C at (8, 4) and D at (4, 1).

3. On squared paper, using the side of one square as 1 unit, draw x and y axes scaled from -3 to 7

    Mark the points A(-2, 4), B(6, 4), C(6, -2). Draw the quadrilateral ABCD so that the perpendicular bisectors of AB and BC are both lines of symmetry.

    (a) Write down the coordinates of D.

    (b) Does ABCD have rotational symmetry ? If it does, give the coordinates of the centre of rotation and the order of symmetry.

4. The diagram shows a rectangle PQRS and three of its images. Describe a transformation that maps PQRS to each image.

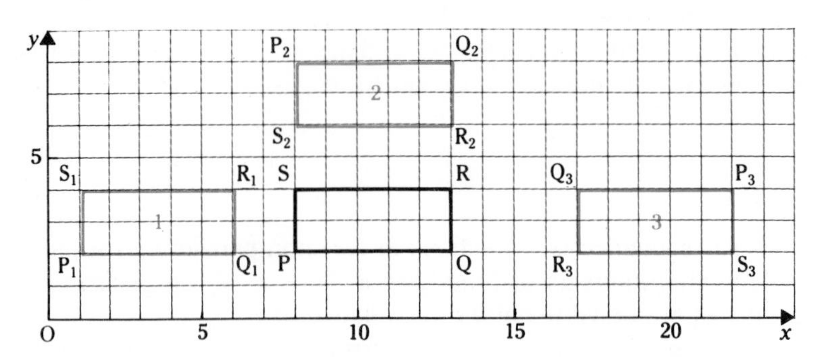

5. Copy the diagram and draw the image given by reflecting the object in each mirror line.

(a)

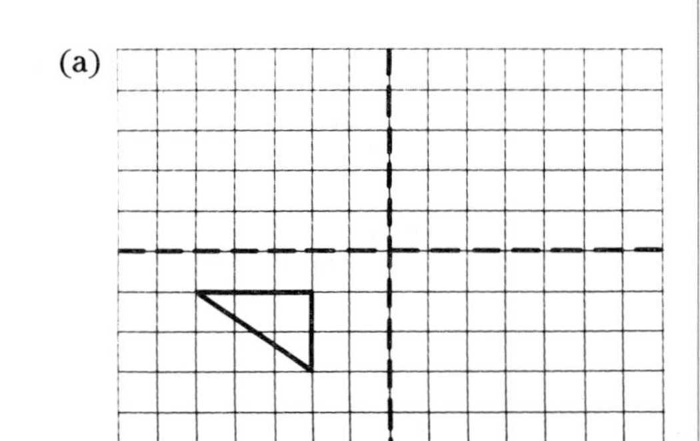

(b)

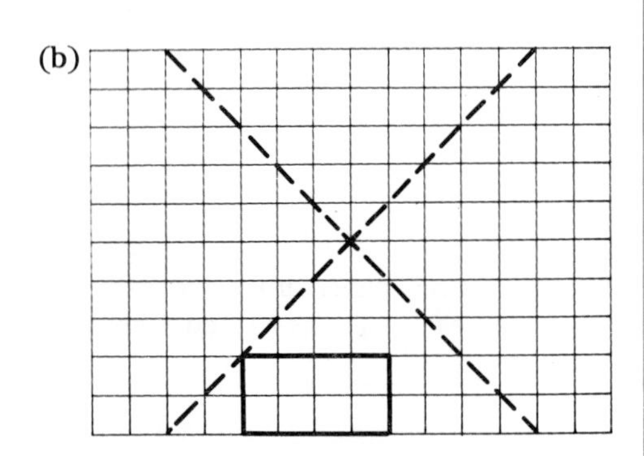

6. On squared paper draw the triangle with vertices at A(4, 2), B(1, 6) and C(2, 0). A second triangle has vertices $A_1(6,2)$, $B_1(9,6)$ and $C_1(8,0)$. Find the mirror line if $\triangle A_1B_1C_1$ is the image of $\triangle ABC$ by reflection.

7. In each part state whether or not the two shapes are congruent.

(a)

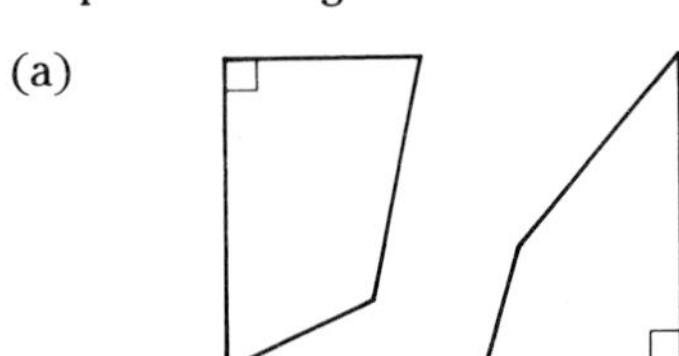

(b)

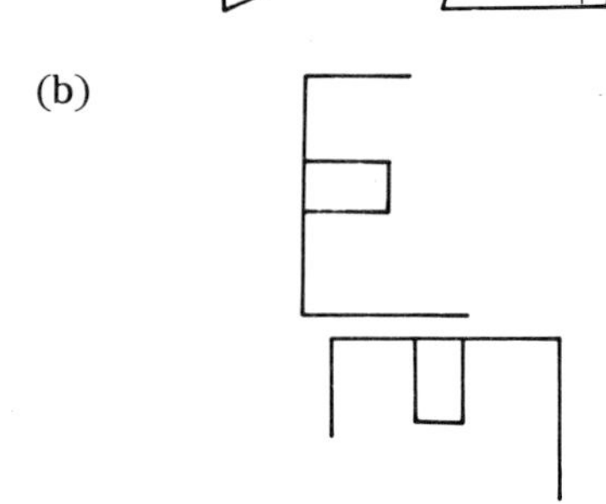

(c)

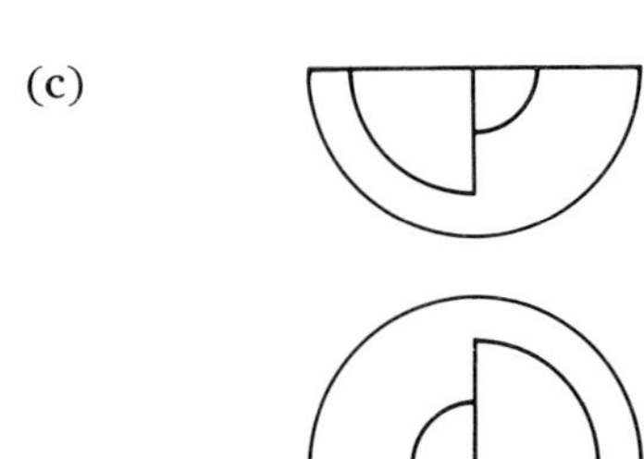

8. Describe the transformations used to produce this border pattern from the element shown.

9. Copy the diagram, in which the purple triangle is the image of the black one. Find the angle of rotation and the centre of rotation.

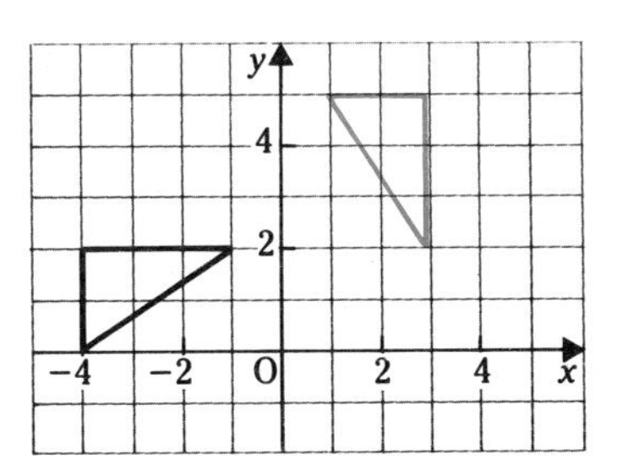

10. Draw on squared paper the triangle whose vertices are the points A(2, 1), B(5, 1) and C(5, 4).

(a) Draw $\triangle A_1B_1C_1$, which is the image given when $\triangle ABC$ is reflected in the *y*-axis.

(b) Draw $\triangle A_2B_2C_2$, the image of $\triangle A_1B_1C_1$ reflected in the *x*-axis. What single transformation maps $\triangle ABC$ to $\triangle A_2B_2C_2$?

(c) When $\triangle ABC$ is rotated through 180° about B, the image is $\triangle A_3B_3C_3$. What transformation maps $\triangle A_2B_2C_2$ to $\triangle A_3B_3C_3$?

BASIC MEASUREMENT

BASIC UNITS

Certain quantities, such as length and mass, have a fundamental place in everyday life. Because we need to be able to measure these, it is necessary to have a standard amount of each as a unit.

Length

The metric units of length are based on the metre, which is roughly the length of a man's stride. One metre is written 1 m. So that smaller lengths can be measured conveniently, a metre is divided into 100 parts, each of which is a centimetre (cm). An even smaller unit is given when 1 m is divided into 1000 parts, each of which is a millimetre (mm);
hence 1 cm = 10 mm.

Clearly it would not be convenient to measure distances between towns in metres so a much larger unit, the kilometre (km), is used, where 1 kilometre is equal to 1000 metres.

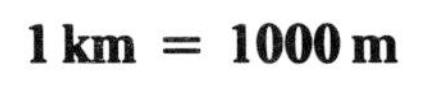

$$\mathbf{1\,km = 1000\,m}$$

$$\mathbf{1\,m = 100\,cm}$$

$$\mathbf{1\,cm = 10\,mm}$$

For example:

$$4\,\text{km} = 4 \times 1000\,\text{m} = 4000\,\text{m} \quad \text{and} \quad 376\,\text{m} = \frac{376}{1000}\,\text{km} = 0.376\,\text{km}$$

$$8.7\,\text{m} = 8.7 \times 100\,\text{cm} = 870\,\text{cm} \quad \text{and} \quad 59\,\text{cm} = \frac{59}{100}\,\text{m} = 0.59\,\text{m}$$

$$2.3\,\text{cm} = 2.3 \times 10\,\text{mm} = 23\,\text{mm} \quad \text{and} \quad 472\,\text{mm} = \frac{472}{10}\,\text{cm} = 47.2\,\text{cm}$$

Note that when changing from a large unit to a smaller one there are *more* of the smaller units so we *multiply* by the appropriate factor.
When changing from a small unit to a larger one, there are *fewer* of the large units so we *divide*.

It is useful to recognise the meaning of the prefixes used in front of the basic unit, in this case the metre:

kilo means 'one thousand times as big'
centi means 'one hundredth part of'
milli means 'one thousandth part of'

Mass

When a quantity of a commodity is bought, we usually ask for a certain weight but what we really want is a certain *mass*. The *weight* of an object is the pull of gravity on it and this varies from place to place. Weight can be measured by using a spring balance or similar weighing machine.
Weight also depends upon the amount of material in the object. This is the *mass* of the object and it does not vary.

The basic unit of mass is the gram (a very small unit: about the mass of one average sized crisp). Using some of the same prefixes as for length units gives further units of mass:

1 kilogram (kg) = 1000 grams (g)

1 gram (g) = 1000 milligrams (mg)

A centigram is not in common use.

Because the biggest of the units above, the kilogram, is not a very large one (1 kg is the mass of an ordinary bag of sugar), a much bigger unit is needed to measure, say, building materials. This unit is the tonne where 1 tonne (t) = 1000 kg.

Exercise 5a

Express (a) 47 tonnes in kilograms (b) 1227 mm in centimetres.

(a) Change from large unit to smaller unit — multiply.

1 t = 1000 kg

$$47\text{ t} = 47 \times 1000\text{ kg} = 47\,000\text{ kg}$$

(b) Change from small unit to larger one — divide.

1 cm = 10 mm

$$1227\text{ mm} = \frac{1227}{10}\text{ cm} = 122.7\text{ cm}$$

1. Express each quantity in the unit given in brackets.

(a) 4 kg (g)
(b) 81 mm (cm)
(c) 2.1 m (cm)
(d) 2024 g (kg)
(e) 5 km (m)
(f) 7.3 g (mg)
(g) 21 t (kg)
(h) 121 mg (g)
(i) 35 mm (cm)
(j) 5670 kg (t)
(k) 140 cm (m)
(l) 23 m (mm)

Express
(a) 2 m 37 cm in centimetres
(b) 1 kg 79 g in kilograms.

(a) Only the 2 m must be changed into centimetres.

$2\text{ m} = 2 \times 100\text{ cm} = 200\text{ cm}$

$\therefore \quad 2\text{ m } 37\text{ cm} = 200\text{ cm} + 37\text{ cm} = 237\text{ cm}$

(b) Change the 79 g into kilograms.

$79\text{ g} = \frac{79}{1000}\text{ kg} = 0.079\text{ kg}$

$\therefore \quad 1\text{ kg } 79\text{ g} = 1\text{ kg} + 0.079\text{ kg} = 1.079\text{ kg}$

2. Express each quantity in the unit given in brackets.

(a) 3 cm 5 mm (mm)
(b) 3 t 250 kg (kg)
(c) 8 km 36 m (m)
(d) 3 km 450 m (km)
(e) 7 m 88 cm (m)
(f) 9 g 77 mg (g)

3. Sally had two pieces of tape. One piece measured 2 m and the other piece measured 62 cm. Give the total length of tape in
(a) metres (b) centimetres.

PERIMETER

The total distance round the boundary of a shape is its *perimeter.* When the dimensions of a simple shape are known, its perimeter can be found very easily.

The perimeter of this square is

$3\text{ cm} + 3\text{ cm} + 3\text{ cm} + 3\text{ cm} = 12\text{ cm}$

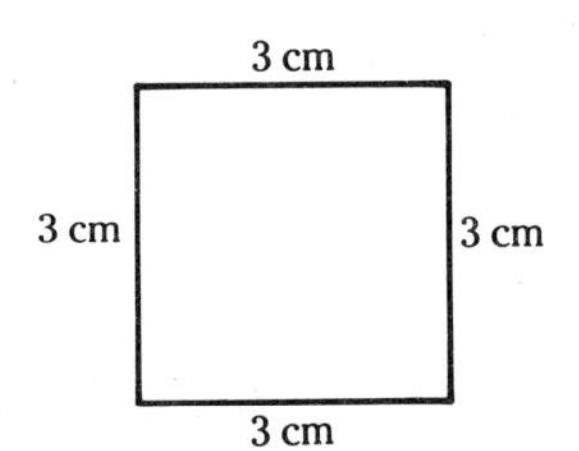

In general the perimeter of a square is given by
4 × length of one side

For this rectangle the perimeter is

$7\text{ cm} + 4\text{ cm} + 7\text{ cm} + 4\text{ cm}$

$= 2 \times 7\text{ cm} + 2 \times 4\text{ cm}$

$= 22\text{ cm}$

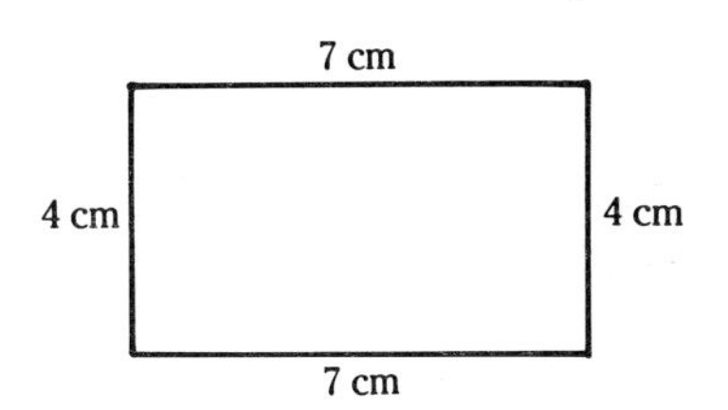

In general, the perimeter of a rectangle is given by
2 × length + 2 × breadth

The perimeter of any shape can be found by adding the lengths of all its sides, provided that all these lengths are either given or can be deduced,

e.g.

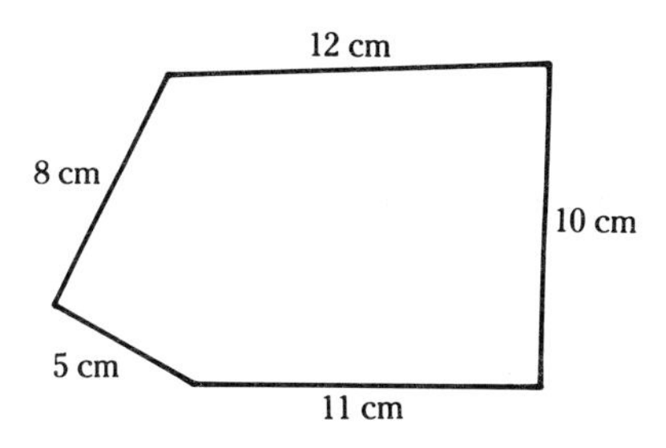

Perimeter $= (5 + 8 + 12 + 10 + 11)\text{ cm} = 46\text{ cm}$

Exercise 5b

Find the perimeter of the shape given in each question.

1. A square of side (a) 6.2 cm (b) 0.71 m

2. A rectangle measuring (a) 4.5 m by 3 m (b) 11 mm by 6.1 mm

3.

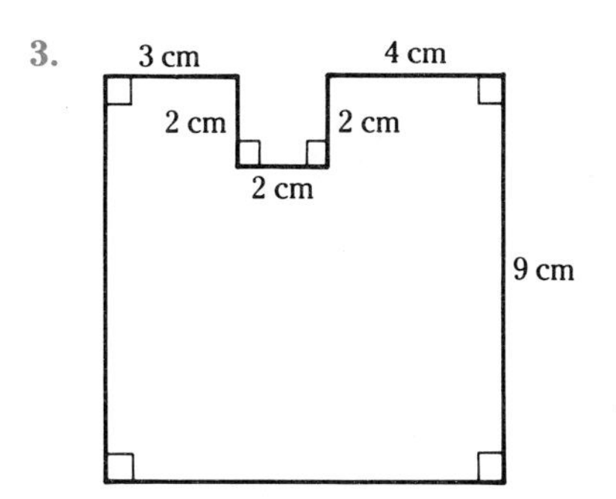

4.

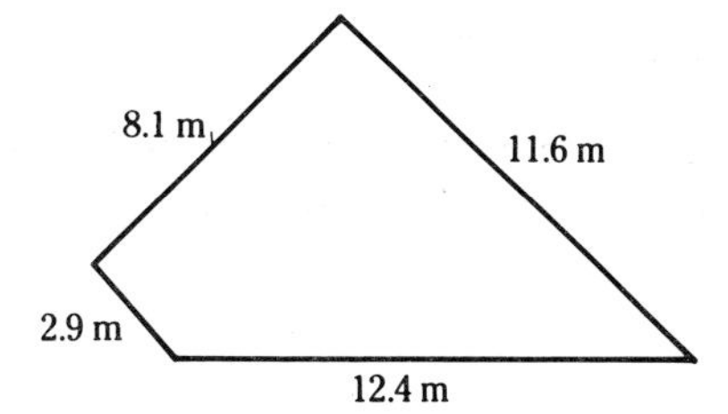

5. A rectangle that measures 10 cm by 16 cm and has a square of side 2 cm cut from each corner.

6. (a) An equilateral triangle of side 7.3 m.
   (b) A rhombus of side 0.42 cm.

Find the perimeter of this shape:

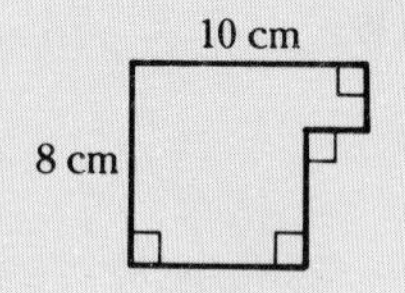

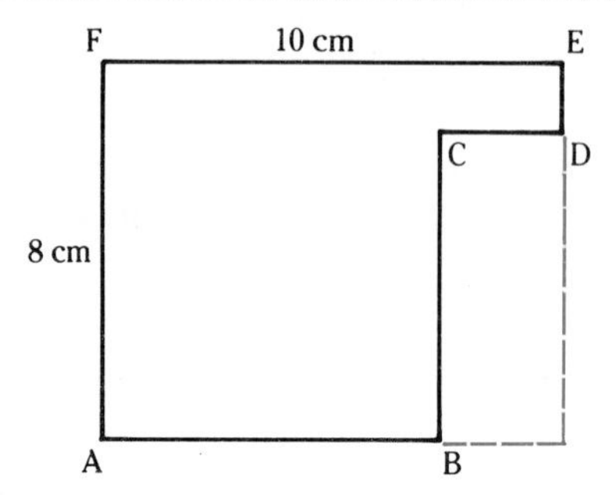

Although there are four sides whose lengths are not given, it is clear that combining some sides gives a known length.

$$AB + CD = FE = 10\,\text{cm}$$

and

$$BC + DE = AF = 8\,\text{cm}$$

The perimeter is given by

$$AB + BC + CD + DE + EF + FA$$

$$= AB + CD + BC + DE + EF + FA$$

$$= 10\,\text{cm} + 8\,\text{cm} + 10\,\text{cm} + 8\,\text{cm} = 36\,\text{cm}$$

Find the perimeter of each shape.

7.

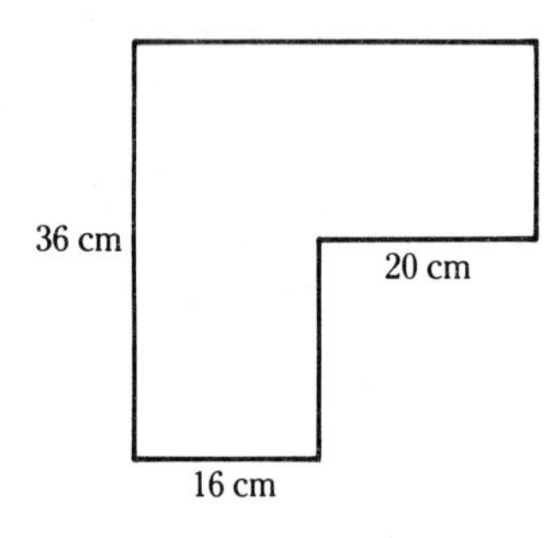

8.

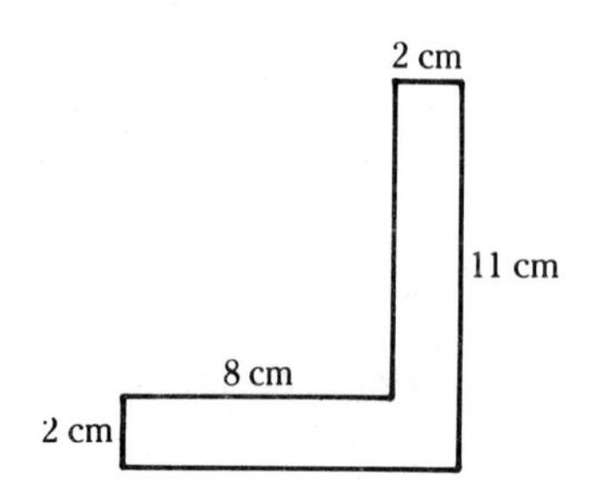

9.

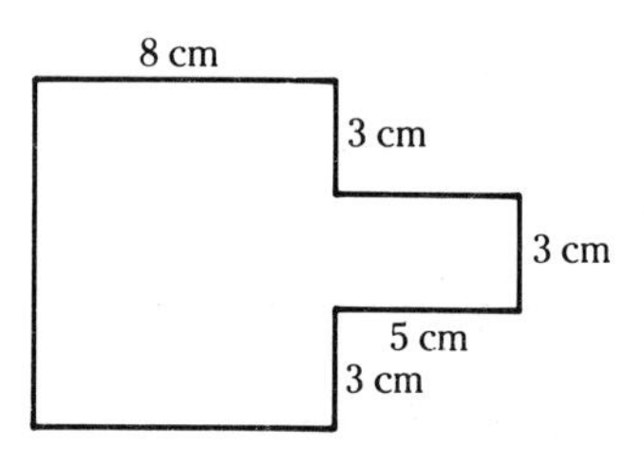

10.

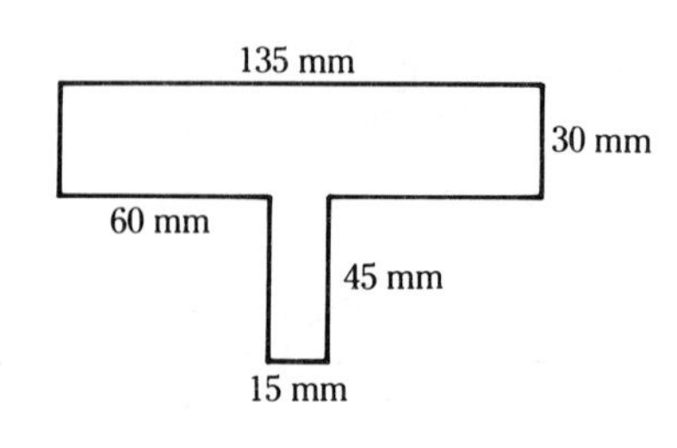

AREA

Counting Squares

The area of a shape drawn on a flat surface is the amount of surface enclosed within the boundary lines.
If the shape is drawn on a squared grid, the area can be assessed by counting the squares inside the boundary.

Exercise 5c

In this exercise, give each area as a number of grid squares.

1. What is the area of each shape ?

(a) 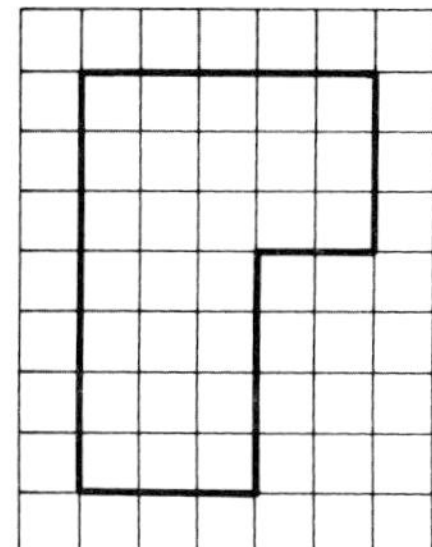 (b) 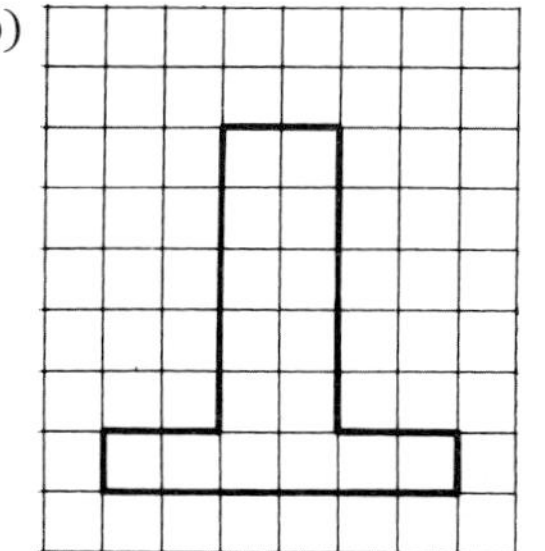 (c) 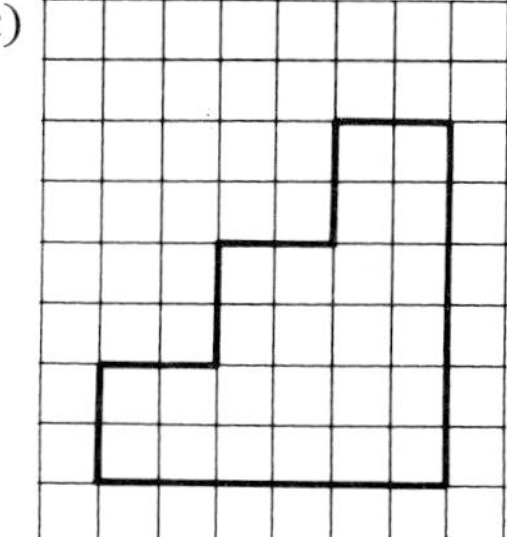

The boundary of a figure may not lie exactly on a grid line. In this case a square is counted if half or more of it is inside the figure but excluded if more than half of it is outside. An area found in this way can only be approximate.

2. Find an approximate value for the area of each shape.

(a) 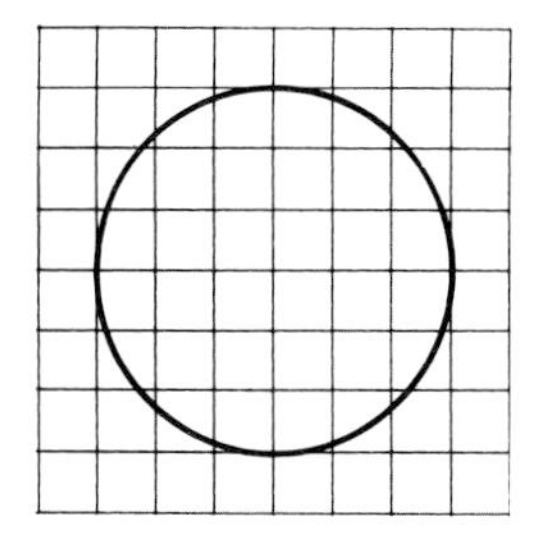

(c) 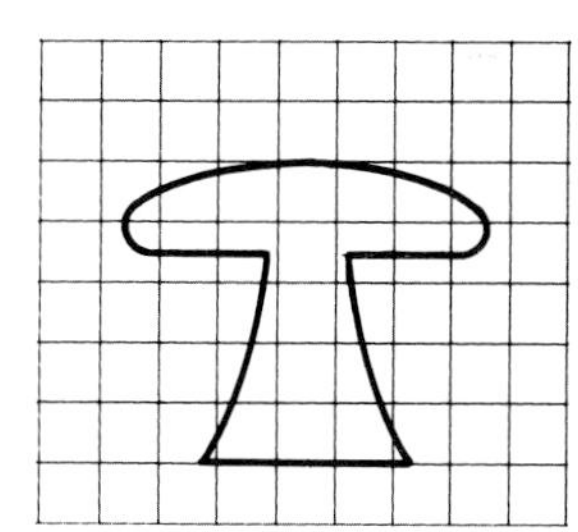

(b) 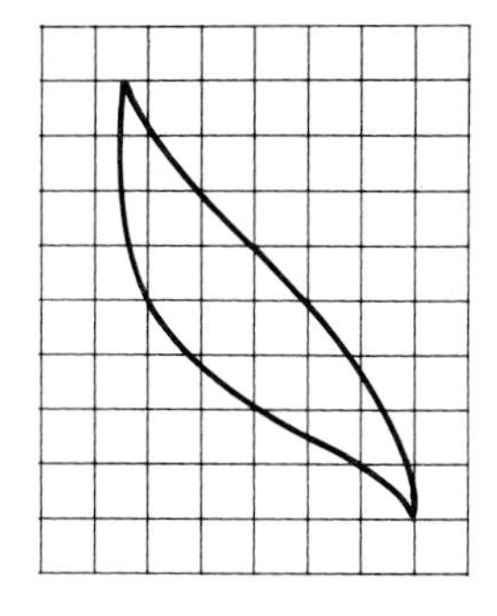

(d) 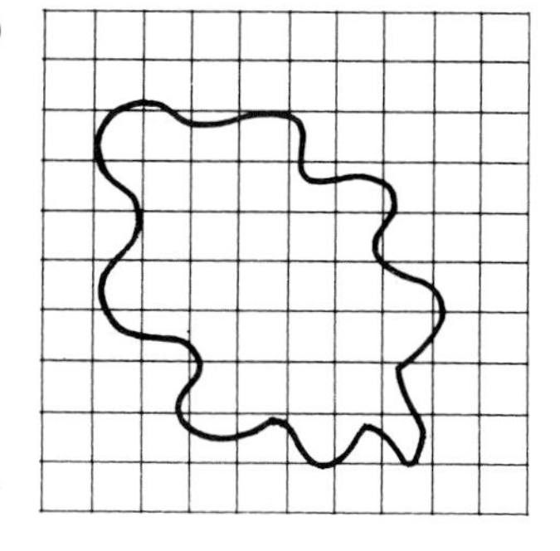

Units of Area

Suppose that the area of a figure is given as 8 squares.
If this is to convey the same size to everybody, the square must be of a standard size which can be clearly defined.
However, large areas are best found from large squares while smaller areas are easier to deal with in smaller squares, so we need a variety of standard squares to measure all types of area.

The side of the square that is useful for working in exercise books is one with a side of 1 centimetre, i.e. 1 cm.

The area of this square is 1 square centimetre, i.e. 1 cm^2

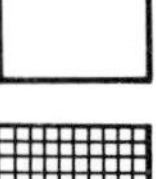

We know that 1 cm = 10 mm, so a square of side 1 cm can be divided into 10×10 squares, i.e. 100 squares, of side 1 mm, each with an area of 1 square millimetre, i.e. 1 mm^2

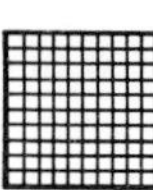

$$\mathbf{1\,cm^2 = 100\,mm^2}$$

Now 100 cm = 1 m, so a square of side 1 m can be divided into 100×100 squares of side 1 cm and area 1 cm^2.

$$\mathbf{1\,m^2 = 100 \times 100\,cm^2 = 10\,000\,cm^2}$$

Similarly, as 1 km is 1000 m, it follows that

$$\mathbf{1\,km^2 = 1000 \times 1000\,m^2 = 1\,000\,000\,m^2}$$

Which of the units given above should be used, depends on the kind of area being measured, e.g. the area of a county could be given in km^2, a garden in m^2, a sheet of paper in cm^2 and a small stamp in mm^2.

Another metric unit in which an area of land can be measured is the hectare where

$$\mathbf{1\,ha = 10\,000\,m^2}$$

CALCULATING AREA

The Area of a Square

If the side of a square is 3 cm, the square is made up of 9 squares, each of side 1 cm, as shown,

i.e. the area of a square of side 3 cm is 9 cm^2.

This can be *calculated* using

$$\text{Area} = 3 \times 3\text{ cm}^2 = 3^2\text{ cm}^2$$

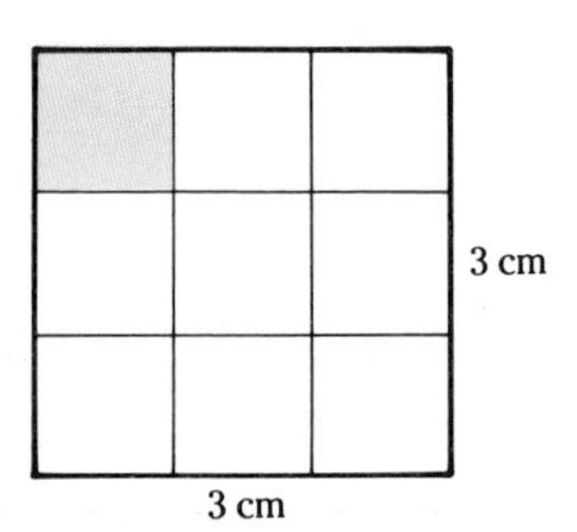

In general the area of a square is given by

area = (length of side)^2

The Area of a Rectangle

A rectangle with a length of 4 m and breadth (or width) of 2 m can be divided into 8 squares of side 1 m, so its area is $8\,\text{m}^2$,

i.e. area $= 4 \times 2\,\text{m}^2$

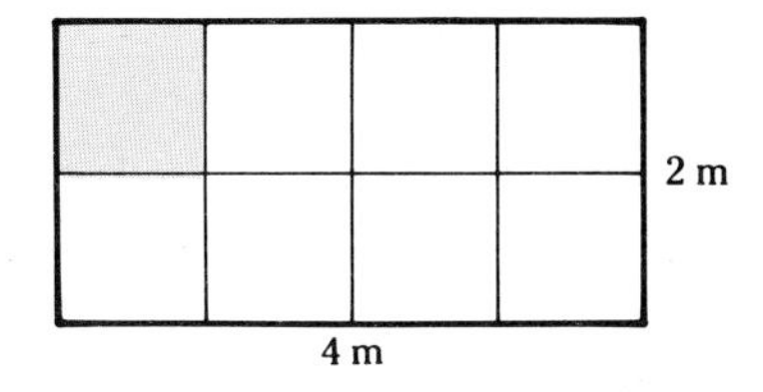

In general, the area of a rectangle is given by

area = length × breadth

Note that both sides must be measured in the same unit.

Exercise 5d

Calculate the area of the shape given in each question.

1. A square of side 9 cm.

2. A rectangle of length 14 mm and width 2 mm.

3.

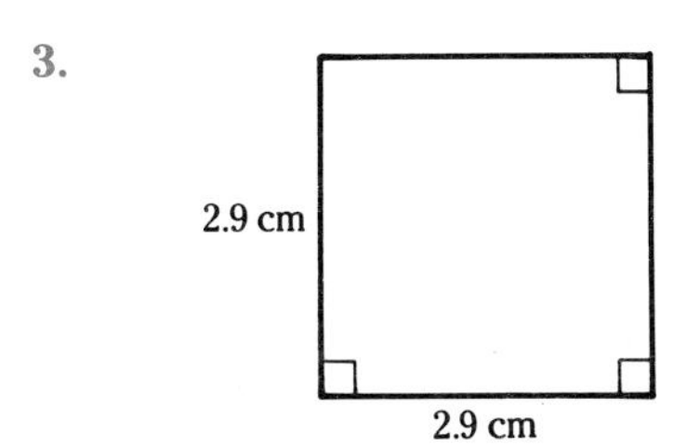

4.

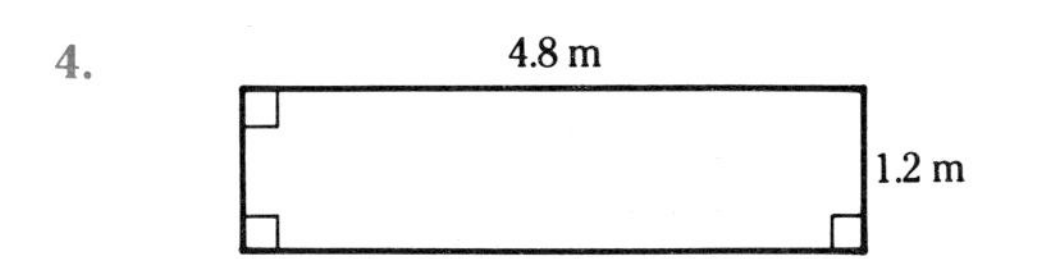

Find the area of a rectangle measuring 1.2 m by 42 cm.

The units must be the same for both sides so change 1.2 m to centimetres.

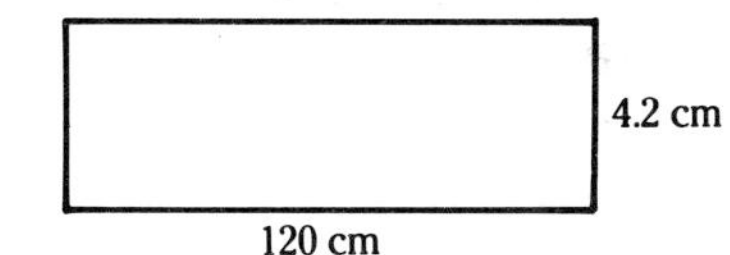

$1.2\,\text{m} = 1.2 \times 100 = 120\,\text{cm}$

Area of rectangle

$= \text{length} \times \text{breadth}$

$= 120 \times 42\,\text{cm}^2$

$= 5040\,\text{cm}^2$

5. (a) (b)

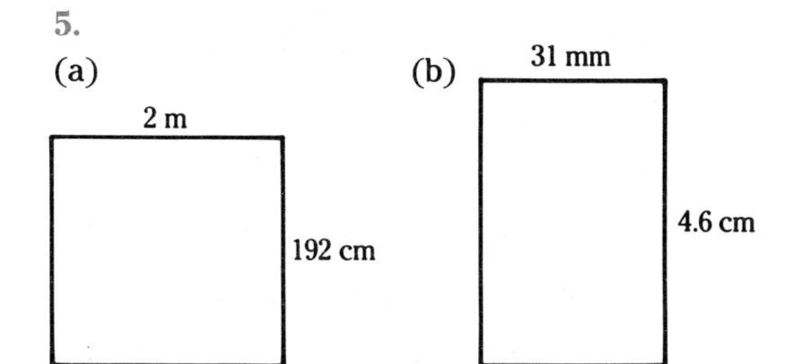

Compound shapes can often be divided into several standard parts whose areas can then be added together or, in some cases, one or more parts can be subtracted from a larger portion.

The diagram shows the floor layout of a workshop. Find the area of the floor.

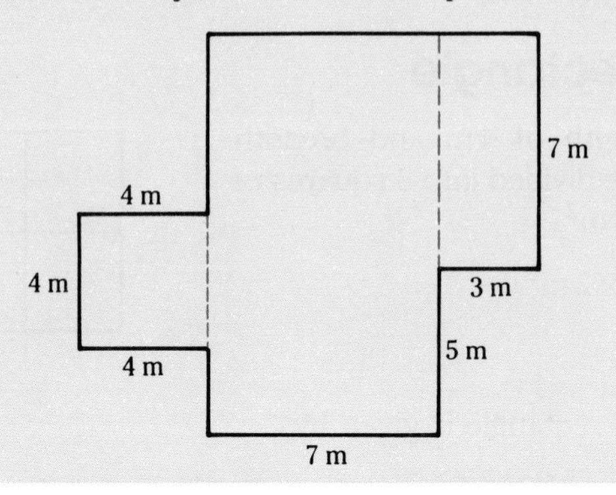

The broken lines split the workshop floor into three sections: a square of side 4 m, a rectangle measuring 7 m by 3 m and a second rectangle whose width is 7 m and whose length is (5 m + 7 m), i.e. 12 m.

Area of square is 4^2 m^2 $= 16$ m^2

Area of first rectangle is 7×3 m^2 $= 21$ m^2

Area of second rectangle is 12×7 m^2 $= 84$ m^2

Total area of workshop floor is $(16 + 21 + 84)$ m^2 $= 121$ m^2

Find the area shown in each diagram.

6.

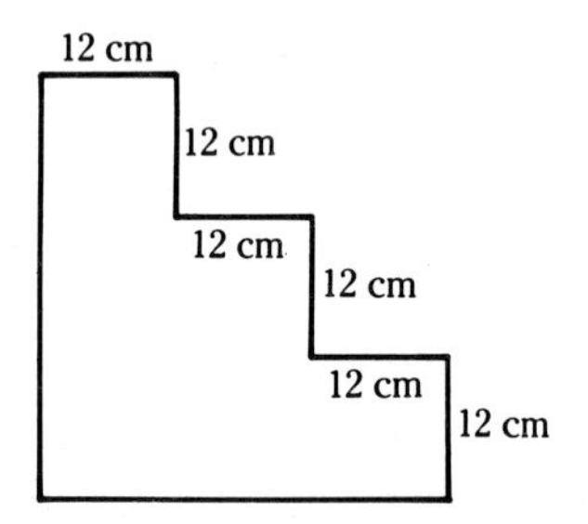

7.

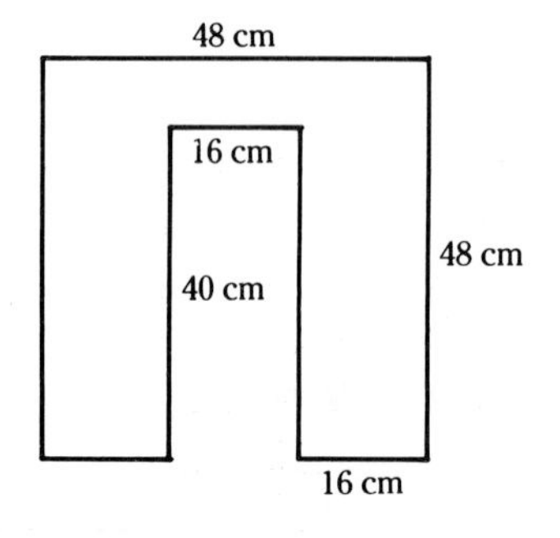

8.

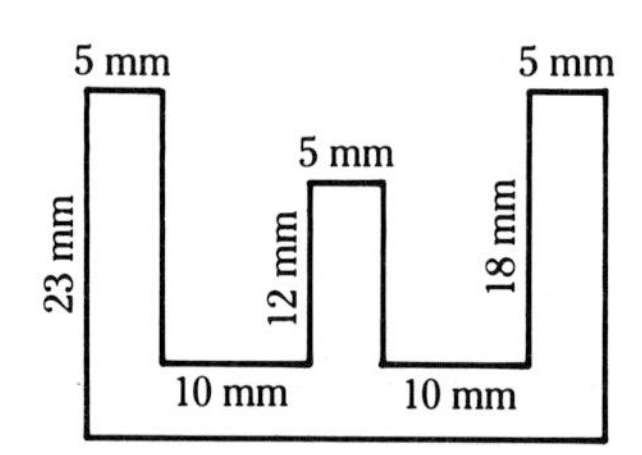

9. This diagram shows the floor plan for a church hall. Find the area of the floor.

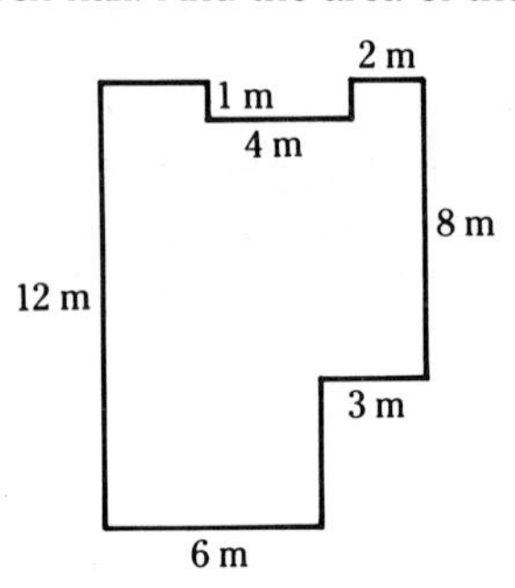

10. A decorative panel is to be set on a wall and the remainder of the wall (shaded in the diagram) will be pebble dashed.
Find the area to be pebble dashed.

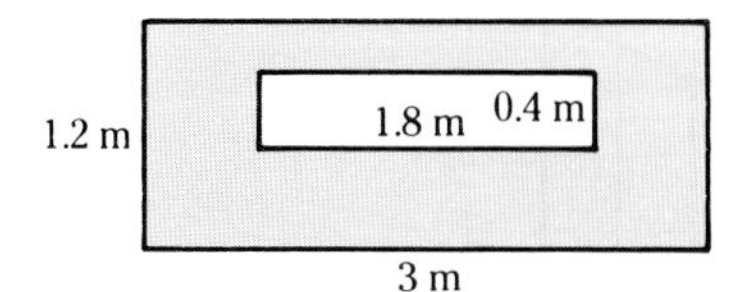

11. A mount for a photograph is in the form of a rectangle measuring 14.5 cm by 20.8 cm. A rectangular hole, 8.9 cm by 15.5 cm, is cut in the card.
Find the area of card left, giving your answer correct to 3 significant figures.

12. A wooden door is made with two glass panels as shown in the diagram. Find
(a) the area of each panel
(b) the area of the wood surface visible on one side of the door
(c) the perimeter of each panel.

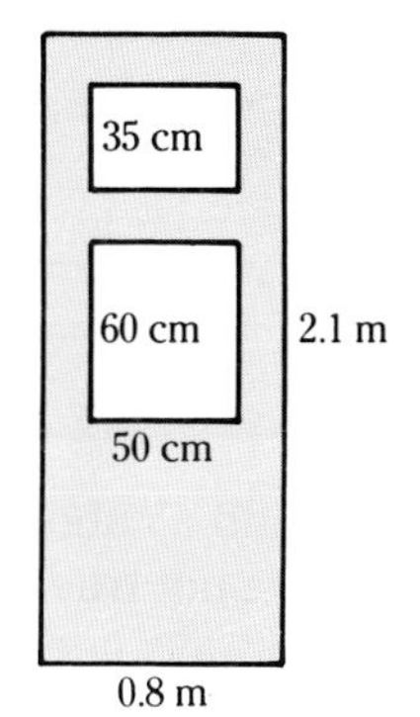

CUBES AND CUBOIDS

The word 'solid' is used rather loosely in this chapter, where 'three-dimensional object' would be a more precise, but clumsier, term. A hollow, closed box, for example, may be called a solid.

The name for a solid whose pairs of opposite faces are parallel rectangles is a *cuboid.* Some of the faces may be square. If all faces are square the cuboid becomes a *cube.*

Drawing Solids

If we look at a three-dimensional object, some of it can be seen but some parts are hidden. It is conventional to use a solid line to draw the parts that are seen and a broken line to show where the hidden parts are.

When a cube is drawn on a flat sheet of paper, only one of its visible faces can be drawn as a square. The other faces look like parallelograms, i.e. their opposite sides are parallel but the angles do not look like right angles.

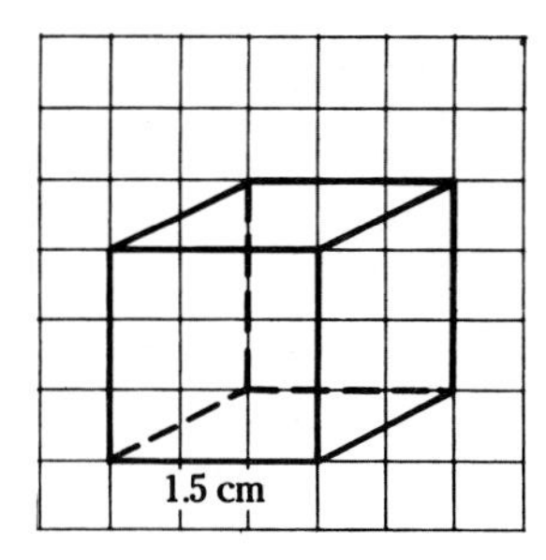

A similar situation applies for cuboids.

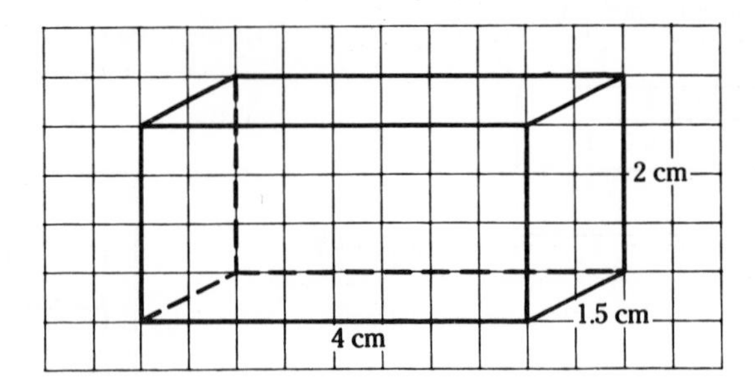

Both for a cube and a cuboid the result of the distortion is that some of the dimensions on the drawing are not true ones and cannot be found by measuring or by counting grid squares. So it is always necessary to mark all lengths on the diagram.

A different way to draw a cube or cuboid is to place one edge in the centre front. Drawn this way none of the angles looks like a right angle and each face is a parallelogram. *Isometric* paper, i.e. a grid of equilateral triangles, provides an easy background for this type of drawing. The advantage is that all the dimensions can be drawn correctly and can be measured from the diagram.

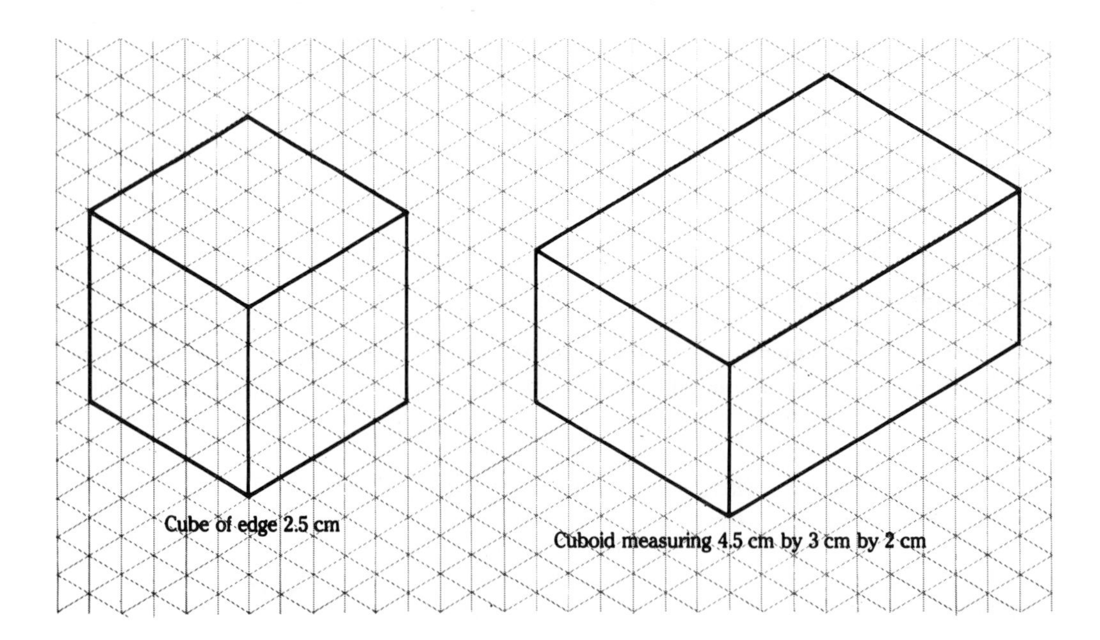

One disadvantage of using isometric paper to draw a cube is that one vertex lies behind another. This does not apply for a cuboid.

THE VOLUME OF A CUBOID

A cuboid can be built up from cubes with edges of length 1 cm. The volume of such a cube is one cubic centimetre, i.e. 1 cm^3.

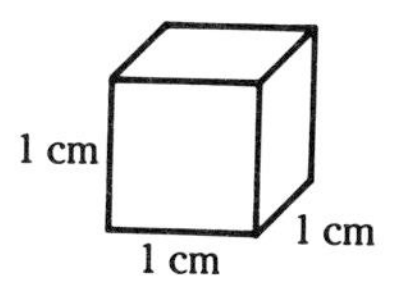

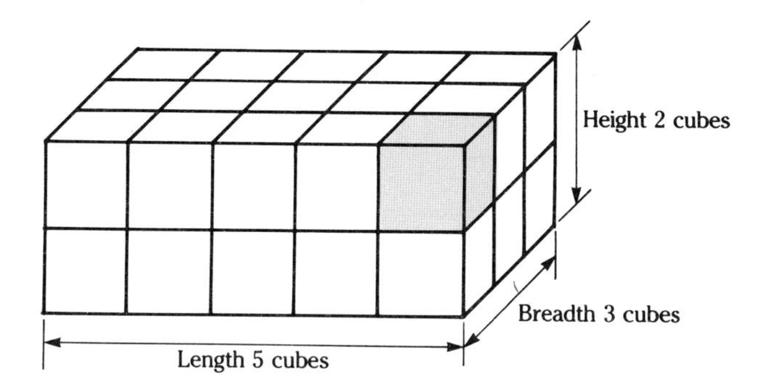

The base of this cuboid contains 5 rows (the length)
of 3 cubes (the breadth or width)
and, building upward, there are 2 layers (the height).

The total number of cubes is $5 \times 3 \times 2 = 30$
so the volume of the cuboid is 30 cm^3 (length × breadth × height).

In general the volume of a cuboid is given by
volume = (length × breadth × height) cubic units

Note that the units used for the three dimensions must be the same.

It follows that the volume of a cube is (length of side)^3 cubic units.

Units of Volume

The common units of volume are based on units of length, i.e. mm, cm, m and km.

Consider a cube of edge 1 cm. The cube can be divided into 10 layers each containing 10×10 cubes of edge 1 mm.

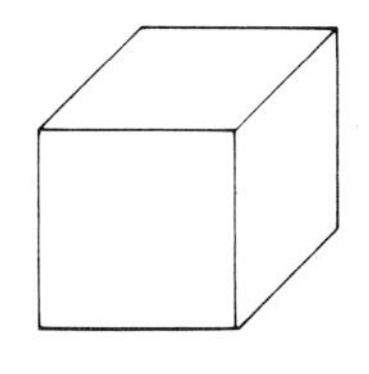

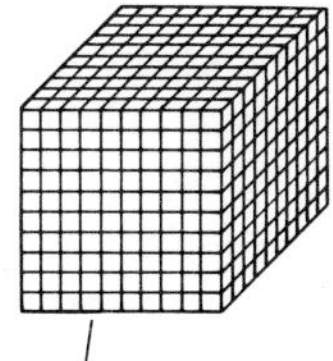

100 cubes, each with a volume of 1 mm^2, in every one of these layers

 i.e.

$$\mathbf{1\,cm^3 = 10 \times 10 \times 10\,mm^3}$$

Similarly, as $1\,\text{m} = 100\,\text{cm}$,

$$\mathbf{1\,m^3 = 100 \times 100 \times 100\,cm^3}$$

and

$$\mathbf{1\,km^3 = 1000 \times 1000 \times 1000\,m^3}$$

As before, when changing from a small unit to a larger unit we divide by the appropriate factor, i.e. the number of units is reduced,

e.g. to convert from mm^3 to cm^3, divide by $10 \times 10 \times 10$,
and to convert from cm^3 to m^3, divide by $100 \times 100 \times 100$.

Exercise 5e

How many cubes of edge 2 cm would be needed to form a cube of edge 8 cm ?

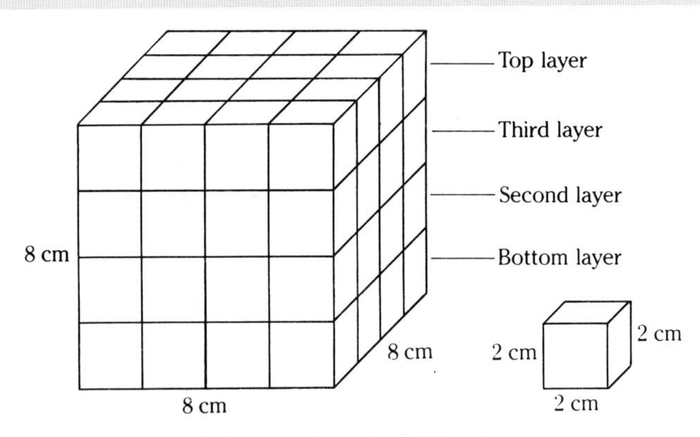

In the bottom layer there are 4×4 cubes, i.e. 16 cubes.

There are 4 layers of cubes altogether.

Therefore 64 cubes are needed.

1. Draw a cube of side 6 cm. How many cubes of side 3 cm would be required to fill it ?

2. How many cubes of side 2 cm would be needed to fill the same space as a cuboid measuring
   (a) 6 cm by 4 cm by 2 cm
   (b) 12 cm by 2 cm by 2 cm ?

3. A cuboid measures 4 cm by 4 cm by 8 cm. If the same space is filled by smaller cubes, how many cubes are needed if their side is
   (a) 1 cm (b) 2 cm (c) 4 cm ?

4. Twenty-four cubes of side 2 cm are arranged to form a cuboid 8 cm high.
   Give a possible length and breadth for the cuboid.

5. Find the volume of each of the following cuboids.

	Length	Breadth	Height
(a)	5 mm	4 mm	3 mm
(b)	6.1 m	3 m	1.2 m
(c)	4 cm	4 cm	4 cm

Find the volume of a cuboid measuring 2 m by 70 cm by 120 mm.
Give the answer in (a) cm^3 (b) m^3.

(a) All measurements must be in centimetres.

$$\text{Length of cuboid is } 2\text{ m} = 2 \times 100\text{ cm}$$
$$= 200\text{ cm}$$
$$\text{Height of cuboid is } 120\text{ mm} = 120 \div 10\text{ cm}$$
$$= 12\text{ cm}$$
$$\text{Volume of cuboid} = \text{length} \times \text{breadth} \times \text{height}$$
$$= 200 \times 70 \times 12\text{ cm}^3$$
$$= 168\,000\text{ cm}^3$$

(b) First convert all measurements to metres.

$$\text{Breadth of cuboid is } 70\text{ cm} = 70 \div 100\text{ m} = 0.7\text{ m}$$
$$\text{Height of cuboid is } 120\text{ mm} = 120 \div 1000\text{ m} = 0.12\text{ m}$$
$$\text{Volume of cuboid} = 2 \times 0.7 \times 0.12\text{ m}^3 = 0.168\text{ m}^3$$

Note that the answer to part (b) can also be obtained directly from the answer to part (a) using $168\,000 \div (100 \times 100 \times 100)\text{ m}^3$.

6. Express in cm^3
   (a) 0.42 m^3
   (b) 292 mm^3
   (c) 0.0063 m^3
   (d) 73.1 mm^3

7. Express in mm^3
   (a) 6.2 cm^3
   (b) 0.092 m^3
   (c) 0.43 cm^3
   (d) 43 cm^3

Find the volume of each cuboid giving the answer in the unit in brackets.

	Length	Breadth	Height	Unit
8.	2 m	70 cm	60 cm	(cm^3)
9.	0.5 cm	4 mm	3 mm	(mm^3)
10.	3.5 cm	25 mm	20 mm	(cm^3)
11.	1 m	40 cm	700 mm	(m^3)

FURTHER PROPERTIES OF SOLIDS

Capacity

Many three-dimensional objects are used for storing liquid and in these cases what we are usually concerned about is the volume of liquid that can be stored, rather than the volume of the container itself. To avoid any confusion between these two quantities we say that the *capacity* of the container is the volume of liquid it can hold and special units are used. The most common unit of capacity in the metric system is the litre (ℓ); petrol is bought in litres.

A *much* smaller unit, suitable for measuring medicine for example, is the millilitre (mℓ), which is one thousandth of a litre. (A teaspoon holds about 5 mℓ.)

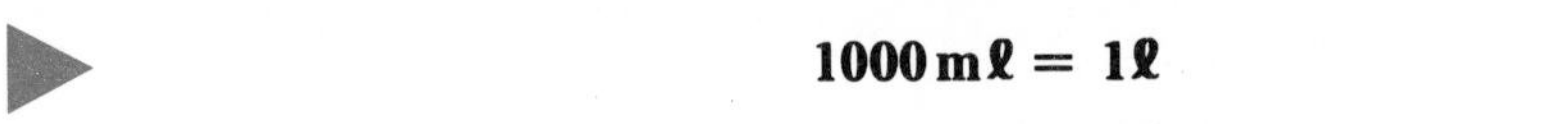

$$\mathbf{1000\,m\ell = 1\ell}$$

Because capacity is a particular form of volume, there is a relationship between the two sets of units.

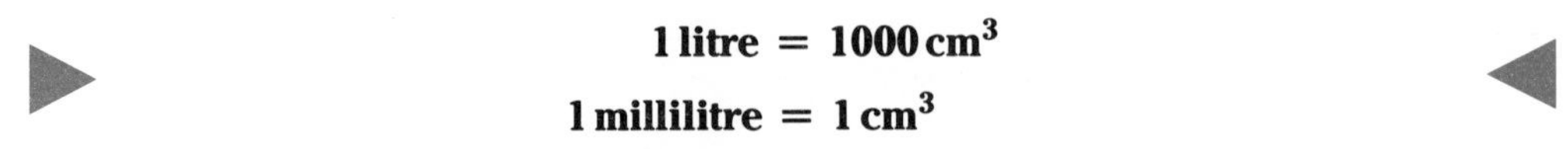

$$\mathbf{1\ litre = 1000\,cm^3}$$

$$\mathbf{1\ millilitre = 1\,cm^3}$$

Strictly speaking, in order to calculate capacity the *inside* measurements of the container should be given. In practice we usually have to *assume* that the given dimensions are internal.

Density

It is often important to know the mass of one unit of volume of the material from which an object is made.
This is sometimes called the *density* of the material, i.e.

$$\textbf{density} = \frac{\textbf{mass}}{\textbf{volume}}$$

A jeweller, for example, might need to know that the mass of 1 cm^3 of silver is 10.5 g, i.e. that the density of silver is 10.5 g/cm^3.

Exercise 5f

In all questions on capacity, assume that inside measurements of the container are given.

1. A cake tin has a square base of side 20 cm. The sides are vertical and 6 cm high. Cake mixture is poured into the tin and levelled off 4 cm above the base. Find
   (a) the capacity of the tin
   (b) the volume of cake mixture in the tin.

2. Find the capacity of a water tank measuring 1.2 m by 80 cm by 90 cm
   (a) in cubic centimetres (b) in litres.

3. A jug contains exactly 1 litre of liquid. All the liquid is poured into a 9 cm high metal box with a rectangular base, 10 cm by 7 cm. Will any of the liquid spill out and, if so, how much?

The volume of a gold ingot is 32 cm^3. Given that the density of gold is 19.3 g/cm^3, find the mass of the ingot.

$$\text{Volume} = 32\,\text{cm}^3$$

$$\text{Mass} = 32 \times 19.3\,\text{g}$$

$$= 617.6\,\text{g}$$

For a substance as valuable as gold, the mass would probably not be corrected to 3 significant figures.

Find the mass of each object. Where necessary decide whether or not the answer should be corrected to 3 s.f.

4. A block of brass with volume 14.3 cm^3, given that the mass of 1 cm^3 of brass is 8.5 g.

5. One litre of milk; the density of milk is $0.98\,\text{g/cm}^3$.

6. A $15\,\text{cm}^3$ block of ice of density $0.92\,\text{g/cm}^3$.

7. A cuboid of platinum measuring 12 cm by 5 cm by 3.2 cm, given that $1\,\text{cm}^3$ of platinum has a mass of 21.5 g.

SPEED, DISTANCE AND TIME

Suppose that a train travels at a steady speed, covering 50 miles in each of 3 consecutive hours, i.e. its speed is 50 m.p.h. The train has travelled 150 miles,

i.e. distance = speed × time

Now suppose that the train goes 40 miles in each of the first two hours and 70 miles in the third hour. The train has again travelled 150 miles in 3 hours which is the same as if it had kept a steady speed of 50 miles in each hour. The steady speed which achieves the same distance in the same time is called the *average speed*, i.e. the *average speed* of the train is 50 miles per hour.

$$\textbf{average speed} = \frac{\textbf{total distance}}{\textbf{total time}}$$

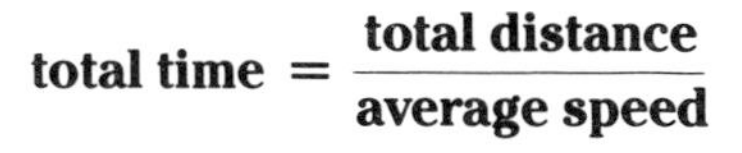

Units of Speed

The common units of speed are

miles per hour (m.p.h.)
kilometres per hour (km/h)
and metres per second (m/s or m s^{-1})

Other units, such as metres per minute or miles per minute, may occur occasionally.

Note that m is used for miles in 'miles per hour'. Apart from this, m always represents metres.

Exercise 5g

Find each unknown quantity, giving it in the correct unit.

	1.	2.	3.	4.	5.
Distance		80 km	350 miles	120 km	
Average speed	10 m.p.h.		70 m.p.h.	30 km/h	84 km/h
Time	4 h	5 h			$\frac{1}{2}$ h

Express (a) 80 m.p.h. in miles per minute
(b) 15 m/s in kilometres per hour.

(a) One minute is $\frac{1}{60}$ of an hour so the number of miles per minute is $\frac{1}{60}$ of the number of miles per hour.

$$80 \text{ m.p.h.} = \tfrac{1}{60} \times 80 \text{ miles per minute}$$
$$= 1.333\ldots \text{ miles per minute}$$
$$= 1.33 \text{ miles per minute} \quad (3 \text{ s.f.})$$

(b) First find the number of metres per hour. One hour is 60×60 seconds so the number of metres per hour is 3600 times the number of metres per second.

$$15 \text{ m/s} = 3600 \times 15 \text{ metres per hour} = 54\,000 \text{ metres per hour}$$

1 km = 1000 m so the number of km/h is $\frac{1}{1000}$ of the number of metres per hour.

$$54\,000 \text{ metres per hour} = \tfrac{1}{1000} \times 54\,000 \text{ km/h}$$
$$= 54 \text{ km/h}$$

In questions 6 and 7 express each speed in the unit given in brackets.

6. (a) 72 m.p.h. (miles per minute)
   (b) 9 miles per second (m.p.h.)

7. (a) 72 km/h (metres per minute)
   (b) 2.1 m/s (km/h)

Katie cycled 3 miles in 20 minutes followed by 5 miles in 30 minutes.
Find her average speed in (a) miles per minute (b) m.p.h.

$$\text{Average speed} = \frac{\text{total distance}}{\text{total time}}$$

$$\text{Total distance} = 3 \text{ miles} + 5 \text{ miles} = 8 \text{ miles}$$

$$\text{Total time taken} = 20 \text{ minutes} + 30 \text{ minutes} = 50 \text{ minutes}$$

(a) Average speed $= \frac{8}{50}$ miles per minute

$= 0.16$ miles per minute

(b) Average speed $= 0.16$ miles per minute $= 60 \times 0.16$ m.p.h.

$= 9.6$ m.p.h.

8. Nick drives 70 miles on a motorway in 52 minutes. He then joins a side road and drives the next 20 miles in 38 minutes. Find his average speed in miles per hour.

9. A train travels 140 miles in 1 hour 20 minutes. During the first hour the train moves at a steady speed of 108 m.p.h.
   (a) What is the average speed for the whole journey?
   (b) How far does the train travel in the final 20 minutes?
   (c) What is the average speed during the last 20 minutes?

10. Susan starts a journey by driving 2 miles through a built-up area, taking 18 minutes. Then she covers 12 miles, on more open road, in 22 minutes. Find her average speed in miles per hour
   (a) for the first 18 minutes
   (b) for the last 22 minutes
   (c) for the whole journey.

11. Susan continues the journey described in question 10 by travelling a further 12 miles on the motorway which takes 14 minutes. Find her average speed for the whole journey.

Investigations

1. Tiles are made in each of the following shapes.

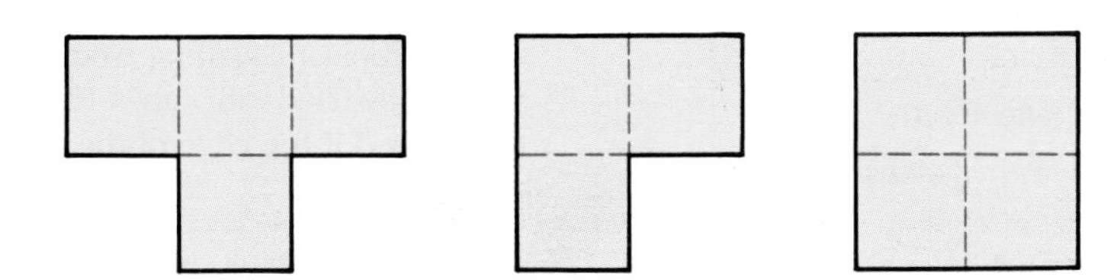

They can be used to tile this shape in various ways without cutting.

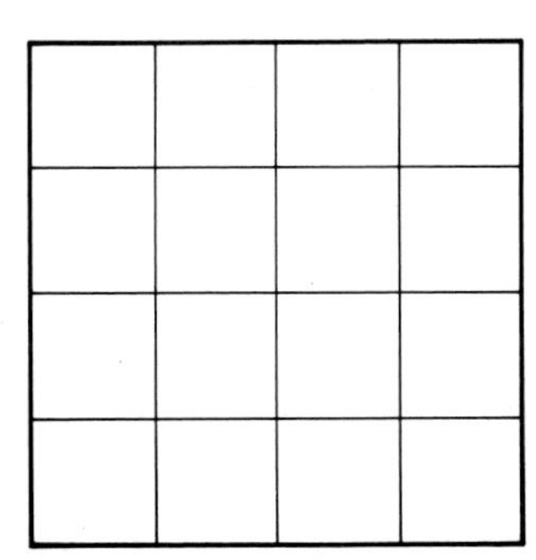

(a) Explain why the middle tile cannot be used to cover the shape on its own.

(b) Investigate different ways in which the tiles can be used to cover the shape.

2. A rectangular floor measuring 3 metres by 5 metres is to be tiled with a mixture of square and rectangular tiles. The diagram shows a corner of the floor.

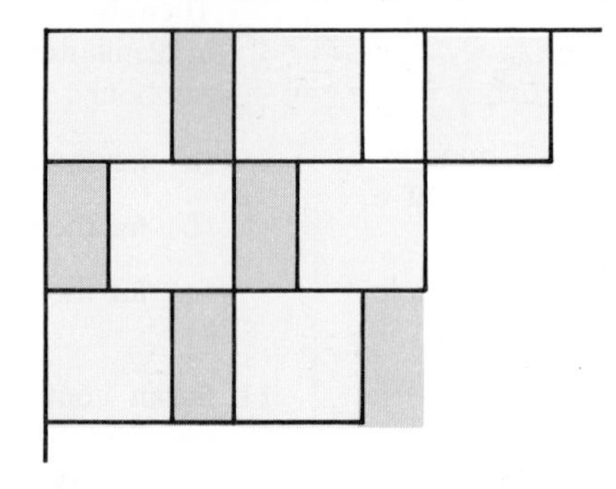

(a) The square tiles measure 15 cm by 15 cm and the rectangular tiles measure 15 cm by 7.5 cm. How many of each are needed to cover the area using the pattern shown ?

(b) Investigate different patterns. Tiles can be cut to fit at the edges of the floor.

Self-Assessment 5

1. Express each quantity in terms of the unit in brackets.

   (a) 588 cm (m) (d) 495 kg (t)

   (b) 588 cm (mm) (e) $8\,m^2$ (cm^2)

   (c) 3.2 g (mg) (f) $5\,cm^3$ (mm^3)

2. Find the perimeter of

   (a) a square of side 4.3 cm

   (b) a rectangle with dimensions 5.1 cm by 22 mm.

3. Find the area of each figure given in question 2.

4. The diagram shows the floor plan of an art gallery. Find the area of the floor.

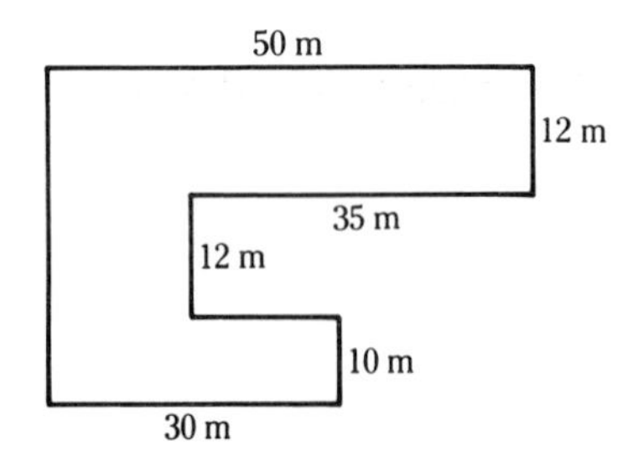

5. A plane is flying at an average speed of 160 m.p.h.

   (a) How far will it fly in $3\frac{1}{2}$ hours ?

   (b) How long will it take to travel 520 miles ?

6. John walks 3 miles in 30 minutes and then 2 miles in 25 minutes. What is his average speed in (a) miles per minute (b) m.p.h. ?

7. On 5 mm squared paper sketch a cube of side 4.7 cm. Calculate its volume.

8. A cuboid measuring 6 cm by 9 cm by 3 cm is to be filled with cubes. How many cubes are needed if the edge of the cube is (a) 1 cm (b) 3 cm ?

9. A storage tank is a cuboid whose inside dimensions are: base 0.8 m by 0.65 m and height 0.75 m. It contains water to a depth of 47 cm.

   (a) What is the capacity of the tank ?

   (b) What is the volume of water in the tank ?

10. A bottle contains exactly 750 mℓ of oil. The oil is poured into a container 12 cm high and with a square base of side 10 cm.

    (a) Will the container hold all the liquid ?

    (b) If the answer to (a) is 'No', how much liquid will be spilt ?

    (c) If the answer to (a) is 'Yes', how much more liquid will the container hold ?

11. What is the density of oak if a block of oak measuring 20 cm by 10 cm by 6.5 cm has a mass of 1.06 kg ?

6 PERCENTAGES AND THEIR APPLICATIONS

WORKING WITH PERCENTAGES

Per cent means 'in each hundred',
e.g. 23% means 23 out of every 100 items being considered.

It follows that $23\% = \frac{23}{100} = 0.23$

Conversely $\frac{74}{100} = 74\%$ and $0.69 = 69\%$

To convert a decimal, or a fraction, to a percentage, multiply by 100.

A fraction whose denominator is not 100, can be expressed as a percentage if it is first converted to a decimal,

e.g. $\frac{3}{4} = 0.75 = 75\%$ and $\frac{7}{13} = 0.5384\ldots = 53.8\%$ (3 s.f.)

Some relationships are worth remembering:

$$\frac{1}{2} = 50\% \quad \frac{1}{4} = 25\% \quad \text{and} \quad 1 = 100\%$$

A decimal that is bigger than 1 converts to a percentage bigger than 100%

e.g. $1.34 = 134\%$

Similarly $2\frac{1}{2} = 250\%$

If, say 37% of the members of a club are female, it follows that 63% (i.e. 100% − 37%) are not female.

In general, if x% of a set of items have a particular property, then $(100 - x)\%$ of the items do not have that property.

Exercise 6a

Complete the following table.

	Percentage	Decimal	Fraction
1.	38 %		
2.		0.07	
3.			$1\frac{1}{2}$
4.		0.61	
5.	5 %		
6.		2.35	
7.			$\frac{9}{10}$
8.	$17\frac{1}{2}$ %		

9. If 23 % of the books in a library are reference books, which are not available for borrowing, what percentage of the books can be borrowed ?

10. Fourteen per cent of the passengers in a bus are men, 53 % are women and the rest are children. What percentage of the passengers are children ?

11. On Wednesday afternoons students at a sixth form college choose one physical activity from swimming, table tennis, badminton and gymnastics. If 24 % choose swimming, 25 % choose table tennis and 37 % choose badminton, what is the percentage who choose gymnastics ?

12. When a committee took a vote on a motion, 41 % voted for the motion and 38 % voted against. What percentage abstained ?

FINDING A PERCENTAGE OF A QUANTITY

A percentage in itself does not often give practical information unless we also know what it is a percentage of, and what its value is in real terms. For example, if a deposit of 15 % is required when buying a TV, the purchaser really wants to know how much money that is, and that depends on the price of the set; or, a school that is instructed to provide places for 5 % more children next year needs to know precisely how many extra children there will be, and that depends on the present number of children.

The value of a percentage of a given quantity is

$$\frac{\textbf{percentage}}{\textbf{100}} \times \textbf{given quantity}$$

or percentage as a decimal × given quantity

For example, if the price of a TV is £396 then a deposit of 15 % is

$$\frac{15}{100} \times £396 \quad \text{or} \quad 0.15 \times £396$$

i.e. £59.40

and if there are 540 pupils in a school at present, 5 % extra places means

$\frac{5}{100} \times 540$ children or 0.05×540 children

i.e. 27 extra children.

Percentage Increase and Decrease

Percentage increases, or percentage reductions, are particularly important in real life. Quoting changes in wages as percentages, for instance, can sometimes be misleading until we find what the value of the change is, in money terms.

For example, a 6% rise in a wage of £150 a week is worth £9 a week extra, whereas a 10% rise in a wage of £80 is worth only £8 extra.

Exercise 6b

Find

1. 13% of 900 pupils
2. 4% of 50 m
3. 125% of 74 kg
4. $12\frac{1}{2}$% of a population of 40 000
5. 20% of £13.25
6. 78% of 200 marks

Lynne earns £14 from her Saturday job. She decides to save 30% towards her holiday and to spend 40% of her pay on clothes. How much money does Lynne

(a) save (b) spend on clothes ?

(a) 30% of £14 is $0.3 \times$ £14 = £4.20
Lynne saves £4.20

(b) 40% of £14 is $0.4 \times$ £14 = £5.60
Lynne spends £5.60 on clothes.

7. A curtain, of length 2.8 m, shrinks by $2\frac{1}{2}$% when it is washed. How much shorter is the curtain after washing ?

8. The cost of a package holiday for an adult is £472. The cost for a child is 70% of the adult price. If two adults and three children book this holiday, what will the total cost be ?

9. A travelling salesman is paid 5% commission on each sale with a value up to £200. For each sale with a higher value the commission is $7\frac{1}{2}$%. If he takes two orders, one worth £160 and the other worth £670, what commission can he expect to receive ?

10. £2600 was raised at the village Fun Day. It was decided to give 45% to Save the Children, 30% to the RSPB and the remainder to village societies. How much did the village societies receive ?

11. A rug is laid on the floor of a room which measures 2.8 m by 3.5 m. The rug covers 45% of the floor.
Find the area of the rug.

12. Of 140 visits made by birds to a bird-table during a six-hour period, 55% were made by blue tits and 35% by chaffinches.
How many visits were made by blue tits and how many by chaffinches?

The list price of a particular car today is \$9650. Next month the price goes up by $7\frac{1}{2}$%. What will it cost next month?

$$\text{Next month's increase is } 7\tfrac{1}{2}\% \text{ of } \$9650$$
$$= \$0.075 \times 9650$$
$$= \$723.75$$
$$\text{So next month's price is } \$9650 + \$723.75$$
$$= \$10\,373.75$$

Alternatively,

$$\text{next month's price is } (100\% + 7\tfrac{1}{2}\%) \text{ of } \$9650$$
$$\text{i.e. } 1.075 \text{ of } \$9650$$
$$= \$10\,373.75$$

13. A necklace that cost \$140 is sold at a profit of 25%. For how much is it sold?

14. An employee earning \$145 a week is offered an increase of 12%. Find

(a) the cash value of the increase

(b) the new weekly wage.

15. Each year the population of Far Island, currently 86 000, is increasing by 7% of the population at the beginning of that year. What, to the nearest hundred, will the population be after

(a) 1 year (b) 2 years?

16. Jane and Alice each have a salary of \$3600. Jane is offered a rise of 8% for this year, with the same percentage increase next year. Alice's increases are to be 7% for this year and 9% for next year. Who is offered the better deal and by how much over the two years?

The calculation when a reduction is made is very similar but the change is subtracted from the original value (or the reduction per cent is subtracted from 100%).

17. In their sale, James Brothers offer a 20% discount on the marked price of all goods. Find the sale price of

(a) a lawnmower marked \$145

(b) a wheelbarrow marked \$67.

18. A Speedy-Ace cycle is on sale in two shops. In Jim's Store it is priced at \$176, with a discount for cash of $7\frac{1}{2}$%. Best Wheels are offering 10% off their marked price of \$181.60. Which is the better bargain?

19. A rectangular poster, measuring 34 cm by 48 cm, is reduced by a photocopier which is set to shorten lines by $12\frac{1}{2}$%. What are the dimensions of the copy of the poster?

20. A motor bike costs £690 when new. If its value decreases by 10% each year, what is it worth after (a) 1 year (b) 2 years?

21. Mr Smith's weekly pay is £160 and 18% of this is deducted by his employer for pension contributions.
   (a) How much is left after pension contributions have been deducted?
   (b) Mr Smith is given a $7\frac{1}{2}$% wage increase. If 18% of his new wage is deducted at source, how much is left?

22. A fan heater is priced at £54. Store A has it on special offer at £5 off. Store B is offering a discount of 5%.
Which is the better bargain and by how much?

23. Between two elections the size of the electorate in Munton Westside fell by 14%. At the first election 31 765 people were entitled to vote.
To the nearest hundred, how many can vote at the second election?

TAXES

Value Added Tax

This is a tax charged on most goods and services. It is calculated at a rate fixed by the Government and (at the time of writing) is $17\frac{1}{2}$%.

The VAT is added to the basic cost.

Income Tax

Income tax is deducted from everyone's *taxable income,* i.e. their earnings over and above the value of their allowances. The lowest rate of income tax is called the *basic rate* and this is what most people pay. Those earning high salaries however have to pay a certain amount of *higher rate* tax.

The rates at which income tax is calculated are announced by the Chancellor of the Exchequer in his Budget. These rates can vary from year to year, as can the allowances that are given before income tax begins to be deducted.

Other Forms of Tax

Direct taxation is applied before any money is spent. Income tax is one example of direct taxation; other direct taxes include capital transfer tax, inheritance tax, capital gains tax and corporation tax.

Indirect taxation takes effect only when money is spent. VAT is an example of an indirect tax because an individual pays only when goods or services are bought. There are other forms of indirect tax: excise duty is a special tax applied to certain goods such as alcohol, tobacco and petrol. These goods also carry VAT. The road fund licence is another indirect tax; every car has to have the licence (payable at regular intervals) before it can be used on public roads.

Exercise 6c

The price of a dining table is given as £860 plus VAT. If the rate of VAT is $17\frac{1}{2}\%$, find the price that a customer must pay for the table.

The value of the VAT is 17.5% of £860

$= £0.175 \times 860$

$= £150.50$

The customer pays £860 + £150.50

$= £1010.50$

Alternatively,

The price including VAT is $(100\% + 17\frac{1}{2}\%)$ of £860

$= 1.175 \times £860$

$= £1010.50$

Note that the second method gives the inclusive price more quickly and if the amount of VAT is wanted it can be found by subtraction.

In questions 1 to 3 find the total purchase price of the item. Take the rate of VAT as 17.5%.

1. An electric cooker marked £626 + VAT.

2. A calculator costing £9.60 + VAT.

3. A van marked £5640 + VAT.

4. The price tag on a television gives £289 plus VAT at 15%. What does the customer have to pay?

5. In March, Nicki looked at a camera costing £160 plus VAT. The VAT rate at that time was $17\frac{1}{2}\%$. How much would the camera have cost in March?

   Nicki decided to wait until June to buy the camera but by then the VAT rate had been raised to 22%. How much did she have to pay?

6. An electric cooker was priced in a showroom at £560 plus VAT at 15%.

   (a) What was the price to the customer?

   Later in the year VAT was increased to 17.5%. The showroom manager placed on the cooker a notice which read:

   Due to the increase in VAT this cooker will now cost you £660.10

   (b) Was the manager correct?

   (c) If your answer is 'Yes', state how the manager calculated the new price.

   (d) If your answer is 'No', give your reason and find the correct price.

7. A wine-merchant buys a certain wine out of bond at a cost of £3.26 a bottle. He adds a mark-up of £1.14 per bottle to what he paid; VAT at 15% is charged. What does one of his customers pay for a bottle of this wine? If VAT was raised from 15% to 20% what would be the increase in cost to the customer?

Ken Watson earns £12 500 per year gross and has allowances of £5480. How much tax does he have to pay if he is liable to tax only at the basic rate of 25% ?

Ken's taxable income is gross income − allowances

= £12 500 − £5480

= £7020

Tax due is 25% of £7020

= £0.25 × 7020

= £1755

8. Find the taxable income in each of the following cases.

	Gross Income	Allowances
(a)	£8600	£4230
(b)	£12 500	£7960
(c)	£5860	£3470

For each case given above, calculate the income tax payable if the basic rate is (i) 25% (ii) 30% (iii) 33% (assume that no higher rate tax is due).

A solicitor has an annual salary of £44 000 and can claim allowances of £9540. The basic rate of income tax is 25% and is payable on the first £23 000 of taxable income. Higher rate tax of 40% is charged on any taxable income over £23 000. Find the total tax payable.

Taxable Income is £44 000 − £9540 = £34 460

Basic tax on £23 000 = 25% of £23 000

= 0.25 × £23 000

= £5750

Higher rate tax is due on £34 460 − £23 000 i.e. on £11 460

Higher rate tax is 40% of £11 460

= 0.4 × £11 460

= £4584

Total tax payable = £5750 + £4584 = £10 334

9. Basic rate tax is payable on taxable income up to £23 000. Any taxable income above this figure is taxed at a higher rate.

   Find the income tax due to be paid in each case.

	Yearly income	Allowances	Basic rate tax	Higher rate tax
(a)	£8650	£4560	30%	
(b)	£34 400	£6820	25%	40%
(c)	£11 500	£7600	30%	
(d)	£45 000	£8600	33%	50%

National Insurance contributions are paid by employers, employees and the self-employed, to provide various benefits such as retirement pensions, unemployment benefit and health care. The rates are expressed as a percentage of earnings; they are determined by the Government and vary from time to time.

Employees' National Insurance contributions (NIC) are calculated at the rates given in the table below.

Gross earnings per month	NIC payable
Up to £234	0%
above £234 up to £1755	2% of £234 plus 9% of gross earnings above £234
over £1755	£141.57

Use this information to calculate the monthly National Insurance contributions payable on earnings of

(a) £230 per month (b) £1600 per month (c) £2000 per month

(a) No contribution is due on monthly earnings of £230

(b) NIC due on first £234 is 2% of £234

$= 0.02 \times £234 = £4.68$

Amount on which 9% is payable is $£1600 - £234 = £1366$

NIC due on £1366 is 9% of £1366

$= 0.09 \times £1366 = £122.94$

Monthly contribution is $£4.68 + £122.94 = £127.62$

(c) NIC on monthly earnings of £2000 is £141.57, i.e. the maximum payable.

Use the National Insurance rates given in the worked example to calculate the National Insurance payable on the given earnings.

10. £1000 per month

11. £206 per month

12. £7600 per year

13. £28 000 per year

SAVING

Most people who do not need to spend their money immediately invest it in some form of savings scheme. Money that is invested is lent to an organisation to use until the owner wants it back. The organisation pays interest to the owner for the use of the money.

Some of the best known forms of saving are building society accounts, National Savings and interest-paying bank accounts. Each of these usually pays interest at an annual percentage rate.

Another, increasingly popular, way to save is to make contributions to a pension scheme. Company schemes are often enhanced by contributions made by the employer. Personal pension schemes are taken out by individuals at their own choice; self-employed people make wide use of these.

There are other forms of investment, such as Unit Trusts and Investment Trusts, Equities (these are shares in public companies) and Gilts or Government Stocks. Investments of this type depend upon many different factors, not least upon the general state of the economy.

The Premier Share Account in a building society pays interest of 10% per annum, added to the account half-yearly. If £1000 is invested in this account and the interest is not withdrawn, find the amount in the account at the end of the first year.

Interest for 1st half year is $\frac{1}{2}$ of 10% of £1000 $= 0.5 \times 0.1 \times$ £1000

$=$ £50

The amount in the account at the end of the first half year is £1050

Interest for second half year is $\frac{1}{2}$ of 10% of £1050 $= 0.5 \times 0.1 \times$ £1050

$=$ £52.50

The amount in the account at the end of the first year is £1102.50

Note that if the interest had been paid at 10% per annum *added yearly,* the interest would have been only £100. To provide £102.50, the rate of interest would have had to be 10.25%. This rate is called the *compounded annual rate* (c.a.r.) and is often quoted by building societies along with their ordinary rate. Interest from investments is called *investment income* and is subject to income tax just as earned income is.

In general, tax is deducted by the building society or bank from the gross interest and paid direct to the Inland Revenue, leaving the net interest to be paid to the investor. In this way standard rate tax-payers are not liable to pay any further tax on their interest.

This is why you often see two rates of interest quoted in building society tables in a form such as

7% p.a. net = 9.33% p.a. gross

(Special arrangements can be made, however, for non-tax-payers to have their interest paid gross.)

Exercise 6d

1. An investment of \$400 is made in a building society account. If neither capital nor interest is withdrawn, find the amount in the account at the end of 1 year if the rate of interest is 12% per annum and is added
   (a) yearly (b) half-yearly (c) quarterly.

2. A savings account pays interest at 8% p.a., added half-yearly. If \$1000 is invested, find
   (a) the amount in the account at the end of the first year
   (b) the compounded annual rate.

3. A lump sum of \$1000 can be invested for two years. Which of the following accounts provides the better investment?
   (i) A savings account paying half-yearly interest at 7% p.a.
   (ii) An account paying yearly interest of 8% p.a. and making a fixed administration charge of \$10 per year.

4. An income bond pays 9% p.a.; the income is payable monthly. If \$6600 worth of bonds are bought, find the monthly income.

The interest earned on an account can be withdrawn each time it is due, leaving the original *investment* unchanged. In this case the account earns *simple interest*. The more usual system however is for the interest to be added to the original deposit so that it too earns interest during the next year. This is called *compound interest*.

An investment of \$580 is made in an account offering a fixed interest rate of 7% per annum. If the interest is left in the account at the end of each year find the total interest earned after three years.

Interest for first year is 7% of \$580 $= \$0.07 \times 580$

$= \$40.60$

Amount in account at end of first year is \$580 + \$40.60

$= \$620.60$

Interest for second year is 7% of \$620.60 = \$43.44

Amount in account at end of second year is \$620.60 + \$43.44

$= \$664.04$

Interest for third year is 7% of \$664.04 = \$46.48

Amount in account at end of third year is \$664.04 + \$46.48

$= \$710.52$

The total interest added is \$710.52 − \$580 = \$130.52

Note how the *value* of the interest rises year by year even though the *rate* of interest is constant.

Find the compound interest earned on

5. \$200 invested for 2 years at 8% per annum.

6. \$500 invested for 3 years at 10% per annum.

7. \$440 invested for 2 years at 9% per annum.

Find the total in the account at the end of the time if

8. \$1200 is invested for 4 years at 10% per annum.

9. \$850 is invested for 2 years at 8% per annum.

10. \$2000 is invested for 3 years at 6% per annum.

Compound Growth Tables

These tables give the multiplying factors for various percentage rates over different periods of time. They can be used to find the growth in sums of money, sales, populations, etc.

The table below gives the multiplying factors for rates of growth from 6% to 15% over a ten-year period.

Rate of growth p.a.	Number of years									
	1	2	3	4	5	6	7	8	9	10
6%	1.060	1.124	1.191	1.262	1.338	1.419	1.504	1.594	1.689	1.791
7%	1.07	1.145	1.225	1.311	1.403	1.501	1.606	1.718	1.838	1.967
8%	1.08	1.166	1.260	1.360	1.469	1.587	1.714	1.851	1.999	2.159
9%	1.090	1.188	1.295	1.412	1.539	1.677	1.828	1.993	2.172	2.367
10%	1.100	1.210	1.331	1.464	1.611	1.772	1.949	2.144	2.358	2.594
11%	1.110	1.232	1.368	1.518	1.685	1.870	2.076	2.305	2.558	2.839
12%	1.120	1.254	1.405	1.574	1.762	1.974	2.211	2.476	2.770	3.106
13%	1.130	1.277	1.443	1.631	1.842	2.082	2.353	2.658	3.004	3.395
14%	1.140	1.300	1.482	1.689	1.925	2.195	2.502	2.853	3.252	3.707
15%	1.150	1.323	1.521	1.749	2.011	2.313	2.660	3.059	3.518	4.046

The table shows that the multiplying factor for a population growing at 8% for 8 years is 1.851 and that the multiplying factor for a sum of money growing at 12% p.a. for 9 years is 2.770.

Exercise 6e

Use the compound growth table above, giving answers correct to 3 s.f.

What sum of money will £350 grow to if it is invested for 5 years at 9%?

The table shows that the multiplying factor is 1.539

So £350 will grow to 1.539 × £350

= £538.65 = £539 (3 s.f.)

1. If £10 is invested for 3 years at 8%, what sum will it amount to?

2. What amount will £20 grow to if it is invested for 6 years at 11%?

3. If £5000 is invested for 5 years at 7%, what sum will it amount to?

4. The population of Brookfield is 1600. If it increases at 7% per year what, to the nearest hundred, will the population be after 10 years?

5. The population of Broadtown has increased at 7% per year for the past 4 years. If the population was 29 600 four years ago, what is it now? (Give the answer to the nearest hundred.)

6. The number of magpies nesting in a wood has increased steadily at 14% each year for the last 5 years.
   If the number of magpies five years ago was 231,
   (a) how many are there now?
   (b) how many will there be in 5 years time?

BORROWING

There are many ways in which money can be borrowed and most people need to borrow at some stage in their lives. Institutions that provide loans charge for the use of their money and the cost of borrowing is often considerable. Some forms of borrowing are more expensive than others, however, and it is wise to understand the language and the systems of the most common forms of lending.

Mortgages

Nearly everybody who wants to buy a house or flat, has to borrow in order to do so. Money borrowed for this purpose is called a *mortgage* and is usually obtained from a building society or bank. The loan is not usually as much as the purchase price of the property; more often it is between 80 % and 95 % of the price.

This form of loan, being for a large sum, is repayable over a long period of time - anything from 10 to 30 years. As a result the amount of interest charged over the whole term of the mortgage is enormous.
The total payments can be more than four times the value of the property!

What most people are most concerned about is the size of the monthly repayments. These are often quoted as an amount per £1000 borrowed and vary with the interest rate and the number of years over which the loan is to be repaid.

For the duration of the mortgage the deeds of the property are held by the lender, who has certain rights over the property and can impose conditions on how it is used.

Failure to keep up the mortgage repayments can, in extreme circumstances, result in the house being repossessed by the lending institution.

Bank Loans, Credit Sales and Credit Cards

There are so many different names for different loan schemes that it is impossible to mention all of them. Also there are frequent changes in legislation, which can affect the operation, and the cost, of any scheme.

The only things that are unchanging in the sphere of borrowing are that it is not cheap and that it is essential to read the small print. Nevertheless it is worth taking a brief look at the main methods.

Bank loans are straightforward loans of money, which are immediately the property of the borrowers to spend as they please. Before it agrees to a loan, a bank may require some form of credit rating.

A bank loan is repaid by monthly instalments, usually over 2 to 5 years. After mortgages, this is said to be the least expensive way of borrowing.

(If the loan is a large one, some form of security, often a house, is required. Failure to maintain the repayments may result in forfeiture of the security.)

In a *credit sale* the goods belong to the purchaser from the time of purchase. Usually a down payment is required, followed by monthly payments over a period of time (anything from 3 months to 3 years). The total repayments are nearly always more, sometimes a lot more, than the cash price. However, it is not uncommon for interest-free credit to be offered for a limited period on items, particularly cars, when unsold stock is building up.

By law the cost of any form of credit, including mortgages, must be clearly displayed as a percentage called the annual percentage rate (APR).

A *credit card* such as a Visa card can be used to pay for goods and services without using money at the time. Each card-holder is given a credit limit, which is the maximum total amount that can be paid for by using the card. If the card-holder attempts to pay for an item when the credit limit has already been reached, the credit card company will refuse to authorise the payment.

A statement showing all purchases made is sent monthly to the card-holder, who then must pay at least the statutory minimum amount, or any other amount up to the total on the statement. Interest is charged on any part of the amount owed which is not paid.

The rate of interest may look reasonable, as it is quoted as a rate per month; but $2\frac{1}{2}$% per month is equivalent to about 34% p.a.!

Other cards, like American Express and some department store cards, operate in a similar way except that the total amount spent in the month must be paid when the bill is presented: payment of part only is not allowed. These are called *charge cards.*

Exercise 6f

A building society offers a twenty-five-year mortgage for monthly repayments of £12.50 per £1000 borrowed.

(a) What are the monthly repayments on a mortgage of £30 000 ?

(b) What is the total of the repayments for the full 25 years ?

(a) The monthly repayment on £1000 is £12.50

The monthly repayment on £30 000 is $30 \times$ £12.50 = £375

(b) The total of 12 monthly repayments over each of 25 years is

$12 \times 25 \times$ £375 = £112 500

Where appropriate give answers correct to the nearest penny.

1. The Central Building Society offers a twenty-five-year mortgage for monthly repayments of £13 per £1000 borrowed.

   (a) What are the monthly repayments on a mortgage of
   (i) £25 000 (ii) £55 000 ?

   (b) If the monthly repayments are £585, how much has been borrowed ?

2. The repayments on a mortgage of £40 000 are calculated at £12.75 per calendar month for each £1000 borrowed. What amount must be paid

   (a) per month

   (b) per year

   (c) over the full twenty-five-year term ?

3. Wai-Ling Yeung obtains a 95% mortgage on a flat whose purchase price is £48 000. How much can she borrow and how much must she herself pay initially towards the cost ?

4. The Patel family buy a house costing $70 000. They negotiate an 80% mortgage on which the monthly repayments are $12.60 for each $1000 borrowed, for 25 years. Find
   (a) the amount borrowed
   (b) the monthly repayments
   (c) the total cost of the house.

5. Winston Armstrong's mortgage repayments are agreed with his building society one year at a time.
   Last year, on a loan of $55 000, his total repayment amounted to $5610.
   What was his monthly repayment per $1000 borrowed ?

The cash price of a washing machine is $360. The credit sale terms are: a deposit of $72 followed by 24 monthly repayments of $15.60. Find
(a) the total credit sale price
(b) the amount that would be saved by paying cash.

(a) Total of monthly repayments is $24 \times \$15.60 = \$374.40$

$$\text{Total credit sale price} = \text{deposit} + \text{repayments}$$
$$= \$72 + \$374.40$$
$$= \$446.40$$

(b) Amount saved if cash were paid is $\$446.40 - \$360$

$$= \$86.40$$

6. A second-hand car is offered for sale either for $1700 cash or on credit where the terms are a deposit of 20% and 18 monthly payments of $101. Find
   (a) the deposit
   (b) the total cost of buying the car on credit
   (c) the difference between the cash price and the credit price.

7. The marked price of a motor bike is $1230. A purchaser who pays cash is offered a discount of 5%. The bike can also be bought on credit by paying a deposit of $300 followed by 24 monthly payments of $47.25.
   (a) How much does a cash customer pay ?
   (b) What is the total cost of buying on credit ?

8. The balance shown on Tariq's credit card statement is $193.67. The minimum payment required is either $5 or 5% of the balance, whichever is the greater. How much must Tariq pay ?

9. A department store arranges its own credit terms on any sale over $150. The terms are: a deposit of 25% of the price, the balance to be increased by 20% and then divided by 12 to give the monthly repayments.
   If these terms are used to buy a range of kitchen units priced at $2400, find
   (a) the deposit
   (b) the increased balance
   (c) the monthly repayment.

10. Mary James wants to buy a car costing $9800 but cannot afford to pay cash. She has a choice of two methods for buying the car over a period of time; they are
    (i) a bank loan for $9800 repayable over 36 months at $327 per month
    (ii) a credit agreement requiring a deposit of 25% of the cash price followed by 30 monthly payments of $332.
    Which is the cheaper way to buy the car and by how much ?

EXPRESSING ONE QUANTITY AS A PERCENTAGE OF ANOTHER

We can always express one quantity as a fraction of another quantity and then convert the fraction to a percentage.

For example:
In a test, one pupil scored 39 out of a possible 60 marks. To express this result as a percentage we use

$$\frac{\text{mark}}{\text{total}} \times 100\,\%$$

i.e. $$\frac{39}{60} \times 100\,\% = 65\,\%$$

When counting the number of tiles left in a box, Tom made the total 27, but there were actually only 25. The percentage error is given by

$$\frac{\text{error}}{\text{correct number}} \times 100\,\%$$

i.e. $$\frac{2}{25} \times 100\,\% = 8\,\%$$

A bike that cost £126 was later sold for £80. The percentage loss is given by

$$\frac{\text{loss}}{\text{purchase price}} \times 100\,\%$$

i.e. $$\frac{46}{126} \times 100\,\%$$

These examples illustrate the way in which one quantity, A, is expressed as a percentage of another, B,

i.e. $$\frac{A}{B} \times 100\,\%$$

Examples of what A might represent are: a mark out of a total (first example above), an error (second example above), a profit or loss (third example above), an increase or decrease, part of a larger quantity, etc.

The quantity called B can represent: a total (first example above), a correct value (second example above), an original price (third example) or value, a workforce, etc.

Exercise 6g

Express 36 g as a percentage of 0.3 kg.

When comparing two quantities in any way, they should be measured in the same unit. So 0.3 kg is converted into 0.3×1000 g, i.e. 300 g.

36 g as a percentage of 300 g is

$$\frac{36}{300} \times 100\% = 12\%$$

Express the first quantity as a percentage of the second.

1. 30 cm, 50 cm

2. 84 p, £1.25

3. 36 min, 1 h

4. 780 g, 3 kg

5. Find the percentage error if
   (a) a three-metre length of fabric is measured as 3.08 m
   (b) £3.15 is rounded to £3
   (c) the value of 5.1^2 is estimated as 25.

6. Find the percentage mark in each case.
   (a) 14 out of 20
   (b) 34 out of 40
   (c) 111 out of 150
   (d) 84 out of 120.

7. During a bank-holiday weekend 29 people were injured in road accidents and 3 of them died. What percentage of the road casualties died?

8. If 2 litres of water are added to 18 litres of milk, what percentage of the mixture is (a) milk (b) water?

9. A boy saved £1.50 out of his Saturday job wage of £5.50. What percentage of his wage did he save?

10. Nina scored 47 out of 60 in a mental test. What was her percentage mark?

11. In a school of eight hundred and fifty pupils, there are five hundred and ten girls. What is the percentage of boys in the school?

12. A small factory employing sixty-four mechanics makes sixteen of them redundant. What percentage of the original workforce is retained?

13. Jason had sold a number of raffle tickets priced at 2 p each. Everyone who bought a ticket had paid with a 2 p coin. Jason counted the coins and reported that the total number was 54. Unfortunately he had dropped 2 coins without noticing, so they were not included in his total.
    What was the percentage error
    (a) in the number of coins
    (b) in the reported takings?

14. A dealer bought what she believed was an antique silver jug for £420. When she discovered that it was a fake she had to sell it for £180.
    What was her percentage loss? (Remember that the original figure is the purchase price.)

15. If an article bought for £60 is sold for £69, what is the percentage profit?

16. In a sale the price of a television set is reduced from £275 to £225. What is the percentage discount?

17. If Kevin's weekly wage goes up from £80 to £84, what is his percentage pay rise?

18. The value of a bicycle drops in the first year from £240 to £170. What is the percentage depreciation in that year?

FINDING THE ORIGINAL QUANTITY

In all the percentage problems so far examined, the calculation has been direct because the original quantity was known. Now we consider the case when the original quantity has to be found.

Fifty-four per cent of the adults living in a particular street own a car. If 162 adults own a car, how many adults live in this street ?

54 % of the total number of adults is 162

i.e. 0.54 of the total number of adults is 162

$\therefore$ the total number of adults is $162 \div 0.54$

$= 300$

Three hundred adults live in the street.

Exercise 6h

1. In a magazine, 65 % of the pages are in colour. If there are 52 coloured pages, what is the total number of pages in the magazine ?

2. The sale price of a television set is £256 which is 80 % of the original selling price. What was the original selling price ?

3. The number of soft-centred chocolates in a box is 18. If 72 % of the chocolates have soft centres, how many chocolates are there in the box ?

4. Rita bought a bag of balloons. Sixteen were red and the rest were green. If 64 % of the balloons were red, how many were green ?

5. When buying a computer and printer, 28 % of the total cost was for the printer. The computer cost £540. How much did the printer cost ?

6. Questions in a test were allocated 1 mark each. Susan achieved a total of 64 %, having correctly answered 16 questions.
   (a) How many questions were there in the test ?
   (b) Andrew got 19 questions right. What percentage mark did he get ?

7. Of the telephone calls Gary received in one week, 87.5% were from friends. If 9 of the calls were not from friends how many calls did he receive altogether ?

A men's outfitter buys in ready-made suits which are sold, with a mark-up of 50 %, for £345 each. For what price did the outfitter buy a suit ?

We do not know the buying price as a sum of money, but we do know that the mark-up is 50 % of the buying price, so the selling price is 150 % of the buying price.

150 % of the buying price is £345

i.e. $1.50 \times$ the buying price = £345

So the buying price = £345 $\div$ 1.5

Therefore the outfitter buys a suit for £230.

Similarly if an item is sold at a loss of 28 %, the selling price represents (100 % − 28 %), i.e. 72 % of the buying price.

By selling his car for £4550, John Roberts made a loss of 21 %. How much did he pay for the car ?

The selling price represents (100 % − 21 %), i.e. 79 %, of his buying price.

79 % of the buying price is £4550

i.e. 0.79 × the buying price = £4550

∴ the buying price = £4550 ÷ 0.79

To the nearest ten pounds, John Roberts paid £5760 for his car.

Where appropriate, give answers correct to the nearest pound, or the nearest penny.

8. Find the original price in each case.

	Selling price	Profit	Loss
(a)	£1008	12 %	
(b)	£445.50		10 %
(c)	£920	15 %	
(d)	£56		30 %
(e)	£252	5 %	
(f)	£1200		40 %

9. A bookseller buys a book, gives it a mark-up of 30 % and sells it for £9.10. What did she pay for the book ?

10. A nearly new, second-hand car is sold for £6440 at a loss of 8 %. What was the original purchase price of the car ?

11. If VAT at 20 % is included, the price of a dining-room suite is £1440.
    (a) What is the price without VAT ?
    (b) By what number would you divide the 'VAT inclusive' price in order to find the price before adding VAT, if the rate of VAT is (i) 15 % (ii) 17.5 % (iii) 22 % ?

12. The engine of a particular car was modified. As a result the number of kilometres covered on one litre of petrol increased by 6 % to 15.9 km/ℓ.
    What was the petrol consumption before modification ?

13. When water freezes its volume increases by 4 %. What volume of water will make 260 cm^3 of ice ?

14. After deductions of 37 %, Ron Jackson's take-home pay is £151.20. What is his gross wage ?

Self-Assessment 6

1. Express
   (a) $3\frac{1}{2}$ as a percentage
   (b) 2.83 as a percentage
   (c) 37 % as a decimal
   (d) 135 % as a mixed number.

2. Find
   (a) 16 % of £40
   (b) 99 % of 14 500 people

3. Two stores sell an identical lawn strimmer at the same basic price of £46.50. Reg's Stores offer a discount of 6 % while Right Tools give a reduction of £3. Which store gives the better deal and by how much ?

4. Last quarter my electricity bill was £52.80. This quarter the bill is £59.40. Find the percentage increase.

5. A plumber presented a bill for £254 plus VAT. Find how much the customer has to pay if the rate of VAT is

   (a) $17\frac{1}{2}$%   (b) 22%

6. Jiten Shah earns £9850 a year and has tax allowances of £4744. How much income tax does she pay at the basic rate of 25%?

7. Copy and complete this bill.

	£
1 bathroom suite 1 shower unit Taps and fittings	192.00 126.00 88.00
Less $2\frac{1}{2}$% trade discount	
Add VAT at 17.5%	
Payment due	

8. 240 boys and 180 girls took an examination. If 65% of the boys passed and 60% of the girls passed, what percentage of the total number of candidates passed?

9. A second-hand car, bought for £6200, depreciates by 8% per year. What is it worth after

   (a) 1 year   (b) 3 years?

10. Express

    (a) 56 marks out of 80 as a percentage

    (b) 72 cm as a percentage of 1.56 m (correct to 3 s.f.).

11. If she sells an article for £45, a dealer loses 10% of the price she paid for the article.

    (a) What price did she pay?

    (b) At what price would she have to sell to make a gain of 12% on her buying price?

12. The repayments on a 25-year mortgage of £46 000 are calculated at 1.25% per calendar month.

    (a) Find the repayment due
        (i) per month   (ii) per year
        (iii) over 25 years.

    (b) Express the total repayment as a percentage of the original mortgage.

13. Jan has £5000 to invest and decides to pay it into a building society account. The Midtown Building Society can offer an account which pays 10.3% per annum, added yearly. At the Reliant West, there is an account which pays interest quarterly at 10% per annum. If Jan does not intend to withdraw any interest during the year, which account should she choose?

14. A certain factory employs 20 mechanics and 2 supervisors. The mechanics earn £250.80 for a 44-hour week and each of the supervisors is paid £315 weekly.

    (a) Find the total cost per week of employing this labour force.

    As a result of automation, it is found that only one supervisor is needed and that the number of mechanics can be reduced by 40%. The remaining mechanics are given an extra 90 p per hour and their working week is reduced to 40 hours. The supervisor is given a rise of 15%.

    (b) How many mechanics are now employed and what do they earn each week?

    (c) Find the reduction in the total weekly wage bill and express it as a percentage of the total found in part (a).

15. Each week the owner of a corner shop buys one thousand pounds worth of food, marks it up by 10% and turns it over (i.e. sells all of it) in the week. Another retailer spends £1000 on buying furniture. His mark-up is 100% but he only turns his stock over every three months. Who makes the bigger profit over a year?

7

BASIC ALGEBRA

THE USE OF LETTERS

There are many situations where the value of a number is unknown.

For example, if a textbook costs £14, then the number of these books that can be bought for £490 is unknown without some calculation. If we use the letter x to represent that number of books, then we can express the information given by using mathematical symbols, i.e. $14 \times x = 490$.

As a second example, consider these instructions for the quantity of rice needed for a meal: allow 50 grams per person. In this case both the number of people and the total mass of rice needed are unknown. If we use the letter n to represent the number of people and the letter w for total number of grams of rice, then again we can use mathematical symbols to express the information, i.e. $w = 50 \times n$

Notice that, in both examples, letters are used to represent numbers, not quantities. Thus w is the *number* of grams of rice whereas 'w grams' is the mass of rice.

Letters that are used to represent unknown numbers are sometimes called *variables* because, without further information, they can have a variety of values.

ALGEBRAIC EXPRESSIONS

An algebraic expression is a set of letters and numbers connected by addition, subtraction, multiplication and/or division.

Examples of algebraic expressions are $2 \times x$, $3 - x$, $a + b$, $\frac{y}{x}$

It is conventional to omit the multiplication sign so, for example,

$2 \times x$ is written as $2x$ and $2ab$ means $2 \times a \times b$

The *terms* in an algebraic expression are the parts separated by a + or − sign. A particular term is usually identified by the letter or combination of letters involved.

For example, in the expression $2a - 3xy + 6$, the terms are $2a$, $-3xy$ and 6; they might be identified individually as 'the term in a', 'the xy term' and 'the number term' respectively.

Like terms contain the same letter or combination of letters. Thus $2xy$ and $5xy$ are like terms, whereas $2xy$ and $3x$ are unlike terms.

An expression can be simplified when it contains two or more like terms, as these terms can be combined.

For example, $2x + 5x$ means '2 lots of x' plus '5 lots of x'

so $2x + 5x$ can be written simply as $7x$

In the same way, $5xy - 2xy$ can be simplified to $3xy$.

When simplifying algebraic expressions, remember that, as letters represent numbers, all the ordinary rules of arithmetic apply. Some of the important facts are as follows:

Brackets are dealt with first, then multiplication and division are done before addition and subtraction.

When directed numbers are multiplied or divided, the same signs give a positive result and different signs give a negative result.

When a string of numbers are multiplied, the order does not matter,
e.g. $2 \times x \times 3$ is the same as $2 \times 3 \times x$, which can be written as $6x$.

Brackets

If we want to multiply both x and 3 by 4, we can group x and 3 together in a bracket and write $4(x + 3)$,

i.e. $4(x + 3) = 4 \times x + 4 \times 3 = 4x + 12$

In the same way, $2(2x - 5) = 2 \times 2x + 2 \times (-5)$

$= 4x - 10$

Indices

Indices applied to letters have exactly the same meaning as when applied to numbers.

Therefore, as 3^2 means 3×3, x^2 means $x \times x$

Similarly, $t \times t \times t$ can be written t^3

Also x^{-2} means $1/x^2$, $x^{1/2}$ means $\sqrt{x}$, $x^0 = 1$

Remember that $(a^3)^2$ means $a^3 \times a^3$

Different powers of the same letter can be multiplied by adding the indices,

e.g. $p^3 \times p^5 = p^8$

However, $p^3 \times q^5$ cannot be simplified (apart from omitting the $\times$ sign and writing p^3q^5) because p and q represent different unknown numbers.

Different powers of the same number can be divided by subtracting the indices,

e.g. $$\frac{p^3}{p^5} = p^{-2}$$

Different powers of the same letter cannot be added or subtracted, e.g. $x^2 + x^3$ cannot be simplified because x^2 and x^3 are unlike terms.

Fractions

The four rules (+, −, ×, ÷) used for numerical fractions are equally valid for fractions involving letters.

For example, we find fractions equivalent to $\frac{2a}{4}$ by multiplying or dividing the numerator and the denominator by the same number (or letter),

i.e. $$\frac{2a}{4} = \frac{6a}{12} = \frac{a}{2} = \frac{ab}{2b} = \frac{a^2}{2a}$$

We can express $\frac{2x}{3} - \frac{x}{6}$ as a single fraction by finding equivalent fractions with a common denominator and then subtracting the numerators,

i.e. $$\frac{2x}{3} - \frac{x}{6} = \frac{4x}{6} - \frac{x}{6} = \frac{4x - x}{6} = \frac{3x}{6} = \frac{x}{2}$$

We can simplify $\frac{2x}{3} \times \frac{x}{6}$ by multiplying the numerators and multiplying the denominators,

i.e. $$\frac{{}^{1}\not{2}x}{3} \times \frac{x}{\not{6}_{3}} = \frac{x^2}{9}$$ (Notice that we cancel the common factor 2.)

To simplify $\frac{2x}{3} \div \frac{x}{6}$ we find the reciprocal of $\frac{x}{6}$ and multiply,

i.e. $$\frac{2x}{3} \div \frac{x}{6} = \frac{2\not{x}^{1}}{{}_{1}\not{3}} \times \frac{\not{6}^{2}}{\not{x}_{1}} = \frac{4}{1} = 4$$

Exercise 7a

Simplify $3x + 4y + x - 7y$

$3x$ and x are like terms so $3x + x = 4x$; similarly $4y - 7y = -3y$

$$3x + 4y + x - 7y = 4x - 3y$$

1. Simplify
   (a) $2x + 3 + 2 + 5x$
   (b) $3a - 2 + 4a + 6$
   (c) $3x + 5y - 2x$
   (d) $5t - 8 - 2t + 3$
   (e) $4 - 5p - 2 - 3p$
   (f) $a - 4b + 3a$

2. Simplify
   (a) $6 - 2x - 4 - 3x$
   (b) $10 - 5y - 7y - 3$
   (c) $2x + y - z + 3x - 2y$
   (d) $-a + 2b - 3a$
   (e) $5s + t - 2s + 6$
   (f) $4p - q + r + 2q - r$

3. Multiply out the brackets

(a) $3(x-3)$

(b) $2(3x+4)$

(c) $2(3x-2)$

4. Multiply out the brackets

(a) $5(x-1)$

(b) $4(3-x)$

(c) $3(a-2b)$

Simplify (a) $2x-3(4-5x)$ (b) $x-2-(5x-4)$

(a) First we multiply out the bracket; $-3(4-5x)$ means multiply both 4 and $-5x$ by -3. Remember that $(-3)\times(-5x) = +15x$

$$2x-3(4-5x) = 2x-12+15x$$
$$= 17x-12$$

(b) $-(5x-4)$ means subtract $5x$ and subtract -4; remember that $-(-4) = +4$

$$x-2-(5x-4) = x-2-5x+4$$
$$= -4x+2$$
$$= 2-4x$$

5. Simplify

(a) $5x+4(5x+3)$

(b) $7-3(4-x)$

(c) $3p+2(4-5p)$

(d) $x-(2-3x)$

(e) $8+3(a-8)$

(f) $b-(5-b)$

(g) $4(2-t)+2(t-3)$

(h) $3b-4(2-5b)$

(i) $3(4-x)-2(1+3x)$

(j) $-2(x-1)-3(x+1)$

(k) $-4(c-2)+6(2-c)$

6. Simplify

(a) $p\times p\times p$

(b) $2a\times 3a$

(c) $2x^2\times x$

(d) $3b\times b^3$

(e) $4x\times 3y$

(f) $x^3\div x$

(g) $a^4\div a^2$

(h) $y^2\div y^3$

(i) $p^3\div p^3$

(j) $4x^2\div 2x$

7. Simplify

(a) $8x\div 2y$

(b) $(-x)\times(-2x)$

(c) $b\times(-b)$

(d) $8x^3\div 2x$

(e) $9y^3\div 6xy$

(f) $(a^2)^3$

(g) $(1/x)^{-1}$

(h) $(pq)^0$

(i) $(1/c)^{-2}$

(j) $(x^{-1})^2$

8. Simplify

(a) $3x+x(2+x)$

(b) $a(a+b)+b(a-b)$

(c) $x(x-2)-x(2x-4)$

(d) $a(b-c)-(ab+c)$

(e) $x^2-3x(4-x)$

(f) $x^2(1-x^2)-x(1-x)$

(g) $x-x(1-x)$

(h) $a(b-c)-b(a-c)$

(i) $x(x-3)+2(x-3)$

(j) $4p(q+r)-2p(q-r)$

(k) $x^3(x+1)-x^2(x-1)$

Simplify (a) $\frac{x}{4}+\frac{5x}{6}$ (b) $\frac{x}{4}\div\frac{5x}{6}$ (c) $\frac{6x}{5}\times\frac{2x}{3y}$

(a)
$$\frac{x}{4}+\frac{5x}{6}=\frac{3x+10x}{12}$$
$$=\frac{13x}{12}$$

(b)
$$\frac{x}{4}\div\frac{5x}{6}=\frac{{}^{1}\not{x}}{{}_{2}\not{4}}\times\frac{\not{6}^{3}}{5\not{x}_{1}}$$
$$=\frac{3}{10}$$

(c)
$$\frac{{}^{2}\not{6}x}{5}\times\frac{2x}{\not{3}_{1}y}=\frac{2x}{5}\times\frac{2x}{y}$$
$$=\frac{4x^2}{5y}$$

9. Simplify

(a) $\frac{x}{2}+\frac{2x}{3}$

(b) $\frac{2a}{5}-\frac{a}{4}$

(c) $\frac{y}{3}\times\frac{y}{2}$

(d) $\frac{2x}{5}\div\frac{15}{4x}$

(e) $\frac{4y}{3}\times\frac{15z}{8y}$

(f) $\frac{3b}{7}\div\frac{9ab}{14}$

(g) $\frac{3}{x}\div\frac{6}{y}$

(h) $\frac{x^2}{2}+\frac{x^3}{4}$

(i) $\frac{x^2}{2}\times\frac{x^3}{4}$

(j) $\frac{x^2}{2}\div\frac{x^3}{4}$

10. Find the value of $3x+2$ when
(a) $x = 4$, (b) $x = -3$

11. Find the value of $3-2x$ when
(a) $x = 1$, (b) $x = -1$

12. Find the value of x^2+1 when
(a) $x = 2$, (b) $x = -1$

13. Find the value of $\frac{2x-1}{3}$ when
(a) $x = 5$, (b) $x = -4$

14. Find the value of $\frac{2+x^2}{x}$ when
(a) $x = 1$, (b) $x = -1$

EQUATIONS

When two *different* algebraic expressions are equal, we have an equation.

For example, $x = 2x-1$ is an equation.

However, $x+x = 2x$ is not an equation because $2x$ is another way of expressing $x+x$, i.e. the two expressions are not different.
($x+x = 2x$ is an example of an *identity*.)

The Solution of an Equation

The solution of an equation is the number or set of numbers which the letters represent in that equation.

A problem can sometimes be solved if we can use algebra to relate the given information to form an equation and then solve it. This chapter started off with a problem which we interpreted as the equation $14x = 490$. This was a simple problem with an obvious solution, but it illustrates the potential of equations as a powerful problem-solving tool. We will start with methods for solving the simplest category of equations.

LINEAR EQUATIONS IN ONE UNKNOWN

Linear equations in one unknown contain just one letter to the power 1, e.g. $2x-5 = 7$, $5-3a = a+2$ are linear equations, but $x^2-2 = 2x$ is not a linear equation.

Sometimes the solution is obvious. For example, if $x+1 = 3$, then clearly x represents 2 and we say that $x = 2$ is the solution of the equation.
However the solution of $3x+6 = 2(4-x)$ is not so obvious and an organised approach is necessary.

The two sides of an equation can be thought of as the contents of the two pans on a pair of scales which are exactly balanced. The equality will remain true (the scales will stay balanced) *provided that we do the same thing to both sides.* The aim is to end up with 'letter' = 'number' and we can achieve this by adding, subtracting, multiplying or dividing by anything except zero, as long as we do it to both sides.

It is sensible to proceed in the following order

1. remove any brackets
2. collect like terms
3. collect letter terms on one side (choose the side where the result will be positive, remembering that $-2 > -3$ and that $-2 < 0$)
4. collect the number terms on the other side.

Therefore to solve $3x+6 = 2(4-x)$, we proceed as follows:

Remove bracket $\quad 3x+6 = 8-2x$

Add $2x$ to both sides $\quad 3x+6+2x = 8-2x+2x$

i.e. $\quad 5x+6 = 8$

Take 6 from both sides $\quad 5x = 2$

Divide both sides by 5 $\quad x = \frac{2}{5}$

As a check, see if the original equation is true when $x = \frac{2}{5}$,

i.e. $\quad \text{LHS} = 3\times\frac{2}{5}+6 = 7\frac{1}{5}, \quad \text{RHS} = 2(4-\frac{2}{5}) = 2\times 3\frac{3}{5} = 7\frac{1}{5}$

Therefore $x = \frac{2}{5}$ is the correct solution.

Exercise 7b

Find x if $5-3x = 2$

First we add $3x$ to both sides to give a positive x term.

$$5-3x+3x = 2+3x$$

$$5 = 2+3x$$

$$5-2 = 2+3x-2$$

$$3 = 3x$$

i.e. $$x = 1$$

Sometimes the letter represents a negative number.

1. Solve the equations
   (a) $3x+2 = 11$
   (b) $2x-5 = 9$
   (c) $7-2x = 3$
   (d) $13-2t = 21$
   (e) $3p-5 = 7$
   (f) $1.5-x = 0.7$

2. Solve the equations
   (a) $x+5 = 4x-4$
   (b) $3x-2 = 5-4x$
   (c) $7-5x = 4x-11$
   (d) $x+2.5 = 3.6-x$
   (e) $2t-1.6 = 4t-2.8$
   (f) $3-2(x-2) = 10$

3. Solve the equations
   (a) $5-(4-a) = 2a$
   (b) $4x-3(x+1) = 7$
   (c) $6y = 4-3(y-5)$
   (d) $4x-(x-9) = 0$
   (e) $1-(3-4b) = 0$
   (f) $2(x-1.5) = 3x$

Solve the equation $\frac{x}{5}+\frac{x}{4} = 3$

Remember that, provided we keep the equality true, we can do anything we choose to an equation. An equation is easier to deal with if it does not contain fractions, so we choose to get rid of them; we can do this by multiplying both sides by the lowest common multiple of the denominators.

$$\frac{x}{5}+\frac{x}{4} = 3$$

Multiply both sides by 20 $$20\left(\frac{x}{5}+\frac{x}{4}\right) = 20\times 3$$

i.e. $$\frac{\overset{4}{\cancel{20}}}{1}\times\frac{x}{\cancel{5}_1}+\frac{\overset{5}{\cancel{20}}}{1}\times\frac{x}{\cancel{4}_1} = 60$$

$\Rightarrow$ $$4x+5x = 60$$

$$9x = 60$$

$\therefore$ $$x = \frac{60}{9} = 6\tfrac{2}{3}$$

Solve the equation $\dfrac{2}{y} = 8$

$$\frac{2}{y} = 8$$

i.e. $$\frac{2}{y} = 8 = \frac{8}{1}$$

This time the unknown is in the denominator. The lowest common multiple of y and 1 is y, so we multiply both sides by y.

$$y \times \frac{2}{y} = y \times 8$$

i.e. $$\frac{\not{y}^1}{1} \times \frac{2}{\not{y}_1} = 8y$$

$\Rightarrow$ $$2 = 8y$$

$\Rightarrow$ $$\frac{2}{8} = y \quad \text{i.e.} \quad y = \frac{1}{4}$$

4. Solve the equations

(a) $\dfrac{2x}{3} = 5$

(b) $\dfrac{2x}{3} = \dfrac{1}{4}$

(c) $\dfrac{x}{3} + \dfrac{2}{5} = \dfrac{1}{2}$

(d) $\dfrac{x}{3} + \dfrac{2x}{5} = 4$

(e) $\dfrac{3x}{2} - \dfrac{x}{4} = 2$

(f) $\dfrac{x}{2} + \dfrac{1}{3} = \dfrac{x}{3}$

(g) $\dfrac{3}{x} = 1$

(h) $\dfrac{4}{a} = 2$

(i) $\dfrac{6}{y} = 3$

(j) $\dfrac{1}{x} = 3$

(k) $\dfrac{2}{x} = \dfrac{3}{4}$

(l) $\dfrac{3}{z} = \dfrac{2}{5}$

The perimeter of a rectangular sheet is 9 m and the length is $\frac{1}{2}$ m more than the width. Find the width of the sheet by forming an equation and solving it.

Let x m represent the width of the sheet.

The length of the sheet is $(x + \frac{1}{2})$ m.

The perimeter is twice the width plus twice the length,

$\therefore$ $$2x + 2(x + \tfrac{1}{2}) = 9$$

$\Rightarrow$ $$2x + 2x + 1 = 9$$

$\Rightarrow$ $$4x = 8$$

so $x = 2$

The width of the sheet is 2 m.

In each of the following questions form an equation from the information given. Then solve the equation. State clearly, either in words or on a diagram, what your letter represents. End your solution by answering the questions asked.

Most of these problems are simple enough for you to answer without the help of an equation: use this to check the validity of your equation.

5. A group of people is divided into three smaller but equal-sized groups. There are 15 people in one of the smaller groups. How many were in the original group ?

6. The perimeter of an equilateral triangle is 81 cm. What is the length of one of the sides ?

7. A twenty per cent increase in my weekly wage will give me an extra £27 a week. What is my present weekly wage ?

8. I asked John to think of a number and then divide it by three. He said that the result was two less than the number he thought of. What number did he think of ?

9. I want to make a rectangular lawn with a perimeter of 60 m so that its length is twice its width. How wide should it be ?

10. The volume of a cardboard box is ten times that of a carton. The box will hold eight cartons with 36 cm^3 of space to spare. Find the volume of one carton.

11. I am ten years older than my sister and I am now twice her age. How old is my sister now ?

12. The length of a rectangle is 6 cm more than its width and its perimeter is 48 cm. Find the length of the rectangle.

INEQUALITIES

The use of letters to represent unknown numbers is not restricted to problems that can be represented as an equation.

For example, suppose that fewer than 50 students enrol for a course at a college.

The number of students enrolling is unknown but if we represent it by x, then using the symbol $<$ to mean 'is less than', we can write

$$x < 50$$

This is an inequality and it is true when x represents any number less than 50, i.e. x represents a range of numbers and this range can be illustrated on a number line.

The open circle at the right-hand end of the range indicates that 50 is not included in the range.

The number of students who enroll cannot be negative so a further inequality is implied, i.e. x must be greater than or equal to zero, which is written $x \geqslant 0$.

The other symbols that are used to represent inequalities are

$>$ means 'is greater than' and $\leqslant$ means 'is less than or equal to'

The range given by $x \geqslant 0$ can also be illustrated on a number line.

The solid circle at the left-hand end of the range indicates that 0 *is* included in the range.

When a variable has to satisfy two inequalities we have a double inequality.

For example x, the number of students enrolling on the course, is restricted in two ways, i.e. $x < 50$ and $x \geqslant 0$ (i.e. $0 \leqslant x$).

Because the values of x lie between two boundaries, these two facts can be combined into one statement, $0 \leqslant x < 50$.

This number line illustrates the double inequality:

THE RANGE IN WHICH A CORRECTED NUMBER CAN LIE

Suppose that the length of a piece of string is given as 23 cm to the nearest centimetre.

The smallest number that can be rounded up to 23 is 22.5, and the largest number that can be rounded down to 23 is just less than 23.5. Therefore the string can have any length from 22.5 cm up to, but not including, 23.5 cm and is not restricted to integer values.

This gives a range of numbers which can be illustrated on a number line.

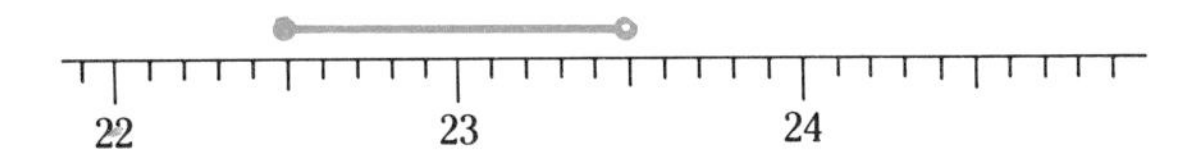

If the length of the string is denoted by x cm then we can say that

$$22.5 \leqslant x < 23.5$$

Exercise 7c

1. Each of the following numbers is given to the nearest whole number. Illustrate on a number line the range in which the number lies.
   (a) 12 (b) 8 (c) 100

2. Each of the following numbers is correct to 1 decimal place. Illustrate on a number line the range within which the number lies.
   (a) 2.7 (b) 34.4 (c) 5.0

3. Each of the following numbers is correct to 2 significant figures. Use a number line to illustrate the range within which the number lies.
   (a) 2.2 (b) 0.15 (c) 120

4. The weight of sugar in a bag is given as 254 g to the nearest gram. What is the least possible weight of the sugar ?

5. The number of people attending a football match is given as 5400 to the nearest hundred. What is the greatest number of people that could have been there ?

6. The width of a fridge is given as 96 cm, to the nearest centimetre. Is it safe to assume that it will fit into a gap that is 96 cm wide ? Explain your answer.

7. Carpet tiles are square in shape, with sides that are 30 cm long, to the nearest millimetre.

   (a) Ten tiles are placed end to end. What is range of the length of this row of tiles ?

   (b) A square room measures 300 cm by 300 cm, to the nearest centimetre. How many tiles should be bought to make sure that the floor of this room can be carpeted wall to wall ?

8. A digital weighing machine shows the weight of an object placed on it correct to the nearest gram. When one metal washer is weighed, the display shows 12 g. When 10 identical washers are placed on it, the display shows 116 g.

   (a) Give the least possible weight of one washer.

   (b) Explain how the weighing machine could be used to give the weight of one washer correct to 2 decimal places.

OPERATIONS ON INEQUALITIES

Consider the true inequality $2 < 5$

If we add or subtract the same number on both sides, we find that the inequality remains true, e.g. $2+5 < 5+5$, $2-8 < 5-8$

If we multiply (or divide) both sides by the same positive number, we also find that the inequality remains true, e.g. $2 \times 2 < 5 \times 3$

However, multiplication (or division) by a negative number destroys the truth of the inequality, e.g. $2 < 5$ but $2 \times (-2)$ is *not* less than $5 \times (-2)$, i.e.

an inequality remains true when the same number is added to, or subtracted from, both sides and when both sides are multiplied or divided by the same positive number.

However, *multiplication or division by a negative number must be avoided.*

Solving Inequalities

Consider the inequality $3 - 2x \geqslant 5$

The range of values of x for which the inequality is true is not immediately obvious. Finding this range of values of x is called solving the inequality.

Now we can add $2x$ to both sides of $\quad 3 - 2x \geqslant 5$

giving $\quad 3 \geqslant 5 + 2x$

Subtracting 5 from both sides gives $\quad -2 \geqslant 2x$

Dividing both sides by 2 gives $\quad -1 \geqslant x$

i.e. $x \leqslant -1$ is the solution of the inequality, and it can be illustrated on a number line.

i.e.

Notice that the procedure for solving inequalities is very similar to that for solving equations; always collect the x terms on the side with the greater number of xs as this avoids ending up with a negative letter term.

Exercise 7d

1. Solve the inequalities and illustrate the solution on a number line.

(a) $4x-5>3$
(b) $1+3x<4$
(c) $7>3+2x$
(d) $1+2x>0$
(e) $5<7+x$
(f) $3>4-x$
(g) $4x-1\geqslant 3$
(h) $2+3x\leqslant 11$
(i) $3-5x\geqslant 18$
(j) $3(x-2)\geqslant 4$
(k) $2(3x-1)\leqslant 3$
(l) $3(2-x)>5$

2. Give the largest integer that satisfies

(a) $2x-3<5$
(b) $4-x\geqslant 2$
(c) $3(2x+1)<10$
(d) $5(2-x)\geqslant 4$

3. Give the smallest integer that satisfies

(a) $5+3x\geqslant 14$
(b) $0<3-x$
(c) $2(x-3)>12$
(d) $0\leqslant 4(2x-5)$

Find the range of values of x for which (a) $x\geqslant 2$ and $x>1$
(b) $4<2x+1\leqslant 9$

(a) If we illustrate both given ranges on a number line, then we can see the values of x where the ranges overlap.

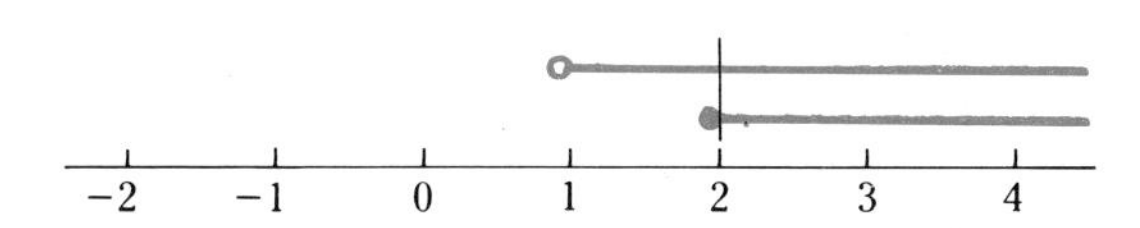

$x\geqslant 2$ and $x>1$ are both satisfied for $x\geqslant 2$

(b) $4<2x+1\leqslant 9$ represents two inequalities, i.e. $4<2x+1$ and $2x+1\leqslant 9$

We solve each inequality and then find the values of x that satisfy both of them.

$$4<2x+1 \quad\Rightarrow\quad 3<2x \quad\Rightarrow\quad 1\tfrac{1}{2}<x$$
i.e. $x>1\frac{1}{2}$

$$2x+1\leqslant 9 \quad\Rightarrow\quad 2x\leqslant 8 \quad\Rightarrow\quad x\leqslant 4$$

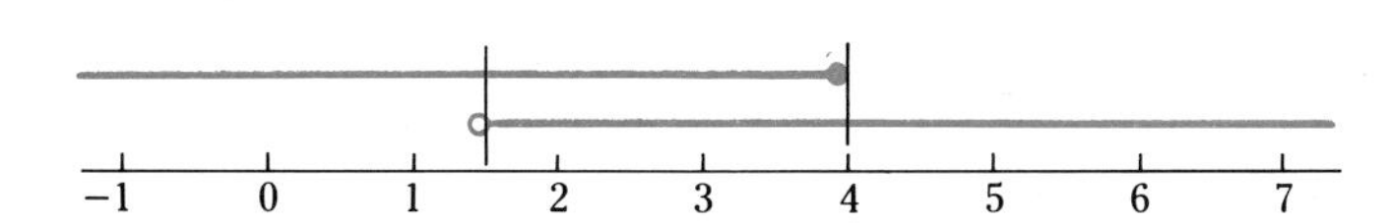

Values of x greater than $1\frac{1}{2}$ and less than or equal to 4 satisfy both the given inequalities, i.e. $1\frac{1}{2}<x\leqslant 4$

4. Find the range of values of x which satisfy both the inequalities.
   (a) $3 < 3x \leqslant 6$
   (b) $4 \leqslant 2x \leqslant 13$
   (c) $9 \leqslant 2x < 20$
   (d) $6 < 3x < 20$
   (e) $x \leqslant 1$ and $x < 2$
   (f) $2 + x \geqslant 3$ and $3 - x \geqslant 1$
   (g) $5 > x + 1 > 2$
   (h) $7 \leqslant 3 - x \leqslant 12$

5. For each part of question 4 give (i) the smallest integer, (ii) the largest integer, that satisfies each double inequality.

6. Find (i) the smallest integer, (ii) the largest integer, that satisfies each of the following sets of inequalities.
   (a) $x + 1 < 2$ and $x - 1 > -6$
   (b) $5 < 3a < 6$
   (c) $2 < x + 1 < 5$
   (d) $2n < 3$ and $n + 1 > 6$

A computer supplier has to sell more than ten computers a week to stay financially viable. The manufacturer can let the supplier have a maximum of 50 computers each week. Use inequalities to represent the number of computers that can be sold each week.

Let the letter n represent the number of computers sold each week.

We know that n is greater than 10 but less than or equal to 50,

i.e. $n > 10$ and $n \leqslant 50$

We also know that n is a whole number. All this information can be written briefly as

$$10 < n \leqslant 50, \quad \text{where } n \text{ is an integer}$$

Construct an inequality to represent the information about the unknown quantity in each of questions 7 to 12. Remember to state clearly what number your letter represents. If your letter can have only whole number values, this must also be stated.

7. The minimum weight of popcorn that can be bought from a wholesaler is 15 kg.

8. No more than 56 passengers can be carried on a coach.

9. The temperature will remain above 0 °C overnight.

10. I think of a number, double it and then add two. The result is less than one hundred.

11. A packet of pins contains 250 pins to the nearest 10 pins. What is the largest number of pins possible in a packet ?

12. The length of a room is given as 355 cm to the nearest 5 cm. What is the shortest possible length of the room ?

FORMULAE

A formula is a set of instructions for solving a problem. For example, the formula for finding the area of a rectangle can be written in words as follows.

The area of a rectangle is found by multiplying its length by its width.

This formula works for any rectangle, i.e. the length and the width of the rectangle can each be any number of units. Using letters for these unknown numbers, we can express the formula algebraically.

If the length of a rectangle is l units and its width is b units, its area, A square units, is given by

$$A = lb$$

Notice that the letters in the formula represent numbers, i.e. if a rectangle is 12 cm long then l is 12.

Making Formulae

To make an algebraic formula for solving a general problem, we need to be able to express the solution in words. Then we can identify the variable quantities and allocate letters to represent the unknown numbers.

For example, Sam makes earrings and sells them at markets and craft fairs.
Each pair of earrings costs £1 to make and is sold for £2.50.
She keeps her accounts on a computer spreadsheet and needs a formula for the gain or loss made on each occasion.

In words this formula is

The gain made is equal to the difference between the selling price and the cost of each pair, multiplied by the number of pairs of earrings sold less the rent of the sales pitch.

The variables are: the number of pairs of earrings sold, and the rent.

If n is the number sold and £R is the rent, then money made on each pair is £2.5 − £1, i.e. £1.50 so the money made on sales is £$1.5 \times n$.

If the gain made is £P, we can now write a formula for P in terms of n and R, i.e.

$$P = 1.5n - R$$

Many people find that making a formula is quite difficult; in this situation it can be helpful to consider a numerical version first. In the problem above, for example, if 20 pairs are sold and the rent is £10, then the gain is given by £$(1.5 \times 20 - 10)$.

Exercise 7e

1. A club has F full-time members and P part-time members. Give a formula for the total number, T, of members.

2. Grit and salt are mixed for salting icy roads. If x tonnes of grit are mixed with y tonnes of salt, to give a total mass, m tonnes, of the mixture, write down a formula for m.

3. Write down a formula for A where $A\text{ m}^2$ is the area of a square of side a m.

4. Write down a formula for d where d km is the distance travelled by a car moving at a steady speed of s km/h for t hours.

5. The lengths of the sides of a triangle are a cm, b cm and c cm. Write down a formula for p where p cm is the perimeter of the triangle.

6. A greengrocer starts the day with a stock of S boxes of strawberries. During the day he sells T boxes and R boxes are wasted and thrown away. Give a formula for the number of boxes, N, left at the end of the day.

7. Here are the instructions for roasting a chicken.
   Roast at a high oven setting for 35 minutes per pound plus 30 minutes.
   Give a formula for T where T minutes is the cooking time for a chicken weighing p lbs.

8. A garage repair bill is made up of the cost of spare parts and labour charges at £20 an hour. Find a formula for T where £T is the bill for a repair needing x hours of labour and y pounds-worth of spare parts.

9. Tins of fruit, weighing p grams each, are packed into boxes. If an empty box weighs x grams, find a formula for W when W grams is the weight of a box containing N tins of fruit.

10. A roll of newsprint is L m long. Give a formula for N when N m is the length left on the roll after n pieces, each of length p m, have been cut off the roll.

Find a formula for p where p metres is the perimeter of a rectangle whose length is x metres and whose width is y centimetres.

If p is a number of metres, then the formula for p must also give a number of metres, i.e. the width must be expressed as a number of metres.

$$\text{Width} = \frac{y}{100}\text{ m}$$

The perimeter of a rectangle is equal to twice its length plus twice its width,

i.e.
$$p = 2x + 2\left(\frac{y}{100}\right)$$

$$p = 2x + \frac{y}{50}$$

11. One tin of paint weighs W grams and n of these tins are packed into a carton that weighs c grams. Find a formula for K where K kg is the weight of the carton when full of tins.

12. A letter costs x pence to post. Find a formula for C when £C is the cost of posting n such letters.

13. One pair of shoes can be cleaned in 4 minutes. Find a formula for T where T hours is the time taken to clean n pairs of shoes.

14. Give a formula for A where A cm^2 is the area of a rectangle measuring l m by c cm.

15. There are L m of tape on a roll. The length of tape left on the roll after n pieces each of length l cm have been cut from it, is k m. Give a formula for k.

16. A common room contains s sofas that each seat two people and c chairs. Give a formula for N, the total number of people who can be seated.

USING FORMULAE

The formula for the area, A square units, of a rectangle is given by

$$A = lb$$

where l units is the length of the rectangle and b units is its width. This formula can be used to find the area of a particular rectangle by substituting numbers for the letters.

For example, for a rectangle 12 cm long and 8 cm wide, $l = 12$ and $b = 8$

Using $A = lb$ gives $A = 12 \times 8 = 96$

Therefore the area of this rectangle is 96 cm^2.

Note that, to use the formula for the area of a rectangle both the length and the width must be expressed in the same unit; if a rectangle is 2 m long and 25 cm wide, then 2 m must be expressed as 200 cm (or 25 cm as 0.25 m). Then we can use $l = 200$ and $b = 25$ which gives the area in cm^2 (or $l = 2$ and $b = 0.25$ giving the area in m^2).

Exercise 7f

In questions 1 to 3, give the numbers that are being substituted for the letters and end each question with a sentence giving the answer. 1(a) is done for you.

1. A length, l cm, of wire is bent into a triangle whose sides are a cm, b cm and c cm long, with the wire along the a cm side doubled.

   The formula for l is $l = 2a + b + c$.

   Use this formula to find the length of wire used to make each triangle.

(a)

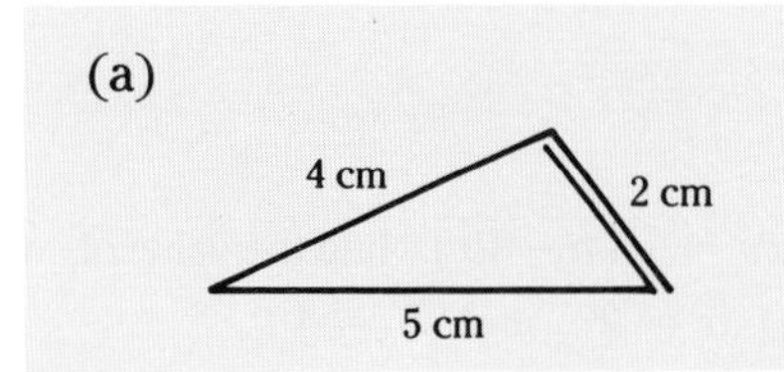

When $a = 2,\ b = 5,\ c = 4,$

using $l = 2a + b + c$

gives $l = 4 + 5 + 4$

$l = 13$

The length of wire used is 13 cm.

(b)

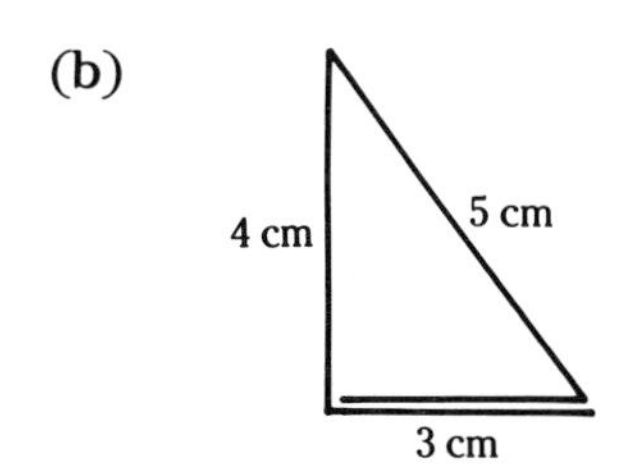

(c)

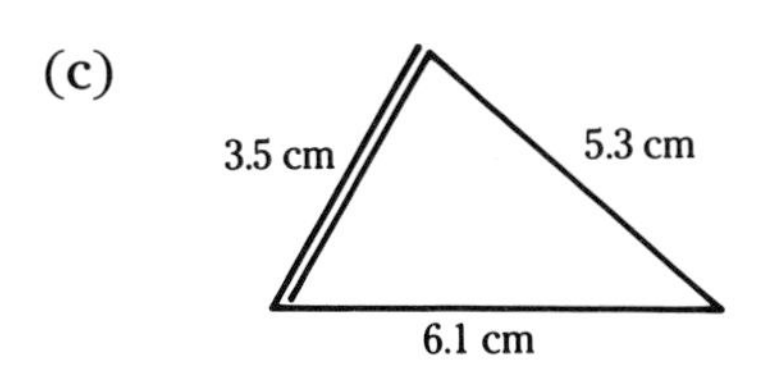

(d)

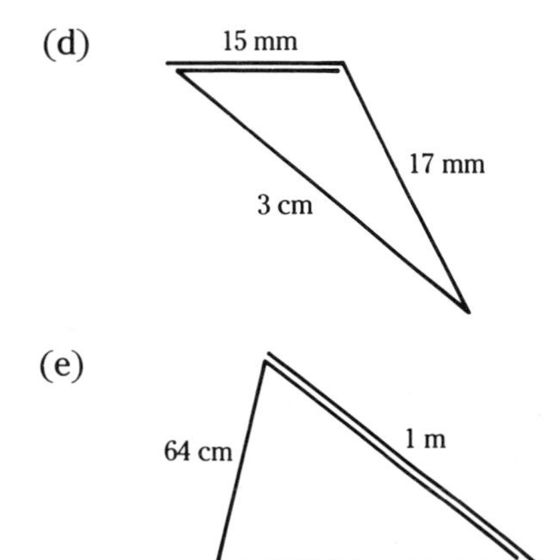

(e)

2. The formula for the distance, d units, covered when moving at a constant speed of s units per hour for t hours is $d = st$.

   Use the formula to find the distance moved by

   (a) a car travelling at 75 km/h for 2 hours
   (b) a train moving at 120 m.p.h. for 3 hours
   (c) a bus travelling at 30 km/h for 30 minutes
   (d) a rocket moving at 300 km/h for 10 seconds
   (e) a boat moving at 15 knots (nautical miles per hour) for 30 minutes
   (f) a bullet moving at 100 m/s for 2.83 seconds.

3. Most shops sell goods at a price which includes value added tax (VAT). The amount, £T, of this tax can be calculated from the selling price, £P, by using the formula $T = \dfrac{rP}{100 + r}$ where r% is the rate at which VAT is charged.

   Find, to the nearest penny, the VAT charged on

   (a) a calculator sold for £6 when the VAT rate is 18%
   (b) a suit sold for £120 when the VAT rate is 12%
   (c) a ream of paper sold for £6.50 when the VAT rate is 20%
   (d) a packet of pencils sold for 75 p when the VAT rate is 17.5%.

We do not need to know what a formula is for in order to find the number represented by one of the letters, provided that we are given the numerical values of the other letters.

Given that $v = u - at$, find v when $a = -2$, $t = 5$ and $u = 17$

$$v = u - at$$

when $a = -2$, $t = 5$, $u = 17$,

$$v = 17 - (-2) \times 5$$
$$= 17 - (-10)$$
$$= 17 + 10$$
$$= 27$$

Notice that the negative number has been put in brackets. This is a sensible precaution against mistakes.

4. If $S = n(a+b)$, find S when
   (a) $n = 6$, $a = 3$ and $b = 6$
   (b) $n = 4$, $a = -3$ and $b = 5$
   (c) $n = 2.4$, $a = 3.6$ and $b = -1.5$

5. If $a = b^2 + c^2$, find the value of a when
   (a) $b = 3$ and $c = 4$
   (b) $b = 1.7$ and $c = 2.4$
   (c) $b = -5$ and $c = -12$

6. If $v = \sqrt{(a - 3b)}$, find the value of v when
   (a) $a = 27$ and $b = 4$
   (b) $a = 0.18$ and $b = 0.05$
   (c) $a = -1.5$ and $b = -2.6$

7. Given that $f = \frac{1}{u} + \frac{1}{v}$, find the value of f when
   (a) $u = 16$ and $v = 25$
   (b) $u = 0.5$ and $v = 0.8$
   (c) $u = -1.25$ and $v = 0.97$

Sometimes we need to find the value of a letter on the right-hand side of a formula. This can be done by substituting numbers for the letters whose values are known and then solving the resulting equation.

If $v = u + at$, find the value of a when $v = 25$, $u = 11$ and $t = -7$

$$v = u + at$$

when $v = 25$, $u = 11$, $t = -7$, $\quad 25 = 11 + a \times (-7)$

$\Rightarrow \quad 25 = 11 - 7a$

add $7a$ to both sides $\quad 25 + 7a = 11$

take 25 from both sides $\quad 7a = -14$

$\Rightarrow \quad a = -2$

8. Given that $y = mx + c$, find

   (a) x when $y = 3$, $m = 2$ and $c = 1$

   (b) x when $y = -3$, $m = 2$ and $c = -5$

   (c) c when $y = 4$, $m = 2$ and $x = 1$

9. If $a = \frac{1}{2}(b + c + d)$, find

   (a) b when $a = 3$, $c = 1$ and $d = \frac{1}{2}$

   (b) d when $a = 1.7$, $b = -4$ and $c = 12.5$

10. If $f = \frac{u}{2} + \frac{v}{3}$, find

    (a) u when $f = 5$ and $v = 9$

    (b) u when $f = 2$ and $v = -1$

    (c) v when $f = 0.5$ and $u = 2$

    (d) v when $f = -10$ and $u = \frac{1}{2}$

11. Given that $T = \frac{2w - 1.5}{s}$, find s when $T = 3.8$ and $w = 4.8$

In most practical situations we have to supply the formula ourselves.

The area of a rectangle is 36 cm^2 and its length is 9 cm. What is (a) its breadth (b) its perimeter ?

9 cm

36 cm^2

b cm

(a) $A = l \times b$

$36 = 9 \times b$

$\frac{36}{9} = b$

The breadth of the rectangle is 4 cm.

(b) $p = 2l + 2b$

$p = 18 + 8$

The perimeter is 26 cm.

12. In each question find the unknown dimension. Remember that units must be consistent.

(a) a cm, 22.09 cm^2, a cm

(b) 16 cm, 112 cm^2, b cm

(c) 11 mm, b cm, 4.95 cm^2

Calculate the values missing from the following table. Each question refers to a rectangle.

	Length	Width	Area	Perimeter
13.		2.6 cm	9.88 cm^2	
14.	5.4 cm		648 mm^2	
15.		18 mm		86.8 mm

Find the values missing from the following table. Each question refers to a cuboid.

	Length	Breadth	Height	Volume
16.	1 m	4 m		800 cm^3
17.	6 cm		8 mm	5760 mm^3
18.		35 mm	2 cm	28 cm^3

19. Ball-point pens cost x p each. Find a formula for C where £C is the cost of n of these pens. Use the formula to find
    (a) the cost of 50 pens at 25 p each
    (b) the number of pens bought at 30 p each if the total cost is £12.

CHANGING THE SUBJECT OF A FORMULA

The formula for finding the VAT, £T, due on a telephone bill is given by

$$T = \frac{Sr}{100}$$

where £S is the total bill excluding VAT and r% is the rate at which VAT is charged.

This is a formula for finding T, so T is called the *subject of the formula.*

Now suppose we want a formula to find the value of r; this means that we want a formula in the form $r = \dots$, i.e. a formula in which r is the subject.

We can derive this from $T = \dfrac{Sr}{100}$ by thinking of it as an equation to solve for values of r,

i.e. $$T = \frac{Sr}{100}$$

Multiply both sides by 100 $$100T = Sr$$

Divide both sides by S $$\frac{100T}{S} = r$$

i.e. $$r = \frac{100T}{S}$$

This process is called *changing the subject of a formula.*

Since changing the subject of a formula involves 'solving' the formula for the required letter, the methods used for solving linear equations apply, i.e. get rid of fractions and brackets; collect the terms containing the required letter on one side; collect all other terms on the other side; divide both sides by the number in front of the required letter.

Exercise 7g

1. Make the letter in the bracket the subject of the formula.

   (a) $c = x + y$ (x)

   (b) $V = s - t$ (s)

   (c) $r = t + u$ (u)

   (d) $D = y - x$ (x)

2. Make the letter in the bracket the subject of the formula.

   (a) $s = a + 2b$ (a)

   (b) $b = p + q + r$ (p)

   (c) $v = u + rt$ (u)

   (d) $r = 2\pi - R$ (R)

Make T the subject of the formula (a) $P = \dfrac{T}{r}$ (b) $l = 2t - 3T$

In each case we need to 'solve' the formula for T.

(a) $$P = \frac{T}{r}$$

Multiply both sides by r $$Pr = T$$

i.e. $$T = Pr$$

(b) $$l = 2t - 3T$$

Add $3T$ to both sides $$l + 3T = 2t$$

Take l from both sides $$3T = 2t - l$$

Divide both sides by 3 $$T = \frac{2t - l}{3}$$

3. Change the subject of the formula to the letter in the bracket.

   (a) $C = rt$ (t)

   (b) $S = 2t - d$ (t)

   (c) $b = \frac{1}{2}(a + c)$ (a)

   (d) $v = u - 3t$ (t)

   (e) $x = \dfrac{3y}{4}$ (y)

   (f) $A = P + \frac{1}{10}I$ (I)

   (g) $V = \dfrac{2R}{I}$ (R)

   (h) $p = q + \dfrac{r}{5}$ (r)

4. Rearrange the formula to make the letter in the bracket the subject.

   (a) $y = c - 2x$ (x)

   (b) $p = 2(q - r)$ (q)

   (c) $p = \frac{1}{4}(s + t)$ (t)

   (d) $C = 2\pi r$ (r)

   (e) $ab - d = c$ (a)

   (f) $c = a(x + b)$ (x)

   (g) $R = 3(P + Q)$ (P)

   (h) $I = \dfrac{PRT}{100}$ (R)

5. (a) Find a formula for the sum, S, of the three consecutive whole numbers n, $n+1$, $n+2$.

   (b) Change the subject of the formula found in (a) to give a formula for n, the first of three consecutive whole numbers whose sum is S.

   (c) Find the first of three consecutive whole numbers whose sum is 336.

6. (a) Find a formula for the cost, £C, of taking n children by coach to a swimming pool when the cost of the coach hire is £P and the entry charge is £S for each child.

   (b) Change the subject of the formula found in (a) to give a formula for the number of children.

   (c) Find the number of children that can be taken to the swimming pool for a total cost of £108 when the cost of coach hire is £60 and the entry charge is £1.20 per child.

7. (a) A dealer bought x pens for £y and sold them all for z pence each. His profit was £P. Give a formula for P in terms of x, y and z.

   (b) Make x the subject of the formula.

   (c) Make y the subject of the formula.

Investigations

1. In the following addition, each letter represents a different digit.

$$\begin{array}{r} \text{PAD} \\ +\text{GAD} \\ \hline \text{EGGS} \\ \hline \end{array}$$

(a) Explain why E must be 1

(b) What is the value of P ?

2. It is known that if the sum of the digits in a number is divisible by three, then the number itself is also divisible by three.

Consider the number 72 for example.

$7+2=9$ and 9 is divisible by 3, so 72 is also divisible by 3.

Start with any two digit number; if the tens digit is a and the units digit is b then the number can be written as $10a+b$.

You have to show that if $a+b$ will divide by 3 then so will $10a+b$.

If you can argue successfully that the test works for any two digit number, try extending your argument to a three digit number.

Investigate the test for divisibility by 9.

Self-Assessment 7

1. Simplify $6x - 2(y - 5x)$

2. Solve the equation
   (a) $4 - (x + 2) = 7$ (b) $5 = \frac{2}{y}$

3. Simplify $\frac{2x}{15} \div \frac{x}{5}$

4. Illustrate on a number line the values of x for which $3x - 7 < 8$

5. The length of a table is given as 2.56 m correct to three significant figures. If the length of the table is x m, write a double inequality satisfied by x and illustrate it on a number line.

6. Simplify
   (a) $(-2b) \times (-3b)$ (c) $x - x(x - 4)$
   (b) $6p \div 3p$

7. Find the range of values of x for which $5 < 2x - 1 < 15$

8. Express $\frac{x}{4} + \frac{5x}{12}$ as a single fraction.

9. Simplify
   (a) $x^9 \div x^5$ (b) $(w^{-2})^2$

10. Find a formula for W where W kg is the total mass of ballast produced when c kg of sand is mixed with d kg of gravel.

11. Find A when $r = 2$ and $h = 5$ if $A = 3rh$

12. Find f when $v = -1$ and $u = 2$ given that $f = \frac{1}{u} + \frac{1}{v}$

13. Make p the subject of the formula $r = a(p + q)$

14. The cost of one floppy disc is d pence.
    (a) Find a formula for P if £P is the cost of n of these floppy discs.
    (b) Use your formula to derive a formula for d in terms of P and n.

8 SOCIAL ARITHMETIC

PERSONAL FINANCE

We all require money to buy food and clothes, to pay the rent or the mortgage, and to settle our electricity or gas bills, etc. When we work, we can get paid in various ways.

Hourly Pay

Many people, such as production workers in a factory, get paid an hourly rate up to an agreed number of hours each week, i.e. their basic working week. Any extra hours are usually paid at a higher overtime rate. This rate may be 'time-and-a-half' or even 'double time', i.e. twice the basic rate.

Commission

Workers such as sales staff and representatives, may be paid a fairly low basic wage, plus a commission on every order they secure. The commission is usually a percentage of the value of the order.

Piece-work

Some workers are paid for the 'amount' of work they do. In a factory, for instance, a person's earnings can be based on the number of components made in a shift. This type of payment is called *piece-work*. Sometimes a worker's earnings are made up partly of a basic wage and partly of a piece-work payment.

Exercise 8a

Last week Sonia Morris worked 50 hours, 14 of which were overtime. If the basic hourly rate is \$5 and overtime is paid at time-and-a-quarter, find her gross wage for the week.

Basic working week is $(50 - 14)$ hours $=$ 36 hours

Payment for 36 hours at \$5 per hour $= \$36 \times 5$

$= \$180$

Overtime rate at time-and-a-quarter is $\$5 \times 1.25 = \$6.25$

Payment for 14 hours overtime at \$6.25 per hour is $14 \times \$6.25 = \$87.50$

Gross wage for the week is $\$180 + \$87.50$

$= \$267.50$

1. The hourly rate at ABC Electronics for a 38-hour week is £4. Overtime is paid at time-and-a-half.
   (a) Find the hourly overtime rate of pay.
   (b) One week Sally works 42 hours. Calculate her gross pay.
   (c) In the same week Ian works 45 hours. Find his gross wage.
   (d) The following week Sally works 49 hours. Find her gross wage for this week. How much more does she earn this week than last week ?
   (e) Six months later Ian's hourly rate was increased to £4.80. How much would he earn in a week when he worked 48 hours ?

2. Jim and George Tranter work in different factories. Jim is paid £5.20 per hour for a basic working week of 35 hours and receives time-and-a-half for any overtime.

   George is paid £5.50 per hour for a basic working week of 39 hours and receives double-time for any overtime.

   Find
   (a) Jim's basic weekly wage
   (b) Jim's overtime rate per hour
   (c) George's basic weekly wage
   (d) George's overtime rate per hour
   (e) who receives the greater gross pay in a week when they both work for 43 hours.

3. Amer Hussein's time-sheet for a week is shown below.

Name Amer Hussein
Works No. 63
Week No. 23

Day	AM		PM	
	in	out	in	out
Monday	8.00	12.00	12.59	4.32
Tuesday	8.02	12.01	1.00	4.30
Wednesday	8.00	12.03	1.00	4.30
Thursday	7.58	12.00	1.15	4.31
Friday	8.00	12.01	1.00	3.32

   Use this time-sheet to answer the following questions.
   (a) What time is 'clocking-on' time ?
   (b) What time does work normally end for the day ?
   (c) How long is the lunch break ?
   (d) How long should Amer work (i) each morning (ii) each afternoon ?
   (e) On which day of the week did Amer have an extended lunch break ?
   (f) How long is the basic working week if the time-sheet shows that Amer worked the required time on the Friday ?
   (g) Calculate his gross wage when he works a full week if the basic hourly rate is £4.80.

In addition to a basic weekly wage of £45, Eleanor Brett receives a commission of 1 % for selling second-hand motor cars. Calculate her gross wage for a week when she sells cars to the value of £18 000.

Basic wage is £45

Commission on £18 000 at 1 % is $\frac{1}{100} \times £18\,000$

$= £180$

Gross wage for the week is £45 + £180

$= £225$

4. Calculate the commission earned on sales of
   (a) £8000 at 5 % (b) £6500 at 2 % (c) £26 000 at $1\frac{1}{2}$ %

5. Clive Hannah receives a basic wage of \$80 per week and receives a commission of $2\frac{1}{2}$% on all sales over \$500. Find his income for a week when he sells goods to the value of \$7700.

6. Anne Lewis is paid a basic wage of \$60 per week plus a commission of $1\frac{1}{2}$% on her sales over \$2000. Find her income for a week when she sells goods to the value of \$15 300.

7. Steve Cross sells double glazing. Apart from a basic wage of \$40 he is paid commission at the following rates

Up to \$1000	none
From \$1001 to \$5000	5%
Above \$5000	3%

Calculate his income in a week when he sells double glazing to a value of \$15 500.

Vicki Jones receives a guaranteed weekly wage of \$135 plus a bonus of 20 p for every component she completes each day after the first 25. During a particular week the numbers of components she completes are:

Monday 56, Tuesday 47, Wednesday 58, Thursday 46, Friday 52.

Calculate her gross wage for the week.

Guaranteed weekly wage is \$135

Bonus payments are paid on (31 + 22 + 33 + 21 + 27), i.e. 134 components

Bonus payment is 134×20 p

= \$26.80

Gross wage for the week is \$135 + \$26.80

= \$161.80

8. The table shows the number of 24-hour electric plug timers produced by three production workers each day for a week.

	Mon	Tues	Wed	Thurs	Fri
Mrs Adcroft	35	38	34	39	42
Mr Barnard	37	40	37	44	-
Ms Curtis	34	40	42	38	38

The rate of payment is 50 p for each plug up to 20 per day and 65 p for each plug above 20 per day.

(a) How many plugs does each person produce in the week?

(b) For each person find how many plugs are paid for at
 (i) 50 p each
 (ii) 65 p each.

(c) Find each person's income for the week.

(d) On which day of the week does this group of workers produce the greatest number of plugs?

9. Colin Perry wants to earn money to buy a video-recorder costing \$216 by washing cars at 80 p a time.

(a) How many cars must he wash?

(b) How many days would it take if he washes 18 cars each day?

10. A team of factory workers assemble front brakes for Volvo cars. For each unit they produce in a day, up to 150 units, the team receives a bonus payment of 40 p; above this figure they receive 45 p. Find the bonus paid to the team for a week in which the number of units produced is

Mon	Tues	Wed	Thurs	Fri
330	375	354	387	352

11. In a second week, the factory workers described in question 10 assemble over 150 units a day. The team bonus for the week is \$683.40
How many units do they assemble during the week?

GROSS AND NET WAGES

The amount you earn in a week or a month is called your *gross wage*. Your 'take-home' pay is usually considerably less than this since there can be deductions for income tax, National Insurance contributions (NIC), pension contributions, etc. When all the agreed deductions have been subtracted from your gross wage, what remains is called your *net wage* or *take-home pay*.

National Insurance contributions and income tax, together with the employee's pension contribution, make up the greater part of any deductions (see Chapter 6).

Exercise 8b

Edna Barker earns £190 per week. She pays £7.64 in National Insurance contributions, £11.40 towards her pension fund and her income tax amounts to £31.45. Calculate her take-home pay.

Total deductions = £7.64 + £11.40 + £31.45

= £50.49

Net pay = gross pay − deductions

= £190 − £50.49

= £139.51

Copy and complete the following table, which gives details of the pay earned by several employees of a large company during one week last March.

	Employee	Gross pay	Deductions			Net pay
			NIC	Income tax	Pension fund	
1.	Munn	£125	£7.56	£15.65	£7.50	
2.	Squires	£235	£15.43	£39.78		£165.69
3.	Furnell	£183		£38.52	£10.98	£117.03
4.	Waters	£242	£21.78		£14.52	£156.98

Sheila Kelly earns £240 per week. She pays 9 % National Insurance contributions and 6 % for her pension, both calculated on her gross wage. If income tax amounts to £46.70, calculate her net wage.

HOUSEHOLD BILLS

The total cost for all three types of bill is found by adding a fixed or standing charge to the cost of the actual number of units used.

Electricity Bills

The unit of electricity is the kilowatt hour (kWh). It is the amount of electricity used in 1 hour by an appliance with a rating of 1 kilowatt. A 3 kW electric fire would use 1 unit in 20 minutes, whereas a 100 W bulb (1 kW = 1000 W) would burn for 10 hours on the same amount of electricity. The number of units used in any given quarter (of the year) is the difference between the readings at the end and beginning of that quarter.

Gas Bills

Units

The amount of gas used is measured by volume and recorded by a meter in units, each unit being 100 cubic feet. This figure is converted into cubic metres by multiplying by 2.83. Since equal volumes of gas can have different amounts of useful heat, the Gas Boards charge for their gas in the units of heat used throughout the European Community, namely kilowatt hours (kWh). The volume of gas recorded by the meter is converted into kilowatt hours using the formula

$$\text{number of kilowatt hours} = \frac{\text{number of cubic metres} \times \text{calorific value}}{3.6}$$

Tariffs

Various quarterly tariffs are available, each of them consisting of a fixed or standing charge together with a charge for each therm used.

Exercise 8c

The electricity meter readings for the Parry household at the beginning and end of the last quarter were 37 459 and 39 007. If electricity costs 7.43 p per unit and there is a standing charge of £11.75, find the cost of electricity for the quarter.

Number of units used is $39\,007 - 37\,459 = 1548$

Cost of 1548 units at 7.43 p per unit is $1548 \times 7.43\,\text{p}$

$= 11\,501.64\,\text{p}$

$= £115.02$ (to the nearest penny)

Total cost $=$ standing charge $+ £115.02$

$= £11.75 + £115.02$

$= £126.77$

Find the quarterly electricity bill for each of the following households.

	Name	Meter reading		Number of units used	Standing charge	Cost per unit
		At beginning of quarter	At end of quarter			
1.	Mr Kilner	22 926	23 792		£13.45	7.66 p
2.	Mrs Dix	35 447	36 413		£18.21	9.88 p
3.	Mr Shaw	18 937	19 784		£17.75	11.5 p

4. (a) Complete the following table which refers to meter readings in the Rehman household for a year.

Date	Meter reading	Number of units used in the specified quarter	
9 February	38 294		
8 May		First:	847
10 August		Second:	346
9 November	39 689	Third:	
10 February		Fourth:	1015

(b) Find the cost of electricity for the first quarter if the standing charge is £14.66 and electricity costs 9.66 p per unit.

(c) Find the cost of electricity for the third quarter if the standing charge is £13.88 and electricity costs 8.73 p per unit.

(d) Find the total cost of electricity for the year if the standing charge is £15.94 per quarter and the cost of electricity throughout the year is kept fixed at 9.34 p per unit.

Calculate the quarterly gas bill for each of the following households.

	Name	Number of kWh used	Standing charge	Cost of gas per kWh
5.	Mr Angel	4373	£ 9.40	1.5 p
6.	Mrs White	9622	£10.55	1.8 p
7.	Ms Chant	6656	£14.73	1.74 p
8.	Mr Deats	13 712	£17.21	1.566 p

Mrs Khan uses on average 8750 kWh each quarter (91 days). She can pay for this gas using one of two tariffs:

(a) a Credit Tariff, which charges 1.566 p per kWh plus a standing charge of 10.3 p per day

(b) the Domestic Prepayment Tariff, which charges 2.02 p per kWh for the first 1500 kilowatt hours

plus 1.566 p per kWh for additional kilowatt hours

plus a standing charge of £6

Which method of payment should she use ?

(a) If she uses the Credit Tariff

Cost of 8750 kWh at 1.566 p per kWh is 8750×1.566 p

$= £137.03$

Standing charge is 91×10.3 p

$= £9.37$

Total cost $= £146.40$

(b) If she uses the Domestic Prepayment Tariff

Cost of the first 1500 kWh at 2.02 p per kWh is 1500×2.02 p

$= £30.30$

Cost of remaining 7250 kWh at 1.566 p per kWh is 7250×1.566 p

$= £113.54$

Total cost $= £30.30 + £113.54$

$= £149.84$

Method (a) costs £3.44 less than method (b). It would therefore be cheaper to pay using the Credit Tariff.

For each of the following customers calculate which tariff is the cheaper and by how much:

	Name	Number of kWh used	Credit Tariff		Domestic Prepayment Tariff		
			Standing charge	Cost per	Standing charge	Price per kWh for initial usage	Price per kWh for further usage
9.	Eyles	12 000	£14	1.58 p	£5	1.8 p for first 1500	1.59 p
10.	Yates	15 000	£16	1.70 p	£6	2.3 p for first 1500	1.73 p
11.	Fish	11 250	£15	1.82 p	£7	2.5 p for first 1200	1.82 p

There are some accounts, such as telephone bills, that are not as straight forward as domestic gas and electricity bills. The next questions illustrate some of them.

12. This is part of a telephone bill.

Phone bill *for 081-010-2112*

Your bill is £	3.61	Call charges		
		£	1.638	for direct-dialled calls of less than 10 units:
		£	2.10	for direct-dialled calls of 10 units and over:
		£	−0.126	for calls via the operator:
minus £	−2.11	Rebate for low usage 'Low usage' means using less than 120 units or making less than £5.04 worth of calls each quarter. You made £3.61 worth this quarter which equals 86 units so we are giving you a rebate of 6.2 p for each of the 34 unused units.		
plus £	27.14	Advance charges from 1 Jan 93 to 31 Mar 93		
£	28.64	Subtotal excluding VAT		
plus £	5.01	VAT at 17.5 %		
£	**33.65**	**Total amount now due**		

(a) How much is the rebate for low usage ?

Read the paragraph below the heading 'Rebate for low usage' before answering the next three questions.

(b) How many units were used this quarter ?

(c) How much was charged for these units after the rebate ?

(d) What, in pence, does this work out at per unit used ?

(e) What percentage of the subtotal excluding VAT, are the advanced charges ?

13. This table gives information about the market for mobile telephones.

HOW MUCH WILL IT COST ?								
	Vodafone LowCall			**Cellnet Lifetime**		**Vodafone and Cellnet Business Services**		
Handsets	Motorola NEC, Nolda and Panasonic promise £250 handsets			Deal with Sony for £299 handset		£4–500		
Call charges: (per minute)	peak	off-peak	w/e	peak	all other times	week-days	all other times	Sunday
Inside M25	54 p	15 p	27 p	50 p	20 p	33 p	10 p	10 p
Outside M25	46 p	15 p	23 p	50 p	20 p	25 p	10 p	10 p
Monthly rental*	£15			£15		£25		
Connection fee*	£30			£25		£60		

All call charges, connection fees and monthly rentals are RECOMMENDED prices.

(a) What is the connection charge for Vodafone LowCall ?

(b) What is the price for a Cellnet Lifetime telephone ?

Petra calculates that, on average, in a month, she will make 20 peak time calls, 5 off-peak calls and 8 weekend calls, all inside the M25, and all lasting less than one minute.

(c) Find the total monthly charge she would expect from Vodafone LowCall.

(d) How does this compare with the expected monthly cost from Cellnet Lifetime ?

14. This is a table of the charges made for photocopies of various types.

PHOTOCOPYING CHARGES

Paper size	Type	No. of copies	Price per copy Single side	Price per copy Double sided
A4	White	Up to 10	9 p	16 p
		Over 10	8 p	15 p
		Over 20	7 p	13 p
	Coloured	Up to 10	10 p	18 p
		Over 10	9 p	16 p
		Over 20	8 p	14 p
A3	White	Up to 10	15 p	24 p
		Over 10	13 p	21 p
		Over 20	11 p	18 p

Enlargement and reduction: Cost of copy + 10 p

(a) Find the cost of
   (i) 14 white single-sided A4 copies
   (ii) 3 double-sided blue A4 copies and 1 single-side A3 reduction copy.

(b) John wants 19 white double-sided A3 copies. What is the cheapest way to obtain them ?

IMPERIAL UNITS

As Imperial units are still part of our everyday vocabulary it is sensible to be familiar with those in common use. These are given below.

Units of length: the inch (in), the foot (ft), the yard (yd), the furlong and the mile

$$1\text{ ft} = 12\text{ inches}$$

$$1\text{ yd} = 3\text{ ft}$$

$$1\text{ furlong} = 220\text{ yd}$$

$$1\text{ mile} = 1760\text{ yd}$$

1 inch

Units of area: the square yard, the acre, the square mile (occasionally the square inch and square foot)

Units of volume: cubic feet and cubic yards

Units of capacity: pints and gallons

$$1\text{ gallon} = 8\text{ pints}$$

Units of mass: the ounce (oz), the pound (lb), and the ton; occasionally the stone and the hundredweight (cwt)

$$1\text{ lb} = 16\text{ oz}$$

$$1\text{ stone} = 14\text{ lb}$$

$$1\text{ cwt} = 112\text{ lb}$$

$$1\text{ ton} = 2240\text{ lb}$$

Exercise 8d

Express the given quantity in terms of the unit in brackets.

1. 4 ft (in)
2. $\frac{1}{2}$ lb (oz)
3. 36 in (ft)
4. 15 ft (yd)
5. $6\frac{1}{2}$ stones (lb)
6. $2\frac{1}{2}$ gallons (pints)
7. 20 oz (lb)
8. 12 pints (gallons)
9. $\frac{1}{6}$ yd (in)
10. 2 sq ft (sq in)
11. $\frac{3}{4}$ lb (oz)
12. 5280 yd (miles)
13. A dripping tap fills a 1 pint milk bottle in 3 minutes. How many gallons of water drip from the tap in 24 hours?
14. A rectangular room is 12 ft wide and 15 ft long. What is the floor area in square yards?
15. A recipe asks for $\frac{1}{2}$ gill of cream. One pint is 20 fluid ounces and 1 gill is $\frac{1}{4}$ pint. How many fluid ounces of cream are required?
16. One acre is 4840 sq yd. A farmer buys a square field of 40 acres. What is the perimeter of the field?

EQUIVALENCE BETWEEN METRIC AND IMPERIAL UNITS

In supermarkets it is not unusual to find apples, say, in priced prepacked bags of 500 g or 1 kg but to find loose apples sold by the pound.

This mixture of imperial and metric units in everyday use means that we should all know rough equivalents for corresponding units.

Length: 8 km ≈ 5 miles

1 metre ≈ 39 inches (1 m is roughly 1 yd)

10 cm ≈ 4 inches

Area: 1 hectare ≈ 2.5 acres

Mass: 1 tonne ≈ 1 ton (1 tonne is slightly less than 1 ton)

1 kg ≈ 2.2 lb

100 g ≈ 3.5 oz (100 g is roughly a quarter of a lb)

Capacity: 1 litre ≈ 1.75 pints

1 gallon ≈ 4.5 litres

Exercise 8e

The use of rough equivalents cannot give exact answers, so bear this in mind when giving answers.

The cost of posting a first class letter is 24 p for a letter weighing not over 60 g and 36 p for a letter weighing not over 100 g. A letter weighs 1.5 oz on my kitchen scales. What is the value of the stamps I should put on it ?

$$3.5\text{ oz} \approx 100\text{ g}$$

$$1\text{ oz} \approx \frac{100}{3.5}\text{ g}$$

so

$$1.5\text{ oz} \approx \frac{100 \times 1.5}{3.5}\text{ g}$$

$$= 43\text{ g} \quad \text{(to the nearest g)}$$

A 24 p stamp is enough.

1. The petrol tank on my car holds 12 gallons. How many litres is this ?

2. After an excise duty increase, the price of petrol is quoted on the radio as £2.10 a gallon. How much is this per litre ?

3. An old dressmaking pattern states that the seam allowance is $\frac{5}{8}$ inch. How many millimetres is this ?

4. An old knitting pattern requires twenty 1 oz balls of double knitting yarn. How many 50 g balls are needed to make up this pattern ?

5. A farm is advertised for sale as 140 hectares. How many acres is this ?

6. Floorboards are sold in units of 30 cm. (30 cm is sometimes called a metric foot!) What length of floorboard should be bought to replace one that is 12 ft long ?

7. A recipe for jam requires 20 lb of sugar. How many 1 kg bags of sugar are needed ?

8. A particular brand of carpet is priced at £8.75 per square yard in a local shop and at £9.60 per m^2 in a department store. Which is cheaper ?

RATES OF CONSUMPTION

The rate at which quantities are consumed is usually expressed as an amount of one quantity with respect to one unit of another.

Speed is the rate at which a moving object covers distance and it is given as the distance covered in one unit of time, e.g. kilometres per hour (km/h).

Fuel consumption is the rate at which fuel is used. For vehicles it is usually expressed as distance covered on one unit quantity of fuel, e.g. miles per gallon (m.p.g.), kilometres per litre (km/ℓ). It is also often given as litres per 100 km.

When vast quantities of fuel are used the consumption is given as the fuel used in covering a unit of distance or time, e.g. gallons per mile or litres per second.

Coverage of paint, fertilizer, spray, etc., describes how the liquid covers (or should cover) area, so it is expressed in quantity of liquid per unit of area; for example, litres per square metre (ℓ/m^2) or if the quantity used is small, square metres per litre.

Pressure describes the force per unit area when one substance is pressing on another, e.g. air in a car tyre pressing on the inside of the tyre. It can be measured in N/m^2 or lb/in^2.

To change from, say, m.p.g. to km/ℓ, we need to think first about changing one unit, and then about changing the other; m.p.g. is equivalent to $\frac{\text{miles}}{\text{gallons}}$ so we *multiply* by the number of kilometres in a mile and *divide* by the number of litres in a gallon.

Exercise 8f

Express a speed of 60 m.p.h. in m/s using $8\,\text{km} \approx 5$ miles.

$$\begin{aligned} 60\text{ m.p.h.} &= \frac{60 \times 8}{5}\text{ km/h} \\ &= \frac{60 \times 8 \times 1000}{5}\text{ m/h} \\ &= \frac{60 \times 8 \times 1000}{5 \times 60 \times 60}\text{ m/s} \\ &= \frac{80}{3}\text{ m/s} = 26.7\text{ m/s} \quad (3\text{ s.f.}) \end{aligned}$$

i.e. $60\text{ m.p.h.} \approx 27\text{ m/s}$.

In questions 1 to 6 give answers correct to 3 s.f. when possible. When that degree of accuracy is not possible, give to 2 s.f.

1. Express 40 km/h in m.p.h.

2. Express 70 m.p.h. in km/h.

3. Express 500 litres/second in litres/hour.

4. Express 50 m.p.g. in (a) kilometres/gallon.
   (b) km/litre, using your answer to (a).

5. Express 50 m^2/litre in (a) sq ft/litre.
   (b) sq ft/gallon, using your answer to (a).

6. Express 4 kg/cm^2 in (a) lb/cm^2.
   (b) lb/sq. in., using the answer to (a).

In questions 7 to 13 use your own judgement, with regard to the context of the question, as to the accuracy required for the answer.

7. The average petrol consumption of a car is 35 m.p.g. The driver puts 25 litres of petrol into the tank. How far can the car be expected to travel ?

8. To cover an area of 30 m^2, 2.5 litres of paint are needed.
   Give the coverage in
   (a) ℓ/m^2
   (b) litres per square yard.

9. A petrol pump can deliver petrol at the rate of $\frac{1}{2}$ litre/second. How long does it take to fill a tank that holds 20 gallons ?

10. A car manual states that the front tyre pressures should be 3.5 kg/cm^2, and the pressure gauge at the local garage measures pressure in lb/sq in. What should the gauge read to give the correct pressure ?

11. A firm uses packaging cartons that are cubes of side 2 ft. The full cartons are lifted into containers at the rate of 5 cartons per minute. How long does it take to fill a container measuring 3.5 m by 5 m by 10 m ?

12. A bottle of liquid insecticide contains 500 mℓ. The instructions state that it should be diluted in the ratio 2.5 mℓ of insecticide to 2 litres of water and the diluted mixture applied at the rate of 250 mℓ/m^2. What area will the contents of the bottle treat ?

13. The density of gold is given as 19.3 g/cm^3. Using 1 oz = 28.3 g and 1 inch = 2.54 cm, find the density of gold in oz/in^3.

TIME AND TIMETABLES

There are two systems for giving the time of day.

One system uses two periods of twelve hours. The first starts at midnight and continues to noon; times within this period are referred to as 'a.m.'. The second period goes from noon to midnight and times are referred to as 'p.m.'.

The other system has one period of twenty-four hours, starting at midnight and continuing through to the next midnight.

Thus 1 hour after noon is 1 p.m. in the first system and 1300 hours (read as 'thirteen hundred hours') or 13.00 in the second system.

Most clocks and watches with dials use the a.m./p.m. system whereas many digital clocks and watches, and timetables, use the 24-hour system.

Exercise 8g

1. Give the equivalent times on a 24-hour clock.
   (a) 8.30 a.m.
   (b) 8.30 p.m.
   (c) 5.42 a.m.
   (d) 2.36 p.m.

2. Give the equivalent time on a 12-hour clock, using a.m. or p.m.
   (a) 03.00
   (b) 19.42
   (c) 08.51
   (d) 22.43

Find the elapsed time between 9.20 a.m. and 3.52 p.m.

Method 1
Elapsed time from 9.20 a.m. to noon is

$$12\text{ h} - 9\text{ h } 20\text{ min} = 2\text{ h } 40\text{ min}$$

Elapsed time from noon to 3.52 p.m. is 3 h 52 min.

$\therefore$ elapsed time from 9.20 a.m. to 3.52 p.m. is

$$2\text{ h } 40\text{ min} + 3\text{ h } 52\text{ min} = 6\text{ h } 32\text{ min}$$

Method 2
9.20 a.m. = 09.20 and 3.52 p.m. = 15.52
Elapsed time is from 09.20 to 15.52

i.e. 6 h 32 min

(Remember that 15.52 means 15 hours 52 minutes.)

3. Find the elapsed time between
   (a) 03.20 and 15.08 hours on the same day
   (b) 11.30 a.m. and 5.42 p.m. on the same day
   (c) 20.35 and 09.40 on the next day
   (d) 10.40 a.m. and 7.52 a.m. on the next day.

Here is part of a timetable for trains from Paddington to Bristol and Weston-super-Mare.

Paddington*	*d*	**00 50**	**06 35**	**06 55**	**07 25**	**07 35**	**08 00**	**08 05**	**08 35**	**09 00**	**09 05**	**09 35**
Slough	*d*	___	**06 48**	**07 08**	**07 38**	**07 48**	___	___	**08 48**	___	___	**09 48**
Reading C*	*d*	___	**07 03**	**07 23**	**07 53**	**08 03**	**08 24**	**08 30**	**09 03**	**09 24**	**09 30**	**10 03**
Didcot	*d*	___	**07 17**	**07 34**	**08 06**	**08 16**	___	___	**09 16**	___	___	**10 16**
Swindon	*a*	**02 17**	**07 37**	**07 54**	**08 27**	**08 37**	___	___	**09 37**	___	___	**10 37**
Chippenham	*a*	___	**07 51**	___	**08 40**	**08 50**	___	___	**09 50**	___	___	___
Bath Spa	*a*	___	**08 09**	___	**08 52**	**09 02**	___	**09 16**	**10 02**	___	**10 16**	___
Bristol Parkway	*a*	___	___	**08 21**	___	___	**09 12**	___	___	**10 12**	___	**11 01**
Bristol Temple Meads	*a*	___	**08 25**	___	**09 07**	**09 17**	___	**09 31**	**10 17**	___	**10 31**	___
Nailsea & Backwell	*a*	___	___	___	09 25	___	___	10 11	___	___	___	___
Yatton	*a*	___	___	___	09 32	___	___	10 18	___	___	___	___
Weston-super-Mare	*a*	___	___	___	09 41	___	___	10 32	**10 38**	___	11 12	___

Paddington*	*d*	**10 05**	**10 35**	**11 00**	**11 05**	**11 35**	**12 05**	**13 00**	**13 05**	**13 35**	**13 35**	**14 00**
Slough	*d*	___	**10 48**	___	___	**11 48**	___	12 25	___	**13 48**	**13 48**	___
Reading C*	*d*	___	**10 03**	**11 24**	**11 30**	**12 03**	___	**13 24**	**13 30**	**14 03**	**14 03**	___
Didcot	*d*	___	**11 16**	___	___	**12 16**	___	___	___	**14 16**	**14 16**	___
Swindon	*a*	**10 55**	**11 37**	___	___	**12 37**	**12 55**	___	**14 00**	**14 37**	**14 37**	**14 49**
Chippenham	*a*	___	**11 50**	___	___	___	**13 08**	___	___	___	**14 50**	___
Bath Spa	*a*	**11 17**	**12 02**	___	**12 16**	___	**13 20**	___	**14 22**	___	**15 02**	___
Bristol Parkway	*a*	___	___	**12 12**	___	**13 01**	___	**14 12**	___	___	___	**15 14**
Bristol Temple Meads	*a*	**11 32**	**12 17**	___	**12 31**	___	**13 35**	___	**14 37**	___	**15 17**	___
Nailsea & Backwell	*a*	12 11	___	___	13 21	___	14 21	___	15 22	___	16 26	___
Yatton	*a*	12 18	___	___	13 28	___	14 28	___	15 29	___	16 33	___
Weston-super-Mare	*a*	12 34	**12 38**	___	13 42	___	14 42	___	15 42	___	16 45	___

Heavy type indicates through trains and light type indicates connecting trains.

If I catch the 11.05 from Paddington, to go to Weston-super-Mare, do I have to change trains, and if so where? How long should the journey take? (Use the timetable above.)

The 11.05 is in heavy type to Bristol Temple Meads and in light type beyond there, so I have to change trains at Bristol Temple Meads.

Arrival time in Weston-super-Mare is 13.42, so the journey should take 13 h 42 min − 11 h 5 min

i.e. 2 h 37 min

Use the timetable above to answer questions 4 to 9.

4. What is the earliest through train from Paddington to Weston-super-Mare, and how long does it take?

5. Mrs Angelon has an appointment in Swindon at 2.00 p.m. She wants to travel by train from Slough and has to arrive at Swindon at least 15 minutes before 2.00 p.m. What is the time of the latest train she can catch? How long will she have in Swindon before her appointment if the train is on time?

6. Which train from Paddington gives the quickest journey to Weston-super-Mare? Is this a through train?

7. How long do the fastest trains take to go from Paddington to Bristol Temple Meads?

8. How long do the fastest trains take to go from Paddington to Bristol Parkway?

9. Mr Black wanted to go to Bath Spa but mistakenly caught the 09.00 from Paddington instead of the 09.05.
   (a) If Mr Black realises his mistake soon enough he can change trains and still arrive in Bath Spa when he originally intended. Where does he have to make the change and how long should he have to wait there to catch the correct train?
   (b) If Mr Black does not realise that he is on the wrong train soon enough to make the change in (a), where does he next have the opportunity to get off the train?

POSTAGE AND OTHER STEP FUNCTIONS

The table below gives the postal rates (March 1992) for inland letters.

Weight not over	First class	Second class	Weight not over	First class	Second class
60 g	24 p	18 p	500 g	£ 1.20	93 p
100 g	36 p	28 p	600 g	£ 1.50	£ 1.15
150 g	45 p	34 p	700 g	£ 1.80	£ 1.35
200 g	54 p	41 p	750 g	£ 1.95	£ 1.40
250 g	64 p	49 p	800 g	£ 2.05	Not
300 g	74 p	58 p	900 g	£ 2.25	admissible
350 g	85 p	66 p	1000 g	£ 2.40	over
400 g	96 p	75 p	Each extra 250 g or		750 g
450 g	£ 1.08	84 p	part thereof 60 p		

Considering just first class post, we see that the cost goes up in steps, depending on the weight. For example, a letter weighing up to 60 g costs 24 p, but when the weight exceeds 60 g the cost jumps to 36 p, and so on.

This graph, showing cost against weight, illustrates the 'step' nature of the postal rates.

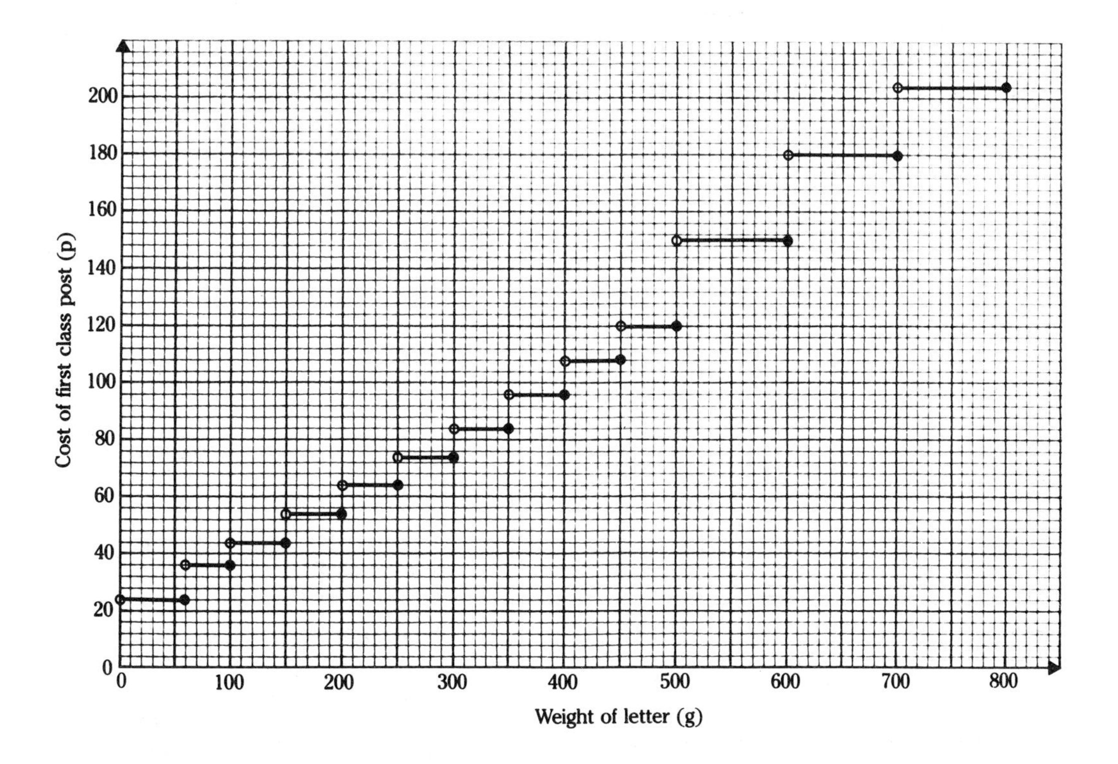

Notice that the 'open' circle at the left-hand end of each line indicates that the point is not included. The closed circle at the right-hand end of each line indicates that the point is included. Many of the charges for services have this 'step' structure. Other examples are parking charges and telephone charges.

Exercise 8h

Use the table for postal rates on page 151 to find the cost of sending a packet weighing 1.26 kg by

(a) first class letter post (b) second class letter post.

(a) The cost of the first 1 kg (1000 g) is £2.40
The cost of the remaining 0.26 kg or 260 g is £1.20
The total cost is £3.60

(b) Since the package weighs more than 750 g it cannot be sent by second class letter post.

Use the table on page 151 to answer questions 1 to 5.

1. Find the cost of first class letter post for a package weighing
   (a) 280 g (b) 102 g (c) 396 g (d) 1.44 kg (e) 4.2 kg

2. Find the cost of second class letter post for a letter weighing
   (a) 75 g (b) 250 g (c) 745 g (d) 55 g

3. Find the total cost of sending five 80 g letters and three 540 g packages by first class letter post.

4. Find the total cost of sending twelve 72 g letters by first class letter post and six 645 g packages by second class letter post.

5. What is the maximum number of packages weighing 275 g that Nicky Woodman can send by first class letter post if the total bill must be less than £10 ?

6. Draw a graph to show the cost of second class post against weight, similar to that for first class post on the page opposite.

7. A multistorey car-park in a city centre has the following charge tariff:

up to 1 hour	80 p
up to 2 hours	120 p
up to 3 hours	165 p
up to 4 hours	220 p
up to 5 hours	340 p
up to 6 hours	480 p

each additional hour or part thereof 140 p.

How much does it cost to park for

(a) $1\frac{1}{2}$ hours (b) $2\frac{1}{4}$ hours (c) $4\frac{3}{4}$ hours (d) 8 hours ?

8. Photocopies of particular pages are charged at the following rates:

Number of copies	Cost per copy
1–20	10 p
21–100	8 p
101 upwards	5 p

(a) Find the total cost of 8 copies of one page and 48 copies of a second page.

(b) Together with the copies in (a), how many copies of a third page can be made if the money spent is to be less than £7 ?

(c) If 18 copies are required what is the cheapest way to do it ?

The table below gives the charge rates for inland dialled telephone calls. Calls are charged in whole units of 4.2 p, e.g. a local call of $3\frac{1}{2}$ minutes (i.e. 3.5×60 seconds) at the standard rate of 80 seconds to a unit takes $\frac{3.5 \times 60}{80.00} = 2.625$ units; so the charge is for 3 units, which is 3×4.2 p, i.e. 12.6 p.

Time allowed in seconds for each unit

	Peak rate	Standard rate	Cheap rate
Local calls	57.50	80.00	220.00
National calls up to 56.4 km outside the local call area	27.00	36.15	80.80
National calls over 56.4 km connected over low cost routes	23.95	32.00	50.35
National calls over 56.4 km and calls to Channel Islands	19.20	25.60	37.95
Calls to mobile telephones	7.61	7.61	11.40

9. Find the cost of a local telephone call lasting 18 minutes at
   (a) peak rate (b) standard rate (c) cheap rate.

10. Find the cost of a call (not low cost) of 85 km lasting $4\frac{1}{2}$ minutes at
    (a) peak rate (b) standard rate (c) cheap rate.

11. Find the cost of a mobile telephone call lasting 4 minutes 34 seconds at the standard rate.

12. How much more would it cost me to make an 8 minute 22 second telephone call to London, which is a low cost route and is 120 km away, at 10 a.m. (peak rate) than at 10 p.m. (cheap rate) ?

INSURANCE

Although all property and people are at risk, relatively few suffer loss. Insurance works by spreading the cost of loss among all who are insured.

Some forms of insurance are legal requirements. For example, any driver using a car or motor cycle on a public road must, by law, be insured for third party risks. Third party risk covers damage caused to other people or their property. Other forms of insurance are sensible precautions against possible loss or damage.

The payment for insurance is called the *premium*. The premium may be given in a form such as £2 per £100 insured value, or the premium may be quoted as a total amount for a particular insurance. Premiums are usually payable yearly.

Some insurances give a discount if the insured person bears part of the risk. For example a householder may agree to pay the first £50 of any loss. This has the misleading name of 'an *excess*'.

Car insurances usually offer discounts for several consecutive years in which no claims have been made. This form of discount is called a *no claims bonus*.

Exercise 8i

The premium for insuring a building worth £86 000 is £4.30 per £1000 value. Find the premium to be paid.

Premium is £4.30 × 86

= £369.80

The table gives the premiums for insuring buildings and contents as quoted by Northern Star Insurance Co.

	Buildings/ £1000	Contents/ £1000
Area A	£1.80	£ 6.50
Area B	£2.10	£ 8.00
Area C	£2.20	£10.80
Area D	£2.80	£12.90

Use this table to answer questions 1 to 7.

1. Find the premium for insuring a house worth £150 000 (building only) in area D.

2. Find the premium for insuring a house worth £80 000 and its contents worth £9000 in area B.

3. Mr and Mrs Hadinsky live in Area A and value the contents of their house at £12 000. This includes a piano worth £850, a ring worth £700 and a watch worth £350. One condition of the insurance cover is that all items whose value is greater than 5% of the total insured must be listed.
   (a) Find the premium to be paid.
   (b) State the items that have to be listed.

4. The Scott family move from a house worth £70 000 in area A, to a house worth £120 000 in area C. What is the increase in the premium for insuring their house?

5. The premium paid for insuring the contents of Mr and Mrs Coles home is £320. If they live in area B, what is the value of the contents of their house?

6. A house in area D is valued at £140 000 and its contents at £50 000.
   (a) What is the premium for insuring house and contents?
   (b) If an excess of £100 is accepted on the building insurance a discount of 4% is given and an excess of £50 on the contents earns a discount of 5% on the contents premium. What is the revised total premium, to the nearest pound?

7. A householder living in area C has a house valued at £75 000 with contents worth £8000. The discount on the buildings premium is 2% for an excess of £500 and on the contents the discount is 5% for an excess of £200. Find the premium for insuring house and contents if
   (a) no excess is agreed
   (b) both excesses are agreed.

8. (a) The insurance premium for comprehensive cover on a small family car in Liverpool is £350. Daniel Kirby wants to insure himself to drive such a car but finds that because he is under 25 years of age, there is a 50% surcharge on the premium. What premium does he have to pay?
   (b) Three years later, when Daniel is over 25 years old, he no longer has to pay the surcharge and because he has made no claims on his insurance, finds that he is entitled to a 40% no claims bonus. However, the basic premium has increased to £420. Find the premium he has to pay now.
   (c) Six years later the basic premium is £490 but Daniel pays only £196. What percentage is his no claims bonus now?

Insurance is only one part of the cost of running a car. In addition there are the annual road fund licence, repairs and maintenance, petrol and, lastly, payment for the vehicle itself. Some people also add in the depreciation of the value of the car.

9. Maya Liang wants to take out a loan to buy herself a second-hand car and decides to estimate what it will cost her for a year. The repayments on the loan are £94 a calendar month. Maya has been quoted £250 premium for insurance. The road tax is £125 and she estimates that she will do 10 000 miles at an average of 40 m.p.g. Petrol is £2.00 a gallon. Maya also estimates that she will need one service costing about £100.

   How much does her estimate for 1 year's motoring come to?
   How much is this a week?

10. Derek James buys a new car costing £10 000 and decides to work out the cost of running the car for its first year. He includes repayments of £350 per month, depreciation of 25% of the purchase price, £500 for insurance, £125 road tax, a service charge of £200 and £14 a week for petrol.

    How much does it cost him each week to run his car?

MONEY

In many respects money is similar to any other commodity. Foreign currencies can be bought and sold in much the same way that cars can be bought and sold. Money can be lent and borrowed in a manner similar to hiring out or renting, say, a scaffold tower.

Exchange Rates

When we shop abroad, prices quoted in the local currency often give us little idea of value so we tend to convert prices into sterling (£). To do this we need to know the exchange rate, i.e. how many units of the local currency are equivalent to one pound sterling.

For example, using an exchange rate of 10.10 French francs (Ff) to £1

means that $\pounds 100 = 100 \times 10.10\,\text{Ff} = 1010\,\text{Ff}$

and that $101\,\text{Ff} = \pounds\frac{101}{10.1} = \pounds 10$

A reasonable idea of the cost is given by rounding off the exchange rate to make the arithmetic easy, but skill in mental arithmetic is useful!

For example, a price of 250 Ff could be approximately converted into sterling by rounding $10.10\,\text{Ff} \equiv \pounds 1$ to $10\,\text{Ff} \equiv \pounds 1$.

Then $250\,\text{Ff} \approx \pounds\frac{250}{10} = \pounds 25$ to the nearest pound

A more accurate conversion can be made using a conversion graph or a calculator.

Exercise 8j

If £1 is equivalent to 2195 Italian lire (L), estimate the sterling equivalent of

(a) 10 000 L (b) 500 L.

(a) Approximating the exchange rate to 2000 L = £1 makes the arithmetic easier.

$$10\,000\,\text{L} \approx £\frac{10\,000}{2\,000} = £5$$

(b)

$$500\,\text{L} \approx £\frac{500}{2000} = £\frac{1}{4} = 25\,\text{p}$$

The following table gives the equivalent of £1 in various currencies.

£	French franc (Ff)	Spanish peseta (pta)	Italian lira (L)	Irish punt (pt)
1	10.04	182	2205	1.20

Use this table (a) to estimate

(b) to calculate (to the nearest penny), the sterling equivalent of

1. 200 Ff
2. 60 Ff
3. 40 pta
4. 3810 pta
5. 900 L
6. 250 pt
7. 3000 L
8. 5354 Ff
9. 450 L

Use the table given above to find how many pesetas are equivalent to 1 Ff.

From the table 10.04 Ff = 182 pta

$$\therefore\quad 1\,\text{Ff} = \frac{182}{10.04}\,\text{pta}$$

$$= 18.13\,\text{pta}$$

Use the table given at the beginning of the exercise to make the following conversions. Use your own judgement on how accurately your answers should be given.

10. 100 pta to Ff
11. 100 L to pta
12. 800 pta to L
13. 350 pta to Ff
14. 8.50 pt to Ff
15. 550 pta to pt

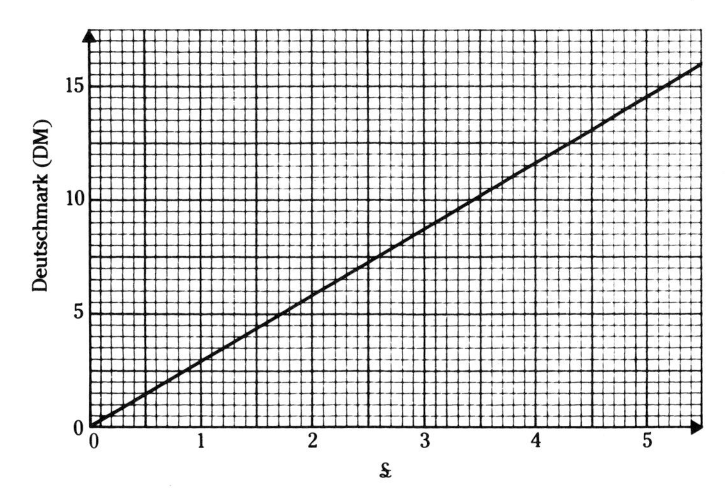

Use this conversion graph to find

16. £3 in DM
17. £2.50 in DM
18. £1.40 in DM
19. 9 DM in £
20. 8 DM in £
21. 2.50 DM in £

SOME MEDIA MISUSES

Sometimes when items appearing in the press or on radio or television contain an element of mathematics, insufficient care is taken to use the correct terminology. What is worse is that there are cases of deliberate misrepresentation in an attempt to make an argument appear to be stronger. It is therefore vital that we do not accept everything we read or hear without carefully considering its true meaning and implications, its accuracy and its honesty.

Here are two examples of careless terminology:

(a) In mathematics the word 'plus' is used only when collecting two quantities together, one on either side of 'plus'. However, advertisements often include phrases such as 'Send in your order today and you will have the chance to win £1000. PLUS Steve Stardust will present the cheque to the winner.' (To express this correctly, although in a less eye-catching way, we could say 'Send in your order today and you will have the chance to win £1000 plus the chance to have it presented by Steve Stardust'.)
This particular misuse is both grammatically and mathematically wrong. Grammar, however, does tend to change with time and no doubt 'plus' will continue to be used in this way. This does *not* mean, though, that the mathematical definition of 'plus' can be changed, so take care.

(b) We often hear a news item saying, for instance, that 'the rate of inflation has fallen by one percentage point'. What is meant is that 'the rate of inflation has fallen by one per cent'. The misuse of 'percentage point' can be very confusing, especially when a decimal point is involved, e.g. if the fall in the rate of inflation is from 4.7 % to 3.7 %.

Keep your eyes and ears open, and see if you can spot more examples of misuse – there are a good many.

Misconceptions

The wrong interpretation of information given in the media can often arise, either from misleading presentation or from misuse of words or from lack of care in reading and considering the information.

Therefore we will now consider the importance of careful reading and thoughtful weighing up of news items with a mathematical content.

Take, for example, the statement 'the rate of inflation is falling'. Some people think that this means that prices are coming down, but it doesn't. Inflation means rising prices; the rate of inflation measures how fast they are rising. If the *rate* goes down it simply means that prices do not rise so quickly - but they still keep on rising.

There are areas where conflicting figures are given to represent what is apparently the same thing. In wage negotiations, for example, the pay of a 'typical employee' might vary considerably; a union official might choose the basic wage of the lowest-paid after all possible deductions, whereas the employer might quote the earnings (including overtime) of a higher-paid employee before any deductions are made. Clearly neither of these is typical and anyone reading only one version would be misled.

These are merely examples of a much wider problem and there are many pitfalls for the unwary in pseudo-mathematical reporting. The best way to avoid any of these is to have a background of precise language, cautious, careful reading and a strong objection to believing everything you hear or read - even in textbooks.

Investigation

For most holiday and business travel purposes it is reasonable to work with a single exchange rate. However, when changing sterling into foreign currency before going on holiday and then changing what is left of that currency back into sterling on return, we find that we have to deal with two exchange rates. High street banks offering exchange display their rates under two headings: 'Bank Buys' and 'Bank Sells', (exchange rates vary slightly from bank to bank in much the same way that the cost of a packet of tea varies from shop to shop). A typical display of exchange rates looks like this.

	Bank buys	Bank sells
Belgian franc	52.40	48.00
French franc	8.55	7.88
Deutschmark	2.53	2.33
Italian lira	2385	2220
Spanish peseta	191	178
Swiss franc	2.335	2.155
US dollar	1.543	1.417

This means that if we are exchanging French francs and sterling,
the bank will sell us French francs at 7.88 Ff to £1
the bank will buy French francs from us at 8.55 Ff to £1

In addition, banks usually charge a commission on each transaction; typically this is 1% of the sterling value.

(a) Miss Peters was told on Monday that she would have to go to Germany the following week to attend a meeting. She decided to change £100 into Deutschmarks for her own use. On Friday of that week she was told that the meeting had been cancelled and she would no longer be required to go. She returned to the bank and changed the Deutschmarks back into sterling.

The bank charged 1 % commission on each transaction. Use the table opposite to find how much Miss Peters lost on each transaction.

(b) Repeat part (a) assuming that Miss Peters was to go to Spain instead of Germany.

(c) Mr Jones wants to rent a flat in Spain for one month. The rent is 200 000 pta and has to be paid to the owners in Spain in pesetas. Collect up-to-date information and investigate the various ways in which this can be done and what each method costs in sterling.

Self-Assessment 8

1. Which is the greater pay packet, and by how much ?
   (a) The payment for 46 hours, including 9 hours overtime, if the basic hourly rate is £4.80 and time-and-a-half is paid for overtime.
   (b) A basic wage of £50 plus commission of $1\frac{1}{2}$ % on sales of £18 000, if the commission is not paid on the first £2500.

2. Phil Strand's telephone account shows that he has used 847 units at 4.80 p per unit. If the rental charge is £21.45 and value added tax at $17\frac{1}{2}$ % is added to the total, find the payment due.

3. (a) The price of petrol is £2.20 a gallon. How much is this a litre ?
   (b) Express 40 m/s in (i) km/h (ii) m.p.h.

4. A petrol pump can deliver petrol at the rate of $\frac{1}{3}$ litre per second. How long does it take to fill a tank that holds 12 gallons ?
   (1 litre ≈ 1.75 pints)

5. The Budds live in a house valued at £95 000 and have contents valued at £26 000. The Makegood Insurance Co. charge £2.40 per thousand pounds for insuring buildings and £11.20 per thousand for insuring contents. The discount on the building premium is $2\frac{1}{2}$ % for an excess of £500 and on the contents the discount is 5 % for an excess of £250. Find the total premium for insuring house and contents if
   (a) no excess is agreed
   (b) both excesses are agreed.

9 QUADRILATERALS, POLYGONS AND TESSELLATIONS

SPECIAL QUADRILATERALS

In Chapter 3 we saw that a general quadrilateral has four sides and the sum of its interior angles is 360°; unless told otherwise, no sides are equal and no angles are equal. However there are several special cases.

Square

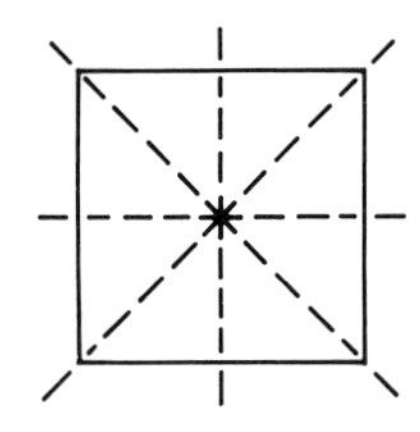

In a square, all four sides are equal and all four angles are right angles. A square has four lines of symmetry.

Rectangle

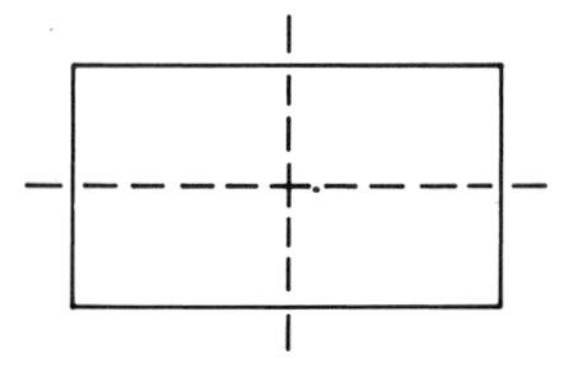

In a rectangle, the opposite sides are equal and all four angles are right angles. A rectangle has two lines of symmetry.

Parallelogram

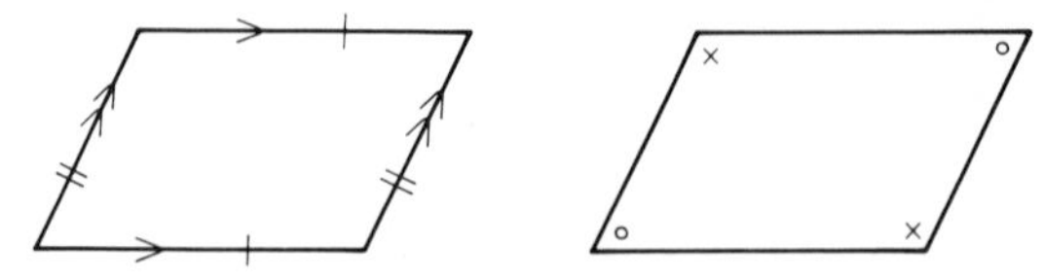

A parallelogram has opposite sides that are equal and parallel, and opposite angles that are equal.

A parallelogram has no lines of symmetry but it does have rotational symmetry of order 2.

Rhombus

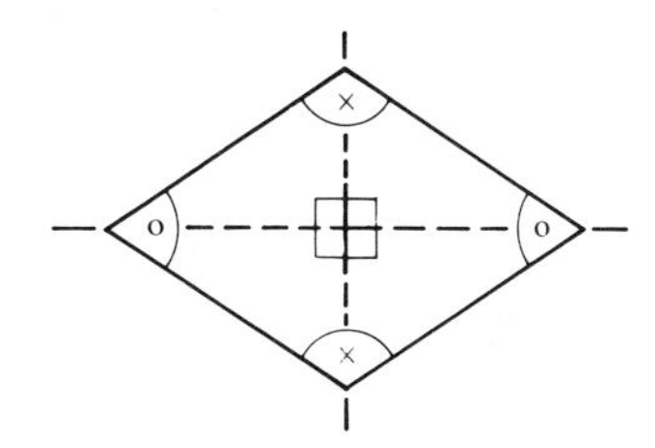

In a rhombus the opposite angles are equal, the opposite sides are parallel and all four sides are the same length.

A rhombus has two lines of symmetry (the diagonals).

Kite

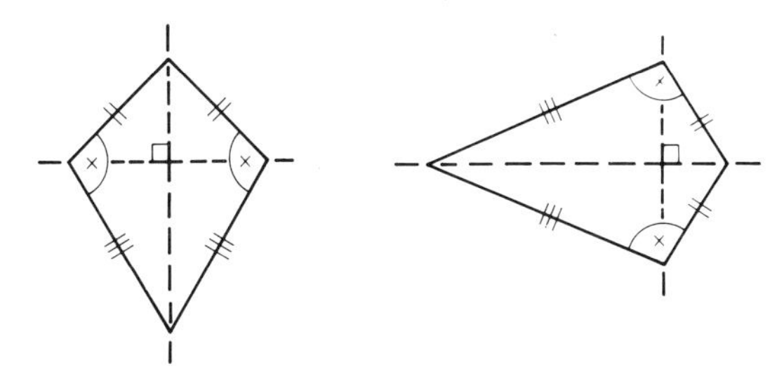

A kite has one pair of opposite angles equal and two pairs of adjacent sides equal.

A kite has one line of symmetry. It has no rotational symmetry.

Trapezium

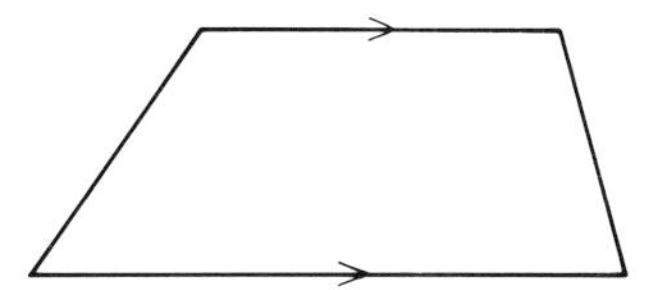

A trapezium has one pair of opposite sides parallel. Usually it has no line of symmetry.

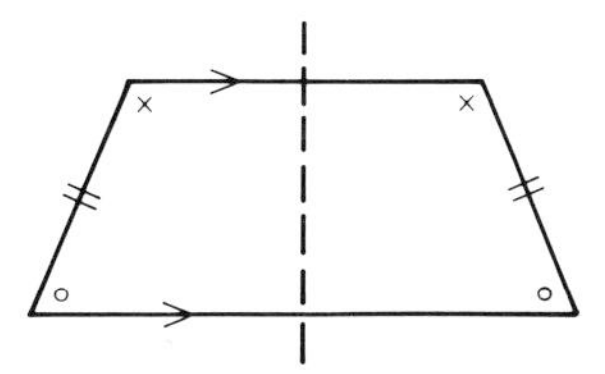

However, in the special case when the two sloping sides are the same length there is one line of symmetry. This is called an isosceles trapezium. Its non-parallel sides are equal and two pairs of adjacent angles are equal.

Exercise 9a

In each question from 1 to 6

(a) name the type of quadrilateral (some may be *general*)

(b) find the size of each marked angle.

1.

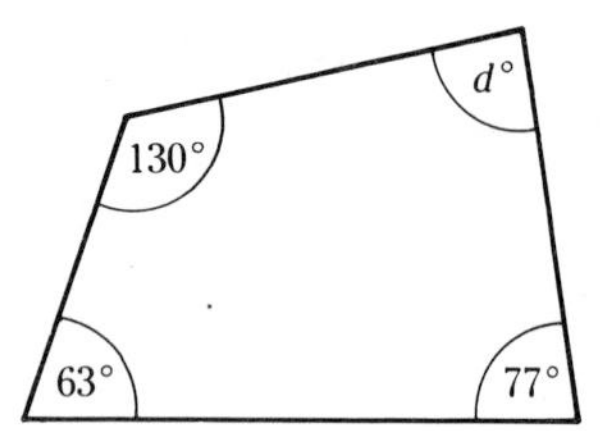

2.

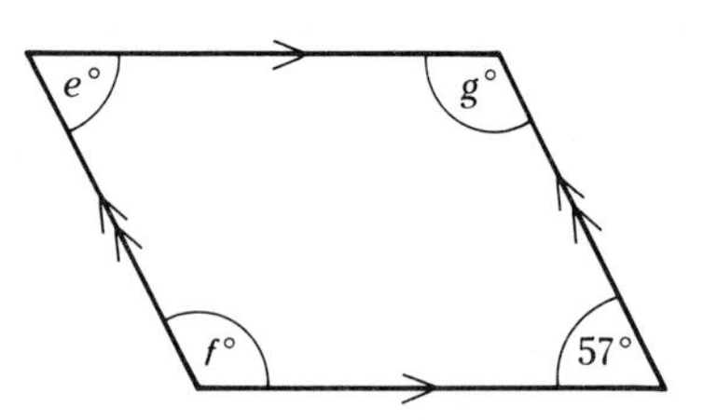

3.

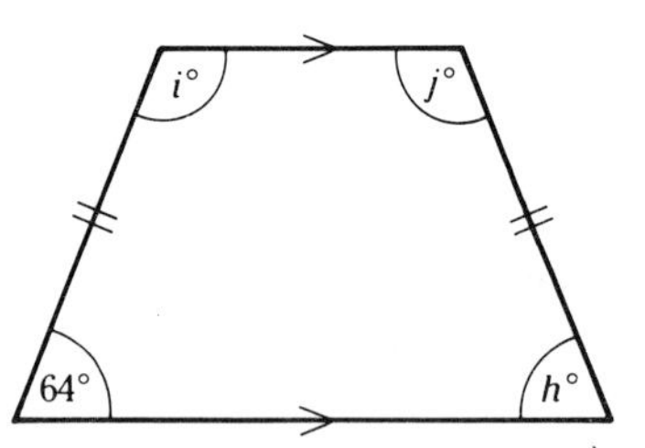

4.

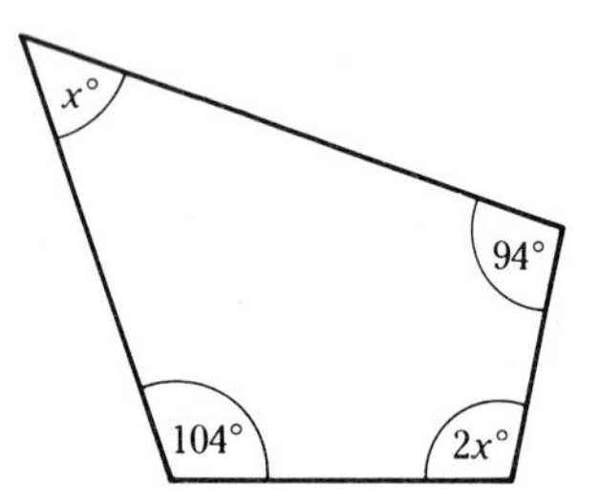

5.

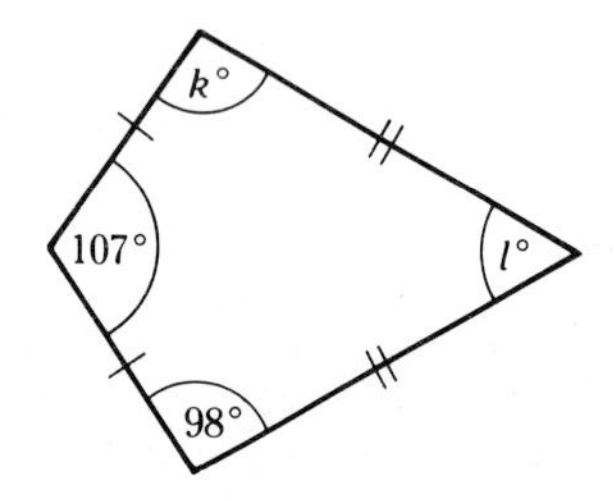

6.

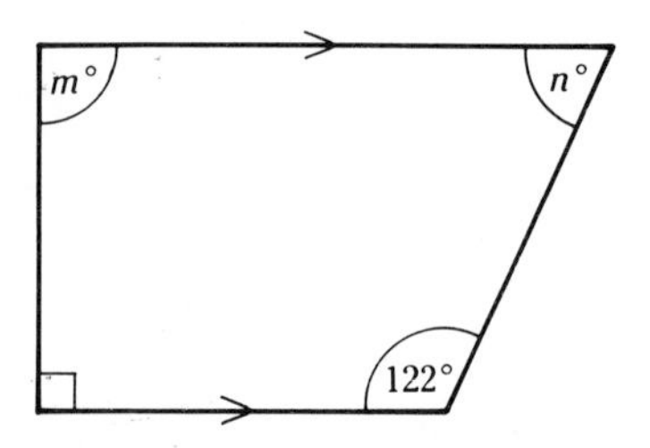

In questions 7 to 12 some of the diagrams contain more than one quadrilateral. Name each quadrilateral and find the size of each marked angle.

7.

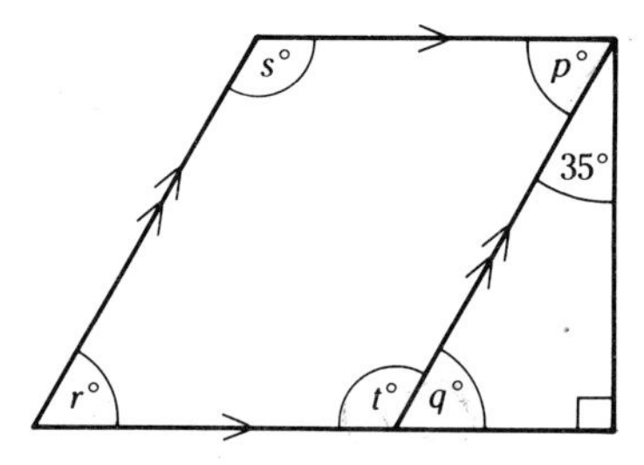

8.

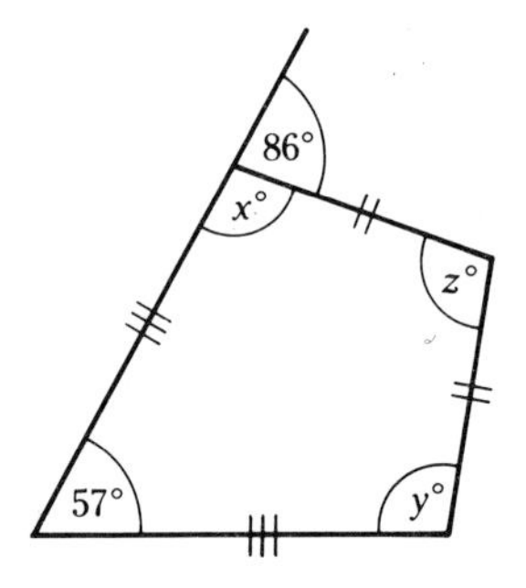

9.

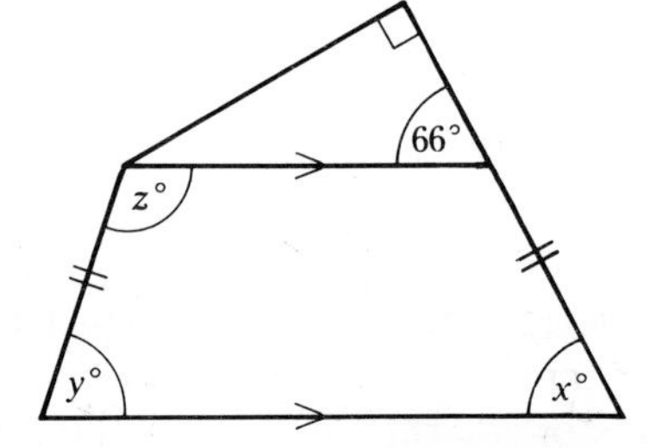

10.

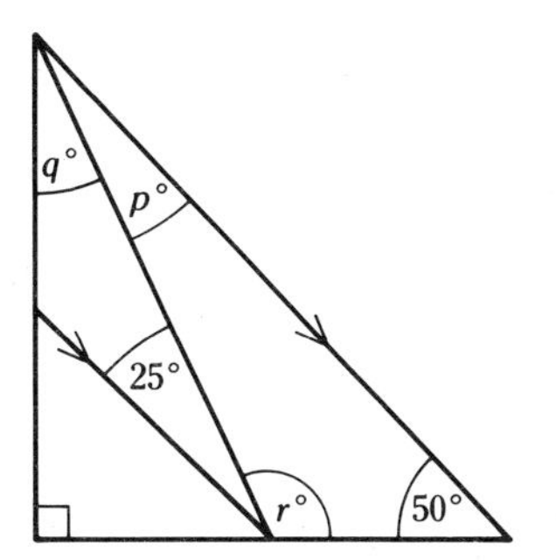

11.

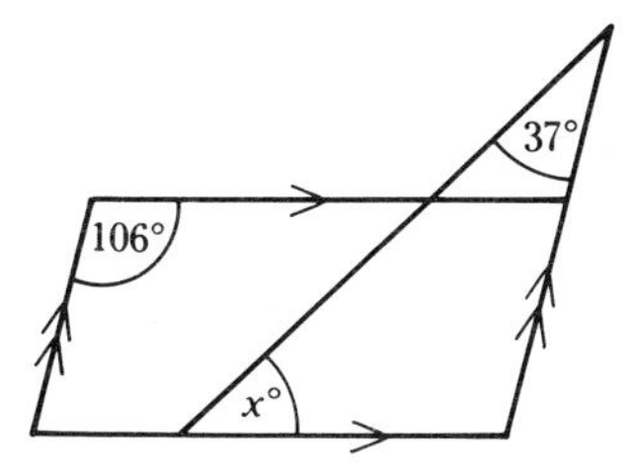

12.

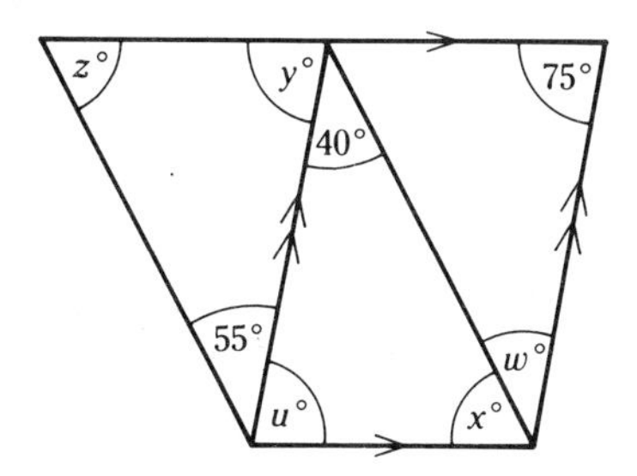

13.

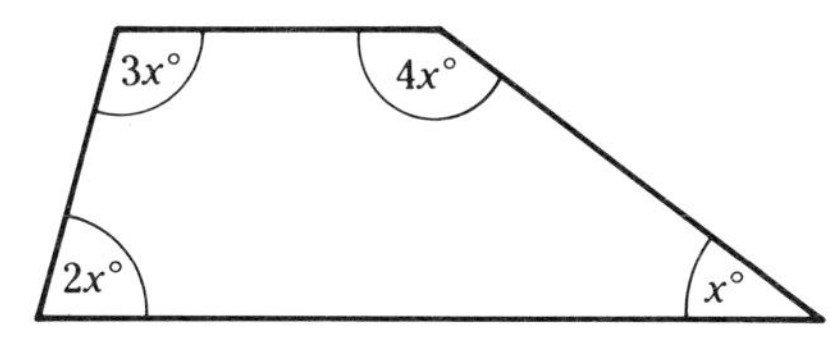

(a) Find the value of x.

(b) Prove that ABCD is a trapezium.

14.

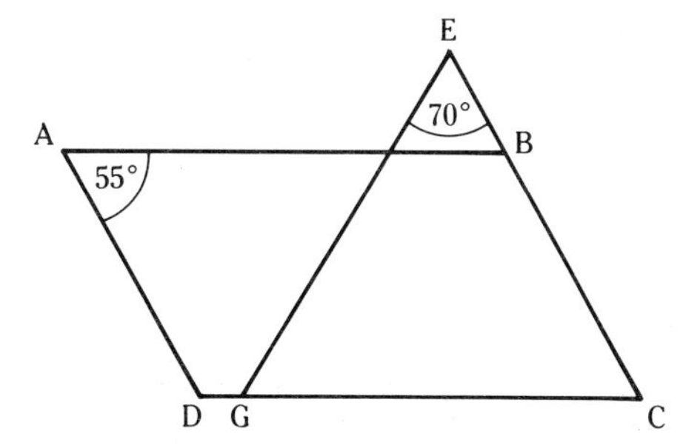

ABCD is a parallelogram. Find the size of

(a) $D\hat{C}B$ (b) $E\hat{G}C$

What sort of triangle is triangle GEC ?

15.

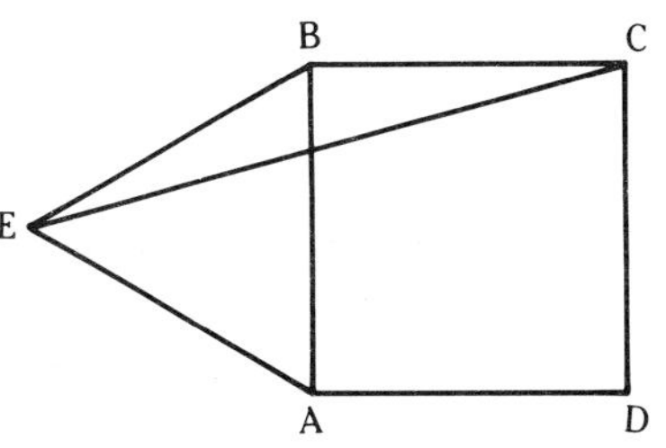

ABCD is a square and ABE is an equilateral triangle. Find

(a) $B\hat{A}E$ (c) $B\hat{E}C$

(b) $E\hat{B}C$ (d) $E\hat{C}D$.

16. Four rods are placed, in the given order, to make a quadrilateral. Name the special quadrilaterals that can be made if the lengths of the rods are

(a) 5 cm, 10 cm, 5 cm, 10 cm

(b) 5 cm, 5 cm, 10 cm, 10 cm

(c) 5 cm, 5 cm, 5 cm, 10 cm

(d) 5 cm, 5 cm, 5 cm, 5 cm.

17. ABCD is a trapezium with AD parallel to BC. $A\hat{B}C = 58°$ and $B\hat{C}D = 64°$.
BA and CD are produced (i.e. extended) to meet at E.

(a) Calculate the angles in ABCD and $\triangle$ADE.

(b) What type of triangle is $\triangle$ADE ?

(c) Draw a line through D parallel to AB to meet BC at F. What type of quadrilaterals are EBFD and ADFB ?

(d) Join AF. If it is possible, calculate the angles of $\triangle$ABF. If it is not possible, give a reason.

18. PQRS is a parallelogram. $S\hat{P}Q = 72°$ and $R\hat{P}Q = 48°$. RP is produced to T so that PT = PQ and SP is produced to meet QT at U.

(a) Find the angles of $\triangle$s QPT and UPT.

(b) What type of triangle is $\triangle$UPT ?

(c) What type of quadrilateral is PUQR ?

(d) What type of triangle is $\triangle$RQT ?

POLYGONS

A polygon is a plane (flat) figure bounded by straight lines.

When all the vertices (corners) of a polygon point outward, the polygon is convex, but if one or more of the vertices point inward, the polygon is concave.

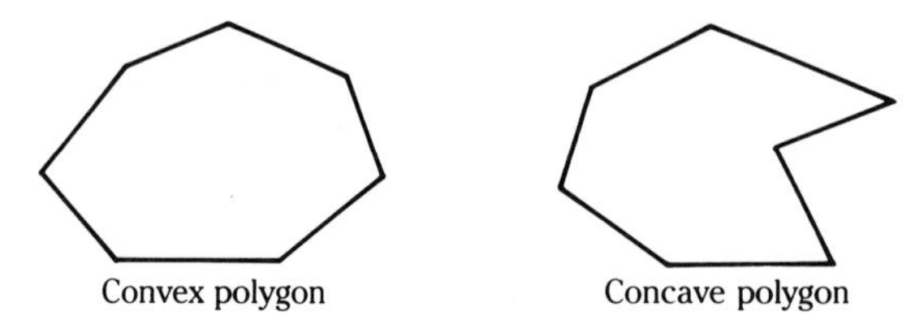

Convex polygon　　Concave polygon

Some polygons have names that you already know. They are included in the table given below.

Number of sides	3	4	5	6	8
Name of polygon	triangle	quadrilateral	pentagon	hexagon	octagon

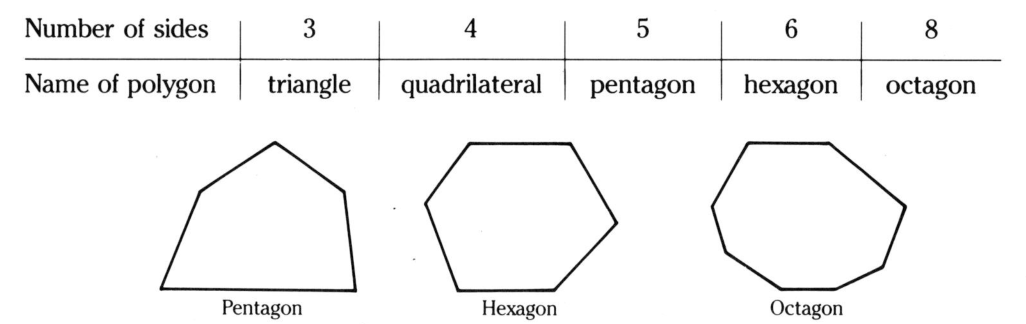

Pentagon　　Hexagon　　Octagon

The work that follows applies to convex polygons only.

Exterior Angles

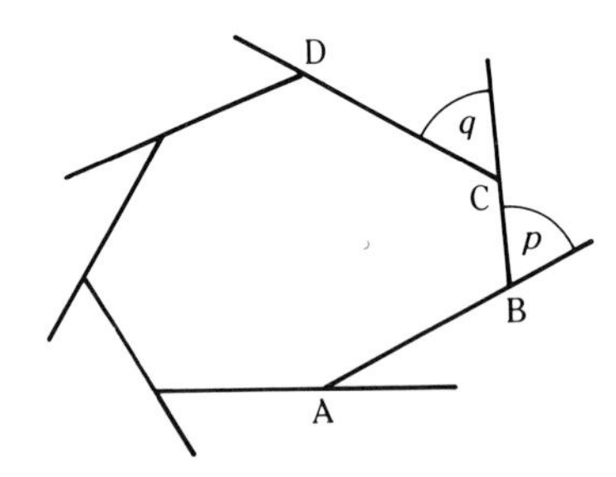

Consider walking around this polygon. Start at A and walk along AB. At B turn through an angle p and walk along BC to C. At C turn through an angle q and walk along CD to D . . . and so on. By the time you get back to A and face along the direction AB you will have turned through one complete revolution, i.e.

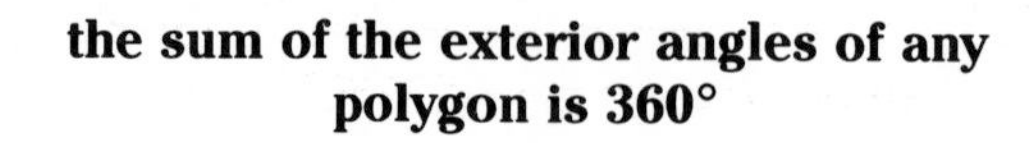

the sum of the exterior angles of any polygon is 360°

Exercise 9b

Find the angle marked $x°$

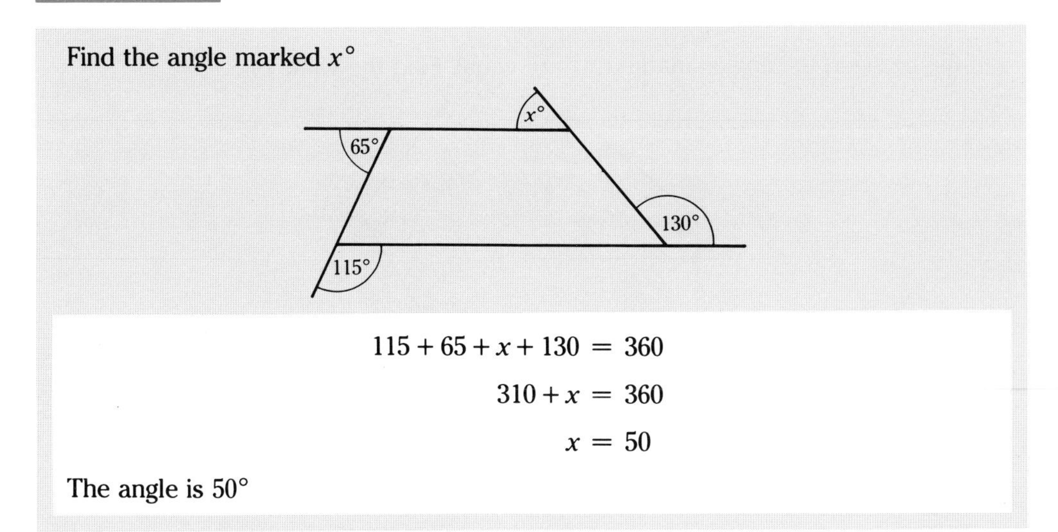

$$115 + 65 + x + 130 = 360$$
$$310 + x = 360$$
$$x = 50$$

The angle is 50°

In each question find the angle marked $x°$

1.

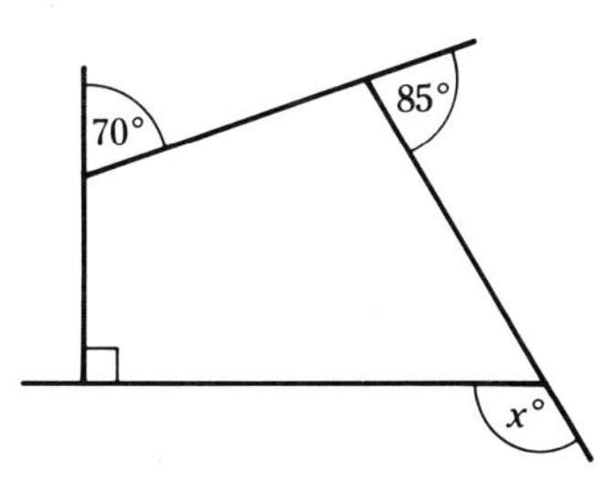

2.

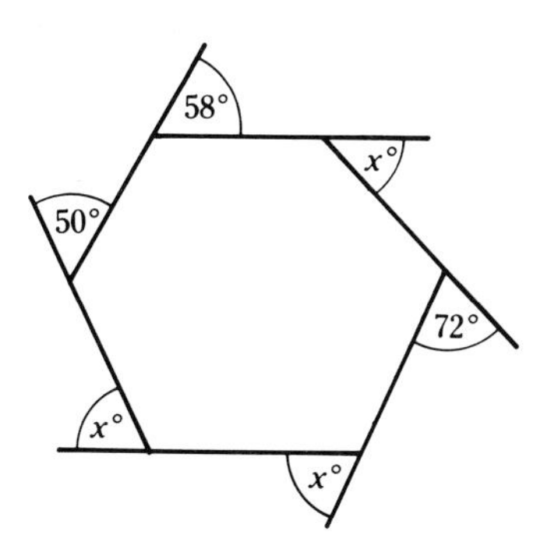

3.

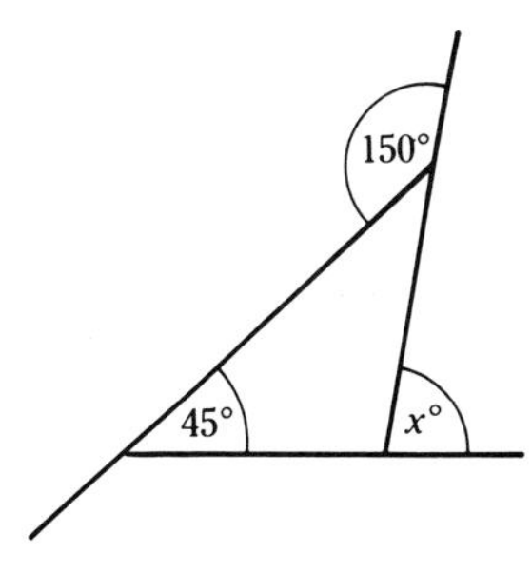

4.

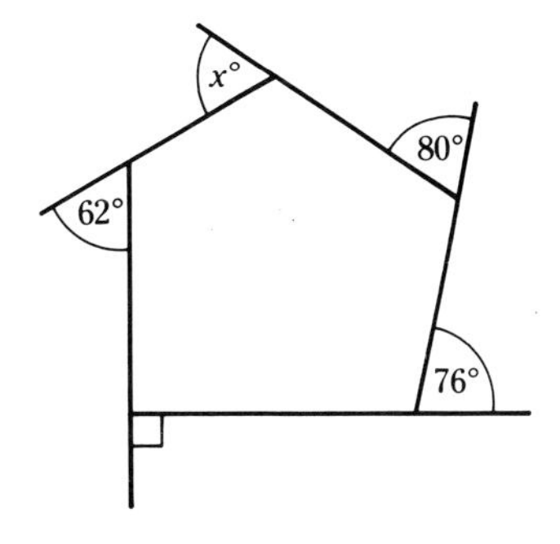

Interior Angles

At any vertex of a convex polygon the sum of the interior and the exterior angles is 180°. If the polygon has n sides, the sum of all the interior and exterior angles is $n \times 180°$, i.e. $180n°$.

Since the sum of all the exterior angles is 360° the sum of all the interior angles is $180n° - 360°$, which can be written $(n-2)180°$.

Exercise 9c

In the hexagon the angles marked $x°$ are equal. Find the value of x.

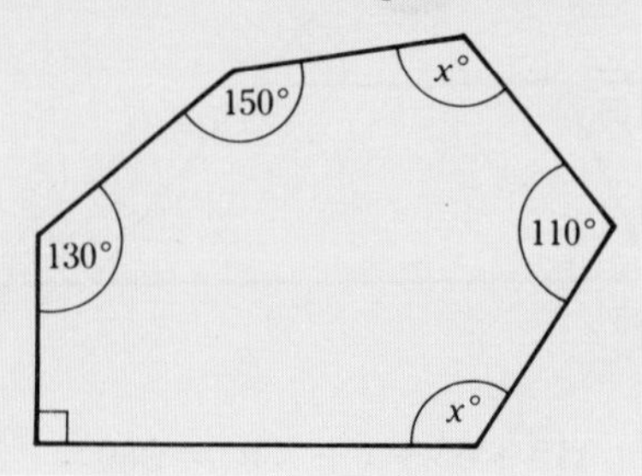

$$\begin{aligned}\text{The sum of the interior angles is } 180° \times 6 - 360° &= 720° \\ 90 + x + 110 + x + 150 + 130 &= 720 \\ 480 + 2x &= 720 \\ 2x &= 240 \\ x &= 120\end{aligned}$$

In each question find the angle(s) marked $x°$.

1.

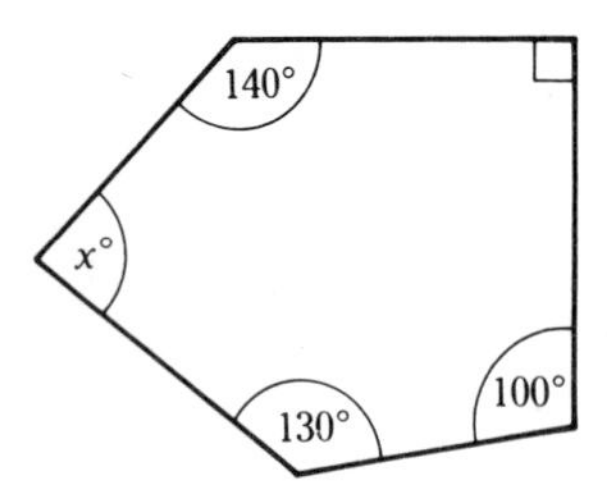

2.

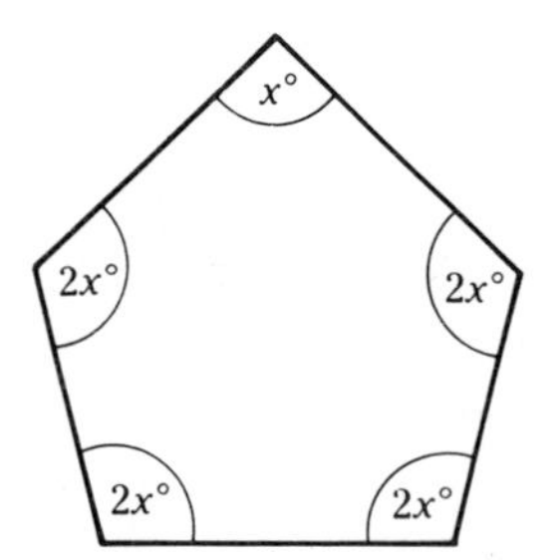

3.

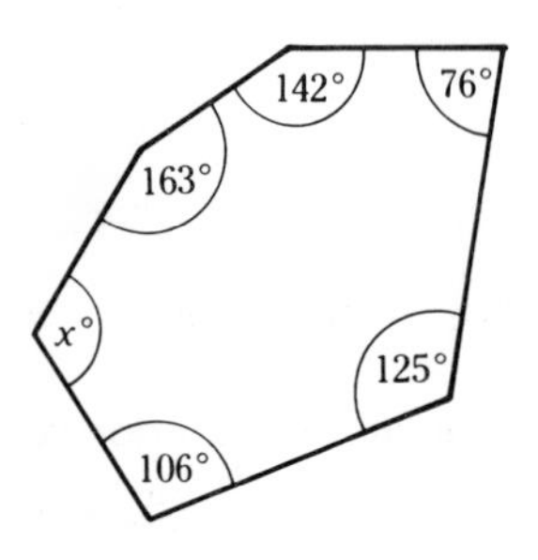

4.

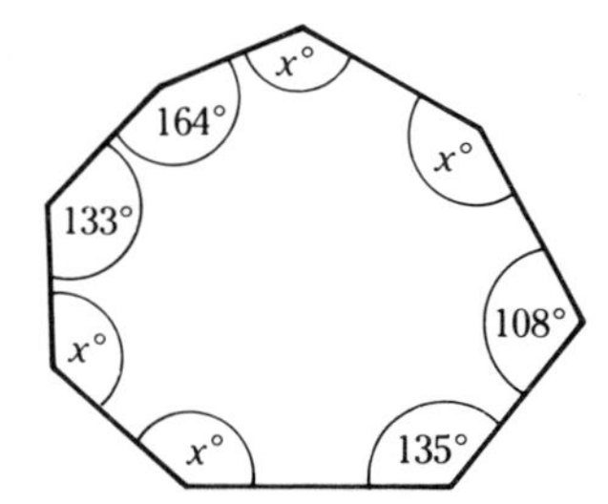

5. (a) Draw a large pentagon (to fill half a sheet of A4 paper). Measure its interior angles and add your results.

   (b) *Calculate* the sum of the interior angles of a pentagon.

   (c) Do your answers to (a) and (b) agree ? If they differ by 1 or 2 degrees, explain why this might be.

6. Repeat question 5 for polygons with

   (a) 6 sides

   (b) 8 sides.

REGULAR POLYGONS

A polygon is regular when its sides are all the same length and its angles are all the same size.

All the polygons shown below are regular.

Square

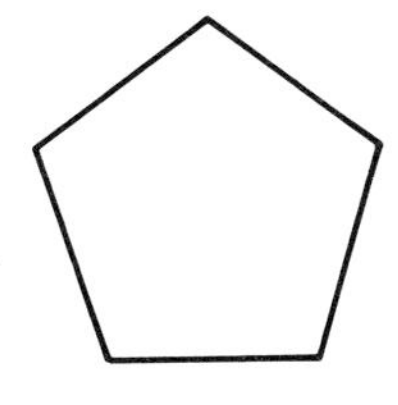

Pentagon

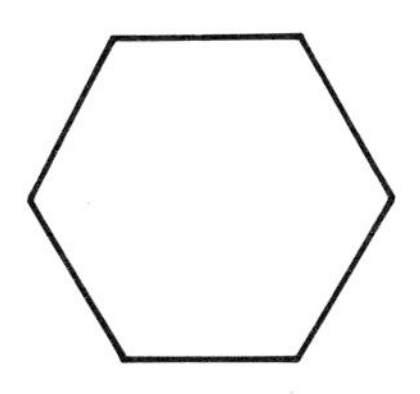

Hexagon

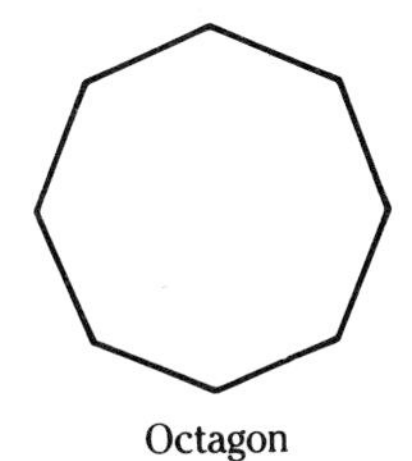

Octagon

Exercise 9d

Find the angles of a regular octagon.

An octagon is a polygon with 8 sides.
To find an exterior angle of a regular polygon we divide 360° by the number of sides, since all exterior angles are equal.

An exterior angle of a regular octagon is

$$360^\circ \div 8 = 45^\circ$$

An interior angle and an exterior angle together make 180°

An interior angle of a regular octagon is

$$180^\circ - 45^\circ = 135^\circ$$

1. Find the size of each exterior angle of a regular polygon with
   (a) 5 sides (d) 10 sides
   (b) 6 sides (e) 18 sides
   (c) 7 sides (f) 20 sides.

2. Find the size of each interior angle of a regular polygon with
   (a) 9 sides (c) 24 sides
   (b) 12 sides (d) 36 sides.

3. How many sides has a regular polygon if each exterior angle is
   (a) 30° (b) 20° (c) 24° ?

4. How many sides has a regular polygon if each interior angle is
   (a) 120° (b) 156° (c) 162° ?

5. Is it possible for the exterior angle of a regular polygon to be
   (a) 40° (c) 60°
   (b) 50° (d) 80° ?

6. Is it possible for the interior angle of a regular polygon to be
   (a) 90° (c) 170°
   (b) 135° (d) 180° ?

The remaining questions are mixed problems on polygons.

In questions 7 to 10 find the angle marked $x°$.

7.

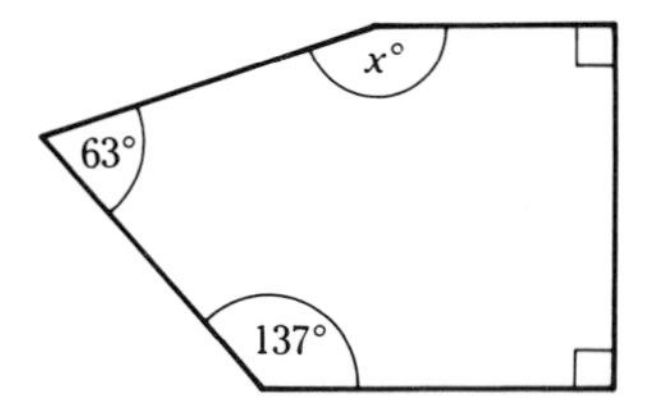

8.

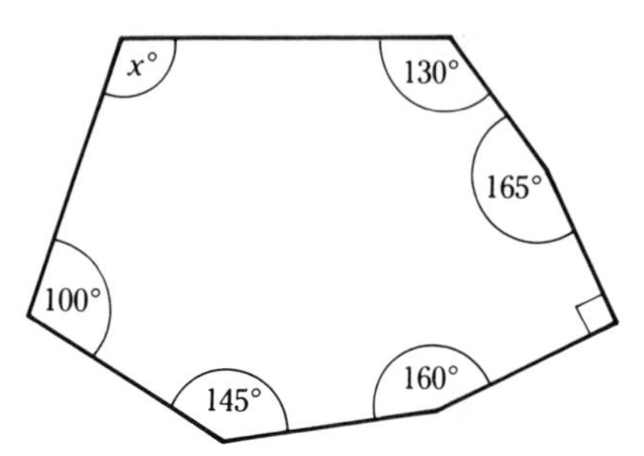

9.

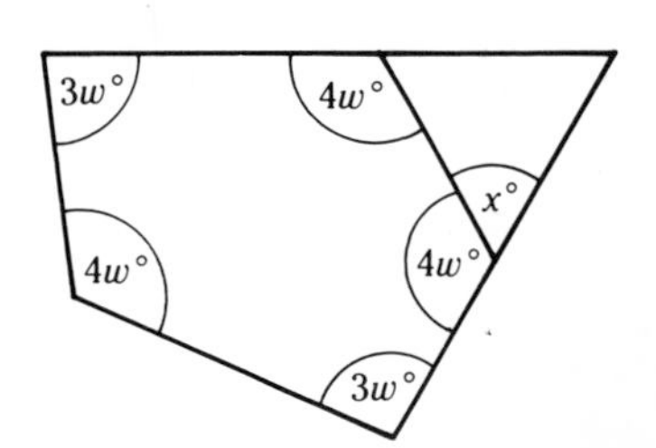

10.

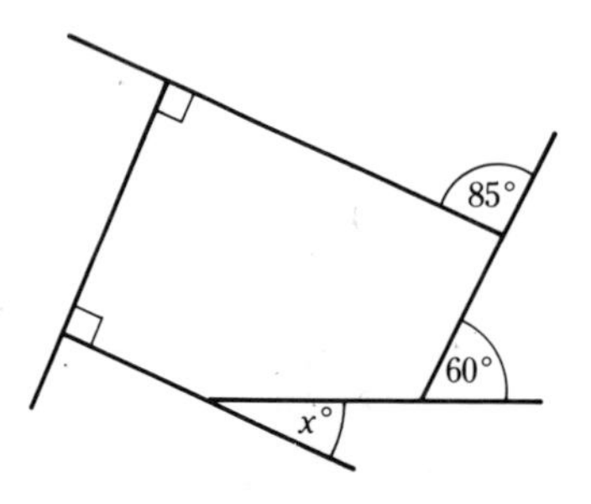

In questions 11 to 14 find the value of x.

11.

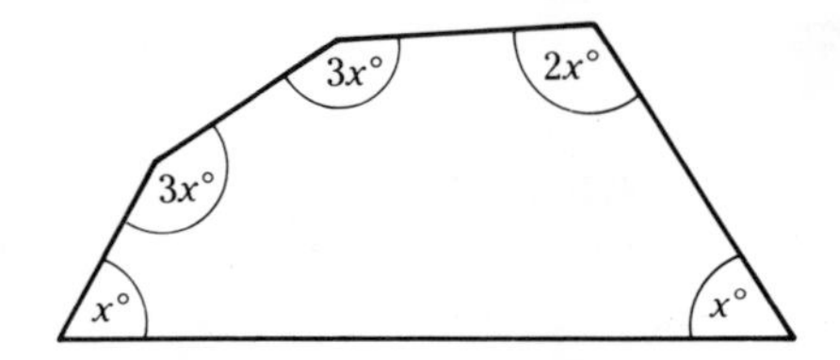

12.

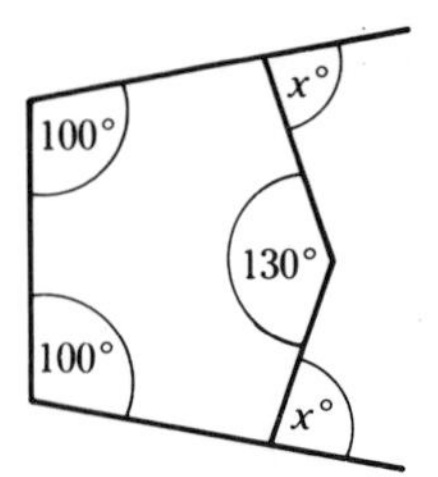

13.

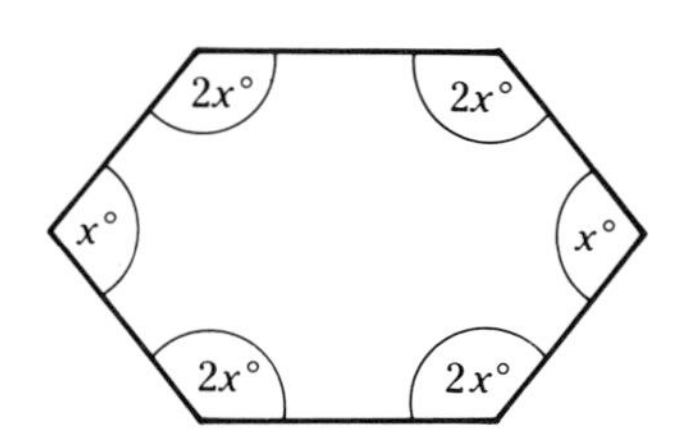

14.

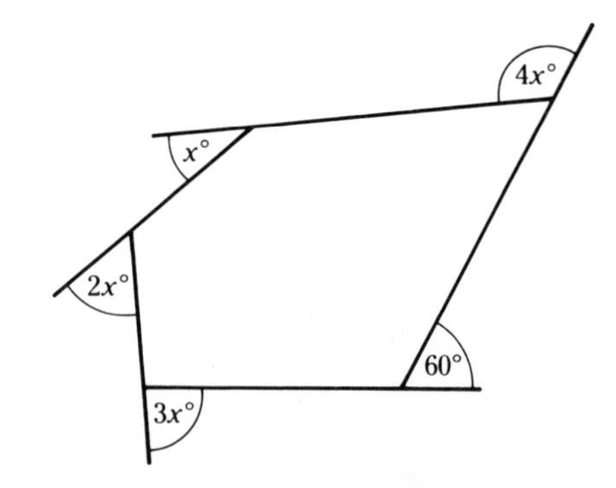

15. ABCD is a regular pentagon. BC and ED are produced (i.e. extended) and meet in F. Find each of the angles in triangle CDF.

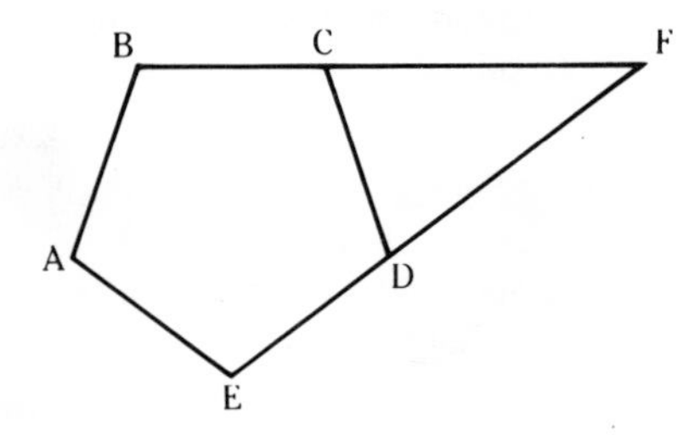

16. (a) For a regular hexagon, find the size of (i) an exterior angle, (ii) an interior angle.

(b) ABCDEF is a regular hexagon. Find the size of (i) $F\hat{A}E$ (ii) $E\hat{A}B$ (iii) $B\hat{E}F$ (iv) $A\hat{E}B$.

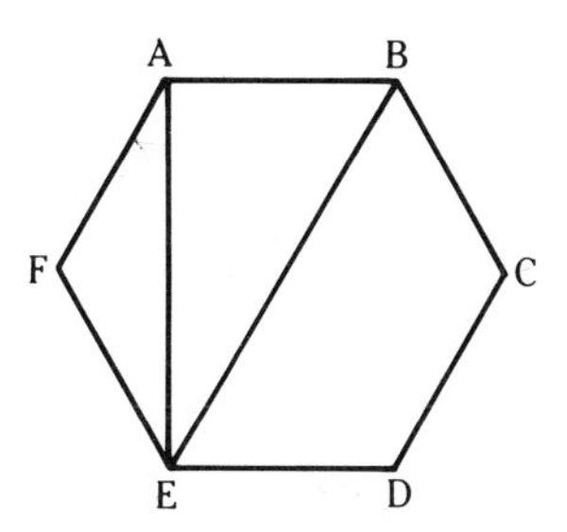

17. The diagram shows a hexagon with just two lines of symmetry. These are marked PQ and RS. Find the values of x, y and z.

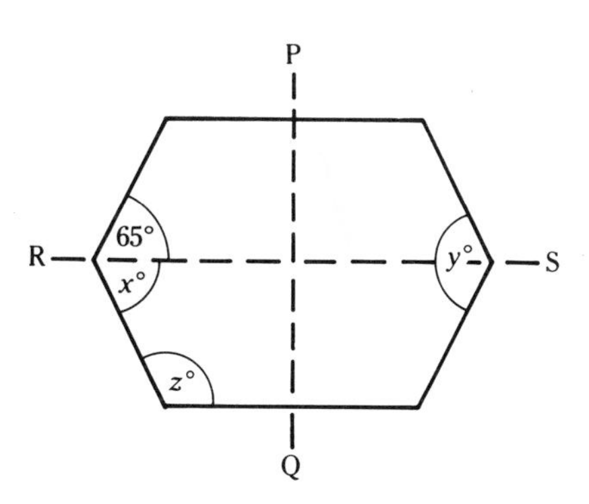

18. ABCDEFGH is a regular octagon and O is equidistant from all the vertices. Find the angles in triangle AOB.

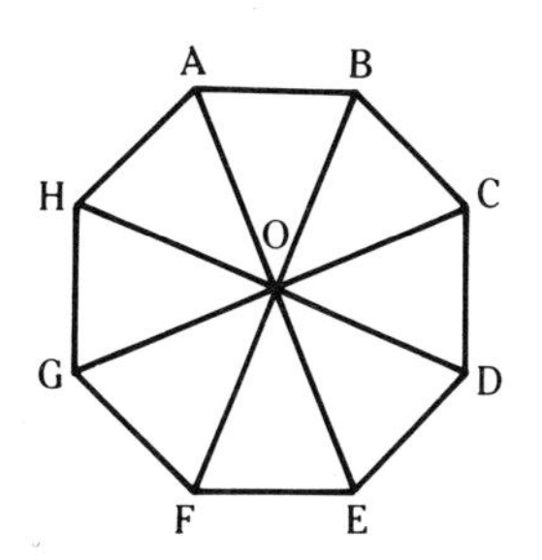

In questions 19 to 21, each polygon is regular. Give answers correct to 1 decimal place where necessary.

19.

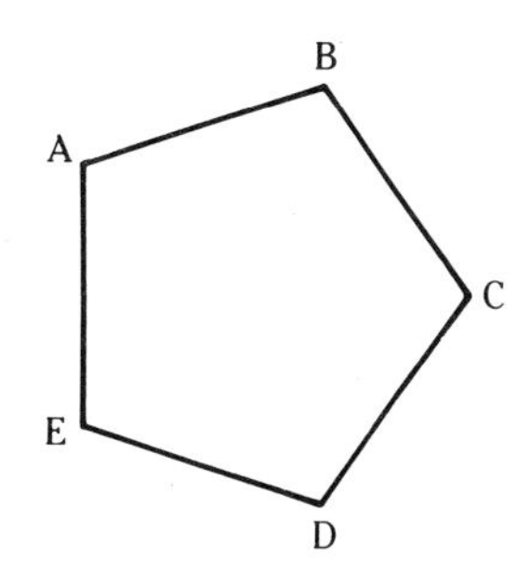

Find

(a) $A\hat{B}E$ (b) $D\hat{B}E$.

20.

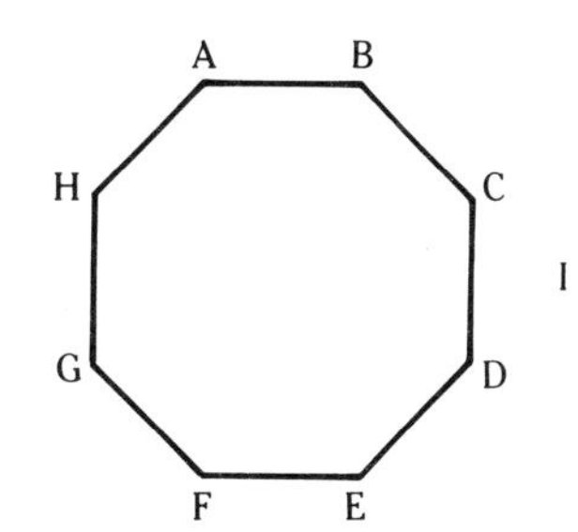

Find the angles in triangle CDI.

21.

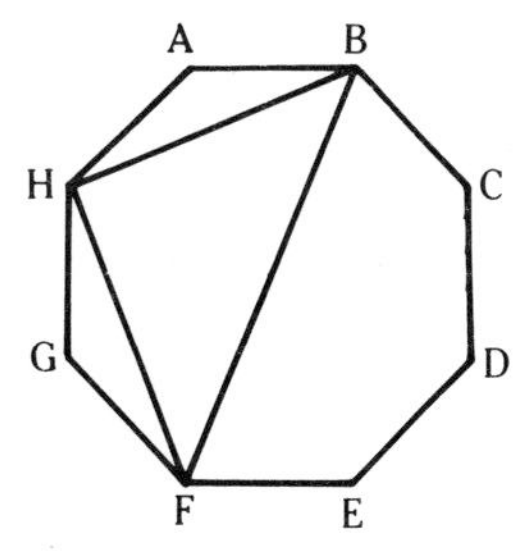

Find

(a) $B\hat{A}H$ (c) $A\hat{B}F$ (e) $H\hat{F}B$

(b) $A\hat{B}H$ (d) $H\hat{B}F$ (f) $F\hat{H}B$.

What kind of triangle is HBF ?

TESSELLATIONS

Congruent shapes (though not reflections) that fit together, without gaps, to cover a flat surface are said to tessellate. Some examples are given below.

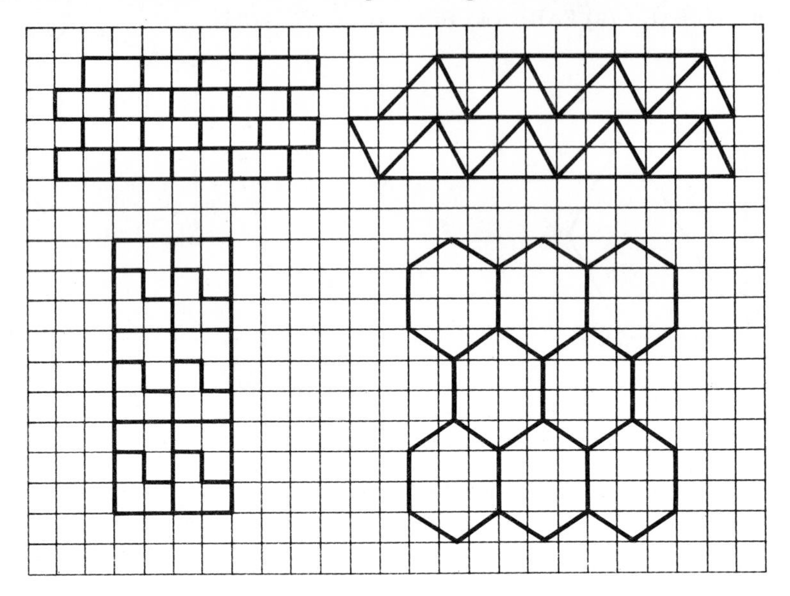

Tessellations can also be made using a combination of regular shapes, for example octagons and squares as shown below.

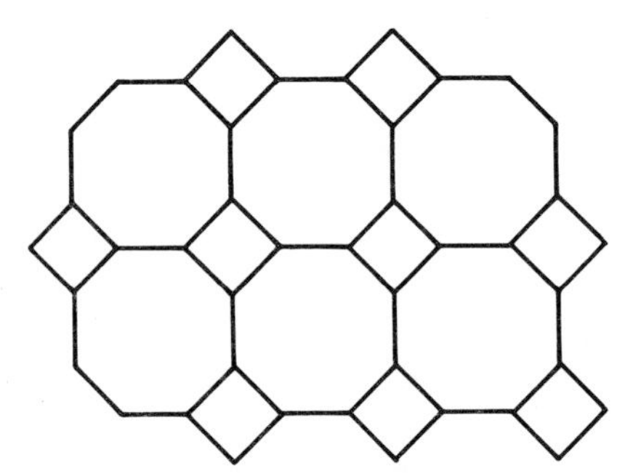

Other interesting shapes that tessellate can be formed by taking a piece away from a square and attaching it to the opposite side, for example

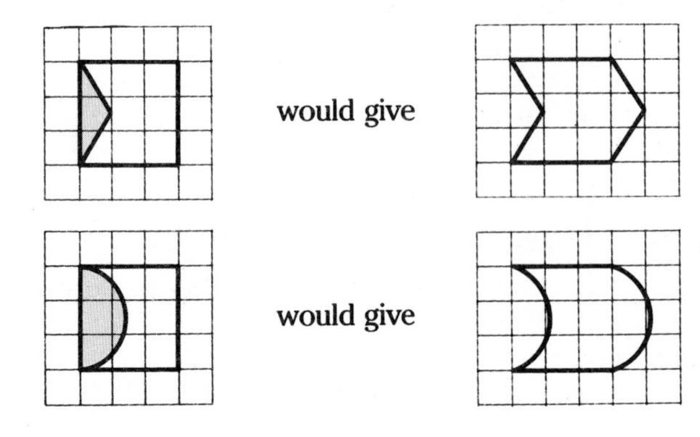

Exercise 9e

1. Use squared paper to show that each of the shapes given below tessellates.

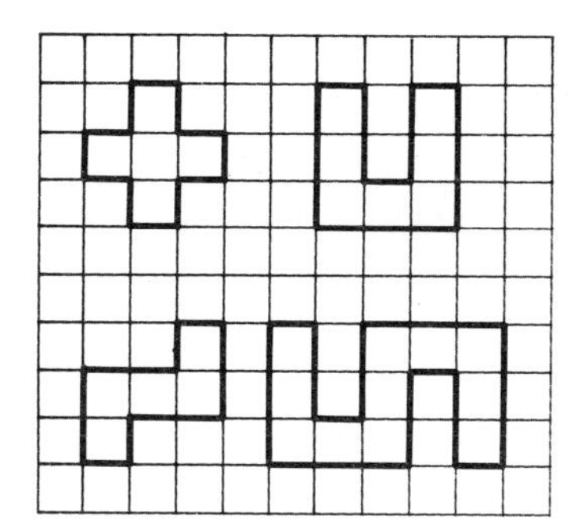

2. Use squared paper to investigate the statement that 'all parallelograms tessellate'. Do you think that the statement is true ? If not, give an example of a parallelogram that will not tessellate.

3. Repeat question 2 for any triangle.

4. Simon has a supply of tiles of the same size and shape. In each case from (a) to (f), can he use them to cover a floor and get a green floor if one side only of each tile is green ?

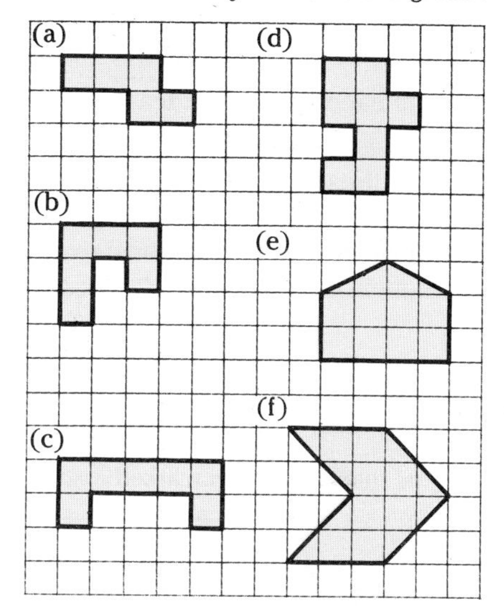

Investigations

1. Draw a series of polygons starting with four sides and increasing the number of sides each time by one. Draw all the diagonals. For each polygon write down
   (a) the number of sides
   (b) the number of diagonals
   (c) the number of intersections of these diagonals.
   Can you find any relationship between your answers to
   (i) (a) and (b) (ii) (b) and (c) ?

2. (a) Three equal squares can be arranged like this and like this
   Can you find any other arrangements ? Squares must come together along complete edges. How many of each of these arrangements will tessellate ? Show your tessellations on sketches.
   (b) Repeat (a) using 4 squares.
   (c) Repeat (a) using 5 squares, then 6 squares, and so on.
   (d) Can you find any relationship between the number of squares used and
   (i) the number of possible arrangements
   (ii) the number that will tessellate
   (iii) the number that will not tessellate ?

3. The diagrams show some polygons.

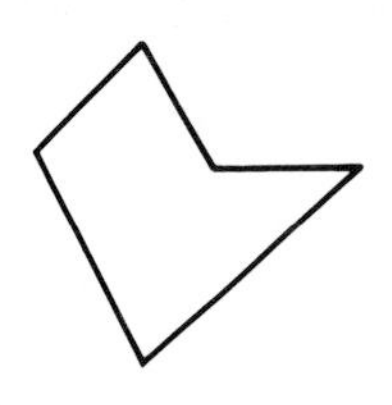

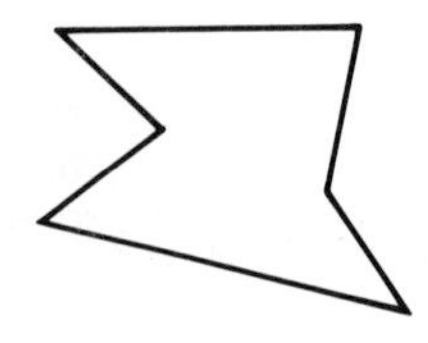

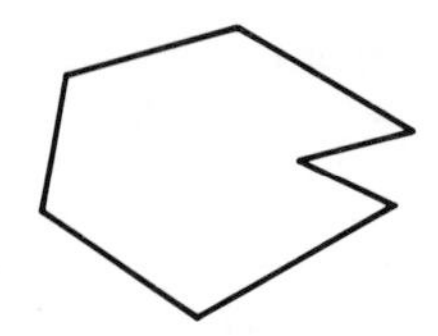

In each polygon at least one interior angle is a reflex angle.

Does the formula for the sum of the interior angles of a polygon hold for polygons such as these ?

4. Investigate the relationship between the number of sides and the number of reflex interior angles that are possible.

Self-Assessment 9

1. Find the size of each marked angle.

(a)

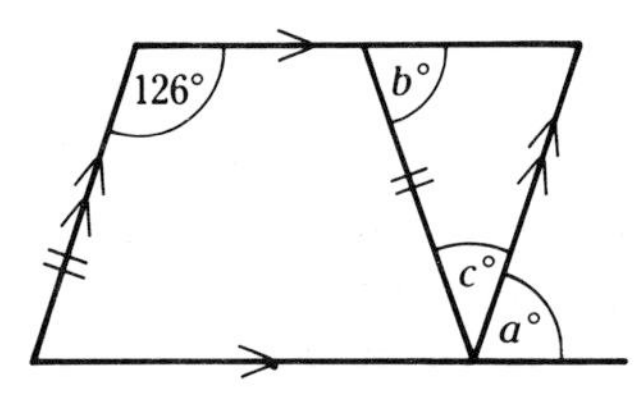

(b)

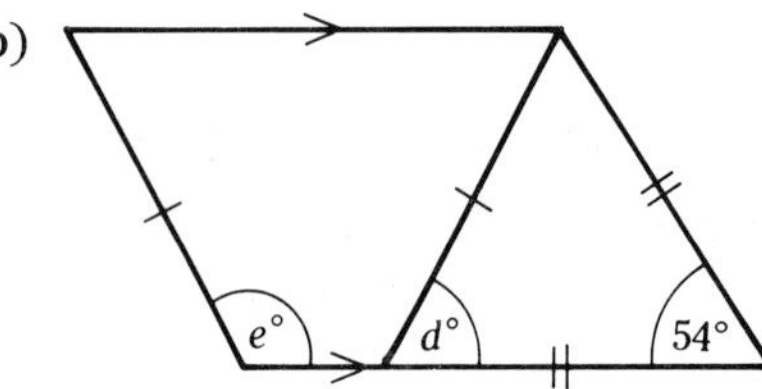

2. Find the interior angle of a regular polygon with 9 sides.

3. The exterior angles of a hexagon are 72°, 59°, 118°, 63°, $x°$ and $x°$. Find the value of x.

4. Is it possible to have a regular polygon with an interior angle of

(a) 132° (b) 156° ?

5.

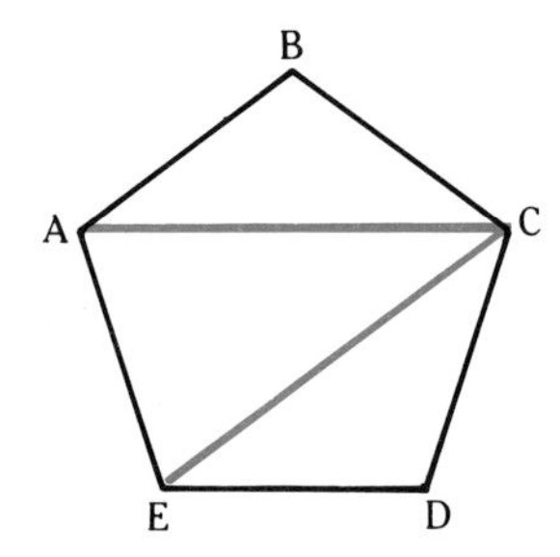

ABCDE is a regular pentagon. Find the angles in $\triangle ACE$.

6. Which of the following shapes tessellate ? Illustrate your answers with sketches.

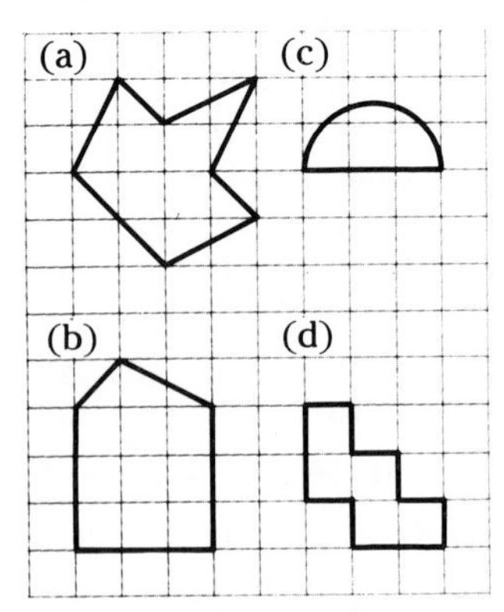

10 PYTHAGORAS' THEOREM

SQUARES AND SQUARE ROOTS

All scientific calculators have squaring and square root functions and practice in using them is given in Chapter 2. Check the instruction manual if you have any doubt about how to use them.

PYTHAGORAS' THEOREM

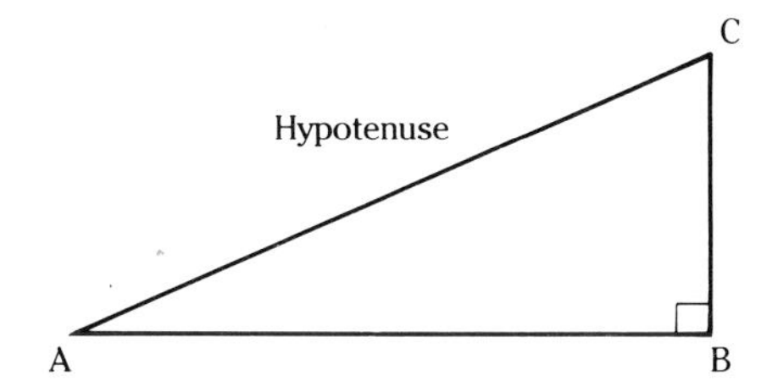

Pythagoras' theorem states that, in a right-angled triangle, the square of the hypotenuse is equal to the sum of the squares of the other two sides,

i.e. $$AC^2 = AB^2 + BC^2$$

If any two sides of a right-angled triangle are given, the third side can be found.

Conversely, if the square of one side of a triangle is equal to the sum of the squares of the other two sides, the triangle contains a right angle. The right angle is opposite the longest side.

There are many special triangles where the lengths of the three sides have whole number values. The most important of these are the 3, 4, 5 triangle and the 5, 12, 13 triangle, together with multiples of these.

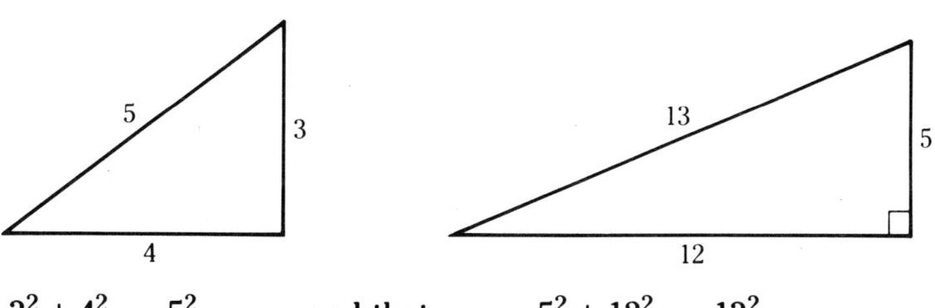

Check that $3^2 + 4^2 = 5^2$ and that $5^2 + 12^2 = 13^2$

Three whole numbers, such that the square of one of them is equal to the sum of the squares of the other two, form a *Pythagorean triad*. Their study leads to many interesting and unexpected results.

Exercise 10a

For each of the following numbers, use a calculator to find (i) the square (ii) the square root. Where appropriate, give answers correct to four significant figures.

1. (a) 13.2 (b) 763 (c) 0.9 (d) 0.006 73
2. (a) 56.7 (b) 3370 (c) 0.82 (d) 0.0005

(a) In triangle ABC, $\hat{B} = 90°$, AB = 56 cm and BC = 37 cm. Find AC.

(b) In triangle ABC, $\hat{B} = 90°$, AC = 8.15 cm and BC = 4.89 cm. Find AB.

Give each answer correct to 3 significant figures.

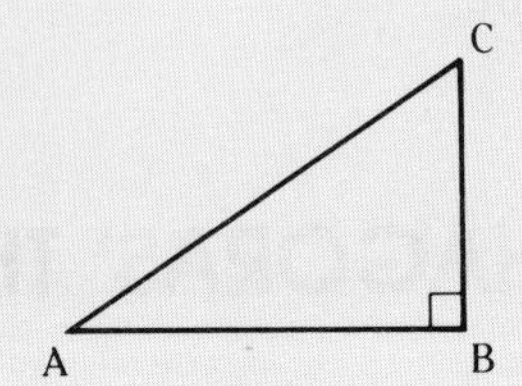

(a)

$$
\begin{aligned}
AC^2 &= AB^2 + BC^2 \quad \text{(Pythagoras)} \\
&= 56^2 + 37^2 \\
&= 3136 + 1369 \\
&= 4505 \\
AC &= \sqrt{4505} \\
&= 67.119 \text{ cm} \\
&= 67.1 \text{ cm} \quad \text{(3 s.f.)}
\end{aligned}
$$

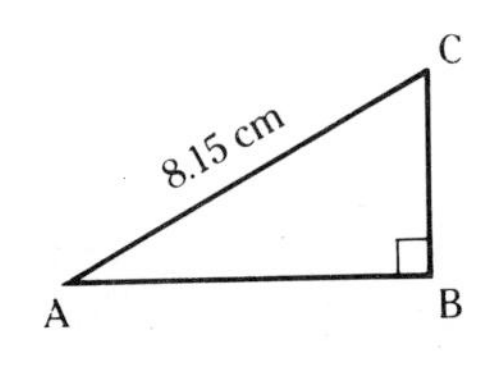

(b)

$$
\begin{aligned}
AC^2 &= AB^2 + BC^2 \quad \text{(Pythagoras)} \\
8.15^2 &= AB^2 + 4.89^2 \\
66.4225 &= AB^2 + 23.9121 \\
42.5104 &= AB^2 \\
AB &= \sqrt{42.5104} \\
&= 6.52 \text{ cm}
\end{aligned}
$$

C
8.15 cm
A
B

Use the information in the diagrams to find the required lengths, giving your answers correct to 3 significant figures.

3. Find AC.

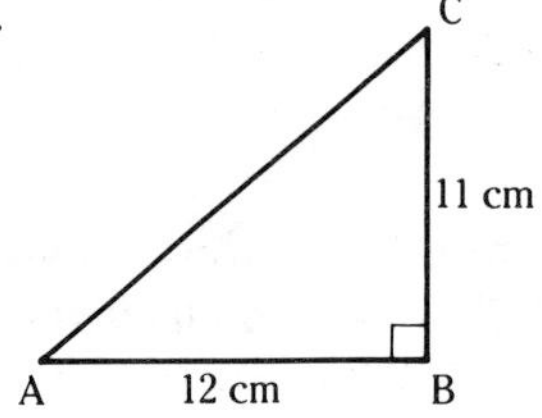

4. Find PR.

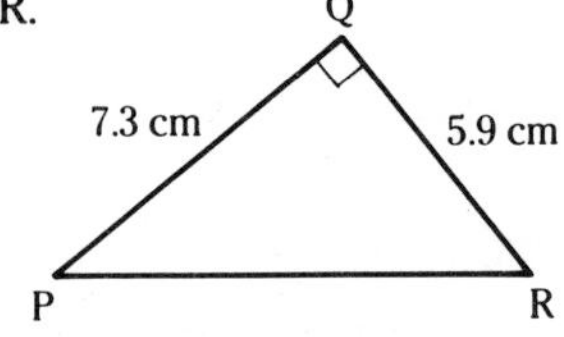

5. Find YZ.

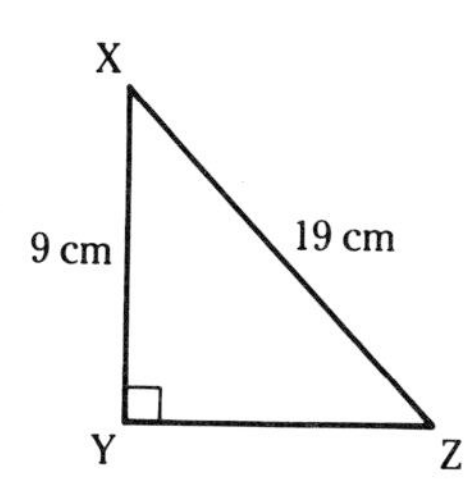

6. Find PQ.

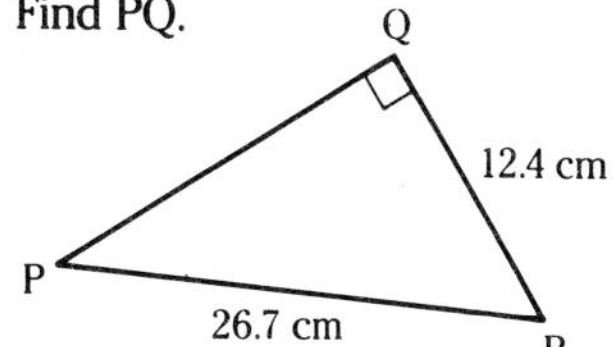

In $\triangle ABC$, $\hat{B} = 90°$, $AC = 4.5$ cm and $AB = 3.6$ cm.
Find BC.

It is worthwhile looking for a 3, 4, 5$\triangle$ or a 5, 12, 13$\triangle$ to make the calculation simpler.

$AC = 5 \times 0.9$ cm

$AB = 4 \times 0.9$ cm

$\therefore$ $\triangle ABC$ is a 3, 4, 5$\triangle$

$\therefore$ $BC = 3 \times 0.9$ cm

$= 2.7$ cm

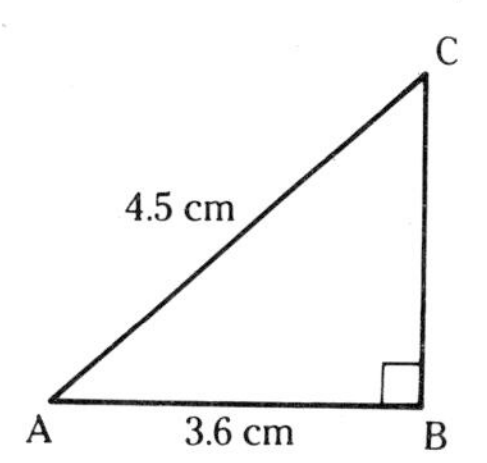

7. Find AC and DC.

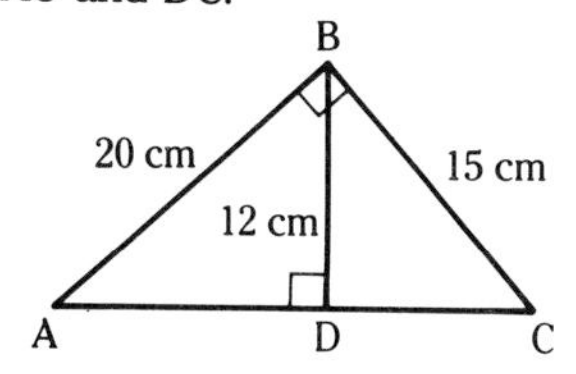

8. Find RS and PR.

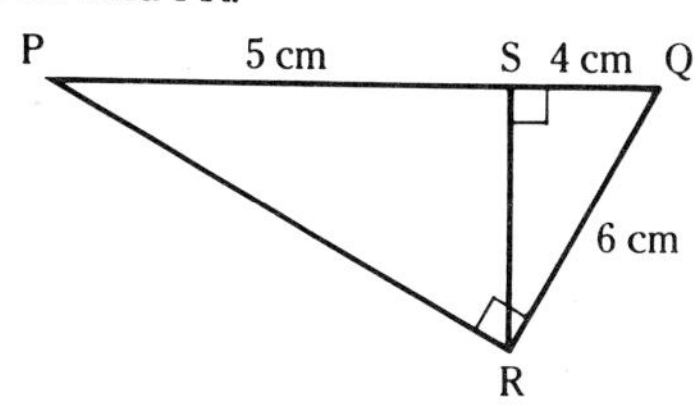

9. Find DC

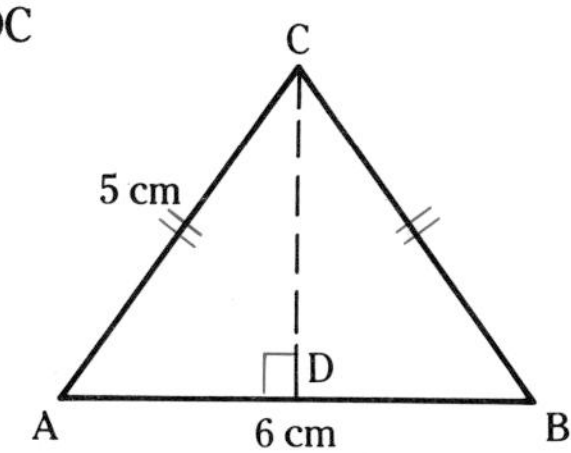

10. Find (a) AE (b) ED

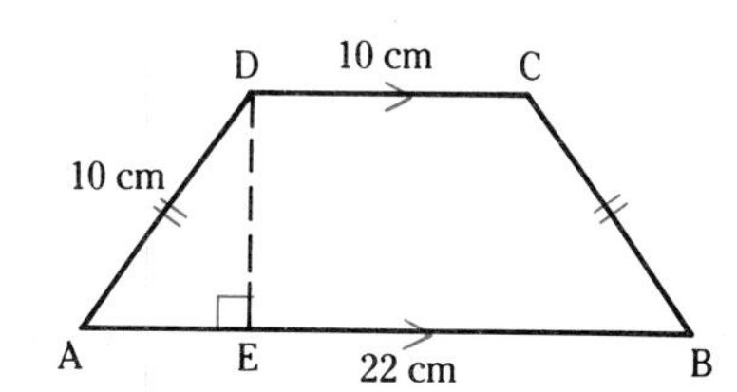

11. In $\triangle XYZ$, $\hat{X} = 90°$, $XY = 3.9$ cm and $XZ = 4.9$ cm.

(a) Find YZ.

(b) YX is extended to W so that $XW = 2.5$ cm.
Find ZW.

12. Are the following triangles right-angled? If so, write down the angle that is 90°.

(a) $\triangle ABC$ in which $AB = 11$ cm, $BC = 61$ cm and $AC = 60$ cm.

(b) $\triangle XYZ$ in which $XY = 2.8$ cm, $YZ = 3.5$ cm and $XZ = 2.1$ cm.

(c) $\triangle DEF$ in which $DE = 13$ cm, $DF = 18$ cm and $EF = 27$ cm.

(d) $\triangle PQR$ in which $QR = 570$ cm, $PR = 950$ cm and $PQ = 760$ cm.

13. In a triangle XYZ, $X\hat{Y}Z = 90°$ and W is the foot of the perpendicular from Y to XZ. XY = 32 cm, YZ = 16 cm and WZ = 7.16 cm. Find the length of
(a) XZ (b) WX (c) WY.

14. In $\triangle PQR$, PQ = PR = 9 cm and QR = 10 cm. S is the midpoint of QR. Find the height of $\triangle PQR$.

Find the distance between the points A(1, 2) and B(7, 4).

Draw a diagram to see clearly what is going on.

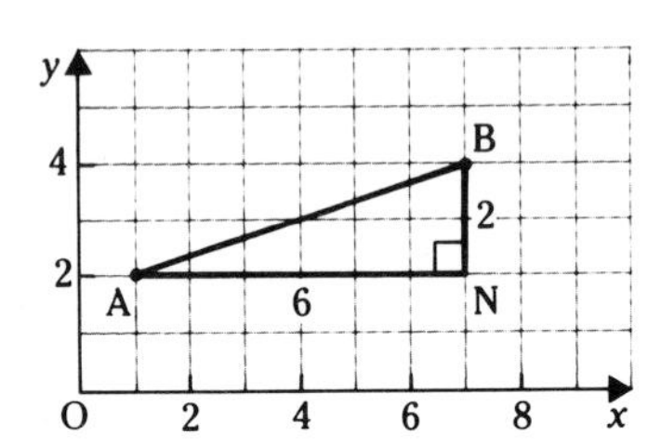

N is the point such that AN is parallel to the x-axis and BN is parallel to the y-axis. It follows that $A\hat{N}B = 90°$

AN = (7 − 1), i.e. 6 units and BN = (4 − 2), i.e. 2 units

Applying Pythagoras' theorem to $\triangle ANB$

$$AB^2 = 6^2 + 2^2$$
$$= 36 + 4$$
$$= 40$$

∴ AB is 6.32 units (3 s.f.)

15. Find the distance between each of the following pairs of points:
(a) A(3, 1) and B(6, 7)
(b) X(1, 2) and Y(10, 9)
(c) P(−2, 2) and Q(9, 5)
(d) A(2, −4) and B(7, 8)
(e) P(−3, −3) and Q(9, 6)
(f) D(−4, 6) and E(2, −5)

COORDINATES IN THREE DIMENSIONS

Just as an ordered pair of coordinates is used to determine the position of a point in a plane, i.e. in two dimensions, so an ordered triple of coordinates is used to define the position of a point in space, i.e. in three dimensions (3-D for short). The coordinates give the distances, in order, from a fixed point O, along or parallel to three mutually perpendicular axes, Ox, Oy and Oz.

Mutually perpendicular means that each axis is perpendicular to the other two.

There are several different formations in which the axes can be drawn. The one we use most frequently in this book is shown in the diagram below.

If Ox and Oy are drawn as they were for two dimensions, then Oz comes 'out of the page'.

A point P is then located by giving its distances from O in the positive directions of these axes. These distances are called the *coordinates* of P.

For example, if P is the point (2, 3, 4) then P is

2 units from O in the direction Ox
3 units from O in the direction Oy
4 units from O in the direction Oz

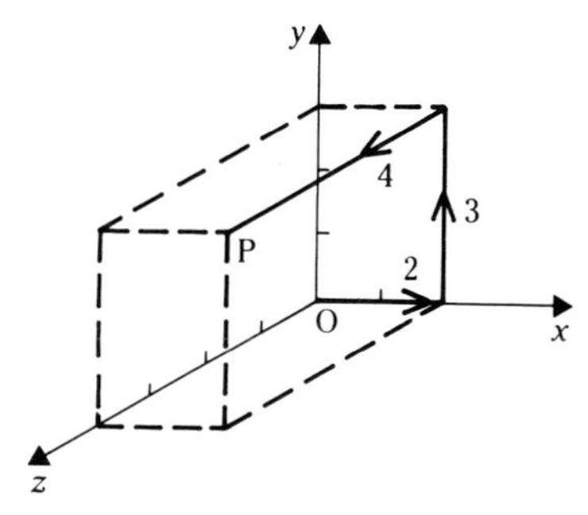

To find the position of P(2, 3, 4) start at O, move 2 units along the x-axis, then 3 units up parallel to the y-axis, followed by 4 units parallel to the z-axis.

Exercise 10b

In this exercise the origin is at one vertex of the solid and the axes lie along three of its edges. Each axis is graduated in units. When diagrams are drawn it is an advantage to use squared paper.

1. For each diagram write down the coordinates of A.

(a)

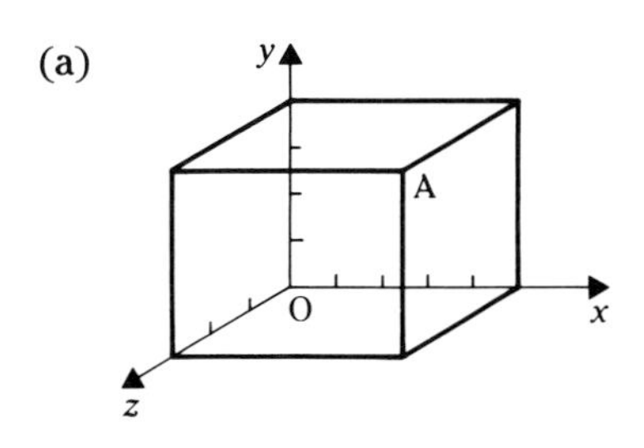

(c)

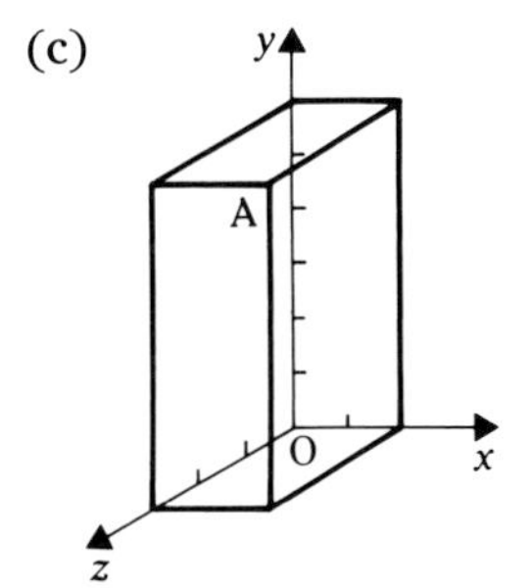

(b)

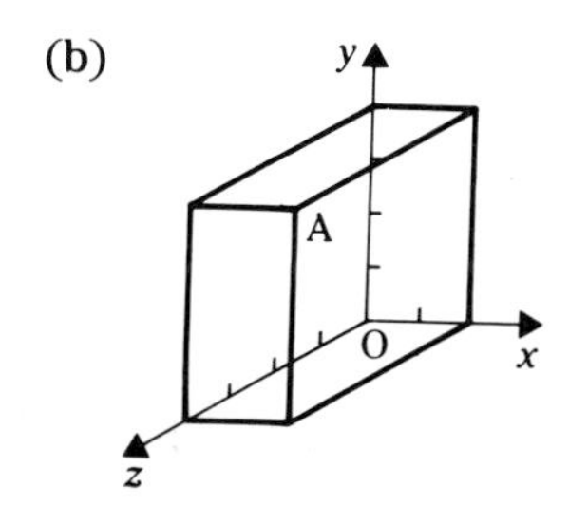

(d)

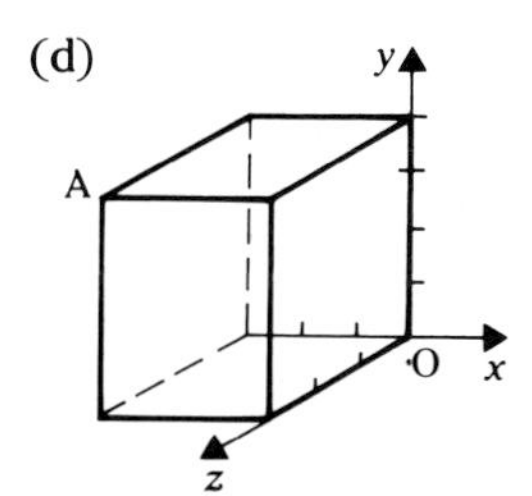

2. Draw diagrams, similar to those given in question 1, to show the position of A, when A has each of the following sets of coordinates

(a) (2, 2, 4) (b) (5, 3, 2) (c) (1, 3, 4) (d) (4, 4, 4)

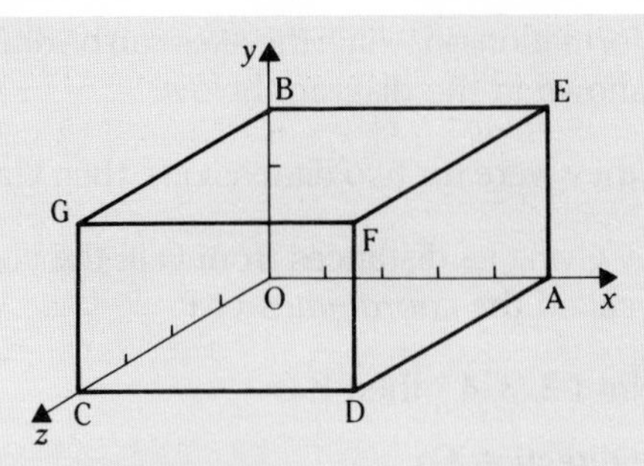

The diagram shows a cuboid where OA = 5 units, OB = 3 units and OC = 4 units. Find the coordinates of

(a) E (b) D (c) F.

(a) To get to E, start at O and move 5 units in the direction Ox followed by 3 units in the direction Oy. There is no movement in the direction Oz.

The coordinates of E are (5, 3, 0).

(b) D is 5 units in the direction Ox
no units in the direction Oy
4 units in the direction Oz.

D is the point (5, 0, 4).

(c) Similarly F is the point (5, 3, 4).

3.

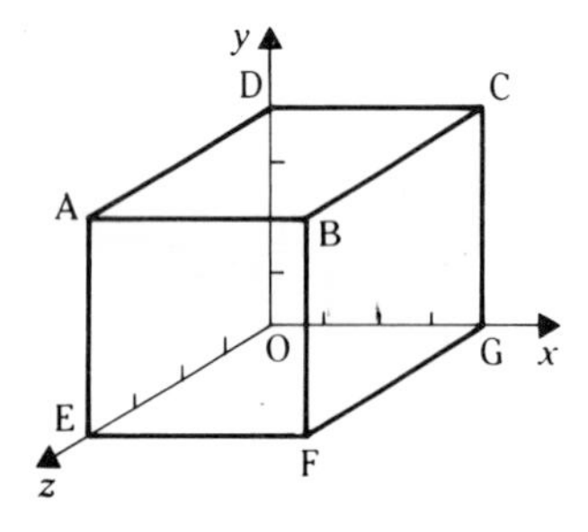

The diagram shows a cube of edge 4 units. Find

(a) the coordinates of all eight vertices

(b) the coordinates of the midpoints of the edges
(i) OG (ii) OD (iii) BC (iv) BF
(v) DC (vi) AD.

(c) the coordinates of the centre of the square
(i) ODCG (ii) ABFE (iii) BCGF
(iv) ABCD.

Questions 4 to 6 refer to the diagram given below.

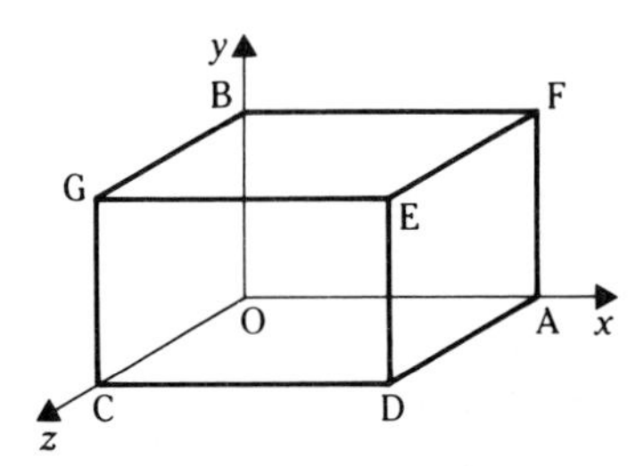

4. If OA = 3, OB = 5 and OC = 4 write down the coordinates of
(a) A (b) F (c) D (d) E.

5. If the diagram represents a cube of edge 3 units, write down the coordinates of each vertex.

6. If E is the point (3, 6, 4) write down the coordinates of each of the other vertices.

There are many ways in which axes in three dimensions can be drawn. Look carefully at the following diagrams; make sure that you know which axis is which. When *you* draw diagrams it is sensible to keep to one standard position for the axes.

7.

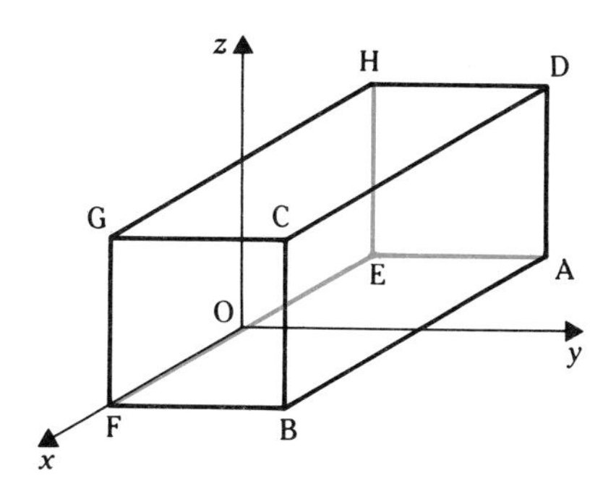

The diagram shows a cuboid labelled A to H. The coordinates of B are (3, 4, 0) and the coordinates of D are (−5, 4, 2).

(a) Write down the coordinates of the other vertices.

(b) Write down the coordinates of the midpoint of (i) AB (ii) CD.

(c) If the origin is moved along the x-axis to F and the directions of Oy and Oz remain unchanged, write down the new coordinates of the eight vertices.

In questions 8 and 9 the units are centimetres.

8. A, B and C are the points (6, 0, 0), (6, 4, 0) and (6, 4, 8) respectively.

(a) Draw a diagram showing clearly the points A, B and C.

(b) How far does a spider walk if it goes from A to C via B ?

9. A, B and C are the points (3, 0, 0), (3, 4, 0) and (3, 4, 12) respectively.

(a) Draw a diagram showing clearly the points A, B and C

(b) How far is it from O to C via A and B ?

(c) How far is it directly from
(i) O to B (ii) O to C ?

10. Four of the vertices of a cuboid are at the points (0, 2, 0), (0, 4, 0), (0, 2, 4) and (6, 2, 4). Find the coordinates of the other four vertices.

11.

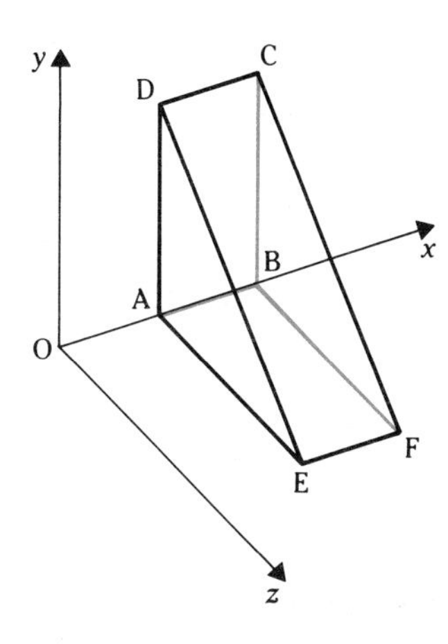

A is the point (2, 0, 0), B is the point (5, 0, 0), C is the point (5, 4, 0) and F is the point (5, 0, 4).

(a) Write down the coordinates of the points D and E.

(b) Find the area of triangle BCF.

12.

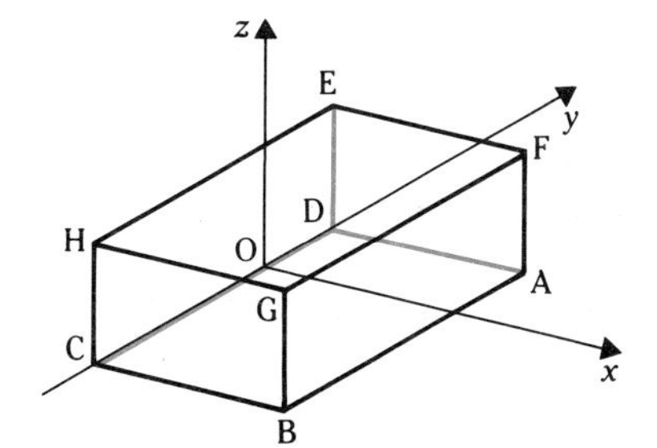

ABCDEFGH is a cuboid. A is the point (5, 2, 0). AB is 7 units long and AF is 3 units long. Find the coordinates of

(a) B (b) H (c) F

PROBLEMS

The first step towards solving any geometric problem should be to draw a clear diagram showing all the information that is given in the question.

If one length is found first and used to find a second length or an angle, use the exact value for the first length or, if that is not possible, use at least 4 significant figures. Unless otherwise stated, all answers should be given correct to 3 significant figures.

Exercise 10c

1. A ship sails 26 nautical miles due north then 34 nautical miles due east. How far is it from its starting point ?

2. Find the length of a diagonal of a square of side 17 cm.

3. Find the length of the side of a rhombus whose diagonals measure 10 cm and 24 cm.

4.

B
A
C
5.4 m
4 m
3.7 m
3 m
E
D
12.5 m

The diagram shows the cross-section of a workshop. Find the length of each sloping edge of the roof.

5.

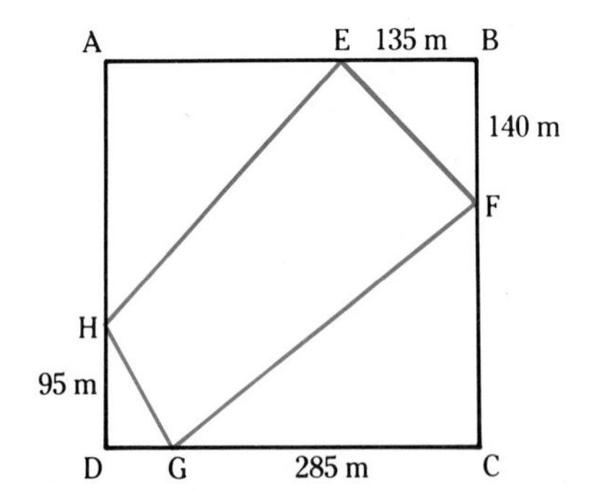

The diagram shows a square field, ABCD, of side 350 m, which has been divided into five enclosures by erecting a fence EFGHE.

Calculate the length of this fence.

6.

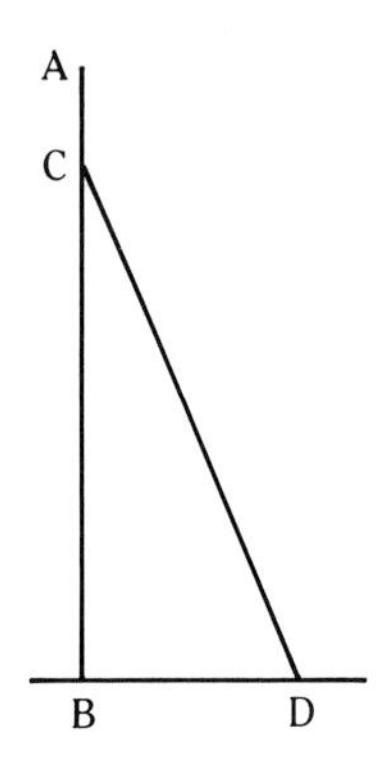

A vertical pylon, AB, is 40 m high, and stands on level ground. It is supported by a wire, CD, 38 m long which is attached to a point 7 m from the top of the pylon, the other end being anchored to a point on the ground. How far is this point from the base of the pylon ?

7.

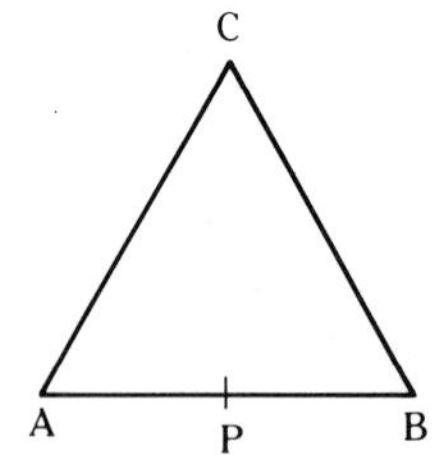

ABC is a table top in the shape of an equilateral triangle and AB = 1.2 m. P is the midpoint of AB.

(a) Find the length of CP.

(b) X is a point on CP such that PX = $\frac{1}{3}$CP. Find the length of XB.

8.

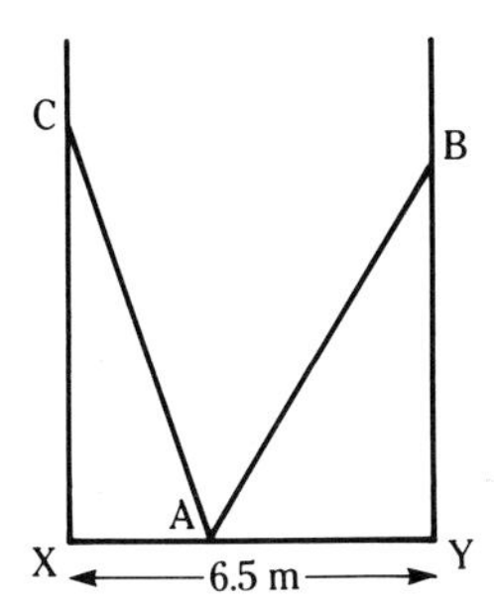

The diagram shows a ladder, AB, resting on horizontal ground, XY, in a narrow street 6.5 m wide. The foot, A, of the ladder is 3.5 m from the base of the vertical wall BY and rests against this wall at a distance 7.5 m above the ground. How long is the ladder ?

The ladder is now turned about A so that it rests, at a point C, against a vertical building on the opposite side of the street. How far up this wall does the ladder reach ?

9.

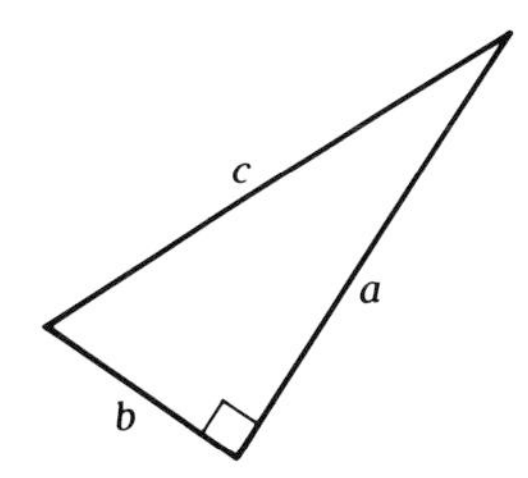

(a) In the diagram, c is the hypotenuse of a right-angled triangle, the other two sides being a and b.

(i) Find c if $a = 3$ and $b = 4$.

(ii) Find b if $a = 5$ and $c = 13$.

(iii) Find a if $b = 24$ and $c = 25$.

(b) (i) Use your answers to (a) to complete the following table

a	b	c
3	4	
5		13
	24	25
9	40	41

(ii) If the next value of b is 60, find the corresponding values for c and a and complete the fifth row of the table.

(iii) Add two more rows to the table, following the same pattern.

10.

(a) A carpenter checks that a rectangular window frame is 'square' by measuring the diagonals, which should be the same length. A frame is 185 cm by 105 cm. What should be the length of each diagonal ? Give your answer correct to the nearest millimetre.

(b) Use some rectangular objects that you have available, e.g. a picture frame, a door, the cover of a book, etc., to test whether or not they are 'square'.

11.

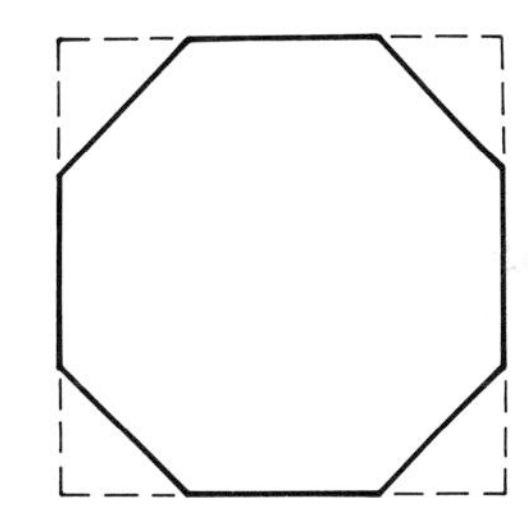

A mirror is in the shape of an octagon. It is formed by starting with a square of side 90 cm and cutting an isosceles triangle from each corner. The two equal sides of each triangle are of length 30 cm.

(a) Find the lengths of the sides of the octagon.

(b) Find the distance of each vertex from the centre of the octagon.

12.

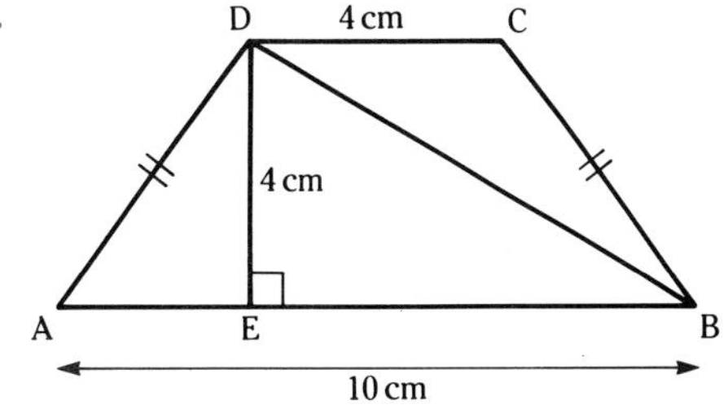

The diagram shows a trapezium ABCD in which BC = AD, AB = 10 cm and CD = 4 cm. DE is perpendicular to AB and is 4 cm long.

Find the length of

(a) AE (b) AD (c) BD.

THREE-DIMENSIONAL PROBLEMS

If a line is perpendicular to a plane, then it is perpendicular to any line in that plane.

For example, GC is perpendicular to the plane ABCD.

Therefore GC is perpendicular to CB, CD and CA.

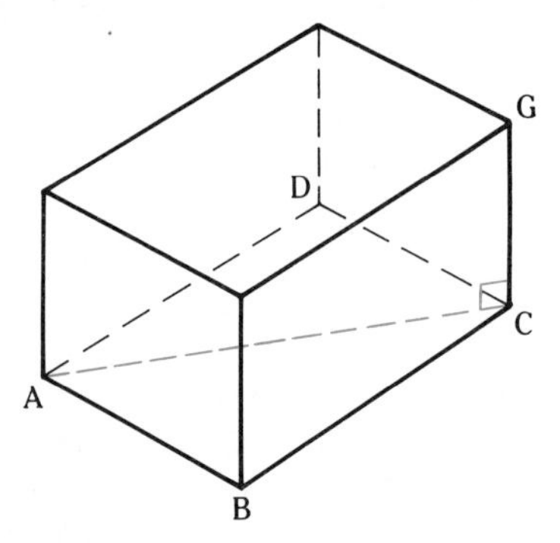

The following hints may be helpful in drawing a good diagram.

(a) Vertical lines should be drawn vertically on your diagram.

(b) All angles that are 90° in three dimensions should be marked as right angles on the diagram. This is particularly important for those angles that do not *appear* to be 90°.

(c) Lines that are parallel should be shown as parallel on the diagram.

(d) Show sides that cannot be seen by broken lines.

(e) It is often helpful to draw a separate diagram for an individual triangle in which calculations are needed. Mark any right angle.

Exercise 10d

The sketch shows a rectangular box measuring 10 cm by 9 cm by 6 cm, where AE = 10 cm, AD = 6 cm and DC = 9 cm.

Calculate the length of (a) AC (b) DG

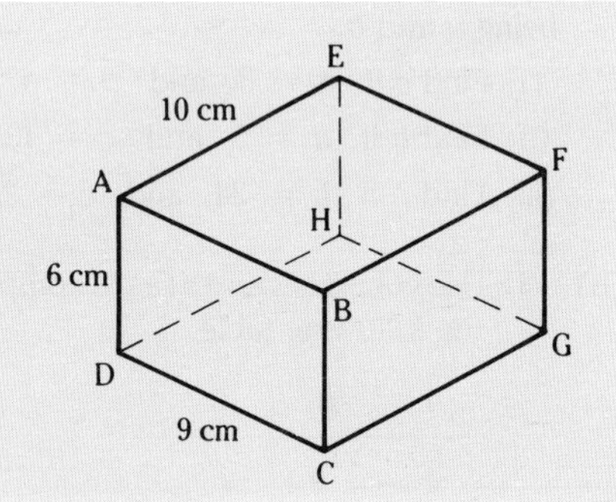

(a) To find AC, we use triangle ADC

$$AC^2 = AD^2 + DC^2$$
$$= 36 + 81$$
$$= 117$$
$$AC = 10.81\ldots$$

The length of AC is 10.8 cm correct to 3 s.f.

(b) DG is the diagonal of the bottom face of the box; we can use triangle DCG.

Similarly
$$DG^2 = DC^2 + CG^2$$
$$= 81 + 100$$
$$= 181$$
$$DG = 13.45\ldots$$

The length of DG is 13.5 cm correct to 3 s.f.

1.

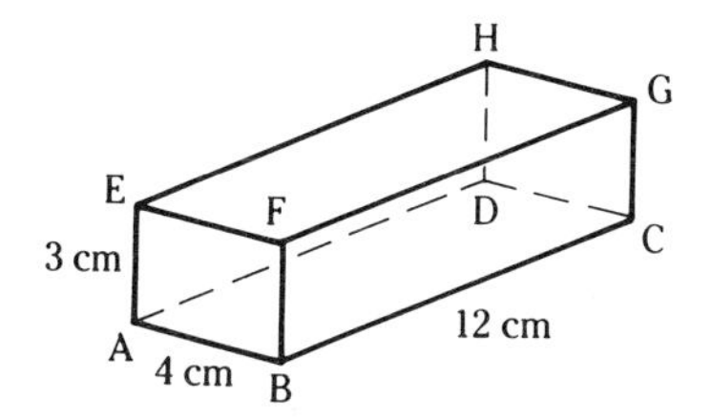

The sketch shows a cuboid. Each of the six faces is a rectangle.

(a) Copy the diagram. Notice that in the drawing the rectangular faces look like parallelograms.

(b) Name all the edges that are equal in length to (i) AB (ii) EA (iii) BC.

(c) Draw triangle EHG and find the length of EG.

2.

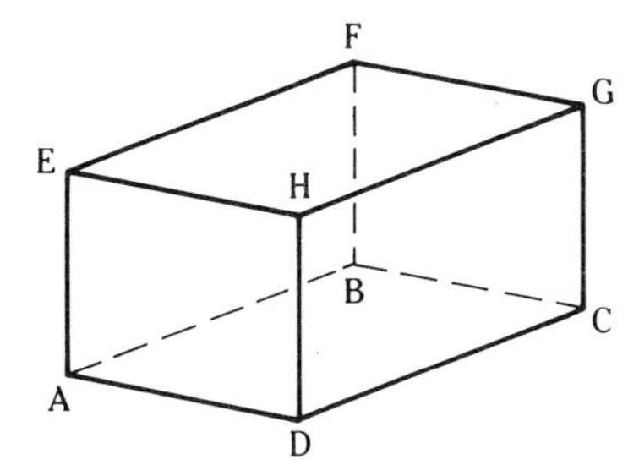

In this cuboid AB = 12 cm, AE = 8 cm and BC = 9.5 cm.

Find the length of (a) AH (b) DG.

3. Sketch a cube of edge 6 cm.

(a) Find the length of a diagonal of a face.

Now imagine that the cube is cut in half to give a cuboid measuring 6 cm by 6 cm by 3 cm. Sketch the cuboid and find the length of

(b) a diagonal of the smallest face.

4.

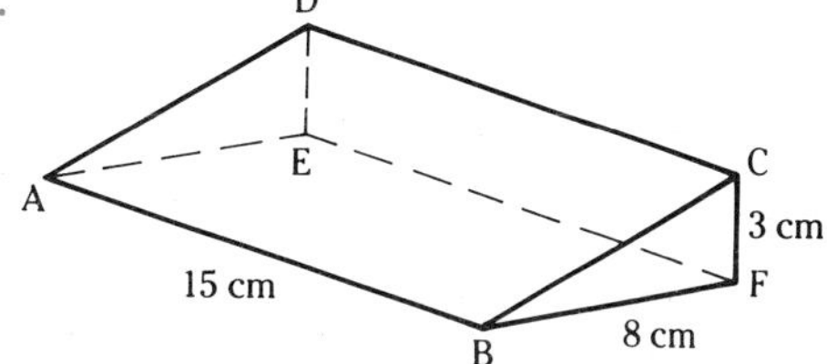

The diagram represents a large wedge-shaped piece of cheese ABCDEF resting on a flat horizontal table. The rectangular face DCFE is vertical. A small mouse approaches the cheese.

Use the information on the diagram to find the distance travelled by the mouse if it walks

(a) the length of the edge BC

(b) in a direct line from A to C across the face ABCD.

5. The coordinates of three points are A(0, 4, 0), B(−3, 0, 0) and C(0, 0, 6). Find the length of
(a) AC (b) AB (c) BC

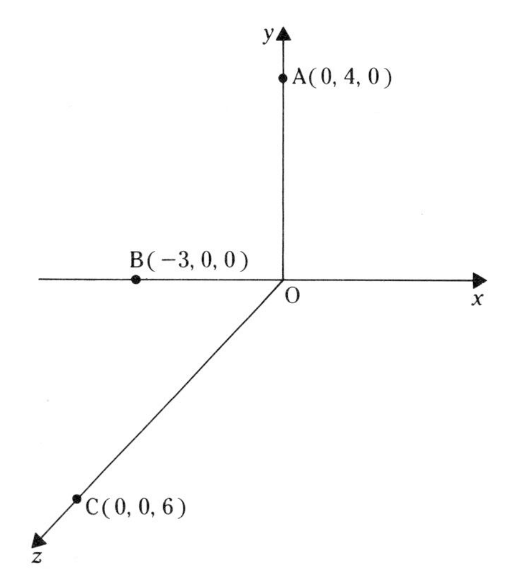

Self-Assessment 10

1.

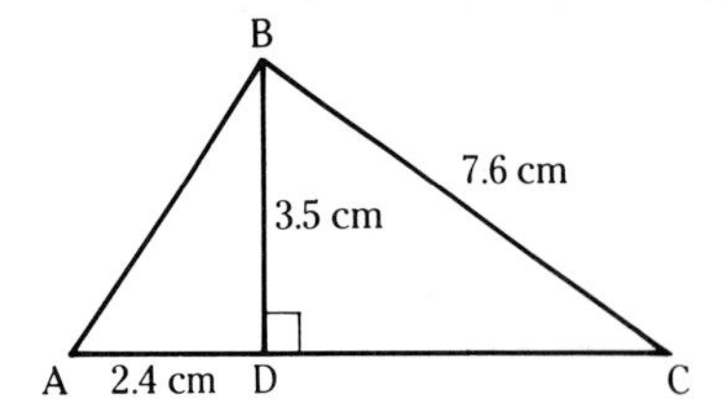

(a) Use the information given on the diagram to find
(i) AB (ii) DC.

(b) Use your results to determine whether or not triangle ABC is a right-angled triangle.

2. Find the distance between the points A(4, 1) and B(8, −5).

3. In △ABC, $\hat{B} = 90°$, AC = 40 cm and AB = 24 cm. Without using a calculator, find BC.

4. Find the length of a diagonal of a rectangle measuring 4.2 cm by 7.8 cm.

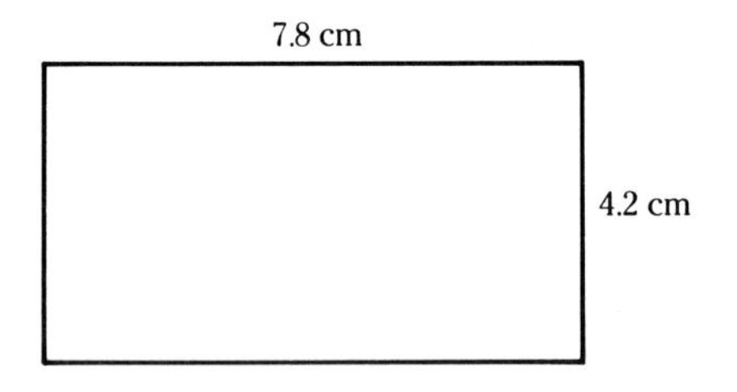

5.

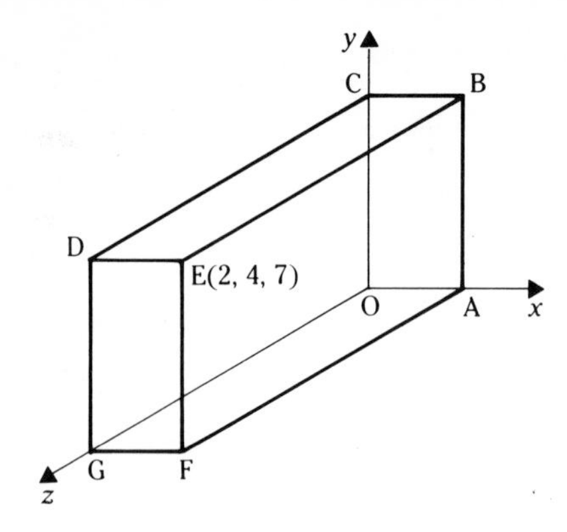

Use the information given in the diagram

(a) to write down the coordinates of
(i) A (ii) B (iii) D (iv) F

(b) to find the lengths of (i) GE (ii) FB.

6. The diagram shows a box with a ribbon round it.

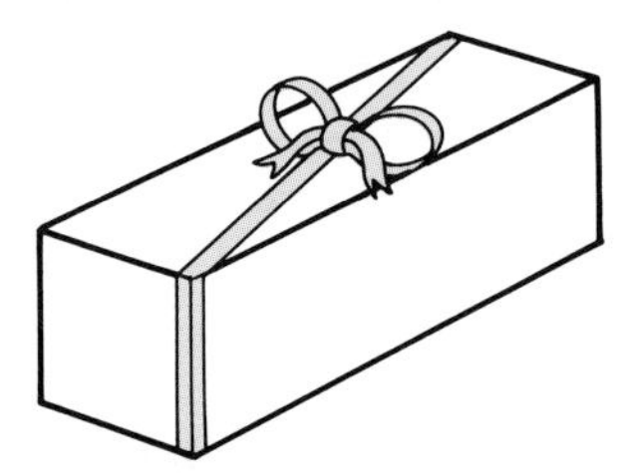

The box is 10 cm deep, 10 cm high and 30 cm long. The ribbon goes up one edge, diagonally across the top, down an edge and diagonally across the bottom. The bow uses 60 cm of ribbon. How long is the ribbon ?

AREAS AND VOLUMES

CALCULATING AREAS

In Chapter 5 we saw that the area of any shape made up of squares and rectangles can be calculated exactly. For other shapes the method used was to superimpose a squared grid and count squares. The result, however, is only an approximation.

There are a number of such figures for which there is a way to *calculate* the area; these are considered in this chapter.

The Area of a Parallelogram

We know that a parallelogram is a quadrilateral in which both pairs of opposite sides are parallel and equal. Using these properties it is easy to obtain a rectangle equal in area to a parallelogram.

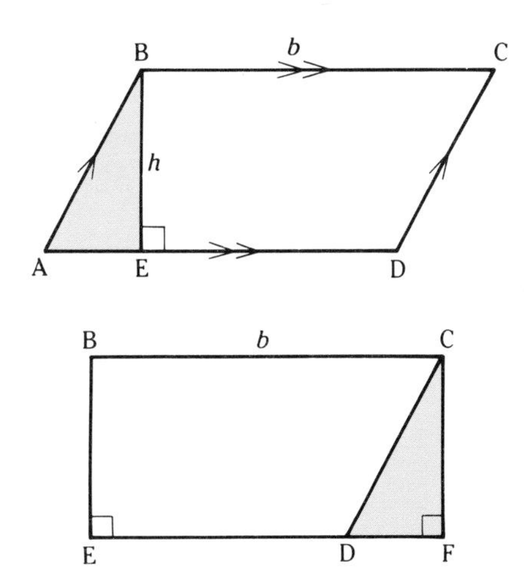

From the given parallelogram ABCD, the shaded right-angled triangle can be cut off and placed with AB along DC as shown. This forms a rectangle EBCF with length b and width h and therefore with an area given by $b \times h$, which is the same as the area of ABCD.

In the parallelogram, h is the perpendicular height; usually we just say *height* because this is understood to mean perpendicular height.

Area of a parallelogram = base × height

Note that the side AB of the parallelogram is the *slant height* and is *not* equal to the perpendicular height.

Exercise 11a

Find the area of this parallelogram.

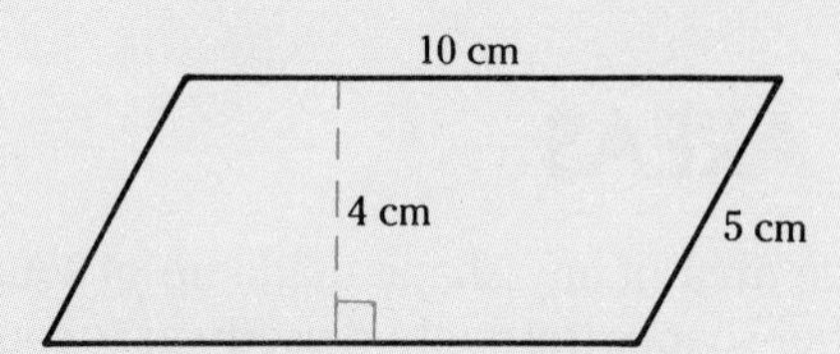

The given length of 5 cm is the slant height and is not needed to find the area.

$$\begin{aligned} \text{Area} &= \text{base} \times \text{height} \\ &= 10 \times 4 \text{ cm}^2 \\ &= 40 \text{ cm}^2 \end{aligned}$$

Find the area of each parallelogram.

1.

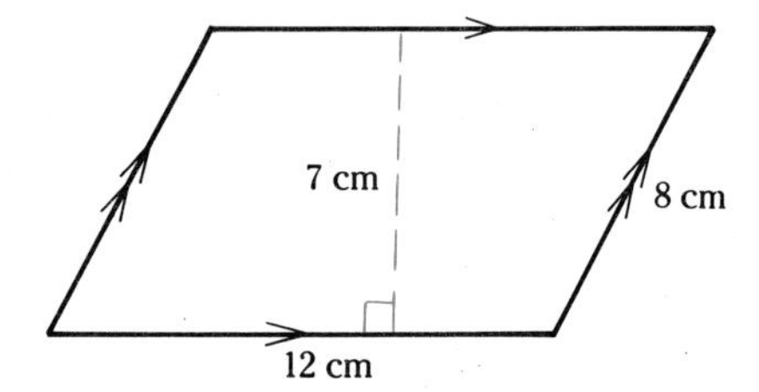

2.

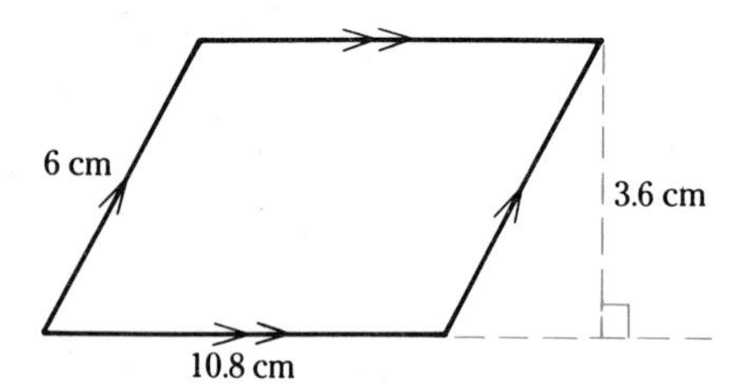

3.

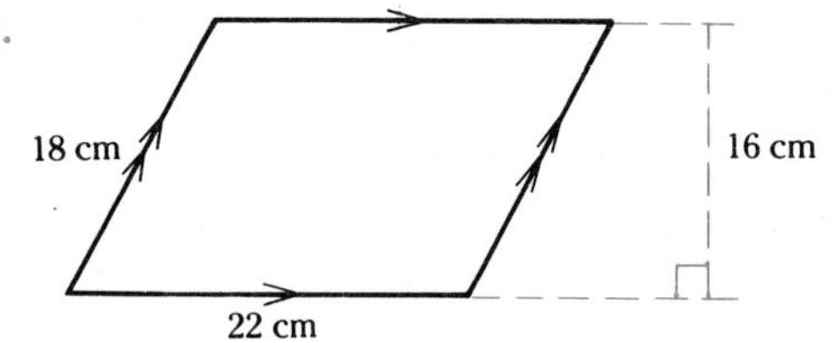

4.

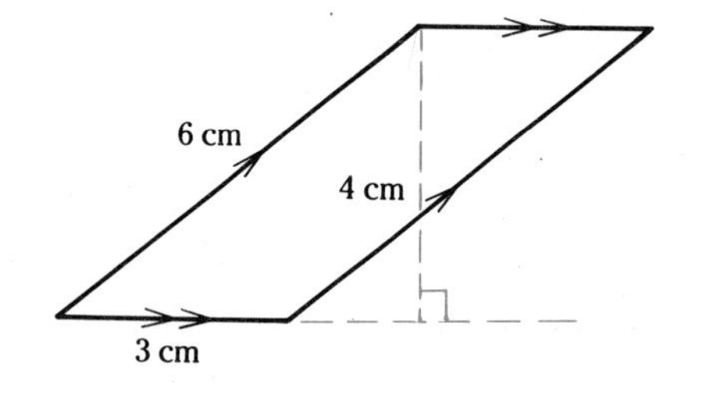

It is not always obvious which side of a parallelogram is the base as it is not necessarily the bottom line. The base may be identified more easily if the parallelogram is viewed from a different direction.

5.

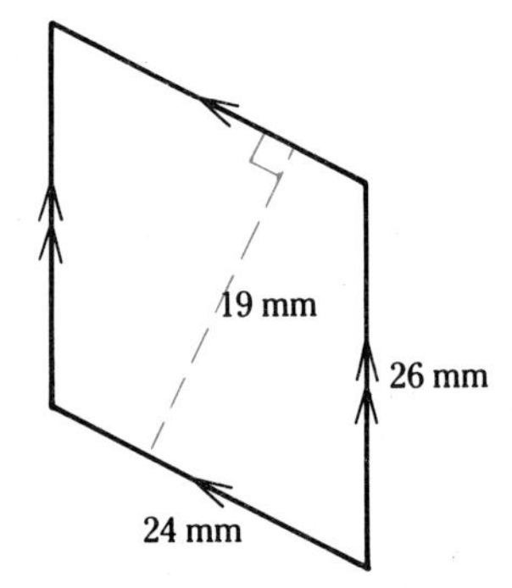

6.

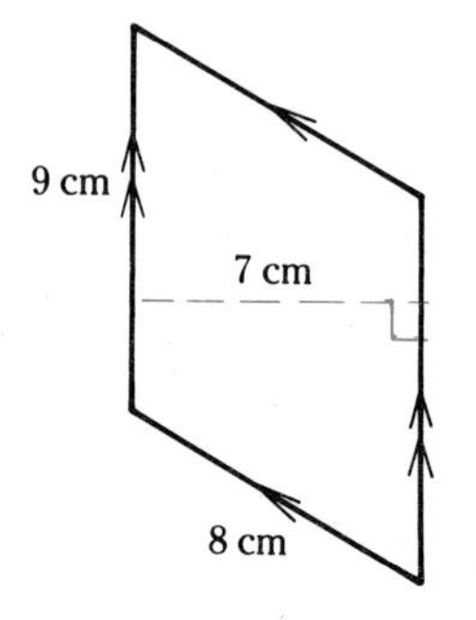

7.

7.2 cm
5 cm
7 cm

8.

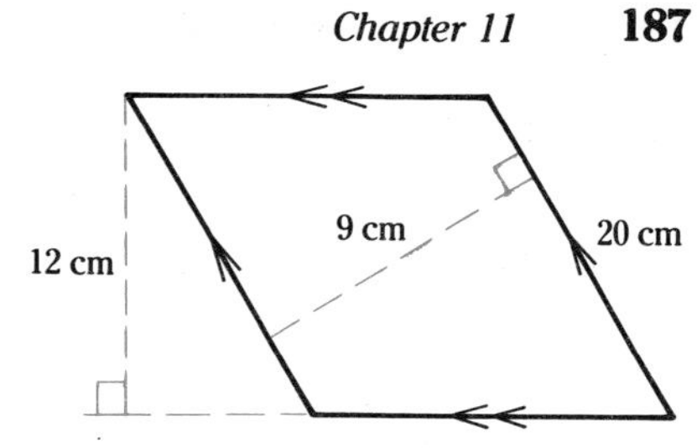

Find the area of parallelogram ABCD.

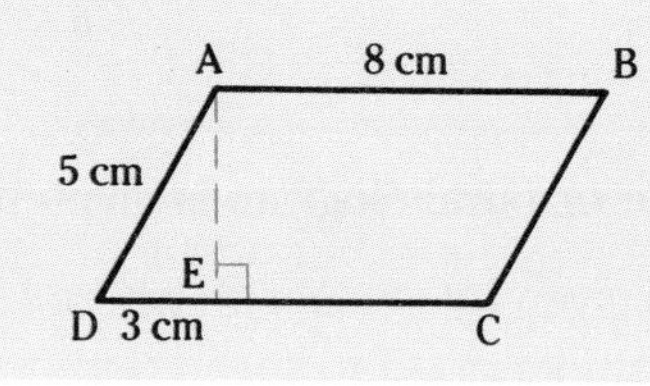

A B
5 cm
h
D 3 cm E C

First we find the perpendicular height.

In triangle ADE,

$$5^2 = 3^2 + h^2 \quad \text{(Pythagoras)}$$

$$h^2 = 25 - 9$$

$$h = 4$$

$$\text{Area of parallelogram} = b \times h$$

$$= 8 \times 4\ \text{cm}^2$$

$$= 32\ \text{cm}^2$$

Find the area of each parallelogram.

9.

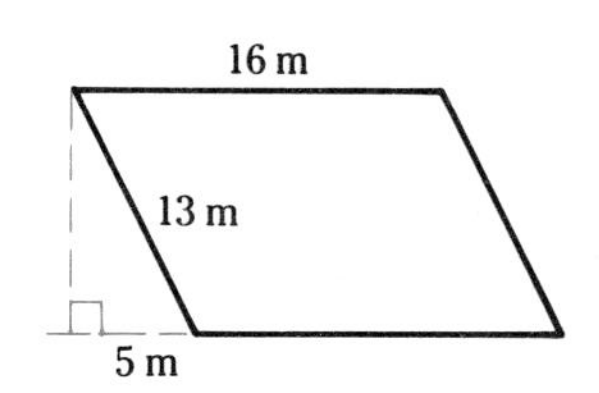

10.

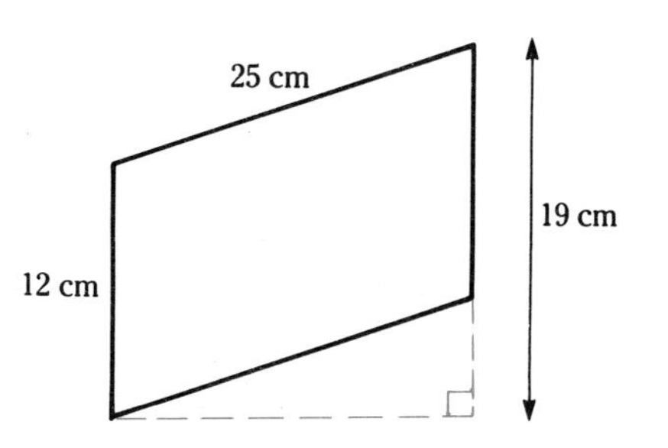

11.

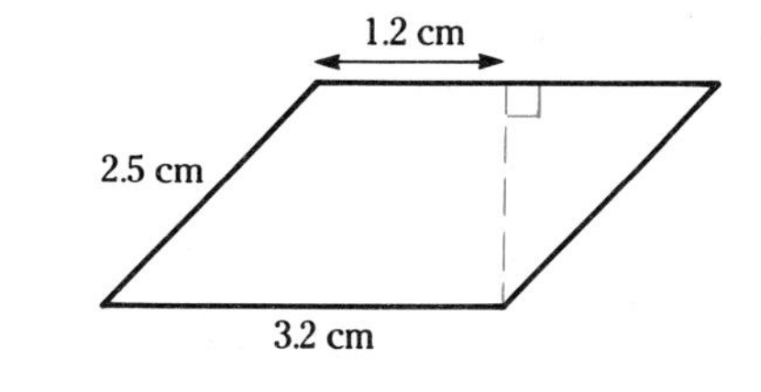

12.

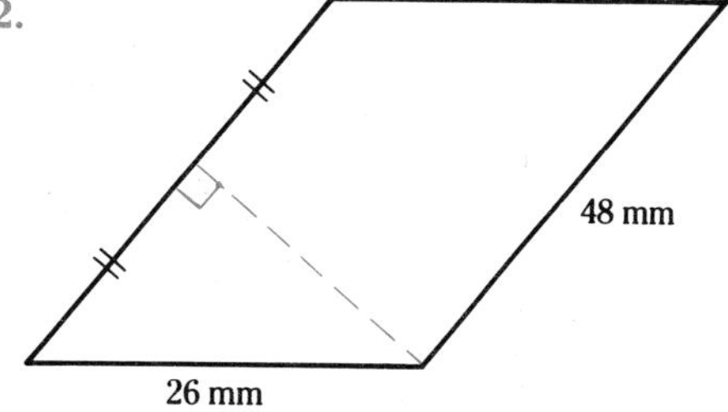

THE AREA OF A TRIANGLE

Any rectangle or parallelogram can be divided, by drawing a diagonal, into two triangles with the same shape and size and therefore with equal areas.

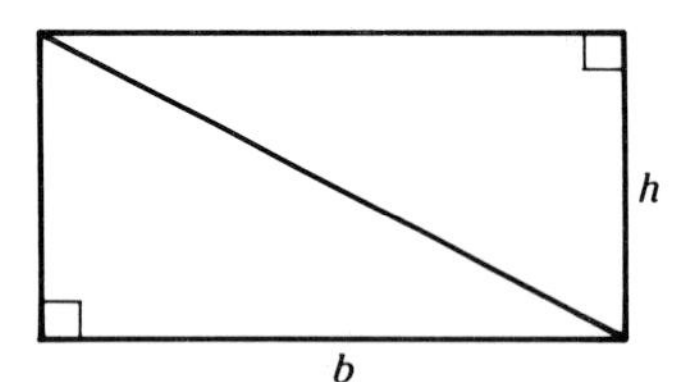

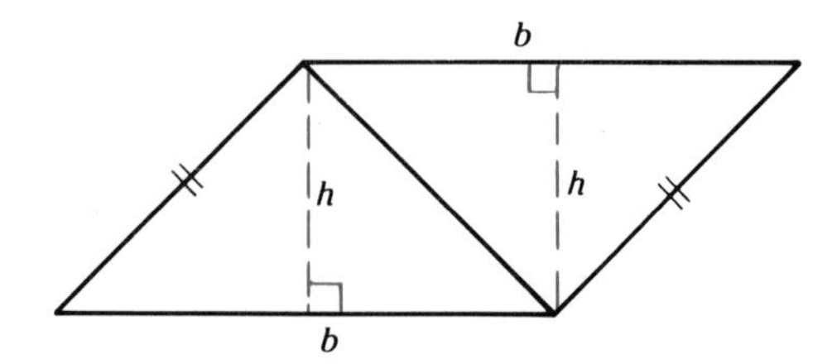

The area of the original rectangle or parallelogram is given by $b \times h$

Therefore the area of a triangle is given by $\frac{1}{2} \times b \times h$ where h is the height of the triangle. As for a parallelogram, height is understood to mean perpendicular height.

Area of a triangle $= \frac{1}{2} \times$ **base** $\times$ **height**

Exercise 11b

Find the area of this triangle.

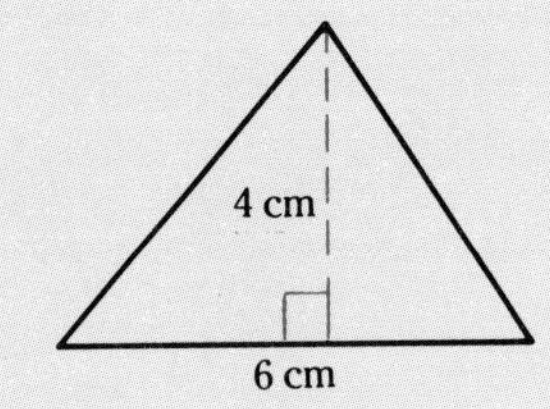

$$\text{Area} = \tfrac{1}{2}\ \text{base} \times \text{height}$$
$$= \tfrac{1}{2} \times 6 \times 4\ \text{cm}^2$$
$$= 12\ \text{cm}^2$$

Find the area of each triangle.

1.

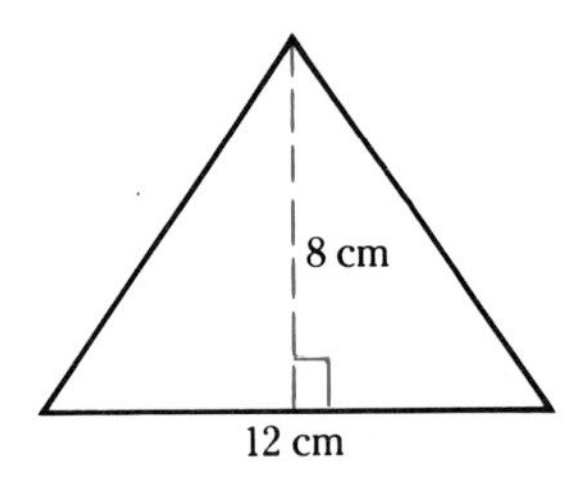

2.

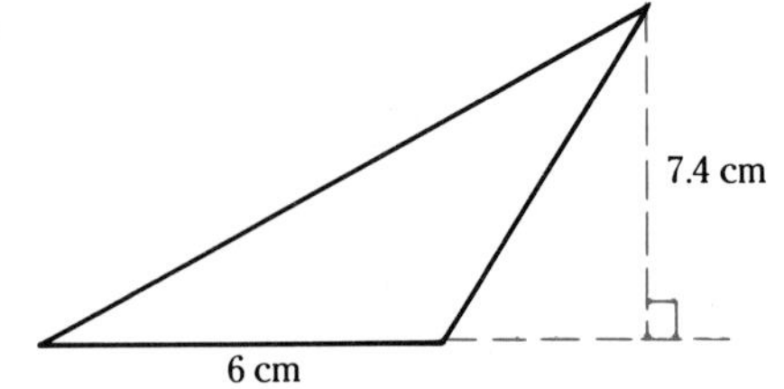

3.

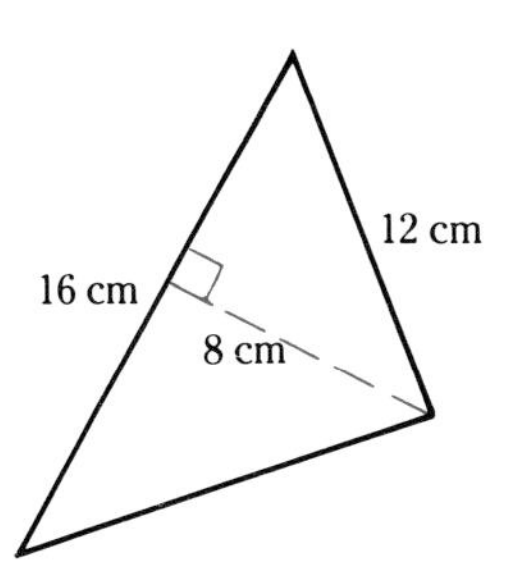

4.

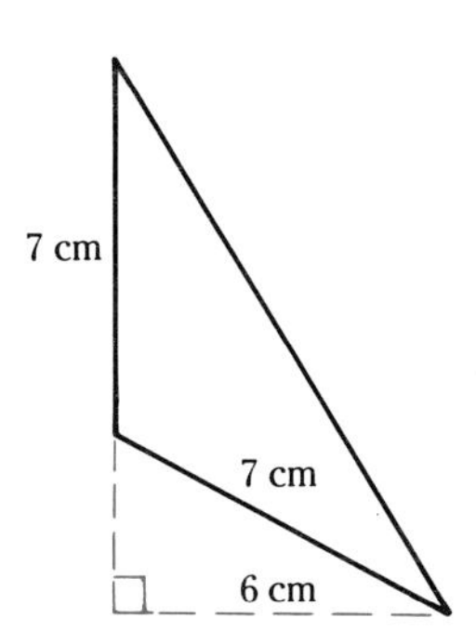

5.

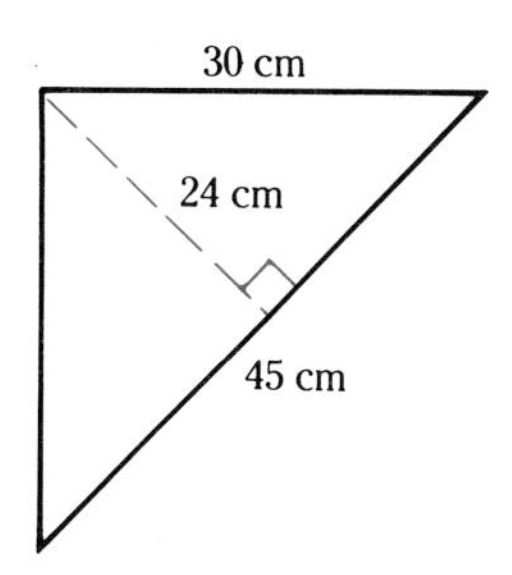

6.

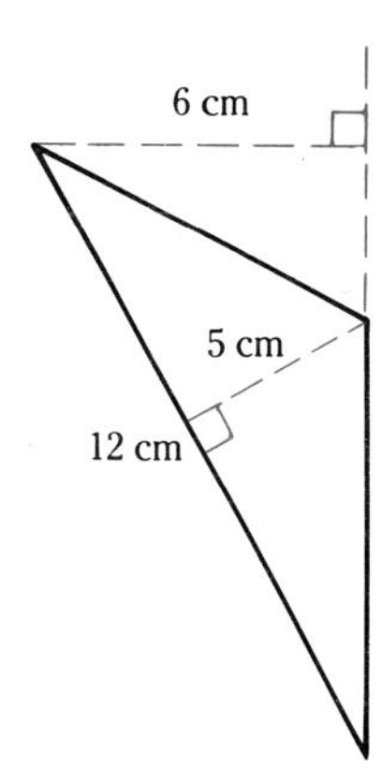

The units must be consistent.

Find the area of a triangle whose base is 12 cm and whose height is 46 mm.

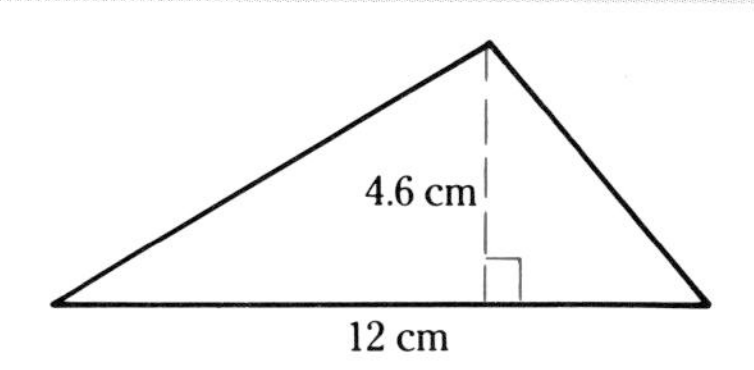

The units must be the same; 46 mm = 4.6 cm

$$\text{Area of triangle} = \tfrac{1}{2} \times 12 \times 4.6\ \text{cm}^2$$
$$= 27.6\ \text{cm}^2$$

Alternatively, 12 cm could be expressed as 120 mm and the area found in mm^2

Find the area of each triangle (a) in m^2 (b) in cm^2

	Base	Height
7.	2.7 m	140 cm
8.	76 cm	0.4 m
9.	0.76 m	230 mm

	Base	Height
10.	7.2 m	47 cm
11.	9.1 cm	58 mm
12.	0.04 m	16 cm

Find the area of a triangle whose vertices are at the points (1, 1), (4, 4) and (7, 0). Take 1 unit on each axis as 1 cm.

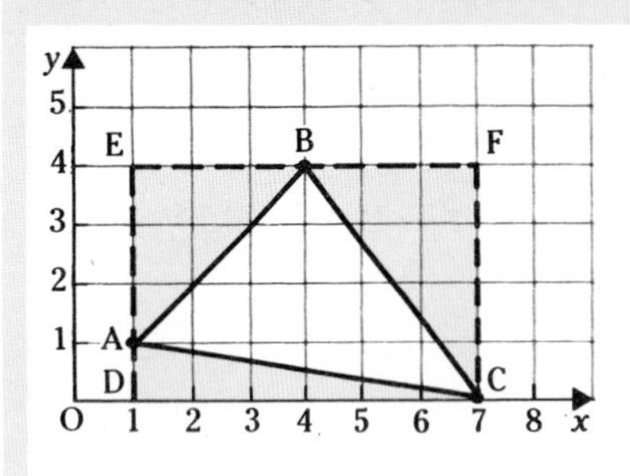

The triangle can be enclosed by the rectangle DEFC as shown.

The area of $\triangle ABC$ can be found from the area of this rectangle less the areas of the three shaded triangles.

Area rectangle DEFC $= 6 \times 4\ \text{cm}^2 = 24\ \text{cm}^2$

Area $\triangle ADC = \frac{1}{2} \times 6 \times 1\ \text{cm}^2 = 3\ \text{cm}^2$

Area $\triangle BFC = \frac{1}{2} \times 3 \times 4\ \text{cm}^2 = 6\ \text{cm}^2$

Area $\triangle ABE = \frac{1}{2} \times 3 \times 3\ \text{cm}^2 = 4\frac{1}{2}\ \text{cm}^2$

$\therefore$ area $\triangle ABC = (24 - 3 - 6 - 4\frac{1}{2})\ \text{cm}^2$

$= 10\frac{1}{2}\ \text{cm}^2$

Taking 1 unit on each axis as 1 cm, find the area of the triangle with the given coordinates.

13. (0, 2), (6, 0), (6, 4)

14. (−2, 1), (3, 2), (5, 6)

15. (3, −3), (6, 1), (−1, 5)

16. (6, 4), (−8, 6), (−3, −6)

The vertices of a quadrilateral are at the points (2, 4), (6, 0), (−1, 3) and (0, −5). Find its area taking 1 unit as 1 cm on each axis.

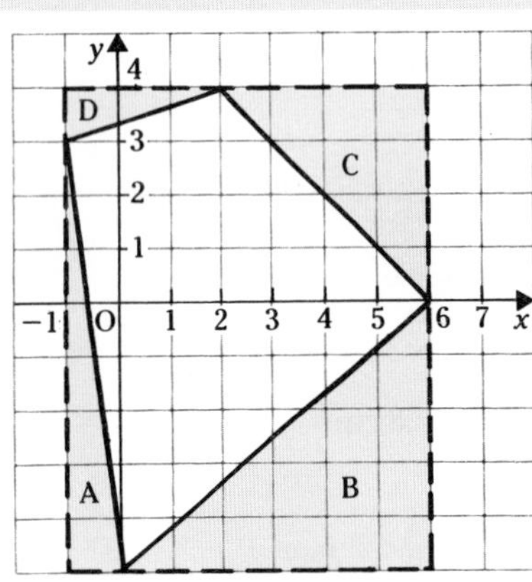

The quadrilateral can be enclosed in a simple rectangle by drawing horizontal or vertical lines through the given points.

Area of quadrilateral = area of rectangle
− area of triangle A
− area of triangle B
− area of triangle C
− area of triangle D

$= (63 - 4 - 15 - 8 - 1\frac{1}{2})\ \text{cm}^2$

$= 34\frac{1}{2}\ \text{cm}^2$

In each question find the area of the quadrilateral with vertices at the given points. Take 1 unit on each axis as 1 cm.

17. $(-2, -1), (1, 6), (7, 6), (1, -4)$

18. $(-3, 0), (0, -2), (4, 0), (3, 6)$

19. $(-1, -3), (5, -1), (3, 3), (-1, 4)$

20. $(6, 1), (3, 7), (-2, 6), (0, -3)$

The area of a triangle is 48 mm^2. If its height is 6 mm, what is the length of its base ?

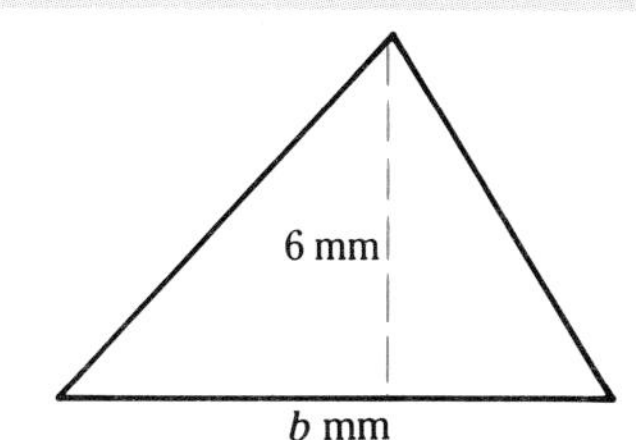

$$\text{Area} = \tfrac{1}{2} \times \text{base} \times \text{height}$$
$$48 = \tfrac{1}{2} \times b \times 6$$
$$48 = 3b$$
$$b = 16$$

The length of the base is 16 mm.

Find the missing measurement for each triangle. Remember that units must be consistent.

	Area	Base	Height
21.	30 mm^2	10 mm	
22.	108 cm^2		6 cm
23.	75 mm^2	3 cm	
24.	1.28 m^2		64 cm

In $\triangle ABC$, $AB = BC = 10$ cm and $AC = 12$ cm. Find the area of $\triangle ABC$.

$\triangle ABC$ is isosceles so BD divides the triangle into two equal shapes.

$BD = 8$ cm ($\triangle ABD$ is a 3, 4, 5 triangle)

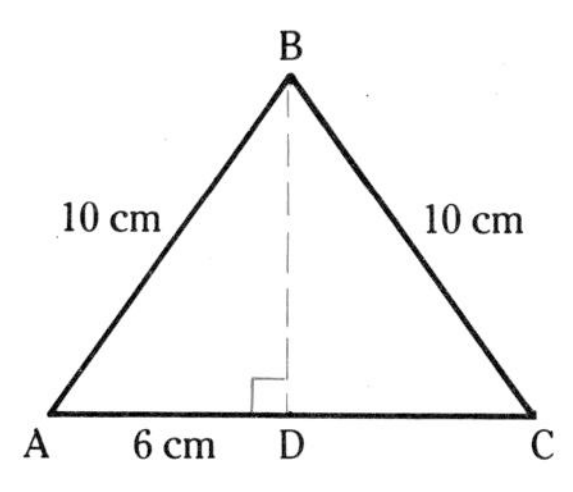

$$\text{Area of } \triangle ABD = \tfrac{1}{2}\text{ base} \times \text{height}$$
$$= \tfrac{1}{2} \times 12 \times 8\text{ cm}^2$$
$$= 48\text{ cm}^2$$

25. Find the area of triangle PQR in which $PQ = PR = 15$ cm and $QR = 24$ cm.

26. Find the area of triangle DEF in which $DE = EF = DF = 4$ cm.

27. In triangle PQR, $PQ = QR = 5$ cm and $PR = 8$ cm. QS is perpendicular to PR. Find
    (a) the length of QS.
    (b) the area of triangle PQR.

28.

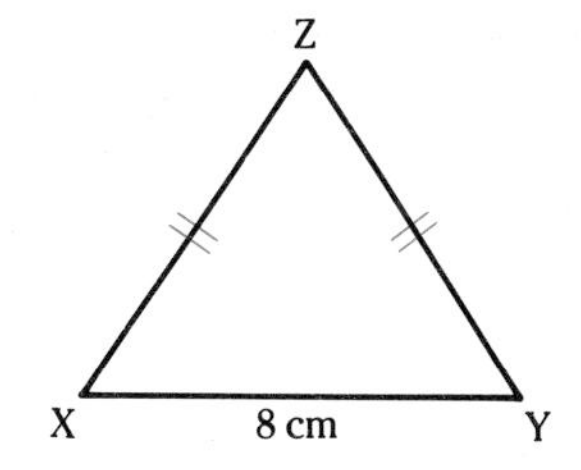

The area of this triangle is 24 cm^2. Find the height of the triangle and hence the length of XZ.

AREAS OF COMPOUND SHAPES

The Area of a Trapezium

A trapezium is a quadrilateral with *one* pair of opposite sides parallel.

Consider the trapezium given in the following diagram. By drawing a diagonal we can divide the trapezium into two triangles.

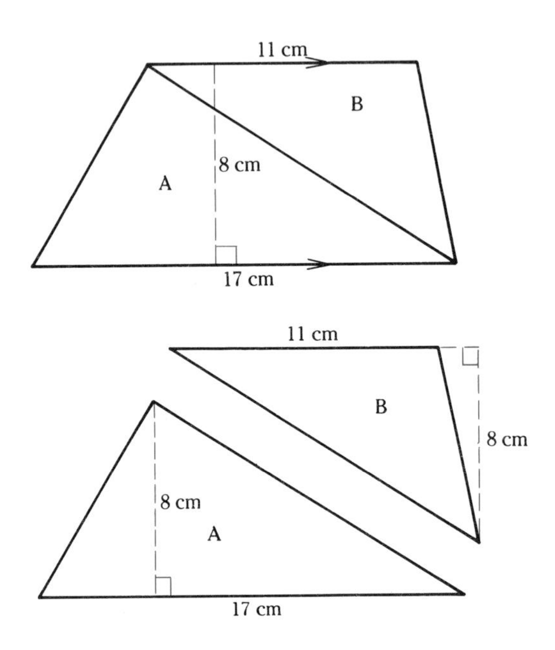

For triangle A the height is 8 cm and the base is 17 cm.
Therefore its area is $\frac{1}{2} \times 8 \times 17\,\text{cm}^2$.
For triangle B the height is 8 cm and the base is 11 cm.
Therefore its area is $\frac{1}{2} \times 8 \times 11\,\text{cm}^2$.

The area of the trapezium is the sum of the areas of the triangles,

i.e. $$\tfrac{1}{2} \times 8 \times 17\,\text{cm}^2 + \tfrac{1}{2} \times 8 \times 11\,\text{cm}^2 = \tfrac{1}{2} \times 8 \times (17 + 11)\,\text{cm}^2$$

and we note that $(17 + 11)$ is the sum of the parallel sides.

Any trapezium can be divided in a similar way into two triangles with equal heights so, in general,

 **Area of trapezium** $= \frac{1}{2} \times$ **height** $\times$ **sum of parallel sides** 

If the two non-parallel sides of a trapezium are equal in length it is called an isosceles trapezium.

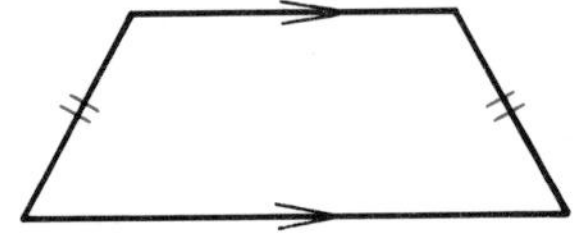

Exercise 11c

1. Find the area of each trapezium.

(a)

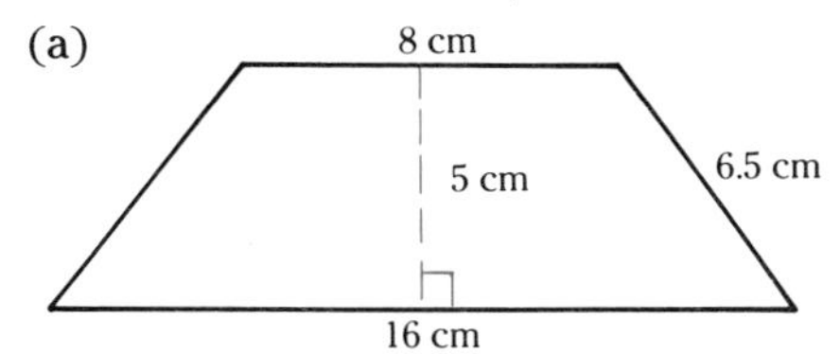

(b)

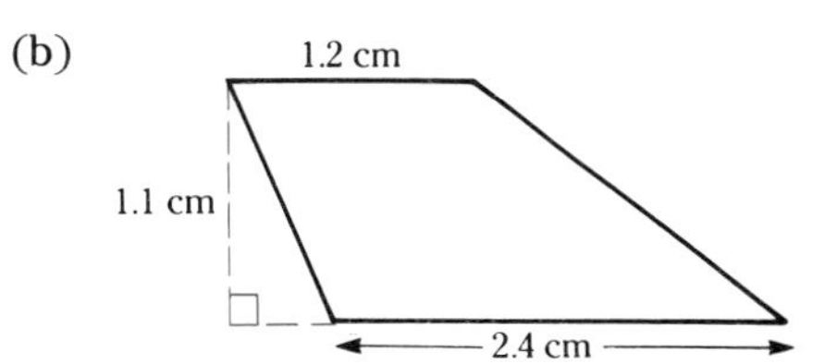

2. Find the area of a trapezium given that
   (a) its parallel sides, which are of lengths 6 cm and 7 cm, are 6 cm apart
   (b) its parallel sides are of lengths 120 cm and 1.5 m and its height is 2.3 m. (Remember that units must be consistent.)

The area of a trapezium is 345 cm^2. If the height is 15 cm and the length of one of the parallel sides is 22 cm, find the length of the other parallel side.

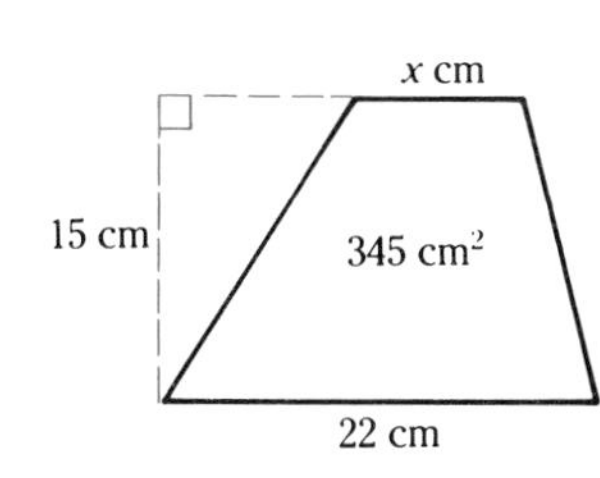

$$\text{Area} = \tfrac{1}{2} \times \text{height} \times (\text{sum of parallel sides})$$

$$345 = \tfrac{1}{2} \times 15 \times (22 + x)$$

$$= 7.5 \times (22 + x)$$

$$\frac{345}{7.5} = 22 + x$$

$$46 = 22 + x$$

$$\therefore \ x = 24$$

The length of the required side is 24 cm.

A trapezium has parallel sides of lengths a cm and b cm, which are h cm apart. Find the unknown dimension.

	a	b	h	Area (cm^2)
3.	14	8		143
4.		6	8	64
5.	15		22	385
6.	40	24		480
7.		2	3	18

8.

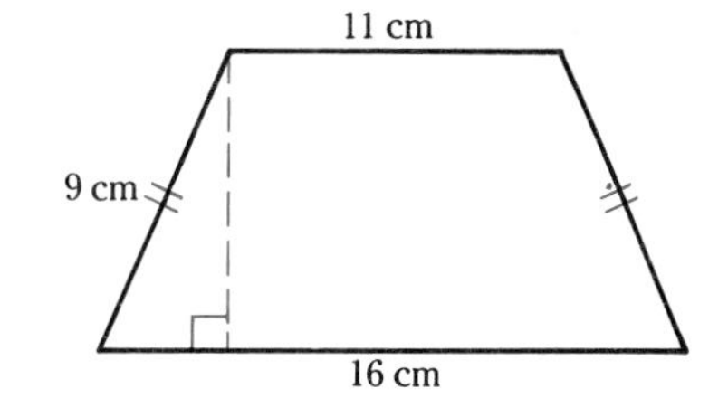

Find (a) the height of the trapezium
(b) the area of the trapezium.

The areas of compound shapes can be calculated if they are made up of squares, rectangles, triangles and trapeziums.

The diagram shows the end wall of a bungalow. The wall is entirely brick-built except for the two windows. Find the area of the brickwork.

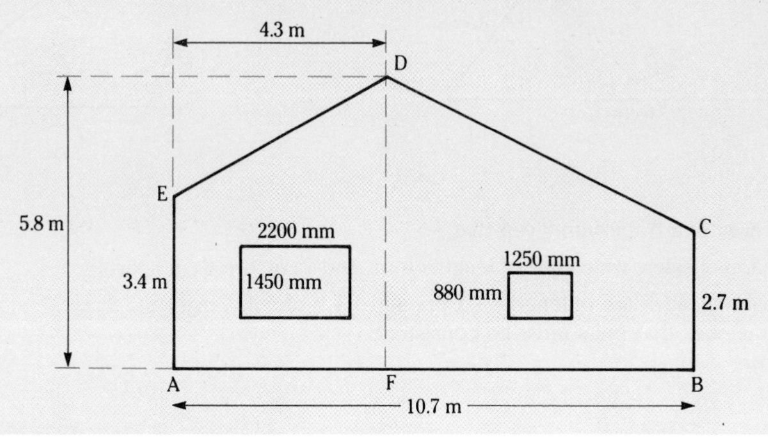

DF divides ABCDE into 2 trapeziums.

Area of AEDF $= \frac{1}{2}(3.4 + 5.8) \times 4.3\,\text{m}^2 = 19.78\,\text{m}^2$

FB $= 10.7\,\text{m} - 4.3\,\text{m} = 6.4\,\text{m}$

Area of FBCD $= \frac{1}{2}(2.7 + 5.8) \times 6.4\,\text{m}^2 = 27.2\,\text{m}^2$

Total area of wall $= (19.78 + 27.2)\,\text{m}^2 = 46.98\,\text{m}^2$

Take the dimensions of the windows in metres

Area of larger window $= 1.450 \times 2.200\,\text{m}^2 = 3.19\,\text{m}^2$

Area of smaller window $= 1.250 \times 0.880\,\text{m}^2 = 1.1\,\text{m}^2$

Area of brickwork $= (46.98 - 3.19 - 1.1)\,\text{m}^2 = 42.69\,\text{m}^2 = 42.7\,\text{m}^2$ (3 s.f.)

Find the area of each shape. If necessary split the figure into parts whose areas can be calculated.

9.

18 cm

7 cm

11 cm

10.

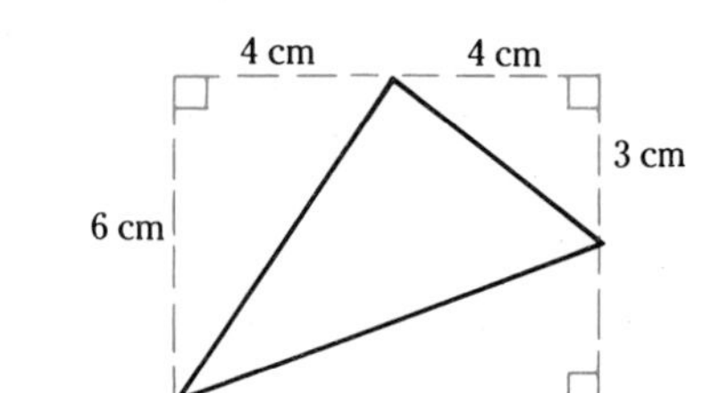

11.

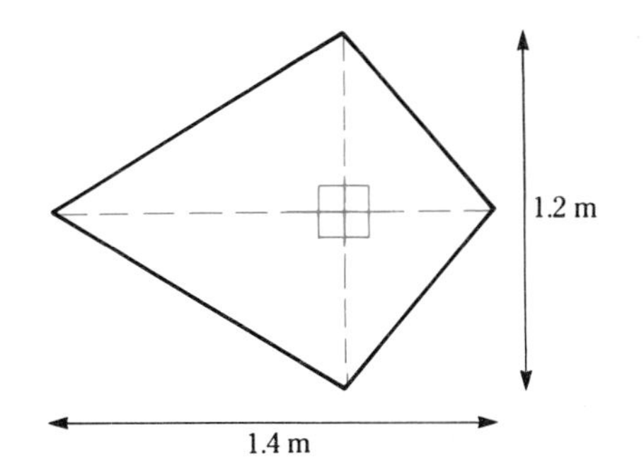

12.

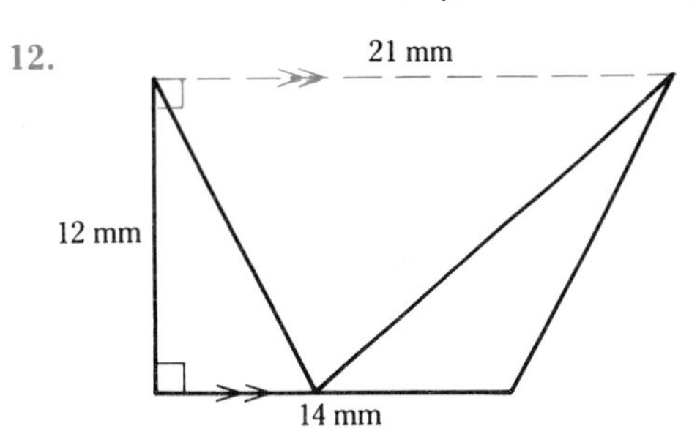

13. A landscape gardener designs a layout for a garden with an awkward shape. The diagram shows his plan.

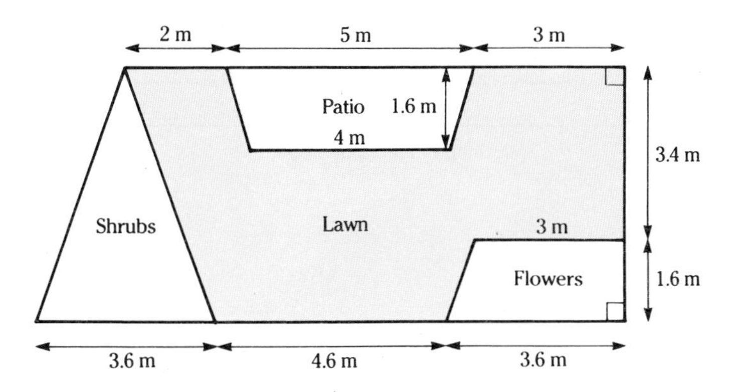

Find the area of the lawn.

14. The front view of a frame tent is shown in the diagram. Find the area of canvas, given that the window and door are made from nylon net.

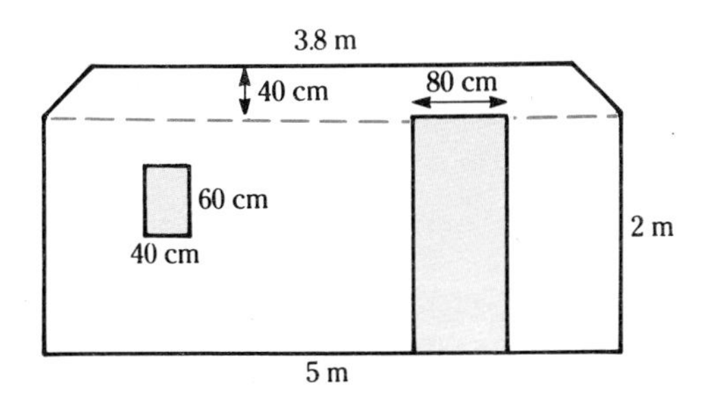

15. The floor of a restaurant is to be carpeted with the exception of the bar area and the dance floor. Find the area of the carpeted section.

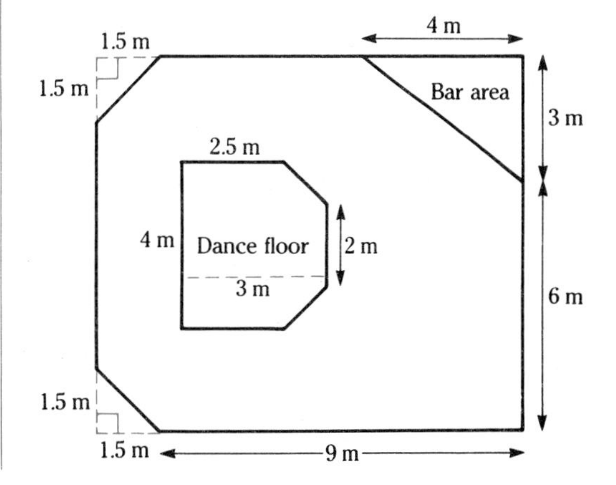

16. The stonework, shown shaded, on the front of an office needs specialist cleaning.

(a) Find the area to be treated.

(b) If the cleaning firm charges \$85 for each square metre or part of a square metre, find the cost of the renovation.

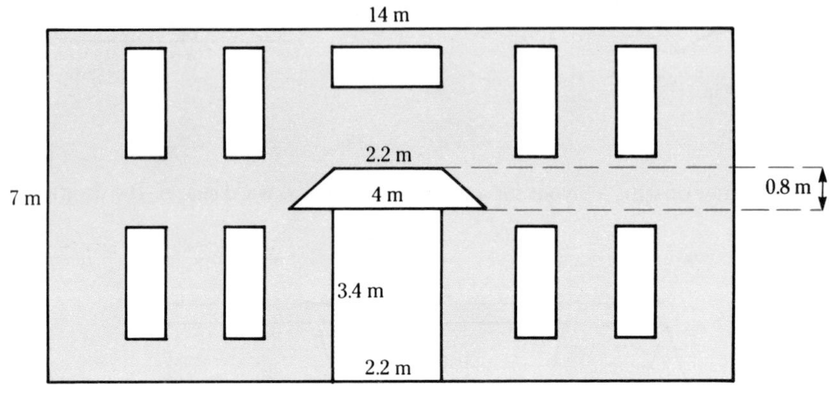

All windows are 2.2 m × 0.8 m

THE SURFACE AREA OF A CUBOID

A cuboid has six faces of which opposite pairs are identical. The total surface area of a cuboid is therefore given by adding the areas of three different faces and doubling the result.

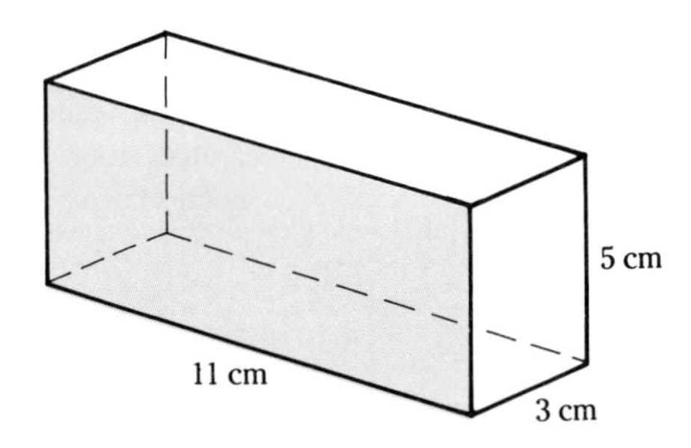

For the cuboid shown,

the area of the top (or the base) is $11 \times 3\,\text{cm}^2 = 33\,\text{cm}^2$

the area of the front face (shaded) is $11 \times 5\,\text{cm}^2 = 55\,\text{cm}^2$

the area of an end is $3 \times 5\,\text{cm}^2 = 15\,\text{cm}^2$

Therefore the total surface area is $2 \times (33 + 55 + 15)\,\text{cm}^2 = 206\,\text{cm}^2$

This can be seen very clearly if we draw a *net* of the cuboid, i.e. the flat shape obtained when the cuboid is cut along some of its edges and flattened out.

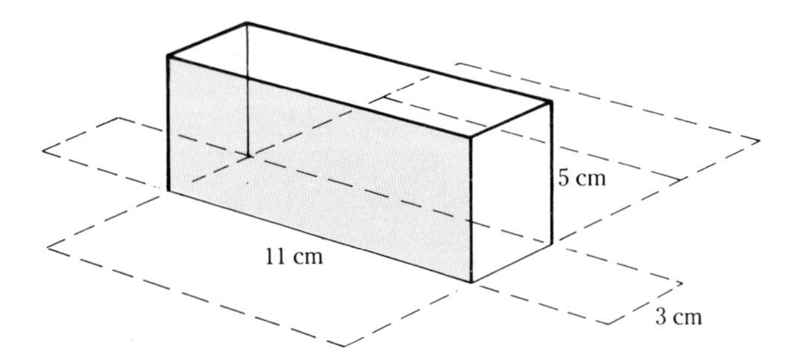

For example if the cuboid above is cut along the thick edges and opened up, this net is produced.

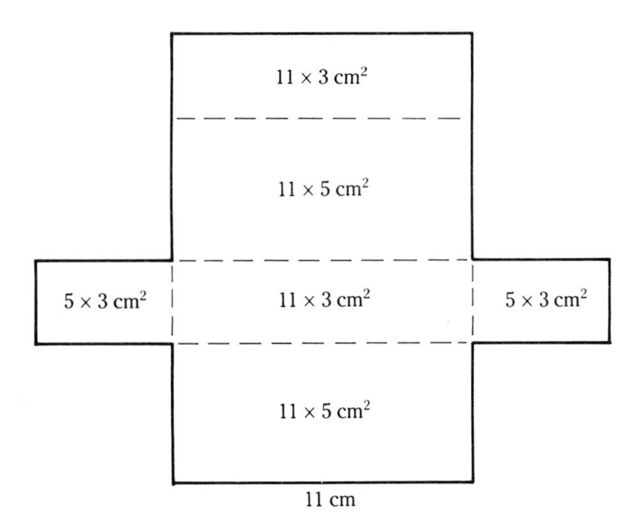

Exercise 11d

In questions 1 and 2 find the surface area and volume of the cuboid given by the net.

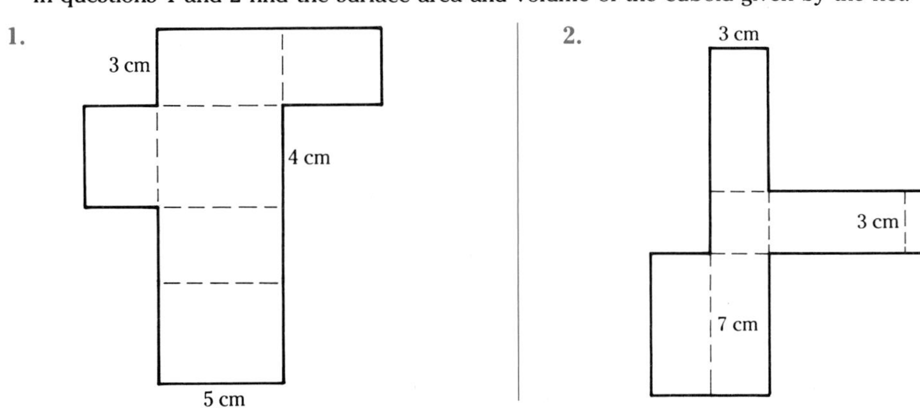

In questions 3 and 4 draw a suitable net for the cuboid with the given dimensions and find the surface area of the cuboid.

3. 7 cm by 4 cm by 3 cm

4. 4 cm by 3.5 cm by 2.5 cm

5. Draw as many different nets as you can for a 3 cm cube. Each net should be in one piece.

6. This net will make a cuboid.

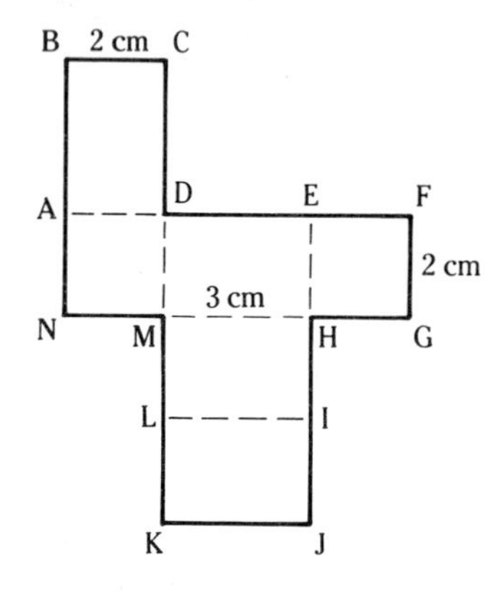

(a) *Sketch* the cuboid and mark its dimensions on the sketch.

(b) Which corners meet with B ?

(c) Which edge joins with EF ?

7.

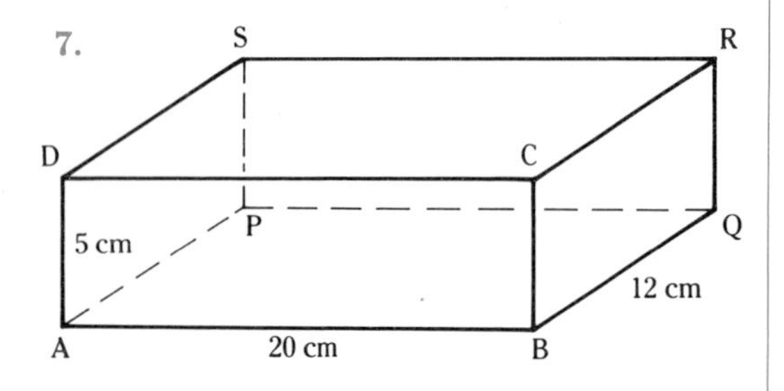

(a) Find the length of BR.

(b) Find the least distance from A to R if the distance is to be measured only along edges of the cuboid.

(c) Draw the net for the cuboid formed by cutting along BC, CR and RQ, and along AD, DS, SP and SR.

(d) Find the least distance from A to R if the distance can be measured anywhere on the surface of the cuboid.

8.

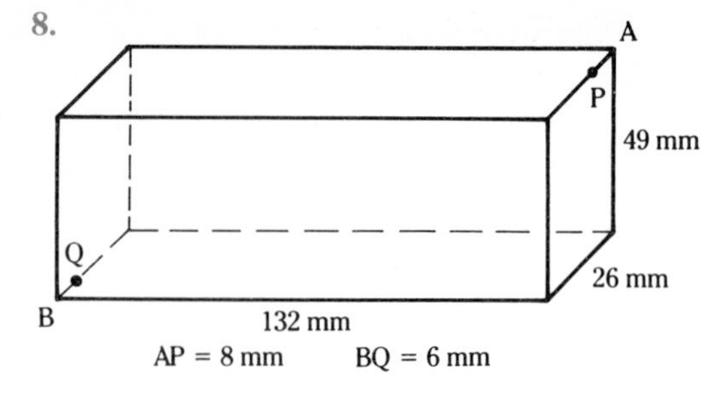

(a) Using only the given diagram, find what you think is the shortest distance from P to Q on the surface of this cuboid.

(b) Draw a net for the cuboid and again find the shortest distance on the surface from P to Q. (To form the net, start at A and cut along the longest edge first.)

(c) Did you get the same distance both times and which do you think was the better way to find the distance ?

9. Which of these nets will make a cuboid ?

(a)

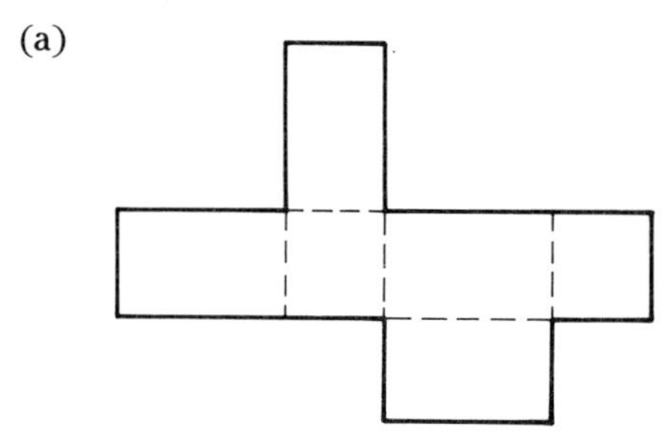

(b)

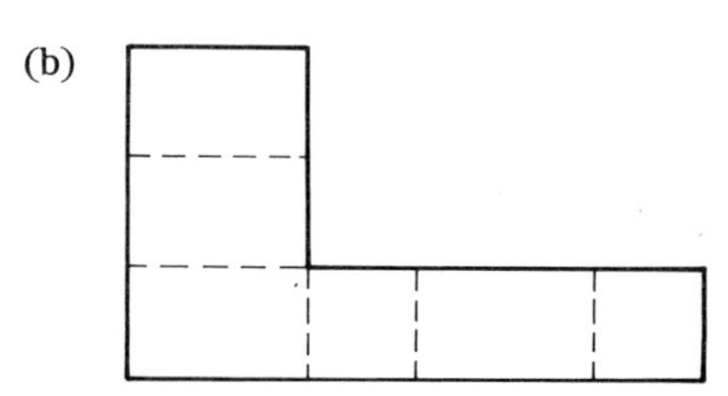

(c)

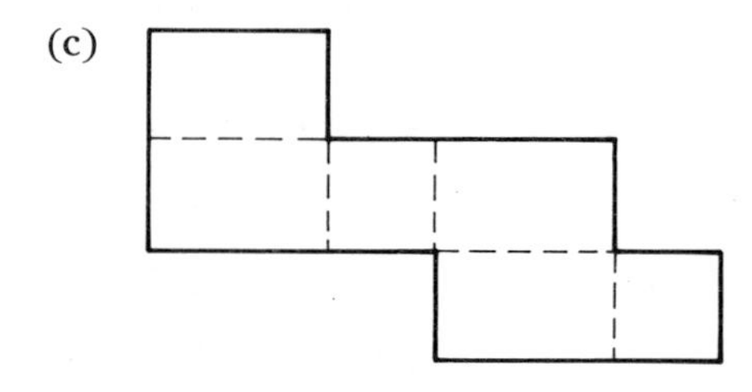

PRISMS

In Chapter 5 the volumes of a cube and a cuboid were investigated. Now we consider ways to calculate the volumes of other solids with interesting shapes.

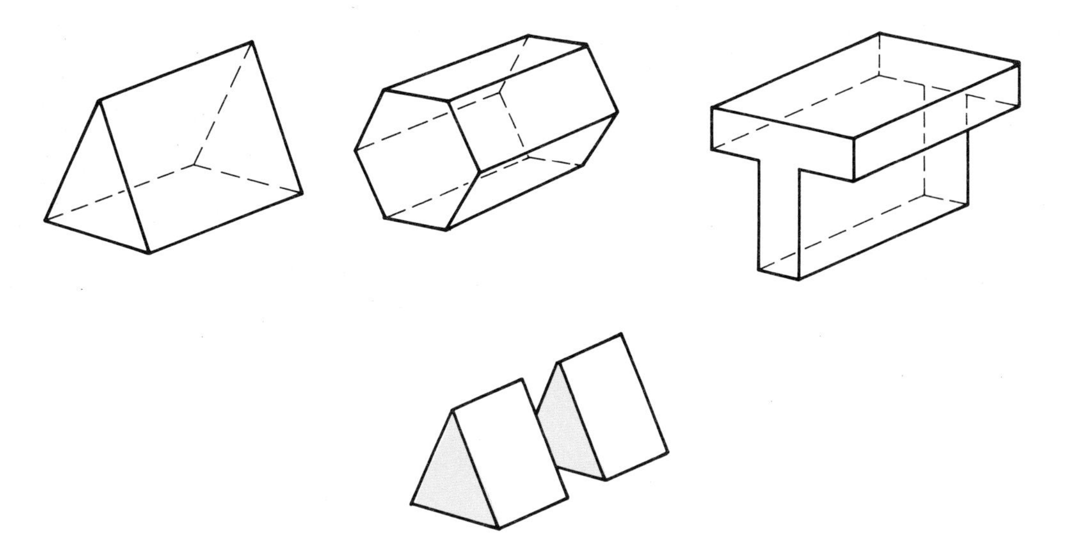

When any one of the solids above is cut through, parallel to the ends, the *cross-section* produced always has the same shape and size as the ends have; the cross-section is said to be *uniform* (i.e. constant). Solids with this property are called *prisms.* One of the simplest prisms is a cuboid; it is called a rectangular prism because its uniform cross-section is a rectangle. Other prisms also are known by their cross-section when this is a simple shape, e.g. the first two solids in the diagram above are a triangular prism and a hexagonal prism.

The Volume of a Prism

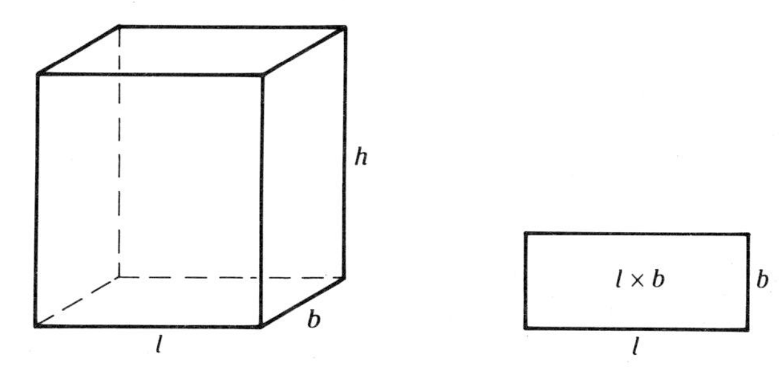

For the rectangular prism shown above, the volume is known to be given by:

volume = length × breadth × height

Now breadth × height gives the area of the uniform cross-section so we can say:

volume = area of cross-section × length

This property is true for all prisms, i.e., in general,

volume of a prism = cross-sectional area × length

Note that, if a prism is standing on one of its ends the base is a cross-section, and in this case:

volume = area of base × height

Note also that the term 'right prism' means that the prism can stand upright on its base with its sides vertical, e.g.

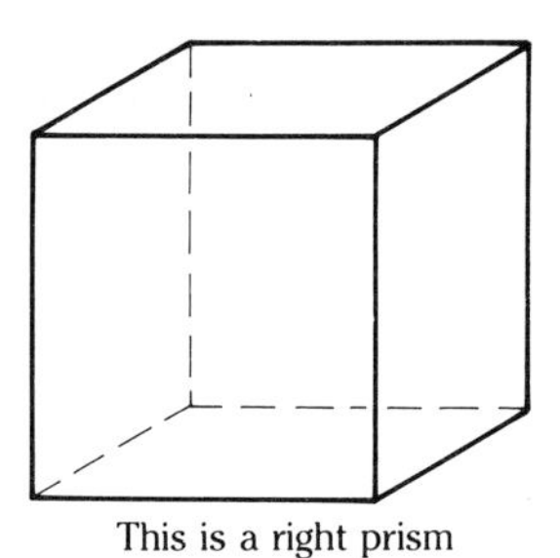

This is a right prism

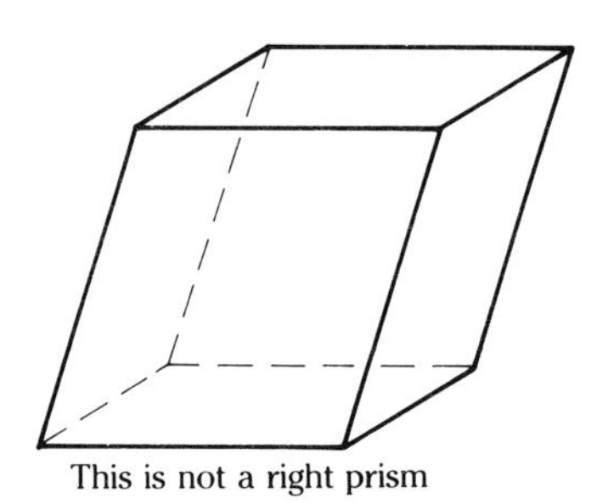

This is not a right prism

In this book we shall deal only with right prisms.

EDGES, FACES AND VERTICES

In examining each of the solids in this chapter we have referred to its edges, its faces and its vertices.
Each flat side is a face; the line where two faces meet is an edge; the point where edges meet is a vertex (i.e. a corner).

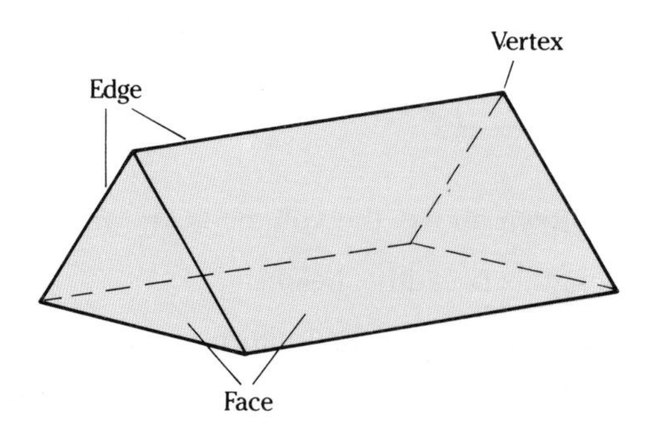

Exercise 11e

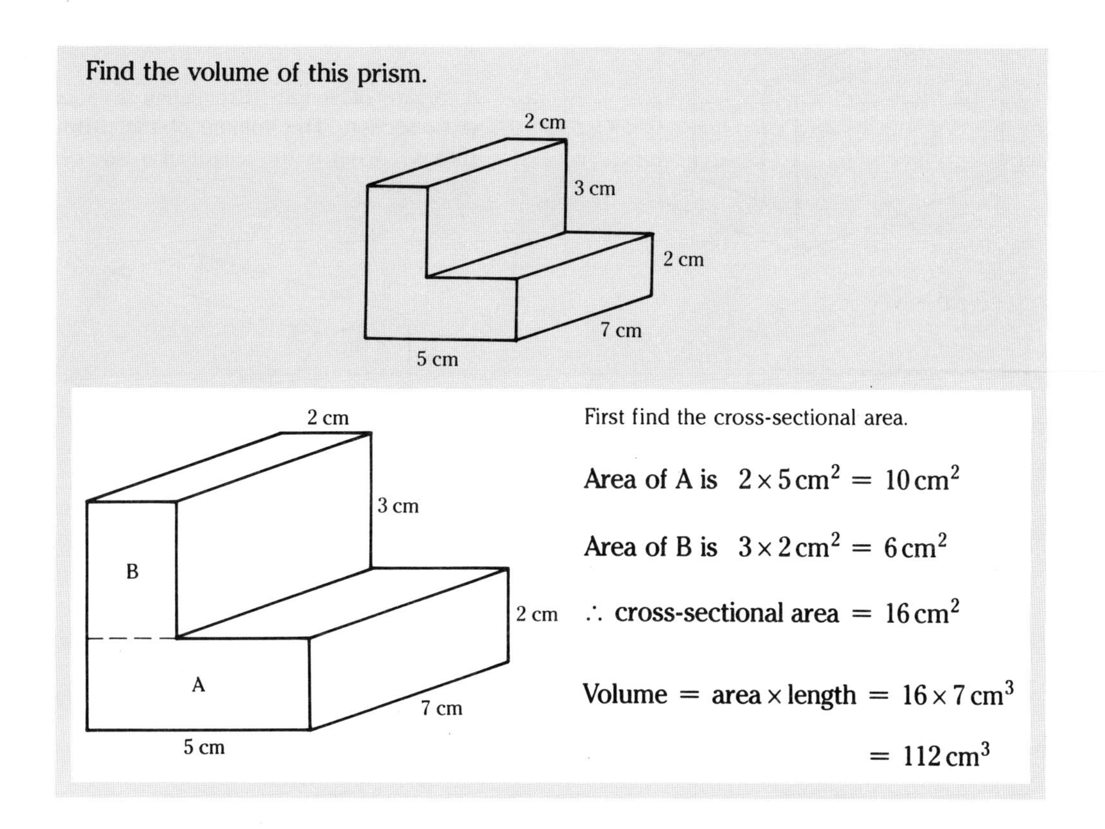

Find the volume of this prism.

First find the cross-sectional area.

Area of A is $2 \times 5\,\text{cm}^2 = 10\,\text{cm}^2$

Area of B is $3 \times 2\,\text{cm}^2 = 6\,\text{cm}^2$

$\therefore$ cross-sectional area $= 16\,\text{cm}^2$

Volume $=$ area $\times$ length $= 16 \times 7\,\text{cm}^3$

$= 112\,\text{cm}^3$

Find the volume of each of the following prisms.

1.

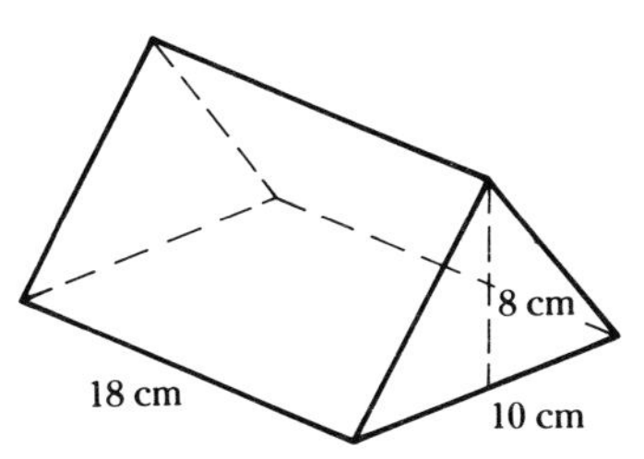

2.

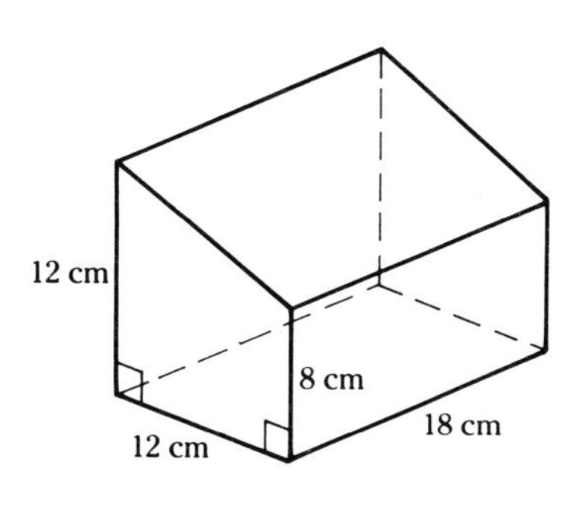

3.

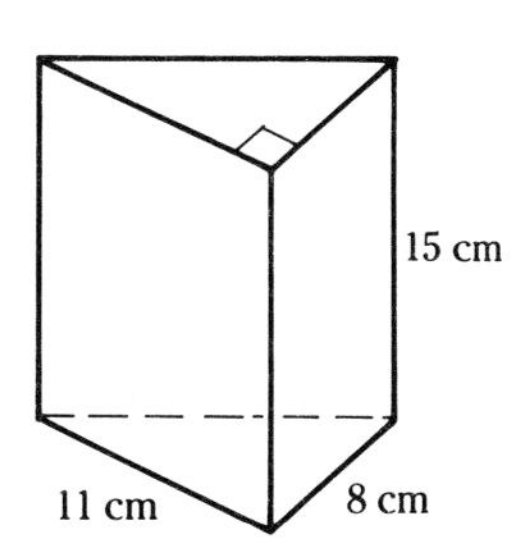

4.

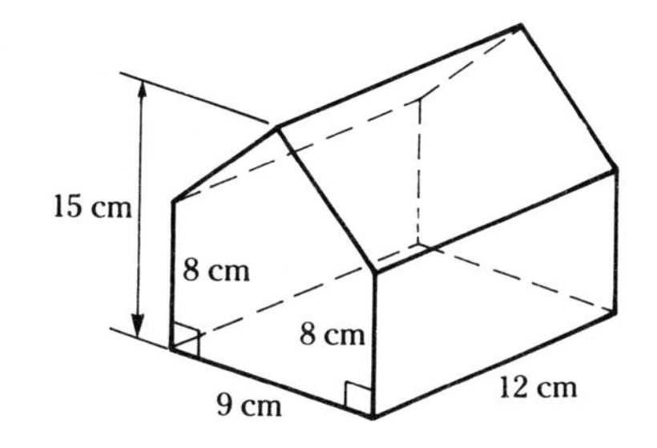

5.

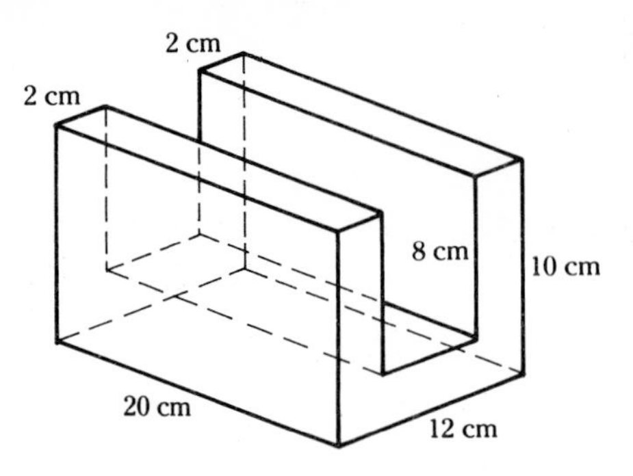

6.

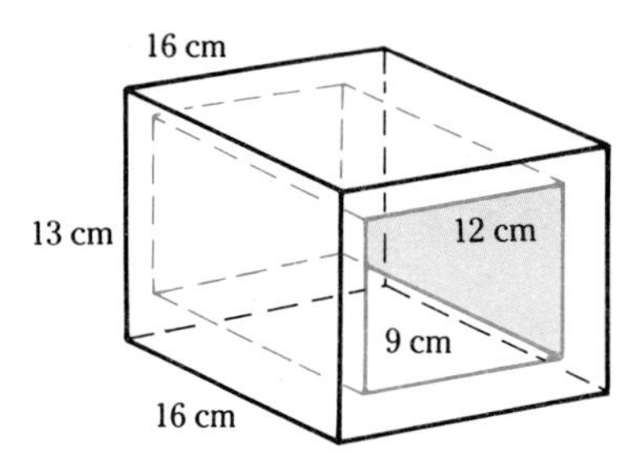

7. A scout's tent has the shape of a triangular prism. It is 2.6 m long and the triangular end is 2.5 m wide and 1.9 m high.

(a) Find the volume inside the tent.

(b) What is the area of canvas, including the ground sheet, used to make this tent ?

8.

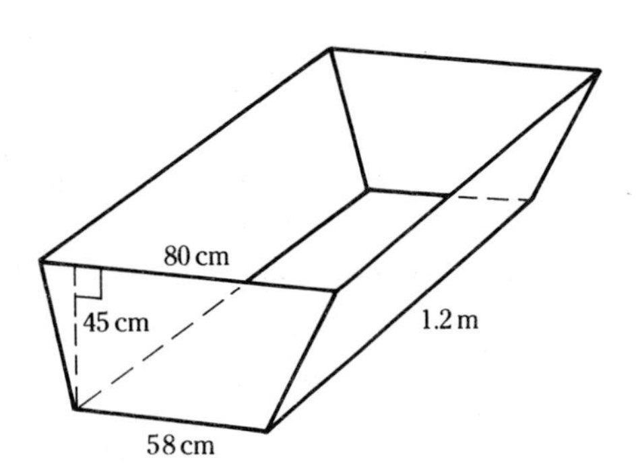

The uniform cross-section of a water trough is a trapezium 80 cm wide at the top, with a 58 cm wide base; the trough is 45 cm deep and 1.2 m long. Find the capacity of the trough.

9. The volume of a solid with uniform cross-section is $65\,\text{cm}^3$. If the area of its cross-section is $13\,\text{cm}^2$, find its length.

10. A prism of length 12 cm has a square cross-section. The volume of the prism is $108\,\text{cm}^3$. What is the length of a side of its square base ?

11.

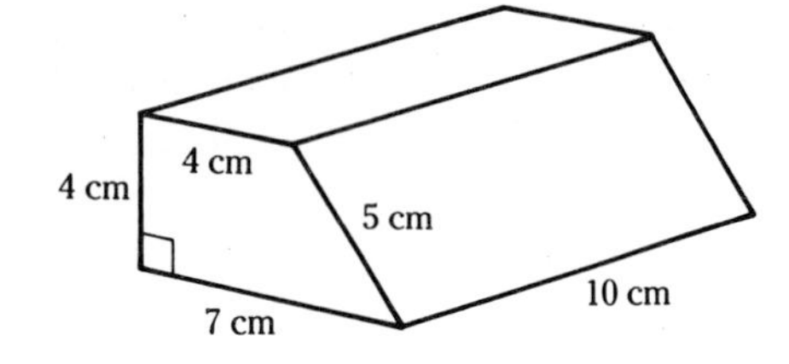

(a) Sketch a net for the given prism.

(b) Find the total surface area of the prism.

12.

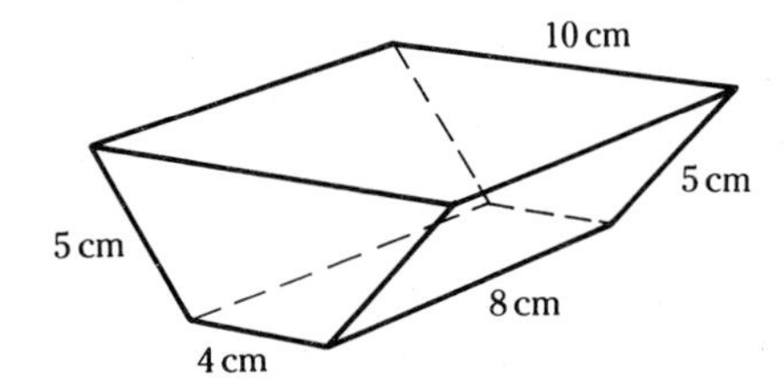

(a) Sketch a net for the given prism.

(b) Calculate the height of the cross-section.

(c) Find the total surface area.

13.

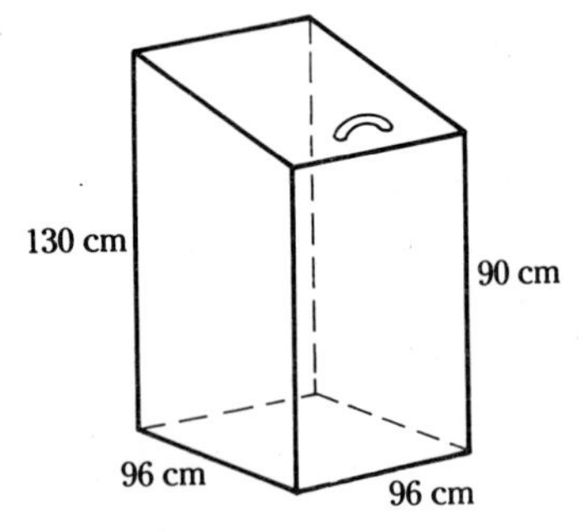

For the storage bin shown in the diagram, find

(a) the length of the sloping top edge of the side of the bin

(b) the volume of the bin

(c) the total external surface area including the base.

PLANS AND ELEVATIONS

Plans

This is a sketch of a set of three cake tins; it attempts to show them as three-dimensional.

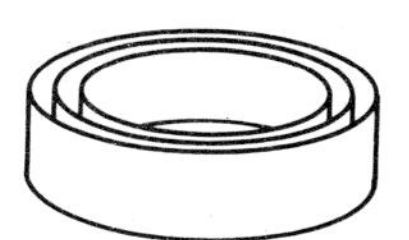

When they are viewed from directly above, what we see is the *plan* of the tins. The plan is two-dimensional and shows only the concentric circular rims of the three tins.

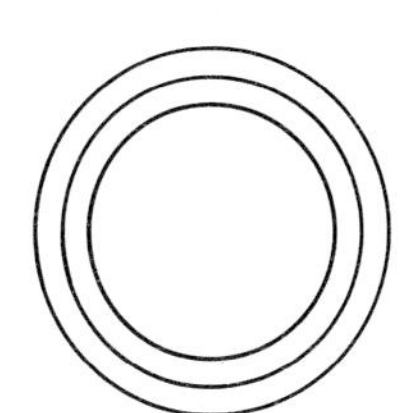

If the set of tins were turned upside down, all that could be seen from above would be the base of the largest tin.
When we draw the plan, however, broken lines are used to show the circumferences of the 'hidden' bases of the two smaller tins.

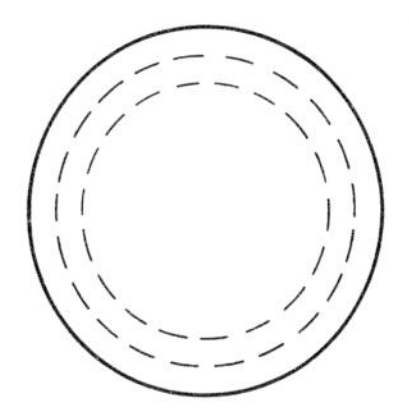

Elevations

An elevation of an object is the view seen when the object is viewed from the front, side or back. As for plans, any hidden shapes are drawn with broken lines. A diagram of an elevation should indicate the direction of viewing.

In the case of the set of cake tins (right way up), the elevation is the same in all directions. The outer tin is seen fully and the two inner tins are shown by broken lines.

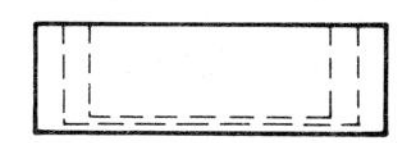

Sections

When an object is sliced into two parts (real or imaginary), the shape of the cut surface is called a *section.*
For some objects the section may be uniform, as is the case for any prism cut parallel to its ends.
In other cases the section depends upon where and how the cut is made, e.g.

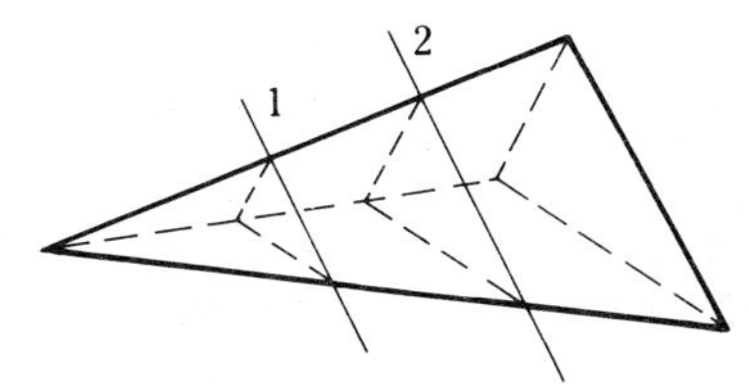

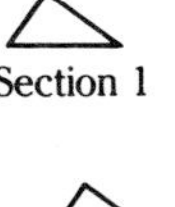

Section 1

Section 2

Exercise 11f

The diagram shows a component used for building a stage.

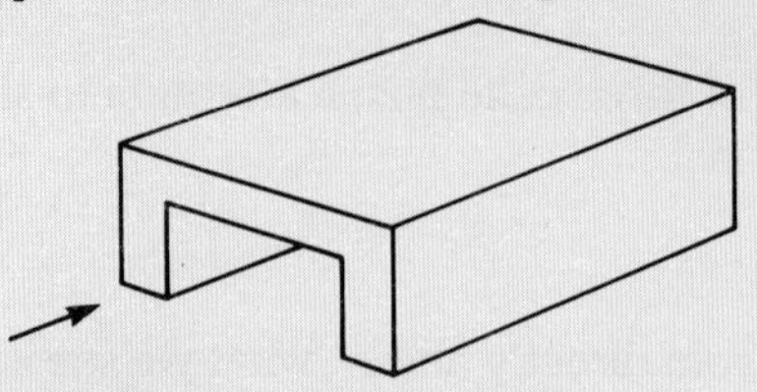

(a) Sketch a plan of the component.
(b) Sketch the elevation in the direction of the arrow.

(a)

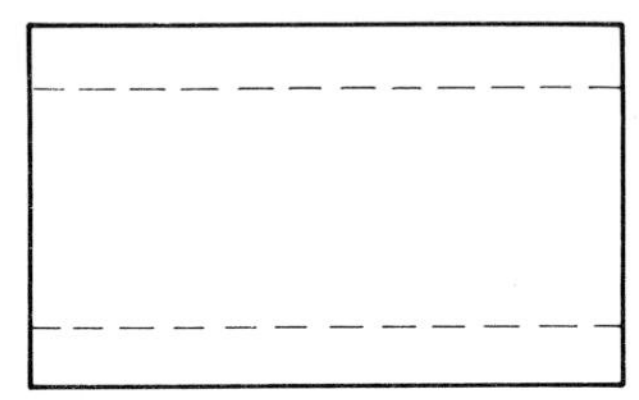

Broken lines show the hidden edges.

(b)

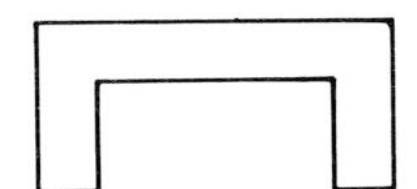

1. Sketch the plan of each object.

(a)

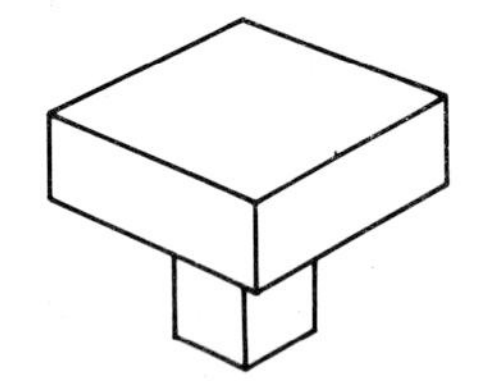

(b)

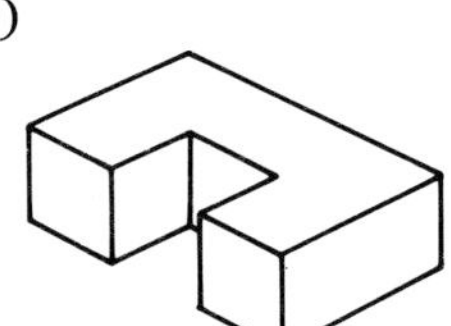

(c)

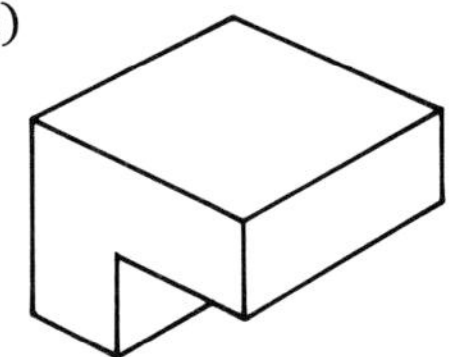

2. Sketch the elevations of each solid, viewed in the directions of the arrows.

(a)

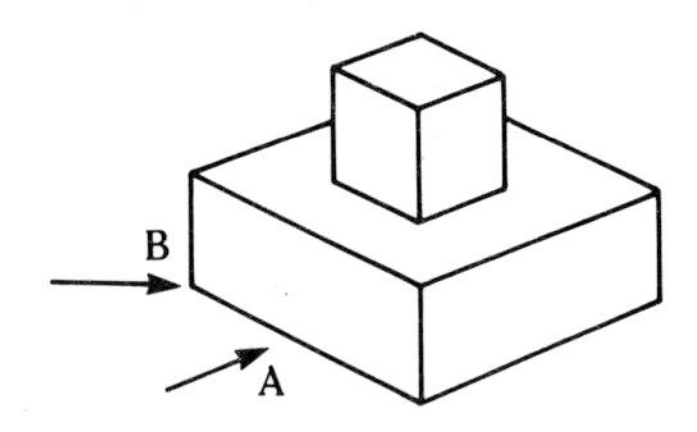

(c)

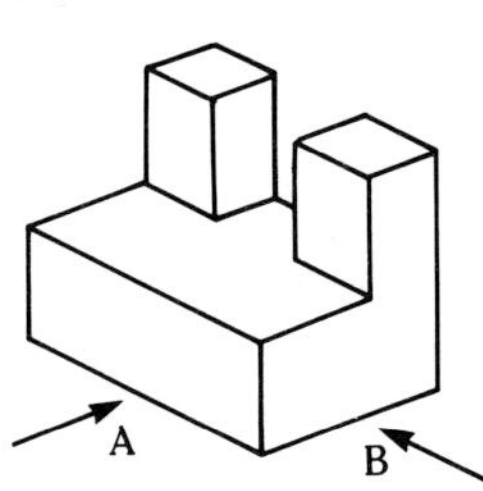

(b)

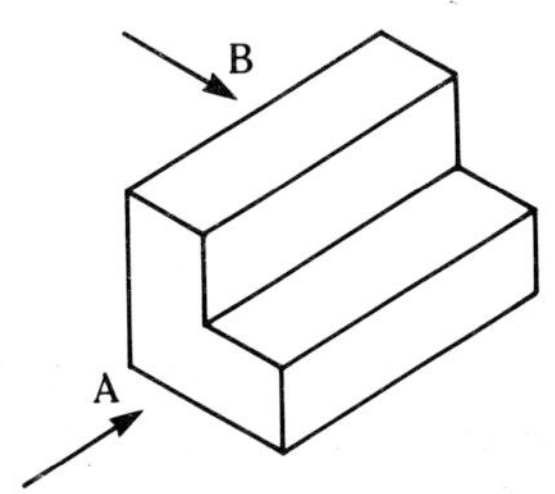

(d)

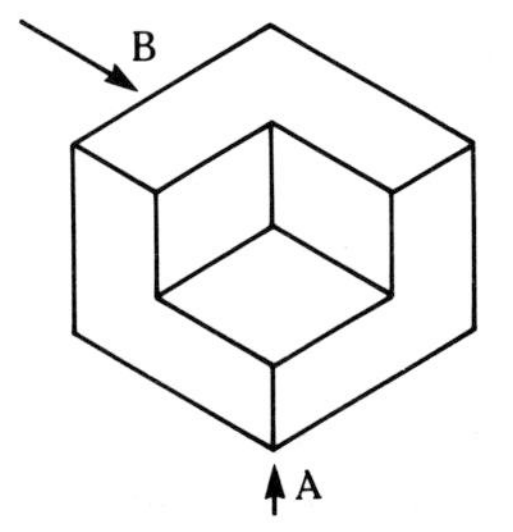

3. The plan and the elevation in the direction of the arrow are given for a solid. In each case sketch the solid.

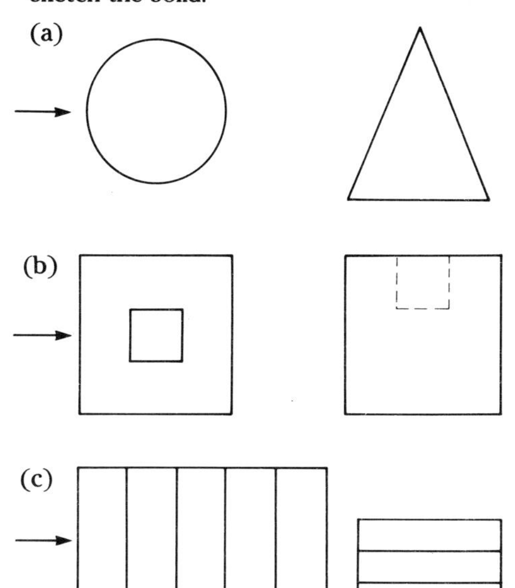

4.

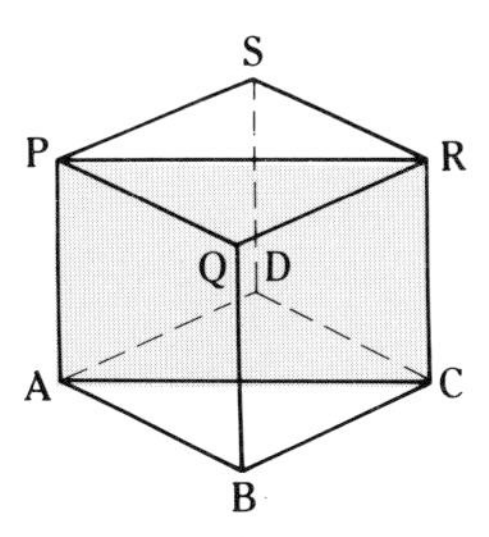

The cube in the diagram has an edge of length 6 cm.

(a) Sketch the shaded section and find its area.

(b) Sketch the section PBCS and compare it with the section drawn in (a). What do you notice?

5. The diagram shows a box in the shape of a cuboid.

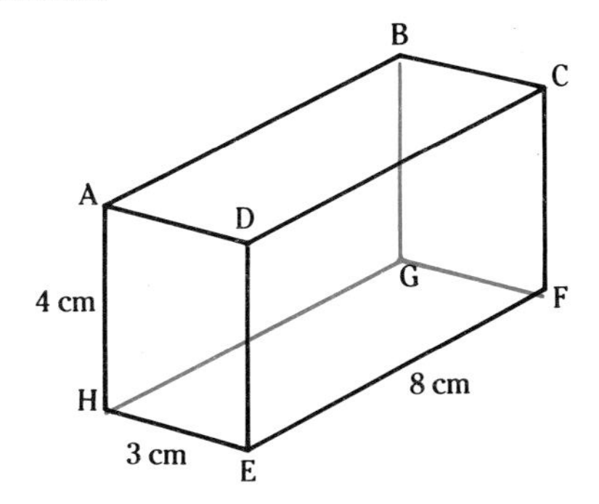

(a) Calculate the length of HF.

(b) Draw the section AHFC and mark the lengths of its sides.

(c) Use the section AHFC to draw a triangle from which the length of AF can be found. Use this triangle to calculate the length of the longest stick that will just fit inside the box.

6.

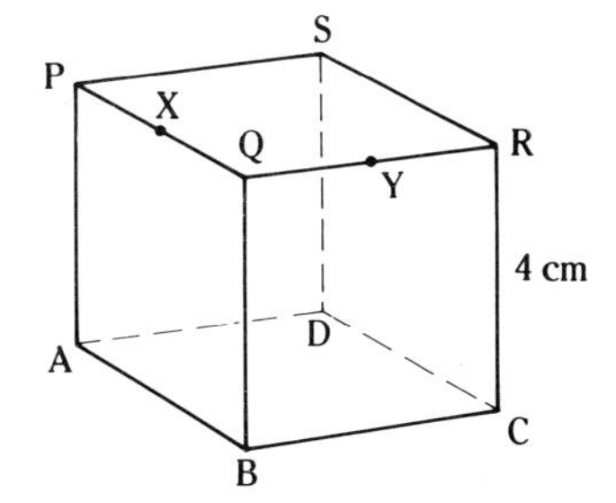

The base of the cube in the diagram is horizontal. The midpoints of PQ and QR are X and Y. The cube is divided into two parts by a vertical cut through XY.

(a) Sketch the section.

(b) Find the length of XY and the area of the section.

(c) Find the volume of each of the two parts into which the cube has been cut.

Investigations

1. A cube can be made from a net of six squares.
   Investigate the possible arrangements of these six squares.

2. Advertisements in magazines often include a pre-paid return form which can be folded and tucked in to form an 'envelope' without any sticking required. It is possible to use this idea to make a cube in a similar way. Investigate.

Self-Assessment 11

1.

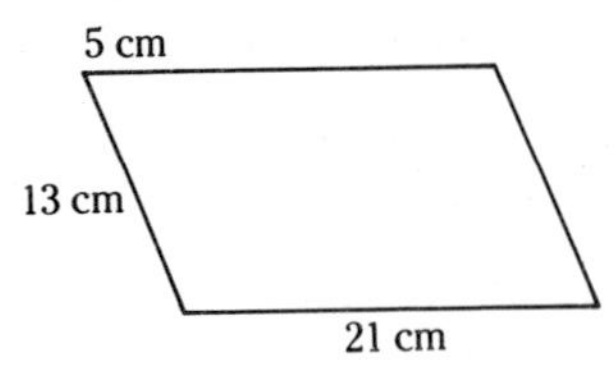

(a) Find the area of a parallelogram with one pair of opposite sides of length 14.7 cm, and 11.3 cm apart.

(b) Find
  (i) the height
  (ii) the area
  of the parallelogram in the diagram.

2. Find the area of each triangle.

(a)

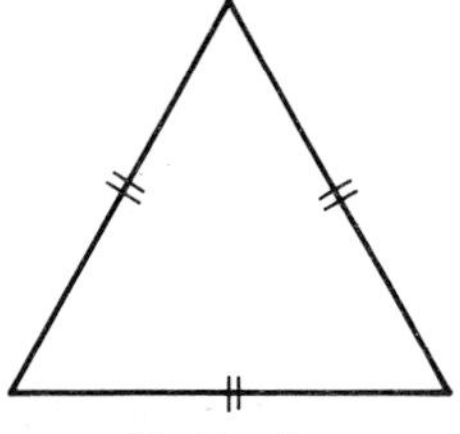

(b)

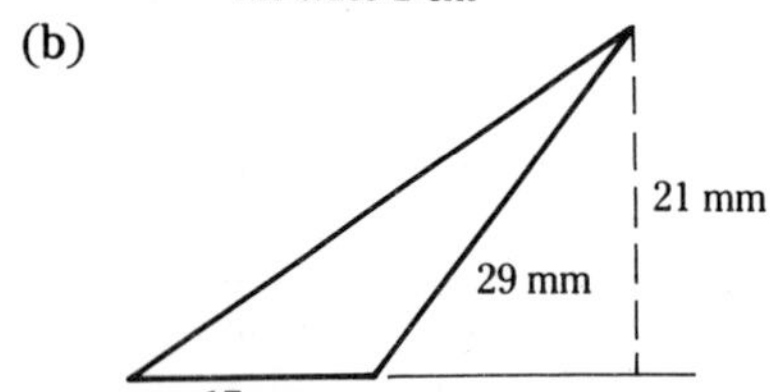

3. On squared paper, using the side of one square to represent 1 cm, draw a triangle with vertices at $(4, -3)$, $(-1, 4)$ and $(3, 6)$. Find its area by enclosing it in a rectangle.

4. In the diagram the side of each grid square represents 1 cm. Find the shaded area. (Look for the quickest method, in which only two separate areas need be calculated.)

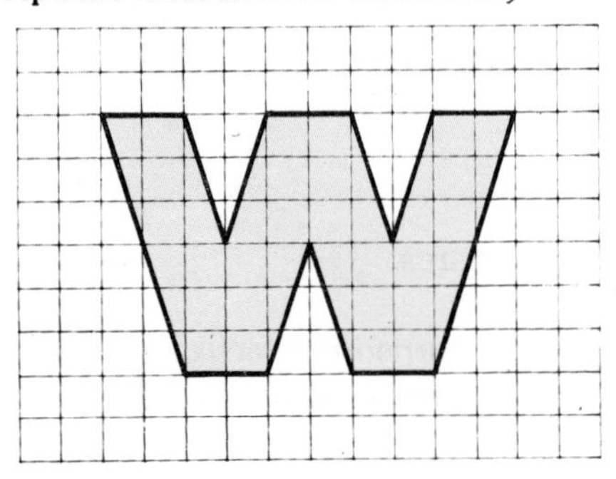

5. Find
   (a) the height of $\triangle ABC$
   (b) the area of the trapezium shown in the diagram.

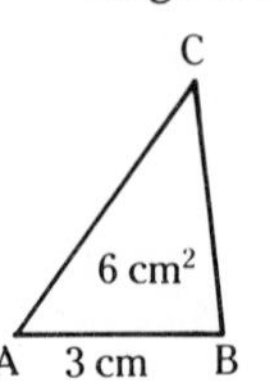

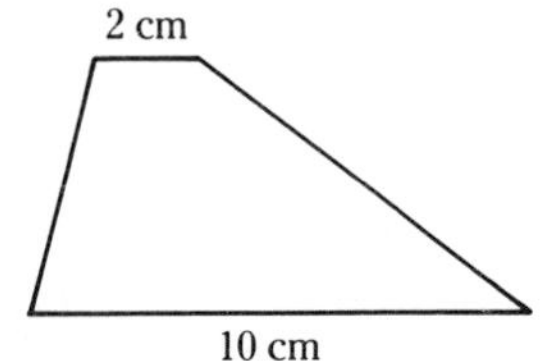

6. Find the area of this shape.

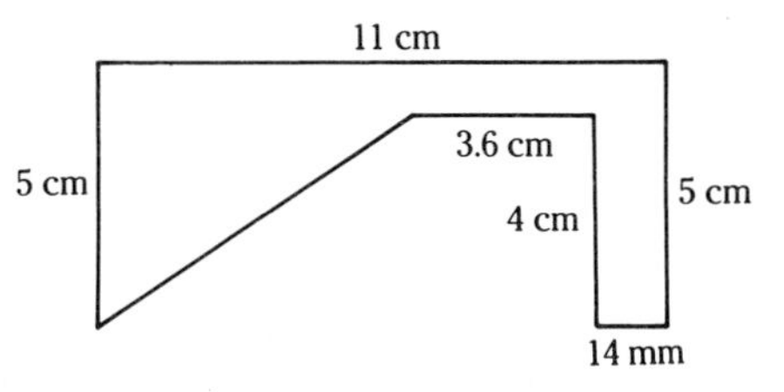

7. The floor plan of a conservatory is shown in the diagram. The floor is symmetrical and is to be tiled except for the carpeted area which is shaded. Find the area to be tiled.

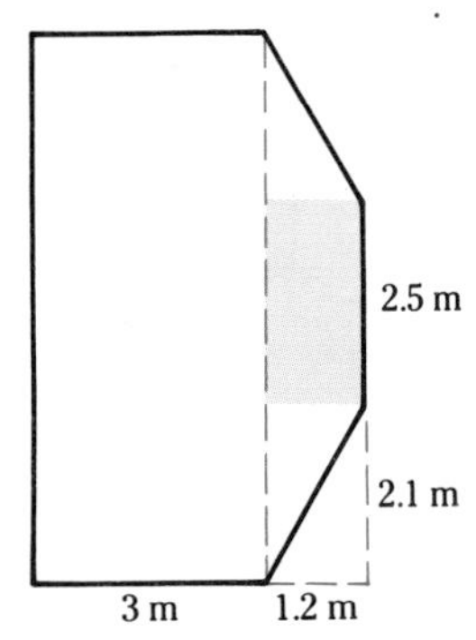

8. (a) Draw a net for the cuboid shown in this diagram.

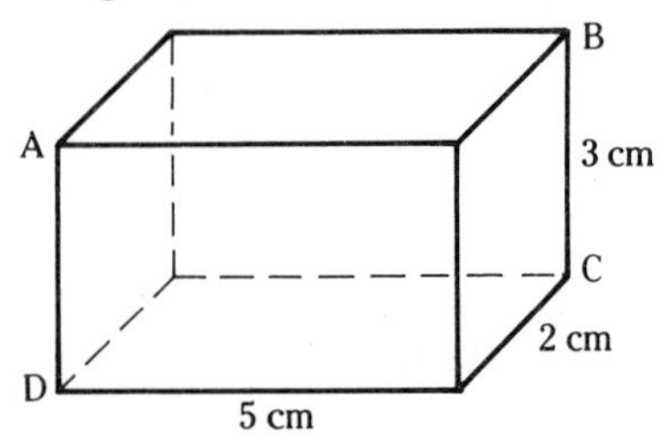

(b) Find the surface area of the cuboid.

(c) Draw the section ABCD. Hence find the longest diagonal of the cube.

9.

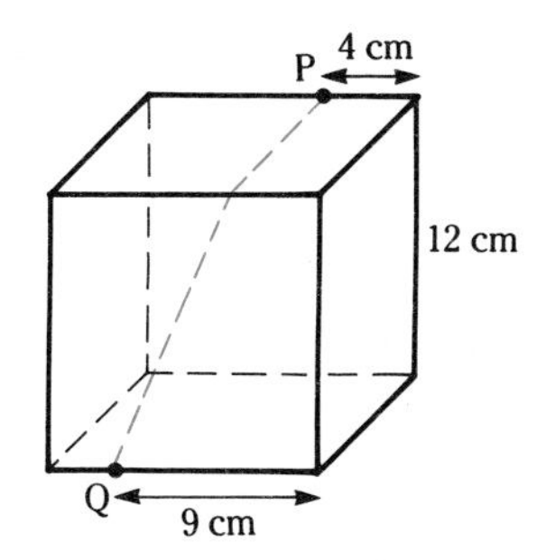

Two points, P and Q, are on the edges of the cube shown in the diagram. A fly starts at P. Find how far it moves to get to Q

(a) if it walks only along edges of the cube

(b) if it takes the shortest route on the surface of the cube. *Hint:* Draw a net and mark the points P and Q on it.

10. A three-dimensional drawing of a machine component is shown in the diagram. Sketch

(a) the plan of the component

(b) the elevation in the direction of the arrow.

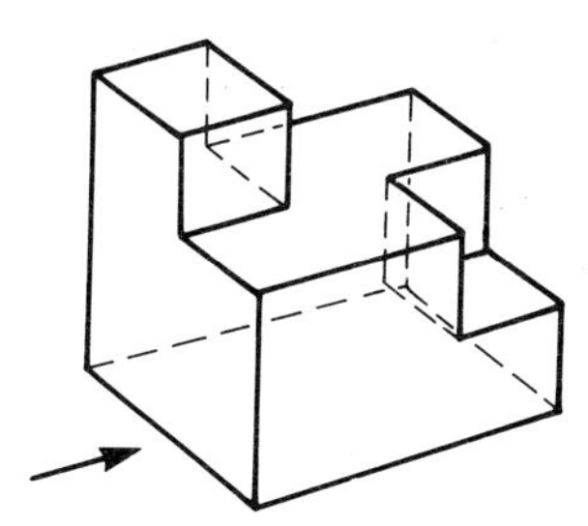

11. The cube shown in the diagram has edges of length 6 cm.

(a) Sketch the section PBR.

(b) Find the lengths of the sides of this section.

(c) Find the area of the section.

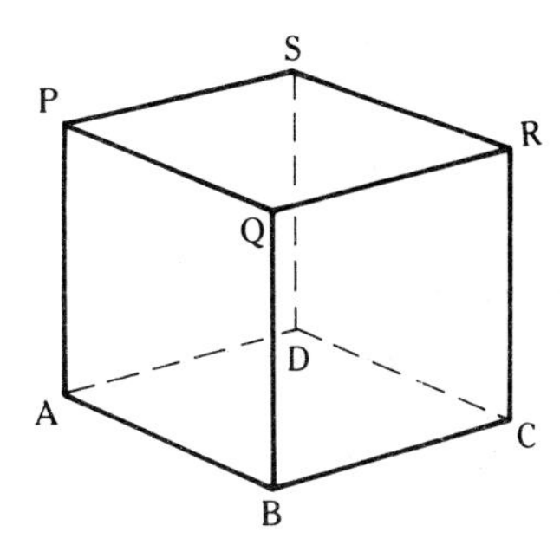

12. For the cube given in question 11

(a) find the area of $\triangle PQB$

(b) draw the section PBCS and use it to help find the length of the diagonal PC.

13. A hole with square cross-section of side 2 cm is cut through the cube given in question 11, from the middle of the face BCRQ to the middle of the face ADSP. Find the volume of the remaining solid.

12 CIRCLES AND CYLINDERS

PARTS OF A CIRCLE

The names of the principal parts of a circle are shown in the diagrams.

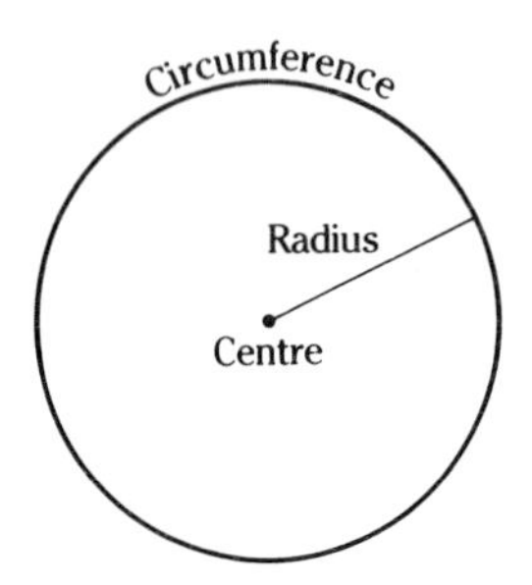

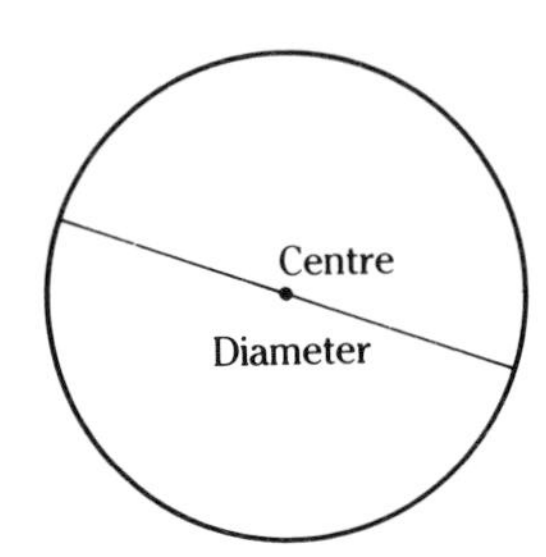

A diameter goes through the centre and is twice as long as the radius.

After measuring the diameter and circumference of a few different circles, it becomes clear that the circumference is given by multiplying the diameter by a number that is a little bigger than 3.

This number cannot be written exactly using figures so is represented by the symbol π.

Circumference = π × diameter

$$C = \pi d \quad \text{or} \quad C = 2\pi r$$

The value of π has been calculated to a vast number of decimal places; in fact there is no end to the number of decimal places and no number pattern emerges. Numbers of this type are called irrational.

In practice no more than three decimal places are usually used and, to this degree of accuracy,

$$\pi = 3.142 \text{ (3 d.p.)}$$

Even this approximation is not needed very often, as most calculators have a π button which can be used in circle calculations. In all the exercises in this chapter, unless instructed otherwise, use the π button if your calculator has one; if it hasn't, take $\pi = 3.142$. In either case give answers to 3 significant figures whenever it is appropriate.

In situations where only a very rough idea of the circumference of a circle is wanted, taking $\pi \approx 3$ is quite useful. It must be remembered that the result is *less* than the true value however, especially if calculating, say, the length of trim needed to go round a circular table.

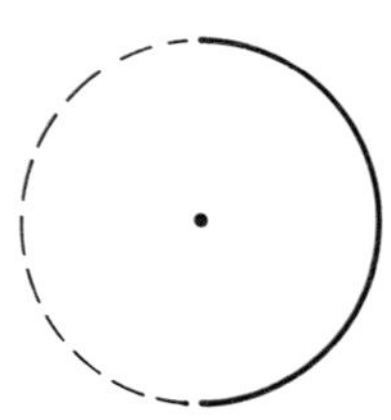

This is a semicircle. Its length is half of the circumference of the whole circle.

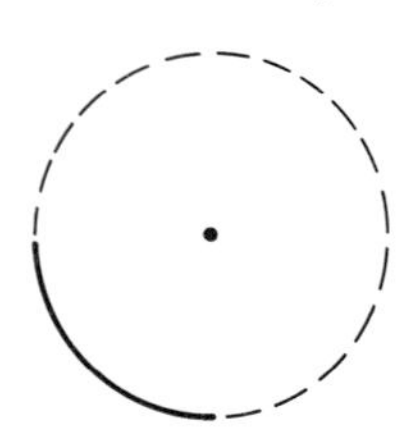

This is a quadrant. Its length is one quarter of the circumference of the whole circle.

Exercise 12a

1. Use $\pi \approx 3$ to find an approximate value for the circumference of the given circle.

   (a) radius 6 cm
   (b) radius 3.2 mm
   (c) radius 3 m
   (d) diameter 11 cm
   (e) diameter 8 m
   (f) diameter 4 mm

For the following questions use a calculator and give answers correct to three significant figures.

2. Find the circumference of a circle of radius

   (a) 38 mm
   (b) 4.4 m
   (c) 10.5 mm
   (d) 0.25 m
   (e) 1.03 m
   (f) 7.2 cm

3. Find the circumference of a circle whose diameter is

   (a) 56 cm
   (b) 14 m
   (c) 6.3 cm
   (d) 9.8 m
   (e) 0.84 m
   (f) 3.04 cm

The goal area of a hockey pitch is marked out by a line in the shape of a semicircle of radius 16 yards. Find the length of this line.

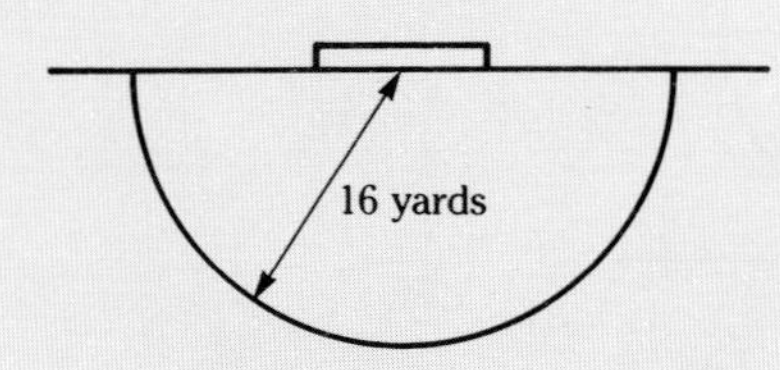

Circumference of a circle $= 2\pi r$

The curved goal line is a semicircular arc.

Length of line round goal area is $\frac{1}{2} \times 2\pi r = \pi r$

$= \pi \times 16$ yards

$= 50.26\ldots$ yards

Length of goal line, correct to 3 s.f., is 50.3 yards.

Note that the *perimeter* of the goal area was not asked for, so the base line diameter was not included.

4. Find the perimeter of each of the following shapes.

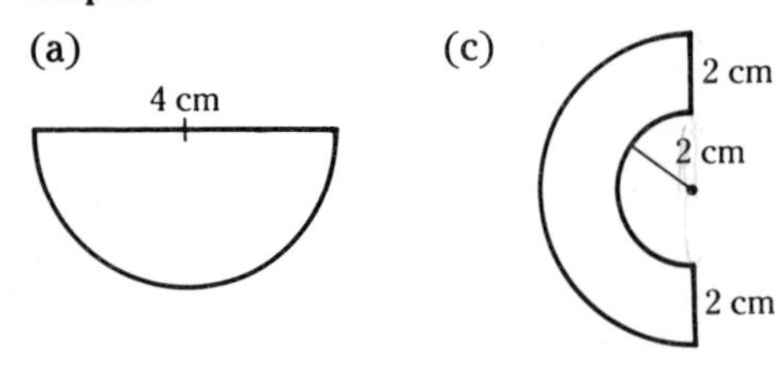

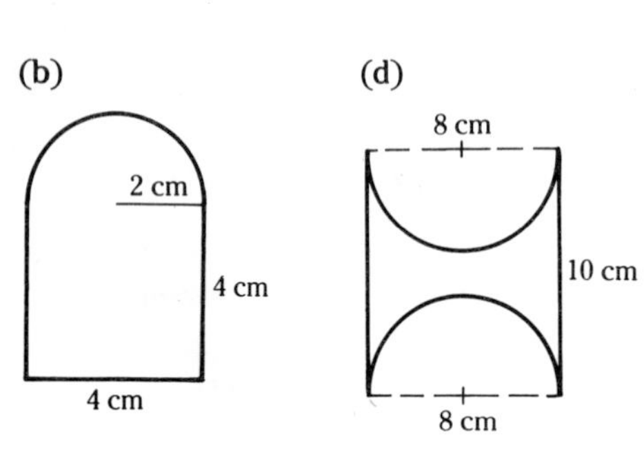

5. A circular flower bed has a diameter of 1.5 m. A metal edging is to be placed round it. Find the length of edging needed and the cost of the edging if it is sold at £6.50 per metre and only a whole number of metres can be bought.

6.

A bicycle wheel has a radius of 28 cm.

(a) What is the circumference of the wheel ?

(b) How far does the wheel travel in one complete revolution ?

(c) If the bicycle travels a distance of 352 m, how many times has the wheel revolved ?

(d) One revolution of the bicycle pedals produces four revolutions of the bicycle wheel. How many revolutions of the pedal make the bicycle travel 106 m ?

7. The sides of a square sheet of metal are of length 30 cm. A quadrant of radius 15 cm is cut from each of the four corners. Sketch the shape that is left and find its perimeter.

8. A boy flies a model aeroplane on the end of a wire 10 m long. If he keeps the wire horizontal, how far does his aeroplane fly in one revolution ?

9. If the aeroplane described in question 8 takes 1 second to fly 10 m, what is the time taken for 1 revolution ? If the aeroplane has enough power to fly for 1 minute, how many revolutions can it perform ?

10. A cotton reel has a diameter of 3 cm. If there are 500 turns of thread on the reel, how long is the thread ?

11.

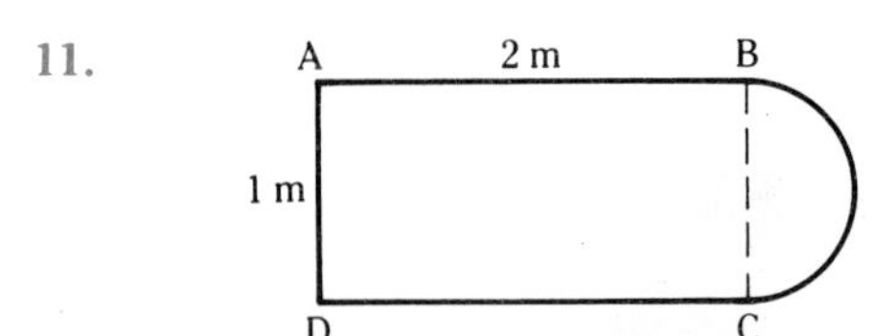

The diagram shows a rectangular breakfast bar with a semicircular flap at the end. Find

(a) the length of BC
(b) the radius of the semicircle
(c) the length of the arc BC
(d) the perimeter of the breakfast bar.

12.

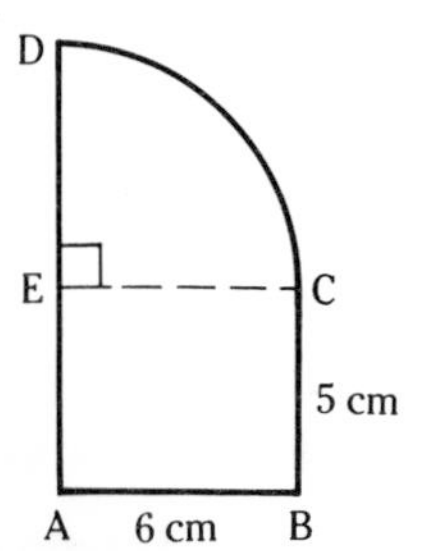

The diagram shows the cross-section of a plinth for a cupboard. Find

(a) the length of EC
(b) the length of the AD
(c) the length of the arc DC
(d) the perimeter of the figure.

The circumference of a circle is 28 cm.
Find the radius of the circle.

Using $C = 2\pi r$
gives $28 = 2 \times \pi \times r$

$\therefore \quad \dfrac{28}{2 \times \pi} = r$

So $r = 4.456\ldots$

Correct to 3 s.f. the radius is 4.46 cm

13. Find the radius of the circle whose circumference is

(a) 44 cm
(b) 121 mm
(c) 831 cm
(d) 550 m
(e) 36.2 mm
(f) 0.3 m
(g) 4512 mm
(h) 10.1 cm

14. A roundabout, which is to be built at a major road junction, has to have a minimum circumference of 192 m. What is the minimum diameter ?

15. The turning circle of a car has a circumference of 63 m. What is the narrowest road in which the car can make a U-turn without going on to the pavement ?

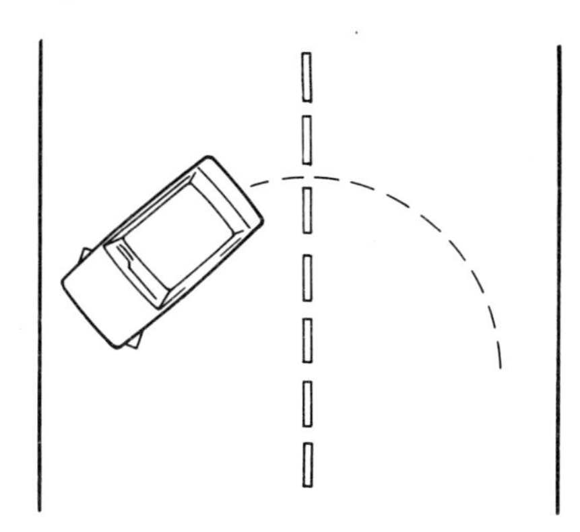

THE AREA OF A CIRCLE

Consider a circle of radius r, and therefore of circumference $2\pi r$.

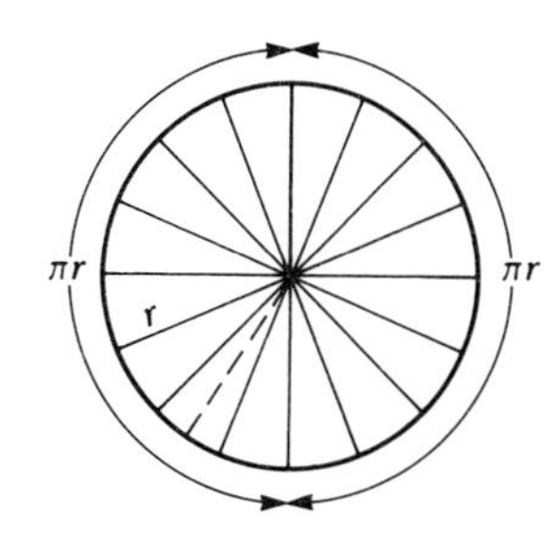

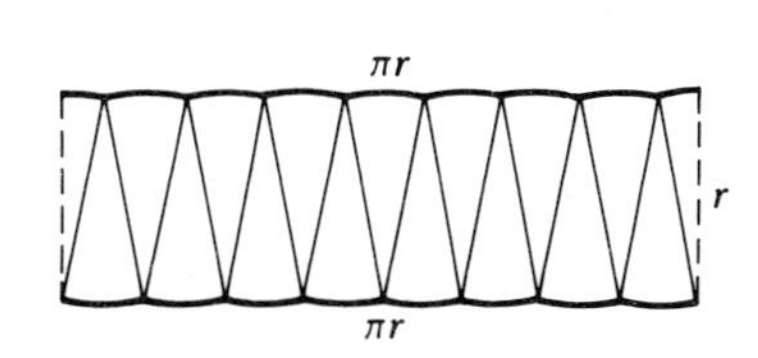

If this circle is cut up into narrow slices (called *sectors*) which are placed together as shown, then a shape that is nearly a rectangle of length πr and width r is produced.

The narrower the sectors are, the nearer the shape becomes to a rectangle.

The area of the 'rectangle' is $\pi r \times r$, i.e. πr^2, and this is the same as the area, A, of the circle from which it was made.

Hence, for a circle of radius r

$$A = \pi r^2$$

Exercise 12b

Find the area of

(a) a circle of radius 3.5 cm
(b) a semicircle of radius 5 mm

(a)

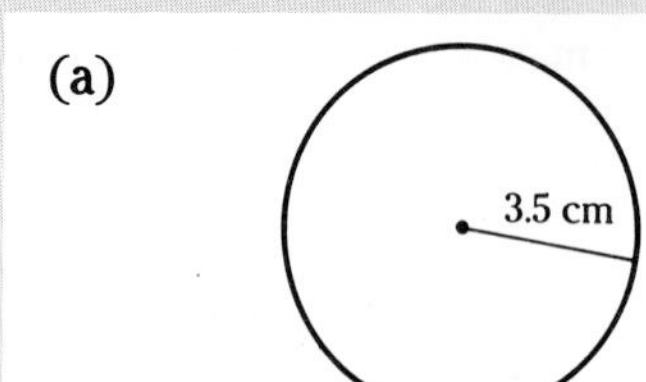

$$\text{Area} = \pi r^2$$
$$= \pi \times 3.5^2 \text{ cm}^2$$
$$= 38.48\ldots \text{ cm}^2$$
$$= 38.5 \text{ cm}^2 \quad (3 \text{ s.f.})$$

(b)

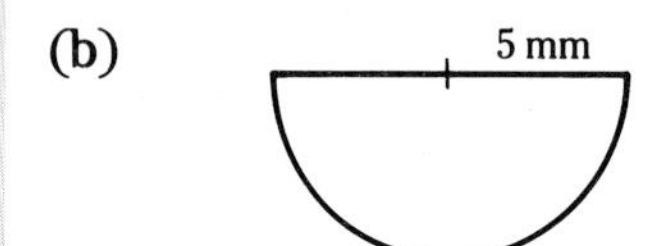

$$\text{Area} = \text{half area of circle}$$
$$= \tfrac{1}{2} \times \pi r^2$$
$$= \tfrac{1}{2} \times \pi \times 5^2 \text{ mm}^2$$
$$= 39.26\ldots \text{ mm}^2$$
$$= 39.3 \text{ mm}^2 \quad (3 \text{ s.f.})$$

1. Find the area of each circle.

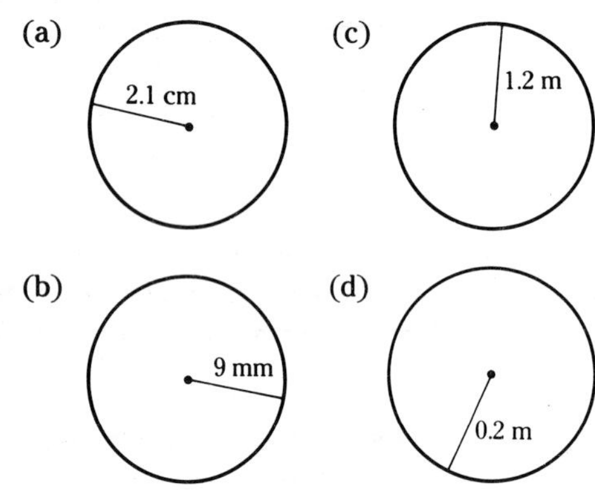

2. The shape of this flower bed is a semicircle of diameter 6 m.

   Find (a) its radius (b) its area.

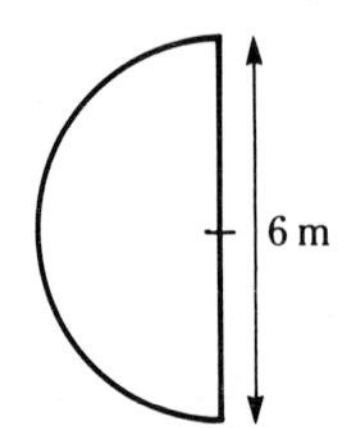

3. This diagram shows the cross-section of a window moulding. Find its area.

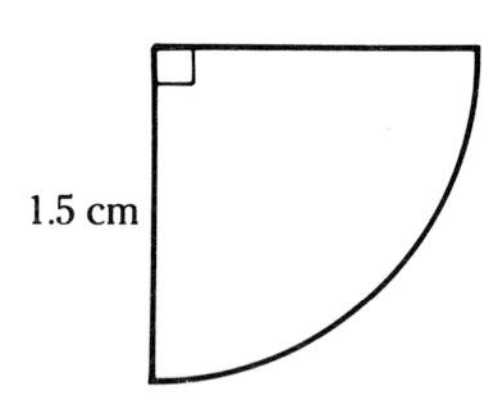

4. The floor of a concert hall is square and the stage is a semicircle. Find

   (a) the area of the floor

   (b) the area of the stage

   (c) the total area.

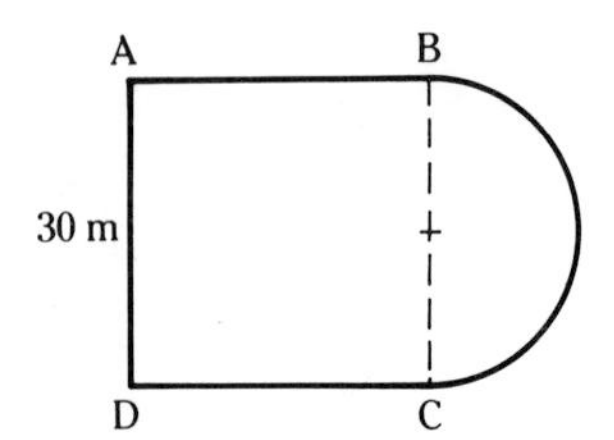

5. The diagram shows a quadrant on one side of a square. Find
   (a) the area of the square
   (b) the area of the quadrant
   (c) the area of the whole figure.

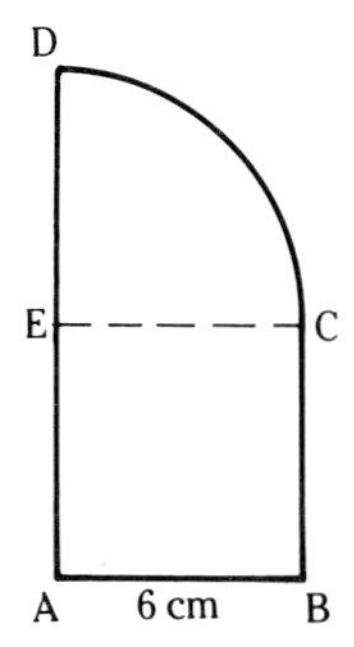

6. Find the area of the shaded shape.

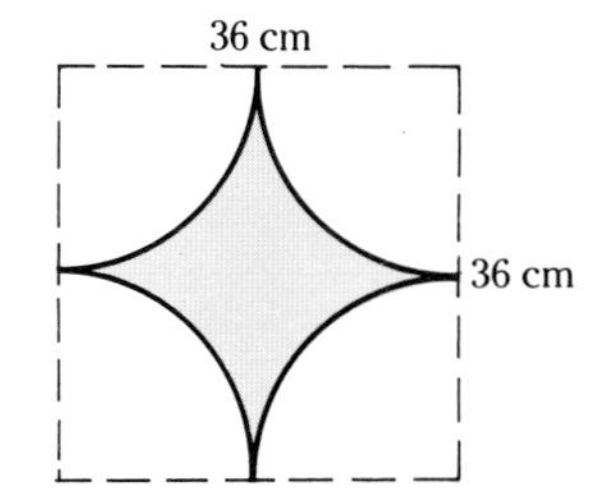

7. Find the area of each shaded shape.

(a)

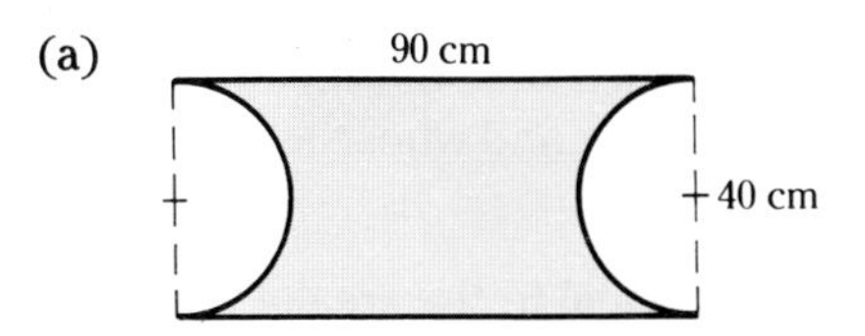

(b)

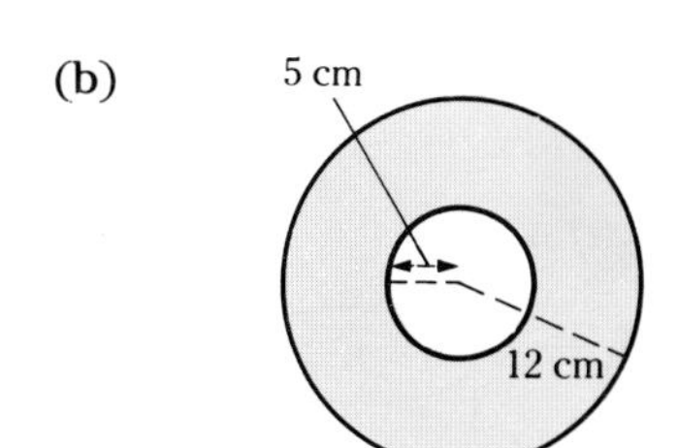

(c)

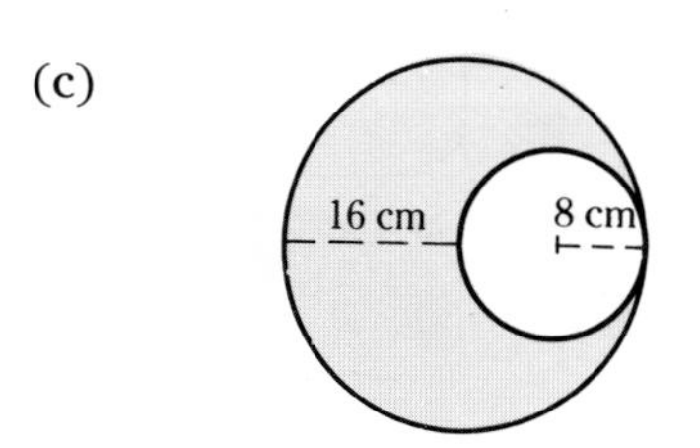

8. A circular bandstand has a diameter of 7 m. The floor is to be sealed.
   (a) Find the area of the floor of the bandstand.
   (b) If one tin of the sealant covers $3\,m^2$, how many tins will have to be bought?

9. A rectangular patio has a circular pond in the middle. Find
   (a) the area of the whole plot
   (b) the area of the pond
   (c) the area of the paved part of the patio
   (d) the circumference of the pond.

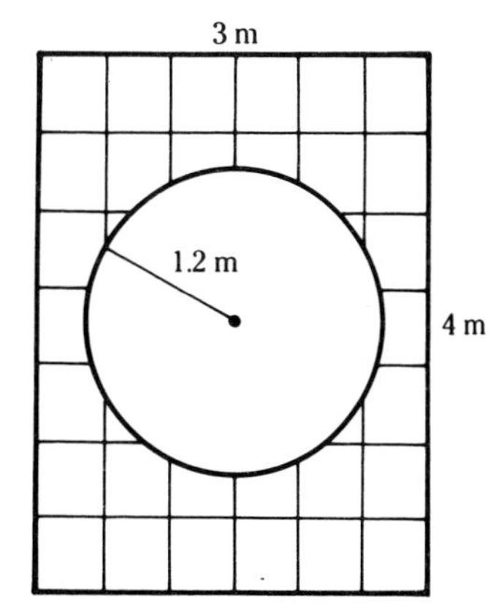

10. The diagram shows the section through a drainage pipe. The bore of the pipe is 14 cm and the wall of the pipe is 11 mm thick. Find
    (a) the area of cross-section of the bore
    (b) the cross-sectional area of the clay from which the pipe is made, i.e. the shaded area.

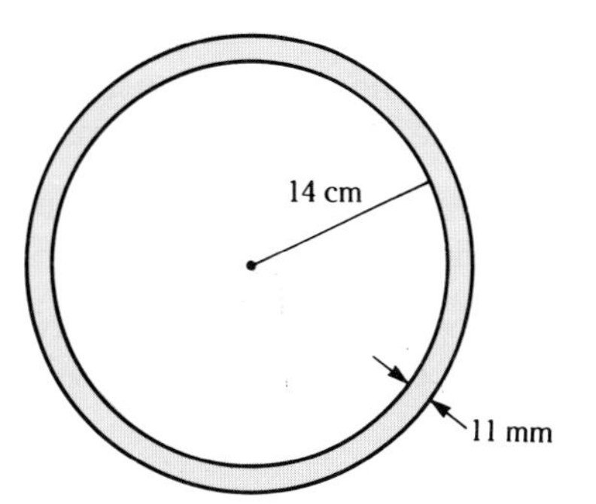

11. The diagram shows a circular engine gasket, of radius 9 cm. The gasket has four circular holes of diameters 5 cm, 5 cm, 6 cm and 8 cm.

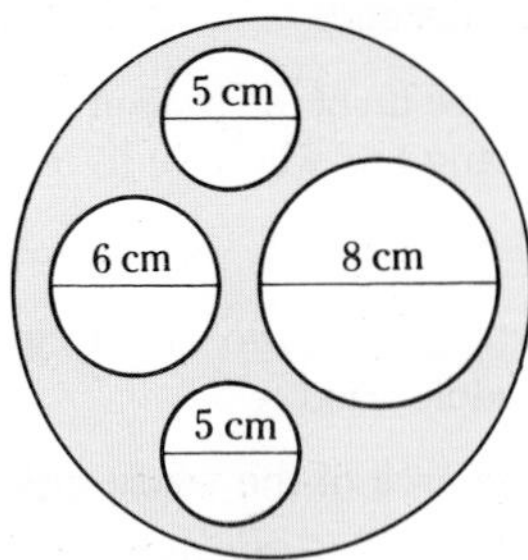

Find, correct to 3 s.f.,

(a) the area of material removed from the circle to make the gasket

(b) the area of the gasket.

12. A sheet of metal is in the shape of a circle of radius 26 cm. From it is to be cut the largest possible square.

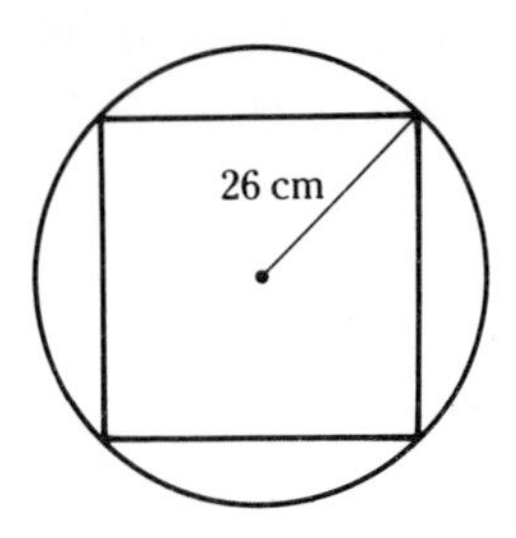

Find

(a) the area of the largest square

(b) the percentage reduction in perimeter

(c) the percentage of metal wasted.

CYLINDERS

Curved Surface Area

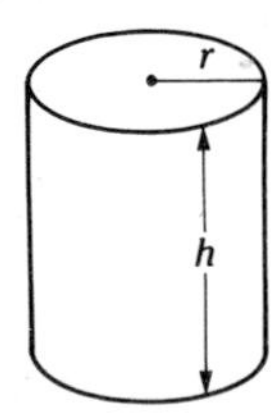

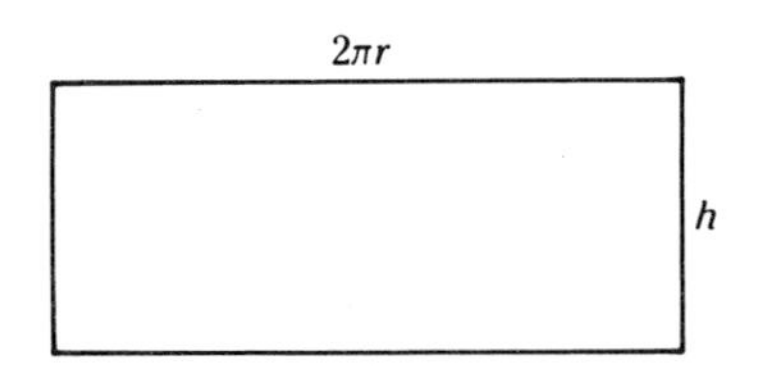

Imagine that a thin metal cylinder, without ends, is cut open and the metal flattened. A rectangle is obtained whose width is the height of the cylinder and whose length is equal to the circumference of the cylinder.

The area of the rectangle is therefore $2\pi r \times h$ and this is equal to the area of the curved surface from which it was formed. Hence the area, A, of the curved surface of the cylinder is given by

$$\boldsymbol{A = 2\pi rh}$$

Volume

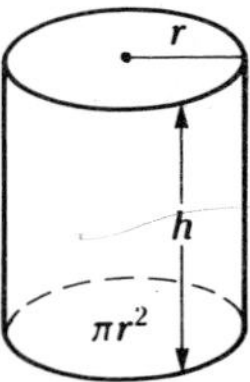

A solid cylinder has a constant circular cross-section and is therefore a circular prism.

The volume of any prism is given when the base area is multiplied by the height.

Therefore the volume, V, of a cylinder of height h and base radius r is given by $\pi r^2 \times h$, i.e. for a cylinder

$$\boldsymbol{V = \pi r^2 h}$$

Exercise 12c

1. Find the curved surface area of the cylinder whose height, h cm, and radius, r cm, are

   (a) $r = 2, \quad h = 6$

   (b) $r = 2.5, \quad h = 5.8$

   (c) $r = 30, \quad h = 9$

   (d) $r = 5.2, \quad h = 7.8$

2. Find the area of the paper label covering the outside of a soup tin (not the top or base) of height 13.6 cm and radius 3.9 cm, given that there is an overlap of 1 cm.

3. A garden roller is in the form of a cylinder of radius 0.24 m and width 0.65 m. What area is rolled by four revolutions of the roller?

A cylindrical canister is closed (i.e. has a top and a base). It is 18 cm high and the radius of the base is 3 cm. Find the area of the base and the curved surface area. Hence find the total surface area of the canister.

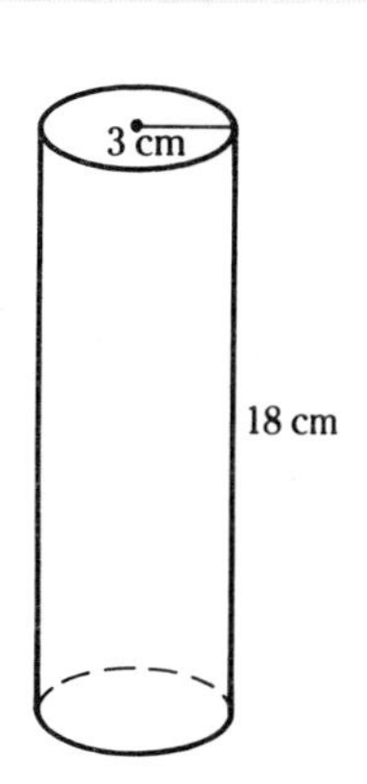

$$\text{Area of base} = \pi r^2$$
$$= \pi \times 3^2 \text{ cm}^2$$
$$= 28.27\ldots \text{ cm}^2 = 28.3 \text{ cm}^2 \quad (3 \text{ s.f.})$$

$$\text{Curved surface area} = 2\pi rh$$
$$= 2 \times \pi \times 3 \times 18 \text{ cm}^2$$
$$= 339.29\ldots \text{ cm}^2 = 339 \text{ cm}^2 \quad (3 \text{ s.f.})$$

$$\text{The total surface area} = \text{top} + \text{base} + \text{curved surface area}$$
$$= (28.27 + 28.27 + 339.29) \text{ cm}^2$$
$$= 395.8\ldots \text{ cm}^2 = 396 \text{ cm}^2 \quad (3 \text{ s.f.})$$

4. The radius of a closed cylinder is 2.1 cm and its height is 10 cm.

   Find (a) the area of its curved surface

   (b) the area of its base

   (c) the total outer surface area.

5. A cylindrical water butt has a diameter of 70 cm and is 92 cm high. It has a removable flat circular lid. What is the outer surface area of the water butt

   (a) without the lid (b) with the lid on?

The inside of a cylindrical water tank is 1.26 m high and its radius is 62 cm. Find correct to 3 s.f. the volume inside the tank in cubic centimetres and give the capacity of the tank in litres.

Both dimensions must have the same unit so use 1.26 m = 126 cm

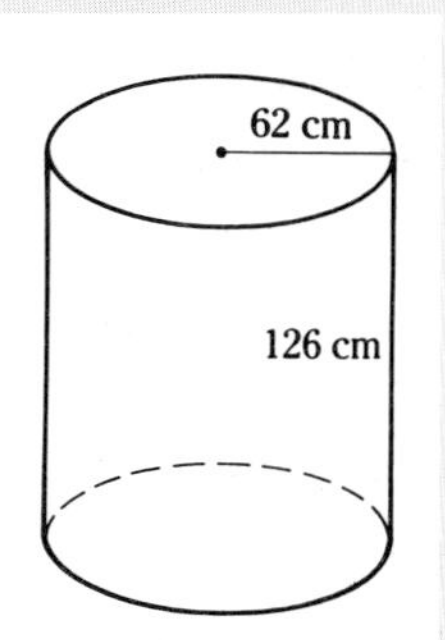

$$\text{Volume inside tank} = \pi r^2 h$$
$$= \pi \times 62^2 \times 126 \text{ cm}^3$$
$$= 1\,521\,611 \text{ cm}^3 = 1\,520\,000 \text{ cm}^3 \quad (3 \text{ s.f.})$$

$$1000 \text{ cm}^3 = 1 \text{ litre}$$

$$\text{Capacity of tank} = \frac{1\,521\,611}{1000} \text{ litres} = 1520 \text{ litres} \quad (3 \text{ s.f.})$$

6. Find the volume of each cylinder whose dimensions are given. Make sure that the units are consistent.
   (a) Radius 1.2 m, height 64 cm.
   (b) Radius 150 cm, height 2 m.
   (c) Radius 0.8 cm, height 22 mm.

7. The internal radius of a cylindrical water tank is 32 cm.
   Find (a) in cm^3 (b) in litres,
   the amount of water in the tank when the depth of water is 18 cm.

8. A solid cylinder of silver has radius 2 cm and length 6.4 cm.
   (a) Find the volume of the cylinder.
   (b) If one cubic centimetre of silver has a mass of 10.5 g, find the mass of the cylinder.

Find the radius of a cylinder with height 5.3 cm and volume 150 cm^3, giving the answer to the nearest centimetre.

$$V = \pi r^2 h$$

$$\therefore \quad 150 = \pi \times r^2 \times 5.3$$

$$\frac{150}{5.3\,\pi} = r^2$$

$$r^2 = 9.008\ldots$$

$$r = \sqrt{9.008\ldots} = 3.00\ldots$$

To the nearest centimetre the radius is 3 cm.

9. The table gives information about a cylinder. Find each missing measurement giving height to 3 s.f. and radius to the nearest whole unit.

	Radius	Height	Volume
(a)	11 cm		1024 cm^3
(b)	3.8 mm		760 mm^3
(c)		1.3 m	17 m^3
(d)		0.12 cm	1.56 cm^3

10. One cubic metre of oil fills a cylindrical drum of radius 40 cm. What is the height of the drum ?

11. A cylindrical pot of emulsion paint holds 5 litres when full. The pot is 25 cm high.

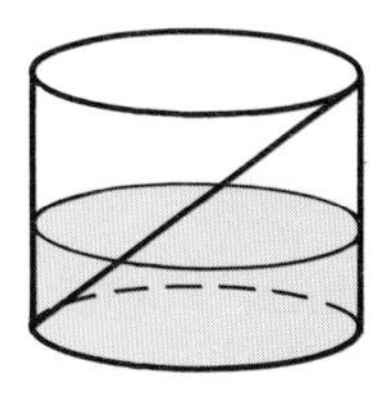

   (a) Find the diameter of the pot.
   (b) Draw the shape of a vertical section through a diameter. Hence calculate the length of the longest stirring stick that will just fit inside the pot.

12. A metal cylinder of length 18 cm and diameter 3 cm is melted down and cast into a cylindrical metal rod of diameter 1 cm. How long is the rod ?

13. A cylindrical water butt, of radius 30 cm and height 80 cm, is exactly half full of water. If 60 litres of water are used, what depth of water is left in the butt ?

14. A cylindrical jar contains 462 g of marmalade. If the mass of 1 cubic centimetre of marmalade is 1.16 g, find the volume of marmalade in the jar. If the jar is full and its radius is 3.5 cm, find the height of the jar.

15. The diagram shows a spacing collar for a spindle. It is in the form of a metal cylinder with a cylindrical hole drilled through the centre.

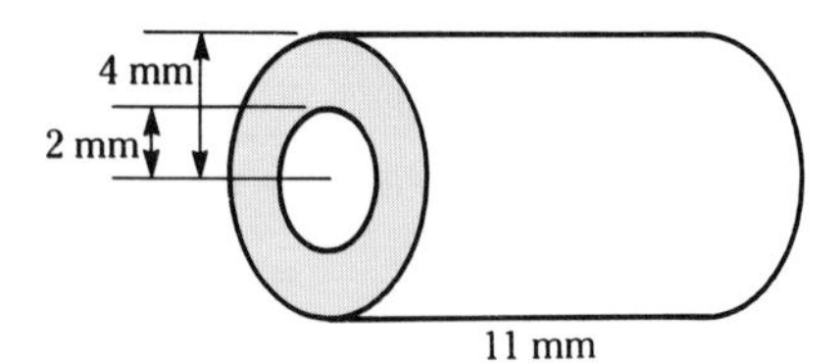

   Use the given dimensions to find
   (a) the volume of metal removed by the drill
   (b) the volume of metal in the collar
   (c) the density of the metal, in g/cm^3, given that the collar has a mass of 3.32 g.

DIMENSIONS OF LENGTH, AREA AND VOLUME

The formulae for finding the lengths, areas and volumes of various objects all contain letters that represent numbers of length units (or area units or volume units). Some of the formulae also contain numbers, and symbols that represent numbers, such as π. An expression that contains only one symbol representing a number of length units is *one-dimensional*. Its value must be given in cm, km, feet, etc.

An expression containing the product of two length unit symbols gives an area. It is *two-dimensional* and its value must be a number of (length)^2 units, e.g. m^2, mm^2.

Three length unit symbols multiplied together (or an area symbol multiplied by a length symbol) give a *three-dimensional* formula. The result is a volume, which is measured in (length)^3 units, e.g. cm^3, m^3.

A number or symbol that does not represent a number of units of length, area or volume, has no effect on the dimension of an expression.
For example, if d is a number of length units and a is a number of area units, then

$4d$ is one-dimensional (length)

$3d^2$ is two-dimensional (area)

πa is two-dimensional

$2\pi d^3$ is three dimensional (volume)

ad is three-dimensional

Checking dimensions and units helps to identify whether a quantity represents length, area or volume, e.g. a quantity given as x cm^2 must be an area.

Applying the same check helps in spotting an incorrect formula. Suppose, for example, that a formula for the volume, V, of an object is given as $V = \frac{1}{3}\pi xy$ where x and y are numbers of length units.
Volume is three-dimensional, whereas $\frac{1}{3}\pi xy$ is only two-dimensional, so the formula cannot be correct.

Exercise 12d

1. State whether each of the following quantities is a length, an area or a volume.

   (a) 10 cm
   (b) 21 cm^3
   (c) 85 cm^2
   (d) 9 km^2
   (e) 630 mm
   (f) 4π mm^3
   (g) 2π cm
   (h) 3 m

2. State whether each of the following quantities should be measured in length, area or volume units.

   (a) The diameter of a circle.
   (b) The region inside a square.
   (c) The space inside a sphere.

3. State whether each of the following quantities should be measured in length, area or volume units.

   (a) A perimeter.
   (b) The amount of air in a room.
   (c) The surface of a cone.

4. The letters a, b and c each represent a number of centimetres. Write down a suitable unit (e.g. cm^2) for the subject of each of the following formulae.

   (a) $N = a + b$
   (b) $R = 4\pi ab$
   (c) $X = 4\pi a^2$
   (d) $Y = \pi a^3$
   (e) $P = 2\pi c$
   (f) $S = abc$

In questions 5 and 6, a and b represent numbers of length units, A and B represent numbers of area units and V represents a number of volume units.

5. State whether X represents a number of units of length, area or volume.

(a) $X = \pi ab$
(b) $X = a + b$
(c) $X = \pi B$
(d) $X = \pi ab^2$
(e) $X = \dfrac{\pi V}{a}$
(f) $X = 2Ab$
(g) $X = a^2 + b^2$
(h) $X = \dfrac{V}{ab}$

6. Some of the following formulae are wrongly constructed. State, with a reason, which are incorrect.

(a) $B = ab$
(b) $A = \pi b^2$
(c) $A = a^2 + b^3$
(d) $V = 2a^2b$
(e) $V = a + B$
(f) $A = a(a + b)$

7. Emma looked up in her notes to find the formula she was supposed to use to find the volume of a certain solid. What she found was $V = \pi x^? y$ and she couldn't read the index number. She knew that x and y were units of length. What was the index number ?

8. Peter was asked to find the area of a circle with diameter 18 cm. He wrote down:

$$\text{Area} = 2\pi r$$
$$= 2 \times \pi \times 9\,\text{cm}^2$$
$$= 56.5\,\text{cm}^2$$

Louise did not know any circle formulae but she knew that Peter was wrong. How did she know ?

9. This is a marker buoy used for showing the course for a power boat race.

Which of these formulae could give the surface area ?

A $A = \pi r^2 + 2\pi h$

B $A = 2\pi r^2 h$

C $A = 2\pi r + 2h$

D $A = 2\pi rh + 4\pi r^2$

Investigation

Pencils are to be sold in packs of ten. Each pencil (unsharpened) is a cylinder which is 20 cm long and 0.6 cm in diameter.

Investigate different ways in which the pencils can be boxed for sale, and indicate the advantages and disadvantages of each of your solutions.

Self-Assessment 12

In this exercise give answers that are not exact to 3 s.f. unless a different instruction is given.

1.

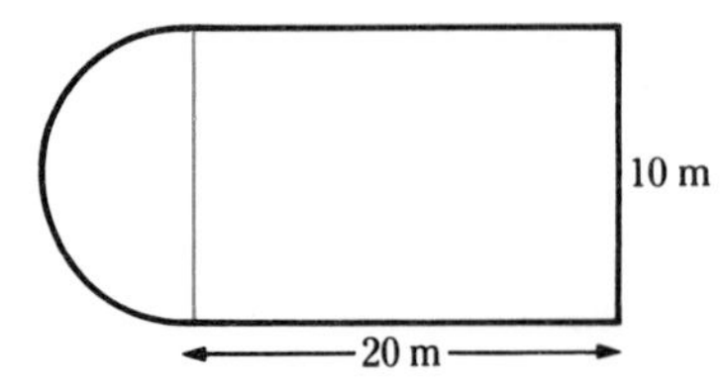

The diagram shows the layout for a lawn. The shape is a rectangle with a semicircle at one end. Find its area.

2. The circumference of a tin is 28 cm. What is its radius ?

3. A tin of fruit is a cylinder. The diameter of the top is 4 cm and the tin is 6 cm high.

(a) Find the volume of the tin.

(b) How long does the label need to be made if 0.5 cm is allowed for an overlap ?

4. A square PQRS is drawn inside a circle of radius 16 cm as shown.

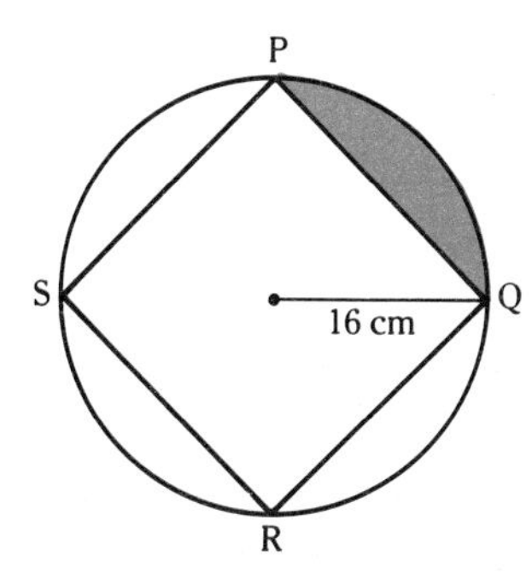

Find the complete perimeter of the shaded part.

5. Referring to the diagram in question 4 find, to the nearest square centimetre,
   (a) the area of the circle
   (b) the area of the shaded part.

6. Sticks of chalk, 8 cm long and 1 cm in diameter, are sold in packets each containing two rows of five sticks. The packet is a cuboid measuring 8.5 cm by 5.5 cm by 2.2 cm. Calculate
   (a) the total volume of ten sticks of chalk
   (b) the volume of the packet
   (c) the percentage of the volume of the packet that is wasted.

7. Biscuits are sold in cylindrical tins 7 cm high and with a radius of 12 cm. A paper label covers the curved surface of the tin and overlaps by 4 mm. Find the volume of the tin and the area of the label.

8. The diagram shows a metal window frame consisting of a rectangle surmounted by a semicircle. The rectangle is bisected by a vertical bar. Find the total length of metal used to make the frame.

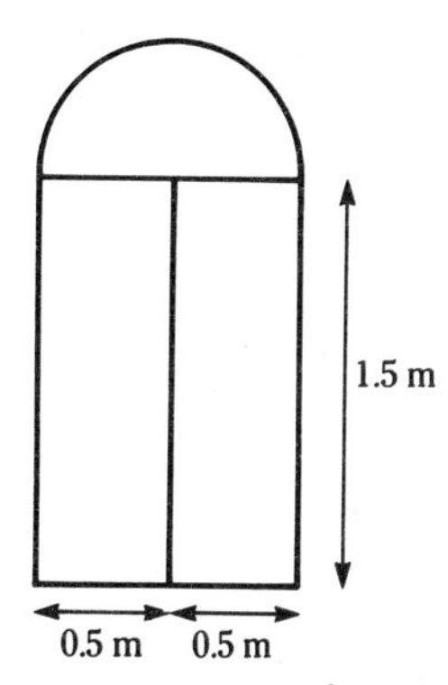

9. Looking at the dimensions, which of the following formulae might be used to find the surface area of a closed cylindrical can ?

A $A = \pi r^2 h$

B $A = 2\pi r^2 + h$

C $A = \pi r + h$

D $A = 2\pi r^2 + 2\pi rh$

13 RATIO AND PROPORTION

RATIO

Ratio is a form of comparison.

'The ratio of 4 g to 12 g' means '4 g compared with 12 g'

A ratio can often be simplified, i.e. expressed in smaller numbers,

e.g. 4 g compared with 12 g is the same as 1 g compared with 3 g
which is the same as 1 compared with 3

Rather than write 'compared with' every time, we use the symbol :
So 1 compared with 3 is written 1 : 3

Exercise 13a

1. Using the symbol : write each sentence as an equation.
   (a) 16 m compared with 24 m is the same as 2 compared with 3.
   (b) 12 p compared with 48 p is the same as 1 compared with 4.
   (c) 8 kg compared with 14 kg is the same as 4 compared with 7.

2. Write each statement as a sentence.
   (a) 36p : 18p = 2 : 1
   (b) 18g : 20g = 9 : 10
   (c) 240 : 180 = 4 : 3

Simplify the ratio
(a) £75 : £60 (b) 10 : 18 : 24

(a) £75 : £60 = 75 : 60 = 5 : 4
dividing by 15

(b) 10 : 18 : 24 = 5 : 9 : 12
(The only number that divides into all three numbers is 2.)

Simplify each ratio.

3. (a) 32 : 96 (b) 7 : 21 (c) 16 : 28 (d) 108 : 48

4. (a) 20 : 8 : 32 (b) 9 : 15 : 27 (c) 14 : 21 : 35 (d) 12 : 30 : 42

5. (a) 35p : 42p (b) 18m : 42m (c) 72g : 150g (d) £18 : £14

Express in its simplest form the ratio 4 m : 75 cm

The given units are not the same. It is usually best to change the larger unit to the smaller one.

4 m = 400 cm

4 m : 75 cm = 400 cm : 75 cm
= 400 : 75
= 16 : 3

Simplify each ratio.

6. (a) 60p : £1.40 (b) 1.25 kg : 850 g (c) 36 mm : 1.2 cm (d) 45 min : 2 h

7. (a) 950 m : 1.5 km (b) £2.40 : 96p (c) 550 m : 1.1 km (d) 40 g : 0.56 kg

8. (a) 3 m : 12 m : 9 m (b) 15 g : 9 g : 6 g (c) £28 : £18 : £8 (d) 12p : £1 : 72p

We have seen that some ratios are simplified if both parts are divided by a common factor. To simplify ratios which include fractions we *multiply* both parts by the same number.

Simplify the ratio (a) $2:\frac{2}{3}$ (b) $\frac{1}{2}:\frac{2}{3}$

(a) $2:\frac{2}{3} = 6:2$ multiplying by 3

$= 3:1$

(b) $\frac{1}{2}:\frac{2}{3} = 3:4$ multiplying by 6, the common denominator of 2 and 3

Express each ratio in its simplest form.

9. (a) $2:\frac{1}{2}$ (b) $3:\frac{4}{3}$ (c) $\frac{4}{5}:5$ (d) $4:\frac{7}{8}$

10. (a) $\frac{1}{5}:\frac{5}{6}$ (b) $\frac{1}{4}:\frac{1}{7}$ (c) $\frac{4}{3}:\frac{5}{6}$ (d) $6:4\frac{1}{2}$

In the following problems, express all ratios in their simplest form.

11. A man earns $5500 and pays income tax of $860. What is the ratio of tax to earnings ?

12. A snack bar sells 84 cans of cola and 54 cans of lemonade. Write down and simplify the ratio of the sales of cola to lemonade.

13. There are 280 vehicles in a car park; 42 are vans and the rest are cars. Find the ratio of the number of cars to the number of vans.

14. In a group of 32 students, 18 are female. Find the ratio of

(a) the number of female students to the number of male students

(b) the number of female students to the total number of students.

15. One rectangle is 8 cm long by 4.5 cm wide and another one is of length 7 cm and width 5 cm. Taking them in the order given, find the ratio of their

(a) lengths (b) widths (c) perimeters (d) areas.

16. Find

(a) the cost of 11 m^2 of vinyl flooring at $8.40 per square metre

(b) the cost of 44 vinyl tiles at $2.40 each

(c) the ratio of the cost of the vinyl flooring to the cost of the tiles.

17. The diagram shows the design of a garden.

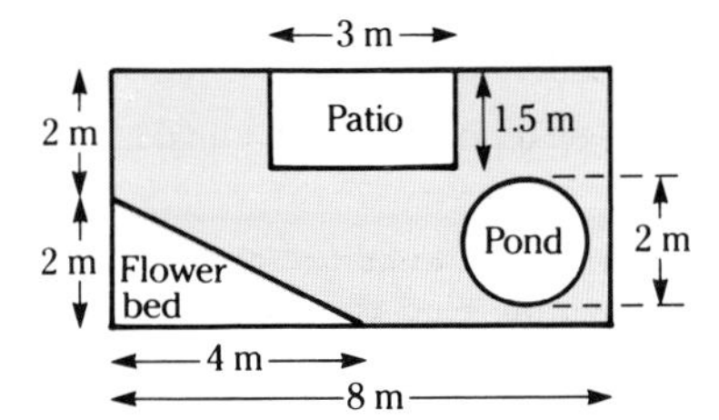

Find the ratio of the areas of

(a) the patio to the lawn

(b) the pond to the patio

(c) the flower bed to the lawn.

Take $\pi \approx 3$.

18.

12 cm

6 cm

The cylinder and the box are the same height. The box has a square cross-section with a side equal to the diameter of the cylinder. Find the ratio of the volume of the cylinder to the volume of the box.

RELATIVE SIZES OF RATIOS

One way to compare the sizes of two or more ratios, is to express them as fractions with the same denominator.

Exercise 13b

Which is the larger ratio,
$4:5$ or $5:6$?

First express $4:5$ as $\frac{4}{5}$ and $5:6$ as $\frac{5}{6}$.
Then make the denominators the same; 30 has both 5 and 6 as factors.

$$\frac{4}{5} = \frac{24}{30} \quad \text{and} \quad \frac{5}{6} = \frac{25}{30}$$

So $5:6$ is larger than $4:5$

1. Find the larger of the two given ratios.
   (a) $3:4$ or $5:7$
   (b) $8:5$ or $13:8$
   (c) $3:5$ or $2:3$
   (d) $3:7$ or $4:9$

2. In each of the following sets of ratios, some are equal. Find them.
   (a) $1:\frac{3}{4}$, $8:6$, $20:15$
   (b) $\frac{2}{5}:3$, $4:30$, $\frac{1}{10}:\frac{3}{4}$
   (c) $\frac{2}{3}:\frac{3}{4}$, $240:360$, $8:9$
   (d) $1\frac{1}{2}:2\frac{1}{2}$, $\frac{3}{10}:\frac{1}{2}$, $8:15$

When a ratio is used to describe the scale of a map, the first number in the ratio is very often 1, i.e. the ratio is given in the form $1:n$

Write in the form $1:n$ the ratio
(a) $3:10$ (b) 5 cm : 2 km

(a) $3:10 = 1:\frac{10}{3} = 1:3.33$ (3 s.f.)

(b) 2 km = 200 000 cm
5 cm : 2 km = 5 : 200 000
= 1 : 40 000

3. Find each ratio in the form $1:n$, giving n to 3 s.f. where necessary.
   (a) $25:10\,000$
   (b) $5:8$
   (c) $2:15$
   (d) $8:25$

4. A certain map is drawn so that 5 cm represents 100 km.
   (a) Express this map ratio in the form $1:n$.
   (b) What distance is represented by 17 cm on the map?

5. John is considering which of two road map books to buy. They both have the same page size but map book A uses a scale of 1 : 10 000 while the scale of the maps in book B is 1 : 50 000. John wants the one that gives the larger area of the country on each page. Which should he choose?

If $x:3 = 6:5$, find x.

$x:3 = 6:5$ gives $\frac{x}{3} = \frac{6}{5}$

$\therefore \quad 3\times\frac{x}{3} = 3\times\frac{6}{5}$

$\therefore \quad x = \frac{18}{5}$

Hence $x = 3\frac{3}{5}$

Note that if x is the second number in the ratio it is usually easier to reverse both ratios before trying to calculate x,

e.g. if $3:x = 7:5$

then $x:3 = 5:7$

6. Find x if

(a) $x:4 = 3:5$ (d) $3:2 = 5:x$

(b) $x:7 = 1:2$ (e) $7:3 = x:1\frac{1}{2}$

(c) $4:3 = x:4$ (f) $3:7 = 2:x$

7. In a school the ratio of girls to boys is $5:4$. If there are 360 boys how many girls are there ? (Let x be the number of girls.)

8. In a certain road there are 16 bungalows. If the ratio of the number of houses to the number of bungalows is $3:2$, find the number of houses.

9. The distance 'as the crow flies' between Apton and Bendale is 12 km. The scale of a map of this area is $1:250\,000$. What is the distance between Apton and Bendale on the map ?

Express the ratios in the form $1:n$.
(a) $4.2\times10^{-3}:0.08$ (b) $1.8\times10^{-6}:4.2\times10^{-3}$

(a) $4.2\times10^{-3}:0.08$

Multiply by 10^3 $= 4.2:80$

$= 1:19.0$ correct to 3 s.f.

(b) $1.8\times10^{-6}:4.2\times10^{-3}$

Multiply by 10^6 $= 1.8:4200$

$= 1:2333.3\ \ldots$

$= 1:2.33\times10^3$ correct to 3 s.f.

10. The wave length of a television signal is about 0.6 m. The wave length of sodium light (ordinary street lights) is about 5.9×10^{-7} m. The wave length of X-rays is about 1×10^{-10} m. Find, in the form $1:n$, the ratio of

(a) the wave length of sodium light to the wave length of a television signal

(b) the wave length of X-rays to the wave length of sodium light.

DIVISION IN A GIVEN RATIO

Suppose that £450 is to be divided among Tom, Dick and Harry in the ratio $2:3:4$. This means that Tom gets 2 portions, Dick gets 3 portions and Harry gets 4. Before the money can be shared out we need to know what one portion is, so we divide £450 into $(2+3+4)$ parts, i.e. 9 parts, then one part is £50. Then Tom gets $2\times£50 = £100$, Dick gets $3\times£50 = £150$ and Harry gets $4\times£50 = £200$.
Any quantity can be divided in this way into any number of shares in a given ratio.

The total of the calculated shares should always be checked. In the case above, $£100+£150+£200 = £450$, which is correct.

Exercise 13c

Divide \$120 into two parts in the ratio 5 : 3

The number of portions is 5 + 3, i.e. 8

$$\text{The larger part is } \tfrac{5}{8} \text{ of } \$120 = 0.625 \times \$120$$
$$= \$75$$
$$\text{The smaller part is } \tfrac{3}{8} \text{ of } \$120 = 0.375 \times \$120$$
$$= \$45$$

Check: \$75 + \$45 = \$120

1. (a) Divide 48 kg into two parts in the ratio 5 : 1
   (b) Divide 40 minutes into two parts in the ratio 3 : 2

2. (a) Divide 128 g into three parts in the ratio 4 : 3 : 1
   (b) Divide \$84 into three parts in the ratio 2 : 2 : 3

3. Find the length of AP if P divides the line AB in the ratio 3 : 1 and AB is 28 cm long.

4. On a map the direct distance between Lowburgh and Benchurch is 6.5 cm. The village of Winton divides the line joining these towns internally in the ratio 9 : 4. Find the distances on the map between Lowburgh and Winton and between Winton and Benchurch.

5. Teresa weighs 52 kg and Dawn weighs 48 kg. Divide 200 g of chocolate between them in the ratio of their weights.

6. Share 45 sweets among three children in the ratio 3 : 5 : 7

7. A village Fun Day raised \$3500, which was divided in the ratio 2 : 3 between the Village Hall Fund and Cancer Research. How much was given to Cancer Research ?

8. A garage repair bill came to \$217. The ratio of the cost of parts to the cost of labour was 3 : 4. What was the labour cost ?

9. Mr Hill decides to give \$12 000 to his two daughters, to be divided between them in the ratio of their ages. The girls have the same birthday and at present they are 14 and 16 years old. How much money will each daughter receive if the money is given
   (a) today
   (b) in five years' time
   (c) in fifteen years' time ?
   After how many years do you think the daughters would receive equal amounts ?

10. A fruit cake contains flour, sugar, butter and dried fruit. The ratio of the weights of these ingredients is 4 : 2 : 2 : 3. If this cake mixture weighs 1.76 kg, what is the weight of each ingredient ?

11. The angles of a triangle are in the ratio 4 : 5 : 6. Find each angle.

DIRECT PROPORTION

Another word that is used for comparing quantities is *proportion*. For example, if a number of identical books are purchased, the total cost is proportional to the number of books bought; double the number of books and the cost doubles, treble the number and the cost trebles and so on.

Two varying quantities that are always in the same ratio are said to be *in proportion*. This type of relationship is called *direct proportion*.

Solving Problems

A. By the Unitary Method

A machine labels 640 bottles in 4 minutes. How many will it label in 1 hour ?

First find the number of labels applied in 1 minute.

In 4 minutes the machine labels 640 bottles

In 1 minute the machine labels $\frac{640}{4}$ bottles

i.e. the machine labels 160 bottles in 1 minute

1 hour = 60 minutes

In 60 minutes the machine labels 160×60 bottles

i.e. 9600 bottles.

In the example above the method used was to find first the 'unit' quantity; in this case the number of labels per minute, i.e. in one unit of time. This way of dealing with proportion problems is called the *unitary method*. It is usually obvious which quantity to take one unit of but, if in doubt, remember that it is the quantity of which different amounts are mentioned. In the example, two different times are mentioned, so what happens in a unit of time is needed.

B. By the Ratio Method

An alternative method uses direct proportion, i.e. two equal ratios, and is explained by solving the same problem again.

A machine labels 640 bottles in 4 minutes. How many will it label in 1 hour ?

Let x be the number of bottles labelled in 60 minutes.

The number of bottles is in direct proportion to the time taken.

$$\frac{x}{60} = \frac{640}{4}$$

$$\cancel{60}^{1} \times \frac{x}{\cancel{60}_{1}} = 60 \times \frac{640}{4} = 9600$$

In 60 minutes the machine labels 9600 bottles.

Note that when using this method the ratios should be arranged so that x is in the numerator. In the solution above, for example, it would not be so easy if the ratios were written in the form $\frac{60}{x} = \frac{4}{640}$

Exercise 13d

Which of the methods on the previous page is used is a matter of personal choice. In this exercise use the method you prefer.

1. A car uses 40 litres of petrol in travelling 280 miles. How much will be used on a journey of 84 miles?

2. Working on his own, a bricklayer building a wall can lay 288 bricks in 4 hours. How many bricks can he lay in $6\frac{1}{2}$ hours?

3. If it costs £9.60 to feed a dog for 11 days, how much will it cost to feed the same dog for 14 days?

4. A wire 33 cm long has a mass of 561 g. What is the mass of 13 cm of this wire?

5. On a hundred-mile trial, a cyclist covers 65 miles in 4 hr 20 min. If she continues at the same speed, how long will she take for the complete course?

6. This recipe is meant to make 12 scones.

240 g flour	40 g sultanas
60 g margarine	75 mℓ milk
24 g sugar	Pinch of salt

   Convert this recipe so that 16 scones can be made.

7. Flying at an average speed of 780 km/h, an aircraft covers 9360 km in a given time. How far can it travel in the same time at an average speed of 720 km/h?

In a mix for making mortar, 70 kg of sand are mixed with 20 kg of cement.

(a) How much sand is needed to mix with 30 kg of cement?

(b) How much cement is needed to mix with 1400 kg of sand?

In the two parts of this question the order of the given and required quantities is reversed. In this situation a different starting point is needed for each part, whichever method is used.

Unitary Method

(a) In this part we work with one unit of cement.

20kg of cement are mixed with 70 kg of sand

1 kg of cement is mixed with $\frac{70}{20}$ kg, i.e. 3.5 kg of sand

$\therefore$ 30 kg of cement are mixed with 30×3.5 kg, i.e. 105 kg of sand

(b) Now we work with one unit of sand.

70 kg of sand are mixed with 20 kg of cement

1 kg of sand is mixed with $\frac{20}{70}$ kg, i.e. $\frac{2}{7}$ kg of cement

1400 kg of sand are mixed with $1400 \times \frac{2}{7}$ kg, i.e. 400 kg of cement

Ratio Method

To use the ratio method for part (a), where the quantity of sand is to be found, we take x kg as the amount of sand. In part (b) however, the quantity of cement is required so we take this quantity as y kg.

Note that the information in examples of this type is sometimes expressed in a different form e.g. 'sand and cement are mixed in the ratio 7 : 2'. The methods of solution are just the same.

8. If a fan-heater consumes 6 units of electricity in $2\frac{1}{2}$ hours,
   (a) how many units will be consumed in 10 hours
   (b) for how many hours will the heater run on 15 units ?

9. A farmer is using a tractor to plough a square field. He can drive the tractor 13 times across the field in $45\frac{1}{2}$ minutes.
   (a) How long will it take to cross the field 27 times ?
   (b) How many times can he cross the field in $66\frac{1}{2}$ minutes ?

10. For an area of $18\,\text{m}^2$, the amount of a fertiliser required is 675 g.
    (a) How much is needed to fertilise $11\,\text{m}^2$?
    (b) What area will 862.5 g fertilise ?

11. The cost of $14\,\text{m}^2$ of carpet is \$176.40.
    (a) How much will $11\,\text{m}^2$ cost ?
    (b) How much carpet can be bought for \$113.40 ?

12. Among the ingredients given in a recipe for sponge cake are: 500 g flour, 300 g butter and 4 eggs. The recipe can be adapted to make larger or smaller cakes. If someone wanted to make a cake using 100 g of butter, what decision could be made about the number of eggs ?

13. Copper and tin are mixed in the ratio 3 : 7 to form an alloy.
    (a) How much copper is needed to mix with 42 g of tin ?
    (b) How much tin should be mixed with 15 g of copper ?
    (c) How much of each metal is there in 1 kg of alloy ?

INVERSE PROPORTION

There are some cases where one quantity varies in a way that is linked to another quantity but where an increase in one quantity causes a *decrease* in the other.
Consider, for example, the times that a cyclist would take to cover a distance of 48 miles at various steady speeds.

Speed in miles per hour	4	6	8	12	16
Time taken in hours	12	8	6	4	3

Notice that as the speed goes up the time taken for the journey goes down.
This is an example of *inverse proportion*.
Notice also that speed × time always has the same value.

In general

the product of
two inversely proportional quantities is constant

WARNING Although many quantities are either directly or inversely proportional, a great many more are not. Always be prepared to think carefully before assuming that either of these relationships applies to quantities being considered – or in fact whether there is any relationship at all.

Exercise 13e

A farmer has enough feed to last his 36 cows 30 days from today. If he buys an extra 12 cows today, how long will the feed last ?

Unitary Method

36 cows can be fed for 30 days

1 cow can be fed for 30×36 days (a longer time)

48 cows can be fed for $\frac{30 \times 36}{48}$ days

i.e. for $22\frac{1}{2}$ days

Constant Product Method

Let x be the required number of days

Then $48 \times x = 36 \times 30 = 1080$

$\therefore \quad x = \frac{1080}{48} = 22\frac{1}{2}$

The feed will last $22\frac{1}{2}$ days.

1. Which of the following quantities are
   (i) directly proportional
   (ii) inversely proportional
   (iii) not simply related ?
   (a) The number of a particular make of ball-point pen bought and the total cost.
   (b) The number of people doing a job and the time taken to finish it.
   (c) The thickness of a pad of notepaper and the number of sheets in it.
   (d) The ages of students and their mathematics marks.
   (e) The length of a trench and the time taken by one man to dig it.
   (f) A woman's age when she married and the number of children she has.
   (g) The steady speed of a car and the time it takes to cover a fixed distance.
   (h) The steady speed of a car and the distance it covers in a fixed time.

2. The length of an essay, typed at an average of 10 words per line, is 204 lines long. How many lines will it occupy if it is retyped at an average of 12 words to the line ?

3. A library has funds to buy 280 books that cost \$15 each. How many books costing \$10.50 could be bought instead ?

4. When nine hikers share out their packs of sandwiches equally they get 5 each. If three of the hikers didn't want any sandwiches, how many would each of the others get ?

5. A plane takes 4 hours to fly a certain distance at 750 m.p.h.
   (a) How long would the flight take at 800 m.p.h. ?
   (b) At what speed should the plane fly to complete the flight in 4 hours 10 minutes ?

6. If the students on a course are split into tutorial groups of 8, there will be 15 groups.
   (a) How many groups of 10 would there be ?
   (b) If only 6 tutors are available, how many students will be in each group ?

7. A supplier delivers a regular quantity of bulk feed to a chicken farm. The quantity lasts for 14 days when there are 500 chickens.
   (a) How long does the quantity last when the number of chickens is 420 ?
   (b) How many chickens can be fed for 20 days ?

8. A contractor estimates that he can carry out the fencing of a large estate in 9 days if he employs 4 labourers.
   (a) How many labourers would be needed to complete the work in 6 days ?
   (b) How long would 3 labourers take to do the job ?

   Assume that all the labourers work at the same rate!

The remaining questions in this exercise include cases where there is no simple relationship between the quantities, as well as some involving direct proportion or inverse proportion. Where you think there is no link, briefly explain why.

9. If 2 ounces of flour are needed for 10 pancakes, how many pancakes can be made with 12 ounces of flour ?

10. Twelve tins of cat food are enough to feed three cats for four days. For how many days would the same amount of food feed two cats ?

11. A baby's weight increased by 3 kg in 6 weeks. By how much did it increase in a year ?

12. Carpet to cover a floor of area 9 m^2 cost \$162.
   (a) How much would it cost to cover 15 m^2 with the same carpet ?
   (b) At a cost of \$243, what area could be covered with the same carpet ?

13. A class of 22 pupils uses 77 exercise books in a term. If the number in the class is reduced to 18, how many exercise books are likely to be used in a term ?

14. A group of 6 hikers walk 10 miles in 3 hours. How long would 14 hikers take to walk 10 miles ?

15. The seating in a concert room was arranged in 4 rows of 21 chairs. A different arrangement uses the same number of chairs in 7 rows. How many chairs per row are there in the second arrangement ?

16. A decorator with twenty years' experience can hang 3 rolls of wallpaper an hour. How long will it take a decorator with ten years' experience to do the same job ?

THE INVERSE SQUARE LAW

We have seen that some everyday quantities are directly proportional to each other and others are inversely proportional. There are, however, other relationships between quantities.

For example, the gravitational pull of the earth on an object depends upon the distance of that object from the earth's centre in the following way:

if the distance, d metres, is doubled then the gravitational pull, g newtons, is divided by 4 (i.e. 2^2)
if the distance is trebled, the pull of gravity is divided by 9 (i.e. 3^2).

These two cases illustrate the general relationship between g and d which is

$$g = \frac{k}{d^2}, \quad \text{where } k \text{ is a constant}$$

We say that g is inversely proportional to the square of d.

This kind of relationship is known as the *inverse square law*.

Exercise 13f

The distance between a subject being photographed and the intensity of light from the flash falling on it are related by the inverse square law, such that the intensity of light is inversely proportional to the square of the distance. If the flash is moved from 2 m to 2.5 m from the subject, what happens to the light falling on the subject ?

The distance has increased by a factor $\frac{2.5}{2}$, i.e. 1.25

Therefore the light falling on the subject is divided by a factor $(1.25)^2$
$= 1.56$ (3 s.f.)

1. Two quantities, x and y, obey the inverse square law so that x is inversely proportional to the square of y. When x is 10, y is 4. If y is increased to 8, what happens to x and what is its new value ?

2. 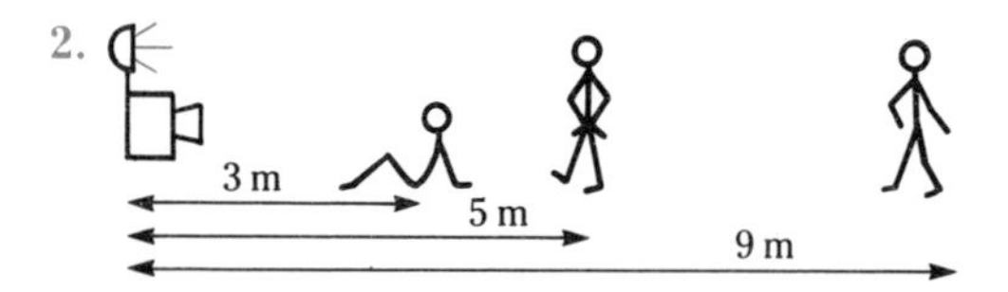

The diagram shows Carla being photographed in three different positions. The light from the flash that falls on Carla and the distance of Carla from the flash obey the inverse square law as described in the worked example.

What fraction of the light that falls on Carla when she is nearest the camera, falls on her when she is

(a) furthest from the camera

(b) in the middle position ?

3. The gravitational pull of the earth on an object is inversely proportional to the square of the distance of the object from the centre of the earth. The orbit of a satellite is changed from 6000 miles above the centre of the earth to 5000 miles above. What happens to the gravitational pull on the satellite ?

4. The signal strength received from a radio transmitter is inversely proportional to the distance from the transmitter. Stella is 6 kilometres from the transmitter and Scott is 8 kilometres from it. How many times stronger is the signal strength where Stella lives than where Scott lives ?

5. The capacity of a cylindrical tank is fixed but its radius and height can vary, so the height is inversely proportional to square of the radius.

(a) If the height is increased from 1.5 m to 2 m, what happens to the radius ?

(b) If the radius is reduced from 50 cm to 25 cm, what happens to the height ?

Self-Assessment 13

1. Express in its simplest form the ratio
   (a) 25 p to 80 p
   (b) 45 seconds to $1\frac{1}{2}$ hours
   (c) 65 : 26 : 39

2. A box of biscuits contains 15 chocolate, 10 cream and 25 plain biscuits.
   What is the ratio of
   (a) chocolate to plain biscuits
   (b) cream biscuits to all the others ?

3. Which is the bigger ratio, 1.2 : 1.4 or 7 : 8 ?

4. Express in the form $1 : n$
   (a) the ratio 25 : 375
   (b) 5 cm to 100 m

5. Find x if
   (a) $3 : 8 = x : 56$
   (b) $2 : 7 = 11 : x$

6. Elaine finds that the ratio of the time she spends watching television to the time she spends doing homework is 3 : 2. If she has 10 hours to herself one weekend, how many hours' homework is she likely to do ?

   If she doubles her homework time will she double her viewing time that weekend ?

7. A hotel bill for £840 is divided between Nick, Gary and Winston in the ratio of their annual salaries. Nick earns £12 500, Winston earns £15 000 and Gary's salary is £7500. How much does each man pay ?

8. A pile of 72 identical books weighs 21 kg.
   (a) How many of the same books weigh 35 kg ?
   (b) What is the weight of 48 of these books ?

9. Thirty-five workmen build a house in 16 days. At the same rate
   (a) how long would it take 28 workmen to build the house
   (b) how many workmen would be needed to build the house in 14 days ?

14 SCALE DRAWING

COMPASS DIRECTIONS

Compass directions use the eight points of the compass.

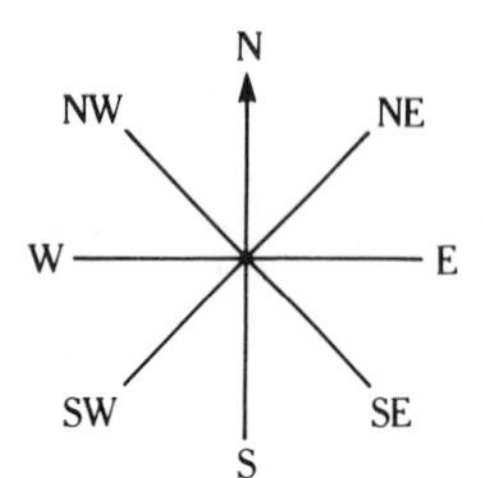

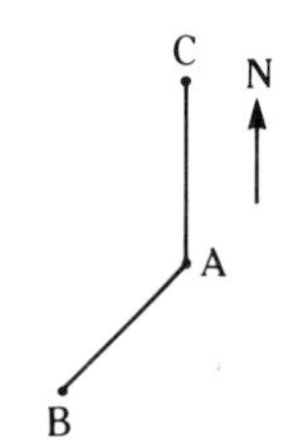

B is south west of A and C is north of A.

Sometimes the direction of one point from another is not exactly one of the eight directions shown above. If it is not, the direction is measured first from north or south, whichever is the nearer, and then towards the east or the west. For example

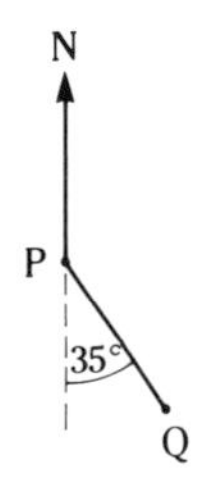

The direction of Q from P is S 35°E

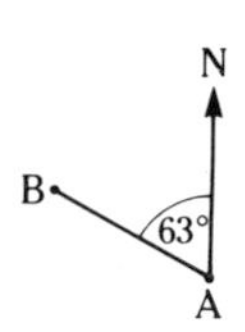

The direction of B from A is N 63°W

Three-Figure Bearings

The modern method of giving the direction of one point from another is to use a three-figure bearing. To find the bearing of B from A, stand at A and look north; then turn clockwise until you are looking at B. The angle you have turned through is the three-figure bearing.

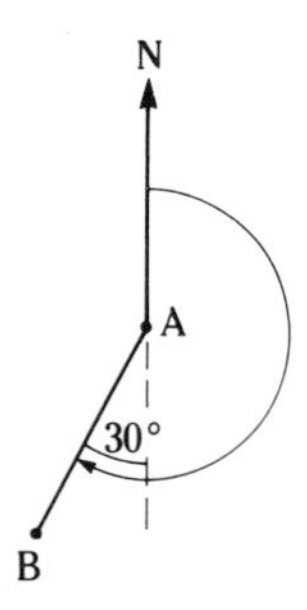

From A, the bearing of B is 210°

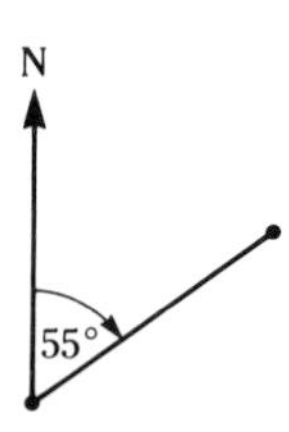

If the angle is less than 100°, it is made into a three-figure bearing by putting a zero in front, e.g. 55° becomes 055°

Exercise 14a

1. Use compass directions to give
   (a) the bearing of each letter from A
   (b) the bearing of A from each of the other marked points,

   e.g. the bearing of B from A is N 62°E and the bearing of A from B is S 62°W

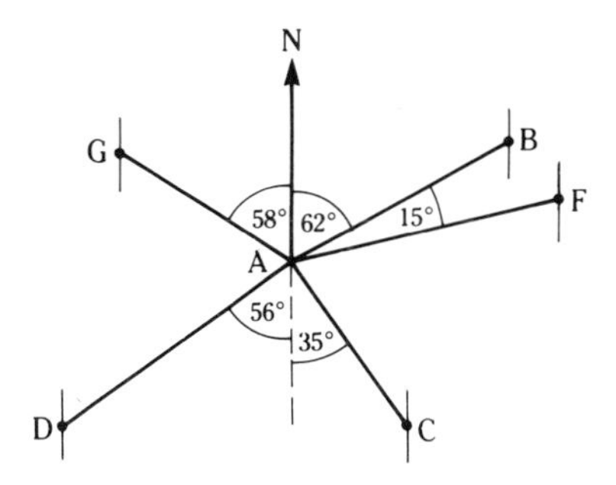

2. Use the diagram in question 1 to write down the three-figure bearing of
   (a) each point from A
   (b) A from each of the other letters.

A man walks 2 km from P to Q on a bearing of 148°. He then walks 3 km on a bearing of 052° to R. Draw a diagram to represent his journey.

Draw a north pointing line each time you use a bearing. Start with the north line at P, draw PQ then add a north line at Q before drawing QR.

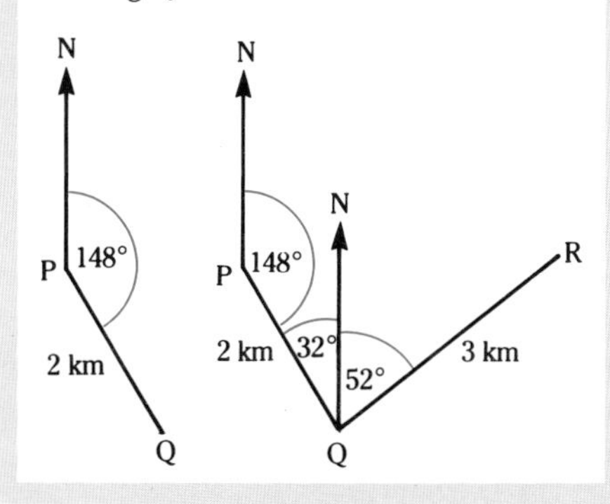

3. Jane starts from A and walks 5 km to B on a bearing of 114°. She then walks 3 km to C on a bearing of 256°. Find $A\widehat{B}C$.

4. Draw a rough sketch to illustrate each of the following bearings. Mark an angle in your sketch.
   (a) The bearing of a ship, S, from a lighthouse, L, is 072°
   (b) From town T, the bearing of another town, S, is 330°
   (c) From an aircraft A, the bearing of an airport C, is 126°
   (d) The bearing of the church, C, from the town hall, H, is 215°.

5. Draw diagrams to represent the information given below:
   (a) A town, X, is 50 km from a town Y. The bearing of X from Y is 240°
   (b) A man walks 3 km from A, on a bearing of 285°, to B. Then he walks 3 km due east to C
   (c) ABC is a triangular field. B is 200 m from A on a bearing of 133° and C is 260 m from B on a bearing of 240°
   (d) Ship P is 10 km due east of ship Q. The bearing of ship R from P is 333° and the bearing of R from Q is 046°.

6. A is 20 km due west of B. The bearing of C from A is 044° and the bearing of C from B is 314°. Find the angles of triangle ABC.

7. Use this sketch to answer the questions that follow:

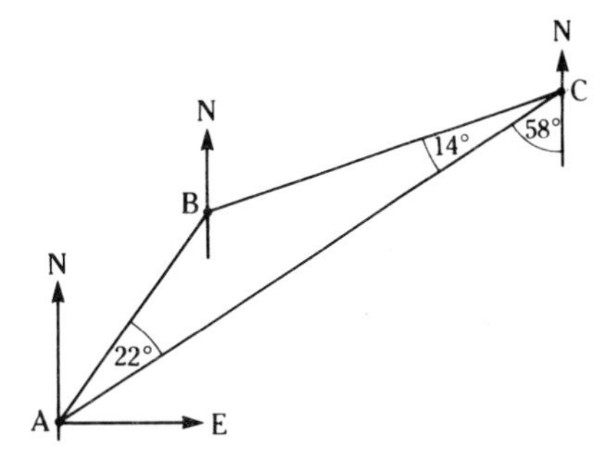

   (a) What is the bearing of B from C ?
   (b) What is the angle between AC and due east ?
   (c) What is the bearing of B from A ?
   (d) What is the angle between BC and due north ?

ANGLES OF ELEVATION AND DEPRESSION

The *angle of elevation* is the angle through which you raise your line of view from the horizontal to look up at something.

The *angle of depression* is the angle through which you lower your line of view from the horizontal to look down at something.

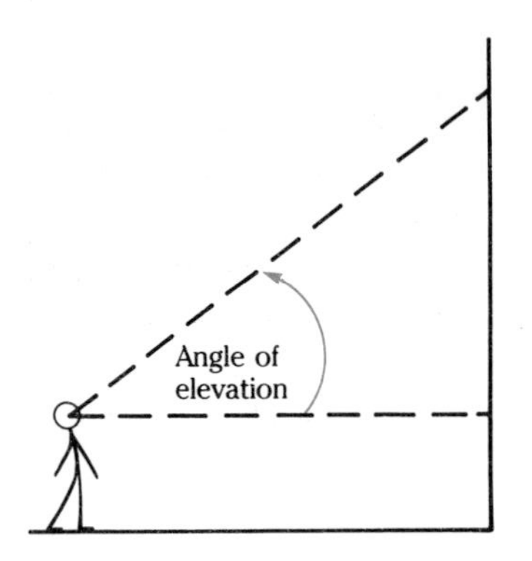

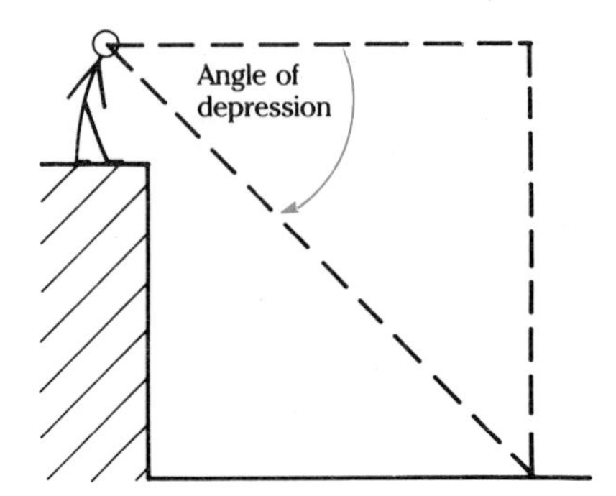

SCALE DRAWINGS

The construction of a scale drawing usually requires the choice of a scale and the calculation of the lengths to be used.

If you are asked to draw a car park that is a rectangle measuring 100 m by 50 m, you cannot draw it full size. To fit it on to your page you will have to scale down the measurements. In this case you could use 1 cm to represent 10 m on the car park. This is called the scale, and can be written $1\text{ cm} \equiv 10\text{ m}$ or $1\text{ cm} : 10\text{ m}$. Sometimes the scale is given as a map ratio, e.g. $1 : 50\,000$. This means that 1 cm represents 50 000 cm, i.e. $1\text{ cm} \equiv \frac{1}{2}\text{ km}$. The scale must always be written on any scale drawing.

If you have access to a computer aided design system (CAD) you may like to use it to produce some of the scale drawings in the following exercise.

Exercise 14b

1.

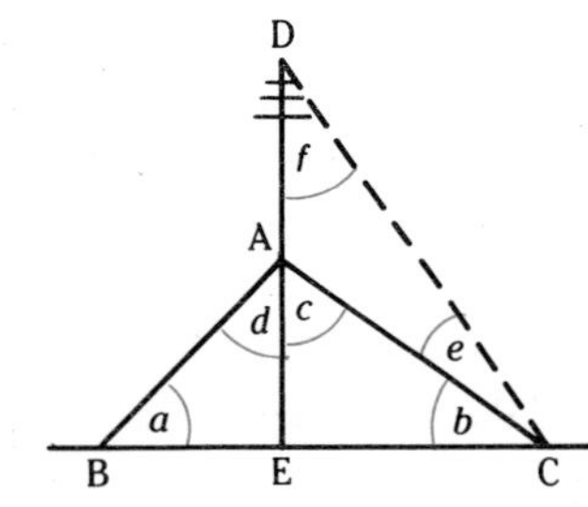

The diagram shows a radio transmitter DE supported by stays AB and AC.

(a) Which letter represents the angle of elevation of
  (i) A from B (ii) D from C ?

(b) Which letter represents the angle of depression of
  (i) C from A (ii) C from D ?

In questions 2 to 12 give measurements correct to the nearest millimetre.

2. Draw a sketch of the following situations.
   (a) From the opposite side of the road, the angle of elevation of the top of the roof of my house is 37°. The horizontal distance from the point where I measured the angle to the point on the ground immediately beneath the ridge of the roof is 12 m.
   (b) From the top of Blackpool Tower, which is 158 m high, the angle of depression of a ship that I can see directly out to sea is 25°.

3. Suggest a suitable scale if you are to make a scale drawing for each of the situations given in question 2.

4.

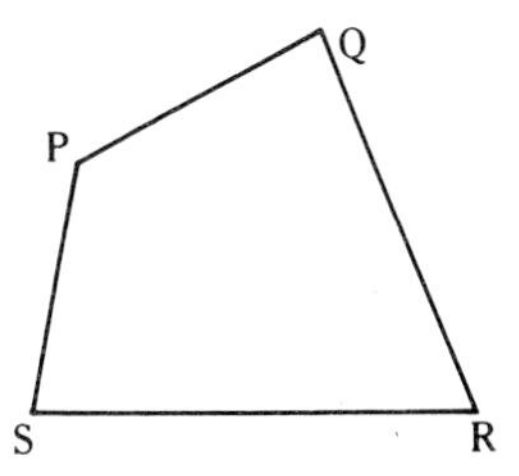

Above is a sketch of a field PQRS in which PQ = 38 m and QR = 52 m.
The field is to be drawn using a scale of 1 cm to 5 m.
   (a) What should be the lengths of PQ and QR on the scale drawing?
   (b) On the drawing SR is 13 cm. How long is the side SR of the field?

5. The map shows part of the north of England. Scale 1 cm : 10 miles
Trace the map carefully, adding any lines needed to answer the questions that follow.

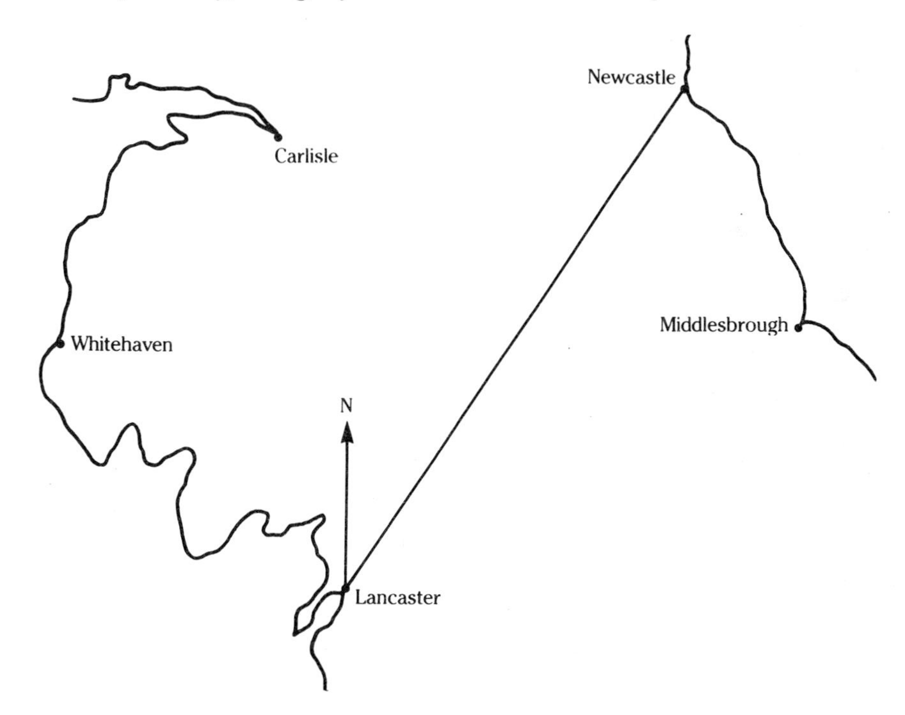

   (a) An aeroplane flies in a straight line from Newcastle to Lancaster.
      (i) What is the distance travelled by the aeroplane?
      (ii) What is the bearing on which the aeroplane flies?
   (b) A helicopter flies from Carlisle to Middlesbrough. How far is this?
   (c) What is the bearing of Newcastle from Whitehaven?

To make a scale drawing start by making a rough sketch of the object you are asked to draw. Mark on the sketch all angles and all full size measurements. Next draw another sketch and put the scaled measurements on this one. (It may be necessary to calculate more angles.) Then do the accurate drawing.

A stained glass window in the town hall is a rectangle with an equilateral triangle on the top. The rectangle measures 10 m wide by 7 m high. Each side of the triangle is equal to the width of the rectangle. Using a scale of 1 cm to 2 metres, make a scale drawing of the window. Use your drawing to find, to the nearest tenth of a metre, the height of the window.

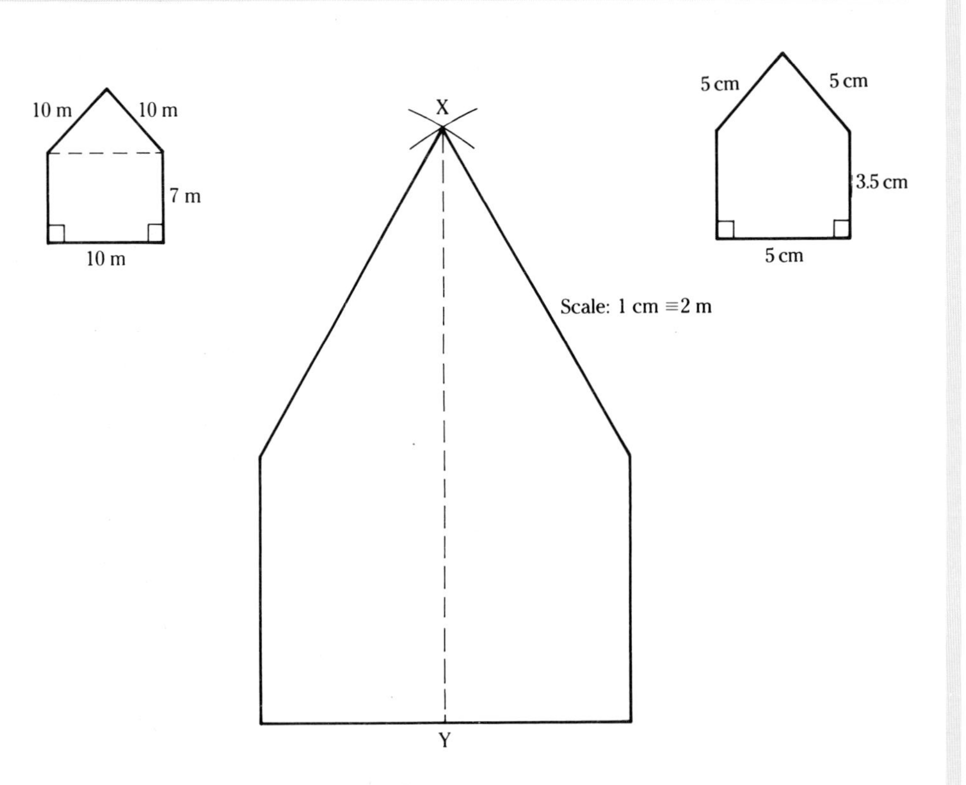

Y is the midpoint of the base.

From the drawing XY measures 7.85 cm, so the height of the window is 15.7 m.

We have chosen a small scale to save space. A more satisfactory scale for this drawing is 1 cm to 1 m.

6. (a) Taking the information given in question 2(a) and using 1 cm to represent 1 m, make a scale drawing to show my position relative to my house. Use your drawing to determine the height of the top of the roof above the ground.

   (b) Use the information given in question 2(b), and a scale of 1 cm : 20 m, to make a scale drawing that will enable you to find the distance from the ship to the base of Blackpool Tower.

7. 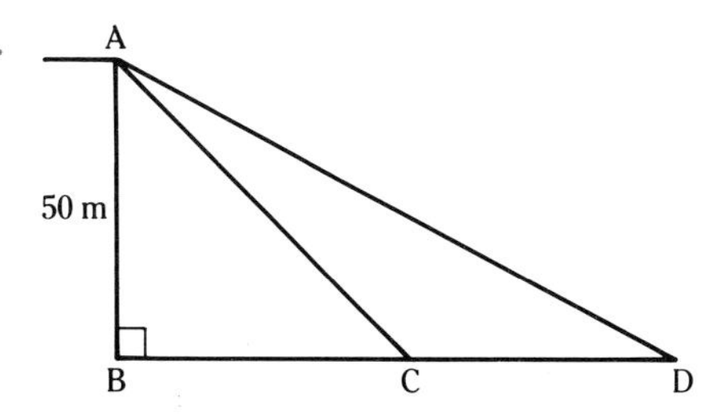

AB represents a vertical cliff 50 m high. C and D are two marker-buoys on the sea such that angle BAC is 40° and angle BAD is 55°. If all four points lie in the same vertical plane draw a scale diagram taking 1 cm to represent 5 m.

(a) What is the angle of depression of D from A ?

(b) What is the angle of elevation of A from C ?

(c) Measure the lengths of BC and CD, each correct to the nearest millimetre. Hence find the distance of (i) B from C (ii) C from D.

8. 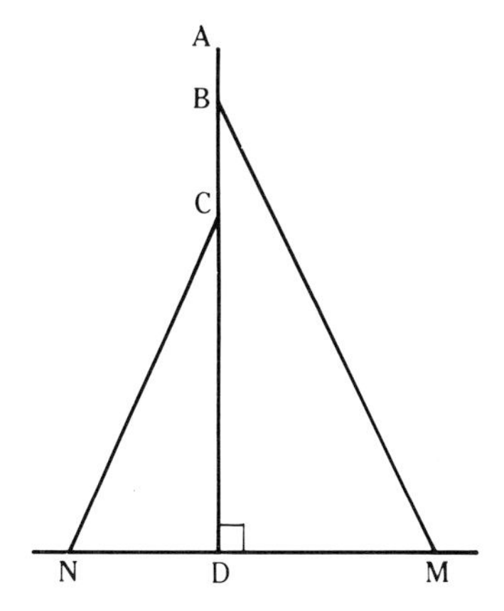

ABCD represents a vertical television mast 75 m high. BM and CN are supporting wires with anchorage points such that NDM is horizontal. ND = 15 m, DM = 30 m, angle BMD = 60° and angle CND = 65°.

(a) Draw a scale diagram using 1 cm to represent 5 m.

(b) Measure the lengths of CN and BM, each correct to the nearest millimetre. What is the length of each supporting wire ?

(c) How far is B below the top of the mast ?

9. The diagram shows the positions of three British cities: London, Nottingham and Birmingham.

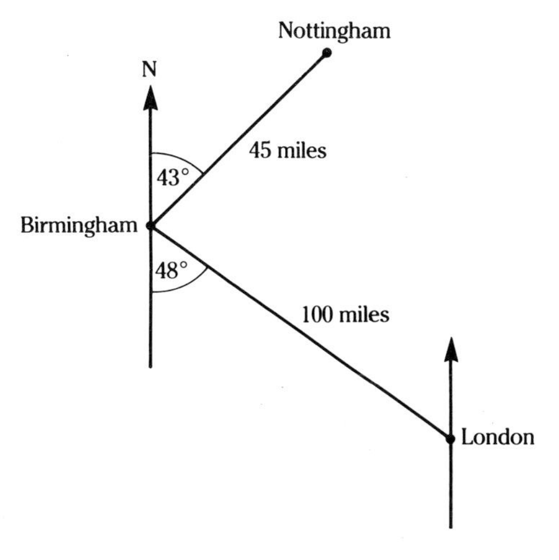

(a) What is the bearing of
   (i) Nottingham from Birmingham
   (ii) London from Birmingham
   (iii) Birmingham from Nottingham ?

(b) Using 1 cm to represent 10 miles and the distances given on the diagram, make a scale diagram to show the positions of the three cities.

(c) Join London to Nottingham and measure the length of your line to the nearest millimetre. Hence find the distance from London to Nottingham.

10. 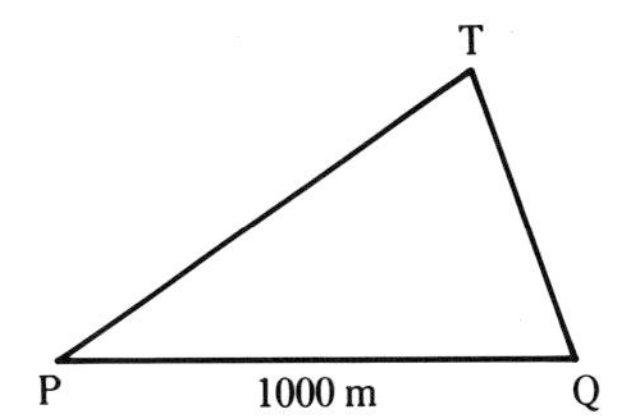

(a) Ship P is 1000 m due west of another ship Q. From P the bearing of a trawler T is 056 ° and from Q the bearing of the trawler is 340 °. Use a scale of 1 cm to 100 m to make a scale drawing and use it to find the distance of the trawler from P and from Q.

(b) A second trawler, V, lines up exactly half way between T and Q. Show the position of V on your diagram and find the distance and bearing of V from P.

11.

• P

Scale 1 : 4 000 000

This scale drawing shows the positions of Washington (W), Philadelphia (P), and Pittsburgh (B). Trace the diagram carefully.

(a) (i) Measure BP, giving its length to the nearest millimetre.
(ii) How far is it from Pittsburgh to Philadelphia ?

(b) How far is it, in kilometres,
(i) from Washington to Philadelphia
(ii) from Washington to Pittsburgh ?

(c) (i) What is the bearing of Philadelphia from Pittsburgh ?
(ii) What is the bearing of Pittsburgh from Philadelphia ?

(d) By measuring a suitable line on your diagram find
(i) how far Washington is east of Pittsburgh
(ii) how far Pittsburgh is north of Philadelphia.

12.

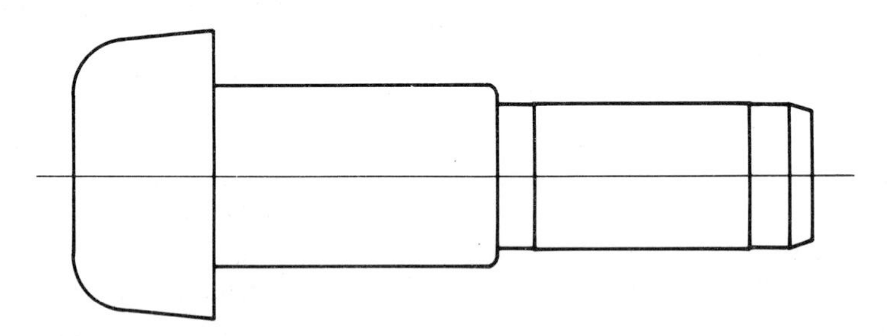

The diagram shows a drawing of a machine pin produced on a CAD program. It is shown here using a scale of 4 : 1. Use the drawing to find the actual measurements of

(a) the length of the pin

(b) the diameter of the thicker part of the shank

(c) the diameter of the narrower part of the shank

(d) the diameter of the head

(e) the thickness of the head.

Investigations

1. Make a scale drawing of the plan and one elevation of the object (chair, desk, bed, or whatever) on which you do your homework.

2. These diagrams show the elevation from the side and the plan as seen from above of a cylindrical telescope on a stand. The scale is 1 : 10.

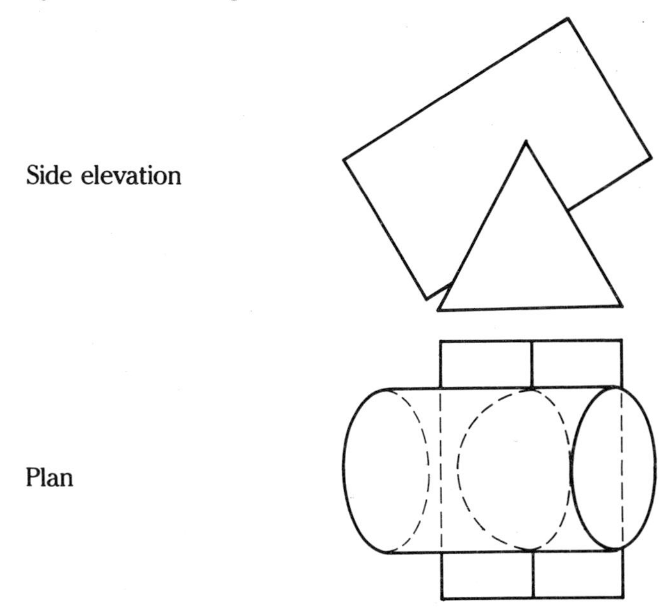

Make a free-hand sketch showing a three-dimensional view of the telescope and stand.

Self-Assessment 14

1.

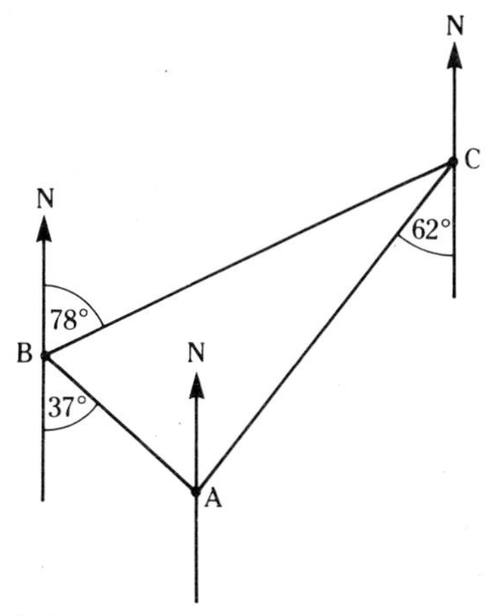

(a) Find the bearing of
 (i) C from B (ii) A from B
 (iii) B from A (iv) B from C.

(b) Find the angles in triangle ABC.

2. The bearing of a ship X from a lighthouse Y is 098°. Ship Z is due west of X. The bearing of Z from Y is 240°. Find the angles of triangle XYZ.

3. A triangle ABC is to be drawn to scale. AB = 120 m and AC = 95 m.
 (a) Find what the drawn lengths of AB and AC should be if the scale is 1 cm to 10 m.
 (b) If the measured length of BC is 10.2 cm, what is the real length of BC ?

4. An aircraft controller observes that the angle of elevation of an approaching aircraft, which is 1.8 km horizontally from the control building, is 20°. Using a scale of 10 cm to represent 1 km, make a scale drawing of this situation and use it to find the height of the aeroplane at this instant.

5. A helicopter flies 12 km on a bearing of 125°. It then changes course and flies 22 km on a bearing of 025°.

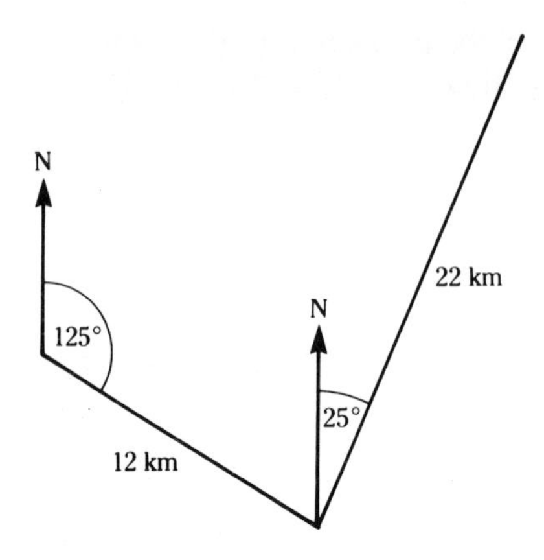

(a) Draw a scale diagram using 1 cm to represent 2 km.

(b) How far is the helicopter due east of its starting point?

(c) How far is the helicopter due north of its starting point?

15 SIMULTANEOUS EQUATIONS AND FORMULAE

COEFFICIENTS

We identify a particular term in an expression by using the letter, or combination of letters, involved.

The number in front of a letter is called the *coefficient*.

For example, for the term $3x$, we say that 3 is the coefficient of x,
for the term $4pq$, we say that 4 is the coefficient of pq.

If no number is written in front of a term, the coefficient is 1 or -1, depending on the sign of the term,

e.g. in $3+x-x^2$, the coefficient of x is 1 and the coefficient of x^2 is -1.

SIMULTANEOUS LINEAR EQUATIONS

Sometimes a problem involves two unknown quantities and gives rise to an equation with two variables.

Consider the equation $2x+y = 8$

A solution of this equation is a pair of values of x and y that satisfy the equation. Hence one solution is $x = 2$ and $y = 4$. Another solution is $x = 1$ and $y = 6$. In fact we can give x any value we choose and then find the corresponding value of y, e.g. if $x = 4.5$, then $y = -1$.

Thus a solution to an equation with two unknowns is a pair of values and there is an infinite set of solutions.

If, however, we *also* know that $x+y = 5$
then we find that only one of the solutions of the first equation satisfies the second equation,

e.g. $x = 2$ and $y = 4$ satisfy $2x+y = 8$ but do not satisfy $x+y = 5$ whereas $x = 3$ and $y = 2$ satisfy both equations.

The two equations together form a pair of *simultaneous* equations. In this context, simultaneous means that x and y represent the same numbers in both equations; the solution must be a pair of numbers that satisfies *both* equations.

Solving Simultaneous Equations

Consider the equations $2x + y = 8$ [1]

and $x + y = 5$ [2]

We know how to solve an equation with one letter term only, so we will try to eliminate either x or y from these two equations.

Combining the left-hand sides and the right-hand sides of two equations in the *same* way produces another equality. In this case, subtracting the LHS and the RHS of [2] from the LHS and the RHS of [1] gives

$$(2x + y) - (x + y) = 8 - 5$$

giving $x = 3$

Then substituting 3 for x in equation [2] gives $y = 2$.

As a check we see whether $x = 3$ and $y = 2$ satisfy equation [1]

$$\text{LHS of [1]} = 2(3) + 2 = 8 = \text{RHS of [1]}$$

Therefore the solution of the pair of equations is $x = 3$ and $y = 2$

Choosing this combination made the y terms disappear but, if the x terms are the same in two equations subtracting one from the other will eliminate the x terms.

Sometimes one letter can be eliminated by adding the equations. As an example

consider $4x + y = 8$ [1]

and $2x - y = 6$ [2]

[1] + [2] gives $6x = 14$

$\Rightarrow$ $x = \frac{7}{3} = 2\frac{1}{3}$

Substituting $\frac{7}{3}$ for x in [1] gives

$$\frac{28}{3} + y = 8$$

$\Rightarrow$ $y = -\frac{4}{3}$

Note that the symbol $\Rightarrow$ means 'giving'.

To eliminate a letter from a pair of equations,
***subtract* when the coefficients are the same,**
***add* when the coefficients are equal and opposite**
(i.e. same number but one positive and one negative).

Exercise 15a

1. Solve the following simultaneous equations.

(a) $x - y = 2$
$3x + y = 10$

(b) $4x + 3y = 7$
$2x + 3y = 5$

(c) $3a + b = 8$
$a + b = 4$

(d) $2x - y = 6$
$3x + y = 14$

(e) $4a + b = 17$
$2a + b = 11$

(f) $5x - 2y = 4$
$3x + 2y = 12$

(g) $5x + y = 14$
$3x + y = 10$

(h) $5p + 3q = 5$
$4p - 3q = 4$

(i) $4a + b = 37$
$2a - b = 17$

Solve the equations $x + 2y = 7$ and $3x + 2y = 9$

$$x + 2y = 7 \quad [1]$$

$$3x + 2y = 9 \quad [2]$$

It is easier to subtract the first equation from the second. A mistake is less likely if the equations are rewritten with equation [2] on top, i.e.

$$3x + 2y = 9 \quad [2]$$

$$x + 2y = 7 \quad [1]$$

[2] − [1] gives $2x = 2 \quad \Rightarrow \quad x = 1$

Substituting 1 for x in [1] gives $1 + 2y = 7$ so $y = 3$

Checking in [2]: LHS $= 3(1) + 2(3) = 9 =$ RHS

Therefore the solution is $x = 1$ and $y = 3$

2. Solve the simultaneous equations.

(a) $x + y = 5$
$3x + y = 7$

(b) $5x + 2y = 14$
$7x + 2y = 22$

(c) $9x + 5y = 50$
$12x + 5y = 65$

Solve the equations $2x - y = 11$ and $x - y = 8$

$$2x - y = 11 \quad [1]$$

$$x - y = 8 \quad [2]$$

As $-y - (-y) = -y + y = 0$, subtraction eliminates y.

[1] − [2] gives $x = 3$

From [2] $3 - y = 8$

$\Rightarrow$ $y = -5$

Check in [1]: LHS $= 2(3) - (-5)$

$= 6 + 5 = 11 =$ RHS

Therefore $x = 3$ and $y = -5$

3. Solve the simultaneous equations.

(a) $3x - y = 5$
$x - y = 1$

(b) $3x - 2y = 14$
$x - 2y = 4$

(c) $3p - 5q = -3$
$4p - 5q = 1$

Solve the equations $4a - 3b = 5$ and $4a - 5b = 2$

$$4a - 3b = 5 \quad [1]$$

$$4a - 5b = 2 \quad [2]$$

The a terms are the same, so subtraction eliminates a.

[1] − [2] gives $-3b - (-5b) = 3$

$\Rightarrow$ $-3b + 5b = 3$

$\Rightarrow$ $2b = 3$

$\Rightarrow$ $b = \frac{3}{2}$

From [1] $4a - 3(\frac{3}{2}) = 5$

$\Rightarrow$ $4a = \frac{19}{2}$

$\Rightarrow$ $a = \frac{19}{8}$

Check in [2]: LHS $= \frac{19}{2} - \frac{15}{2} = 2 =$ RHS

Therefore $a = \frac{19}{8}$ and $b = \frac{3}{2}$

4. Solve the simultaneous equations.

(a) $x + 3y = 0$
$x - y = 4$

(b) $4x - y = 8$
$4x + 2y = 20$

(c) $a - b = 8$
$2a + b = 7$

(d) $2p + 3q = 0$
$2p - 5q = -4$

(e) $2a + 3b = 7$
$2a - b = -1$

(f) $3x - 2y = 14$
$x + 2y = 10$

(g) $3p - 5q = 7$
$4p + 5q = -14$

(h) $3s + 5t = 35$
$4s - 5t = 0$

(i) $3x + 2y = 12$
$3x - y = 9$

(j) $3u + 5v = 17$
$4u + 5v = 16$

(k) $3c - d = 10$
$c + d = -2$

(l) $2f + r = 8$
$2f - 4r = 3$

Harder Simultaneous Equations

Sometimes the coefficients of neither of the letter terms are the same. In this case one or both of the equations can be multiplied to produce the same letter term.

Consider the equations $x - y = 5$ [1]
and $3x + 4y = 8$ [2]

We can multiply both sides of equation [1] by 3, which gives $3x - 3y = 15$ [3]
Then [2] − [3] will eliminate the x terms.

Alternatively we can multiply [1] by 4, which gives $4x + 4y = 20$ [3]
and then [2] + [3] will eliminate the y terms. Because mistakes are less likely when adding equations, we will choose this second approach, i.e.

$$x - y = 5 \quad [1]$$

$$3x + 4y = 8 \quad [2]$$

[1] × 4 gives $4x - 4y = 20$ [3]

[2] + [3] gives $7x = 28$ so $x = 4$

From [1] $y = -1$

Therefore the solution is $x = 4$ and $y = -1$

Exercise 15b

1. Solve the simultaneous equations.

(a) $2x + y = 7$
$3x + 2y = 11$

(b) $5x - 4y = -3$
$3x + y = 5$

(c) $9x + 7y = 10$
$3x + y = 2$

(d) $5a + 3b = 21$
$2a + b = 3$

(e) $3s - 2t = -2$
$s + t = 1$

(f) $5x + 3y = 11$
$4x + 6y = 16$

(g) $4a + 3b = 1$
$16a - 5b = 21$

(h) $2x + 5y = 1$
$4x + 3y = 9$

(i) $7r + 2s = 22$
$3r + 4s = 11$

Sometimes both equations need to be altered before we add or subtract.

Solve the equations $3x + 5y = 6$ and $2x + 3y = 5$

$$3x + 5y = 6 \quad [1]$$

$$2x + 3y = 5 \quad [2]$$

[1] × 2 gives $6x + 10y = 12$ [3]

[2] × 3 gives $6x + 9y = 15$ [4]

Then [3] − [4] gives $y = -3$

From [1] we have $3x - 15 = 6$

$\Rightarrow$ $3x = 21$, so $x = 7$

Checking in [2] gives LHS $= 2(7) + 3(-3) = 5 =$ RHS

Therefore the solution is $x = 7$ and $y = -3$

2. Solve the simultaneous equations.

(a) $2x + 3y = 12$
$5x + 4y = 23$

(b) $3x - 2y = -7$
$4x + 3y = 19$

(c) $2x - 5y = 1$
$5x + 3y = 18$

(d) $6x + 5y = 9$
$4x + 3y = 6$

(e) $14a - 3b = -18$
$6a + 2b = 12$

(f) $6s - 7t = 25$
$7s + 6t = 15$

(g) $3p + 4q = 5$
$2p + 10q = 18$

(h) $7x - 3y = 20$
$2x + 4y = -4$

(i) $10x + 3y = 12$
$3x + 5y = 20$

3. The remaining questions are mixed types of simultaneous equations.

(a) $x+2y = 9$
$2x-y = -2$

(b) $x+y = 4$
$x+2y = 9$

(c) $2x+3y = 0$
$3x+2y = 5$

(d) $3x-y = -10$
$4x-y = -4$

(e) $3x+2y = -5$
$3x-4y = 1$

(f) $5x+2y = 16$
$2x-3y = -5$

(g) $3p+2q = -4$
$3p-4q = 8$

(h) $a+b = 6$
$a-b = 1$

(i) $3s-5t = 13$
$2s+5t = -8$

(j) $x+2y = 7$
$y-x = 1$

Problem Solving

Problems can often be expressed in terms of equations and hence solved. It is important, however, to realise that the solutions may not all give reasonable answers to the problem, so this must be checked.

Many people, though, would be delighted to get to the point where solutions need checking. It is often getting started that is difficult, so here are some hints on problem solving.

1. Make sure that you understand the problem, i.e. that you know what all the words mean and that you know what has to be found.
   - Identify the information that is given in the problem; if the problem is about an object, draw a diagram and put all the information that you can on the diagram.
   - Decide what is unknown and use letters to identify unknown quantities. If you have a diagram, put the letters on it.
   - If there is more than one unknown, are there any conditions linking them ? If there are, write them down. (This will often help to reduce the number of unknowns.)

2. Look for relationships between the unknowns and the given information. To help find such relationships, try going through the following sequence.
   - Can you use your experience of solving a similar problem ?
   - Can you think of a related, but simpler problem, having the same kind of unknown, that you can solve ? You may then be able to work up from there.
   - Are there any other facts that may be useful ?
   - Try replacing given information/unknowns with simple numbers and see if this helps you to spot a method.
   - Can you break the problem down into smaller parts ?

Most of this advice applies to a wide variety of problems, not only those that can eventually be expressed in terms of an equation.

Exercise 15c

One angle in a triangle is 90° and the difference between the other two angles is 36°. Find the larger of the two unknown angles.

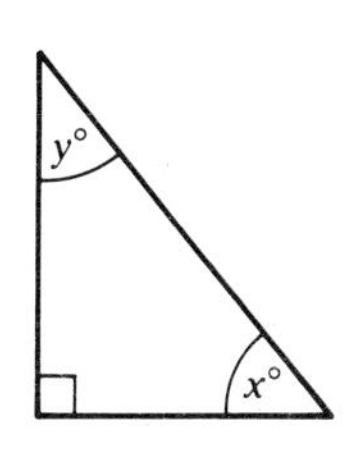

Let $x°$ be the larger angle.

The sum of the three angles is 180°

Therefore $x + y = 90$ [1]

The difference between x and y is 36,

Therefore $x - y = 36$ [2]

[1] + [2] $\Rightarrow$ $2x = 126 \Rightarrow x = 63$

The larger of the two unknown angles is 63°

Form two equations from the information given in each of the following problems. In those cases where the letters are not given, state clearly, either in words or in a diagram, what your letters represent. Solve the equations and end your solution by answering the question asked.

1. Two numbers x and y are such that x is the larger number.
   (a) The sum of the two numbers is 27. Express this as an equation involving x and y.
   (b) The difference between the two numbers is 15. Write this statement as an equation in x and y.
   (c) Solve the two equations simultaneously to find the smaller number.

2. The angles in a triangle are 60°, $x°$ and $y°$.
   (a) Write down a relationship between x and y.
   (b) If the difference between the unknown angles is 45°, write down another relationship between x and y.
   (c) What is the size of the largest angle in the triangle ?

3. A cup costs x pence and a saucer costs y pence.
   (a) One cup and one saucer cost £2.05. Write down an equation in x and y.
   (b) One cup and two saucers cost £2.70. Write down another equation in x and y.
   (c) Find the cost of one cup and the cost of one saucer.

4. A rectangle is a cm long and b cm wide. The perimeter of the rectangle is 48 cm and the length is 5 cm more than the width.
   (a) Draw a diagram showing this information and write down two different equations involving a and b.
   (b) Hence find the length of the rectangle.

5. A brand of pain reliever comes in two forms of pill; red pills and white pills. Red pills cost x pence each and white pills cost y pence each. A pack containing 10 red pills and 40 white pills costs 250 pence and a pack containing 5 red pills and 30 white pills costs 175 pence.
   Find
   (a) an expression involving x that gives the cost of 10 red pills
   (b) the cost of one red pill.

6. The sum of two numbers is 38 and their difference is 12. The larger number is x and the smaller number is y. Find the numbers.

7. Given that 5 pens and 4 pencils cost 348 pence and that 4 pens and 8 pencils cost 336 pence, find the cost of
   (a) 2 pens and 4 pencils
   (b) 3 pens (c) 1 pencil.

8. Find two numbers such that twice the first added to the second is 26 and the first added to three times the second is 28.

9. In 9 years time a father will be twice as old as his son. Three years ago he was four times as old as his son. How old is each of them now?

10. When a car travels at a steady speed of v km/h on a flat road, it covers a distance s km in 2 hours. If the same car travels at a steady speed of $2v$ km/h it covers $(s+5)$ km in 2 hours. Find the value of v. (Remember that 'distance = speed × time'.)

FORMULAE INVOLVING SQUARES AND SQUARE ROOTS

Consider the equation $x^2 = 4$

The solutions of this equation are the values of x which, when multiplied by themselves, make 4, i.e. the square roots of 4.

Now $2 \times 2 = 4$ *and* $(-2) \times (-2) = 4$, so the solutions of $x^2 = 4$ are

$x = 2$ or $x = -2$ which is abbreviated to $x = \pm 2$

Similarly, if $x^2 = 3$ then $x = \pm\sqrt{3}$

and if $x^2 = a$ then $x = \pm\sqrt{a}$

Now consider the equation $\sqrt{x} = 5$

To get rid of the square root, we must square both sides.

This gives $x = 25$

Similarly, if $\sqrt{x} = a$ then $x = a^2$

Therefore, when changing the subject of a formula,

if the letter required is squared, isolate that letter on one side of the formula and take the square root of both sides, remembering that both the positive and the negative square root must be considered;

if the formula involves a square root, isolate the term containing the square root on one side and then square both sides.

Note that the square of $\sqrt{a+b}$ is $a+b$

Exercise 15d

If $P = a^2 + b^2$ find a when $P = 2.7$ and $b = 0.9$

$P = a^2 + b^2$

When $P = 2.7$ and $b = 0.9$, $2.7 = a^2 + (0.9)^2$

i.e. $2.7 = a^2 + 0.81$

$1.89 = a^2$

Taking the square root of both sides gives $a = \pm 1.37$ (3 s.f.)

1. Given that $V = 4\pi r^2$, find, correct to 3 s.f.
   (a) V when $r = 4$
   (b) V when $r = 2.7$
   (c) r when $V = 16$
   (d) r when $V = 4.87$

2. If $a^2 = b^2 + c^2$, find, correct to 3 s.f.
   (a) a when $b = 4$ and $c = 3$
   (b) a when $b = 1.6$ and $c = 2.1$
   (c) b when $a = 8$ and $c = 4$
   (d) c when $a = 3.5$ and $b = 2.8$

If $v = \sqrt{u^2 - 5t}$ find u when $v = 12$ and $t = 6$

When $v = 12$ and $t = 6$, $v = \sqrt{u^2 - 5t}$ gives

$$12 = \sqrt{u^2 - 30}$$

We now need to square both sides to get rid of the square root sign.

$$144 = u^2 - 30$$

$$\Rightarrow \quad 174 = u^2$$

$$\therefore \quad u = \pm 13.2 \text{ (3 s.f.)}$$

3. If $r = \sqrt{x^2 + y^2}$, find, correct to 3 s.f.
   (a) r when $x = 3$ and $y = 4$
   (b) r when $x = 2$ and $y = 1$
   (c) x when $r = 13$ and $y = 5$

4. If $r = \sqrt{p^2 + q^2}$, find, correct to 3 s.f.
   (a) p when $r = 8$ and $q = 2$
   (b) q when $r = 25$ and $p = 7$
   (c) q when $r = 2.4$ and $p = 1.7$

Make u the subject of the formula $v^2 = u^2 - 2as$

$$v^2 = u^2 - 2as$$

Add $2as$ to both sides $\quad v^2 + 2as = u^2$

i.e. $\quad u^2 = v^2 + 2as$

Take the square root of both sides $\quad u = \pm\sqrt{v^2 + 2as}$

In questions 5 and 6 change the subject of the formula to the letter in the bracket.

5. (a) $c = x^2 + y^2$ $\quad (x)$
   (b) $a^2 = b^2 + c^2$ $\quad (b)$
   (c) $p = t + r^2$ $\quad (r)$
   (d) $g = 2x^2 - y^2$ $\quad (y)$
   (e) $v = \frac{1}{2}gt^2$ $\quad (t)$

6. (a) $A = \pi r^2$ $\quad (r)$
   (b) $V = \pi r^2 h$ $\quad (r)$
   (c) $x^2 = 5 - y^2$ $\quad (y)$
   (d) $R = a^3 - at^2$ $\quad (t)$
   (e) $z^2 = x^2 - y^2$ $\quad (y)$

Make l the subject of the formula $T = 2\pi\sqrt{\frac{l}{g}}$

$$T = 2\pi\sqrt{\frac{l}{g}}$$

Divide both sides by 2π $\quad \frac{T}{2\pi} = \sqrt{\frac{l}{g}}$

Square both sides $\quad \frac{T^2}{4\pi^2} = \frac{l}{g}$

Multiply both sides by g $\quad \frac{gT^2}{4\pi^2} = l \quad$ i.e. $\quad l = \frac{gT^2}{4\pi^2}$

In questions 7 and 8 make the letter in the bracket the subject of the formula.

7. (a) $p = \sqrt{2q}$ $\quad (q)$
   (b) $x = \frac{1}{2}\sqrt{y}$ $\quad (y)$
   (c) $q = p\sqrt{r}$ $\quad (r)$

8. (a) $b = a + \sqrt{c}$ $\quad (c)$
   (b) $V = \sqrt{3 - t}$ $\quad (t)$
   (c) $v = \sqrt{rt}$ $\quad (t)$

9. The formula for the volume, V cubic units, of a cylinder whose height is h units and whose radius is r units is given by $V = \pi r^2 h$.
   (a) Use the formula to find the volume of a cylinder whose height is 12 cm and whose radius is 5 cm.
   (b) Find h when $V = 120$ and $r = 6.25$

10. The formula for finding the length, d units, of the diagonal of a rectangle a units long and b units wide is $d = \sqrt{a^2 + b^2}$
    (a) Find d when $a = 4$ and $b = 8$
    (b) Use the formula to find the length of the diagonal of a rectangle that is 1.2 m long and 75 cm wide.
    (c) Use the formula to find a when $b = 15$ and $d = 25$

11. Standing on a level plain, with the height of your eyes x feet above ground level, you can see for y miles.

    If y is given approximately by the formula $y = \sqrt{1.5x}$.
    (a) Find how far you can see if your eyes are 5 feet above ground level
    (b) If you climb a scaffold tower until you can see for 5 miles, what is the height of your eyes ?

THE LANGUAGE OF MATHEMATICS

The further anyone progresses in mathematics, the more vital it becomes to express ideas precisely and accurately. You may so far have taken the view that if *you* know what you mean, and your answer is right, then that is all that matters. Sooner or later, however, some of you will need to communicate more advanced ideas to other people so that *they* know *exactly* what you mean.

The ability to use clear, correct, unambiguous mathematical language cannot be acquired overnight. It depends, first of all, on a frame of mind that sees the necessity for meticulous care in expression, and then it must be developed steadily and consistently until it becomes second nature.

For those who are thinking of taking mathematics further, now is the time to begin to develop the skill of using mathematical language correctly. Because this is done by starting at the beginning, inevitably we shall initially be looking at examples that seem almost too trivial to bother with. This should not deter an interested student, for the introduction to rigour which these simple cases give can create the attitude of mind required to use the language fully.

The language of mathematics is a combination of words and symbols, each symbol being the shorthand form for a word or phrase. When the words and symbols are correctly used, a piece of mathematical reasoning can be read, as prose can, in properly constructed sentences.

You have already used a fair number of symbols but not, perhaps, always with enough care for their precise meaning. As we now take a look at some familiar symbols we find that some can be translated correctly in more than one way.

The Use and Misuse of Symbols and Words

First consider the elementary symbol $+$.
This can be read as 'plus' or 'and' or 'together with' or 'positive'.

e.g. $3+2$ means 3 plus 2 or 3 and 2

The symbol $-$ has a similar variety of translations.

e.g. $5-4$ means 5 minus 4
$5-(-4)$ means 5 minus 'negative 4'

Now consider $\times$ which can be read as 'multiplied by' or 'times' or 'of'.

e.g. 7×5 means 7 multiplied by 5 or 7 times 5

$\frac{1}{100}\times x$ means one hundredth of x

Note. When 'times' is used for $\times$, it really means 'lots of', e.g. 3×8 means 3 lots of 8. It is quite incorrect, therefore, to say, 'times 3 by 8' a phrase that teachers often hear, because, clearly it is nonsense to write 'lots of 3 by 8'. (This emphasises that 'times' is not a verb.) If we want to use $\times$ as an instruction, we have to use the word 'multiply', e.g. the instruction to 'work out 3×8' is 'multiply 3 by 8'.

The next sign we consider is $=$ which means 'is equal to'. This symbol should be used *only* to link two quantities that are equal in value. Used in this way a short complete sentence is formed, e.g.

$x = 3$ is read as 'x is equal to 3'.

It is very easy to slip into the habit of saying 'equals' or 'equal' instead of 'is equal to'. For instance it is not good English to write 'Let $x = 3$' because this really translates to 'Let x is equal to 3'. While this sort of misuse may seem (and, up to this level, is) trivial it can be serious at a more advanced level and is better avoided altogether.

It is also bad practice to use $=$ in place of the word 'is'. For instance, when defining a symbol such as the radius of a circle we should say 'the radius of the given circle is r cm' and *not* 'the radius of the given circle $= r$ cm', because r cm and the radius are not two separate quantities of equal value; r cm *stands for* the radius.

Of course, if the radius is later found to be 4 cm, it *is* then correct to say '$r = 4$'.

Exercise 15e

Here are some problems followed by solutions which, although sometimes ending with the correct answer, contain nonsense on the way. These solutions have been taken from actual students' work and are examples of very common misuses of language.

Criticise these solutions.

1. Simplify $2\frac{1}{2} + 1\frac{1}{4} - 2\frac{1}{3}$

$$2\tfrac{1}{2} + 1\tfrac{1}{4} = 3\tfrac{3}{4} - 2\tfrac{1}{3}$$
$$= 1\tfrac{5}{12}$$

2. Solve the equation $6x + 5 = 3x + 11$

$$6x + 5 = 3x + 11$$
$$= 3x + 5 = 11$$
$$= \quad 3x = 6$$
$$= \quad x = 2$$

3. Write down the formula for the circumference of a circle.

The formula for the circumference of a circle is $2\pi r$.

4. Make r the subject of the formula

$P = r + 2t$

$$P = r + 2t = P - 2t = r$$
$$\therefore \quad r = P - 2t$$

5. Two angles of a triangle measure $60°$ and $80°$. Find the size of the third angle.

$$60° + 80° = 180° - 140°$$
$$= \text{third angle} = 40°$$

6. Three buns and two cakes cost 54 p and five buns and one cake cost 62 p. Find the cost of one bun and of one cake.

$$\text{Buns} = x\,\text{p} \quad \text{Cakes} = y\,\text{p}$$
$$3x + 2y = 54\,\text{p}$$
$$5x + y = 62\,\text{p}$$
$$10x + 2y = 124\,\text{p}$$
$$7x = 70\,\text{p}$$
$$x = 10\,\text{p} \quad \text{and} \quad y = 12\,\text{p}$$

Symbols that Connect Statements

The symbol $\therefore$, meaning 'therefore', introduces a fact, complete in itself, which follows from a previous complete fact. It is correct to write

$$x^2 = 9$$
$$\therefore \quad x = \pm 3$$

Note that $\Rightarrow$ can correctly be used as an alternative to $\therefore$, e.g.

$$x^2 = 9 \quad \Rightarrow \quad x = \pm 3$$

but the converse is not necessarily true.

There are occasions when none of these symbols is absolutely correct, a very simple example being

$$3 = x$$
$$x = 3$$

These two statements give exactly the same information; in this situation it is best to use 'i.e.' ('that is'):

$$3 = x$$

i.e. $$x = 3$$

It is quite common to see the word 'or' where we have used 'i.e.'. Although this is not actually wrong it should be treated with caution because 'or' strongly suggests that an *alternative result* is being given, and not just the same result rearranged.

A similar criticism of bad practice can be levelled at the way some people try to give their reasons for steps in a solution. In the solution of a pair of simultaneous equations, for example, we sometimes see

$$3x - 4y = 5 \qquad \times 2$$

$$2x + 7y = 13 \qquad \times 3$$

$$6x - 8y = 10$$

$$6x + 21y = 39$$

These four lines are disjointed, do not really explain what is happening and cannot be read sensibly in words. It is much better to present this piece of work in the following way:

$$3x - 4y = 5 \qquad [1]$$

$$2x + 7y = 13 \qquad [2]$$

$$2 \times [1] \quad \Rightarrow \quad 6x - 8y = 10$$

$$3 \times [2] \quad \Rightarrow \quad 6x + 21y = 39$$

After the initial definition of equations [1] and [2] this now reads '2 times equation [1] gives $6x - 8y = 10$' and '3 times equation [2] gives $6x + 21y = 39$'.

Investigation

(a) Choose any two-digit number whose digits are not the same. (For example, 25 is allowed, but 22 is not.) Now reverse the digits to give another two digit number and then find the difference between your chosen number and this one.

(b) Using the result of part (a) as your chosen number, repeat the process given above. Carry on repeating the process until you end up with a single digit number.

(c) Start again with a different number and repeat (a) and (b).

(d) Investigate other numbers.

(e) If your chosen number is x, the tens digit is a and the units digit is b, we can write $x = 10a + b$. If the number formed by reversing the digits is y, write a formula for y in terms of a and b.

(f) Use the formulae for x and y to explain why you get the results found in (d).

Self-Assessment 15

1. Solve the simultaneous equations
   $x - 2y = 8$ and $x + 2y = 12$

2. Solve the simultaneous equations
   $3x - 5y = -4$ and $x + 2y = 6$

3. Make r the subject of the formula

   (a) $2as + r^2 = t$ (b) $L = \sqrt{\dfrac{r}{g}}$

4. A pendulum of length l metres takes T seconds to swing from one side to the other and back again.

   The formula for T is $T = 2\pi\sqrt{\dfrac{l}{g}}$

   where $g\,\text{m/s}^2$ is the acceleration due to gravity.

   (a) Find T when $l = 4$ and $g = 10$

   (b) How long does it take a pendulum 6 metres long to swing from side to side when $g = 9.8$?

5. The formula for finding the length, d cm, of a diagonal of a cuboid whose dimensions are a cm, b cm and c cm is $d = \sqrt{a^2 + b^2 + c^2}$

   (a) Find d when $a = 2.4$, $b = 3.6$ and $c = 1.8$

   (b) How long is the diagonal of a cuboid whose dimensions are 2 m by 2.5 m by 80 cm?

   (c) The diagonal of a cuboid is 25 cm long. The cuboid is 8 cm long and 12 cm wide. What is its depth?

6. If James gives Thomas \$3, Thomas will have twice as much money as James. If Thomas gives James \$5, James will have twice as much as Thomas. How much money does each boy have?

16 SEQUENCES

Enjoying and succeeding in mathematics depends to some extent on recognising patterns. Some patterns are visual and geometric but others involve numbers or algebraic expressions. We start by looking at some that involve numbers.

SEQUENCES

A *sequence* is a set of numbers arranged in a particular order, e.g. $2, 5, 8, 11, \ldots$
In this example 11 is the 4th term of the sequence.

If, however, a set of numbers such as 4, 8, 9, 10 are not in any particular order (e.g. could be given as 9, 4, 8, 10 or 8, 10, 4, 9), the numbers are not a sequence.

Notation

We use u_1 to denote the first term of a sequence, u_2 to denote the second term, and so on. If we want to refer to a general term of a sequence, without specifying which term, we call it the nth term and denote it by u_n.

Note that n can have any of the values $1, 2, 3, \ldots,$ i.e. n is a positive integer.

Defining a Sequence

A sequence may be defined by giving the connection between one term and the next. This connection can be given in words, e.g. in the sequence above we can see that 3 is added to each term to give the following term.

This can be written as a formula because, if the nth term is u_n, the next term, i.e. the $(n+1)$th term or u_{n+1} is given by $u_{n+1} = u_n + 3$

If the first term, u_1, is known then the second term can be found from the formula,

i.e. if $u_1 = 2$ then $u_2 = u_1 + 3 = 2 + 3 = 5$

The second term can now be used to find the third term,

i.e. $u_3 = u_2 + 3 = 5 + 3 = 8$

and so on.

Another way to define a sequence is to relate a term to its position in the sequence, i.e. to n, and then give a formula for the nth term.

For example, if the nth term is 2^{n+1} then the 1st, 2nd and 3rd terms can be found by replacing n by 1, 2 and 3 respectively, giving 2^2, 2^3 and 2^4, i.e. 4, 8 and 16.

Exercise 16a

Give the next two terms in each sequence and state in words the rule you used to find them.

1. 2, 6, 10, 14, ...
2. 20, 17, 14, 11, ...
3. 4, 12, 36, 108, ...
4. 32, 16, 8, 4, ...
5. 1, 2, 4, 7, ...
6. 7, 13, 19, 25, ...
7. 5, 25, 125, 625, ...
8. 81, 27, 9, 3, ...

In each question from 9 to 15 you are given the first two terms of a sequence and the rule for finding other terms. Write down the next three terms.

9. 2, 6, ... multiply by 3
10. 2, −4, ... multiply by −2
11. 2, 4, ... add 2
12. 4, 2, ... divide by 2
13. 2, 4, ... add two more each time
14. 2, 4, ... add the previous two terms
15. 2, 3, ... add 1 more than was added last time

The nth term of a sequence, u_n, is given by the formula $u_n = 2^n + 1$. Find the third term and the ninth term.

$$u_n = 2^n + 1$$

The third term, u_3, is $2^3 + 1 = 8 + 1 = 9$

The ninth term, u_9, is $2^9 + 1 = 512 + 1 = 513$

In each question from 16 to 21 one of the terms of a sequence and the formula for finding the nth term are given. Check that the value of the given term is correct and write down the first four terms and the tenth term.

16. nth term $= 2 + 2n$; 6th term $= 14$
17. nth term $= 2^n$; 5th term $= 32$
18. nth term $= 3 \times 2^{n-1}$; 7th term $= 192$
19. nth term $= n(n-1)$; 7th term $= 42$
20. nth term $= (n-1)^2$; 6th term $= 25$
21. nth term $= n^2 - 1$; 4th term $= 15$

The first term of a sequence is 3 and $u_{n+1} = 3u_n - 4$
Write down the next 3 terms of the sequence.

$$u_1 = 3$$
$$u_2 = 3u_1 - 4 = 3\times 3 - 4 = 5$$
$$u_3 = 3u_2 - 4 = 3\times 5 - 4 = 11$$
$$u_4 = 3u_3 - 4 = 3\times 11 - 4 = 29$$

In each question from 22 to 27, the nth term of the sequence is denoted by u_n and the first term is given. Give the next four terms.

22. $u_1 = 2, \quad u_{n+1} = 3u_n$

23. $u_1 = 3, \quad u_{n+1} = u_n + 2$

24. $u_1 = -2, \quad u_{n+1} = u_n - 2$

25. $u_1 = 1, \quad u_{n+1} = 2u_n - 1$

26. $u_1 = 9, \quad u_{n+1} = \sqrt{u_n + 2}$

27. Give u_{n+1} in terms of u_n for the sequences in questions 1 to 4.

Finding a Formula for the *n*th Term

If we are given the first few terms of a sequence then we may be able to find a formula for the nth term in terms of n.

One way of trying to spot the relationship is to write out a table, e.g. for the sequence 2, 5, 8, 11,...

n	1	2	3	4
nth term	2	5	8	11

We can see that we add 3 to the first term to get the second, add another 3 to get the third and so on, so to find the 4th term we start with 2 and add $(4-1)$ threes. To find the nth term we add $(n-1)$ threes; hence the nth term $= 2 + 3(n-1)$
Multiplying out, the nth term $= 3n - 1$

Once a formula has been found it is sensible to check that it does generate the given terms.

Exercise 16b

In each question from 1 to 10 find a formula for the nth term in terms of n; write down the next two terms and the tenth term.

1. 3, 8, 13, 18, ...

2. 1, 4, 9, 16, ...

3. 2, 6, 18, 54, ...

4. $1, \frac{1}{2}, \frac{1}{3}, \frac{1}{4}, \ldots$

5. $1, \frac{1}{2}, \frac{1}{4}, \frac{1}{8}, \ldots$

6. $1\times 2,\ 2\times 3,\ 3\times 4,\ 4\times 5, \ldots$

7. 2, 5, 10, 17, 26, ...

8. $\frac{1}{2}, \frac{2}{3}, \frac{3}{4}, \frac{4}{5}, \ldots$

9. 5, 8, 11, 14, ...

10. 1, 8, 27, 64, ...

DIFFERENCES

Sometimes the rule or formula is too difficult to spot; in this case a *difference table* may help us to continue the sequence. The first difference sequence is found by subtracting u_1 from u_2, u_2 from u_3 and so on.

This is a simple example: 1, 2, 5, 10, 17, ...

Terms	1		2		5		10		17		26		37
1st difference		1		3		5		7 →		9 →		11	

We can see that the first difference row will continue with 9 and 11 and hence we can continue the sequence, i.e. $17 + 9$ gives 26 and $26 + 11$ gives 37.

The sequence is now 1, 2, 5, 10, 17, 26, 37, ...

A less obvious example is 2, 6, 22, 56, 114, ... We find that we need a second difference row before the pattern becomes clear.

Terms	2		6		22		56		114		202		326
1st difference		4		16		34		58		88		124	
2nd difference			12		18		24 →		30 →		36		

In some cases it may be necessary to add a third difference line before being able to see the pattern.

Notice that a difference table does not always help because there are some sequences whose first differences, second differences, and so on, do not show an obvious pattern.

CHOICE OF RULE

If a few terms only are given it is not possible to be certain that the only possible rule has been found.

For instance, if a sequence starts 1, 2, 4, ... we might think that we must multiply each term by 2 to obtain the next and hence get 1, 2, 4, 8, 16, ...

However it is possible that the rule is to add one more each time, in which case we get 1, 2, 4, 7, 11, ...

Even if we are given four terms it is sometimes possible to find alternative rules to define the sequence; we give the simplest or most obvious one but you may find a different, equally acceptable, rule.

Exercise 16c

For the following sequences make difference tables and use them to find two more terms of each sequence.

1. 11, 12, 16, 23, 33, ...
2. 2, 3, 7, 15, 28, ...
3. 11, 17, 33, 71, 143, 261, ...
4. 0, 1, −2, −6, −8, −5, ...
5. 0, −1, 4, 27, 80, 175, ...

For each of the following sequences there are at least two possible rules or formulae for generating it. Find two possibilities and in each case give three more terms.

6. 2, 6, 18, ...
7. 0, 1, 4, ...
8. 3, 6, 12, ...

Use any method to continue each of the following sequences for three more terms. Give a rule or formula if possible.

9. 1, 8, 27, 64, ...
10. $\frac{1}{2}, \frac{2}{3}, \frac{3}{4}, \frac{4}{5}, \ldots$
11. 1, 2, 3, 5, 9, ...
12. 0, 3, 8, 15, ...
13. 100, 99, 95, 79, 15, ...
14. 1.3, 2.4, 3.5, 4.6, ...
15. 2, 3, 2, 4, 2, 5, 2, ...
16. 2, 3, 5, 7, 11, ...
17. 1, −2, 4, −8, ...
18. 2, 5, 10, 17, 26, ...

Questions 19 to 24 are concerned with the sequence 3, 7, 11, 15, ...

19. Write down the next two terms and the rule used to obtain them.
20. Give the formula for the nth term in terms of n.
21. Why are there no even terms ?
22. Give the first five terms of the sequence formed by multiplying each term of the given sequence by the term following it. (The first term is 3×7, i.e. 21.)
23. Use a difference table on the five terms of the new sequence formed in question 22, to find the sixth and seventh terms.
    Check that you are correct by using the rule given in question 22.
24. Give the first five terms of the sequence formed by adding each term of the original sequence to the term following it.
25. Give the formula for the nth term of the sequence in question 24.

26. (a) Copy and complete the following difference table.

Given sequence	2		5		12		27		54		97
1st difference		3		7		15		27			
2nd difference											
3rd difference											

(b) Use your table to extend each of the 3rd, 2nd and 1st difference rows by three more terms.

(c) Find the next three terms of the given sequence.

Fibonacci Sequences

One of the sequences in the first exercise, i.e. 2, 4, 6, 10, ... was generated by starting with two terms and obtaining the rest by adding the previous two terms. This is called a Fibonacci sequence.

The simplest Fibonacci sequence is 1, 1, 2, 3, 5, 8, ... and this crops up in natural objects; for instance, if you count the number of spirals in the seedhead of a sunflower you will find that it is one of the numbers in this sequence, e.g. 55 or 89.

Other Fibonacci sequences can be found by starting with different pairs of numbers.

Pascal's Triangle

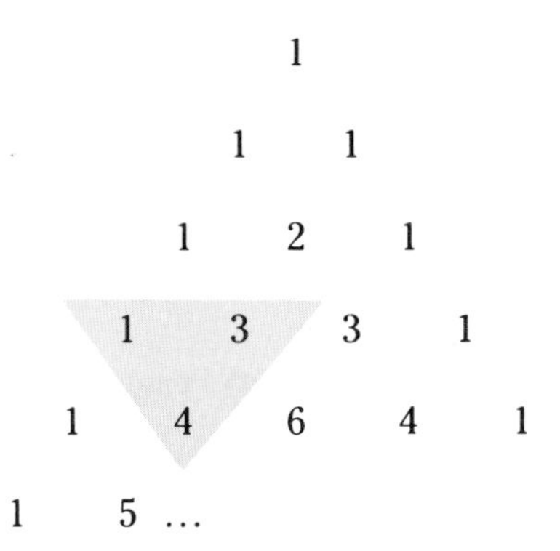

Each number in Pascal's Triangle is formed by adding together the two numbers just above it: for instance, $4 = 1 + 3$
(You may imagine that the triangle is surrounded by zeros, so $0 + 1 = 1$)

The numbers in this arrangement appear in unexpected contexts in mathematics, such as in probability calculations and in expanding brackets.

Exercise 16d

1. Form a Fibonacci sequence from each of the following pairs of numbers. Give six terms.
   (a) 1, 3 (b) 2, 3 (c) 1, 4

2. Form a difference table for the sequence in question 1(a). What do you notice?

3. (a) Give the first eight terms of the Fibonacci sequence that begins 1, 1, ...
   (b) Form a sequence by expressing each term of the sequence in (a) as a fraction of its following term. Give the first eight terms.
   (c) Give the fractions in (b) as decimals correct to 4 decimal places. What do you notice?

4. Copy Pascal's triangle. Complete the sixth row and add two more rows.

5. Find 11^0, 11^1, 11^2, ... and compare the figures with the numbers in Pascal's Triangle. How do you explain the discrepancy in the sixth line?

6. (a) Find the exact value of each of the first four terms of the sequence
   9^2, 99^2, 999^2, ...
   (b) Guess the value of the fifth term and check it by calculation.

FLOW CHARTS

When the relationship between the terms of a sequence is known, it can be used to generate the terms of the sequence. The process of generating the terms requires a logical order of operations which can be shown visually in a flow chart.

This flow chart finds the 10th term of the sequence whose nth term is $3n - 1$

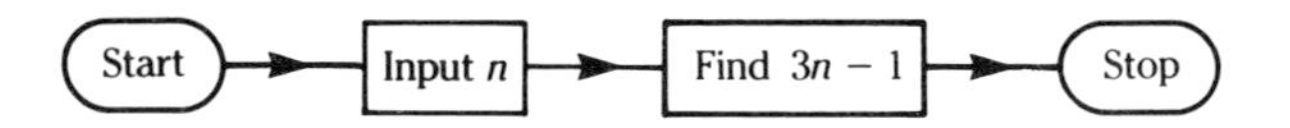

We need a more elaborate version if, instead of requiring one particular term, we want, say, the first five terms.

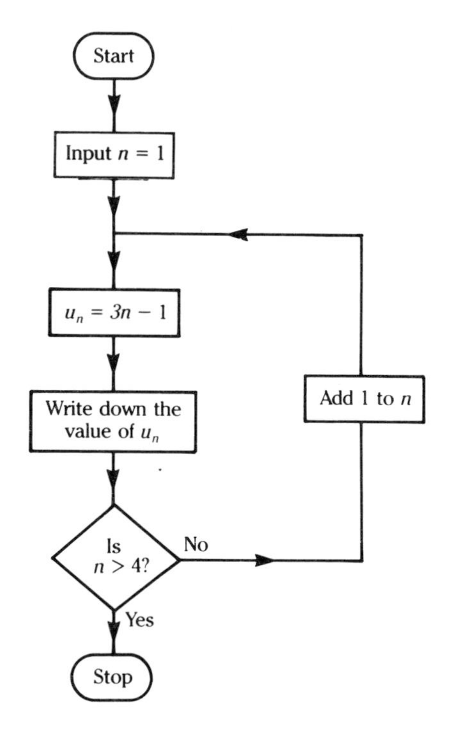

In this flow chart we have an example of a decision box (diamond-shaped and containing a question) and a loop that takes us back to work out the next term.

We now need to work through the flow chart to make sure that it is giving the correct terms.

Flow charts can be used to show the order in which operations have to be done for any process, not necessarily a mathematical process. The following exercise shows some other uses of flow charts.

Using a Computer

If we have a rule or a formula for generating a sequence then it is possible to write a simple program for a computer.
The following programs are in Basic and will run on most machines. They both produce the same sequence.

```
10 PRINT "Rule: Start with 1 and add 4 to each term."
20 PRINT TAB(9); "N" TAB(15); "Nth TERM"
30 X = 1
40 N = 1
50 PRINT N, X
60 N = N+1
70 X = X+4
80 IF N < 11 THEN GOTO 50
```

```
10 PRINT "Nth term = 1+4(N-1)"
20 PRINT TAB(9); "N" TAB(15); "Nth TERM"
30 FOR N = 1 TO 10
40 X = 1+4*(N-1)                (or X = 4*N-3)
50 PRINT N, X
60 NEXT N
```

There may be more refined ways of writing a program but these are simple and self-explanatory and if you have not tried writing a program before, they could act as an introduction. Type RUN (and press Return) and you should see ten terms of the sequence appear on the screen. Either program can be adapted for other rules and formulae and to give any number of terms. Try producing some of the sequences in Exercise 16a.

Two textbooks that are helpful in this context are:

132 Short Programs for the Mathematics Classroom, published by the Mathematical Association in conjunction with Stanley Thornes;
BBC Basic Programming for Schools and Colleges, by Mark Brindley, published by Stanley Thornes.

Using a Spreadsheet

A more sophisticated approach to calculating terms is to use a *spreadsheet*. In this case the program is already prepared and all you have to do is to specify the rule or formula and say how many terms you want.

You will need to consult the manual for your particular spreadsheet in order to discover how to enter the numbers and labels and formulae, but the simple use of a spreadsheet is easy if you follow the instructions.

The following sequence was produced using *Viewsheet* on the BBC Master but spreadsheets are all very much the same.

To start with you will see the following display.

```
Slot = A 1

Contents = *Blank*

      ......A......B......C......D......E......F......G..

.......1>

.......2

.......3

.......4
```

Put N in A1, Nth in A2 and TERM in B2. These are the *labels.* Then put 1 in C1 and use the replicating facility (consult your manual) to add 1 to the previous entry so that 2 appears in D1, 3 in E1 and so on as far as K1.

Now write the formula $4*N-3$ in C2 and replicate this in boxes D2 to K2.

Press ESCAPE and most of the terms of the sequence should appear on the screen. (The width of the columns may need adjusting to get all ten terms on the screen.)

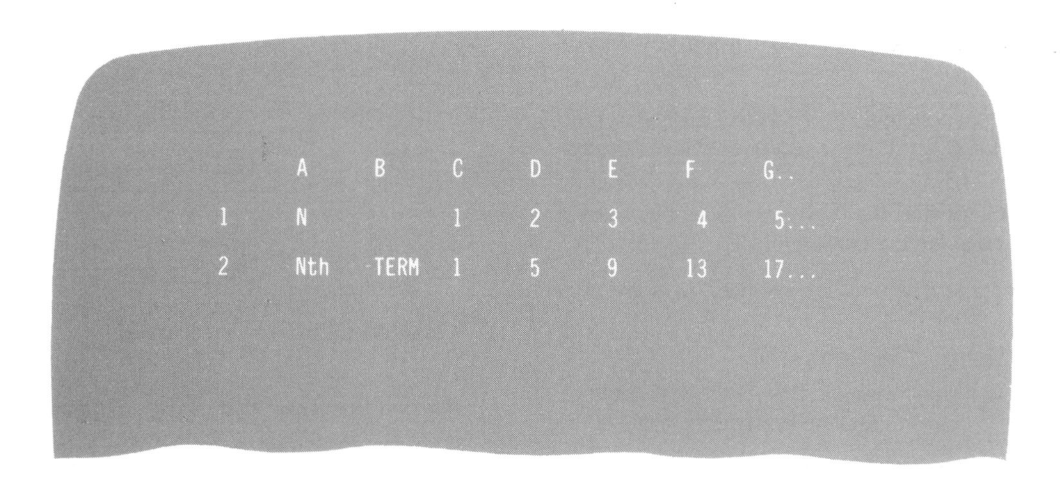

The spreadsheet could be used to calculate over two hundred terms if you wished, though you would have to adjust the viewing window to see them all. It could also produce a large number of different sequences at once, using the other rows, but the labelling would need adjusting so that you would know which sequence was which.

Exercise 16e

1.

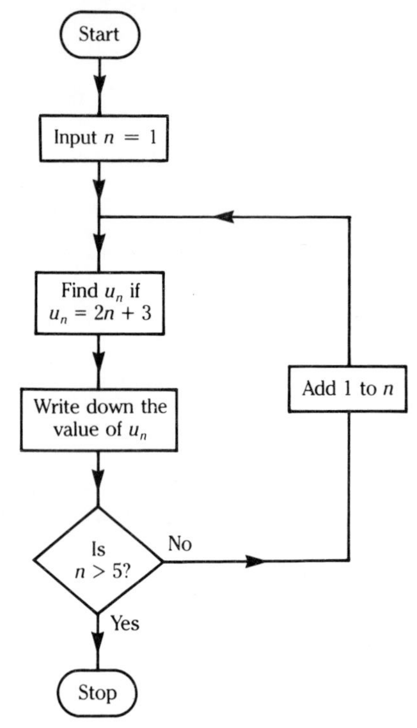

Write down the terms given by this flow chart.

2. What change would you make to the flow chart given in question 1 if ten terms were required?

3. Draw a simple flow chart for working out the first 12 terms of the sequence whose nth term is $2 + 2n$.

   Check that the flow chart gives the correct value for the tenth term.

4. The nth term of a sequence, u_n, is given by $u_n = n^2 - 1$.
   (a) Find the eighth term.
   (b) Draw a simple flow chart that could be used to find the first twenty terms of the sequence.
   (c) Use the flow chart to find the eighth term and check that your answers to parts (a) and (c) agree.

5. Draw a flow chart with a decision box and a loop for working out the first five terms of the sequence whose nth term is $(n-1)^2$

6. Copy this diagram. Make the line about 10 cm long.

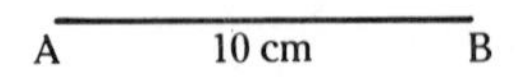

Now follow the process given in this flow chart.

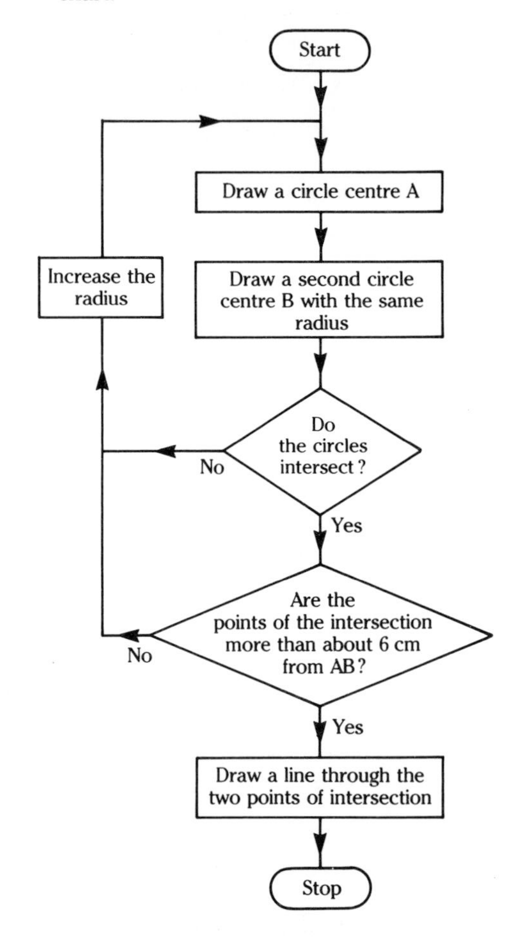

What does this process achieve?

7. Draw a flow chart that gives
   (a) the first four terms of the sequence where

   $$u_{n+1} = 2u_n + 1 \quad \text{and} \quad u_1 = 1$$

   (b) the first six terms of the sequence for which

   $$u_{n+1} = u_n - 2 \quad \text{and} \quad u_1 = 3$$

8. (a) There is a box missing from this flow chart. Copy and correct the flow chart.

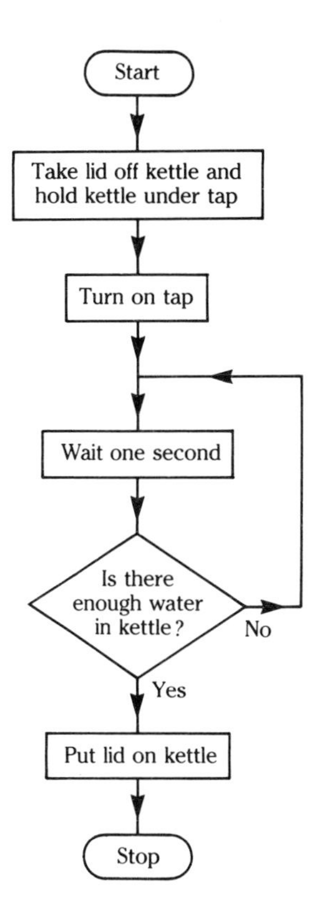

(b) Take another simple process that needs a decision to be made at some point and draw a flow chart to illustrate the steps needed to complete the process.

In a flow chart it is possible to have more than one decision box and hence more than one loop. The next question illustrates such a situation.

9. Draw a flow chart to illustrate the steps needed to pick enough primroses, and then enough bluebells, to make a mixed bunch.

10. Draw a flow chart to illustrate another process that needs two decision boxes.

11. This is a computer program written in BASIC. It is simpler than those given before this exercise and you should be able to follow the computer instructions.

```
10 FOR N = 1 TO 4
20 PRINT 2*N+3
30 NEXT N
```

(a) What does the symbol * mean? (Read the programs before this exercise carefully.)

(b) How many terms of the sequence does this program give?

(c) Explain what line 20 does when `N = 1`

(d) What is the third number that is printed on the screen?

(e) What is the formula for the nth term of the sequence?

(f) If you wanted the first 12 terms printed on the screen, what would need to be changed?

12. This BASIC program performs a well-known operation.

```
10 PRINT "Type a number"
20 INPUT Y
30 FOR N = 1 TO 10
40 PRINT N; "x"; Y; "="; N*Y
50 NEXT N
```

(a) What do the quotation marks mean?

(b) Explain exactly what line 40 does when `N = 1`

(c) What does this program do?

13. This is a another BASIC program that gives a sequence.

```
10 FOR N = 1 TO 6
20 PRINT N*N+1
30 NEXT N
```

(a) How many terms of the sequence does this program give?

(b) Give the last term printed on the screen.

(c) What is the formula for the nth term of the sequence?

(d) Change line 20 to `PRINT (N*N+1)/2`. (Note that / is used instead of ÷ for 'divided by'.) Give the terms of the new sequence.

SEQUENCES GIVEN BY VISUAL PATTERNS

If we write down the number of dots in each of the squares above we find we have a familiar sequence, i.e. the *square* numbers, 1, 4, 9, 16, ...

Dots can also be arranged in triangles.

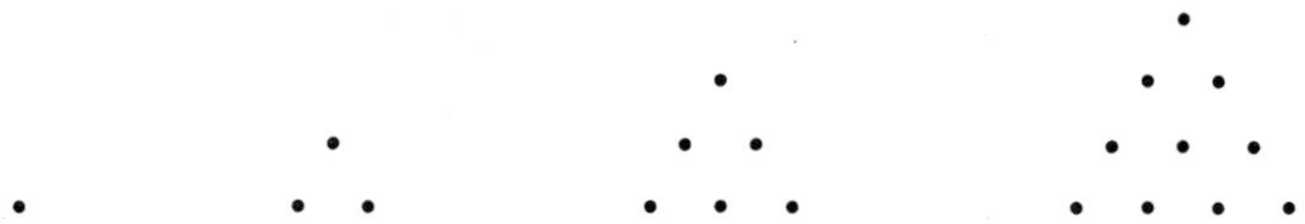

The sequence given by the number of dots is 1, 3, 6, 10, ...
These are the *triangular* numbers.

Number sequences are also generated by other visual sequences of arrangements of dots and lines and shapes.

Exercise 16f

In each question from 1 to 4,

(a) add two more diagrams to the sequence

(b) give the associated number sequence

(c) give a rule or a formula for generating the number sequence.

1.

2.

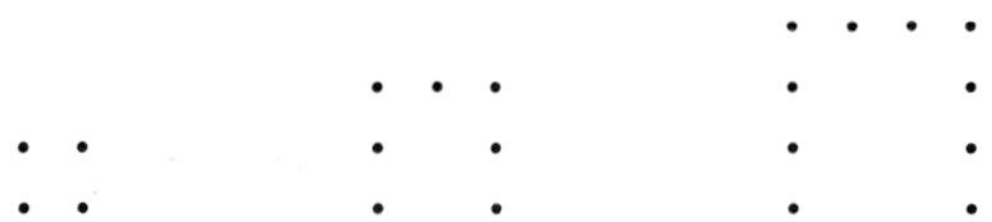

3.

The associated number sequence is given by the *total* number of rectangles of all sizes (including squares) in each diagram.

4.

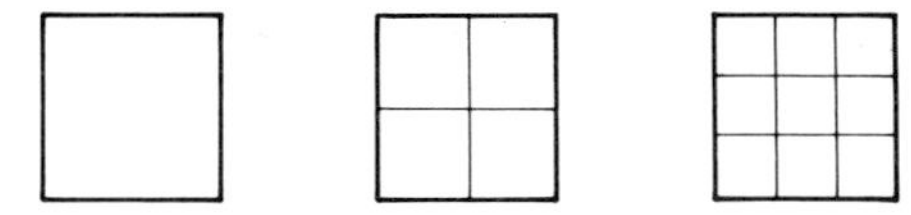

The associated number sequence is given by the total number of squares in each diagram.

In the following questions it is neither necessary nor helpful to draw the next two patterns. Write down the first five terms of the associated number sequence and give the rule or formula.

5.

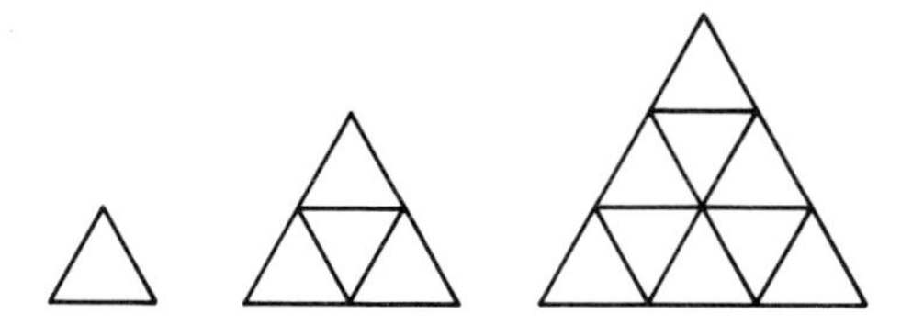

The number sequence is given by the number of small triangles in each diagram.

6. Cannon balls are piled up in a triangular pyramid. Each ball (apart from those at the bottom) rests on the three underneath.

   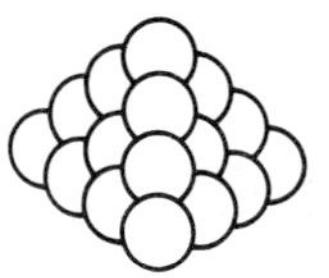

The number sequence is given by the number of cannon balls in each pile.

7. Each line passes through the centre of the circle.

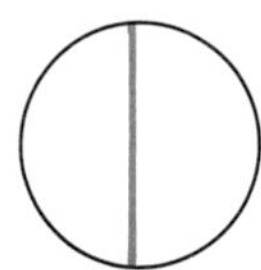 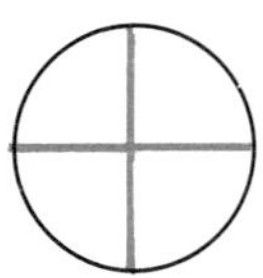 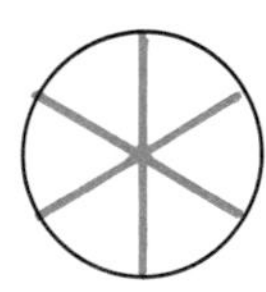

The number sequence is given by the number of sectors.

8. The lines are positioned to give the maximum number of regions.

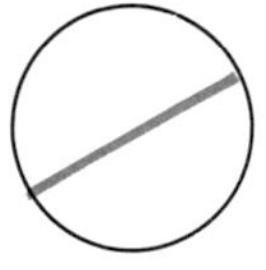 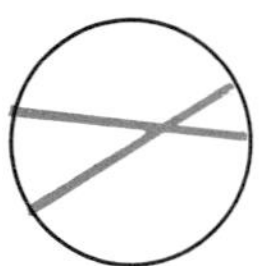 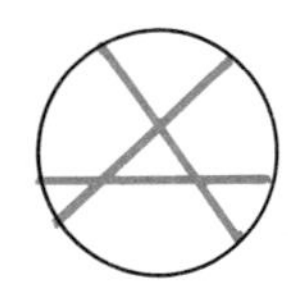

The number sequence is given by the number of regions.

9.

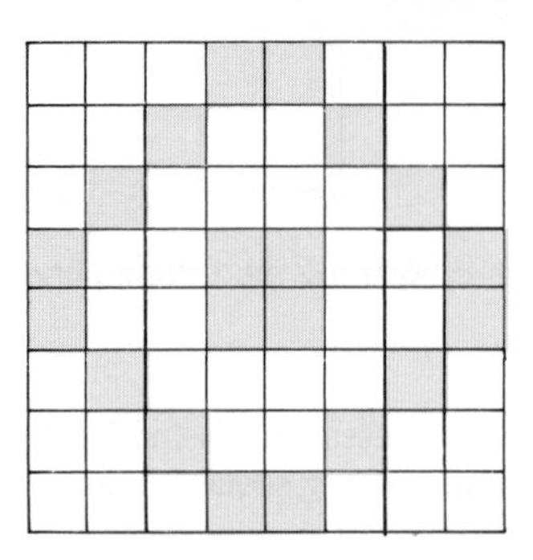

A square pattern is made up of 1 cm purple and white square tiles.
The centre four tiles are purple.
The middle two tiles on each edge are purple and so are the tiles that run diagonally from one group of purple edge tiles to the next.
A square of side 8 cm is shown.

(a) Draw and mark the purple tiles for a square with a side of
(i) 6 cm (ii) 4 cm

(b) Is it possible to draw this pattern in a square of side 7 cm ? What limitations are there on the size of the square ?

(c) Copy and fill in the following table, adding two more columns. If necessary, draw more diagrams.

Length of side in cm	4	6	8		
Number of purple tiles			20		
Number of white tiles					

(d) Give the formula for the number of purple tiles used in a square of side n cm, where n is even and greater than 2.

(e) How many tiles are there in a square of side n cm ($n \geqslant 4$ and even)?
How many white tiles are there ?

USE OF A COUNTER EXAMPLE

In this chapter we have seen how identifying the pattern in a sequence can lead to the general result, i.e. an expression for the nth term. Seeing patterns in other aspects of mathematics often leads to similar generalisations. For example, drawing a few different triangles, and for each of them adding up the three angles, reveals this pattern: the sum of the angles is 180° whatever the shape or size of the triangle drawn. This leads us to say that the result is true for all possible triangles.

There are pitfalls in drawing an overall conclusion based on a pattern seen from a few examples. Looking at the prime numbers 3, 5, 7, 11 could lead to the generalisation that 'all prime numbers are odd'. This is not true however as 2 is a prime number and 2 is not an odd number. We have given an example that does not fit the pattern 'all prime numbers are odd' so that pattern is not valid. An example used to show that a generalisation is faulty is called a *counter example*.

Investigations

1. Find a counter example to show that each of the following generalisations is incorrect.

(a) The diagonals of a quadrilateral bisect each other, i.e. cut each other in half.

(b) The square root of a number is always less than the number.

(c) The first three terms of a series are 2, 4, 8, so the nth term must be $n^2 - n + 2$

(d) The sum of two prime numbers is always even.

2. Alex was asked to investigate the relationship between the number of lines drawn across a circle and the number of regions that the circle is divided into by those lines. Alex drew these diagrams.

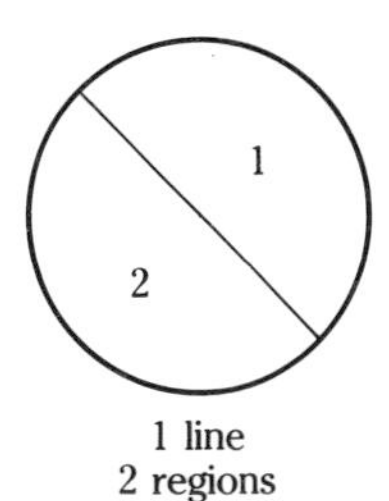

1 line
2 regions

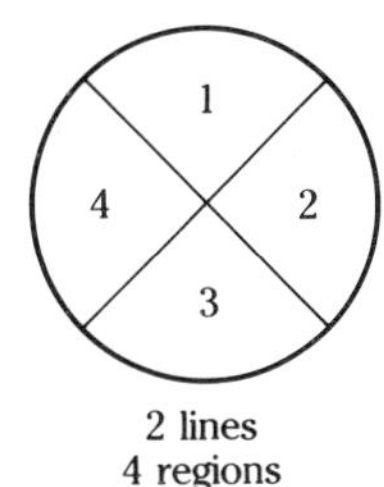

2 lines
4 regions

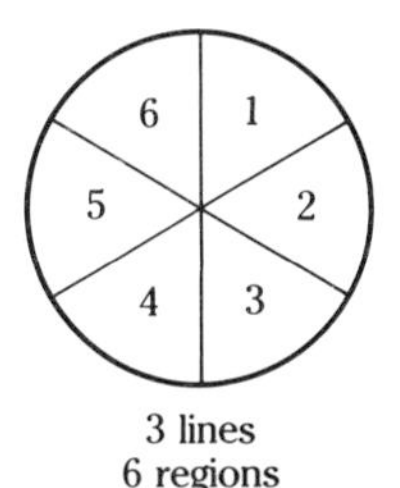

3 lines
6 regions

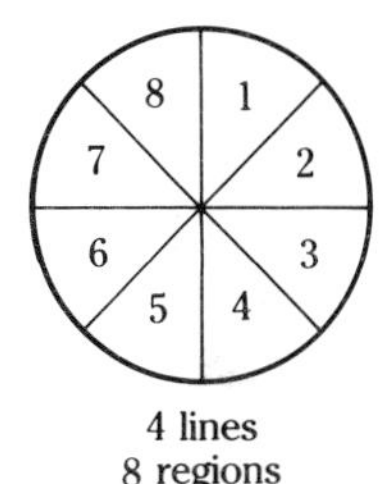

4 lines
8 regions

From these diagrams Alex made the statement that 'n lines drawn across a circle produces $2n$ regions'.

Draw an example to show that Alex's statement is not always true.

3. Each of the following statements makes a general assertion, i.e. they state that a fact is true in all cases.

For each of these statements find an example
(i) for which it is true (ii) for which it is false.

(a) When a number is divided, the result is less than the original number.

(b) When three consecutive numbers are multiplied together the result can be divided by 4.

(c) A square number can be written as the sum of two consecutive prime numbers.

4. The natural (counting) numbers form a simple sequence: 1, 2, 3, 4, . . .

Make a new sequence by adding the first n natural numbers (the fourth term will be $1 + 2 + 3 + 4$, i.e. 10). Give ten terms.

Now double each of the numbers in the second sequence. What is the connection between this third sequence and the first sequence ?

Use your conclusions to find the sum of the first 15 natural numbers without adding them all up (but check afterwards).

If you obtained the correct sum, does this prove that you will always get the correct sum of the first n natural numbers if you use your rule ?

5. The diagram shows a system for making road barriers of any length by adding extensions to a basic framework made of rods. Each extension is made of four rods.

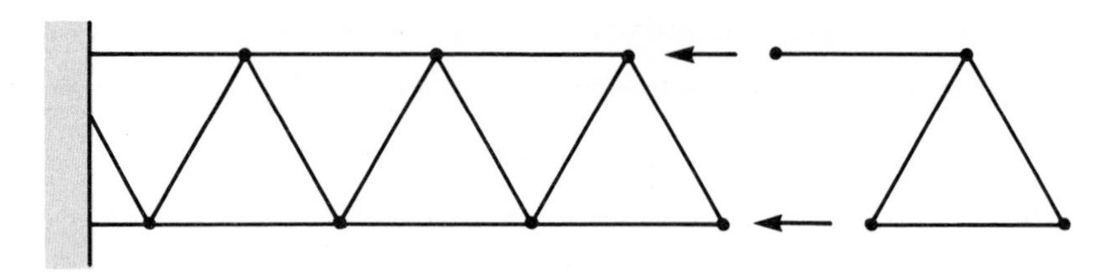

(a) If the basic framework with 3 extension pieces uses a total of 23 rods, how many rods are used for the basic framework ?

(b) How many rods are used for a barrier with (i) 6 extensions (ii) n extensions ?

(c) Barriers are supplied pre-assembled in packs. Pack 1 contains one basic framework. Pack 2 contains one basic framework and another basic framework with 1 extension. Pack 3 contains one basic framework, one basic framework with 1 extension and one basic framework with 2 extensions, and so on for Pack 4, Pack 5, ... How many rods are needed to make up Pack 3 ?

(d) How many rods are needed to make up Pack 10 ?

(e) Find a connection between the pack number, P, and the number, n, of rods in the pack.

Self-Assessment 16

1. Give the next two terms of the following sequence and a rule for obtaining them. 3, 8, 15, 24, ...

2. Give the first four terms of the sequence whose nth term is $5n-2$

3. The first term, u_1, of a sequence is 3. Give the next four terms if $u_{n+1} = 2u_n + 1$

4. Give the formula in terms of n for the nth term of the sequence $-1, 3, 7, 11, \ldots$

5. Find, in terms of n, the nth term of the sequence: $\frac{1 \times 3}{4}, \frac{2 \times 4}{9}, \frac{3 \times 5}{16}, \frac{4 \times 6}{25}, \ldots$

6. Use a difference table to find the next two terms of the sequence 2, 7, 18, 38, 70, ...

7.

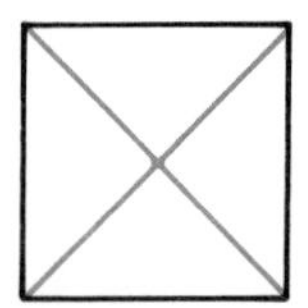

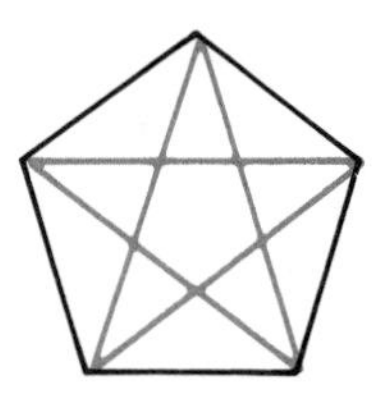

(a) Draw two more diagrams in this sequence.

(b) Give the first seven terms of the number sequence given by the number of diagonals in each diagram.

8.

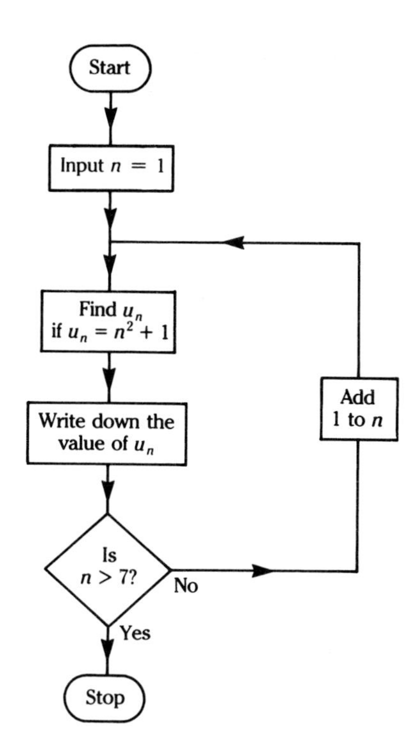

a) Write down the terms given by this flow chart.

b) If ten terms of the sequence were required how would the flow chart have to be altered ?

17

STRAIGHT LINE GRAPHS

PROPERTIES OF A LINE

In Chapter 6 we saw that a point can be located in a plane by means of its coordinate distances from the origin O in the directions of the x and y axes. Now we can investigate various properties of a line that passes through two points with known coordinates.

Consider the line that passes through the points A(2, 4) and B(5, 8).

Length

To find the length of the line between A and B, we first make a sketch.

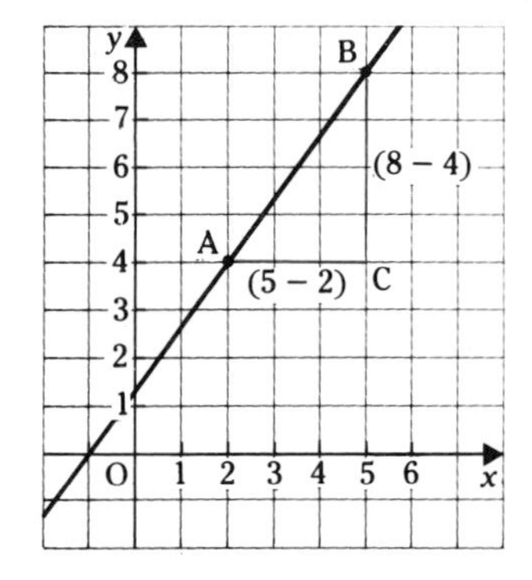

Using Pythagoras' theorem in triangle ABC shows that

$$\begin{aligned} AB^2 &= AC^2 + BC^2 \\ &= (8-4)^2 + (5-2)^2 \\ &= 25 \end{aligned}$$

i.e. $\quad AB = 5$

Midpoint

The midpoint, M(x, y), of AB is halfway, in the directions of both Ox and Oy, from A towards B,

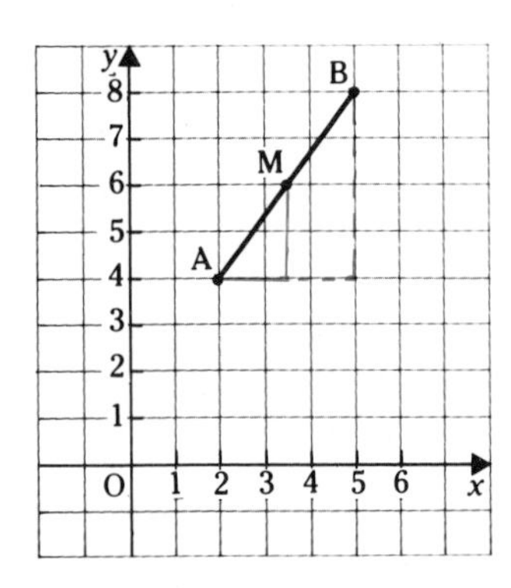

i.e. at M, $\quad x = 2 + \frac{1}{2}(5-2) = 3\frac{1}{2}$

which is equal to $\frac{1}{2}(2+5)$

Similarly, $\quad y = 4 + \frac{1}{2}(8-4) = 6$

which is equal to $\frac{1}{2}(4+8)$

Note that the coordinates of M are the averages of the coordinates of A and B so a quick look at a diagram is often all that is needed to find a midpoint.

Gradient

The *gradient*, or slope, of a line is a measure of how fast the line is rising or falling. It is defined as the rate at which y increases compared with x between *any* two points on that line. Using A(2, 4) and B(5, 8) as the two points, the gradient, which is usually represented by m, can be calculated.

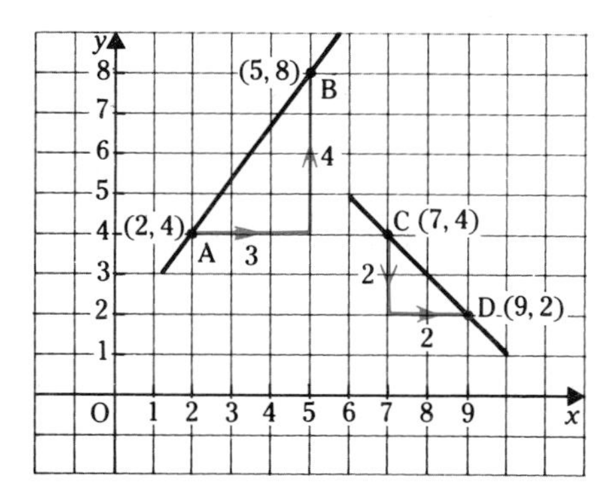

For the line AB $m = \dfrac{y \text{ at B} - y \text{ at A}}{x \text{ at B} - x \text{ at A}} = \dfrac{8-4}{5-2} = \dfrac{4}{3}$

For the line CD $m = \dfrac{y \text{ at D} - y \text{ at C}}{x \text{ at D} - x \text{ at C}} = \dfrac{2-4}{9-7} = \dfrac{-2}{2} = -1$

The differences between the y coordinates and the x coordinates must be found in the same order. This may give a negative result, as for the line CD; in these cases the line 'slopes downward'.

Exercise 17a

1. For each pair of points draw a sketch and find the length of the line joining them.
   (a) (3, 6) and (5, 2)
   (b) (−2, 4) and (2, 1)
   (c) (5, 1) and (7, 9)
   (d) (−3, −4) and (−6, 2)

2. Write down the coordinates of the midpoint of the line joining each pair of points in question 1.

3. Find the gradient of the line joining each pair of points in question 1.

4. Sketch the line through the points (−4, 2) and (7, 2). At what rate is y increasing? What happens if you try to calculate the gradient? Is there a definite value for m?

5. Sketch the line through the points A(4, −2) and B(4, 5). What is the increase in x from A to B? Describe the rate at which y is increasing. What happens if you try to calculate the gradient? Is there a definite value for m?

6. Without drawing a diagram state which, if any, of the lines joining the following points are parallel to the x-axis and which are parallel to the y-axis.
   (a) (3, 0) and (−10, 0)
   (b) (0, −1) and (0, 1)
   (c) (99, 0) and (0, 0)
   (d) (0, 5) and (5, 0)

THE EQUATION OF A STRAIGHT LINE

If, for every point on a line, the coordinates satisfy a particular relationship, this relationship is known as the equation of the line.

A Line Parallel to an Axis

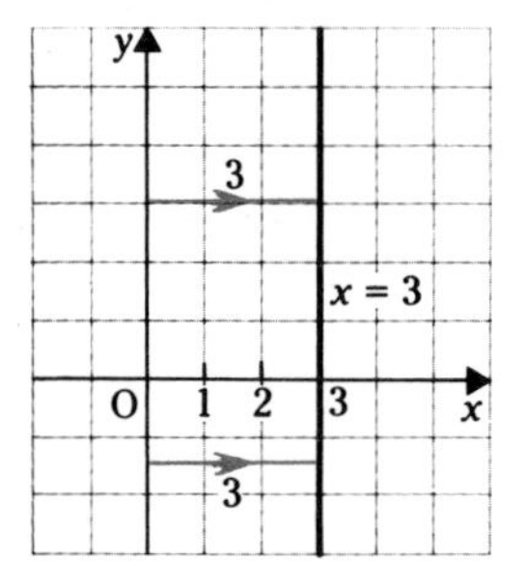

For every point on this line the x coordinate is 3.
The equation of the line is $x = 3$

Any line with equation $x = a$ is parallel to the vertical axis.

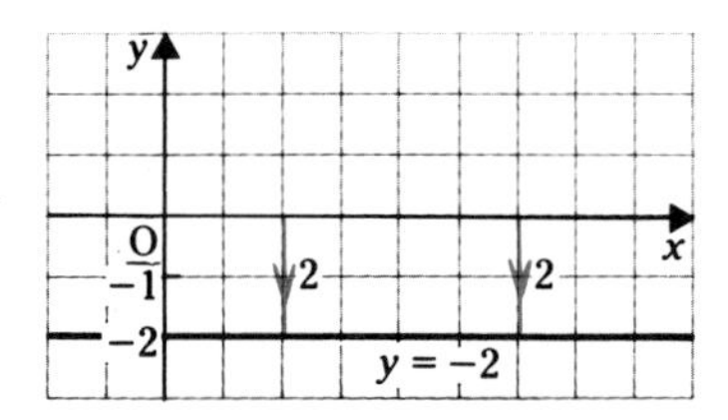

The y coordinate of every point on this line is -2.
The equation of the line is $y = -2$

Any line with equation $y = b$ is parallel to the horizontal axis.

A Slant Line Through the Origin

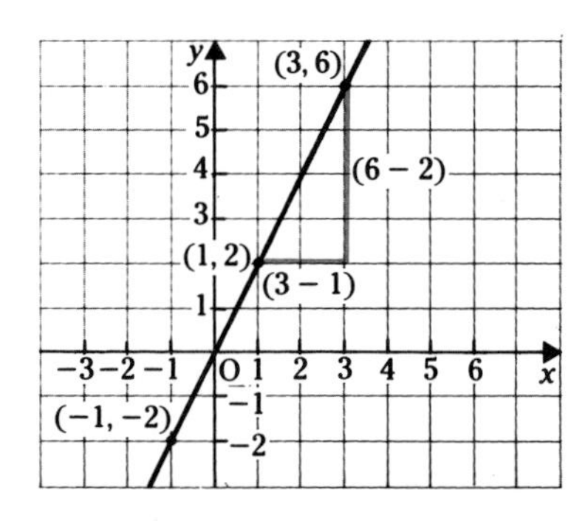

The y coordinate of every point on this line is twice the x coordinate.
The equation of the line is $y = 2x$

Also, considering any two points, we see that the gradient of the line is 2,
i.e. the gradient of the line gives the coefficient of x in the equation of the line.

The equation $y = mx$ represents any straight line through the origin and m is its gradient.

The larger the value of m, the steeper is the line. If m is positive the line rises from left to right and if m is negative the line falls.

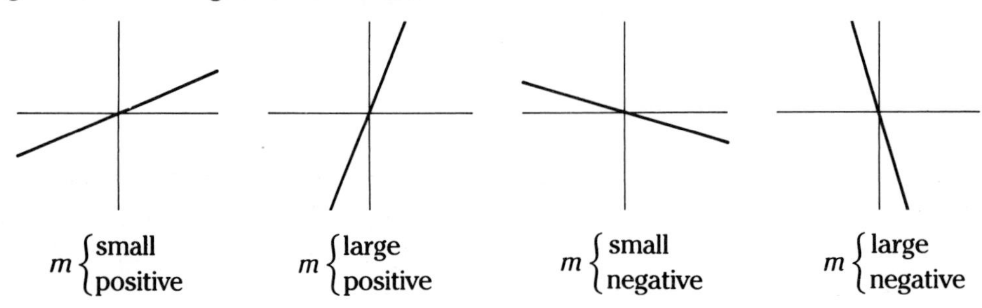

$m \begin{cases} \text{small} \\ \text{positive} \end{cases}$ $m \begin{cases} \text{large} \\ \text{positive} \end{cases}$ $m \begin{cases} \text{small} \\ \text{negative} \end{cases}$ $m \begin{cases} \text{large} \\ \text{negative} \end{cases}$

A General Slant Line

Consider a translation of 3 units upward, applied to the line with equation $y = 2x$. This produces a line where each y coordinate is given by adding 3 to the corresponding x coordinate; therefore its equation is $y = 2x + 3$

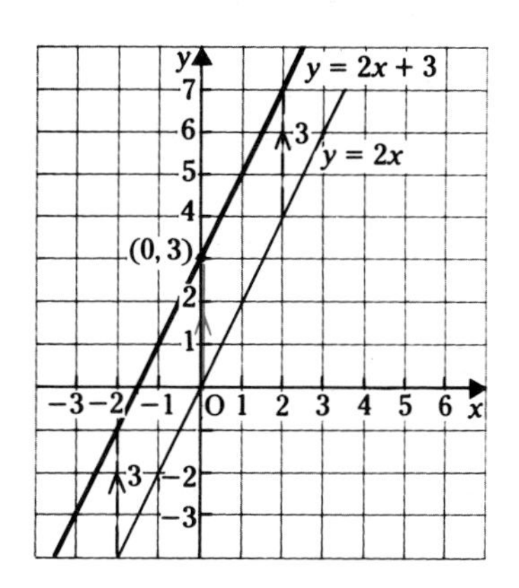

The amount of translation is called the y-intercept and this gives the number term, or constant term, in the equation of the line.

In general, for a line with a gradient m and y-intercept c, the equation is $y = mx + c$.
If c is positive, the line crosses the y-axis above the origin.
If c is negative, the line crosses the y-axis below the origin.

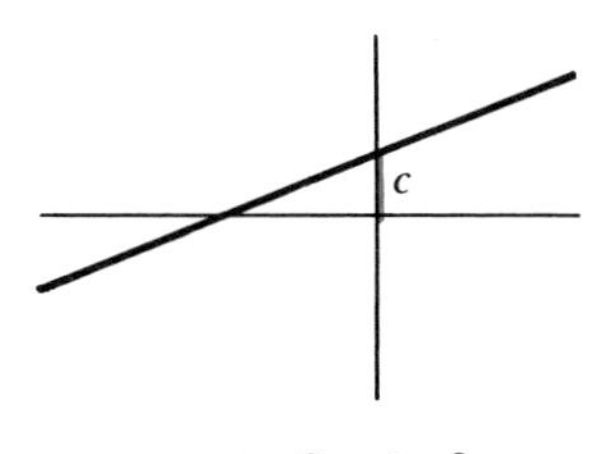

$m > 0, c > 0$

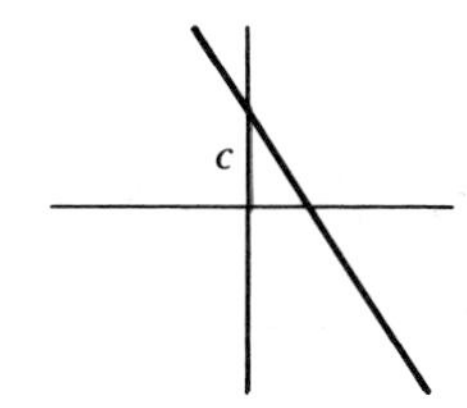

$m < 0, c > 0$

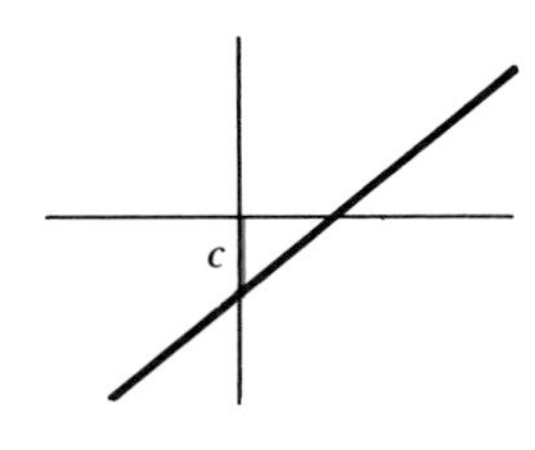

$m > 0, c < 0$

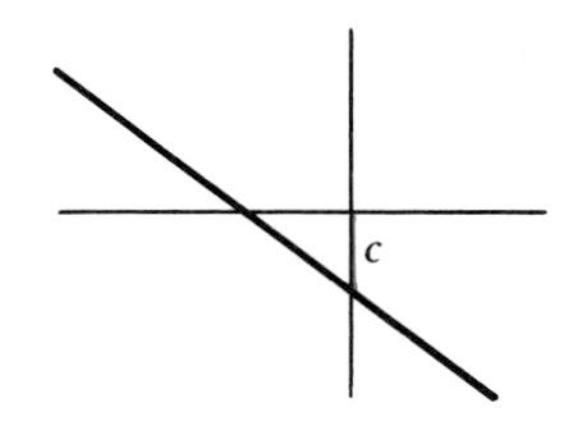

$m < 0, c < 0$

Exercise 17b

1. On squared paper sketch the line with equation
   (a) $x = -5$
   (b) $y = 1$
   (c) $y = -4$
   (d) $x = 0$

2. Write down the gradient of each line.
   (a) $y = 5x - 1$
   (b) $y = -7x + 3$
   (c) $y = x + 3$
   (d) $y - 4x = 6$

3. Write down the y-intercept for each line given in question 2 and sketch the line on squared paper.

4. Write down the equation of the line whose gradient and y-intercept respectively are
   (a) 2 and 6
   (b) 4 and -1
   (c) -3 and 2
   (d) 1 and 0

5. (i) Find the gradient and y-intercept for each of the following lines.
   (ii) Write down the equation of each line.

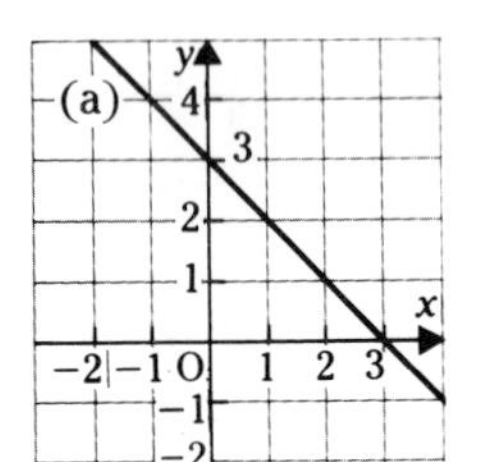

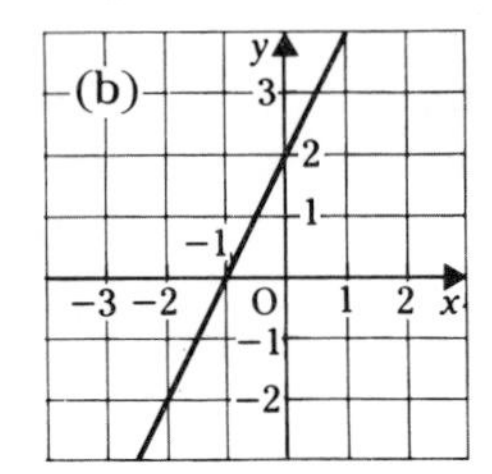

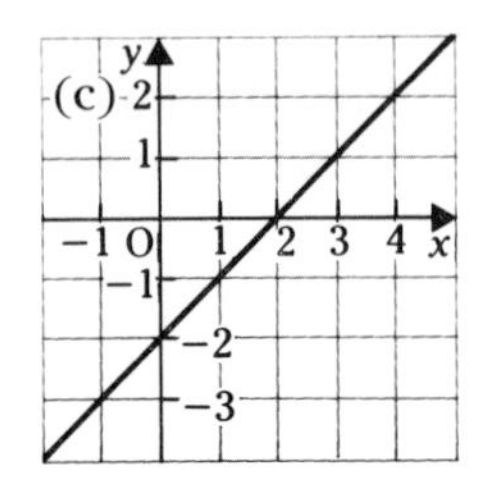

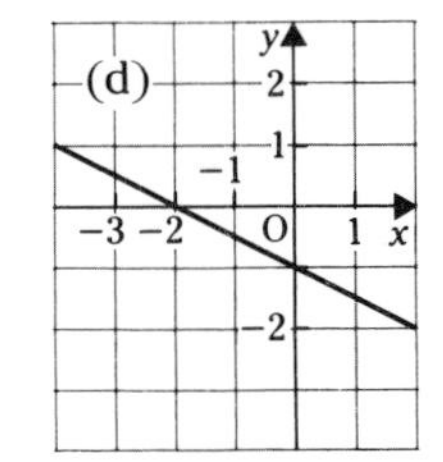

(a) Determine whether the point A is on the line with equation $y = 7 - 2x$ if the coordinates of A are (i) $(7, 1)$ (ii) $(3\frac{1}{2}, 0)$.

(b) Find also the coordinates of the point on this line where $y = -3$

(a) (i) When $x = 7$, $\quad y = 7 - 2(7)$, $\quad$ i.e. $y = -7$

Therefore the point $(7, 1)$ is not on the line.

(ii) When $x = 3\frac{1}{2}$, $\quad y = 7 - 2(3\frac{1}{2})$, $\quad$ i.e. $y = 0$

Therefore the point $(3\frac{1}{2}, 0)$ is on the line.

(b) When $y = -3$, $\quad -3 = 7 - 2x$,

i.e. $\quad 2x = 7 + 3 = 10 \Rightarrow x = 5$

The point where $y = -3$ is $(5, -3)$

6. Find the y-coordinate of the point on the line $y = 7x - 4$, whose x-coordinate is
   (a) 6 (b) -4 (c) 0

7. Find the x-coordinate of the point on the line $y = 7x - 4$, whose y-coordinate is
   (a) 10 (b) -11 (c) 1

8. Find whether or not the given point lies on the given line.
   (a) $(3, 4)$; $2x + 3y = 18$
   (b) $(1, -8)$; $x - 2y = 15$
   (c) $(0, 5)$; $4x + 3y = 20$
   (d) $(-2, 2)$; $5x - 4y + 18 = 0$

9. Find the x and y intercepts for each line given in question 8 (i.e. find the points where each line crosses the x-axis and the y-axis).

For questions 10 to 12 draw x and y axes, each scaled from -6 to 6.

10. Plot the point $(3, 2)$ and through it draw the straight line with gradient 2.

11. Plot the point $(-2, 1)$ and through it draw the straight line with gradient $\frac{1}{2}$.

12. Sketch the line passing through the point $(-5, 5)$ and with gradient -2.

Find the equation of the straight line that passes through the point $(-5, 4)$ and has a gradient of -2.

Taking $y = mx + c$ as the equation of the line, the value of m is -2

Therefore the equation of the line is $y = -2x + c$

The point $(-5, 4)$ is on the line so $4 = -2(-5) + c$

$c = -6$

The equation of the line is $y = -2x - 6$

13. Find the equation of the straight line passing through the given point and with the given gradient.
    (a) $(1, 3)$; $\frac{1}{2}$ (b) $(7, -2)$; -1 (c) $(-1, -3)$; 3 (d) $(2, 6)$; $-\frac{1}{2}$.
14. Given that the line with equation $y = 4x + c$ passes through the point $(-1, -5)$, find c and sketch the line.
15. If a line with equation $y = mx - 3$ passes through the point $(2, -1)$, find the gradient and sketch the line.

Different Forms for the Equation of a Line

So far we have used the equation of a line in the form $y = mx + c$ which is the standard form. Its advantage is that the gradient and y-intercept can be read from the equation.

However the equation $y = mx + c$ can be presented in a variety of ways, e.g.

$y - 3x = 6$, $3x - y + 6 = 0$ and $x - \frac{y}{3} = 2$ are all forms of the same straight line.

In fact, any equation with an x term, and/or a y term and a number, is the equation of a straight line and it can be rearranged so that it is in standard form.

Consider, for example, $x - \frac{y}{3} = 2$

Multiplying both sides by 3 to eliminate the fraction gives

$$3 \times x - 3 \times \frac{y}{3} = 3 \times 2 \quad \text{i.e} \quad 3x - y = 6$$

Now we need to isolate y on one side, i.e. to 'solve' the equation for y.

$$3x = 6 + y$$

$$3x - 6 = y \quad \text{i.e.} \quad y = 3x - 6$$

Now we can 'read off' the gradient, 3, and the y-intercept, -6.

Parallel Lines

As parallel lines go in the same direction, their gradients are equal,

i.e. if two lines with equations $y = m_1x + c_1$ and $y = m_2x + c_2$ are parallel, then

$$m_1 = m_2$$

Exercise 17c

Find the gradient and y-intercept of the line with equation $4y - 2x = 3$. Hence *sketch* the line.

We need the equation in the form $y = mx + c$ so we must isolate y.

$$4y - 2x = 3$$

$$\therefore \quad 4y = 2x + 3$$

$$\therefore \quad y = \tfrac{1}{2}x + \tfrac{3}{4}$$

The gradient of the line is $\frac{1}{2}$ and the y-intercept is $\frac{3}{4}$

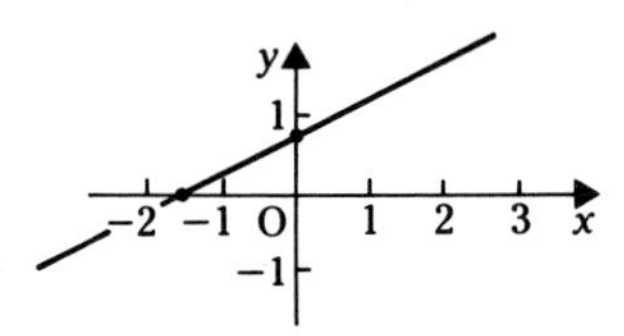

1. Find the gradient and y-intercept for each of the following lines and sketch the line.
   (a) $3y + 6 = x$
   (b) $4y + 3x = 8$
   (c) $2x + 6y = 12$
   (d) $2x - y - 7 = 0$
   (e) $y + 3x + 1 = 0$
   (f) $2 + x = 4y$

2. Sketch the line representing the given equation. Find the gradient of each line.
   (a) $x + \dfrac{y}{3} = 1$
   (b) $\dfrac{x}{5} + y = 2$
   (c) $x - \dfrac{y}{2} = 1$
   (d) $y - \dfrac{x}{4} = 3$

3. Sketch the line with equation $x + y = 1$ and find its gradient.

Find the equation of the straight line that passes through the points $(2, 1)$ and $(6, -3)$.

The gradient of the line is

$$\frac{-3-1}{6-2} = -1$$

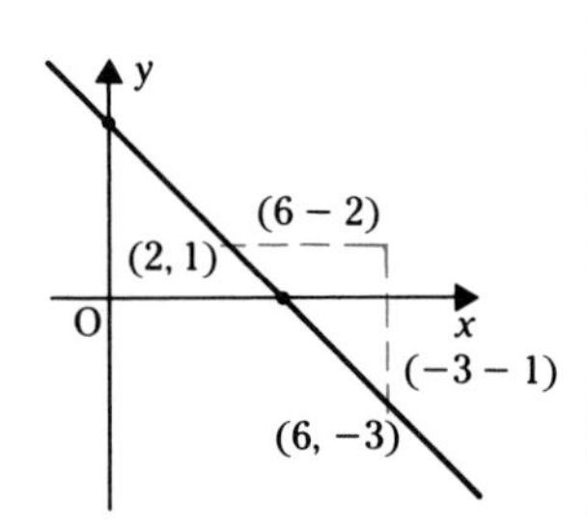

Let the equation of the line be

$$y = -x + c$$

The point $(2, 1)$ is on the line so

$$1 = -2 + c$$

i.e. $\quad c = 3$

Therefore the equation of the line is $y = -x + 3$ or $x + y = 3$

(Check: when $x = 6$, $y = -6 + 3 = -3$ which is correct.)

In questions 4 to 6 find the equation of the line through the two given points.

4. (a) $(3, 0)$ and $(0, 8)$ (b) $(2, 0)$ and $(0, 2)$

5. (a) $(4, -1)$ and $(3, -6)$ (b) $(3, 2)$ and $(1, 7)$

6. (a) $(-9, -3)$ and $(6, 0)$ (b) $(5, -2)$ and $(-4, 7)$

7. State which of the following equations represent lines that are parallel.

$$y = 2x+3, \quad y = 4-2x, \quad y = 4+2x, \quad 2y = x+1, \quad y = x+3$$

8. There are two pairs of parallel lines represented in the following set of equations. Which are they and what, for each pair, is the gradient ?

$$2x+y = 2 \quad y = 2x-4 \quad 3y-4x = 5 \quad y = 7-2x \quad 4x = 3y \quad 2y+x = 1$$

Find the equation of the straight line that is
(a) parallel to the line $y = 5x-2$ and passes through the point $(-2, 6)$
(b) parallel to the line $3x+4y = 1$ and cuts the x-axis where $x = -1$

(a) The gradient of the line $y = 5x-2$ is 5 so the gradient of a parallel line is also 5.

Let the equation of the required line be $y = 5x+c$

The point $(-2, 6)$ is on this line, so

$$6 = 5(-2)+c$$

$$c = 16$$

The equation of the parallel line is $y = 5x+16$

(b) The gradient of the line is found from the terms $3x$ and $4y$. The equation of any line with the same gradient will therefore contain the same coefficients of x and y.

Let the equation of the required line be $3x+4y+c = 0$

The line crosses the x-axis at the point $(-1, 0)$

$\therefore$ $$3(-1)+0+c = 0$$

i.e. $$c = 3$$

The equation of the required line is $3x+4y+3 = 0$

9. Give the equations of any three lines that are parallel to the line with equation
(a) $y = 2x-6$ (b) $5x-2y-7 = 0$ (c) $2x = 4-3y$

10. Give the equations of the lines that pass through the point $(0, 4)$ and are parallel to the line with equation
(a) $y = 4x+1$ (b) $y+3x = 6$ (c) $2y-x = 1$

11. Find the gradients and the intercepts on the y-axis of the lines with equations $y = 5 - 2x$ and $y = 5x - 2$. What is the equation of the line that is parallel to the first line and cuts the y-axis at the same point as the second line ?

DRAWING A LINE FROM ITS EQUATION

Consider the line with equation $2x + 3y - 12 = 0$.
The coordinates of three points on the line can be found by making a table as shown, choosing three values of x (we usually include $x = 0$), and then calculating the corresponding values of y from the equation of the line.

x	-3	0	3
y	6	4	2

These three points can now be plotted and the required line drawn through them.

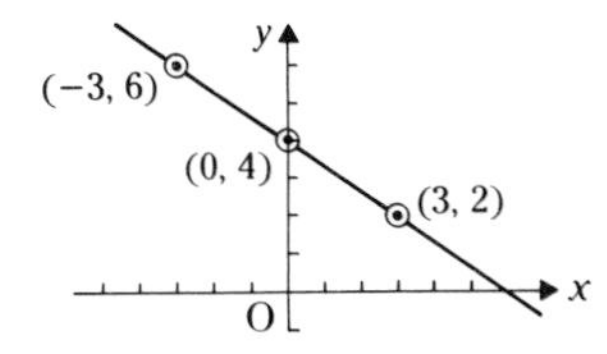

Although only two points are needed in order to draw a particular line, we use a third point as a check. If the three points do not all lie on one line, check the calculations.

Exercise 17d

On graph paper draw each of the following lines. Use 1 cm to represent 1 unit. The range of values of x is given; find the range for y. Find the gradient of each line.

1. $x - 4y = 8, \quad 0 \leqslant x \leqslant 8$
2. $x + y = 6, \quad 0 \leqslant x \leqslant 7$
3. $x + \dfrac{y}{3} = 1, \quad 0 \leqslant x \leqslant 6$
4. $3x + 5y = 15, \quad 0 \leqslant x \leqslant 6$
5. $2x - y = 3, \quad -2 \leqslant x \leqslant 2$
6. $\dfrac{x}{3} - y = 1, \quad -2 \leqslant x \leqslant 5$

GRAPHICAL SOLUTION OF SIMULTANEOUS EQUATIONS

The equation of a straight line is a linear equation, i.e. it is made up of an x term, a y term and a number. For every point on the line the x and y coordinates satisfy the equation of the line. If we have two linear equations, each gives a straight line and, unless the lines are parallel, these two lines will cross somewhere.

At their point of intersection the x and y coordinates satisfy both linear equations, i.e. these values of x and y are the solutions of the simultaneous equations that represent the two lines.

Exercise 17e

The value of x that satisfies the pair of equations $x+y=4$ and $y=1+x$ is known to be in the range $0 \leqslant x \leqslant 5$. Solve the equations graphically.

First draw the lines, for $0 \leqslant x \leqslant 5$, representing the two equations.

$x+y=4$

x	0	4	5
y	4	0	-1

$y=1+x$

x	0	2	5
y	1	3	6

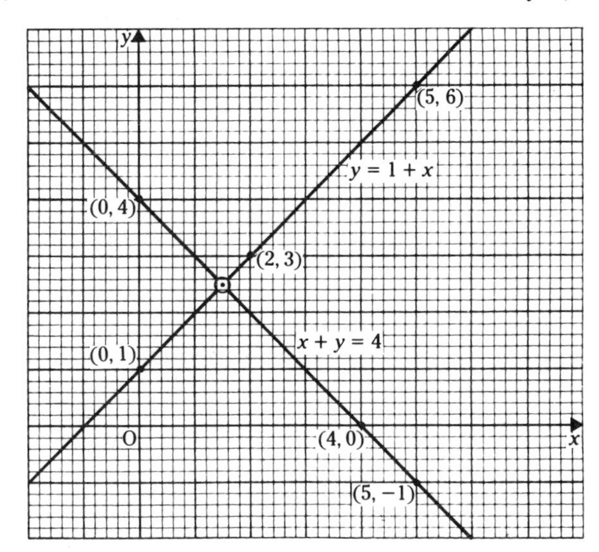

The point where the lines cross has coordinates $(1\frac{1}{2}, 2\frac{1}{2})$.

Therefore the solution of the given pair of equations is

$$x = 1\tfrac{1}{2} \quad \text{and} \quad y = 2\tfrac{1}{2}$$

In questions 1 to 3 the range of values of x and y is given within which the solution of the pair of equations lies. Taking a scale of 2 cm to 1 unit, use graphs to solve each pair of equations.

1. $\left.\begin{array}{l} y = 5-x \\ y = 2+x \end{array}\right\}$ $0 \leqslant x \leqslant 5, \quad 0 \leqslant y \leqslant 7$

2. $\left.\begin{array}{l} x+y = 1 \\ y = x+2 \end{array}\right\}$ $-3 \leqslant x \leqslant 2, \quad -2 \leqslant y \leqslant 4$

3. Try to solve

   $\left.\begin{array}{l} x+y = 9 \\ y = 4-x \end{array}\right\}$ $0 \leqslant x \leqslant 9, \quad 0 \leqslant y \leqslant 9$

   Why do you think the method fails ?

Use squared paper for questions 4 and 5.

4. Sketch the lines with equations

   $$y = 2.4x - 3.1$$
   $$\text{and} \quad y = -3.7x + 2.4.$$

   Hence show that the value of x that satisfies both equations simultaneously is in the range $0 \leqslant x \leqslant 1$.

5. By sketching the lines represented by

   $$2.1x - y = 5.5$$
   $$\text{and} \quad 3.8y + 2x = 5.9$$

   find a range, spanning two integers, within which lies the value of x that satisfies both equations simultaneously. Find a similar range for the corresponding value of y.

STRAIGHT LINE GRAPHS IN PRACTICAL SITUATIONS

In a variety of real-life situations, use can be made of straight line graphs in which the coordinates of points represent practical quantities. A particularly useful application is for converting one set of units to another.

For instance when on holiday abroad it can help if a distance in kilometres can be converted immediately to an equivalent number of miles.

It is also useful to be able to convert between the currencies of different countries.

Exercise 17f

Given that £1 converts to 11.2 Norwegian kroner, draw a graph to convert values up to £100 into kroner.

Use your graph to find

(a) the cost in pounds of a pair of shoes priced at 760 kroner

(b) how many kroner correspond to £46.

£1 ≡ 11.2 kroner

so £50 ≡ 560 kroner

and £100 ≡ 1120 kroner

Plotting the last two points and (0, 0) gives the required conversion graph.

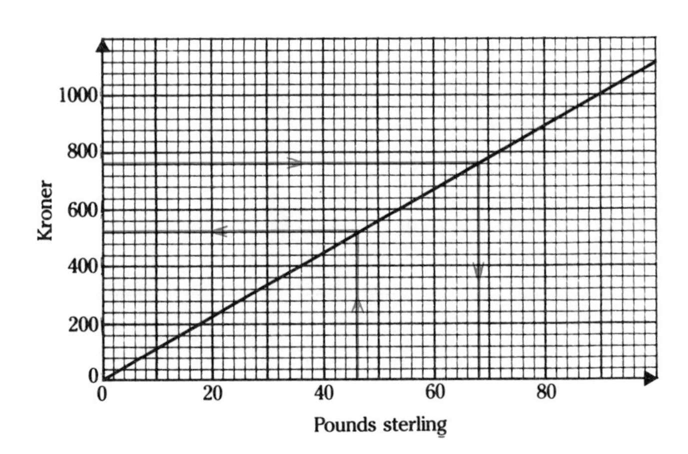

From the graph:

(a) the shoes cost £68

(b) £46 corresponds to 520 kroner.

1. This graph can be used to convert speeds from m.p.h. to km/h and conversely.

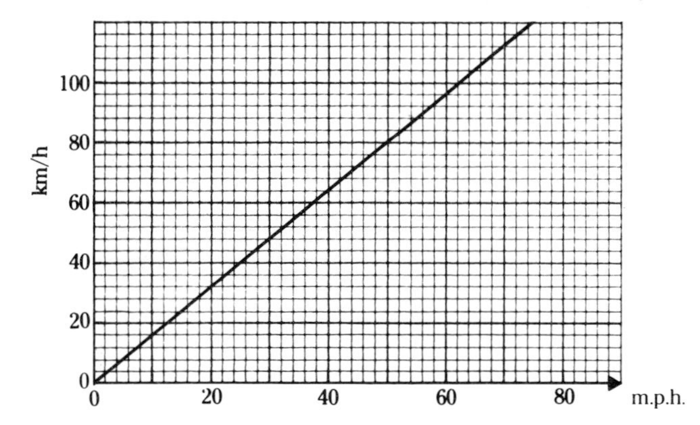

Use the graph to find a speed of:

(a) 52 m.p.h. in km/h (b) 100 km/h in m.p.h. (c) 72 m.p.h. in km/h (d) 52 km/h in m.p.h.

2. The table shows how many US dollars correspond to several amounts of British currency.

Pounds sterling	25	75	112.50
US dollars	42	126	189

Using 4 cm to represent 50 units on both axes, draw a straight line graph through the three points.

Use the graph to convert:

(a) 78 dollars to pounds (b) £54 to dollars (c) 140 dollars to pounds (d) £100 to dollars

3. Some temperatures in degrees Fahrenheit (°F) and the equivalent values in degrees Celsius (°C) are given in the table below.

Temperature in °F	53	115	158
Temperature in °C	12	46	70

Using 2 cm to represent 20 units on each axis, with ranges from 0 to 90 °C and −40 °F to 180 °F, draw the line through the given points and use it to convert

(a) 170 °F into °C (b) 35 °C into °F

Water freezes at 0 °C. What is the freezing point of water in °F ?

4. This table shows the distances a girl walked in various times.

Time in hours	0	1	$2\frac{1}{2}$	4	5
Distance in kilometres	0	6	15	24	30

Use these results to draw a graph and find the gradient.

(a) What does the gradient represent ?

(b) How far did she walk in 3 hours 45 minutes ?

(c) How long did it take her to walk 21 km ?

5. An examination is marked out of 65 (i.e. 100 % is 65). Draw a graph which shows the marks from 0 to 65 as percentages from 0 to 100 %. Use the graph

(a) to express marks of 32 and 57 as percentages

(b) to find the marks given to a candidate who scored 82 %.

THE MEANING OF THE GRADIENT AND THE y-INTERCEPT

For a straight line with equation $y = mx + c$ the gradient m tells us the increase in y when x increases by 1 unit, (i.e. the rate of increase of y compared with x).

This is often abbreviated to

gradient is the rate of increase of y with respect to x

For a straight line graph that results from plotting real quantities, the gradient represents the increase in the quantity on the vertical axis as the quantity on the horizontal axis increases by one unit. For example, in this graph, the gradient represents the increase in temperature per unit increase in time, i.e. a number of degrees Celsius per second.

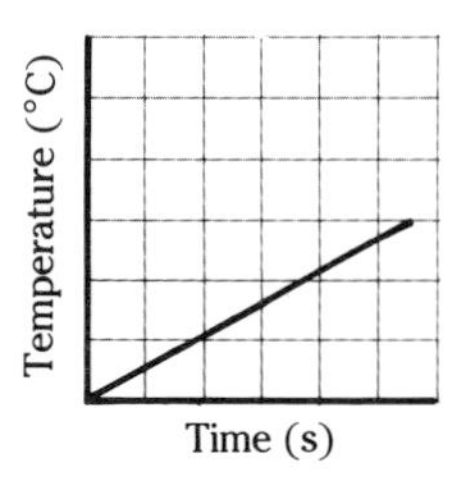

The value of the gradient is found, as before, from the coordinates of any two points on the graph *but* as the scales on the two axes are unlikely to be equal, the distances between the two points must be taken from the appropriate scale and not by counting graph squares, i.e.

$$\text{gradient} = \frac{\text{increase in quantity on vertical axis}}{\text{increase in quantity on horizontal axis}}$$

This graph, for example, shows the cost to a householder of consuming different quantities of gas.

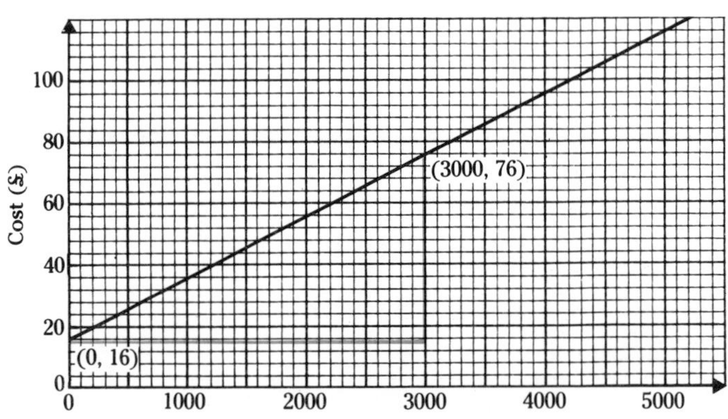

The gradient of the graph is given by

$$\frac{76-16}{3000-0} = \frac{60}{3000} = \frac{1}{50}$$

It represents the increase in the cost for an increase of one unit of consumption, i.e. £0.02 per kilowatt hour.

The y-intercept is 16 and this represents what the customer has to pay before any gas has been used, i.e. the standing charge is £16.

Exercise 17g

1. For each graph give (i) the value of the gradient (ii) a meaning for the gradient.

(a)

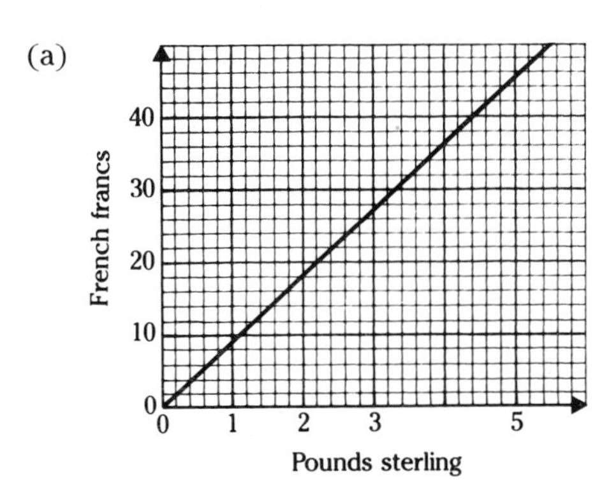

(c)

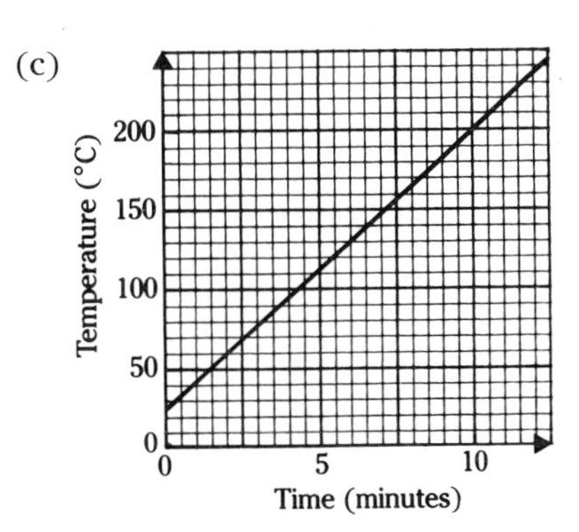

(b)

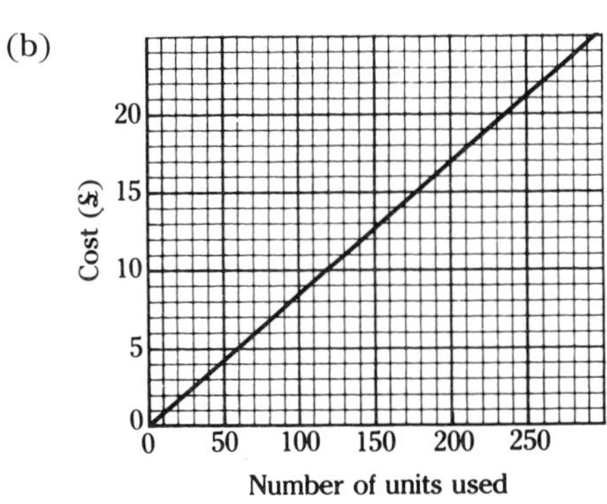

(d)

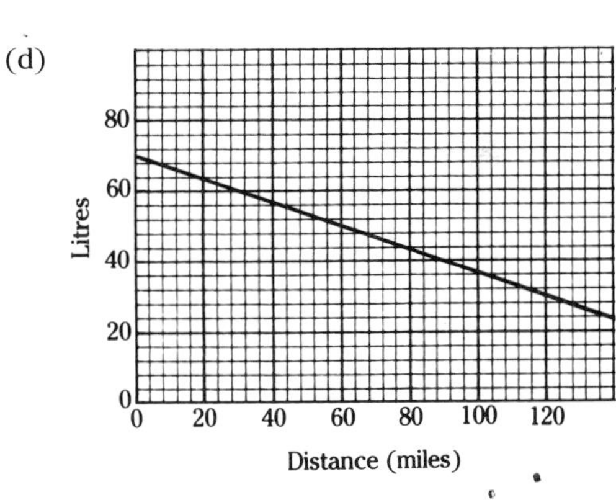

2. This graph shows how the quantity of water in a reservoir varies with time. When full it contains 2 000 000 gallons.

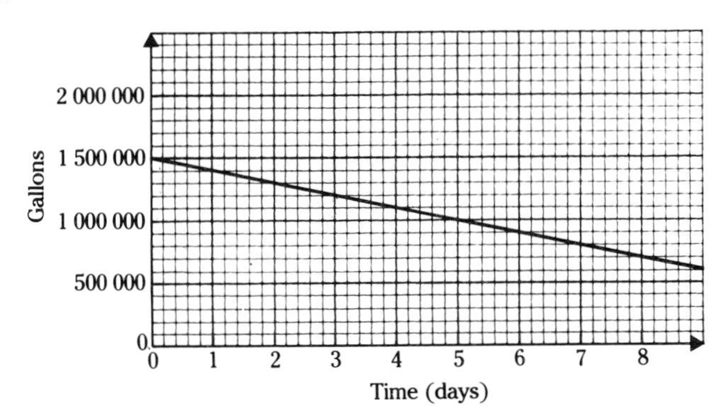

(a) Use the graph to find
  (i) the volume of water in the reservoir after three days
  (ii) after how many days the reservoir is half empty.

(b) What is the gradient of the graph and what does it represent?

(c) What is the value of the intercept on the vertical axis and what does it represent?

3. A householder can choose to buy electricity either on Tariff A or on Tariff B. The graph below shows the costs incurred in using each of these tariffs.

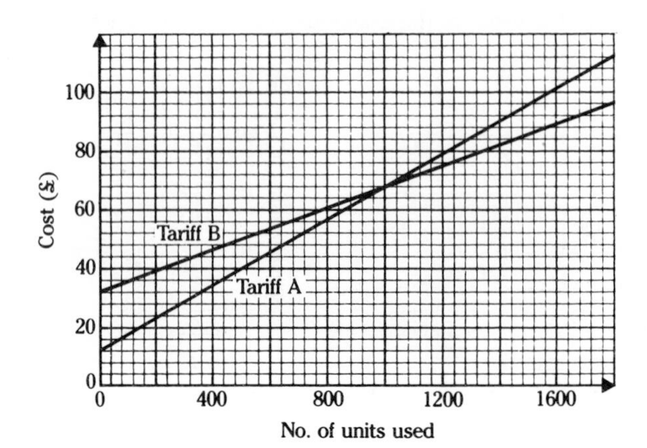

(a) Find the gradient of the line representing each tariff and attach a meaning to each of these values.

(b) Write down the value of the vertical intercept in each case and give it a meaning.

(c) Which is the more economical tariff to choose if the household consumes (i) 560 units (ii) 1400 units ?

4. Details of three families' quarterly telephone bills are given in the table.

Name	No. of units used (n)	Total cost (£x)
Smith	500	44
Jones	850	59.40
Robinson	1200	74.80

Represent this information on a straight line graph using 1 cm ≡ 100 units on the horizontal n-axis and 1 cm ≡ £10 vertically.

Use the graph to find (a) the gradient and vertical intercept

(b) the cost of one unit

(c) the quarterly rental charge.

Self-Assessment 17

1. For the line joining each of the following pairs of points find (i) the length (ii) the midpoint (iii) the gradient.

(a) $(6, -3)$ and $(1, 9)$ (b) $(-2, 5)$ and $(4, -3)$

2. On squared paper sketch the line represented by each equation.

(a) $y = -5$ (b) $x = 2$ (c) $y = 3x - 4$ (d) $y + x = 5$

3. Find the gradient and y-intercept of each line.

(a)

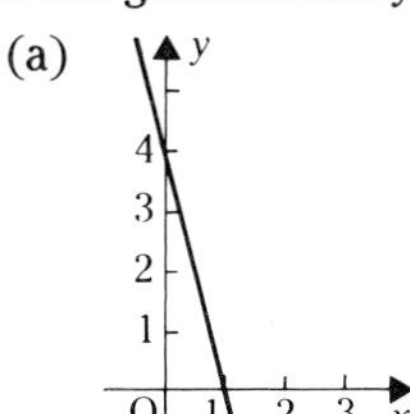

(b)

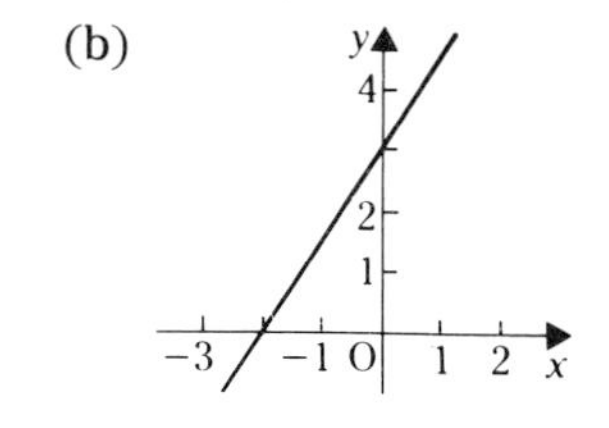

(c)

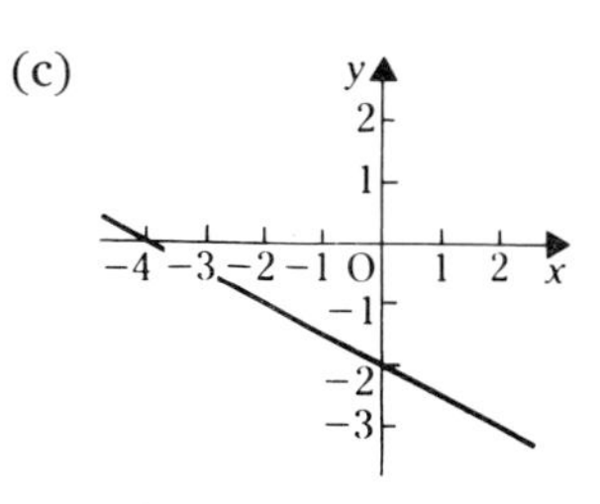

4. Find the equation of the line that
   (a) passes through the point $(4, -1)$ and has a gradient of 2
   (b) passes through the origin and is parallel to the line with equation $y = 3x - 1$

5. Find the equation of the line through the points $(-1, 3)$ and $(5, -5)$.

6. On the line given in question 5, find
   (a) x when $y = -1$ (b) y when $x = 8$ (c) the y-intercept

7. Draw, on the same graph, using $-2 \leqslant x \leqslant 4$ and $-1 \leqslant y \leqslant 5$, the lines with equations $y = 2x + 1$ and $3y + x = 10$.

   Use your graph to solve the pair of equations.

8. Given that £1 is equivalent to 2.46 Deutschmarks, construct a graph, from 0 to £100, to be used for converting between these two currencies.

   Use the graph to give the value of
   (a) £34 in DM (b) 215 DM in £s

9. This graph shows the cost of producing a magazine as the number of pages in it varies.

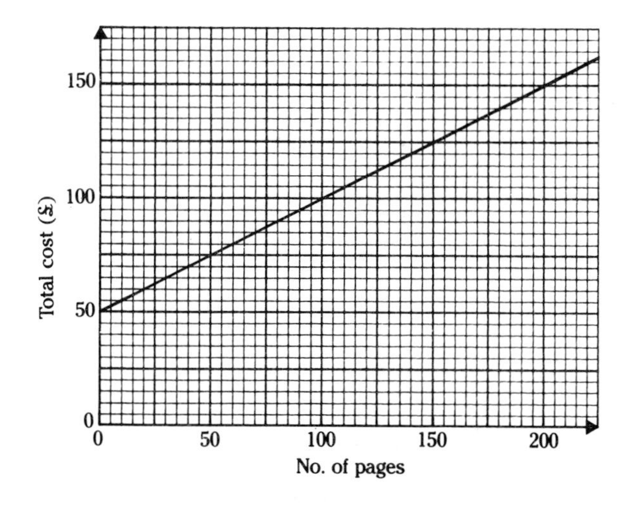

   (a) What is the cost of the magazine when it contains 130 pages ?
   (b) Find the gradient of the graph and say what it represents.
   (c) Suggest a meaning for the vertical intercept.

INEQUALITIES IN A PLANE

INEQUALITIES IN TWO DIMENSIONS

In an earlier chapter the inequalities considered involved only one variable; they were discussed in algebraic terms and illustrated by number lines.

Two-dimensional space, with x and y axes, can also be used to illustrate the meaning of inequalities.

For instance, the inequality $x \geqslant 3$ can be illustrated in the xy plane by all the points with an x coordinate equal to or greater than 3.

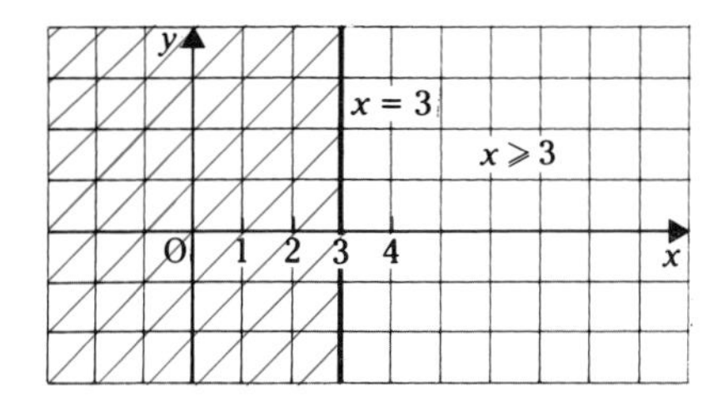

The boundary line, which represents all the points for which $x = 3$, is a solid line to show that it is included in the given inequality. The region to the right of it contains all the points with x coordinates greater than 3. To indicate the region that satisfies an inequality, we usually shade the area we do *not* want, in this case the area to the left of the line $x = 3$. This leaves clear the region we *do* want.

The inequality $x > 3$ is represented by the same area but points on the boundary line are *not* included this time; this is indicated by a broken line.

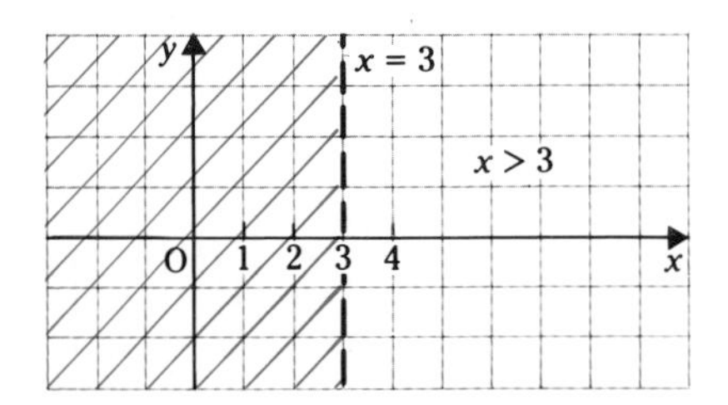

Inequalities involving y can be illustrated in a similar way.

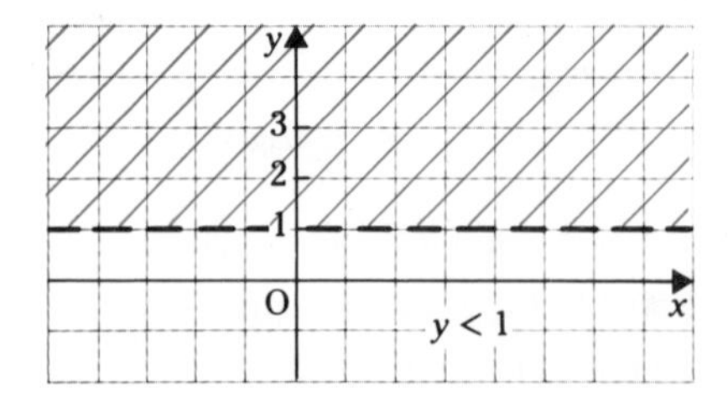

Exercise 18a

Draw on an xy plane the region that represents $-2 \leqslant x < 3$ and state whether or not the points $(1, 1)$, $(3, 2)$ and $(-2, 4)$ lie in this region.

$$-2 \leqslant x < 3 \quad \text{gives} \quad -2 \leqslant x \quad \text{and} \quad x < 3$$

The boundary lines of the required region are $x = -2$ (included), $x = 3$ (not included)

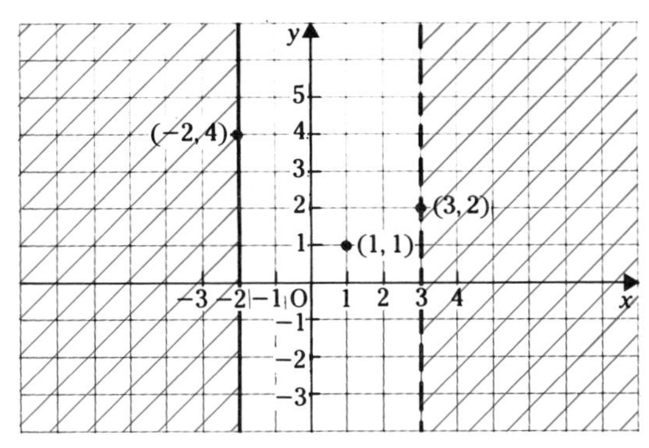

The unshaded region represents $-2 \leqslant x < 3$

$(1, 1)$ lies in this region, $(3, 2)$ is not in this region, $(-2, 4)$ lies in this region.

On an xy plane draw diagrams to represent the following inequalities. In each case state whether the point $(-1, 1)$ lies in the given region.

1. $1 < x < 4$
2. $-2 \leqslant x \leqslant 2$
3. $5 \geqslant x > 3$
4. $0 > y > -3$
5. $2 > y > -1$
6. $-5 \leqslant x < 0$

What inequality is represented by the unshaded region?

(a)

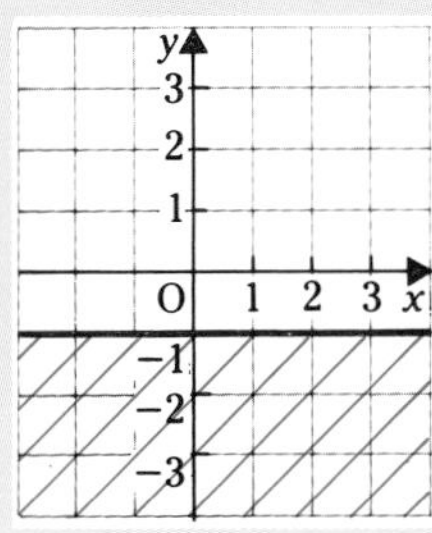

(b)

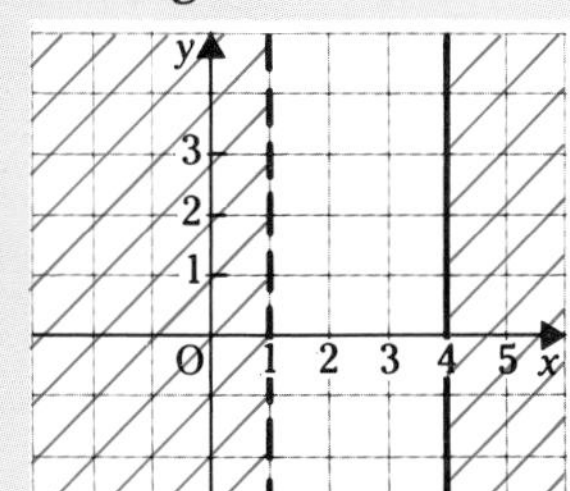

(a) The boundary line is $y = -1$ and is included.

The inequality is $y \geqslant -1$

(b) The boundary lines are $x = 1$ (not included)

and $x = 4$ (included)

The inequality is $1 < x \leqslant 4$

In questions 7 to 12 give inequalities that define each unshaded region.
In each case state whether or not the point $(1, 3)$ lies in this region.

7.

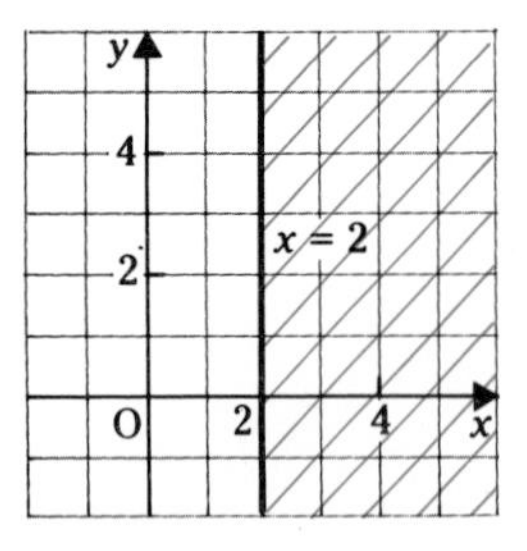

8.

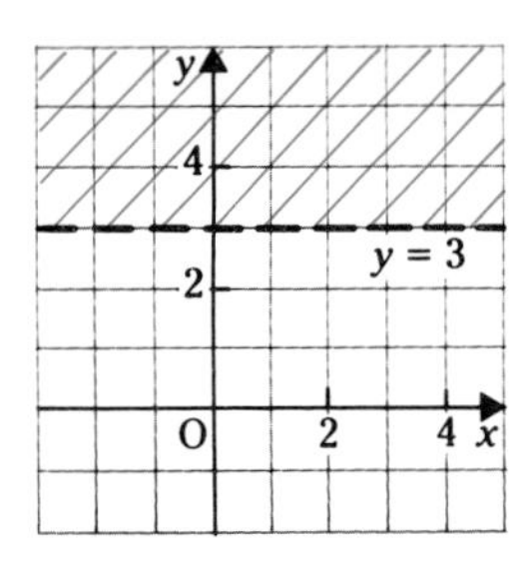

9.

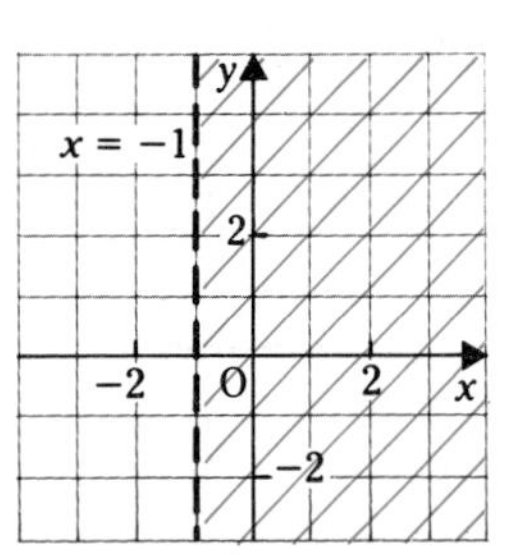

10.

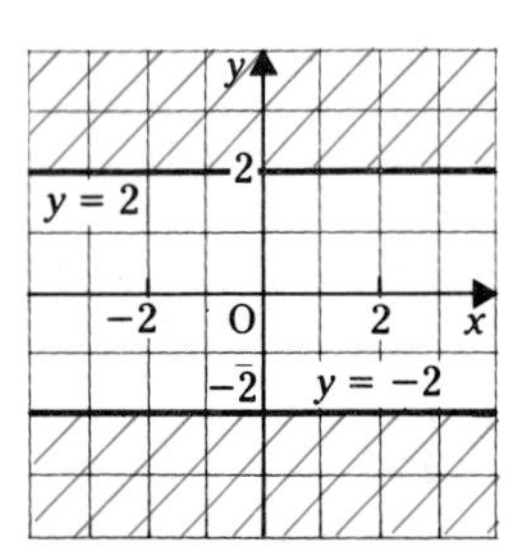

11.

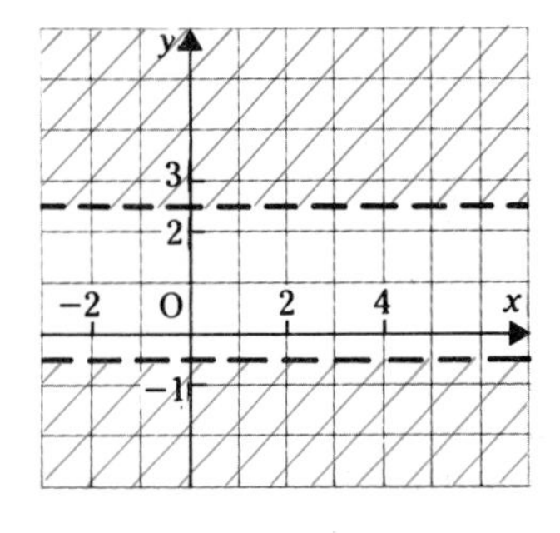

12.

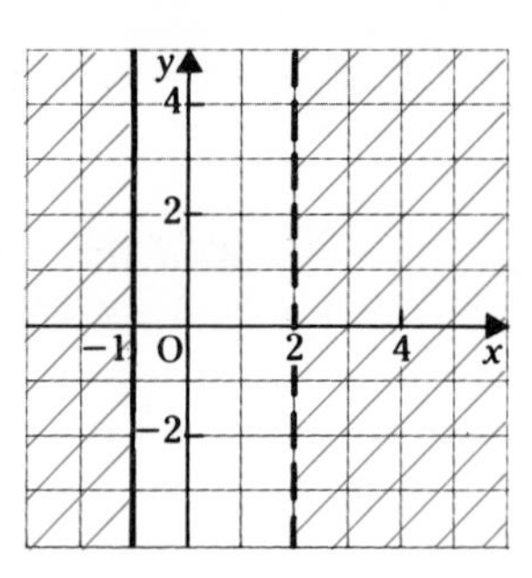

Although in this book we usually shade the region that is not wanted, this is not a hard and fast rule and there may be occasions when the *required* region is shaded. Always check carefully what the shading represents and always *state clearly* on your own work whether the region asked for is shaded or unshaded.

Find inequalities to define each shaded region.

13.

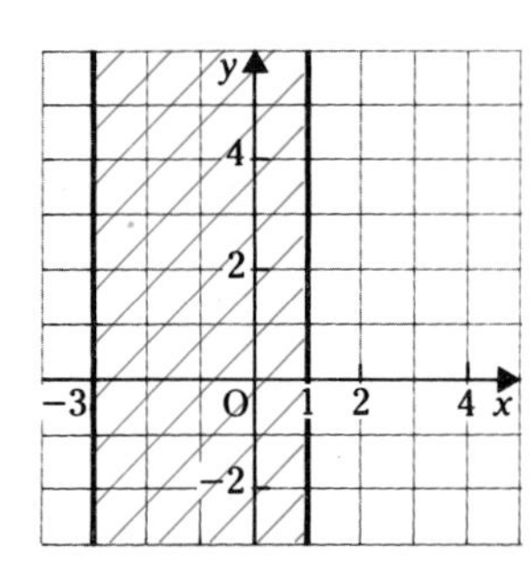

14.

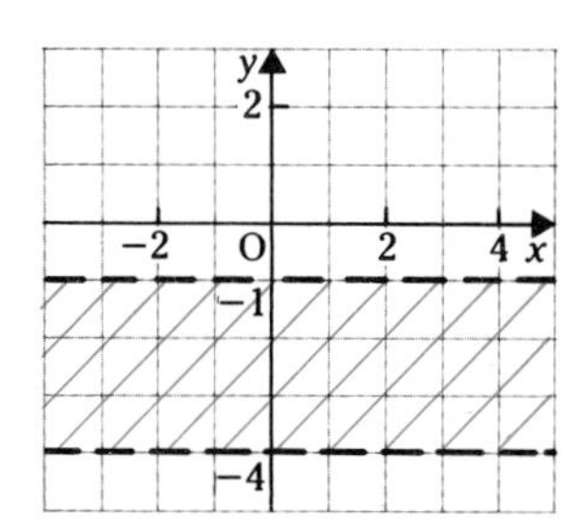

15.

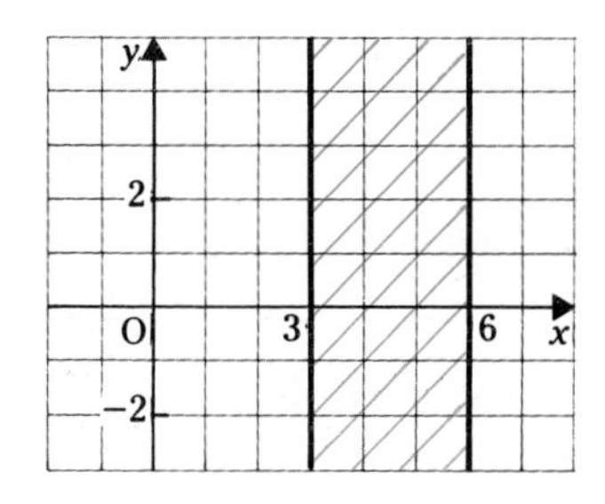

The remaining questions in this exercise use regions of an xy plane that are defined by a number of inequalities.

Draw a diagram to represent the region defined by the set of inequalities

$$-1 \leqslant x \leqslant 2 \quad \text{and} \quad -5 \leqslant y \leqslant 0$$

The boundary lines are $x = -1, \; x = 2, \; y = -5, \; y = 0$

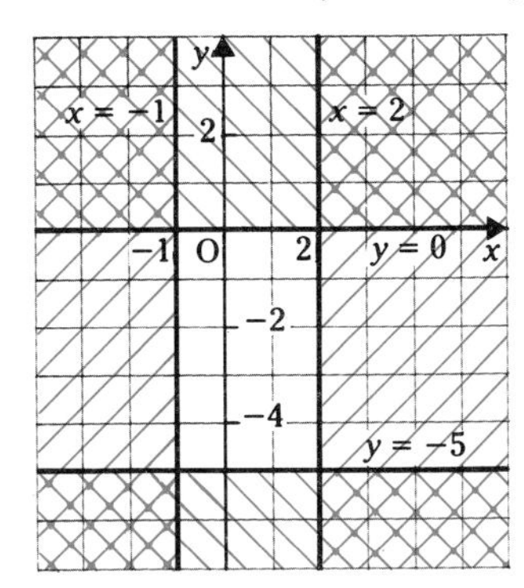

The unshaded region represents the inequalities.

Draw diagrams to represent the regions described by the following sets of inequalities. In each case, draw axes for values of x and y from -5 to 5.

16. $2 \leqslant x \leqslant 4, \quad -1 \leqslant y \leqslant 3$

17. $-2 < x < 2, \quad -2 < y < 2$

18. $0 \leqslant x \leqslant 4, \quad 0 \leqslant y \leqslant 3$

19. $-4 < x < 0, \quad -2 < y < 2$

20. $-1 < x < 1, \quad -3 < y < 1$

21. $x \geqslant 1, \quad -1 \leqslant y \leqslant 2$

Give the sets of inequalities that describe the unshaded regions.

22.

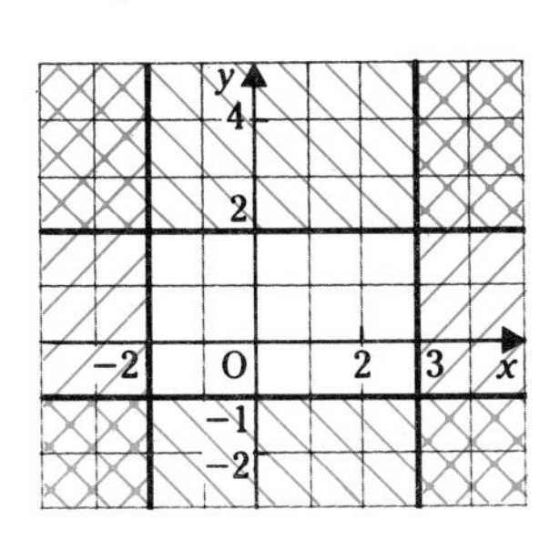

23.

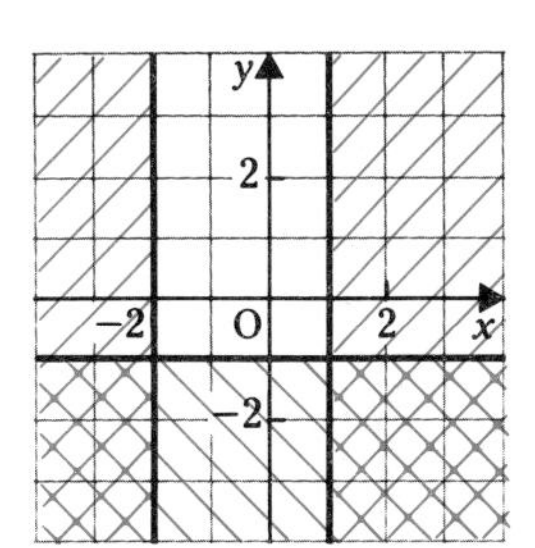

24.

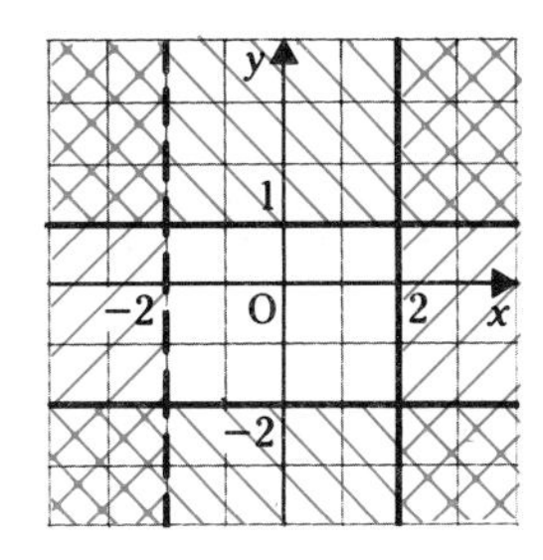

25.

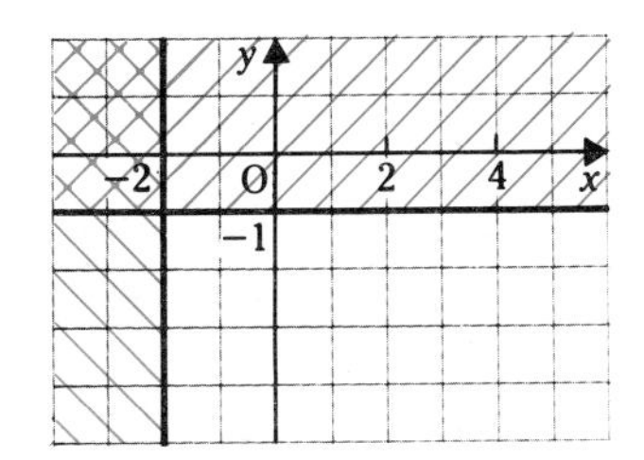

INEQUALITIES INVOLVING TWO VARIABLES

The equation $2x + y = 4$ is represented in the xy plane by a sloping line.

It follows that the inequality $2x + y < 4$ is represented by an area bounded by that sloping line.

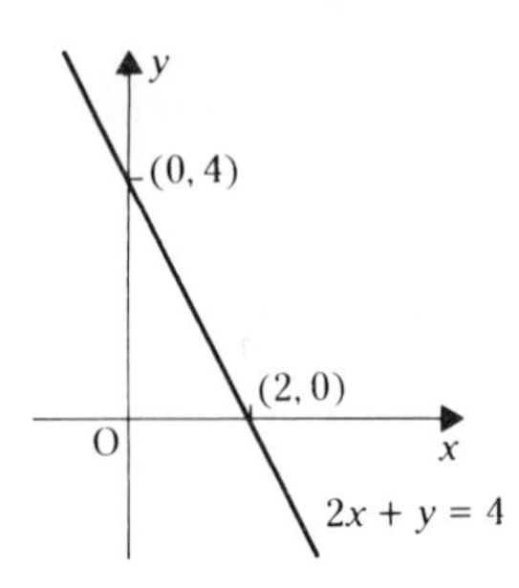

The boundary line divides the space into two regions. To decide which of these regions represents the given inequality we can use a check point that is not on the line.

The easiest point to use is the origin.

When $x = 0$ and $y = 0$, $2x + y = 0$ which is less than 4.
So the origin is in the region that represents $2x + y < 4$.

Alternatively, converting the inequality into the form $y < 4 - 2x$ we see that the required region contains all the points that are *below* the line $y = 4 - 2x$.

Now we can shade the region that is not required; the boundary line is not included so a broken line is used as before.

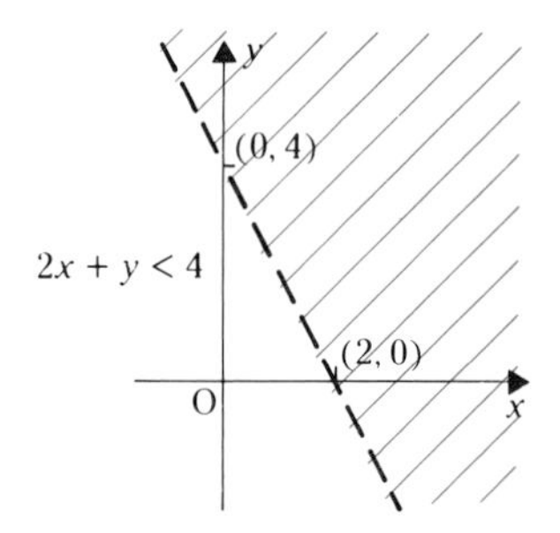

Exercise 18b

Leave unshaded the region defined by the inequality $3x - 2y \leqslant 6$

The boundary line is $3x - 2y = 6$
and it is included in the inequality.

x	0	2	4
y	−3	0	3

When $x = 0$ and $y = 0$,
$3x - 2y = 0$ which is less than 6.
So the origin is in the required region and we shade the area on the other side of the line.

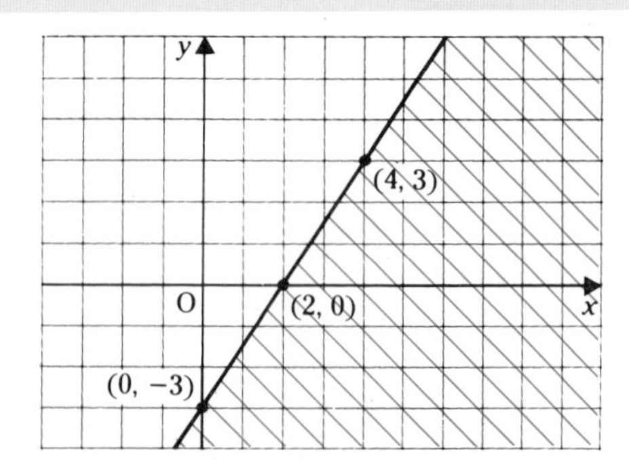

Alternatively $3x - 2y \leqslant 6 \;\Rightarrow\; 2y \geqslant 3x - 6 \;\Rightarrow\; y \geqslant \frac{3}{2}x - 3$
So the required region is above the line.

The unshaded region represents the inequality $3x - 2y \leqslant 6$

Using x and y axes scaled from -6 to 6, leave unshaded the regions defined by the given inequalities.

1. $x+y<3$
2. $3x-2y<6$
3. $2x+4y\leqslant 7$
4. $2x-y\leqslant 3$
5. $x+2y\leqslant 4$
6. $3x-5y>15$

Find the inequality that defines the unshaded region.

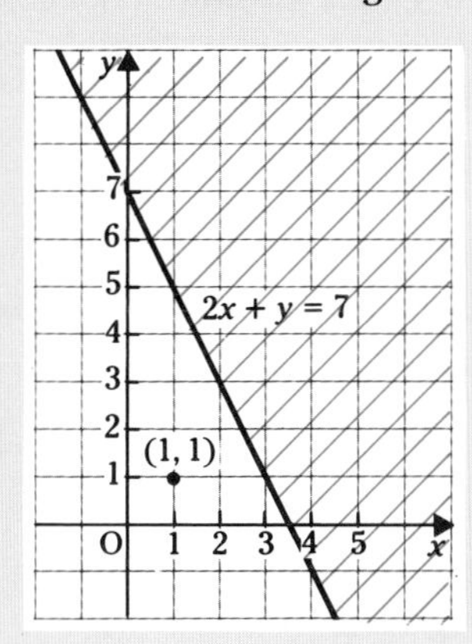

The boundary line, $2x+y=7$, is solid and is therefore included.

Check a point that is in the unshaded region, e.g. $(1, 1)$

When $x=1$ and $y=1$, $2x+y=3$ which is less than 7

So the inequality is $2x+y\leqslant 7$

Alternatively, writing the equation of the boundary line as $y=7-2x$ and noting that the given region is below the boundary line, we see that the inequality is $y\leqslant 7-2x$ or $2x+y\leqslant 7$

Find the inequality that defines each unshaded region.

7.

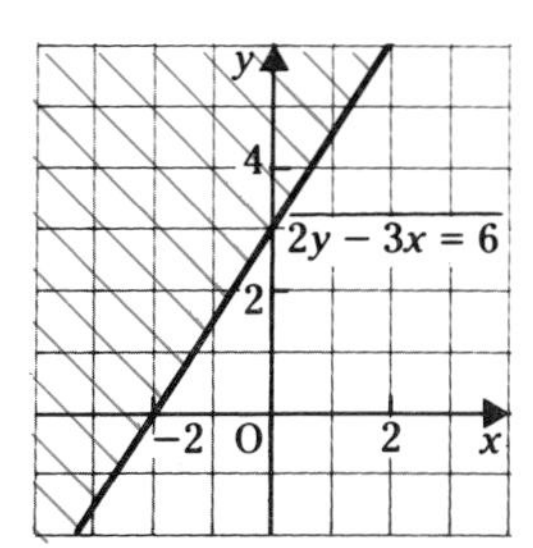

8.

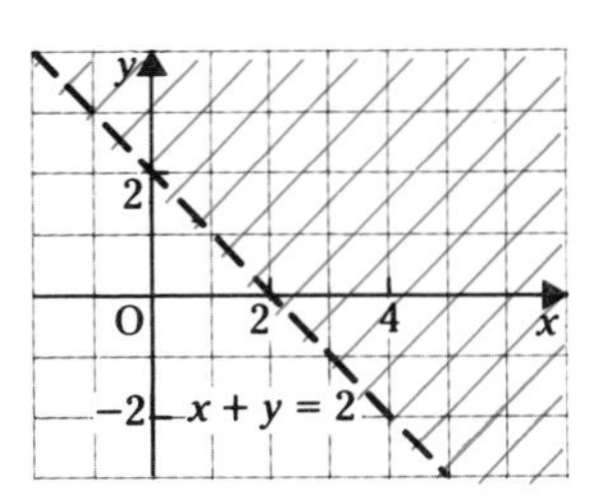

9.

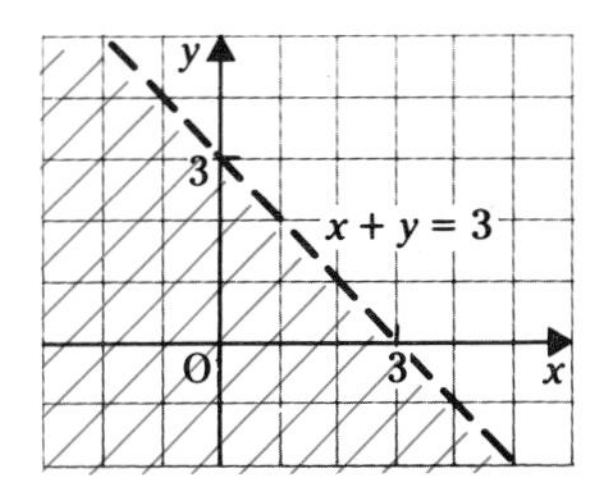

First find the equation of the boundary line.

10.

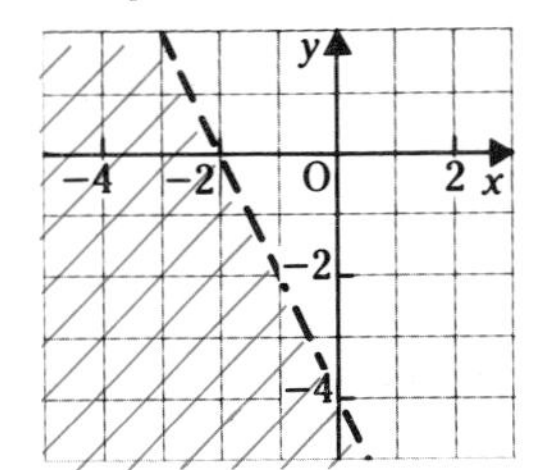

Regions with more than one sloping line boundary can be illustrated in a similar way. Each of the boundary lines is drawn and the unwanted region shaded.

Leave unshaded the region defined by the set of inequalities

$$x+y<4,\quad x\geqslant 0\quad \text{and}\quad x+2y\geqslant 2$$

1st boundary line (not included) $x+y=4$

x	4	0	2
y	0	4	2

2nd boundary line (included) $x=0$

3rd boundary line (included) $x+2y=2$

x	0	2	4
y	1	0	-1

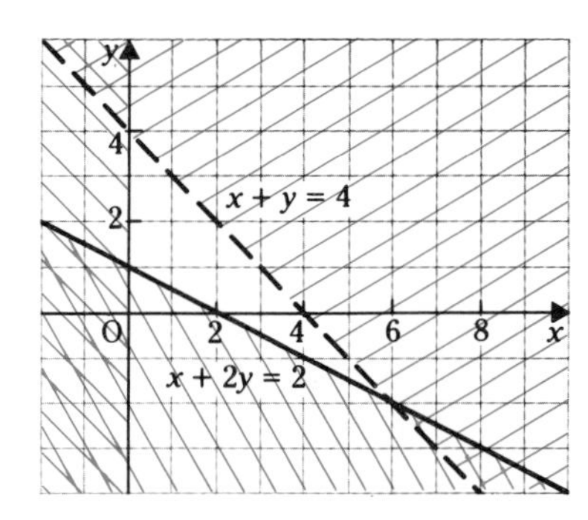

The unshaded region is defined by the given inequalities.

Leave unshaded the regions defined by the following sets of inequalities:

11. $x\geqslant -3,\quad y\geqslant -2,\quad x+y\leqslant 3$

12. $y\leqslant 0,\quad x\leqslant 0,\quad x+y\leqslant -4$

13. $y<3,\quad 2x+3y\geqslant 6,\quad y>x-2$

14. $y>x,\quad y<4x,\quad x+y<5$

15. $x\geqslant 0,\quad y\geqslant x-1,\quad 2y+x<4$

16. What can you say about the region defined by $x+y>4,\ x+y<1,\ x>0$ and $y>0$?

17. Do the regions defined by the following sets of inequalities exist?
    (a) $x+y\geqslant 3,\quad y\leqslant 2,\quad y\geqslant 2x$
    (b) $x+y>3,\quad y<2,\quad y>2x$

Shading a Required Region

In some simple cases you might be asked to shade the region defined by the inequality, instead of leaving it unshaded.

Occasionally, you may be asked to shade the required region when it is defined by several inequalities. If you try to do it by shading the required side of each boundary line, you will find yourself with overlapping shadings, resulting in a confused diagram.

For instance, if $y \geqslant 0$, $x \geqslant 0$ and $x+y \leqslant 3$, the diagram looks like this and the required region disappears in a muddle.

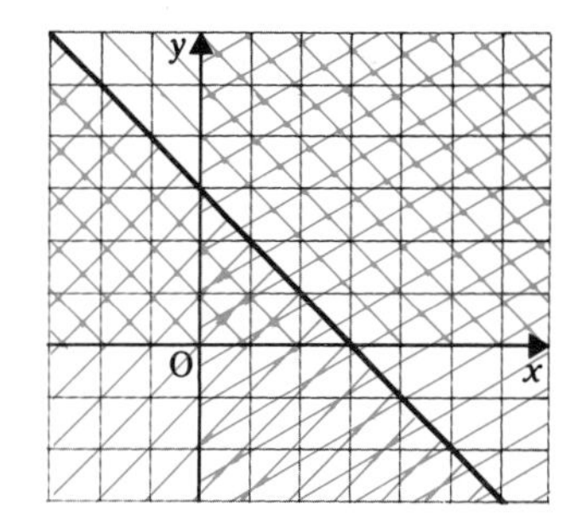

A better method is to do the shading as before so that the required region is left unshaded, then draw a second diagram on which you shade the required area.

1st diagram

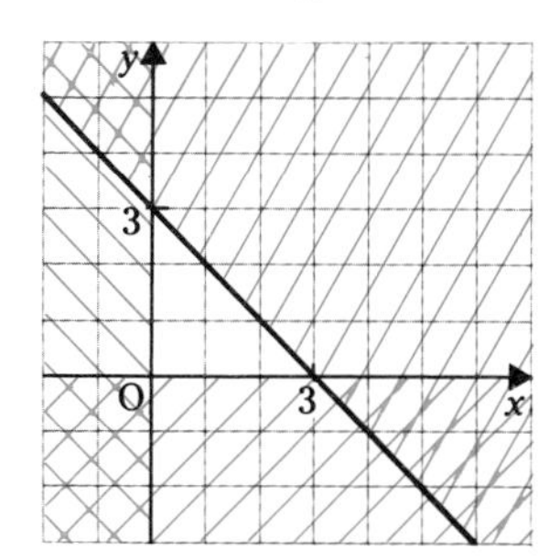

2nd diagram
The required region is shaded.

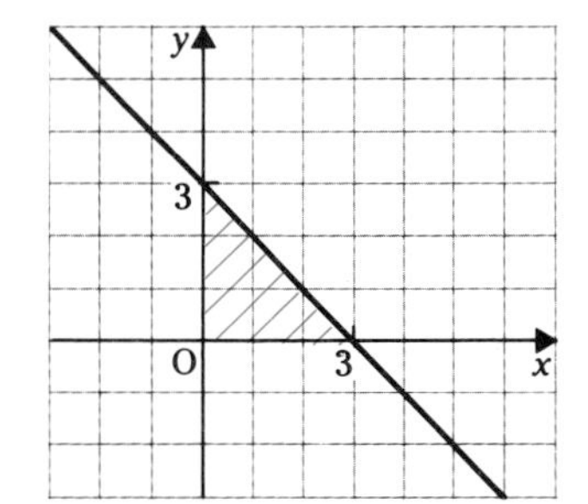

Exercise 18c

Shade the regions defined by the sets of inequalities.

1. $x \leqslant 4, \quad y \leqslant 3, \quad x+y \geqslant 0$

2. $2x+y \geqslant 4, \quad y \leqslant 0, \quad x \leqslant 4$

3. $\dfrac{x}{2}+\dfrac{y}{3} \geqslant 1, \quad \dfrac{x}{2}-\dfrac{y}{3} \geqslant 1, \quad x \leqslant 8$

4. $y \geqslant x, \quad y-x \leqslant 2, \quad y \leqslant 2$

5. $2y \leqslant 3-x, \quad 2y \geqslant x-3, \quad x \geqslant 1$

If you need to use diagrams for solving problems, it is best to leave the required regions unshaded.

Give the inequalities that define the unshaded region.

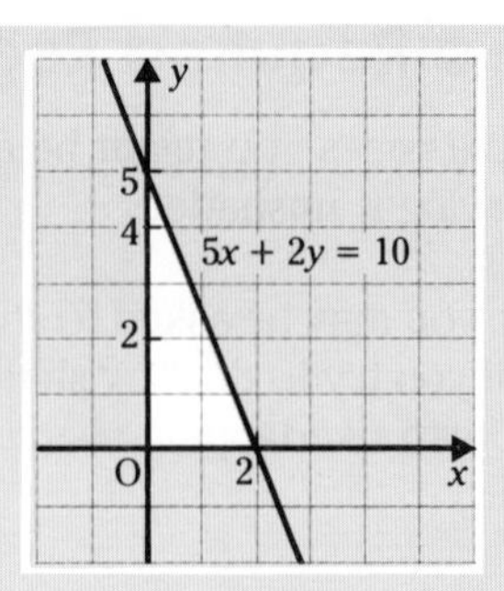

The first two inequalities are $x \geqslant 0,\ y \geqslant 0$
The 3rd boundary line is $5x + 2y = 10$

Test the point $(1, 1)$
When $x = 1$ and $y = 1$, $5x + 2y = 7$
As $7 < 10$ the 3rd inequality is $5x + 2y \leqslant 10$

In questions 6 to 9, give the sets of inequalities that define the unshaded regions.

6.

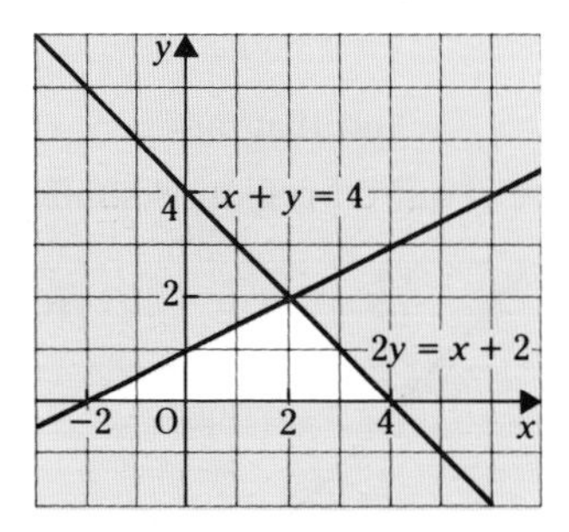

7.

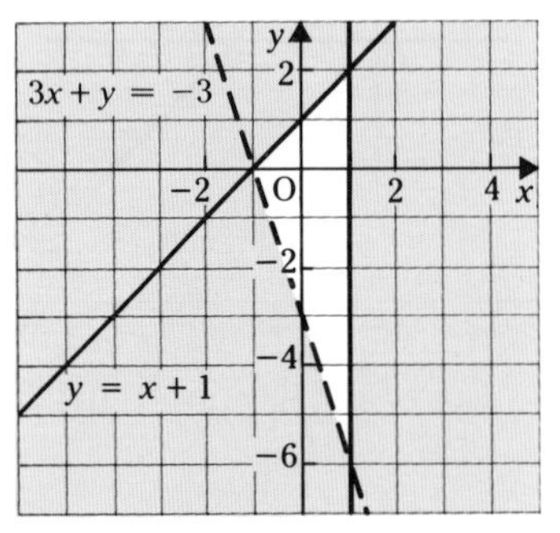

First find the equations of the boundary lines.

8.

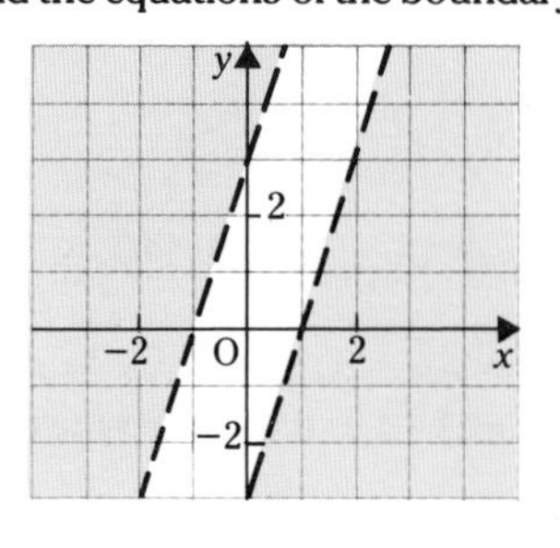

9.

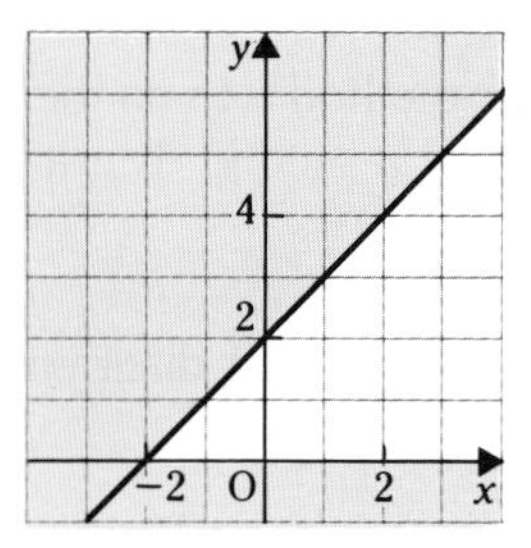

10.

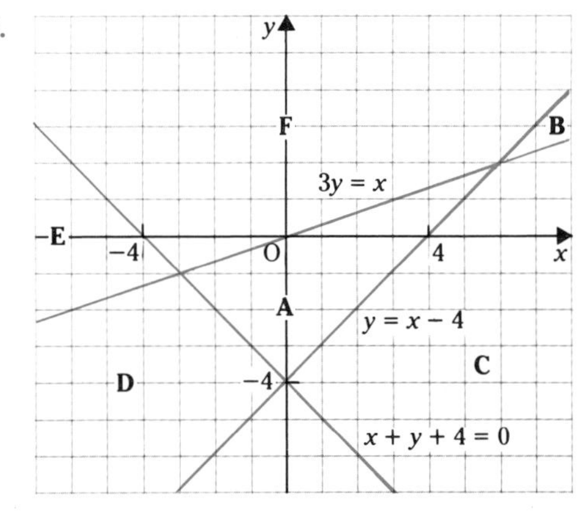

Use inequalities to describe the regions bounded by purple lines.

(a) A

(b) B

(c) C

(d) E

(e) A + D

(f) A + F

11.

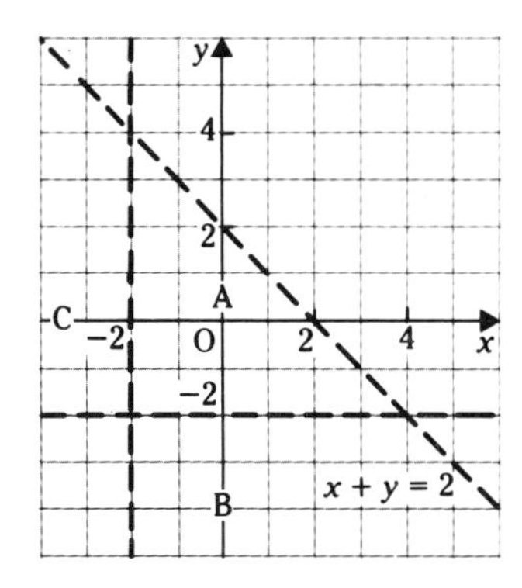

Write down the region, A, B or C, defined by each set of inequalities.

(a) $x+y<2, \quad x<-2, \quad y>-2$

(b) $x+y<2, \quad x>-2, \quad y>-2$

(c) $x+y<2, \quad x>-2, \quad y<-2$

12. Write down the coordinates of the vertices of the unshaded regions.

(a)

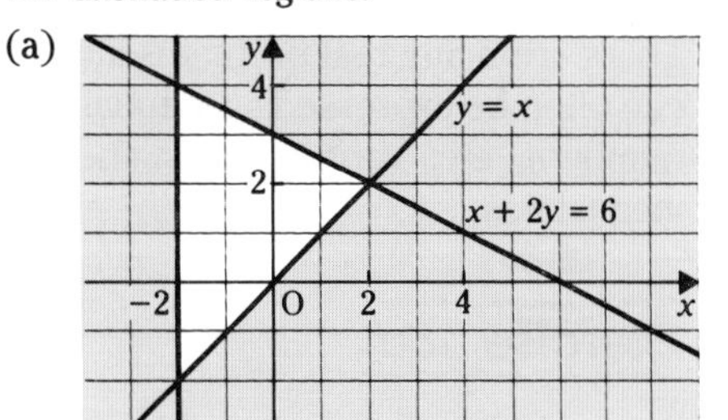

(b)

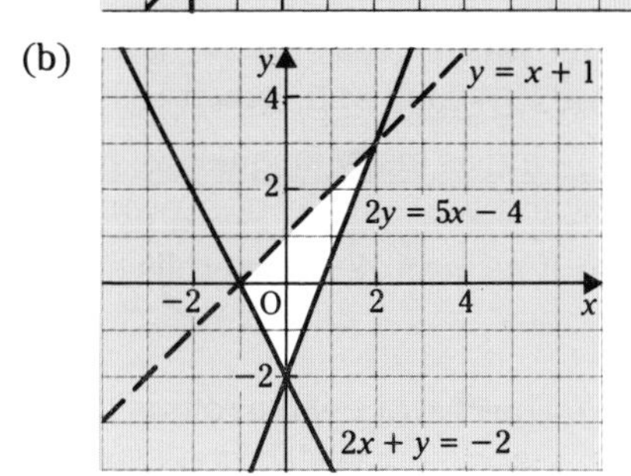

Give the points whose coordinates are integers and that lie in the region given in the diagram.

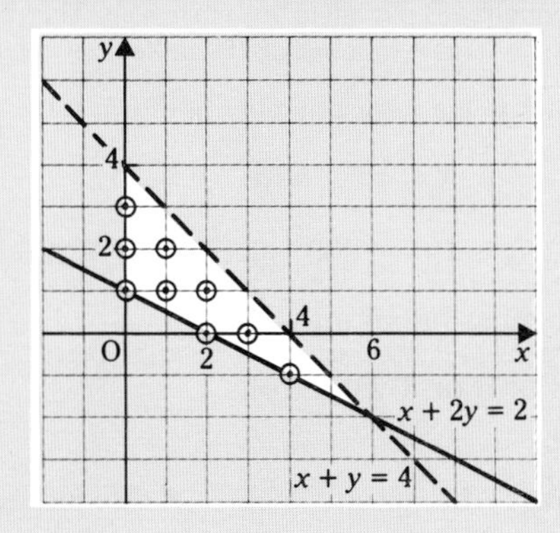

Notice that points on the broken line are *not* in the region.

Points are

$(0,1)$, $(0,2)$, $(0,3)$, $(1,1)$, $(1,2)$, $(2,0)$, $(2,1)$, $(3,0)$ and $(4,-1)$.

13. Draw a diagram and give the coordinates of the points whose coordinates are integers and that lie in the region defined by the inequalities $y \leqslant 3x+6$, $y > x-2$, $x+y > -2$ and $x+y \leqslant 3$

14. Draw a diagram and give the points with coordinates that are integers, on the boundaries of the region defined by the inequalities $x \geqslant 2$, $y \geqslant -1$ and $x+y \leqslant 4$

USING INEQUALITIES TO MODEL REAL SITUATIONS

There are many real problems in which quantities have to be limited in some way. These can often be expressed as inequalities if letters are used to represent unknown quantities, numbers, etc. Various facts about these quantities can then be deduced from the inequalities.

Exercise 18d

Peter was given £3 to buy a mixture of white and brown bread rolls. White rolls cost 15 p each and brown rolls cost 19 p each.

(a) Find as many inequalities as you can involving the number of white rolls (x) and the number of brown rolls (y).

(b) If he buys 12 brown rolls find the possible numbers of white rolls that he can buy.

(a) The cost of x white rolls is $15x$ pence and the cost of y brown rolls is $19y$ pence.

Peter cannot spend more than £3, so the total cost of the rolls must not exceed 300 pence

$$15x + 19y \leqslant 300$$

As a mixture of rolls is to be bought, at least one white roll and at least one brown roll are required

$$x \geqslant 1 \quad \text{and} \quad y \geqslant 1$$

If only one brown roll is bought, 281 p is left to buy white rolls. Therefore the greatest possible number of white rolls is the largest number of 15s in 281, i.e. 18.

A similar argument applies to the largest number of brown rolls.

$$x \leqslant 18 \quad \text{and} \quad y \leqslant 15$$

(b) Using $y = 12$ in $15x + 19y \leqslant 300$ gives $15x + 228 \leqslant 300$ i.e. $15x \leqslant 72$

Hence $x \leqslant 4$ (as x must be an integer)

Peter can buy 1 or 2 or 3 or 4 white rolls.

In questions 1 to 3 express the given information by inequalities.

1. A rectangle is to have a perimeter of not more than 20 cm and an area of at least 12 cm^2. Taking x cm for the length and y cm for the width, write down two inequalities involving x and y (other than $x > 0$ and $y > 0$).

2. In a cash box there are x £1 coins and y 50 p coins. It is known that there are at least twice as many £1 coins as 50 p coins and that the total value of the coins is less than £100.

3. A disc jockey plans to play x pop songs and y rock singles during his programme. A pop song takes 3 minutes of air-time and a rock single takes 4 minutes. The programme must last for less than 45 minutes and there must not be more rock tracks than pop.

4. Barbara is x years old and Christa is y years old. Barbara is three times as old as Christa and the sum of their ages is less than 20 years. Find

   (a) as many relationships as you can for x and y to represent these conditions

   (b) a possible age range for Christa.

Investigation

A firework manufacturer is planning a special display pack containing roman candles and rockets. The details of each firework are given in the table.

	No. in pack	Display time (s)	Weight (g)	Profit (£)
Rocket	x	50	120	1.50
Roman candle	y	25	100	1.00

(a) The pack must contain at least 20 roman candles. Express this as an inequality involving y.

(b) There must be enough fireworks for a display of at least 35 minutes. Show that $2x + y \geqslant 84$

(c) The weight of the pack must not be more than 9 kg. Show that $6x + 5y \leqslant 450$

(d) Use a scale of 1 cm for 20 fireworks on each axis and draw graphs to show the region of the xy plane that satisfies the three inequalities.

(e) If £P is the profit made from x rockets and y roman candles, give a formula for P in terms of x and y.

(f) Investigate possible values of x and y when (i) $P = 80$ (ii) $P = 100$

(g) Investigate ways of finding a pair of values for x and y which will give the most profit.

Self-Assessment 18

Where regions of the xy plane are required, sketches on squared paper are adequate.

1. Write down the inequalities that define each unshaded region.

(a)

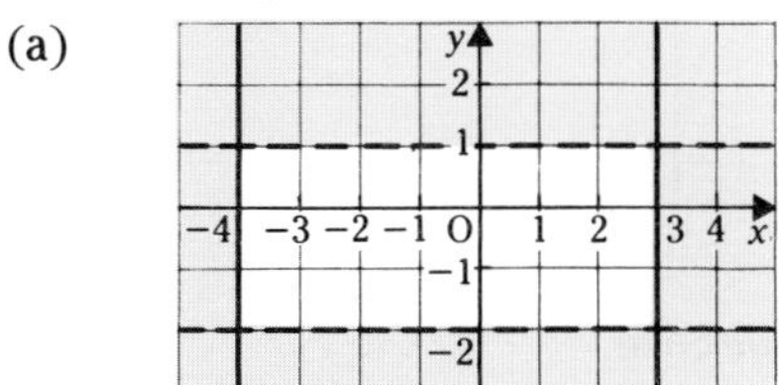

(b)

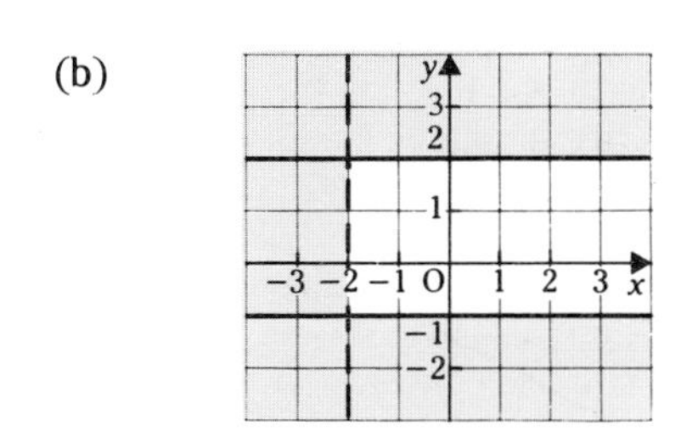

2. Leave unshaded in the xy plane the regions that represent the inequalities.

(a) $1 < x \leqslant 3$ (b) $y < 0$ and $y > 5$

3. *Shade* in the xy plane the region representing

$$x \geqslant 1 \quad \text{and} \quad 1 < y \leqslant 4$$

4. Write down the set of inequalities that define the unshaded region.

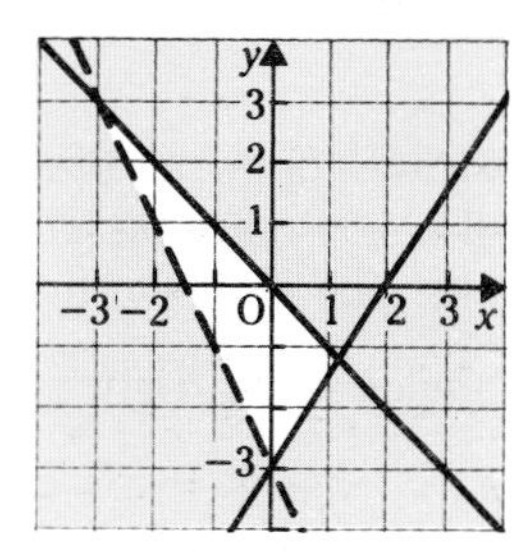

5. Give the coordinates of every point within the unshaded region given in question 4, whose coordinates are integers.

6. Represent by an unshaded region in the xy plane, the set of inequalities $2y + x \geqslant 2$, $x - y + 2 \geqslant 0$, $x \leqslant 3$

19 TRIGONOMETRY IN RIGHT-ANGLED TRIANGLES

THE USES OF TRIGONOMETRY

Simple trigonometry is concerned with the relationships between the sizes of angles and lengths of sides of triangles.
Trigonometry can be used in a practical way to find, for example, the height of an unclimbable tree PQ.

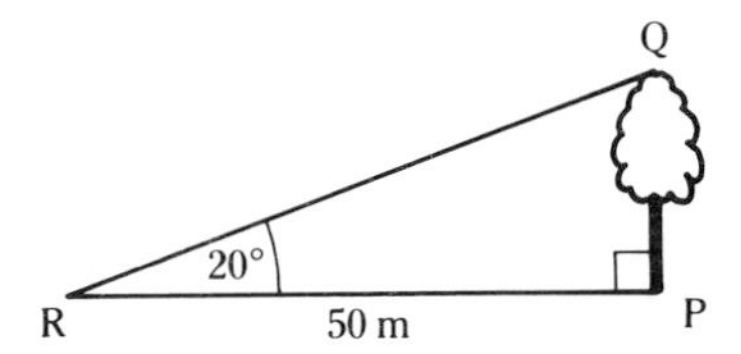

If the distance of a point R from the base of the tree PQ is known and the angle of elevation of the top is found, then the height can be calculated by trigonometry.

RIGHT-ANGLED TRIANGLES

Notation

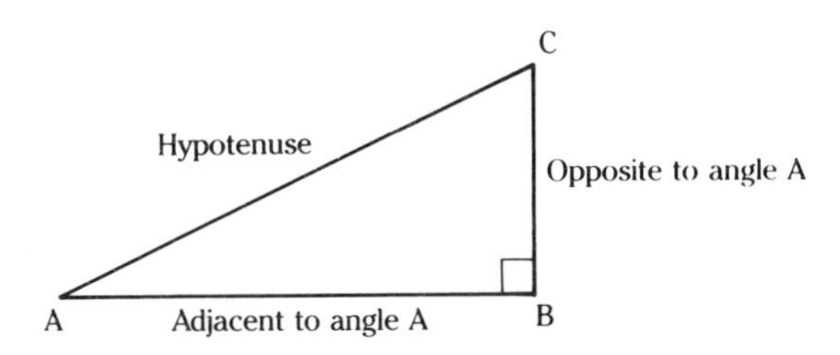

The side AC, opposite the right angle B, is the *hypotenuse*.
BC is the side *opposite* to angle A.
AB is the side *adjacent* to A.

All triangles with a right angle and an angle equal to A are similar.

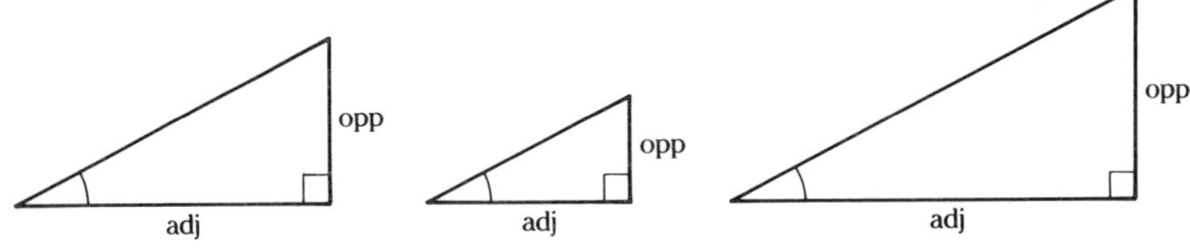

For all these triangles, the ratio $\frac{\text{opp}}{\text{adj}}$ is the same.

THE TANGENT OF AN ANGLE

For any given angle the ratio $\frac{\text{opp}}{\text{adj}}$ has been calculated and is called the *tangent* of the angle.

(The name is due to the fact that the original definition was based on circle work and was linked with the tangent to a circle. There is no chance of any confusion however.)

In a right-angled triangle,

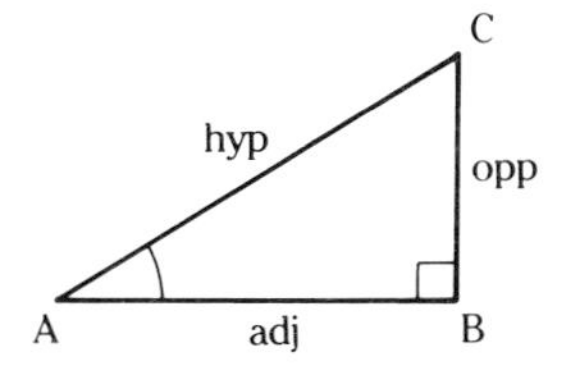

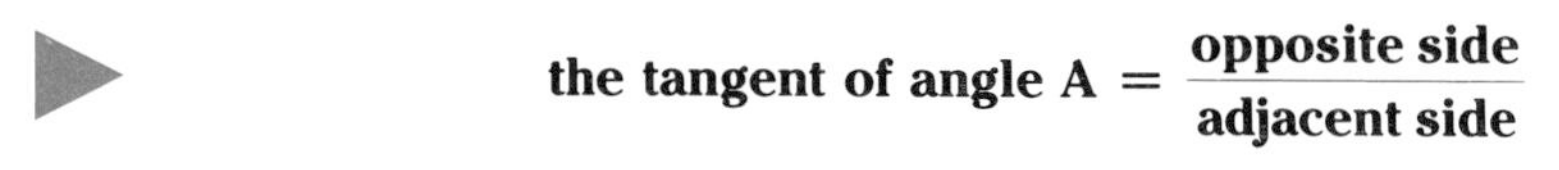

the tangent of angle A $=$ $\frac{\textbf{opposite side}}{\textbf{adjacent side}}$

or, briefly, $\tan A = \frac{\text{opp}}{\text{adj}}$

The values of the tangents of all angles are stored in scientific calculators, e.g. the tangent

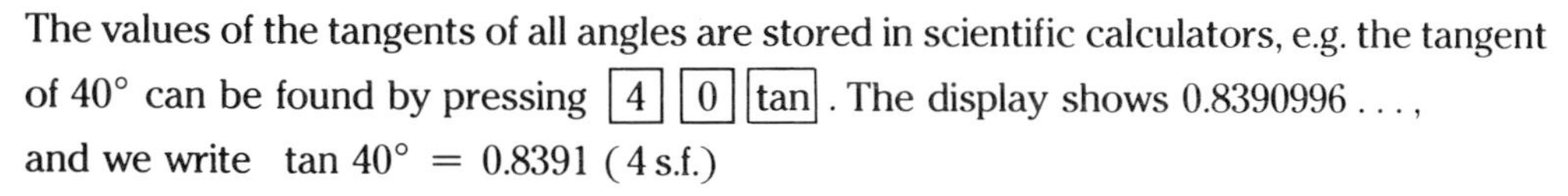

of 40° can be found by pressing [4] [0] [tan]. The display shows 0.8390996 . . . ,
and we write $\tan 40° = 0.8391$ (4 s.f.)

Similarly, if the tangent ratio is known, the angle can be found.

Note that scientific calculators will give angles in various units. Make sure that your calculator is in the correct mode; it should be showing 'deg' on the display.

Using Tangents

Angles are usually given correct to 1 decimal place, tangents to 4 significant figures and lengths to 3 significant figures. Use this convention unless it is inappropriate or you are told to do otherwise.

Using the Tangent Ratio to Find an Angle

When we know the lengths of the sides of a right-angled triangle then, with respect to one angle (not the right angle), the ratio $\frac{\text{opp}}{\text{adj}}$ can be calculated. The value of this ratio can then be used to find the size of the angle.

Exercise 19a

Find the tangents of the following angles.

1. 37°
2. 72.6°
3. 6.5°
4. 32.4°

Find the angle whose tangent is 0.78

$\tan X = 0.78$

Press [·] [7] [8] [INV] [tan] The display shows 37.95423 . . .

$\hat{X} = 37.95\ldots^\circ$

The angle is 38.0° (1 d.p.)

Find the angles whose tangents are given in questions 5 to 8.

5. 0.75 6. 1.457 7. 0.04 8. 3.92

9. Is there any limit to the value of a tangent for which an angle can be found ?

In $\triangle ABC$, $\hat{B} = 90°$, $BC = 6.2$ cm and $AB = 8.9$ cm. Find $\hat{A}$.

C
6.2 cm (opp)
A 8.9 cm (adj) B

Make a habit of labelling the sides 'opp', 'adj', etc.

$$\tan A = \frac{\text{opp}}{\text{adj}} = \frac{6.2}{8.9}$$

$= 0.69662\ldots$ press [INV] [tan]

$\hat{A} = 34.9°$ (1 d.p.)

Find the marked angle in each of the following triangles.

10.

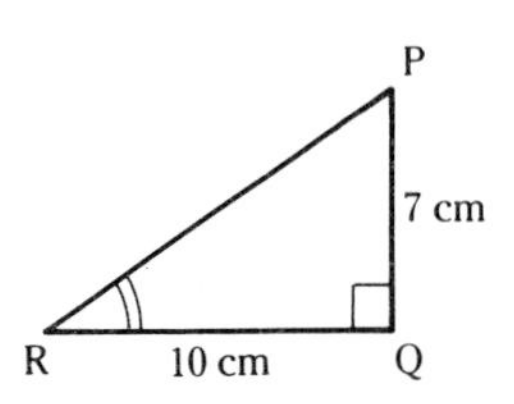

11.

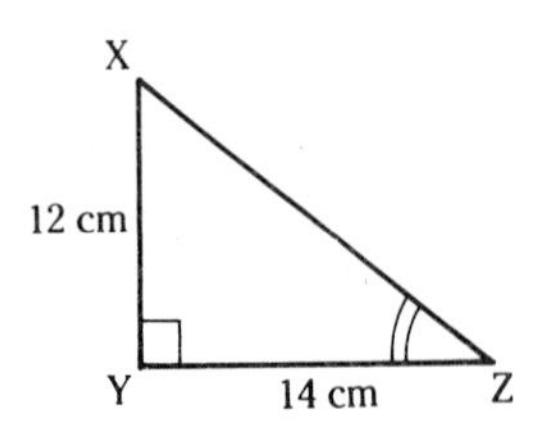

12.

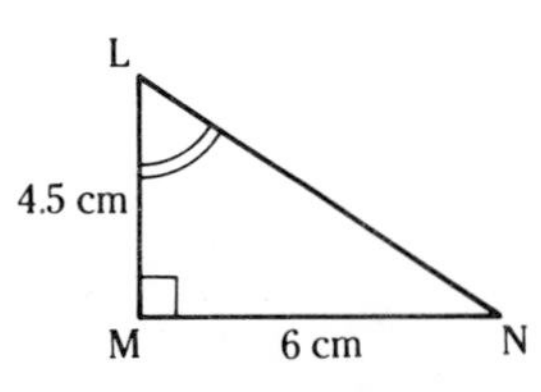

13.

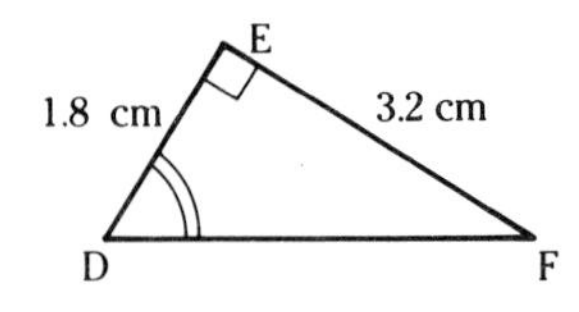

14. In $\triangle ABC$, $\hat{C} = 90°$, $AC = 56$ cm and $BC = 60$ cm. Find $\hat{B}$.

15. In $\triangle PQR$, $\hat{Q} = 90°$, $PQ = 7.2$ cm and $QR = 8$ cm. Find $\hat{R}$.

16. In $\triangle LMN$, $\hat{N} = 90°$, $LN = 14$ cm and $MN = 12$ cm. Find $\hat{M}$.

17. In $\triangle XYZ$, $\hat{Z} = 90°$, $XZ = 5.34$ m and $ZY = 5$ m. Find $\hat{X}$.

18. In $\triangle ABC$, $\hat{B} = 90°$, $\hat{A} = 45°$ and $AB = 10$ cm. Without using a calculator, write down the tangent of 45°.

Finding the Length of a Side

If, in a right-angled triangle, we know one side other than the hypotenuse, and an angle, then we can use the tangent ratio to find another side of the triangle.

Exercise 19b

In $\triangle$LMN, $\hat{L} = 90°$, LM = 9.3 cm and $\hat{M} = 35°$. Find LN.

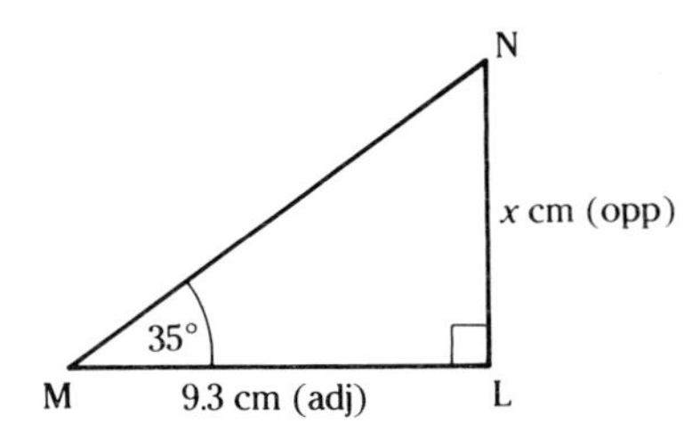

Note that we use the angle opposite to the unknown side. Label the unknown side x cm.

$$\frac{x}{9.3} = \frac{\text{opp}}{\text{adj}}$$

i.e.
$$\frac{x}{9.3} = \tan 35°$$

Multiply both sides by 9.3

$$9.3 \times \frac{x}{9.3} = 9.3 \times \tan 35°$$

$$x = 9.3 \times \tan 35°$$ Press [9] [·] [3] [×] [3] [5] [tan] [=]

$$x = 6.5119\ldots$$

LN = 6.51 cm (3 s.f.)

In each question from 1 to 4, find the required side.

1. Find DE.

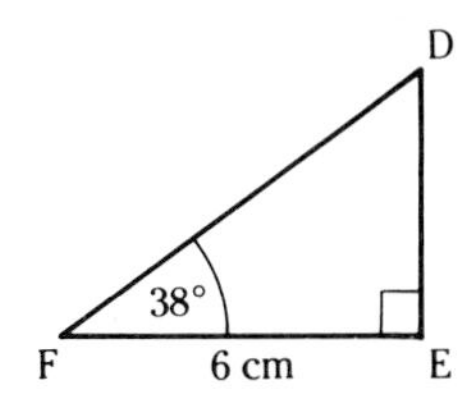

2. Find PQ.

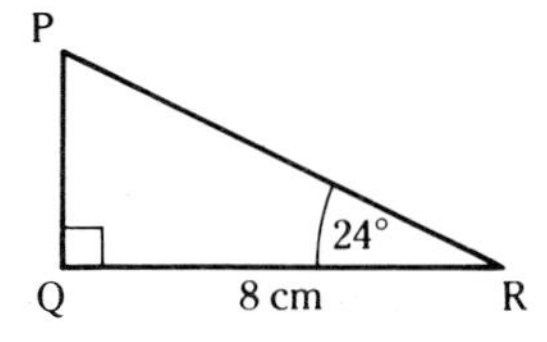

3. Find DE.

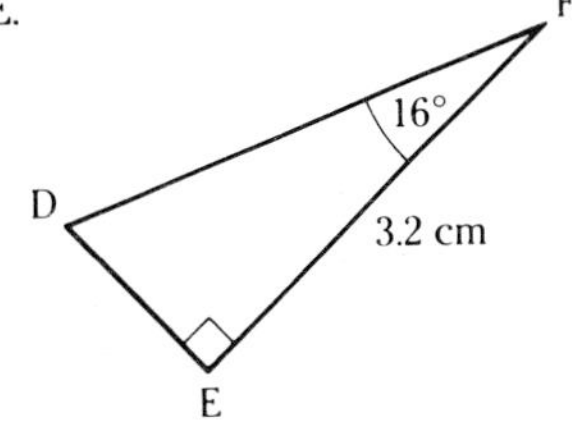

4. Find XY.

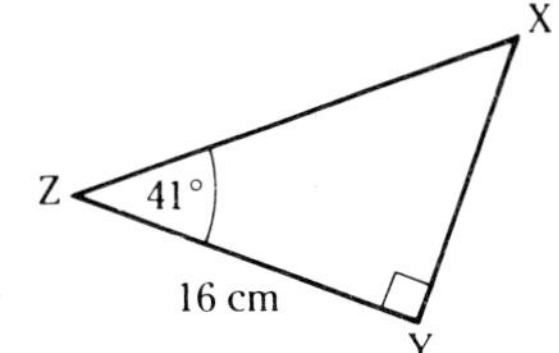

In $\triangle XYZ$, $\hat{Z} = 90°$, $\hat{Y} = 42°$ and $ZX = 9$ cm. Find YZ.

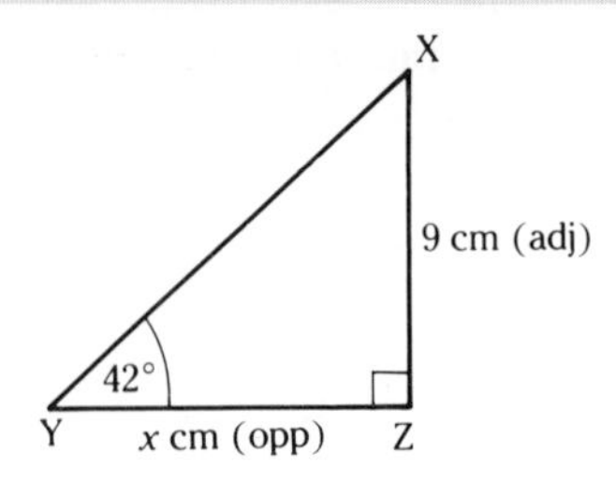

The unknown side is adjacent to the given angle in this case so we need to start by finding the angle *opposite* to the unknown side

$\hat{Y} = 42°$ so $\hat{X} = 48°$

$$\frac{x}{9} = \frac{\text{opp}}{\text{adj}}$$

i.e.
$$\frac{x}{9} = \tan 48°$$

$$9 \times \frac{x}{9} = 9 \times \tan 48°$$

$$x = 9.9955\ldots$$

YZ = 10.0 cm (3 s.f.)

5. In $\triangle JKL$, $\hat{K} = 90°$, $JK = 5$ cm and $\hat{J} = 61°$. Find KL.

6. In $\triangle ABC$, $\hat{A} = 90°$, $\hat{B} = 39°$ and $AC = 3$ cm. Find AB.

In some of the following questions, the third angle may need to be found.

7. In $\triangle PQR$, $\hat{Q} = 90°$, $\hat{R} = 31.5°$ and $QR = 7.2$ cm. Find QP.

8. In $\triangle FGH$, $\hat{G} = 90°$, $\hat{H} = 16.7°$ and $FG = 13$ cm. Find GH.

9. In $\triangle DEF$, $\hat{F} = 90°$, $\hat{E} = 32°$ and $FD = 6$ cm. Find FE.

10. In $\triangle ABC$, $\hat{A} = 90°$, $AB = 45$ m and $\hat{B} = 34°$. Find AC.

11. A triangular field is to be sown with winter wheat. The farmer needs to know how much seed to buy so he makes a rough survey of the field and draws this sketch, which is not drawn accurately.

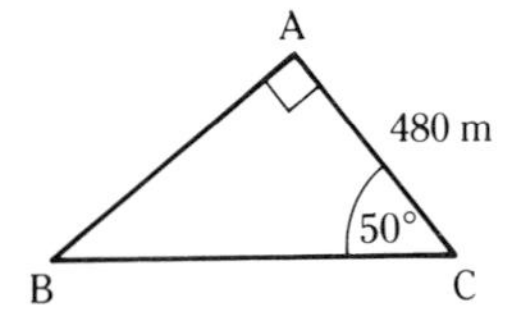

The side AC is measured to the nearest metre and angle C is measured to the nearest degree. Angle A is exactly 90°.

(a) Find the length of the side AB giving your answer to a sensible degree of accuracy bearing in mind the accuracy of the given measurements.

(b) Which of the following values is the best estimate for the area of the field?
(i) $300\,000\ \text{m}^2$ (ii) $150\,000\ \text{m}^2$
(iii) $50\,000\ \text{m}^2$

Find the height of the cross-section of this prism.

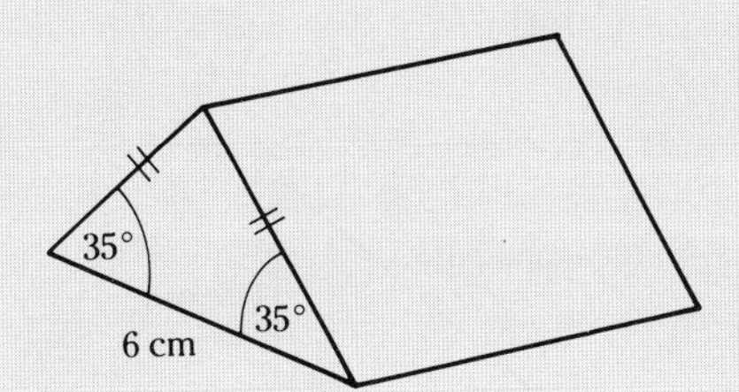

All the information, together with any facts that can be deduced, should be put on to a diagram.

Any isosceles triangle can be divided through the middle into two congruent right-angled triangles.

AD is the height of the cross-section.

Using $\triangle$ADC,

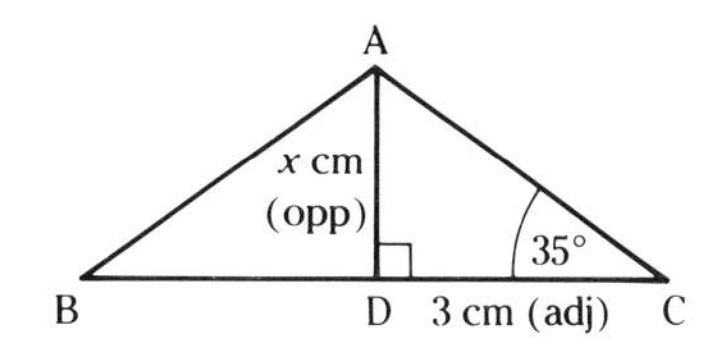

$$\frac{x}{3} = \tan 35°$$

$$x = 3 \tan 35°$$

$$= 2.100\ldots$$

Height of cross-section is 2.10 cm (3 s.f.)

Note that we named the triangle we used. This is important so that the reasoning can be followed easily.

12. A tower PQ is 20 m high.
Point R is 45 m from Q on level ground.
What is the angle of elevation of P from R?

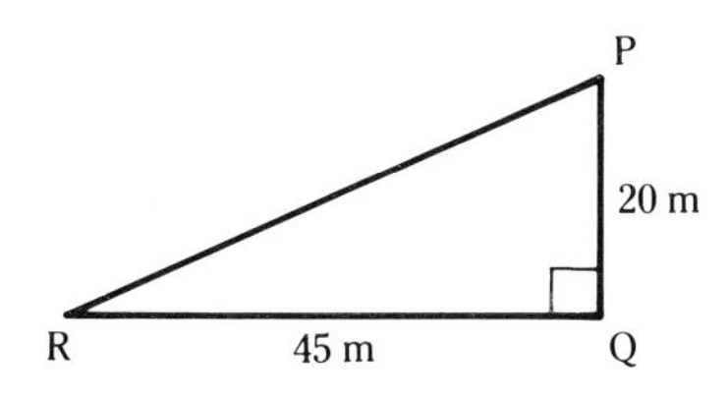

13. The coordinates of A, B and C are (5, 4), (1, 1) and (5, 1) respectively. Find $A\widehat{B}C$.

14. From A, John walks 8 km north to B, then east to C. The bearing of C from A is 052°. How far is B from C?

15. A is the point (6, 5) and O is the origin. Find the angle between the line OA and the x-axis.

16. Find the height of triangle ABC and hence its area.

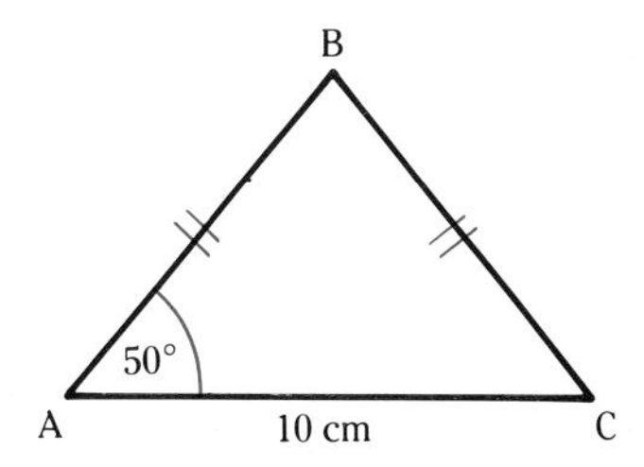

17. The coordinates of the vertices of a triangle are A(1, 1), B(2, 4) and C(8, 2).

(a) Find the lengths of AB, BC and AC.

(b) Show that one of the angles of triangle ABC is 90°.

(c) Find angle ACB.

SINE AND COSINE

Two more useful ratios can be found using two sides of a right-angled triangle.

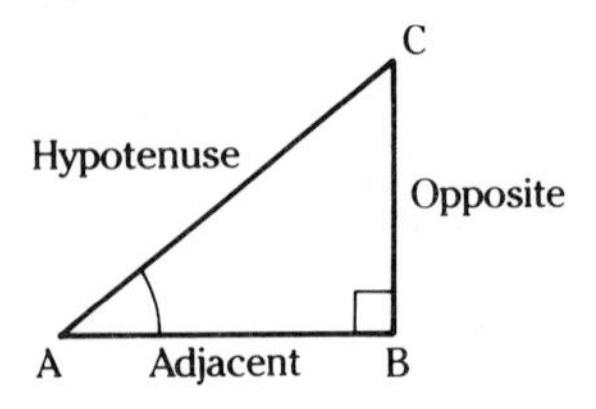

In a right-angled triangle,

$$\text{the sine of angle A} = \frac{\text{opposite side}}{\text{hypotenuse}}$$

$$\text{the cosine of angle A} = \frac{\text{adjacent side}}{\text{hypotenuse}}$$

The sine of angle A is abbreviated to sin A and the cosine of angle A to cos A.

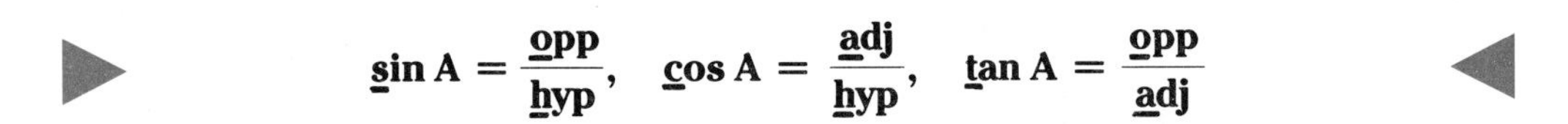

$$\mathbf{\underline{s}in\ A} = \frac{\mathbf{\underline{o}pp}}{\mathbf{\underline{h}yp}}, \quad \mathbf{\underline{c}os\ A} = \frac{\mathbf{\underline{a}dj}}{\mathbf{\underline{h}yp}}, \quad \mathbf{\underline{t}an\ A} = \frac{\mathbf{\underline{o}pp}}{\mathbf{\underline{a}dj}}$$

A possible memory aid is the word SOHCAHTOA, whose letters stand for the underlined initial letters above.

Calculations are done in a way similar to those involving the tangent.

Exercise 19c

1. Find the sines of the following angles.
   (a) 76° (b) 11.3° (c) 22.5°

2. Find the cosines of the following angles.
   (a) 64° (b) 31.6° (c) 3°

3. Find the angles whose sines are given below.
   (a) 0.731 (b) 0.926 (c) $\frac{3}{10}$

4. Find the angles whose cosines are given below.
   (a) 0.12 (b) 0.385 (c) $\frac{4}{9}$

5. For each of the triangles write down sin A, then find $\widehat{A}$.

   (a)

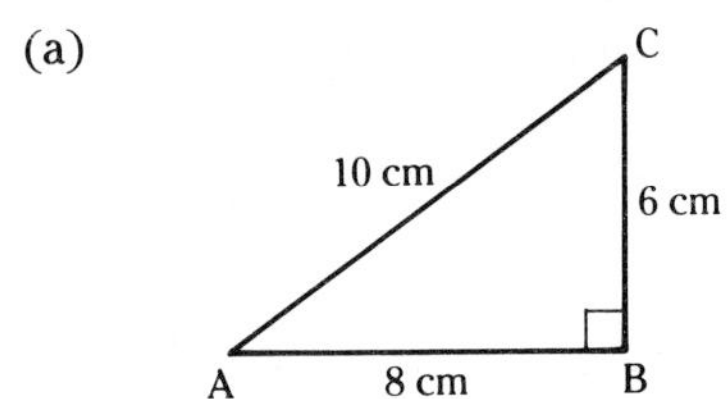

   (b)

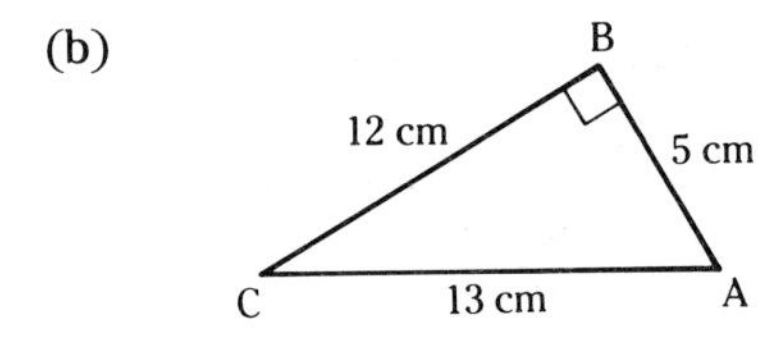

6. Write down cos L for each of the triangles, then find $\hat{L}$.

(a)

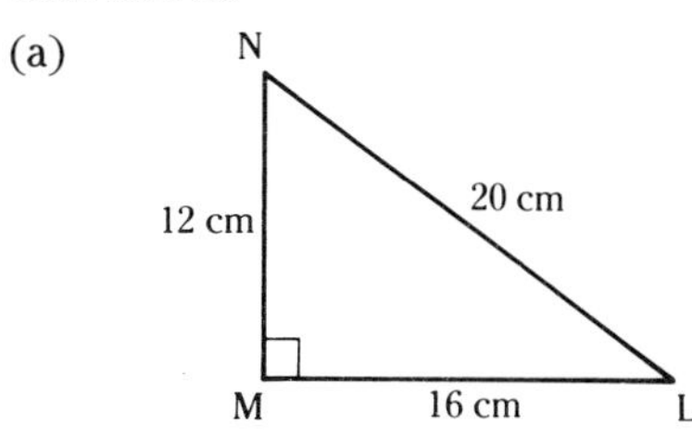

(b)

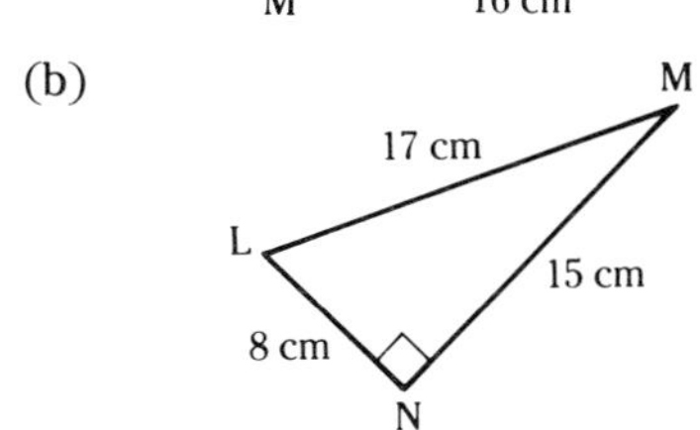

7. In each of the following triangles state which ratio should be used to find the marked angle. The first one is done for you. Remember to label the sides 'opp', 'adj' and 'hyp' to help you to decide which ratio to use.

(a)

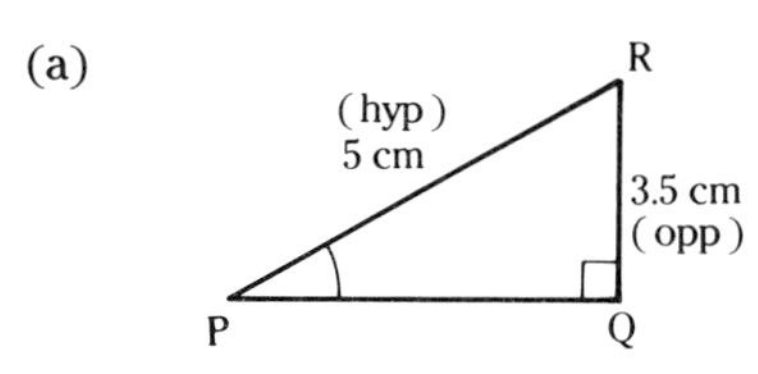

We are given the hypotenuse and the side opposite P, so we use sin P.

(b)

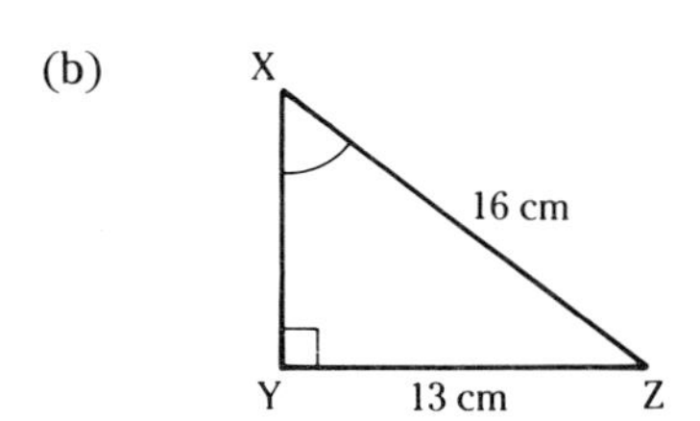

(c)

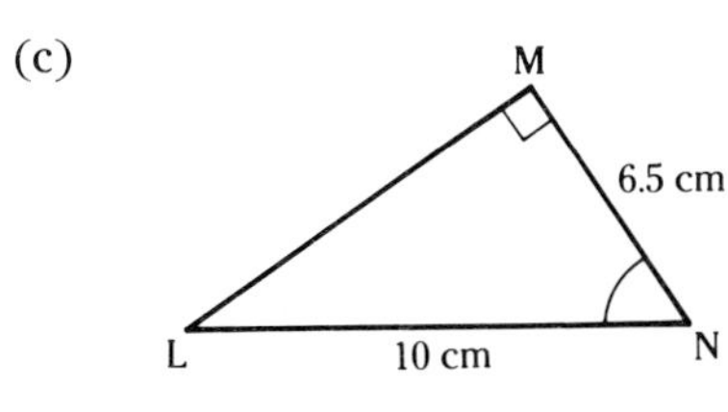

(d)

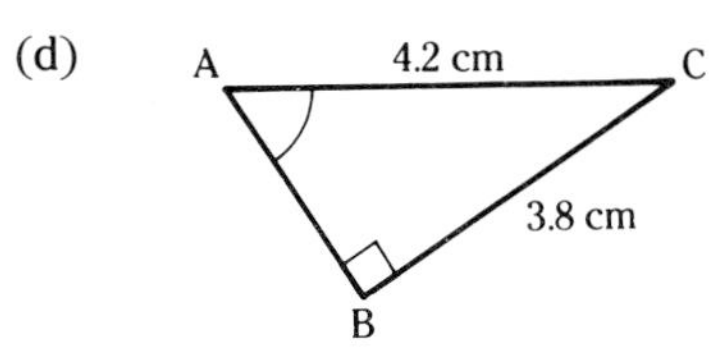

8. For each triangle in question 7, calculate the required angle.

Questions 9 to 12 involve tangents, sines and cosines.

9. In $\triangle ABC$, $\hat{B} = 90°$, $AB = 6\text{ cm}$ and $AC = 10\text{ cm}$. Find $\hat{A}$.

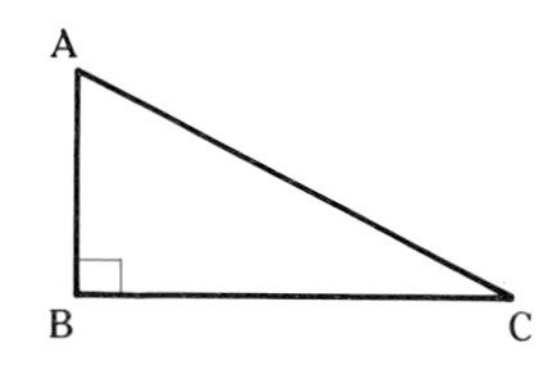

10. In $\triangle LMN$, $\hat{N} = 90°$, $LN = 5.2\text{ cm}$ and $MN = 4.5\text{ cm}$. Find $\hat{M}$.

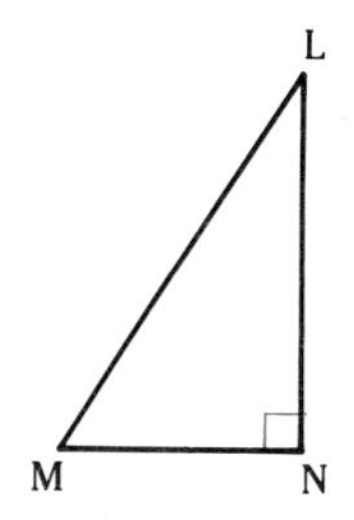

11. In $\triangle PQR$, $\hat{Q} = 90°$, $PQ = 3\text{ cm}$ and $PR = 6\text{ cm}$. Find $\hat{P}$.

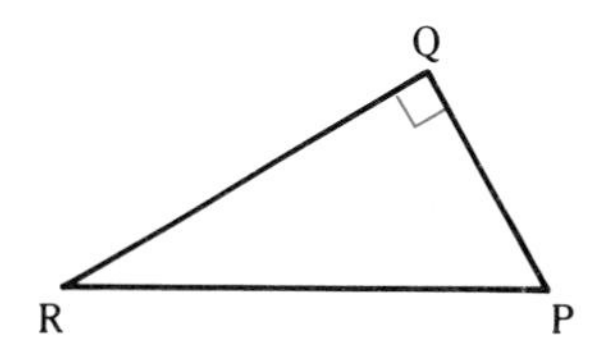

12. In $\triangle XYZ$, $\hat{X} = 90°$, $XY = 7.3\text{ cm}$ and $YZ = 9.8\text{ cm}$. Find $\hat{Z}$.

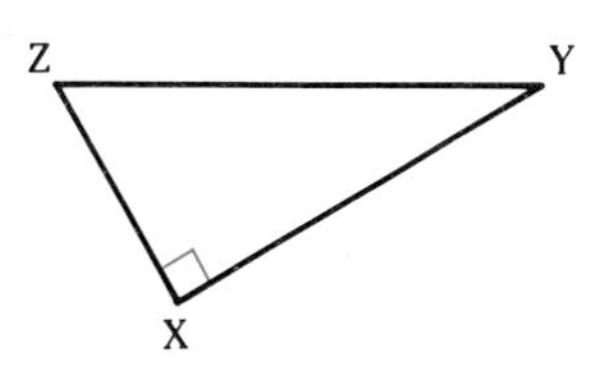

13. In the triangle with sides 3 cm, 4 cm and 5 cm, the smallest angle is A. Write as fractions, tan A, sin A and cos A.

Using Sine and Cosine to Find a Side

Sines and cosines can be used to find the lengths of sides in a similar way to using tangents. It is also possible to find the length of a hypotenuse if suitable information is given.

Problems Involving Sine, Cosine or Tangent

The solution to any problem concerning triangles, involves deciding which of sine, cosine or tangent should be used. When a diagram has been drawn with the information given and required, it becomes clear which pair of sides are involved in relation to an angle and hence which of the three ratios should be used.

Remember that if more than one triangle appears in the diagram, the triangle you are using should be named.

Remember also that an isosceles triangle can be divided into two congruent right-angled triangles.

Problems Involving Circles

When a problem involves a circle, the following facts are useful. In the diagram, O is the centre of the circle. A and B are points on the circumference and the line joining them is called a *chord*.

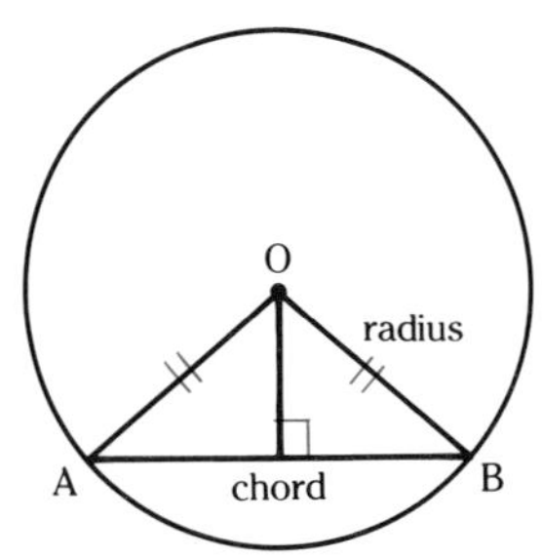

As OA and OB are radii, they are equal. Therefore $\triangle AOB$ is isosceles, and a line drawn from O perpendicular to the chord AB forms two congruent right-angled triangles. We can then use trigonometry to find lengths and angles in either of these triangles.

Exercise 19d

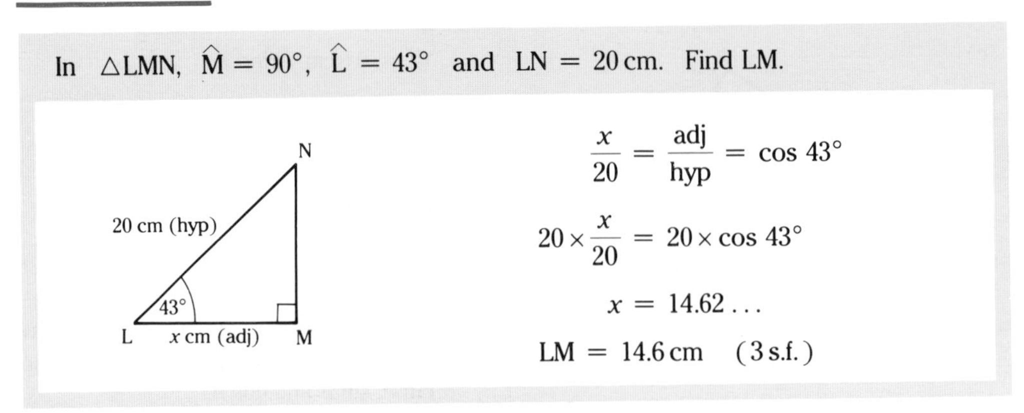

In $\triangle LMN$, $\widehat{M} = 90°$, $\widehat{L} = 43°$ and $LN = 20$ cm. Find LM.

$$\frac{x}{20} = \frac{\text{adj}}{\text{hyp}} = \cos 43°$$

$$20 \times \frac{x}{20} = 20 \times \cos 43°$$

$$x = 14.62\ldots$$

$$LM = 14.6 \text{ cm} \quad (3 \text{ s.f.})$$

1. In $\triangle ABC$, $\hat{A} = 90°$, $\hat{B} = 36°$ and $BC = 5\text{ cm}$. Find CA.

2. In $\triangle XYZ$, $\hat{Z} = 90°$, $\hat{X} = 72°$ and $XY = 2.68\text{ cm}$. Find ZY.

The following questions involve tangents as well as sines and cosines.

3. In $\triangle DEF$, $\hat{F} = 90°$, $\hat{E} = 30°$ and $DE = 98\text{ cm}$. Find EF.

4. In $\triangle PQR$, $\hat{Q} = 90°$, $\hat{R} = 14°$ and $PR = 12\text{ cm}$. Find PQ.

5. In $\triangle BCD$, $\hat{B} = 90°$, $\hat{D} = 25°$ and $CD = 20\text{ m}$. Find BD.

6. In $\triangle LMN$, $\hat{M} = 90°$, $\hat{N} = 14°$ and $MN = 32\text{ cm}$. Find LM.

7. In $\triangle XYZ$, $\hat{X} = 90°$, $\hat{Y} = 54.3°$ and $XY = 3\text{ cm}$. Find XZ.

8. In $\triangle ABC$, $\hat{C} = 90°$, $\hat{A} = 42°$ and $AB = 9.2\text{ cm}$. Find BC.

9. In $\triangle EFG$, $\hat{E} = 90°$, $\hat{F} = 10°$ and $FG = 16\text{ cm}$. Find EF.

In $\triangle ABC$, $\hat{B} = 90°$, $AB = 6\text{ cm}$ and $\hat{C} = 32°$. Find the hypotenuse.

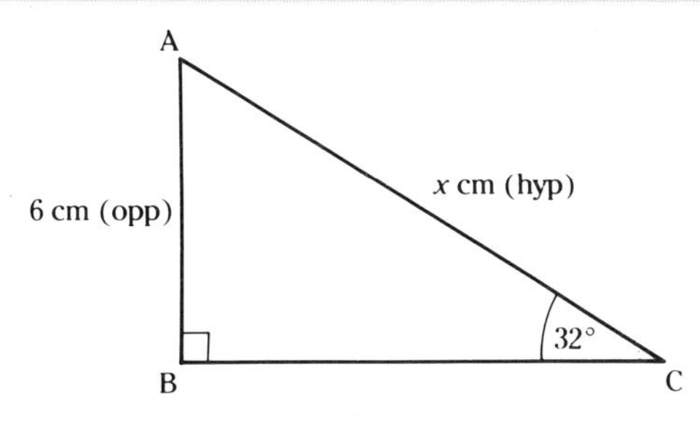

$$\frac{6}{x} = \frac{\text{opp}}{\text{hyp}} = \sin 32°$$

$$x \times \frac{6}{x} = x \times \sin 32°$$

i.e. $$x \times \sin 32° = 6$$

$\therefore$ $$x = \frac{6}{\sin 32°}$$

$$= 11.32\ldots$$

The hypotenuse is 11.3 cm (3 s.f.)

In each question from 10 to 13, find the length of the hypotenuse.

10. In $\triangle ABC$, $\hat{A} = 90°$, $\hat{B} = 31°$ and $AC = 4\text{ cm}$.

11. In $\triangle DEF$, $\hat{F} = 90°$, $\hat{D} = 14°$ and $DF = 7\text{ cm}$.

12. In $\triangle LMN$, $\hat{L} = 90°$, $\hat{M} = 48°$ and $LM = 10\text{ cm}$.

13. In $\triangle PQR$, $\hat{R} = 90°$, $\hat{Q} = 31°$ and $PR = 4.2\text{ cm}$.

In a circle with centre O, AB is a chord. The radius of the circle is 8 cm and the length of the chord is 12 cm. Find $\hat{AOB}$.

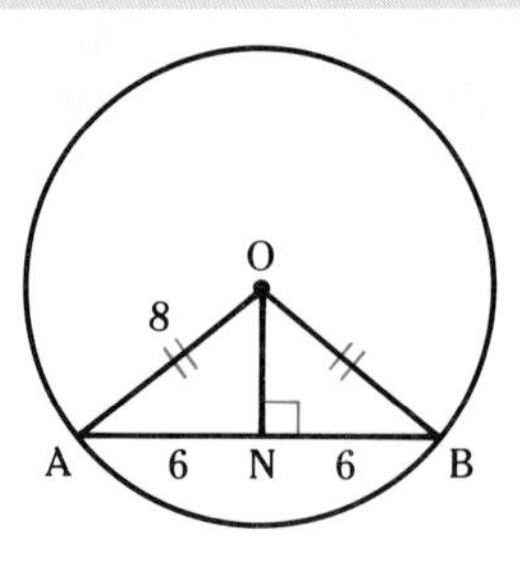

A chord of a circle is a line joining two points on the circumference. OA and OB are radii of the circle, so $\triangle AOB$ is isosceles and can be divided into two right-angled triangles.

Using $\triangle AON$, $\quad \sin A\hat{O}N = \frac{6}{8} = 0.75$

$$A\hat{O}N = 48.59\ldots^\circ$$

$A\hat{O}B = 2\,A\hat{O}N$, $\quad \therefore \quad A\hat{O}B = 97.18\ldots^\circ = 97.2^\circ$ correct to 1 d.p.

14. In a circle with centre O, PQ is a chord of length 12 cm. The chord is 4 cm from O. Find the size of $P\hat{O}Q$.

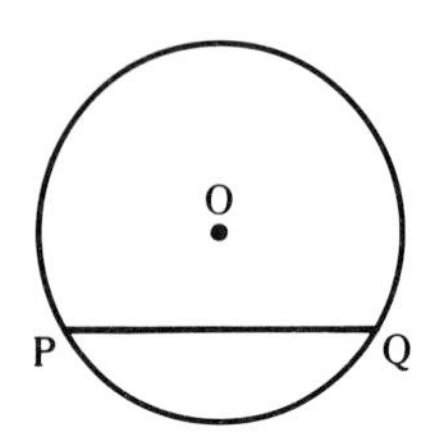

15. In the diagram, C is the centre of the circle. The chord PQ is 12 cm long. Find
    (a) the distance of the chord from the centre of the circle.
    (b) the radius of the circle.

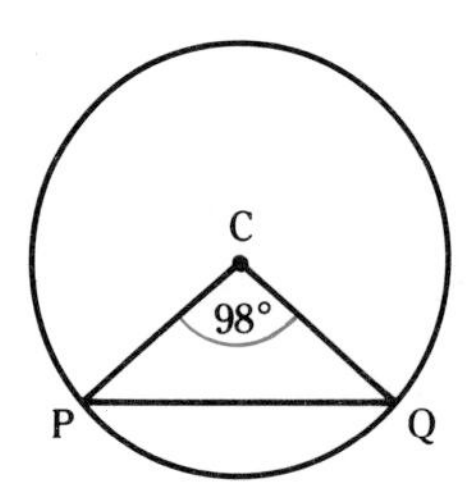

16.

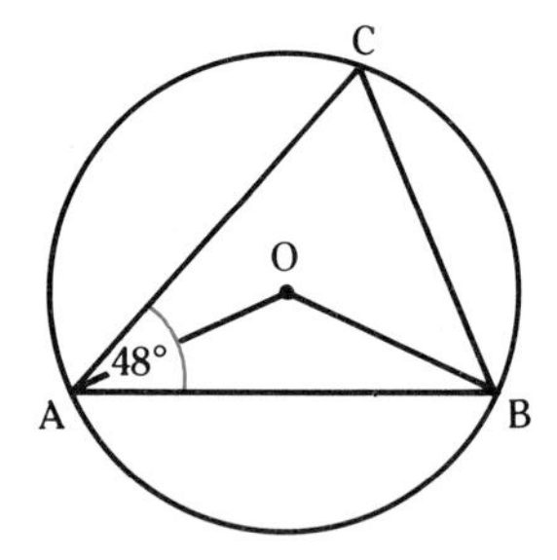

In the diagram, O is the centre of the circle and $\triangle ABC$ is isosceles. AB = AC = 10 cm and $B\hat{A}C = 48^\circ$.

(a) Assuming that AO is a line of symmetry, write down the size of $O\hat{A}B$.

(b) By dividing $\triangle OAB$ into two congruent right-angled triangles, find
   (i) the distance of O from AB
   (ii) the radius of the circle.

(c) Extend AO to meet BC at D
   (i) Write down the sizes of $O\hat{D}B$ and $O\hat{B}D$
   (ii) Using $\triangle ODB$, find DB

(d) Using $\triangle ADB$, find DB. Does your answer agree with the result of (c)(ii)

A plane starts from A and flies 150 km north east to B, then 100 km south east to C.

(a) How far east of A is C ?
(b) How far north of A is C ?
(c) What is the bearing of C from A ?

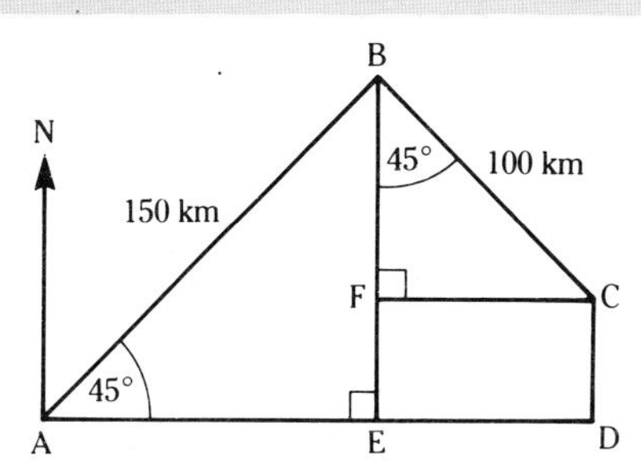

(a) AD is the distance C is east of A.

AD = AE + ED and ED = FC

We need to find AE from $\triangle$AEB and FC from $\triangle$BFC.

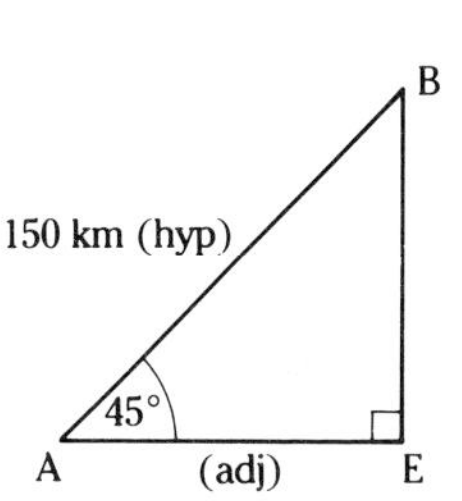

In $\triangle$AEB, $\hat{E} = 90°$ and $\dfrac{AE}{150} = \cos 45°$

$\therefore$ AE $= 150 \times \cos 45° = 106.06\ldots$

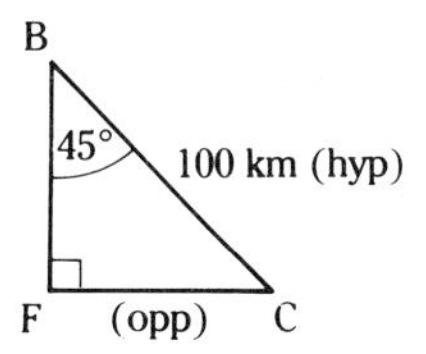

In $\triangle$BFC, $\hat{F} = 90°$ and $\dfrac{FC}{100} = \sin 45°$

i.e. FC $= 100 \times \sin 45° = 70.71\ldots$

$\therefore$ AD $= 106.06 + 70.71 = 176.77\ldots$

C is 176.8 km east of A, correct to 1 d.p.

(b) CD is the distance C is north of A.

CD = BE − FB

BE = AE = 106.06 $\triangle$ABE is isosceles

FB = FC = 70.71 $\triangle$FBC is isosceles

$\therefore$ CD $= 106.06 - 70.71 = 35.35$

C is 35.4 km north of A, correct to 1 d.p.

(c) The bearing is given by $N\hat{A}C$, so we need to find $C\hat{A}D$

In $\triangle$CAD, $\hat{D} = 90°$

$$\tan CAD = \frac{35.35}{176.77} = 0.1999\ldots$$

$C\hat{A}D = 11.30\ldots°$, $\therefore$ $N\hat{A}C = 78.70\ldots°$,

The bearing of C from A is 078.7° (1 d.p.)

When there is more than one triangle in a diagram, state which triangle you are using and which angle is the right-angle. Remember that Pythagoras' theorem can be used to find a third side if two sides are given.

17.

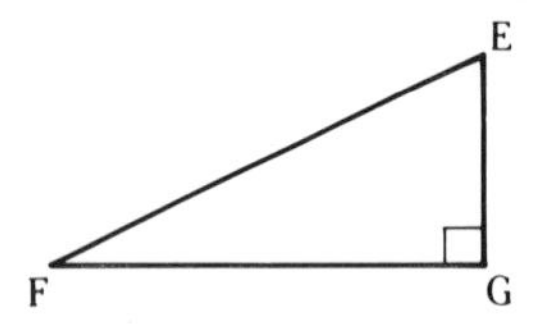

A vertical cliff EG is 30 m high. From a point F, on a level with the foot of the cliff, the angle of elevation of the top of the cliff is 15°.
How far is F from G?

18.

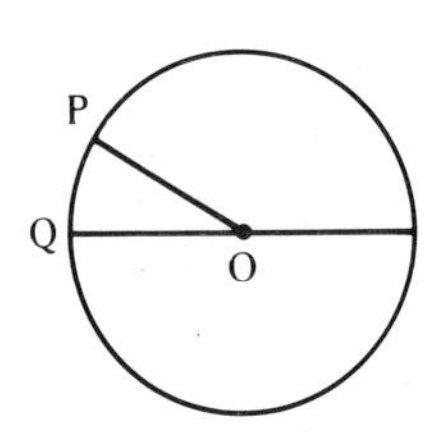

The chairoplane at a fair has a radius, OQ, of length 10 m.
A point P is 4 m above OQ.
Find angle POQ.

19. From A, Emma cycles 4 miles north east to B, then 6 miles north west to C.

(a) Find $B\hat{A}C$.

(b) How far is C from A?

(c) What is the bearing of C from A?

20.

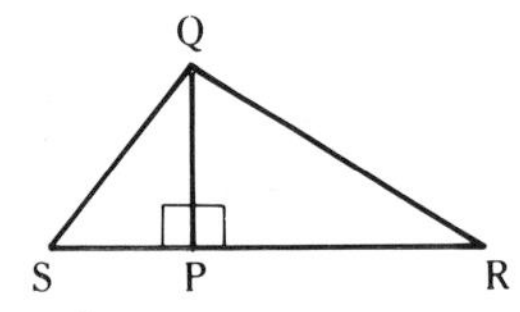

A flagpole PQ is 10 m high. S, P and R are on level ground. From R the angle of elevation of Q is 32°. From S the angle of elevation of Q is 50°. Find the distance from S to R.

21. From a point A on the shore, a boat B can be seen on a bearing of 060°. The bearing from A of a second boat C is 330°. B is 100 m from C and 70 m from A.

Find

(a) $B\hat{C}A$ (b) the bearing of B from C.

22. From A, a ship sails 60 km on a bearing of N 60 °W to B. It then changes course and sails 40 km on a bearing of N 30 °E to C.

(a) How far west of A is C?

(b) How far north of A is C?

(c) Find the bearing of C from A.

(d) How far is C from A?

23.

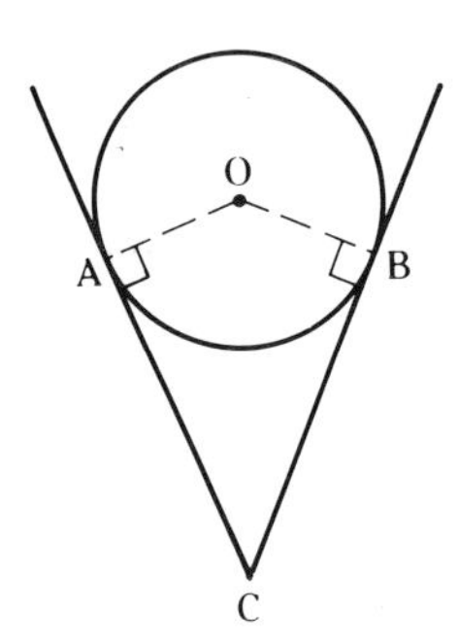

A sphere, of radius 4 cm and centre O, fits into a hollow cone, and $B\hat{C}A = 46°$.

Find

(a) AC (b) OC (c) AB.

24.

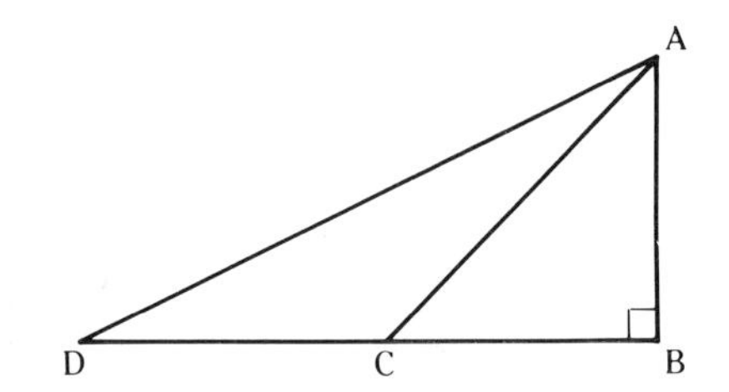

From A the angle of depression of C is 54° and of D is 39°. AB is 24 feet.

Find

(a) BC (b) DC (c) AD.

25. The points A(2, 2), B(6, 5), C(8, 1) are joined to form a triangle. Draw lines through A and C parallel to the x-axis and draw a line through B parallel to the y-axis to form several right-angled triangles.

Use two of these triangles to find $A\hat{B}C$.

26. The diagram shows a cross-section through an underground water main.

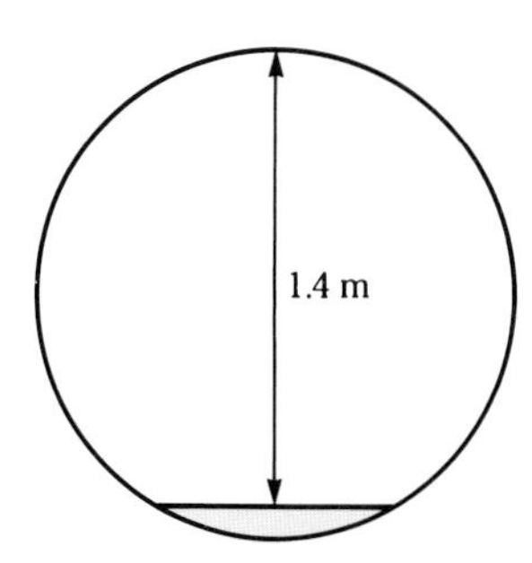

The pipe has a flat platform built into it to make maintenance easier. The cross-section is a circle whose diameter is 1.5 m.
Find the width of the platform.

27. The diagram shows a section through an underground railway tunnel.

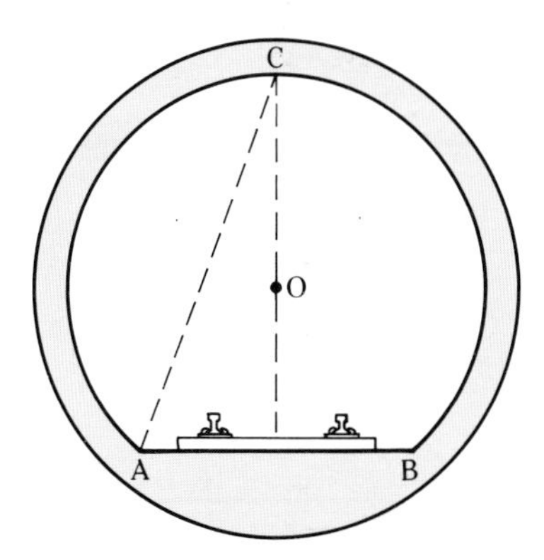

The 'floor' of the tunnel is 2 m wide and the angle of elevation of the highest point of the tunnel (C) from the edge of the floor (A) is 69 °.

(a) Draw a diagram showing just the inside wall and floor of the tunnel. Mark the points A, B, C and O which is the centre of the circle forming the inside wall.

(b) Calculate the height of the tunnel.

(c) Join AO and hence find the radius of the circular cross-section forming the inside of the tunnel.

28. The diagram shows the pack for a bar of chocolate. It is a prism whose cross-section is an isosceles right-angled triangle.

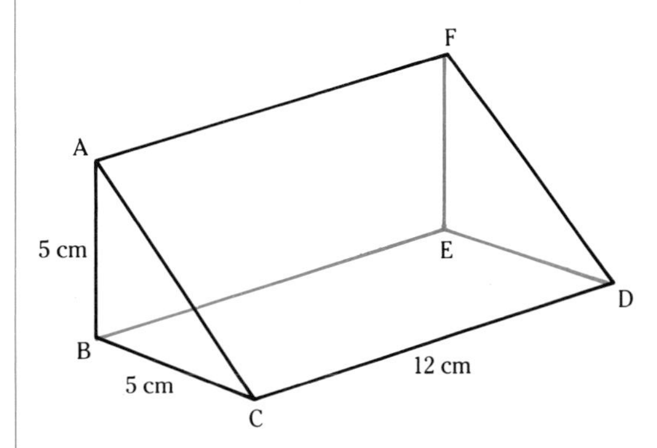

(a) Draw the base EBCD and find the length of BD.

(b) Draw the section through ABD and use it to find $A\hat{D}B$.

29.

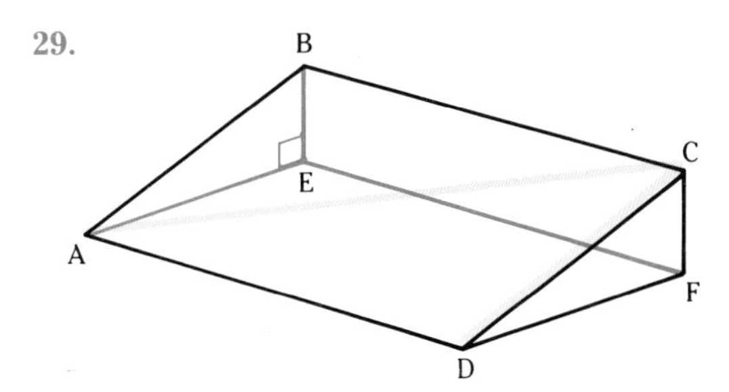

The diagram shows a prism which represents part of a hillside with two paths running to C; one path starts from A and the other path starts from D.
AD = 50 m, DF = 24 m, and CF = 8 m.

(a) (i) Draw ADFE
(ii) Find the length of AF.

(b) (i) Draw $\triangle$CDF
(ii) Find angle CDF.

(c) (i) Draw $\triangle$CAF
(ii) Find angle CAF.

(d) If you were walking up this hillside which path would you prefer to use to get to C and why ?

Self-Assessment 19

1. Give the sine, cosine and tangent of 58.4°

2. Find the angle
   (a) whose cosine is 0.382
   (b) whose sine is 0.741

3. In $\triangle ABC$, find $\widehat{A}$.

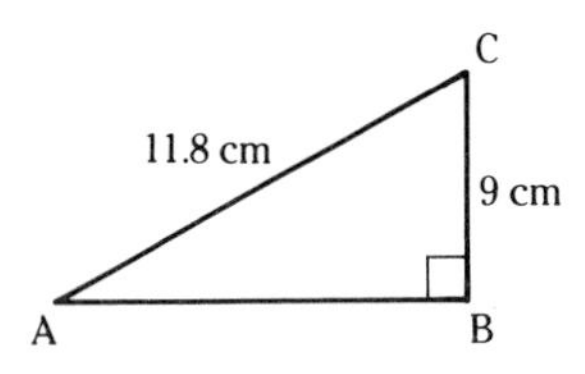

4. In $\triangle ABC$, $\widehat{A} = 90°$, $\widehat{C} = 62°$ and $AC = 5$ cm. Find AB.

5. In $\triangle LMN$, $LN = LM = 7$ cm and $MN = 6$ cm. Find $\widehat{M}$.

6. 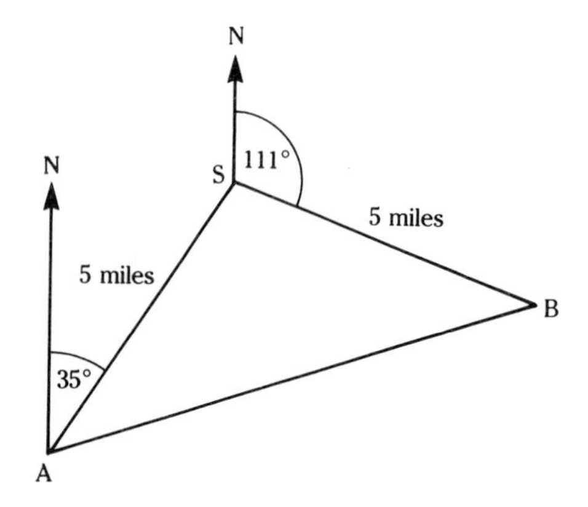

The bearing of ship S from point A is 035° and the bearing of point B from S is 111°. The ship is 5 miles both from A and from B.

Find
   (a) $A\widehat{S}B$
   (b) the distance of B from A
   (c) the bearing of B from A.

7. Town P is 30 miles north east of town Q and 20 miles north west of town R.
   (a) How far west of R is Q ?
   (b) How far south of R is Q ?
   (c) Give the bearing of Q from R.

8. 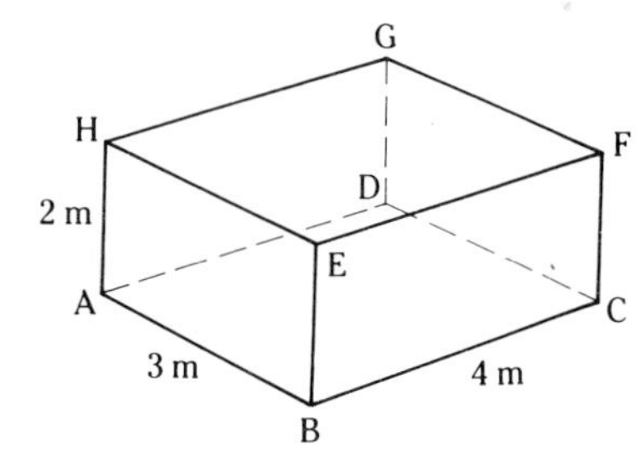

The dimensions of a cuboid are 2 m, 3 m and 4 m.
   (a) Find the length of AC.
   (b) Draw the section through A, C, F and H.
   (c) Hence find the angle between the diagonal HC and AC.

9. 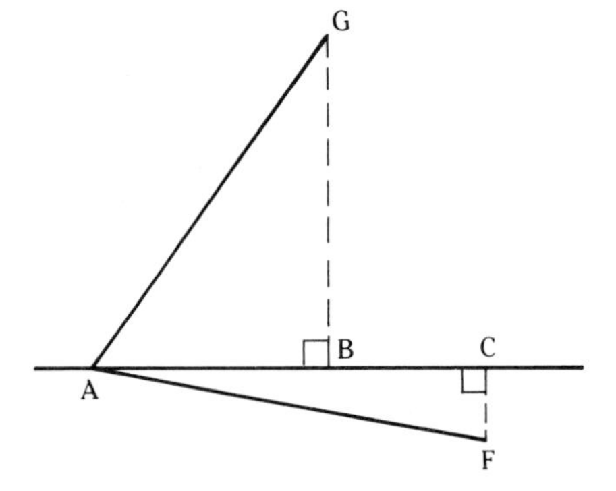

Anne is in a boat A, watching a gannet at G and a fish at F. At the instant when the angle of elevation of G from A is 52°, the angle of depression of F from A is 10° and $AG = AF = 30$ m, the gannet dives straight at the fish.

Find
   (a) AB and AC and hence BC
   (b) GB and CF and hence the vertical height of the gannet above the fish
   (c) Draw a suitable right angled triangle and find the angle of slope of the gannet's dive.

10. A company logo is in the shape of a symmetrical arrowhead and the designer has set it in a circle of radius 3 cm. The centre of the circle is O and $A\hat{O}B = 100°$.

(a) Find the distance between A and B.

(b) Find the length of (i) OD (ii) DE

(c) Find $C\hat{O}A$.

(d) Explain why $\triangle AOC$ is isosceles.

(e) Find the length of AC.

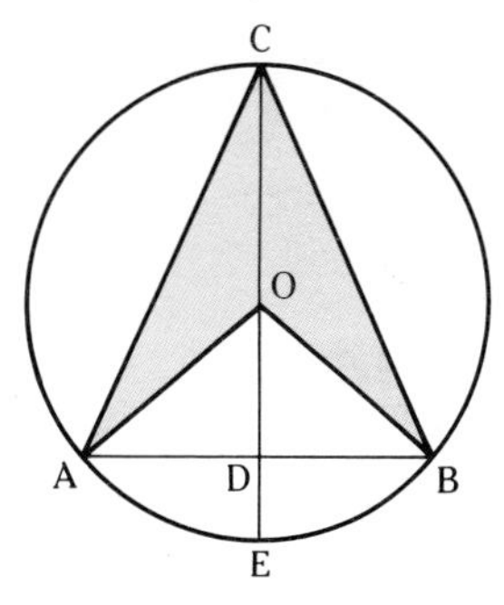

20 PRODUCTS AND FACTORS

PRODUCTS

We know that $2(x+4)$ means that both terms in the bracket are to be multiplied by 2, i.e. $2(x+4) = 2x+8$

In the same way, $x(x+4)$ means that both terms in the bracket are to be multiplied by x, i.e. $x(x+4) = x \times x + x \times 4 = x^2+4x$

Therefore an expression such as $3(x-2)-x(x-4)$ can be simplified by multiplying out the brackets and collecting like terms, i.e.

$$\begin{aligned} 3(x-2)-x(x-4) &= 3x-6-x^2-x(-4) \\ &= 3x-6-x^2+4x \\ &= 7x-6-x^2 \end{aligned}$$

THE PRODUCT OF TWO BRACKETS

Consider this problem.

A flat sheet of card measuring 8 cm by 10 cm is made into an open box by cutting out a square from each corner of the sheet and folding up the edges. The area of the base of the box depends on the size of the squares that are cut out, but if we take x cm as the length of the sides of these squares, we can find a formula for the area, $A\text{ cm}^2$, of the base.

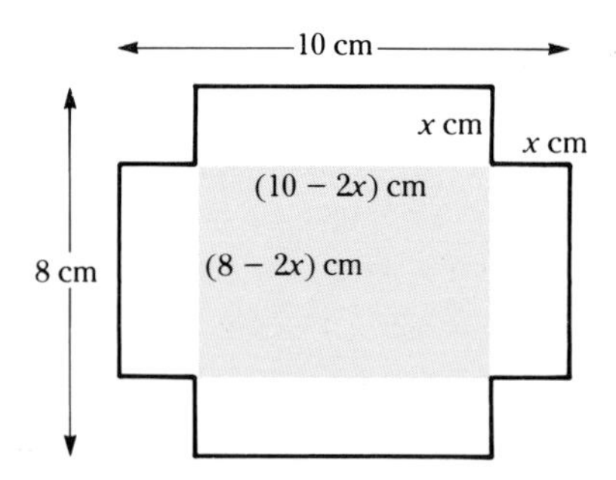

From the diagram, the length of the base is $(10-2x)$ cm and the width is $(8-2x)$ cm, so $A = (10-2x)(8-2x)$

Expressions such as $(10-2x)(8-2x)$ mean that each term in the second bracket is multiplied by each term in the first bracket, i.e.

$$\begin{aligned} (10-2x)(8-2x) &= 10(8-2x)-2x(8-2x) \\ &= 80-20x-16x+4x^2 \\ &= 80-36x+4x^2 \end{aligned}$$

The first line of working can be left out, but it is sensible to keep to this order, i.e. multiply

1. the first terms in each bracket
2. the outside terms
3. the inside terms
4. the second terms in each bracket.

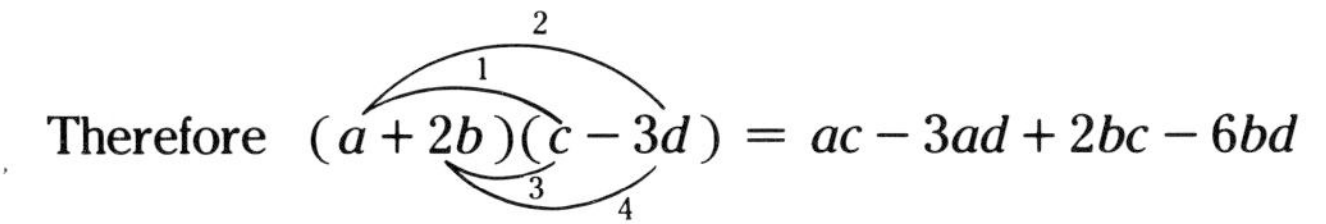

Therefore $(a+2b)(c-3d) = ac - 3ad + 2bc - 6bd$

Exercise 20a

1. Expand (i.e. multiply out the brackets)
   (a) $x(x-2)$
   (b) $3x(2-x)$
   (c) $2x(5-3x)$
   (d) $a(2a-5)$
   (e) $2p(1-p)$
   (f) $5a(2-3a)$
   (g) $2s(2s+5)$
   (h) $-x(x+2y)$
   (i) $2x(x+y)$
   (j) $-p(2q-3p)$
   (k) $2a(a-2b)$
   (l) $4s(3t-2s)$

2. Expand and simplify where possible
   (a) $2(x+3)+x(x-3)$
   (b) $3x(x-3)-4(2x+6)$
   (c) $4x-x(2+x)$
   (d) $2a(b+c)-2(b+2c)$
   (e) $2x(x-1)-x(2x+1)$
   (f) $-x(2-x)+2x(3-2x)$

3. Expand and simplify where possible
   (a) $(x+2)(x+3)$
   (b) $(x-2)(x+4)$
   (c) $(2x+3)(x-5)$
   (d) $(3x+1)(2x+4)$
   (e) $(2x-3)(x-7)$
   (f) $(a+b)(a-c)$
   (g) $(p+q)(s-t)$
   (h) $(x-y)(x-2z)$
   (i) $(x-2y)(x-3y)$
   (j) $(a+2b)(a-b)$
   (k) $(2p-q)(2p+q)$
   (l) $(3x+2y)(2x+z)$

In question 3 above, some expansions simplify and some do not. The terms in the brackets of those that do simplify involve the same letters. The following expansions all simplify.

4. Expand and simplify
   (a) $(x+4)(x+1)$
   (b) $(x+1)(x+2)$
   (c) $(a+1)(a+5)$
   (d) $(a+3)(a+5)$
   (e) $(t+7)(t+3)$
   (f) $(p+5)(p+2)$
   (g) $(x+6)(x+8)$
   (h) $(x+10)(x+3)$

5. Expand and simplify
   (a) $(x-2)(x-3)$
   (b) $(x-4)(x-3)$
   (c) $(x-2)(x-5)$
   (d) $(a-1)(a-4)$
   (e) $(s-4)(s-5)$
   (f) $(x-6)(x-7)$
   (g) $(p-4)(p-6)$
   (h) $(t-8)(t-4)$

6. Expand and simplify
   (a) $(x-2)(x+6)$
   (b) $(x+3)(x-2)$
   (c) $(x-4)(x+3)$
   (d) $(x-3)(x+5)$
   (e) $(t+6)(t-8)$
   (f) $(p+3)(p-5)$
   (g) $(a+3)(a-7)$
   (h) $(x-4)(x+9)$
   (i) $(x+7)(x-3)$
   (j) $(y-2)(y+1)$

7. (a) $(3x+5)(x-2)$
   (b) $(2x-7)(3x+1)$
   (c) $(2s+3)(2s-5)$
   (d) $(4x-3)(2x+7)$
   (e) $(3x+1)(3x-1)$
   (f) $(7x-5)(2x+1)$
   (g) $(5x-1)(7x+1)$
   (h) $(3x+1)(5x-1)$
   (i) $(2a+5)(2a-5)$

8. (a) $(5t+3)(3t+2)$
   (b) $(4x-3)(3x+8)$
   (c) $(8x+1)(2x-5)$
   (d) $(5a-3)(2a-7)$
   (e) $(3-x)(2-x)$
   (f) $(5+2y)(1+y)$
   (g) $(12+x)(2-3x)$
   (h) $(2+x)(5-2x)$
   (i) $(6-5y)(4-3y)$

Squaring a Bracket

$$(x+3)^2 \quad \text{means} \quad (x+3)(x+3)$$

Similarly $\quad (x+a)^2 = (x+a)(x+a)$

$= x^2 + xa + ax + a^2$

$= x^2 + 2ax + a^2 \quad$ since xa is the same as ax

Therefore $\quad (x+3)^2 = x^2 + 6x + 9$

Also $\quad (x-a)^2 = (x-a)(x-a)$

$= x^2 - xa - ax + a^2$

$= x^2 - 2ax + a^2$

Therefore $\quad (x-5)^2 = x^2 - 10x + 25$

The Difference Between Two Squares

When two brackets have the same terms but different signs, their product simplifies to just two terms, i.e.

$$(x+a)(x-a) = x^2 - xa + ax - a^2$$
$$= x^2 - a^2$$

This expression is called the difference between two squares.

Exercise 20b

1. Expand
   (a) $(x+1)^2$
   (b) $(x+2)^2$
   (c) $(y+4)^2$
   (d) $(a+7)^2$
   (e) $(x+y)^2$
   (f) $(a+b)^2$
   (g) $(p+q)^2$
   (h) $(x+8)^2$

2. Expand
   (a) $(x-1)^2$
   (b) $(x-5)^2$
   (c) $(t-9)^2$
   (d) $(p-6)^2$
   (e) $(x-y)^2$
   (f) $(a-b)^2$
   (g) $(y-7)^2$
   (h) $(x-9)^2$

3. Expand
   (a) $(x+1)(x-1)$
   (b) $(x-4)(x+4)$
   (c) $(c+2)(c-2)$
   (d) $(y-5)(y+5)$
   (e) $(x+y)(x-y)$
   (f) $(a+b)(a-b)$
   (g) $(x-7)(x+7)$
   (h) $(t-6)(t+6)$

Expand $\quad (2x-5)^2$

$(2x-5)^2$
$= (2x)^2 - (2x)(5) - (2x)(5) + 5^2$
$= 4x^2 - 20x + 25$

4. Expand
   (a) $(3x+1)^2$
   (b) $(5x-2)^2$
   (c) $(3y+2)^2$
   (d) $(2a-3)^2$
   (e) $(3x-1)^2$
   (f) $(4x+3)^2$

5. Expand
   (a) $(2x-7)(2x+7)$
   (b) $(3x-1)(3x+1)$
   (c) $(4x+5)(4x-5)$
   (d) $(2a+7)(2a-7)$

FACTORISING

So far in this chapter we have started with a product and multiplied it out. It is often necessary to reverse this process, i.e. to express an algebraic expression as a product of factors. This is called *factorising*.

Common Factors

Consider the expression $2x+6y$

The first term can be written as $2\times x$ and the second term as $2\times 3y$

i.e. $2x+6y = 2\times x + 2\times 3y$ [1]

Thus 2 is a factor of each term in the expression, and we say that 2 is a *common factor*.

It is known that $2(x+3y) = 2\times x + 2\times 3y$ [2]

Therefore $2x+6y = 2(x+3y)$

i.e. we have *factorised* $2x+6y$ by 'taking out' the common factor.
Note that a factorisation can (and should) be checked by expanding the brackets.

Exercise 20c

1. Factorise

(a) $3x+6$	(c) $6a-9$	(e) $10p-5$	(g) $6-15a$	(i) $12x-9y$
(b) $4y-8$	(d) $2a+4b$	(f) $8-12x$	(h) $2a+4b$	(j) $8q-18p$

Factorise (a) y^2+3y (b) $6xy-4yz$ (c) x^3-x^2+x

(a) $y^2+3y = y\times y + 3\times y = y(y+3)$

(b) $6xy-4yz = 2y\times 3x - 2y\times 2z = 2y(3x-2z)$

(c) $x^3-x^2+x = x\times x^2 - x\times x + x\times 1 = x(x^2-x+1)$

Note that the middle step can be done mentally; it is written down here to help explain the thinking involved.

Note also that when an expression has more than one common factor, as is the case in (b), it may be that only one of these factors is noticed. A check for further common factors in the expression in the bracket should reveal any that have been overlooked. The working might then look like this:

$$6xy-4yz = 2(3xy-2yz) = 2y(3x-2z)$$

2. Factorise

(a) x^2+3x	(c) y^2-2y	(e) $4a-a^2$	(g) $4b^2-b$
(b) b^2+6b	(d) $3x^2+2x$	(f) x^2-4x	(h) $p-p^2$

3. Factorise
   (a) $3x^2+6x+9$
   (b) $10x^2-5x-20$
   (c) $16-12x-20x^2$
   (d) $5xy-2xz+3x$
   (e) $ab-2ac+4ad$
   (f) $3y^3+6y^2-9y$

4. Factorise
   (a) $2x^2-4x$
   (b) $5xy+10xz$
   (c) x^2+x^3
   (d) $8abc-12bcd$
   (e) $3xy+6y^2-9y$
   (f) $5ab+10bc-5bd$

5. Factorise
   (a) $mg-ma$
   (b) $2\pi r+\pi rh$
   (c) $\pi R^2-\pi r^2$
   (d) $2rh_1-2rh_2$
   (e) $\frac{1}{2}mu^2-\frac{1}{2}mv^2$
   (f) $2\pi rh+\pi r^2$
   (g) ax^2-bx^2
   (h) $\frac{1}{2}ah-\frac{1}{2}bh$
   (i) πr^2+4r+r^2
   (j) ax^2+a^2x
   (k) $P+\dfrac{PRT}{100}$
   (l) $mgh-\frac{1}{2}mv^2$

CHANGING THE SUBJECT OF A FORMULA

Sometimes when changing the subject of a formula, the required letter appears in more than one term. In this case it may be possible to collect the terms containing that letter on one side of the formula and then take it out as a common factor.

For example, to make r the subject of the formula $A=\pi rl+\pi rh$, we see that r is a common factor of the terms on the right-hand side. We can factorise that side to give

$$A=r(\pi l+\pi h)$$

Now we can divide both sides by $(\pi l+\pi h)$, i.e. $\pi(l+h)$, to give

$$\frac{A}{\pi(l+h)}=r,\quad \text{i.e.}\quad r=\frac{A}{\pi(l+h)}$$

When changing the subject of a formula, start by expanding any brackets and eliminating any fractions. Then collect terms containing the required letter on one side and all other terms on the other side.

Exercise 20d

1. Make the letter in the bracket the subject of the formula.
   (a) $T=2p+ph$ (p)
   (b) $M=Cn-3C$ (C)
   (c) $g=hl-\pi hr$ (r)
   (d) $V=a^2r+\pi ahr$ (r)
   (e) $r^2=v(h-a)$ (a)
   (f) $A=2\pi r(h_1-h_2)$ (h_1)

2. Solve these equations for x (i.e. make x the subject).
   (a) $ax=b-cx$
   (b) $ax-r=bx+q$
   (c) $a-bx=c+dx$
   (d) $x(b-c)=ax+b$
   (e) $a-b(x-a)=ax$
   (f) $x(a-b)=a(b-x)$

The formulae in question 3 are a mixture of the types considered in Chapters 7 and 15 as well as those considered here.

It is important to realise that the square of an expression such as $a+b$ is $(a+b)^2$; conversely $\sqrt{(a^2+b^2)}$ is *not* $a+b$.

3. Make the letter in the bracket the subject.
(a) $A = \pi r^2 + \pi rh$ (h)
(b) $v^2 = u^2 + 2as$ (u)
(c) $s = ut + \frac{1}{2}at^2$ (a)
(d) $R = r - \frac{1}{p}$ (p)
(e) $s = \frac{t}{2}(u+v)$ (v)
(f) $X = a + \sqrt{y}$ (y)

Investigation

A triangle has sides of lengths n^2+1, n^2-1 and $2n$.

If we give n the value 4, we get a triangle whose sides are 17, 15 and 8 units long.

(a) Use Pythagoras' theorem to show that this triangle is right-angled.

(b) Give other values to n and investigate the resulting triangles.

(c) Comment on your results to (b).

(d) Investigate triangles whose sides are of lengths n^2+4, n^2-4 and $4n$.

Self-Assessment 20

1. Expand and simplify
(a) $4x(3-2x)$
(b) $2(3-x)-x(x-8)$
(c) $(3x-4)(2x+3)$
(d) $(2x-3)^2$
(e) $(2a-b)(2a+b)$
(f) $(12+x)(4-3x)$

2. Factorise
(a) $10a-5b$
(b) $3xy-9yz$
(c) $2\pi r_1 - 2\pi r_2$
(d) $4p-36q$
(e) $\pi rh - \pi r^2$
(f) $7b^2-14b$

3. Make v the subject of the formula
(a) $T = \dfrac{d}{v-u}$
(b) $2v = 5v - at$
(c) $2vt = a(v+t)$
(d) $u^2 = v^2 + 2as$

21 CURVED GRAPHS

GRAPHS FROM TABLES

Graphs are used to give a visual representation of information about two, related, varying quantities.

Before a graph can be drawn it is necessary to know how the quantities vary. Sometimes this information is given in a table, while at other times a formula is given that connects the varying quantities. The following example shows how to draw a clear, informative graph.

The staff at a botanical garden collected data for one of their trees. This data is given in the following table:

Age of tree in years	0.8	1.6	2.4	3.8	5	6.8	7.9
Girth of tree in cm	14	19.9	25.1	32.2	38	44.1	47.5

To draw a graph to represent this data we must:

(a) draw axes that intersect at 90° in the bottom left-hand corner of the graph paper

(b) mark the scale used on each axis (Put time along the horizontal axis and the girth along the vertical axis.)

(c) name the axes

(d) plot carefully the points representing the data given in the table (Use a dot for each point.)

(e) draw a smooth curve to pass through the points

(f) give the graph a title.

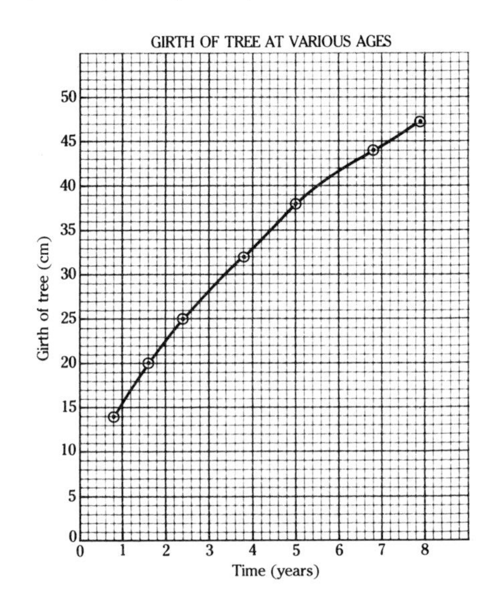

This graph can be used to find various facts relating the girth (distance round the tree) of the tree to time. For example, when the tree is one year old its girth is 15.5 cm; the time taken for its girth to double from the time of the first measurement is another 2.2 years, etc.

Points to Remember when Drawing Graphs

When curved graphs are being drawn the following advice should be kept clearly in mind.

1. Do not take too few points. About eight or ten are usually required.
2. To decide where to draw the y-axis look at the range of x-values, and vice versa.

3. In some questions you will be given most of the y-values but you may have to calculate a few more for yourself. If so, always plot first those points that you were given and, from these, get an idea of the shape of the curve. Then you can plot the points you calculated and see if they fit on to the curve you have in mind. If they do not, go back and check your calculations. Always have a clear idea of the shape of the resulting curve before you begin to draw it.

4. When you draw a smooth curve to pass through the points, always turn the page into a position where your wrist is on the inside of the curve.

Exercise 21a

1. An agricultural research centre experimented with fertilizer to find how varying rates of application (lb/acre) affected the weight of the crop of wheat. The results are illustrated in the graph.

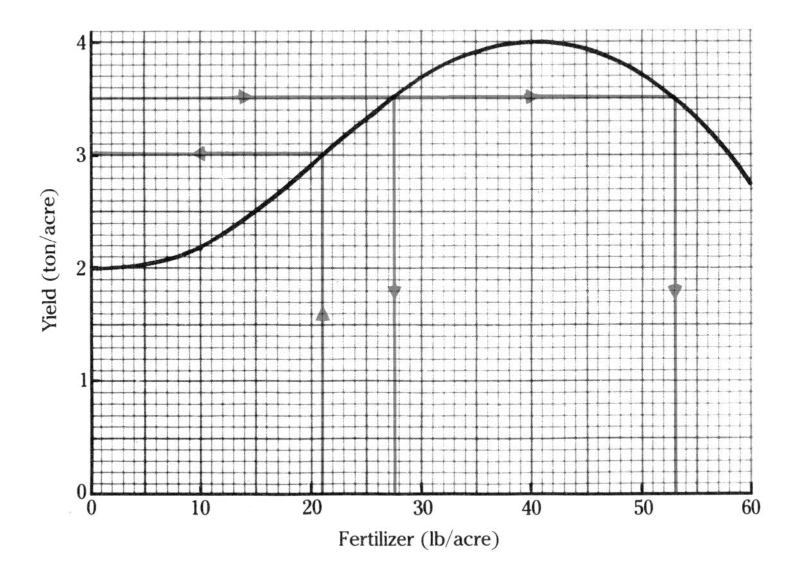

Use the guide lines to find

(a) the number of tons of wheat per acre that can be expected when fertilizer is applied at the rate of 21 lb/acre

(b) the quantity of fertilizer in lb/acre that gives a yield of 3.5 tons/acre.

Lay a transparent ruler on the graph to act as a guide line to find

(c) the yield when fertilizer is used at the rate of 35 lb/acre

(d) the rate at which fertilizer is applied to give a yield of 3.7 tons/acre.

(e) Why do you think that the yield decreases when more than a certain quantity of fertilizer is used ?

2. When a sum of money is invested, the interest added to the original value gives an increased value called the amount. The table shows the amount (A) when £100 has been invested for T years at 12% per year compound interest.

T	0	1	2	3	4	5	6	7	8	9
A	100	112	125	140	157	176	197	221	248	277

Draw the graph connecting A and T. Take 2 cm as 1 unit for T and 5 cm as 50 units for A. From your graph find

(a) the amount after (i) $4\frac{1}{2}$ years (ii) $8\frac{1}{4}$ years

(b) the time, in years, in which £100 will double in value.

3. The table shows the weight, W tonnes, which a multi-fibre wire of diameter d centimetres will support before breaking.

d	1.2	1.8	2.2	2.6	2.8	3	3.4	3.8
W	72	162	242	338	392	450	578	722

Draw a graph for values of d from 0 to 4. Take 4 cm as 1 unit for d and 1 cm as 50 units for W. Use your graph to find

(a) the greatest weight that a wire of diameter 2 cm will support

(b) the smallest diameter of wire that will support a load of 500 t.

4. The table gives values for the total external surface area, A cm^2, of a closed rectangular packing case, which has square ends of side b cm.

b (cm)	1	1.5	2	3	4	5	6
A (cm^2)	110	76.5	62	54	59	71.6	90

Draw a graph connecting A and b taking 4 cm to represent 1 unit on the b-axis and 1 cm to represent 5 units on the A-axis. Let 40 (instead of 0) be the lowest value on the A-axis.
Use your graph to find

(a) the value of b that gives the lowest value of A

(b) the value of A when b is (i) 2.2 (ii) 5.3

Water in a saucepan cools down. The graph shows how its temperature is changing.

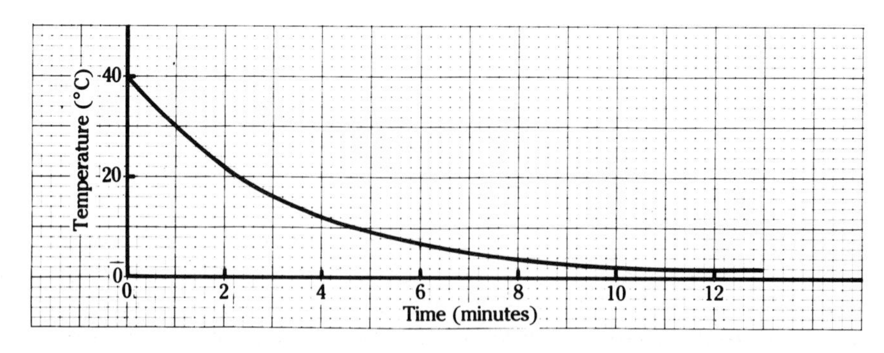

(a) What is the temperature of the water after (i) 4 minutes (ii) 8 minutes?

(b) How long does it take to cool down to 14°C?

CONSTRUCTING A TABLE FROM A FORMULA

In each question in the exercise above the data was given in a table. Sometimes, however, a formula connecting the variables is given and from it a table has to be constructed.

Consider a coin that is dropped, from rest, down a vertical mine shaft such that after t seconds it has fallen s metres. Suppose that the formula connecting s and t for the first 6 seconds of the fall is $s = 5t^2$ and a graph is required to show this relationship. Before a graph can be drawn, we must work out some corresponding values of s and t.

Taking half-unit values of t from 0 to 6 gives the values in the following table. Each value of s is calculated correct to the nearest whole number, for example if $t = 4.5$, $s = 5 \times 4.5^2 = 5 \times 20.25 = 101.25 = 101$ to the nearest integer.

t	0	0.5	1	1.5	2	2.5	3	3.5	4	4.5	5	5.5	6
s	0	1	5	11	20	31	45	61	80	101	125	151	180

We plot time (t) along the horizontal and distance (s) on the vertical axis.

When all the points have been plotted, draw a smooth curve through them. The resulting graph is shown in the diagram. From this graph we can find s for any given value of t from 0 to 6, e.g. the distance the coin falls in 3.7 s is 68 m. Similarly, the time to fall 135 m is 5.2 s.

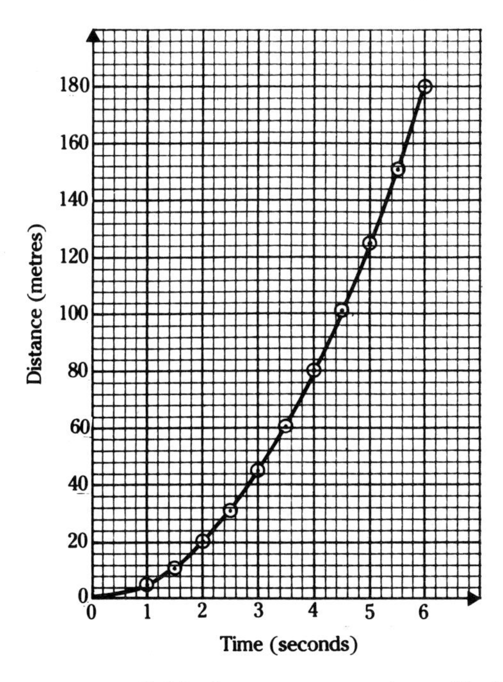

There are graphics programs available for computers that will plot curves and give the coordinates of points of intersection as accurately as anyone could want. There are even pocket calculators on the market which have this facility. If you have access to one of these, you may like to use it to answer some of the following questions. If you explore these graphics capabilities further, you will find that you can do many of the remaining questions in this chapter far more accurately than it is possible to do by drawing.

Exercise 21b

1. Copy and complete the following table giving values of y for values of x from 1 to 5 where $y = 3x^2$.

x	1	2	3	4	5
y	3	12			75

Using a scale of 2 cm for 1 unit on the horizontal x-axis and a scale of 2 cm for 10 units on the vertical y-axis, draw the graph $y = 3x^2$ for values of x from 1 to 5

Use your graph to find the value of y when $x = 2.5$ and the value of x when $y = 8$

2. The area, $A\text{ cm}^2$, covered by mould growing on a culture dish is measured daily and for the first six days it is found that $A = \frac{1}{2}d^2$ where d is the number of days that have passed since the culture was seeded.

Copy and complete the following table.

d	0	1	2	3	4	5	6
A	0	$\frac{1}{2}$	2			12.5	

Using a scale of 2 cm for 1 unit on the horizontal axis for d and a scale of 1 cm for 1 unit on the vertical axis for A, draw the graph of $A = \frac{1}{2}d^2$ and use it to find d when $A = 4$
If 1 day is 24 hours, in how many hours does the area of mould increase from 2 cm^2 to 4 cm^2?

3. A car starts from rest and travels a distance D metres in t seconds, where $D = 40\sqrt{t}$. Construct a table to show the corresponding values of D and t, for values of t from 0 to 10, at unit intervals. Use these values to draw a graph, and use your graph to find

(a) how far the car travels in the first 4.4 seconds

(b) the time taken to travel 100 m.

4. Copy and complete the following table, which shows values of $\dfrac{6}{Q}$ for values of Q from 1 to 6 at unit intervals.

Q	1	2	3	4	5	6
$6/Q$	6		2	1.5		1

Hence draw the graph of $P = \dfrac{6}{Q}$ within the given range taking 2 cm as 1 unit on both axes.

Use your graph to write down

(a) the value of P when $Q = 2.8$

(b) the value of Q when $P = 4.6$

5. Draw the graph of $y = x^3 + 4$ for values of x from -4 to 4 at half-unit intervals. Mark your y-axis from -60 to 70. Use your graph to find

(a) the value of y when $x = 2.7$

(b) the value of x when $y = 40$

(c) the value of y when $x = -1.5$

(d) the value of x when $y = -30$

Make a table to show the values of $x^2 - 3x - 4$ for whole number values of x from -2 to 5. Hence draw the graph of $y = x^2 - 3x - 4$ for this range of values of x.

Use your graph to find

(a) the lowest value of $x^2 - 3x - 4$ and the corresponding value of x

(b) the value of x when $x^2 - 3x - 4$ is (i) 0 (ii) 4.

(c) the value of $x^2 - 3x - 4$ when $x = 2.5$

Calculate the value of $x^2 - 3x - 4$ when $x = 2.5$ and compare your answer with the reading you took from the graph in part (c).

x	-2	-1	0	1	2	3	4	5
x^2	4	1	0	1	4	9	16	25
$-3x$	6	3	0	-3	-6	-9	-12	-15
-4	-4	-4	-4	-4	-4	-4	-4	-4
$x^2 - 3x - 4$	6	0	-4	-6	-6	-4	0	6

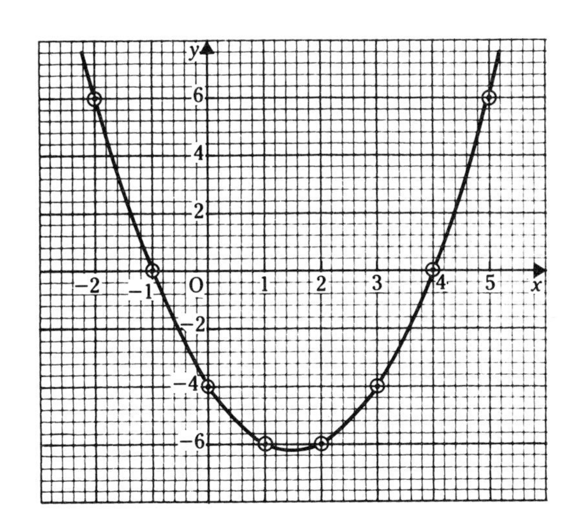

(a) From the graph, the lowest value of $x^2 - 3x - 4$ is -6.25. This occurs when $x = 1.5$

(b) (i) The values of x when $x^2 - 3x - 4$ is 0 are -1 and 4

(ii) The values of x when $x^2 - 3x - 4$ is 4 are -1.70 and 4.70

(c) From the graph: when $x = 2.5$, $x^2 - 3x - 4 = -5.2$

When $x = 2.5$

$$\begin{aligned} x^2 - 3x - 4 &= 2.5^2 - 3 \times 2.5 - 4 \\ &= 6.25 - 7.5 - 4 \\ &= -5.25 \end{aligned}$$

This value is very close to the reading taken in part (c).

Keep the following graphs as you may need them in later exercises.

6. Complete the following table, which gives the values of $x(3-x)$ for values of x in the range -1 to 4 at half-unit intervals.

x	-1	-0.5	0	0.5	1	1.5	2	2.5	3	3.5	4
$3-x$	4			2.5		1.5					-1
$x(3-x)$	-4			1.25		2.25					-4

Hence draw the graph of $y = x(3-x)$ within the given range taking 2 cm as the unit on both axes. Use your graph to write down

(a) the highest value of $3x - x^2$ and the value of x for which it occurs

(b) the values of x where the graph crosses the x-axis

(c) the values of x when $x(3-x) = 1$ (i.e. when $y = 1$).

7. Copy and complete the following table, which gives the values of $(x+1)(x-1)(x-3)$ for values of x between -2 and $+4$.

x	-2	-1.5	-1	-0.5	0	0.5	1	1.5	2	2.5	3	3.5	4
$(x+1)(x-1)(x-3)$	-15	-5.6	0	2.6	3	1.9		-1.9	-3			5.6	15

Hence draw the graph of $y = (x+1)(x-1)(x-3)$ for values of x between -2 and $+4$. Use your graph to find

(a) the values of x where the graph crosses the x-axis

(b) the value(s) of x when y is (i) 1 (ii) -8

(c) the highest value of $(x+1)(x-1)(x-3)$ within the range $-1 \leqslant x \leqslant 3$ and the value of x for which this highest value occurs.

(d) Are there any values of x for the graph you have drawn for which $(x+1)(x-1)(x-3)$ is greater than the highest value you have given for (c)? If so, give one.

8. Copy and complete the following table, which gives values of $\frac{8}{x}$ for values of x from -8 to -1 and from 1 to 8.

x	-8	-7	-6	-5	-4	-3	-2	-1	1	2	3	4	5	6	7	8
$\frac{8}{x}$	-1	-1.1	-1.3	-1.6							2.67	2				

Hence draw the graph of $y = \frac{8}{x}$ within the given ranges. Use 1 cm to represent 1 unit on both axes.

(a) How many lines of symmetry does this curve have?
Show any lines of symmetry on your diagram.

(b) Why is there no point on the graph when $x = 0$?

(c) Use your graph to find the value of y when x is (i) 4.2 (ii) -3.4

(d) Use your graph to find the value of x when y is (i) 4.2 (ii) -3.4

Draw the graph of $y = x^2 + 4x + 3$ for half-unit values of x from -4 to 0. Use your graph to find the lowest value of $x^2 + 4x + 3$, and the corresponding value of x.
Draw, on the same axes, the graph of $y = x + 2$. Write down the values of x at the points of intersection of the two graphs. Use your graphs to find the range of values of x for which $x^2 + 4x + 3$ is less than $x + 2$.

x	-4	-3.5	-3	-2.5	-2	-1.5	-1	-0.5	0
$y = x^2 + 4x + 3$	3	1.25	0	-0.75	-1	-0.75	0	1.25	3

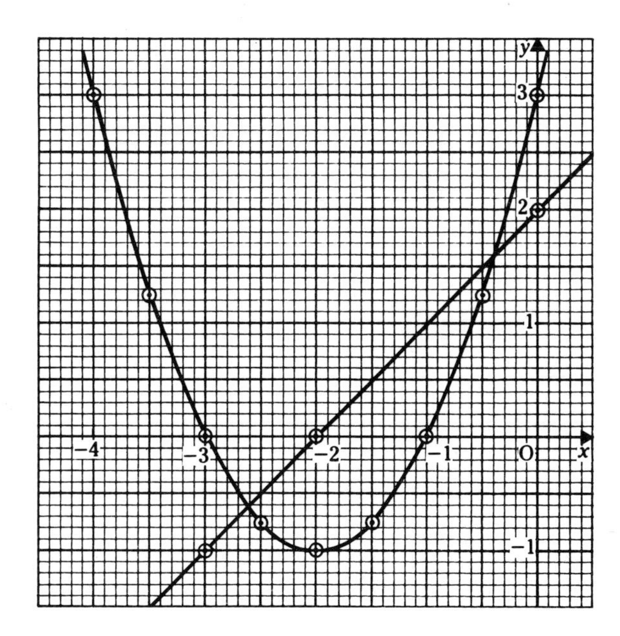

From the graph the lowest value of $x^2 + 4x + 3$ is -1, which occurs when $x = -2$.

The graph of $y = x + 2$ is a straight line so we take only three values of x and find the corresponding values of y.

x	-3	-2	0
$y(= x + 2)$	-1	0	2

The graphs intersect when $x = -2.6$ and -0.4

From -2.6 to -0.4 the curve, which has equation $y = x^2 + 4x + 3$, is below the straight line $y = x + 2$

Therefore $x^2 + 4x + 3 < x + 2$ for x greater than -2.6 but less than -0.4

9. Copy and complete the following table, which gives values of $9x - x^2$ for values of x in the range -2 to 10.

x	-2	-1	0	1	2	3	4	5	6	7	8	9	10
$9x - x^2$	-22		0	8	14	18	20		18	14			-10

Using 1 cm as 1 unit for x and 2 cm as 5 units for y, draw the graph of $y = 9x - x^2$
On the same axes draw the graph of $y = 5x - 10$
Write down the range of values of x for which $9x - x^2$ is greater than $5x - 10$

10. Use the graph of $y = \frac{8}{x}$, drawn for question 8 for this question.
On the same axes draw the graph of $y = 8 - x$

(a) Write down the values of x at the points where the graphs intersect.

(b) For what values of x on your graph is $8 - x$ greater than $\frac{8}{x}$?

CURVE SKETCHING

Quadratic Graphs

The most important family of curves we consider are given by equations of the form

$$y = ax^2 + bx + c \quad (a \neq 0)$$

These are quadratic curves and all have the same basic shape and are called *parabolas*.

We have seen that if a is positive the vertex is at the bottom and there is no highest point. On the other hand, if a is negative the vertex is at the top and there is no lowest point.

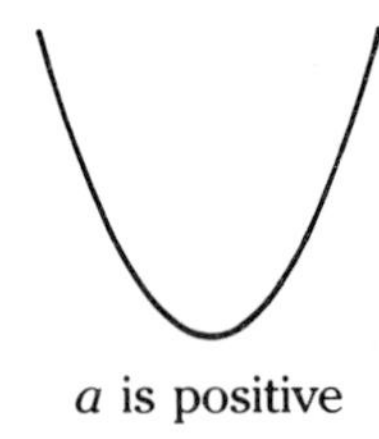

a is positive

a is negative

Cubic Graphs

All graphs that have equations of the type

$$y = ax^3 + bx^2 + cx + d \quad (a \neq 0)$$

are curves of the same general shape.
They are called *cubic curves*.

If a is positive they look

like this

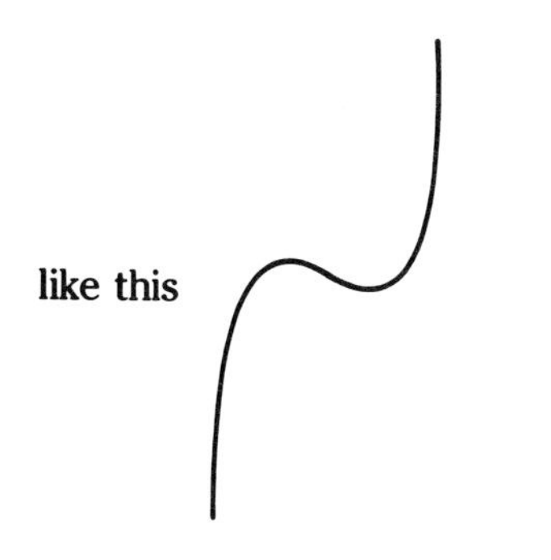

or this or

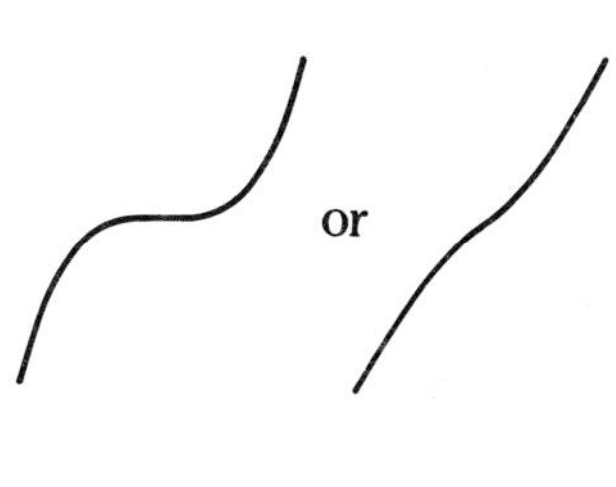

while if a is negative they look

like this

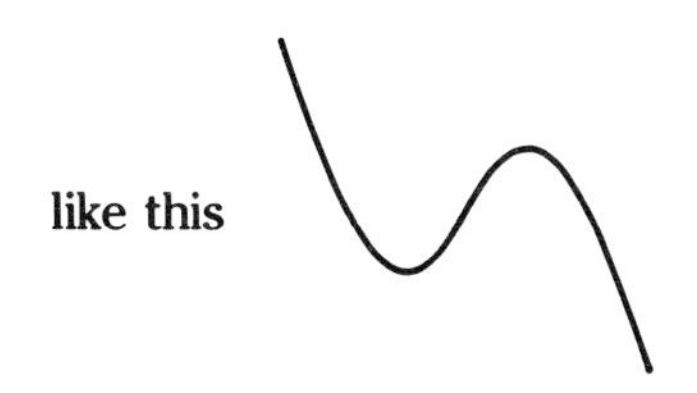

or this

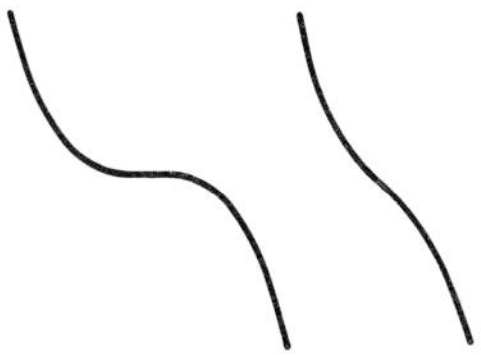

Notice that every cubic curve has a kink in it. Sometimes the kink is a double bend like the diagrams on the left. Sometimes the kink is hardly noticeable, like the diagrams on the right.

Equations of the Form $y = \frac{a}{x}$

Equations of the form $y = \frac{a}{x}$ give distinctive 'two part' curves.

There is no value of y when $x = 0$.

If a is positive the curve looks like this

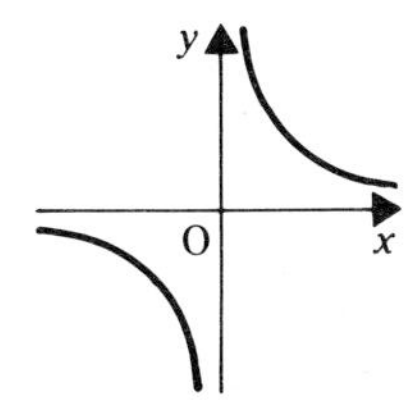

while if a is negative it looks like this

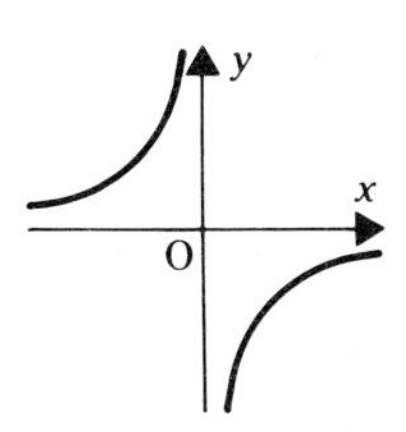

A curve of this type is called a *hyperbola*.

Exercise 21c

This sketch shows the graph of $y = x^2 + 8x + 12$

Find the coordinates of C.

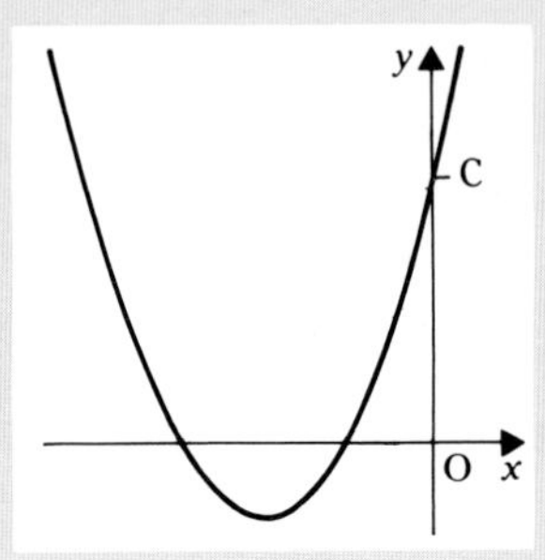

The graph cuts the y-axis where $x = 0$

When $x = 0$, $y = (0)^2 + 8(0) + 12 = 12$

The coordinates of C are $(0, 12)$.

1.

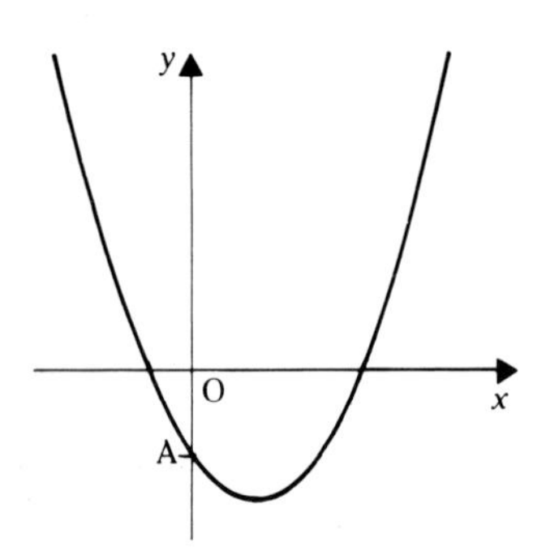

The sketch shows the graph of

$$y = x^2 - 2x - 8$$

Find the coordinates of A.

2. Sketch, on the same axes, the graphs of

   (i) $y = x^2$

   (ii) $y = x^2 - 4$

   (iii) $y = 4 - x^2$,
   clearly distinguishing between them.

   Describe a transformation that

   (a) maps the first curve to the second

   (b) maps the second curve to the third.

3.

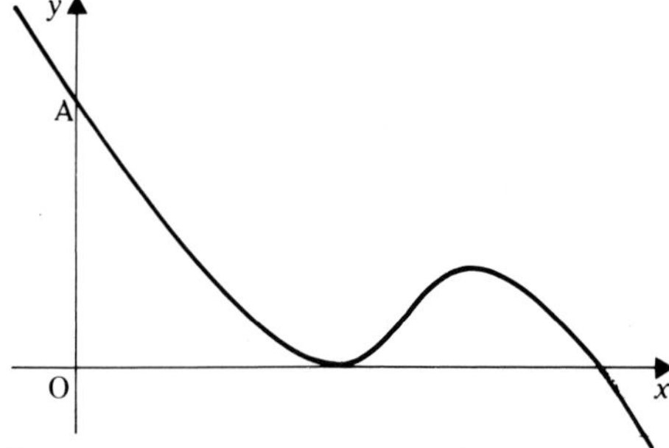

The sketch shows the graph of
$$y = (4 - x)(x - 2)^2$$
Find the coordinates of A.

4. Sketch the graph of $y = \frac{1}{x}$ for values of x from -10 to $-\frac{1}{10}$ and from $\frac{1}{10}$ to 10.

   (a) What happens to the value of y as the value of x increases beyond 10 ?

   (b) Is there a value of y for which $x = 0$?

   (c) Is there a value of x for which $y = 0$?

5. Sketch, on separate axes, the graphs of (i) $y = \frac{8}{x}$ (ii) $y = -\frac{8}{x}$. Show clearly the two parts of each curve.

In questions 6 to 9 several possible answers are given. Write down the letter that corresponds to the correct answer.

6. The graph of $y = x(1-x^2)$ could be

A
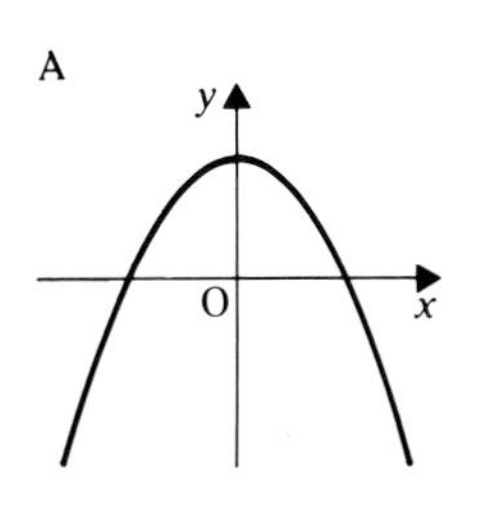

B
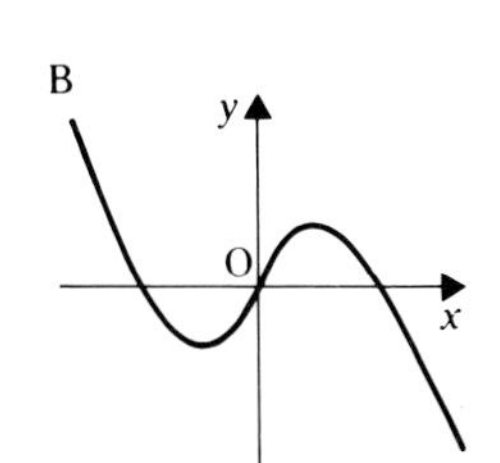

C
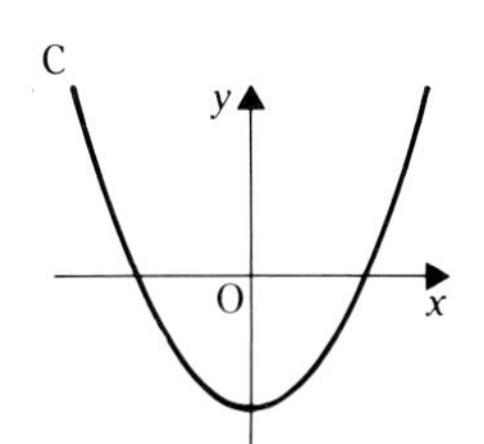

D
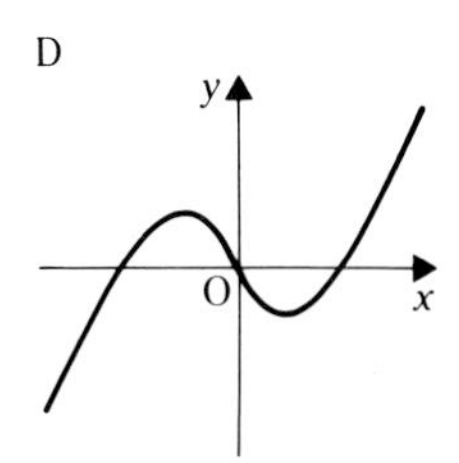

7. The graph of $y = 12+4x-x^2$ could be

A
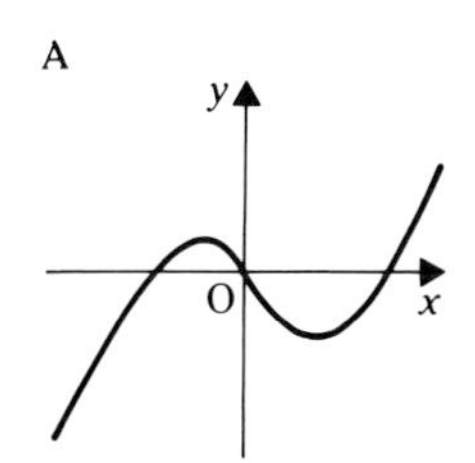

B
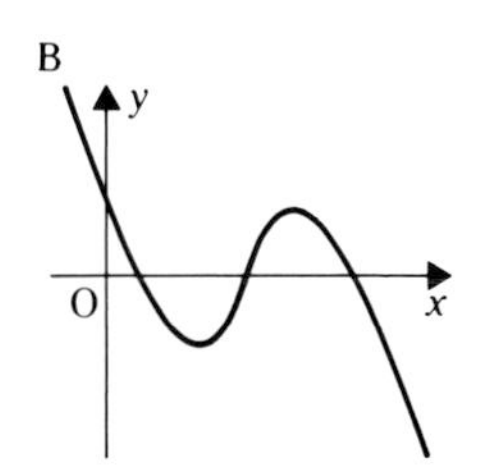

C
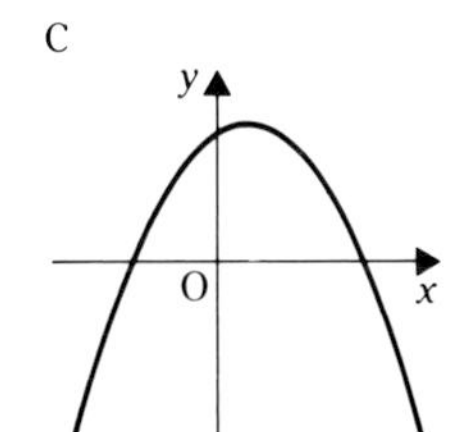

D
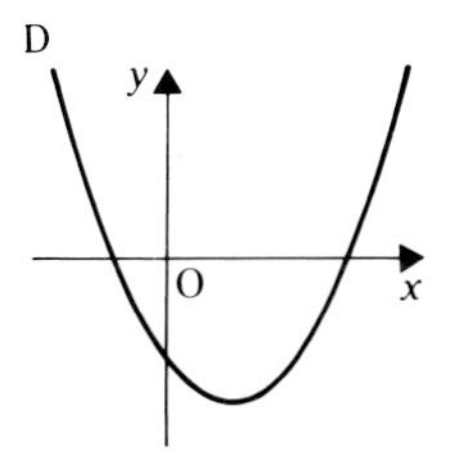

8. The graph of $y = x^3 - 2$ could be

A
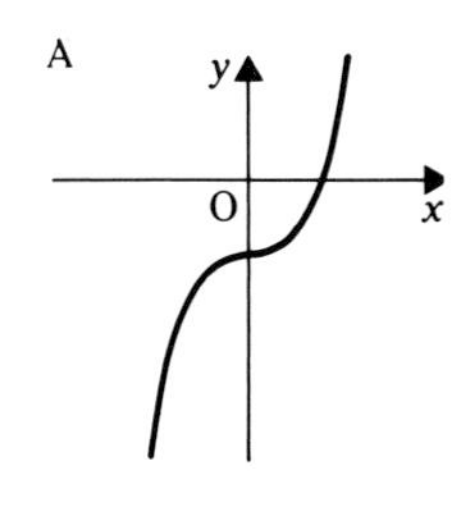

B
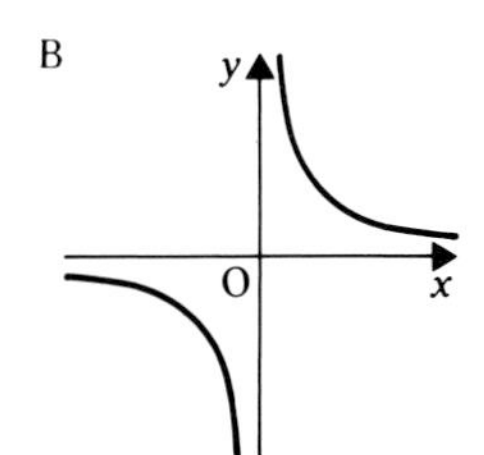

C
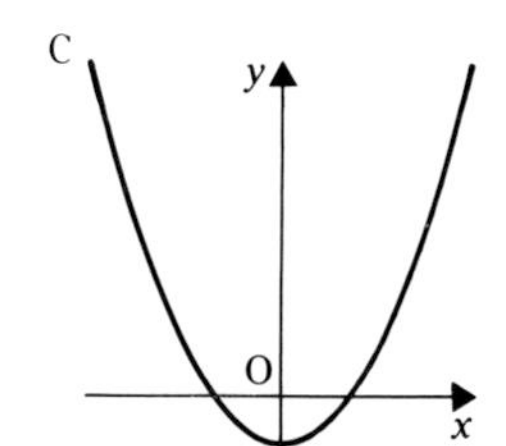

D
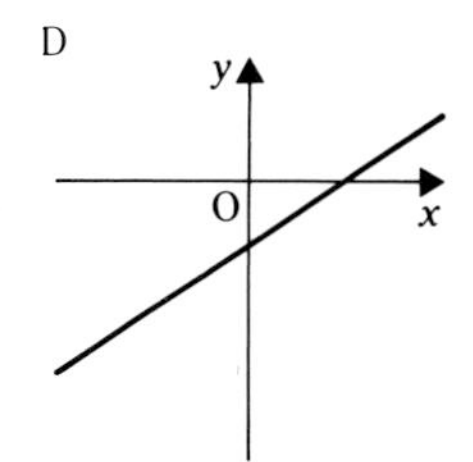

9. The graph of $y = 2+\dfrac{1}{x}$ could be

A
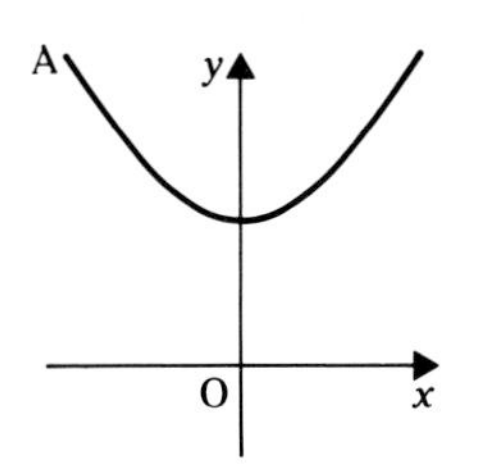

B
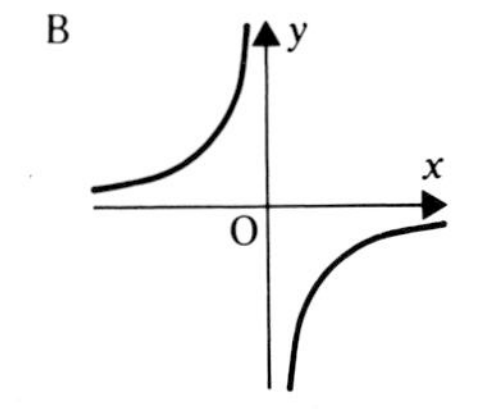

C
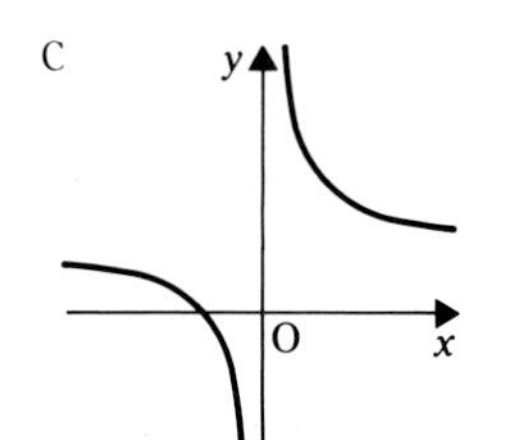

D
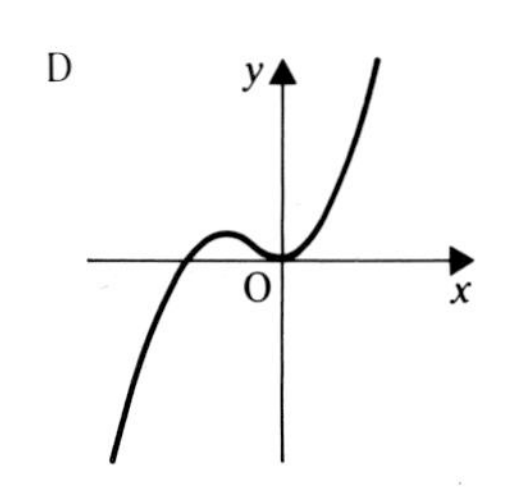

PROBLEM SOLVING

The graphs studied in previous sections can help in the solution of several different types of problem. First we consider some real-life situations.

Exercise 21d

1. An open box with a square base is cut from a square sheet of card measuring 40 cm by 40 cm. The side of the square base of the box can vary from 0 to 40 cm.

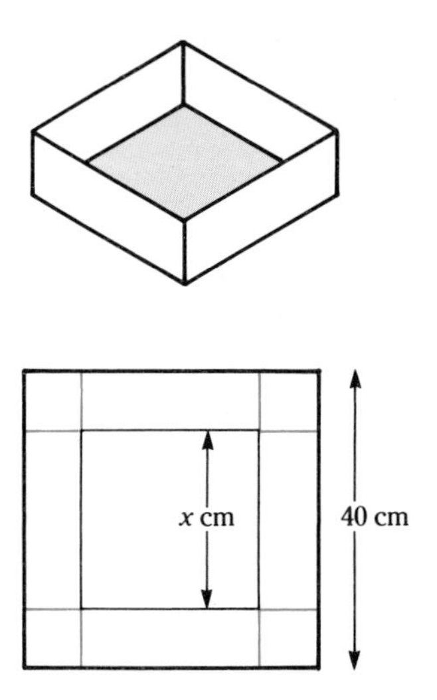

The table shows how the capacity of the box changes as the side of the base increases.

Length of base (cm)	0	5	10	15	20	25	30	35	40
Capacity (cm^3) (to nearest 100 cm^3)	0	400	1500	2800	4000	4700	4500	3100	0

Plot these points and draw a smooth curve through them.

From the graph find the estimated length of side which will give the box with greatest capacity.

2. The table shows the capacity, C litres, for jugs that are mathematically similar, but have different heights, H cm.

H (cm)	5	7	8.5	11.25	14.5	18
C (litres)	0.09	0.26	0.46	1.07	2.29	4.38

Draw a graph to represent this data using 1 cm = 1 unit on the H-axis and 4 cm = 1 unit on the C-axis. Use your graph to find

(a) the height of a similar jug with a capacity of (i) 1.5 litres (ii) 3.5 litres

(b) the capacity of a similar jug that is (i) 10 cm high (ii) 17.5 cm high.

3.

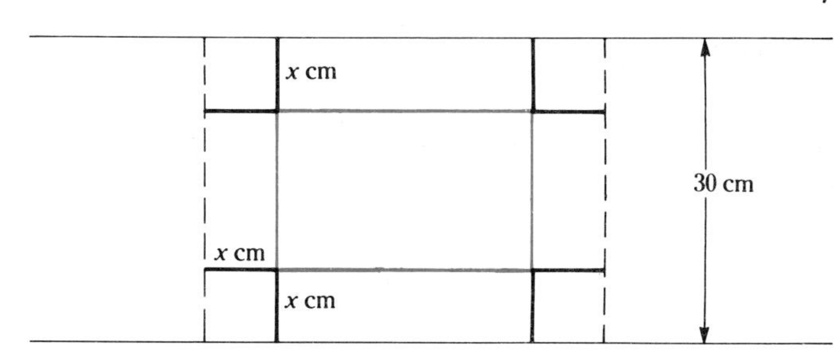

Rectangular pieces are cut from a continuous roll of thin card which is 30 cm wide. Squares of side x cm are removed from the corners of each piece and the sides are folded to form an open rectangular box whose length is twice its width.

(a) What are the dimensions of the base of the box?

(b) Show that the capacity of the box, $C\,\text{cm}^3$, is given by the equation

$$C = 8x(15-x)^2$$

(c) Draw the graph of $C = 8x(15-x)^2$ for values of x between 0 and 15. Use 1 cm to represent 1 unit on the x-axis and 1 cm to represent 500 units on the C-axis. Hence find the maximum capacity of the box and the value of x that provides it.

(d) What percentage of each rectangular piece of card is wasted if it is decided to manufacture rectangular boxes with the maximum capacity?

4. The total length, P metres, of metal required to make a metal framework of height h metres is given by the formula $P = 5h + \frac{2}{h}$

(a) Copy and complete the following table.

h	0.25	0.3	0.4	0.5	0.6	0.7	0.8	0.9	1	1.1	1.2	1.3
P	9.25	8.17	7		6.3	6.36	6.5	6.72		7.32	7.67	8.04

(b) Plot these points on a graph and join them with a smooth curve. Use 2 cm to represent 0.1 on the h-axis and 2 cm to represent 1 unit on the P-axis.

(c) Use your graph to find
(i) the length of metal required for a framework 1.06 m high
(ii) the heights of the two frameworks that can be made from 8 m of metal.

(d) What is the height of the framework that uses the shortest length of metal?

5. An open rectangular tank with a square base of side x m, is to have a fixed capacity of $36\,\text{m}^3$. Find, in terms of x, an expression for the depth of the tank. If the total external surface area is $A\,\text{m}^2$, show that

$$A = x^2 + \frac{144}{x}$$

Find the values of A for whole number values of x from 2 to 7 inclusive. Hence draw the graph of $y = x^2 + \frac{144}{x}$ for values of x between 2 and 7.

Scale the x-axis from 2 to 7 and the y-axis from 0 to 80.

Use your graph to estimate the dimensions of the tank when the total external surface area is least.

6. The graph below shows the price of Brited plc shares at the close of business each week-day over a twelve-week period.
   (a) During which periods is the price of the share rising?
   (b) During which periods is the price of the share falling?
   (c) After week 3, when would the best time have been (i) to buy (ii) to sell?
   (d) What do you think is likely to happen to the price of the share during week 13?
   (e) 'The price of the share doubled in the first six weeks.' Is this statement true or false?

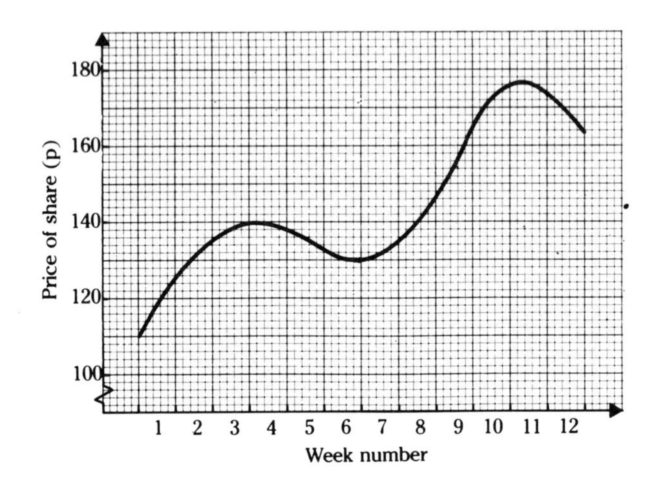

SOLVING QUADRATIC INEQUALITIES

The inequality $x^2 < 9$ is called a quadratic inequality because it contains an x^2 term.

Quadratic inequalities can sometimes be solved by sketching graphs. To solve $x^2 < 9$ we sketch the graphs of $y = x^2$ and $y = 9$ on the same axes.

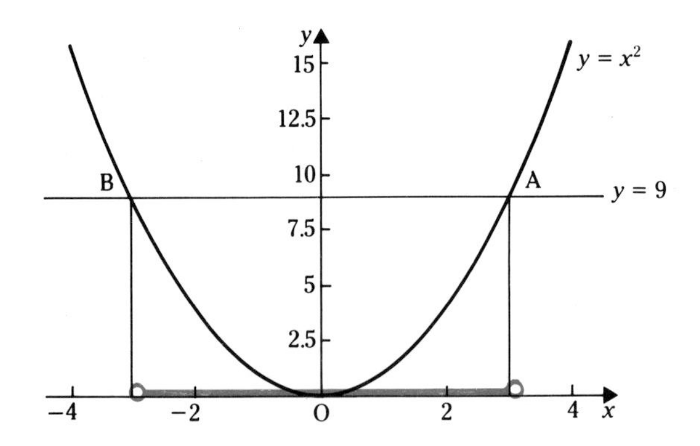

We can see that the graph of $y = x^2$ is below the graph of $y = 9$, i.e. $x^2 < 9$, for the values of x between A and B.

At A and B, $x^2 = 9$ so $x = \pm 3$

Therefore $x^2 < 9$ for $-3 < x < 3$

Exercise 21e

Find the ranges of values of x for which $x^2 - 3 \geqslant 1$

First rearrange $x^2 - 3 \geqslant 1$ so that the x^2 term is isolated.

Adding 3 to each side of $x^2 - 3 \geqslant 1$ gives $x^2 \geqslant 4$

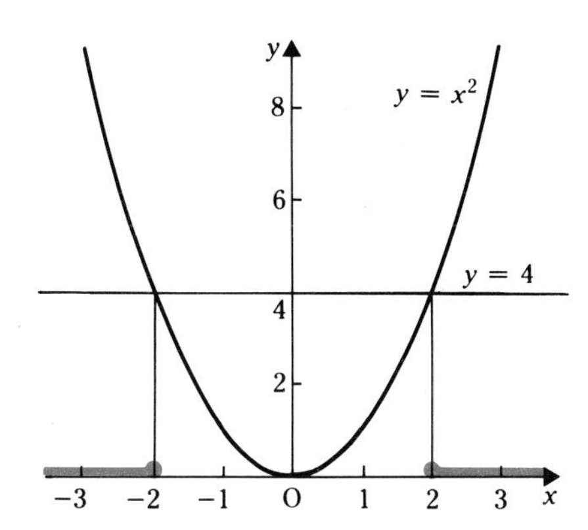

$x^2 = 4$ when $x = \pm 2$

$x^2 \geqslant 4$ when $x \leqslant -2$ and $x \geqslant 2$

Find the range of values of x that satisfy each inequality.

1. $x^2 \geqslant 1$

2. $x^2 < 16$

3. $x^2 \leqslant 25$

4. (a) Sketch the graph of $y = x^2 - 4$
   (b) Give the coordinates of the points where $y = 0$
   (c) Write down the range of values of x for which $x^2 - 4 < 0$

5. (a) Sketch the graph of $y = 1 - x^2$
   (b) Give the coordinates of the points where the graph crosses the x-axis.
   (c) Hence find the range of values of x for which $1 - x^2 < 0$

6. (a) Arrange $x^2 - 2 \geqslant 7$ in the form $x^2 \geqslant a$. What is the value of a?
   (b) Hence find the range of x for which $x^2 - 2 \geqslant 7$

SOLVING EQUATIONS BY TRIAL AND IMPROVEMENT

A solution of an equation can be found by estimating a solution and trying it in the equation. Then, in the light of what happens, improving on the estimate. A systematic approach is needed to keep track of results, and we start by finding two consecutive whole numbers between which the solution lies.

Consider the equation $x^2 + x - 3 = 0$

First we will try 1 (0 is obviously too small) by substituting 1 for x in the LHS (left hand side) of the equation and comparing it with the RHS (which is 0 in this case).

When $x = 1$, LHS $= 1^2 + 1 - 3 = -1$ which is less than 0

We will now try the next whole number, i.e. 2
When $x = 2$, LHS $= 2^2 + 2 - 3 = 3$ and this is greater than 0

These results show that the solution is between 1 and 2 and we can illustrate this on a number line.

LHS < 0 1 2 LHS > 0

Now we can try a value of x between 1 and 2 and use this to narrow the interval in which we know the solution lies. Any value can be chosen but comparing the differences between 0 and the LHS for the two values we have tried shows that the solution is nearer to 1 than to 2; so we choose to try $x = 1.3$
When $x = 1.3$, LHS $= (1.3)^2 + 1.3 - 3 = -0.01$ which is less than 0, but close.

We can add this value to the number line.

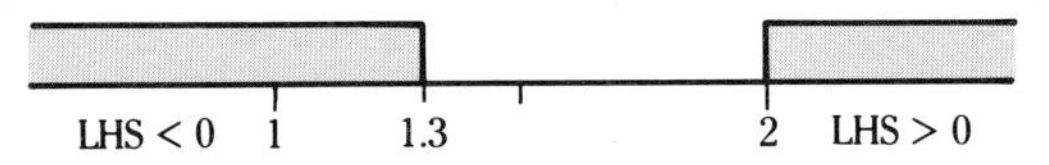

We will try $x = 1.4$ next;
when $x = 1.4$, LHS $= (1.4)^2 + 1.4 - 3 = 0.36$ which is greater than 0

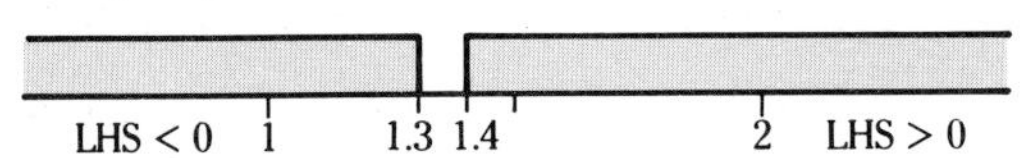

Adding the last result to the number line, we can now see that the solution lies between $x = 1.3$ and $x = 1.4$ and, comparing the differences again, we can say that the solution is nearer to 1.3 than to 1.4, i.e., the solution is $x = 1.3$ correct to 1 decimal place.

To get a result correct to 2 decimal places, we repeat the process in the interval 1.3 to 1.4; as there is not much space left on the number line already used, it is sensible to draw it again.

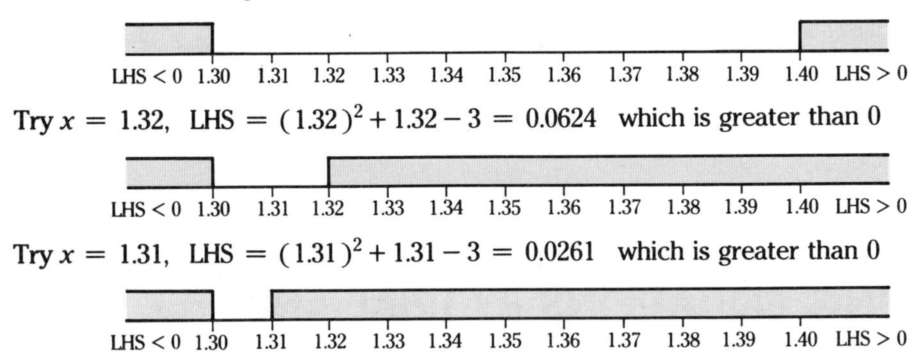

Try $x = 1.32$, LHS $= (1.32)^2 + 1.32 - 3 = 0.0624$ which is greater than 0

Try $x = 1.31$, LHS $= (1.31)^2 + 1.31 - 3 = 0.0261$ which is greater than 0

Now we can see that the solution lies between 1.30 and 1.31 and is nearer to 1.30, i.e. the solution is 1.30 correct to 2 decimal places.

This process can be repeated to give three decimal places, and again to give four decimal places, and so on.

Exercise 21f

1. Show that the equation $x^2+x-1=0$ has a solution between $x=0$ and $x=1$. Find this solution correct to 1 decimal place.

2. Find two positive integer values of x between which $x^2+6x-8=0$ has a solution.

   Find this solution correct to 1 decimal place.

3. Arrange the equation $2x^2=4x-1$ in a form where the left-hand side is zero. Show that this equation has a solution between $x=1$ and $x=2$ and find it correct to 2 decimal places.

4. (a) Arrange the equation $x=x^3-1$ in a form where the left-hand side is zero.

   (b) Find two consecutive positive values of x between which a solution lies.

   (c) Find this solution correct to 2 decimal places.

5. Repeat question 4 for the equation

$$\frac{2}{x+1}=x-3$$

Computer Investigation

When we found a solution of an equation by trial and improvement, the successive numbers we chose for trial solutions were based on the closeness of previous trials. This requires a judgement to be made at each step. We can remove the need for this judgement by imposing the rule 'for the next trial solution, use the value of x that bisects the interval'. In this form, the process is known as the *interval bisection method* and it is suitable for a straightforward BASIC program which can be run on a computer.

The following program uses the interval bisection method to find the solution of the equation $x^3-2x+1=0$

First you need to find two whole numbers, A and B, between which a solution lies.

Type in the programme and run it, entering the values for A and B found above.

```
10 INPUT A,B
20 LET C=A*A*A-2*A+1
30 LET X=(A+B)/2
40 LET Y=X*X*X-2*X+1
50 IF Y>0 AND C>0 OR Y<0 AND C<0 THEN PRINT TAB(5) X; TAB(20) B
60 IF Y<=0 AND C>0 OR Y>=0 AND C<0 THEN PRINT TAB(5) A; TAB(20) X
70 IF Y<0 AND C<0 OR Y>0 AND C>0 THEN A=X
80 IF Y<=0 AND C>0 OR Y>=0 AND C<0 THEN B=X
90 IF ABS(Y)>=0.0001 THEN GOTO 20
```

(a) How accurate an answer can you give for the solution of the equation?

(b) If the figure in line 90 is changed, this will alter the width of the final interval printed. Try altering it to 0.000 001. How accurate an answer does this give?

(c) Alter lines 20 and 40 of the program, to solve the equation $x^2-\frac{1}{x}-2=0$ (replace the expression in X by the LHS of the equation, using X, not x).

(d) Try using this program for some of the questions in Exercise 21f, rearranging them where necessary so that the RHS is zero.

Self-Assessment 21

1. Draw the graph of $y = x^2 + 5x - 10$ for values of x from -7 to 2. Take 2 cm as 1 unit on the x-axis and 1 cm as 1 unit on the y-axis.

   Use your graph to find

   (a) the lowest value of $x^2 + 5x - 10$ and the corresponding value of x.

   (b) the values of x when $x^2 + 5x - 10 = -5$

2. Sketch, on the same axes, the graphs of $y = \dfrac{12}{x}$ and $y = x^2 + 5$

   Estimate the values of x where the graphs intersect.

3. On separate axes, sketch the graphs of

   (a) $y = x^3$ (c) $y = -x^3$

   (b) $y = x^2 - 2$ (d) $y = 2 - x^2$

   Show clearly where each graph crosses the axes.

4. (a) Copy and complete the following table which gives values of $x^2 - 4x + 4$ for values of x from 0 to 4

x	0	1	1.5	2	2.5	3	4
$x^2 - 4x + 4$	4	1	0.25				4

   (b) Draw the graph of $y = x^2 - 4x + 4$ for these values of x. Use a scale of 2 cm for 1 unit on each axis.

   (c) On the same axes, draw the line $y = 3$

   (d) Give the range of values of x for which $x^2 - 4x + 4 < 3$

5. In this question several possible answers are given. Write down the letter that corresponds to the correct answer.

   The graph of $y = (3 - x)(4 + x)^2$ could be

A

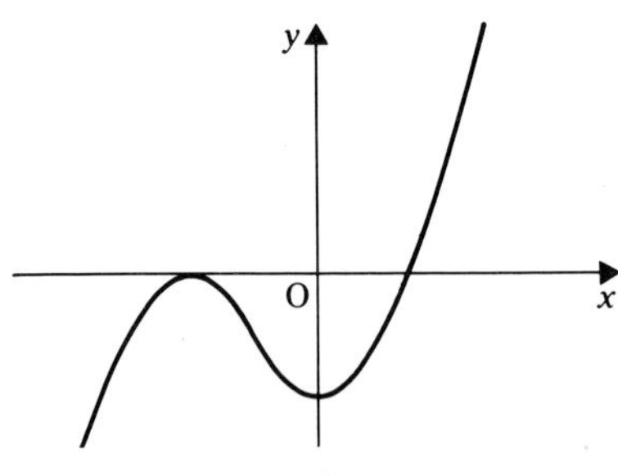

B

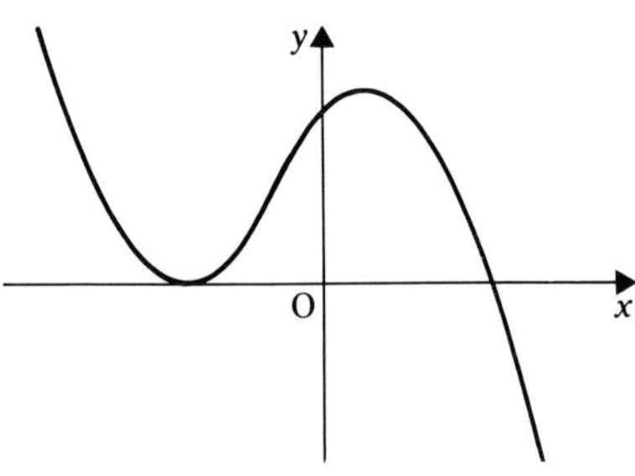

C

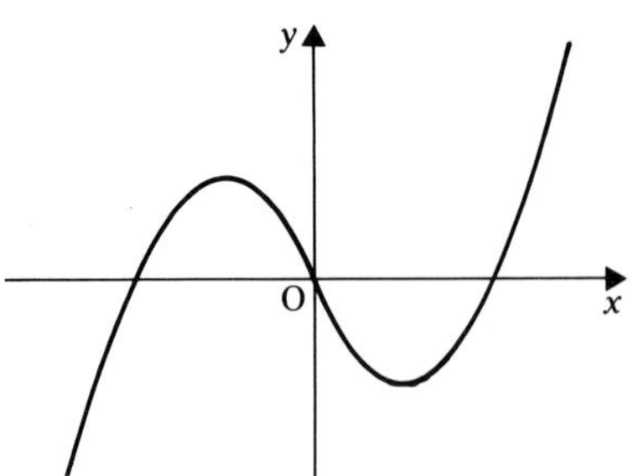

D

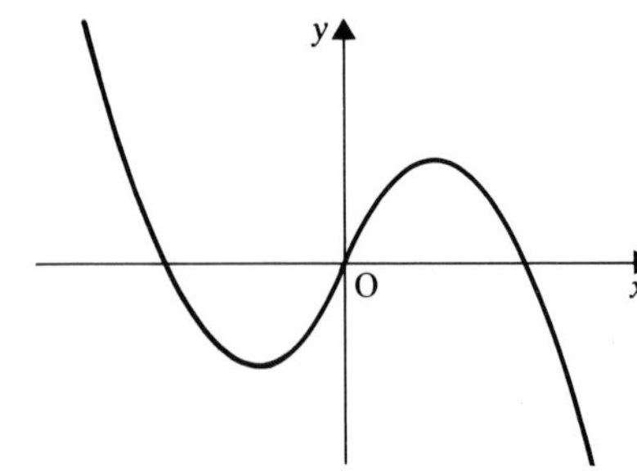

6. When a low-loader transports a piece of heavy equipment at a speed of v m.p.h., the cost of a journey of 100 miles is £$\left(\frac{6000}{v} + 20v\right)$

   Complete the following table, which shows the cost in pounds (C) for values of v from 10 to 30.

v	10	13	15	18	20	22	25	27	30
C	800	721		693		713		762	800

   Draw a graph to show how the cost varies for speeds between 10 m.p.h. and 30 m.p.h. Take 4 cm to represent 5 m.p.h. on the horizontal axis and £100 on the vertical axis starting at £500.

   Use your graph to estimate (a) the cost of the journey at a speed of 12.4 m.p.h.
   (b) the speeds at which the journey will cost £780
   (c) the speed at which the cost of the journey is least.

7. Find the range of values of x that satisfy the inequality $x^2 + 4 < 29$

8. Show that there is a root of the equation $x^2 + x - 9 = 0$ between $x = 2$ and $x = 3$
   Use trial and improvement to find this solution correct to 2 d.p.

22 TRAVEL GRAPHS

DISTANCE, SPEED AND TIME

The relationship between speed, distance and time is introduced in Chapter 5.

As a reminder, distance = speed × time and, for a given distance, the average speed is equivalent to the steady speed at which the distance is covered in the same time.

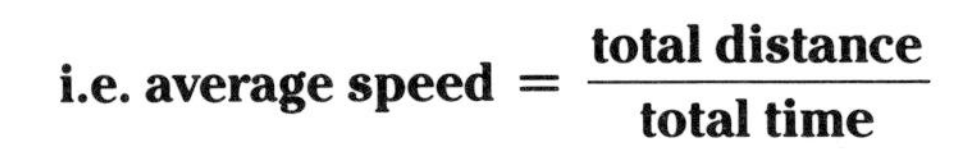

$$\textbf{i.e. average speed} = \frac{\textbf{total distance}}{\textbf{total time}}$$

Distance–Time Graphs

If an object is moving at a steady speed its motion can be represented in a *distance-time graph* by a straight line.

For example, if an object moves at a steady speed of 2 m/s, then its distance from a fixed point increases by 2 m each second. Plotting this distance against time gives the following graph.

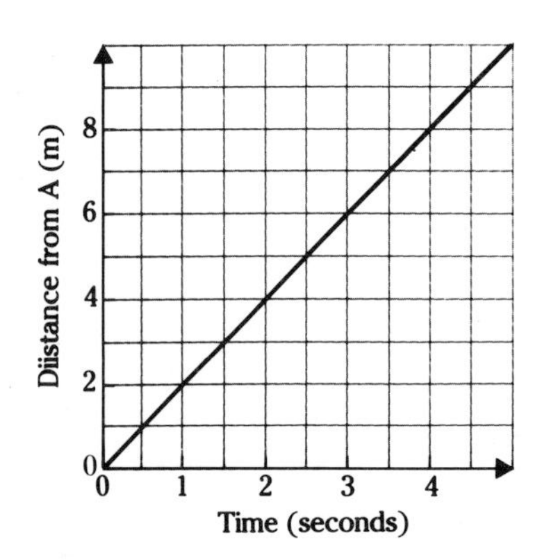

This graph shows that the object travels 8 m in 4 s at a speed of 2 m/s.

Notice that when time is involved in a graph, it is marked on the horizontal axis unless there is a special reason for changing this convention.

Exercise 22a

1. Find the average speed of an object that moves
   (a) 42 m in 6 s
   (b) 144 miles in 8 hours.

2. Find the distance covered by an object that moves in each of the following ways. Make sure that the units are consistent.
   (a) $6\,\mathrm{m\,s^{-1}}$ over 12 s.
   (b) $17\,\mathrm{km\,h^{-1}}$ over $3\frac{1}{2}$ hours.

3. Find the time taken by a moving object if it travels
   (a) 15 m at $5\,\mathrm{m\,s^{-1}}$
   (b) 17 km at $3.6\,\mathrm{km\,h^{-1}}$.

4. A train travels for 2 hours at 50 m.p.h. and then for 3 hours at 60 m.p.h.
   (a) Find the total distance travelled.
   (b) Find the average speed for the whole journey.
   (c) Find the average of 50 and 60. Does this give the average speed for the journey?

Express $4\,\mathrm{m\,s^{-1}}$ in $\mathrm{km\,h^{-1}}$

1 h = 60 × 60 s
1 km = 1000 m

In 1 s the object moves 4 m

In 1 h it moves 4 × 60 × 60 m

i.e. $\dfrac{4 \times 60 \times 60}{1000}$ km

= 14.4 km

So $4\,\mathrm{m\,s^{-1}} = 14.4\,\mathrm{km\,h^{-1}}$

5. Express each speed in the unit indicated.
   (a) $6\,\mathrm{m\,min^{-1}}$ in $\mathrm{m\,s^{-1}}$
   (b) $10\,\mathrm{km\,h^{-1}}$ in m/min
   (c) $30\,\mathrm{km\,h^{-1}}$ in $\mathrm{m\,s^{-1}}$
   (d) $9\,\mathrm{m\,s^{-1}}$ in $\mathrm{km\,h^{-1}}$

6. From each of the following distance–time graphs, give the distance travelled, the time taken and the speed.

(a)

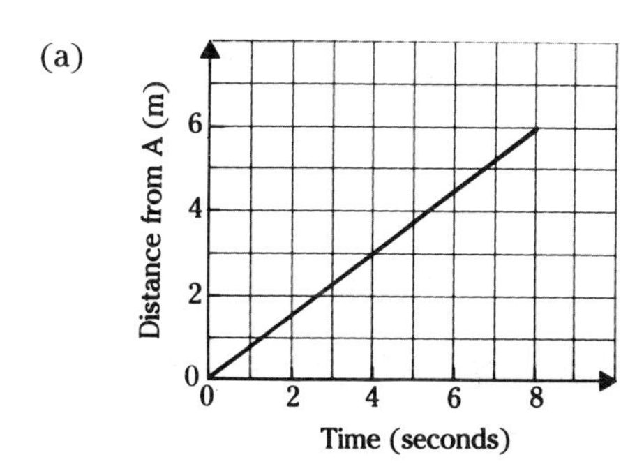

(b)

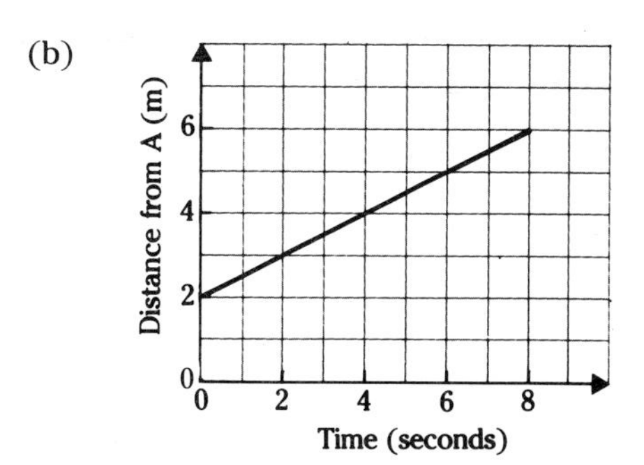

(c)

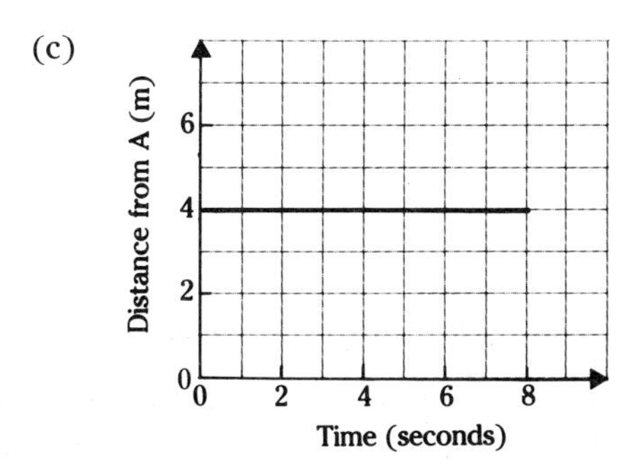

DISPLACEMENT

Distance travelled is independent of the direction in which an object moves.
Displacement is defined as the distance of the object, measured from a given point in a given direction.

C 3 m A 4 m B

An object moves from A to B and back to A. The distance it has travelled is 8 m but its *displacement* from A is zero.
If the object carries on moving to C it will have travelled a distance of 11 m but its displacement from A is -3 m.

We use the convention that displacement to the right (or up) is positive and to the left (or down) is negative.

Displacement–Time Graphs

If, in the example described above, the speed is 2 m/s, we can use a displacement–time graph to show the motion.

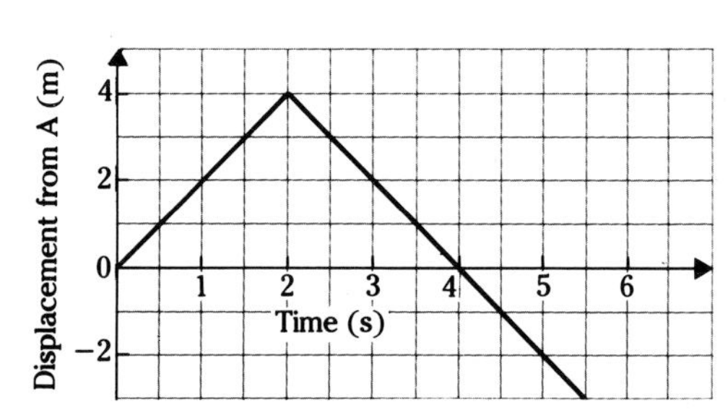

A displacement–time graph can be used to show more complicated motion.

A *Sprinter* train runs between two stations A and B. The motion is shown in the graph below.

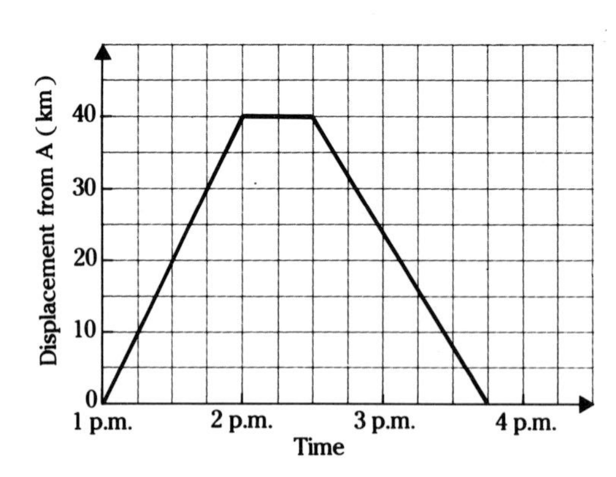

The train runs at a speed of $\frac{40}{1}$ km h^{-1}, i.e. 40 km h^{-1}, from A to B, stops at B for half an hour,

then returns to A at $\frac{40}{1.25}$ km h^{-1}, i.e. 32 km h^{-1}.

Notice that, at 3 p.m. the displacement from A is 24 km but the distance travelled since 1 p.m. is 56 km.

The graphs of two train journeys can be drawn on the same axes.
Here are two examples.

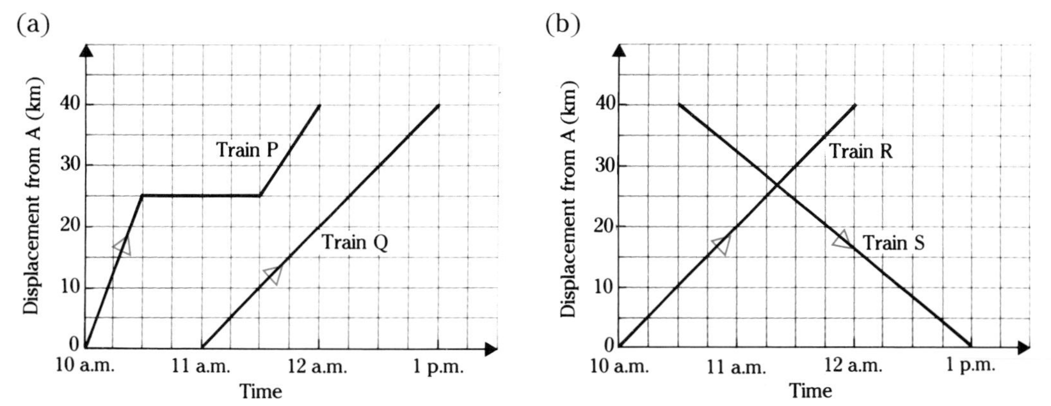

In (a), P and Q take the same time to travel from A to B; P travels faster, but stops at an intermediate station. The slope of the graph for P during motion is greater than that for Q. In (b), R is travelling from A to B and S from B to A. They pass 27 km from A, at approximately 11.20 a.m.

Graphs of this type, illustrating a journey made by a person or vehicle, are called *Travel Graphs*.

SPEED AND VELOCITY

Consider a train P travelling from A to B at 60 km/h and another train Q travelling from B to A also at 60 km/h.

Both trains have the same speed but they are travelling in opposite directions so, to specify the motion of either train we have to give the speed *and* the direction of travel.

The quantity that specifies both speed and direction of motion is called *velocity*.

Taking the direction from A to B as positive, we can give the velocity of P as +60 km/h and the velocity of Q as −60 km/h.

Exercise 22b

1. State whether each of the following quantities is a distance, a displacement, a speed or a velocity.

   (a) 30 m.p.h.

   (b) 43 km

   (c) $4\,\text{m s}^{-1}$ vertically downward.

   (d) 6 miles due north.

   (e) $3\,\text{cm s}^{-1}$ towards the opposite corner of the room.

   (f) 10 km round the M25.

2. In each of the following displacement–time graphs, describe the motion and give the distances, times and velocities in the different sections.

(a)

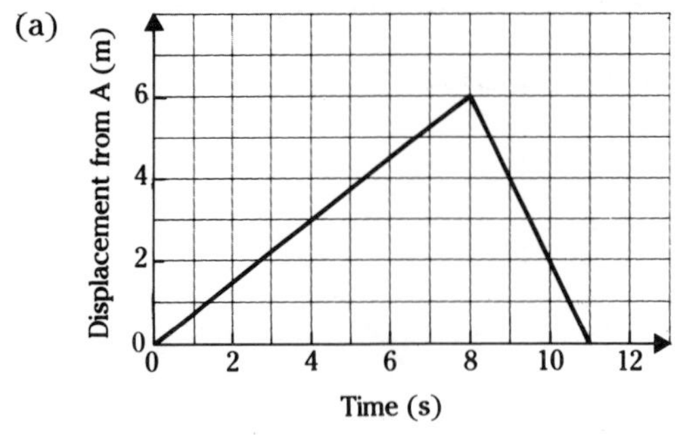

(c)

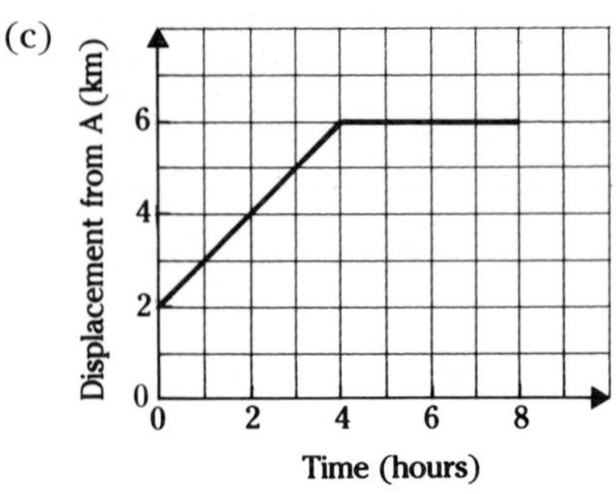

(b)

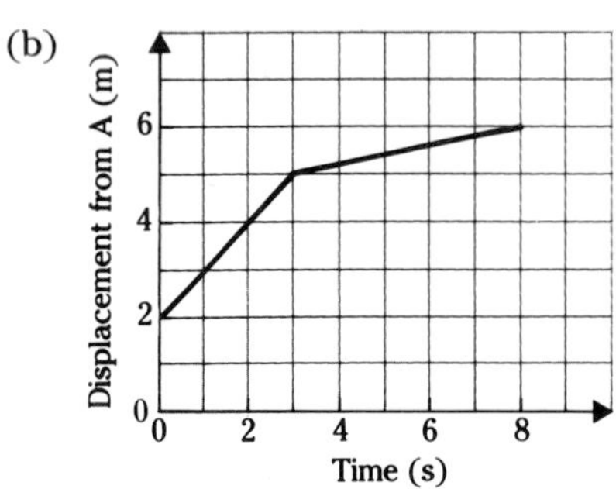

(d)

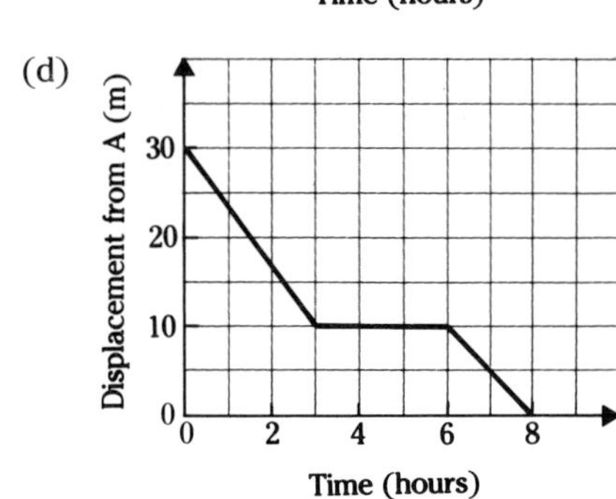

3. Sketch a displacement–time graph to show the following motion, marking in relevant displacements and times.

   (a) A car moves at a steady speed from A to B, a distance of 30 km, in 40 minutes. It stops at B for 30 minutes, then returns to A at $30\,\text{km}\,\text{h}^{-1}$.

   (b) A train starts from station C and travels to D at a constant speed of 60 m.p.h., taking 50 minutes. A second train starts from C half an hour after the first and takes 40 minutes to get to D.

4.

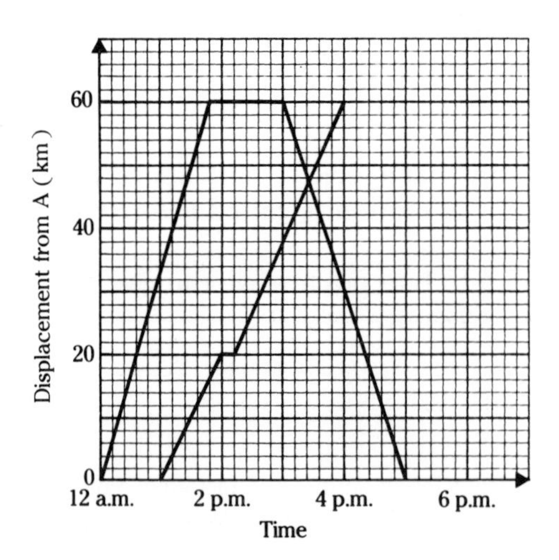

Two trains travel between stations A and B. Describe their movements, giving details of distances, velocities and times. Does one overtake the other or do they pass one another moving in opposite directions ?

5. (a) On graph paper and using scales of 4 cm to 1 hour and 1 cm to 5 km, draw lines to represent the motion of two trains P and Q travelling between two stations A and B, 60 km apart.
Starting at noon, P travels at a steady 60 km h^{-1} from A to B, stops there for 18 minutes, then returns to A, taking 72 minutes.
Q starts from A as P reaches B, and reaches B as P reaches A.

(b) At what speed does Q travel ?

(c) At what time, and where, do the two trains pass ?

(d) Draw an appropriate line on the graph to determine the speed at which Q would have to travel if the two trains were to pass at 1.30 pm. Assume that Q starts from A at the same time as before.

Finding Velocity from a Displacement–Time Graph

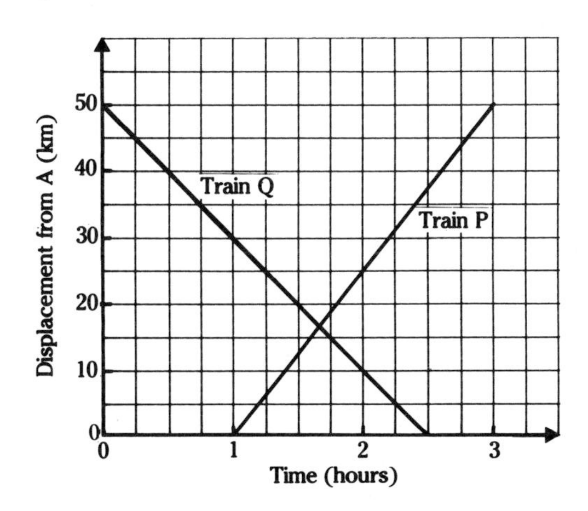

The graph shows two trains moving between stations A and B.

Train P is moving from A to B at $\frac{50}{2}$ km/h, i.e. the velocity of train P is 25 km/h.

The gradient of the line representing P's motion is $\frac{50}{2}$, i.e. 25, which is the same value as the velocity.

Train Q is moving from B to A at $\frac{50}{2.5}$ km/h, i.e. the velocity of Q is -20 km/h because we are taking the direction A to B as positive.

The gradient of the line representing Q's motion is $\frac{-50}{2.5}$ and this is the same value as the velocity of Q.

In both cases, the gradient of the line gave the velocity. This is true in general.

The gradient of a displacement-time graph gives the velocity.

CURVED DISPLACEMENT–TIME GRAPHS

Objects seldom move at a steady speed and a curved graph represents a more realistic situation.

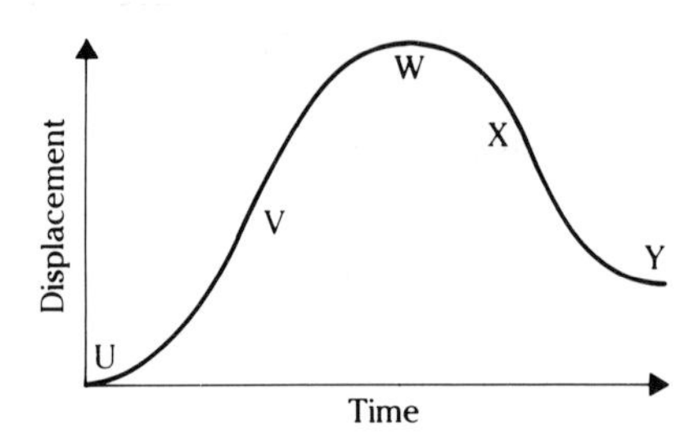

The object starts from rest (the gradient is zero at U) and gradually reaches a maximum speed (the gradient is greatest at V). It slows down again until, for an instant at W, it is at rest, then speeds up in the opposite direction (X) and comes to rest (Y).

Exercise 22c

1. The graph shows the motion of a stone thrown vertically upward from a point A.

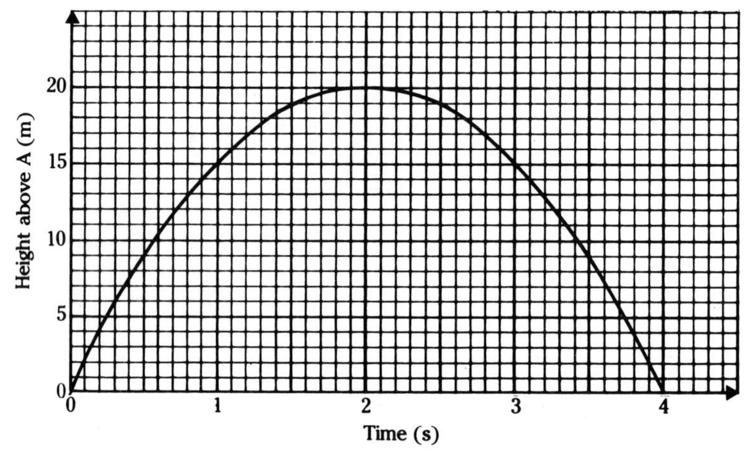

   (a) Give the height above A after (i) 0.5 s (ii) 1.75 s (iii) 3.2 s.

   (b) When is the stone at its greatest height ?

   (c) When is the upward velocity at its greatest ?

   (d) After what time does the stone return to A ?

2. The distance, d m, travelled in t s by a marble rolling down a groove, is given in the table.

t	0	1	2	3	4	5
d	0	0.5	2	4.5	8	12.5

   (a) On graph paper, using scales of 2 cm to 1 second and 1 cm to 1 m, draw a graph of distance against time.

   (b) How far has the marble travelled after 2.5 s ?

3. A rubber ball is dropped into a swimming pool and sinks to the bottom. The table shows the height, h m, of the ball above the bottom of the pool after t s.

t	0	0.5	1	1.5	2	2.5	3	3.5	4
h	3	2.9	2.7	2.45	2.15	1.8	1.4	0.8	0

(a) Draw a graph to show this information. Use scales of 4 cm to 1 m and 4 cm to 1 s.

(b) How far has the ball fallen through the water after 1.25 s ?

(c) When is the velocity greatest ?

4.

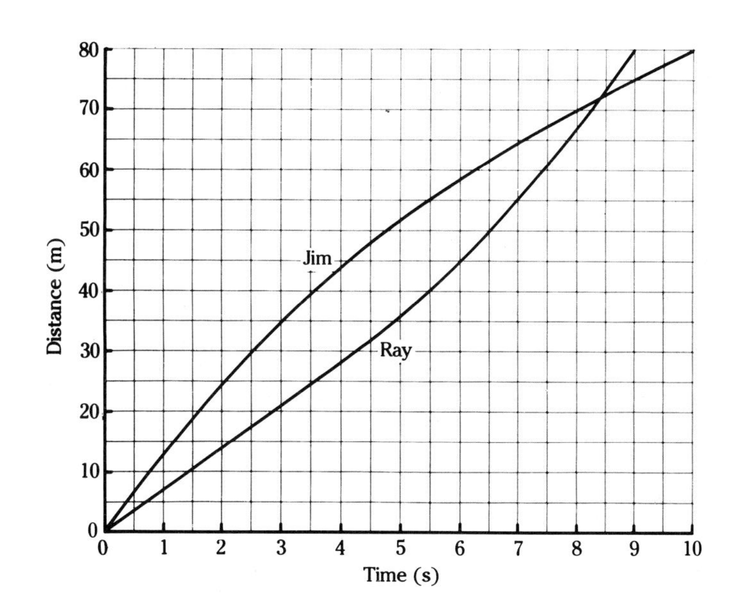

The graph shows an 80 m race between Jim and Ray.

(a) How far ahead was Jim after 5 seconds ?

(b) When did Ray overtake Jim ?

(c) Who came second ?

(d) When the winner crossed the finishing line, how many metres behind him was the loser ?

5. Ann and Cheryl both ran in their first marathon (26 miles). Ann started off fairly fast, covering the first 8 miles in 2 hours, but then gradually slowed down to complete the race in 9 hours. Cheryl ran the race at a fairly steady speed and finished in 7 hours.

(a) Sketch, on the same axes, graphs illustrating the two runs.

(b) Use your sketch to estimate how far Cheryl had run when she overtook Ann.

6. A car stops at one set of lights, A, and at the next set of lights, B. The graph shows the journey between the two sets of lights.

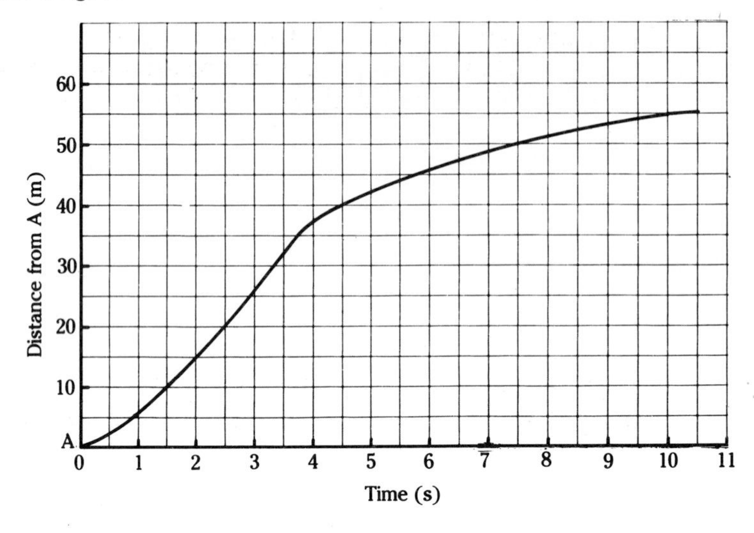

(a) What is the distance between the two sets of lights ?

(b) How long did it take the car to cover the first 10 m from A ?

(c) How long did it take the car to cover the second 10 m from A ?

(d) For about how long was the car accelerating (increasing its speed) ?

(e) About how far from B was the car when it started to slow down ?

7. A train leaves London at midday to travel non-stop to Coventry, a distance of 100 miles. It takes about 15 minutes to reach its steady speed of 90 m.p.h. Half-an-hour after leaving London, the train has to reduce speed to 50 m.p.h. for a distance of ten miles. It then accelerates back to 90 m.p.h. before slowing down for 10 minutes and then stopping at Coventry.

(a) Sketch a distance–time graph to illustrate this journey.

(b) Estimate the time that the journey takes.

GROWTH AND DECAY

Travel graphs are concerned with changes in motion; similar methods can be applied to changes in other quantities, such as population, temperature or the growth of a tree.

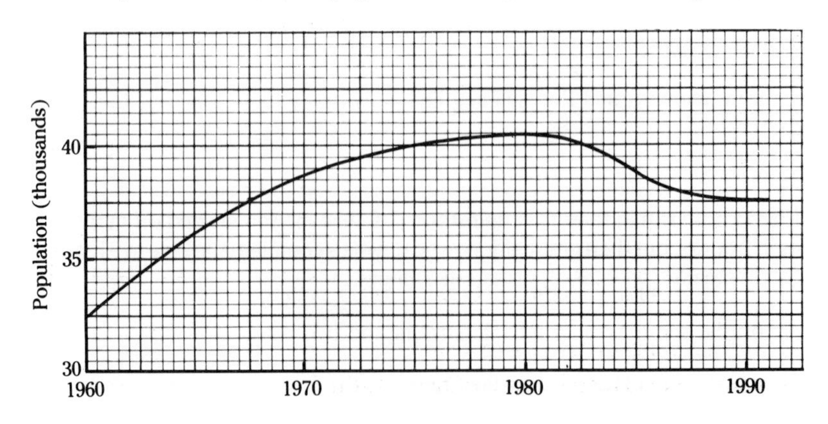

The population of a town is shown in the graph. From it we can find the population at a given time; we can also find when the population was growing or declining or was steady.

For example, in 1970 the population was 38 800; the curve is going up there so the population was growing then. In 1980 the curve is flat so the population was neither growing nor shrinking, i.e. it was steady. For a few years after that the curve goes down so the population was decreasing.

Exercise 22d

Use graph paper in this exercise.

1. Interpret the following population graphs, commenting on these points.
   Is the population increasing or decreasing ? Is the population constant at any time ?

(a)

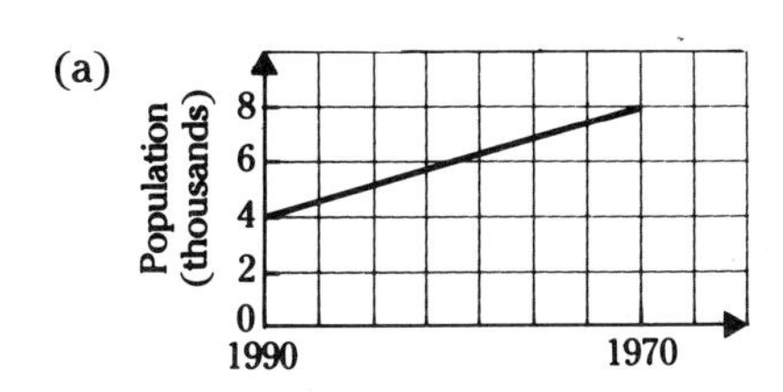

(c)

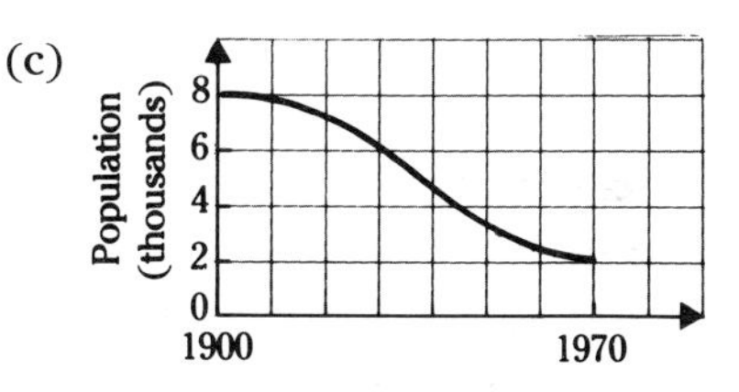

(b)

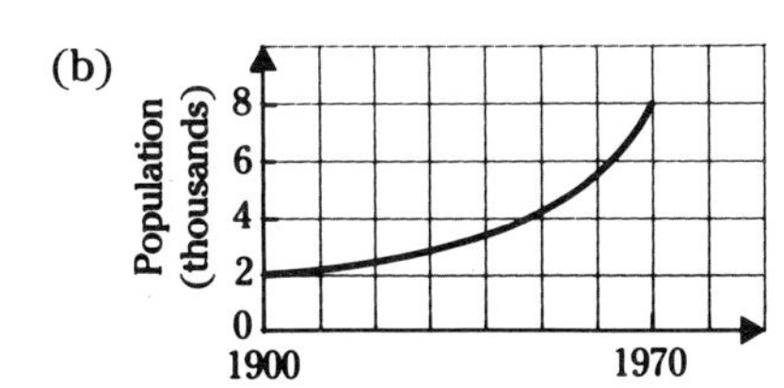

(d)

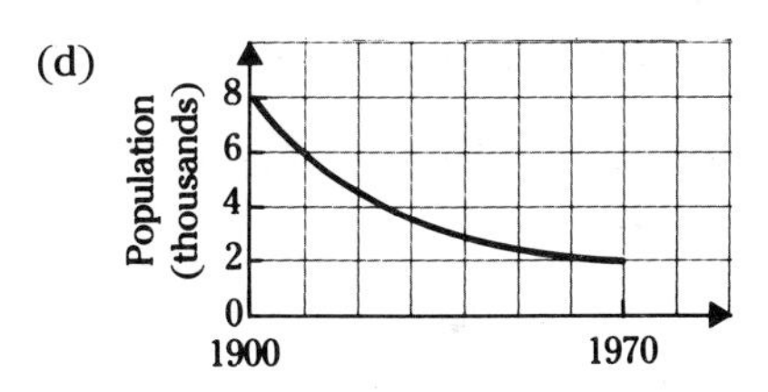

2. The graph shows the population of a small country. (Notice that the population scale starts at 1 thousand.)

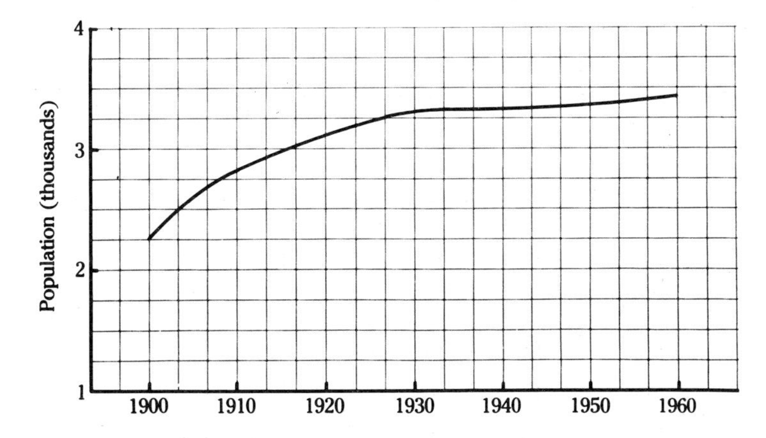

   (a) When was the population at its greatest ?
   (b) When was the population increasing most rapidly ?

3. The table shows the retail price index at the end of each year from 1978 to 1985.

Year	1978	1979	1980	1981	1982	1983	1984	1985
Index	100	106	123	140	162	171	178	185

(a) Draw a graph to show this information. Choose suitable scales and start the retail price index scale at 100.

(b) Between which two years was the retail price index increasing most quickly ?

(c) Did the retail price index fall at any time ?

4. The diagram shows some grain storage tanks with different shapes. Grain is drawn off at the same constant rate from each tank.

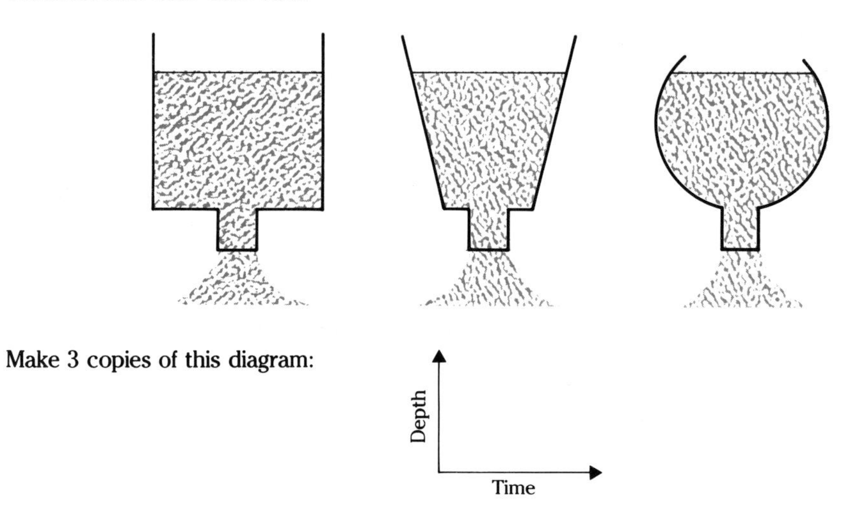

Make 3 copies of this diagram:

Sketch a graph, one on each diagram, showing how the depth of grain in the tank varies with time.

Self-Assessment 22

1. A train travels 60 km in $1\frac{1}{2}$ hours. What is its average speed ?

2. In each case state whether a velocity or a speed is given.

(a) 2 m/s upward

(b) 16 m.p.h.

3.

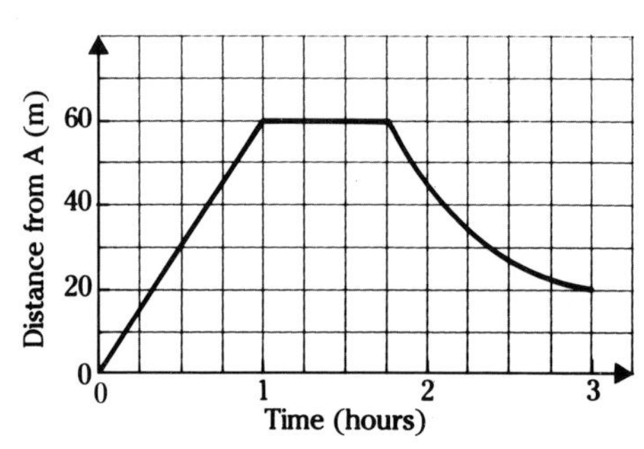

(a) Describe the motion of the train represented on this displacement-time graph.

(b) Give the velocity after $\frac{1}{2}$ hour.

4.

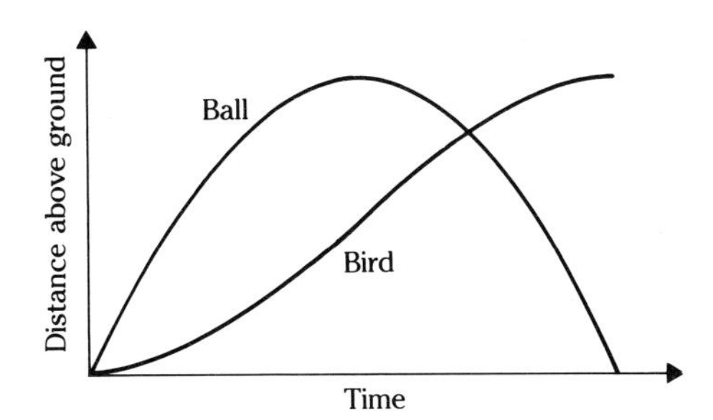

The graph shows the distance above the ground level of a ball thrown straight up and a bird that flies off at the same instant.

(a) Describe what happens to the speed of the ball.

(b) Describe what happens to the speed of the bird.

(c) Can you tell from the graph whether the ball hits the bird ?

5. Water is pumped into a swimming pool at a steady rate. The top of the pool is a rectangle and the sides are vertical. The floor of the pool slopes down from a depth of 1 metre at one end to a depth of 5 metres at the other end.

(a) Draw a sketch of the constant cross-section of the pool.

(b) Sketch a graph showing how the depth of water in the pool varies with time as it fills with water

(i) until the floor of the pool is covered

(ii) subsequently until the pool is full.

23 COLLECTING AND ILLUSTRATING DATA

STATISTICS

Statistics is concerned with the collection and analysis of large quantities of information. In this chapter we are going to look at the collection of information and at ways of grouping and illustrating it.

Data is the collective noun for pieces of information.
We require data for all kinds of purposes, e.g. assessing the performance of organisations or products, planning, producing opinion polls.
There are (very roughly) two categories of data: facts and opinions.

Collecting Information

There are various ways of collecting and recording information, the most common being to ask people to fill in forms. If the information is to be of any use then the forms need to be designed carefully. Take the apparently simple request to fill in a name; if a form has just NAME followed by an empty box then anything from a single first name, to all first names plus surname and title, is likely to appear. Thus the exact information required must be considered and then asked for precisely.

Observation Sheets

Some data can be collected directly by counting or measuring and the data can then be recorded on an observation sheet. Some methods for doing this are more efficient than others.
Consider, for example, recording the results of a count of the number of occupants in each car going into a town centre in the morning rush hour. This could be done simply by writing down the numbers as they are observed, e.g. 1, 3, 1, 1, 2, 1, 4, ...
A little forethought would indicate that, because there are only a few possibilities, the results could be recorded in a simple table using tally marks, e.g.

Number of occupants per car	1	2	3	4	5	6 or more
	IIII	I	I	I		

Notice that tally marks are easier to total if they are grouped in fives. This can be done several ways, e.g. ~~IIII~~ or a square of four sides crossed by a diagonal

When two, or more, pieces of information are required about a person or an object, a two-way table can be used.

Suppose, for example, that we want to collect information about the number of living rooms (not including kitchens, bathrooms, etc.) and the number of people living in each house in a road. We could use a table like one of those given below.

	Living rooms	People
No. 1		
No. 2		
No. 3		
.		
.		
.		

Living rooms People	1	2	3	4	5...
1					
2					
3					
4					
5					
.					
.					
.					

The information can be recorded simply in the top table. This table has the advantage that individual houses can be identified, but it could be a long table. The lower table gives the information more compactly but it is not possible to record the information about a particular house in this table.

Suppose, as another example, you offer to get the orders from a group of people for food from a fast food take-away. The information could be collected in a table like the one below.

	Burger	Cheese burger	Fries	Coke	Milk shake...
Andy					
Rajiv					
Coral					
.					
.					
.					

Questionnaires

Questionnaires are typically used for collecting several pieces of information about a particular subject; for example the use made by employees of a works canteen. The information required is usually a mixture of fact and opinion.

When data is required from individuals, the best method is to use a form with the information required written on it. The advantage of this is that each person is asked for the same information in the same way.
We have already seen that a request for precise information, e.g. name, weight, should be asked for unambiguously. Some data however is not precise, e.g. eye colour, opinion about a proposed road development.
It is sensible to ask for such information in predetermined categories or possible responses. For example, a question asking for eye colour could be in the form

Tick the box that most closely corresponds to the colour of your eyes:

Brown ☐ Hazel/Green ☐ Blue ☐

A question asking for an opinion could be in the form:

Private cars should be banned from city centres.

Agree ☐ Disagree ☐ Undecided ☐

If you need to compile a questionnaire it is sensible to try it out on a few people first, to find out whether any questions are not clear.

Exercise 23a

1. A market research firm wants to carry out a survey into how long people take to eat lunch. Make an observation sheet on which the information can be collected.

2. Jaye is going to ask each of her classmates how many children live in their household.
   (a) Make a simple chart on which she can record the answers.
   (b) Suggest some difficulties she might face when asking for the information.
   (c) Jaye decides to extend her study to investigate where each of her classmates fits in the household, i.e. only child, elder of two, and so on. Suggest a simple way of classifying this information.
   (d) Draw up a two-way table in which she can record the information.

3. Brendan operates a delivery service for bread. He takes the order one day for delivery the next day. He offers to deliver any of the following varieties of bread: white sliced, wholemeal sliced, white split-tin, granary, wholemeal, white rolls, brown rolls.

   Suggest a way to record the orders from which he can easily find how much of each type of bread he needs to take, as well as the specific order for each customer.

4. At the market garden where Jocelyn works, three different varieties of lettuce are grown: Golden Crisp, Red Curl and Salad Bowl. She plants out seedlings and after a fortnight any weak plants are discarded.
   (a) Suggest a way in which Jocelyn can record the number of plants of each variety that are discarded.
   (b) If lettuce seedlings are planted out at weekly intervals, suggest a way in which the date of planting can also be recorded.

5. Petra works in a restaurant and her job involves taking the orders for drinks, getting them and then giving each one to the right person without asking them to remind her what they had ordered.

   For a table of four people, she takes the order like this:

   Blond man: white wine
   Bald man: d coke
   Tall woman: gin & t (ice, no lemon)
   Woman: fiz mineral water

   (a) Give reasons why this may not be a good way of recording an order.

   (b) Suggest other ways in which she could record an order.

6. Peter wanted to investigate the attitude of pupils in his school to school uniform. Write down two questions he could ask, each question having three or more responses.

7. Shona wanted to investigate the use made of an automatic drinks machine in the college entrance lobby.

   (a) Write a question seeking factual information with three or more responses.

   (b) Write a question asking for an opinion with three or more responses.

FREQUENCY TABLES

The following list of figures shows the number of occupants in each car travelling towards London on the M4. The numbers were recorded for each car passing the observation point during a ten-minute period so they are in random order.

1 2 1 4 2 1 1 2 1 2 4 1 5 3 1 2 1 1 2 1 4 3
5 2 3 1 1 2 2 1 3 1 1 1 4 2 1 5 1 2 3 1 2 1
2 1 2 3 3 1 2 4 1 3 1 2 1 3 2 1 5 3 6 2 1 1
3 2 4 1 6 3 3 3 2 3 3 1 1 2 4 1 2 4 4 1 1 3
3 4 3 2 4 3 2 3 1 1 2 1 2 1 3 2 1 1 1 1 4 2

Data in this form is called raw data. Before any sense can be made of this data, it needs to be sorted into categories.
There are six categories here: 1, 2, 3, 4, 5 and 6 occupants.
Using a table, each item can be recorded under its appropriate category using tally marks.
The total number of items in a category is the *frequency*.

Number of occupants per car	1	2	3	4	5	6	
Tally	𝍸 𝍸 𝍸 𝍸 𝍸 𝍸 𝍸 𝍸 ||	𝍸 𝍸 𝍸 𝍸 𝍸 |||	𝍸 𝍸 𝍸 𝍸 ||	𝍸 𝍸 ||	||||	||	
Frequency	42	28	22	12	4	2	Total: 110

This is called a frequency table.

Bar Charts

The frequency table above can be illustrated by a bar chart.

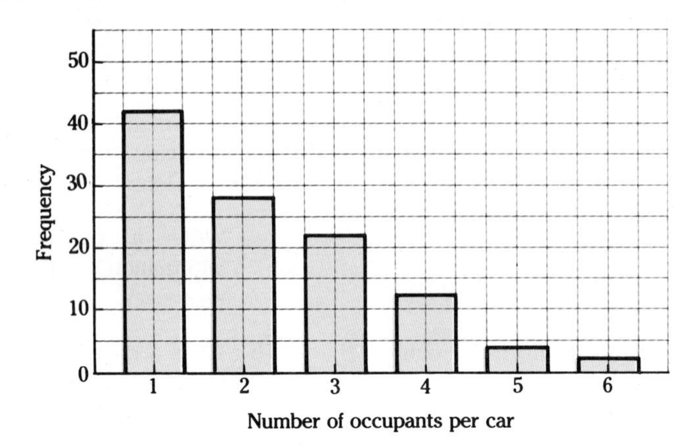

Notice that each bar covers one category, so all bars are the same width. The height of each bar gives the frequency of that category.

Lines can be used instead of bars, in which case the diagram is sometimes called a line graph. An example of a line graph is shown in Chart 1 on page 370.

GROUPING DATA

The following list of numbers gives the bill in pounds of each of the first 50 people going through the express check-out in a supermarket.

15.60	5.95	31.22	3.02	6.60	24.70	15.45	32.50	12.45	4.43
12.65	10.09	52.86	12.88	2.53	31.79	9.86	25.79	18.28	32.05
14.87	24.65	15.70	8.65	4.42	17.20	8.53	0.45	0.95	4.44
7.45	5.82	45.20	2.70	10.04	15.70	32.20	12.43	36.75	32.50
16.87	3.78	0.56	33.67	9.67	25.50	33.06	7.56	2.63	45.80

These figures range from 0.45 to 52.86 and there are 49 different values. Arranging them in order of size would not give much more clarity, but organising them into groups would give a better idea of the pattern of these bills.

We will group them as follows:

0.01–10.00, 10.01–20.00, 20.01–30.00, 30.01–40.00, 40.01–50.00, 50.01–60.00

Counting the number of bills in each group gives this frequency table.

Bill (£)	0.01–10.00	10.01–20.00	20.01–30.00	30.01–40.00	40.01–50.00	50.01–60.00
Frequency	20	14	4	9	2	1

Now we can draw this bar chart.

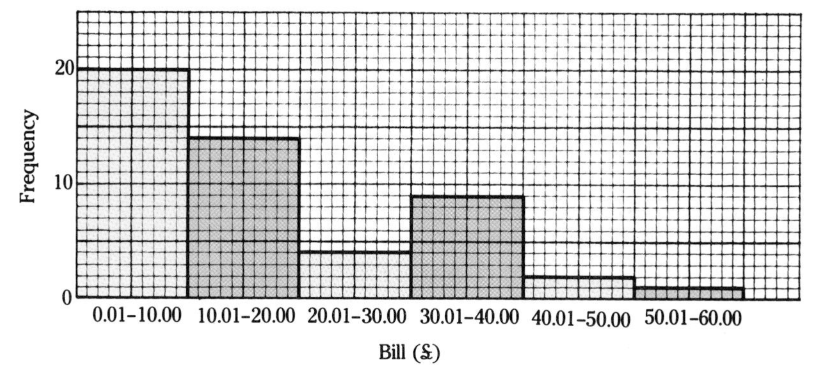

Notice that we can now see a pattern in the overall distribution of the bills, e.g. bills between \$0.01 and \$10 were most frequent and bills over \$40 were a small proportion of the total number. We cannot tell from the bar chart what the distribution of bills is within a group however, e.g. it is not possible to judge whether more than half of the bills between \$10.01 and \$20 are less than \$15. Therefore grouping data enables overall patterns to be seen but detail is lost.

Using Computer Databases

Computer database programs are powerful data-processing tools. Whan data is entered into a database, the program can sort the data into, say, numerical or alphabetical order. Most programs have several further functions, for example grouping the data and producing a variety of diagrams including bar charts.

Exercise 23b

1. The bar chart shows the numbers of different pets kept by households in a block of flats.

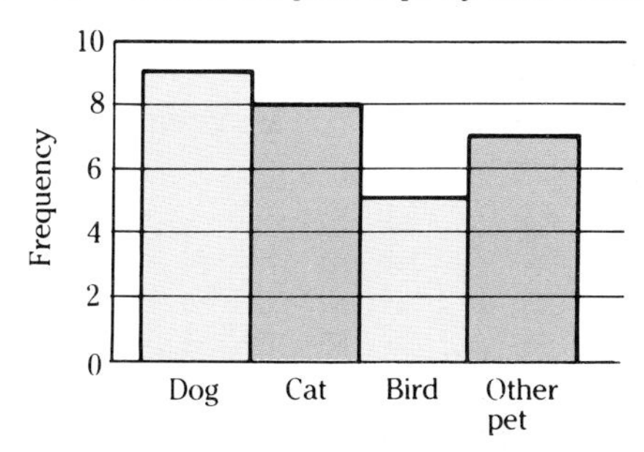

(a) How many dogs are owned by households in the flats ?

(b) How many birds are owned by households in the flats ?

(c) Copy and complete the following frequency table.

Type of pet	Dog	Cat	Bird	Other pet
Frequency				

(d) How many pets are there altogether ?

(e) Do any of the households have two dogs ?

2. The passengers getting onto a bus during its journey were placed in one of four categories: man (M), woman (W), boy (B), girl (G). This list shows the information as it was collected.

M W W W B G W M G G G M B M G M
B G B B M M G B W W W W M M W M

(a) Make a frequency table from this information.

(b) Draw a bar chart illustrating the information.

(c) How many males were on the bus and how many females?

(d) How many more girls than boys were there on the bus?

(e) How many passengers are there altogether?

3. This bar chart comes from an analysis of the sizes of shoes sold in the children's shoe department of a large store.

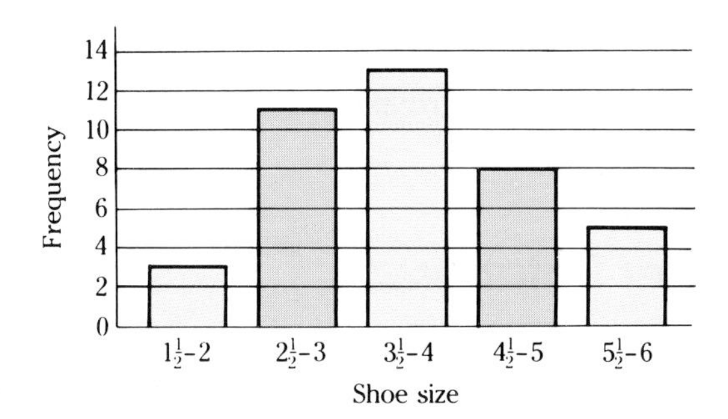

Use the bar chart to answer these questions.

(a) Which group of shoe sizes is the most common?

(b) Which group of shoe sizes is the least common?

(c) Can you tell from the bar chart how many people take size 5 shoes?

(d) How many pairs of shoes are included in this distribution?

4. The marks gained by students in an examination are given below. They have been extracted from a database and are in numerical order.

30	39	47	52	56	59	63	69	79	86
30	40	47	52	56	59	63	70	79	86
31	42	48	53	57	60	64	72	80	87
31	44	48	53	57	60	65	74	81	87
38	45	49	55	58	61	65	75	85	88
39	46	51	56	59	62	68	77	86	89
39	46	51	56	59	62	68	79	86	89

(a) What are the lowest and highest marks?

(b) Form a frequency table using the groups 30–39, 40–49, 50–59, 60–69, 70–79 and 80–89.

(c) Draw a bar chart to illustrate this information. For the heights of the bars use 1 cm to represent one pupil.

(d) Which group contains the greatest number of students?

(e) How many more students were in the group with the highest marks than in the group with the lowest marks?

CONTINUOUS DATA

The number of occupants in a car is a whole number (2.5 people is not possible!).

On the other hand, a person's height is not an exact whole number of centimetres. An adult's height is likely to be between 150 cm and 200 cm and could be marked anywhere along this section of a tape measure.

110 120 130 140 150 160 170 180 190 200 210 cm

Because height can be anywhere on a continuous scale, it is not possible to have a gap in the scale and say that no person's height can be in that gap.

A collection of heights is an example of *continuous data*.

Grouping Continuous Data

This is a list of the heights of 55 children. It was extracted from a database which has sorted the heights into numerical order. Each height was rounded *up* to the next whole centimetre, so a recorded height of 131 cm means that the child's height, h cm, is in the range $130 < h \leqslant 131$

131	134	136	137	139	141	142	144	145	147	149
132	134	136	137	139	141	142	144	145	148	150
132	134	136	138	140	142	143	144	146	148	150
133	135	136	138	140	142	143	144	147	149	152
133	135	137	139	140	142	144	145	147	149	153

The heights given range from 131 cm to 153 cm.

This information needs grouping to make more sense of it, so we will use groups of width 5 cm, ending the first group at 135 cm and so on. This gives five groups which, using h cm for the actual height, can be written

$$130 < h \leqslant 135, \quad 135 < h \leqslant 140, \quad 140 < h \leqslant 145, \quad 145 < h \leqslant 150, \quad 150 < h \leqslant 155$$

Notice that all groups have the *same width*.
Notice also that a height which is more than 135 cm belongs in the second group whereas a height of 135 cm belongs in the first group.

Looking down the list of heights we see that there are 10 children whose heights are in the first group, 15 children whose heights are in the second group, and so on, and a frequency table can be produced.

Height, h cm	Frequency
$130 < h \leqslant 135$	10
$135 < h \leqslant 140$	15
$140 < h \leqslant 145$	17
$145 < h \leqslant 150$	11
$150 < h \leqslant 155$	2
Total	55

Bar Charts for Continuous Data

We can use the frequency table above to draw a bar chart.

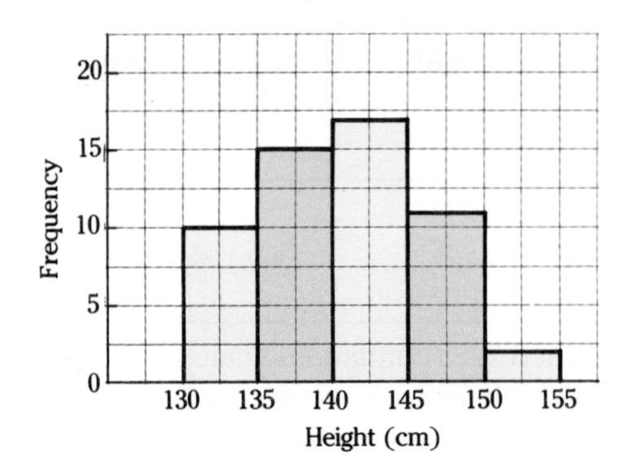

Notice that the horizontal axis gives the heights on a continuous scale, like part of a tape measure, so *there are no gaps between the bars.*

A bar chart illustrating continuous data has no gaps between the bars.

Exercise 23c

1. State whether the following sets of data can take distinct values only or are continuous.
   (a) The populations in parliamentary constituencies.
   (b) The journey times to work of employees at a factory.
   (c) The number of heads showing when four coins are tossed.
   (d) The lengths of sticks of spaghetti in a packet.
   (e) The weights of parcels sent by parcel post.
   (f) The capacities of hand-blown glass bottles.
   (g) The diameters of ball bearings produced by a machine.
   (h) Shoe sizes.

2. Emma kept a record of the time she had to wait for the bus to work each morning for four weeks. The results are shown in this frequency table.

Time, t (in minutes)	Tally	Frequency
$0 \leqslant t < 5$	~~||||~~ ||	7
$5 \leqslant t < 10$	~~||||~~ ||||	9
$10 \leqslant t < 15$	|||	3
$15 \leqslant t < 20$	|	1

   (a) On how many mornings did Emma have to wait for 15 minutes or longer ?
   (b) How often did Emma wait less than 5 minutes ?
   (c) On how many mornings did Emma record the length of her wait ?
   (d) Did Emma ever have to wait for 20 minutes ?

3. Here is a frequency table showing the times, in minutes, taken by a group of commuters to travel from home to work on a particular morning.

Time, t (in minutes)	Frequency
$0 < t \leqslant 10$	2
$10 < t \leqslant 20$	9
$20 < t \leqslant 30$	5
$30 < t \leqslant 40$	4
$40 < t \leqslant 50$	2
$50 < t \leqslant 60$	1

Copy and complete this bar chart, using the table.

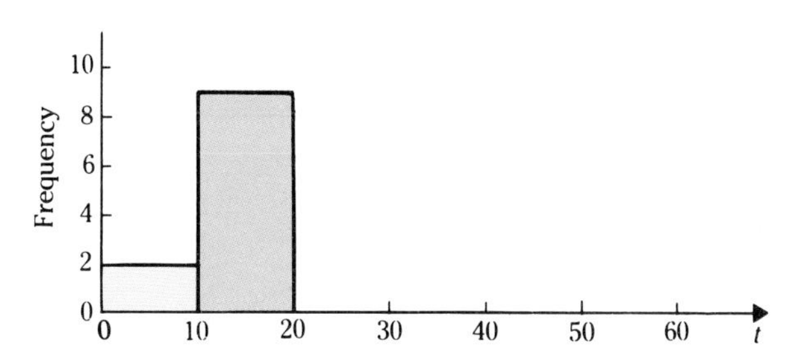

4. Use the bar chart on page 405 to answer the following questions.
   (a) How many children had a height over 145 cm ?
   (b) How many children had a height less than or equal to 140 cm ?
   (c) In which group did the heights of most children lie ?
   (d) How many children had a height of 138 cm ?

5. This is a list of the weights, each correct to the nearest kilogram, of 100 adults. The list is in numerical order.

47	50	52	54	60	63	63	64	66	66	68	69	70	70	72	78	79	80	90	104
48	51	53	55	60	63	63	64	66	67	68	69	70	71	73	78	80	82	92	110
49	51	53	58	61	63	63	65	66	67	68	70	70	71	73	78	80	83	94	112
49	51	53	58	62	63	64	65	66	68	69	70	70	72	74	79	80	85	95	115
49	52	54	59	62	63	64	65	66	68	69	70	70	72	75	79	80	88	100	118

   (a) What is the smallest recorded weight ?
   (b) If a person's weight is recorded as 60 kg, what is the range in which their actual weight, w kg, lies ?
   (c) Copy and complete this frequency table.

Weight, w kg	Frequency
$39.5 \leqslant w < 59.5$	
$59.5 \leqslant w < 79.5$	
$79.5 \leqslant w < 99.5$	
$99.5 \leqslant w < 119.5$	
Total	

   (d) How many people have a weight less than 79.5 kg ?
   (e) Explain why it is not possible to obtain from the table the number of people whose weights are greater than 100 kg.

Frequency Polygons

Another method of illustrating grouped data is to plot the middle point of the top of each bar, (but not the bar itself) and join these points with straight lines. The middle of a bar is halfway through the group that it represents and it is easier to keep track of the points if we add a row to a frequency table to give these halfway values.

For example, to make a frequency polygon for this frequency table we add the row to the table, and can then draw the graph.

Marks	1-9	10–19	20–29	30–39	40–49
Halfway values	5	15	25	35	45
Frequency	5	8	12	10	9

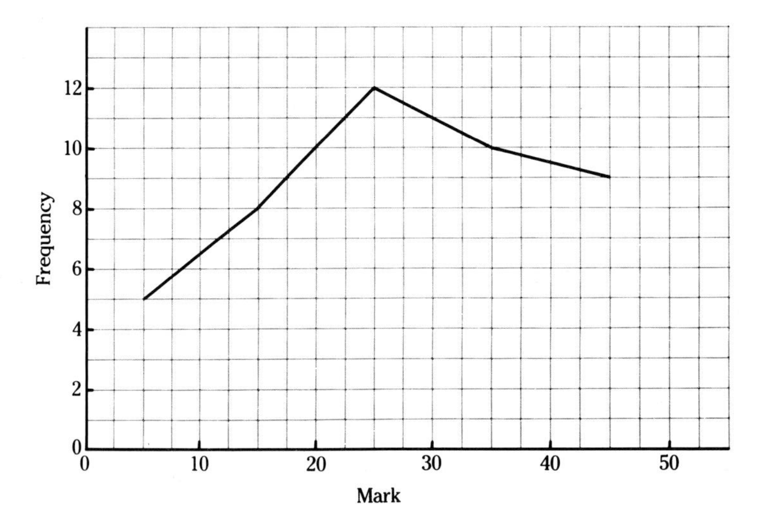

Exercise 23d

1. Copy the grid for this bar chart, but do not draw the bars. On your grid, draw a frequency polygon giving the same information.

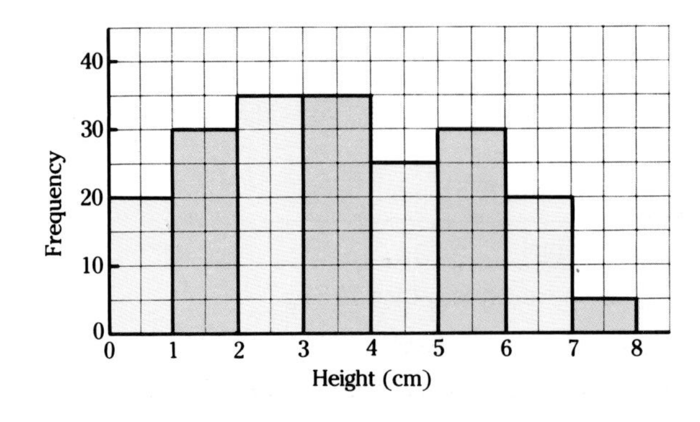

2. Draw a frequency polygon for the information given in the bar chart on page 362.

3. This frequency table gives the heights of a batch of tomato seedlings two weeks after the seeds were sown.

Height, h cm	$0 \leqslant h < 1$	$1 \leqslant h < 2$	$2 \leqslant h < 3$	$3 \leqslant h < 4$	$4 \leqslant h < 5$
Mid-way value	0.5				
Frequency	5	10	25	4	1

(a) Copy the table and complete the middle row.
(b) Draw a frequency polygon illustrating this distribution of heights.

4. This frequency table gives the distribution of the weights of tomatoes picked from plants grown in a greenhouse.

Weight, w grams	$0 \leqslant w < 10$	$10 \leqslant w < 20$	$20 \leqslant w < 30$	$30 \leqslant w < 40$	$40 \leqslant w < 50$
Mid-way value					
Frequency	20	25	60	65	40

(a) Copy the table and fill in the middle row.
(b) Draw a frequency polygon illustrating this distribution of heights.

5. Draw a frequency polygon to illustrate the distribution of the amount of money spent by customers of a sweet shop using the information given in the table.

Money spent	0–99 p	£1–£1.99	£2–£2.99	£3–£3.99
Frequency	25	12	5	2

6. A batch of lettuce seeds are sown and the heights of the seedlings are measured after three weeks. The frequency polygon illustrates the distribution of these heights.

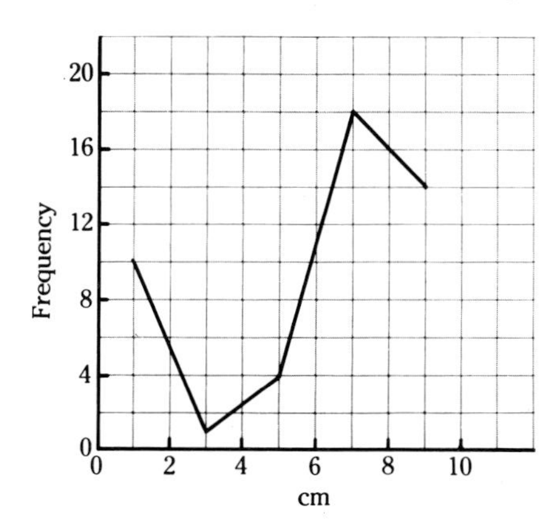

(a) How many plants are there in the first group ?
(b) How many plants were measured altogether ?
(c) What is the span of heights in the first group ?
(d) Make a frequency table from this polygon.
(e) Why do you think that there was such a large number of plants in the first group ?

7. In a cider-apple orchard the number of apples harvested from each tree was recorded. This frequency polygon summarises the results.

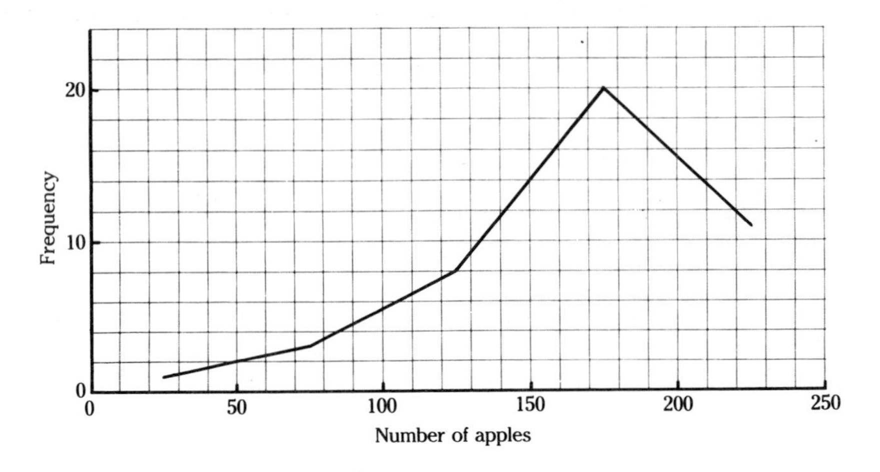

(a) Make a frequency table from the polygon.

(b) How many trees are there in the orchard ?

(c) If the orchard owner decides to get rid of trees that yielded less than 100 apples, how many trees will he dig up ?

(d) Sketch the shape of a frequency polygon that the owner might prefer to see.

PIE CHARTS

Bar charts are good for showing the overall pattern of the distribution of the numbers of items in each group. However to show the *proportion* that each group is of the whole, we use a diagram called a *pie chart.*
A pie chart is a circle cut into slices so that the size of each slice represents the proportion of each group to the whole.

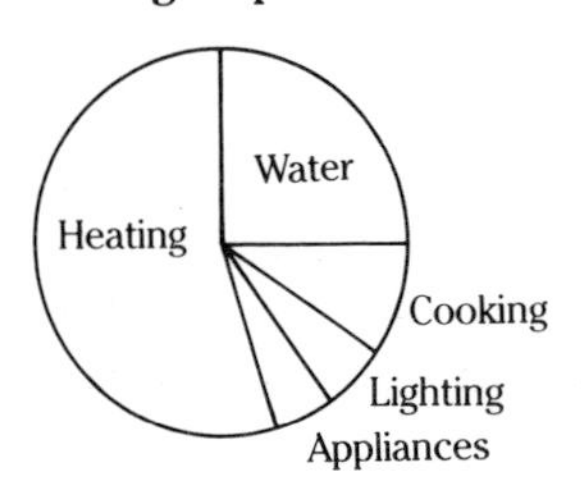

This pie chart shows what proportion of the total fuel consumption is used for different purposes in an average house.
The slice representing hot water is a quarter of the circle, so one quarter of the fuel is used to provide hot water.

Constructing Pie Charts

This frequency table summarises the number of videos out on rental, by recommended viewing classification.

Classification	U	PG	12	15	18	
Frequency	24	16	9	25	36	Total: 110

To construct a pie chart we first find the number in each category as a fraction of the total. For the U classification this is $\frac{24}{110}$ (i.e. 21.8 %). Therefore this slice occupies $\frac{24}{110}$ of the circle and its angle is $\frac{24}{110}$ of 360°, i.e. 79° to the nearest degree. Doing this for the other slices gives this table.

Classification	U	PG	12	15	18
Fraction of total	$\frac{24}{110}$	$\frac{16}{110}$	$\frac{9}{110}$	$\frac{25}{110}$	$\frac{36}{110}$
Angle	79°	52°	29°	82°	118°

Note that when angles are calculated to the nearest degree the total is not always exactly 360°. Note also that tables sometimes give each category as a percentage of the total; the percentage is then used to find the angle.

We can now draw the pie chart.

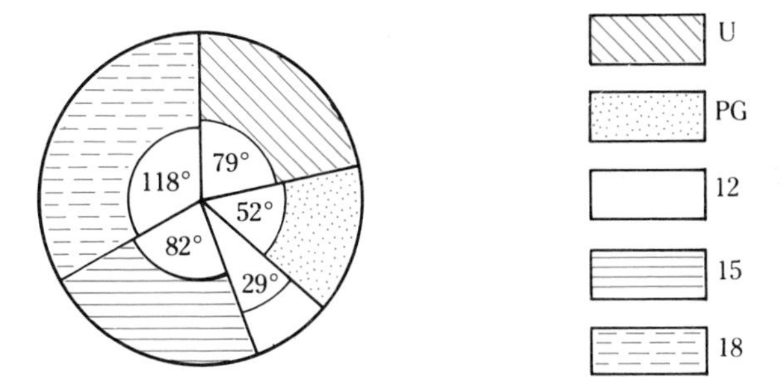

Notice that the size of each slice can be indicated either by giving the angle at the centre or, as is more usual in officially prepared pie charts, the percentage of the total that the slice represents. Also a key is needed when the slices are not labelled.

Interpreting Pie Charts

When a pie chart is marked to show the size of each slice and if the total number of items represented is also given, then the number of items represented by each slice can be found. If the size of each slice is not given, all we can do is to estimate what fraction of the total is represented by that slice.

For example, this slice represents 4.5 % of an annual budget of £2 500 000 allocated to promotions.

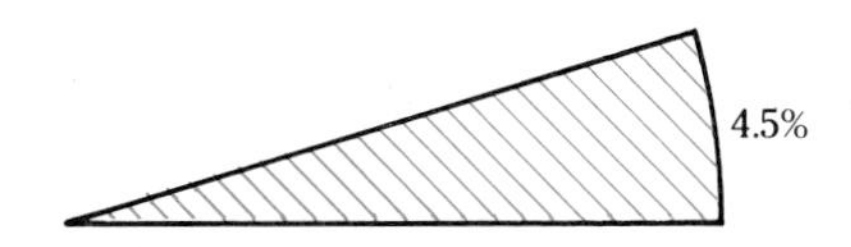

Therefore, 4.5 % of £2 500 000 is spent on promotion, i.e. £$0.045 \times 2\,500\,000 =$ £112 500

Exercise 23e

These books were taken out one evening in the public library:

12 detective stories, 9 thrillers, 4 science fiction, 12 novels and 18 others.

A pie chart is to be drawn to represent this information. Find the angle of the slice representing thrillers.

Total number of books is 55

Fraction representing thrillers is $\frac{9}{55}$

Angle representing thrillers is $\frac{9}{55} \times 360° = 58.9\ldots°$

$= 59°$ to the nearest degree

For questions 1 to 3 draw a pie chart to represent the information.

1. A box of 60 coloured balloons contains the following numbers of balloons of each colour:

Colour	Red	Yellow	Green	Blue	White
Number of balloons	16	22	10	7	5

2. Ninety people were asked how they travelled to work and the following information was recorded:

Transport	Car	Bus	Train	Motorcycle	Bicycle
Number of people	32	38	12	6	2

3. Three hundred people were asked whether they lived in a flat, a house, a bedsit, a bungalow or in some other type of accommodation and the following information was recorded:

Type of accommodation	Flat	House	Bedsit	Bungalow	Other
Frequency	90	150	33	15	12

4.

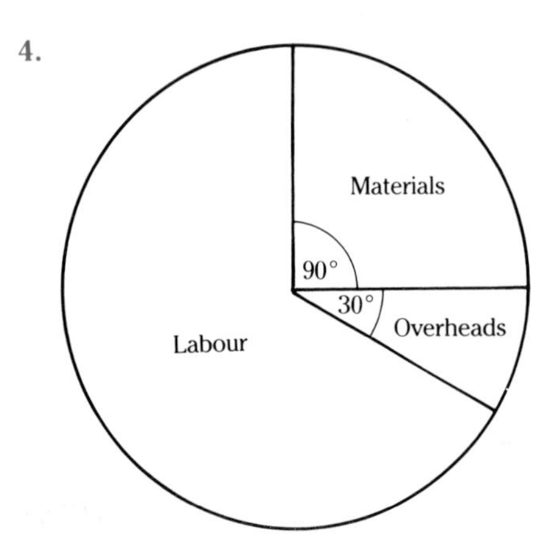

This pie chart shows the costs involved in making a television set. The total cost is £180.

(a) What fraction of the total cost is the cost of materials ?

(b) What fraction of the total cost is the cost of overheads ?

(c) What is the cost of materials ?

(d) What is the cost of overheads ?

(e) What are the labour costs ?

5. This pie chart shows the different methods of transport used by the children of Wiley School.

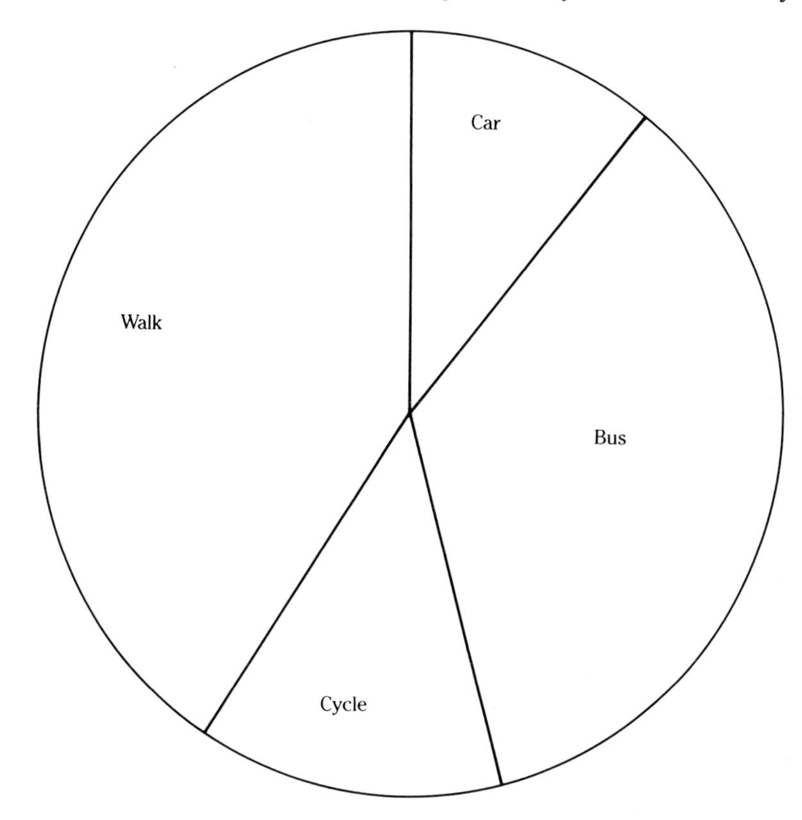

(a) Measure the angle at the centre of the circle for each sector and write each angle as a fraction of a complete revolution (e.g. $48° = \frac{48}{360}$ of a revolution).

(b) If there were 1080 children in the school how many would walk?

(c) If there were 540 children in the school how many would arrive by bus?

(d) If there were 630 children in the school how many would cycle?

(e) What percentage of the children arrived by car?

6. This pie chart shows the age distribution of the population of Green Island, in years, in 1991:

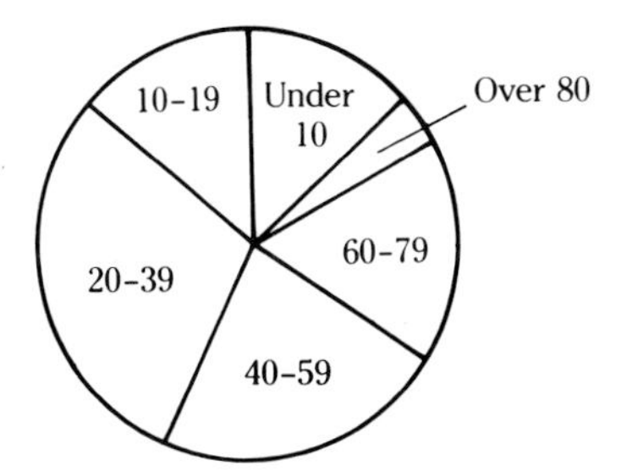

(a) Estimate the *percentage* of the population in the age groups
(i) under 10 years (ii) 60–79 years.

(b) State which groups are of roughly the same size.

Chart 1 Crimes recorded by police (1876–1990)

Total crimes (millions)

Source: Criminal Statistics, England and Wales (HMSO)

Chart 2 Victims of personal crime

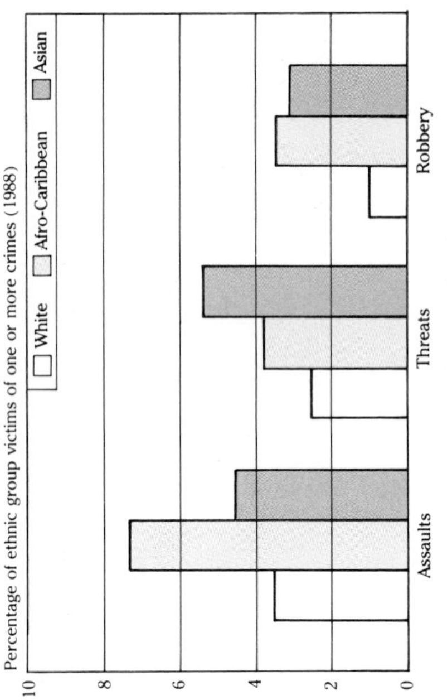

Percentage of ethnic group victims of one or more crimes (1988)

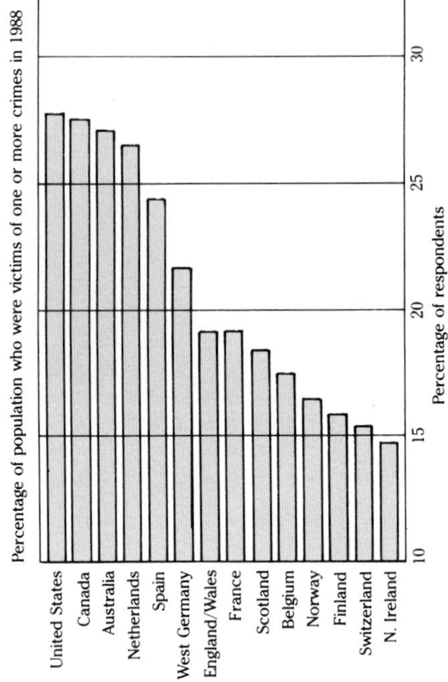

Source: The British Crime Survey 1988 (Home Office Research Study No 111)

Chart 3 Recorded and unrecorded crime

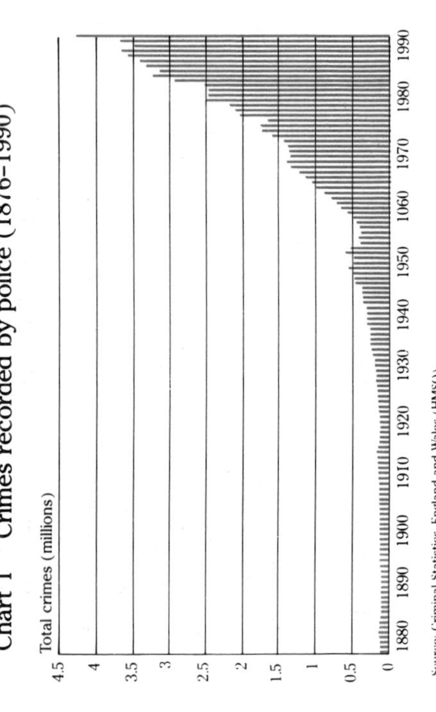

Source: The British Crime Survey 1988 (Home Office Research Study No 111)

Chart 4 International comparisons

Percentage of population who were victims of one or more crimes in 1988

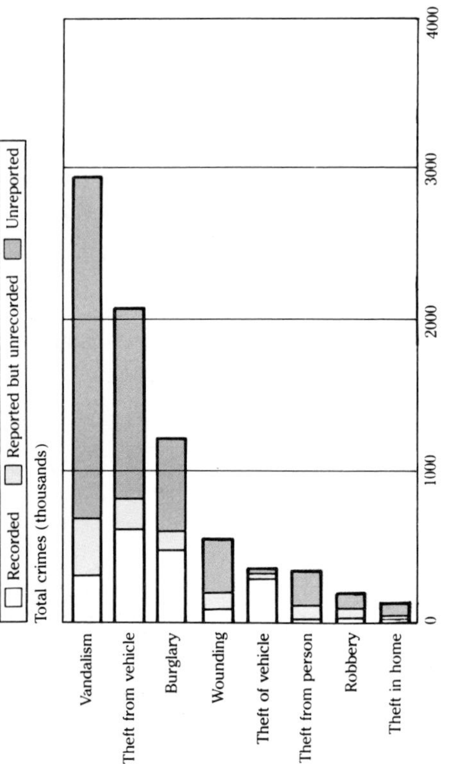

Source: Experience of crime across the world. J. Van Dijk, P. Mayhew, M. Killas (Kluwer 1990)

Chart 5 Risk of assault by age and gender

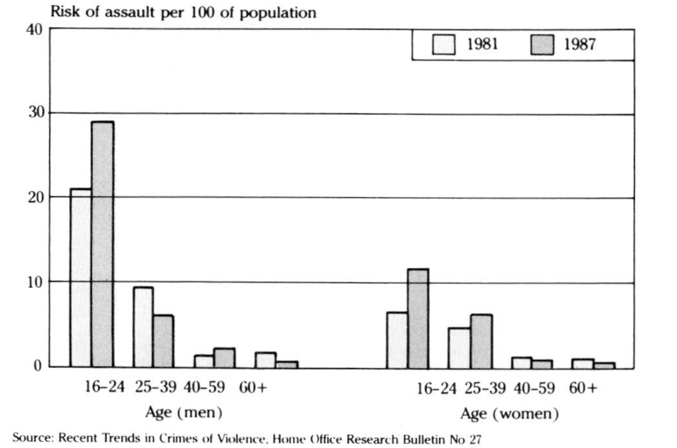

Source: Recent Trends in Crimes of Violence, Home Office Research Bulletin No 27

Chart 6 Crimes recorded by the police (1990)

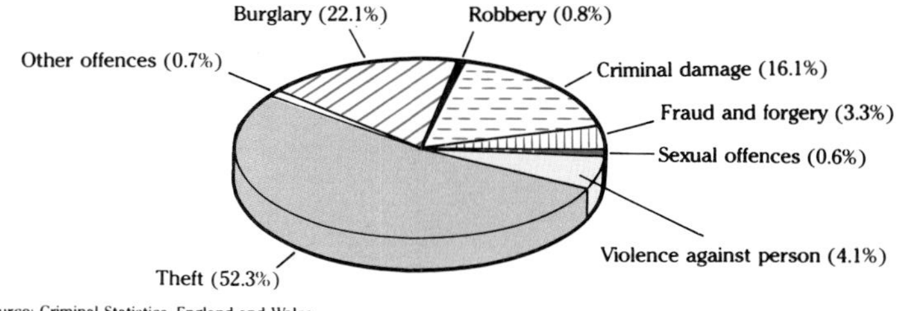

Source: Criminal Statistics, England and Wales

Chart 7 Crimes measured by British Crime Survey (1987)

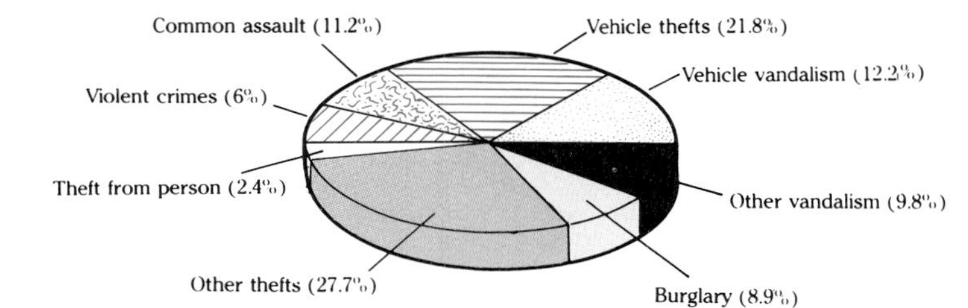

Source: Home Office Research Study No 111

7. This question refers to the charts above.

Charts 1, 2, 3, 4 and 5 are all bar charts and they show the variety of ways in which bar charts can be drawn, e.g. horizontally (chart 4), showing two or more sets of information (charts 2, 3 and 5).

(a) Use chart 1 to find the approximate number of crimes reported to the police in 1980 and in 1990. Hence find the percentage increase in reported crimes from 1980 to 1990.

(b) Use chart 3 to find the approximate number of recorded thefts from vehicles and the number of unreported thefts from vehicles.

(c) Use chart 5 to find which age group of the population is most at risk of assault. Who is more likely to be assaulted, a twenty-year old male or a seventy-year old female?

(d) What percentage of crimes recorded by the police in 1990 were fraud and forgery? Combine this information with the information found in (a), to find the actual number of recorded fraud and forgery crimes in 1990.

(e) What percentage of the Asian ethnic group were victims of assault in 1988?

(f) Which country had the smallest percentage of the population as criminal victims in 1988?

(g) Which category of crime formed the smallest percentage of all crimes measured by the British Crime Survey in 1987?

MISLEADING ILLUSTRATIONS

The following graph shows the variation in the exchange rate of sterling against the Deutschmark. It is typical of many that appear in the financial pages of newspapers.

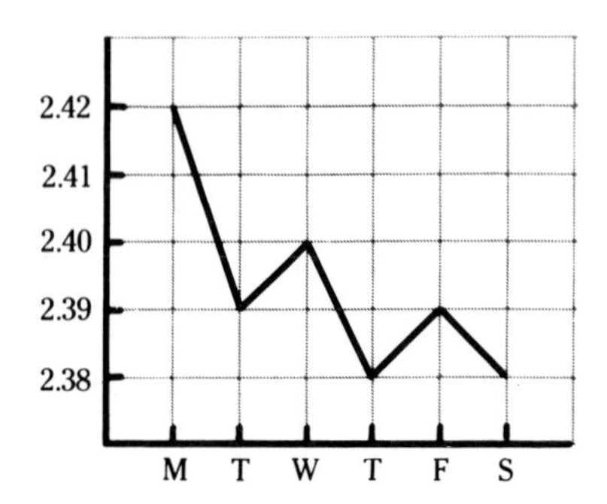

Because the vertical scale does not start at zero, the graph gives the impression of an enormous fall in the value of Sterling. In fact, the value has fallen from 2.42 Dm on Monday to 2.38 Dm on Friday, which is a fall of 0.04 Dm. This is $\frac{0.04}{2.42}$ of its value on Monday, i.e. just under 2 %.

Not many graphs are drawn deliberately to mislead, but may be given this way to save space. Some however are drawn in such a way as to emphasise a change, so look carefully at any bar chart or graph before basing judgements on it.

Exercise 23f

1. Michael took the following bar chart to show his bank manager in support of his request for doubling his overdraft limit.

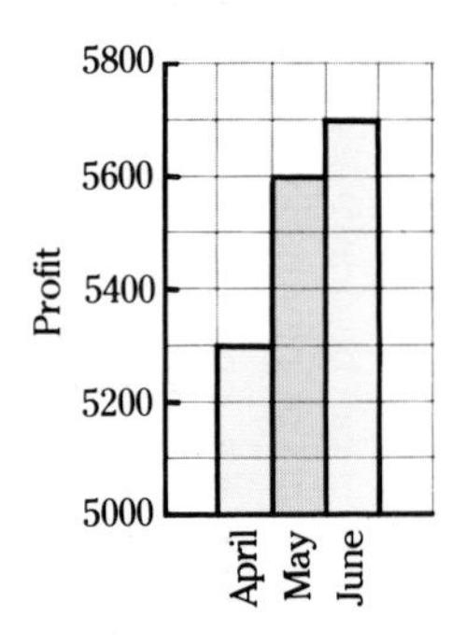

   (a) Explain why Michael's bank manager was not impressed.

   (b) What was the percentage increase in sales from April to June ?

2. This is part of a proposed advertisement for a slimming product.

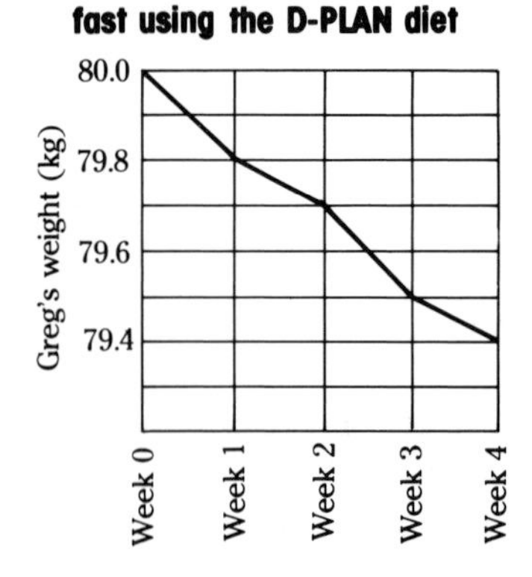

   (a) Do you think that this would form the basis for a fair advertisement ? Give reasons for your comments.

   (b) What percentage of his weight at the start of the four weeks had Greg lost at the end of the four weeks ?

3. Avril produced this 'pie chart' to illustrate a poster asking pupils to buy cards produced at school where 25% of the income from each card would go to charity.

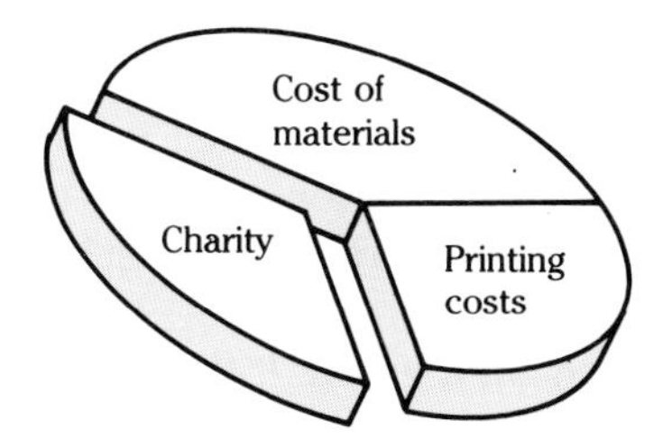

(a) Can you work out from the illustration what percentage of the price covers printing costs?

(b) Is the illustration reasonable? Give reasons for your answer.

4. The illustration is part of some promotional material aimed at persuading doctors to prescribe a new medicine that was introduced last May.

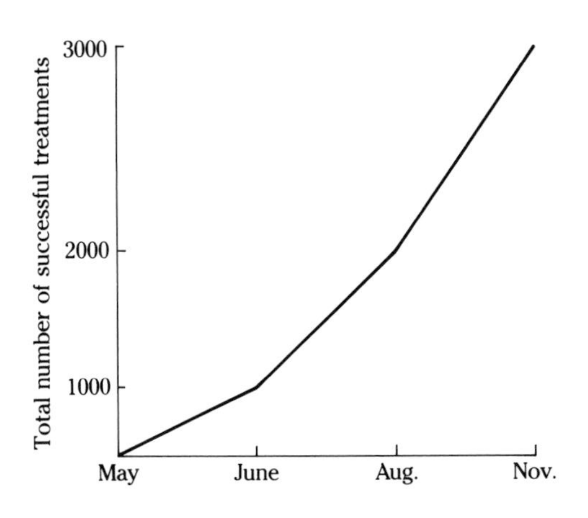

(a) What impression do you get from this illustration?

(b) Is the monthly number of successful treatments increasing?

(c) Name two factors that would appear to distort the data.

(d) Give an illustration that represents this data fairly.

5. This graph is not misleading; it shows how the annual change in the retail price index varied over a few years. Study it carefully and then answer the questions that follow.

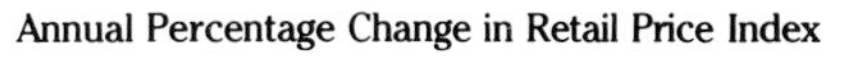

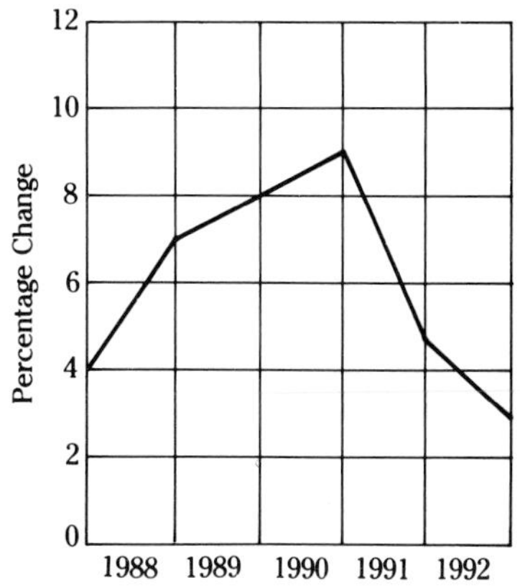

(a) What was the annual percentage change in the retail price index during 1989?

(b) If a table cost £100 at the end of 1988, what would it cost at the end of 1989, assuming that its price changed in line with the retail price index?

(c) What was happening to prices in 1991?

(d) If a games machine cost £100 at the beginning of 1991, what would it cost at the end of 1991, assuming that the price changed in line with the retail price index?

6. The following illustration was used to impress upon people the need to be vaccinated during a flu epidemic.

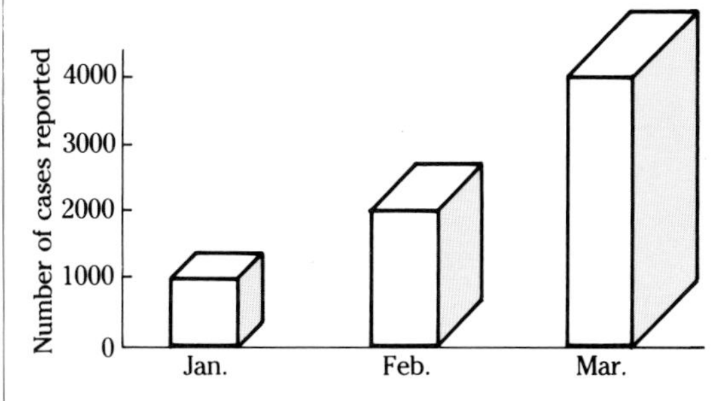

(a) How many cases were reported in March?

(b) Does this illustration give a true impression of the facts? Give reasons for your answer.

SCATTER DIAGRAMS

Sometimes we need to investigate whether a relationship exists between two attributes. For example, is there a relationship between a person's height and shoe size, or between the cost of a book and the number of pages in it ?

In other situations it may appear that two quantities are directly proportional, so the graph relating them would be a straight line. A purchaser may think, for example, that the secondhand value of a particular model of a car is directly related to the mileage it has done.

To test hypotheses such as these, points can be plotted on a graph. If there is a direct relationship, the points should lie on a straight line. Because we can expect there to be slight variations in any practical situation, the points will be scattered a little. If there is not a direct relationship, the points will be very scattered.

A graph in which the plotted points do not lie *exactly* on a straight line is called a *scatter diagram*.

For example, this table lists the heights and the shoe sizes of 12 women.

Height (cm)	158	160	161	163	164	166	166	167	168	170	171	174
Shoe size (continental)	37	36	38	39	37	40	38	37	39	42	41	40

Plotting the points gives this graph.

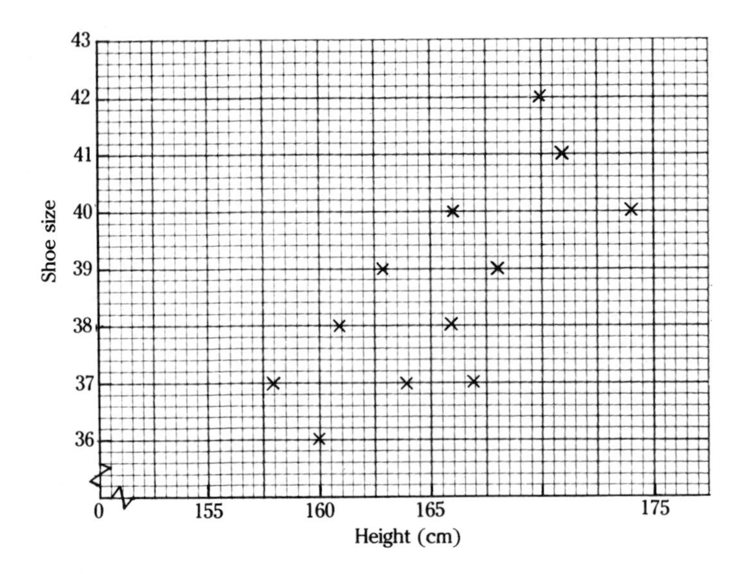

Now we can see that taller people tend to have larger feet but the relationship between height and shoe size is not strong enough to say that there is a direct (i.e. linear) relationship.

Line of Best Fit and Correlation

Looking again at the scatter graph opposite, we can see that the points are scattered loosely about a straight line, which we can draw by eye. This is called *the line of best fit.*

When drawing this line, the aim is to get the points evenly distributed about the line, so that the sum of the distances from the line to points that are above it, is roughly equal to the sum of the distances from the line to points that are below it. This may mean that none of the points lies on the line. It is sensible to use a transparent ruler.

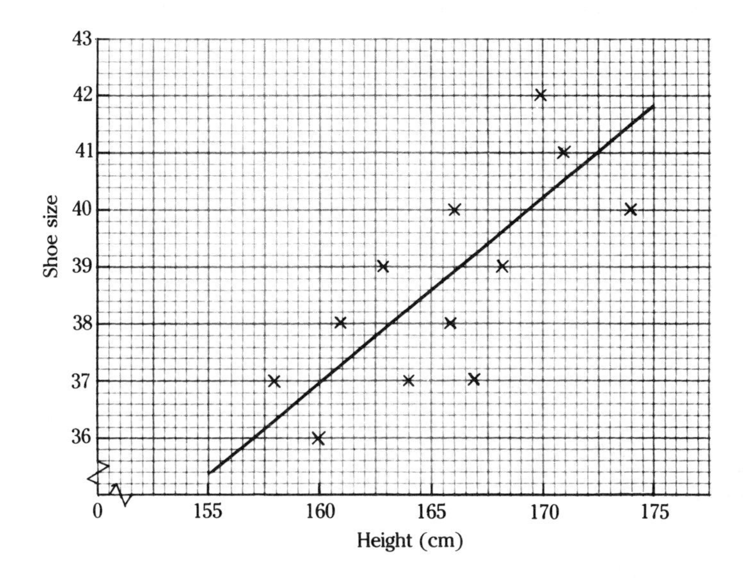

The less scatter there is about the line, the stronger is the relationship between the two quantities. We use the word *correlation* for the strength of the relationship.

If the points are close to the line, there is a strong correlation. In this case it is reasonable to use the line to predict the value of one quantity, given the other.

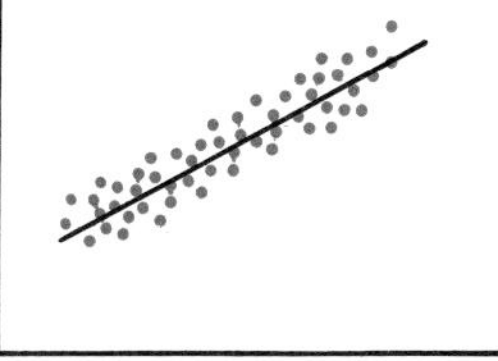

If the points are loosely scattered about the line, there is moderate correlation. Any predictions made from the line would be rough estimates (very rough if the points were widely scattered).

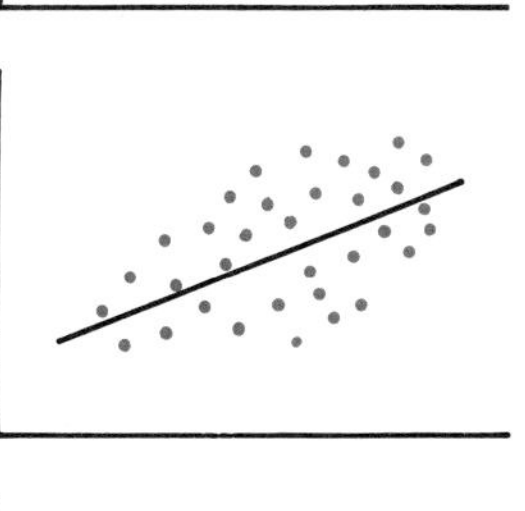

Sometimes the points are so scattered that there is no obvious line and we say that there is no correlation.

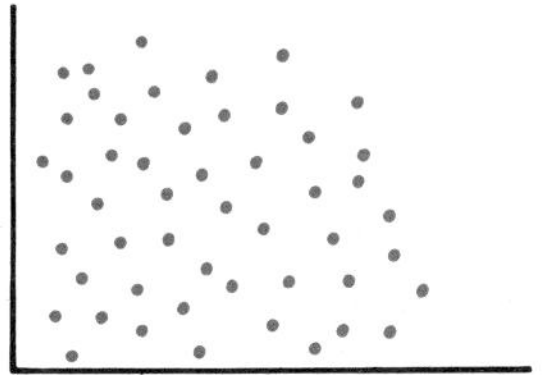

Exercise 23g

The prices and mileages of secondhand *Sarrion* cars were checked with a number of dealers and the data obtained is shown in the table.

Price (\$)	6100	3300	850	8350	5400	3400	5950
Mileage	26 500	68 900	92 000	16 800	52 600	81 700	43 400

Plot the information on graph paper and draw the best line you can to fit these points.

(a) Do you think there is a reasonable correlation between the mileage and the secondhand value of Sarrion cars ?

Use the line to estimate

(b) the price of a Sarrion that has 18 000 miles on the clock

(c) the mileage of a Sarrion that costs \$3200.

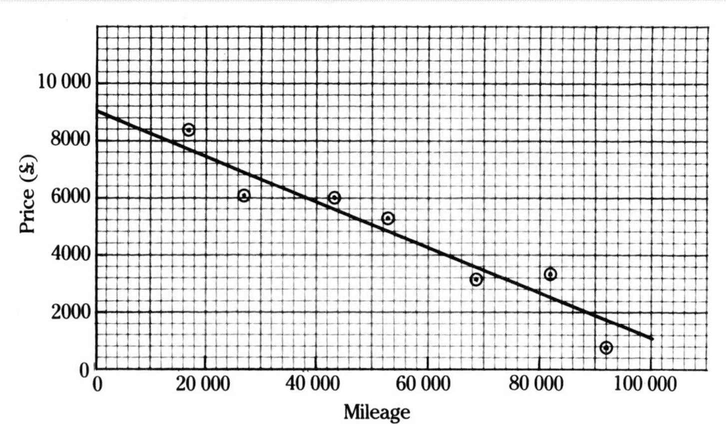

(a) The correlation is quite strong. (b) \$7600 (c) 73 000

The scatter of the points is about \$ 200 above and below the line, so these estimates are subject to an error of about ±\$ 200.

In each question, plot the information on a graph using the suggested scales where given. If the correlation is good enough to justify doing so, draw a line of best fit. Then answer the specific questions.

1. This table shows the number of bad oranges per box after different delivery times.

No. of bad oranges	0	2	5	4	2
No. of hours in transit	4	10	18	14	6

Use 1 cm ≡ 2 hours and 1 cm ≡ 1 orange

How many bad oranges could be expected after a 12-hour delivery ? Give an indication of the margin of error of your answer.

2. A breeder of exotic fish carried out a survey over eight years to investigate the average weight of koi carp at various ages. The data he collected are given in the table.

Age of koi (years)	1	2	3	4	5	6	7	8
Average weight (g)	90	230	495	610	1050	1090	1280	1560

Use 1 cm ≡ 1 year and 1 cm ≡ 200 g

(a) Do you think that a mistake was made in calculating one of the average weights? If so, which weight is suspect?

(b) What might a 9-year-old koi be expected to weigh?

(c) If the line were extended to 20 years, could it be used to estimate the weight of a 20-year-old koi? Give a reason for your answer.

3. This table shows the heights and weights of 12 people.

Height (cm)	150	152	155	158	158	160	163	165	170	175	178	180
Weight (kg)	56	62	63	64	57	62	65	66	65	70	66	67

Use 2 cm ≡ 5 cm for height, starting the scale at 145 cm, and 2 cm ≡ 5 kg, starting the scale at 55 kg.

(a) Comment on the correlation between the heights and weights.

(b) Carlos weighs 65 kg. What can you say about his height?

4. This table shows the number of rooms and the number of people living in each of 15 houses.

Number of rooms	3	4	4	5	5	5	6	6	6	6	7	7	7	8	8
Number of people	3	2	5	4	2	1	6	2	3	4	4	5	3	2	6

Cheryl lives in a house with four other people. Is the house likely to have more than four rooms?

5. From the scatter graph on page 375 suggest a range for the height of a woman with shoe size 40.

Investigation

You are invited to criticise a questionnaire and to consider the design of some questions.

A student designed this questionnaire to gather evidence for a project on the acceptability of school uniform to the pupils in a school.

1. Name (as it appears in the register) ____________________

2. Age ____________________

3. Sex ____________________

4. Religion (tick the correct box) Christian ☐ Muslim ☐ Jewish ☐ Other ☐

5. School uniform should be worn by every pupil in the school.
Tick the box which most closely matches your opinion.

Agree ☐ Neither agree nor disagree ☐ Disagree ☐

(a) One problem associated with requests for personal information is a reluctance to tell the truth. Are any of the above questions likely to generate untruthful answers ? Can you re-word them so that a truthful answer is more likely ?

(b) What problems do you think question 4 will pose ?

(c) Why do you think question 4 is there ?

(d) Do you think that a different result would come from this survey if question 5 was worded 'School uniform should be abolished' ?

(e) Do you think that there should be more categories from which to choose a response to question 5, e.g. Agree/Disagree strongly ?

(f) Why do you think that questions 2 and 3 are included ?

(g) Design a questionnaire to find peoples' views on whether uniform should be worn by bank counter staff. Remember that it is rarely possible to foresee all the problems, so any questionnaire that you design should be tried out on a few people and then adapted if necessary.

(h) Find a questionnaire (either one you have had to fill in or one from a magazine) and criticise it for suitability of questions and purpose.

Self-Assessment 23

1. A list of the number of heads obtained when five coins were tossed repeatedly is given below.

   0 3 1 0 3 2 4 2 5 0 1 3 2 5 4 3 2 2 3 3 3 2 2 4 1 1 3 2 5 3 2 4 3 1 3 2 2 0

   Form a frequency table and then draw a bar chart to illustrate this information.

2. Here is a list showing the times, in seconds, taken by a group of people to calculate 125×36 in their heads. The list has been sorted into numerical order.

   7 9 10 15 23 24 24 27 29 30 30 31 32 33 34 35 35 36 39 42 45 46 47 47 49 50 50 55 56 58 59 60
   60 61 62 68 70 72 79 80 88 90 95 110 125 159

   Use groups $0 \leqslant t < 40$, $40 \leqslant t < 80$, $80 \leqslant t < 120$, and $120 \leqslant t < 160$ to make a frequency table. Illustrate this information by drawing a frequency polygon.

3. Use the data in question 1 to draw a pie chart showing the percentage of tosses that resulted in 0, 1, 2, 3, 4, or 5 heads.

4. The table shows the score obtained on a verbal reasoning test (VR) and on a pattern recognition test (PR) by twelve different people.

VR score	15	12	20	17	10	13	18	12	18	5	9	14
PR score	6	2	8	5	2	6	8	7	9	4	8	9

(a) Draw a scatter graph to illustrate this information and use it to comment on the degree of correlation between the two scores.

(b) Draw a line of best fit.

(c) If Clarrie got a score of 19 on the verbal reasoning test, what can you say about her likely score on the pattern recognition test ?

5. Study the bar chart before answering the following questions.

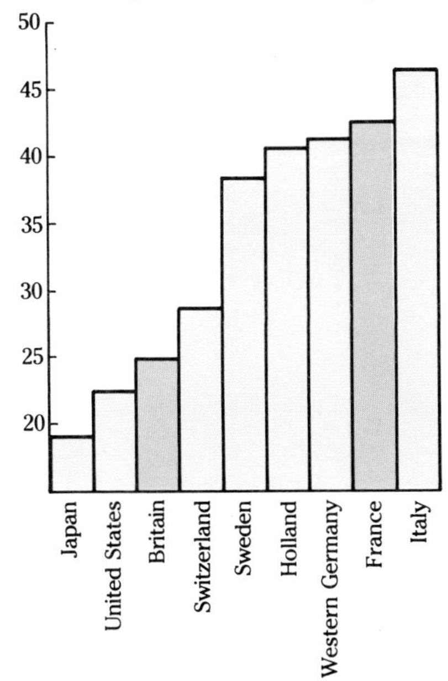

(a) Describe what this graph is illustrating.

(b) Which country has the lowest percentage social cost per worker ?

(c) If you compare the social cost per worker in France and Britain by looking only at the heights of the bars, what impression is given ?

(d) Reading the scale on the left-hand side of the graph carefully, how do the social costs per worker compare in France and Britain ?

6.

BOOK MARKET – UK

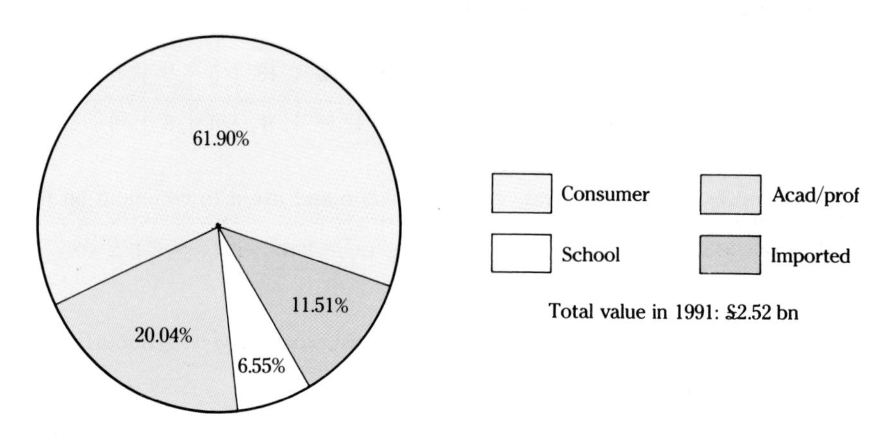

This pie chart illustrates an article about the book trade.

(a) Which year are these figures for ?

(b) What was the total value of the U.K. book market in that year ?

(c) What percentage of the market did imported books account for ?

(d) What was the value of the school sector of this market ?

24 NETWORKS

NETWORKS

A network is any diagram where lines represent the links between items. The items are represented by points. For example, a road map or a family tree is a network.

Road Maps

This road map is drawn to scale so that distances and directions can be determined. The letters represent junctions.

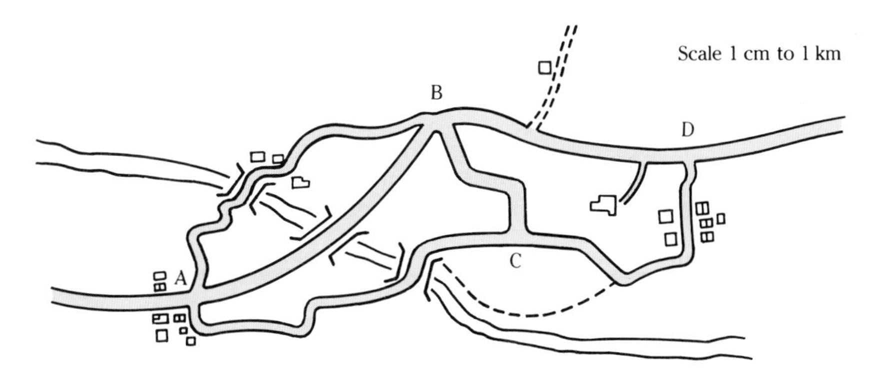

If the measurements are marked, and a rough idea only of the direction is needed, the map can be simplified. A possible network is shown below.

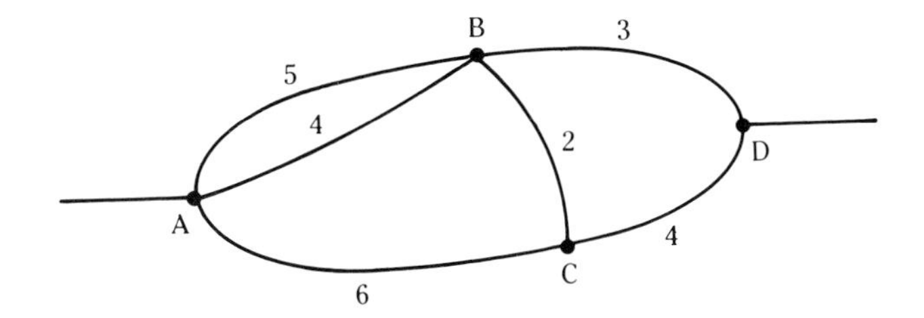

The London Underground map and the British Rail network are examples of simplified networks; accurate distances and directions are not needed, simply the order in which stations lie and the cross-linking of the various rail lines.

Simplified networks are useful when planning routes.

Road and rail networks show relationships between geographical locations but networks can be used to illustrate other relationships, some of which are illustrated in the next section and the following exercise.

Networks Showing Relationships

Anne, Bob and Cathy are three cousins. This can be represented in a network marked with arrows, so that the line with an arrow means 'is a cousin of',
e.g.

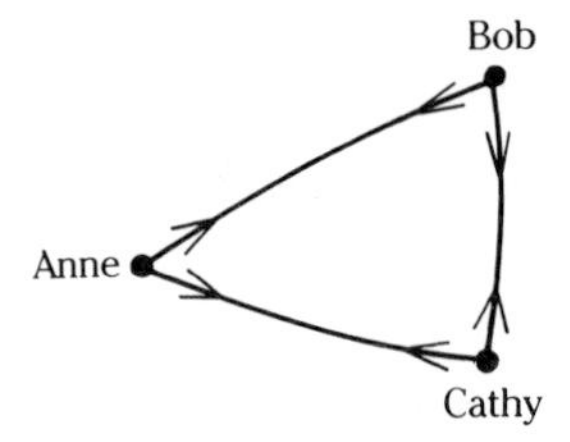

On the other hand suppose that Jane likes Susan but Susan doesn't like Jane; Susan and Martine like each other. This time the line with an arrow means 'likes';

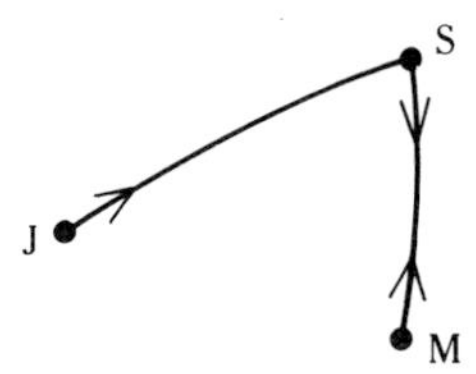

Notice that there is no information about Jane and Martine's relationship; they may not know each other or they may be acquainted and not like each other.

Networks of this type can be used for all sorts of relationships other than family links, such as those between numbers.

Exercise 24a

1.

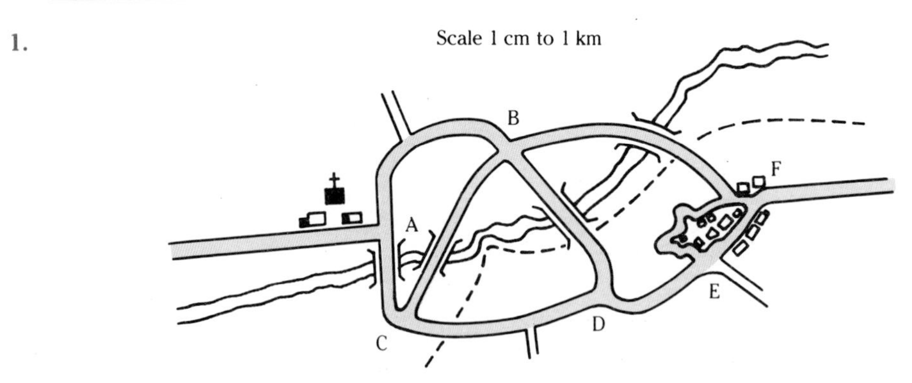

This road map shows buildings, lanes, side roads and bridges.

(a) Draw a simplified network showing only the roads marked in purple and the points A to F. Mark the estimated distances between points.

(b) Find the shortest route from A to F that passes through each of the other points once only.

(c) If CD is a one-way street and it is not possible to drive from C to D, is it possible to find a route as required in part (b) ?

2.

In this road system the distances between villages are marked in kilometres.

Find

(a) the shortest route from A to F

(b) the longest route from A to F that does not require any road to be covered more than once

(c) the longest route that does not require any road to be covered more than once but with any chosen starting and finishing points. (These two points could be the same.)

3.

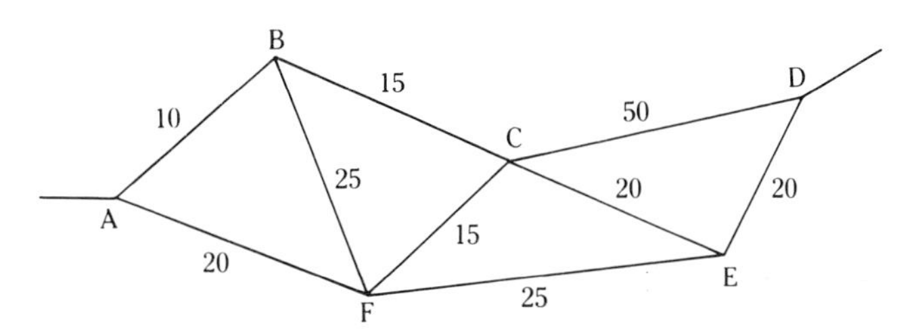

This road network is marked with the time it takes in minutes to get from one village to another.

(a) Find the quickest route from A to D.

(b) Find the slowest route from A to D that does not go through any village more than once.

(c) A delivery van has to visit all the villages, starting from A and finishing at A. Plan a route for the driver, minimising his travel time.

4.

Britair operates a passenger air service flying between London and each of the other cities on the map. It also flies on the routes between G (Glasgow) and D (Dublin), G and B (Brussels), M (Manchester) and B, M and F (Frankfurt), M and P (Paris).

Draw a network to show all the routes that Britair offers.

5. (a)

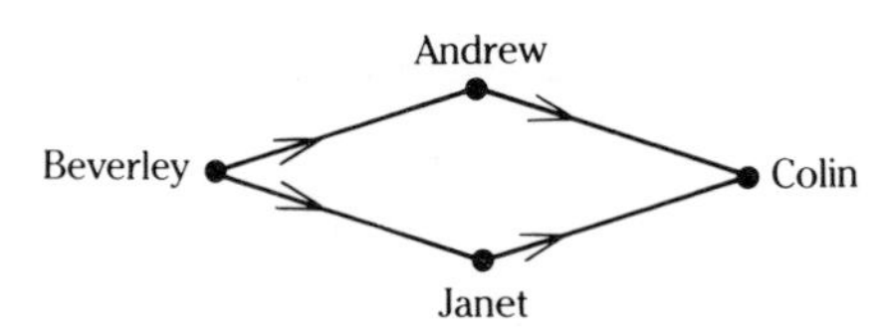

A line with an arrow means 'is older than'. List the age relationships shown. Is Janet older than Andrew?

(b) Copy the network and add lines to show the following information. Hitesh is older than Janet but younger than Andrew; Graham is older than the other five.

6.

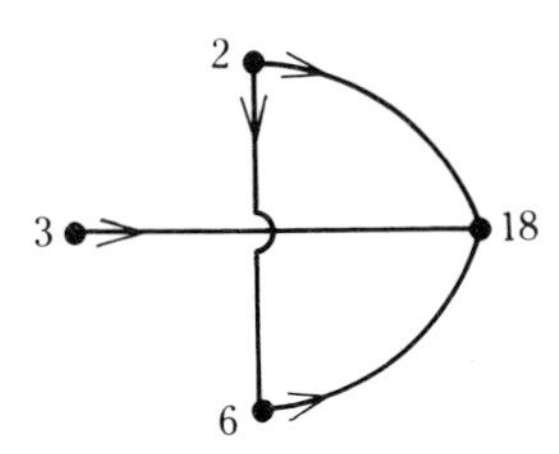

In this incomplete network concerning 18 and its factors, a line with an arrow means 'is a factor of'. One point representing a number and some lines are missing.

(a) What is the missing number? (Do not count 1 or 18 as factors.)

(b) Copy and complete the network.

(c) Draw a similar network for the factors of 20.

(d) If you wanted to count a number as a factor of itself, describe what you would have to add to the diagram.

7. In this network a line with an arrow means 'is a parent of'.

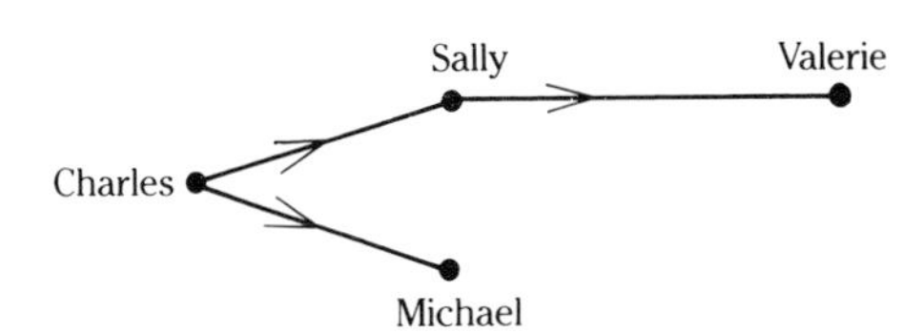

(a) Who is Sally's parent?

(b) What relation is (i) Michael to Sally, (ii) Michael to Valerie, (iii) Valerie to Charles?

8. Draw a network to represent the following information. State the meaning of a line with an arrow. (Notice that 'is taller than' is not a suitable meaning to use for part (a) so another relationship should be chosen.)

(a) Ahmet and Sally are the same height.

(b) Nell and Sally are taller than Tim.

(c) Malcolm is taller than Nell and Raj.

(d) Penny is shorter than Tim.

(e) Raj is taller than Penny and Ahmet.

9.

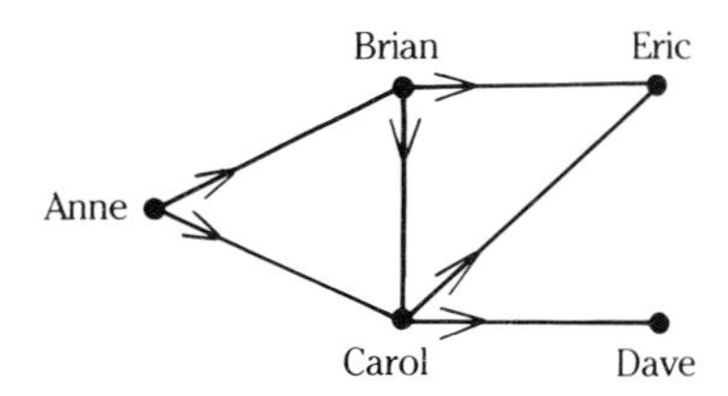

In the diagram above the line with an arrow means 'has a higher mark than'.

(a) Who has the highest mark ?

(b) Which two people have the lowest marks ? Who has the lower mark of the two ?

10. Draw a network to show the relationship 'is a multiple of' between the numbers 2 to 12 inclusive. A line with an arrow means 'is a multiple of'.

11.

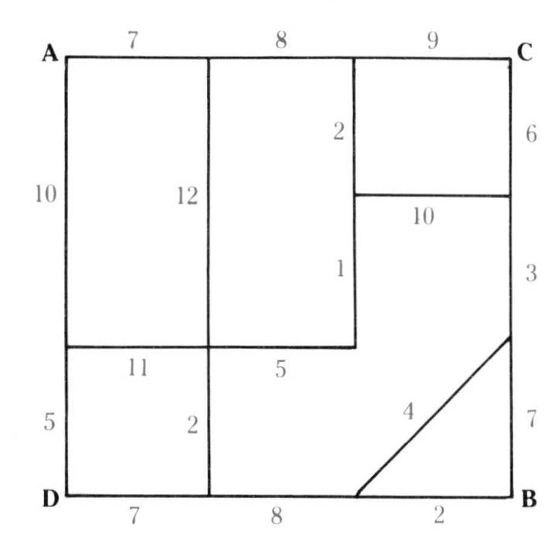

The network shows the time taken in minutes to get from one point to another. Find the quickest route to get from

(a) A to B (b) C to D

Investigations

1. (a) Use a local street map to draw a network showing the streets in the area where you live.

(b) Choose two points on your network. Find how many routes there are between these two points that do not involve having to walk down a street more than once.

(c) Estimate the time it takes to walk along each street and add this information to your network.

(d) Find the route between your points that takes (i) the least time (ii) the most time.

(e) Plan a route for a postman along all the streets in your network.

2. (i)

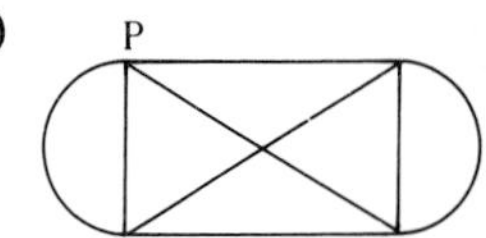

(ii)

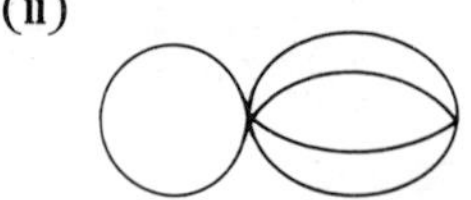

(iii)

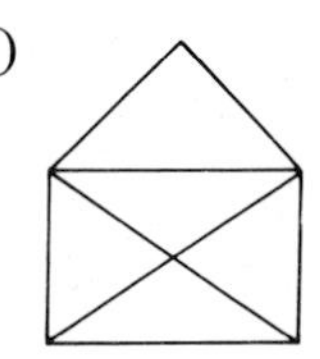

(a) Copy diagram (i) by starting at point P; do not lift your pen from the paper and do not go over any line twice. This is a *traversable* network.

(b) Repeat for diagrams (ii) and (iii), choosing for yourself where to start. (Some points cannot be used as starting points.)

(c) Which of the following networks cannot be drawn in the way described in part (a)?

A

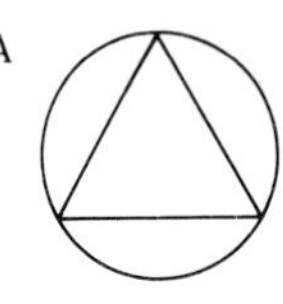

C

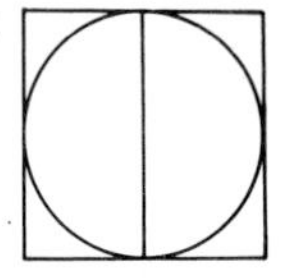

E

B

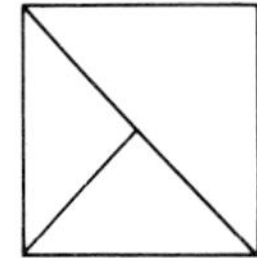

D

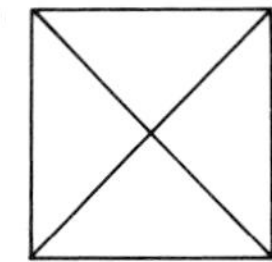

F

(d) Can you tell whether a network is traversable without trying all the possibilities?

3. It is said that in the eighteenth century, a mathematician called Euler became interested in the discussion about the bridges of Königsberg. Was it possible to take a walk, crossing each bridge once and only once and returning to the starting point?

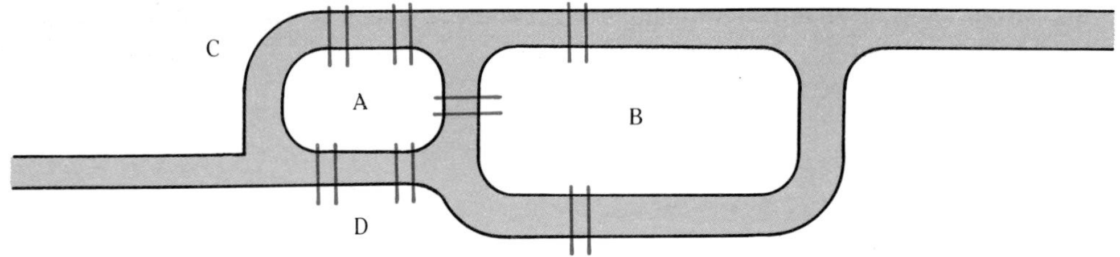

He redrew the map as a simple network, with points for areas A, B, C and D, and lines for bridges.

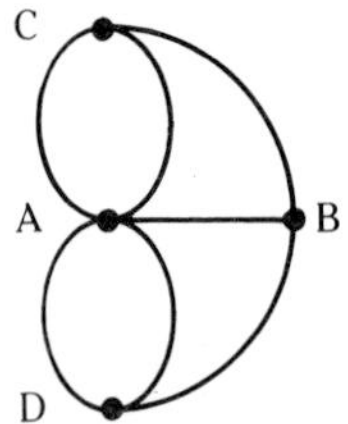

(a) Is the walk possible? Give your reason.

(b) If the walk is possible, take away one bridge to make it impossible. If it is impossible, add or take away one bridge to make it possible.

25

ENLARGEMENT AND SIMILARITY

ENLARGEMENTS

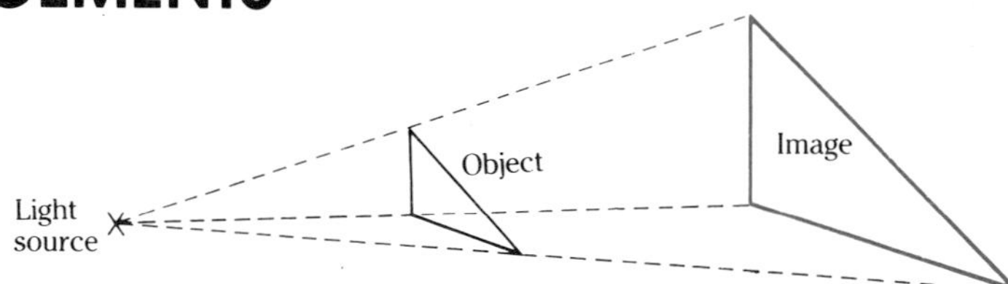

When a projector throws an image on to a screen, the image is the same shape as the object but larger. If each side of the image is twice as long as the corresponding side of the object, then we say that the *scale factor* is 2.

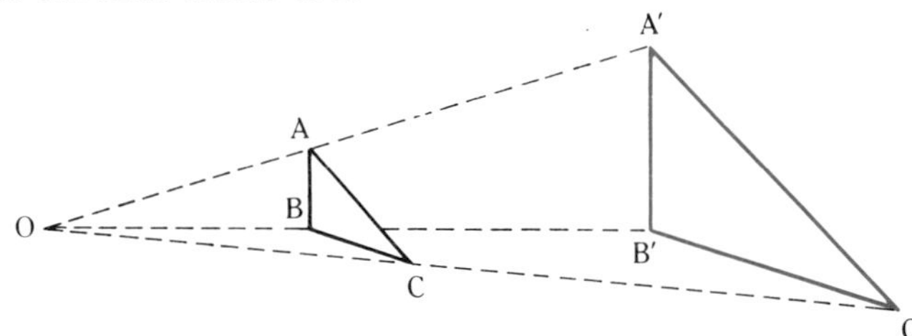

The point O, corresponding to the light source, is called the *centre of enlargement*. Lines drawn from O through AA', BB' and CC' are *guide lines* and, when the scale factor is 2, $OA' = 2OA$, $OB' = 2OB$ and $OC' = 2OC$.

The same idea can be used to enlarge any shape. Suppose we wish to enlarge a given quadrilateral so that the lengths of the enlarged version are three times those of the original.

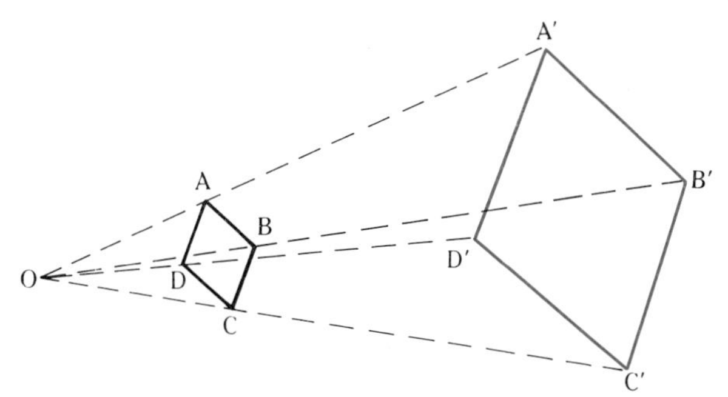

First mark O, the centre of enlargement, at any convenient point. Then draw the guide lines from O through the vertices of the object. The amount by which we extend the guide lines depends on the size of the image required. In this case we want the lines on the image to be three times as long as the corresponding lines on the object, i.e. OA is extended to A' so that $OA' = 3OA$, OB to B' so that $OB' = 3OB$ and so on.
Note that all the lengths are measured from O.

If the scale factor is less than 1 it is unnecessary to extend the guidelines beyond the vertices of the original figure. For example, if triangle ABC is enlarged using a scale factor of $\frac{1}{2}$ then A′ is the point on OA such that $OA' = \frac{1}{2}OA$. Similarly $OB' = \frac{1}{2}OB$ and $OC' = \frac{1}{2}OC$.

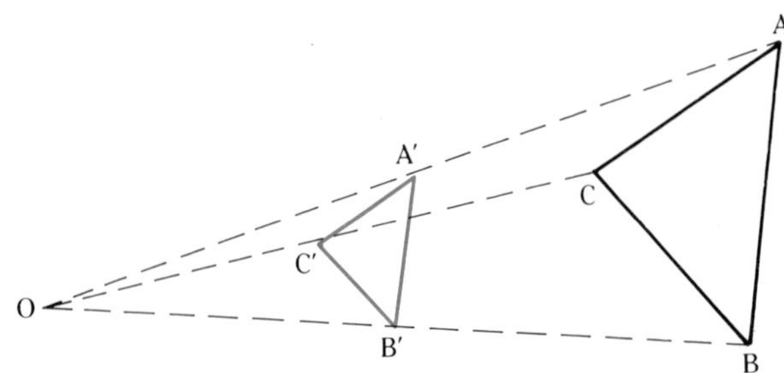

Notice that a scale factor that is less than 1 produces an image that is *smaller* than the object, although the word enlargement is often still used to describe this transformation.

Exercise 25a

1. (a) A source of light O is placed behind a rectangular picture ABCD, held vertically. It casts a shadow A′B′C′D′ on the wall. What is the scale factor ?

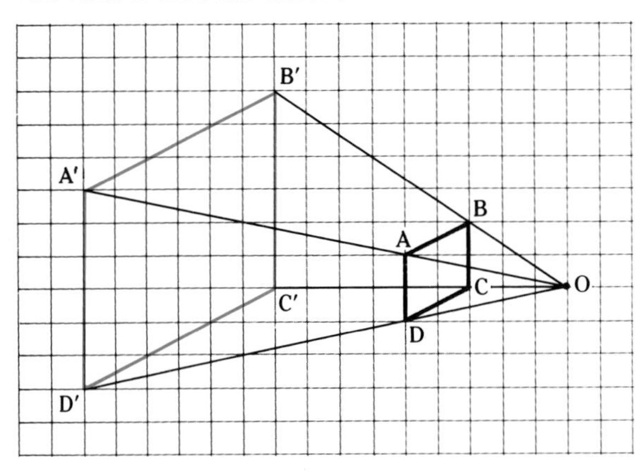

(b) A powerful floodlight at ground level casts a shadow on a nearby building, of a free-standing end-wall of a house that is being demolished. The two walls are parallel. Find the scale factor.

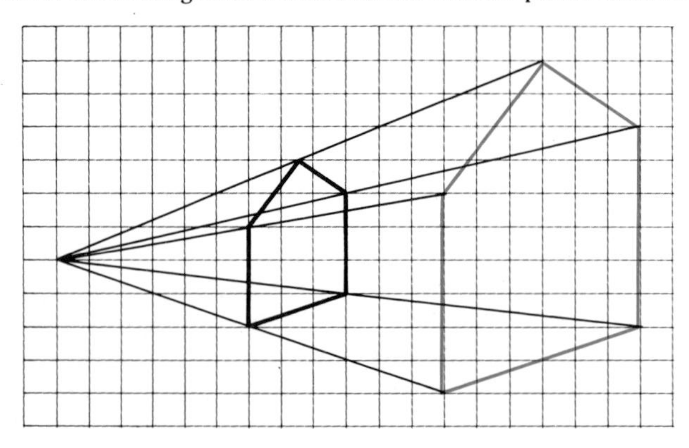

2. 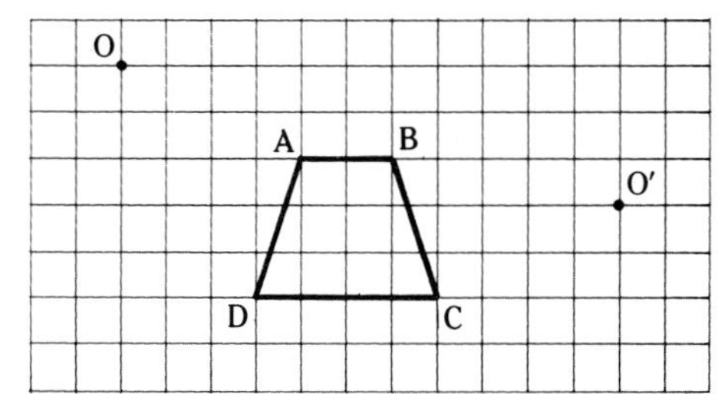

   (a) Copy the diagram on squared paper. Using O as the centre of enlargement and a scale factor of 2, draw the enlargement of ABCD. Label the vertices A′B′C′D′. Check that the enlarged shape has sides twice as long as the original.

   (b) Repeat part (a) but this time use O′ as the centre of enlargement. Is it true that the enlarged shape has sides twice as long as the original ? What is the effect on the image of changing the centre of the enlargement ?

3. Repeat question 2 using a scale factor of

   (a) 3 (b) $\frac{1}{2}$ (c) $1\frac{1}{2}$ (d) $\frac{3}{4}$

4. 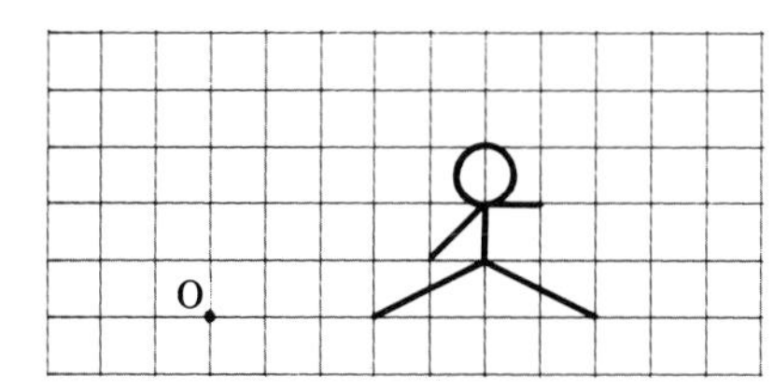

   Copy the figure on squared paper allowing plenty of space above and to the right. Use O as the centre of enlargement and, on the same diagram, draw an enlarged figure using a scale factor of (a) $1\frac{1}{2}$ (b) 3

5. Plot the points A(3, 5), B(6, 2), C(3, −1) and D(0, 2). Join them to give the quadrilateral ABCD.

   (a) Using the point E(3, 2) as the centre of enlargement and a scale factor of 2, draw the enlargement of ABCD. Label the vertices A_1, B_1, C_1, D_1 and write down their coordinates.

   (b) Repeat part (a) but this time using B as the centre of enlargement and a scale factor of $\frac{1}{3}$. Label the vertices A_2, B_2, C_2, D_2 and write down their coordinates.

   (c) How does the length of A_1D_1 compare with the length of A_2D_2 ?

In questions 6 and 7, the purple figure is an enlargement of the black figure. Copy the diagram on squared paper. Draw the guide lines for the enlargement. The point where these lines meet is the centre of enlargement. Give the coordinates of this point, and the scale factor of the enlargement.

6. 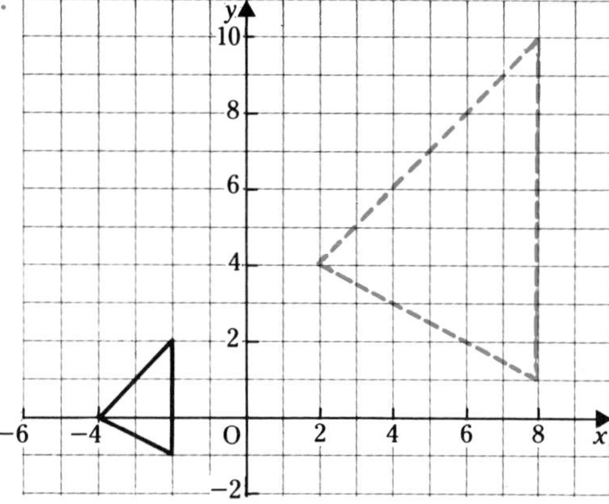

7. 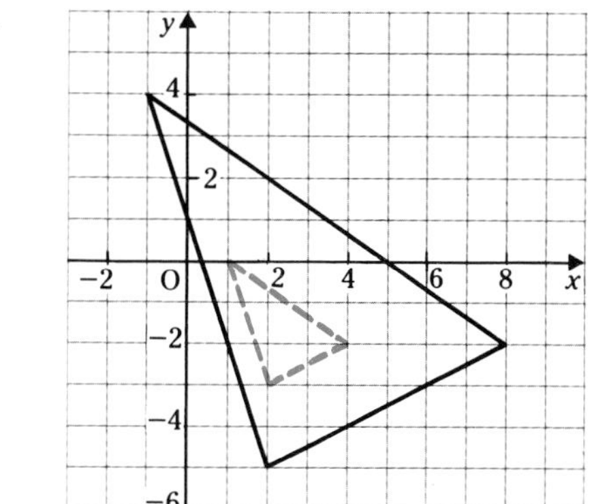

8. 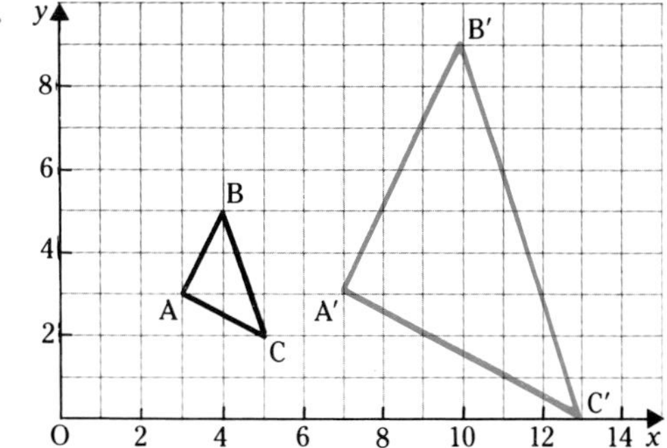

   △A′B′C′ is an enlargement of △ABC. Copy the diagram on to squared paper, draw the guidelines through the corresponding vertices of the two triangles and give the coordinates of the point where these guidelines meet. What special point is this ?

SIMILAR FIGURES

Two figures are similar if they have the same shape, but not necessarily the same size, i.e. one figure is an enlargement of the other.

Enlarging a figure does not alter the angles. It does change the lengths of the lines, but all the lengths change in the same ratio, e.g. if one line is trebled in length, all lines are trebled in length, and the scale factor of the enlargement is 3.

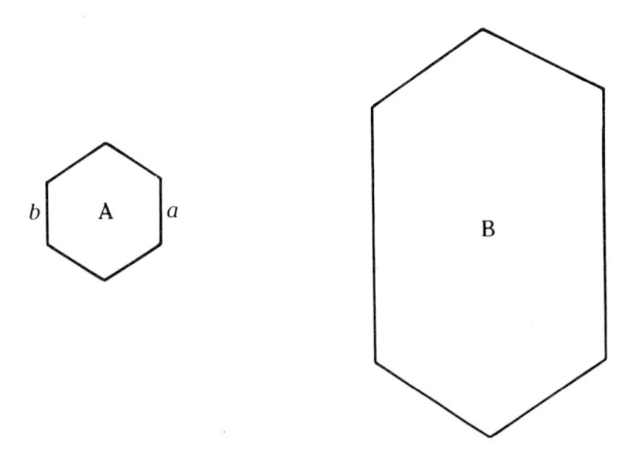

Suppose that a hexagon, A, is enlarged, the sides marked a and b being four times as long, while the other sides are doubled in length. The resulting hexagon, B, contains the same angles as A but the two shapes are obviously different. Not all the lengths have changed in the same ratio. The hexagons are not similar. (Hexagon B is an enlarged *and* stretched version of hexagon A.)

Many practical problems can be solved by using similar figures. Some examples are considered in the next exercise.

Exercise 25b

This logo was drawn and then reduced photographically by setting the machine at 35%.

Take measurements from the diagram and hence find the length of the sides of the outside triangle on the original drawing.

The length of a side on the diagram is 5 cm.

The scale factor of the reduction is 35%, i.e. 0.35, so 5 cm is 0.35 of the original length.

Let the original length be x cm, then 0.35 of $x = 5$

Therefore $0.35 \times x = 5$

i.e. $x = \frac{5}{0.35}\ldots$

$= 14.28$

On the original drawing, the length of the sides are 14.3 cm (3 s.f.)

1.

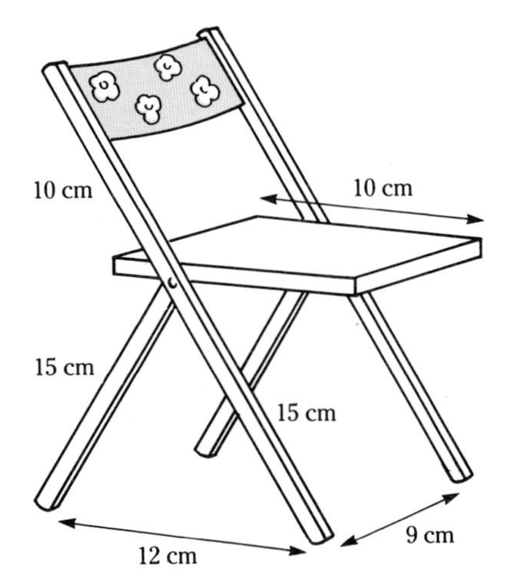

A school-girl had to design a chair. She intended making a quarter size model and she started with this drawing.

(a) What will the width of the proposed full size chair be ?

(b) The chair is intended to fold flat with the front of the seat going up and the legs coming together. What will be the height of the folded up proposed chair ?

2. The diagram shows a design for a company logo. It is a circle with a square inside the circle as shown.

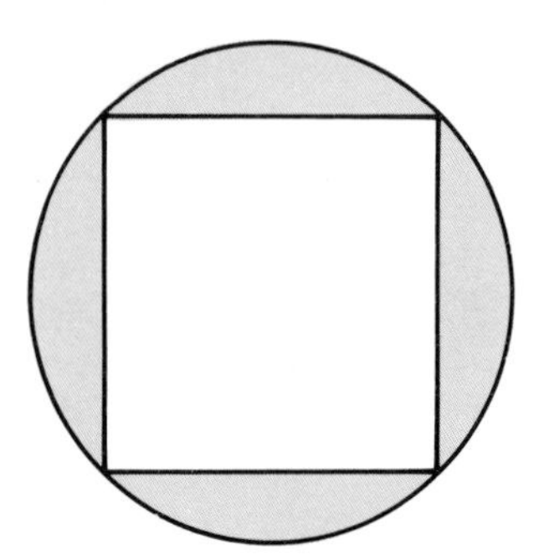

   (a) The logo is drawn so that the radius of the circle is 4 cm. Find the area of the shaded part.
   (b) Draw the logo when it is enlarged by a factor of 3.

3. A designer makes a model of a proposed new table. The model is made to a scale of 1 : 5.

   (a) The model is 25 cm long. How long will the real table be ?
   (b) If the real table is to be 1.5 m long, how long should the model be ?
   (c) The legs on the real table have to be inclined at 60 ° to the horizontal. At what angle to the horizontal should the legs on the model be inclined ?

The diagram shows a scale model of a multi-storey car park.

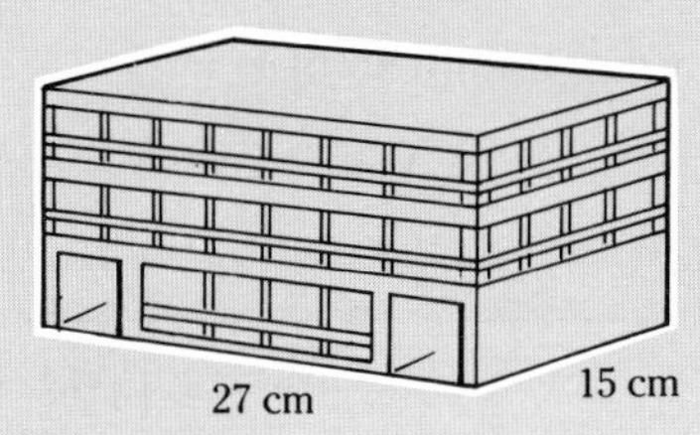

The actual building is 54 metres long.

(a) What is the width of the actual building ?

(b) If the building is 12 metres high, how tall is the model ?

First we need the enlargement factor; to find this we compare corresponding lengths on the actual building and the model. Remember that the lengths must be given in the same unit before we can compare them.

(a) The length of the building is 54 m, i.e. 5400 cm, and the length of the model is 27 cm.

Therefore the enlargement factor is $\frac{5400}{27} = 200$

The width of the model is 15 cm,
so the width of the building is 200×15 cm $=$ 3000 cm $=$ 30 m.

(b) The building is 12 m high, so the height of the model is $\frac{12}{200}$ m $=$ 6 cm.

4. A ladder is leaning against a wall and its foot is 1 m from the bottom of the wall.

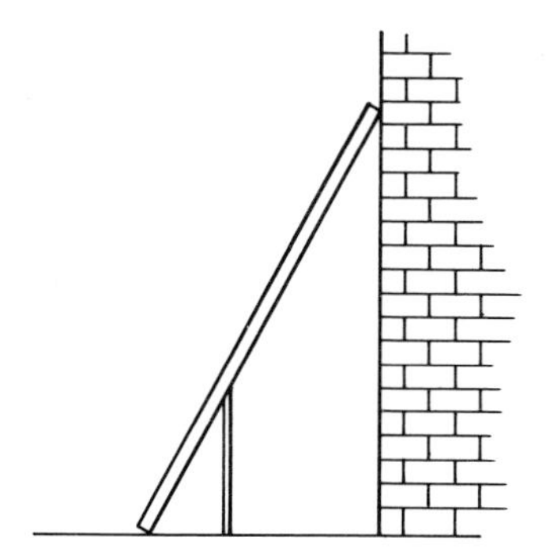

A vertical stick, which touches the ladder and the ground is 65 cm long and its lower end is 20 cm from the foot of the ladder. How far up the wall is the top of the ladder ?

5. This is a pair of similar cuboids. Find the height of the larger one.

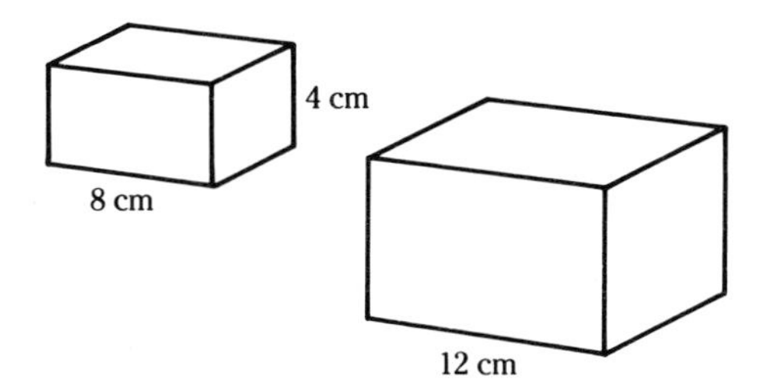

6. (a) These two triangles are similar. Find the length of (i) EF (ii) AB

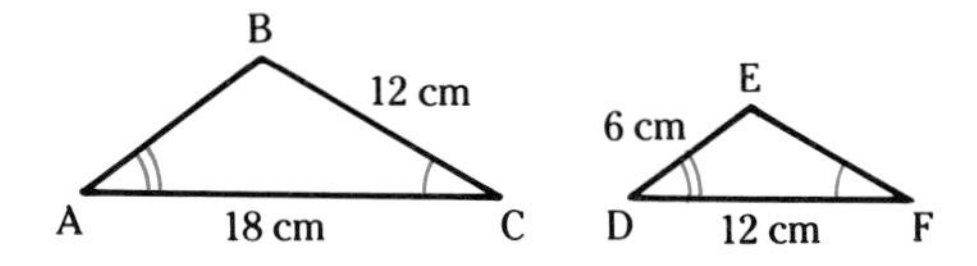

(b) Triangles ABC and ADE are similar. Find the length of DE.

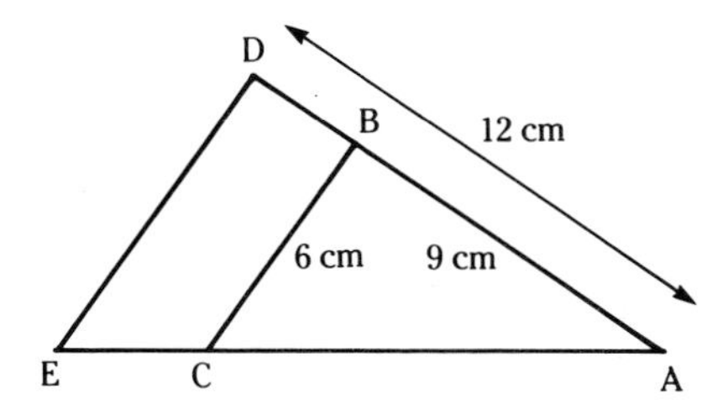

7.

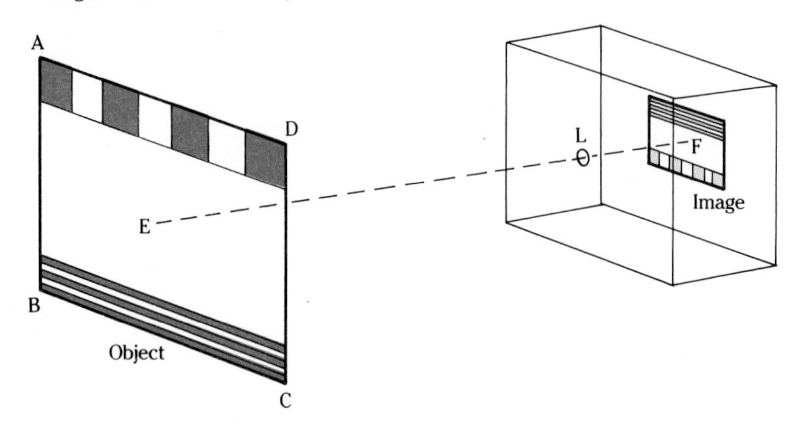

The diagram shows a rectangular card with a pattern on it, and the image of the card produced at the back of a camera. L is the lens of the camera. The centre, E, of the card is 8 cm from L and the centre, F, of the image is 4 cm from L.

(a) The length, AD, of the card is 6 cm and the height, AB, is 4 cm. What are the length and height of the image ?

(b) Sketch the image and label its corners A′, B′, C′ and D′ to correspond to the corners A, B, C and D of the card.

(c) Why is the image of the card upside down ?

8.

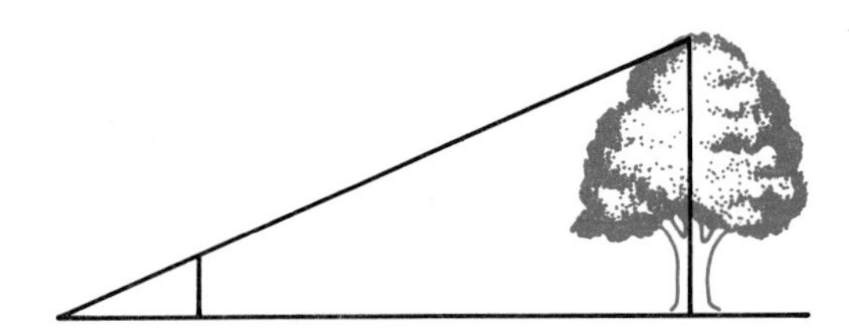

Sally wishes to find, with a little help from a 6 foot pole, the height of an oak tree that stands on level ground. She walks away from the base of the tree, with the Sun directly behind her, until she reaches a point 100 ft from its base. At this point she stands the pole on the ground and finds that the top of the shadow of the pole coincides with the top of the shadow of the tree at a point a further 10 feet away. How tall is the tree ?

9.

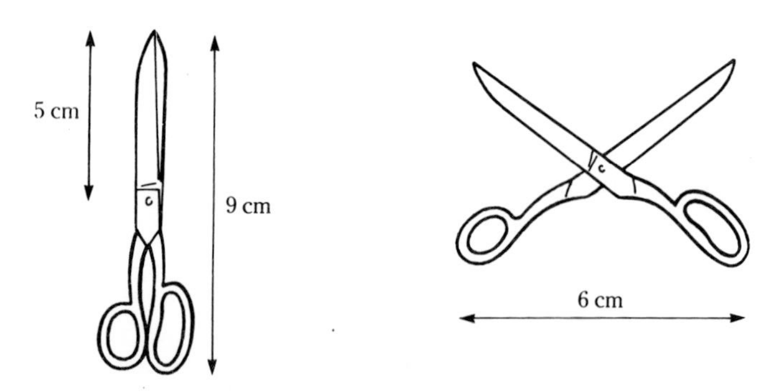

A closed pair of scissors is 9 cm long, the pivot being 5 cm from the points. The maximum distance apart that Paul can open the scissors using his thumb and first finger, is 6 cm. When he does this, what is the distance between the points ?

Self-Assessment 25

1. 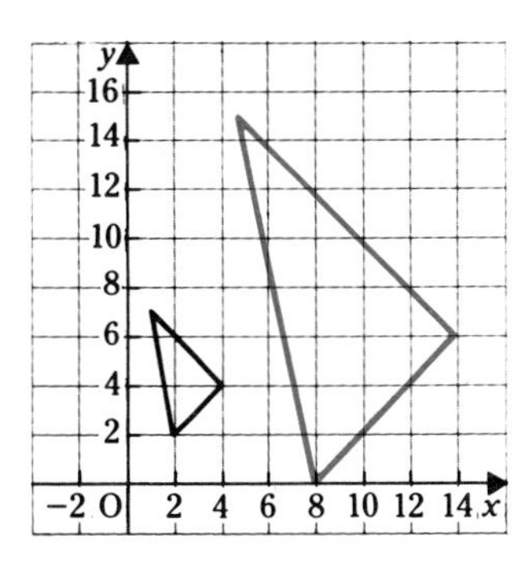

The purple triangle is an enlargement of the black triangle. Copy the diagram on squared paper. Find the coordinates of the centre of enlargement and state the scale factor.

2. These two triangles are similar.

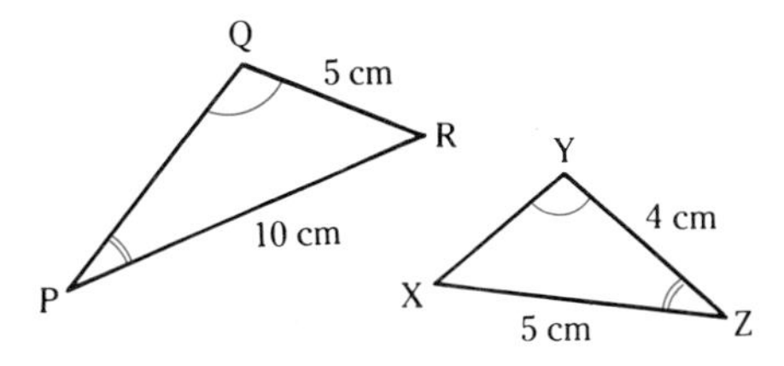

Find the length of (a) PQ (b) XY

3. The lengths of the edges of two cubes are in the ratio 2 : 3.

If an edge of the larger cube is 12 cm what is the length of an edge of the smaller cube ?

4. Use the information in the diagram to find the lengths of

(a) YC (b) BC.

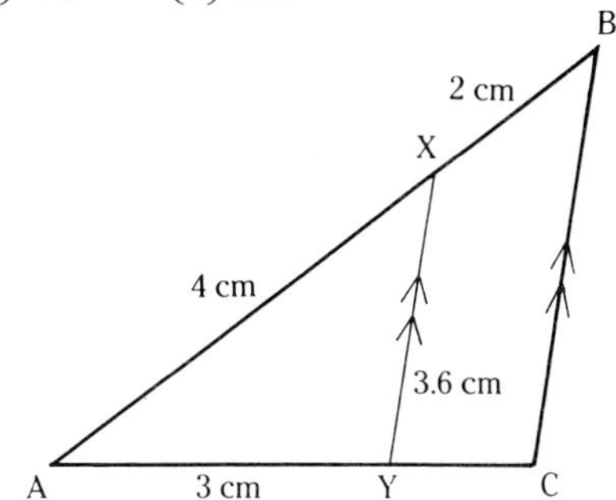

5. 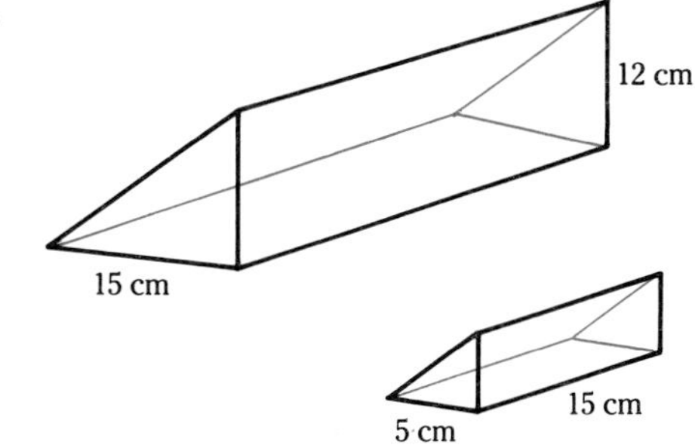

The prisms in the diagram are similar. Find

(a) the length of the larger prism

(b) the height of the smaller prism.

26 LOCI

'Locus' is the Latin word for 'position' or 'place' but it is used in mathematics to mean not just one point, but a set of points whose positions satisfy a given rule.

Every point on a locus must obey the given conditions or rule and every point that obeys the rule lies on the locus.

If the rule is that a point P on a sheet of paper is to be 3 cm from a fixed point O (also on the paper), then a few possible positions can be marked to give an idea of the shape of the complete locus.

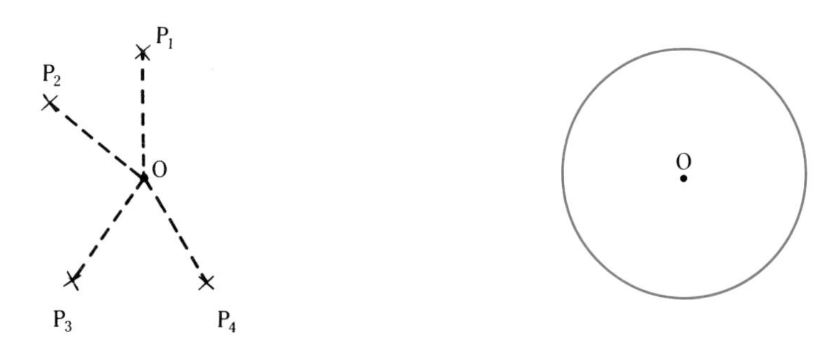

Mark as many positions of P as you need to deduce the shape of the locus.

It can now be seen that the locus is the circle, centre O, radius 3 cm.

It is sometimes helpful to think of a locus as the path traced out by a moving point.

For example, suppose that a goat is tethered by a rope with one end fixed at O. If the goat moves so that the rope is always taut, the path is a circle.

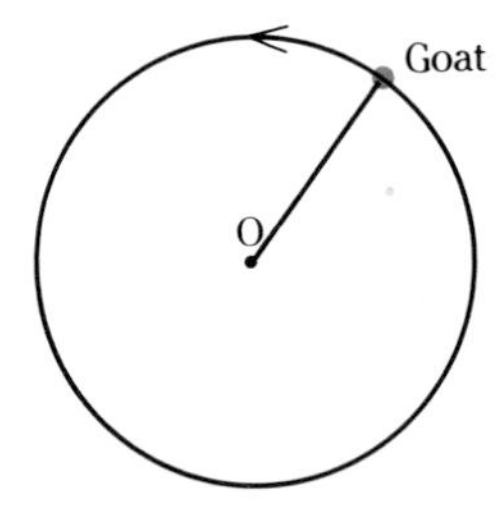

In two dimensions a locus can be a set of separate points, a set of lines or curves, or a region.

The plural of locus is *loci*.

Exercise 26a

One end of a chain 2 m long is attached to the collar of a dog and the other end to a ring that can slide on a fixed rail 4 m long. Assuming that the dog's collar remains 0.5 m from the ground, sketch the locus of the point of attachment on the collar.

To find a region, find its boundary first, in this case by thinking of the chain as being taut. Mark a few possible positions.

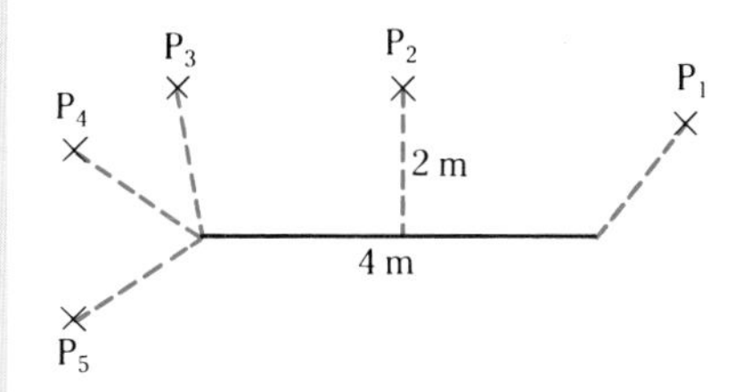

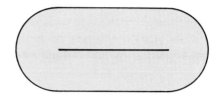

The boundary is part of the locus so it is drawn with a solid line, not a broken one.

Sketch the locus in each of the following questions. In some cases the sketch will have to be approximate but if a straight line or a circle is involved it should be described where possible, e.g. by giving the centre and radius of the circle.

1. The end of a hand of a clock.

2. (a) A ball thrown vertically upwards
   (b) A ball thrown up at an angle.

3. The red 7 on a roulette wheel.

4. A bicycle is ridden in a straight line along a level road.
   (a) A point on the saddle.
   (b) A point on the rim of the bicycle wheel.
   (c) The midpoint of a spoke.

5. A lower corner of an up-and-over garage door.

6. A goat tethered by a rope 6 m long to a point in the centre of a field.

7. A dog on a long rope, tethered to a tree trunk. The dog walks clockwise round the tree, keeping the rope taut.

8. A point that is equidistant from two fixed points A and B whose distance apart is 6 cm.

9. A point that is always 2 cm from a fixed line.

10. A point that is equidistant from two fixed intersecting lines AB and AC.

11. A door handle on an opening door.

12. 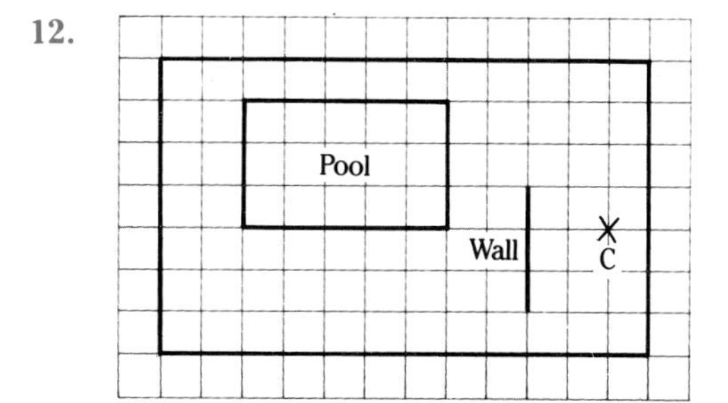

The diagram shows a swimming pool and a wall in a garden. Carol is sitting behind the wall at point C. Alan is walking about on the other side of the wall in such a way that Carol is unable to see him. Copy the diagram and shade the locus of the point representing Alan.

STANDARD LOCI

The more important loci previously discussed are now listed.

1. The locus of a point that moves in such a way that it is always at a fixed distance r from a fixed point C, is called a circle. C is the centre of the circle, and r is its radius.

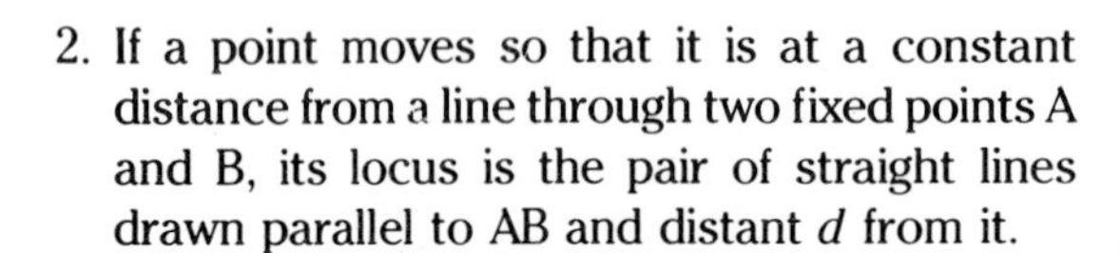

2. If a point moves so that it is at a constant distance from a line through two fixed points A and B, its locus is the pair of straight lines drawn parallel to AB and distant d from it.

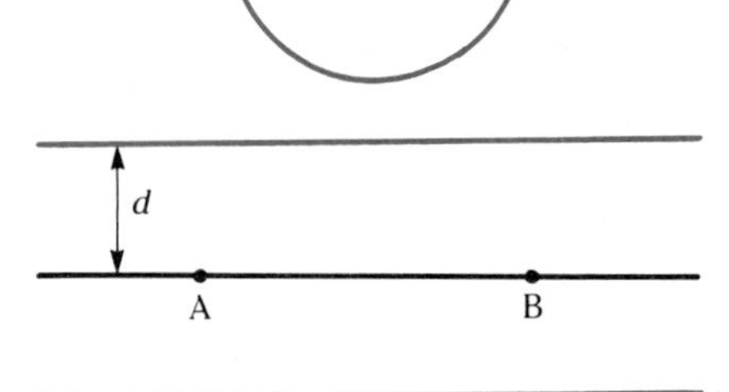

3. The locus of a point that is equidistant from two fixed points A and B, is the perpendicular bisector of AB.

4. The locus of a point that is equidistant from two fixed intersecting lines XOY and ZOW, is the pair of bisectors of the angles between the fixed lines. These bisectors are always at right angles to each other.

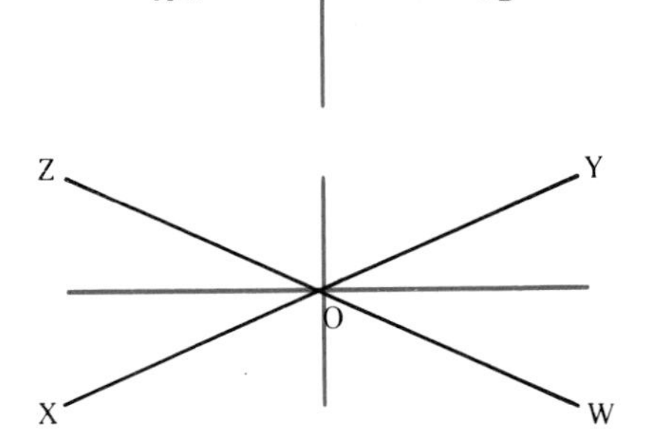

When drawing a locus accurately, draw a rough sketch and use it to find the shape of the locus and to calculate any necessary information. The accurate drawing should be as simple and as clear of unnecessary clutter as possible.

Exercise 26b

For each question sketch the locus of P and then draw the locus accurately, using whatever instruments are appropriate. If the locus is a region, draw the boundary accurately and shade the region lightly. If possible describe the locus briefly.

1.

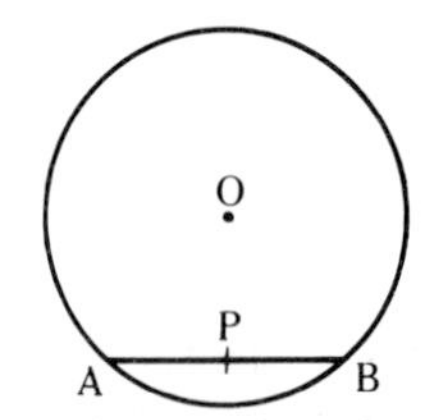

AB is a chord of variable length in a circle centre O, radius 5 cm, and P is the midpoint of AB. AB moves so that it is always parallel to its original position.

2. AB is a chord of length 6 cm of a circle, centre O, radius 5 cm, and P is the midpoint of AB. AB moves round the circle.

3. A is a fixed point. P is such that $AP < 4$ cm.

4. A and B are fixed points 8 cm apart. P is a point such that $AP \leqslant BP$.

5. A is a fixed point. P is the centre of a circle of radius 6 cm that passes through A.

6. P is such that it is less than 4 cm from a fixed line.

In the square ABCD, AB = 8 cm. A point E is 6 cm from A and also equidistant from B and C. Draw a sketch showing all the possible positions of E.

The locus of a point 6 cm from A is a circle and the locus of a point equidistant from B and C is the perpendicular bisector of BC. E lies at the intersection of these two loci.

From this sketch we see that there are two positions for E, i.e. E_1 and E_2.

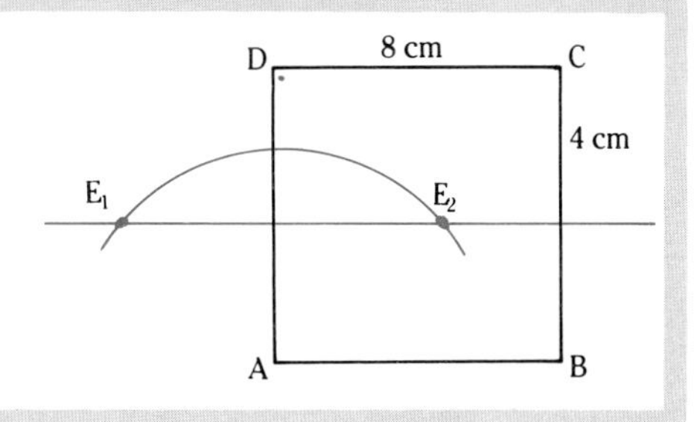

In the following questions, a rough sketch and an accurate drawing are required.

7. In triangle PQR, PQ = 10 cm, $\widehat{Q} = 90°$ and $\widehat{P} = 50°$. Find a point T within the triangle such that T is equidistant from PQ and QR, and T is 7.5 cm from P. (There may be more than one possible position for T.) Measure TQ.

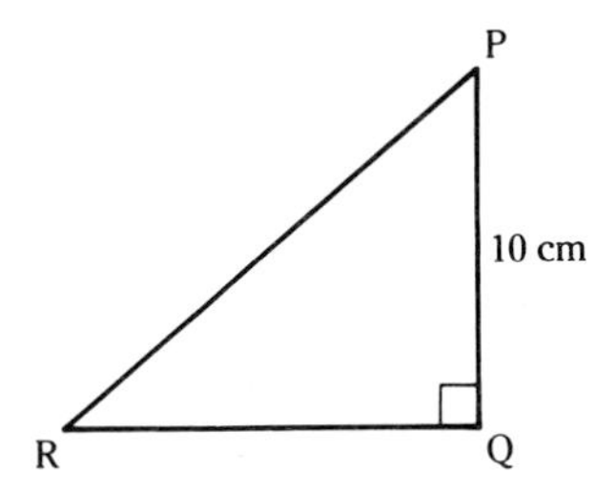

8. ABCD is a rectangle such that AB = 8 cm and BC = 12 cm. Find all the possible positions of a point E, if E is 5 cm from AB and 8 cm from D. Measure EC in each case.

9. 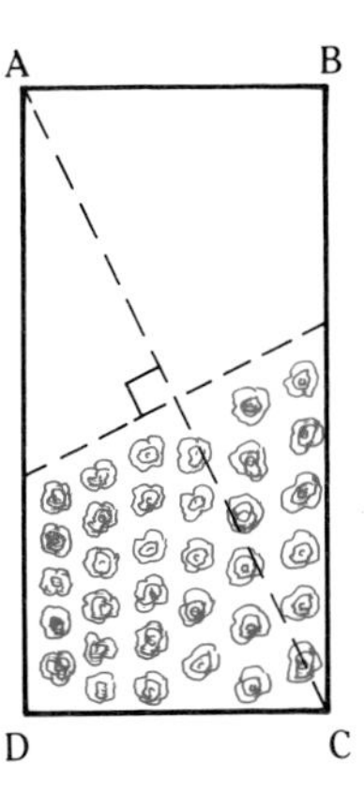

ABCD is a rectangular enclosure where AB = 8 m and BC = 16 m. A donkey is tethered by a rope 9.5 m long attached to the corner A. The owner has divided the enclosure into two sections by a line that is the perpendicular bisector of AC and has planted the part further from A with cabbages. Sketch a diagram and shade the planted region that the donkey can reach.

(a) Use an accurate drawing to find the length of the straight line boundary of this region.

(b) How long a rope *should* the donkey have to keep it out of the cabbage patch?

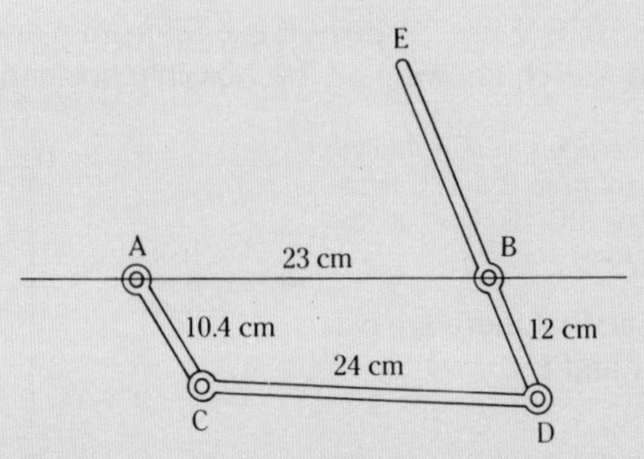

This linkage is a simplified version of a windscreen wiper mechanism. A and B are fixed points and AC rotates through 360° about A. C is linked to a point D on the wiper.

(a) Sketch the loci of C and D.

(b) Using an accurate drawing, mark the positions of D when AC is in line with AB. Hence find the angle through which the wiper turns.

(b) Using an accurate drawing, find the extreme positions of D. Hence find the angle through which the wiper turns.

(a) The locus of D is part of a circle, radius 12 cm.

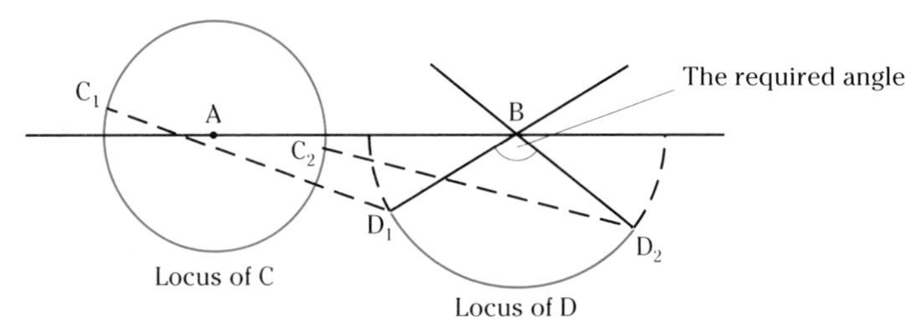

$C_1D_1 = C_2D_2 = 24$ cm

(b) Draw the line AB, circle and semi-circle. With compasses set at a radius of 24 cm, use trial and error to find D_1 and D_2. It should become clear that C_1AD_1 and AC_2D_2 are straight lines. We have used a scale of 1 cm to 6 cm to save space but this is too small for accuracy. A better scale to use is 1 cm to 2 cm.

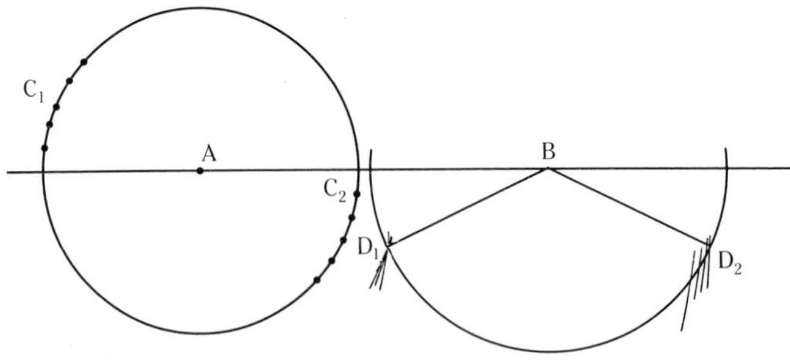

The angle turned through is about 130°

10.

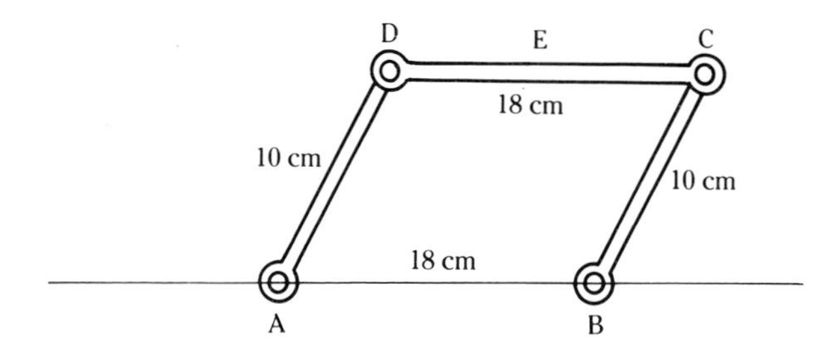

In the linkage above, A and B are fixed points. DA rotates about A. D starts on AB and AD turns through 180°. Sketch and describe the locus of

(a) D

(b) C

(c) E, the midpoint of DC.

(d) Sketch the locus of F, the midpoint of AC and make an accurate drawing to find four possible positions of F.

11.

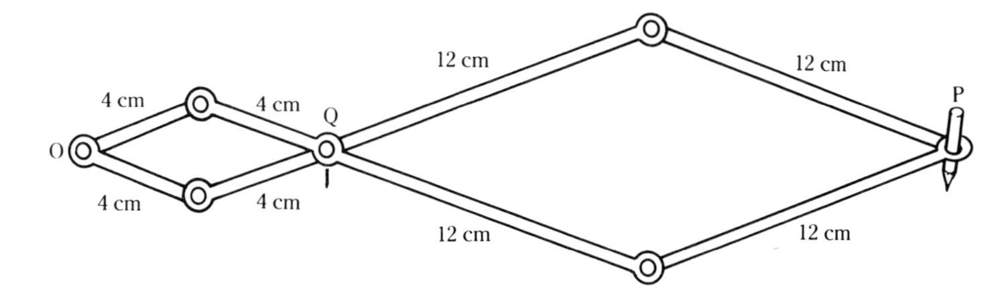

This linkage is a pantograph, which is used in drawing. O is a fixed point. If Q is moved round a drawing of a square, the mechanism moves the pen at P so that it draws a shape. Describe the shape. How does it compare with the original drawing ?

12.

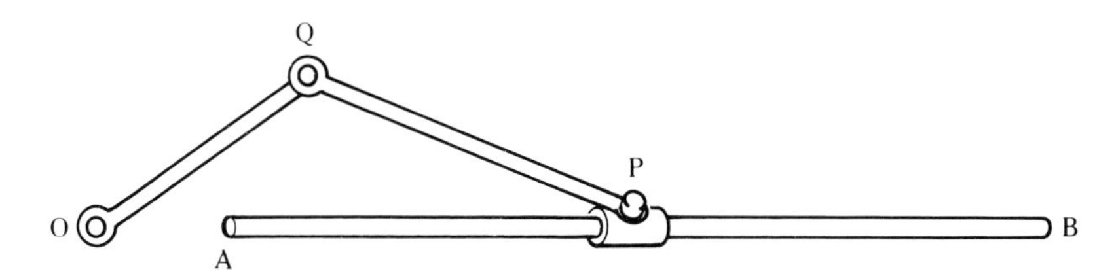

In this linkage, OQ is constrained to rotate about O, which is a fixed point. A sleeve P is linked to Q. P is free to slide along the fixed bar AB.

OQ = 5 cm, QP = 10 cm, OA = 3 cm and AB = 16 cm.

(a) Sketch the locus of Q.

(b) Sketch the locus of P as OQ rotates.

(c) Make an accurate drawing and mark four possible positions of Q and the corresponding positions of P. Find the greatest and least distances of P from O.

LOCI IN THREE DIMENSIONS

The ideas and methods developed to deal with loci in two dimensions can be extended to three dimensions.

In three dimensions a locus can be a line or a surface or a region contained by a surface. The locus of the possible positions of a fly trapped in a box is the space enclosed by the box.

Two other examples of loci in three dimensions are given below.

The locus of a point that is at a given distance r from a fixed point A, is a sphere, centre A, radius r.

The locus of a point P that is equidistant from two fixed points A and B is the plane bisecting AB at right angles. (Only part of this plane is shown in the diagram. Two possible positions of P are shown, marked P_1 and P_2.)

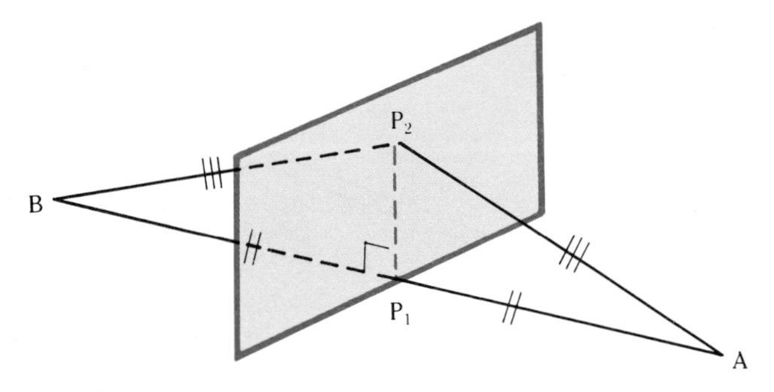

Exercise 26c

For each question give either a sketch or a full description of the locus of P, or both if it helps to make the situation clear.

1. A door measures 1 m by 2 m, and it rotates through 80° as it opens. P is the top outer corner.

2. A square table 1 m high can be placed anywhere in a room. P is a point on a corner of the table.

3. P is the end of a rod PQ, of length 80 cm. The rod can swing in any direction about the fixed point Q, though P never rises above the level of Q.

4. P is 4 cm from the floor.

5. Q is the centre of a sphere of radius 4 cm. The distance of P from the surface of the sphere is

(a) 6 cm, (b) 2 cm, (c) 4 cm.

6. P is 2 cm from a wire stretched horizontally between two walls.

7. P is a bee that flies no more than 40 m from its hive and no more than 1 m from the ground, which is level.

8. Two sticklebacks have their nests 1 m apart. When the two fish meet they fight but the one nearer its own nest will win. P is a point at which neither is dominant.

The rest of this exercise consists of mixed questions.

9. (a) A square WXYZ is rolled along a fixed line. Sketch and describe the locus of X.

   (b) Repeat the question for an equilateral triangle XYZ.

10. 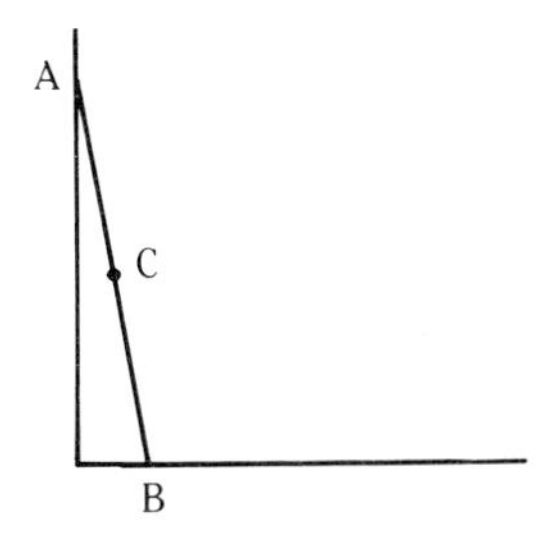

A ladder AB is propped at a very steep angle against a wall. It slides down, its ends staying in contact with the wall and the floor, until it is flat on the floor. C is the midpoint of AB.

Sketch the locus of (a) A (b) B (c) C.

11. 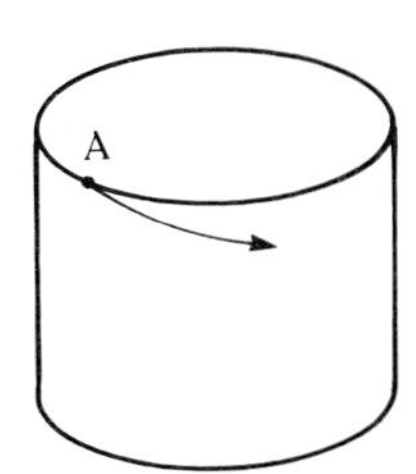

A spider crawls from top to bottom down the outside of a cylinder in such a way that its path is always at 30° to the horizontal.

(a) Sketch or describe the locus of the spider in three dimensions.

(b) If the curved surface of the cylinder were unrolled and flattened out, sketch the spider's path.

(c) The height of the cylinder is 6 cm and the radius 8 cm. How long is the spider's path ?

(d) If the radius of the cylinder were 1 cm, how would the length of the path differ from that found in (c) ?

12. 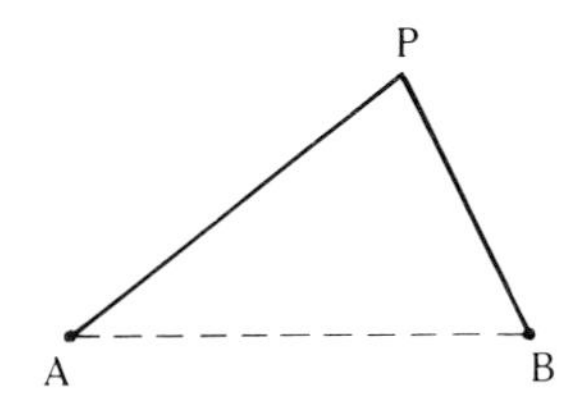

A and B are two fixed points 6 cm apart. A thread 10 cm long has one end fixed at A and the other fixed at B. A pencil placed in the loop of thread pulls it taut and the pencil point P is marked. Plot as many positions of P as convenient and find the shape of the locus of P. (This locus may also be drawn by putting the pencil into the loop of the thread and moving it, keeping the thread taut; the pencil then draws the locus. This method works better on a larger scale.)

13. (a) P moves so that the sum of its distances from two fixed perpendicular lines is 8 cm. Use graph paper to draw the locus of P.

    (b) Draw the locus of P if the two fixed lines are at 60° to each other. (Use isometric paper.)

14. AOB and COD are two lines that cut at 60°. The locus of a point P that is equidistant from AB and CD is the pair of lines XY and ZW.

    (a) Find angle XOZ.

    (b) If P is also 8 cm from O find all four possible positions of P. Give the distances between adjacent positions of P.

15. 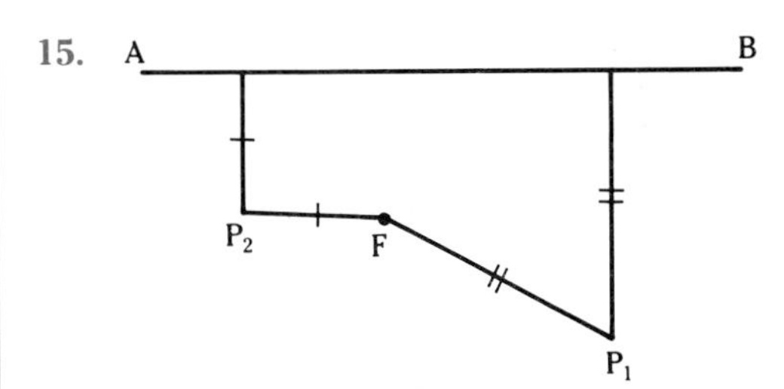

A farmer wishes to erect a fence to divide the land between his farmhouse F and a straight road AB. Each post is to be the same distance from the farmhouse as it is from the road. The possible positions of two posts are shown at P_1 and P_2. Plot other possible positions where posts could be erected, to obtain the locus of points that are equidistant from the farmhouse and the road.

Investigations

1. Up-and-over garage doors, mechanical weighing machines and similar mechanisms have interesting linkages controlling movement. Investigate as many as you can find, drawing the locus of a point on a moving part, e.g. a garage door, giving both a sketch and an accurate drawing where possible.

2. In Exercise 26c, question 9, a square and a triangle were rolled along a straight line and the locus of a vertex was considered. This situation can be further investigated.
   (a) Other polygons or circles can be rolled.
   (b) The locus of a point other than a vertex can be traced. The point can even be inside the figure.
   (c) The figure can be rolled on a curve or inside a square.

Self-Assessment 26

Assume that all the questions refer to two-dimensional situations unless you are told otherwise.

1. (a) A circle of radius 2 cm rolls round the inside of a square of side 6 cm. Sketch the locus of the centre of the circle.
   (b) A circle of radius 1 cm rolls round the outside of a square of side 6 cm. Sketch the locus of the centre of the circle.

2. A circle of radius 1 cm rolls round the inside of a circle of radius 4 cm. Sketch the locus of the centre of the circle with radius 1 cm.

3. A speedboat passes between two marker buoys, travelling so that it is equidistant from the two buoys. Describe the locus of the speedboat.

4. A moth is fascinated by a candle flame and flies all round it, keeping at a distance of 8 cm from the centre of the flame. Describe in words the three-dimensional locus of the moth.

5. A is a fixed point. Illustrate the locus of P if
   (a) $4\text{ cm} < AP < 6\text{ cm}$
   (b) $AP \geqslant 3\text{ cm}$.

6. Point P lies within a square ABCD of side 6 cm so that it is 5 cm from B and 3 cm from CD.

   Use an accurate drawing to find how far P is from A.

7. The diagram shows a fenced yard with a lorry parked inside.

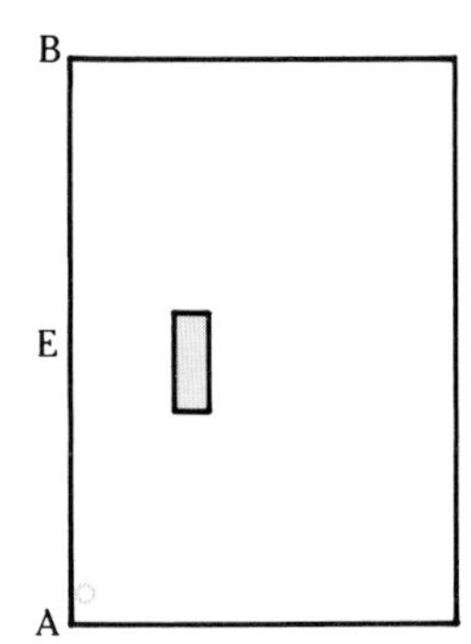

   A security guard walks along the fence AB from the corner A to the middle of the fence at E.
   (a) Make a copy of the diagram. Shade the region of the yard that the guard can see from A.
   (b) Shade the region of the yard that the guard can see from two intermediate positions on his walk and from E.
   (c) Mark the region of the yard that the guard cannot see from any point on his walk.
   (d) If he continued his walk to the other end, B, of the fence, would he be able to see the whole of the yard at some point on his walk ?

8.

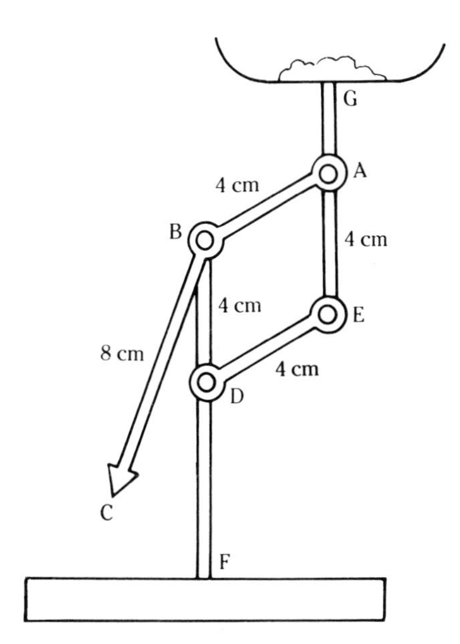

The diagram shows the linkage in a miniature weighing machine with a tray at G on which an object can be placed. C is a heavy pointer, BDF, GAE and ABC are rigid, $A\hat{B}C = 150°$ and F is fixed to a heavy base. The linkage is freely jointed at A, B, D and E. With nothing on the tray, BC is vertical. When an object is placed on the tray, the tray descends a short distance. Describe the locus of

(a) A (b) E (c) C (d) the midpoint of BE.

27 VECTORS AND TRANSFORMATIONS

VECTORS

A vector quantity is one that has both *magnitude* (i.e. size) and *direction.*

The simplest example of a vector is *displacement,* i.e. change of position. Both the distance moved and the direction are needed to describe it.

We can describe a displacement as, for example, 10 km on a bearing of 065°, or as the result of moving 4 m parallel to a wall followed by 3 m at right angles to the wall.

In either case the displacement can be represented by a directed line, i.e. a line with an arrow.

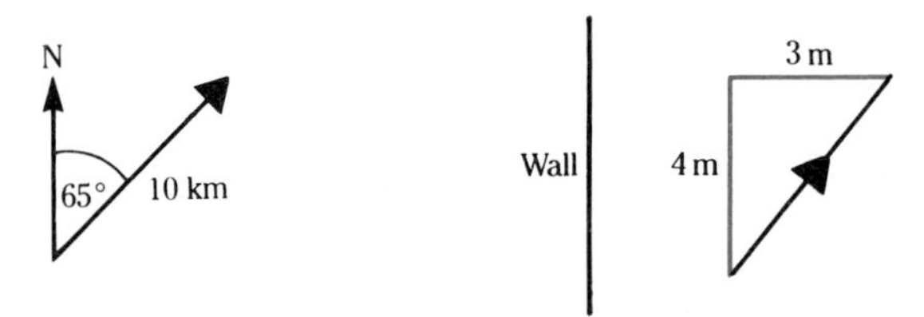

Other examples of vectors are
force, e.g. 5 newtons acting downward
and velocity, e.g. 4 m.p.h. due north.
(Speed is the word used when no direction is given, so speed is *not* a vector.)

An example of a quantity that is not a vector is the mass of an object: it has magnitude but no direction. The word *scalar* is used for quantities of this kind.

Notation

A directed line representing a vector can be drawn on squared paper.

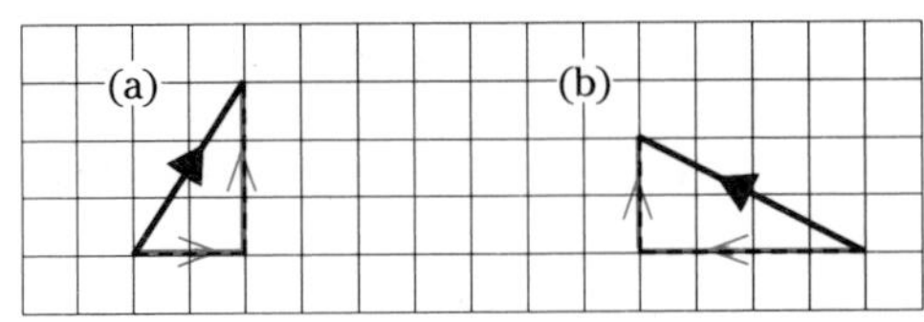

In (a) the displacement is 2 units to the right (+ve) and 3 units up, and is written $\begin{pmatrix} 2 \\ 3 \end{pmatrix}$

In (b) the displacement is 4 units to the left (−ve) and 2 units up, and is written $\begin{pmatrix} -4 \\ 2 \end{pmatrix}$

Note that the top number represents the movement parallel to the x-axis
and the bottom number the movement parallel to the y-axis.

We can identify the vector either by using the capital letters indicating its end points, with an arrow over the top, ($\overrightarrow{AB}$), or by a small letter in heavy type (**a**) or, if handwritten, a small letter with a line underneath i.e. $\underline{a}$.

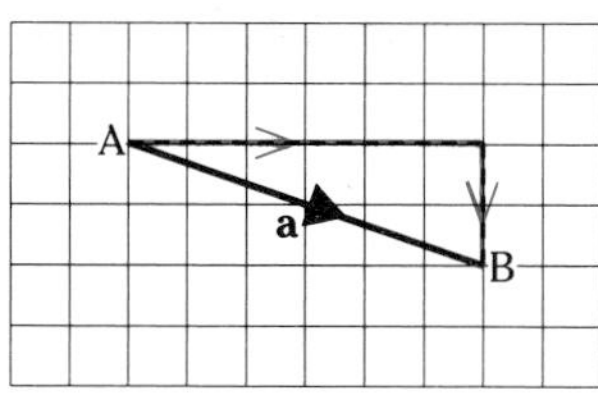

e.g. $$\overrightarrow{AB} = \mathbf{a} = \underline{a} = \begin{pmatrix} 6 \\ -2 \end{pmatrix}$$

Exercise 27a

1. State whether each of the following quantities is a vector or a scalar.
   (a) The length of a mat.
   (b) A velocity of 7 km per hour due east.
   (c) An acceleration of $1\,\text{m s}^{-2}$ downwards.
   (d) The flight of a bird in a straight line from bird-table to window-sill.
   (e) The mass of a bag of sugar.
   (f) The time it takes to read this sentence.
   (g) The flight path of an aeroplane.
   (h) The force needed to move a lift.

2. 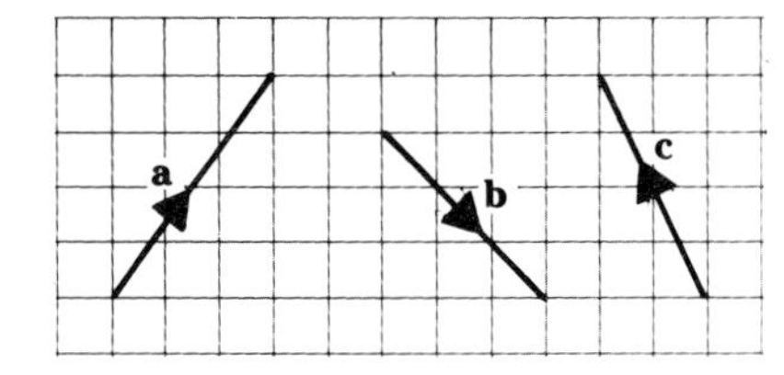

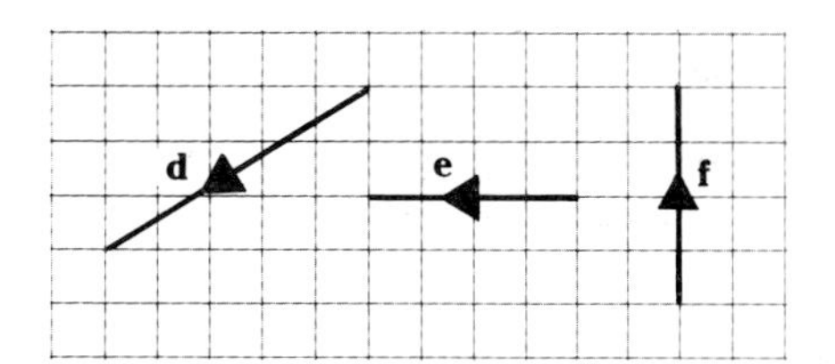

   Give in the form $\begin{pmatrix} p \\ q \end{pmatrix}$ the vectors shown in the diagrams above.

3. On squared paper, draw directed lines to represent the following vectors.

   (a) $\mathbf{a} = \begin{pmatrix} 4 \\ 5 \end{pmatrix}$ (c) $\mathbf{c} = \begin{pmatrix} -6 \\ 1 \end{pmatrix}$ (e) $\mathbf{e} = \begin{pmatrix} 0 \\ 2 \end{pmatrix}$

   (b) $\mathbf{b} = \begin{pmatrix} 2 \\ -5 \end{pmatrix}$ (d) $\mathbf{d} = \begin{pmatrix} -4 \\ -5 \end{pmatrix}$ (f) $\mathbf{f} = \begin{pmatrix} -3 \\ 0 \end{pmatrix}$

4. Draw lines representing the following vectors.

   (a) $\mathbf{a} = \begin{pmatrix} 3 \\ 4 \end{pmatrix}$ (c) $\mathbf{c} = \begin{pmatrix} 0 \\ 6 \end{pmatrix}$ (e) $\mathbf{e} = \begin{pmatrix} 2 \\ 1 \end{pmatrix}$

   (b) $\mathbf{b} = \begin{pmatrix} -4 \\ 0 \end{pmatrix}$ (d) $\mathbf{d} = \begin{pmatrix} -5 \\ 12 \end{pmatrix}$ (f) $\mathbf{f} = \begin{pmatrix} -3 \\ -2 \end{pmatrix}$

Translations

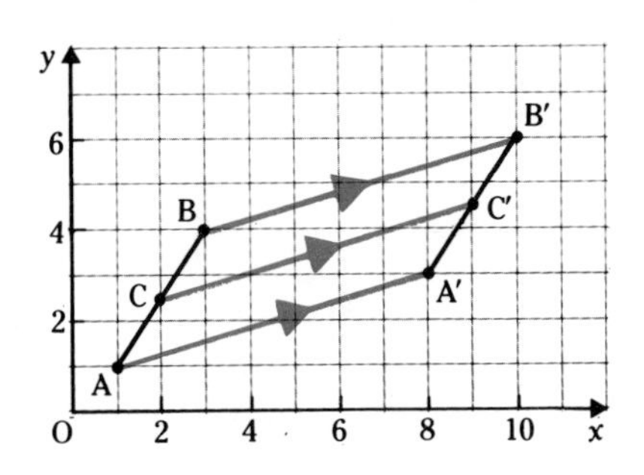

The translation that maps AB to A′B′ can be described by the vector $\overrightarrow{AA'}$ (from A to A′),

i.e. $\begin{pmatrix} 7 \\ 2 \end{pmatrix}$

Notice that this is the same as $\overrightarrow{BB'}$ or $\overrightarrow{CC'}$ because any point on the line AB is translated in the same way.

Exercise 27b

For each of the following questions, give the vector that describes the translation that maps A to B.

1.

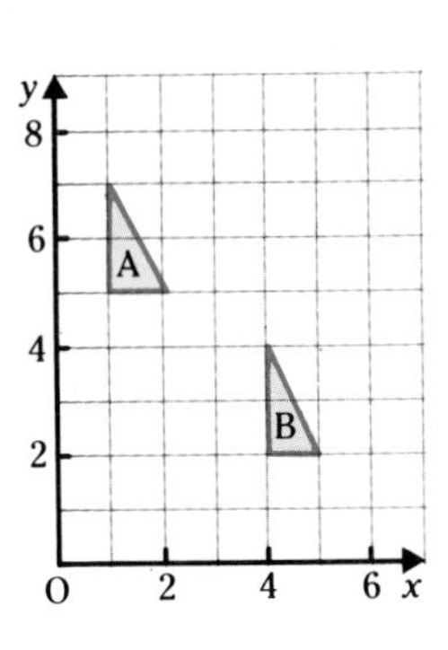

2.

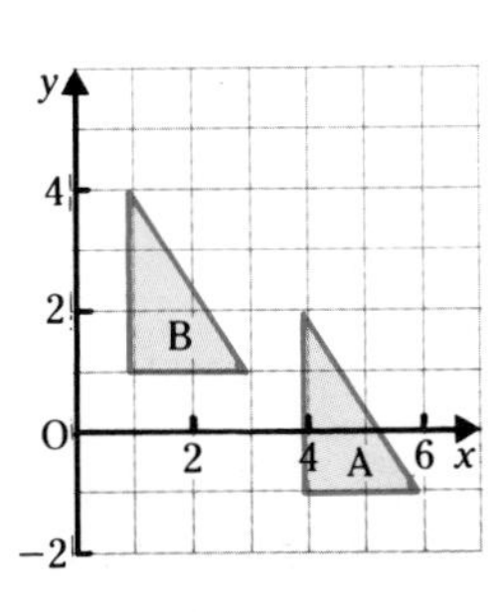

3.

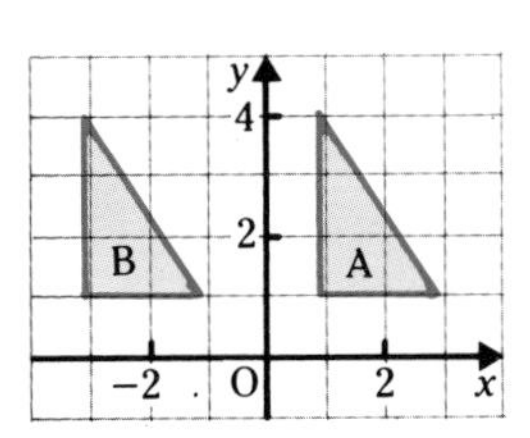

4.

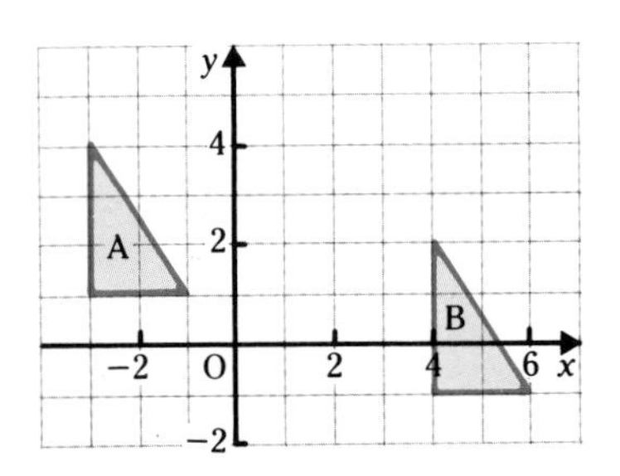

A translation is described by the vector $\begin{pmatrix} 2 \\ -3 \end{pmatrix}$. A, B and C are the points (2, 1), (1, 5) and (−2, 2). Find the images of A, B and C under the given translation.

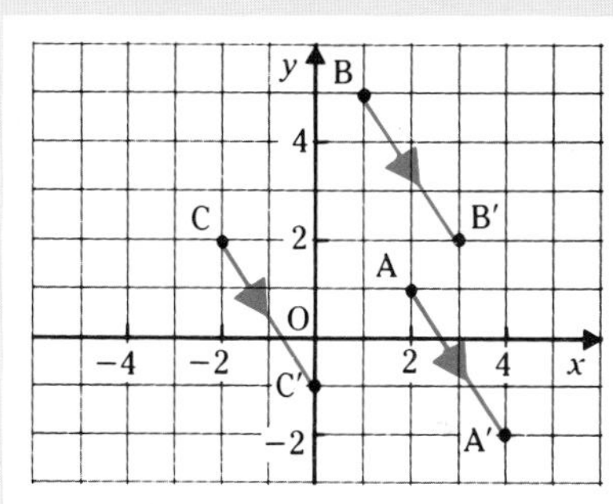

From the diagram,

the image of A is (2 + 2, 1 − 3), i.e. (4, −2),

the image of B is (1 + 2, 5 − 3), i.e. (3, 2)

the image of C is (−2 + 2, 2 − 3), i.e. (0, −1)

5.

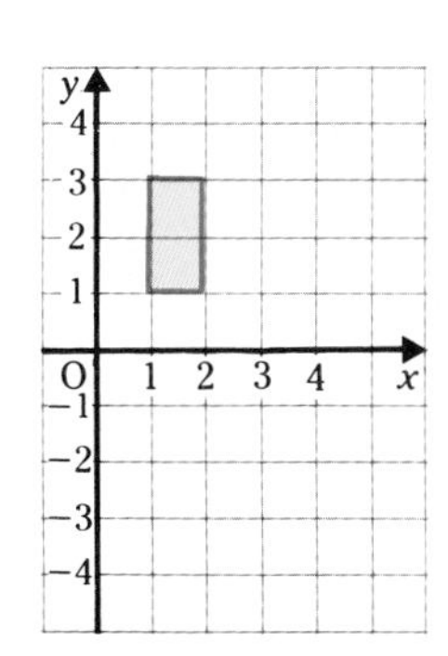

Copy the diagram and draw the image of the rectangle when it is translated by the vector $\begin{pmatrix} -1 \\ -3 \end{pmatrix}$.

6. Copy the diagram and draw the image of the shape labelled A when it is translated by the vector $\begin{pmatrix} 5 \\ -4 \end{pmatrix}$.

Label the image B. What is the vector that will translate B to A?

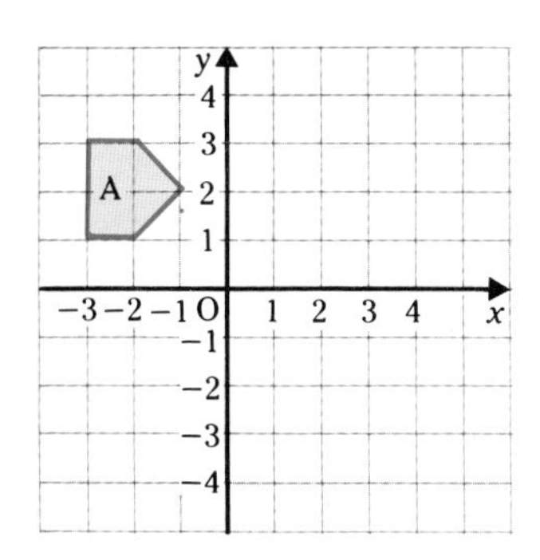

7. Draw axes for values of x and y from −8 to 8. In △PQR, P, Q and R are the points (0, 4), (1, 3) and (−1, 1) respectively.

(a) P_1, Q_1 and R_1 are the points (3, 8), (4, 7) and (2, 5) respectively. Give the vector describing the translation that maps △PQR to $\triangle P_1Q_1R_1$.

(b) △PQR is mapped to $\triangle P_2Q_2R_2$ by the translation given by the vector $\begin{pmatrix} -3 \\ 1 \end{pmatrix}$.

What vector describes the translation that maps $\triangle P_1Q_1R_1$ to $\triangle P_2Q_2R_2$?

(c) What is the connection between the two vectors in part (b) and the vector in part (a)?

8. Draw axes as for question 4. In △ABC, A, B and C are the points (1, 1), (4, 2) and (3, 6) respectively.

(a) Find the image $A_1B_1C_1$ of ABC under the translation described by $\begin{pmatrix} 4 \\ 2 \end{pmatrix}$

(b) Find the image $A_2B_2C_2$ of ABC under the translation described by $\begin{pmatrix} -6 \\ 1 \end{pmatrix}$

(c) Find the image $A_3B_3C_3$ of ABC under the translation described by $\begin{pmatrix} 0 \\ -4 \end{pmatrix}$

(d) Find the vector describing the translation that maps $\triangle A_1B_1C_1$ to $\triangle A_2B_2C_2$.

TRANSFORMATIONS

A *reflection* is defined by the mirror line.

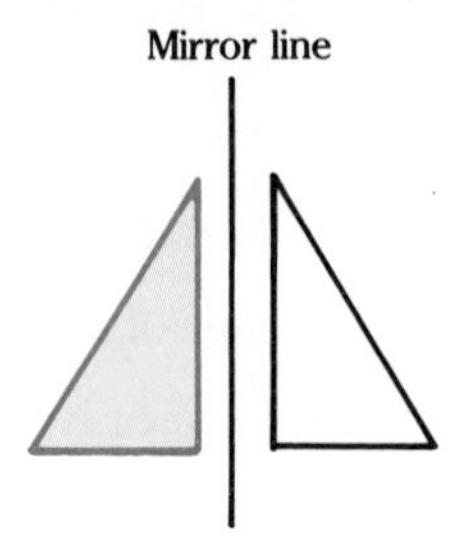

A *rotation* is defined by the centre, the angle and direction of rotation.

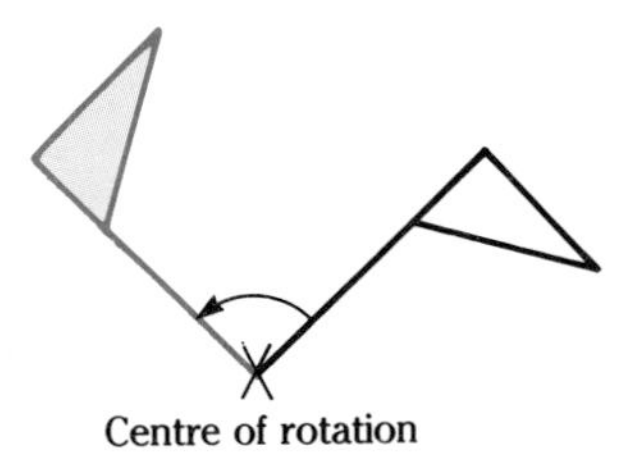

A *translation* is defined by a description of the displacement, usually in the form of a vector.

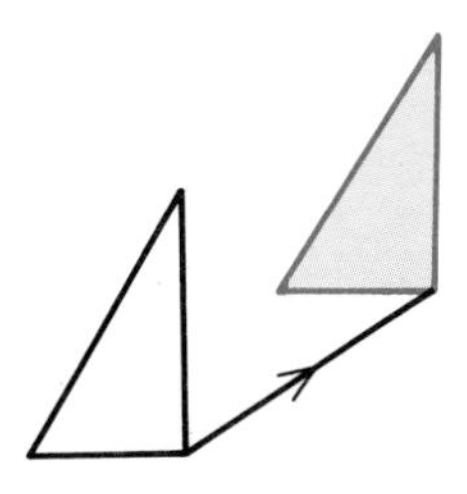

An *enlargement* is defined by the centre of enlargement and the scale factor.

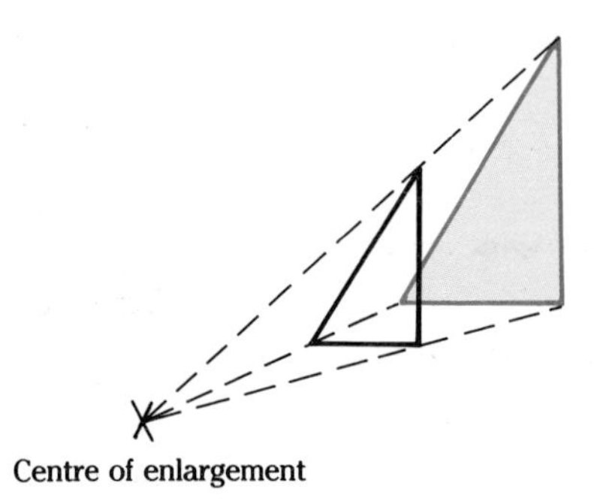

Exercise 27c

1.

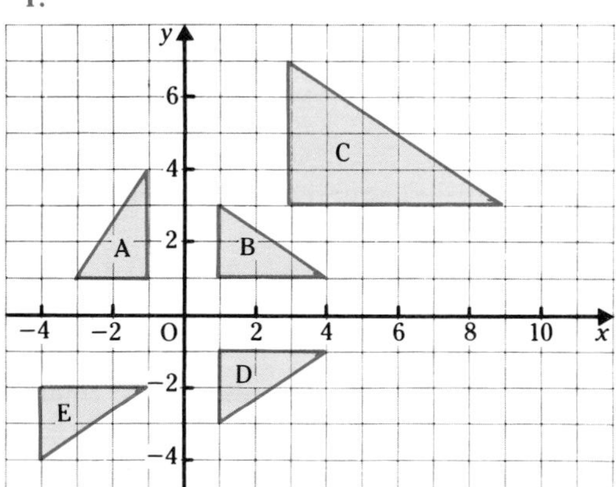

Describe fully the transformation that maps

(a) A to B

(b) B to D

(c) B to C

(d) D to E

2.

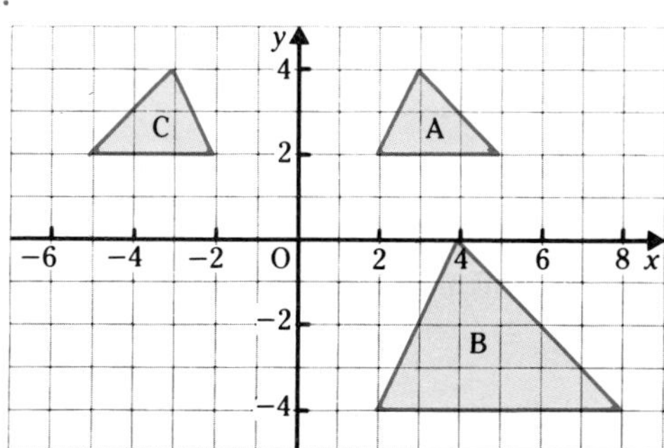

(a) Find the image of A when it is translated using the vector $\begin{pmatrix} -1 \\ -4 \end{pmatrix}$.

Label the image D.

(b) Describe fully the transformation that maps

(i) D to A

(ii) D to B

(iii) A to C

(iv) C to A.

Draw $\triangle ABC$ with vertices A(1, 1), B(4, 1) and C(4, 5), and the image of $\triangle ABC$ when it is rotated anticlockwise through 90 ° about O. Label the image A′B′C′.

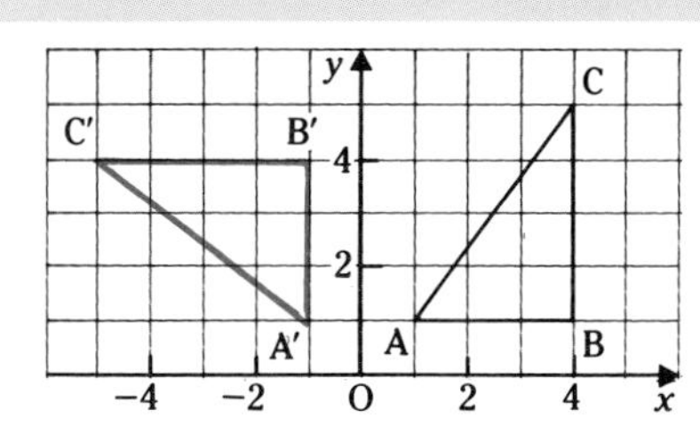

For question 3 to 8 draw x and y axes, each for values from −6 to 6.

3. P, Q and R are the points (2, 1), (5, 1) and (5, 3).

Draw $\triangle PQR$ and label it A. Then draw and label the following images of A

(a) rotation of A through 90 ° anticlockwise about O

(b) rotation of A through 180 ° about O

(c) rotation of A through 90 ° clockwise about O.

4. P is the triangle with vertices (−5, 0), (−3, 0) and (−3, 2).

Q is the triangle with vertices (1, 0), (3, 0) and (1, 2).

R is the triangle with vertices (−2, −6), (0, −6) and (0, −4).

Draw and label the translation given by the vector $\begin{pmatrix} 2 \\ 3 \end{pmatrix}$ of

(a) P (b) Q (c) R.

5. A, B and C are the points $(-2, 1)$, $(-4, 1)$ and $(-2, 5)$.

   Draw $\triangle$ABC and label it Q.

   Draw and label the following images

   (a) The reflection of Q in the x-axis.

   (b) The reflection of Q in the y-axis.

6. A is a triangle with vertices $(1, 2)$, $(4, 2)$ and $(4, 4)$. Find

   (a) the image when A is reflected in the line $y = x + 2$

   (b) the image when A is reflected in the line $y = -x + 2$

7. B is a triangle with vertices $(-2, 1)$, $(-5, 1)$ and $(-2, 2)$. Find

   (a) the image of B when it is rotated anticlockwise through $90°$ about the point $(1, 1)$

   (b) the image of B when it is rotated clockwise through $90°$ about the point $(0, -1)$.

   X is a triangle with vertices $(0, 0)$, $(1, 3)$ and $(-3, 0)$. Find

   (a) the image of X when it is reflected in
      (i) the x-axis
      (ii) the y-axis

   (b) the image of X when it is rotated clockwise through $90°$ about
      (i) the point $(1, 3)$
      (ii) the point $(-3, 0)$

Self-Assessment 27

1. Draw a diagram on squared paper to show the vectors

   (a) $\begin{pmatrix} 2 \\ 4 \end{pmatrix}$ (b) $\begin{pmatrix} 0 \\ 3 \end{pmatrix}$ (c) $\begin{pmatrix} -2 \\ 5 \end{pmatrix}$ (d) $\begin{pmatrix} -3 \\ 0 \end{pmatrix}$

2. Give each of the vectors in the diagram in the form $\begin{pmatrix} x \\ y \end{pmatrix}$.

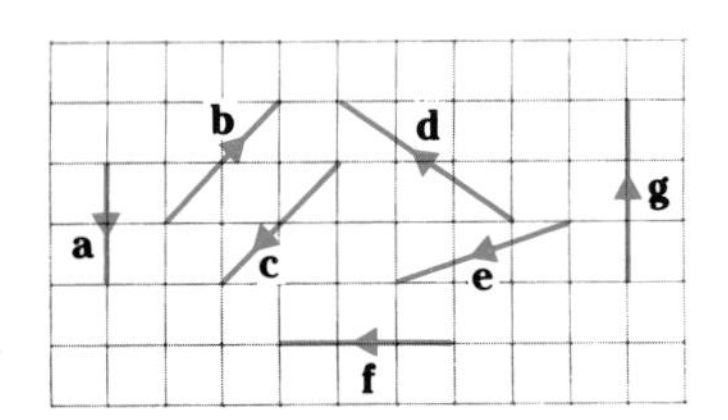

3. Describe the transformation that maps
   (a) A to B (b) A to C (c) B to C

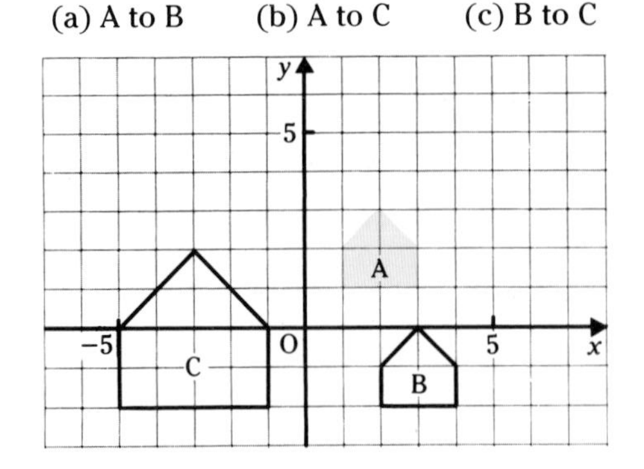

4. On squared paper, draw the triangle A whose vertices are P$(1, 0)$, Q$(3, 0)$, R$(2, 3)$. Draw the image of A when it has been

   (a) translated by the vector $\begin{pmatrix} -1 \\ 4 \end{pmatrix}$

   (b) enlarged by a factor 2, centre the origin

   (c) reflected in the x-axis.

5. Which of the following quantities are vectors ?

   (a) A speed of 30 m.p.h.

   (b) A force of 30 N upward.

   (c) A change of position of 45 km due east.

6. A and B are the points $(4, 5)$ and $(-3, 6)$. A and B are mapped to the points A′ and B′ by the translation described by the vector $\begin{pmatrix} -2 \\ -1 \end{pmatrix}$. Give the points A′ and B′.

28 PROBABILITY

EXPERIMENTAL PROBABILITY

If you throw an ordinary dice there are six possible scores, namely 1, 2, 3, 4, 5 or 6.

The act of throwing the dice is called an *experiment.*
The score that you get is called an *outcome* or *event.*
The set $\{1, 2, 3, 4, 5, 6\}$ is called the set of all possible outcomes.

The probability of obtaining a particular score is the number of ways of getting that score divided by the total number of possibilities.

For example, the probability of scoring 3 is $\frac{1}{6}$, since out of the six equally likely outcomes, only one is 'successful', i.e. is a 3.

We write $\qquad P(3) = \frac{1}{6}$

and $P(1 \text{ or } 2 \text{ or } 3 \text{ or } 4 \text{ or } 5 \text{ or } 6) = 1$ since the outcome *must* show one of these scores.

Similarly, the probability of scoring a 7 is 0, for out of the six equally likely scores, not one of them is 7.

When we get the result we seek, we say that the outcome is a successful event.

Generally

$$\textbf{P(successful event)} = \frac{\textbf{number of successful outcomes}}{\textbf{total number of possible outcomes}}$$

$$\textbf{P(certainty)} = \textbf{1}$$

$$\textbf{P(impossibility)} = \textbf{0}$$

If A stands for a particular event, the probability of A happening is written $P(A)$, and

$$0 \leqslant P(A) \leqslant 1$$

The probability that an event A does not happen is written $P(\bar{A})$, and

$$P(\bar{A}) = 1 - P(A)$$

In some experiments an event can happen more than once.

For example, since there are four Jacks in an ordinary pack of 52 playing cards

$$P(\text{a Jack}) = \frac{4}{52} = \frac{1}{13}$$

Similarly, if a bag contains 7 white discs and 9 black discs

$$P(\text{choosing a white disc}) = \frac{7}{16}$$

and $\qquad P(\text{choosing a black disc}) = \frac{9}{16}$

Exercise 28a

A card is drawn at random from a pack of 52 playing cards. What is the probability that the card is

(a) red
(b) a king
(c) a red jack, queen or king
(d) a card that is lower than 8 ? (An ace is higher than 8.)

(a) There are 26 red cards in the pack

$$\therefore \qquad P(\text{red}) = \tfrac{26}{52} = \tfrac{1}{2}$$

(b) There are 4 kings in the pack

$$\therefore \qquad P(\text{king}) = \tfrac{4}{52} = \tfrac{1}{13}$$

(c) Since there are 2 red jacks, 2 red queens and 2 red kings in the pack

$$P(\text{red jack, queen or king}) = \tfrac{6}{52} = \tfrac{3}{26}$$

(d) Similarly, $P(\text{lower than } 8) = \tfrac{24}{52} = \tfrac{6}{13}$

1. A card is drawn at random from a pack of 52 playing cards. Find the probability that it is
   (a) a club
   (b) a heart, a spade or a club
   (c) the ace of spades
   (d) a five
   (e) a red four.

2 A dice is rolled on the table. Find the probability that the number on top is
   (a) 4
   (b) more than 4
   (c) less than four.
   (d) What do you notice about your answers to parts (a), (b) and (c)?

3. A letter is picked at random from the letters of the English alphabet. Find the probability that the letter
   (a) is a consonant
   (b) comes from the part of the alphabet from G to N inclusive
   (c) appears in the word GEOMETRY.

4. The aces and picture cards have been removed from a pack of playing cards leaving just the number cards from 2 to 10 of each suit. A card is drawn at random from these 36 cards. What is the probability that it is
   (a) black
   (b) a heart
   (c) a three
   (d) the four of clubs
   (e) even
   (f) a prime number
   (g) an ace
   (h) a number less than 11 ?

5. A two-figure number is written down at random. Find the probability that
   (a) the number is greater than 44
   (b) the number is less than 100.

6. A letter is picked at random from the English alphabet. Find the probability that
   (a) the letter is a vowel
   (b) the letter comes in the first half of the alphabet
   (c) the letter is one that appears in the word PROBABILITY.

A pin-board is marked as shown and a pin is stuck into the board at random. Find the probability that

(a) the pin is stuck into the shaded area
(b) the pin is not stuck into the shaded area.

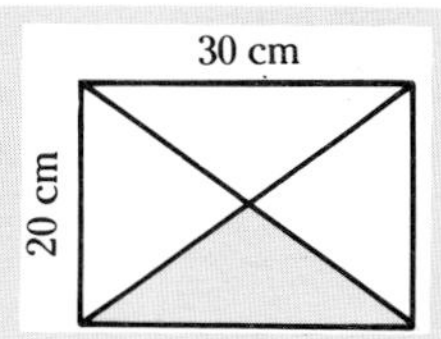

Area of board $= 20 \times 30\ \text{cm}^2$

Area of triangle is $\frac{1}{2}$ base $\times$ perpendicular height $= \frac{1}{2} \times 30 \times 10\ \text{cm}^2 = 150\ \text{cm}^2$

(a) $P(\text{pin in shaded area}) = \frac{150}{600} = \frac{1}{4}$

(b) The unshaded area is $(600 - 150)\ \text{cm}^2 = 450\ \text{cm}^2$

$\therefore \quad P(\text{pin in unshaded area}) = \frac{450}{600} = \frac{3}{4}$

7. A rectangular board measuring 30 cm by 40 cm is marked as shown in the diagram. A pin is stuck into the board at random. Find the probability that

(a) the pin is stuck into the shaded area

(b) the pin is stuck into the unshaded area.

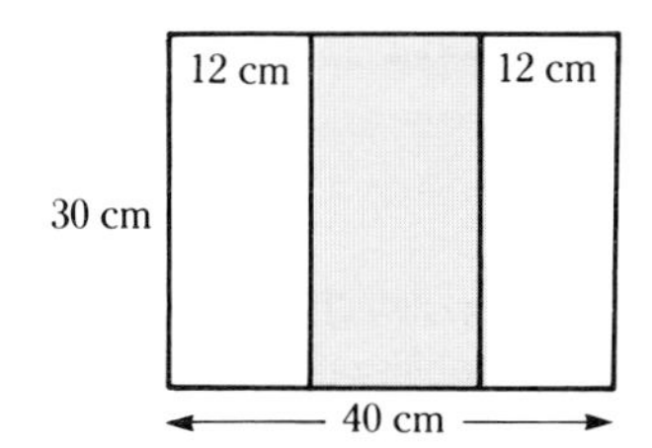

8. When Fiaz drops a coin on the board shown in the diagram its centre is equally likely to fall anywhere on the board. Find the probability that the centre of the coin falls

(a) on the shaded area

(b) on the unshaded area.

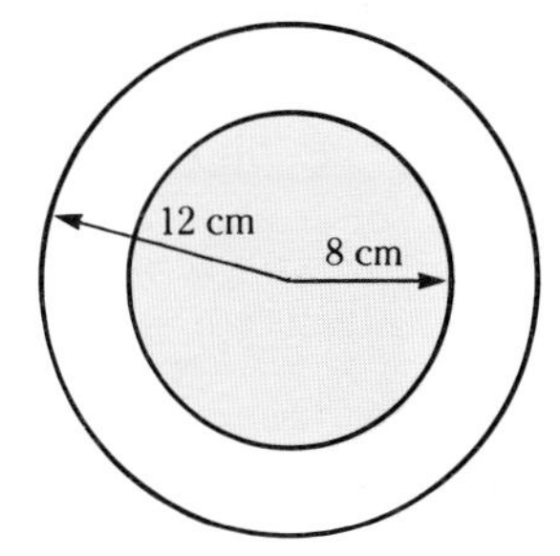

The probability of drawing a diamond from a pack of 52 playing cards is $\frac{13}{52}$, i.e. $\frac{1}{4}$. What is the probability of drawing a card that is not a diamond?

$P(\text{card is not a diamond}) = 1 - \frac{1}{4} = \frac{3}{4}$

9. A bag contains black, blue and red counters. The probability of drawing a red counter is $\frac{2}{5}$. If Ali draws a counter from this bag what is the probability that it is not red?

10. In a raffle 750 tickets are sold. If you buy 10 tickets what is the probability that

(a) you will win first prize

(b) you will not win first prize?

11. A letter is chosen at random from the letters of the word SUCCESSION. What is the probability that the letter is

(a) N (b) S (c) a vowel (d) not S?

12. A bag contains a set of snooker balls (i.e. 15 reds and 1 each of white, yellow, green, brown, blue, pink and black). What is the probability that one ball removed at random is

(a) red
(b) not red
(c) black
(d) not red or white?

13. A bag of sweets contains 4 caramels, 3 fruit centres and 5 mints. If one sweet is taken out, what is the probability that it is
    (a) a mint (b) a caramel (c) not a fruit centre ?

Of a class of 21, 10 altogether learn French, 6 learn both French and German and 6 learn neither. What is the probability that a pupil chosen at random learns only German ?

We can represent this information on a diagram. Suppose that the left-hand circle represents those pupils studying French and that the right-hand circle represents those studying German. Six study neither so are placed outside both circles. If 10 learn French and 6 learn both languages then 4 study only French. Since the total is 21 the number studying only German is 5.

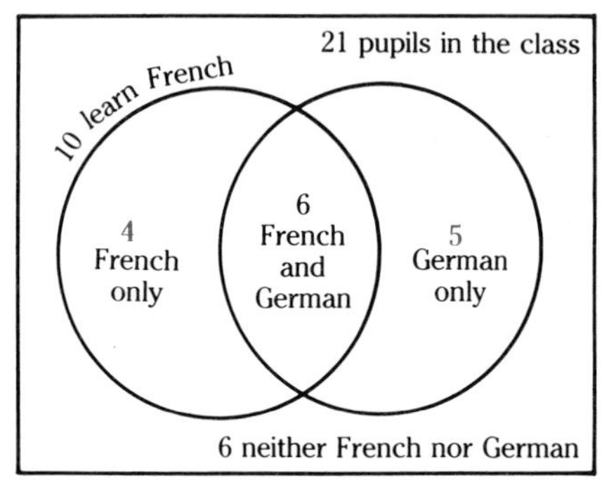

$P(\text{pupil picked at random studies only German}) = \frac{5}{21}$

14. A group of 50 television addicts were asked if they watched BBC and/or ITV. The replies revealed that 21 watched both channels but 9 watched only ITV. What is the probability that one of these people chosen at random watches only BBC ?

15. Of the 24 pupils in a class 20 have a television set and 12 have a video recorder. If every pupil has at least one of these items what is the probability that a pupil chosen at random has both ?

16. In a group of 30 children, all but 5 had a dog or a cat or both. If 18 kept a dog and 5 of these also kept a cat, what is the probability that one pupil, chosen at random,
    (a) keeps both a dog and a cat
    (b) keeps only a cat ?

17. During November, 36 cars were taken to a Testing Station for an MOT certificate. The results showed that 8 had both defective brakes and defective lights, 10 altogether had defective brakes, and 13 altogether had defective lights. If one car had been chosen from these at random what is the probability that
    (a) it had defective brakes
    (b) it had defective lights
    (c) it passed the test ?

The Expected Number of Successes

The converse of what we considered in the last exercise is also important. If we know the probability that an event will occur on one occasion, we can find the likely number of times it will occur on a given number of similar occasions.
We do this by multiplying the probability that it happens once by the number of times on which it could happen.

For example, we know that if we toss an unbiased dice, the probability that it will score six is $\frac{1}{6}$. So, if we toss the dice 36 times, then we are likely to get $\frac{1}{6} \times 36$ sixes, i.e. 6 sixes. (We are of course unlikely to get exactly 6 sixes, but there should be roughly that number if the dice is fair.)

Exercise 28b

In a television audience if one person is picked at random the probability that it is a man is $\frac{3}{8}$. There are 360 people in the audience. How many are likely to be men ?

$$\text{Likely number of men} = 360 \times \tfrac{3}{8}$$
$$= 135$$

1. A dice is rolled 180 times. How many times would you expect to get
   (a) 5 (b) an even number (c) 1, 2 or 3 ?

2. A card is drawn at random, 260 times, from an ordinary pack of 52 playing cards. How many times would you expect to get
   (a) an Ace (c) a black card
   (b) a heart (d) a red 7 ?

3. The probability that it will rain in Sunbrook on any given day in August is $\frac{2}{7}$. How many rainy days can you expect if you go to Sunbrook for 14 days in August ?

4. In a car park there is a probability of $\frac{3}{8}$ that a car picked at random is British made. There are 184 cars in the car park. How many of them
   (a) are British made
   (b) are not British made ?

5. The probability that you will get a yellow disc when you draw a disc at random from a box is $\frac{2}{5}$. How many yellow discs will you expect to get if you do this with each of 40 such boxes ?

6. At a school canteen, the estimated probabilities that a pupil asks for milk, cola or squash are $\frac{3}{12}$, $\frac{5}{12}$ and $\frac{4}{12}$ respectively. Next week it is estimated that there will be 1800 pupil customers. How many of each type of drink does the canteen expect to sell ?

7. An opinion poll used a sample of 1000 randomly selected voters to find voting intentions in a general election. Of these voters, 360 said that they would vote Conservative at the next general election and 75 said that they would vote for the Raving Looney party.
   (a) If a voter is selected at random from the sample, what is the probability that he/she stated an intention to vote Conservative ?
   (b) If there are 20 000 000 voters in the general election, how many are likely to vote
   (i) Conservative (ii) Raving Looney
   assuming that candidates for each party are standing in all constituencies ?

ADDITION OF PROBABILITIES

If we select a card at random from a pack of 52, the probability of drawing a king is $\frac{4}{52}$ and the probability of drawing a black ten is $\frac{2}{52}$.

There are 4 kings and 2 black tens so if we want to find the probability of drawing either a king or a black ten there are 6 cards that we would count as 'successful'.

$\therefore$ $\qquad P(\text{king or a black ten}) = \frac{6}{52}$

Now $\qquad P(\text{king}) = \frac{4}{52}$ and $P(\text{black ten}) = \frac{2}{52}$

i.e. $\qquad P(\text{king or black ten}) = P(\text{king}) + P(\text{black ten})$

We *add* the probabilities if there are several mutually exclusive possibilities (i.e. separate and independent possibilities) that we count as successful.

Sometimes two events are not completely separate, i.e. mutually exclusive. Consider, for example, the probability of drawing either a red card or a king. There are 26 red cards and 4 kings, but 2 of the kings are also red cards. There are therefore a total of 28 possible successful cards.

$$P(\text{red card or king}) = \frac{28}{52} = \frac{7}{13}$$

If two events are not mutually exclusive we cannot add the separate probabilities.

Exercise 28c

1. A card is drawn at random from an ordinary pack of 52. What is the probability that the card is

   (a) a red ace (b) a black king

   (c) a red ace or a black king ?

2. Joy rolls an ordinary dice. What is the probability that the number shown is

   (a) 2 (b) 3 or 4 (c) 2, 3 or 4 ?

3. A card is drawn at random from the 12 court cards (jacks, queens and kings). What is the probability that the card is

   (a) a black jack

   (b) a red queen

   (c) either a black jack or a red queen ?

4. Graham is looking for his house key. The probability that it is in a pocket is $\frac{5}{9}$, while the probability that it is in the car is $\frac{1}{3}$. What is the probability that

   (a) the key is either in a pocket or in the car

   (b) the key is somewhere else ?

5. When Mrs Greene goes shopping the probability that she returns by bus is $\frac{4}{7}$, in a taxi $\frac{1}{7}$, on foot $\frac{3}{14}$. What is the probability that she returns

   (a) by bus or taxi (b) by bus or on foot ?

6. Karl has a bag containing some coloured discs. When a disc is drawn from the bag the probability of getting a red disc is $\frac{2}{5}$, a blue disc $\frac{2}{7}$ and a yellow disc $\frac{1}{4}$. Karl offers the bag to Sandra who draws one disc. Find the probability that the colour of this disc is

   (a) red or blue

   (b) blue or yellow

   (c) red, blue or yellow

   (d) some other colour.

7. Sengha rolls an ordinary dice. What is the probability that the number on the dice is

   (a) an even number

   (b) a prime number

   (c) either even or prime ?

POSSIBILITY SPACE FOR TWO EVENTS

Any two-dimensional array that shows all the possible outcomes is called a *possibility space.*

When two coins are tossed the possible outcomes are HH, HT, TH, TT

Each outcome is equally likely so $P(2 \text{ heads}) = \frac{1}{4}$

By listing the possible equally likely outcomes the required probability can be found. However if two dice are rolled there are many possible outcomes. We must set out the list in an organised way so that there is no risk of missing any.

We can list the outcomes in the following table.

First dice

Second dice		1	2	3	4	5	6
	1	(1, 1)	(1, 2)	(1, 3)	(1, 4)	(1, 5)	(1, 6)
	2	(2, 1)	(2, 2)	(2, 3)	(2, 4)	(2, 5)	(2, 6)
	3	(3, 1)	(3, 2)	(3, 3)	(3, 4)	(3, 5)	(3, 6)
	4	(4, 1)	(4, 2)	(4, 3)	(4, 4)	(4, 5)	(4, 6)
	5	(5, 1)	(5, 2)	(5, 3)	(5, 4)	(5, 5)	(5, 6)
	6	(6, 1)	(6, 2)	(6, 3)	(6, 4)	(6, 5)	(6, 6)

The table shows that there are 36 possible outcomes.

To find the probability of getting a total score of 5, ring the entries that indicate a total score of 5, i.e. $1+4$, $2+3$, and so on.

Hence $P(5) = \frac{4}{36} = \frac{1}{9}$

Similarly, we can find the probability of scoring, say, 8. Put squares around the outcomes that total 8. Thus $P(8) = \frac{5}{36}$

Exercise 28d

In each question from 1 to 3, draw a possibility space to show the outcomes when two ordinary dice are rolled. Use this possibility space to find the required probabilities. Use different marks such as a ring or a square, or different colours, for the parts of each question.

1. Find the probability that
   (a) the sum of the two numbers is 7
   (b) the difference between the scores is 2
   (c) the sum is 7 and the difference is 2
   (d) the sum is greater than 4.

2. Find the probability that
   (a) the sum of the two numbers is 7 or more
   (b) the difference between the two numbers is 3 or less
   (c) the sum of the two numbers is 7 or more and their difference is 3 or less.

3. Find the probability that
   (a) prime numbers appear on both dice
   (b) at least one prime number appears
   (c) only one prime number appears.

4. A four-sided spinner has the numbers 1 to 4 marked on it. It is spun twice and the two scores are noted. Draw a possibility space table to show the outcomes. Find the probability that
   (a) the total score is even
   (b) the two separate scores are both even
   (c) the product of the scores is even.

5. I have two bags each containing four hyacinth bulbs and I know that each bag contains a pink, a blue, a yellow and a white bulb. If I take one bulb at random from each bag, find the probability that
   (a) the hyacinths will be the same colour
   (b) the hyacinths will be of different colours.

PROBABILITY TREES

Another method for dealing with two independent events, such as tossing two coins, is to draw a probability tree.

When the first coin is tossed, the probability that it lands head up is $\frac{1}{2}$ and the probability that it lands tail up is $\frac{1}{2}$.

We can show this in a diagram.

P(H) = $\frac{1}{2}$
P(T) = $\frac{1}{2}$

If the first coin lands head up then the second coin can land either head up or tail up. The probabilities are shown in this diagram.

P(H) = $\frac{1}{2}$
P(T) = $\frac{1}{2}$

Similarly if the first coin lands tail up, the second coin can land either way up.

P(H) = $\frac{1}{2}$
P(T) = $\frac{1}{2}$

First coin | Second coin

These three diagrams can be combined in one diagram, called a *tree diagram*.

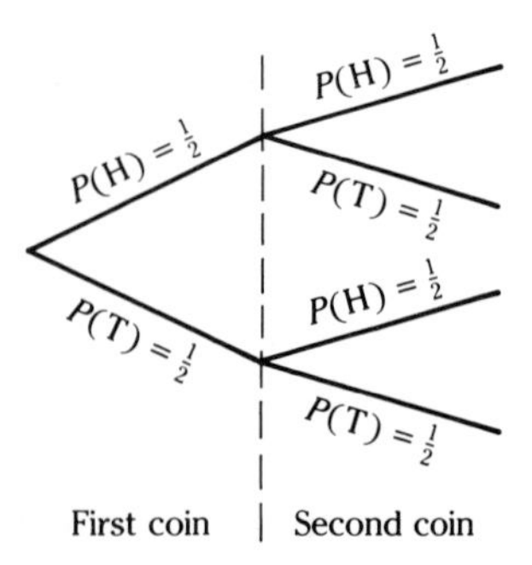

When two coins are tossed, the possible outcomes are (HH, HT, TH, TT) so the probability of getting two heads is $\frac{1}{4}$.

This result can be obtained from the tree diagram. Follow a path along the required branches (i.e. head first, head second) and *multiply together the probabilities on the two branches*. This gives $\frac{1}{2}\times\frac{1}{2}=\frac{1}{4}$.

The probability of getting just one head (i.e. HT or TH) is $\frac{1}{4}+\frac{1}{4}$, i.e. $\frac{1}{2}$.

This can also be obtained from the tree diagram by following two paths and *adding together the probabilities from the two paths.*

The advantage of probability trees is that they can be used in more complicated situations when we are interested in only one outcome. Suppose, for example, that two dice are tossed and we are interested only in sixes. We then need only two branches for one throw, one for 'a six' and one for 'not a six'.

Another advantage of probability trees is that they can be used for more than two events. For example, if three coins are tossed, we can add another set of branches to the ends of the tree opposite.

Exercise 28e

A dice is tossed twice. What is the probability of getting

(a) a six on the first throw and not on the second throw

(b) at least one six from the two throws ?

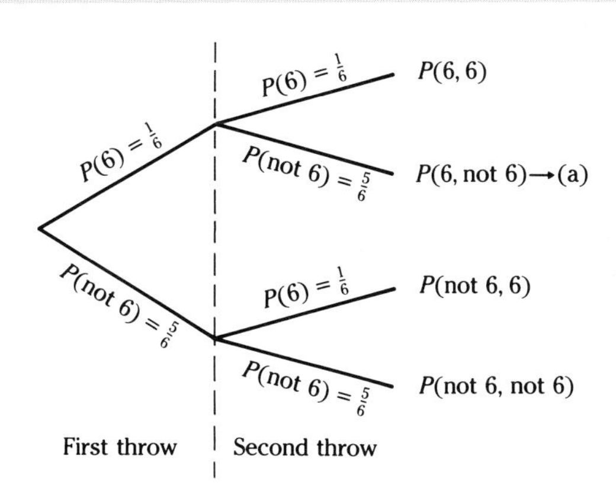

(a) Six first and not second comes from following one path.

$$P(6 \text{ first, not } 6 \text{ second}) = \tfrac{1}{6}\times\tfrac{5}{6} = \tfrac{5}{36}$$

(b) At least one six comes from following the top three paths.

$$P(\text{at least one six}) = \tfrac{1}{6}\times\tfrac{1}{6}+\tfrac{1}{6}\times\tfrac{5}{6}+\tfrac{5}{6}\times\tfrac{1}{6} = \tfrac{11}{36}$$

1. Use the probability tree in the worked example to find the probability
   (a) that two sixes are thrown
   (b) just one six is thrown.

2. Three dice are thrown. Copy the probability tree and fill in the remaining probabilities.

   Use your tree diagram to find the probability that
   (a) no sixes are thrown
   (b) just one six is thrown
   (c) at least two sixes are thrown.

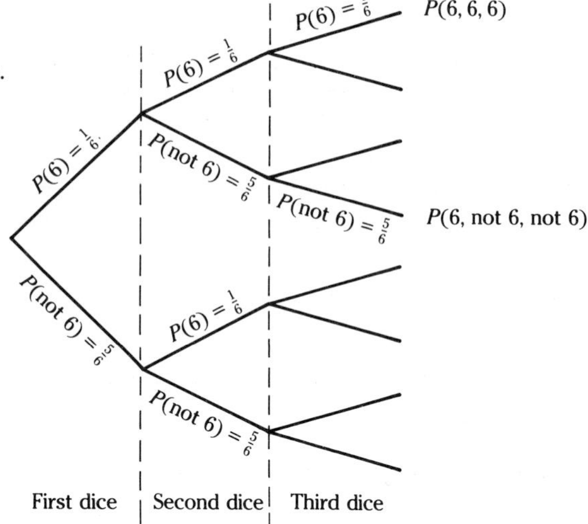

3. The weather forecast suggests that the probability that it will rain on Monday is $\frac{2}{25}$ and the probability that it will rain on Tuesday is $\frac{1}{9}$.

   (a) On which of these two days is it more likely to rain ? Give a reason for your answer.

   (b) Copy and complete this tree diagram.

   (c) Use your tree diagram to find the probability that it will rain on

      (i) both days
      (ii) just one of the days.

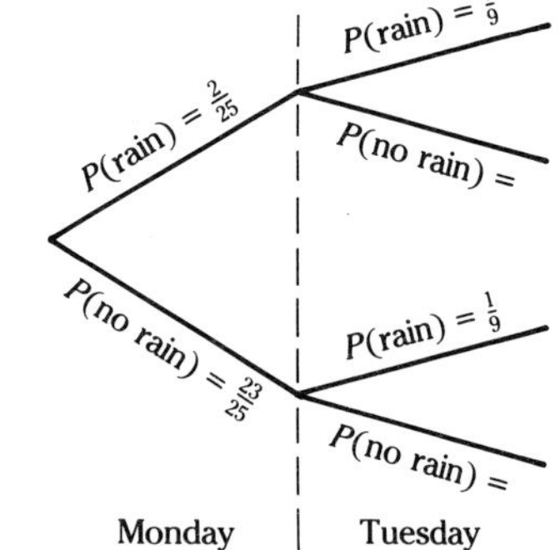

   The probability that it will rain on Wednesday is $\frac{1}{2}$.
   Add more branches to your tree to include Wednesday.

   (d) Use your new tree to find the probability that it will rain on

      (i) none of the three days
      (ii) at least one of the three days.

4. A dice has been loaded so that, when it is tossed, the probability of scoring six is 20 %. The chances of scoring one, two, three, four and five are equal.

   (a) What is the probability of scoring five with this dice ?

   (b) If the dice is tossed twice, draw a probability tree to show all the possible outcomes of scoring six or not six.

   (c) Use your tree to find the probability of scoring
      (i) two sixes (ii) at least one six (iii) no sixes.

5. A coin is tossed three times. Draw a tree diagram to show the probabilities and use it to find the probability of getting

   (a) a head and two tails (b) exactly one tail (c) at least one head.

6. On the way home Larry passes through three sets of traffic lights. The probability that the first set is green when he reaches them is $\frac{3}{5}$, the probability that the second set is green is $\frac{2}{3}$ and the probability that the third set is green is $\frac{3}{4}$. Draw a probability tree and use it to find the probability that he has to stop at

   (a) just one set of traffic lights

   (b) at least one set of traffic lights

   (c) exactly two sets of traffic lights.

7. In a packet of lupin seeds, $\frac{2}{3}$ of the seeds are for blue flowers and the others are for pink flowers.

   (a) If two seeds are planted, what is the probability that both are for blue flowered lupins?

   (b) The probability that a seed for a blue flower germinates is $\frac{4}{5}$ and the probability that a seed for a pink flower germinates is $\frac{9}{11}$. If a seed does not germinate, it fails.

   Copy and complete this tree diagram to show all the possible outcomes when two seeds are planted.

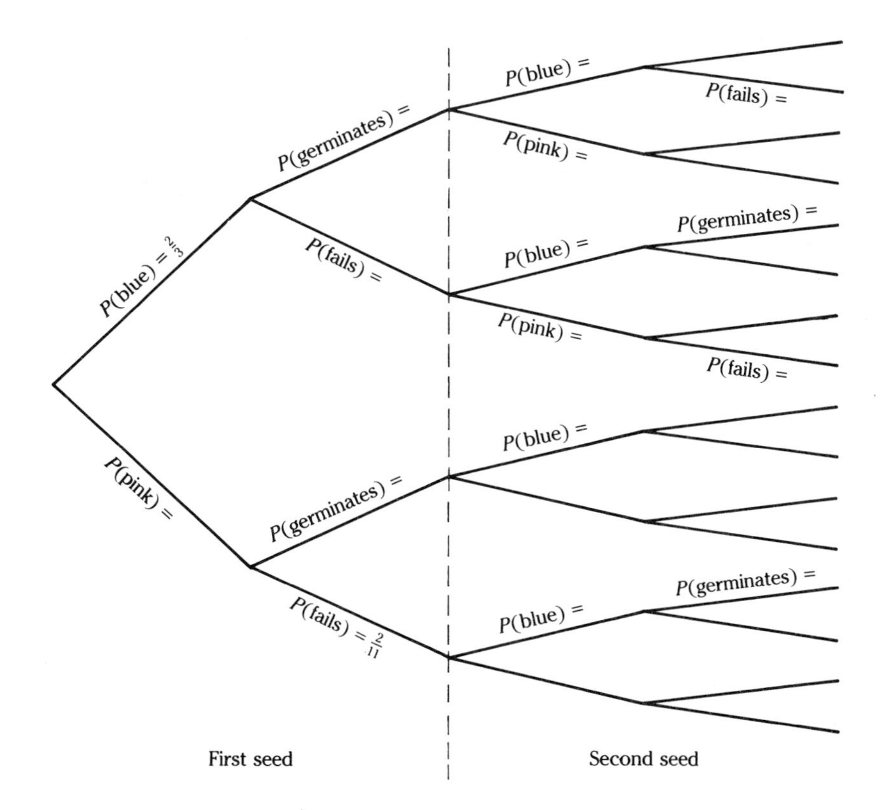

   (c) Use your tree to find the probability that both seeds germinate and produce one blue and one pink lupin.

Investigation

1. (a) What is the probability that, if a dice is rolled, the score is 5 or 6 ?

(b) Roll a dice 20 times and record the number of times a 5 or 6 is scored.

Work out the fraction $\dfrac{\text{number of times 5 or 6 is scored}}{\text{number of times dice is rolled}}$

Roll it another 20 times and find the value of this fraction for the 40 outcomes. Carry on another 20 times, and another 20, and so on. Does the fraction, correct to two decimal places, settle down to a steady value ? How does this value compare with the answer you got for part (a) ?

2. (a) What is the probability that the next person you meet was born in one of the summer months June, July or August ?

(b) Conduct an experiment. Ask at least 100 people:
In which month were you born ?

Calculate the fraction $\dfrac{\text{number born in June, July or August}}{\text{total number of people you have asked}}$

Compare your answers for (a) and (b).

3. Pick out a card from a well shuffled pack of 52 playing cards. Replace the card, shuffle the pack and then pick out another card. Write *Y* if at least one of the cards was an ace, king, queen or jack. Write *N* otherwise. Replace the cards, shuffle the pack and do the same thing again. Repeat this at least 100 times.

Work out the fraction $\dfrac{\text{number of } Y\text{s}}{\text{total number of outcomes}}$

Work out the theoretical probability that at least one card out of two cards drawn at random is an ace, king, queen or jack and compare this with your experimental value.

Repeat this procedure for other selections of your own choice from the pack. Do your results convince you that the theoretical results give a good indication of what is likely to happen ?

Self-Assessment 28

1. A card is drawn at random from an ordinary pack of 52 playing cards. What is the probability that it is
(a) a red 3 (b) the Ace of spaces ?

2. A dice is rolled 360 times. How many times would you expect to get
(a) 6
(b) 1 or 2 ?

3. (a) What is the probability that, if a dice is rolled, the score is 5 or 6 ?

(b) Roll a dice 20 times and record the number of times a 5 or 6 is scored.

Work out the fraction

$$\frac{\text{number of times 5 or 6 is scored}}{\text{number of times dice is rolled}}$$

Roll it another 20 times and find the value of this fraction for the 40 outcomes.
Carry on another 20 times, and another 20, and so on. Does the fraction, correct to two decimal places, settle down to a steady value ? How does this value compare with the answer you got for part (a) ?

4. (a) What is the probability that the next person you meet was born in one of the summer months June, July or August ?

(b) Conduct an experiment. Ask at least 100 people: In which month were you born ?

Calculate the fraction

$$\frac{\text{number born in June, July or August}}{\text{total number of people you have asked}}$$

Compare your answer for (a) and (b).

5. Andy and Coral both enter for a skating examination. Andy estimates that the probability that he will pass is 0.8 and Coral estimates that the probability that she will pass is 0.9.

(a) On these estimates, who is more likely to pass ?

By drawing a tree diagram, estimate the probability that

(b) Andy will pass but Coral will fail

(c) they both pass.

6. The number of brothers and sisters of each child in a class was noted. The table shows the results.

Sisters \ Brothers	0	1	2	3	4
0	3	6	4	0	1
1	5	3	2	2	0
2	2	1	0	0	1
3	0	1	1	0	0

(a) How many pupils have two brothers ?

(b) How many pupils have at least 1 sister ?

(c) What is the probability that a pupil chosen at random has one brother and one sister ?

29 STATISTICAL CALCULATIONS

AVERAGES

It is sometimes necessary to describe how a set of data is distributed. For example, the distribution of the weights of two thousand people could be described by a value representative of most of these weights, i.e. an average value, together with an indication of how far the weights are spread about this value.

The Shape of a Bar Chart

It is possible to get an impression of the distribution of a set of data by looking at its bar chart.

Consider these two bar charts; they show the scores obtained in a general knowledge quiz by two different groups of 250 people.

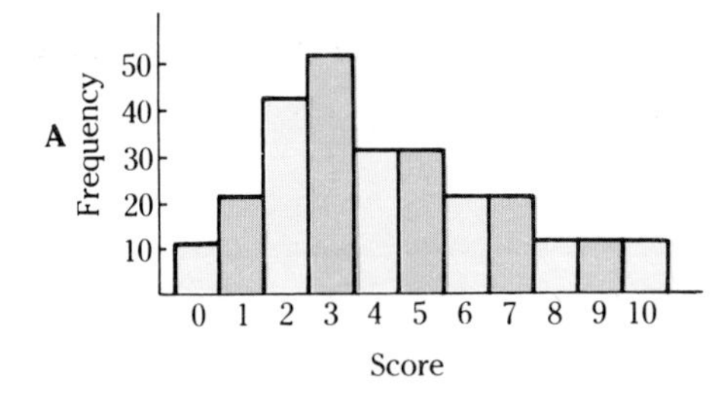

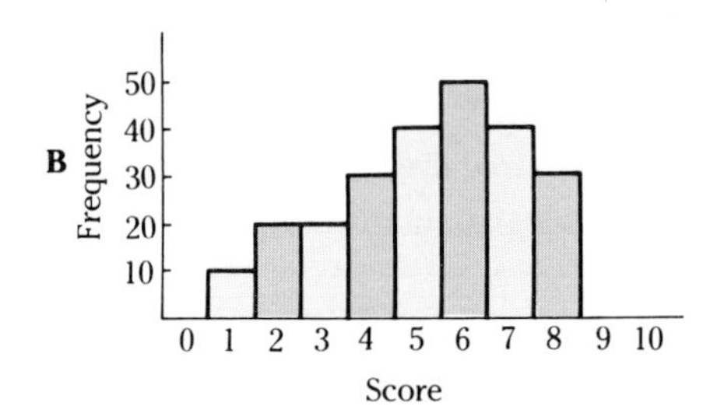

From the bar charts it is apparent that the bulk of the scores of group A is lower than the bulk of scores of group B. It is also clear that the spread of scores for group B is less than that for group A. We will look at this aspect of distributions later in this chapter.

Both 'average' and 'bulk' are vague ways of referring to the centre of a distribution. There are three more precise ways of giving a central value for a set of numbers and we will define each in turn.

Mode

 **The mode is the number that occurs most often.** 

For example, for the set 1, 3, 3, 5, 6, 7, 8, 8, 8 the mode is 8.

For the scores for group A, the modal score is 3 and for group B, the modal score is 6.

Sometimes there are two or more numbers that occur equally often; in this case there are two or more modes. When the numbers are all different, there is no mode.

Median

When numbers are arranged in order of size, the median is the number in the middle.

There are nine numbers in the set 1, 3, 3, 5, 6, 7, 8, 8, 8, so the middle number, or median, is the 5th number, i.e. the $\frac{9+1}{2}$th number. Hence the median of this set is 6.

If there is an even number of numbers in the set, then the median is the value halfway between the two middle values.

Find the median of these sums of money: £2.50, £1.85, £3.54, £2.60

First the items must be arranged in ascending size order.

£1.85, £2.50, £2.60, £3.54

There are four items here, so the middle ones are £2.50 and £2.60

The median sum of money is halfway between £2.50 and £2.60, i.e. £2.55

In general, if there are n numbers in a set, the median is the value of the $\frac{(n+1)}{2}$th number. when the numbers are arranged in size order.

The Mean

The mean, or arithmetic average, of a set of *n* numbers is the sum of the numbers divided by *n*.

For example, the mean of the set 1, 3, 3, 5, 6, 7, 8, 8, 8 is

$$\frac{1+3+3+5+6+7+8+8+8}{9} = \frac{49}{9} = 5\frac{4}{9}$$

To give an interpretation of the mean, suppose that the numbers in this set are the scores obtained from 9 balls on a pinball machine. If it were possible to even out the scores, i.e. to get an equal score from each ball to give the same total, then this equal score would be the mean; we would say that the average score is $5\frac{4}{9}$. The mean value does not have to be one of the given values or even, as in this case, a *possible* value.

The mean is the most frequently used central measure, so much so that the mean value is often called 'the average'.
However, each of the mean, mode and median has advantages in different situations.

Consider, as one example, a shoe retailer who records the size of each pair of shoes sold. The modal size (i.e. the most common size) would be of most interest in this case because it would be sensible to stock most of that size.

On the other hand suppose that the following sums of money are the daily earnings of a group of people in a small company: \$5, \$52, \$58, \$59 \$60

The mean sum is \$46.80 which is lower than all but one of these sums. This is because one very low sum has affected the mean and in this case the mean sum of money does not give a fair impression of the daily earnings. It would be better to use the median sum of \$58 as representative of these daily earnings.

In general, if the median is greater than the mean then more than half the numbers are greater than the mean. Conversely, if the median is less than the mean then more than half of the numbers are less than the mean. In the context of a set of test marks with mean 6.3 and median 5, we can say that more than half the students got a mark below the mean.

Exercise 29a

1. Find the mean, median and mode of each of the following sets of numbers. Give answers correct to three significant figures where necessary.
   (a) 3, 6, 2, 5, 9, 2, 4
   (b) 1.6, 2.4, 3.9, 1.7, 1.6, 0.2, 1.3, 2
   (c) 4, 3, 4, 5, 2, 5, 4, 3
   (d) 0.8, 0.7, 0.6, 0.7, 0.8, 0.8, 0.9, 0.5

2. A small firm employs nine people. The annual salaries of the employees are \$60 000, \$25 000, \$20 000, \$12 000, \$10 000, \$10 000, \$10 000, \$9 000, \$8 000.
   Find the mean, modal and median salaries. Which of these three figures would you be most interested in if you were involved in negotiating salary increases and were (a) the boss (b) a union official.
   Give brief reasons for your answer.

3. Five students got mean marks of 52, 45.5, 63, 73.6 and 85.7 respectively for ten tests. Find the total marks obtained by each student.

4. The mean daily takings in a shop from Monday to Friday were \$580, while the mean daily takings from Monday to Saturday were \$680.50.
   (a) How much was taken over the five days Monday to Friday ?
   (b) How much was taken over the six days Monday to Saturday ?
   (c) How much was taken on Saturday ?

In a game of darts, three throws make one turn. On 15 turns, John had a mean score of 25. How much does he need to score on his next turn to raise his mean score to 26 ?

The total made for the first 15 turns is

$$15 \times 25 = 375$$

To get a mean score of 26 on 16 turns, John needs to make a total score of

$$16 \times 26 = 416$$

Therefore John needs to score $416 - 375$, i.e. 41 on his 16th turn.

5. In a boat race the average weight of the eight oarsmen was 75.3 kg and the average weight of the crew including the cox was 73.2 kg. How heavy was the cox ?

6. The average weight of the fifteen players in a rugby team was 81.9 kg, while the average weight of the team plus a reserve was 82.7 kg. How heavy was the reserve ?

7. In five visits to a dart board, a dart player's average score was 65. After a further visit his average fell to 61. What did he score on his sixth visit ?

This bar chart shows the scores obtained by a group of people (Group A, p. 426) in a quiz. Find the mean score.

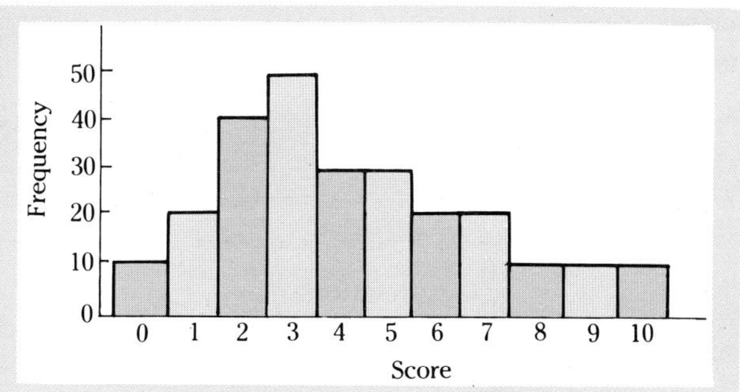

To find the mean score, we first have to find the total value of all the scores, i.e. to find $10 \times 0 + 20 \times 1 + 40 \times 2 + \ldots$ and so on: It is easier to keep track of these calculations if we first make a frequency table from the bar chart, and add an extra column to accommodate 'frequency $\times$ score'. Using f for frequency and x for the score gives

	x	f	fx
	0	10	0
	1	20	20
	2	40	80
	3	50	150
	4	30	120
	5	30	150
	6	20	120
	7	20	140
	8	10	80
	9	10	90
	10	10	100
Total		250	1050

From the table, we see that 250 people got a total score of 1050.

Therefore the mean score is $\dfrac{1050}{250} = 4.2$

8. Use these bar charts to find the mean value of the distribution.

(a)

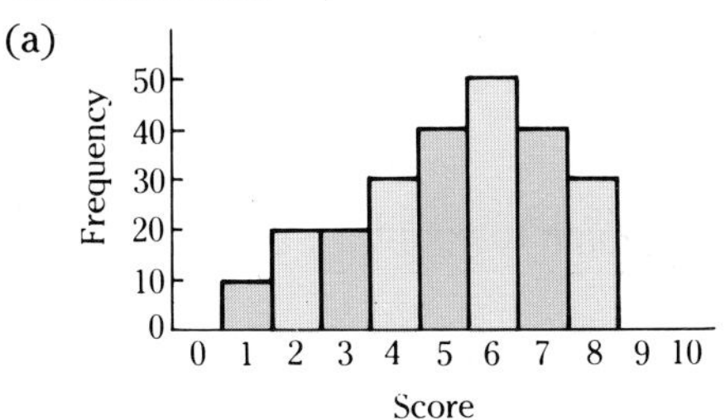

(b)

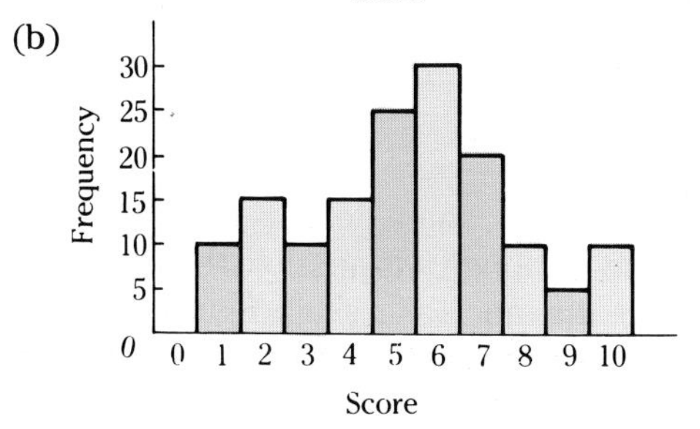

9. An ordinary dice was thrown 50 times. The table gives the number of times each score was obtained.

Score	1	2	3	4	5	6
Frequency	7	8	10	8	5	12

Find the mean score per throw.

10. Three coins were tossed together 30 times and the number of heads per throw was recorded.

Number of heads	0	1	2	3
Frequency	3	12	10	5

Find the mean number of heads per throw.

It is also possible to find the median from a frequency distribution. This is illustrated in the next worked example.

Use this histogram from the worked example on page 429 to find the median score.

x	f	
0	10	
1	20	30 scores
2	40	70 scores
3	50	120 scores
4	30	150 scores
5	30	
6	20	
7	20	
8	10	
9	10	
10	10	
Total	250	

There are 250 scores so the median score is halfway between the 125th and 126th score when they are arranged in order of size.

By adding the frequencies, as shown above, we see that the 125th and 126th score are both in the 5th row of the table, i.e. **the median score is 4.**

11. This table gives the distribution of marks obtained in a test. Find the median mark.

Mark	0	1	2	3	4	5
Frequency	1	5	9	12	15	8

12. Find the median of the distribution given in question 9.

FINDING AVERAGES FROM GROUPED FREQUENCY TABLES

This frequency table shows the results of asking some men to count the number of items in their pockets.

Number of items	0–4	5–9	10–14	15–19	20–24
Frequency	6	11	6	4	3

Mode and Median

Because the number of items have been placed in groups, some detail is lost. We do not know how many men had 3 items in their pockets so, although it is possible that more men had 3 items than any other number, we cannot give the mode as a single figure. It is clear, however, that more men had 5 to 9 items in their pockets than any other group; this is called the *modal group*.

It is also possible to find the group in which the median of the distribution lies, by counting up frequencies as before. The distribution shows, in order of size, the number of items in the pockets of 30 men, so the median is the average number of items in the pockets of the 15th and 16th men. These are both in the second group, so the best that we can say at this stage is that the median number of items is in the 5–9 items group.

Mean

As we have seen, we do not know the exact number of items that each man had so it is not possible to find the total number of items exactly. However if we *assume* that the mean number of items per group is the halfway value of the group, we can find an approximate total.

Consider, for example, the first group; assuming that the mean number of items is 2, there is an approximate total of 12 items in that group.

Doing the same calculation for the other groups and arranging the results in a table gives

No. of items per man	Frequency, f	Halfway value, x	No. of items in this group, fx
0–4	6	2	12
5–9	11	7	77
10–14	6	12	72
15–19	4	17	68
20–24	3	22	66
Total	30	Total	295

Therefore the mean number of items is approximately $\frac{295}{30} = 9.8$ to 1 d.p.

For continuous data, the calculation is performed in the same way. This table gives the heights of tomato plants four weeks after seeds were planted.

Height, h cm	f	Halfway value, x	fx
$0 \leqslant h < 3$	2	1.5	3
$3 \leqslant h < 6$	5	4.5	22.5
$6 \leqslant h < 9$	10	7.5	75
$9 \leqslant h < 12$	3	10.5	31.5
Total	20	Total	132

Therefore the mean height is approximately $\frac{132}{20}$ cm $= 6.6$ cm

Exercise 29b

Keep all your solutions and graphs from this exercise; they are needed for later exercises.

Estimate the mean value of each distribution.

1. Fifty boxes of oranges were examined and the number of damaged oranges in each box was recorded with the following result.

No. of damaged oranges	0–4	5–9	10–14	15–19
Frequency	34	11	4	1

2. Twenty beans were planted in a seed tray. The table shows the distribution of the heights of the resulting plants three weeks later.

Height, h cm	$1 \leqslant h < 4$	$4 \leqslant h < 7$	$7 \leqslant h < 10$	$10 \leqslant h < 13$
Frequency	2	5	10	3

3. The table shows the distribution of the heights of 50 adult females.

Height, h cm	$149.5 \leqslant h < 154.5$	$154.5 \leqslant h < 159.5$	$159.5 \leqslant h < 164.5$	$164.5 \leqslant h < 169.5$
Frequency	4	21	18	7

4. The bar chart shows the result of an examination of 20 boxes of screws. Start by making a frequency table.

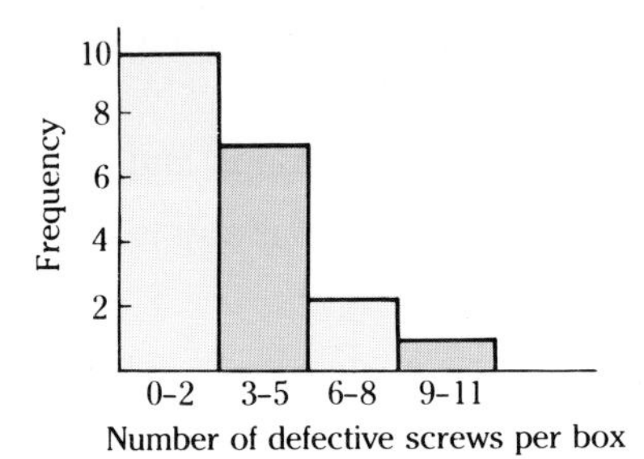

5. The entrance to a supermarket needed to be rebuilt. A survey was carried out to investigate the numbers of customers entering during a one minute period so that sensible decisions could be made about the size and type of entrance to build. The table shows the result of the survey.

No. of customers per minute	0–2	3–5	6–8	9–11	12–14	15–17
Frequency	100	200	150	90	40	20

CUMULATIVE FREQUENCY

In Exercise 29a the median of a frequency distribution was found by adding the frequencies to find the value of the middle item. Adding the frequencies in this way gives *cumulative frequencies* which are best set out in a table. Using again the frequency distribution of scores for group A (p. 429) gives this table.

Score x	f	Score	Cumulative frequency
0	10	0	10
1	20	$\leqslant 1$	30
2	40	$\leqslant 2$	70
3	50	$\leqslant 3$	120
4	30	$\leqslant 4$	150
5	30	$\leqslant 5$	180
6	20	$\leqslant 6$	200
7	20	$\leqslant 7$	220
8	10	$\leqslant 8$	230
9	10	$\leqslant 9$	240
10	10	$\leqslant 10$	250

From this table, as well as being able to find the median, we can also find the number of people who got less than, say, a score of 5. The table shows that 150 people got 4 or less, i.e. less than 5.

We can also give the number of people who got a score greater than, say, 6. From the table, 200 people got a score of 6 or less; there were 250 scores altogether, so 250 − 200, i.e. 50 people, got a score greater than 6.

We can also make a cumulative frequency table for a grouped frequency distribution which, for the number of items in mens' pockets, looks like this.

No. of items	f	No. of items	Cumulative frequency
0–4	6	$\leqslant 4$	6
5–9	11	$\leqslant 9$	17
10–14	6	$\leqslant 14$	23
15–19	4	$\leqslant 19$	27
20–24	3	$\leqslant 24$	30

For the distribution of heights of tomato plants on page 431, the table looks like this.

Height, h cm	f	h	Cum f
$0 \leqslant h < 3$	2	< 3	2
$3 \leqslant h < 6$	5	< 6	7
$6 \leqslant h < 9$	10	< 9	17
$9 \leqslant h < 12$	3	< 12	20

Exercise 29c

1. Make a cumulative frequency table for the distribution of damaged oranges per box given in Exercise 29b, question 1. Use it to find the number of boxes that contained
   (a) at least 10 damaged oranges
   (b) fewer than 15 damaged oranges.

2. Use the information given in Exercise 29b, question 2 to make a cumulative frequency table. Three weeks after planting, how many bean plants were
   (a) at least 7 cm high
   (b) between 4 and 10 cm high ?

3. Make a cumulative frequency table for the heights of females as described in Exercise 29b, question 3. How many of the women are less than 159.5 cm tall ? Hence find the probability that one of these women chosen at random is less than 159.5 cm tall.

CUMULATIVE FREQUENCY CURVES

Using a grouped frequency distribution and plotting the cumulative frequency against the *upper value* of each group gives a graph. If the points are joined by straight lines, the graph is called *a cumulative frequency polygon.* If a smooth curve is drawn through the points, the graph is called a *cumulative frequency curve.*

The two grouped distributions discussed in the last section give these cumulative frequency curves.

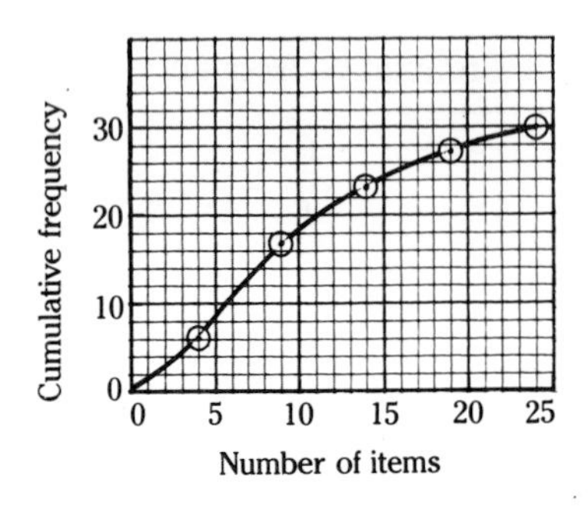

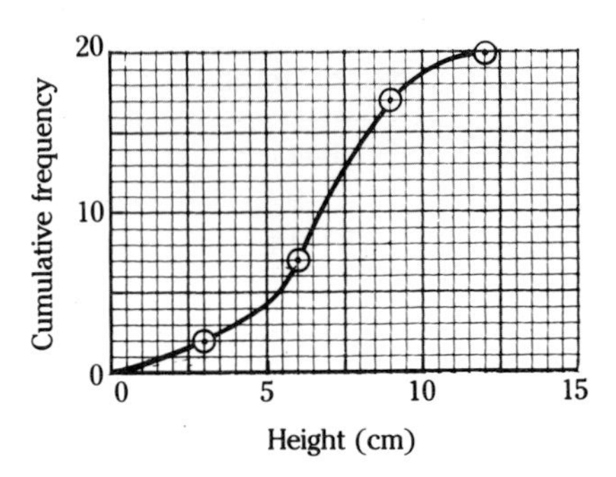

Note that we start the curve at the lower end of the first group. The curve always starts at zero on the cumulative frequency axis.

Finding the Median of a Grouped Frequency Distribution

When we discussed the median number of items in pockets, we said that we could not give a precise value. A good approximation to the median however can easily be read off the cumulative frequency curve. At the middle value of the cumulative frequency, a line is drawn across, to meet the curve, and then down to give the corresponding number of items.

The middle value of the cumulative frequency is the 15.5th value.

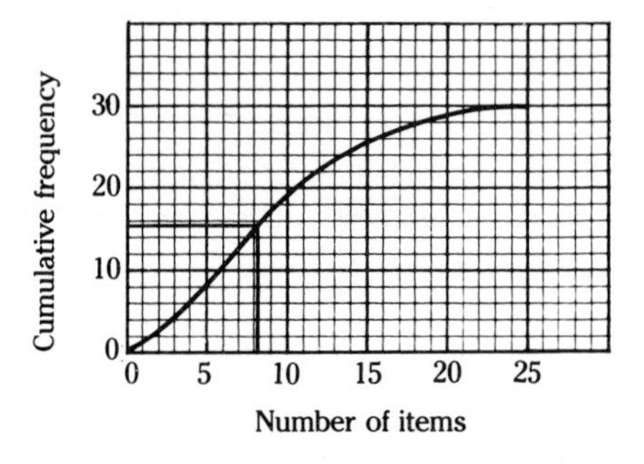

From the graph, the median is approximately 8.

Exercise 29d

This cumulative frequency curve shows the number of people arriving for a meeting from the time when the doors were opened. The meeting started 15 minutes after the doors opened.

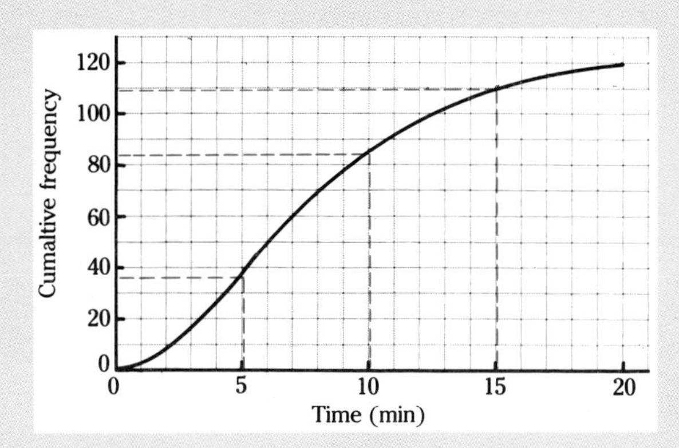

Use the curve to find

(a) the number of people who arrived in time

(b) the number of people who arrived during the first five minutes

(c) the number of people who arrived after 10 minutes

(d) the number of people who arrived after the meeting started

(e) the probability that someone picked at random had arrived late.

(a) The number of people who arrived in time were those who arrived in the first 15 minutes. Drawing a line up from 15 on the time axis to meet the curve and then across to the cumulative frequency axis gives this number.

110 people arrived in time.

(b) 38 people arrived in the first five minutes.

(c) The curve goes up to 120 on the cumulative frequency axis, so 120 people attended the meeting.

The number of people who arrived after 10 minutes is $120 - 86 = 34$

(d) The number of people who arrived after the meeting started, i.e. after 15 minutes is $120 - 110 = 10$

(e) 120 people attended the meeting.

10 people arrived late

$\therefore$ P(one person picked at random arrived late) $= \frac{10}{120} = \frac{1}{12}$

1. Use the cumulative frequency tables made in Exercise 29c to draw a cumulative frequency curve for each distribution. Hence give, approximately, the median of each of these distributions.

2. This cumulative frequency curve illustrates the journey times to college of some students.

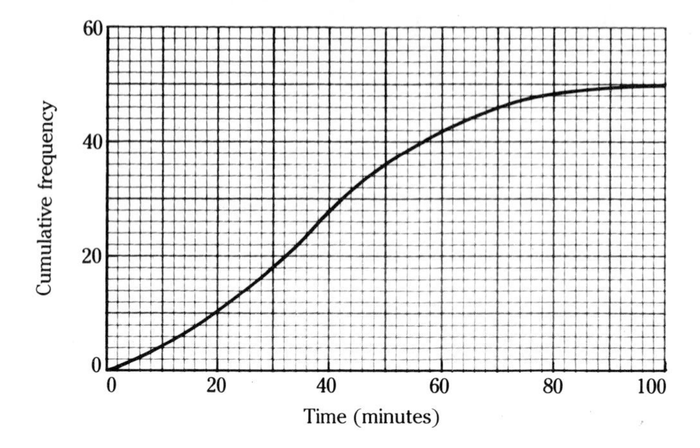

Use the curve to find

(a) the number of students who took part in the survey
(b) the median journey time
(c) the number of students who took less than 10 minutes to get to college
(d) the number of students who had journey times greater than 30 minutes
(e) the number of students who took between 40 minutes and one hour to get to college
(f) the probability that a student chosen at random had a journey time of between 20 and 30 minutes.

3. Using the curve given for question 2, copy and complete this frequency table.

Journey time, t minutes	Number of students, f	Halfway value of t, x	fx
$0 \leqslant t < 10$			
$10 \leqslant t < 20$			
$20 \leqslant t < 40$			
$40 \leqslant t < 60$			
$60 \leqslant t < 80$			
$80 \leqslant t < 100$			

Use the table to

(a) calculate an approximate value for the mean journey time
(b) draw a histogram to illustrate the data.

4. Use your results from questions 2 and 3 to compare the median journey time and the mean journey time.
A student chosen at random from this group is found to have a journey time greater than the mean journey time. Is the probability that this should happen greater or less than 0.5 ?

COMPARING THE MEAN AND THE MEDIAN

This diagram illustrates the results of a test taken by some children.

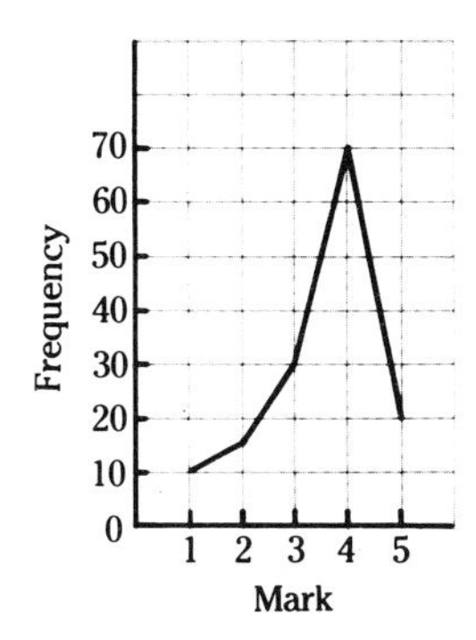

The marks range from 1 to 5. The frequency polygon has a peak greater than halfway through the range so we would expect the mean mark and the median mark to be greater than 2.5

Calculating from the polygon, the number of children is $(10 + 15 + 30 + 70 + 20)$, i.e. 145 and the total number of marks is $(10 + 30 + 90 + 280 + 100)$, i.e. 510. So the mean mark is $510 \div 145 = 3.52$

The median mark is the 73rd mark in order; and this is 4

Remember that the median mark is the middle mark, i.e. half the people taking the test get the median mark or more. In this test the median mark is higher than the mean, so *more than half* the people taking it got more than the average mark.

It is important to realise that in any distribution it is possible that more than half of the distribution can be above (or below) the mean, so when you hear a news item such as 'In this year's tests for seven-year-olds, the average result was Level 2 and half of those taking the test achieved Level 2 or higher', you do not respond (as many people do), 'Of course they would'.

Exercise 29e

1. Pauline got the following marks (each out of 100) in a series of tests: 15, 58, 60, 66, 69, 75, 76
   (a) Find her mean mark and her median mark.
   (b) What fraction of her marks were greater than the mean ?

2. The table shows the distribution of weekly income of a group of students.

Weekly income (£)	1–30	31–60	61–90	91–120
Frequency	30	100	20	110

   (a) Find the mean income.
   (b) Draw a frequency polygon to illustrate the distribution.
   (c) Draw a cumulative frequency polygon and give the median income.
   (d) Mark the mean and the median income on the cumulative frequency curve and find, approximately, the percentage of students who have less than the mean income.

3. The mean life of 'Logman' clock batteries is stated to be 18 months. The office manager bought a batch of these batteries and found that more than half of them failed in less than 18 months. Did he have cause to complain to the manufacturers ?

   Give reasons for your answer.

4. Two groups of students took the same examination. The mean mark for each group was the same at 52 %. The median mark for group A was 49% and the median mark for group B was 56 %. Compare the performance of the two groups.

5. In a village of 200 inhabitants the distribution of the ages is as given in the table.

Age (years)	0–9	10–19	20–29	30–39	40–49	50–59	60–69	70–79	80–89
Frequency	22	28	32	39	30	20	18	9	2
Halfway value	5								

   (a) Explain why the halfway value of the 0–9 group is 5
   (b) Find the mean age.
   (c) Draw a frequency polygon to illustrate this distribution.
   (d) Draw a cumulative frequency polygon and give the median age.
   (e) Approximately what percentage of the inhabitants are above the mean age ?

DISPERSION

An aspect of a set of data that often has to be assessed is the spread of the items in the set. Dispersion is the name for the spread of a distribution and there are several ways of measuring it.

Range

The range of a distribution is defined as the difference between the extreme values. Consider the two distributions of scores at the start of this chapter;
for group A, the lowest score is 0 and the highest score is 10, so the range is $10 - 0$, i.e. 10 and for group B, the range is $8 - 1$, i.e. 7.

For a grouped frequency distribution, we do not know the precise extreme values, so in this case we give the range as the difference between the highest and lowest possible values. For the distribution of heights of tomato plants, these extreme values are 0 cm and 12 cm, so the range is 12 cm.

The range is a crude measure of dispersion since it tells us nothing about the intermediate values and it can be distorted by one or two extreme values. Consider a student who scores 8, 52, 56, 60, 68, 70, 75, 77, 80 in nine examinations. The range of marks is from 8 to 80, whereas every mark apart from 8 is over 50.

Inter-quartile Range

A much better measure of spread is given by using the range of the middle half of the values.

The middle half lies between the value that is one-quarter of the way through a distribution and the value that is three-quarters of the way through. These two values are called the *quartiles.*

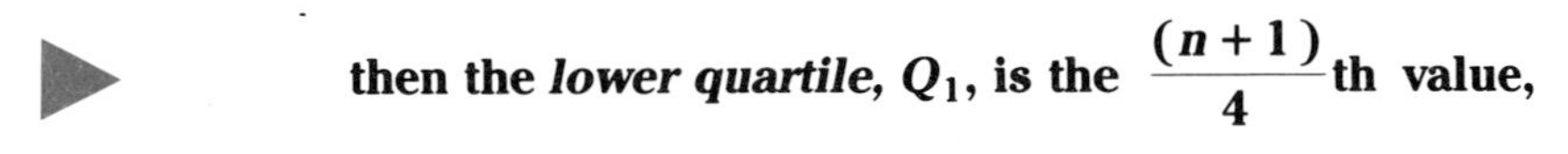

If there are n values, in ascending order,

then the *lower quartile,* Q_1, is the $\frac{(n+1)}{4}$th value,

and the *upper quartile,* Q_3, is the $\frac{3(n+1)}{4}$th value.

The difference between the upper quartile and the lower quartile is called the *inter-quartile range,* i.e.

the inter-quartile range is $Q_3 - Q_1$

The inter-quartile range can be found easily from a cumulative frequency curve.

This is the cumulative frequency curve for the heights of tomato plants.

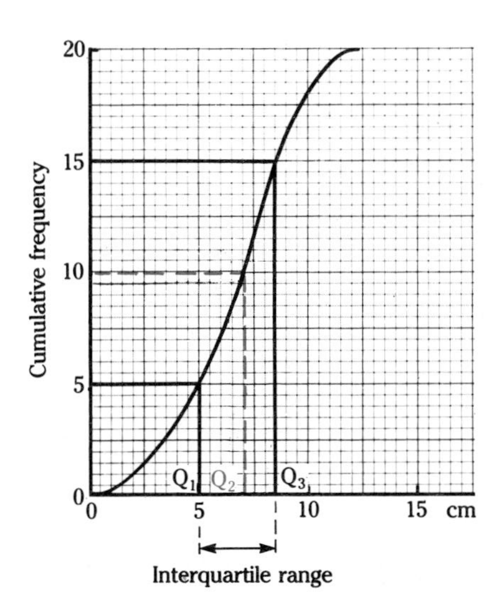

From the graph, the inter-quartile range is $(8.4 - 5)$ cm, i.e. 3.4 cm

Exercise 29f

1. Use the cumulative frequency curves drawn for question 1 in Exercise 29d to find the inter-quartile range of each distribution.

2. The cumulative frequency curve given below shows the weekly earnings, in pounds, of a group of teenagers.

   Use the graph to find (a) the median (b) the upper and lower quartiles.
   Hence find the inter-quartile range.

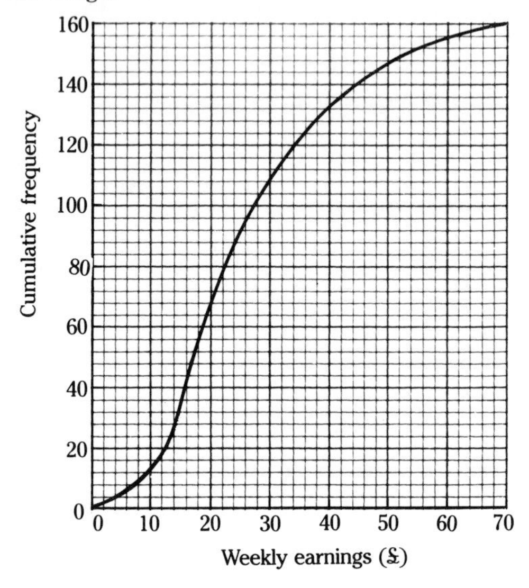

3. Two brands, X and Y, of AA batteries were investigated by a consumer magazine. A sample of 50 of each brand was tested. Each battery was run in a personal cassette player until it failed. The results were

   Brand X: mean life = 20 hours, inter-quartile range = 4 hours
   Brand Y: mean life = 19.5 hours, inter-quartile range = 2 hours

   Which brand of battery was more reliable ?

COMPARING DISTRIBUTIONS

The diagram shows four frequency polygons. They illustrate the results of four different tests.

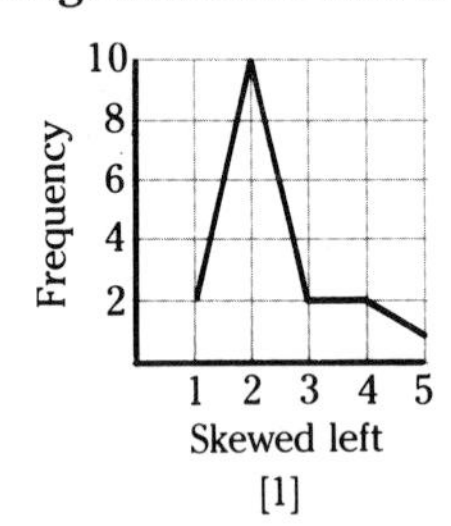

Skewed left
[1]

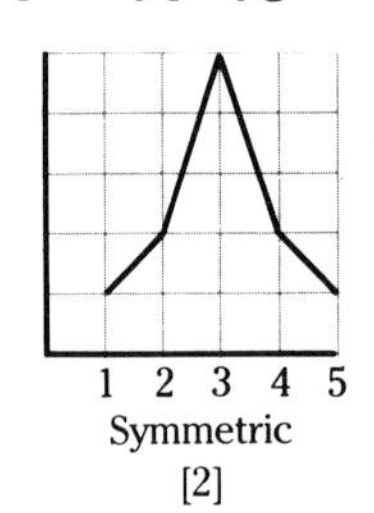

Symmetric
[2]

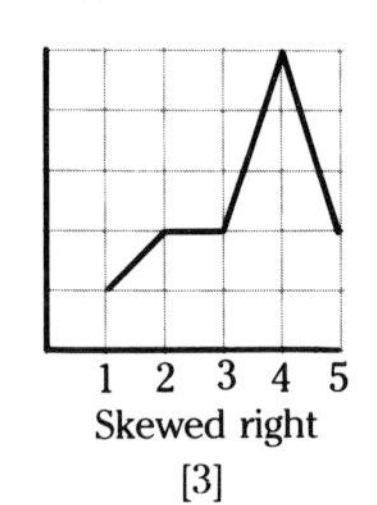

Skewed right
[3]

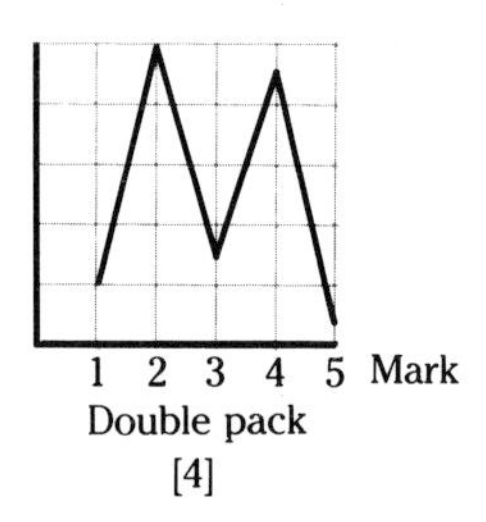

Double pack
[4]

In all the distributions the range of marks is 1 to 5, and 3 is the middle of the range. In diagram [2], the peak is in the middle of the range and the polygon is symmetrical. In any polygon that is roughly symmetrical, we would expect the mean and median to be about the same as the peak mark.

If we compare [1] and [3], we can say that the mean mark in [1] is lower than the mean mark in [3]. If these diagrams illustrate tests taken by the same class of children we might be tempted to give reasons for the results being as they are.
It could be that test [1] was easier than test [3], or that the person marking test [1] was a harder marker than the person marking test [3], or that some of the more able children were not there when test [1] was taken, or one or more of several other possibilities.
Be careful when trying to interpret statistical figures; there are often complex reasons for their form.
If we consider test [4], the mean mark is 3 (to the nearest whole number). If we had not seen the frequency polygon and knew just the mean mark and the range, we might think the distribution of marks looked a bit like that for test [2]. In fact, the distribution for test [4] has a double peak. This shows that it is dangerous to assume anything about a distribution without further information.

Exercise 29g

1.

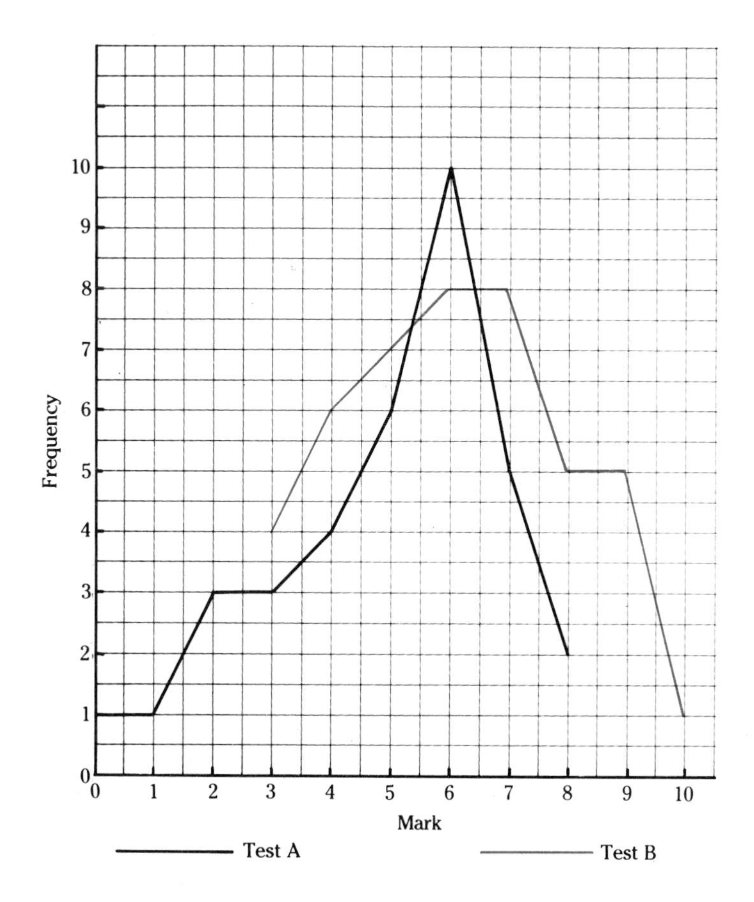

The diagram shows the distribution of marks for the same test taken by two groups of students. Comment on the differences between the distributions. Give at least three different possible reasons for these differences.

2. This table shows the distribution of the heights of a batch of tomato plants three weeks after planting.

Height, h cm	$0 \leqslant h < 5$	$5 \leqslant h < 10$	$10 \leqslant h < 15$	$15 \leqslant h < 20$	$20 \leqslant h < 25$
Frequency	2	4	9	12	1

(a) Find the mean height.

(b) Draw a frequency polygon to illustrate the information.

(c) A second batch of tomato plants are planted and their heights are measured after three weeks. The information is illustrated in this frequency polygon.

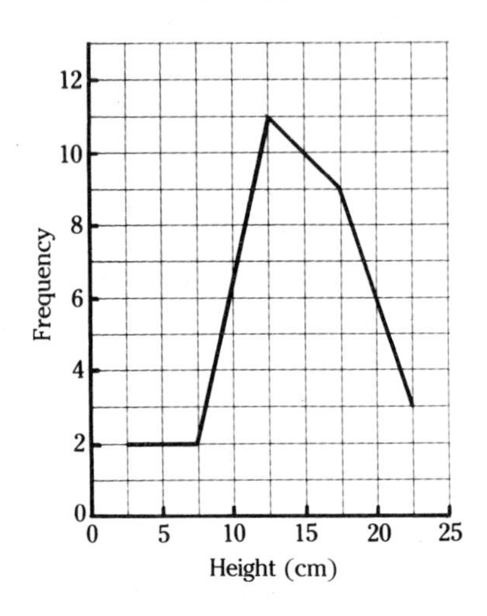

Compare the heights of the two batches of plants.

3. The diagram shows the cumulative frequency curve for the distribution of the lengths of pegs made by machine A and for the distribution of lengths of pegs made by machine B.

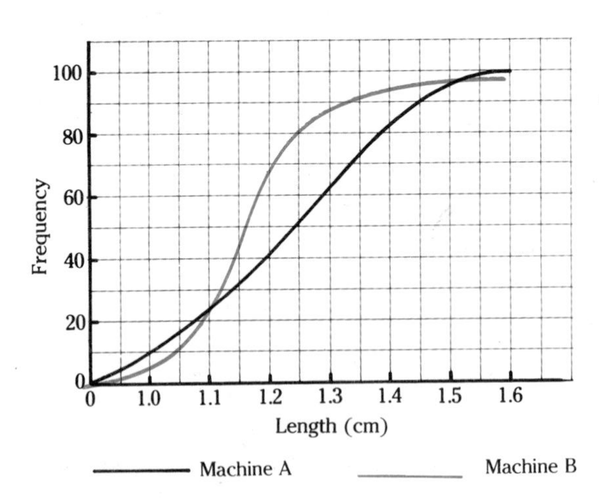

(a) Find the inter-quartile range of each distribution.

(b) Which machine would you say is more consistent ?

Give reasons for your answer.

4. (a) If an ordinary dice is rolled 60 times, write down the number of occasions on which you would expect to get a score of 1, a score of 2, a score of 3, a score of 4, a score of 5 and a score of 6.
   (b) Draw a frequency polygon to illustrate your answers to (a).
   (c) Make an observation sheet on which you can record the results of actually tossing an ordinary dice.
   (d) Toss an ordinary dice 60 times and draw another frequency polygon to illustrate your results.
   (e) Find the mean and the median score both for the expected distribution of scores and for the actual distribution of scores.
   (f) Compare your results with the expected frequencies.

Investigation

A machine turns out ball-bearings whose diameters vary a little. This is a list of the diameters, measured in millimetres to one decimal place, of a sample of 48 ball-bearings.

12.1	12.1	12.2	12.2	12.3	12.3	12.3	12.4	12.4	12.4	12.4	12.4
12.4	12.4	12.4	12.4	12.5	12.5	12.5	12.5	12.5	12.5	12.5	12.5
12.5	12.5	12.5	12.5	12.5	12.6	12.6	12.6	12.6	12.6	12.6	12.6
12.6	12.6	12.7	12.7	12.7	12.7	12.8	12.8	12.8	12.8	12.9	13.0

It is thought that the diameters have a symmetrical distribution. Use the list to test this hypothesis as best you can.

You will need access to a computer database and a statistical package for the remainder of this investigation.

Many quantities vary; any list of values of a variable, such as times, prices, etc., can be investigated statistically and the shape of the distribution examined. Large quantities of data are stored in computer databases and the functions built into the database and/or statistical package can be used to sort and group information, draw bar charts and cumulative frequency curves, and to find means and medians.

Find some data from a database and investigate it, comparing it if possible with other similar data. A few examples of data that may be available are: weights of machine packed goods, examination results, birthdates, sales figures, times taken to cover a fixed distance in athletics, stock exchange prices.

Self-Assessment 29

1. Find the mode, the median and the mean of this set of numbers.

   2, 4, 4, 5, 6.5, 6.8, 7, 7, 7, 8, 9.5

2. This frequency table shows the distribution of lengths of screws made by a machine.

Length, l mm	$4.5 \leqslant l < 5.0$	$5.0 \leqslant l < 5.5$	$5.5 \leqslant l < 6.0$	$6.0 \leqslant l < 6.5$	$6.5 \leqslant l < 7.0$
Frequency	5	20	14	3	2

   Find the mean length.

3. The table shows the number of employees working overtime each day for a period of one month.

Number of employees	0	1	2	3	4	5	6
Frequency	3	4	8	9	4	2	1

(a) Find the mean number of employees working overtime each day.

(b) Draw a cumulative frequency curve and use it to find the median and the inter-quartile range.

4. This table shows the distribution of lengths of screws made by the same machine as that in question 2, but on a different day.

Length, mm	$4.5 \leqslant l < 5.0$	$5.0 \leqslant l < 5.5$	$5.5 \leqslant l < 6.0$	$6.0 \leqslant l < 6.5$	$6.5 \leqslant l < 7.0$
Frequency	10	12	15	5	3

(a) On the same axes, draw the frequency polygons for this distribution and for the distribution given in question 2.

(b) Compare the two frequency polygons.

(c) Give at least two possible reasons for the difference.

ANSWERS

Where answers are given correct to a number of significant figures, you may find a difference between the last figure of your answer and that given here. This situation can arise when a calculated value is used in its corrected form to calculate a further value. Wherever possible uncorrected values should be used for further calculation.

When answers come from measurements from drawn diagrams, it is not possible to give exact answers, nor is it sensible to expect complete agreement with answers given here.

Some diagrams are included in these answers. They are small and not fully labelled and are only intended to provide a check on shape. Your diagrams should be fully labelled and very much larger.

CHAPTER 1

Exercise 1a page 3

5. (a) 54 (b) 1200 (c) 99 (d) 2100 (e) 8000 (f) 132 (g) 7 (h) 63 (i) 50 (j) 108 (k) 8 (l) 25 (m) 80 (n) 62 (p) 40 (q) 55 (r) 1440 (s) 51 (t) 7 (u) 45

6. (a) 85 (b) 246 (c) 96 (d) 722 (e) 650 (f) 105 (g) 24 (h) 260 (i) 60 (j) 21 (k) 128 (l) 12 (m) 69 (n) 29 (p) 12 (q) 126 (r) 442 (s) 138 (t) 27 (u) 21

7. (a) 3 (b) 1 (c) 1 (d) 1 (e) 3 (f) 6 (g) 1 (h) 1 (i) 4 (j) 1 (k) 4 (l) 4 (m) 5 (n) 11 (p) 8 (q) 3

8. (a) 8 (b) 14 (c) 6 (d) 3 (e) 4 (f) 8 (g) 14 (h) 41 (i) 29 (j) 13 (k) 22 (l) 5

9. (a) 45 (b) 910 (c) 22 (d) 35 (e) 8 (f) 16 (g) 6000 (h) 2500

10. (a) 2, 4 (b) 11, 4 (c) 5, 7

11. (a) 6, 3 (b) 11, 1 (c) 10

12. 102

13. 10 p

14. 122

15. 27

16. The end result is 99 or 0.

Exercise 1b page 5

1. 13 284
2. 18 078
3. 53 710
4. 6840
5. 23 352
6. 112 194
7. 144 432
8. 240 165
9. 31, r 10
10. 31, r 17
11. 11, r 24
12. 18, r 4
13. 32, r 9
14. 389, r 9
15. 31, r 117
16. 15, r 235

Exercise 1c page 7

1. (a) 1, 2, 3, 6
(b) 1, 2, 4, 8
(c) 1, 3, 7, 21
(d) 1, 2, 3, 5, 6, 10, 15, 30
(e) 1, 2, 4, 8, 16
(f) 1, 2, 4, 5, 10, 20
(g) 1, 11
(h) 1, 5, 25
(i) 1, 2, 3, 6, 9, 18
(j) 1, 2, 3, 4, 6, 9, 12, 18, 36
(k) 1, 3, 9, 27
(l) 1, 3, 5, 9, 15, 45

2. 2, 3, 5, 7, 11, 13, 17, 19, 23, 29, 31, 37, 41, 43, 47, 53, 59, 61, 67, 71, 73, 79, 83, 89, 97

3. (a) 2, 4, 6, 8 (b) 4, 8, 12, 16 (c) 5, 10, 15, 20 (d) 3, 6, 9, 12 (e) 12, 24, 36, 48 (f) 8, 16, 24, 32

4. (a) 1 (b) 2 (c) 4 (d) 9 (e) 3 (f) 13 (g) 3 (h) 6 (i) 6 (j) 2 (k) 13 (l) 6

5. (a) 6 (b) 12 (c) 15 (d) 36 (e) 30 (f) 20 (g) 60 (h) 72 (i) 90 (j) 72 (k) 36 (l) 48

6. (a) 27 (b) 32 (c) 125 (d) 1 (e) 64 (f) 16 (g) 9 (h) 81 (i) 11 (j) 81 (k) 64 (l) 196 (m) 153 (n) 192 (p) 729 (q) 4

7. (a) $2^3 \times 17$ (b) $2^4 \times 3^2 \times 5$ (c) $2^3 \times 3^3$ (d) $2 \times 3^2 \times 5^2$ (e) $2^2 \times 3 \times 7$ (f) $2^4 \times 3 \times 11$ (g) $2 \times 3 \times 11^2$ (h) 2×157 (i) $2^4 \times 7^2$ (j) $3^4 \times 5$

8. (a) 3, 5, 11, 17 (b) 3, 6, 15, 21, 27 (c) 1, 3, 4, 5, 6, 10, 15

9. (a) 9 (b) 8 (c) 25 (d) 64

10. 24 m

11. 60 s

12. 50 cm

13. £100

14. 45 cm

15. 110 cm

16. Thursday, 25th February (i.e. 24 days later)

Exercise 1d page 11

1. (a) $<$ (d) $>$ (g) $>$ (j) $<$
   (b) $>$ (e) $>$ (h) $>$ (k) $<$
   (c) $<$ (f) $>$ (i) $>$ (l) $>$
2. (a) -7 (e) 3 (i) 0 (m) 8
   (b) -1 (f) 1 (j) -5 (n) -14
   (c) 1 (g) -3 (k) -3 (p) -4
   (d) -9 (h) -13 (l) 3 (q) -9
3. (a) -6 (d) -1 (g) 2 (j) 10
   (b) 4 (e) -9 (h) 15 (k) -6
   (c) 7 (f) 5 (i) -3 (l) 1

Exercise 1e page 12

1. (a) 10 (d) 1 (g) -4 (j) 12
   (b) -8 (e) 7 (h) -6 (k) 16
   (c) 2 (f) 23 (i) -8 (l) -288
2. (a) -26 (c) 1 (e) -8
   (b) 1 (d) 17 (f) -22
3. 5 and -5
4. -7
5. One number is -3 times the preceding number.
6. (a) One number is -2 times the preceding number.
   (b) $-1, 2, \ldots, 128, -256$
7. (b) $5-(-2) = 7$ (e) $-1+(-2) = -3$
   (c) $2+3 = 5$ (f) $5-(-4) = 9$
   (d) $2-(-2) = 4$
8. e.g. $8-(-2) = 5\times 2$

Exercise 1f page 14

1. (a) 5, 6 (c) 15, 21
   (b) 5, 7 (d) 13, 17
2. (a) natural numbers (c) triangular numbers
   (b) odd integers (d) prime numbers
3. (a) 1, 0, -1, -2 (b) 13, 17, 19, 23
4. (a) 1, 3, 5, 7, 9 (e) 1, 4, 9, 16, 25
   (b) 1, -2, 4, -8, 16 (f) 3, 6, 9, 12, 15
   (c) 96, -48, 24, -12, 6 (g) 1, 2, 2, 4, 8
   (d) 1, 3, 4, 7, 6 (h) 2, 3, 5, 10, 20

Self-Assessment 1 page 16

1. (a) 27 (b) 22
2. (a) 6 (b) 36
3. (a) 17 (b) 72
4. 13
5. 162, -486
6. (a) 36 (b) 37 (c) 235
   and other possible answers
   (d) 62 (e) 25 and other possible answers
7. 38 430
8. 37
9. (a) 3600 (b) 40 (c) 12
10. 14, 10
11. 51
12. -3, 9, -12, 21, -33
13. 3 cm

CHAPTER 2

Exercise 2a page 19

1. (a) $\frac{4}{8}$ (b) $\frac{2}{8}$ (c) $\frac{6}{8}$
2. (a) $\frac{6}{12}$ (b) $\frac{8}{12}$ (c) $\frac{9}{12}$ (d) $\frac{10}{12}$
3. $\frac{2}{5} = \frac{4}{10} = \frac{6}{15} = \frac{10}{25} = \frac{40}{100}$
4. (a) $\frac{1}{3}$ (d) $\frac{2}{7}$ (g) $\frac{3}{4}$
   (b) $\frac{1}{3}$ (e) $\frac{3}{4}$ (h) $\frac{5}{23}$
   (c) $\frac{1}{12}$ (f) $\frac{4}{7}$
5. (a) $2\frac{1}{2}$ (d) $7\frac{2}{5}$ (g) $5\frac{3}{8}$
   (b) $1\frac{2}{3}$ (e) $5\frac{3}{10}$ (h) $6\frac{3}{11}$
   (c) $2\frac{1}{4}$ (f) $6\frac{3}{4}$
6. (a) $\frac{5}{4}$ (d) $\frac{13}{4}$ (g) $\frac{17}{5}$
   (b) $\frac{7}{3}$ (e) $\frac{8}{3}$ (h) $\frac{27}{4}$
   (c) $\frac{7}{5}$ (f) $\frac{15}{8}$
7. (a) $6\frac{1}{4}$ (d) $4\frac{1}{6}$ (g) $4\frac{1}{5}$
   (b) $4\frac{1}{3}$ (e) $4\frac{1}{8}$ (h) $1\frac{8}{9}$
   (c) $7\frac{1}{5}$ (f) $4\frac{1}{2}$
8. $\frac{5}{7} = \frac{15}{21}$, $\frac{2}{3} = \frac{14}{21}$; $\frac{5}{7}$
9. $\frac{2}{3} = \frac{10}{15}$, $\frac{4}{5} = \frac{12}{15}$; $\frac{2}{3}$
10. (a) $\frac{1}{60}$ (b) $\frac{1}{6}$ (c) $\frac{5}{6}$
11. $\frac{1}{5}$
12. $\frac{1}{4}$
13. $\frac{9}{16}$
14. (a) $\frac{11}{30}, \frac{1}{2}, \frac{3}{5}, \frac{2}{3}$ (b) $\frac{3}{8}, \frac{2}{5}, \frac{7}{10}, \frac{17}{20}$
15. (a) $\frac{5}{6}, \frac{7}{12}, \frac{1}{2}, \frac{1}{3}$ (b) $\frac{3}{4}, \frac{7}{10}, \frac{17}{25}, \frac{3}{5}$
16. (a) $\frac{14}{5}, \frac{17}{6}, 2\frac{7}{8}, 3$ (b) $\frac{12}{7}, \frac{27}{14}, 2\frac{1}{6}, \frac{7}{3}$

Exercise 2b page 23

1. (a) $\frac{13}{20}$ (c) $\frac{1}{5}$ (e) $\frac{8}{15}$ (g) $\frac{1}{6}$
   (b) $\frac{19}{20}$ (d) $\frac{1}{6}$ (f) $\frac{11}{12}$ (h) $\frac{13}{56}$
2. (a) $\frac{5}{6}$ (c) $\frac{5}{6}$ (e) $4\frac{9}{20}$ (g) $3\frac{1}{20}$
   (b) $2\frac{5}{6}$ (d) $3\frac{1}{4}$ (f) $1\frac{5}{6}$ (h) $\frac{7}{12}$
3. (a) $\frac{17}{20}$ (c) $\frac{1}{2}$ (e) $\frac{3}{5}$ (g) $\frac{1}{8}$
   (b) $\frac{53}{100}$ (d) $\frac{29}{30}$ (f) 0 (h) $6\frac{7}{15}$
4. (a) \$6 (e) \$32 (i) 27 cm
   (b) 20 min (f) 34 kg (j) $22\frac{1}{2}$ ft
   (c) \$7 (g) 2 days (k) 219 days
   (d) 3 cm (h) 40 s (l) \$72
5. (a) $\frac{2}{15}$ (e) $\frac{9}{14}$ (i) $\frac{2}{9}$
   (b) $\frac{5}{24}$ (f) $\frac{6}{25}$ (j) $\frac{1}{7}$
   (c) $\frac{1}{6}$ (g) $\frac{6}{49}$ (k) $1\frac{3}{4}$
   (d) $\frac{4}{7}$ (h) $\frac{1}{15}$ (l) $11\frac{1}{5}$
6. (a) $1\frac{2}{3}$ (e) $4\frac{1}{2}$ (i) $\frac{2}{5}$
   (b) $2\frac{1}{2}$ (f) $2\frac{2}{5}$ (j) $\frac{4}{13}$
   (c) $1\frac{2}{7}$ (g) $\frac{1}{4}$ (k) $\frac{4}{11}$
   (d) $1\frac{1}{3}$ (h) $\frac{1}{6}$ (l) $\frac{2}{3}$
7. (a) $\frac{3}{4}$ (e) $\frac{2}{3}$ (i) $32\frac{1}{7}$
   (b) $\frac{1}{12}$ (f) $\frac{3}{10}$ (j) $\frac{5}{6}$
   (c) $\frac{2}{5}$ (g) 6 (k) $\frac{4}{27}$
   (d) $\frac{2}{3}$ (h) 5 (l) $4\frac{5}{6}$
8. (a) 1 (c) $\frac{3}{2}$
   (b) $\frac{8}{15}$ (d) $\frac{27}{50}$
9. (a) $\frac{9}{20}$ (c) 10
   (b) $\frac{4}{5}$ (d) $\frac{5}{13}$

10. (a) $1\frac{1}{18}$ (b) $\frac{5}{24}$ (c) $1\frac{5}{8}$ (d) $\frac{7}{12}$ (e) $2\frac{9}{14}$ (f) $\frac{7}{10}$ (g) $\frac{21}{40}$ (h) $1\frac{1}{2}$ (i) $\frac{21}{34}$

11. 6

12. $\frac{3}{4}$

13. $\$135$

14. $2\frac{2}{5}$

15. (a), (b)

16. 23, $\frac{1}{2}$ cm

17. $1\frac{1}{4}$ seconds

18. $7\frac{1}{2}$ minutes

19. (a) $4\frac{1}{2}$ inches (b) 32

20. $\frac{9}{32}$ inches

21. (a) $\frac{7}{12}$ (b) $\frac{5}{12}$

Exercise 2c page 28

1. (a) $\frac{7}{100}$ (b) $\frac{7}{10}$ (c) 70 (d) 7 (e) $\frac{7}{100}$ (f) $\frac{7}{1000}$

2. (a) $\frac{1}{5}$ (b) $\frac{1}{2}$ (c) $\frac{1}{4}$ (d) $\frac{2}{25}$ (e) $\frac{1}{1000}$ (f) $\frac{7}{10}$ (g) $1\frac{2}{5}$ (h) $\frac{1}{8}$ (i) $1\frac{1}{20}$ (j) $\frac{1}{400}$ (k) $2\frac{3}{50}$ (l) $5\frac{1}{200}$

3. (a) 1.9 (b) 1.8 (c) 4.5 (d) 1.3 (e) 2.8 (f) 1.4 (g) 11.7 (h) 3.2

4. (a) 1.94 (b) 0.46 (c) 1.64 (d) 1.66 (e) 2.77 (f) 0.18 (g) 5.67 (h) 0.7 (i) 8 (j) 2.47 (k) 2.331 (l) 1.437

5. (a) 250 (b) 0.66 (c) 2.44 (d) 1.2 (e) 0.0035 (f) 4.4 (g) 0.032 (h) 2660

6. (a) 90 (b) 0.08 (c) 36 (d) 140 (e) 0.03 (f) 0.12 (g) 240 (h) 0.021

7. (a) 3 (c) 10 (c) 20 (d) 0.3 (e) 10 (f) 0.2 (g) 40 (h) 500

8. (a) 0.12 (b) 0.01 (c) 0.45 (d) 0.0001 (e) 0.125 (f) 0.25 (g) 0.21 (h) 0.008

9. (a) 3.072 (b) 0.266 (c) 0.135 (d) 4.41 (e) 0.126 (f) 0.63 (g) 0.32 (h) 0.2

10. (a) 4 (b) 30 (c) 3 (d) 0.07 (e) 12 (f) 30 (g) 0.012 (h) 2220

11. (a) 0.55 (b) 1.08 (c) 110 (d) 23.7 (e) 0.000 32 (f) 3.7 (g) 900 (h) 19.8 (i) 4.69 (j) 1480

12. (a) 0.0002 (b) 45.01 (c) 12 (d) 2.07 (e) 1.25 (f) 3240 (g) 2.81 (h) 0.0054 (i) 0.064 (j) 5.1

13. (a) 0.2 (b) 0.125 (c) 0.75 (d) 0.6 (e) 0.15 (f) 0.25 (g) 0.875 (h) 0.24

14. 6.4

15. 0.251 m

16. 3.68

17. 0.045

Exercise 2d page 32

1. (a) 2180 (b) 2600 (c) 27 (d) 4000 (e) 21 (f) 0 (g) 300 (h) 400 (i) 140 (j) 910 (k) 13 (l) 400

2. (a) 0.69 (b) 13.5 (c) 1.00 (d) 2.253 (e) 0.058 (f) 28.8 (g) 40.38 (h) 77.998 (i) 0.050 77 (j) 1.0028

3. (a) 2200 (b) 2600 (c) 27 (d) 3500 (e) 21 (f) 0.48 (g) 300 (h) 440 (i) 140 (j) 910 (k) 13 (l) 380

4. (a) 0.694 (b) 13.5 (c) 1.00 (d) 2.25 (e) 0.0581 (f) 28.8 (g) 40.4 (h) 78.0 (i) 0.0508 (j) 1.00

5.
(a) (i) 6 (ii) 0.667
(b) (i) 142857 (ii) 0.143
(c) (i) 6 (ii) 0.167
(d) (i) 2 (ii) 0.222
(e) (i) 09 (ii) 0.0909
(f) (i) 3 (ii) 0.0333
(g) (i) 6 (ii) 0.267
(h) (i) 384615 (ii) 0.385
(i) (i) 7 (ii) 0.778

6. and **7.** It is not possible to give definitive answers but your approximations should, in general, agree with the answers for question 8 as far as the first significant figure.

8. For question 6
(a) 17.5 (b) 5.46 (c) 19.2 (d) 0.368 (e) 0.002 12 (f) 0.007 76 (g) 5.03 (h) 2.15

For question 7
(a) 5.77 (b) 1.37 (c) 0.0274 (d) 1.04 (e) 0.309 (f) 0.0841 (g) 0.0162 (h) 0.535

9. $1\frac{2}{7}, \frac{15}{11}$, 1.49, 1.57, $\frac{5}{3}$

10. $\frac{6}{25}, \frac{3}{16}, \frac{2}{13}$, 0.105, 0.05

11. 49.6 m

12. 0.15 m

13. 566

14. 1.72

15. 14

16. $\$8.19$

17. 29 kg (29 000 g)

18. 540 cm

19. 6804 kg

Exercise 2e page 37

1. (a) 16 (b) $\frac{1}{16}$ (c) 1 (d) $\frac{1}{32}$ (e) $\frac{1}{2}$ (f) 729 (g) 1 (h) $\frac{1}{3}$ (i) $\frac{1}{25}$ (j) $\frac{1}{64}$ (k) $\frac{1}{27}$ (l) 1

2. (a) 5.20 (b) 4.47

3. (a) 4.24 (b) 2.38

4. (a) 1200 (b) 0.0314 (c) 317 000 (d) 0.009 55 (e) 907 040 (f) 0.000 760 5 (g) 0.000 000 000 115 (h) 2 800 000 000 000

5. (a) 4 (b) $\frac{4}{25}$ (c) 1 (d) $\frac{64}{27}$ (e) $\frac{3}{2}$ (f) 1

6. (a) 5 (b) 3 (c) 2 (d) 2 (e) 3 (f) 5 (g) 7 (h) 25 (i) 4 (j) 11 (k) 5 (l) 12

7. (a) 24.1 (b) 1.71 (c) 0.0514 (d) 2.29 (e) 0.135 (f) 1.78 (g) 1.48 (h) 1.36 (i) 38.7 (j) 2.41 (k) 0.000 005 69 (l) 0.708

8. (a) 0.786 (b) 7.19

9. (a) 0.454 (b) 1.66

10. (a) 2.65×10^4 (b) 8.23×10^{-3} (c) 2.04×10^5 (d) 5.099×10^{-2} (e) 2.21×10^{-3} (f) $1.070\,03 \times 10^6$ (g) 6.2×10^0 (h) 4.788×10^3

11. (a) 6.36×10^{10} (b) 1.08×10^0 (c) 3×10^2 (d) 5×10^2 (e) 1.92×10^3 (f) 7.47×10^{-1}

12. (a) 8.64×10^{12} (b) $6.\dot{6} \times 10^{-3}$ (c) 3.624×10^7 (d) 6×10^2 (e) 1.44×10^{10} (f) -3.576×10^7

13. (a) 64 (b) 1 (c) 216 (d) 64

14. (a) 6.738×10^9 km (b) 5.162×10^9 km

Self-Assessment 2 page 39

1. (a) $\frac{4}{3}$ (b) $\frac{2}{3}$

2. (a) 6 (b) $1\frac{1}{9}$ (c) $3\frac{1}{2}$

3. $\frac{3}{14}$

4. $\frac{6}{35}$, 60

5. $\frac{5}{9}$, 0.65, $\frac{2}{3}$, 0.7

6. $2\frac{13}{14}$

7. 5.11

8. 0.25

9. (a) 1.62 (b) 0.35 (c) 10 (d) 2.33 (e) 0.09 (f) 0.05

10. (a) 64 (b) 1 (c) $\frac{1}{16}$ (d) $2\frac{1}{2}$ (e) 9

11. (a) 4.5×10^6 (b) 2.4×10^{-3}

12. (a) 12.7 (b) 0.004 71 (c) 9.98

CHAPTER 3

Exercise 3a page 43

1. (a) 180° (b) 270° (c) 720° (d) 240°

2. (a) 30° (b) 180° (c) 36° (d) 153°

3. (a) 30°, acute (b) 270°, reflex

4. (a) (i) acute, 30° (ii) acute, 60° (iii) reflex, 230° (iv) obtuse, 111° (v) acute, 26°

5. $a = 48°$, $b = 132°$

6. $c = 36°$

7. $p = 180°$, $q = 145°$

8. $x = 80°$

9. $y = 148°$

10. $z = 147°$

Exercise 3b page 48

1. (a) b (b) g

2. (a) d (b) h (c) c (d) b

3. (a) b (b) c

4. (a) c and f, b and e (b) c and g, b and d (c) e and d, c and f (d) c and g, b and h

5. $a = 100°$, $b = 80°$

6. $c = 105°$, $d = 105°$, $e = 105°$, $f = 105°$

7. $g = 110°$, $h = 110°$, $i = 120°$, $j = 60°$

8. $k = 45°$, $l = 135°$

9. $m = 28°$, $n = 118°$

10. $p = 75°$, $q = 105°$

11. $p = 70°$

Exercise 3c page 49

1. $a = 60°$, $b = 60°$, $c = 60°$

2. $d = 68°$, $e = 68°$, $f = 112°$

3. $g = 90°$, $h = 90°$, $i = 117°$

4. $j = 75°$, $k = 105°$, $l = 150°$

5. $m = 120°$

6. $n = 60°$

7. $p = 50°$

8. $x = 55°$, $y = 125°$

9. $q = 34°$, $r = 34°$, $s = 112°$

10. $t = 72°$, $u = 43°$, $v = 115°$

11. $w = 64°$, $x = 52°$, $y = 52°$, $z = 76°$

12. $a = 149°$, $b = 31°$

13. $c = 55°$, $d = 35°$, $e = 29°$

14. $f = 67°$, $g = 46°$, $h = 23°$

15. $i = 51°$

16. $j = 122°$, $k = 78°$, $l = 102°$

17. (a) (i) 68°
(ii) $B\widehat{C}D = 60°$, $C\widehat{B}D = C\widehat{D}B = 60°$
(b) equilateral

18. (a) (i) 64° (ii) 76° (iii) 28°
(b) $\triangle$ACE (c) right-angled $\triangle$ (d) no

19. (a) $z = 65°$, $w = 115°$
(b) $y = 56°$, $z = 72°$
(c) $x = 56°$, $w = 126°$
(d) $x = 66°$, $z = 56°$

20. (a) $2x = 84°$, $3x = 126°$, $y = 108°$, $z = 72°$
(b) $x = 37°$, $2x = 74°$, $3x = 111°$, $z = 42°$
(c) $y = 114°$, $x = 41°$, $2x = 82°$, $3x = 123°$
(d) $x = 36°$, $2x = 72°$, $3x = 108°$, $y = 144°$, $z = 36°$

21. 78°, 22°

22. 108°

23. 90°, 66°, 24°

24. (a) 30°
(b) 150°, 15°, 15°
(c) 75°, 30°, 75°
(d) Not possible. $A\widehat{E}D = 105°$

Exercise 3d page 54

1. 5.07 cm

2. 9.63 cm

3. 70°

4. 4.31 cm

5. $\widehat{A} = 56°$, $\widehat{B} = 40°$, $\widehat{C} = 84°$

6. $\widehat{D} = 45°$, $\widehat{E} = 52°$, $\widehat{F} = 83°$

7. Two triangles are possible for part (a), one only for part (b) and none for part (c).
   When two sides and an angle are given and the angle is not the included angle, there may be one or two triangles satisfying the given data or it may be impossible to draw any triangle at all.
8. AC = 7.4 cm
9. PR = 7.4 cm
10. WZ = 6.4 cm, YZ = 6.0 cm

Self-Assessment 3 page 56

1. 150°
2. (a) $p = 53°$ (b) $q = 72°$
3. (a) c (c) c and f
   (b) d and h (d) f and h
4. (a) $a = 37°$, $b = 74°$, $c = 32°$
   (b) $d = 44°$, $e = 56°$, $f = 80°$, $g = 136°$
5. BC = 5.5 cm
6. QR = 7.8 cm
7. $\widehat{D} = 41°$, $\widehat{E} = 56°$
8. $x = 57°$, $2x = 114°$, $y = 66°$

CHAPTER 4

In this chapter, re means reflection, ro means rotation and tr means translation

Exercise 4a page 57

1. A(1, 3) B(−2, 1) C(6, 2) D(2, −3)
   E(−5, −4) F(0, −2) G(4, 0)
2.

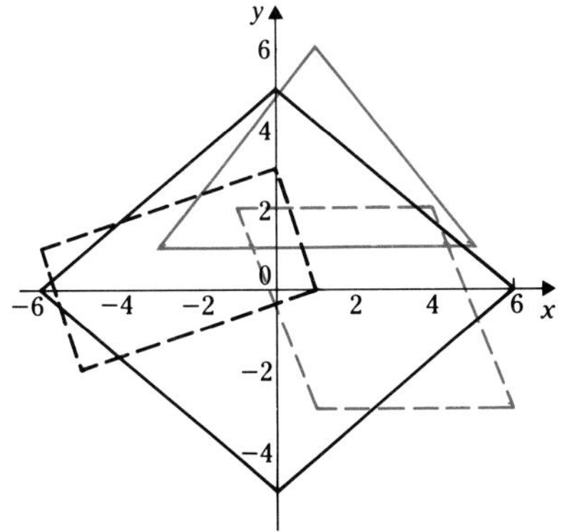

(a) black outline; rhombus
(b) black broken outline; rectangle
(c) green outline; isosceles triangle
(d) green broken outline; parallelogram
(e) kite

Exercise 4b page 59

1. (a)

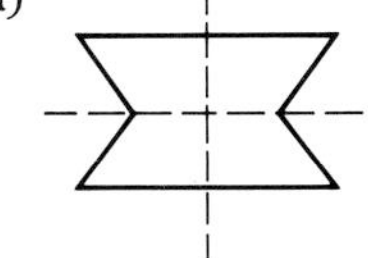

(d)

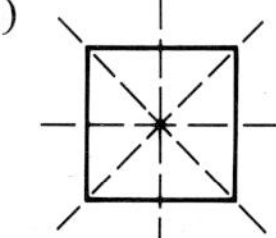

(c)

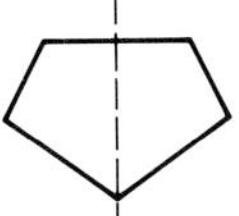

(f)

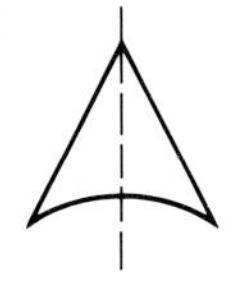

2. (a)

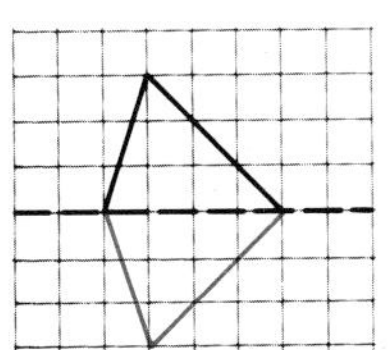

(c)

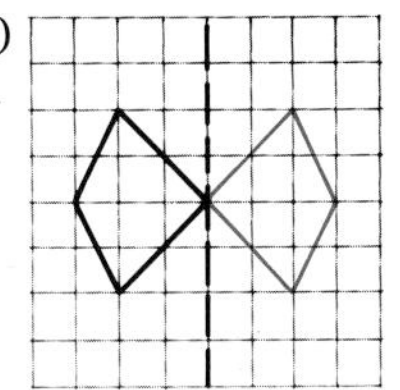

(b)

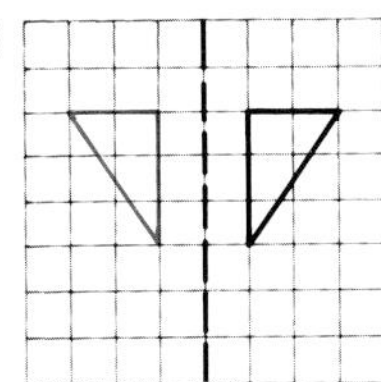

(d)

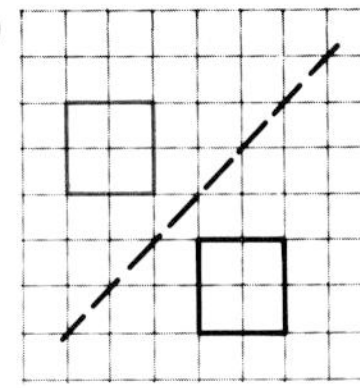

3. (a) 2 (b) 2 (d) 4

4. (i) (e)
   (ii) (a), (c), (d)
   (iii) (b), (f)

5.

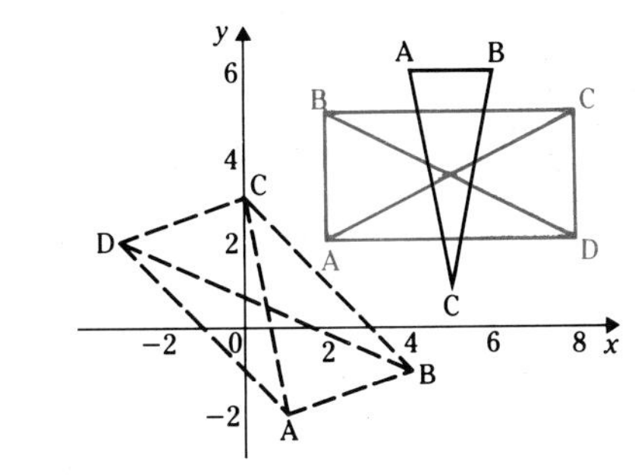

(a) black outline; (i)
(b) green outline; (iii)
(c) black broken outline; (ii)

6. (a) (−1, −3), (6, −1) or (8, −1), (8, −3) etc.
   (b) (4, −3), (6, 4)

Exercise 4c page 61

1. (a)

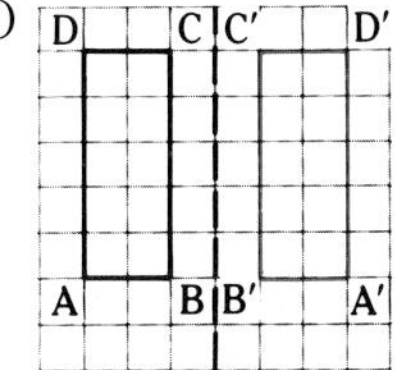

(c)

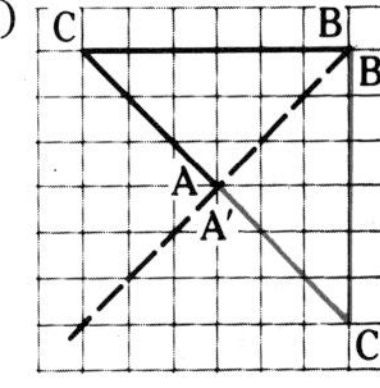

(b)

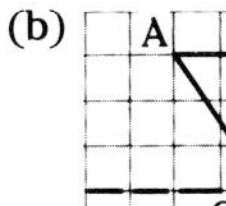

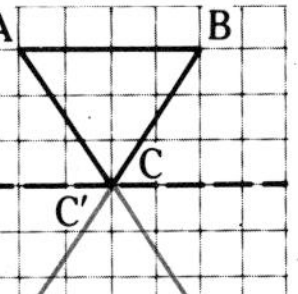

(d)

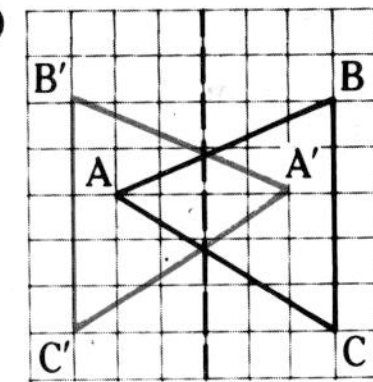

2.

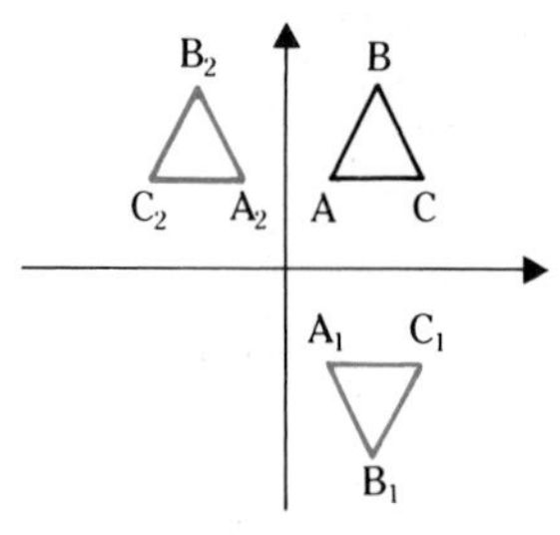

3.

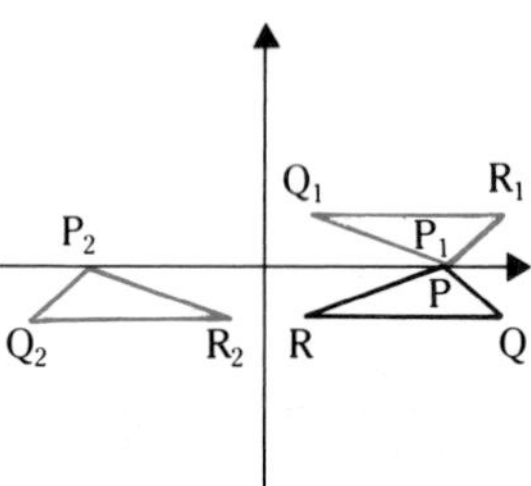

4.

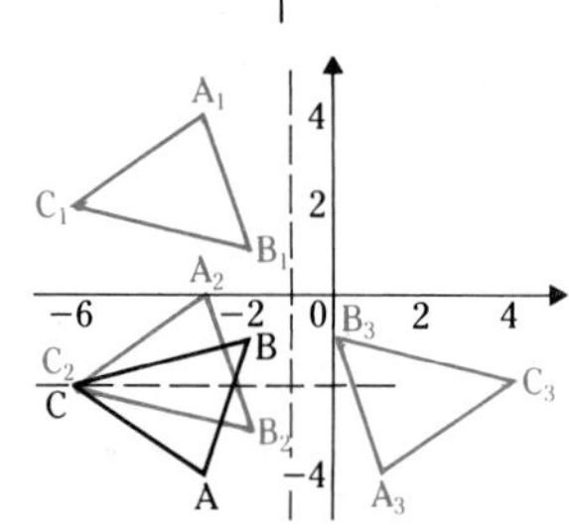

5. (d) re in x-axis

6. (a)

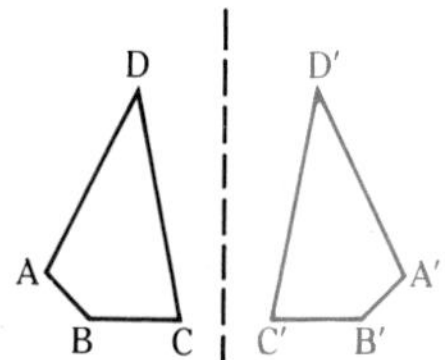

(b)

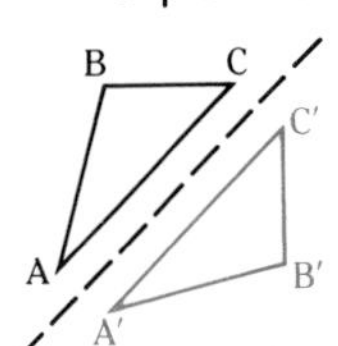

(c)

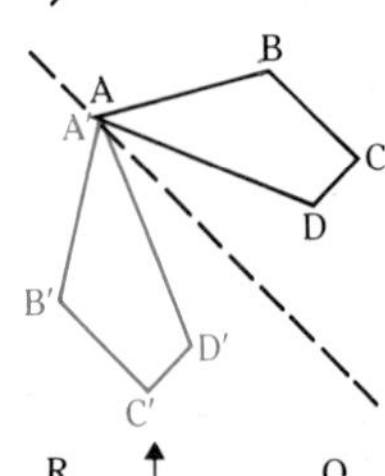

7.

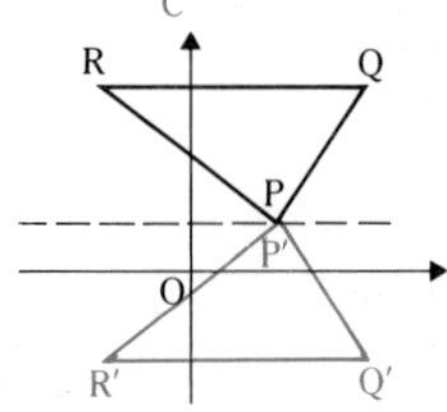

Exercise 4d page 63

1. (a) re (b) tr (c) re (d) tr (e) tr (f) re

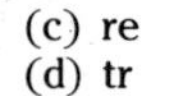

2.

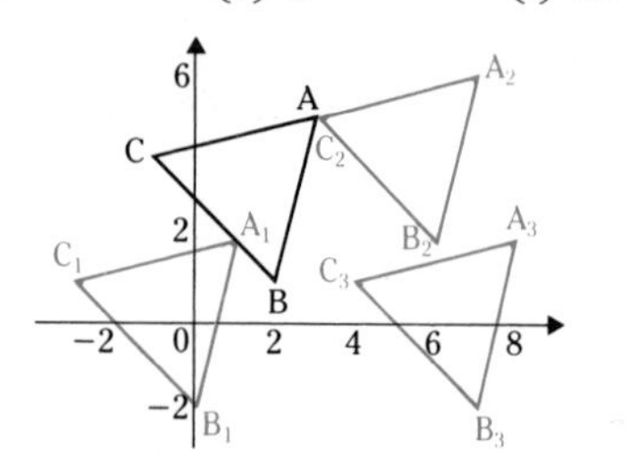

3. (a) 3 right, 3 down
(b) 4 left, 2 down
(c) 2 left, 8 down

4.

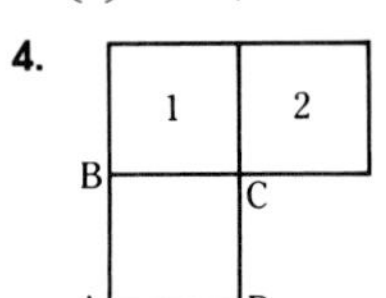

(c) tr; distance equal to BC in the direction BC

5. (d) tr; 5 left, 1 up

Exercise 4e page 64

1. (a) 90° (b) 90° (c) 180° (d) 90°

2. (a) A′(3, 2), B′(3, −2)
(b) A′(−2, −1), B′(1, 2)
(c) A′(1, 2), B′(−1, 2)
(d) A′(1, −1), B′(−3, −3)

3. (a)

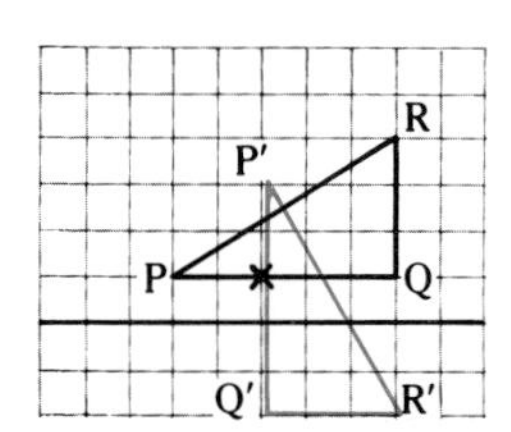

(b)

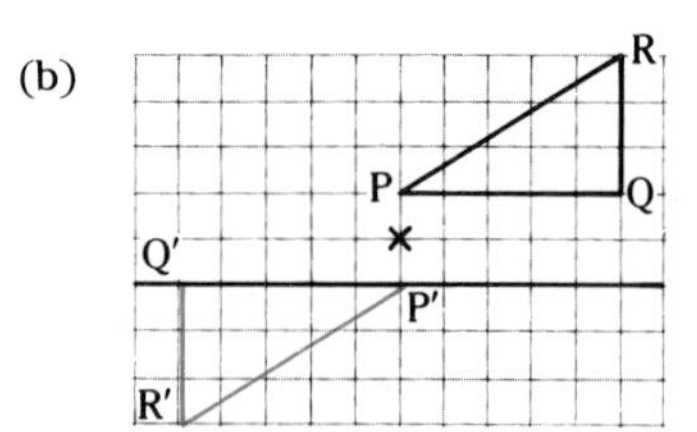

(c)

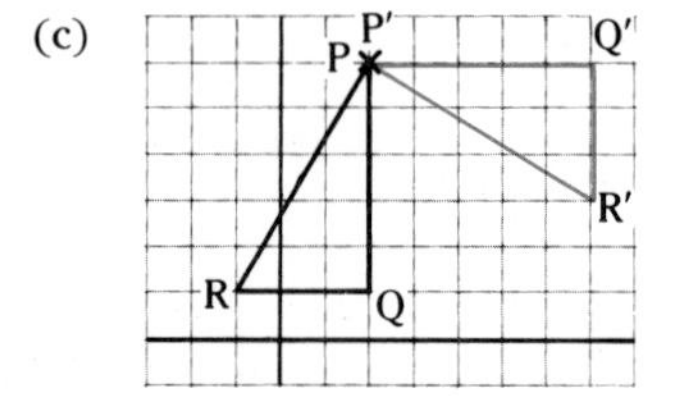

(d)

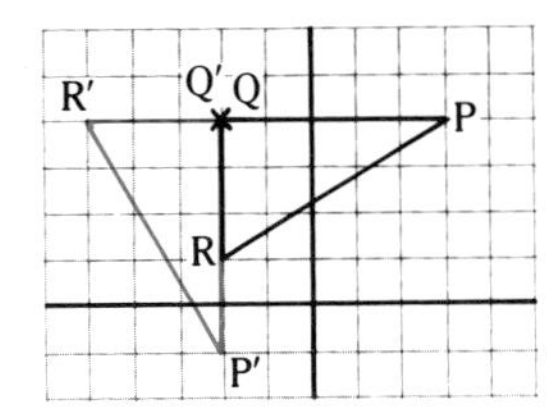

Exercise 4f page 66

1.

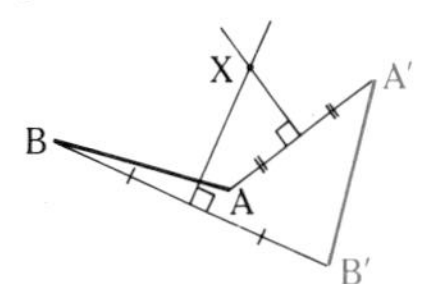

2.

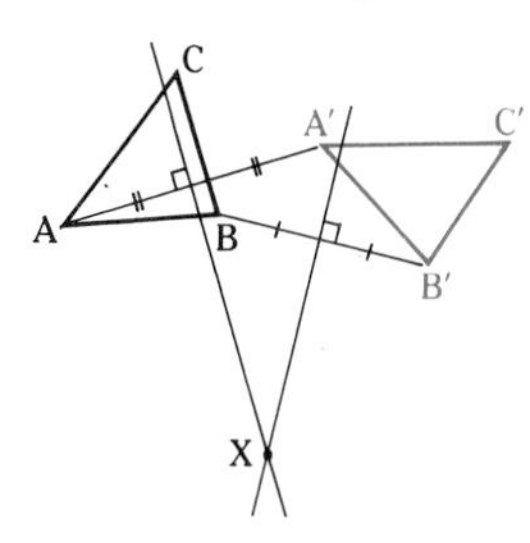

3. tr; 4 left 2 up
4. re in horizontal line through (0, 1)
5. re in line through (1, 2) and (2, 3)
6. tr; 3 left
7. re in line through (3, 2) and (5, 0)
8. ro of 180° about (3, 2)
9. re in *y*-axis, tr 8 right, ro of 180° about (0, $1\frac{1}{2}$)
10. re in *y*-axis, ro of 90° about O
11. re in *y*-axis, tr 4 left, ro of 90° about O, ro of 180° about (0, 2), ro of 90° about (0, 4)
12. re in *y*-axis, tr 4 right, ro of 120° about O, ro of 120° about *X*
13. re, tr and ro

Exercise 4h page 71

1. yes, re
2. no
3. yes, ro
4. yes, ro
5. no
6. no
7. (a) tr or re or ro (b) yes
8. (a) ro (b) yes
9. (a) ro (b) yes
10. (a) re (b) yes

Self-Assessment 4 page 73

1. (a) line, 1
(b) rotational, 2
(c) rotational, 3
(d) neither
(e) both, 3, 3
(f) both, 5, 5
(g) rotational, 2
(h) neither
2. (a) yes, AC and BD
(b) yes, ($1\frac{1}{2}$, $2\frac{1}{2}$)
(c) no line symmetry; yes, ($2\frac{1}{2}$, $2\frac{1}{2}$)
3. (a) (−2, −2) (b) yes, (2, 1), 2

4. (1) tr; 7 left
(2) re in horizontal line on which $y = 5$
(3) ro about (15, 3)
5. (a)

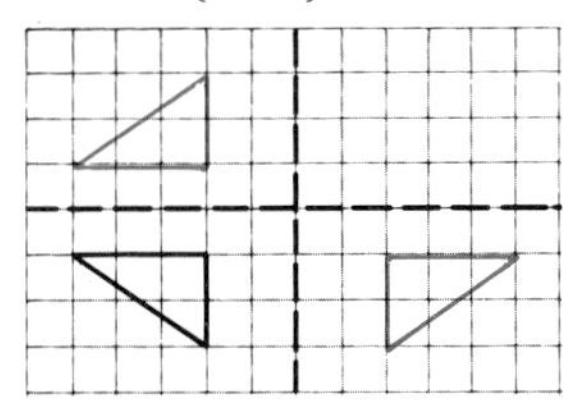

(b)

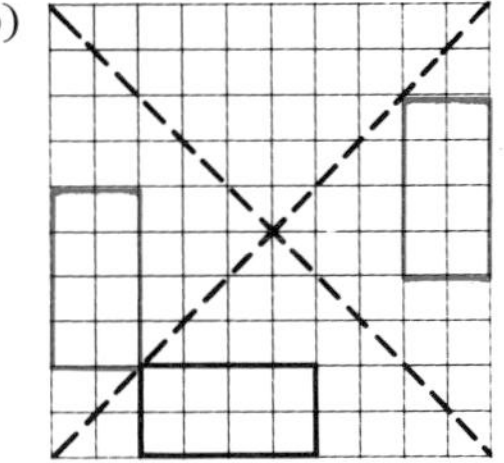

6. The vertical line through (5, 0)
7. (a) no (b) yes (c) yes
8. reflection
9. 90° clockwise; (1.0)
10.

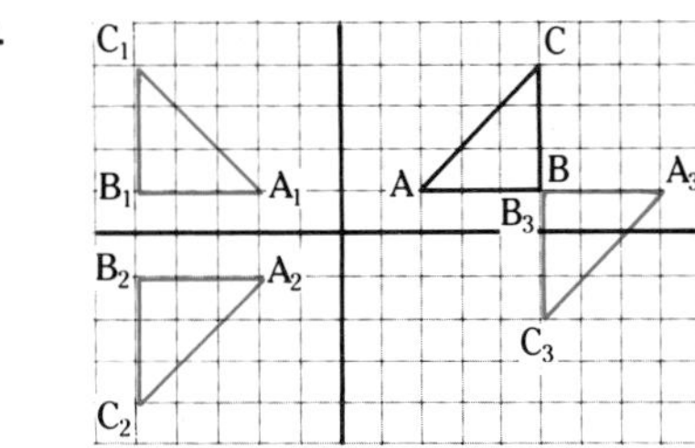

(b) ro of 180° about O
(c) tr; 10 right, 2 up

CHAPTER 5

Exercise 5a page 77

1. (a) 4000 g
(b) 8.1 cm
(c) 210 cm
(d) 2.024 kg
(e) 5000 m
(f) 7300 mg
(g) 21 000 kg
(h) 0.121 g
(i) 3.5 cm
(j) 5.67 t
(k) 1.4 m
(l) 23 000 mm
2. (a) 35 mm
(b) 3250 kg
(c) 8036 m
(d) 3.45 km
(e) 7.88 m
(f) 9.077 g
3. (a) 2.62 m (b) 262 cm

Exercise 5b page 79

1. (a) 24.8 cm (b) 2.84 m
2. (a) 15 m (b) 34.2 mm
3. 40 cm
4. 35 m
5. 52 cm
6. (a) 21.9 m (b) 1.68 cm
7. 144 cm
8. 42 cm
9. 44 cm
10. 420 mm

Exercise 5c page 81

1. (a) 27 squares (b) 16 squares (c) 24 squares
2. (a) 28 squares (b) 12 squares (c) 15 squares (d) 33 squares

Exercise 5d page 83

1. 81 cm^2
2. 28 mm^2
3. 8.41 cm^2
4. 5.76 m^2
5. (a) 3.84 m^2 or 38 400 cm^2
   (b) 14.26 cm^2 or 1426 mm^2
6. 864 cm^2
7. 1664 cm^2
8. 415 mm^2
9. 92 m^2
10. 2.88 m^2
11. 164 cm^2
12. (a) 0.3 m^2 and 0.175 m^2 or 3000 cm^2 and 1750 cm^2
    (b) 1.205 m^2 or 12 050 cm^2
    (c) 220 cm and 170 cm

Exercise 5e page 88

1. 8
2. (a) 6 (b) 6
3. (a) 128 (b) 16 (c) 2
4. 4 cm by 6 cm or 2 cm by 12 cm
5. (a) 60 mm^3 (b) 21.96 m^3 (c) 64 cm^3
6. (a) 420 000 cm^3 (b) 0.292 cm^3 (c) 6300 cm^3 (d) 0.0731 cm^3
7. (a) 6200 mm^3 (b) 92 000 000 mm^3 (c) 430 mm^3 (d) 43 000 mm^3
8. 840 000 cm^3
9. 60 mm^3
10. 17.5 cm^3
11. 0.28 m^3

Exercise 5f page 90

1. (a) 2400 cm^3 (b) 1600 cm^3
2. (a) 864 000 cm^3 (b) 864 litres
3. yes, 370 mℓ
4. 122 g (3 s.f.)
5. 980 g
6. 13.8 g
7. 4128 g

Exercise 5g page 91

1. 40 miles
2. 16 km/h
3. 5 h
4. 4 h
5. 42 km
6. (a) 1.2 miles/minute (b) 32 400 m.p.h.
7. (a) 1200 metres/minute (b) 7.56 km/h
8. 60 m.p.h.
9. (a) 105 m.p.h. (b) 32 miles (c) 96 m.p.h.
10. (a) $6\frac{2}{3}$ (6.67) m.p.h. (b) 32.7 m.p.h. (c) 21 m.p.h.
11. 28.9 m.p.h. (3 s.f.)

Self-Assessment 5 page 94

1. (a) 5.88 m (b) 5880 mm (c) 3200 mg (d) 0.495 t (e) 80 000 cm^2 (f) 5000 mm^3
2. (a) 17.2 cm (b) 14.6 cm or 146 mm
3. (a) 18.49 cm^2
   (b) 11.22 cm^2 or 1122 mm^2
4. 1080 m^2
5. (a) 560 miles
   (b) 3 hours 15 minutes
6. (a) 0.0909 miles/minute ($\frac{1}{11}$)
   (b) 5.45 m.p.h. ($5\frac{5}{11}$)
7. 104 cm^3 (3 s.f.) (103.823 cm^3)
8. (a) 162 (b) 6
9. (a) 0.39 m^3 or 390 000 cm^3
   (b) 0.2444 m^3 or 244 400 cm^3
10. (a) yes (c) 450 mℓ
11. 0.815 g/cm^3 (3 s.f.)

CHAPTER 6

Exercise 6a page 96

1. 0.38, $\frac{19}{50}$
2. 7%, $\frac{7}{100}$
3. 150%, 1.5
4. 61%, $\frac{61}{100}$
5. 0.05, $\frac{1}{20}$
6. 235%, $2\frac{7}{20}$
7. 90%, 0.9
8. 0.175, $\frac{7}{40}$
9. 77%
10. 33%
11. 14%
12. 21%

Exercise 6b page 97

1. 117
2. 2 m
3. 92.5 kg
4. 5000
5. ＄2.65
6. 156
7. 0.07 m = 7 cm
8. ＄1935.20
9. ＄58.25
10. ＄650
11. 4.41 m^2
12. 77, 49
13. ＄175
14. (a) ＄17.40 (b) ＄162.40
15. (a) 92 000 (b) 98 500
16. Jane, by 36 p
17. (a) ＄116 (b) ＄53.60
18. Jim's store, by 64 p
19. 29.75 cm by 42 cm
20. (a) ＄621 (b) ＄558.90
21. (a) ＄131.20 (b) ＄141.04
22. A by ＄2.30
23. 27 300

Exercise 6c page 100

1. ＄735.55
2. ＄11.28
3. ＄6627
4. ＄332.35
5. ＄188; ＄195.20
6. (a) ＄644 (b) no
   (d) He calculated the extra 2½% on ＄644 instead of on ＄560; ＄658
7. ＄5.06, 22 p
8. (a) ＄4370 (i) ＄1092.50 (ii) ＄1311 (iii) ＄1442.10
   (b) ＄4540 (i) ＄1135 (ii) ＄1362 (iii) ＄1498.20
   (c) ＄2390 (i) ＄597.50 (ii) ＄717 (iii) ＄788.70
9. (a) ＄1227 (b) ＄7582 (c) ＄1170 (d) ＄14 290
10. ＄73.62 per month
11. Nil
12. ＄487.44 per year
13. ＄1698.84 per year

Exercise 6d page 104

1. (a) ＄448 (b) ＄449.44 (c) ＄450.20
2. (a) ＄1081.60 (b) 8.16%
3. Account (i) by ＄1.12
4. ＄49.50
5. ＄33.28
6. ＄165.50
7. ＄82.76
8. ＄1756.92
9. ＄991.44
10. ＄2382.03

Exercise 6e page 105

1. £12.60
2. £37.40
3. £7015
4. 3100
5. 38 800
6. (a) 445 (b) 857

Exercise 6f page 107

1. (a) (i) £325 (ii) £715 (b) £45 000
2. (a) £510 (b) £6120 (c) £153 000
3. £45 600, £2400
4. (a) £56 000 (b) £705.60 (c) £225 680
5. £8.50
6. (a) £340 (b) £2158 (c) £458
7. (a) £1168.50 (b) £1434
8. bank loan by £9.68
9. (a) £600 (b) £2160 (c) £180
10. bank loan by £638

Exercise 6g page 110

Non-exact answers are given to 3 s.f.

1. 60%
2. 67.2%
3. 60%
4. 26%
5. (a) 2.7% (b) 4.76% (c) 3.88%
6. (a) 70% (b) 85% (c) 74% (d) 70%
7. 10.3%
8. (a) 90% (b) 10%
9. 27.27%
10. 78.3%
11. 40%
12. 75%
13. (a) 3.57% (b) 3.57%
14. 57.1%
15. 15%
16. 18.2%
17. 5%
18. 29.2%

Exercise 6h page 111

1. 80
2. £320
3. 25
4. 9
5. £210
6. (a) 25 (b) 76%
7. 72
8. (a) £900 (b) £495 (c) £800 (d) £80 (e) £240 (f) £2000
9. £7
10. £7000
11. (a) £1200
(b) (i) 1.15 (ii) 1.175 (iii) 1.22
12. 15 km/litre
13. 250 cm^3
14. £240

Self-Assessment 6 page 112

1. (a) 350% (b) 283% (c) 0.37 (d) $1\frac{7}{20}$
2. (a) £6.40 (b) 14 355
3. Right Tools, by 21 p
4. 12.5%
5. (a) £298.45 (b) £309.88
6. £1276.50
7. £406; £10.15; £395.85; £69.27; £465.12
8. 62.9%
9. (a) £5704 (b) £4828
10. (a) 70% (b) 46.2%
11. (a) £50 (b) £56
12. (a) (i) £575 (ii) £6900 (iii) £172 500
(b) 375%
13. Reliant West (£4 better)
14. (a) £5646 (b) 12, £264 each (c) 37.5%
15. Corner Shop by £1200

CHAPTER 7

Exercise 7a page 116

1. (a) $7x+5$ (b) $7a+4$ (c) $x+5y$ (d) $3t-5$ (e) $2-8p$ (f) $4a-4b$
2. (a) $2-5x$ (b) $7-12y$ (c) $5x-y-z$ (d) $2b-4a$ (e) $3s+t+6$ (f) $4p+q$
3. (a) $3x-9$ (b) $6x+8$ (c) $6x-4$
4. (a) $5x-5$ (b) $12-4x$ (c) $3a-6b$
5. (a) $25x+12$ (b) $3x-5$ (c) $8-7p$ (d) $4x-2$ (e) $3a-16$ (f) $2b-5$ (g) $2-2t$ (h) $23b-8$ (i) $10-9x$ (j) $-5x-1$ (k) $20-10c$
6. (a) p^3 (b) $6a^2$ (c) $2x^3$ (d) $3b^4$ (e) $12xy$ (f) x^2 (g) a^2 (h) y^{-1} (ii) 1 (j) $2x$
7. (a) $\dfrac{4x}{y}$ (b) $2x^2$ (c) $-b^2$ (d) $4x^2$ (e) $\dfrac{3y^2}{2x}$ (f) a^6 (g) x (h) 1 (i) c^2 (j) $\dfrac{1}{x^2}$
8. (a) $5x+x^2$ (b) $a^2+2ab-b^2$ (c) $2x-x^2$ (d) $-ac-c$ (e) $4x^2-12x$ (f) $2x^2-x^4-x$ (g) x^2 (h) $bc-ac$ (i) x^2-x-6 (j) $2pq+6pr$ (k) x^4+x^2
9. (a) $\dfrac{7x}{6}$ (b) $\dfrac{3a}{20}$ (c) $\dfrac{y^2}{6}$ (d) $\dfrac{8x^2}{75}$ (e) $\dfrac{5z}{2}$ (f) $\dfrac{2}{3a}$ (g) $\dfrac{y}{2x}$ (h) $\dfrac{(2x^2+x^3)}{4}$ (i) $\dfrac{x^5}{8}$ (j) $\dfrac{2}{x}$
10. (a) 14 (b) -7
11. (a) 1 (b) 5
12. (a) 5 (b) 2
13. (a) 3 (b) -3
14. (a) 3 (b) -3

Exercise 7b page 120

1. (a) 3 (b) 7 (c) 2 (d) -4 (e) 4 (f) 0.8
2. (a) 3 (b) 1 (c) 2 (d) 0.55 (e) 0.6 (f) $-\frac{3}{2}$

3. (a) 1 (b) 10 (c) $\frac{19}{9}$ (d) -3 (e) $\frac{1}{2}$ (f) -3
4. (a) $\frac{15}{2}$ (b) $\frac{3}{8}$ (c) $\frac{3}{10}$ (d) $\frac{60}{11}$ (e) $\frac{8}{5}$ (f) -2 (g) 3 (h) 2 (i) 2 (j) $\frac{1}{3}$ (k) $2\frac{2}{3}$ (l) $7\frac{1}{2}$
5. $\frac{x}{3} = 15$; 45 people
6. $3x = 81$; 27 cm
7. $\frac{20x}{100} = 27$; £135
8. $\frac{x}{3} = x - 2$; 3
9. $2x + 2(2x) = 60$; 10 m
10. $10x = 8x + 36$; 18 cm^3
11. $x + 10 = 2x$; 10 years old
12. e.g. $4x - 12 = 48$; 15 cm

Exercise 7c page 123

1. (a) 11.5 — 12.5 (b) 7.5 — 8.5 (c) 99.5 — 100.5
2. (a) 2.65 — 2.75 (b) 34.35 — 34.45 (c) 4.95 — 5.05
3. (a) 2.15 — 2.25 (b) 0.145 — 0.155 (c) 115 — 125
4. 253.5 g
5. 5449
6. no, can be up to, but below, 96.5 wide
7. (a) $229.5 \leqslant l < 300.5$ where l cm is the length of 10 tiles
   (b) 102 if the direction matters, 101 if it does not
8. (a) 11.55 g (b) weigh 100

Exercise 7d page 125

1. (a) $x > 2$ (b) $x < 1$ (c) $x < 2$ (d) $x > -\frac{1}{2}$ (e) $x > -2$ (f) $x > 1$ (g) $x \geqslant 1$ (h) $x \leqslant 3$ (i) $x \leqslant -3$ (j) $x \geqslant 3\frac{1}{3}$ (k) $x \leqslant \frac{5}{6}$ (l) $x < \frac{1}{3}$
2. (a) 3 (b) 2 (c) 1 (d) 1
3. (a) 3 (b) 2 (c) 10 (d) 3
4. (a) $1 < x \leqslant 2$ (b) $2 \leqslant x \leqslant 6\frac{1}{2}$ (c) $4\frac{1}{2} \leqslant x < 10$ (d) $2 < x < 6\frac{2}{3}$ (e) $x \leqslant 1$ (f) $1 \leqslant x \leqslant 2$ (g) $1 < x < 4$ (h) $-9 \leqslant x \leqslant -4$
5. (a) 2, 2 (b) 2, 6 (c) 5, 9 (d) 3, 6 (e) none, 1 (f) 1, 2 (g) 2, 3 (h) -9, -4
6. (a) -4, 0 (b) none, none (c) 2, 3 (d) none, none
7. $w \geqslant 15$, w kg is weight of popcorn
8. $0 \leqslant n \leqslant 56$, n is an integer (the number of passengers)
9. $t > 0$, t °C is the temperature
10. $2x + 2 < 100$, x is the number
11. 254
12. 352.5 cm

Exercise 7e page 127

1. $T = F + P$
2. $m = x + y$
3. $A = a^2$
4. $d = st$
5. $p = a + b + c$
6. $N = S - T - R$
7. $T = 35p + 30$
8. $T = 20x + y$
9. $W = Np + x$
10. $N = L - np$
11. $K = \frac{(nW + c)}{1000}$
12. $C = \frac{nx}{100}$
13. $T = \frac{n}{15}$
14. $A = 100lc$
15. $k = L - \frac{nl}{100}$
16. $N = 2s + c$

Exercise 7f page 129

1. (b) 15 cm (c) 18.4 cm (d) 77 mm (e) 359 cm
2. (a) 150 km (b) 360 miles (c) 15 km (d) 0.833 km (to 3 s.f.) (e) $7\frac{1}{2}$ nautical miles (f) 283 m
3. (a) 92 p (b) £12.86 (c) £1.08 (d) 11 p
4. (a) 54 (b) 8 (c) 5.04
5. (a) 25 (b) 8.65 (c) 169
6. (a) 3.87 (b) 0.173 (c) 2.51
7. (a) 0.103 (b) 3.25 (c) 0.231
8. (a) 1 (b) 1 (c) 2
9. (a) $4\frac{1}{2}$ (b) -5.1
10. (a) 4 (b) $\frac{14}{3}$ (c) -1.5 (d) $-\frac{123}{4}$
11. 2.13
12. (a) 4.7 cm (b) 7 cm (c) 4.5 cm
13. 3.8 cm, 12.8 cm
14. 12 mm, 13.2 cm
15. 25.4 mm, 457.2 mm^2
16. 0.02 cm
17. 12 mm
18. 4 cm
19. $C = \frac{nx}{100}$ (a) £12.50 (b) 40

Exercise 7g page 133

1. (a) $x = c - y$ (b) $s = V + t$ (c) $u = r - t$ (d) $x = y - D$
2. (a) $a = s - 2b$ (b) $p = b - q - r$ (c) $u = v - rt$ (d) $R = 2\pi - r$
3. (a) $t = \frac{C}{r}$ (b) $t = \frac{(S + d)}{2}$ (c) $a = 2b - c$ (d) $t = \frac{(u - v)}{3}$ (e) $y = \frac{4x}{3}$ (f) $I = 10A - 10P$ (g) $R = \frac{VI}{2}$ (h) $r = 5p - 5q$
4. (a) $x = \frac{(c - y)}{2}$ (b) $q = \frac{p}{2} + r$ (c) $t = 4p - s$ (d) $r = \frac{C}{2\pi}$ (e) $a = \frac{(c + d)}{b}$ (f) $x = \frac{c}{a} - b$ (g) $P = \frac{R}{3} - Q$ (h) $R = \frac{100I}{PT}$

5. (a) $S = 3n + 3$ (c) 111
   (b) $n = \dfrac{(S-3)}{3}$
6. (a) $C = P + nS$ (c) 40
   (b) $n = \dfrac{(C-P)}{S}$
7. (a) $P = \dfrac{zx}{100} - y$ (c) $y = \dfrac{zx}{100} - P$
   (b) $x = \dfrac{100P + 100y}{z}$

Self-Assessment 7 page 135

1. $16x - 2y$
2. (a) -5 (b) $\frac{2}{5}$
3. $\frac{2}{3}$
4. 
5. $2.555 \leqslant x < 2.565$
6. (a) $6b^2$ (b) 2 (c) $5x - x^2$
7. $3 < x < 8$
8. $\dfrac{2x}{3}$
9. (a) x^4 (b) w^{-4}
10. $W = c + d$
11. 30
12. $-\frac{1}{2}$
13. $p = \dfrac{r}{a} - q$
14. (a) $P = \dfrac{nd}{100}$ (b) $d = \dfrac{100P}{n}$

CHAPTER 8

Exercise 8a page 136

1. (a) £6 (d) £218, £42
   (b) £176 (e) £254.40
   (c) £194
2. (a) £182 (d) £11
   (b) £7.80 (e) George, by £14.10
   (c) £214.50
3. (a) 8.00 a.m. (e) Thursday
   (b) 4.30 p.m. (f) $36\frac{1}{2}$ h
   (c) 1 h (g) £175.20
   (d) (i) 4 h (ii) $3\frac{1}{2}$ h
4. (a) £400 (b) £130 (c) £390
5. £260 6. £259.50 7. £555
8.

	(a)	(b)		(c)
	No. plugs	(i)	(ii)	
Mrs A	188	100	88	£107.20
Mr B	158	80	78	£ 90.70
Ms C	192	100	92	£109.80

   (d) Thursday, 121
9. 270, 15 10. £771.60 11. 1602

Exercise 8b page 139

1. £94.29 3. £16.47 5. £157.30
2. £14.10 4. £48.72

Exercise 8c page 140

1. £79.79 2. £113.65 3. £115.16
4. (a) 39 141, 39 487, 202, 40 704 (c) £31.51
   (b) £96.48 (d) £288.85
5. £75 7. £130.54
6. £183.75 8. £231.94
9. Domestic Prepayment tariff by £4.65
10. Credit tariff by £3.05
11. Credit tariff by 16 p
12. (a) £2.11 (d) 1.74 p
    (b) 86 (e) 94.8%
    (c) £1.50
13. (a) £30 (c) £28.71 including rental
    (b) £299 (d) £1.11 more expensive
14. (a) £1.12
    (b) 69 p
    (c) Better to buy 21 at 18 p (£3.78) than 19 at 21 p (£3.99)

Exercise 8d page 145

1. 48 in 9. 6 in
2. 8 oz 10. 288 sq in
3. 3 ft 11. 12 oz
4. 5 yd 12. 3 miles
5. 91 lb 13. 480 pints or 60 gallons
6. 20 pints 14. 20 sq yd
7. $1\frac{1}{4}$ lb 15. $2\frac{1}{2}$ fluid oz
8. $1\frac{1}{2}$ gall 16. 1 mile (1760 yd)

Exercise 8e page 146

All answers are approximate.

1. 54 ℓ 3. 16 mm
2. 47 p 4. 12
5. 350 acres
6. 360 cm (390 required to be certain)
7. 10 (to use 9.09 kg)
8. The department store by 67 p per m^2

Exercise 8f page 148

1. 25 m.p.h.
2. 112 km/h
3. 1 800 000 litres/h
4. (a) 80 km/gall (b) 18 km/litre
5. (a) 528 sq ft/litre (b) 2400 sq ft/gall
6. (a) 8.8 lb/cm^2 (b) 55 lb/sq in
7. 194 miles
8. (a) 0.083 (2 s.f.) (b) 0.071 (2 s.f.)
9. 3 min
10. 1.23 lb/sq in
11. 2.13 h (approx)
12. 1600 m^2
13. 11.1 oz/in^3

Exercise 8g page 149

1. (a) 0830 (c) 0542
   (b) 2030 (d) 1436
2. (a) 3.00 a.m. (c) 8.51 a.m.
   (b) 7.42 p.m. (d) 10.43 p.m.
3. (a) 11 h 48 min (c) 13 h 5 min
   (b) 6 h 12 min (d) 21 h 12 min

4. (a) 0835, 2 h 3 min
5. 11.35, 1 h 23 min
6. The 0835 and the 1035 both take 2 h 3 min. Both are through trains.
7. The 0905 and the 1105 both take 1 h 26 min.
8. 1 h 12 min
9. (a) Reading, 6 min (b) Bristol Parkway

Exercise 8h page 152

1. (a) 74 p (b) 45 p (c) 96 p (d) £3.60 (e) £10.20
2. (a) 28 p (b) 49 p (c) £1.40 (d) 18 p
3. £6.30
4. £12.42
5. 13
7. (a) 120 p (b) 165 p (c) 340 p (d) 760 p
8. (a) £4.64 (b) 29 (c) make 21 copies
9. (a) 79.8 p (b) 58.8 p (c) 21 p
10. (a) 63 p (b) 46.2 p (c) 33.6 p
11. 155.4 p
12. 46.2 p

Exercise 8i page 154

1. £420
2. £240
3. (a) £78 (b) piano, ring
4. £138
5. £40 000
6. (a) £1037 (b) £989
7. (a) £251.40 (b) £243.78
8. (a) £525 (b) £252 (c) 60%
9. £2103, £40.44
10. £158.71

Exercise 8j page 156

1. (a) £20 (b) £19.92
2. (a) £6 (b) £5.98
3. (a) 20 p (b) 22 p
4. (a) £19 (b) £20.93
5. (a) 45 p (b) 41 p
6. (a) £200 (b) £208.33
7. (a) £1.50 (b) £1.36
8. (a) £540 (b) £533.27
9. (a) 25 p (b) 20 p
10. 5.52 Ff
11. 8 ptas
12. 9692 L
13. 19.31 Ff
14. 71.12 Ff
15. 3.63 pt
16. 8.7 DM
17. 7.3 DM
18. 4 DM
19. £3.10
20. £2.73
21. 84 p

Self-Assessment 8 page 159

1. (b) by £40.10
2. £72.97
3. (a) 49 p (b) (i) 144 km/h (ii) 90 m.p.h.
4. 165 seconds
5. (a) £519.20 (b) £498.94

CHAPTER 9

The answers for marked angles are given in alphabetical order.

Exercise 9a page 162

1. (a) general (b) 90°
2. (a) parallelogram (b) 57°, 123°, 123°
3. (a) isosceles trapezium (b) 64°, 116°, 116°
4. (a) general (b) 54°
5. (a) kite (b) 98°, 57°
6. (a) trapezium (b) 90°, 58°
7. parallelogram, trapezium; 55°, 55°, 55°, 125°, 125°
8. kite; 94°, 94°, 115°
9. isosceles trapezium, general; 66°, 66°, 114°
10. trapezium; 25°, 15°, 105°
11. parallelogram, trapezium; 37°
12. parallelogram, two trapeziums; 75°, 40°, 65°, 75°, 50°
13. (a) 36 (b) since $5x = 180$
14. (a) 55° (b) 55°, isosceles
15. (a) 60° (b) 150° (c) 15° (d) 75°
16. (a) parallelogram (b) kite (c) trapezium (d) rhombus
17. (a) 122°, 116°, 58°, 64°, 58°
    (b) isosceles
    (c) isosceles trapezium, parallelogram
    (d) not possible; position of F is not fixed by the given information
18. (a) 24°, 24°, 132° in each triangle
    (b) isosceles
    (c) trapezium
    (d) isosceles

Exercise 9b page 165

1. 115°
2. 60°
3. 75°
4. 52°

Exercise 9c page 166

1. 80°
2. 60°
3. 108°
4. 135°
5. (a) 540° (b) 540°
6. (a) 720°, 720° (b) 1080°, 1080°

Exercise 9d page 167

1. (a) 72° (b) 60° (c) $51\frac{3}{7}°$ (d) 36° (e) 20° (f) 18°
2. (a) 140° (b) 150° (c) 165° (d) 170°
3. (a) 12 (b) 18 (c) 15
4. (a) 6 (b) 15 (c) 20
5. (a) yes (b) no (c) yes (d) no
6. (a) yes (b) yes (c) yes (d) no
7. 160°
8. 110°
9. 60°
10. 35°
11. 54
12. 75
13. 72
14. 30
15. 72°, 72°, 36°
16. (a) (i) 60° (ii) 120°
    (b) (i) 30° (ii) 90° (iii) 60° (iv) 30°
17. $x = 65$, $y = 130$, $z = 115$
18. $O\widehat{A}B = O\widehat{B}A = 67.5°$, $A\widehat{O}B = 45°$
19. (a) 36° (b) 36°
20. $C\widehat{D}I = D\widehat{C}I = 45°$, $C\widehat{I}D = 90°$
21. (a) 135° (b) 22.5° (c) 67.5° (d) 45° (e) 45° (f) 90° right-angled isosceles

Exercise 9e page 171

1. (a)

(c)

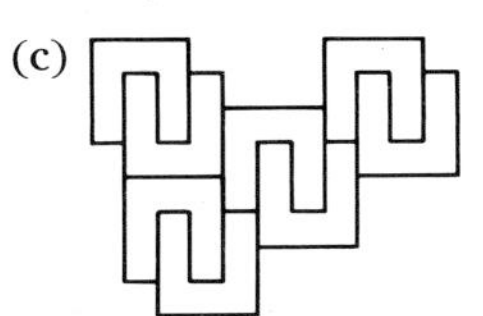

(b)

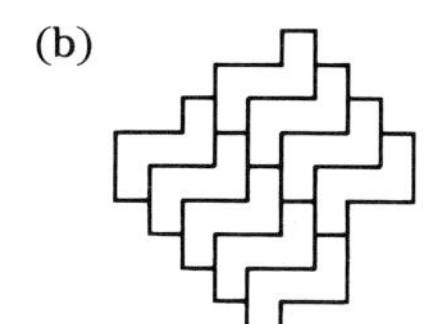

(d)

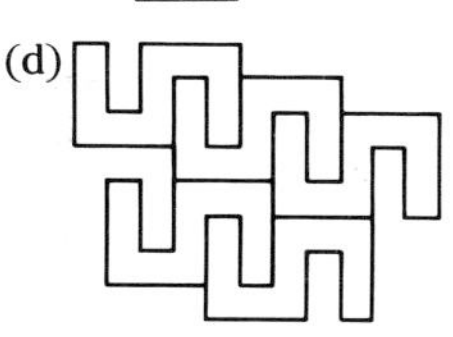

2. yes
3. yes
4. (a) yes (c) no (e) yes
   (b) yes (d) yes (f) yes

Self-Assessment 9 page 172

1. (a) 54°, 54°, 72° (b) 63°, 117°
2. 140
3. 24
4. (a) no (b) yes
5. $\widehat{AEC} = \widehat{EAC} = 72°$, $\widehat{ACE} = 36°$
6. All except (c) will tessellate.

(a)

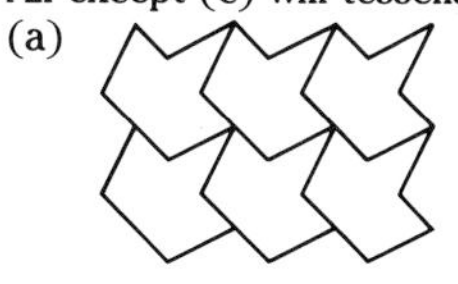

(d)

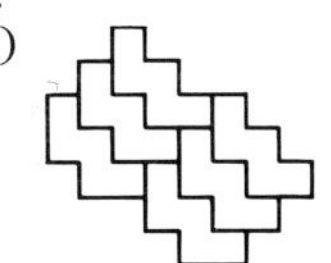

(b)

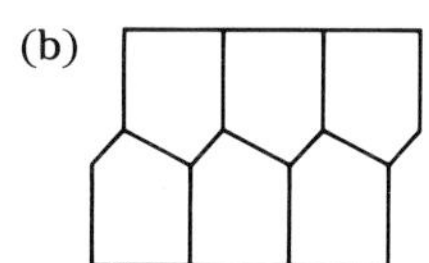

CHAPTER 10

Exercise 10a page 174

1. (a) (i) 174.2 (ii) 3.633
   (b) (i) 582 200 (ii) 27.62
   (c) (i) 0.81 (ii) 0.9487
   (d) (i) 0.000 004 529 (ii) 0.082 04
2. (a) (i) 3215 (ii) 7.530
   (b) (i) 11 360 000 (ii) 58.05
   (c) (i) 0.6724 (ii) 0.9055
   (d) (i) 0.000 000 25 (ii) 0.022 36
3. 16.3 cm
4. 9.39 cm
5. 16.7 cm
6. 23.6 cm
7. AC = 25 cm, DC = 9 cm
8. RS = 4.47 cm, PR = 6.71 cm
9. 4 cm
10. (a) 6 cm (b) 8 cm
11. (a) 6.26 cm (b) 5.50 cm
12. (a) yes, A (c) no
    (b) yes, X (d) yes, Q
13. (a) 35.8 cm (c) 14.3 cm
    (b) 28.6 cm
14. 7.48 cm
15. (a) 6.71 (c) 11.4 (e) 15
    (b) 11.4 (d) 13 (f) 12.5

Exercise 10b page 177

1. (a) (5, 4, 3) (c) (2, 6, 3)
   (b) (2, 4, 4) (d) (−3, 4, 3)
2. (a)

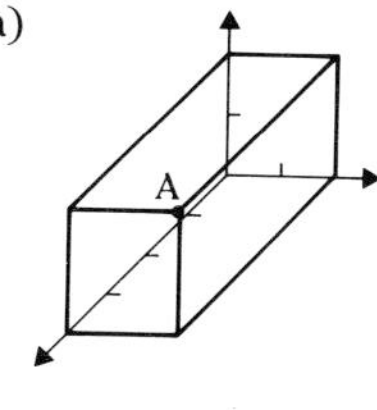

(c)

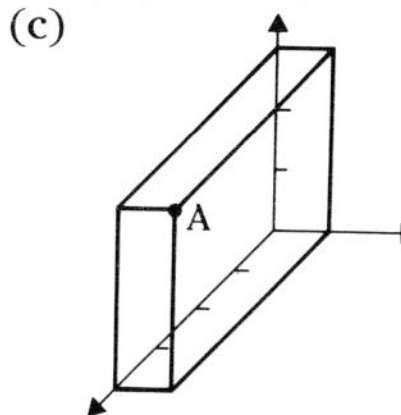

(b)

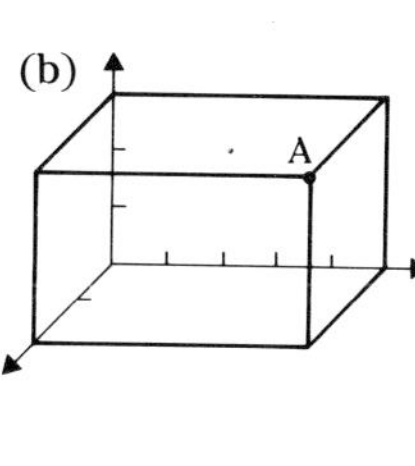

(d)

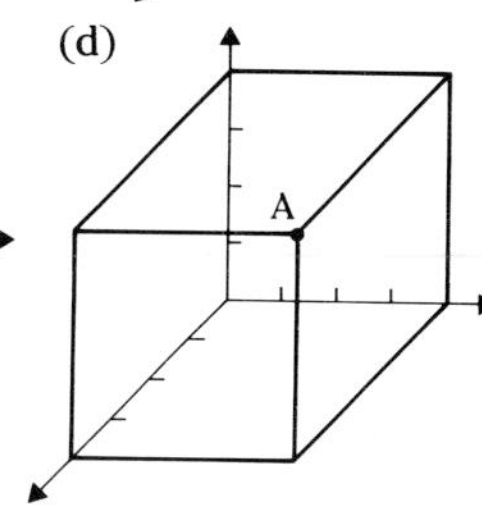

3. (a) A(0, 4, 4), B(4, 4, 4), C(4, 4, 0), D(0, 4, 0), E(0, 0, 4), F(4, 0, 4), G(4, 0, 0), O(0, 0, 0)
   (b) (i) (2, 0, 0) (ii) (0, 2, 0) (iii) (4, 4, 2)
   (iv) (4, 2, 4) (v) (2, 4, 0) (vi) (0, 4, 2)
   (c) (i) (2, 2, 0) (ii) (2, 2, 4) (iii) (4, 2, 2)
   (iv) (2, 4, 2)
4. (a) (3, 0, 0) (c) (3, 0, 4)
   (b) (3, 5, 0) (d) (3, 5, 4)
5. O(0, 0, 0), A(3, 0, 0), B(0, 3, 0), C(0, 0, 3), D(3, 0, 3), E(3, 3, 3), F(3, 3, 0), G(0, 3, 3)
6. O(0, 0, 0), A(3, 0, 0), B(0, 6, 0), C(0, 0, 4), D(3, 0, 4), F(3, 6, 0), G(0, 6, 4)
7. (a) A(−5, 4, 0), C(3, 4, 2), E(−5, 0, 0), F(3, 0, 0), G(3, 0, 2), H(−5, 0, 2)
   (b) (i) (−1, 4, 0) (ii) (−1, 4, 2)
   (c) A(−8, 4, 0), B(0, 4, 0), C(0, 4, 2), D(−8, 4, 2), E(−8, 0, 0), F(0, 0, 0), G(0, 0, 2), H(−8, 0, 2)
8. (a)

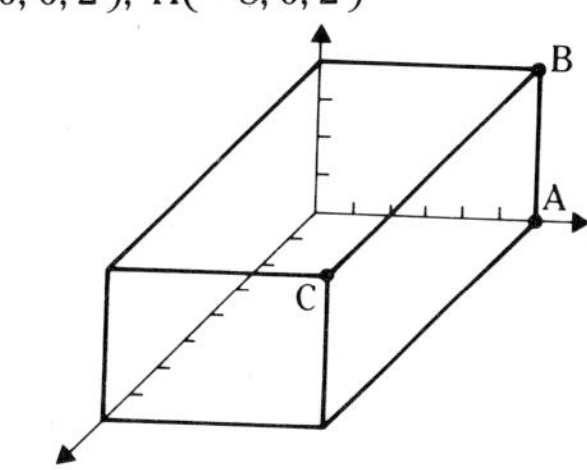

   (b) 12 units
9. (a)

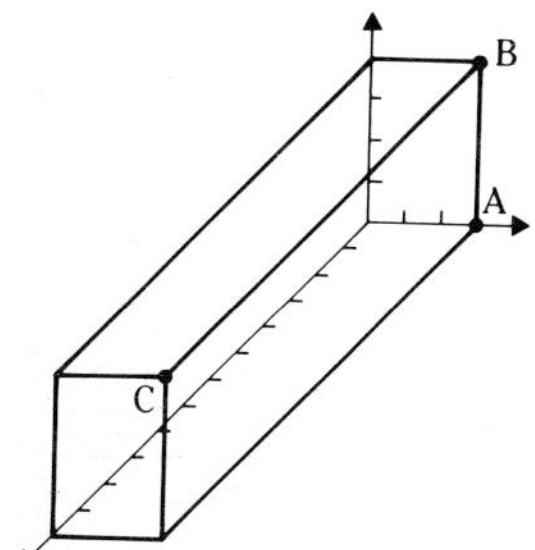

   (b) 19 units
   (c) (i) 5 units (ii) 13 units

10. (6, 2, 0), (0, 4, 4), (6, 4, 4), (6, 4, 0)
11. (a) D(2, 4, 0), E(2, 0, 4) (b) 8 sq units
12. (a) (5, −5, 0) (b) (0, −5, 3) (c) (5, 2, 3)

Exercise 10c page 180

1. 42.8 nautical miles
2. 24.0 cm
3. 13 cm
4. AB = 3.96 m, BC = 9.12 m
5. 997 m to nearest m
6. 18.8 m
7. (a) 1.04 cm (b) 0.693 cm^2
8. 8.28 m, 7.71 m
9. (a) (i) 5 (ii) 12 (iii) 7
   (b) (ii) $a = 11, c = 61$
   (iii) 13, 84, 85; 15, 112, 113
10. (a) 212.7 cm or 2127 mm
11. (a) 30 cm, 42.4 cm (b) 47.4 cm

Exercise 10d page 182

1. (b) (i) EF, DC, HG (ii) FB, GC, HD
   (iii) AD, EH, FG
   (c) 12.6 cm
2. (a) 12.4 cm (b) 14.4 cm
3. (a) 8.49 cm (b) 6.71 cm
4. (a) 8.54 cm (b) 17.3 cm
5. (a) 7.21 units (b) 5 units (c) 6.71 units

Self-Assessment 10 page 184

1. (a) (i) 4.24 cm (ii) 6.75 cm
   (b) no
2. 7.21
3. 32 cm
4. 8.86 cm
5. (a) (i) (2, 0, 0) (ii) (2, 4, 0) (iii) (0, 4, 7)
   (iv) (2, 0, 7)
   (b) (i) 4.47 (ii) 8.06
6. 143 cm

CHAPTER 11

Exercise 11a page 186

1. 84 cm^2
2. 38.88 cm^2
3. 352 cm^2
4. 12 cm^2
5. 456 mm^2
6. 63 cm^2
7. 36 cm^2
8. 180 cm^2
9. 192 m^2
10. 288 cm^2
11. 4.8 cm^2
12. 480 mm^2

Exercise 11b page 188

1. 48 cm^2
2. 22.2 cm^2
3. 64 cm^2
4. 21 cm^2
5. 540 cm^2
6. 30 cm^2
7. (a) 1.89 m^2 (b) 18 900 cm^2
8. (a) 0.152 m^2 (b) 1520 cm^2
9. (a) 0.0874 m^2 (b) 874 cm^2
10. 1.69 m^2, 16 900 cm^2
11. 0.002 64 m^2, 26.4 cm^2
12. 0.0032 m^2, 32 cm^2
13. 12 cm^2
14. 9 cm^2
15. 20 cm^2
16. 79 cm^2
17. 45 cm^2
18. 28 cm^2
19. 28 cm^2
20. 47.5 cm^2
21. 6 mm
22. 36 cm
23. 0.5 cm or 5 mm
24. 4 m or 400 cm
25. 108 cm^2
26. 6.93 cm^2
27. (a) 3 cm (b) 12 cm^2
28. 6 cm, 7.21 cm

Exercise 11c page 193

1. (a) 60 cm^2 (b) 1.98 cm^2
2. (a) 39 cm^2 (b) 3.105 m^2
3. 13 cm
4. 10 cm
5. 20 cm
6. 15 cm
7. 10 cm
8. (a) 8.65 cm (b) 117 cm^2
9. 101.5 cm^2
10. 18 cm^2
11. 0.84 m
12. 84 mm^2
13. 33.02 m^2
14. 9.92 m^2
15. 74.75 m^2
16. (a) 72.2 m^2 (b) \$6205

Exercise 11d page 197

1. 94 cm^2, 60 cm^3
2. 102 cm^2, 63 cm^3
3. 122 cm^2
4. 65.5 cm^2
6. (b) F and J (c) BC
7. (a) 13 cm (d) 26.2 cm (3 s.f.)
   (b) 37 cm
8. (b) 151 mm (3 s.f.)

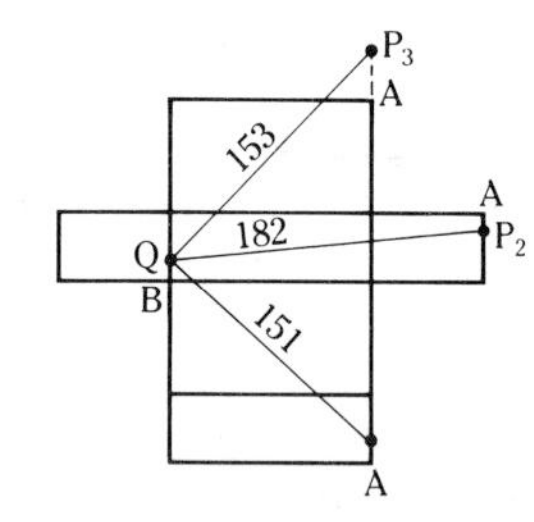

   (c) (b)
9. (a) and (c)

Exercise 11e page 201

1. 720 cm^3
2. 2160 cm^3
3. 660 cm^3
4. 1242 cm^3
5. 1120 cm^3
6. 1600 cm^3
7. (a) 6.175 m^3 (b) 23.1 m^2 (3 s.f.)
8. 0.3726 m^3
9. 5 cm
10. 3 cm

11. (a)

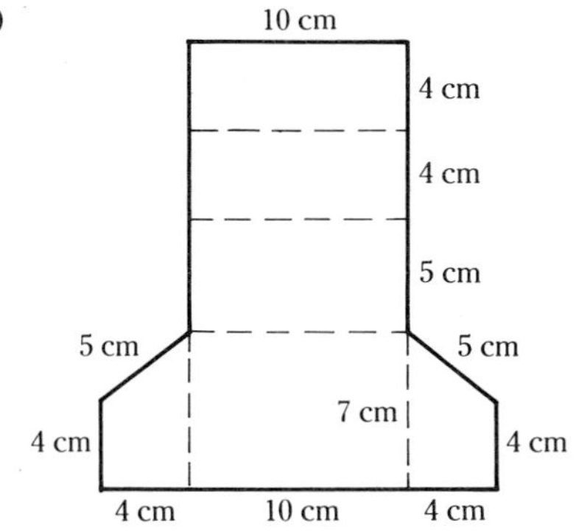

(b) 244 cm^2

12. (a)

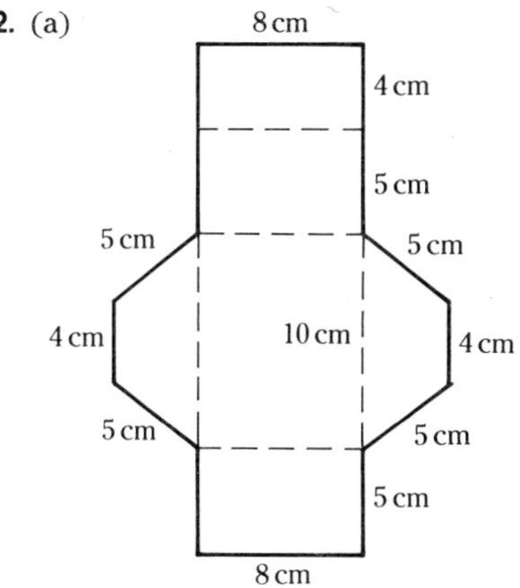

(b) 4 cm (c) 248 cm^2

13. (a) 104 cm
(b) 1.014 m^3 (1 013 160 cm^3)
(c) 6.144 m^2 (61 440 cm^2)

Exercise 11f page 204

1. (a) (b) (c)

2. (a) (b) (c) (d)

3. (a) (b)

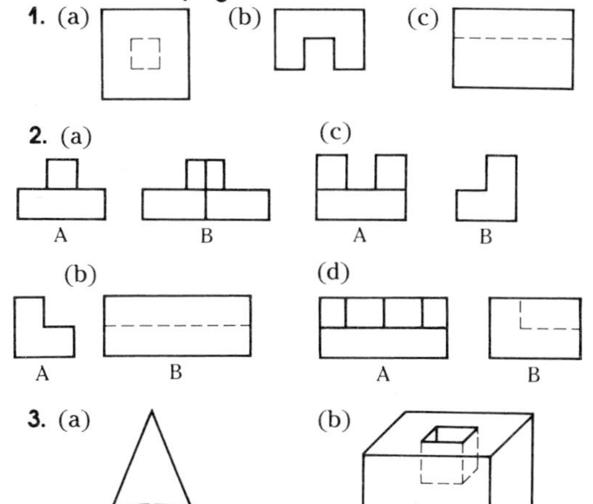

(c)

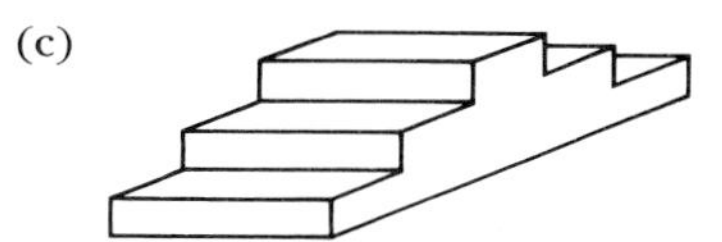

4. (a)

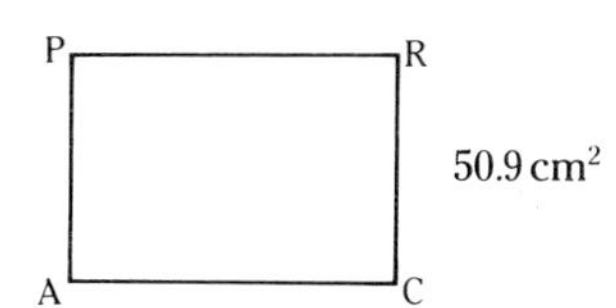

(b) P S B C

They are identical in shape and size.

5. (a) 8.54 cm
(b)

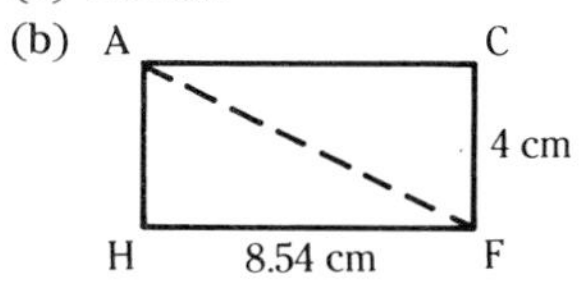

(c) 9.43 cm

6. (a)

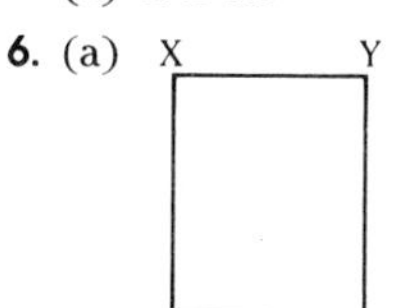

(b) 2.83 cm; 11.3 cm^2
(c) 8 cm^3, 56 cm^3

Self-Assessment 11 page 206

1. (a) 166 cm^2 (3 s.f.)
(b) (i) 12 cm (ii) 252 cm^2
2. (a) 1.73 cm^2 (3 s.f.)
(b) 178.5 cm^2
3. 19 cm^2
4. 39 cm^2
5. (a) 4 cm (b) 24 cm^2
6. 28.6 cm^2
7. 22.62 m^2
8. (b) 62 cm^2 (c) 6.16 cm
9. (a) 35 cm (b) 24.5 cm (3 s.f.)
10.

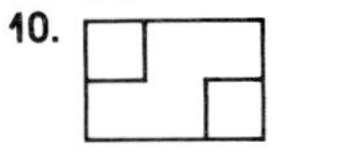

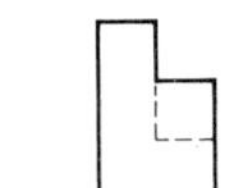

11. (b) Each 8.49 cm (3 s.f.)
(c) 31.2 cm^2 (3 s.f.)
12. (a) 18 cm^2 (b) 10.4 cm
13. 192 cm^3

CHAPTER 12

Exercise 12a page 209

1. (a) 36 cm (b) 19.2 mm (c) 18 m (d) 33 cm (e) 24 cm (f) 12 mm
2. (a) 239 mm (b) 27.6 m (c) 66.0 cm (d) 1.57 m (e) 6.47 m (f) 45.2 cm
3. (a) 176 cm (b) 44.0 m (c) 19.8 cm (d) 30.8 mm (e) 2.64 m (f) 9.55 m
4. (a) 10.3 cm (b) 18.3 cm (c) 22.8 cm (d) 45.1 cm
5. 4.71 m; £32.50
6. (a) 176 cm (b) 176 cm (c) 200 (d) 15
7. 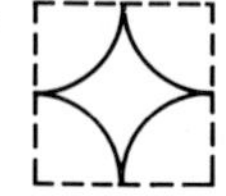 94.2 cm
8. 62.8 m
9. 6.28 seconds, 9.55
10. 47.1 m
11. (a) 1 m (b) 0.5 m (c) 1.57 m (d) 6.57 m
12. (a) 6 cm (b) 11 cm (c) 9.42 cm (d) 31.4 cm
13. (a) 7.00 cm (b) 19.3 mm (c) 132 cm (d) 87.5 m (e) 5.76 mm (f) 4.77 cm (g) 718 mm (h) 1.61 cm
14. 61.1 m
15. 20 m

Exercise 12b page 212

1. (a) 13.9 cm^2 (b) 254 mm^2 (c) 4.52 m^2 (d) 1260 cm^2 or 0.126 m^2
2. (a) 3 m (b) 14.1 m^2
3. 1.77 cm^2
4. (a) 900 m^2 (b) 353 m^2 (c) 1253 m^2
5. (a) 36 cm^2 (b) 28.3 cm^2 (c) 64.3 cm^2
6. 278 cm^2
7. (a) 2340 cm^2 (b) 374 cm^2 (c) 603 cm^2
8. (a) 38.5 m^2 (b) 13
9. (a) 12 m^2 (b) 4.52 m^2 (c) 7.48 m^2 (d) 7.54 m
10. (a) 615 cm^2 (b) $\pi(15.1^2 - 14^2)\text{ cm}^2 = 101\text{ cm}^2$
11. (a) 118 cm^2 (b) 137 cm^2
12. (a) 1352 cm^2 (b) 9.97 % (c) 36.3 %

Exercise 12c page 215

1. (a) 75.4 cm^2 (b) 91.1 cm^2 (c) 1700 cm^2 (d) 255 cm^2
2. 347 cm^2
3. 3.92 m^2
4. (a) 132 cm^2 (b) 13.9 cm^2 (c) 160 cm^2
5. (a) 24 100 cm^2 (b) 27 900 cm^2
6. (a) 2.90 m^3 (b) 14.1 m^3 (c) 4.42 cm^3
7. (a) 57 900 cm^3 (b) 57.9 litres
8. (a) 80.4 cm^3 (b) 844 g
9. (a) 2.69 cm (b) 16.8 mm (c) 2 m (d) 2 cm
10. 1.99 m
11. (a) 16.0 cm (b) 29.7 cm
12. 1.62 m
13. 18.8 cm
14. 398 cm^3; 10.3 cm
15. (a) 138 mm^3 (b) 415 mm^3 (c) 8 g/cm^3

Exercise 12d page 217

1. (a) length (b) volume (c) area (d) area (e) length (f) volume (g) length (h) length
2. (a) length (b) area (c) volume
3. (a) length (b) volume (c) area
4. (a) cm (b) cm^2 (c) cm^2 (d) cm^3 (e) cm (f) cm^3
5. (a) area (b) length (c) area (d) volume (e) area (f) volume (g) area (h) length
6. (c) b^3 is volume, others are area
   (e) V(vol), a(length), B(area)
7. 2
8. $2\pi r$ is a length, not measured in cm^2
9. D

Self-Assessment 12 page 218

1. 239 m^2
2. 4.46 cm
3. (a) 75.4 cm^3 (b) 13.1 cm
4. 47.8 cm
5. (a) 804 cm^2 (b) 73.1 cm^3
6. (a) 62.8 cm^3 (b) 103 cm^3 (c) 39%
7. 3170 cm^3, 531 cm^2
8. 8.07 m
9. D

CHAPTER 13

Exercise 13a page 220

1. (a) 16 m : 24 m = 2 : 3
   (b) 12 p : 48 p = 1 : 4
   (c) 8 kg : 14 kg = 4 : 7
2. (a) 36 p compared with 18 p is the same as 2 compared with 1.
   (b) 18 g compared with 20 g is the same as 9 compared with 10.
   (c) 240 compared with 180 is the same as 4 compared with 3.
3. (a) 1 : 3 (b) 1 : 3 (c) 4 : 7 (d) 9 : 4
4. (a) 5 : 2 : 8 (b) 3 : 5 : 9 (c) 2 : 3 : 5 (d) 2 : 5 : 7
5. (a) 5 : 6 (b) 3 : 7 (c) 12 : 25 (d) 9 : 7
6. (a) 3 : 7 (b) 25 : 17 (c) 3 : 1 (d) 3 : 8
7. (a) 19 : 30 (b) 5 : 2 (c) 1 : 2 (d) 1 : 14

8. (a) 1 : 4 : 3 (b) 5 : 3 : 2 (c) 14 : 9 : 4 (d) 3 : 25 : 18
9. (a) 4 : 1 (b) 9 : 4 (c) 4 : 25 (d) 32 : 7
10. (a) 6 : 25 (b) 7 : 4 (c) 8 : 5 (d) 4 : 3
11. 43 : 275 **12.** 14 : 9 **13.** 17 : 3
14. (a) 9 : 7 (b) 9 : 16
15. (a) 8 : 7 (b) 9 : 10 (c) 25 : 24 (d) 36 : 35
16. (a) \$92.40 (b) \$105.60 (c) 7 : 8
17. (a) 9 : 41 (b) 2 : 3 (c) 8 : 41
18. π : 4 (1 : 1.27)

Exercise 13b page 222

1. (a) 3 : 4 (b) 13 : 8 (c) 2 : 3 (d) 4 : 9
2. (a) all equal (b) all equal (c) $\frac{2}{3} : \frac{3}{4} = 8 : 9$ (d) $1\frac{1}{2} : 2\frac{1}{2} = \frac{3}{10} : \frac{1}{2}$
3. (a) 1 : 400 (b) 1 : 1.6 (c) 1 : 7.5 (d) 1 : 3.13
4. (a) 1 : 2 000 000 (b) 340 km
5. B
6. (a) $2\frac{2}{5}$ (b) $3\frac{1}{2}$ (c) $5\frac{1}{3}$ (d) $3\frac{1}{3}$ (e) $3\frac{1}{2}$ (f) $4\frac{2}{3}$
7. 450 **8.** 24 **9.** 4.8 cm
10. (a) 1 : 1 020 000 (b) 1 : 5900

Exercise 13c page 224

1. (a) 40 kg, 8 kg (b) 24 min, 16 min
2. (a) 64 g, 48 g, 16 g (b) \$24, \$24, \$36
3. 21 cm **4.** 4.5 cm, 2 cm
5. Teresa 104 g, Dawn 96 g
6. 9, 15, 21 **7.** \$2100 **8.** \$124
9. (a) \$5600, \$6400 (b) \$5700, \$6300 (c) \$5800, \$6200; never
10. flour 640 g, sugar and butter 320 g, fruit 480 g
11. 48°, 60°, 72°

Exercise 13d page 226

1. 12 **2.** 468 **3.** \$12.22 **4.** 221 g
5. 6 hours 40 minutes
6. 320 g flour, 80 g marg, 32 g sugar, 53 g sultanas (to nearest gram), 100 mℓ of milk, pinch of salt
7. 8640 km **8.** 24; $6\frac{1}{4}$
9. (a) $94\frac{1}{2}$ minutes (b) 19
10. (a) 412.5 g (b) 23 m^2
11. (a) \$138.60 (b) 9 m^2
12. Use 1 very large egg.
13. (a) 18 g (b) 35 g (c) 300 g copper, 700 g tin

Exercise 13e page 228

1. (a) i (b) ii (c) i (d) iii (e) i (f) iii (g) ii (h) i
2. 170 to nearest line
3. 400 **4.** $7\frac{1}{2}$
5. (a) $3\frac{3}{4}$ hours (b) 720 mph
6. (a) 12 (b) 20
7. (a) $16\frac{2}{3}$ days (b) 350
8. (a) 6 (b) 12 days
9. 60 **10.** 6
11. No link; babies' weight does not increase steadily.
12. (a) \$270 (b) 13.5 m^2
13. 63 **14.** About 3 hours **15.** 12
16. No direct link between experience and rate of working.

Exercise 13f page 230

1. x decreases by a factor 4, 2.5
2. (a) $\frac{1}{9}$ (b) $\frac{9}{25}$
3. increases by a factor of 1.44
4. 1.78 ($\frac{16}{9}$)
5. (a) decreases to 0.87 of the original radius
(b) increases to 4 times the original height

Self-Assessment 13 page 231

1. (a) 5 : 16 (b) 1 : 120 (c) 5 : 2 : 3
2. (a) 3 : 5 (b) 1 : 4
3. (a) 7 : 8
4. (a) 1 : 15 (b) 1 : 2000
5. (a) 21 (b) 38.5
6. 4 hours; no, total time does not increase
7. Nick \$300, Winston \$360, Gary \$180
8. (a) 120 (b) 14 kg
9. (a) 20 days (b) 40

CHAPTER 14

Exercise 14a page 233

1. (a) B, N62°E; C, S35°E; D, S56°W; F, N77°E; G, N58°W
(b) B, S62°W; C, N35°W; D, N56°E; F, S77°W; G, S58°E
2. (a) B, 062°; C, 145°; D, 236°; F, 077°; G, 302°
(b) B, 242°; C, 325°; D, 056°; F, 257°; G, 122°
3. (a) 72° S (c) 126° C

(b)

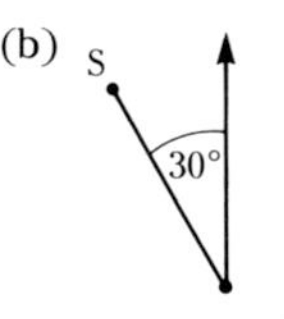

(d)

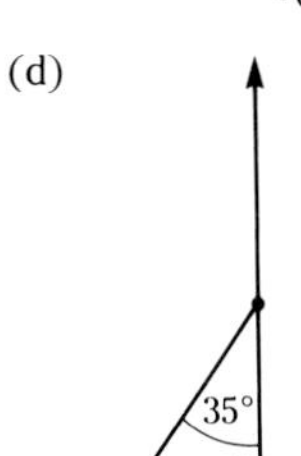

4. (a)

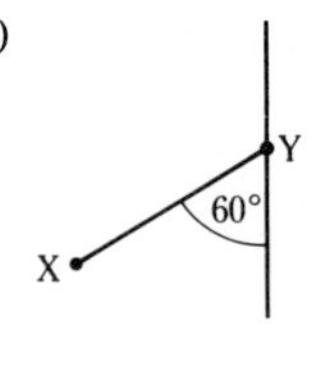

(c)

(b)

(d)

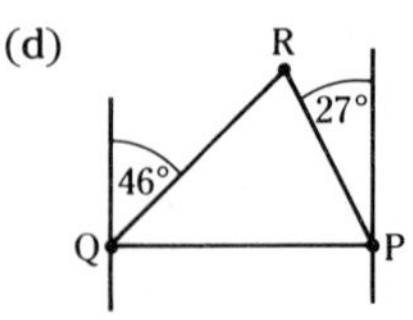

5. 38°
6. A = 46°, B = 44°, C = 90°
7. (a) 252° (b) 32° (c) 036° (d) 72°

Exercise 14b page 236

1. (a) (i) a (ii) $(b+e)$
   (b) (i) $90-c=b$ (ii) $90-f=b+e$
2. (a)

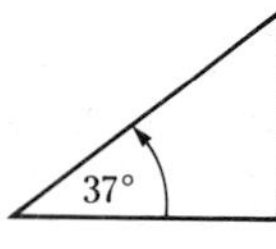

(b)

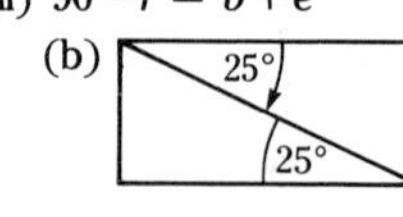

3. (a) 1 cm ≡ 1 m (b) 1 cm ≡ 20 m
   (These are only suggestions; other scales could be chosen.)
4. (a) PQ, 7.6 cm; QR, 10.4 cm (b) 65 m
5. (a) (i) 80 miles (ii) 214°
   (b) 75 miles (c) 067°
6. (a) 9 m (b) 340 m
7. (a) 35° (b) 50° (c) (i) 42 m (ii) 29 m
8. (b) CN = 7.1 cm, BM = 12.0 cm; 35.5 m and 60 m
   (c) 23 m
9. (a) (i) 043° (ii) 132° (iii) 223°
   (c) 109 miles
10. (a) PT = 968 m, QT = 576 m
    (b) 941 m in a bearing of 073° (to nearest degree)
11. (a) (i) 8.2 cm (ii) 328 km
    (b) (i) 120 km (ii) 268 km
    (c) (i) 100° (ii) 280°
    (d) (i) 232 km (ii) 56 km
12. (a) 21 mm (c) 4 mm (e) 4 mm
    (b) 5 mm (d) 8 mm

Self-Assessment 14 page 239

1. (a) (i) 078° (ii) 143° (iii) 323° (iv) 258°
   (b) $\widehat{A}=99°$, $\widehat{B}=65°$, $\widehat{C}=16°$
2. $\widehat{X}=8°$, $\widehat{Y}=142°$, $\widehat{Z}=30°$.
3. (a) AB, 12 cm; AC, 9.5 cm; (b) 102 m
4. 655 m
5. (b) 19.1 km (c) 13.1 km

CHAPTER 15

Exercise 15a page 243

1. (a) $x=3, y=1$ (f) $x=2, y=3$
   (b) $x=1, y=1$ (g) $x=2, y=4$
   (c) $a=2, b=2$ (h) $p=1, q=0$
   (d) $x=4, y=2$ (i) $a=9, b=1$
   (e) $a=3, b=5$
2. (a) $x=1, y=4$ (c) $x=5, y=1$
   (b) $x=4, y=-3$
3. (a) $x=2, y=1$ (c) $p=4, q=3$
   (b) $x=5, y=\frac{1}{2}$
4. (a) $x=3, y=-1$ (g) $p=-1, q=-2$
   (b) $x=3, y=4$ (h) $s=5, t=4$
   (c) $a=5, b=-3$ (i) $x=\frac{10}{3}, y=1$
   (d) $p=-\frac{3}{4}, q=\frac{1}{2}$ (j) $u=-1, v=4$
   (e) $a=\frac{1}{2}, b=2$ (k) $c=2, d=-4$
   (f) $x=6, y=2$ (l) $f=\frac{7}{2}, r=1$

Exercise 15b page 245

1. (a) $x=3, y=1$ (f) $x=1, y=2$
   (b) $x=1, y=2$ (g) $a=1, b=-1$
   (c) $x=\frac{1}{3}, y=1$ (h) $x=3, y=-1$
   (d) $a=-12, b=27$ (i) $r=3, s=\frac{1}{2}$
   (e) $s=0, t=1$
2. (a) $x=3, y=2$ (f) $s=3, t=-1$
   (b) $x=1, y=5$ (g) $p=-1, q=2$
   (c) $x=3, y=1$ (h) $x=2, y=-2$
   (d) $x=\frac{3}{2}, y=0$ (i) $x=0, y=4$
   (e) $a=0, b=6$
3. (a) $x=1, y=4$ (f) $x=2, y=3$
   (b) $x=-1, y=5$ (g) $p=0, q=-2$
   (c) $x=3, y=-2$ (h) $a=\frac{7}{2}, b=\frac{5}{2}$
   (d) $x=6, y=28$ (i) $s=1, t=-2$
   (e) $x=-1, y=-1$ (j) $x=2\frac{2}{3}, y=3\frac{2}{3}$

Exercise 15c page 247

1. (a) $x+y=27$
   (b) $x-y=15$
   (c) 6
2. (a) $x+y=120$
   (b) $x-y=45$ $(x>y)$
   (c) 82.5°
3. (a) $x+y=205$
   (b) $x+2y=270$
   (c) cup: £1.40, saucer: 65 p
4. (a)

   b cm

   a cm

   $a+b=24$, $a-b=5$
   (b) 14.5 cm
5. (a) $10x$ p (b) 5 p
6. 13 and 25
7. (a) 168 p (b) 180 p (c) 12 p
8. 6 and 10
9. 27 years, 9 years
10. $\frac{5}{2}$

Exercise 15d page 248

1. (a) 201 (b) 91.6 (c) ± 1.13 (d) ± 0.623
2. (a) ± 5 (b) ± 2.64 (c) ± 6.93 (d) ± 2.1 (exactly)
3. (a) 5 (b) 2.24 (c) ± 12
4. (a) ± 7.75 (b) ± 24 (c) ± 1.69
5. (a) $x = \pm\sqrt{c-y^2}$ (b) $b = \pm\sqrt{a^2-c^2}$ (c) $r = \pm\sqrt{p-t}$ (d) $y = \pm\sqrt{2x^2-g}$ (e) $t = \pm\sqrt{2u/v}$
6. (a) $r = \pm\sqrt{A/\pi}$ (b) $r = \pm\sqrt{V/\pi h}$ (c) $y = \pm\sqrt{5-x^2}$ (d) $t = \pm\sqrt{(a^3-r)a}$ (e) $y = \pm\sqrt{x^2-z^2}$
7. (a) $q = p^2/2$ (b) $y = 4x^2$ (c) $r = q^2/p^2$
8. (a) $c = (b-a)^2$ (b) $t = 3-V^2$ (c) $t = v^2/r$
9. (a) $942\,\text{cm}^3$ (b) 0.978
10. (a) 8.94 (b) 1.42 m (c) 20 (a cannot be negative)
11. (a) 2.7 miles (2 s.f.) (b) 17 ft (2 s.f.)

Self-Assessment 15 page 254

1. $x = 10, y = 1$
2. $x = 2, y = 2$
3. (a) $r = \pm\sqrt{t-2as}$ (b) $r = gL^2$
4. (a) 3.97 (b) 4.92 seconds
5. (a) 4.69 (b) 3.3 m (c) 20.4 cm
6. James £11, Thomas £13

CHAPTER 16

Exercise 16a page 256

1. 18, 22; add 4 to previous term.
2. 8, 5; take 3 from previous term.
3. 324, 972; multiply previous term by 3.
4. 2, 1; divide previous term by 2.
5. 11, 16; add one more than was added to obtain the previous term.
6. 31, 37; add 6 to previous term
7. 3125, 15 625; multiply previous term by 5
8. $1, \frac{1}{3}$; divide previous term by 3
9. 18, 54, 162, . . .
10. 8, -16, 32, . . .
11. 6, 8, 10, . . .
12. $1, \frac{1}{2}, \frac{1}{4}, \ldots$
13. 8, 14, 22, . . .
14. 6, 10, 16, . . .
15. 5, 8, 12, . . .
16. 4, 6, 8, 10, . . ., 22
17. 2, 4, 8, 16, . . ., 1024
18. 3, 6, 12, 24, . . ., 1536
19. 0, 2, 6, 12, . . ., 90
20. 0, 1, 4, 9, . . ., 81
21. 0, 3, 8, 15, . . ., 99
22. 6, 18, 54, 162, . . .
23. 5, 7, 9, 11, . . .
24. $-4, -6, -8, -10, \ldots$
25. 1, 1, 1, 1, . . .
26. 3.316 . . ., 2.305 . . ., 2.075 . . ., 2.018, . . .
27. $u_{n+1} = u_n + 4$; $u_{n+1} = u_n - 3$; $u_{n+1} = 3u_n$; $u_{n+1} = \dfrac{u_n}{2}$

Exercise 16b page 257

1. nth term $= 3+5(n-1) = 5n-2$; 23, 28, . . ., 48
2. nth term $= n^2$; 25, 36, . . ., 100
3. nth term $= 2\times 3^{n-1}$; 162, 486, . . ., 39366
4. nth term $= \dfrac{1}{n}$; $\frac{1}{5}, \frac{1}{6}, \ldots, \frac{1}{10}$
5. nth term $= \dfrac{1}{2^{n-1}}$; $\frac{1}{16}, \frac{1}{32}, \ldots, \frac{1}{512}$
6. nth term $= n(n+1)$; 5×6, 6×7, . . ., 10×11
7. nth term $= n^2+1$; 37, 50, . . ., 101
8. nth term $= \dfrac{n}{n+1}$; $\frac{5}{6}, \frac{6}{7}, \ldots, \frac{10}{11}$
9. nth term $= 3n+2$; 17, 20, . . ., 32
10. nth term $= n^3$; 125, 216, . . ., 1000

Exercise 16c page 259

1. 46, 62
2. 47, 73
3. 437, 683
4. 6, 28
5. 324, 539
6. e.g. multiply previous term by 3; 54, 162, 486
   or add 8 more than previously added; 38; 66, 102
7. e.g. add 3 times the previous addition; 13, 40, 121
   or nth term $= (n-1)^2$; 9, 16, 25
8. e.g. multiply previous term by 2; 24, 48, 96
   or add 3 more than previously added; 21, 33, 48
9. 125, 216, 343, . . .; nth term $= n^3$
10. $\frac{5}{6}, \frac{6}{7}, \frac{7}{8}, \ldots$; nth term $= \dfrac{n}{(n+1)}$
11. 16, 27, 43, using a difference table
12. 24, 35, 48; add 2 more than added to obtain previous term.
13. $-241, -1265, -5361$; subtract 4 times the number subtracted to obtain the previous term.
14. 5.7, 6.8, 7.9; add 1.1 to previous term.
15. 6, 2, 7; odd terms are all 2; for even terms add 1 to previous even term.
16. 13, 17, 19; prime numbers.
17. 16, -32, 64; $u_n = (-2)^{n-1}$
18. 37, 50, 65; $u_n = n^2+1$
19. 19, 23; add 4 to previous term.
20. nth term $= 4n-1$
21. $4n$ is even so $4n+1$ is odd.
22. 21, 77, 165, 285, 437, . . .
23. 621, 837
24. 10, 18, 26, 34, 42, . . .
25. nth term $= 8n+2$
26.

```
2   5   12   27   54   97   160   247   362
  3   7   15   27   43   63   87   115
    4   8   12   16   20   24   28
      4   4   4   4   4   4
```

Exercise 16d page 260

1. (a) 1, 3, 4, 7, 11, 18, . . .
   (b) 2, 3, 5, 8, 13, 21, . . .
   (c) 1, 4, 5, 9, 14, 23, . . .

2. 1 3 4 7 11 18
2 1 3 4 7
Apart from the first term, 1st differences form the same sequence.

3. (a) 1, 1, 2, 3, 5, 8, 13, 21, . . .
(b) $1, \frac{1}{2}, \frac{2}{3}, \frac{3}{5}, \frac{5}{8}, \ldots$
(c) 1, 0.5, 0.6667, 0.6, 0.625, 0.6154, 0.6190, . . .
Converges (to 0.6180 . . .)

5. 1, 11, 121, 1331, 14641, . . .
Second 10 in sixth line represents number of 100s in 10^5, so 0 appears in hundreds column and 1 must be carried to next column.

6. (a) 81, 9801, 998 001, 99 980 001
(b) 9 999 800 001

Exercise 16e page 264

1. 5, 7, 9, 11, 13, 15, . . .

2. In decision box change 5 to 9

3. **4.**

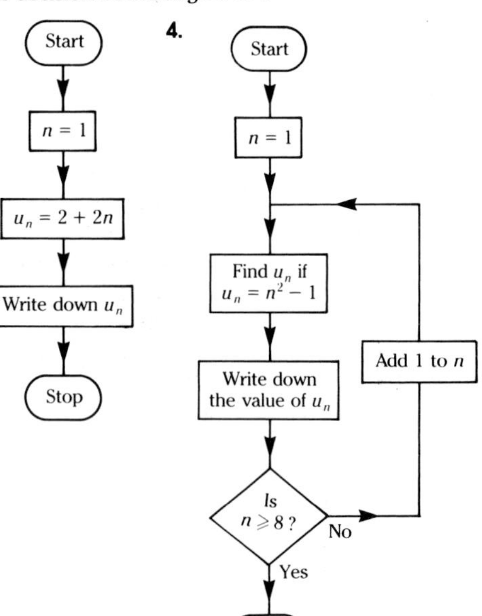

5.

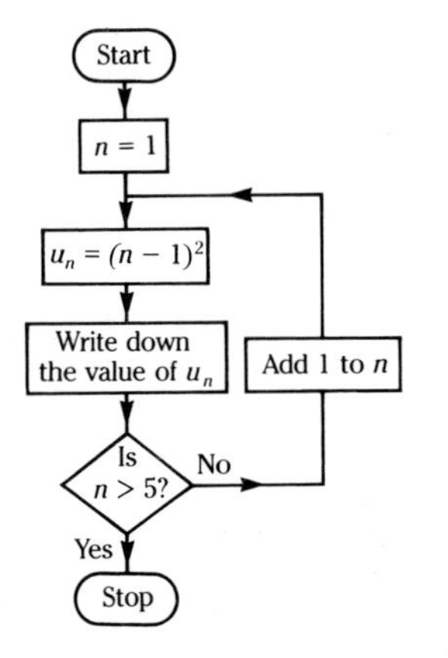

6. Constructs the perpendicular bisector of AB

7. (a)

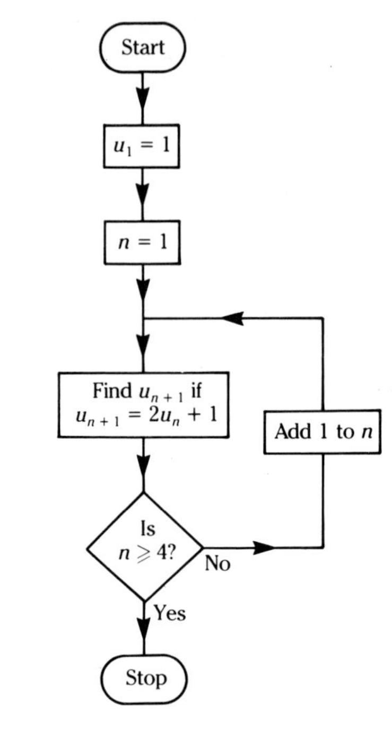

(b)

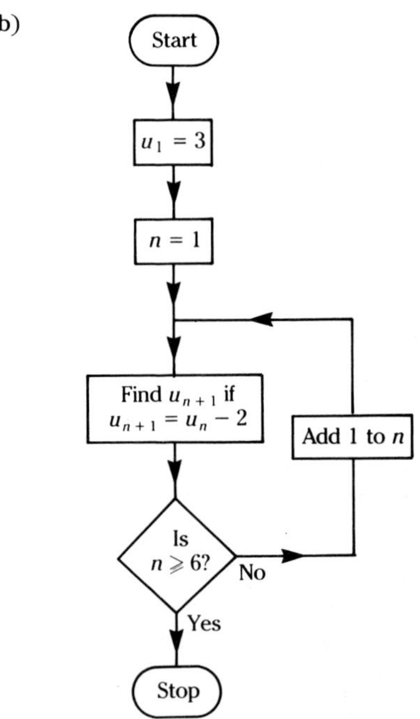

8. Turn off the tap after Wait one second

9.

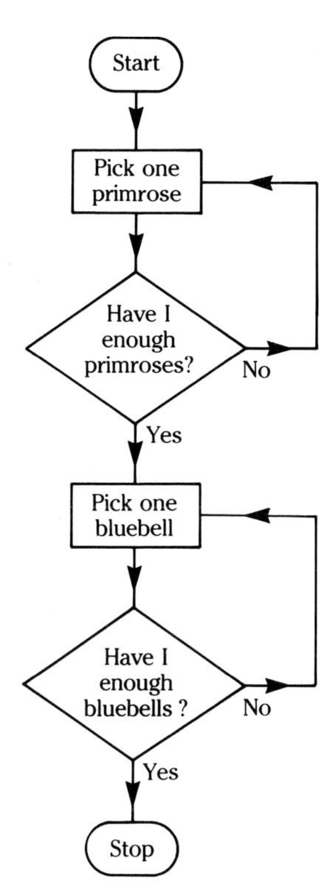

11. (a) multiply
    (b) 4
    (c) gives $2 \times 1 + 3$ i.e. 5
    (d) 9
    (e) nth term $= 2n + 3$
    (f) 10 FOR N = 1 TO 12
12. (a) They show what will be printed.
    (b) If 6, say, is chosen value $1 \times 6 = 6$
    (c) Prints multiplication table.
13. (a) 6
    (b) 37
    (c) $u_n = n^2 + 1$
    (d) 1, 2.5, 5, 8.5, 13, 18.5

Exercise 16f page 266

1. (b) 4, 8, 12, 16, 20, . . .
   (c) nth term $= 4n$
2. (a) 4, 7, 10, 13, 16, . . .
   (c) nth term $= 3n + 1$
3. (b) 1, 3, 6, 10, 15, 21, . . .
   (c) nth term $= \frac{1}{2}n(n+1)$
4. 30, 55; nth term $= 1^2 + 2^2 + 3^2 + \ldots + n^2$
5. 1, 4, 9, 16, 25, . . .; $u_1 = 1, u_n = n^2$
6. 1, 4, 10, 20, 35, . . .; $u_1 = 1$,
   $u_n = u_{n-1} + \frac{1}{2}n(n+1)$
   (u_n = sum of first n triangular numbers.)
7. 2, 4, 6, 8, 10, . . .; nth term $= 2n$
8. 2, 4, 7, 11, 16, . . .; add 1 more than was added to obtain the previous term,
   or nth term $= \frac{1}{2}n(n+1) + 1$
9. (b) With 2 tiles in the middle of an edge, number of tiles along an edge must be even. 4 cm is the smallest.

(c)

4	6	8	10	12
12	16	20	24	28

(d) $2(n+2)$
(e) n^2; $n^2 - 2n - 4$

Self-Assessment 16 page 270

1. 35, 48, . . .; add 2 more than was added to obtain the previous term.
2. 3, 8, 13, 18, . . .
3. 7, 15, 31, 63, . . .
4. nth term $= 4n - 5$
5. nth term $= \dfrac{n(n+2)}{(n+1)^2}$
6. 117, 182
7. 0, 2, 5, 9, 14, 20, 27, . . .
8. (a) 2, 5, 10, 17, 26, 37, 50
   (b) Change Is $n > 7$? to Is $n > 10$?

CHAPTER 17

Exercise 17a page 273

1. (a) $\sqrt{20}$ (b) 5 (c) $\sqrt{68}$ (d) $\sqrt{45}$
2. (a) $(4, 4)$ (b) $(0, 2\frac{1}{2})$ (c) $(6, 5)$ (d) $(-4\frac{1}{2}, -1)$
3. (a) -2 (b) $-\frac{3}{4}$ (c) 4 (d) -2
4. 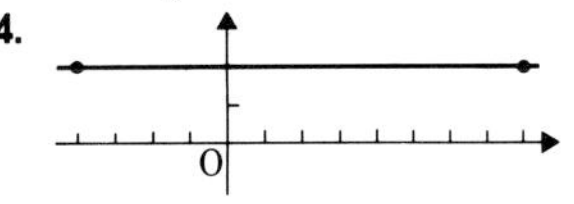

   zero; $\frac{0}{11} = 0$; yes, 0
5. zero; infinitely large; $\frac{7}{0}$; no
6. (a) ∥ to x-axis (b) ∥ to y-axis (c) ∥ to x-axis (d) not ∥ to either.

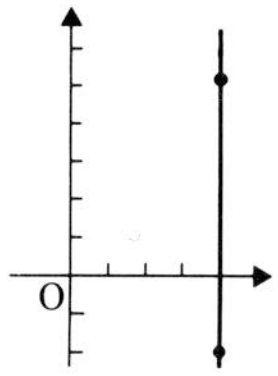

Exercise 17b page 275

1. (a)

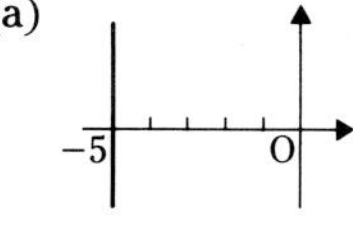

(c)

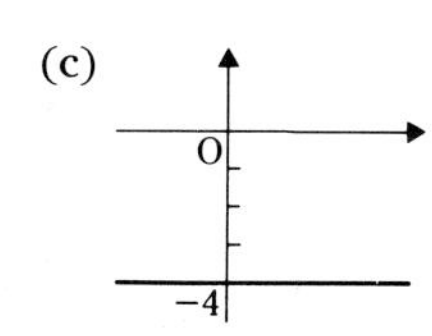

(b)

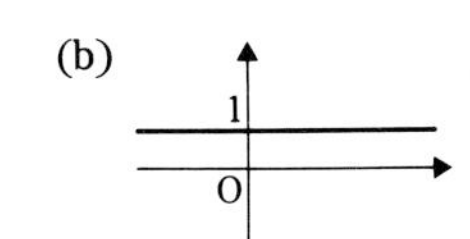

(d)

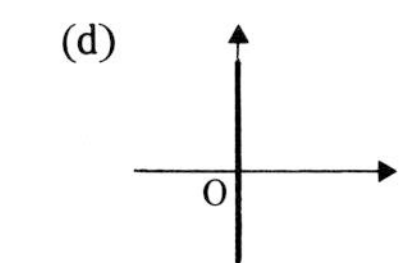

2. (a) 5 (b) −7 (c) 1 (d) 4

3. (a) −1

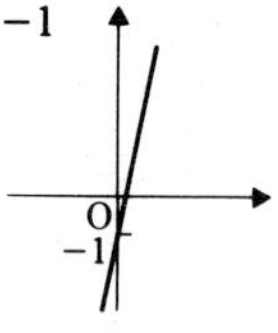

(c) 3

(b) 3

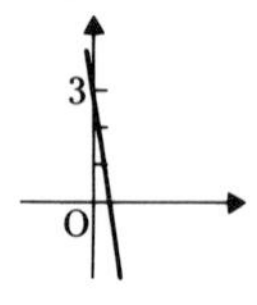

(d) 6

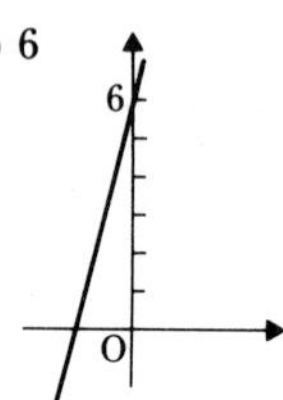

4. (a) $y = 2x+6$ (c) $y = -3x+2$
(b) $y = 4x-1$ (d) $y = x$

5. (a) (i) −1, 3 (ii) $x+y = 3$
(b) (i) 2, 2 (ii) $y = 2x+2$
(c) (i) 1, −2 (ii) $y = x-2$
(d) (i) $-\frac{1}{2}$, −1 (ii) $2y+x+2 = 0$

6. (a) 38 (b) −32 (c) −4

7. (a) 2 (b) −1 (c) $\frac{5}{7}$

8. (a) yes (c) no
(b) no (d) yes.

9. (a) 9, 6 (c) 5, $6\frac{2}{3}$
(b) 15, $-7\frac{1}{2}$ (d) $-3\frac{3}{5}$, $4\frac{1}{2}$

10.

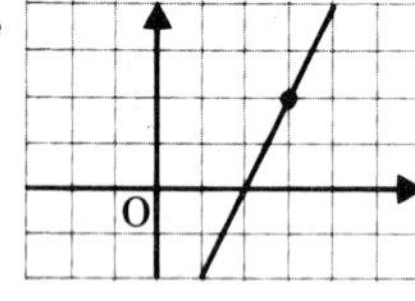

11.

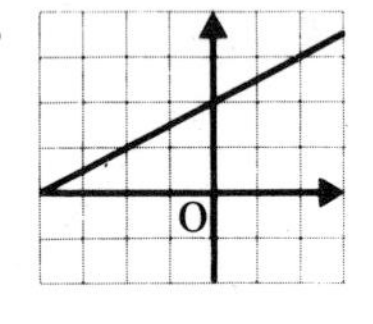

12.

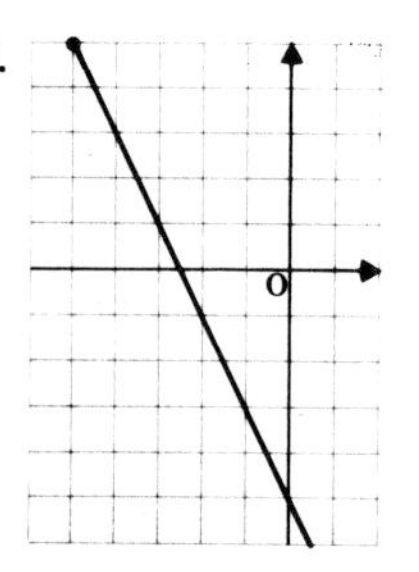

13. (a) $2y = x+5$ (c) $y = 3x$
(b) $y+x = 5$ (d) $2y+x = 14$

14. −1;

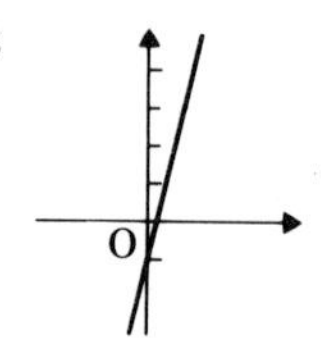

15. 1;

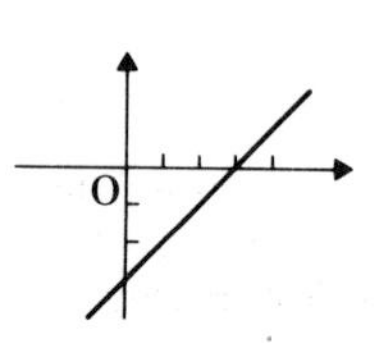

Exercise 17c page 278

1. (a) $\frac{1}{3}$, −2

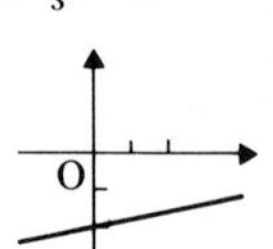

(d) 2, −7

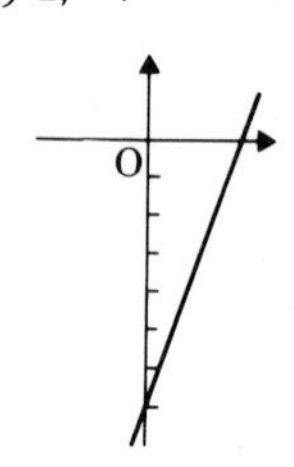

(b) $-\frac{3}{4}$, 2

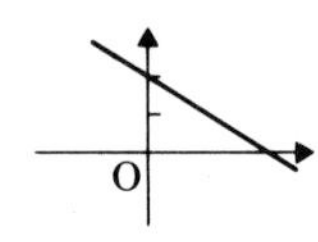

(e) −3, −1

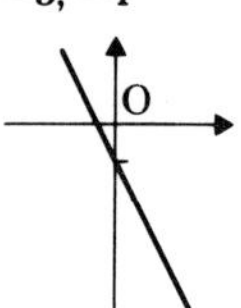

(c) $-\frac{1}{3}$, 2

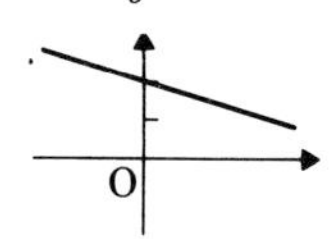

(f) $\frac{1}{4}$, $\frac{1}{2}$

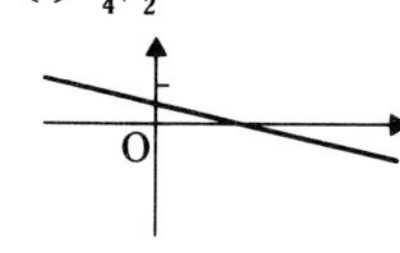

2. (a) −3

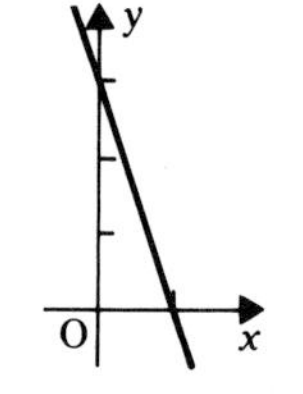

(b) $-\frac{1}{5}$

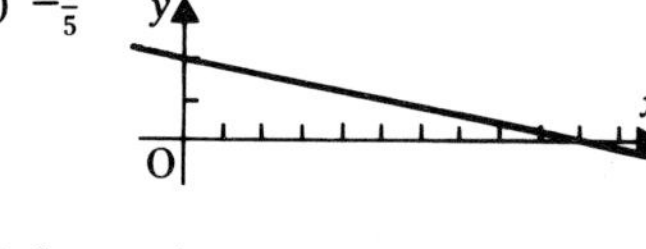

(c) 2

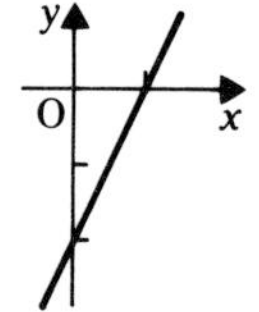

(d) $\frac{1}{4}$

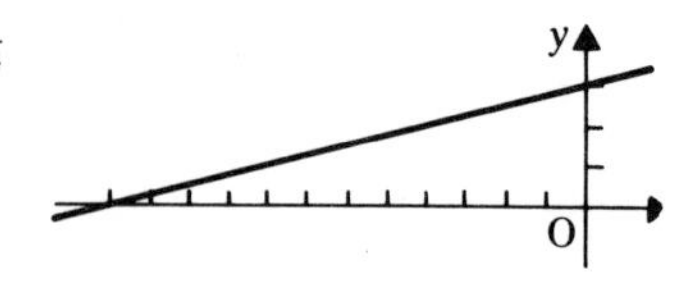

3.

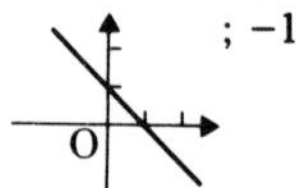

; −1

4. (a) $\frac{x}{3} + \frac{y}{8} = 1$; $m = -\frac{8}{3}$

(b) $\frac{x}{2} + \frac{y}{2} = 1$; $m = -1$

5. (a) $y = 5x - 21$ (b) $5x + 2y = 19$
6. (a) $5y = x - 6$ (b) $y + x = 3$
7. $y = 2x + 3$ and $y = 4 + 2x$
8. $2x + y = 2$ and $y = 7 - 2x$; $m = -2$
   $3y - 4x = 5$ and $4x = 3y$; $m = \frac{4}{3}$
9. (a) $y = 2x \pm$ any number
   (b) $5x - 2y \pm$ any number $= 0$
   (c) $2x = \pm$ any number $- 3y$
10. (a) $y = 4x + 4$ (c) $2y - x = 8$
    (b) $y + 3x = 4$
11. $y = 5 - 2x$: $m = -2, c = 5$;
    $y = 5x - 2$: $m = 5, c = -2$;
    $y + 2x + 2 = 0$

Exercise 17d page 280

1. $\frac{1}{4}$

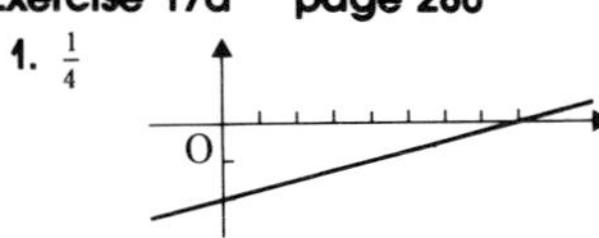

2. -1

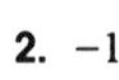

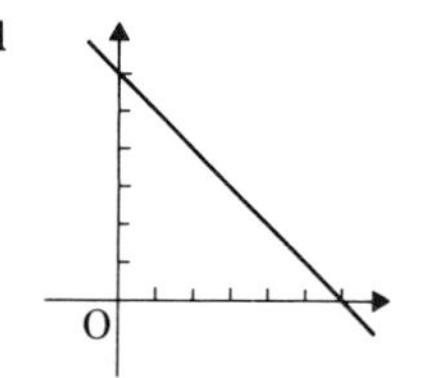

3. -3

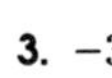

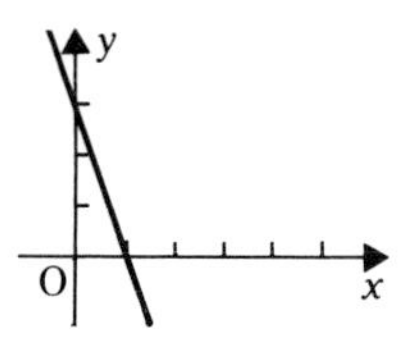

4. $-\frac{3}{5}$

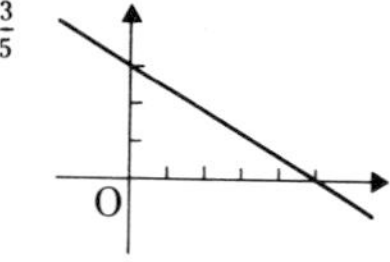

5. 2

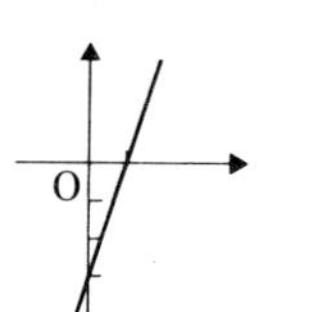

6. $\frac{1}{3}$

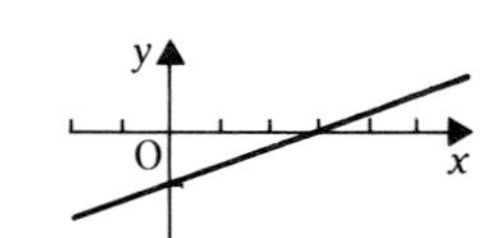

Exercise 17e page 281

1. $x = 1\frac{1}{2}$, $y = 3\frac{1}{2}$ 2. $x = -\frac{1}{2}$, $y = 1\frac{1}{2}$
3. The lines are parallel.
5. e.g. $2 \leqslant x \leqslant 4$, $-1 \leqslant y \leqslant 1$
   ($x \approx 2.7$, $y \approx 0.2$)

Exercise 17f page 282

1. (a) 84 km/h (c) 116 km/h
   (b) 62 m.p.h. (d) 32 m.p.h.
2. (a) £46 (c) £83
   (b) $91 (d) $168
3. (a) 77 °C (b) 95 °F; 32 °F
4. (a) speed (c) $3\frac{1}{2}$ hours
   (b) 22.5 km
5. (a) 49%, 88% (b) 53

Exercise 17g page 285

1. (a) (i) 9
   (ii) number of francs per pound
   (b) (i) 0.085
   (ii) cost in £/unit
   (c) (i) 17.5
   (ii) rise in temperature per minute
   (d) (i) −0.33
   (ii) number of litres consumed per mile
2. (a) (i) 1 200 000 gallons
   (ii) 5 days
   (b) −100 000; number of gallons used per day
   (c) 1 500 000; number of gallons in reservoir on 1st day
3. (a) A, 0.055; B, 0.036; cost in £/unit
   (b) A, 12; B, 32; standing charge
   (c) (i) A (ii) B
4. (a) 0.044, 22 (c) £22
   (b) 4.4 p

Self-Assessment 17 page 286

1. (a) (i) 13 (ii) $(3\frac{1}{2}, 3)$ (iii) $-\frac{12}{5}$
   (b) (i) 10 (ii) $(1, 1)$ (iii) $-\frac{4}{3}$
2. (a)

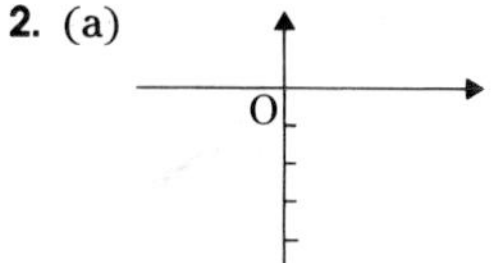

(c)

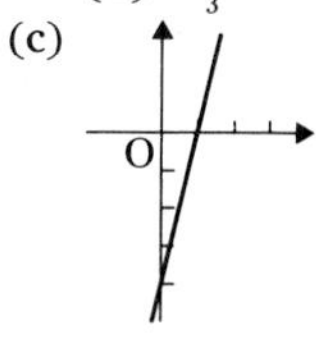

(b)

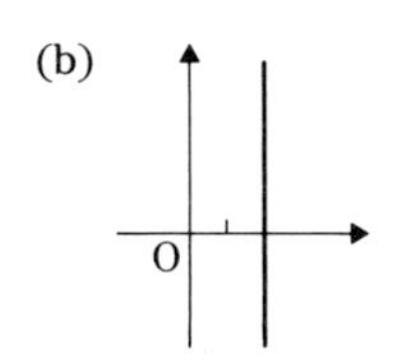

(d)

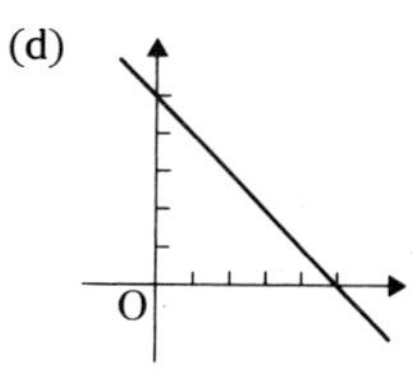

3. (a) −4, 4 (b) $1\frac{1}{2}$, 3 (c) $-\frac{1}{2}$, −2
4. (a) $y = 2x - 9$ (b) $y = 3x$
5. $3y + 4x = 5$
6. (a) 2 (b) −9 (c) $\frac{5}{3}$
7.

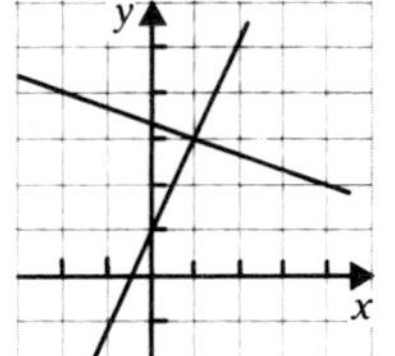

$x = 1, y = 3$

8. (a) 83.64 DM (b) £87.40
9. (a) £115 (b) $\frac{1}{2}$; cost per page
   (c) production costs before printing

CHAPTER 18

Exercise 18a page 289

1. 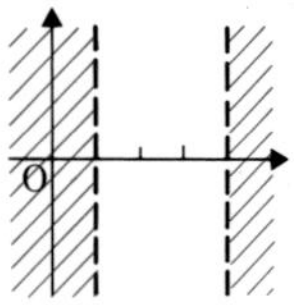 no

2. 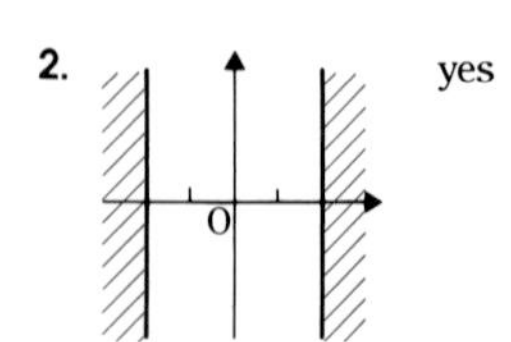

yes

3. 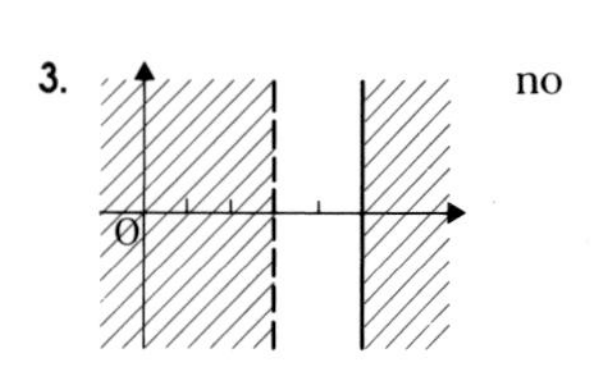

no

4. 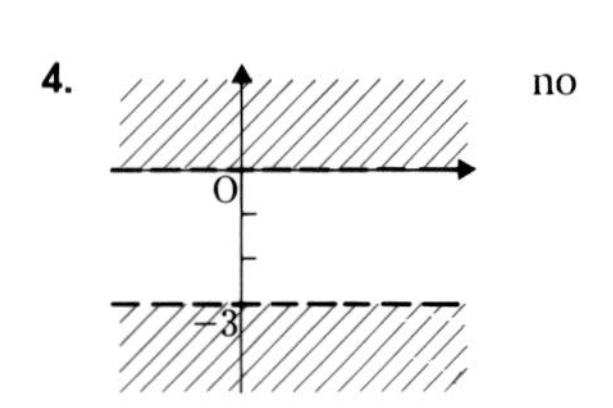

no

5. 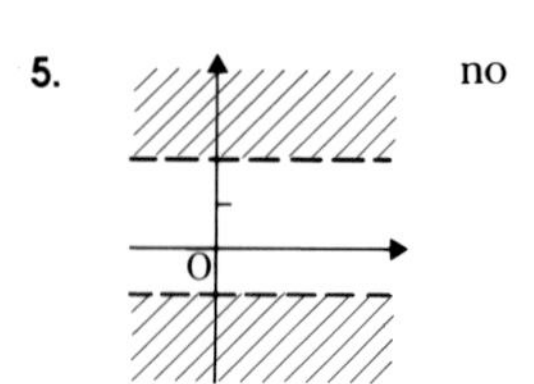

no

6. 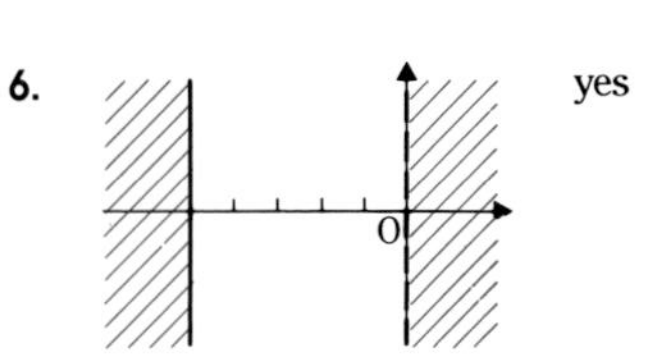

yes

7. $x \leqslant 2$, yes
8. $y < 3$, no
9. $x < -1$, no
10. $-2 \leqslant y \leqslant 2$, no
11. $-\frac{1}{2} < y < 2\frac{1}{2}$, no
12. $-1 \leqslant x < 2$, yes
13. $-3 \leqslant x \leqslant 1$
14. $-4 < y < -1$
15. $3 \leqslant x \leqslant 6$

16. 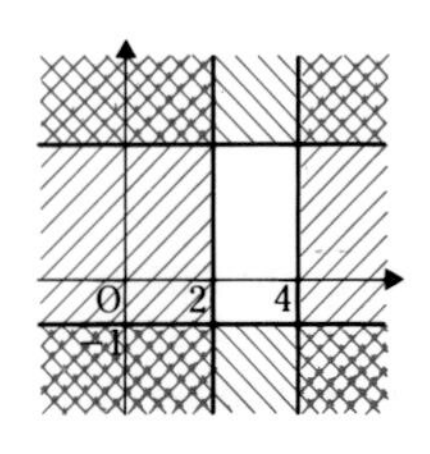

17. 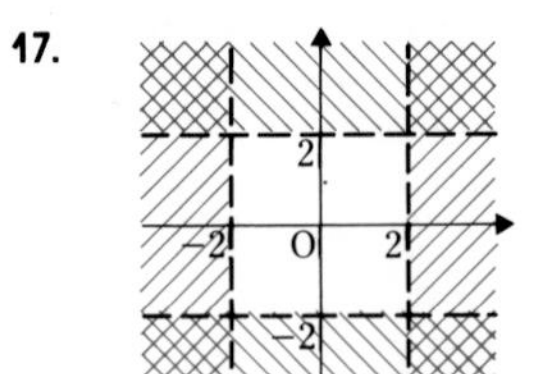

18. 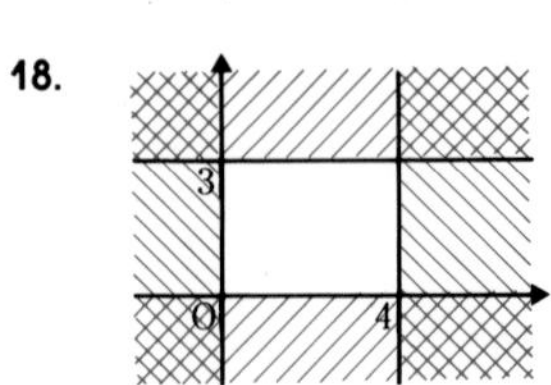

19. 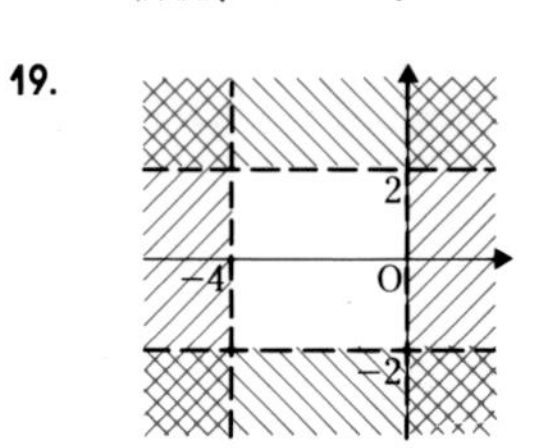

20. 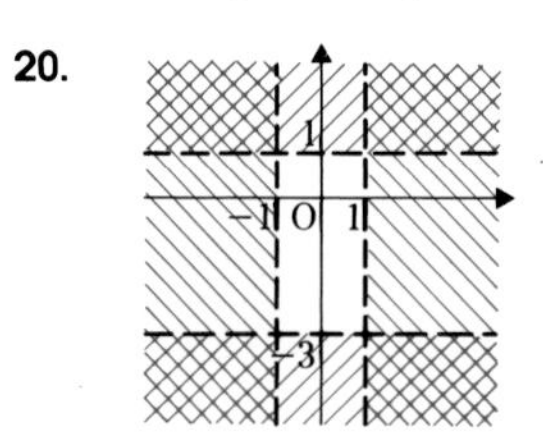

21. 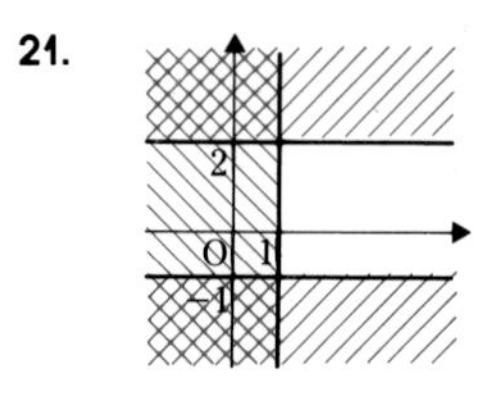

22. $-2 \leqslant x \leqslant 3, \quad -1 \leqslant y \leqslant 2$
23. $-2 \leqslant x \leqslant 1, \quad y \geqslant -1$
24. $-2 < x \leqslant 2, \quad -2 \leqslant y \leqslant 1$
25. $x \geqslant -2, \quad y \leqslant -1$

Exercise 18b page 292

1. 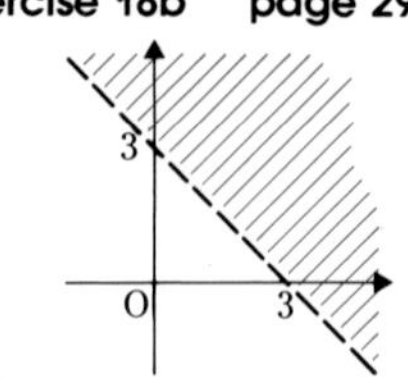

2. 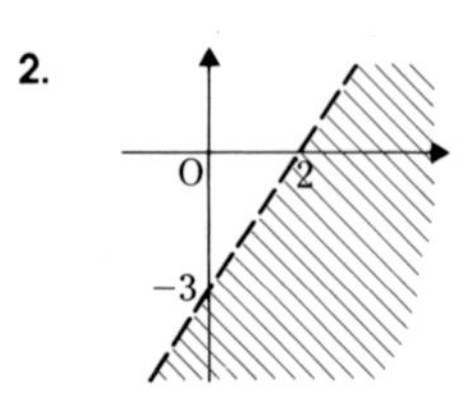

3.

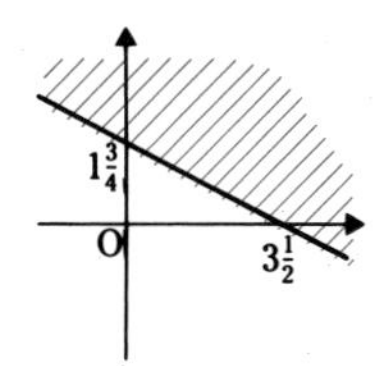

4.

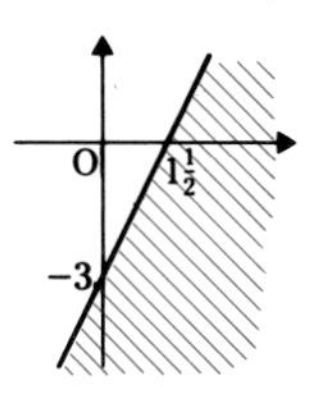

5.

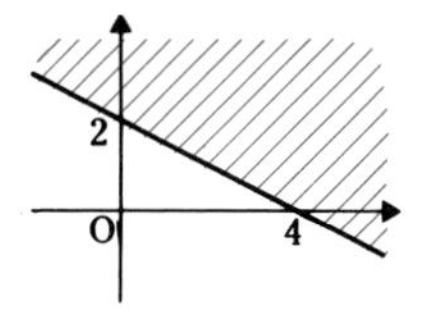

6.

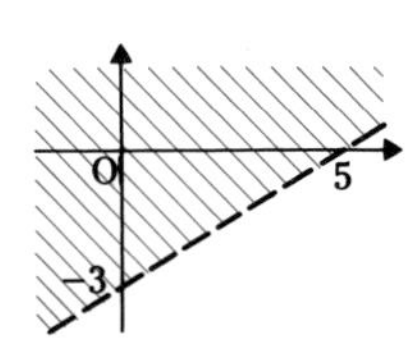

7. $2y-3x \leqslant 6$
8. $x+y<2$
9. $x+y>3$
10. $2x+y+4>0$

11.

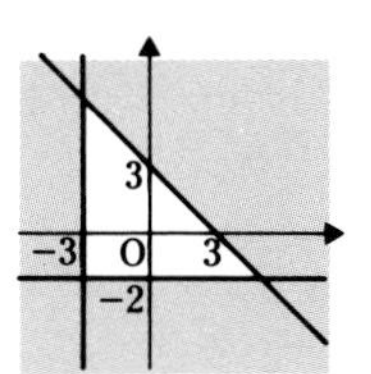

12.

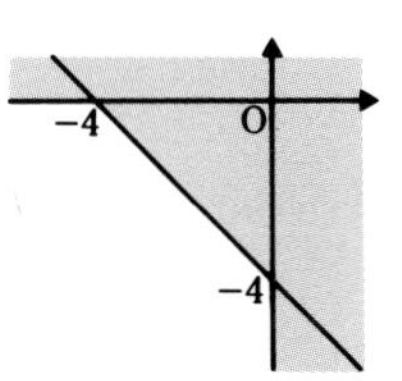

13.

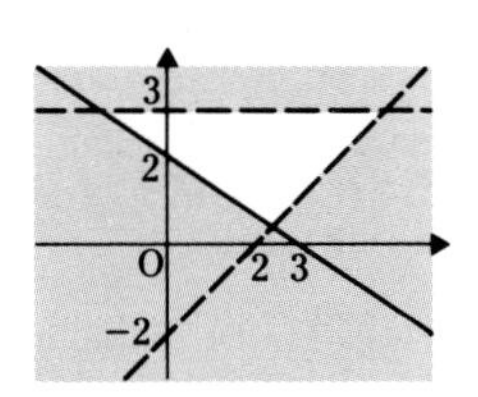

14.

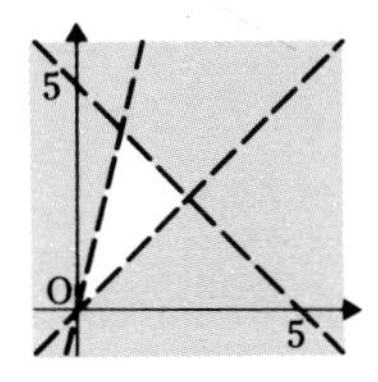

15.

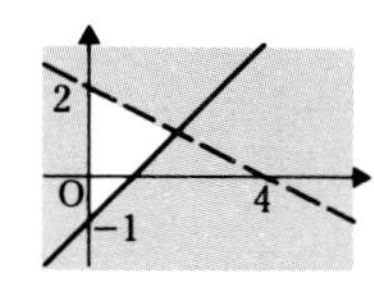

16. Does not exist
17. (a) Region consists of only one point (1, 2).
(b) Does not exist

Exercise 18c page 295

1.

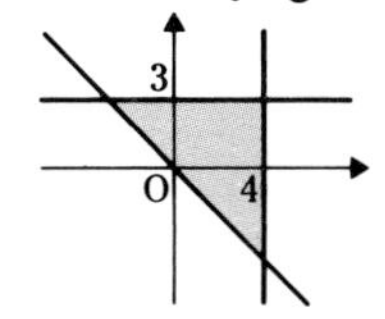

2.

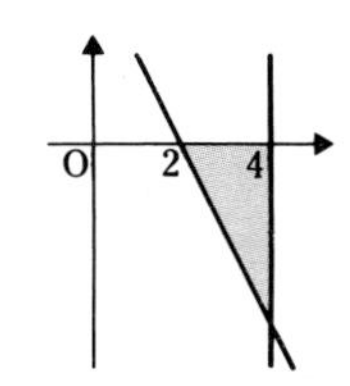

3.

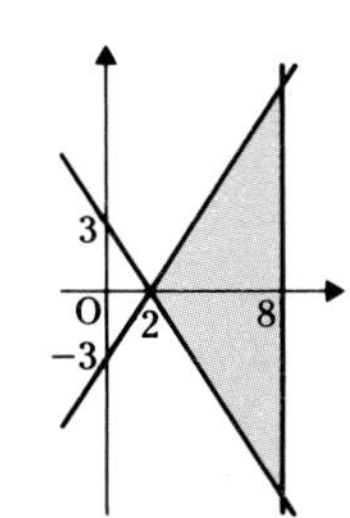

4.

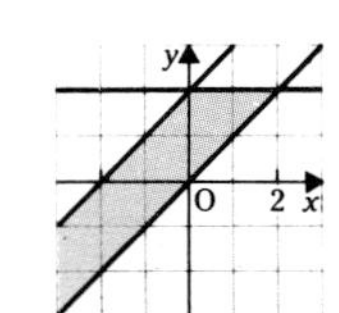

5.

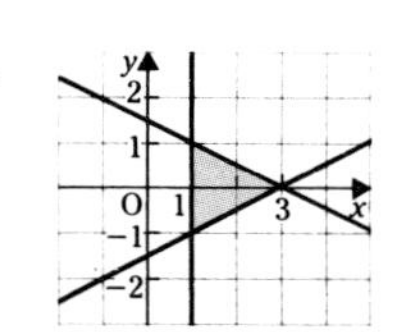

6. $y \geqslant 0,\quad 2y \leqslant x+2,\quad x+y \leqslant 4$
7. $x \leqslant 1,\quad y \leqslant x+1,\quad 3x+y>-3$
8. $y<3x+3,\quad y>3x-3$

9. $y \geqslant 0, \quad y \leqslant x+2$
10. (a) $x+y+4 \geqslant 0, \quad 3y \leqslant x, \quad y \geqslant x+4$
    (b) $3y \geqslant x, \quad y \leqslant x+4$
    (c) $3y \leqslant x, \quad y \leqslant x+4, \quad x+y+4 \geqslant 0$
    (d) $x+y+4 \leqslant 0, \quad 3y \geqslant x$
    (e) $3y \leqslant x, \quad y \geqslant x+4$
    (f) $x+y+4 \geqslant 0, \quad y \geqslant x+4$
11. (a) C (b) A (c) B
12. (a) (2, 2), (−2, 4), (−2, −2)
    (b) (2, 3), (−1, 0), (0, −2)
13. (−1, 0), (−1, 1), (−1, 2), (−1, 3), (0, −1), (0, 0), (0, 1), (0, 2), (0, 3), (1, 0), (1, 1), (1, 2), (2, 1)
14. (2, −1), (2, 0), (2, 1), (2, 2), (3, 1), (4, 0), (5, −1), (4, −1), (3, −1)

Exercise 18d page 298

1. $2x+2y \leqslant 20, \quad xy \geqslant 12$
2. $x \geqslant 2y, \quad x+\frac{1}{2}y < 100$
3. $3x+4y < 45, \quad y \leqslant x$
4. Barbara x years old, Christa y years old.
   (a) $x = 3y \quad x+y < 20$
   (b) 1, 2, 3 or 4 years old

Self-Assessment 18 page 299

1. (a) $-4 \leqslant x \leqslant 3$ and $-2 < y < 3$
   (b) $x > -2$ and $-1 \leqslant y \leqslant 2$
2. (a) 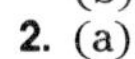

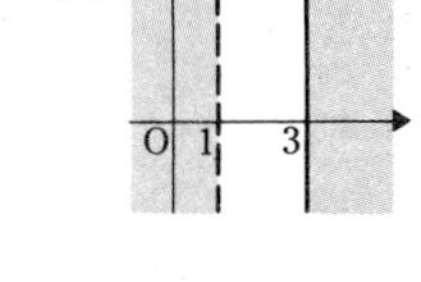

(b)

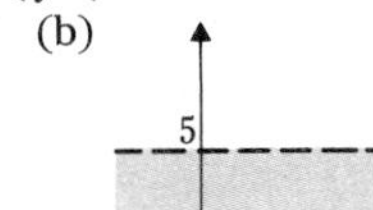

3.

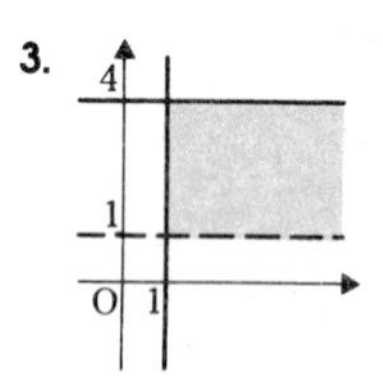

4. $y+2x > -3, \quad y+x \leqslant 0, \quad 3x-2y \leqslant 6$
5. (−2, 2), (−1, 0), (−1, 1), (0, 0), (0, −1), (0, −2), (1, −1)
6. 

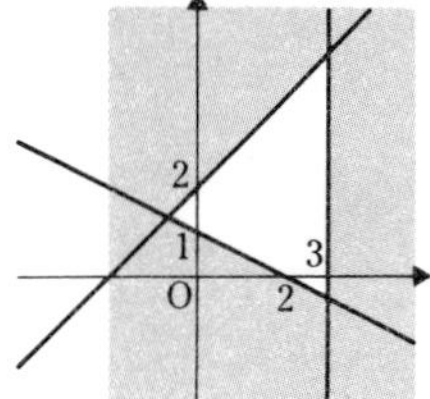

CHAPTER 19

Exercise 19a page 301

1. 0.7536
2. 3.1910
3. 0.1139
4. 0.6346
5. 36.9°
6. 55.5°
7. 2.3°
8. 75.7°
9. no
10. 35.0°
11. 40.6°
12. 53.1°
13. 60.6°
14. 43.0°
15. 42.0°
16. 49.4°
17. 43.1°
18. 1

Exercise 19b page 303

1. 4.69 cm
2. 3.56 cm
3. 0.918 cm
4. 13.9 cm
5. 9.02 cm
6. 3.70 cm
7. 4.41 cm
8. 43.3 cm
9. 9.60 cm
10. 30.4 m
11. (a) about 570 m (±30 m) (b) (ii)
12. 24.0°
13. 36.9°
14. 10.2 km
15. 39.8°
16. 5.96 cm, 29.8 cm^2
17. (a) 3.16, 6.32, 7.07 (c) 26.6°
    (b) $\widehat{B} = 90°$

Exercise 19c page 306

1. (a) 0.9703 (b) 0.1959 (c) 0.3827
2. (a) 0.4384 (b) 0.8517 (c) 0.9986
3. (a) 47.0° (b) 67.8° (c) 17.5°
4. (a) 83.1° (b) 67.4° (c) 63.6°
5. (a) $\frac{6}{10}$; 36.9° (b) $\frac{12}{13}$; 67.4°
6. (a) $\frac{16}{20}$; 36.9° (b) $\frac{8}{17}$; 61.9°
7. (a) sine (b) sine (c) cosine (d) sine
8. (a) 44.4° (b) 54.3° (c) 49.5° (d) 64.8°
9. (cos) 53.1°
10. (tan) 49.1°
11. (cos) 60°
12. (sin) 48.2°
13. $\tan A = \frac{3}{4}, \quad \sin A = \frac{3}{5}, \quad \cos A = \frac{4}{5}$

Exercise 19d page 308

1. 2.94 cm
2. 2.55 cm
3. 84.9 cm
4. 2.90 cm
5. 18.1 m
6. 7.98 cm
7. 4.17 m
8. 6.16 cm
9. 15.8 cm
10. 7.77 cm
11. 7.21 cm
12. 14.9 cm
13. 8.15 cm
14. 112.6°
15. 7.95 cm
16. (a) 24°
    (b) (i) 2.23 cm (ii) 5.47 cm
    (c) (i) 90°, 42° (ii) 4.07 cm
    (d) 4.07 cm, yes
17. 112 m
18. 23.6°
19. (a) 56.3° (b) 7.21 miles (c) 348.7°
20. 24.4 m
21. (a) 44.4° (b) 105.6°
22. (a) 32.0 km (b) 64.6 km (c) N26.3°W (d) 72.1 km
23. (a) 9.42 cm (b) 10.2 cm (c) 7.36 cm
24. (a) 17.4 ft (b) 12.2 ft (c) 38.1 ft
25. 79.7°
26. 0.75 m
27. (b) 2.61 m (c) 1.49 m
28. (a) 13 cm (b) 21.0°
29. (a) 55.5 m (b) 18.4° (c) 8.20°
    (d) AC gives the easier walk but DC is the more direct.

Self-Assessment 19 page 314

1. 0.8517, 0.5240, 1.625
2. (a) 67.5° (b) 47.8°
3. 49.7°
4. 9.40 cm
5. 64.6°
6. (a) 104° (b) 7.88 miles (c) 073°
7. (a) 35.4 miles (b) 7.07 miles (c) 258.7°
8. (a) 5 cm (c) 21.8°
9. (a) 18.5 m, 29.5 m, 11 m
   (b) 23.6 m, 5.21 m, 28.8 m
   (c) 69° with the horizontal.
10. (a) 4.60 cm
    (b) (i) 1.93 cm (ii) 1.07 cm
    (c) 130°
    (d) OA = OC (radii)
    (e) 5.44 cm

CHAPTER 20

Exercise 20a page 317

1. (a) x^2-2x (b) $6x-3x^2$ (c) $10x-6x^2$ (d) $2a^2-5a$ (e) $2p-2p^2$ (f) $10a-15a^2$ (g) $4s^2+10s$ (h) $-x^2-2xy$ (i) $2x^2+2xy$ (j) $-2pq+3p^2$ (k) $2a^2-4ab$ (l) $12st-8s^2$
2. (a) x^2-x+6 (b) $3x^2-17x-24$ (c) $2x-x^2$ (d) $2ab+2ac-2b-4c$ (e) $-3x$ (f) $4x-3x^2$
3. (a) x^2+5x+6 (b) x^2+2x-8 (c) $2x^2-7x-15$ (d) $6x^2+14x+4$ (e) $2x^2-17x+21$ (f) $a^2+ab-ac-bc$ (g) $ps-pt+qs-qt$ (h) $x^2-2xz-xy+2yz$ (i) $x^2-5xy+6y^2$ (j) $a^2+ab-2b^2$ (k) $4p^2-q^2$ (l) $6x^2+3xz+4xy+2yz$
4. (a) x^2+5x+4 (b) x^2+3x+2 (c) a^2+6a+5 (d) $a^2+8a+15$ (e) $t^2+10t+21$ (f) $p^2+7p+10$ (g) $x^2+14x+48$ (h) $x^2+13x+30$
5. (a) x^2-5x+6 (b) $x^2-7x+12$ (c) $x^2-7x+10$ (d) a^2-5a+4 (e) $s^2-9s+20$ (f) $x^2-13x+42$ (g) $p^2-10p+24$ (h) $t^2-12t+32$
6. (a) $x^2+4x-12$ (b) x^2+x-6 (c) x^2-x-12 (d) $x^2+2x-15$ (e) $t^2-2t-48$ (f) $p^2-2p-15$ (g) $a^2-4a-21$ (h) $x^2+5x-36$ (i) $x^2+4x-21$ (j) y^2-y-2
7. (a) $3x^2-x-10$ (b) $6x^2-19x-7$ (c) $4s^2-4s-15$ (d) $8x^2+22x-21$ (e) $9x^2-1$ (f) $14x^2-3x-5$ (g) $35x^2-2x-1$ (h) $15x^2+2x-1$ (i) $4a^2-25$
8. (a) $15t^2+19t+6$ (b) $12x^2+23x-24$ (c) $16x^2+38x-5$ (d) $10a^2-41a+21$ (e) $6-5x+x^2$ (f) $5+7y+2y^2$ (g) $24-34x-3x^2$ (h) $10+x-2x^2$ (i) $24-38y+15y^2$

Exercise 20b page 318

1. (a) x^2+2x+1 (b) x^2+4x+4 (c) $y^2+8y+16$ (d) $a^2+14a+49$ (e) $x^2+2xy+y^2$ (f) $a^2+2ab+b^2$ (g) $p^2+2pq+q^2$ (h) $x^2+16x+64$
2. (a) x^2-2x+1 (b) $x^2-10x+25$ (c) $t^2-18t+81$ (d) $p^2-12p+36$ (e) $x^2-2xy+y^2$ (f) $a^2-2ab+b^2$ (g) $y^2-14y+49$ (h) $x^2-18x+81$
3. (a) x^2-1 (b) x^2-16 (c) c^2-4 (d) y^2-25 (e) x^2-y^2 (f) a^2-b^2 (g) x^2-49 (h) t^2-36
4. (a) $9x^2+6x+1$ (b) $25x^2-20x+4$ (c) $9y^2+12y+4$ (d) $4a^2-12a+9$ (e) $9x^2-6x+1$ (f) $16x^2+24x+9$
5. (a) $4x^2-49$ (b) $9x^2-1$ (c) $16x^2-25$ (d) $4a^2-49$

Exercise 20c page 319

1. (a) $3(x+2)$ (b) $4(y-2)$ (c) $3(2a-3)$ (d) $2(a+2b)$ (e) $5(2p-1)$ (f) $4(2-3x)$ (g) $3(2-5a)$ (h) $2(a+2b)$ (i) $3(4x-3y)$ (j) $2(4q-9p)$
2. (a) $x(x+3)$ (b) $b(b+6)$ (c) $y(y-2)$ (d) $x(3x+2)$ (e) $a(4-a)$ (f) $x(x-4)$ (g) $b(4b-1)$ (h) $p(1-p)$
3. (a) $3(x^2+2x+3)$ (b) $5(2x^2-x-4)$ (c) $4(4-3x-5x^2)$ (d) $x(5y-2z+3)$ (e) $a(b-2c+4d)$ (f) $3y(y^2+2y-3)$
4. (a) $2x(x-2)$ (b) $5x(y+2z)$ (c) $x^2(1+x)$ (d) $4bc(2a-3d)$ (e) $3y(x+2y-3)$ (f) $5b(a+2c-d)$
5. (a) $m(g-a)$ (b) $\pi r(2+h)$ (c) $\pi(R^2-r^2)$ (d) $2r(h_1-h_2)$ (e) $\frac{1}{2}m(u^2-v^2)$ (f) $\pi r(2h+r)$ (g) $x^2(a-b)$ (h) $\frac{1}{2}h(a-b)$ (i) $r(\pi r+4+r)$ (j) $ax(x+a)$ (k) $P\left(1+\frac{RT}{100}\right)$ (l) $m(gh-\frac{1}{2}v^2)$

Exercise 20d page 320

1. (a) $p=\frac{T}{(2+h)}$ (b) $C=\frac{M}{(n-3)}$ (c) $r=\frac{(hl-g)}{\pi h}$ (d) $r=\frac{V}{(a^2+\pi ah)}$ (e) $a=\frac{(vh-r^2)}{v}$ (f) $h_1=\frac{(A+2\pi rh_2)}{2\pi r}$
2. (a) $\frac{2a}{(4a-3b)}$ (b) $\frac{2q}{(p-q)}$ (c) $\frac{1}{a}$ (d) $\frac{3}{a}$

3. (a) $h = \dfrac{(A-\pi r^2)}{\pi r}$ (d) $P = \dfrac{1}{(r-R)}$

(b) $u = \pm\sqrt{(v^2-2as)}$ (e) $v = \dfrac{(2s-ut)}{t}$

(c) $a = \dfrac{(2s-2ut)}{t^2}$ (f) $y = (X-a)^2$

Self-Assessment 20 page 321

1. (a) $12x-8x^2$ (d) $4x^2-12x+9$
(b) $6+6x-x^2$ (e) $4a^2-b^2$
(c) $6x^2+x-12$ (f) $48-32x-3x^2$

2. (a) $5(2a-b)$ (d) $4(p-9q)$
(b) $3y(x-3z)$ (e) $\pi r(h-r)$
(c) $2\pi(r_1-r_2)$ (f) $7b(b-2)$

3. (a) $v = \dfrac{(d+Tu)}{T}$ (c) $v = \dfrac{at}{(2t-a)}$

(b) $v = \dfrac{at}{s-2}$ (d) $v = \pm\sqrt{u^2-2as}$

CHAPTER 21

Exercise 21a page 323

1. (a) 3 tons/acre
(b) $27\frac{1}{2}$ lb/acre
(c) 3.9 tons/acre
(d) 30 lb/acre or 50 lb/acre

2. (a) (i) \$166.5 (ii) \$254.7
(b) about 6 yr 1 month

3. (a) 200 t (b) 3.16 cm

4. (a) 3 (b) (i) 59 (ii) 76.5

5. (a) (i) 12 °C (ii) 4 °C
(b) $3\frac{1}{2}$ min

Exercise 21b page 326

1. Graphs drawn to half scale

x	1	2	3	4	5
y	3	12	27	48	75

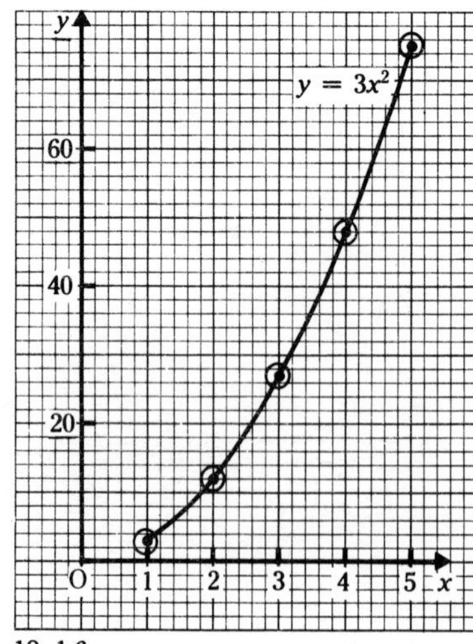

19, 1.6

2.

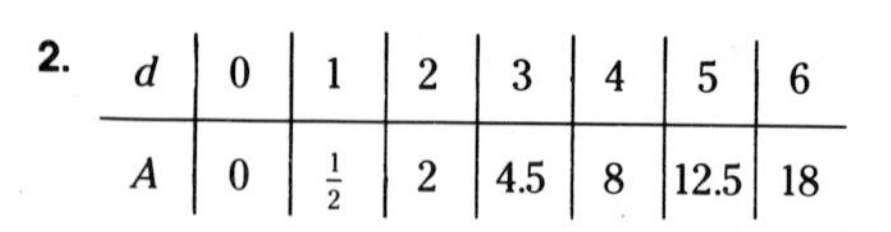

d	0	1	2	3	4	5	6
A	0	$\frac{1}{2}$	2	4.5	8	12.5	18

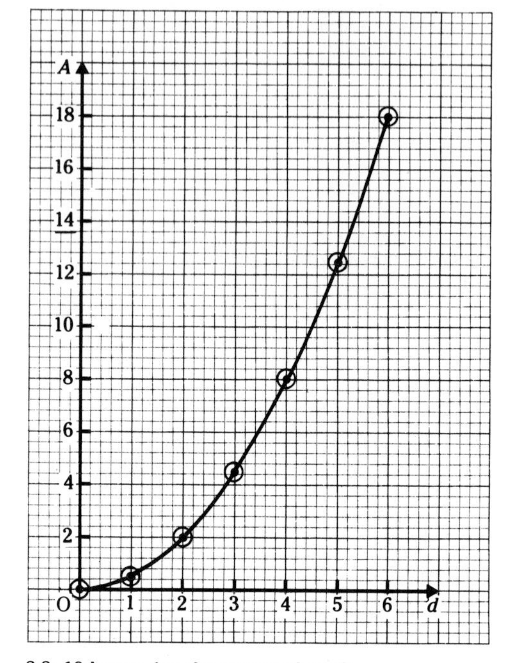

2.8; 19 hours (to the nearest hour)

3. (a) 84 m (b) 6.25 s

4. (a) 2.1 (b) 1.3

5. (a) 23.7 (b) 3.3 (c) 0.6 (d) −3.2

6. (a) 2.25 when $x = 1.5$ (c) 0.38 and 2.62
(b) 0 and 3

7. (a) −1, 1, 3
(b) (i) −0.9, 0.75, 3.1 (ii) −1.6
(c) 3.1 when $x = -0.15$
(d) any value of x greater than 3.31

8. (a) 2
(b) 8/0 is indeterminate
(c) (i) 1.9 (ii) −2.35
(d) (i) 1.90 (ii) −2.35

9. From −1.74 to 5.74

10. (a) 1.17, 6.83 (b) From 1.17 to 6.83

Exercise 21c page 332

1. A(0, −8)

2. vertex at (0, 0);
through (−2, 0), (2, 0) and (0, −4);
through (−2, 0), (2, 0) and (0, 4)

(a) a translation 4 units vertically downward
(b) reflection in the x-axis

3. A(0, 16)

4. (a) $y \to 0$ (b) no (c) no

5.

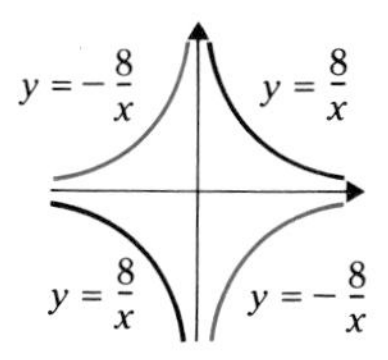

6. B
7. C
8. A
9. C

Exercise 21d page 334

1. $26\frac{2}{3}$ cm
2. (a) (i) 12.6 cm (ii) 16.7 cm
(b) (i) 0.75 ℓ (ii) 4.03 ℓ
3. (a) $(30-2x)$ cm and $2(30-2x)$ cm $= (60-4x)$ cm
(c) 4000 cm^3 when $x = 5$
(d) $6\frac{2}{3}$%
4. (a) 6.5, 7
(c) (i) 7.19 m (ii) 1.29 m or 0.31 m
(d) 0.63 m
5. base 4.16 m by 4.16 m, depth 2.08 m
6. (a) Beginning of wk 1 to end of wk 3, and from beginning of wk 7 to the early part of wk 11.
(b) Beginning of wk 4 to the end of wk 6 and from the middle of wk 11 on.
(c) (i) end of wk 6 (ii) early in wk 11
(d) probably a fall in price
(e) false

Exercise 21e page 337

1. $x \leqslant -1$ and $x \geqslant 1$
2. $-4 < x < 4$
3. $-5 \leqslant x \leqslant 5$
4. (a)

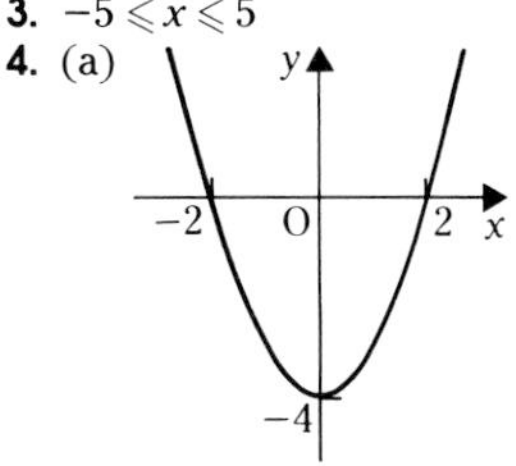

(b) $(-2, 0)$ and $(2, 0)$
(c) $-2 < x < 2$

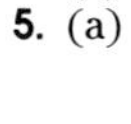

5. (a)

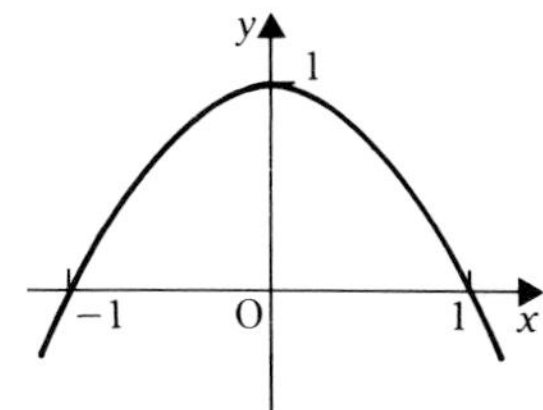

(b) $(-1, 0)$, $(1, 0)$
(c) $x < -1$ and $x > 1$
6. (a) 9 (b) $x \leqslant -3$ and $x \geqslant 3$

Exercise 21f page 339

1. 0.6
2. 1 and 2, 1.1
3. 1.71
(a) $x^3 - x - 1 = 0$
(b) 1 and 2
(c) 1.32
5. (a) $0 = x - 3 - \frac{2}{x+1}$
(b) 3, 4
(c) 3.45

Self-Assessment 21 page 364

1. (a) -16.25 when $x = -2.5$
(b) -5.85, 0.85
2. 1.6
3. (a)

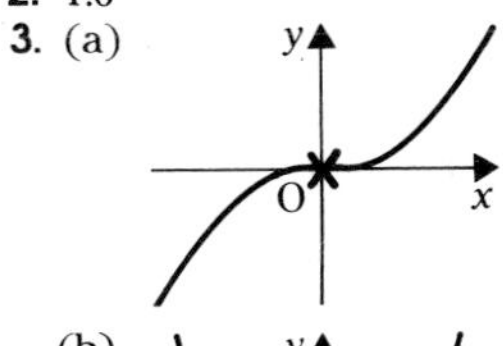

(b)

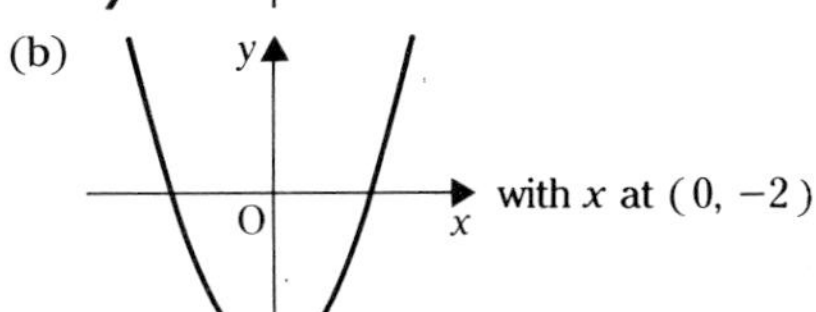

(c)

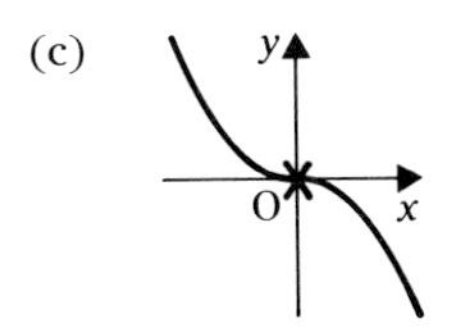

(d)

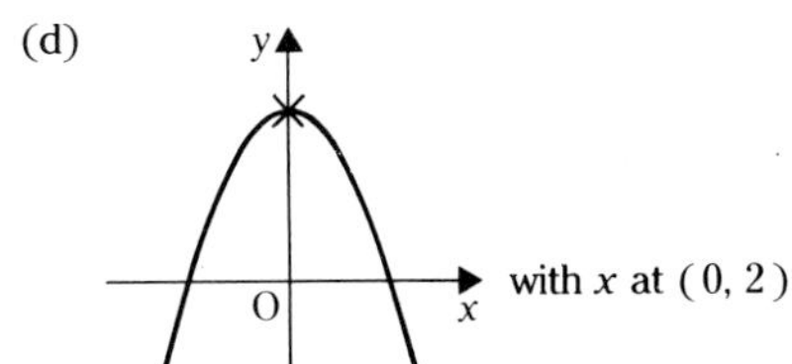

4. (a)

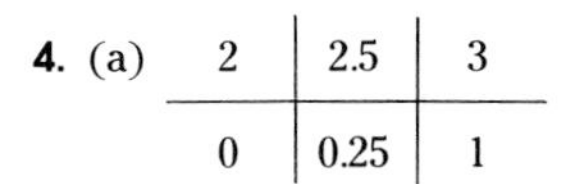

2	2.5	3
0	0.25	1

(b) & (c)

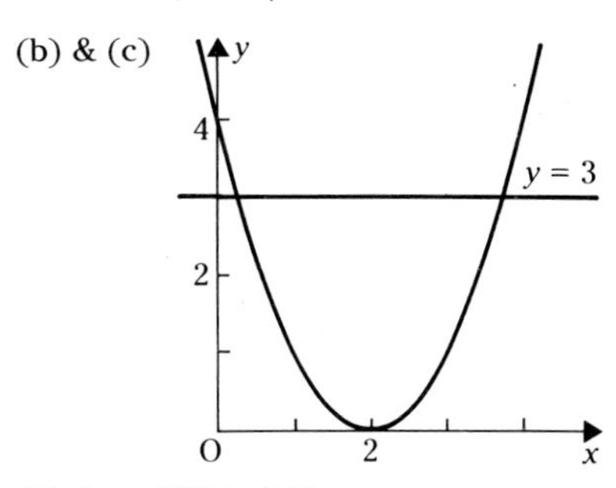

(d) from 0.27 to 3.73
5. B

6. (a) £732
   (b) 10.5 m.p.h. and 28.5 m.p.h.
   (c) 17.3 m.p.h.
7. $-3 < x < 2$
8. 2.54

CHAPTER 22

Exercise 22a page 343

1. (a) 7 m/s (b) 18 m.p.h.
2. (a) 72 m (b) 59.5 km
3. (a) 3 s (b) 4.72 h (3 s.f.)
4. (a) 280 miles
   (b) 56 m.p.h.
   (c) No, the speeds are not equally important.
5. (a) $0.1\,\text{m s}^{-1}$ (c) $8.33\,\text{m s}^{-1}$ (3 s.f.)
   (b) 167 m/min (3 s.f.) (d) 32.4 km/h
6. (a) Steady speed of 0.75 m/s, distance 6 m.
   (b) Steady speed of 0.5 m/s, distance 4 m.
   (c) At rest 4 m from A.

Exercise 22b page 345

1. (a) speed (d) displacement
   (b) distance (e) velocity
   (c) velocity (f) speed
2. (a) Starts from A and moves 6 m in 8 s at 0.75 m/s, then returns to A in 3 s at 2 m/s, i.e. with velocity -2 m/s.
   (b) Starts 2 m from A and moves 3 m in 3 s at 1 m/s then 1 m in 5 s at 0.2 m/s.
   (c) Starts 2 km from A and moves 4 km in 4 h at 1 km/h, is then stationary 6 km from A for 4 h.
   (d) Starts 30 m from A and moves 20 m back towards A in 3 h at 6.67 m/h then remains at rest for 3 h before moving 10 m back to A in 2 h with velocity -5 m/h.
3. (a)

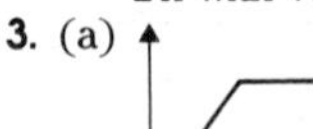

(b)

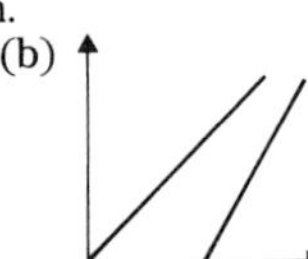

4. 1st train: leaves A at 12 noon, travels 60 km in 1 h 48 m at 33.3 km/h; rests 1 h 12 m; returns to A in 2 h with velocity -30 km/h.
   2nd train: leaves A at 1 p.m., travels 20 km in 1 h at 20 km/h; rests 12 m; continues in same direction, travelling 40 km in 1 h 48 m at 22.2 km/h. They pass travelling in opposite directions.
5. (a)

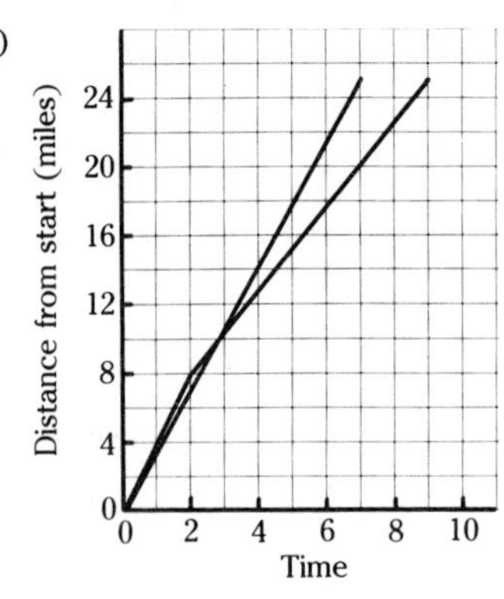

   (b) 40 km/h
   (c) At about 1.50 p.m., 33 km from A
   (d) 100 km/h

Exercise 22c page 348

1. (a) (i) 9 m (ii) 19.7 m (iii) 13 m
   (b) after 2 s
   (c) at the start
   (d) 4 s
2. (b) 3.1 m
3. (b) 0.4 m (c) when $t = 4$
4. (a) 17 m (c) Jim
   (b) after 8.3 s (d) 5 m
5. (a)

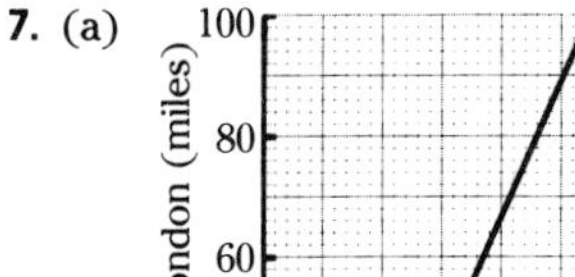

   (b) 10 miles
6. (a) 55 m (c) 1 s (e) 24 m
   (b) $1\frac{1}{2}$ s (d) 3.75 s
7. (a)

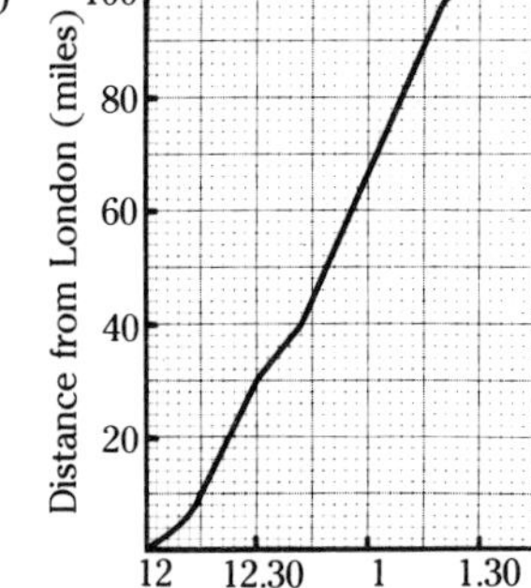

   (b) $1\frac{1}{2}$ h

Exercise 22d page 351

1. (a) Population increasing at constant rate.
   (b) Population increasing, slowly at first then faster.
   (c) Population decreasing, slowly at first then faster then more slowly again.
   (d) Population decreasing fast at first, but ultimately not at all.
2. (a) 1960 (b) 1900–5
3. (b) 1981–2 (c) no
4. (a)

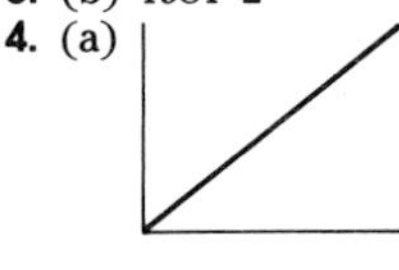

(b)

(c)

Self-Assessment 22 page 352

1. 40 km/h
2. (a) velocity (b) speed
3. (a) Starting from A it travels at a steady speed for 1 h. It is stationary for $\frac{3}{4}$ h, then travels back, fast to start with, then gradually slowing down to come to rest after $1\frac{1}{4}$ h, 20 km from A.
   (b) 60 km/h
4. (a) Decreases as it rises until it becomes zero at its highest point, then increases as it falls to the ground.
   (b) It gradually increases from zero then decreases to zero.
   (c) no
5. (a)

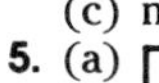

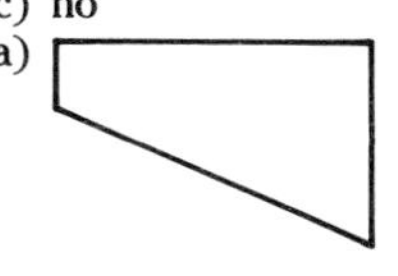

(b)

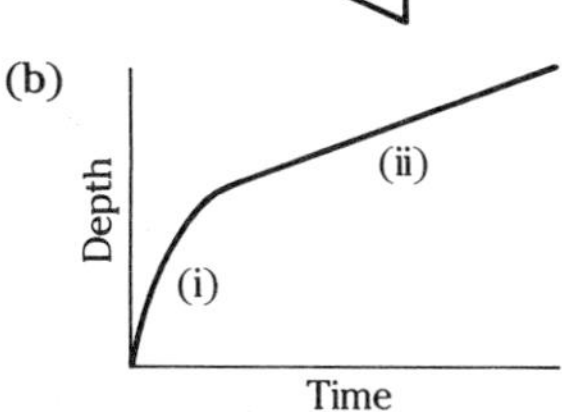

CHAPTER 23

Exercise 23b page 359

1. (a) 9
   (b) 5
   (c) dog 9; cat 8; bird 5; other pet 7
   (d) 29
   (e) not possible to know
2. (a) M 10; W 9; B 6; G 7
   (b)

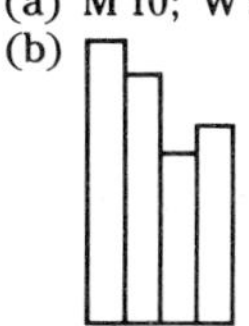

   (c) 16 of each
   (d) 1
   (e) 32
3. (a) $3\frac{1}{2}$–4 (b) $1\frac{1}{2}$–2 (c) no (d) 40
4. (a) 30, 89
   (b)

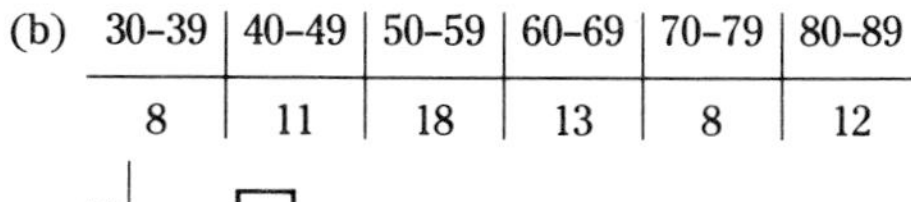

30–39	40–49	50–59	60–69	70–79	80–89
8	11	18	13	8	12

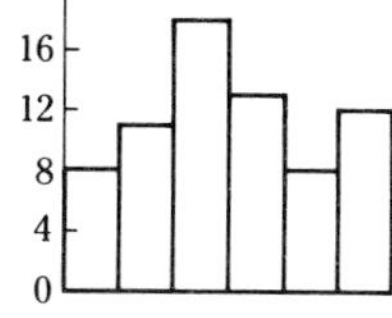

   (d) 50–59 (18)
   (e) 4

Exercise 23c page 362

1. (a) can take distinct values only
   (b) continuous
   (c) can take distinct values only
   (d) continuous
   (e) continuous
   (f) continuous
   (g) continuous
   (h) can take distinct values only
2. (a) 1 (b) 7 (c) 20 (d) no
3.

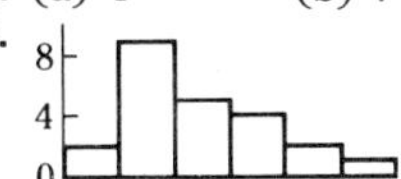

4. (a) 13 (c) $140 < h \leqslant 145$
   (b) 25 (d) cannot tell from bar chart
5. (a) 47 kg
   (b) $59.5 \leqslant w < 60.5$
   (c) 20, 61, 13, 6: Total 100
   (d) 81
   (e) Because 100 kg is in the middle of a group.

Exercise 23d page 364

1.

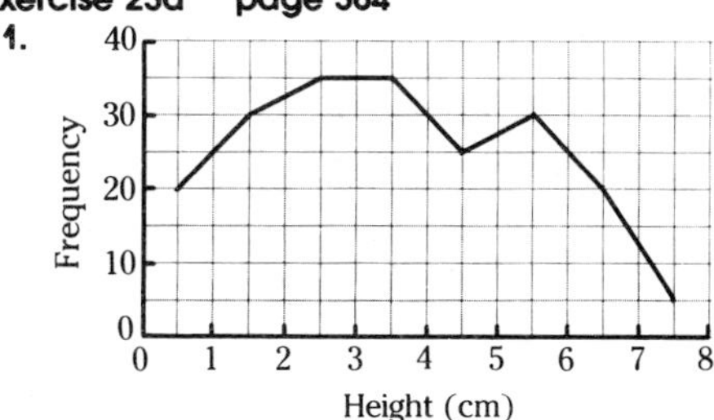

2.

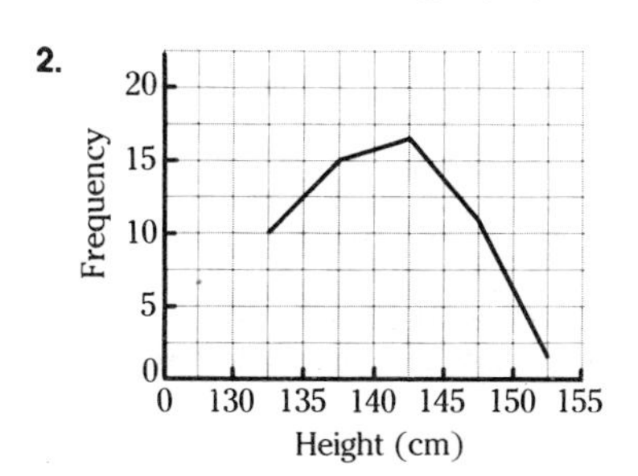

3. (a) Midway value | 0.5 | 1.5 | 2.5 | 3.5 | 4.5

   (b)

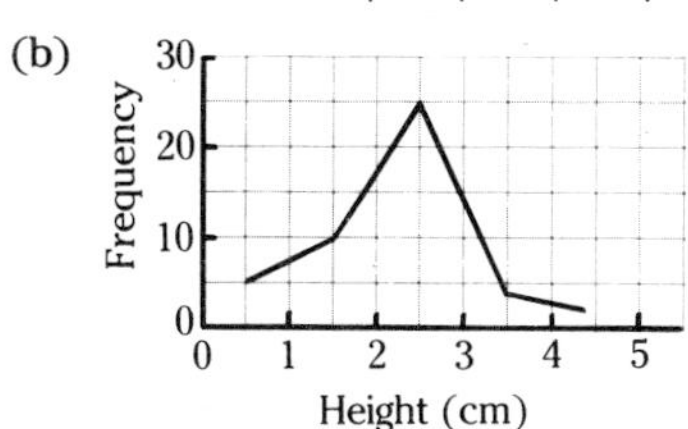

4. (a)

Mid-way values	5	15	25	35	45

(b)

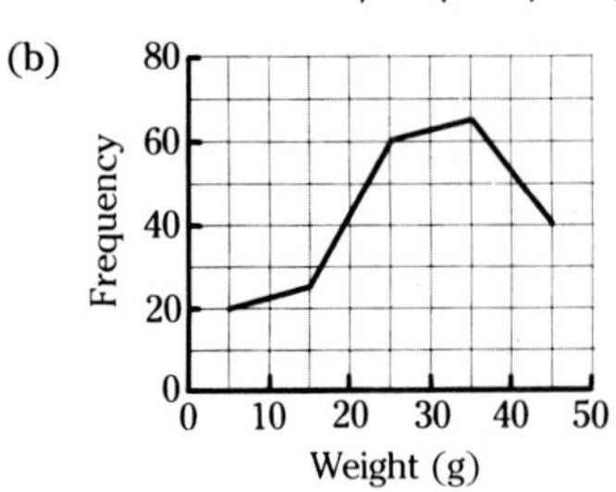

5.

6. (a) 10 (b) 47 (c) 0 to 2 cm

(d)

Height, cm	$0 \leqslant h < 2$	$2 \leqslant h < 4$	$4 \leqslant h < 6$	$6 \leqslant h < 8$	$8 \leqslant h < 10$
Frequency	10	1	4	18	14

(e) This includes failures

7. (a)

Number of apples, x	$0 \leqslant x < 50$	$50 \leqslant x < 100$	$100 \leqslant x < 150$	$150 \leqslant x < 200$	$200 \leqslant x < 250$
Frequency	1	3	8	20	11

(b) 43
(c) 4
(d) e.g.

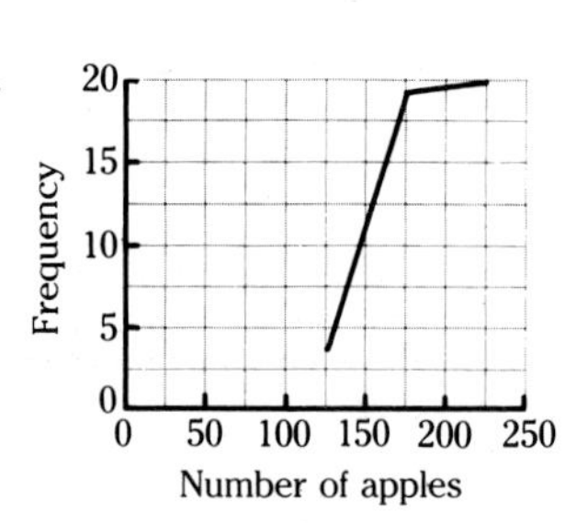

Exercise 23e page 369

1. 96°, 132°, 60°, 42°, 30°
2. 128°, 152°, 48°, 24°, 8°
3. 108°, 180°, 40°, 18°, 14°
4. (a) $\frac{1}{4}$ (c) £45 (e) £120
(b) $\frac{1}{12}$ (d) £15
5. car $\frac{13}{120}$, cycle $\frac{2}{15}$, bus $\frac{63}{180}$, walk $\frac{49}{120}$
(b) 441 (d) 84
(c) 189 (e) 10.8%
6. (a) (i) 10% (ii) 14%
(b) under 10 and 10–19 years
7. (a) 2.6 million, 4.3 million, 65%
(b) 600, 1300
(c) 16–24 year-olds, 20 year-old male
(d) 3.3%, 142 000
(e) 4.5%
(f) Northern Ireland
(g) theft from person

Exercise 23f page 372

1. (a) The base line is drawn at too high a level. Profits are fairly flat.
(b) about $7\frac{1}{2}$%
2. (a) no. The base line is drawn at such a high figure that the weight loss appears grossly exaggerated.
(b) $\frac{3}{4}$% (0.75%)
3. (a) no
(b) no, exaggerates the percentage given to charity.
4. (a) Successful treatment is rising faster and faster.
(b) no
(c) Vertical scale not equally spaced, horizontal scale not based on the same number of months.
(d)

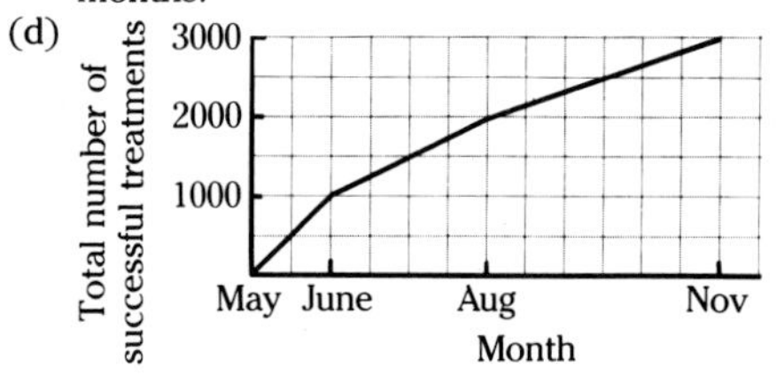

5. (a) 8%
(b) £108
(c) They were not rising as quickly as in 1989 and 1990.
(d) £105
6. (a) 4000
(b) no; because we 'see' the *volume* of the blocks, not just their height, the monthly increase is exaggerated.

Exercise 23g page 376

1. 3, + or − 1 orange
2. (a) no (?) (b) about 1800 g
(c) No, because koi don't grow indefinitely at the same rate.

3. (a) fairly good
   (b) His height is likely to be between 160 cm and 175 cm, but this is a wide range so the information is not very useful.
4. Too much scatter to give an opinion.
5. about 165 cm to 174 cm

Self-Assessment 23 page 378

1.

Number of heads	0	1	2	3	4	5
Frequency	4	5	11	11	4	3

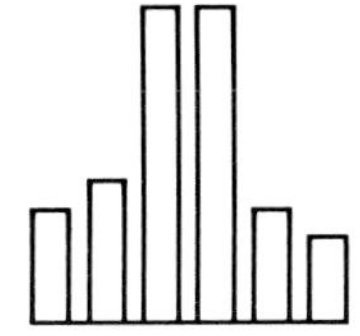

2.

Time, t sec	Frequency
$0 \leqslant t < 40$	19
$40 \leqslant t < 80$	20
$80 \leqslant t < 120$	5
$120 \leqslant t < 160$	2

3.

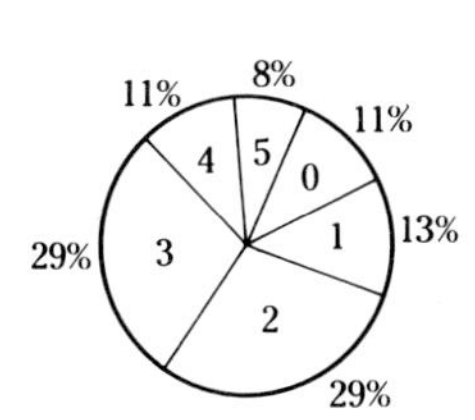

4. (a)

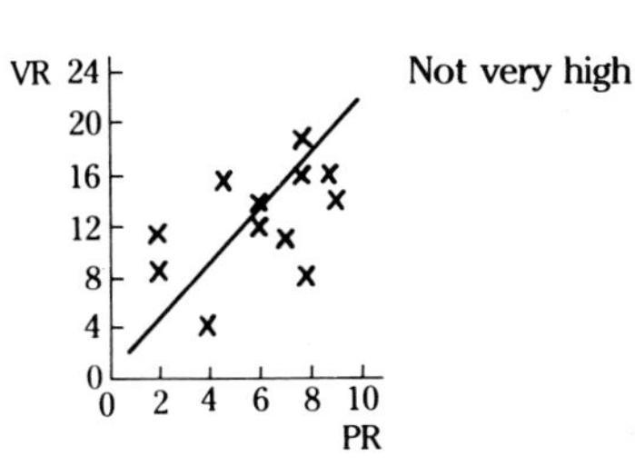

Not very high

   (c) She is likely to score 6 or higher.

5. (a) Costs that an employer must pay in addition to the pay per worker.
   (b) Japan
   (c) That it is $2\frac{1}{2}$ times as much in France as in Britain.
   (d) They are about half as much again, i.e. $1\frac{1}{2}$ times.

6. (a) 1991
   (b) £2.52 billion
   (c) 11.51%
   (d) £0.165 billion

CHAPTER 24

Exercise 24a page 382

1. (a)

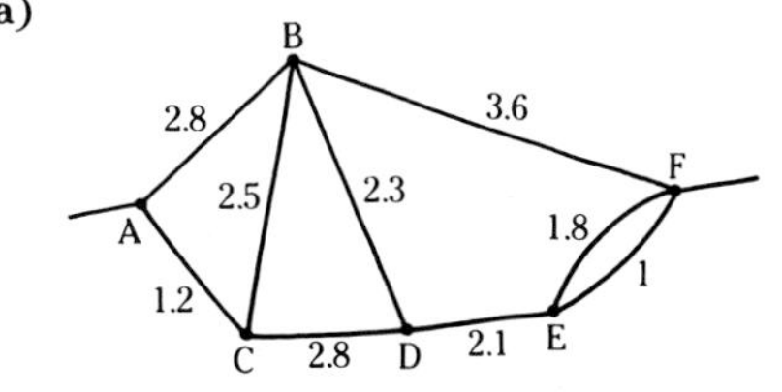

   (b) ACDBEF; 9 km approximately
   (c) no
2. (a) ADECF or ABCF 29 km
   (b) ADBCEF 48 km
   (c) e.g. CEFCBADE 71 km
3. (a) AFED or ABCED 65 min
   (b) ABFECD 130 min
   (c) AFEDECBA or ABCEDEFA 130 min
4.

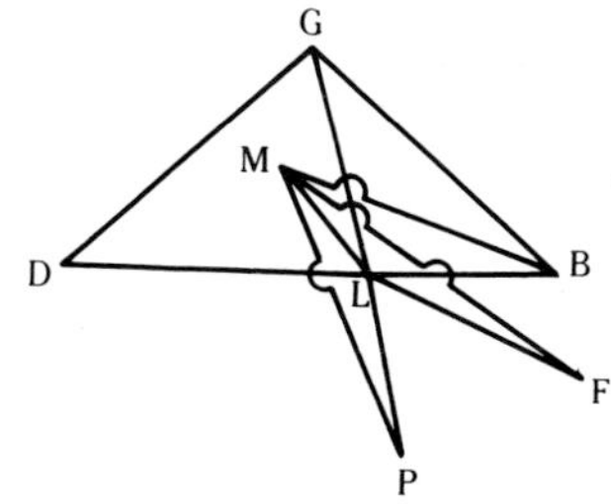

5. (a) Beverley is the oldest, Colin the youngest, Andrew and Janet in between. There is no information about Janet's and Andrew's relative ages.
   (b) e.g.

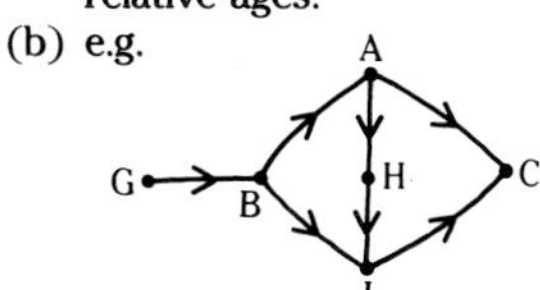

6. (a) 9
   (b)

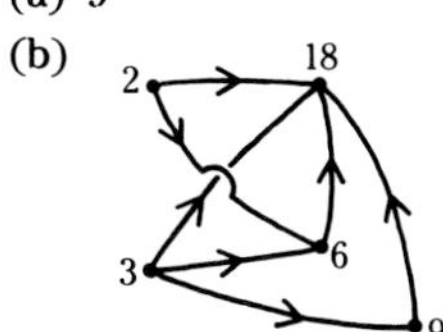

   (c)

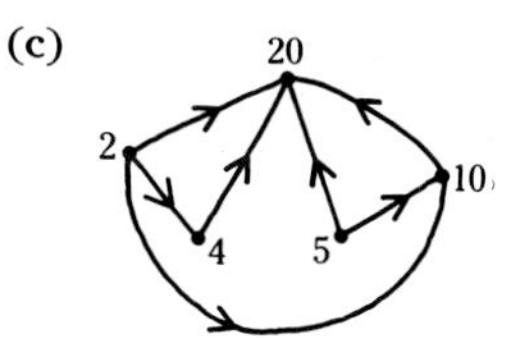

   (d) A loop at each point, e.g.

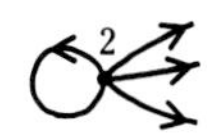

7. (a) Charles
   (b) (i) Brother (ii) Uncle
   (iii) Granddaughter

8. 'is not shorter than'

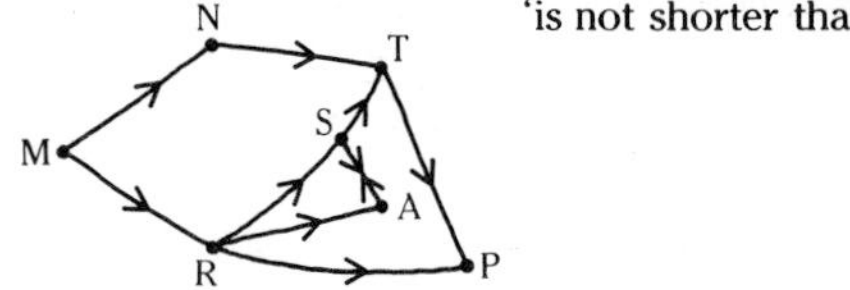

9. (a) Anne
   (b) Dave and Eric; not possible to tell
10. e.g.

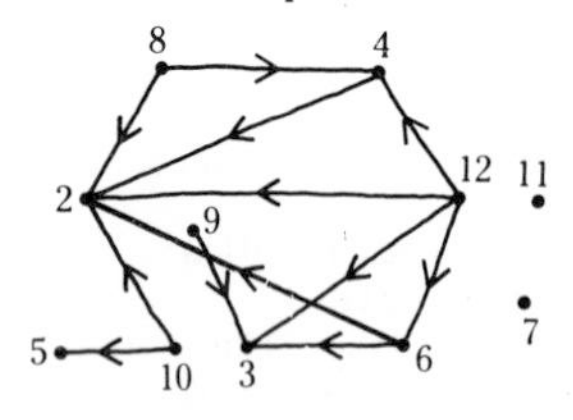

11. (a) $7 + 12 + 2 + 8 + 2 = 31$
    (b) $9 + 2 + 1 + 5 + 2 + 7 = 26$

CHAPTER 25

Exercise 25a page 388

1. (a) 3 (b) 2
2.

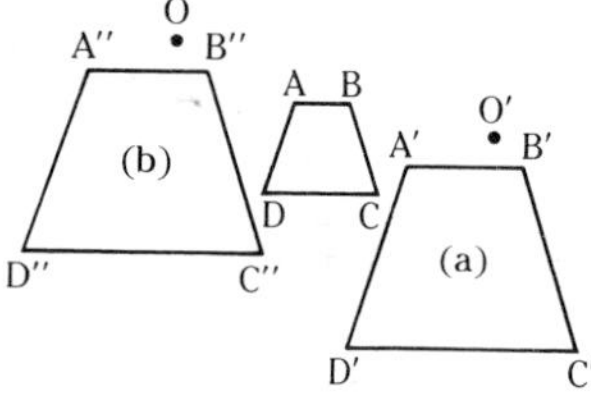

5. (a) $A_1(3, 8)$, $B_1(9, 2)$, $C_1(3, -4)$, $D_1(-3, 2)$
   (b) $A_2(5, 3)$, $B_2(6, 2)$, $C_2(5, 1)$, $D_2(4, 2)$
   (c) $A_1D_1 = 6A_2D_2$
6. $(-7, -2)$, 3
7. $(2, -2)$, $\frac{1}{3}$
8. $(1, 3)$, the centre of enlargement

Exercise 25b page 391

1. (a) 9 cm in the model becomes 36 cm full size.
   (b) 1 m
2. (a) 18.3 cm^2
3. (a) 1.25 m (b) 30 cm (c) 60°
4. 3.25 m
5. 6 cm
6. (a) (i) 8 cm (ii) 9 cm (b) 8 cm
7. (a) 3 cm and 2 cm
   (b)

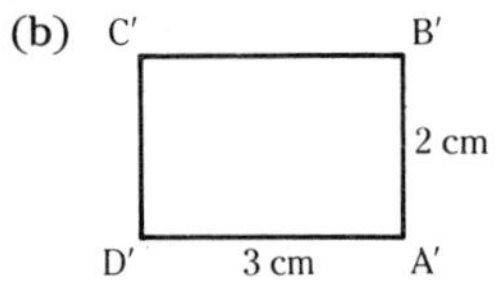

   (c) Each of ALA', etc must be a straight line
8. 66 ft
9. $7\frac{1}{2}$ cm

Self-Assessment 25 page 395

1. $(-1, 3)$, 3
2. (a) 8 cm (b) $2\frac{1}{2}$ cm
3. 8 cm
4. (a) 1.5 (b) 5.4 cm
5. (a) 45 cm (b) 4 cm

CHAPTER 26

Exercise 26a page 397

1. a circle
2. (a) vertical straight line
   (b)

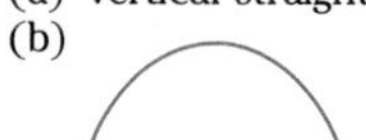

3. arc of a circle
4. (a) straight line parallel to road
   (b)
   (c)

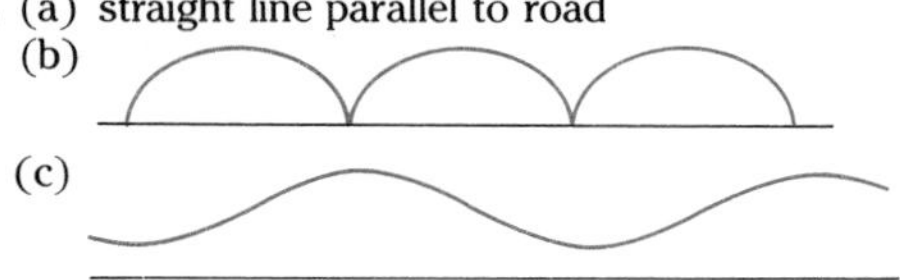

5.

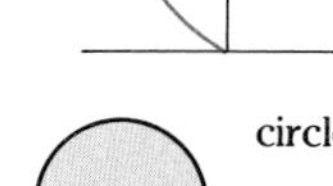

6. circle and its interior, radius 6 m
7.
8. perpendicular bisector of AB
   A B
9. pair of parallel lines
10. pair of angle bisectors
11. arc of a circle
12.

Exercise 26b page 398

1. diameter perpendicular to AB
2. circle centre C radius 4 cm
3. 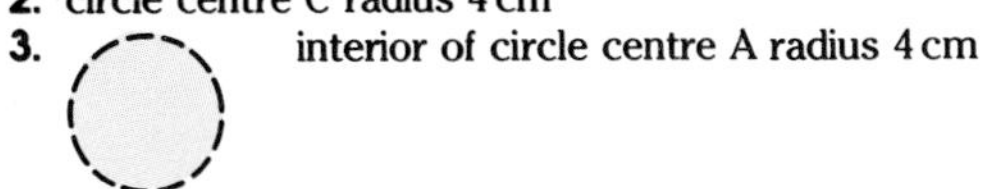 interior of circle centre A radius 4 cm
4. boundary is perpendicular bisector of AB
5. circle centre A radius 6 cm
6. boundaries are parallel lines
7. 4.6 cm
8. 8.1 m, 13.8 m
9. 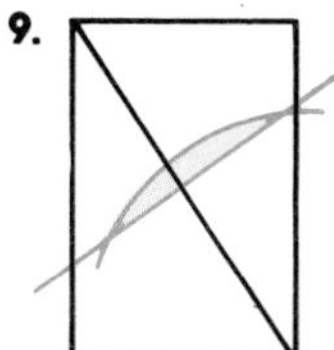
   (a) 6.4 m
   (b) less than 8.9 m
10. (a) semicircle centre A
    (b) semicircle centre B
    (c) semicircle centre midpoint of AB
    (d) semicircle centre midpoint of AB, radius 5 cm
11. Square, four times the size of the original drawing
12. (a) and (b) 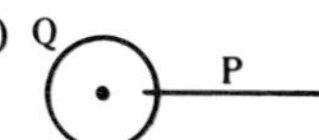

    (c) 15 and 5 cm

Exercise 26c page 402

1. horizontal arc of 80°, radius 1 m
2. plane parallel to the floor, 1 m up
3. hemisphere centre Q, radius 80 cm
4. pair of planes parallel to the floor
5. (a) sphere centre Q, radius 10 cm
   (b) two spheres centre Q, radii 6 and 2 cm
   (c) sphere centre Q, radius 8 cm, and point Q
6. curved surface of cylinder with same axis as the wire and radius 2 cm more than the radius of the wire
7. part of sphere, centre the hive, between the ground and a plane parallel to the ground and 1 m from it
8. plane perpendicular to line joining the nests, through the midpoint
9. (a) arcs of circles of radii WX and WY
   (b) 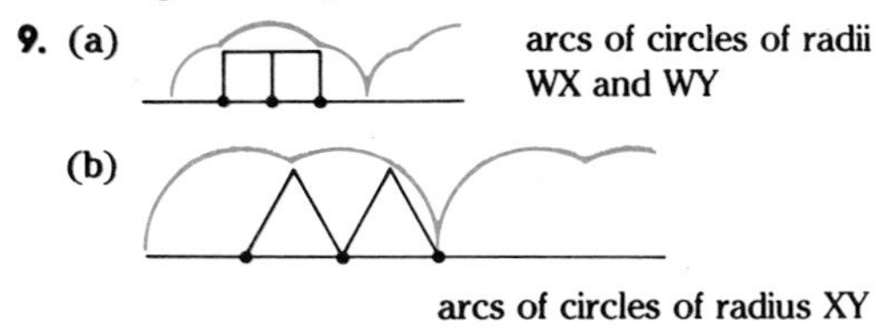
   arcs of circles of radius XY
10. (a) (b) 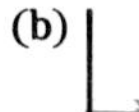 (c) 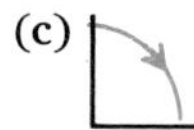

11. (a) part of a helix 
    (b) 30°
    (c) 12 cm
    (d) It is the same.
12. (Ellipse)
13. (a) 8 cm
    (b) 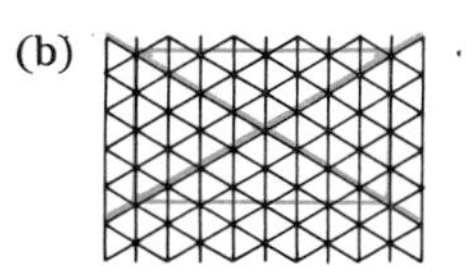
14. (a) 90° 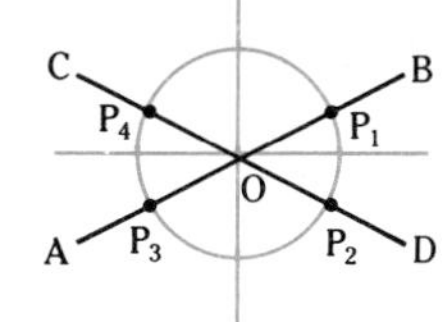

    (b) 8, 16 and 13.9 cm
15. 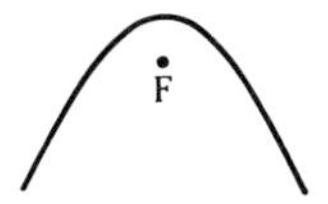

Self-Assessment 26 page 404

1. (a) square of side 2 cm (b) 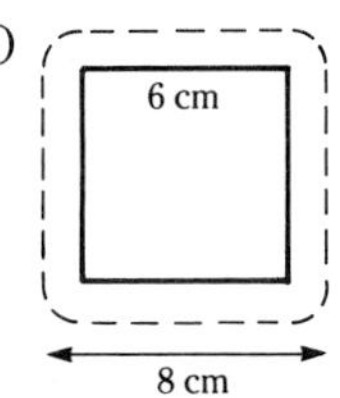

2. 4 cm, 5 cm

3.

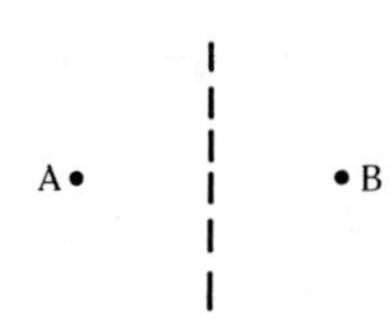

4. The surface of a sphere radius 8 cm with centre at the centre of the flame.

5. (a)

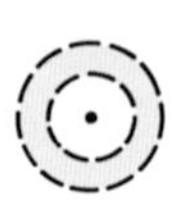

(b)

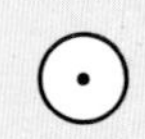

6. 3.6 cm

7. (a)

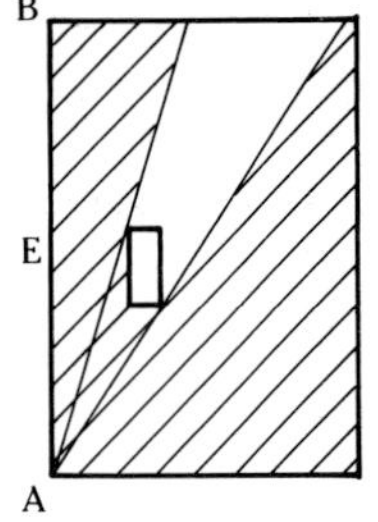

(b)

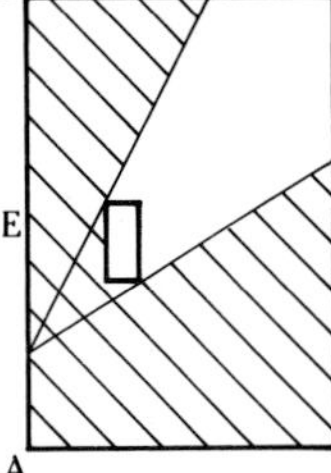

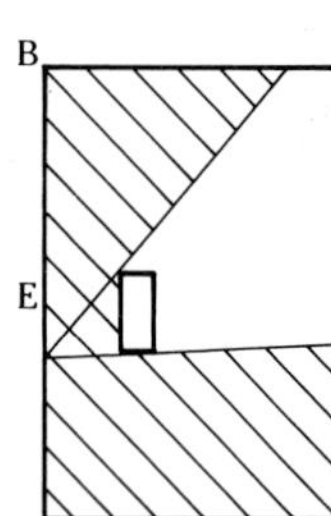

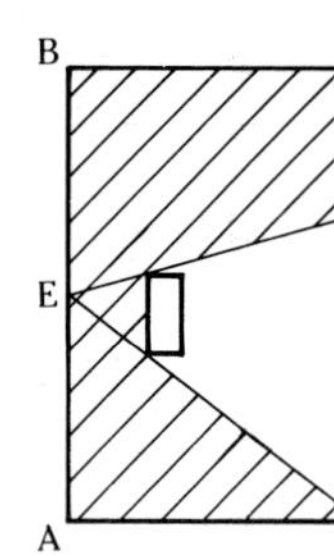

(c)

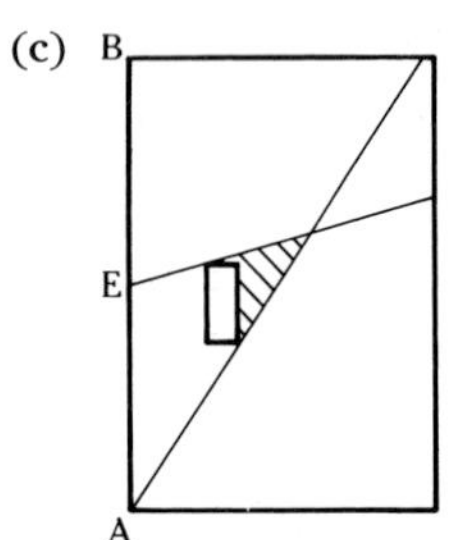

(d) no

8. Part of a circle with
   (a) centre B, radius 4 cm
   (b) centre D, radius 4 cm
   (c) centre B, radius 8 cm
   (d) centre midpoint of BD, radius 2 cm

CHAPTER 27

Exercise 27a page 407

1. (a) scalar (e) scalar
   (b) vector (f) scalar
   (c) vector (g) vector
   (d) vector (h) vector

2. $\mathbf{a} = \begin{pmatrix} 3 \\ 4 \end{pmatrix}$, $\mathbf{b} = \begin{pmatrix} 3 \\ -3 \end{pmatrix}$, $\mathbf{c} = \begin{pmatrix} -2 \\ 4 \end{pmatrix}$,
   $\mathbf{d} = \begin{pmatrix} -5 \\ -3 \end{pmatrix}$, $\mathbf{e} = \begin{pmatrix} -4 \\ 0 \end{pmatrix}$, $\mathbf{f} = \begin{pmatrix} 0 \\ 4 \end{pmatrix}$

3.

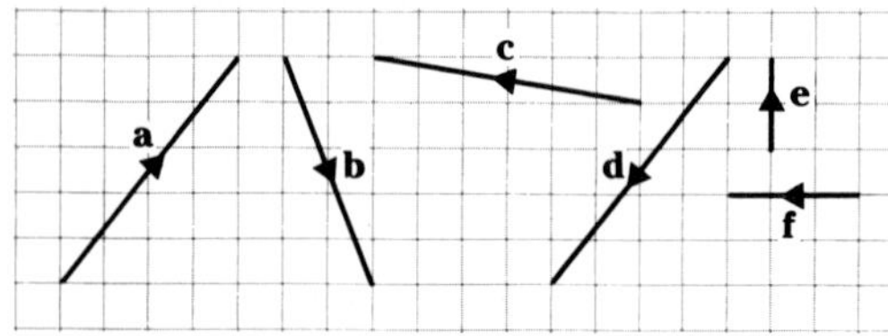

4.

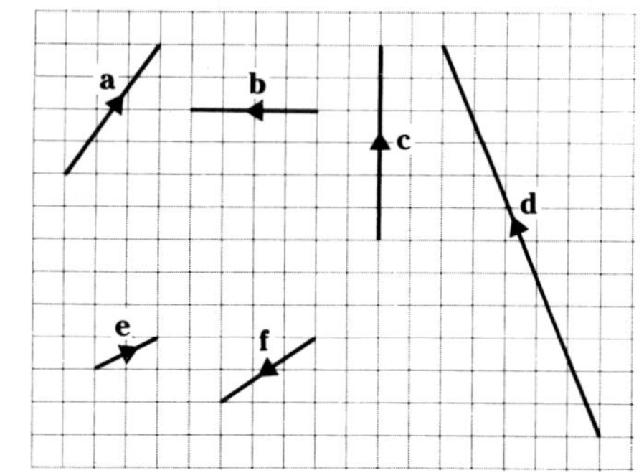

Exercise 27b page 408

1. $\begin{pmatrix} 3 \\ -3 \end{pmatrix}$ 2. $\begin{pmatrix} -3 \\ 2 \end{pmatrix}$ 3. $\begin{pmatrix} -4 \\ 0 \end{pmatrix}$ 4. $\begin{pmatrix} 7 \\ -2 \end{pmatrix}$

5.

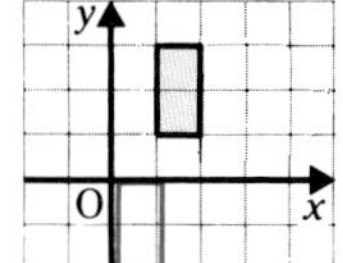

6.

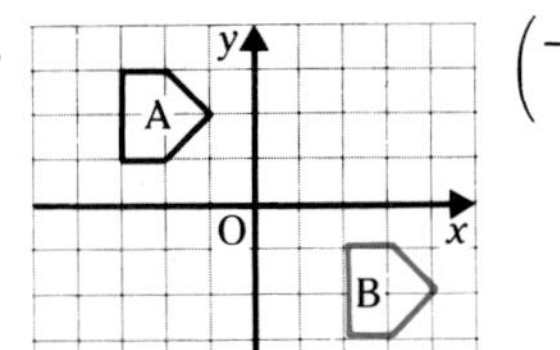

$\begin{pmatrix} -5 \\ 4 \end{pmatrix}$

7. (a) $\begin{pmatrix} 3 \\ 4 \end{pmatrix}$ (c) $\begin{pmatrix} -3 \\ 1 \end{pmatrix} - \begin{pmatrix} 3 \\ 4 \end{pmatrix} = \begin{pmatrix} -6 \\ -3 \end{pmatrix}$
   (b) $\begin{pmatrix} -6 \\ -3 \end{pmatrix}$

8. (a) $A_1(5, 3)$, $B_1(8, 4)$, $C_1(7, 8)$
   (b) $A_2(-5, 2)$, $B_2(-2, 3)$, $C_2(-3, 7)$
   (c) $A_3(1, -3)$, $B_3(4, -2)$, $C_3(3, 2)$
   (d) $\begin{pmatrix} -10 \\ -1 \end{pmatrix}$

Exercise 27c page 411

1. (a) A rotation through 90° clockwise about O.
   (b) A reflection in the x-axis.
   (c) An enlargement, scale factor 2, centre $(-1, -1)$
   (d) A translation by the vector $\begin{pmatrix} -5 \\ -1 \end{pmatrix}$.

2. (a)

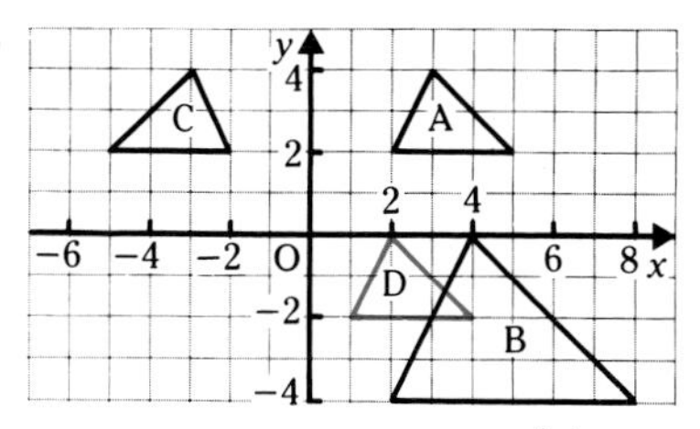

(b) (i) translation by the vector $\begin{pmatrix}1\\4\end{pmatrix}$

(ii) enlargement, scale factor 2, centre the origin

(iii) reflection in the y-axis

(iv) reflection in the y-axis

3.

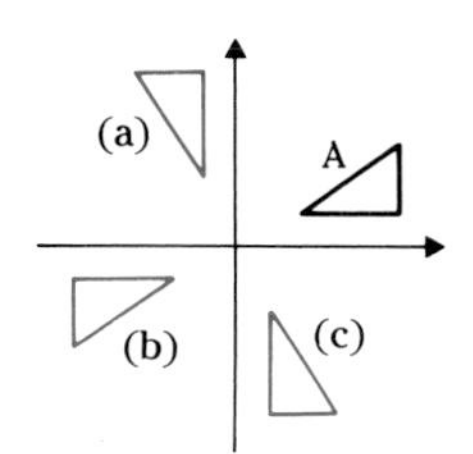

4.

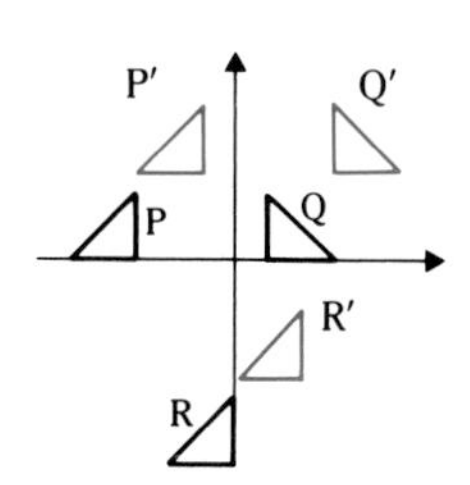

5.

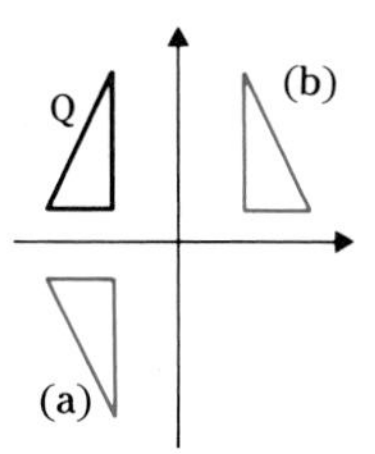

6.

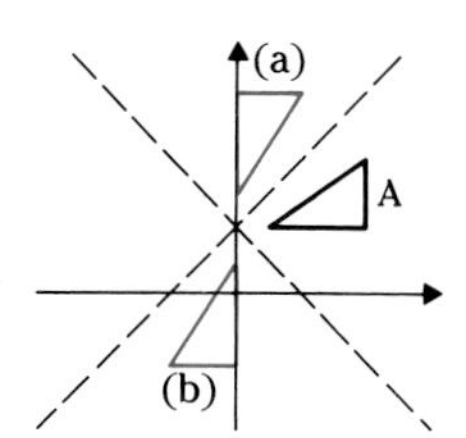

7.

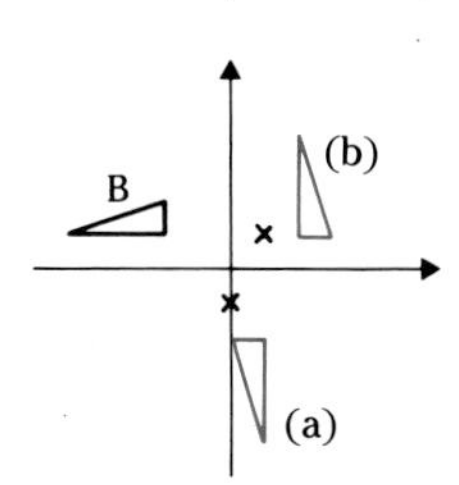

Self-Assessment 27 page 412

1.

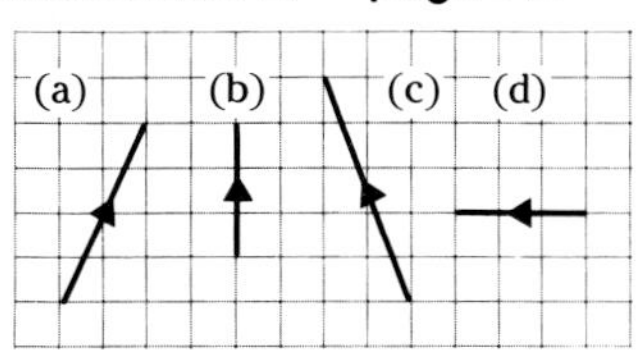

2. (a) $\begin{pmatrix}0\\-2\end{pmatrix}$ (d) $\begin{pmatrix}-3\\2\end{pmatrix}$ (g) $\begin{pmatrix}0\\3\end{pmatrix}$

(b) $\begin{pmatrix}2\\2\end{pmatrix}$ (e) $\begin{pmatrix}-3\\-1\end{pmatrix}$

(c) $\begin{pmatrix}-2\\-2\end{pmatrix}$ (f) $\begin{pmatrix}-3\\0\end{pmatrix}$

3. (a) Translation denoted by the vector $\begin{pmatrix}1\\-3\end{pmatrix}$.

(b) Enlargement, scale factor 2, centre of enlargement (7, 4).

(c) Enlargement, scale factor 2, centre of enlargement (9, −2).

4.

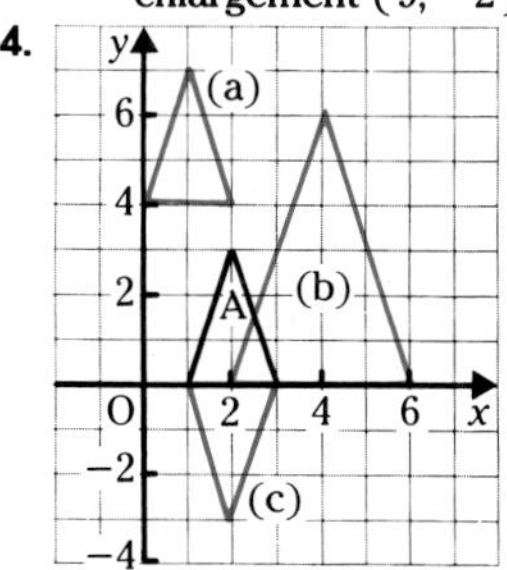

5. (b) and (c)

6. (2, 4), (−5, 5)

CHAPTER 28

Exercise 28a page 414

1. (a) $\frac{1}{4}$ (b) $\frac{3}{4}$ (c) $\frac{1}{52}$ (d) $\frac{1}{13}$ (e) $\frac{1}{26}$

2. (a) $\frac{1}{6}$ (c) $\frac{1}{2}$

(b) $\frac{1}{3}$ (d) they total 1

3. (a) $\frac{21}{26}$ (b) $\frac{4}{13}$ (c) $\frac{7}{26}$

4. (a) $\frac{1}{2}$ (d) $\frac{1}{36}$ (g) 0

(b) $\frac{1}{4}$ (e) $\frac{5}{9}$ (h) 1

(c) $\frac{1}{9}$ (f) $\frac{4}{9}$

5. (a) $\frac{11}{18}$ (b) 1

6. (a) $\frac{5}{26}$ (b) $\frac{1}{2}$ (c) $\frac{9}{26}$

7. (a) $\frac{2}{5}$ (b) $\frac{3}{5}$

8. (a) $\frac{4}{9}$ (b) $\frac{5}{9}$

9. $\frac{3}{5}$

10. (a) $\frac{1}{75}$ (b) $\frac{74}{75}$

11. (a) $\frac{1}{10}$ (b) $\frac{3}{10}$ (c) $\frac{2}{5}$ (d) $\frac{7}{10}$

12. (a) $\frac{15}{22}$ (b) $\frac{7}{22}$ (c) $\frac{1}{22}$ (d) $\frac{3}{11}$

13. (a) $\frac{5}{12}$ (b) $\frac{1}{3}$ (c) $\frac{3}{4}$

14. $\frac{2}{5}$
15. $\frac{1}{3}$
16. (a) $\frac{1}{6}$ (b) $\frac{7}{30}$
17. (a) $\frac{5}{18}$ (b) $\frac{13}{36}$ (c) $\frac{7}{12}$

Exercise 28b page 417

1. (a) 30 (b) 90 (c) 90
2. (a) 20 (b) 65 (c) 130 (d) 10
3. 4
4. (a) 69 (b) 115
5. 16
6. 450 milk, 750 cola and 600 squash
7. (a) 0.36 (b) (i) 7 200 000 (ii) 1 500 000

Exercise 28c page 418

1. (a) $\frac{1}{26}$ (b) $\frac{1}{26}$ (c) $\frac{1}{13}$
2. (a) $\frac{1}{6}$ (b) $\frac{1}{3}$ (c) $\frac{1}{2}$
3. (a) $\frac{1}{6}$ (b) $\frac{1}{6}$ (c) $\frac{1}{3}$
4. (a) $\frac{8}{9}$ (b) $\frac{1}{9}$
5. (a) $\frac{5}{7}$ (b) $\frac{11}{14}$
6. (a) $\frac{24}{35}$ (b) $\frac{15}{28}$ (c) $\frac{131}{140}$ (d) $\frac{9}{140}$
7. (a) $\frac{1}{2}$ (b) $\frac{1}{2}$ (c) $\frac{5}{6}$

Exercise 28d page 419

1. (a) $\frac{1}{6}$ (b) $\frac{2}{9}$ (c) 0 (d) $\frac{5}{6}$
2. (a) $\frac{7}{12}$ (b) $\frac{5}{6}$ (c) $\frac{17}{36}$
3. (a) $\frac{1}{4}$ (b) $\frac{3}{4}$ (c) $\frac{1}{2}$
4. (a) $\frac{1}{2}$ (b) $\frac{1}{4}$ (c) $\frac{3}{4}$
5. (a) $\frac{1}{4}$ (b) $\frac{3}{4}$

Exercise 28e page 421

1. (a) $\frac{1}{36}$ (b) $\frac{5}{18}$
2. (a) $\frac{125}{216}$ (b) $\frac{25}{72}$ (c) $\frac{2}{27}$
3. (a) Tuesday ($\frac{1}{9} > \frac{2}{25}$)
(b)

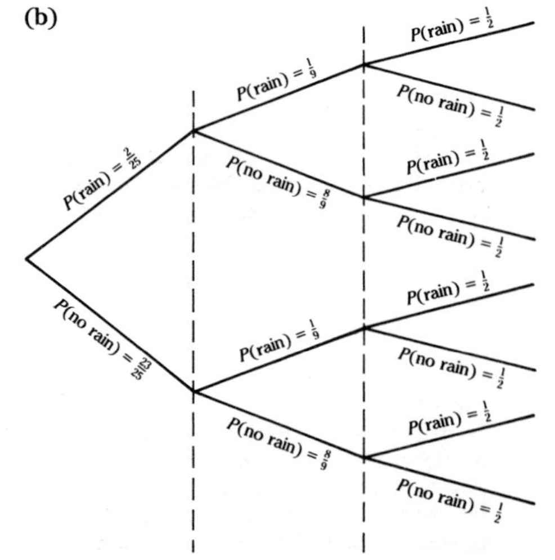

(c) (i) $\frac{2}{225}$ (ii) $\frac{13}{75}$ (d) (i) $\frac{92}{225}$ (ii) $\frac{133}{225}$

4. (a) $\frac{4}{25}$ (16%)
(b)

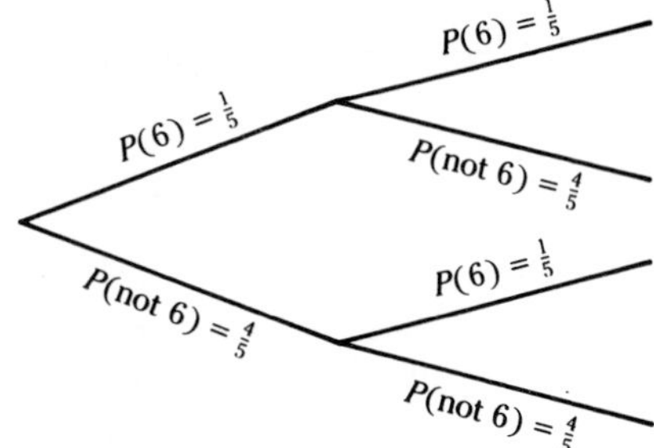

(c) (i) $\frac{1}{25}$ (4%)
(ii) $\frac{9}{25}$ (36%)
(iii) $\frac{16}{25}$ (64%)

5. (a) $\frac{3}{8}$ (b) $\frac{3}{8}$ (c) $\frac{7}{8}$
6. (a) $\frac{9}{20}$ (b) $\frac{7}{10}$ (c) $\frac{13}{60}$
7. (a) $\frac{4}{9}$ (c) $\frac{16}{55}$

Self-Assessment 28 page 424

1. (a) $\frac{1}{26}$ (b) $\frac{1}{52}$
2. (a) 60 (b) 120
3. (a) $\frac{7}{10}$ (b) $\frac{3}{10}$
4. (a) $\frac{1}{2}$ (b) $\frac{13}{36}$ (c) $\frac{1}{3}$ (d) $\frac{1}{3}$
5. (a) Coral (b) 0.08 (c) 0.72
6. (a) 7 (b) 18 (c) $\frac{3}{32}$

CHAPTER 29

Some of these answers are taken from graphs and some others calculated using statistical functions on a calculator. In these cases your answers may vary slightly from those given here.

Exercise 29a page 428

1. (a) 4.43, 4, 2 (c) 3.75, 4, 4
(b) 1.84, 1.65, 1.6 (d) 0.725, 0.75, 0.8
2. $18 200, $10 000, $10 000
(a) mean (shows employees' pay is high)
(b) median or mode (shows a lower figure for employees' pay)
3. 455, 520, 630, 736, 857
4. (a) $2900 (b) $4083 (c) $1183
5. 56.4 kg
6. 94.7 kg
7. 41
8. (a) 5.21 (b) 5.33
9. 3.64
10. 1.57
11. 3
12. 3.5

Exercise 29b page 431

1. 4.2
2. 7.6

3. 159.8
4. 3.1
5. 6.15 customers

Exercise 29c page 433

1. (a) 5 (b) 49
2. (a) 13 (b) 15
3. (a) 25 (b) 0.5

Exercise 29d page 435

1. 3 oranges 8 cm 159.5 cm

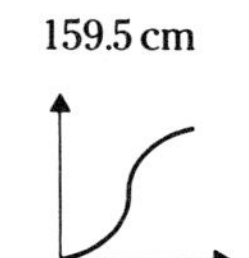

2. (a) 50 (d) 32
   (b) 38 minutes (e) 14
   (c) 4 (f) 0.16
3. (a) 39 minutes (b)
   (b)

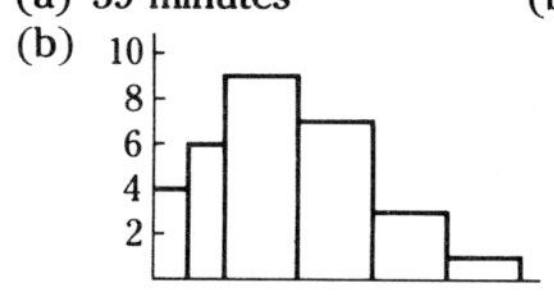

4. median is less than mean; greater than 0.5

Exercise 29e page 438

1. (a) 59.9, 66 (b) $\frac{5}{7}$
2. (a) £69.70
   (b)

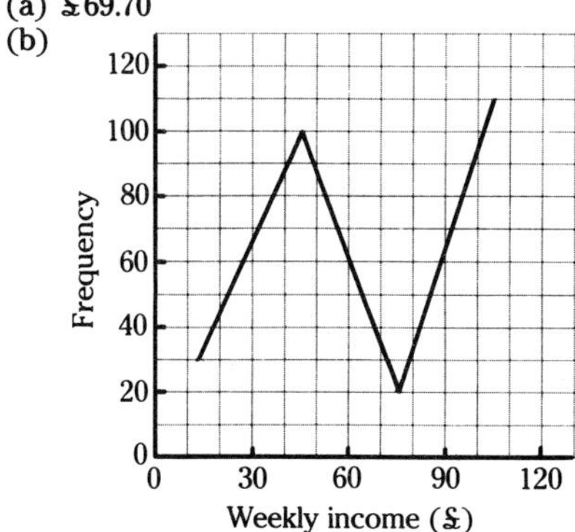

(c) & (d)

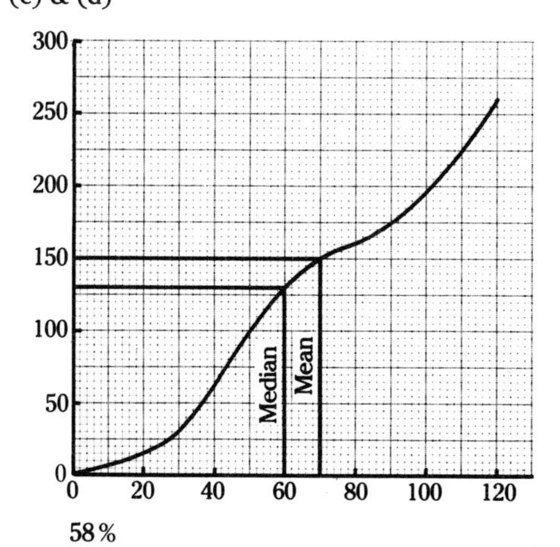

58%

3. No. It is possible for the median to be below the mean as illustrated in question 2.
4. More than half of Group A scored less than the mean value whereas more than half of Group B scored above the same mean value.
5. (a) 0–9 means from 0 up to, but not including, 10
   (b) 35.8 years
   (c)

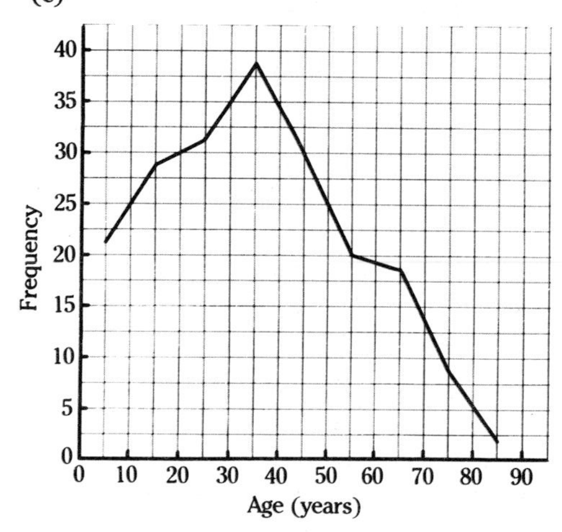

(d)

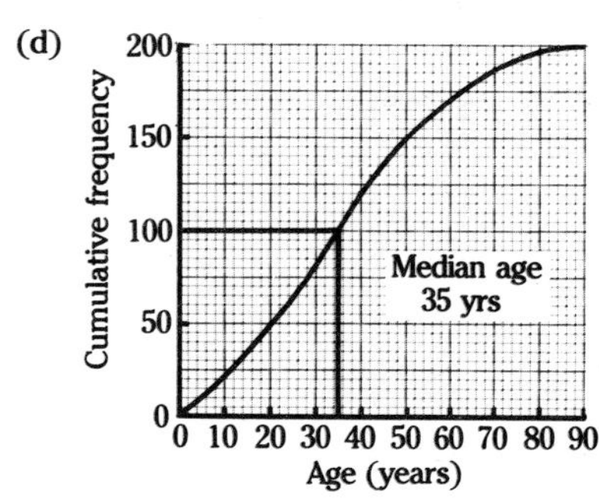

(e) about 47%

Exercise 29f page 439

1. 4 oranges, 3.3 cm, 6.5 cm
2. (a) £22 (b) £16, £34; £18
3. Brand Y; three-quarters of the sample is greater than 18.5 h whereas three-quarters of Brand X is not

Exercise 29g page 441

1. Group B is better overall than Group A. Group B has higher mean and median values. Possible reasons are: Group B is the better group, or has covered the work tested more thoroughly, or is an older group, or has been better taught.

2. (a) 13.6 cm
   (b)

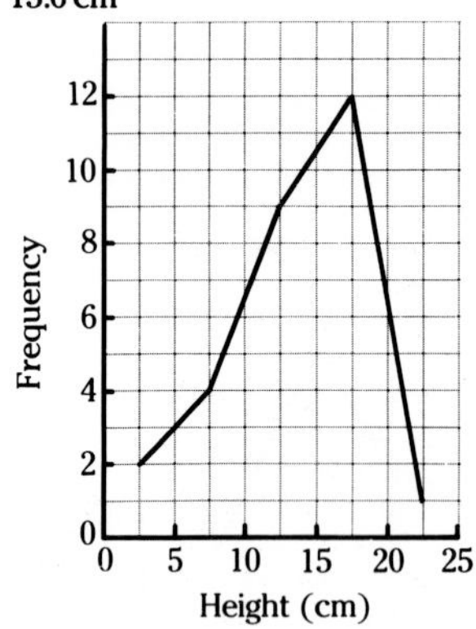

   (c) The second batch has a lower mean.

3. (a) Machine A, 0.25
   Machine B, 0.11
   (b) Machine B; smaller interquartile range

4. (a) 10 times each
   (b)

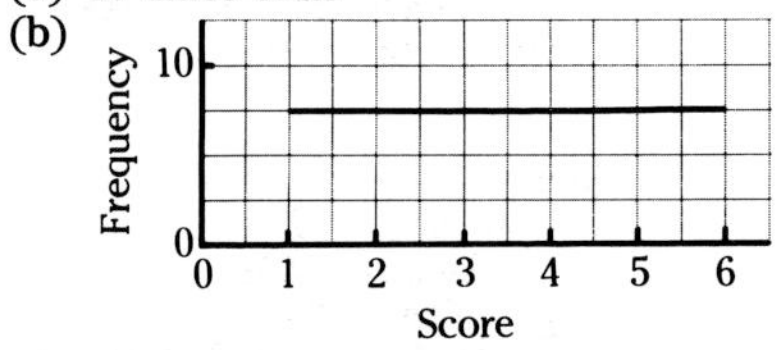

Self-Assessment 29 **page 607**

1. 7, 6.8, 6.1
2. 5.49 mm
3. (a) 2.55 (b) 2.1, 1.8
4. (a)

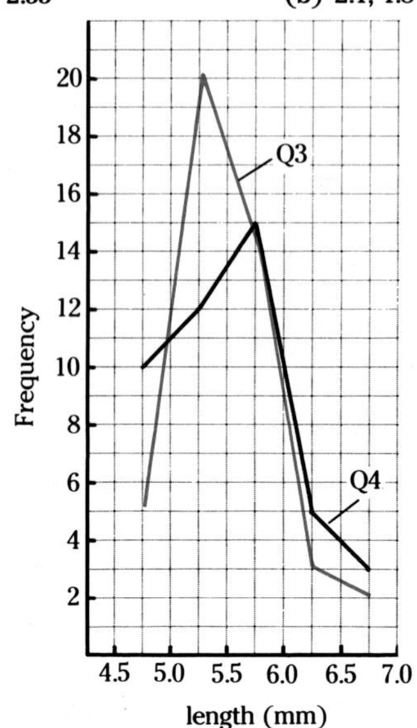

   (b) On the whole the screws are shorter for the batch given in question 3 than in question 4.
   (c) Possibly the machine has been adjusted slightly, as wear could have affected it.

INDEX